T0180698

Lecture Notes in Computer Science 12729

More information about this subseries at http://www.springer.com/series/7412

Aasa Feragen · Stefan Sommer · Julia Schnabel ·
Mads Nielsen (Eds.)

Information Processing in Medical Imaging

27th International Conference, IPMI 2021
Virtual Event, June 28–June 30, 2021
Proceedings

Editors
Aasa Feragen 🆔
Technical University of Denmark
Kgs Lyngby, Denmark

Stefan Sommer 🆔
University of Copenhagen
Copenhagen, Denmark

Julia Schnabel 🆔
King's College London
London, UK

Mads Nielsen 🆔
University of Copenhagen
Copenhagen, Denmark

ISSN 0302-9743   ISSN 1611-3349 (electronic)
Lecture Notes in Computer Science
ISBN 978-3-030-78190-3   ISBN 978-3-030-78191-0 (eBook)
https://doi.org/10.1007/978-3-030-78191-0

LNCS Sublibrary: SL6 – Image Processing, Computer Vision, Pattern Recognition, and Graphics

This Springer imprint is published by the registered company Springer Nature Switzerland AG
The registered company address is: Gewerbestrasse 11, 6330 Cham, Switzerland

Preface

The Information Processing in Medical Imaging (IPMI) conferences have a long history and broad reach. Since 1969, the conferences have taken place on either side of the Atlantic, and the very first IPMI in Asia occurred fifty years later in Hong Kong. IPMI 2021, the twenty-seventh conference in the series, was scheduled to happen in Denmark on the island of Bornholm in the Baltic Sea. However, in the spring and summer of 2021, the COVID-19 pandemic remained a challenge in large parts of the world. Though swift and extensive vaccination programs promised to soon reclaim normality, uncertainty related to international travel made a large physical gathering impossible. Therefore, IPMI 2021 was the first in the conference series to take place not in Asia, the USA, or Europe, but entirely virtually.

All these decades have established traditions that give the IPMI conferences a very special feel and help to promote the series' hallmarks: IPMI places the utmost importance on high-quality submissions coupled with presentations and thorough discussions of the presented contributions. To facilitate this, the venues are often chosen in remote locations and the conferences have discussion groups, social activities, and unlimited discussion time for each presentation. In 2021, we were challenged with organizing a conference that kept as many of these aspects as possible in a virtual venue. We made every effort to retain the IPMI traditions and ideas while navigating the restrictions of a virtual conference.

IPMI 2021 built on the traditional study groups to extend the discussions to both papers presented orally and in poster sessions. The virtual setting allowed study groups to meet before the conference to start the discussions and network in the groups. During the conference, poster sessions ran twice to accommodate time-zone differences. In addition to live talks, oral presenters had posters where participants could meet and discuss the paper and presentations according to their time-zone preference, with no restrictions on duration.

Gitte Moos Knudsen, Professor at the Department of Neurology and Chair of the Neurobiology Research Unit, Copenhagen University Hospital, gave the keynote at IPMI 2021. And of course the conference included the traditional IPMI soccer match, this time without a physical ball.

IPMI 2021 received 204 submissions, of which 200 papers went into peer review and were reviewed by at least 3 reviewers each. Following the reviewing process, each paper that received at least one "accept" was read by one or more members of the Paper Selection Committee, and most of these papers were discussed at the paper selection meeting. 59 submissions were accepted for publication and presentation at the conference, resulting in a 30% acceptance rate. At the conference, 19 oral presentations and 40 posters were presented on topics ranging from brain connectivity, image registration and segmentation, causal models and interpretability, representation learning, computer-assisted intervention, differential geometry, and shape analysis.

One of the defining priorities throughout the organization was diversity. In particular, all committees had at least 40% representation of either gender, and we also strived for a diverse reviewing pool. We are excited to note that among the accepted papers we find first authors from Asia, Africa, North America and Europe – a trend that we hope will continue.

The François Erbsmann Prize is awarded to a young scientist of age 35 or below, who is the first author of a paper, giving his/her first oral presentation at IPMI. The prize was awarded to one of the 18 eligible oral presenters, and awards were given for the best poster presentations.

The IPMI 2021 organizing team would like to send a special thanks to both the Scientific Committee and the Paper Selection Committee: the 166 reviewers did an excellent job in reviewing the submitted papers. The Paper Selection Committee - Polina Golland, Martin Styner, Albert Chung, Ender Konukoglu, Marleen de Bruijne, Dorin Comaniciu, Ipek Oguz, and Demian Wassermann - reached decisions for each paper based on the reviews and thorough discussions in the committee. Due to the pandemic, the paper selection meeting was virtual as well. This, however, proved no obstacle for the work: the committee worked efficiently through a number of long hours on Zoom to decide on the final list of accepted papers.

We would like to thank the IPMI board for giving us the opportunity to host IPMI 2021, and for valuable discussions on how to handle the difficult situation regarding the COVID-19 pandemic. This in particular applies to Albert Chung, who in addition to being chairman of the IPMI board was also the organizer of IPMI 2019. Albert has been invaluable in sharing experiences on organizational aspects and in discussing how to organize the first virtual IPMI.

IPMI 2021 was supported financially by the Carlsberg Foundation, the Lundbeck Foundation, the Otto Mønsted Foundation, and Springer. We are extremely grateful for the support which has allowed us to offer a number of IPMI scholarships for participants needing financial assistance to attend IPMI as well as a general reduction in registration fees. Furthermore, we wish to thank our universities – the University of Copenhagen, the Technical University of Denmark, and King's College London - for generous organizational and administrative support.

We have been delighted to organize IPMI 2021 and present the range of excellent scientific work covered in this volume. We hope IPMI 2021 offered the best possible experience for a first time virtual IPMI. Perhaps IPMI 2021 will be the only virtual conference in the series, or perhaps some form of virtuality will persist or reappear in future IPMIs. We did our very best to organize the conference in a very difficult time.

May 2021

Stefan Sommer
Aasa Feragen
Julia Schnabel
Mads Nielsen

Organization

Conference Chairs

Stefan Sommer	University of Copenhagen, Denmark
Aasa Feragen	Technical University of Denmark, Denmark
Julia Schnabel	King's College London, UK
Mads Nielsen	University of Copenhagen, Denmark

Communications and Local Organization

Nanna Højholt	University of Copenhagen, Denmark

Paper Selection Committee

Polina Golland	Massachusetts Institute of Technology, USA
Martin Styner	University of North Carolina at Chapel Hill, USA
Albert Chung	The Hong Kong University of Science and Technology, Hong Kong
Ender Konukoglu	ETH Zurich, Switzerland
Marleen de Bruijne	Erasmus MC the Netherlands, and University of Copenhagen, Denmark
Dorin Comaniciu	Siemens Healthineers, USA
Ipek Oguz	Vanderbilt, USA
Demian Wassermann	Inria, France

Scientific Committee

Adrian V. Dalca	Massachusetts Institute of Technology, USA
Akshay Pai	Cerebriu, Denmark
Alexis Arnaudon	Imperial College London, UK
Alice Barbara Tumpach	University of Lille, France
Alison Noble	University of Oxford, UK
Anand Joshi	University of Southern California, USA
Andrea Fuster	Eindhoven University of Technology, the Netherlands
Andrew King	King's College London, UK
Anna Calissano	Politecnico di Milano, Italy
Anuj Srivastava	Florida State University, USA
Archana Venkataraman	Johns Hopkins University, USA
Arrate Munoz Barrutia	Universidad Carlos III de Madrid, Spain
Ayushi Sinha	Philips Research, USA

Baba Vemuri	University of Florida, USA
Beatriz Paniagua	Kitware, USA
Ben Glocker	Imperial College London, UK
Bennett A. Landman	Vanderbilt University, USA
Benoit Dawant	Vanderbilt University, USA
Bjoern Menze	Technical University of Munich, Germany
Boklye Kim	University of Michigan, USA
Boudewijn Lelieveldt	Leiden University Medical Center, the Netherlands
Bulat Ibragimov	University of Copenhagen, Denmark
Carl-Fredrik Westin	Harvard University, USA
Carole H. Sudre	University College London, UK
Caroline Petitjean	Université de Rouen, France
Catie Chang	Vanderbilt University, USA
Chantal Tax	Cardiff University, UK
Chao Chen	Stony Brook University, USA
Chen Chen	Imperial College London, UK
Chen Qin	Imperial College London, UK
Christof Seiler	Maastricht University, the Netherlands
Chuyang Ye	Beijing Institute of Technology, China
Claire Cury	Inria, France
Clara Sanchez Gutierrez	Radboud UMC, the Netherlands
Daniel Alexander	University College London, UK
Daniel Rueckert	Imperial College London, UK
Darko Stern	Technical University of Graz, Austria
Diana Mateus	Centrale Nantes, France
Dou Qi	The Chinese University of Hong Kong, Hong Kong
Dzung Pham	Henry M. Jackson Foundation, USA
Ehsan Adeli	Stanford University, USA
Elizabeth A. Krupinski	University of Arizona, USA
Enzo Ferrante	CONICET, Argentina
Erik B. B. Dam	University of Copenhagen, Denmark
Ernst Schwartz	Medical University of Vienna, Austria
Ertunc Erdil	ETH Zurich, Switzerland
Esther E. Bron	Erasmus MC, the Netherlands
Esther Puyol-Antón	King's College London, UK
Francois-Xavier Vialard	University of Paris-Est, France
Frithjof Kruggel	UC Irvine, USA
Gary E. Christensen	University of Iowa, USA
Gemma Piella	Pompeu Fabra University, Spain
Ghada Zamzmi	NIH, USA
Guido Gerig	New York University, USA
Harshita Sharma	University of Oxford, UK
Herve Lombaert	Microsoft Research-Inria Joint Centre, France
Hongzhi Wang	IBM Research, USA
Isabelle Bloch	Télécom Paris, France
Islem Rekik	Istanbul Technical University, Turkey

IPMI 2021 Board

Albert Chung	The Hong Kong University of Science and Technology, Hong Kong
Martin Styner	University of North Carolina, USA
James Duncan	Yale University, USA
Stephen Pizer	University of North Carolina at Chapel Hill, USA
Chris Taylor	University of Manchester, UK
Gary Christensen	University of Iowa, USA
Gabor Szekely	ETH Zurich, Switzerland
Jerry Prince	Johns Hopkins University, USA
William Wells	Harvard Medical School, USA
Sebastien Ourselin	King's College London, UK
Marleen de Bruijne	Erasmus MC, the Netherlands
Randy Brill	Vanderbilt University, USA
Andrew Todd-Pokropek	University College London, UK
Polina Golland	Massachusetts Institute of Technology, USA
Alison Noble	Oxford University, UK
Richard Leahy	University of Southern California, USA

Contents

Sequential Modelling

Learning with Few or Low Quality Labels

Uncertainty Quantification and Generative Modelling

Deep Learning

Registration

HyperMorph: Amortized Hyperparameter Learning for Image Registration

Andrew Hoopes[1(✉)] ⓘ, Malte Hoffmann[1,2] ⓘ, Bruce Fischl[1,2,3] ⓘ,
John Guttag[3] ⓘ, and Adrian V. Dalca[1,2,3] ⓘ

[1] Martinos Center for Biomedical Imaging, MGH, Boston, USA
{ahoopes,mhoffmann,bfischl}@mgh.harvard.edu
[2] Department of Radiology, Harvard Medical School, Boston, USA
[3] Computer Science and Artificial Intelligence Lab, MIT, Cambridge, USA
{guttag,adalca}@mit.edu

Abstract. We present HyperMorph, a learning-based strategy for deformable image registration that removes the need to tune important registration hyperparameters during training. Classical registration methods solve an optimization problem to find a set of spatial correspondences between two images, while learning-based methods leverage a training dataset to learn a function that generates these correspondences. The quality of the results for both types of techniques depends greatly on the choice of hyperparameters. Unfortunately, hyperparameter tuning is time-consuming and typically involves training many separate models with various hyperparameter values, potentially leading to suboptimal results. To address this inefficiency, we introduce amortized hyperparameter learning for image registration, a novel strategy to *learn* the effects of hyperparameters on deformation fields. The proposed framework learns a hypernetwork that takes in an input hyperparameter and modulates a registration network to produce the optimal deformation field for that hyperparameter value. In effect, this strategy trains a single, rich model that enables rapid, fine-grained discovery of hyperparameter values from a continuous interval at test-time. We demonstrate that this approach can be used to optimize multiple hyperparameters considerably faster than existing search strategies, leading to a reduced computational and human burden as well as increased flexibility. We also show several important benefits, including increased robustness to initialization and the ability to rapidly identify optimal hyperparameter values specific to a registration task, dataset, or even a single anatomical region, all without retraining the HyperMorph model. Our code is publicly available at http://voxelmorph.mit.edu.

Keywords: Deformable image registration · Hyperparameter tuning · Deep learning · Amortized learning

ⓒ Springer Nature Switzerland AG 2021
A. Feragen et al. (Eds.): IPMI 2021, LNCS 12729, pp. 3–17, 2021.
https://doi.org/10.1007/978-3-030-78191-0_1

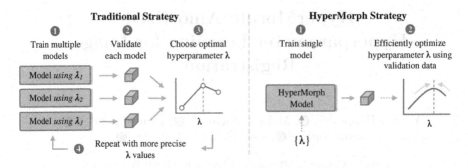

Fig. 1. Hyperparameter optimization strategies. Traditional approaches (left) repeatedly train a registration model, each time with a different hyperparameter value. The proposed HyperMorph approach (right) optimizes a single, richer model once, which approximates a landscape of traditional models.

1   Introduction

Deformable image registration aims to find a set of dense correspondences that accurately align two images. Classical optimization-based techniques for image registration have been thoroughly studied, yielding mature mathematical frameworks and widely used software tools [2, 4, 8, 48, 52]. Learning-based registration methods employ image datasets to learn a function that rapidly computes the deformation field between image pairs [7, 46, 50, 54, 56, 57]. These methods involve choosing registration hyperparameters that dramatically affect the quality of the estimated deformation field. Optimal hyperparameter values can differ substantially across image modality and anatomy, and even small changes can have a large impact on accuracy. Choosing appropriate hyperparameter values is therefore a crucial step in developing, evaluating, and deploying registration methods.

Tuning these hyperparameters most often involves grid or random search techniques to evaluate separate models for discrete hyperparameter values (Fig. 1). In practice, researchers typically perform a sequential process of optimizing and validating models with a small subset of hyperparameter values, adapting this subset, and repeating. Optimal hyperparameter values are selected based on model performance, generally determined by human evaluation or additional validation data such as anatomical annotations. This approach requires considerable computational and human effort, which may lead to suboptimal parameter choices, misleading negative results, and impeded progress, especially when researchers might resort to using values from the literature that are not adequate for their specific dataset or registration task.

In this work, we introduce a substantially different approach, HyperMorph, to tackle registration hyperparameters: amortized hyperparameter learning for image registration. Our contributions are:

Method. We propose an end-to-end strategy to *learn* the effects of registration hyperparameters on deformation fields with a single, rich model, replacing the traditional hyperparameter tuning process (Fig. 1). A HyperMorph model is a hypernetwork that approximates a landscape of registration networks for a range of hyperparameter values, by learning a continuous function of the hyperparameters. Users only need to learn a single HyperMorph model that enables rapid test-time image registration for any hyperparameter value. This eliminates the need to train a multitude of separate models each for a fixed hyperparameter, since HyperMorph accurately estimates their outputs at a fraction of the computational and human effort. In addition, HyperMorph enables rapid, accurate hyperparameter tuning for registration tasks involving many hyperparameters, in which computational complexity renders grid-search techniques ineffective.

Properties. By exploiting implicit weight-sharing, a single HyperMorph model is efficient to train compared to training the many individual registration models it is able to encompass. We also show that HyperMorph is more robust to initialization than standard registration models, indicating that it better avoids local minima while reducing the need to retrain models with different initializations.

Utility. HyperMorph enables rapid discovery of optimal hyperparameter values at *test-time*, either through visual assessment or automatic optimization in the continuous hyperparameter space. We demonstrate the substantial utility of this approach by using a *single* HyperMorph model to identify the optimum hyperparameter values for different datasets, different anatomical regions, or different registration tasks. HyperMorph also offers more precise tuning compared to grid or sequential search.

2   Related Work

Image Registration. Classical approaches independently estimate a deformation field by optimizing an energy function for each image pair. These include elastic models [6], b-spline based deformations [48], discrete optimization methods [16,22], Demons [52], SPM [3], LDDMM [8,13,29,44,58], DARTEL [2], and symmetric normalization (SyN) [4]. Recent learning-based approaches make use of convolutional neural networks (CNNs) to learn a function that rapidly computes the deformation field for an image pair. Supervised models learn to reproduce deformation fields estimated or simulated by other methods [35,46,50,57], whereas unsupervised strategies train networks that optimize a loss function similar to classical cost functions and do not require the ground-truth registrations needed by supervised methods [7,15,26,34,54].

Generally, all these methods rely on at least one hyperparameter that balances the optimization of an image-matching term with that of a regularization or smoothness term. Additional hyperparameters are often used in the loss terms, such as the neighborhood size of local normalized cross-correlation [5] or the number of bins in mutual information [53]. Choosing optimal hyperparameter values for classical registration algorithms is a tedious process since pair-wise registration typically requires tens of minutes or more to compute. While learning-based methods enable much faster test-time registration, individual model *training* is expensive and can require days to converge, causing the hyperparameter search to consume hundreds of GPU-hours [7, 26, 54].

Hyperparameter Optimization. Hyperparameter optimization algorithms jointly solve a validation objective with respect to model hyperparameters and a training objective with respect to model weights [21]. The simplest approach treats model training as a black-box function, including grid, random, and sequential search [9]. Bayesian optimization is a more sample-efficient strategy, leveraging a probabilistic model of the objective function to search and evaluate hyperparameter performance [10]. Both approaches are often inefficient, since the algorithms involve repeated optimizations for each hyperparameter evaluation. Enhancements to these strategies have improved performance by extrapolating learning curves before full convergence [19, 32] and evaluating low-fidelity approximations of the black-box function [30]. Other adaptations use bandit-based approaches to selectively allocate resources to favorable models [28, 36]. Gradient-based techniques differentiate through the nested optimization to approximate gradients as a function of the hyperparameters [38, 40, 45]. These approaches are computationally costly and require evaluation of a metric on a comprehensive, labeled validation set, which may not be available for every registration task.

Hypernetworks. Hypernetworks are networks that output weights of a primary network [25, 33, 49]. Recently, they have gained traction as efficient methods of gradient-based hyperparameter optimization since they enable easy differentiation through the entire model with respect to the hyperparameters of interest. For example, SMASH uses hypernetworks to output the weights of a network conditioned on its architecture [12]. Similar work employs hypernetworks to optimize weight decay in classification networks and demonstrates that sufficiently sized hypernetworks are capable of approximating its global effect [37, 39]. Hyper-Morph extends hypernetworks, combining them with learning-based registration to estimate the effect of hyperparameter values on deformations.

3   Methods

3.1   HyperMorph

Deformable image registration methods find a dense, non-linear correspondence field ϕ between a moving image m and a fixed image f, and can employ a variety of hyperparameters. We follow current unsupervised learning-based registration methods and define a network $g_{\theta_g}(m, f) = \phi$ with parameters θ_g that takes as input the image pair $\{m, f\}$ and outputs the optimal deformation field ϕ.

Our key idea is to model a hypernetwork that learns the effect of *loss* hyperparameters on the desired registration. Given loss hyperparameters Λ of interest, we define the hypernetwork function $h_{\theta_h}(\Lambda) = \theta_g$ with parameters θ_h that takes as input sample values for Λ and outputs the parameters of the registration network θ_g (Fig. 2). We learn optimal hypernetwork parameters θ_h using stochastic gradient methods, optimizing the loss

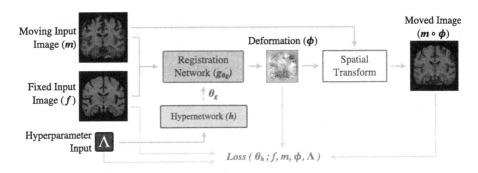

Fig. 2. HyperMorph framework. A hypernetwork (blue) learns to output the parameters of a registration network given registration hyperparameters Λ. HyperMorph is trained end-to-end, exploiting implicit weight-sharing among the full landscape of registration networks within a continuous interval of hyperparameter values. (Color figure online)

$$\mathcal{L}_h(\theta_h; \mathcal{D}) = \mathbb{E}_{\Lambda \sim p(\Lambda)}\Big[\mathcal{L}(\theta_h; \mathcal{D}, \Lambda)\Big], \tag{1}$$

where $\mathcal{D}$ is a dataset of images, $p(\Lambda)$ is a prior probability over the hyperparameters, and $\mathcal{L}(\cdot)$ is a registration loss involving hyperparameters Λ. For example, the distribution $p(\Lambda)$ can be uniform over some predefined range, or it can be adapted based on prior expectations. At every mini-batch, we sample a set of hyperparameter values from this distribution and use these both as input to the network $h_{\theta_h}(\cdot)$ and in the loss function $\mathcal{L}(\cdot)$ for that iteration.

Unsupervised Model Instantiations. Following unsupervised leaning-based registration, we use the loss function:

$$\mathcal{L}_h(\theta_h; \mathcal{D}) = \mathbb{E}_{\Lambda}\Big[\sum_{m, f \in \mathcal{D}} \big((1 - \lambda)\mathcal{L}_{sim}(f, m \circ \phi; \lambda_{sim}) + \lambda\mathcal{L}_{reg}(\phi; \lambda_{reg})\big)\Big], \tag{2}$$

where $m \circ \phi$ represents m warped by $\phi = g_{\theta_g}(m, f)$, $\theta_g = h_{\theta_h}(\Lambda)$. The loss term $\mathcal{L}_{sim}$ measures image similarity and might involve hyperparameters λ_{sim}, whereas $\mathcal{L}_{reg}$ quantifies the spatial regularity of the deformation field and might involve hyperparameters λ_{reg}. The regularization hyperparameter λ balances the relative importance of the separate terms, and $\Lambda = \{\lambda, \lambda_{sim}, \lambda_{reg}\}$.

When registering images of the same modality, we use standard similarity metrics for $\mathcal{L}_{sim}$: mean-squared error (MSE) and *local* normalized cross-correlation (NCC). Local NCC includes a hyperparameter defining the neighborhood size. For cross-modality registration, we use normalized mutual information (NMI), which involves a hyperparameter controlling the number of histogram bins [53].

We parameterize the deformation field ϕ with a stationary velocity field (SVF) v and integrate it within the network to obtain a diffeomorphism, which is invertible by design [1,2,15]. We regularize ϕ using $\mathcal{L}_{reg}(\phi) = \frac{1}{2}\|\nabla v\|^2$.

Semi-supervised Model Instantiation. Building on recent learning-based methods that use additional volume information during training [7, 26, 27], we also apply HyperMorph to the semi-supervised setting by modifying the loss function to incorporate existing training segmentation maps:

$$\mathcal{L}_h(\theta_h; \mathcal{D}) = \mathbb{E}_\Lambda \sum_{m,f \in \mathcal{D}} \Big[(1-\lambda)(1-\gamma)\mathcal{L}_{sim}(f, m \circ \phi; \lambda_{sim})$$

$$+ \lambda\mathcal{L}_{reg}(\phi; \lambda_{reg}) + (1-\lambda)\gamma\mathcal{L}_{seg}(s_f, s_m \circ \phi)\Big], \quad (3)$$

where $\mathcal{L}_{seg}$ is a segmentation similarity metric, usually the Dice coefficient [18], weighted by the hyperparameter γ, and s_m and s_f are the segmentation maps of the moving and fixed images, respectively.

3.2 Hyperparameter Tuning

Given a test image pair $\{m, f\}$, a trained HyperMorph model can efficiently yield the deformation field as a function of important hyperparameters. If no external information is available, optimal hyperparameters may be rapidly tuned in an interactive fashion. However, landmarks or segmentation maps are sometimes available for validation subjects, enabling rapid automatic tuning.

Interactive. Sliders can be used to change hyperparameter values in near real-time until the user is visually satisfied with the registration of some image pair $\{m, f\}$. In some cases, the user might choose different settings when studying specific regions of the image. For example, the optimal value of the λ hyperparameter (balancing the regularization and the image-matching term) can vary by anatomical structure in the brain (see Fig. 7). This interactive tuning technique is possible because of the HyperMorph ability to efficiently yield the effect of λ values on the deformation ϕ.

Automatic. If segmentation maps $\{s_m, s_f\}$ are available for validation, a single trained HyperMorph model enables hyperparameter optimization using

$$\Lambda^* = \arg\max_\Lambda \mathcal{L}(\Lambda; \theta_h, \mathcal{D}, \mathcal{V}) = \arg\max_\Lambda \sum_{\substack{(m,f) \in \mathcal{D}^2 \\ (s_m, s_f) \in \mathcal{V}^2}} \mathcal{L}_{val}(s_f, s_m \circ \phi), \quad (4)$$

where $\mathcal{V}$ is a set of validation segmentation maps and $\phi = g_{h(\Lambda)}(m, f)$, as before. We implement this optimization by freezing the learned hypernetwork parameters θ_h, treating the input Λ as a parameter to be learned, and using stochastic gradient strategies to rapidly optimize (4).

3.3 Implementation

The hypernetwork we use in the experiments consists of four fully connected layers, each with 64 units and ReLu activation except for the final layer, which uses Tanh activations. The proposed method applies to any registration network architecture, and we treat the hypernetwork and the registration network as a single, large network. The only trainable parameters θ_h are those of the hypernetwork. We implement HyperMorph with the open-source VoxelMorph library [7], using a U-Net-like [47] registration architecture. The U-Net in this network consists of a 4-layer convolutional encoder (with 16, 32, 32, and 32 channels), a 4-layer convolutional decoder (with 32 channels for each layer), and 3 more convolutional layers (of 32, 16, and 16 channels). This results in a total of 313,507 convolutional parameters that are provided as output by the hypernetwork. We use the ADAM optimizer [31] during training.

4 Experiments

We demonstrate that a single HyperMorph model performs on par with and captures the behavior of a rich landscape of individual registration networks trained with separate hyperparameter values, while incurring substantially less computational cost and human effort. We test models with one or two registration hyperparameters. Next, we illustrate considerable improvements in robustness to initialization. Finally, we demonstrate the powerful utility of HyperMorph for rapid hyperparameter optimization at validation—for different subpopulations of data, registration types, and individual anatomical structures.

Datasets. We use two large sets of 3D brain magnetic resonance (MR) images. The first is a multi-site dataset of 30,495 T1-weighted (T1w) scans gathered across 8 public datasets: ABIDE [17], ADHD200 [43], ADNI [55], GSP [14], MCIC [24], PPMI [42], OASIS [41], and UK Biobank [51]. We divide this dataset into train, validation, and test sets of sizes 10,000, 10,000, and 10,495, respectively. The second dataset involves a multi-modal collection of 1,558 T1w, T2-weighted (T2w), multi-flip-angle, and multi-inversion-time images gathered from in-house data and the public ADNI and HCP [11] datasets. We divide this dataset into train, validation, and test sets of sizes 528, 515, and 515, respectively. All MRI scans are conformed to a $256 \times 256 \times 256$ 1-mm isotropic grid space, bias-corrected, and skull-stripped using FreeSurfer [20], and we also produce automated segmentation maps for evaluation. We affinely normalize and uniformly crop all images to $160 \times 192 \times 224$ volumes.

Evaluation. For evaluation, we use the volume overlap of anatomical label maps using the Dice metric [18].

Baseline Models. HyperMorph can be applied to any learning-based registration architecture, and we seek to validate its ability to capture the effects of hyperparameters on the inner registration network $g_{\theta_g}(\cdot)$. To enable this insight, we train standard VoxelMorph models with architectures identical to $g_{\theta_g}(\cdot)$ as baselines, each with its fixed set of hyperparameters.

4.1 Experiment 1: HyperMorph Efficiency and Capacity

We aim to evaluate if a single HyperMorph is capable of encapsulating a landscape of baseline models.

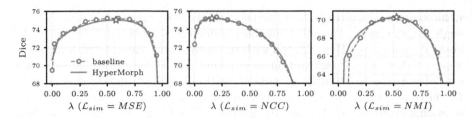

Fig. 3. Mean Dice scores achieved by a single HyperMorph model (blue) and baselines trained for different regularization weights λ (gray) when using each of the MSE, NCC and NMI similarity metrics, respectively. Optima λ^* computed with HyperMorph are indicated by the star markers. (Color figure online)

Setup. We first assess how the accuracy and computational cost of a single HyperMorph model compare to standard grid hyperparameter search for the regularization weight λ. We separately train HyperMorph as well as VoxelMorph baselines using the similarity metrics MSE (scaled by a constant estimated image noise) and NCC (with window size 9^3) for within-modality registration and NMI (with 32 fixed bins) for cross-modality registration, for which we train 13, 13, and 11 baseline models, respectively. We validate the trained networks on 100 random image pairs for visualization. For hyperparameter optimization after training, we use a subset of 20 pairs.

Additionally, we assess the ability of HyperMorph to learn the effect of multiple hyperparameters simultaneously. We first train a HyperMorph model treating λ and the local NCC window size as hyperparameters. We also train a semi-supervised HyperMorph model based on a subset of six labels, and hold out six other labels for validation. In this experiment, the hyperparameters of interest are λ and the relative weight γ of the semi-supervised loss (3). Training baselines requires a two-dimensional grid search on 3D models and is computationally prohibitive. Consequently, we conduct these experiments in 2D on a mid-coronal slice, using baselines for 25 combinations of hyperparameter values.

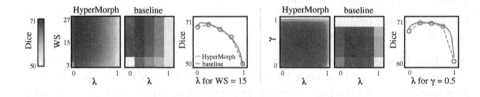

Fig. 4. Two-dimensional hyperparameter search. Left: unsupervised registration with regularization weight λ and local NCC window size WS. Right: semi-supervised registration with hyperparameters λ and segmentation supervision weight γ. For the semi-supervised models, we compute total Dice on both training and held-out labels.

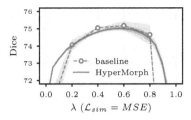 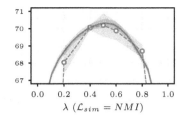

Fig. 5. Variability across several model initializations for HyperMorph and baselines. The shaded areas indicate the standard deviation of registration accuracy, which is substantially more narrow for HyperMorph.

Results. *Computational Cost.* A single HyperMorph model requires substantially less time to convergence than a baseline-model grid search. For single-hyperparameter tests, HyperMorph requires 5.2 ± 0.2 times fewer GPU-hours than a grid search with baseline models (Table 1). For models with two hyperparameters, the difference is even more striking, with HyperMorph requiring 10.5 ± 0.2 times fewer GPU-hours than the baseline models.

Performance. Figures 3 and 4 show that HyperMorph yields optimal hyperparameter values similar to those obtained from a dense grid of baseline models despite the significant computational advantage. An average difference in the optimal hyperparameter value λ^* of only 0.04 ± 0.02 across single-hyperparameter experiments results in a negligible maximum Dice difference of 0.16 ± 0.03 (on a scale of 0 to 100). Similarly, multi-hyperparameter experiments yield a maximum Dice difference of only 0.32 ± 0.02. In practice, fewer baselines might be trained at first for a coarser hyperparameter search, resulting in either suboptimal hyperparameter choice or sequential search leading to substantial manual overhead.

Overall, a *single* HyperMorph model is able to capture the behavior of a range of baseline models individually optimized for different hyperparameters, facilitating optimal hyperparameter choices and accuracy at a substantial reduction in computational cost. We emphasize that the goal of the experiment is not to compare HyperMorph to a particular registration tool, but to demonstrate the effect that this strategy can have on an existing registration network.

Table 1. Comparison between HyperMorph and baseline grid-search techniques for model variability across random initializations (left) and for runtimes (right). We provide runtimes separately for experiments with 1 and 2 hyperparameters (HP).

	Robustness (init SD)		Runtime (total GPU-hours)	
	MSE	NMI	1 HP (3D)	2 HPs (2D)
HyperMorph	**1.97e − 1**	**2.46 − 1**	**146.9 ± 32.0**	**4.2 ± 0.6**
Baseline	5.50e − 1	5.32e − 1	765.3 ± 249.1	44.0 ± 4.6

4.2   Experiment 2: Robustness to Initialization

Setup. We evaluate the robustness of each strategy to network initialization. We repeat the previous, single-hyperparameter experiment with MSE and NMI, retraining four HyperMorph models and four *sets* of baselines each trained for five values of hyperparameter λ. For each training run, we re-initialize all kernel weights using Glorot uniform [23] with a different seed. We evaluate each model using 100 image pairs and compare the standard deviation (SD) across initializations of the HyperMorph and baseline networks.

Results. Figure 5 shows that HyperMorph is substantially more robust (lower SD) to initialization compared to the baselines, suggesting that HyperMorph is less likely to converge to local minima. Across the entire range of λ, the average Dice SD for HyperMorph models trained with MSE is 2.79 times lower than for baseline SD, and for NMI-trained models, HyperMorph SD is 2.16 times lower than baseline SD (Table 1). This result further emphasizes the computational efficiency provided by HyperMorph, since in typical hyperparameter searches, models are often trained multiple times for each hyperparameter value to negate potential bias from initialization variability.

4.3   Experiment 3: Hyperparameter-Tuning Utility

Setup. *Interactive Tuning.* We demonstrate the utility of HyperMorph through an interactive tool that enables visual optimization of hyperparameters even if no segmentation data are available. The user can explore the effect of *continuously varying* hyperparameter values using a single trained model and choose an optimal deformation manually at high precision. Interactive tuning can be explored at http://voxelmorph.mit.edu.

Automatic Tuning. When anatomical annotations are available for validation, we demonstrate rapid, automatic optimization of the hyperparameter λ across a variety of applications. In each experiment, we identify the optimal regularization weight λ^* given 20 registration pairs and use 100 registration pairs for evaluation. First, we investigate how λ^* differs across subpopulations and anatomical regions. We train HyperMorph on a subset of image pairs across the entire T1w training set, and at validation we optimize λ separately for each of ABIDE, GSP, PPMI, and UK Biobank. With this same model, we identify λ^* separately for each of 10 anatomical regions. Second, we explore how λ^* differs between cross-sectional and longitudinal registration; for HyperMorph trained on both within-subject and cross-subject pairs from ADNI, we optimize λ separately for validation pairs within and across subjects.

Results. Figures 6 and 7 show that λ^* varies substantially across subpopulations, registration tasks, and anatomical regions. For example, PPMI and ABIDE require a significantly different value of λ^* than GSP and the UK Biobank. Importantly, with a suboptimal choice of hyperparameters, these datasets would

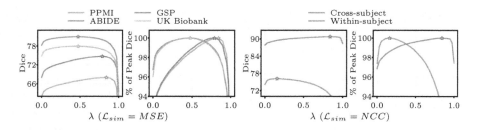

Fig. 6. Registration accuracy across dataset subpopulations (left) and registration tasks (right). The stars indicate the optimal value λ^* as identified by automatic hyperparameter optimization.

have yielded considerably lower registration quality (Dice scores). The variability in the optimal hyperparameter values is likely caused by differences between the datasets; the average age of the ABIDE population is lower than those of other datasets, while the PPMI scans are of lower quality. Similarly, cross-subject and within-subject registration require different levels of regularization. Finally, Fig. 7 illustrates that λ^* varies by anatomical region, suggesting that regularization weights should be chosen by users depending on their tasks downstream from the registration. On average, the automatic hyperparameter optimization takes just 2.8 ± 0.3 min using 20 validation pairs.

The vast majority of existing registration pipelines assume a single hyperparameter value to be optimal for an entire dataset, or even across multiple datasets. Our results highlight the importance of HyperMorph as a rapid, easy-to-use tool for finding optimal hyperparameters, interactively or automatically, for different subpopulations, tasks, or even individual anatomical regions, without the need to retrain models.

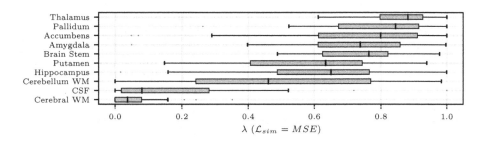

Fig. 7. Optimal regularization weights λ^* across individual anatomical labels. The ranges shown are estimated with HyperMorph for each set of image pairs.

5   Conclusion

The accuracy of deformable image registration algorithms greatly depends upon the choice of hyperparameters. In this work, we present HyperMorph, a learning-based strategy that removes the need to repeatedly train models to quantify the effects of hyperparameters on model performance. HyperMorph employs a hypernetwork which takes the desired hyperparameters as input and predicts the parameters of a registration network tuned to these values. In contrast to existing learning-based methods, HyperMorph estimates optimal deformation fields for arbitrary image pairs and *any* hyperparameter value from a continuous interval by exploiting sharing of similar weights across the landscape of registration networks. A single HyperMorph model then enables fast hyperparameter tuning at test-time, requiring dramatically less compute and human time compared to existing methods. This is a significant advantage over registration frameworks that are optimized across discrete, predefined hyperparameter values in the hope of finding an optimal configuration.

We demonstrate that a single HyperMorph model facilitates discovery of optimal hyperparameter values for different dataset subpopulations, registration tasks, or even individual anatomical regions. This last result indicates a potential benefit and future direction of estimating a spatially varying field of smoothness hyperparameters for simultaneously optimal registration of all anatomical structures. HyperMorph also provides the flexibility to identify the ideal hyperparameter for an individual image pair. For example, a pair of subjects with very different anatomies would benefit from weak regularization allowing warps of high non-linearity. We are eager to explore hypernetworks for a greater number of hyperparameters. We believe HyperMorph will drastically alleviate the burden of retraining networks with different hyperparameter values, thereby enabling efficient development of finely optimized models for image registration.

Acknowledgements. Support for this research was provided by BRAIN U01 MH117023, NIBIB P41 EB015896, R01 EB023281, R01 EB006758, R21 EB018907, R01 EB019956, P41 EB030006, NIA R56 AG064027, R01 AG064027, AG008122, AG016495, NIMH R01 MH123195, NINDS R01 NS0525851, R21 NS072652, R01 NS070963 and NS083534, U01 NS086625, U24 NS10059103, R01 NS105820, NIH BNR U01 MH093765, the HCP, NICHD K99 HD101553, SIG RR023401, RR019307, and RR023043, and the Wistron Corporation. BF has a financial interest in CorticoMetrics which is reviewed and managed by MGH and MGB.

References

1. Arsigny, V., Commowick, O., Pennec, X., Ayache, N.: A log-Euclidean framework for statistics on diffeomorphisms. In: Larsen, R., Nielsen, M., Sporring, J. (eds.) MICCAI 2006, Part I. LNCS, vol. 4190, pp. 924–931. Springer, Heidelberg (2006). https://doi.org/10.1007/11866565_113
2. Ashburner, J.: A fast diffeomorphic image registration algorithm. Neuroimage **38**(1), 95–113 (2007)

3. Ashburner, J., Friston, K.J.: Voxel-based morphometry-the methods. Neuroimage **11**, 805–821 (2000)
4. Avants, B.B., Epstein, C.L., Grossman, M., Gee, J.C.: Symmetric diffeomorphic image registration with cross-correlation: evaluating automated labeling of elderly and neurodegenerative brain. MedIA **12**(1), 26–41 (2008)
5. Avants, B.B., Tustison, N.J., Song, G., Cook, P.A., Klein, A., Gee, J.C.: A reproducible evaluation of ants similarity metric performance in brain image registration. Neuroimage **54**(3), 2033–2044 (2011)
6. Bajcsy, R., Kovacic, S.: Multiresolution elastic matching. Comput. Vis. Graph. Image Process. **46**, 1–21 (1989)
7. Balakrishnan, G., Zhao, A., Sabuncu, M.R., Guttag, J., Dalca, A.V.: VoxelMorph: a learning framework for deformable medical image registration. IEEE TMI **38**(8), 1788–1800 (2019)
8. Beg, M.F., Miller, M.I., Trouvé, A., Younes, L.: Computing large deformation metric mappings via geodesic flows of diffeomorphisms. IJCV **61**(2), 139–157 (2005). https://doi.org/10.1023/B:VISI.0000043755.93987.aa
9. Bergstra, J., Bengio, Y.: Random search for hyper-parameter optimization. JMLR **13**(1), 281–305 (2012)
10. Bergstra, J.S., Bardenet, R., Bengio, Y., Kégl, B.: Algorithms for hyper-parameter optimization. In: NeurIPS, pp. 2546–2554 (2011)
11. Bookheimer, S.Y., et al.: The lifespan human connectome project in aging: an overview. NeuroImage **185**, 335–348 (2019)
12. Brock, A., Lim, T., Ritchie, J.M., Weston, N.: Smash: one-shot model architecture search through hypernetworks. arXiv preprint arXiv:1708.05344 (2017)
13. Cao, Y., Miller, M.I., Winslow, R.L., Younes, L.: Large deformation diffeomorphic metric mapping of vector fields. IEEE TMI **24**(9), 1216–1230 (2005)
14. Dagley, A., et al.: Harvard aging brain study: dataset and accessibility. NeuroImage **144**, 255–258 (2017)
15. Dalca, A.V., Balakrishnan, G., Guttag, J., Sabuncu, M.: Unsupervised learning of probabilistic diffeomorphic registration for images and surfaces. Med. Image Anal. **57**, 226–236 (2019)
16. Dalca, A.V., Bobu, A., Rost, N.S., Golland, P.: Patch-based discrete registration of clinical brain images. In: Wu, G., Coupé, P., Zhan, Y., Munsell, B.C., Rueckert, D. (eds.) Patch-MI 2016. LNCS, vol. 9993, pp. 60–67. Springer, Cham (2016). https://doi.org/10.1007/978-3-319-47118-1_8
17. DI Martino, A., et al.: The autism brain imaging data exchange: towards a large-scale evaluation of the intrinsic brain architecture in autism. Mol. Psychiatry **19**(6), 659–667 (2014)
18. Dice, L.R.: Measures of the amount of ecologic association between species. Ecology **26**(3), 297–302 (1945)
19. Domhan, T., Springenberg, J.T., Hutter, F.: Speeding up automatic hyperparameter optimization of deep neural networks by extrapolation of learning curves. In: Twenty-Fourth International Joint Conference on Artificial Intelligence (2015)
20. Fischl, B.: Freesurfer. Neuroimage **62**(2), 774–781 (2012)
21. Franceschi, L., Frasconi, P., Salzo, S., Grazzi, R., Pontil, M.: Bilevel programming for hyperparameter optimization and meta-learning. arXiv preprint arXiv:1806.04910 (2018)
22. Glocker, B., Komodakis, N., Tziritas, G., Navab, N., Paragios, N.: Dense image registration through MRFs and efficient linear programming. MedIA **12**(6), 731–741 (2008)

23. Glorot, X., Bengio, Y.: Understanding the difficulty of training deep feedforward neural networks. In: AISTATS, pp. 249–256 (2010)
24. Gollub, R.L., et al.: The MCIC collection: a shared repository of multi-modal, multi-site brain image data from a clinical investigation of schizophrenia. Neuroinformatics **11**(3), 367–388 (2013). https://doi.org/10.1007/s12021-013-9184-3
25. Ha, D., Dai, A., Le, Q.V.: Hypernetworks. arXiv preprint arXiv:1609.09106 (2016)
26. Hoffmann, M., Billot, B., Iglesias, J.E., Fischl, B., Dalca, A.V.: Learning image registration without images (2020)
27. Hu, Y., et al.: Weakly-supervised convolutional neural networks for multimodal image registration. MedIA **49**, 1–13 (2018)
28. Jamieson, K., Talwalkar, A.: Non-stochastic best arm identification and hyperparameter optimization. In: AISTATS, pp. 240–248 (2016)
29. Joshi, S.C., Miller, M.I.: Landmark matching via large deformation diffeomorphisms. IEEE TIP **9**(8), 1357–1370 (2000)
30. Kandasamy, K., Dasarathy, G., Schneider, J., Póczos, B.: Multi-fidelity bayesian optimisation with continuous approximations. arXiv preprint arXiv:1703.06240 (2017)
31. Kingma, D.P., Ba, J.: Adam: A method for stochastic optimization. arXiv preprint arXiv:1412.6980 (2014)
32. Klein, A., Falkner, S., Springenberg, J.T., Hutter, F.: Learning curve prediction with Bayesian neural networks (2016)
33. Klocek, S., Maziarka, Ł., Wołczyk, M., Tabor, J., Nowak, J., Śmieja, M.: Hypernetwork functional image representation. In: Tetko, I.V., Kůrková, V., Karpov, P., Theis, F. (eds.) ICANN 2019. LNCS, vol. 11731, pp. 496–510. Springer, Cham (2019). https://doi.org/10.1007/978-3-030-30493-5_48
34. Krebs, J., Delingette, H., Mailhé, B., Ayache, N., Mansi, T.: Learning a probabilistic model for diffeomorphic registration. IEEE TMI **38**(9), 2165–2176 (2019)
35. Krebs, J., et al.: Robust non-rigid registration through agent-based action learning. In: Descoteaux, M., Maier-Hein, L., Franz, A., Jannin, P., Collins, D.L., Duchesne, S. (eds.) MICCAI 2017. LNCS, vol. 10433, pp. 344–352. Springer, Cham (2017). https://doi.org/10.1007/978-3-319-66182-7_40
36. Li, L., Jamieson, K., DeSalvo, G., Rostamizadeh, A., Talwalkar, A.: Hyperband: a novel bandit-based approach to hyperparameter optimization. JMLR **18**(1), 6765–6816 (2017)
37. Lorraine, J., Duvenaud, D.: Stochastic hyperparameter optimization through hypernetworks. arXiv preprint arXiv:1802.09419 (2018)
38. Luketina, J., Berglund, M., Greff, K., Raiko, T.: Scalable gradient-based tuning of continuous regularization hyperparameters. In: ICML, pp. 2952–2960 (2016)
39. MacKay, M., Vicol, P., Lorraine, J., Duvenaud, D., Grosse, R.: Self-tuning networks: Bilevel optimization of hyperparameters using structured best-response functions. arXiv preprint arXiv:1903.03088 (2019)
40. Maclaurin, D., Duvenaud, D., Adams, R.: Gradient-based hyperparameter optimization through reversible learning. In: ICML, pp. 2113–2122 (2015)
41. Marcus, D.S., Wang, T.H., Parker, J., Csernansky, J.G., Morris, J.C., Buckner, R.L.: Open access series of imaging studies (OASIS): cross-sectional MRI data in young, middle aged, nondemented, and demented older adults. J. Cogn. Neurosci. **19**(9), 1498–1507 (2007)
42. Marek, K., et al.: The Parkinson progression marker initiative (PPMI). Prog. Neurobi. **95**(4), 629–635 (2011)

43. Milham, M.P., Fair, D., Mennes, M., Mostofsky, S.H., et al.: The ADHD-200 consortium: a model to advance the translational potential of neuroimaging in clinical neuroscience. Frontiers Syst. Neurosci. **6**, 62 (2012)

44. Miller, M.I., Beg, M.F., Ceritoglu, C., Stark, C.: Increasing the power of functional maps of the medial temporal lobe by using large deformation diffeomorphic metric mapping. PNAS **102**(27), 9685–9690 (2005)

45. Pedregosa, F.: Hyperparameter optimization with approximate gradient. arXiv preprint arXiv:1602.02355 (2016)

46. Rohé, M.-M., Datar, M., Heimann, T., Sermesant, M., Pennec, X.: SVF-net: learning deformable image registration using shape matching. In: Descoteaux, M., Maier-Hein, L., Franz, A., Jannin, P., Collins, D.L., Duchesne, S. (eds.) MICCAI 2017, Part I. LNCS, vol. 10433, pp. 266–274. Springer, Cham (2017). https://doi.org/10.1007/978-3-319-66182-7_31

47. Ronneberger, O., Fischer, P., Brox, T.: U-net: convolutional networks for biomedical image segmentation. In: Navab, N., Hornegger, J., Wells, W.M., Frangi, A.F. (eds.) MICCAI 2015, Part III. LNCS, vol. 9351, pp. 234–241. Springer, Cham (2015). https://doi.org/10.1007/978-3-319-24574-4_28

48. Rueckert, D., Sonoda, L.I., Hayes, C., Hill, D.L., Leach, M.O., Hawkes, D.J.: Nonrigid registration using free-form deformation: Application to breast mr images. IEEE TMI **18**(8), 712–721 (1999)

49. Schmidhuber, J.: A 'self-referential' weight matrix. In: Gielen, S., Kappen, B. (eds.) ICANN 1993, pp. 446–450. Springer, London (1993). https://doi.org/10.1007/978-1-4471-2063-6_107

50. Sokooti, H., de Vos, B., Berendsen, F., Lelieveldt, B.P.F., Išgum, I., Staring, M.: Nonrigid image registration using multi-scale 3D convolutional neural networks. In: Descoteaux, M., Maier-Hein, L., Franz, A., Jannin, P., Collins, D.L., Duchesne, S. (eds.) MICCAI 2017, Part I. LNCS, vol. 10433, pp. 232–239. Springer, Cham (2017). https://doi.org/10.1007/978-3-319-66182-7_27

51. Sudlow, C., et al.: UK biobank: an open access resource for identifying the causes of a wide range of complex diseases of middle and old age. Plos med **12**(3), e1001779 (2015)

52. Vercauteren, T., Pennec, X., Perchant, A., Ayache, N.: Diffeomorphic demons: efficient non-parametric image registration. NeuroImage **45**(1), S61–S72 (2009)

53. Viola, P., Wells III, W.M.: Alignment by maximization of mutual information. Int. J. Comput. Vis. **24**(2), 137–154 (1997). https://doi.org/10.1023/A:1007958904918

54. de Vos, B.D., Berendsen, F.F., Viergever, M.A., Sokooti, H., Staring, M., Išgum, I.: A deep learning framework for unsupervised affine and deformable image registration. MedIA **52**, 128–143 (2019)

55. Weiner, M.W.: Alzheimer's disease neuroimaging initiative (ADNI) database (2003)

56. Wu, G., Kim, M., Wang, Q., Munsell, B.C., Shen, D.: Scalable high-performance image registration framework by unsupervised deep feature representations learning. IEEE Trans. Biomed. Eng. **63**(7), 1505–1516 (2015)

57. Yang, X., Kwitt, R., Styner, M., Niethammer, M.: Quicksilver: fast predictive image registration - a deep learning approach. NeuroImage **158**, 378–396 (2017)

58. Zhan, M., et al.: Frequency diffeomorphisms for efficient image registration. In: Niethammer, M., et al. (eds.) IPMI 2017. LNCS, vol. 10265, pp. 559–570. Springer, Cham (2017). https://doi.org/10.1007/978-3-319-59050-9_44

Deep Learning Based Geometric Registration for Medical Images: How Accurate Can We Get Without Visual Features?

Lasse Hansen[(✉)] and Mattias P. Heinrich

Institute of Medical Informatics, Universität zu Lübeck, Lübeck, Germany
{hansen,heinrich}@imi.uni-luebeck.de

Abstract. As in other areas of medical image analysis, e.g. semantic segmentation, deep learning is currently driving the development of new approaches for image registration. Multi-scale encoder-decoder network architectures achieve state-of-the-art accuracy on tasks such as intra-patient alignment of abdominal CT or brain MRI registration, especially when additional supervision, such as anatomical labels, is available. The success of these methods relies to a large extent on the outstanding ability of deep CNNs to extract descriptive visual features from the input images. In contrast to conventional methods, the explicit inclusion of geometric information plays only a minor role, if at all. In this work we take a look at an exactly opposite approach by investigating a deep learning framework for registration based solely on geometric features and optimisation. We combine graph convolutions with loopy belief message passing to enable highly accurate 3D point cloud registration. Our experimental validation is conducted on complex key-point graphs of inner lung structures, strongly outperforming dense encoder-decoder networks and other point set registration methods. Our code is publicly available at https://github.com/multimodallearning/deep-geo-reg.

Keywords: Deformable registration · Geometric learning · Belief propagation

1 Introduction

Current learning approaches for medical image analysis predominantly consider the processing of volumetric scans as a dense voxel-based task. However, the underlying anatomy could in many cases be modelled more efficiently using only a sparse subset of relevant geometric keypoints. When sufficient amounts of labelled training data are available and the region of interest can be robustly initialised, sparse surface segmentation models have been largely outperformed by dense fully-convolutional networks in the past few years [12]. However, dense learning based image registration has not yet reached the accuracy of conventional methods for the estimation of large deformations where geometry matters

© Springer Nature Switzerland AG 2021
A. Feragen et al. (Eds.): IPMI 2021, LNCS 12729, pp. 18–30, 2021.
https://doi.org/10.1007/978-3-030-78191-0_2

- e.g. for inspiration-expiration lung CT alignment. The combination of iconic (image-based) and geometric registration approaches have excelled in deformable lung registration but they are often time-consuming and rely on multiple steps of pre-alignment, mask-registration, graph-based optimisation and multi-level continuous refinement with different image-based metrics [22]. In this work, we aim to address 3D lung registration as a purely geometric alignment of two point clouds (a few thousand 3D points for inhale and exhale lungs each). While this certainly reduces the complexity of the dense deformable 3D registration task, it may also reduce the accuracy since intensity- and edge-based clues are no longer present. Yet, we demonstrate in our experimental validation that even this limited search range for potential displacements leads to huge and significant gains compared to dense learning based registration frameworks - mainly stemming from the robustness of our framework to implicitly learn the geometric alignment of vessel and airway trees.

1.1   Related Work

Point Cloud Learning: Conventional point cloud registration (iterative closest point, coherent point drift) [18] often focused on the direct alignment of unstructured 3D points based on their coordinates. Newer work on graph convolutional learning has demonstrated that relevant geometric features can be extracted from point clouds with neighbourhood relations defined on kNN graphs and enable semantic labeling or global classification of shapes, object parts and human poses and gestures [3,21]. Graph Convolutional Networks (GCN) [13] define localised filter and use a polynomial series of the graph Laplacian (Tschebyscheff polynomials) further simplified to the immediate neighbourhood of each node. The graph attention networks introduced in [26] are a promising extension based on attention mechanism. Similarly, dynamic edge convolutions [27] achieve information propagation by learning a function that predicts pairwise edge weights based on previous features of both considered nodes.

Learning Based Image Registration: In image registration, learning based methods have surpassed their untrained optimisation-based counterparts in terms of accuracy and speed for 2D optical flow estimation, where millions of realistic ground truth displacement fields can be generated [25]. Advantages have also been found for certain 3D medical registration tasks, for which thousands of scans with pixel-level expert annotations are available and the complexity of deformations is well represented in the training dataset [2,16,28]. As evident from a recent medical registration challenge [11], deep learning has not yet reached the accuracy and robustness for inspiration to expiration CT lung registration, where detailed anatomical labels are scarce (learning lobe alignment might not directly translate into low registration errors [10]) and the motion is large and complex. Even for the simpler case of shallow breathing in 4D CT, few learning-based works have come close to the best conventional methods (e.g. [22]) despite increasingly complex network pipelines [6].

Learning Graphical Registration: More recent research in computer vision has also explored geometric learning for 3D scene flow [14] that aims to register two 3D point clouds by finding soft correspondences. The challenge stems from the difficulty of jointly embedding two irregular point cloud (sub-)sets to enable end-to-end learning of geometric features and correspondence scores. Other recent approaches in point set registration/matching combine deep feature learning with GCNs and classical optimisation techniques, to solve the optimal transport [20] or reformulate traditional matching algorithms into deep network modules [23]. In the medical domain, combining sparse MRF-based registration [24] and multi-level continuous refinement [22] yielded the highest accuracy for two 3D lung benchmarks comprising inspiration and expiration [4,17].

We strongly believe that geometry can be a key element in advancing learning based registration and that the focus on visual features and fully-convolutional networks has for certain applications diverted research from mathematically proven graphical concepts that can excel within geometric networks.

1.2   Contribution

We propose a novel geometric learning method for large motion estimation across lung respiration that combines graph convolutional networks on keypoint clouds with sparse message passing. Our method considers geometric registration as soft correspondence search between two keypoint clouds with a restricted set of candidates from the moving point cloud for each fixed keypoint. **1)** We are the first to combine edge convolutions as end-to-end geometric feature learning from sparse keypoints with differentiable loopy belief propagation (discrete optimisation) for regularisation of displacements on a kNN graph adapted to irregular sets of candidates for each node. **2)** Our compact yet elegant networks, demonstrate surprisingly large gains in accuracy and outperform deep learning approaches that make use of additional visual clues by more than 50% reduced target registration errors for lung scans of COPD patients. **3)** We present a further novel variant of our approach that discretises the sparse correspondence probabilities using differentiable extrapolation for a further six fold gain in computational efficiency and with similar accuracy.

2   Methods

2.1   Loopy Belief Propagation for Regularised Registration of Keypoint Graphs

We aim to align two point clouds, a fixed point cloud P_f ($|P_f| = N_f$) and a moving point cloud P_m ($|P_m| = N_m$). They consist of distinctive keypoints $\mathbf{p}_{f_i} \in P_f$ and $\mathbf{p}_{m_i} \in P_m$. We further define a symmetric k-nearest neighbour (kNN) graph on P_f with edges $(ij) \in E$ that connect keypoints $\mathbf{p}_{f_i}$ and $\mathbf{p}_{f_j}$. A displacement vector $\mathbf{v}_i \in V$ for each fixed keypoint $\mathbf{p}_{f_i}$ is derived from soft correspondences from a restricted set of possible candidates $\mathbf{c}_i^p \in C_i$ (determined by l-nearest

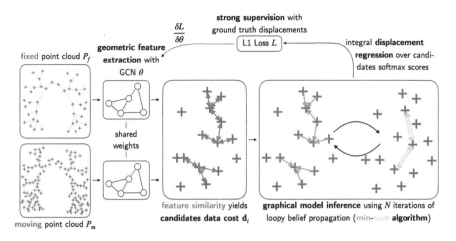

Fig. 1. Overview of our proposed method for accurate point cloud alignment using geometric features combined with loopy belief propagation in an end-to-end trainable deep learning registration framework.

neighbour search ($|C_i| = l$) in the moving point cloud P_m). The regularised motion vector field V is inferred using loopy belief propagation enforcing spatial coherence of motion vectors. The data cost d_i^p ($\mathbf{d}_i = (d_i^1, \ldots, d_i^p, \ldots, d_i^l)$) for a fixed point $\mathbf{p}_{f_i}$ and a single candidate $\mathbf{c}_i^p$ is modeled as

$$d_i^p = \|\theta(\mathbf{p}_{f_i}) - \theta(\mathbf{c}_i^p)\|_2^2, \tag{1}$$

where $\theta(.)$ denotes a general feature transformation of the input point (e.g. deep learning based geometric features, cf. Sect. 2.2). Especially in this case of sparse to sparse inference, missing or noisy correspondences can lead to severe registration errors. Therefore, a robust regularisation between neighbouring fixed keypoints (defined by edges $(ij) \in E$) is enforced by penalizing the deviation of relative displacements. The regularisation cost r_{ij}^{pq} ($\mathbf{r}_{ij}^q = (r_{ij}^{1q}, \ldots, r_{ij}^{pq}, \ldots, r_{ij}^{lq})$) for two fixed keypoints $\mathbf{p}_{f_i}, \mathbf{p}_{f_j}$ and candidates $\mathbf{c}_i^p, \mathbf{c}_j^q$ can then be described as

$$r_{ij}^{pq} = \left\|(\mathbf{c}_i^p - \mathbf{p}_{f_i}) - (\mathbf{c}_j^q - \mathbf{p}_{f_j})\right\|_2^2. \tag{2}$$

To compute the marginal distributions of soft correspondences over the fixed kNN graph we employ N iterations of loopy belief propagation (min-sum algorithm) with outgoing messages $\mathbf{m}_{i \to j}^t$ from $\mathbf{p}_{f_i}$ to $\mathbf{p}_{f_j}$ at iteration t defined as

$$\mathbf{m}_{i \to j}^t = \min_{1, \ldots, q, \ldots l} \left(\mathbf{d}_i + \alpha \mathbf{r}_{ij}^q - \mathbf{m}_{j \to i}^{t-1} + \sum_{(h,i) \in E} \mathbf{m}_{h \to i}^{t-1} \right). \tag{3}$$

The hyperparameter α weights the displacement deviation penalty and thus controls the smoothness of the motion vector field V. Initial messages $\mathbf{m}_{i \to j}^0$ are set to 0. A graphical description of the presented message passing scheme is also

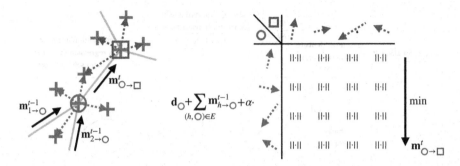

Fig. 2. Illustration of proposed message passing scheme for keypoint registration. The current outgoing message for the considered keypoint is composed of the candidates data cost and incoming messages from the previous iteration. In addition, the squared deviation (weighted by α) of candidate displacements is minimised for a coherent motion across the kNN graph. Reverse messages are not shown for visual clarity.

shown in Fig. 2 and for further in-depth details on efficient belief propagation the reader is referred to [5].

Fast Approximation Using a Discretised Candidates Space: While the proposed message passing approach is easily parallelisable, it still lacks some efficiency as the number of messages to compute for each keypoint is dependent on the number of neighbours k. We propose to reduce the number of message computations per node to 1 by discretising the sparse candidates cost $\mathbf{d}_i$ in a dense cost volume D_i with fixed grid resolution r. Voxelisation of sparse input has been used in point cloud learning to speed up computation [15]. D_i can be efficiently populated using nearest neighbour interpolation at (normalised) relative displacement locations $\mathbf{o_i^P} = (o_{i_x}^p, o_{i_y}^p, o_{i_z}^p) = \mathbf{c}_i^p - \mathbf{p}_{f_i}$, evaluating

$$D_i(u,v,w) = \frac{1}{N_{u,v,w}} \sum_{p=1}^{l} \mathbb{I}\big[\lfloor o_{i_x}^p r \rfloor = u, \lfloor o_{i_y}^p r \rfloor = v, \lfloor o_{i_z}^p r \rfloor = w\big] d_i^p, \qquad (4)$$

where (following notations in [15]) $\mathbb{I}[\cdot]$ denotes a binary indicator that specifies whether the location $\mathbf{o_i^P}$ belongs to the voxel grid (u, v, w) and $N_{u,v,w}$ is a normalisation factor (in case multiple displacements end up in the same voxel grid). By operating on the dense displacement space D_i, we can employ an efficient quadratic diffusion regularisation using min convolutions [5] that are separable in dimensions and also avoid the costly computation of k different messages per node. Approximation errors stem solely from the discretisation step.

2.2   Geometric Feature Extraction with Graph Convolutional Neural Networks

Distinctive keypoint graphs that describe plausible shapes contain inherent geometric information. These include local features such as curvature but also global semantics of the graph (e.g. surface or structure connectivity). Recent work on data-driven graph convolutional learning has shown that descriptive geometric features can be extracted from point clouds with neighbourhood relations defined based on kNN graphs. Edge convolutions [27] can be interpreted as irregular equivalents to dense convolutional kernels. Following notations in [27] we define edge features $\mathbf{e}_{ij} = h_\theta(\mathbf{f}_i, \mathbf{f}_j - \mathbf{f}_i)$, where $\mathbf{f}_i$ denote F-dimensionsal features on points $\mathbf{p}_i \in P$ (first feature layer given as $\mathbf{f}_i = \mathbf{p}_i$). The edge function h_θ computes the Euclidean inner product of the learnable parameters $\theta = (\theta_1, \ldots, \theta_F')$ with $\mathbf{f}_i$ (keypoint information) and $\mathbf{f}_j - \mathbf{f}_i$ (local neigbourhood information). The F'-dimensional feature output $\mathbf{f}'_i$ of an edge convolution is then given by

$$\mathbf{f}_i^{'} = \max_{(i,j)\in E} \mathbf{e}_{ij}, \tag{5}$$

where the max operation is to be understood as a dimension-wise aggregation function. Employing multiple layers of edge convolutions in a graph neural network and applying it to the fixed and moving point clouds (P_f, P_m) yields descriptive geometric features, which can be directly used to compute candidate data costs (see Eq. 1).

2.3 Deep Learning Based End-to-End Geometric Registration Framework

Having described the methodological details, we now summarise the full end-to-end registration framework (see Fig. 1 for an overview). Input to the registration framework are the fixed P_f and moving P_m point cloud. In a first step, descriptive geometric features are extracted from P_f and P_m with a graph convolutional network θ (shared weights). The network consists of three edge convolutional layers, whereby edge functions are implemented as three layers of 1×1 convolutions, instance normalisation and leaky ReLUs. Feature channels are increased from 3 to 64. Two 1×1 convolutions output the final 64-dimensional point feature embeddings. Thus, the total number of free trainable parameters of the network is 26880. In general, the moving cloud will contain more points than the fixed cloud (to enable an accurate correspondence search). To account for this higher density of P_m, the GCN θ acts on the kNN graph for P_f and on the $3k$NN graph for P_m. As described in Sect. 2.1 the geometric features $\theta(P_f)$ and $\theta(P_m)$ are used to compute the candidates cost and final marginal distributions are obtained from N iterations of (sparse or discretised) loopy belief propagation. As all operations in our optimisation step are differentiable the network parameters can be trained end-to-end. The training is supervised with ground truth motion vectors $\hat{\mathbf{v}}_i \in \hat{V}$ (based on 300 available manual annotated and corresponding landmark pairs) using an L1 loss (details on integral regression of the predicted motion vectors V from the marginals in Sect. 2.4).

2.4 Implementation Details: Keypoints, Visual Features and Integral Loss

While our method is generally applicable to a variety of point cloud tasks, we adapted parts of our implementation to keypoint registration of lung CT.

Keypoints: We extract Förstner keypoints with non-maximum suppression as described in [8]. A corner score (distinctiveness volume) is computed using $D(x) = 1/\operatorname{trace}\left((G_\sigma * (\nabla F \nabla F^T))^{-1}\right)$, where G_σ describes a Gaussian kernel and ∇F spatial gradients of the fixed/moving scans computed with a seven-point stencil. Additionally, we modify the extraction to allow for a higher spatial density of keypoints in the moving scan by means of trilinear upsampling of the volume before non-maximum suppression. Only points within the available lung masks are considered.

Visusal Features: To enable a fair comparison to state-of-the-art methods that are based on image intensities, we also evaluate variants of all geometric registration approaches with local MIND-SSC features [9]. These use a 12-channel representation of local self-similarity and are extracted as small patches of size $3 \times 3 \times 3$ with stride $= 2$. The dimensionality is then further reduced from 324 to 64 using a PCA (computed on each scan pair independently).

Integral Loss: As motivated before, we aim to find soft correspondences that enable the estimation of relative displacements, without directly matching a moving keypoint location, but rather a probability for each candidate. A softmax operator over all candidates is applied to the negated costs after loopy belief propagation (multiplied by a heuristic scalar factor). These normalised predictions are integrated over the corresponding relative displacements. When considering a discretised search space (the dLBP variant), final displacements are obtained via integration over the fully quantised 3D displacement space.

To obtain a dense displacement field for evaluation (landmarks do not necessarily coincide with keypoints), all displacement vectors of the sparse keypoints are accumulated in a displacement field tensor using trilinear extrapolation and spatial smoothing. This differentiable dense extrapolation enables the use of an L1 loss on (arbitrary) ground truth correspondences.

3   Experiments and Results

To demonstrate the effectiveness of our novel learning-based geometric 3D registration method, we perform extensive experimental validation on the DIR-Lab COPDgene data [4] that consists of 10 lung CT scan pairs at full inspiration (fixed) and full expiration (moving), annotated with 300 expert landmarks each. Our focus lies in evaluating point cloud registration without visual clues and we extract a limited number of keypoints (point clouds) in fixed ($\approx$2000 each) and moving scans ($\approx$6000 each) within the lungs. Since, learning benefits from a variability of data, we add 25 additional 3D scan pairs showing inhale-exhale CT from the EMPIRE10 [17] challenge, for which no landmarks are publicly

Table 1. Results of methods based on geometric features and optimisation on the COPDgene dataset [4]. We report the target registration error (TRE) in millimeters for individual cases as well as the average distance and standard deviation over all landmarks. The average GPU runtime in seconds is listed in the last row.

	Init	CPD	CPD+GF	sLBP	sLBP+GF (ours)	dLBP+GF (ours)
# 01	26.33	3.02	2.75	2.55	**1.88**	2.14
# 02	21.79	10.83	**5.96**	8.69	6.22	6.69
# 03	12.64	1.94	1.88	1.56	**1.53**	1.68
# 04	29.58	2.89	2.84	3.57	**2.63**	3.01
# 05	30.08	3.01	2.70	3.01	**2.02**	2.42
# 06	28.46	3.22	3.65	2.85	**2.21**	2.69
# 07	21.60	2.52	2.44	1.87	**1.64**	1.83
# 08	26.46	3.85	3.58	2.08	**1.93**	2.14
# 09	14.86	2.83	2.58	1.53	**1.55**	1.82
# 10	21.81	3.57	5.57	3.15	**2.79**	3.72
Avg.	23.36	3.77	3.40	3.08	**2.44**	2.81
Std.	11.86	2.54	1.35	2.09	1.40	1.50
Time		7.63	7.66	2.91	3.05	**0.49**

available and we only include automatic correspondences generated using [8] for supervision. We performed leave-one-out cross validation on the 10 COPD scans with sparse-to-dense extrapolation for landmark evaluation. Training was performed with a batch size of 4 and an initial learning rate of 0.01 for 150 epochs. All additional hyperparamters for baselines and our proposed methods (regularisation cost weighting α, scalar factor for integral loss, etc.) were tuned on case #04 of the COPDgene dataset and left unaltered for the remaining folds.

Overall, we compare five different algorithms that work purely on geometric information, five further methods that use visual input features and one deep-learning baseline for dense intensity registration (the winner of the Learn2Reg 2020 challenge LapIRN [16]). Firstly, we compare our proposed sparse-LBP regularisation with geometric feature learning (sLBP+GF) to a version without geometric learning (sLBP) and coherent point drift [18] without (CPD) and with geometric feature learning (CPD+GF). The non-learning based methods directly use the keypoint coordinates (x, y, z) as input features. In addition, we evaluate the novel discretisation of sparse candidates that is again integrated into an end-to-end geometric learning with differentiable LBP regularisation (dLBP+GF) and leads to substantial efficiency gains. The results clearly demonstrate the great potential of keypoint based registration for the complex task of large deformable lung registration. Numerical and qualitative results are shown in Table 1 and Fig. 3, respectively. Even the baseline methods using no features at all, CPD and sLBP, where inference is based only on optimisation on the extracted keypoint graphs, achieve convincing target registration errors

Table 2. Results of methods based on visual features on the COPDgene dataset [4]. We report the average TRE and standard deviation in millimeters over all landmarks. The average GPU runtime in seconds is listed in the last column. For easier comparison we also add the results of our "geometry only" approaches.

	Avg	Std	Time
init	23.36	11.86	
FLOT+MIND	5.87	1.30	1.63
LapIRN	4.99	1.98	1.08
FE+MIND	3.83	1.21	16.71
sPDD+MIND	3.16	0.69	2.17
CPD+MIND	2.40	0.81	13.12
sLBP+MIND (ours)	**1.74**	0.38	4.65
sLBP+GF (ours)	2.44	1.40	3.05
dLBP+GF (ours)	2.81	1.50	**0.49**

of 3.77 mm and 3.08 mm. Adding learned geometric features within our proposed geometric registration framework leads to relative improvements of 10% (CPD+GF) and 20% (sLBP+GF), respectively. For the efficient approximation of our proposed approach (dLBP+GF) the TRE increases by approximate 0.35 mm but at the same time the average runtime is improved six fold to just below 0.5 s (which is competitive with dense visual deep learning methods such as LapIRN (cf. Table 2)). A statistical test (Wilcoxon signed-rank test calculated over all landmark pairs) with respect to our proposed method (sLBP+GF) shows that improvements on all other comparison methods are highly significant ($p < 0.001$).

We made great efforts to use state-of-the-art learning-based 3D scene flow registration methods and obtained only meaningful results when incorporating the visual MIND features for FLOT [20] and heavily adapting the FlowNet3d embedding strategy [14] (denoted as FE+MIND). FlowNet3d aims to learn a flow embeddings (FE) using a concatenation of two candidate sets (from connected graph nodes), which does not lead to satisfactory results due to the permutation invariant nature of these sparse candidates. Hence, we designed a layer that captures all pairwise combinations and leads to a higher dimensional intermediate tensor that is fed into 1×1 convolutions and is projected (with max-pooling) to a meaningful message vector. For FLOT, we replaced the feature extraction with the handcrafted MIND-PCA embeddings and also removed the refinement convolutions after the optimal transport block (we observed severe overfitting in our training setting when employing the refinement). The sPDD method is based on the probabilistic dense displacement (PDD) network and was modified to operate on the sparse fixed keypoints (instead of a regular grid as in the original published work [7]). Results for the state-of-the-art learning based 3D scene flow registration methods and further comparison experiments using visual input features can be found in Table 2. Our proposed sparse

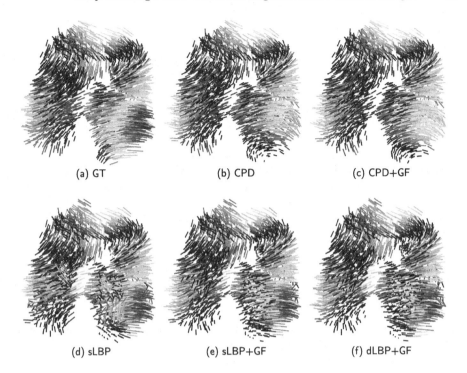

Fig. 3. Qualitative results of different geometric methods ((b)–(f)) on case # 01 of the COPDgene dataset [4]. The ground truth motion vector field is shown in (a). Different colors encode small (blue) and large motion (red). (Color figure online)

registration approach using visual MIND features (sLBP+MIND) achieves a TRE well below 2 mm and thus, improves on the geometry based equivalent (sLBP+GF) by 0.7 mm. However, the extraction of visual features slows down the inference time by 1.6 and 4.1 (dLBP+GF) seconds, respectively. Notably, all proposed geometric registration methods achieve results on par with or significantly better (e.g. more than 50% gain in target registration error w.r.t the dense multi-scale network LapIRN) than the deep learning based comparison methods with additional visual features. Conventional registration methods achieve TREs around 1 to 1.5 mm with runtimes of 3 to 30 min [1,8,22].

4   Discussion and Conclusion

We believe our concept clearly demonstrates the advantages of decoupling feature extraction and optimisation by combining parallelisable differentiable message passing for sparse correspondence finding with graph convolutions for geometric feature learning. Our method enables effective graph-based pairwise regularisation and compact networks for robustly capturing geometric context for large deformation estimation. It is much more capable for 3D medical image registration as adaptations of scene flow approaches, which indicates that these methods may be primarily suited for aligning objects with repetitive semantic object/shape parts that are well represented in large training databases.

We demonstrated that even without using visual features, the proposed geometric registration substantially outperforms very recent deep convolutional registration networks that excelled in other medical tasks. The reason for this large performance gap can firstly lie in the complexity of aligning locally ambiguous structures (vessels, airways) that undergo large deformations and that focusing on relatively few relevant 3D keypoints is a decisive factor in learning meaningful geometric transformations. Our new idea to discretise the sparse candidate displacements into a dense embedding using differentiable extrapolation yields immensive computational gains by reducing the number of message computations (from $k = 9$ to 1 per node) and thereby also enabling future use within alternative regularisation algorithms.

While our experimental analysis was so far restricted to lung anatomies, we strongly believe that graph-based regularisation models combined with geometric learning will play an important role for tackling other large motion estimation tasks, the alignment of anatomies across subjects for studying shape variations and tracking in image-guided interventions. Being able to work independently of visual features opens new possibilities for multimodal registration, where our method only requires comparable keypoints to be found, e.g. using probabilistic edge maps [19]. In addition, the avoidance of highly parameterised CNNs can establish new concepts to gain a better interpretability of deep learning models.

References

1. Avants, B.B., Epstein, C.L., Grossman, M., Gee, J.C.: Symmetric diffeomorphic image registration with cross-correlation: evaluating automated labeling of elderly and neurodegenerative brain. Med. Image Anal. (MedIA) **12**(1), 26–41 (2008)
2. Balakrishnan, G., Zhao, A., Sabuncu, M.R., Guttag, J., Dalca, A.V.: VoxelMorph: a learning framework for deformable medical image registration. IEEE Trans. Med. Imaging (TMI) **38**(8), 1788–1800 (2019)
3. Bronstein, M.M., Bruna, J., LeCun, Y., Szlam, A., Vandergheynst, P.: Geometric deep learning: going beyond Euclidean data. IEEE Signal Process. Mag. (SPM) **34**(4), 18–42 (2017)
4. Castillo, R., et al.: A reference dataset for deformable image registration spatial accuracy evaluation using the COPDgene study archive. Phys. Med. Biol. **58**(9), 2861 (2013)
5. Felzenszwalb, P.F., Huttenlocher, D.P.: Efficient belief propagation for early vision. Int. J. Comput. Vis. (IJCV) **70**(1), 41–54 (2006). https://doi.org/10.1007/s11263-006-7899-4
6. Fu, Y., et al.: LungRegNet: an unsupervised deformable image registration method for 4d-CT lung. Med. Phys. **47**(4), 1763–1774 (2020)
7. Heinrich, M.P.: Closing the gap between deep and conventional image registration using probabilistic dense displacement networks. In: Shen, D., et al. (eds.) MICCAI 2019, Part VI. LNCS, vol. 11769, pp. 50–58. Springer, Cham (2019). https://doi.org/10.1007/978-3-030-32226-7_6

8. Heinrich, M.P., Handels, H., Simpson, I.J.A.: Estimating large lung motion in COPD patients by symmetric regularised correspondence fields. In: Navab, N., Hornegger, J., Wells, W.M., Frangi, A.F. (eds.) MICCAI 2015, Part II. LNCS, vol. 9350, pp. 338–345. Springer, Cham (2015). https://doi.org/10.1007/978-3-319-24571-3_41

9. Heinrich, M.P., Jenkinson, M., Papież, B.W., Brady, S.M., Schnabel, J.A.: Towards realtime multimodal fusion for image-guided interventions using self-similarities. In: Mori, K., Sakuma, I., Sato, Y., Barillot, C., Navab, N. (eds.) MICCAI 2013, Part I. LNCS, vol. 8149, pp. 187–194. Springer, Heidelberg (2013). https://doi.org/10.1007/978-3-642-40811-3_24

10. Hering, A., Häger, S., Moltz, J., Lessmann, N., Heldmann, S., van Ginneken, B.: Constraining volume change in learned image registration for lung CTs. arXiv preprint arXiv:2011.14372 (2020)

11. Hering, A., Murphy, K., van Ginneken, B.: Learn2Reg Challenge: CT Lung Registration - Training Data, May 2020

12. Isensee, F., Jäger, P.F., Kohl, S.A., Petersen, J., Maier-Hein, K.H.: nnU-Net: a self-configuring method for deep learning-based biomedical image segmentation. Nat. Methods 18(2), 203–211 (2020)

13. Kipf, T.N., Welling, M.: Semi-supervised classification with graph convolutional networks. In: International Conference on Learning Representations (ICLR) (2017)

14. Liu, X., Qi, C.R., Guibas, L.J.: Flownet3D: Learning scene flow in 3D point clouds. In: International Conference on Computer Vision and Pattern Recognition (CVPR), pp. 529–537 (2019)

15. Liu, Z., Tang, H., Lin, Y., Han, S.: Point-voxel CNN for efficient 3D deep learning. In: Advances in Neural Information Processing Systems (NeurIPS) pp. 965–975 (2019)

16. Mok, T.C.W., Chung, A.C.S.: Large deformation diffeomorphic image registration with Laplacian pyramid networks. In: Martel, A.L., et al. (eds.) MICCAI 2020, Part III. LNCS, vol. 12263, pp. 211–221. Springer, Cham (2020). https://doi.org/10.1007/978-3-030-59716-0_21

17. Murphy, K., et al.: Evaluation of registration methods on thoracic CT: the EMPIRE10 challenge. IEEE Trans. Med. Imaging (TMI) 30(11), 1901–1920 (2011)

18. Myronenko, A., Song, X.: Point set registration: coherent point drift. IEEE Trans. Pattern Anal. Mach. Intell.(TPAMI) 32(12), 2262–2275 (2010)

19. Murphy, O., et al.: Structured decision forests for multi-modal ultrasound image registration. In: Navab, N., Hornegger, J., Wells, W.M., Frangi, A.F. (eds.) MICCAI 2015, Part II. LNCS, vol. 9350, pp. 363–371. Springer, Cham (2015). https://doi.org/10.1007/978-3-319-24571-3_44

20. Puy, G., Boulch, A., Marlet, R.: FLOT: scene flow on point clouds guided by optimal transport. In: Vedaldi, A., Bischof, H., Brox, T., Frahm, J.-M. (eds.) ECCV 2020, Part XXVIII. LNCS, vol. 12373, pp. 527–544. Springer, Cham (2020). https://doi.org/10.1007/978-3-030-58604-1_32

21. Qi, C.R., Su, H., Mo, K., Guibas, L.J.: PointNet: deep learning on point sets for 3D classification and segmentation. In: International Conference on Computer Vision and Pattern Recognition (CVPR), pp. 652–660 (2017)

22. Rühaak, J., Polzin, T., Heldmann, S., Simpson, I.J., Handels, H., Modersitzki, J., Heinrich, M.P.: Estimation of large motion in lung CT by integrating regularized keypoint correspondences into dense deformable registration. IEEE Trans. Med. Imaging (TMI) 36(8), 1746–1757 (2017)

23. Sarlin, P.E., DeTone, D., Malisiewicz, T., Rabinovich, A.: Superglue: earning feature matching with graph neural networks. In: International Conference on Computer Vision and Pattern Recognition (CVPR), pp. 4938–4947 (2020)
24. Sotiras, A., Ou, Y., Glocker, B., Davatzikos, C., Paragios, N.: Simultaneous geometric - iconic registration. In: Jiang, T., Navab, N., Pluim, J.P.W., Viergever, M.A. (eds.) MICCAI 2010, Part II. LNCS, vol. 6362, pp. 676–683. Springer, Heidelberg (2010). https://doi.org/10.1007/978-3-642-15745-5_83
25. Sun, D., Yang, X., Liu, M.Y., Kautz, J.: PWC-net: CNNs for optical flow using pyramid, warping, and cost volume. In: International Conference on Computer Vision and Pattern Recognition (CVPR), pp. 8934–8943 (2018)
26. Veličković, P., Cucurull, G., Casanova, A., Romero, A., Liò, P., Bengio, Y.: Graph attention networks. In: International Conference on Learning Representations (ICLR) (2018)
27. Wang, Y., et al.: Dynamic graph CNN for learning on point clouds. ACM Trans. Graph. (TOG) **38**(5), 1–12 (2019)
28. Xu, Z., Niethammer, M.: DeepAtlas: Joint Semi-Supervised Learning Of Image Registration And Segmentation. In: Shen, D., et al. (eds.) MICCAI 2019, Part II. LNCS, vol. 11765, pp. 420–429. Springer, Cham (2019). https://doi.org/10.1007/978-3-030-32245-8_47

Diffeomorphic Registration with Density Changes for the Analysis of Imbalanced Shapes

Hsi-Wei Hsieh and Nicolas Charon$^{(\boxtimes)}$

Department of Applied Mathematics and Statistics, Johns Hopkins University,
Baltimore, MD 21218, USA
hhsieh9@jhu.edu, charon@cis.jhu.edu

Abstract. This paper introduces an extension of diffeomorphic registration to enable the morphological analysis of data structures with inherent density variations and imbalances. Building on the framework of Large Diffeomorphic Metric Matching (LDDMM) registration and measure representations of shapes, we propose to augment previous measure deformation approaches with an additional density (or mass) transformation process. We then derive a variational formulation for the joint estimation of optimal deformation and density change between two measures. Based on the obtained optimality conditions, we deduce a shooting algorithm to numerically estimate solutions and illustrate the practical interest of this model for several types of geometric data such as fiber bundles with inconsistent fiber densities or incomplete surfaces.

Keywords: Shape analysis · Diffeomorphic registration · Generalized measures · Density variations

1 Introduction

The field known as computational anatomy [7] has come a long way since its inception several decades ago. Being primarily focused on the development of computational and statistical tools for the analysis of anatomy and its variability, the discipline has thus thrived by benefiting on the one hand from the increasing availability of efficient imaging techniques that can generate large amount of anatomical data and on the other hand from the mathematical advances made in shape analysis that provide the adequate theoretical frameworks and numerical methods for morphological analysis. One of these important theoretical milestones came from the representation of shape spaces as infinite-dimensional Riemannian manifolds which provides the foundations not only to construct relevant families of metrics between geometric structures but also to extend many classical statistics and machine learning tools to those shape spaces.

H.-W. Hsieh and N. Charon—Both authors were supported by NSF grant 1945224.

A. Feragen et al. (Eds.): IPMI 2021, LNCS 12729, pp. 31–42, 2021.
https://doi.org/10.1007/978-3-030-78191-0_3

Among the different Riemannian shape analysis frameworks which have been introduced, deformation-based models [1,12] have found many applications to biomedical data. These are usually referred to as extrinsic (our outer) shape metrics since the distance between two shapes is induced by a metric on the deformation group and measured by how much deformation is needed to map one on the other, which involves solving a registration problem. In particular, the model known as Large Deformation Diffeomorphic Metric Mapping (LDDMM) [1] allows to formulate such a problem as finding an optimal flow map between the two shapes and has been successfully applied to objects such as landmarks, images as well as curves and surfaces. In the latter cases, one additional difficulty is the absence of predefined point to point correspondences between the vertices of the two shapes. Addressing this particular issue motivated new connections with the area of geometric measure theory beginning with the work of [5] and later pursued in e.g. [2–4,9]. These works all share the same guiding principle that shapes such as curves and surfaces are better viewed as elements in certain spaces of measures, which allows to build correspondence free divergences that can be nicely embedded in diffeomorphic registration formulations.

So far, those measure representations have rarely been exploited in shape analysis beyond the pure diffeomorphic transformation setting described above. However, there are important limitations to those methods when dealing with registration of what we term generically as *imbalanced shapes*, namely in the situation where the representing measures display significant variations of mass or density. A motivating example is the case of white matter fiber bundles in which one can expect not only variations in the overall geometry of the bundle but also changes in the number (i.e. density) of fiber curves in each bundle. Diffeomorphic registration of fiber bundles [6] thus typically rely on an ad hoc renormalization/simplification step to compensate for fiber density inconsistencies. Another quite common situation is when a shape, for instance an anatomical surface, is only partially or sparsely known due to acquisition or segmentation issues. We propose to take further advantage of the flexibility of the measure setting by augmenting the diffeomorphic component of LDDMM with a global or local change of density of the source measure to account for potential mass imbalance. We then introduce a generalized registration model in which deformation and density change are estimated jointly. Our model differs from the metamorphosis setting of [10] in that we consider a more general class of measures better adapted to curves and surfaces but also restrict to transformations of the density only, thus avoiding the singularity issues described in [10].

The paper is organized as follows. In Sect. 2, we review the necessary background on diffeomorphic registration and measure representation of shapes. Section 3 introduces our generalized model for diffeomorphic registration with density variations as well as the proposed optimization algorithm. Numerical results on real and synthetic data are presented in Sect. 4.

2   Diffeomorphic Registration of Geometric Measures

The model that we develop in Sect. 3 draws from the concepts of diffeomorphic flows for the modelling of deformations on the one hand and of generalized measures for the representation of shapes on the other. In this section, we give a brief overview of these two mathematical building blocks underlying our paper.

2.1 Diffeomorphisms and Registration

The construction of deformations as flows of vector fields goes back to works such as [1] and [12]. In this paper, we adopt the LDDMM setting of [1]. Let $n \in \mathbb{N}$ with $n \geq 2$ and $\mathbb{R}^n$ be the embedding space of the considered shapes. We will typically have $n = 2$ or $n = 3$ in our examples as we shall primarily be interested in 2D and 3D shapes. We will denote by V a Hilbert space of vector fields of $\mathbb{R}^n$ that is embedded in the space $C_0^1(\mathbb{R}^n, \mathbb{R}^n)$ of C^1 vector fields that vanish at infinity. Then let $L^2([0,1], V)$ be the space of time-varying vector fields such that for all $t \in [0,1]$, $v(t) \in V$ and $\int_0^1 \|v(t)\|_V^2 dt < +\infty$. The flow of $v \in L^2([0,1], V)$ at time $t \in [0,1]$ is defined as the mapping $\varphi_t^v : \mathbb{R}^n \to \mathbb{R}^n$ such that for all $x \in \mathbb{R}^n$, $\varphi_t^v(x) = x + \int_0^t v(s) \circ \varphi_s^v(x) ds$. It follows from the results of [14] (Chap. 7) that φ_t^v belongs to the set $\mathrm{Diff}^1(\mathbb{R}^n)$ of C^1-diffeomorphisms of $\mathbb{R}^n$, namely the bijective maps such that both φ_t^v and its inverse $(\varphi_t^v)^{-1}$ are C^1. Moreover, the term $\int_0^1 \|v(t)\|_V^2 dt$ where $\|\cdot\|_V$ is the norm of the Hilbert space V provides a measure of the energy of the deformation path $t \mapsto \varphi_t^v$ which is related to a right-invariant metric on the diffeomorphism group and is thus often used as a regularization energy for registration problems as we will see next. Furthermore, the embedding assumption on V implies that it is a Reproducing Kernel Hilbert Space (RKHS) of vector fields on $\mathbb{R}^n$. In all this paper, we shall make the additional (and quite common) assumption that the associated matrix kernel is of the form $K_V(x, y) = k_V(x, y) \mathrm{Id}_{n \times n}$ where $k_V : \mathbb{R}^n \times \mathbb{R}^n \to \mathbb{R}$ is a positive definite scalar kernel on $\mathbb{R}^n$.

Shapes can be then transformed by diffeomorphisms by specifying a group action: for instance, the action of a diffeomorphism $\phi \in \mathrm{Diff}^1(\mathbb{R}^n)$ on a set $q = (x_i)_{i=1,...,N}$ of N points of $\mathbb{R}^n$ is typically defined by transporting each point by ϕ i.e. $\phi \cdot q = (\phi(x_i))_{i=1,...,N}$. Registering two such point sets q and q' can be then formulated in this framework as the minimization over all $v \in L^2([0,1], V)$ of a functional like $\frac{1}{2} \int_0^1 \|v(t)\|_V^2 dt + \lambda \sum_{i=1}^N |\varphi_1^v(x_i) - x_i'|^2$ that is a weighted sum of the deformation energy and the squared distances between the corresponding points in $\phi \cdot q$ and q'. This is the problem known as (inexact) landmark registration.

2.2 Geometric Measure Representation of Shapes

In many problems of interest however, shapes cannot be directly described as landmarks. For instance, datasets of triangulated surfaces usually exhibit differences in sampling or do not come automatically with point correspondences across all the dataset. This has motivated the exploration of shape representations from geometric measure theory which allow the comparison and registration of geometric structures without the need for such correspondences. Measure frameworks such as currents or varifolds [5,9] provide a general setting to encode geometric shapes as unlabelled points in $\mathbb{R}^n$ that carry some information of local tangent plane as well. In this paper, we will specifically consider as our shape space $\mathcal{S}$ the set of all objects represented by a discrete measure of the form $\mu = \sum_{i=1}^{N} r_i \delta_{(x_i,T_i)}$ for $N \geq 1$. In this representation, each Dirac $r_i \delta_{(x_i,T_i)}$ can be interpreted as an unlabelled particle of mass $r_i > 0$ (which we shall also refer to as the density of μ at x_i in a discrete sense) located at the position $x_i \in \mathbb{R}^n$ and carrying an oriented d-dimensional subspace T_i. Note that here $0 \leq d \leq n$ is fixed and we will be mostly interested in the cases $d = 1$ and $d = 2$ in practice, i.e. the T_i's are oriented lines or planes. Mathematically, μ is a positive measure on the product of $\mathbb{R}^n$ and the oriented d-dimensional Grassmannian of $\mathbb{R}^n$, and is usually called a d-current or an oriented d-varifold following the definitions and terminology of [8,9]. In practice, it will be more convenient to represent each oriented subspace T_i by an oriented frame of d linearly independent vectors $(u_i^{(k)})_{k=1,\ldots,d}$. Although such a frame is not unique, this will not constitute an issue for the applications considered in this work.

The above space $\mathcal{S}$ of discrete measures provides an effective setting to embed a variety of geometric structures. In particular, curves and surfaces can always be approximated by elements of $\mathcal{S}$ [3,9]. For instance a polygonal curve with edges $[e_i^1, e_i^2]$ for $i = 1,\ldots,N$ can be approximated by the measure of $\mathcal{S}$ (with $d = 1$) $\mu = \sum_{i=1}^{N} r_i \delta_{(x_i,T_i)}$ where r_i is the edge length, $x_i = (e_i^1 + e_i^2)/2$ its midpoint and T_i the oriented line directed by $\overrightarrow{e_i^1 e_i^2}$. Triangulated surfaces can be similarly approached by a 2-dimensional measure in which case r_i is the area of the face, x_i the barycenter of its three points and T_i the oriented plane containing the triangular face. Beyond curves and surfaces, $\mathcal{S}$ is a versatile class of objects represented fundamentally as a distribution of tangent spaces spread at different locations in $\mathbb{R}^n$. One of the key advantage of such measure representations of shapes is that one can easily equip $\mathcal{S}$ with a metric. Among the different classes of metrics between measures that one may choose from, kernel norms (also known as maximum mean discrepancy) are particularly well-suited in our context as they lead to relatively simple and explicit expression of the distance between two measures in $\mathcal{S}$. Specifically, given a positive-definite kernel $K_{\mathcal{S}}$ on the product of $\mathbb{R}^n$ and the set of all oriented d-planes of $\mathbb{R}^n$ (or more simply the set of all oriented d- frames), the associated Hilbert inner product between any $\mu = \sum_{i=1}^{N} r_i \delta_{(x_i,T_i)}$ and $\mu' = \sum_{j=1}^{N'} r'_j \delta_{(x'_j,T'_j)}$ in $\mathcal{S}$ is given by:

$$\langle \mu, \mu' \rangle_{\mathcal{S}} = \sum_{i=1}^{N} \sum_{j=1}^{N'} r_i r'_j K_{\mathcal{S}}(x_i, T_i, x'_j, T'_j). \tag{1}$$

Then the computation of the distance on $\mathcal{S}$ is just obtained from $\|\mu - \mu'\|_{\mathcal{S}}^2 = \|\mu\|_{\mathcal{S}}^2 - 2\langle \mu, \mu' \rangle_{\mathcal{S}} + \|\mu'\|_{\mathcal{S}}^2$ and reduces to evaluations of the kernel function. Note that this provides a notion of distance that does not rely on any correspondence between the Diracs of μ and μ' (and that actually remains well-defined even when the number of Diracs in μ and μ' are different). The properties of these metrics have been studied extensively in [5,8,9] and they provide a convenient notion of discrepancy on our space $\mathcal{S}$ for adequate choices of the kernel $K_{\mathcal{S}}$, such as the one we will specify and use in Sect. 4 for our simulations.

To arrive at a formulation of the LDDMM registration problem for measures in $\mathcal{S}$, the only missing element is the group action of $\mathrm{Diff}(\mathbb{R}^n)$ on $\mathcal{S}$. A standard action is by measure pushforward [5,8] which is given for any $\phi \in \mathrm{Diff}(\mathbb{R}^n)$ and any $\mu = \sum_{i=1}^{N} r_i \delta_{(x_i, T_i)} \in \mathcal{S}$ by

$$\phi \cdot \mu = \sum_{i=1}^{N} |J_{x_i}^{T_i} \phi|.r_i \, \delta_{(\phi(x_i), d_{x_i}\phi(T_i))} \in \mathcal{S} \tag{2}$$

where $d_{x_i}\phi$ denotes the differential of ϕ at x_i, $d_{x_i}\phi(T_i)$ the subspace spanned by the transported frame vectors $(d_{x_i}\phi(u_i^{(k)}))_{k=1,\ldots,d}$ and $|J_{x_i}^{T_i}\phi|$ is the absolute value of the Jacobian determinant of ϕ along T_i at x_i given explicitly by $\sqrt{\det(d_{x_i}\phi(u_i^{(k)}) \cdot d_{x_i}\phi(u_i^{(l)}))_{k,l}}$. This group action happens to be consistent with the usual action of diffeomorphisms on d-dimensional submanifolds of $\mathbb{R}^n$ in the sense that if $\mu \in \mathcal{S}$ is a discrete approximation of a submanifold M then $\phi \cdot \mu$ is typically an approximation of the submanifold $\phi(M)$, c.f. [8] for rigorous statements. This is the main reason for the presence of the mass changes $|J_{x_i}^{T_i}\phi|$ in (2) that represent the local change in d-volume induced by ϕ.

Finally the registration of a given source measure $\mu_0 \in \mathcal{S}$ to a target $\mu' \in \mathcal{S}$ can be framed as minimizing the functional $\frac{1}{2} \int_0^1 \|v(t)\|_V^2 dt + \lambda \|\varphi_1^v \cdot \mu_0 - \mu'\|_{\mathcal{S}}^2$. This class of optimal control problems includes as particular cases the curve and surface registration approaches of [2,5]. We will elaborate on the numerical aspects for the more general framework that we present in the following section.

3 Diffeomorphic Registration with Density Changes

Although the action of diffeomorphisms on $\mathcal{S}$ does allow to transform the mass of measures through the Jacobian determinant of the deformation, registering measures with important inconsistencies or density variations may lead to unnatural or even degenerate optimal deformations as we will show in some of the examples of Sect. 4. Our goal is thus to augment (2) with a complementary process to simultaneously modify the density of the measure. The main focus will be on a global model with a single common density rescaling factor but we will also briefly introduce a preliminary extension of the approach to deal with local changes in density as well.

3.1 An Augmented Optimal Control Problem

Adopting the notations of the previous section, we introduce a complementary rescaling factor $\alpha \in \mathbb{R}^+$, which is a nonnegative number acting as a global multiplicative factor on the measure μ which we write $\alpha.\mu$. Under this extended setting, we formulate the registration of a source μ_0 to a target μ' as the following new optimization problem:

$$\min_{v,\alpha} E(v, \alpha) \doteq \frac{1}{2} \int_0^1 \|v(t)\|_V^2 dt + \frac{\tau}{2}(\alpha - 1)^2 + \lambda \|\alpha.\mu(1) - \mu'\|_{\mathcal{S}}^2 \tag{3}$$

subject to $\mu(t) \doteq (\varphi_t^v) \cdot \mu_0$. The rescaling factor α is here penalized by the simple squared difference with $\alpha = 1$ weighted by a fixed coefficient $\tau > 0$ and one can see formally that letting $\tau \to +\infty$ imposes $\alpha = 1$ and (3) then reduces to the previous LDDMM registration problem.

From now on, let (v, α) be a minimizer of (3) and $q(t)$ the associated optimal trajectory. We shall derive some necessary conditions satisfied by such a minimizer. We write $\mu_0 = \sum_{i=1}^{N} r_i \delta_{(x_i, T_i)}$ and, using the representation of the subspaces T_i by frames of d vectors as explained above, we can alternatively view the state variable of the optimal control problem as $q = ((x_i, u_i^{(k)})_{1 \leq i \leq N, 1 \leq k \leq d})$, where $\mathrm{Span}(u_i^{(1)}, \ldots, u_i^{(d)}) = T_i$ and $|u_i^{(1)} \wedge \cdots \wedge u_i^{(d)}| = \sqrt{\det(u_i^{(k)} \cdot u_i^{(l)})} = r_i$.

We first notice that, as a function of α with v and $\mu(t)$ being fixed, E is quadratic and solving for $\frac{\partial E}{\partial \alpha} = 0$ shows that the optimal α can be expressed with respect to the final measure $\mu(1)$ as:

$$\alpha^* = \frac{\frac{\tau}{2} + \lambda \langle \mu(1), \mu' \rangle_S}{\frac{\tau}{2} + \lambda \|\mu(1)\|_S^2}. \tag{4}$$

where the Hilbert product on S is given by (1). Inserting into (3), this now allows to reduce the problem to an optimal control problem with control v. The optimality conditions on v can be derived similarly to [8,11,13], by introducing the Hamiltonian of the problem which is given by:

$$H(p, q, v) \doteq \sum_{i=1}^{N} \langle p_i^x, v(x_i) \rangle + \sum_{i=1}^{N} \sum_{k=1}^{d} \langle p_i^{u_k}, d_{x_i} v(u_i^{(k)}) \rangle - \frac{1}{2} \|v\|_V^2,$$

where $p_i^x, p_i^{u_k} \in \mathbb{R}^n$ denote the costates of the position x and frame vectors $u_i^{(k)}$. By applying the Pontryagin maximum principle, we find that any optimal trajectory $(x_i(t), u_i^{(k)}(t))$ must satisfy the following Hamiltonian equations:

$$\begin{cases} \dot{x}_i(t) = v(t)(x_i(t)) \\ \dot{u}_i^{(k)}(t) = d_{x_i(t)} v(t)(u_i^{(k)}(t)) \\ \dot{p}_i^x(t) = -d_{x_i(t)} v(t)^T p_i^x(t) - \sum_{k=1}^{d} d_{x_i(t)}^{(2)} v(t)(\cdot, u_i^{(k)}(t))^T p_i^{u_k}(t) \\ \dot{p}_i^{u_k}(t) = -d_{x_i(t)} v(t)^T p_i^{u_k}(t) \end{cases} \tag{5}$$

and, using the RKHS property of V, the optimal control v is given by:

$$v(t)(\cdot) = \sum_{i=1}^{N} k_V(x_i(t), \cdot) p_i^x(t) + \sum_{k=1}^{d} \partial_1 k_V(x_i(t), \cdot)(u_i^{(k)}(t), p_i^{u_k}(t)). \tag{6}$$

Thus, from the above equations, we obtain that the full energy functional to be minimized can be written as a function of the initial costates, namely

$$E(p_i^x(0), p_i^{u_k}(0)) = \frac{1}{2} \sum_{i=1}^{N} \langle p_i^x(0), v(0)(x_i(0)) \rangle + \frac{1}{2} \sum_{i=1}^{N} \sum_{k=1}^{d} \langle p_i^{u_k}(0), d_{x_i(0)} v(0)(u_i^{(k)}(0)) \rangle \tag{7}$$

$$+ \frac{\tau}{2} (\alpha^* - 1)^2 + \lambda \|\alpha^* \cdot \mu(1) - \mu'\|_S^2,$$

where $\alpha^* \cdot \mu(1) = \sum_{i=1}^{N} \alpha^* r_i(1) \delta_{(x_i(1), T_i(1))}$ and $T_i(1) = \mathrm{Span}(\{u_i^{(k)}(1)\})$ is obtained from the Hamiltonian equations (5) and (6).

3.2   Numerical Implementation

The numerical minimization of the energy (7) can be tackled based on an iterative shooting scheme similar to other LDDMM approaches [8,13]. Specifically, given the initial costates $(p_i^x(0), (p_i^{u_k}(0))_{k=1}^d)$ at the current iteration of the algorithm together with the known and fixed initial state variables $(x_i(0), (u_i^{(k)}(0))_{k=1}^d)$, we start by integrating the Hamiltonian equations (5) and (6) based on an RK4 scheme to obtain the measure $\mu(1)$ at the final time. We then compute α^* with (4) from which we obtain the value of the energy (7). In order to update the initial costates, we also need the gradient of E which we can directly compute using automatic differentiation. More precisely, our Python implementation leverages the Pytorch library together with the recently developed KeOps library[1]. The latter allows to generate efficient CUDA subroutines for the computation and automatic differentiation of expressions involving positive definite kernels such as the ones appearing in the Hamiltonian equations and in the inner product of S given by (1). Finally, with E and ∇E being obtained as just explained, the optimization itself is done using the L-BFGS algorithm of the SciPy library.

In what follows, we will refer to this registration algorithm with global density rescaling by the acronym LDDMM+GD. The parameters that need to be set by the user are the kernels k_V and K_S as well as the weighing coefficients λ and τ. The latter controls the relative importance of deformation and mass rescaling in the overall change of density. We illustrate the effect of τ on the simplest example of two single Diracs in Fig. 1 (with $n = 2$ and $d = 1$). The optimal diffeomorphism φ_1^v pictured here via the resulting deformed grid shows a combination of a local rotation effect (in order to match the directions of the frame vectors) and of a local compression (to compensate for the difference in mass). The case $\tau = \infty$ corresponds to the pure diffeomorphic registration setting of the previous section. In sharp contrast, when $\tau = 0$, the deformation reduces to only rotating the directional component of the source Dirac while the transformation of mass is entirely done by the rescaling variable α^*. Intermediate values of τ lead to both φ_1^v and α^* contributing to the change in density.

3.3   Local Density Changes

The model presented in the previous sections is well-suited when a common and global density rescaling effect is expected as the results of Sect. 4 will illustrate but is typically not adapted to the situation of local mass imbalances such as in the case of particular missing parts on the target shape. To tackle this more general case, we briefly discuss a preliminary approach that can be derived as a localized version of the above model. Instead of the single density rescaling variable α, one can introduce N controls $\alpha_i \in \mathbb{R}_+$ associated to each Dirac in μ_0. Writing now $\alpha = (\alpha_1, \ldots, \alpha_N)$ and defining the measure mass rescaling as

---

[1] https://www.kernel-operations.io/.

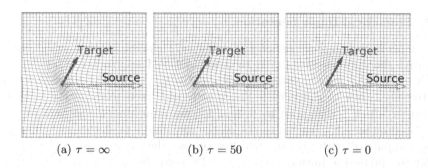

| (a) $\tau = \infty$ | (b) $\tau = 50$ | (c) $\tau = 0$ |

Fig. 1. Registration between the two Diracs $\mu = r_0\delta_{(x_0,T_0)}$ and $\mu' = r'\delta_{(x',T')}$ with $r_0 = 2$, $r' = 4/5$, $x_0 = x' = (0,0) \in \mathbb{R}^2$ and T, T' are the lines spanned by $u_0 = (1,0)$ and $u' = (\cos(\pi/3), \sin(\pi/3))$. The plotted arrows vectors here represent $r_0 u_0$ and $r' u'$ respectively. The figure illustrates the effect of the choice of τ on the registration, with $\tau = \infty$ corresponding to the pure deformation case (i.e. $\alpha^* = 1$). The optimal density rescaling factors in (b) and (c) are $\alpha^* = 0.6773$ and $\alpha^* = 0.4074$ respectively.

$\alpha \cdot \mu = \sum_{i=1}^{N} \alpha_i r_i \delta_{(x_i,T_i)}$, we formulate the registration problem with local density changes as follows:

$$\min_{v,\alpha \in \mathbb{R}_+^N} E(v, \alpha) \doteq \frac{1}{2}\int_0^1 \|v(t)\|_V^2 dt + \frac{\tau}{2}\sum_{i=1}^{N} r_i(\alpha_i - 1)^2 + \lambda\|\alpha \cdot \mu(1) - \mu'\|_S^2 \quad (8)$$

in which the penalty on the density rescaling vector α is now the distance to $(1,\dots,1)$ for the L^2 metric weighed by the density of the initial μ_0. Note that this is only one simple choice of penalty that directly extends (3) but we plan, in future work, to examine other relevant regularizers that would for instance constrain the local variations of the α_i's.

Problem (8) can be solved in similar fashion as in Sect. 3.2. Indeed, the Hamiltonian equations (5) and (6) still hold although the optimality equations on the α_i's are not as straightforward to exploit as (4). In practice, we instead jointly optimize over the initial costates $(p_i^x(0), (p_i^{u_k}(0))_{k=1}^d)$ together with $\alpha = (\alpha_i)$ using L-BFGS, with the gradient of the energy with respect to each α_i being computed by automatic differentiation. We will denote this diffeomorphic registration under local density changes by the acronym LDDMM+LD.

4   Results

As proof-of-concept, we present a few results of the above LDDMM+GD and LDDMM+LD algorithms applied to 3D shapes ($n = 3$), specifically discrete curves ($d = 1$) or surfaces ($d = 2$). Those shapes are converted to elements of $\mathcal{S}$ as explained in Sect. 2.2. For the purpose of visualization however, we shall plot the shapes rather than their associated measures in $\mathcal{S}$ and display the source shape's time evolution along the estimated deformation path φ_t^v. In all experiments, the deformation kernel k_V is a Gaussian and the kernel $K_{\mathcal{S}}$ defining the metric on $\mathcal{S}$ is chosen among the class of kernels discussed in [9], specifically as the tensor product of a Gaussian kernel on $\mathbb{R}^n$ and the Binet kernel between d-dimensional subspaces, i.e. for $T = \mathrm{Span}(u^{(k)})$ and $T' = \mathrm{Span}(u'^{(k)})$ the positive kernel given by $\det((u^{(k)} \cdot u'^{(l)})_{k,l})^2$. We also set τ to a small value so as to put only minimal constraints on the estimation of α.

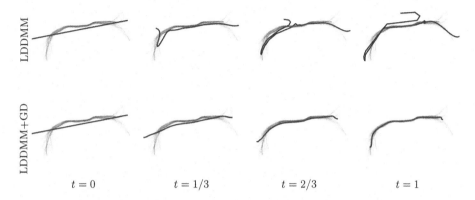

Fig. 2. Registration of single curve to CP fiber bundle (365 curves). The second row shows the deformation at intermediate times for the proposed LDDMM+GD algorithm where the estimated density rescaling is $\alpha^* = 348.80$.

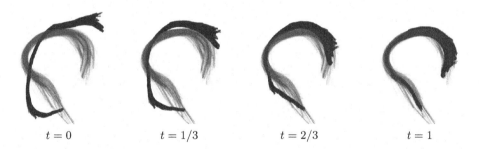

Fig. 3. Registration of CA fiber bundle (431 curves) to Fornix fiber bundle (2151 curves). The estimated α^* is 4.18, close to the fiber density ratio of the bundles.

Fiber Bundles. For our first set of simulations, we consider white matter fiber tracts taken from the publicly available ISMRM 2015 Tractography Challenge repository[2]. In Fig. 2, we show the result of registering a single template curve onto the posterior commissure (CP) bundle containing 365 distinct curves. As can be seen on the first row, regular LDDMM registration generates a folding of the source curve in an attempt to compensate for the difference in total mass.

---

[2] http://www.tractometer.org/ismrm_2015_challenge/.

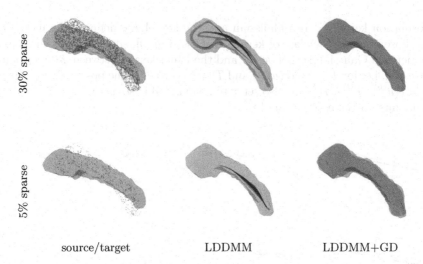

Fig. 4. Registration between two hippocampus surfaces: source (in blue) and target (in red) which has been randomly subsampled to 30% (first row) and 5% (second row) of its total number of triangles. The resulting deformed surface at $t = 1$ obtained with LDDMM (second column) and LDDMM+GD (third column) is compared to the fully sampled target surface. For LDDMM+GD, we obtain $\alpha^* = 0.29$ and $\alpha^* = 0.049$. (Color figure online)

The LDDMM+GD algorithm on the other hand leads to a deformed curve that matches the average geometry of the bundle with an estimated $\alpha^* = 348.80$ consistent with the density of curves in the target. Note that α^* is in fact smaller than 365 which accounts for the spatial spreading and fanning of the bundle. We also consider the registration between two different fiber tracts: the anterior commissure (CA) and fornix which are made of respectively 431 and 2151 individual curves. Once again, standard diffeomorphic registration (not shown here for the sake of space) induces important artifactual folding effects in contrast with the LDDMM+GD registration result of Fig. 3.

Sparse Shapes. Another feature of the LDDMM+GD approach is its robustness under sparse and incomplete observation of the target surface. This is illustrated on the example of hippocampi surfaces (data provided with the Keops library) in Fig. 4 where sparse targets are synthetically generated by keeping only a small number of random faces from the full ground truth target mesh. This mass imbalance results in severe shrinking and twisting of the registered surface estimated with standard LDDMM while LDDMM+GD recovers a surface close to the ground truth and automatically estimates (through α^*) the sparsity rate with good accuracy.

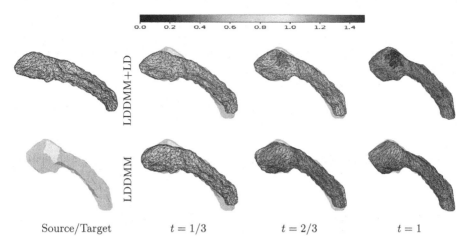

Fig. 5. Registration of two hippocampi surfaces with a missing subregion obtained with the LDDMM+LD and standard LDDMM approach. The colors on the first row correspond to the values of the mass rescaling α_i at each location. One can notice small differences in terms of overlap between the final shape and the ground truth target around that subregion. The Hausdorff distance to the ground truth is 1.5714 (LDDMM+LD) versus 1.9789 (LDDMM). (Color figure online)

Partial Matching. This approach is however not well-suited in the situation where an isolated part of the target shape is locally missing, as with the simulated example of Fig. 5 in which we artificially remove a subregion of the hippocampus surface. In such a case, the LDDMM+LD algorithm allows for local mass changes and is able to estimate, alongside the deformation, the corresponding missing region on the source shape as shown on the first row, where the colors represent the values of the α_i's at the different locations. In contrast, such missing regions can adversely affect registration under the standard LDDMM model. This is evidenced quantitatively by the closer proximity (measured for the usual Hausdorff distance) of the matched surface to the ground truth (i.e. complete) target for our proposed LDDMM+LD approach.

5   Conclusion

We introduced novel frameworks and algorithms for the registration of shapes modelled as discrete measures in which the deformation is coupled with a global or local transformation of the density. The Python implementation will be made openly available in the future and can be currently shared upon request. Our preliminary experiments hint at the potential of those models for the morphological analysis of partial shapes, a recurring issue of deformation models in computational anatomy, and for applications to shape completion. It is also well suited for registration or template estimation of fiber bundle data and could be used in conjunction with other numerical methods in the field, such as the stream-line approximation schemes of [6]. Future work will focus on pushing further those applications and on a more thorough analysis of the LDDMM+LD model, by investigating other possible regularizers on the density change and exploring connections with related unbalanced frameworks in optimal transport [4].

References

1. Beg, M.F., Miller, M.I., Trouvé, A., Younes, L.: Computing large deformation metric mappings via geodesic flows of diffeomorphisms. Int. J. Comput. Vis. **61**, 139–157 (2005)
2. Charon, N., Trouvé, A.: The varifold representation of nonoriented shapes for diffeomorphic registration. SIAM J. Imaging Sci. **6**(4), 2547–2580 (2013)
3. Durrleman, S., Pennec, X., Trouvé, A., Ayache, N.: Statistical models of sets of curves and surfaces based on currents. Med. Image Anal. **13**(5), 793–808 (2009)
4. Feydy, J., Charlier, B., Vialard, F.-X., Peyré, G.: Optimal transport for diffeomorphic registration. In: Descoteaux, M., Maier-Hein, L., Franz, A., Jannin, P., Collins, D.L., Duchesne, S. (eds.) MICCAI 2017, Part I. LNCS, vol. 10433, pp. 291–299. Springer, Cham (2017). https://doi.org/10.1007/978-3-319-66182-7_34
5. Vaillant, M., Glaunès, J.: Surface matching via currents. In: Christensen, G.E., Sonka, M. (eds.) IPMI 2005. LNCS, vol. 3565, pp. 381–392. Springer, Heidelberg (2005). https://doi.org/10.1007/11505730_32
6. Gori, P., et al.: Parsimonious approximation of streamline trajectories in white matter fiber bundles. IEEE Trans Med. Imaging **35**(12), 2609–2619 (2016)
7. Grenander, U., Miller, M.I.: Computational anatomy: an emerging discipline. Q. Appl. Math. **I**(4), 617–694 (1998)
8. Hsieh, H.-W., Charon, N.: Metrics, quantization and registration in varifold spaces. arXiv preprint arXiv:1903.11196 (2019)
9. Kaltenmark, I., Charlier, B., Charon, N.: A general framework for curve and surface comparison and registration with oriented varifolds. In: Computer Vision and Pattern Recognition (CVPR) (2017)
10. Richardson, C., Younes, L.: Computing metamorphoses between discrete measures. J. Geom. Mech. **5**(1), 131 (2013)
11. Sommer, S., Nielsen, M., Darkner, S., Pennec, X.: Higher-order momentum distributions and locally affine LDDMM registration. SIAM J. Imaging Sci. **6**(1), 341–367 (2013)
12. Vercauteren, T., Pennec, X., Perchant, A., Ayache, N.: Diffeomorphic demons: efficient non-parametric image registration. NeuroImage **45**(1), 61–72 (2009)
13. Vialard, F.-X., Risser, L., Rueckert, D., Cotter, C.: Diffeomorphic 3D image registration via geodesic shooting using an efficient adjoint calculation. Int. J. Comput. Vis. **97**(2), 229–241 (2012). https://doi.org/10.1007/s11263-011-0481-8
14. Younes, L.: Shapes and Diffeomorphisms. Springer, Heidelberg (2019). https://doi.org/10.1007/978-3-662-58496-5

Causal Models and Interpretability

Estimation of Causal Effects in the Presence of Unobserved Confounding in the Alzheimer's Continuum

Sebastian Pölsterl$^{(\boxtimes)}$ [iD] and Christian Wachinger [iD]

Artificial Intelligence in Medical Imaging (AI-Med), Department of Child
and Adolescent Psychiatry, Ludwig-Maximilians-Universität, Munich, Germany
{sebastian.poelsterl,christian.wachinger}@med.uni-muenchen.de

Abstract. Studying the relationship between neuroanatomy and cognitive decline due to Alzheimer's has been a major research focus in the last decade. However, to infer cause-effect relationships rather than simple associations from observational data, we need to (i) express the causal relationships leading to cognitive decline in a graphical model, and (ii) ensure the causal effect of interest is identifiable from the collected data. We derive a causal graph from the current clinical knowledge on cause and effect in the Alzheimer's disease continuum, and show that identifiability of the causal effect requires all confounders to be known and measured. However, in complex neuroimaging studies, we neither know all potential confounders nor do we have data on them. To alleviate this requirement, we leverage the dependencies among multiple causes by deriving a substitute confounder via a probabilistic latent factor model. In our theoretical analysis, we prove that using the substitute confounder enables identifiability of the causal effect of neuroanatomy on cognition. We quantitatively evaluate the effectiveness of our approach on semi-synthetic data, where we know the true causal effects, and illustrate its use on real data on the Alzheimer's disease continuum, where it reveals important causes that otherwise would have been missed.

1 Introduction

The last decade saw an unprecedented increase in large multi-site neuroimaging studies, which opens the possibility of identifying disease predictors with low-effect sizes. However, one major obstacle to fully utilize this data is confounding. The relationship between a measurement and an outcome is confounded if the observed association is only due to a third latent random variable, but there is no direct causal link between the measurement and outcome. If confounding is ignored, investigators will likely make erroneous conclusions, because the observed data distribution is compatible with many – potentially contradictory – causal explanations, leaving us with no way to differentiate between the true and false effect on the basis of data. In this case, the causal effect is unidentifiable [24].

© Springer Nature Switzerland AG 2021
A. Feragen et al. (Eds.): IPMI 2021, LNCS 12729, pp. 45–57, 2021.
https://doi.org/10.1007/978-3-030-78191-0_4

It is important to remember that what is, or is not, regarded as a confounding variable is relative and depends on the goal of the study. For instance, age is often considered a confounder when studying Alzheimer's disease (AD), but if the focus is age-related cognitive decline in a healthy population, age is not considered a confounder [20]. Therefore, it is vital to state the causal question being studied.

Causal inference addresses confounding in a principal manner and allows us to determine which cause-effect relationships can be identified from a given dataset. To infer causal effects from observational data, we need to rely on expert knowledge and untestable assumptions about the data-generating process to build the causal graph linking causes, outcome, and other variables [24]. One essential assumption to estimate causal effects from observational data is that of *no unmeasured confounder* [24]. Usually, we can only identify causal effects if we know and recorded all confounders. However, analyses across 17 neuroimaging studies revealed that considerable bias remains in volume and thickness measurement after adjusting for age, gender, and the type of MRI scanner [33]. Another study on confounders in UK Biobank brain imaging data identified hundreds of potential confounders just related to the acquisition process researchers would need to account for [1]. These results suggest that all factors contributing to confounding in neuroimaging are not yet fully understood, and hence the premise of *no unmeasured confounder* is most likely going to be violated.

In this paper, we focus on the problem of estimating causal effects of neuroanatomical measures on cognitive decline due to Alzheimer's in the presence of *unobserved confounders*. To make this feasible, we derive a causal graph from domain knowledge on the Alzheimer's disease continuum to capture known disease-specific relationships. While causal affects are generally unidentifiable in the presence of unobserved confounding, we will illustrate that we can leverage the dependencies among multiple causes to estimate a latent substitute confounder via a Bayesian probabilistic factor model. In our experiments, we quantitatively demonstrate the effectiveness of our approach on semi-synthetic data, where we know the true causal effects, and illustrate its use on real data on the Alzheimer's disease continuum, where our analyses reveal important causes of cognitive function that would otherwise have been missed.

Related Work. Despite the importance of this topic, there has been little prior work on causal inference for estimating causal effects in neuroimaging. In contrast to our approach, most of the previous works assume that all confounding variables are known and have been measured. The most common approach for confounding adjustment is regress-out. In regress-out, the original measurement (e.g. volume or thickness) is replaced by the residual of a regression model fitted to estimate the original value from the confounding variables. In [6], the authors use linear regression to account for age, which has been extended to additionally account for gender in [17]. A Gaussian Process (GP) model has been proposed in [18] to adjust for age, total intracranial volume, sex, and MRI scanner. Fortin et al. [10] proposed a linear mixed effects model to account for systematic differences across imaging sites. This model has been extended in [33] to account for both observed and unobserved confounders. In [29], linear regression is used to regress-out the effect of total brain volume. In addition to the regress-out approach, analyses can be adjusted for confounders by computing instance weights, that are used in a downstream classification or regression model to obtain a pseudo-population that is approximately balanced with respect to the confounders [19,25]. A weighted support vector machine to adjust for age is proposed in [19]. In [25], weighted GP regression is proposed to account for gender and imaging site effects. We note that none of the work above studied whether causal effects can actually be identified from observed data using the theory of causal inference.

2   Methods

Causal inference from observational data comprises multiple steps, (i) defining the causal question and its associated causal graph, (ii) determining under which conditions the question can be answered from real world data, and (iii) estimating the causal effects via modelling. We denote random variables with uppercase letters and specific values taken by the corresponding variables with lowercase letters. We distinguish between real-valued subcortical volume $(X_1^v, \ldots, X_{D_1}^v)$ and cortical thickness $(X_1^t, \ldots, X_{D_2}^t)$ measurements. We denote by $X_1, \ldots, X_D$ all measurements, irrespective of their type $(D = D_1 + D_2)$. Next, we will specify our causal question and determine when the causal effect of a subset of measurements on an outcome is identifiable using Pearl's do-calculus [24].

2.1   The Causal Question and Its Associated Graph

Causal Question. What is the average causal effect of increasing/decreasing the volume or thickness of a subset of neuroanatomical structures on the Alzheimer's Disease Assessment Scale Cognitive Subscale 13 score (ADAS; [23]) in patients with an Alzheimer's pathologic change [13]?

The gold standard to answer this question would be a randomized experiment, where subjects' volumes and thicknesses are randomly assigned. As this is impossible, we have to resort to observational data. To estimate causal effects from observational data, we need to rely on expert knowledge to build the causal graph linking causes, outcome, and other variables [24]. Figure 1 depicts the graph related to our causal question. We explain our reasoning below.

Our causal question already determines that the causal graph needs to comprise ADAS (the outcome), measures $X_1, \ldots, X_D$ (the causes), and the level of beta amyloid 42 peptides $(A\beta)$, which determines whether a patient has an Alzheimer's pathologic change [13]. To link $A\beta$ with the remaining variables, we rely on expert knowledge, namely that $A\beta$ causes levels of Tau phosphorylated at threonine 181 (p-Tau), which in turn causes neurodegeneration that ultimately results in cognitive decline [13,15]. Moreover, we consider that the patient's levels of $A\beta$ and p-Tau are determined by the allelic variant of apolipoprotein E (ApoE; [21]), among other unobserved common causes (dashed line), and that aging influences the neuroanatomy, amyloid and tau pathology [2,4,26]. Beside

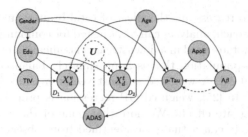

Fig. 1. Causal graph used to estimate the causal effect (red arrow) of subcortical volume (X_d^v) and cortical thickness (X_d^t) on cognitive function (ADAS) in the presence of an unknown and unobserved confounder U. Exogenous variables irrelevant for estimating the causal effect of interest are not shown. Circles are random variables and arrows causal relationships. Filled circles are observed, transparent circles are hidden, bidirectional edges denote unobserved common causes. (Color figure online)

biological relationships, we also include demographic and socio-economic factors. In particular, p-Tau levels, brain size, and the level of education is known to differ in males and females [8]. We model resilience to neurodegeneration by including years of education (Edu) as a proxy for cognitive reserve, and total intracranial volume (TIV) as a proxy for brain reserve, where the latter is only causal for volume measurements $X_1^v, \ldots, X_{D_1}^v$ [30]. Finally, Fig. 1 reflects that age is a known confounder of the relationship between neuroanatomy and cognition [12]. However, as outlined in the introduction, the full set of confounders is extensive and most of them are unmeasured. Therefore, we assume an unknown and unobserved set of additional confounders U.

2.2 Identifiability in the Presence of an Unobserved Confounder

Formally, the causal question states that we want to use the observed data to estimate the average causal effect that a subset $\mathcal{S} \subset \{X_1, \ldots, X_D\}$ of neuroanatomical structures have simultaneously on the ADAS score:

$$\mathbb{E}\left[\text{ADAS} \mid do(X_\mathcal{S} = x_\mathcal{S}')\right] = \int \text{adas} \cdot P(\text{adas} \mid do(x_\mathcal{S}')) \, d\text{adas}. \tag{1}$$

The do-operator states that we are interested in the post-intervention distribution of ADAS, induced by the intervention that sets the neuroanatomical measures $X_\mathcal{S}$ equal to $x_\mathcal{S}'$. The central question in causal inference is that of identification: Can the post-intervention distribution $P(\text{adas} \mid do(x))$ be estimated from data governed by the observed joint distribution over X and ADAS?

Inspecting Fig. 1 reveals that the relationship between any X_d and ADAS is confounded by the known confounder age, but also the unknown confounder U. Knowing that the causal effect of X_d on ADAS is unidentifiable in the presence of unobserved confounding, it initially appears that our causal question cannot be answered [24, Theorem 3.2.5]. Next, we will detail how we can resolve this issue by exploiting the influence that the unknown confounder has on multiple causes simultaneously. The full procedure is outlined in Algorithm 1.

Algorithm 1: Causal inference with unobserved confounding.

Input: Neuroanatomical measures $\mathbf{X} \in \mathbb{R}^{N \times D}$, direct influences on neuroanatomy
$\mathbf{F} \in \mathbb{R}^{N \times P}$, ADAS scores $\mathbf{y} \in \mathbb{R}^{N}$; values for intervention x'_S; τ minimum Bayesian
p-value for model checking.
Output: Estimate of $\mathbb{E}\left[\text{ADAS} \,|\, do(X_S = x'_S)\right]$.

1 Sample a random binary matrix $\mathbf{H} \in \{0; 1\}^{N \times D}$ and split data into $\mathbf{X}^{\text{obs}} = (1 - \mathbf{H}) \odot \mathbf{X}$ and
$\mathbf{X}^{\text{holdout}} = \mathbf{H} \odot \mathbf{X}$.

2 Fit PLFM with parameters θ to $\mathbf{X}^{\text{obs}}$ and $\mathbf{F}$.

3 Simulate M replicates of $\mathbf{x}_i$ by drawing from posterior predictive distribution
$P(\mathbf{x}_i^{\text{sim}} \,|\, \mathbf{x}_i^{\text{obs}}) = \int P(\mathbf{x}_i^{\text{sim}} \,|\, \theta) P(\theta \,|\, \mathbf{x}_i^{\text{obs}}) \, d\theta$.

4 For each observation, estimate Bayesian p-value using test statistic in (5):
$p_{B_i} \approx \frac{1}{M} \sum_{m=1}^{M} I(T(\mathbf{x}_{i,m}^{\text{sim}}) \geq T(\mathbf{x}_i^{\text{holdout}}))$.

5 **if** $\frac{1}{N} \sum_{i=1}^{N} p_{B_i} > \tau$ **then**

6 $\quad$ Estimate substitute confounders $\hat{\mathbf{Z}} = \mathbb{E}\left[\mathbf{Z} \,|\, \mathbf{X}^{\text{obs}}, \mathbf{F}\right]$ by PLFM.

7 $\quad$ Fit a regression model $f: \mathbf{x} \mapsto$ ADAS, using the residuals defined in (12).

8 $\quad$ $\mathbb{E}\left[\text{ADAS} \,|\, do(X_S = x'_S)\right] \approx \frac{1}{N} \sum_{i=1}^{N} f(r(\tilde{\mathbf{x}}_i, \mathbf{f}_i))$, where $\tilde{\mathbf{x}}_i$ equals $\mathbf{x}_i$, except for features
in S, which are set to x'_S.

9 **end**

2.3   Estimating a Substitute Confounder

By assuming that the confounder U is unobserved, we can only attempt to estimate causal effects by building upon assumptions on the data-generating process. Therefore, we assume that the data-generating process is faithful to the graphical model in Fig. 1, i.e., statistical independencies in the observed data distribution imply missing causal relationships in the graph. In particular, this implies that there is a common unobserved confounder U that is shared among all causes X and that there is no unobserved confounder that affects a single cause. Here, causes X are image-derived volume and thickness measurements, and we require that the unknown confounder affects multiple brain regions and not just a single region. This assumption is plausible, because common sources of confounding such as scanner, protocol, and aging affect the brain as a whole and not just individual regions [2,31]. Based on this assumption, we can exploit the fact that the confounder induces dependence among multiple causes.

From Fig. 1 we can observe that U, age, education, gender, and p-Tau are shared among all causes $X_1, \ldots, X_D$. Given these parents, denoted as $PA_{X_1,\ldots,X_D}$, the causes become conditionally independent:

$$P(x_1, \ldots x_D \,|\, PA_{X_1,\ldots,X_D}) = \prod_{d=1}^{D} P(x_d \,|\, PA_{X_1,\ldots,X_D}). \qquad (2)$$

The key realization of our proposed method is that the conditional probability (2), which is derived solely from the causal graph in Fig. 1, has the same form as the conditional distribution of a probabilistic latent factor model (PLFM). Therefore, we can utilize this connection to estimate a substitute confounder $\mathbf{z}$ for the unobserved confounder U via a latent factor model.

The theoretical proof for this approach is due to Wang and Blei [34] who showed that the latent representation of any PLFM does indeed render the relationship between neuroanatomical measures and ADAS unconfounded if (i) the PLFM captures all multi-cause confounders, and (ii) the PLFM estimates the substitute confounder with consistency, i.e., deterministicly, as the number of causes D grows large. To verify whether (i) holds, we rely on posterior predictive checking, as described below, and only proceed with estimation of the causal effect if the check passes.[1] Regarding (ii), [3] showed that estimates of many PLFM are consistent if the number of causes and samples is large. Note, that it does not imply that we need to find the true confounder, just a deterministic bijective transformation of it [34].

Latent Factor Model. Let $\mathbf{f}_i \in \mathbb{R}^P$ be the feature vector describing the observed direct influences on X_d for the i-th patient, except TIV, which we account for by dividing all volume measures $X_1^v, \ldots, X_{D_1}^v$ by it. Then, we can use an extended version of probabilistic principal component analysis (PPCA, [32]) to represent the D causes in terms of the known causes $\mathbf{f}_i$ and the latent substitute confounder $\mathbf{z}_i \in \mathbb{R}^K$:

$$\mathbf{x}_i = \mathbf{W}\mathbf{z}_i + \mathbf{A}\mathbf{f}_i + \boldsymbol{\varepsilon}_i, \quad \boldsymbol{\varepsilon}_i \sim \mathcal{N}(\mathbf{0}, \sigma_x^2 \mathbf{I}_D), \qquad \forall i = 1, \ldots, N, \qquad (3)$$

where $\mathbf{I}_D$ is a $D \times D$ identity matrix, $\mathbf{W}$ a $D \times K$ loading matrix, and $\mathbf{A}$ a $D \times P$ matrix of regression coefficients for the known causes of $\mathbf{x}_i$, excluding TIV.

Our approach is not restricted to PPCA, in fact, any PLFM can be used to infer the substitute confounder. Here, we consider an extended version of probabilistic matrix factorization (BPMF, [27]) as an alternative:

$$x_{ij} = \mathbf{z}_i^\top \mathbf{v}_j + \mathbf{A}_j^\top \mathbf{f}_i + \varepsilon_{ij}, \quad \varepsilon_{ij} \sim \mathcal{N}(0, \sigma_x^2), \quad \forall i = 1, \ldots, N, \ \forall j = 1, \ldots, D, \ (4)$$

where $\mathbf{v}_j$ is a K-dimensional feature-specific latent vector. The full models with prior distributions are depicted in Fig. 2.

Posterior Predictive Checking. To ensure the PLFM can represent the joint distribution over the observed causes well, we employ posterior predictive checking to quantify how well the PLFM fits the data [11, ch. 6]. If the PLFM is a good fit, simulated data generated under the PLFM should look similar to observed data. First, we hold-out a randomly selected portion of the observed causes, yielding $\mathbf{X}^{\text{obs}}$ to fit the factor model, and $\mathbf{X}^{\text{holdout}}$ for model checking. Next, we draw simulated data from the joint posterior predictive distribution. If there is a systematic difference between the simulated and the held-out data, we can conclude that the PLFM does not represent the causes well. We use the expected negative log-likelihood as test statistic to compute the Bayesian p-value p_B – the probability that the simulated is more extreme than the observed data [11]:

$$T(\mathbf{x}_i) = \mathbb{E}_\theta \left[-\log p(\mathbf{x}_i \mid \theta) \mid \mathbf{x}_i^{\text{obs}} \right], \quad p_{B_i} = P(T(\mathbf{x}_i^{\text{sim}}) \geq T(\mathbf{x}_i^{\text{holdout}}) \mid \mathbf{x}_i^{\text{obs}}), \ (5)$$

where θ is the set of all parameters of the PLFM. We estimate p_{B_i} by drawing $\mathbf{x}_i^{\text{sim}}$ repeatedly from the posterior predictive distribution and computing the proportion for which $T(\mathbf{x}_i^{\text{sim}}) \geq T(\mathbf{x}_i^{\text{holdout}})$ (see Algorithm 1). Next, we will prove that the causal effect of neuroanatomical measures on ADAS is identifiable by accounting for the substitute confounder.

---

[1] We follow [34] and use $\bar{p}_B = \mathbb{E}[p_{B_i}] > 0.1$ as criterion.

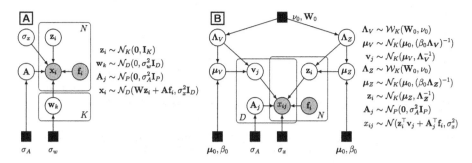

Fig. 2. Probabilistic latent factor models to estimate a K-dimensional substitute confounder z_i from D-dimensional causes x_i. Circles are random variables, filled circles are observed, transparent circles are to be estimated. A: Probabilistic principal component analysis model. B: Bayesian probabilistic matrix factorization model.

2.4   Identifiability in the Presence of a Substitute Confounder

The theoretical results outlined above and described in detail in [34] enable us to treat the substitute confounder $\mathbf{z}$ as if it were observed. We will now prove that the average causal effect (1) that a subset $\mathcal{S}$ of neuroanatomical structures have simultaneously on the ADAS score is identifiable in this modified setting. Therefore, we will again refer to Fig. 1, but replace U with its observed substitute.

Theorem 1. *Assuming the data-generating process is faithful to the graphical model in Fig. 1, the causal effect $\mathbb{E}\left[\mathrm{ADAS}\,|\,do(x'_{\mathcal{S}})\right]$ of a subset $\mathcal{S}$ of neuroanatomical measures on ADAS is identifiable from a distribution over the observed neuroanatomical measures not in $\mathcal{S}$, age, and the substitute confounder $\mathbf{z}$.*

Proof. By assuming that the graph in Fig. 1 is faithful, we can apply the rules of do calculus [24, Theorem 3.4.1] to show that the post-intervention distribution can be identified from observed data and the substitute confounder. We denote by $\bar{\mathcal{S}}$ the complement of the set $\mathcal{S}$:

$$\mathbb{E}\left[\mathrm{ADAS}\,|\,do(x'_{\mathcal{S}})\right] = \mathbb{E}_{age,x_{\bar{\mathcal{S}}},z}\left[\mathbb{E}\left[\mathrm{ADAS}\,|\,do(x'_{\mathcal{S}}),x_{\bar{\mathcal{S}}},age,\mathbf{z}\right]\right] \tag{6}$$

$$= \mathbb{E}_{age,x_{\bar{\mathcal{S}}},z}\left[\mathbb{E}\left[\mathrm{ADAS}\,|\,do(x'_{\mathcal{S}}),x_{\bar{\mathcal{S}}},do(ptau),age,\mathbf{z}\right]\right] \tag{7}$$

$$= \mathbb{E}_{age,x_{\bar{\mathcal{S}}},z}\left[\mathbb{E}\left[\mathrm{ADAS}\,|\,x'_{\mathcal{S}},x_{\bar{\mathcal{S}}},do(ptau),age,\mathbf{z}\right]\right] \tag{8}$$

$$= \mathbb{E}_{age,x_{\bar{\mathcal{S}}},z}\left[\mathbb{E}\left[\mathrm{ADAS}\,|\,x'_{\mathcal{S}},x_{\bar{\mathcal{S}}},ptau,age,\mathbf{z}\right]\right] \tag{9}$$

$$= \mathbb{E}_{age,x_{\bar{\mathcal{S}}},z}\left[\mathbb{E}\left[\mathrm{ADAS}\,|\,x'_{\mathcal{S}},x_{\bar{\mathcal{S}}},age,\mathbf{z}\right]\right] \tag{10}$$

$$\approx \frac{1}{N}\sum_{i=1}^{N}\hat{\mathbb{E}}\left[\mathrm{ADAS}\,|\,x'_{\mathcal{S}},\mathbf{x}_{i,\bar{\mathcal{S}}},age_i,\mathbf{z}_i\right]. \tag{11}$$

Table 1. RMSE × 100 of effects estimated by logistic regression compared to the true causal effects on semi-synthetic data. ROA is the error when only regressing out the observed confounder age, Oracle is the error when including all confounders. Columns with Δ denote the improvement over the 'Non-causal' model.

ν_x/ν_z	Non-causal	ROA	PPCA	BPMF	Oracle	ΔROA	ΔPPCA	ΔBPMF
10/1	20.121	19.416	17.449	18.033	17.917	0.705	2.672	2.087
5/1	21.078	20.436	18.560	18.895	18.781	0.643	2.518	2.183
4/1	21.505	20.889	19.050	19.296	19.169	0.617	2.456	2.210
3/1	22.169	21.590	19.820	19.933	19.782	0.580	2.349	2.236
5/2	22.653	22.097	20.382	20.408	20.233	0.556	2.270	2.244
5/3	23.911	23.417	21.837	21.699	21.438	0.494	2.073	2.212
3/2	24.275	23.798	22.261	22.083	21.796	0.477	2.014	2.192
1/1	25.802	25.391	24.022	23.735	23.319	0.411	1.780	2.067
2/3	27.464	27.116	25.932	25.596	25.040	0.348	1.531	1.867
3/5	27.899	27.567	26.434	26.088	25.502	0.333	1.465	1.811
2/5	29.564	29.284	28.354	28.018	27.307	0.280	1.210	1.546
1/3	30.297	30.037	29.199	28.877	28.124	0.259	1.097	1.419
1/4	31.384	31.153	30.448	30.167	29.354	0.230	0.936	1.216
1/5	32.179	31.967	31.364	31.118	30.266	0.212	0.815	1.060
1/10	34.318	34.154	33.816	33.699	32.778	0.164	0.502	0.620

(left margin annotations: "least confounded" at top pointing to row 10/1, "most confounded" at bottom pointing to row 1/10)

The equality in (6) is due to the factorization given by the graph in Fig. 1, the one in (7) due to rule 3 of do calculus, (8) and (9) are due to rule 2 of do calculus, and (10) is due to ADAS $\perp\!\!\!\perp$ p-Tau $\mid x'_S, x_{\bar{S}}, age, \mathbf{z}$. Finally, we can estimate the outer expectation by Monte Carlo and the inner expectation with a regression model from the observed data alone, if $P(x_S \mid PA_{X_1,\ldots,X_D}) > 0$ for any subset S. This assumption holds for the proposed PLFM in (3) and (4), because their conditional distribution is a normal distribution, which is non-zero everywhere.

2.5   The Outcome Model

Theorem 1 tells us that the average causal effect can be estimated from the observed data and the substitute confounder. The final step in causal inference is to actually estimate the expectation in (11), which we do by fitting a model to predict the ADAS score from neuroanatomical measures, age and the substitute confounder (see Algorithm 1). We will use a linear model, but Theorem 1 holds when using a non-linear model too.

ADAS ranges between 0 and 85 with higher values indicating a higher cognitive decline, hence we convert ADAS to proportions in the interval $(0, 1)$ and use a Bayesian Beta regression model for prediction [7]. Let y_i denote the ADAS score of subject i, then the likelihood function is

$$L(\beta_0, \boldsymbol{\beta}, \phi) = \prod_{i=1}^{N} \frac{y_i^{\mu_i \phi - 1}(1 - y_i)^{(1 - \mu_i)\phi - 1}}{B(\mu_i \phi, (1 - \mu_i)\phi)}, \quad \mu_i = \text{logit}^{-1}(\beta_0 + r(\mathbf{x}_i, \mathbf{f}_i)^\top \boldsymbol{\beta}),$$

where B is the beta function, and ϕ is a scalar scale parameter. To account for unobserved confounding, we replace the original neuroanatomical measures by the residuals with respect to their reconstruction by the PLFM:

$$r(\mathbf{x}_i, \mathbf{f}_i) = \mathbf{x}_i - \mathbb{E}\left[X_1, \ldots, X_D \mid \hat{\mathbf{z}}_i, \mathbf{f}_i\right], \qquad \hat{\mathbf{z}}_i = \mathbb{E}\left[Z \mid \mathbf{x}_i^{\text{obs}}, \mathbf{f}_i\right], \qquad (12)$$

where the expectations are with respect to the selected PLFM.[2]

3 Experiments

Semi-synthetic Data. In our first experiment, we evaluate how well causal effects can be recovered when ignoring all confounders, using only the observed confounder (age), using the observed and unobserved confounders (oracle), and using the observed and substitute confounder computed by (3) or (4). We use T1-weighted magnetic resonance imaging brains scans from $N = 11,800$ subjects from UK Biobank [22]. From each scan, we extract 19 volume measurements with FreeSurfer 5.3 [9] and create a synthetic binary outcome. For each volume, we use age and gender as known causes $\mathbf{f}_i$ and estimate $\hat{x}_{ij} = \mathbb{E}\left[X_{ij} \mid \mathbf{f}_i\right]$ via linear regression. We use age as an observed confounder and generate one unobserved confounder u_k by assigning individuals to clusters with varying percentages of positive labels. First, we obtain the first two principal components across all volumes, scale individual scores to $[0; 1]$, and cluster the projected data into 4 clusters using k-means to assign $u_k \in \{1, 2, 3, 4\}$ and scale σ_k of the noise term. Causal effects follow a sparse normal distribution $(\mathcal{N}_{\text{sp}})$, where all values in the 20–80th percentile range are zero, hence only a small portion of volumes have a non-zero causal effect. Let ν_x, ν_z, $\nu_\varepsilon = 1 - \nu_x - \nu_z$ denote how much variance can be explained by the causal effects, confounding effects, and the noise, respectively, then for the i-th instance in cluster k, we generate a binary outcome y_i as:

$$y_i \sim \text{Bernoulli}(\text{logit}^{-1}(\beta_0 + \hat{\mathbf{x}}_i\boldsymbol{\beta}\tfrac{\sqrt{\nu_x}}{\sigma_x} + u_k \cdot \tfrac{\sqrt{0.9\nu_z}}{\sigma_z} + \text{age}_i\gamma \cdot \tfrac{\sqrt{0.1\nu_z}}{\sigma_{\text{age}}} + \varepsilon_i\tfrac{\sqrt{\nu_\varepsilon}}{\sigma_\varepsilon})),$$

$$\beta_j \sim \mathcal{N}_{\text{sp}}(0, 0.5), \quad \gamma \sim \mathcal{N}(0, 0.2), \quad \sigma_k \sim 1 + \text{InvGamma}(3, 1), \quad \varepsilon_i \sim \mathcal{N}(0, \sigma_k),$$

where σ_x, σ_z, σ_{age}, and σ_ε are standard deviations with respect to $\hat{\mathbf{x}}_i\boldsymbol{\beta}$, u, age_i and ε_i for $i = 1, \ldots, N$. Finally, we choose β_0 such that the positive and negative class are roughly balanced.

Table 1 shows the root mean squared error (RMSE) with respect to the true causal effect of a logistic regression model across 1,000 simulations for various ν_x, ν_z, and $\nu_\varepsilon = 0.1$. We used $K = 5$ substitute confounders and both PLFM passed the posterior predictive check with $\bar{p}_B = 0.269$ (BPMF) and $\bar{p}_B = 0.777$ (PPCA), despite that the true data generation model differs. As expected, by ignoring confounding completely (first column), the RMSE is the highest. When only accounting for the known confounder age (second column), the RMSE decreases slightly. The RMSE reduces considerably when using a substitute confounder and achieves an improvement 2.9–5.5 higher than that of the age-only model. Finally, the results show that there is a cost to using a substitute confounder: using all confounders (Oracle) leads to the lowest RMSE.

---

[2] Code available at https://github.com/ai-med/causal-effects-in-alzheimers-conti nuum.

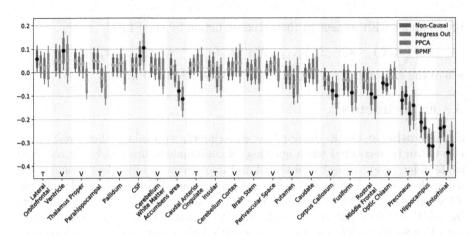

Fig. 3. Mean coefficient (dot), 80% (thick line), and 95% (thin line) credible interval of volume and thickness measures. Significant effects are marked with a black dot. (Color figure online)

Alzheimer's Disease Data. In this experiment, we study the causal effect of neuroanatomical measures on ADAS using data from the Alzheimer's Disease Neuroimaging Initiative [14]. We only focus on effects due to Alzheimer's pathologic change and not other forms of dementia. Therefore, we only include patients with abnormal amyloid biomarkers [13]. We extract 14 volume and 8 thickness measures using FreeSurfer [9] for 711 subjects (highly correlated measures are removed). Since the average causal effect is fully parameterized by the coefficients of the linear Beta regression model, we can compare estimated coefficients of the proposed approach with $K = 6$ substitute confounders, with that of a model ignoring all confounders (Non-causal), and of a model trained on measures where age, gender, and education has been regressed-out.

The BPMF ($\bar{p}_B = 0.293$) and PPCA model ($\bar{p}_B = 0.762$) passed the posterior predictive check; estimated coefficients are depicted in Fig. 3. Lateral orbitofrontal thickness and optic chiasm become non-significant after correcting for unobserved confounding, whereas rostral anterior cingulate thickness, CSF volume, accumbens volume, and corpus callosum volume become significant. The biggest change concerns accumbens volume, which is associated with cognitive *improvement* in the non-causal model, but is a cause for cognitive *decline* in the causal models. This correction is justified, because the accumbens is part of the limbic circuit and thus shares its vulnerability to degenerate during cognitive decline [16]. An analysis based on the non-causal model would have resulted in a wrong conclusion. The result that atrophy of corpus callosum is causal seems to be plausible too, because it is a known marker of the progressive interhemispheric disconnection in AD [5]. While finding literature on the absence of an effect on cognition is difficult, we believe a causal effect of atrophy of the optic nerve to be unlikely, because its main function is to transmit visual information. It is more likely that the non-causal model picked up an association due to aging-related confounding instead. Finally, we want to highlight the change in parahippocampal thickness. Previous research suggests that thinning is common in AD [28], which would only be captured correctly after correcting for unobserved confounding, as indicated by a negative mean coefficient. In contrast, when only accounting for the known confounder age, the estimated mean coefficient remains positive.

4 Conclusion

Inferring causal effects from observational neuroimaging data is challenging, because it requires expressing the causal question in a graphical model, and various unknown sources of confounding often render the causal effects unidentifiable. We tackled this task by deriving a causal graph from the current clinical knowledge on the Alzheimer's disease continuum, and proposed a latent factor model approach to estimate a substitute for the unobserved confounders. Our experiments on semi-synthetic data showed that our proposed approach can recover causal effects more accurately than a model that only accounts for observed confounders or ignores confounding. Analyses on the causal effects on cognitive decline due to Alzheimer's revealed that accounting for unobserved confounding reveals important causes of cognitive decline that otherwise would have been missed.

Acknowledgements. This research was supported by the Bavarian State Ministry of Science and the Arts and coordinated by the Bavarian Research Institute for Digital Transformation, and the Federal Ministry of Education and Research in the call for Computational Life Sciences (DeepMentia, 031L0200A).

References

1. Alfaro-Almagro, F., McCarthy, P., Afyouni, S., Andersson, J.L.R., Bastiani, M., et al.: Confound modelling in UK Biobank brain imaging. Neuroimage **224**, 117002117002 (2021)
2. Barnes, J., Ridgway, G.R., Bartlett, J., Henley, S.M., Lehmann, M., et al.: Head size, age and gender adjustment in MRI studies: a necessary nuisance? Neuroimage **53**(4), 1244–1255 (2010)
3. Chen, Y., Li, X., Zhang, S.: Structured latent factor analysis for large-scale data: Identifiability, estimability, and their implications. J. Am. Stat. Assoc. **115**(532), 1756–1770 (2020)
4. Crary, J.F., Trojanowski, J.Q., Schneider, J.A., Abisambra, J.F., Abner, E.L., et al.: Primary age-related tauopathy (PART): a common pathology associated with human aging. Acta Neuropathol. **128**(6), 755–766 (2014)
5. Delbeuck, X., Van der Linden, M., Collette, F.: Alzheimer's disease as a disconnection syndrome? Neuropsychol. Rev. **13**(2), 79–92 (2003)
6. Dukart, J., Schroeter, M.L., Mueller, K.: Age correction in dementia-matching to a healthy brain. PloS One **6**(7), e22193 (2011)
7. Ferrari, S., Cribari-Neto, F.: Beta regression for modelling rates and proportions. J. Appl. Stat. **31**(7), 799–815 (2004)

8. Ferretti, M.T., Martinkova, J., Biskup, E., Benke, T., Gialdini, G., et al.: Sex and gender differences in alzheimer's disease: current challenges and implications for clinical practice. Eur. J. Neurol. **27**(6), 928–943 (2020)
9. Fischl, B.: FreeSurfer. Neuroimage **62**(2), 774–781 (2012)
10. Fortin, J.P., Cullen, N., et al.: Harmonization of cortical thickness measurements across scanners and sites. Neuroimage **167**, 104–120 (2018)
11. Gelman, A., Carlin, J.B., Stern, H.S., Rubin, D.B., Dunson, D.B.: Bayesian Data Analysis, 3rd edn. Chapman and Hall/CRC, New York (2014)
12. Hedden, T., Gabrieli, J.D.E.: Insights into the ageing mind: a view from cognitive neuroscience. Nat. Rev. Neurosci. **5**(2), 87–96 (2004)
13. Jack, C.R., Bennett, D.A., Blennow, K., Carrillo, M.C., Dunn, B., et al.: NIA-AA research framework: toward a biological definition of alzheimer's disease. Alzheimers Dement **14**(4), 535–562 (2018)
14. Jack, C.R., Bernstein, M.A., Fox, N.C., Thompson, P., et al.: The alzheimer's disease neuroimaging initiative (ADNI): MRI methods. J. Magn. Reson Imaging **27**(4), 685–691 (2008)
15. Jack, C.R., Knopman, D.S., Jagust, W.J., Petersen, R.C., Weiner, M.W., et al.: Tracking pathophysiological processes in alzheimer's disease: an updated hypothetical model of dynamic biomarkers. Lancet Neurol. **12**(2), 207–216 (2013)
16. de Jong, L.W., Wang, Y., White, L.R., Yu, B., Launer, L.J.: Ventral striatal volume is associated with cognitive decline in older people: a population based MR-study. Neurobiol. Aging **33**, 424e1e1–424.10 (2012)
17. Koikkalainen, J., Pölönen, H., Mattila, J., van Gils, M., Soininen, H., Lötjönen, J., et al.: Improved classification of alzheimer's disease data via removal of nuisance variability. PLoS One **7**(2), e31112 (2012)
18. Kostro, D., Abdulkadir, A., Durr, A., Roos, R., Leavitt, B.R., et al.: Correction of inter-scanner and within-subject variance in structural MRI based automated diagnosing. Neuroimage **98**, 405–415 (2014)
19. Linn, K.A., Gaonkar, B., Doshi, J., Davatzikos, C., Shinohara, R.T.: Addressing confounding in predictive models with an application to neuroimaging. Int. J. Biostat. **12**(1), 31–44 (2016)
20. Lockhart, S.N., DeCarli, C.: Structural imaging measures of brain aging. Neuropsychol. Rev. **24**(3), 271–289 (2014)
21. Long, J.M., Holtzman, D.M.: Alzheimer disease: an update on pathobiology and treatment strategies. Cell **179**(2), 312–339 (2019)
22. Miller, K.L., Alfaro-Almagro, F., Bangerter, N.K., Thomas, D.L., Yacoub, E., et al.: Multimodal population brain imaging in the UK Biobank prospective epidemiological study. Nat Neurosci. **19**(11), 1523–1536 (2016)
23. Mohs, R.C., Knopman, D., Petersen, R.C., Ferris, S.H., Ernesto, C., et al.: Development of cognitive instruments for use in clinical trials of antidementia drugs. Alzheimer Dis. Assoc. Disord. **11**, 13–21 (1997)
24. Pearl, J.: Causality: Models, Reasoning, and Inference. Cambridge University Press, Cambridge (2000)
25. Rao, A., Monteiro, J.M., Mourao-Miranda, J.: Predictive modelling using neuroimaging data in the presence of confounds. Neuroimage **150**, 23–49 (2017)
26. Rodrigue, K.M., Kennedy, K.M., Park, D.C.: Beta-amyloid deposition and the aging brain. Neuropsychol. Rev. **19**(4), 436–450 (2009)
27. Salakhutdinov, R., Mnih, A.: Bayesian probabilistic Matrix Factorization Using Markov Chain Monte Carlo. In: ICML, pp. 880–887 (2008)

28. Schwarz, C.G., Gunter, J.L., Wiste, H.J., Przybelski, S.A., Weigand, S.D., et al.: A large-scale comparison of cortical thickness and volume methods for measuring alzheimer's disease severity. Neuroimage Clin. **11**, 802–812 (2016)

29. Snoek, L., Miletić, S., Scholte, H.S.: How to control for confounds in decoding analyses of neuroimaging data. Neuroimage **184**, 741–760 (2019)

30. Stern, Y., Arenaza-Urquijo, E.M., Bartrés-Faz, D., Belleville, S., Cantilon, M., et al.: Whitepaper: defining and investigating cognitive reserve, brain reserve, and brain maintenance. Alzheimer's Dement **16**, 1305–1311 (2020)

31. Stonnington, C.M., Tan, G., Klöppel, S., Chu, C., Draganski, B., Jack, C.R., et al.: Interpreting scan data acquired from multiple scanners: a study with Alzheimer's disease. Neuroimage **39**(3), 1180–1185 (2008)

32. Tipping, M.E., Bishop, C.M.: Probabilistic principal component analysis. J. R. Stat. Soc. Ser. B Stat. Methodol. **61**(3), 611–622 (1999)

33. Wachinger, C., Rieckmann, A., Pölsterl, S.: Detect and correct bias in multi-site neuroimaging datasets. Med. Image Anal. **67**, 101879 (2020)

34. Wang, Y., Blei, D.M.: The blessings of multiple causes. J. Am. Stat. Assoc. **114**, 1–71 (2019)

Multiple-Shooting Adjoint Method for Whole-Brain Dynamic Causal Modeling

Juntang Zhuang$^{(\boxtimes)}$, Nicha Dvornek , Sekhar Tatikonda ,
Xenophon Papademetris , Pamela Ventola , and James S. Duncan

Yale University, New Haven, USA
{j.zhuang,nicha.dvornek,sekhar.tatikonda,xenophon.papademetris,
pamela.ventola,james.duncan}@yale.edu

Abstract. Dynamic causal modeling (DCM) is a Bayesian framework to
infer directed connections between compartments, and has been used to
describe the interactions between underlying neural populations based
on functional neuroimaging data. DCM is typically analyzed with the
expectation-maximization (EM) algorithm. However, because the inversion of a large-scale continuous system is difficult when noisy observations are present, DCM by EM is typically limited to a small number
of compartments (<10). Another drawback with the current method is
its complexity; when the forward model changes, the posterior mean
changes, and we need to re-derive the algorithm for optimization. In this
project, we propose the Multiple-Shooting Adjoint (MSA) method to
address these limitations. MSA uses the multiple-shooting method for
parameter estimation in ordinary differential equations (ODEs) under
noisy observations, and is suitable for large-scale systems such as whole-
brain analysis in functional MRI (fMRI). Furthermore, MSA uses the
adjoint method for accurate gradient estimation in the ODE; since the
adjoint method is generic, MSA is a generic method for both linear and
non-linear systems, and does not require re-derivation of the algorithm
as in EM. We validate MSA in extensive experiments: 1) in toy examples
with both linear and non-linear models, we show that MSA achieves better accuracy in parameter value estimation than EM; furthermore, MSA
can be successfully applied to large systems with up to 100 compartments; and 2) using real fMRI data, we apply MSA to the estimation of
the whole-brain effective connectome and show improved classification
of autism spectrum disorder (ASD) vs. control compared to using the
functional connectome. The package is provided https://jzkay12.github.
io/TorchDiffEqPack.

Keywords: Multiple shoot · Adjoint method · Dynamic causal
modeling

1 Introduction

Autism spectrum disorder (ASD) is a neurodevelopmental disorder that affects
both social behavior and mental health [11]. ASD is typically diagnosed with

© Springer Nature Switzerland AG 2021
A. Feragen et al. (Eds.): IPMI 2021, LNCS 12729, pp. 58–70, 2021.
https://doi.org/10.1007/978-3-030-78191-0_5

behavioral tests, and recently functional MRI (fMRI) has been applied to analyze the cause of ASD [3]. Connectome analysis in fMRI aims to elucidate neural connections in the brain and can be generally categorized into two types: the functional connectome (FC) [21] and the effective connectome (EC) [5]. The FC typically calculates the correlation between time-series of different regions-of-interest (ROIs) in the brain, which is typically robust and easy to compute; however, FC does not reveal the underlying dynamics. EC models the directed influence between ROIs, and is widely used in analysis of EEG [8] and fMRI [19].

EC is typically estimated using dynamic causal modeling (DCM) [5]. DCM can be viewed as a Bayesian framework for parameter estimation in a dynamical system represented by an ordinary different equation (ODE). A DCM model is typically optimized using the expectation-maximization (EM) algorithm [10]. Despite its wide application and good theoretical properties, a drawback is we need to re-derive the algorithm when the forward model changes, which limits its application. Furthermore, current DCM can not handle large-scale systems, hence is unsuitable for whole-brain analysis. Recent works such as rDCM [4], spectral-DCM [17] and sparse-DCM [16] modify DCM for whole-brain analysis of resting-state fMRI, yet they are limited to a linear dynamical system and use the EM algorithm for optimization, hence cannot be used as off-the-shelf methods for different forward models.

In this project, we propose the Multiple-Shooting Adjoint (MSA) method for parameter estimation in DCM. Specifically, MSA uses the multiple-shooting method [1] for robust fitting of an ODE, and uses the adjoint method [15] for gradient estimation in the continuous case; after deriving the gradient, generic optimizers such as stochastic gradient descent (SGD) can be applied. Our contributions are: (1) MSA is implemented as an off-the-shelf method, and can be easily applied to generic non-linear cases by specifying the forward model without re-deriving the optimization algorithm. (2) In toy examples, we validate the accuracy of MSA in parameter estimation; we also validated its ability to handle large-scale systems. (3) We apply MSA in the whole-brain dynamic causal modeling for fMRI; in a classification task of ASD vs. control, EC estimated by MSA achieves better performance than FC.

2   Methods

We first introduce the notations and problem in Sect. 2.1, then introduce mathematical methods in Sect. 2.3–2.4, and finally introduce DCM for fMRI in Sect. 2.5.

2.1   Notations and Formulation of Problem

We summarize notations here for the ease of reading, which correspond to Fig. 1.

- $z(t), \widetilde{z(t)}, \overline{z(t)}$: $z(t)$ is the true time-series, $\widetilde{z(t)}$ is the noisy observation, and $\overline{z(t)}$ is the estimation. If p time-series are observed, then they are p-dimensional vectors for each time t.

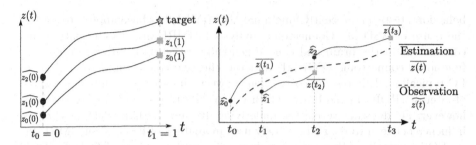

Fig. 1. Left: illustration of the shooting method. Right: illustration of the multiple-shooting method. Blue dots represent the guess of state at split time t_i. (Colour figure online)

- $(t_i, \widehat{z}_i)_{i=0}^N$: $\{\widehat{z}_i\}_{i=0}^N$ are corresponding guesses of states at split time points $\{t_i\}_{i=0}^N$. See Fig. 1. $\widehat{z}_i$ are discrete points, while $\widetilde{z(t)}, z(t), \overline{z(t)}$ are trajectories.
- f_η: Hidden state $z(t)$ follows the ODE $\frac{dz}{dt} = f(z, t)$, f is parameterized by η.
- θ: $\theta = [\eta, z_0, ...z_N]$. We concatenate all optimizable parameters into one vector for the ease of notation, denoted as θ.
- $\lambda(t)$: Lagrangian multiplier in the continuous case, used to derive the adjoint state equation.

The task of DCM can be viewed as a parameter estimation problem for a continuous dynamical system, and can be formulated as:

$$\underset{\eta}{\mathrm{argmin}} \int \left(\overline{z(\tau)} - \widetilde{z(\tau)}\right)^2 d\tau \quad s.t. \quad \frac{d\overline{z(\tau)}}{d\tau} = f_\eta(\overline{z(\tau)}, \tau) \tag{1}$$

The goal is to estimate η from observations $\widetilde{z}$. In the following sections, we first briefly introduce the multiple-shooting method, which is related to the numerical solution of a continuous dynamical system; next, we introduce the adjoint state method, which efficiently determines the gradient for parameters in continuous dynamical systems; next, we introduce the proposed MSA method, which combines multiple-shooting and the adjoint state method, and can be applied with general forward models and gradient-based optimizers; finally, we introduce the DCM model, and demonstrate the application of MSA.

2.2   Multiple-Shooting Method

The shooting method is commonly used to fit an ODE under noisy observations, which is crucial for parameter estimation in ODE. In this section, we first introduce the shooting method, then explain its variant, the multiple-shooting method, for long time-series.

Shooting Method. The shooting method typically reduces a boundary-value problem to an initial value problem [6]. An example is shown in Fig. 1: to find a correct initial condition (at $t_0 = 0$) that reaches the target (at $t_1 = 1$), the shooting algorithm first takes an initial guess (e.g. $\widehat{z_0(0)}$), then integrate the curve to reach point $(t_1, \overline{z_0(1)})$; the error term $target - z_0(1)$ is used to update the initial condition (e.g. $\widehat{z_1(0)}$) so that the end-time value $\overline{z_1(1)}$ is closer to target. This process is repeated until convergence. Besides the initial condition, the shooting method can be applied to update other parameters.

Multiple-Shooting Method. The multiple-shooting method [1] is an extension of the shooting method to long time-series; it splits a long time-series into chunks, and applies the shooting method to each chunk. Integration of a dynamical system for a long time is typically subject to noise and numerical error, while solving short time-series is generally easier and more robust.

As shown in the right subfigure of Fig. 1, a guess of initial condition at time t_0 is denoted as $\widehat{z_0}$, and we can use any ODE solver to get the estimated integral curve $\overline{z(t)}, t \in [t_0, t_1]$. Similarly, we can guess the initial condition at time t_1 as $\widehat{z_1}$, and get $\overline{z(t)}, t \in [t_1, t_2]$ by integration as in Eq. 3. Note that each time chunk is shorter than the entire chunk ($|t_{i+1} - t_i| < |t_3 - t_0|, i \in \{1,2\}$), hence easier to solve. The split causes another issue: the guess might not match estimation at boundary points (e.g. $\overline{z(t_1)} \neq \widehat{z_1}, \overline{z(t_2)} \neq \widehat{z_2}$). Therefore, we need to consider this error of mismatch when updating parameters, and minimizing this mismatch error is typically easier compared to directly analyzing the entire sequence.

The multiple-shooting method can be written as:

$$\underset{\eta, z_0, \dots z_N}{\text{argmin}} \ J = \underset{\eta, z_0, \dots z_N}{\text{argmin}} \sum_{i=0}^{N} \int_{t_i}^{t_{i+1}} \left(\overline{z(\tau)} - \widetilde{z(\tau)} \right)^2 d\tau + \alpha \sum_{i=0}^{N} \left(\overline{z(t_i)} - \widehat{z_i} \right)^2 \quad (2)$$

$$\overline{z(t)} = \widehat{z_i} + \int_{t_i}^{t} f_\eta \left(\overline{z(\tau)}, \tau \right) d\tau, \quad t_i < t < t_{i+1}, \quad i \in \{0, 1, 2, \dots N\} \quad (3)$$

where N is the total number of chunks discretized at points $\{t_0, \dots t_N\}$, with corresponding guesses $\{\widehat{z_0}, \dots \widehat{z_N}\}$. We use $\overline{z(t)}$ to denote the estimated curve as in Eq. 3; suppose t falls into the chunk $[t_i, t_{i+1}]$, $z(t)$ is determined by solving the ODE from $(\widehat{z_i}, t_i)$, where $\widehat{z_i}$ is the guess of initial state at t_i. We use $\widetilde{z(t)}$ to denote the observation. The first part in Eq. 2 corresponds to the difference between estimation $\overline{z(t)}$ and observation $\widetilde{z(t)}$, while the second part corresponds to the mismatch between estimation (orange square, $\overline{z(t_i)}$) and guess (blue circle, $\widehat{z_i}$) at split time points t_i. The second part is weighted by a hyper-parameter α. The ODE function f is parameterized by η. The optimization goal is to find the best η that minimizes loss in Eq. 2, besides model parameters η, we also need to optimize the guess $\widehat{z_i}$ for state at time $t_i, i \in \{0, 1, \dots N\}$. Note that though previous work typically limits f to have a linear form, we don't have such limitations. Instead, multiple-shooting is generic for general f.

2.3   Adjoint State Method

Our goal is to minimize the loss function in Eq. 2. Let $\theta = [\eta, z_0, \dots, z_N]$ represent all learnable parameters. After fitting an ODE, we derive the gradient of loss L w.r.t parameter θ and state guess $\widehat{z_i}$ for optimization.

Adjoint State Equation. Note that different from discrete case, the gradient in continuous case is slightly complicated. We refer to the adjoint method [2,15, 23]. Consider the following problem:

$$\frac{dz(t)}{dt} = f_\theta\left(\overline{z(t)}, t\right), \quad s.t. \quad \overline{z(0)} = x, \quad t \in [0, T], \quad \theta = [\eta, z_0, ...z_N] \tag{4}$$

$$\hat{y} = \overline{z(T)}, \quad J\left(\hat{y}, y\right) = J\left(\overline{z(0)} + \int_0^T f_\theta(\overline{z}, t)dt, y\right) \tag{5}$$

where the initial condition $z(0)$ is specified by input x, output $\hat{y} = \overline{z(T)}$. The loss function J is applied on $\hat{y}$, with target y. Compared with Eq. 1 to Eq. 3, for simplicity, we use θ to denote both model parameter η and guess of initial conditions $\{\widehat{z_i}\}$. The Lagrangian is

$$L = J\left(\overline{z(T)}, y\right) + \int_0^T \lambda(t)^\top \left[\frac{dz(t)}{dt} - f_\theta(\overline{z(t)}, t)\right] dt \tag{6}$$

where $\lambda(t)$ is the continuous Lagrangian multiplier. Then we have the following:

$$\frac{\partial J}{\partial \overline{z(T)}} + \lambda(T) = 0 \tag{7}$$

$$\frac{d\lambda(t)}{dt} + \left(\frac{\partial f_\theta(\overline{z(t)}, t)}{\partial \overline{z(t)}}\right)^\top \lambda(t) = 0 \quad \forall t \in (0, T) \tag{8}$$

$$\frac{dL}{d\theta} - \int_T^0 \lambda(t)^\top \frac{\partial f_\theta(\overline{z(t)}, t)}{\partial \theta} dt = 0 \tag{9}$$

We skip the proof for simplicity. In general, the adjoint method determines the initial condition $\lambda(T)$ by Eq. 7, then solves Eq. 8 to get the trajectory of $\lambda(t)$, and finally integrates $\lambda(t)$ as in Eq. 9 to get the final gradient. Note that Eq. 7 to Eq. 9 is generic for general θ, and in case of Eq. 2 and Eq. 3, we have $\theta = [\eta, z_0, ...z_N]$, and $\nabla\theta = [\frac{\partial L}{\partial \eta}, \frac{\partial L}{\partial z_0}, ... \frac{\partial L}{\partial z_N}]$. Note that we need to calculate $\frac{\partial f}{\partial z}$ and $\frac{\partial f}{\partial \theta}$, which can be easily computed by a single backward pass; we only need to specify the forward model without worrying about the backward, because automatic differentiation is supported in frameworks such as PyTorch and Tensorflow. After deriving the gradient of all parameters, we can update these parameters by gradient descent.

Note that though $J(\overline{z(T)}, y)$ is defined on a single time point in Eq. 6, it can extend to the integral form $\int_{t=0}^T loss(t)dt$. We can defined F as $\frac{dF(t)}{dt} = loss(t)$, $F(0) = 0$, then $F(T)$ (for a single time point T) equals the integral.

Adaptive Checkpoint Adjoint. Equation 7 to Eq. 9 are the analytical form of the gradient in the continuous case, yet the numerical implementation is crucial for empirical performance. Note that $\overline{z(t)}$ is solved in forward-time (0 to T), while $\lambda(t)$ is solved in reverse-time (T to 0), yet the gradient in Eq. 9 requires both $z(t)$ and $\lambda(t)$ in the integrand. Memorizing a continuous trajectory $\overline{z(t)}$ requires much memory; to save memory, most existing implementations forget

---

Algorithm 1: Multiple-shooting adjoint method

Input Observation $\widetilde{z(t)}$, number of chunks N, learning rate lr.
Initialize model parameter η, state $\{\widehat{z_i}\}_{i=0}^{N}$ at discretized points $\{t_i\}_{i=0}^{N}$
Repeat until convergence
    (1) Estimate trajectory $\overline{z(t)}$ from current parameters by the multiple shooting method as in Eq. 3.
    (2) Compute the loss J in Eq. 2, plug J in Eq. 6. Derive the gradient by the adjoint method as in Eq. 7 to Eq. 9.
    (3) Update parameters $\theta \leftarrow \theta - lr \times \nabla\theta$

---

the forward-time trajectory of $\overline{z(t)}$, and instead only record the end-time state $\overline{z(T)}$ and $\lambda(T)$ and solve Eq. 4 and Eq. 7 to Eq. 9 in reverse-time on-the-fly.

While memory cost is low, existing implementations of the adjoint method typically suffer from numerical error: since the forward-time trajectory (denoted as $\overrightarrow{z(t)} = \overline{z(t)}$) is deleted, and the reverse-time trajectory (denoted as $\overleftarrow{z(t)}$) is reconstructed from the end-time state $z(T)$ by solving Eq. 4 in reverse-time, $\overrightarrow{z(t)}$ and $\overleftarrow{z(t)}$ cannot accurately overlap due to inevitable errors with numerical ODE solvers. The error $\overrightarrow{z(t)} - \overleftarrow{z(t)}$ propagates to the gradient in Eq. 9 in the $\frac{\partial f(z,t)}{\partial z}$ term. Please see [23] for a detailed explanation.

To solve this issue, the adaptive checkpoint adjoint (ACA) [23] records $\overrightarrow{z(t)}$ using a memory-efficient method to guarantee numerical accuracy. In this work, we use ACA for its accuracy.

2.4 Multiple-Shooting Adjoint (MSA) Method

Procedure of MSA. MSA is a combination of the multiple-shooting and the adjoint method, which is generic for various f. Details are summarized in Algo. 1. MSA iterates over the following steps until convergence: (1) estimate the trajectory based on the current parameters, using the multiple-shoot method for integration; (2) compute the loss and derive the gradient using the adjoint method; (3) update the parameters based on the gradient.

Advantages of MSA. Previous work has used the multiple-shooting method for parameter estimation in ODEs [13], yet MSA is different in the following aspects: (A) Suppose the parameters have k dimensions. MSA uses an element-wise update, hence has only $O(k)$ computational cost in each step; yet the method in [13] requires the inversion of a $k \times k$ matrix, hence might be infeasible for large-scale systems. (B) The implementation of [13] does not tackle the mismatch between forward-time and reverse-time trajectory, while we use ACA [23] for accurate gradient estimation in step (2) of Algorithm. 1. (C) From a practical perspective, our implementation is based on PyTorch which supports automatic-differentiation, therefore we only need to specify the forward model f without the need to manually compute the gradient $\frac{\partial f}{\partial z}$ and $\frac{\partial f}{\partial \theta}$. Hence, our method is off-the-shelf for general models, while the method of [13] needs to re-implement $\frac{\partial f}{\partial z}$ and $\frac{\partial f}{\partial \theta}$ for different f, and conventional DCM with EM needs to re-derive the entire algorithm when f changes.

2.5 Dynamic Causal Modeling

We briefly introduce the dynamical causal modeling here. Suppose there are p nodes (ROIs) and denote the observed fMRI time-series signal as $s(t)$, which is a p-dimensional vector at each time t. Denote the hidden neuronal state as $z(t)$; then $z(t)$ and $s(t)$ are p-dimensional vectors for each time point t. Denote the hemodynamic response function (HRF) [9] as $h(t)$, and denote the external stimulation as $u(t)$, which is an n-dimensional vector for each t. The model is:

$$f\Big([z(t)\ \ D(t)]\Big) = \begin{bmatrix} dz(t)/dt \\ dD(t)/dt \end{bmatrix} = \begin{bmatrix} D(t)z(t) + Cu(t) \\ Bu(t) \end{bmatrix}, \quad D(0) = A \qquad (10)$$

$$s(t) = \Big(z(t) + \epsilon(t)\Big) * h(t), \quad \widetilde{z(t)} = z(t) + \epsilon(t) = Deconv\Big(s(t), h(t)\Big) \qquad (11)$$

where $\epsilon(t)$ is the noise at time t, which is assumed to follow an independent Gaussian distribution, and $*$ represents convolution operation. $D(t)$ is a $p \times p$ matrix for each t, representing the effective connectome between nodes. A is a matrix of shape $p \times p$, representing the interaction between ROIs. B is a tensor of shape $p \times p \times n$, representing the effect of stimulation on the effective connectome. C is a matrix of shape $p \times n$, representing the effect of stimulation on neuronal state. An example of $n = 1, p = 3$ is shown in Fig. 2.

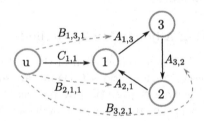

Fig. 2. Toy example of dynamic causal modeling with 3 nodes (labeled 1 to 3). u is a 1-D stimulation signal, so $n = 1, p = 3$. A, B, C are defined as in Eq. 10. For simplicity, though A is a 3×3 matrix, we assume only three elements $A_{1,3}, A_{3,2}, A_{2,1}$ are non-zero.

The task is to estimate parameters A, B, C from noisy observation $s(t)$. For simplicity, we assume $h(t)$ is fixed and use the empirical result from Nitime project [18]. By deconvolution of $s(t)$ with $h(t)$, we get a noisy observation of $z(t)$, denoted as $\widetilde{z(t)}$; $z(t)$ follows the ODE defined in Eq. 10. By plugging f into Eq. 1, and viewing η as $[A, B, C]$, this problem turns into a parameter estimation problem for ODEs, which can be efficiently solved by Algorithm 1. We emphasize that Algo. 1 is generic and MSA can be applied to any form of f, where the linear form of f in Eq. 10 is a special case for a specific model for fMRI.

3   Experiments

3.1   Validation on Toy Examples

We first validate MSA on toy examples of linear dynamical systems, then validate its performance on large-scale systems and non-linear dynamical systems.

A Linear Dynamical System with 3 Nodes. We first start with a simple linear dynamical system with only 3 nodes. We further simplify the matrix A as in Fig. 2, where only three elements in A are non-zero. We set B as a zeros matrix, and $u(t)$ as a 1-dimensional signal. The dynamical system is linear:

$$\begin{bmatrix} dz(t)/dt \\ dD(t)/dt \end{bmatrix} = \begin{bmatrix} D(t)z(t) + Cu(t) \\ 0 \end{bmatrix}, \ D(0) = A, \ u(t) = \begin{cases} 1, & floor(\frac{t}{2})\%2 = 0 \\ 0, & otherwise \end{cases}$$

(12)

$$\widetilde{z(t)} = z(t) + \epsilon(t), \quad \epsilon(t) \sim N(0, \sigma^2)$$

(13)

$u(t)$ is an alternating block function at a period of 2, taking values 0 or 1. The observed function $\widetilde{z(t)}$ suffers from $i.i.d$ Gaussian noise $\epsilon(t)$ with 0 mean and uniform variance σ^2.

   We perform 10 independent simulations and parameter estimations. For estimation of DCM with the EM algorithm, we use the SPM package [14], which is a widely used standard baseline. The estimation in MSA is implemented in PyTorch, using ACA [23] as the ODE solver. For MSA, we use the AdaBelief optimizer [25] to update parameters with the gradient; though other optimizers such as SGD can be used, we found AdaBelief converges faster in practice.

   For each of the non-zero elements in A, we show the boxplot of error in estimation in Fig. 3. Compared with EM, the error by MSA is significantly closer to 0 and has a smaller variance. An example of a noisy observation and estimated curves are shown in Fig. 3, and the estimation by MSA is visually closer to the ground-truth compared to the EM algorithm. We emphasize that the estimated curve is not a simple smoothing of the noisy observation; instead, after estimating the parameters of the ODE, the estimated curve (for $t > 0$) is generated by solving the ODE using only the initial state. Therefore, the match between estimated curve and observation demonstrates that our method learns the underlying dynamics of the system.

Application to Large-Scale Systems. After validation on a small system with only 3 nodes, we validate MSA on large scale systems with more nodes. We use the same linear dynamical system as in Eq. 12, but with the node number p ranging from 10 to 100. Note that the dimension of A and B grows at a rate of $O(p^2)$, and the EM algorithm estimates the covariance matrix of size $O(p^4)$, hence the memory for EM method grows extremely fast with p. For various settings, the ground truth parameter is randomly generated from a uniform distribution between -1 and 1, and the variance of measurement noise is set as $\sigma = 0.5$. For each setting, we perform 5 independent runs, and report the mean squared error (MSE) between estimated parameter and ground truth.

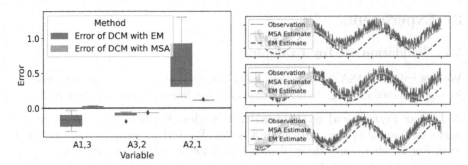

Fig. 3. Results for the toy example of a linear dynamical system in Fig. 2. Left: error in estimated value of connection $A_{1,3}, A_{3,2}, A_{2,1}$, other parameters are set as 0 in simulation. Right: from top to bottom are the results for node 1, 2, 3 respectively. For each node, we plot the observation and estimated curve from MSA and EM methods. Note that the estimated curve is generated by integration of the ODE under estimated parameters with only the initial condition known, not smoothing of noisy observation.

As shown in Table 1, for small-size systems (number of nodes $<= 20$), MSA consistently generates a lower MSE than the EM algorithm. For large-scale systems, since the memory cost of the EM algorithm is $O(p^4)$, the algorithm quickly runs out-of-memory. On the other hand, the memory cost for MSA is $O(p^2)$ because it only uses the first-order gradient. Hence, MSA is suitable for large-scale systems such as in whole-brain fMRI analysis.

Application to General Non-linear Systems. Since neither the multiple-shoot method nor the adjoint state method requires the ODE f to be linear, our MSA can be applied to general non-linear systems. Furthermore, since our implementation is in PyTorch which supports automatic differentiation, we only need to specify f when fitting different models, and the gradient will be calculated automatically. Therefore, MSA is an off-the-shelf method, and is suitable for general non-linear ODEs both in theory and implementation.

We validate MSA on the Lotka-Volterra (L-V) equations [22], a system of non-linear ODEs describing the dynamics of predator and prey populations. The L-V equation can be written as:

$$f\Big([z_1(t), z_2(t)]\Big) = \begin{bmatrix} dz_1(t)/dt \\ dz_2(t)/dt \end{bmatrix} = \begin{bmatrix} \zeta z_1(t) - \beta z_1(t) z_2(t) \\ \delta z_1(t) z_2(t) - \gamma z_2(t) \end{bmatrix}, \quad \begin{bmatrix} \widetilde{z_1(t)} \\ \widetilde{z_2(t)} \end{bmatrix} = \begin{bmatrix} z_1(t) + \epsilon_1(t) \\ z_2(t) + \epsilon_2(t) \end{bmatrix} \quad (14)$$

where $\zeta, \beta, \delta, \gamma$ are parameters to estimate, $\widetilde{z(t)}$ is the noisy observation, and $\epsilon(t)$ is the independent noise. Note that there are non-linear terms $z_1(t)z_2(t)$ in the ODE, making EM derivation difficult. Furthermore, the EM method needs to explicitly derive the posterior mean, hence needs to be re-derived for every different f; while MSA is generic and hence does not require re-derivation.

Besides the L-V model, we also consider a modified L-V model, defined as:

$$dz_1(t)/dt = \zeta z_1(t) - \beta\phi(z_2(t))z_1(t)z_2(t) \tag{15}$$
$$dz_2(t)/dt = \delta\phi(z_1(t))z_1(t)z_2(t) - \gamma z_2(t) \tag{16}$$

where $\phi(x) = 1/(1 + e^{-x})$ is the sigmoid function. We use this example to demonstrate the ability of MSA to fit highly non-linear ODEs.

We compare MSA with LMFIT [12], which is a well-known python package for non-linear fitting. We use L-BFGS solver in LMFIT, which generates better results than other solvers. We did not compare with original DCM with EM because it's unsuitable for general non-linear models. The estimation of the curve for $t > 0$ is solved by integrating using the estimated parameters and initial conditions. As shown in Fig. 4 and Fig. 5, compared with LMFIT, MSA recovers the system accurately. LMFIT directly fits the long sequences, while MSA splits long-sequences into chunks for robust estimation, which may partially explain the better performance of MSA.

3.2 Application to Whole-Brain Dynamic Causal Modeling with fMRI

We apply MSA on whole-brain fMRI analysis with dynamic causal modeling. fMRI for 82 children with ASD and 48 age and IQ-matched healthy controls were acquired. A biological motion perception task and a scrambled motion task

Table 1. Mean squared error ($\times 10^{-3}$, **lower** is better) in estimation of parameters for a linear dynamical system with different number of nodes. "OOM" represents "out of memory".

	10 Nodes	20 Nodes	50 Nodes	100 Nodes
EM	3.3 ± 0.2	3.0 ± 0.2	OOM	OOM
MSA	0.7 ± 0.1	0.9 ± 0.3	0.8 ± 0.1	0.8 ± 0.2

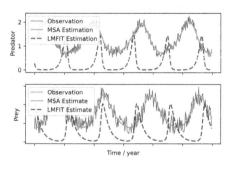

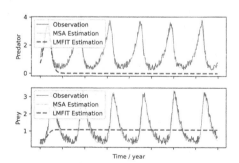

Fig. 4. Results for the L-V model.

Fig. 5. Results for the modified L-V model.

[7] were presented in alternating blocks. The fMRI (BOLD, 132 volumes, TR = 2000 ms, TE = 25 ms, flip angle = 60°, voxel size 3.443.444 mm^3) was acquired on a Siemens MAGNETOM Trio 3T scanner.

Estimation of EC. We use the AAL atlas [20] containing 116 ROIs. For each subject, the parameters for dynamic causal modeling as in Eq. 10 is estimated using MSA. An example snapshot of the effective connectome (EC) during the two tasks is shown in Fig. 6, showing MSA captures the dynamic EC.

Classification Task. We conduct classification experiments for ASD vs. control using EC and FC as input respectively. The EC estimated by MSA at each time point provides a data sample, and the classification of a subject is based on the majority vote of the predictions across all time points. The FC is computed using Pearson correlation. We experimented with a random forest model and InvNet [24]. Results for a 10-fold subject-wise cross validation are shown in Fig. 7. For both models, using EC as input generates better accuracy, F1 score and AUC score (threshold range is [0,1]). This indicates that estimating the underlying dynamics of fMRI helps identification of ASD.

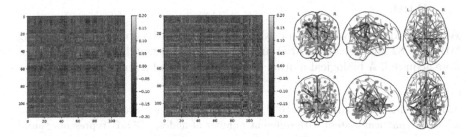

Fig. 6. An example of MSA for one subject. Left: effective connectome during task 1. Middle: effective connectome during task 2. Right: top and bottom represents the effective connectome for task 1 and 2 respectively. Blue and red edges represent positive and negative connections respectively. Only top 5% strongest connections are visualized. (Color figure online)

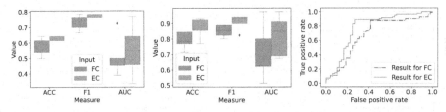

(a) Classification result based on Random Forest.   (b) Classification result based on InvNet.   (c) ROC-AUC curve for results with InvNet.

Fig. 7. Classification results for ASD vs. control.

4 Conclusion

We propose the multiple-shooting adjoint (MSA) method for parameter estimation in ODEs, enabling whole-brain dynamic causal modeling. MSA has the following advantages: robustness for noisy observations, ability to handle large-scale systems, and a general off-the-shelf framework for non-linear ODEs. We validate MSA in extensive toy examples and apply MSA to whole-brain fMRI analysis with DCM. To our knowledge, our work is the first to successfully apply whole-brain dynamic causal modeling in a classification task based on fMRI. Finally, MSA is generic and can be applied to other problems.

Acknowledgment. This research was funded by the National Institutes of Health (NINDS-R01NS035193)

References

1. Bock, H.G., Plitt, K.J.: A multiple shooting algorithm for direct solution of optimal control problems. In: IFAC Proceedings Volumes (1984)
2. Chen, R.T., Rubanova, Y., Bettencourt, J., Duvenaud, D.K.: Neural ordinary differential equations. In; Advances in Neural Information Processing Systems (2018)
3. Di Martino, A., O'connor, D., Chen, B., Alaerts, K., Anderson, J.S., et al.: Enhancing studies of the connectome in autism using the autism brain imaging data exchange. Sci. Data **4**(1), 1–15 (2017)
4. Frässle, S., Harrison, S.J., Heinzle, J., Clementz, B.A., Tamminga, C.A., et al.: Regression dynamic causal modeling for resting-state fMRI. bioRxiv (2020)
5. Friston, K.J., Harrison, L.: Dynamic causal modelling. Neuroimage **19**(4), 1273–1302 (2003)
6. Hildebrand, F.B.: Introduction to Numerical Analysis. Courier Corporation, Chelmsford (1987)
7. Kaiser, M.D., Hudac, C.M., Shultz, S., Lee, S.M., Cheung, C., et al.: Neural signatures of autism. In: PNAS (2010)
8. Kiebel, S.J., Garrido, M.I., Moran, R.J., Friston, K.J.: Dynamic causal modelling for EEG and MEG. Cogn. Neurodyn. **2**, 121 (2008). https://doi.org/10.1007/s11571-008-9038-0
9. Lindquist, M.A., Loh, J.M., Atlas, L.Y., Wager, T.D.: Modeling the hemodynamic response function in fMRI: efficiency, bias and mis-modeling. Neuroimage **45**, S187–S198 (2009)
10. Moon, T.K.: The expectation-maximization algorithm. ISPM (1996)
11. Nation, K., Clarke, P., Wright, B., Williams, C.: Patterns of reading ability in children with autism spectrum disorder. J. Autism Dev. Disord. **36**, 911 (2006)
12. Newville, M., Stensitzki, T., Allen, D.B., Rawlik, M., Ingargiola, A., Nelson, A.: LMFIT: Non-linear least-square minimization and curve-fitting for python (2016)
13. Peifer, M., Timmer, J.: Parameter estimation in ordinary differential equations for biochemical processes using the method of multiple shooting. IET Syst. Biol. **1**(2), 78–88 (2007)
14. Penny, W.D., Friston, K.J., Ashburner, J.T., Kiebel, S.J., Nichols, T.E.: Statistical parametric mapping: the analysis of functional brain images (2011)
15. Pontryagin, L.S.: Mathematical theory of optimal processes (2018)

16. Prando, G., Zorzi, M., Bertoldo, A., Corbetta, M., Chiuso, A.: Sparse DCM for whole-brain effective connectivity from resting-state fMRI data. NeuroImage **208**, 116367 (2020)
17. Razi, A., Seghier, M.L., Zhou, Y., McColgan, P., Zeidman, P., Park, H.J., et al.: Large-scale DCMs for resting-state fMRI. Netw. Neurosci. **1**(3), 222–241 (2017)
18. Rokem, A., Trumpis, M., Perez, F.: Nitime: time-series analysis for neuroimaging data. In: Proceedings of the 8th Python in Science Conference (2009)
19. Seghier, M.L., Zeidman, P., Leff, A.P., Price, C.: Identifying abnormal connectivity in patients using dynamic causal modelling of fMRI responses. Front. Neurosci. **4**, 142 (2010)
20. Tzourio-Mazoyer, N., Landeau, B., Papathanassiou, D., Crivello, F., Etard, O., et al.: Automated anatomical labeling of activations in SPM using a macroscopic anatomical parcellation of the MNI MRI single-subject brain. Neuroimage **15**, 273–289 (2002)
21. Van Den Heuvel, M.P., Pol, H.E.H.: Exploring the brain network: a review on resting-state fMRI functional connectivity. Eur. Neuropsychopharmacol. **20**, 519–534 (2010)
22. Volterra, V.: Variations and fluctuations of the number of individuals in animal species living together. ICES J. Mar. Sci. **3** (1928)
23. Zhuang, J., Dvornek, N., Li, X., Tatikonda, S., Papademetris, X., Duncan, J.: Adaptive checkpoint adjoint for gradient estimation in neural ode. In: ICML (2020)
24. Zhuang, J., Dvornek, N.C., Li, X., Ventola, P., Duncan, J.S.: Invertible network for classification and biomarker selection for ASD. In: Shen, D., et al. (eds.) MICCAI 2019, Part III. LNCS, vol. 11766, pp. 700–708. Springer, Cham (2019). https://doi.org/10.1007/978-3-030-32248-9_78
25. Zhuang, J., Tang, T., Ding, Y., Tatikonda, S.C., Dvornek, N., Papademetris, X., Duncan, J.: Adabelief optimizer: adapting step sizes by the belief in observed gradients. In: NeurIPS (2020)

Going Beyond Saliency Maps: Training Deep Models to Interpret Deep Models

Zixuan Liu[1], Ehsan Adeli[2,3], Kilian M. Pohl[2,4], and Qingyu Zhao[2(✉)]

[1] Department of Electrical Engineering, Stanford University,
Stanford, CA 94305, USA
[2] Department of Psychiatry and Behavioral Sciences, Stanford University,
Stanford, CA 94305, USA
qingyuz@stanford.edu
[3] Department of Computer Science, Stanford University, Stanford, CA 94305, USA
[4] Center for Biomedical Sciences, SRI International, Menlo Park, CA 94025, USA

Abstract. Interpretability is a critical factor in applying complex deep learning models to advance the understanding of brain disorders in neuroimaging studies. To interpret the decision process of a trained classifier, existing techniques typically rely on *saliency maps* to quantify the voxel-wise or feature-level importance for classification through partial derivatives. Despite providing some level of localization, these maps are not human-understandable from the neuroscience perspective as they often do not inform the specific type of morphological changes linked to the brain disorder. Inspired by the image-to-image translation scheme, we propose to train simulator networks to inject (or remove) patterns of the disease into a given MRI based on a warping operation, such that the classifier increases (or decreases) its confidence in labeling the simulated MRI as diseased. To increase the robustness of training, we propose to couple the two simulators into a unified model based on *conditional convolution*. We applied our approach to interpreting classifiers trained on a synthetic dataset and two neuroimaging datasets to visualize the effect of Alzheimer's disease and alcohol dependence. Compared to the saliency maps generated by baseline approaches, our simulations and visualizations based on the Jacobian determinants of the warping field reveal meaningful and understandable patterns related to the diseases.

1 Introduction

In recent years, deep learning has achieved unparalleled success in the field of medical image computing [1] and is increasingly used to classify patients with brain diseases from normal controls based on their Magnetic Resonance Imaging (MRI) data [2]. Compared to traditional machine learning methods, deep models can generally result in superior classification accuracy [3] by training on a large amount of raw imaging data and employing more complex network architectures and learning strategies. However, a primary challenge of applying complex deep networks to 3D MRI data is the lack of *model interpretability*, which arguably

© Springer Nature Switzerland AG 2021
A. Feragen et al. (Eds.): IPMI 2021, LNCS 12729, pp. 71–82, 2021.
https://doi.org/10.1007/978-3-030-78191-0_6

plays a more pivotal role compared to the prediction accuracy itself. For example, when a learning model is used to aid the diagnosis by human experts, one needs to understand how the model reasons its prediction [4]. In other studies where neuroimaging is not a part of the diagnosis workflow (i.e., discovery-oriented analysis), the goal of learning image-based classifiers is solely for revealing the impact of the disease on the brain [5].

Compared to the large body of literature on model development, methods for model interpretation (or model visualization) are either oversimplified or misspecified for neuroimaging studies. For example, the most widely used visualization techniques to date are gradient-based methods [6,7], which aim to generate a *saliency map* for a given MRI. This map encodes the importance of the information contained within each voxel (or local neighborhood) in driving the model prediction. Despite the wide usage in computer vision tasks, the application of gradient-based methods in neuroimaging studies is limited as the saliency maps are generally noisy on the voxel level, imprecise in locating object boundaries, and applicable to only selective network architectures. Most importantly, the saliency maps only indicate the location of brain structures impacted by the disease but do not inform what type of morphological changes are induced (e.g., atrophy of cortical gray matter associated with Alzheimer's disease).

In this work, we propose to interpret a trained classifier by learning two additional simulator networks, which aim to learn human-understandable morphological patterns within an image that can impact the classifier's prediction. Motivated by the image-to-image translation scheme, one simulator warps an MRI of a healthy subject to inject the disease pattern such that the classifier increases its confidence in predicting the MRI as diseased (i.e., logit shift), and the other simulator removes the patterns from the MRI of a diseased subject to decrease the confidence. We then visualize the disease pattern on a subject-level by comparing the image appearance between the raw and simulated image pair or by quantifying the Jacobian map (encoding tissue expansion and shrinkage) of the warping field. To generate robust simulators, we employ a cycle-consistent scheme to encourage the simulators to inject and remove patterns only related to disease while preserving subject-specific information irrelevant to the disease. Furthermore, we propose to couple the two simulators into one coherent model by using the conditional convolution operation. The proposed visualization method was applied to interpret classifiers trained on a synthetic dataset, 1344 T1-weighted MRIs from the Alzheimer's Disease Neuroimaging Initiative (ADNI), and a dataset of 1225 MRIs for classifying individuals with alcohol dependence. We compared our visualization with a number of widely used alternative techniques. Unlike the visualizations from those alternatives, our learning-based method generated images that capture high-level shape changes of brain tissue associated with the disease.

2   Related Work

Most existing methods for model interpretation visualize feature-level or voxel-level saliency scores quantified by partial derivatives [6,7]; i.e., how a small change in feature or voxel values can influence the final prediction. These derivatives can be efficiently computed by back-propagation. However, the voxelwise

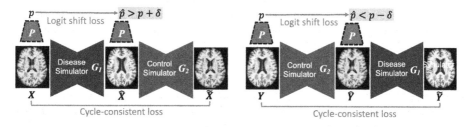

Fig. 1. To interpret a trained classifier ($\mathbb{P}$), the proposed framework trains two separate simulator networks to learn the morphological change that defines the separation between control and diseased cohorts. The disease simulator ($\mathbb{G}_1$) injects the disease pattern into an image X such that the prediction logit $\hat{p}$ for the simulated image $\hat{X}$ increases by a pre-dined threshold δ. The control simulator removes the pattern from an image. The two simulators are trained in a cycle-consistent fashion.

derivatives are generally noisy and non-informative as the variation in a voxel is more related to low-level features rather than the final prediction. One of the exceptions is Grad-CAM [7], which can generate smooth and robust visualization based on deriving feature-level importance but cannot accurately locate object boundaries and is only applicable to certain types of networks. Other than using partial derivatives, occlusion-based methods [8] quantify the importance of a local image neighborhood for prediction by first masking the regional information in the images (zero-out, blur, shuffle, deformation, etc.) and then evaluating the impact on the classifier's prediction accuracy. However, the resulting saliency map can only be defined for the whole population but not for each individual. Recently, Ghorbani [9] has proposed a concept-based interpretation, which aims to directly identify critical image segments that drive the model decision. However, when applied to neuroimaging applications, all the above methods can only locate brain structures that are important for prediction but do not explain the alteration of those structures associated with a disease (Fig. 1).

Recently, image-to-image translation frameworks have achieved marked success in medical applications including denoising, multi-modal image registration, and super-resolution reconstruction [10,11]. The goal of such frameworks is to learn a bijective mapping between two distributions from different image domains. Inspired by this technique, we formulate the two domains as MRIs of healthy and diseased cohorts and learn how an MRI of a healthy subject will be altered if the subject is affected by the disease (and vice versa).

3   Methods

3.1   Cycle-Consistent Image Simulation

Let $\mathcal{X}$ be the set of MRI of controls and $\mathcal{Y}$ the set of diseased participants. We assume a deep classifier $\mathbb{P}$ has been trained on the datasets such that $p = \mathbb{P}(X)$ is the *logit* (value before *sigmoid*) encoding the confidence in labeling image

X as diseased; i.e., X is from a diseased subject if $p > 0$ and from a control subject otherwise. Now our goal is to visualize the model $\mathbb{P}$ to understand how the morphological information in X impacts the final prediction p. To do so, we propose to train two simulator networks $\mathbb{G}_1$ and $\mathbb{G}_2$, where $\mathbb{G}_1(\cdot)$ alters the MRI of a control subject $X \in \mathcal{X}$ to resemble a diseased one $\hat{X} := \mathbb{G}_1(X)$ (adding the disease pattern to X as if the subject was affected by the disease), and $\mathbb{G}_2(\cdot)$ removes the disease pattern from an MRI $Y \in \mathcal{Y}$ so that $\hat{Y} := \mathbb{G}_2(Y)$ resembles the MRI of a healthy control.

Based on existing image-translation methods, one would apply a binary training strategy [12] to learn $\mathbb{G}_1$ and $\mathbb{G}_2$; i.e., to fool the classifier such that $\mathbb{P}(\hat{X}) > 0$ and $\mathbb{P}(\hat{Y}) < 0$. However, the neurological condition linked to a brain disorder may lie in a continuous spectrum as encoded in the predicted logit p. For example, the severity of cognitive impairment can be highly heterogeneous in the AD cohort such that some AD patients should have larger logit values and others having logits closer to 0. As such, the above binary objective may overemphasize the severe AD cases in converting them into controls, thereby implicitly reweighing the importance across subjects during training. To avoid such bias, we enforce the simulators to produce a *logit shift* greater than a pre-defined threshold δ for each subject; i.e., $\mathbb{P}(\hat{X}) - \mathbb{P}(X) > \delta$ and $\mathbb{P}(\hat{Y}) - \mathbb{P}(Y) < -\delta$. This logit shift loss is then formulated as

$$E_{logit} := \mathbf{E}_{X \sim \mathcal{X}}[\max(\mathbb{P}(X) - \mathbb{P}(\hat{X}), -\delta)] + \mathbf{E}_{Y \sim \mathcal{Y}}[\max(\mathbb{P}(\hat{Y}) - \mathbb{P}(Y), -\delta)]. \quad (1)$$

As commonly explored in the literature, we also incorporate the *cycle-consistent* loss to ensure that the simulators can recover the original input from a simulated image. This guarantees that subject-specific information in the image irrelevant to the disease is not perturbed during the simulation, i.e.

$$E_{cycle} := \mathbf{E}_{X \sim \mathcal{X}}[||\mathbb{G}_2(\mathbb{G}_1(X)) - X)||_2] + \mathbf{E}_{Y \sim \mathcal{Y}}[||\mathbb{G}_1(\mathbb{G}_2(Y)) - Y)||_2]. \quad (2)$$

3.2   Coupling Simulators via Conditional Convolution

A drawback of traditional cycle-consistent learning is that the two simulators $\mathbb{G}_1$ and $\mathbb{G}_2$ are designed as independent networks albeit the two simulation tasks are extremely coupled (injecting vs removing disease patterns). In other words, the network parameters between $\mathbb{G}_1$ and $\mathbb{G}_2$ should be highly dependent, and each convolutional kernel at a certain layer should perform related functions. Here, we propose to combine the two simulators into a coherent model whose behavior can be adjusted based on the specific simulation task. We do so by using *conditional convolution* (CondConv) [13] as the fundamental building blocks of the network shown in Fig. 2. Let f and f' be the input and output features of a convolutional operation with activation σ. As opposed to the static convolutional kernel, the CondConv kernel W is conditionally parameterized as a mixture of experts

$$f' := \sigma(\alpha_1 \cdot W_1 \circledast f + ... + \alpha_K \cdot W_K \circledast f), \quad (3)$$

where W is a linear combination of k sub-kernels with weights $\{\alpha_k | k = 1, ..., K\}$ determined via a routing function $r_k(\cdot)$. With t being the task label (e.g., 0 for $\mathbb{G}_1$ and 1 for $\mathbb{G}_2$), we design the following routing function

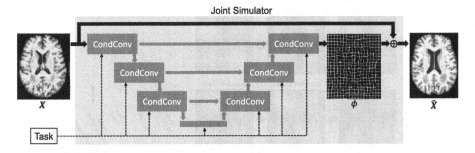

Fig. 2. Two simulators are coupled into one single model by using Conditional Convolution (CondConv), whose parameters are dependent on the specific simulation task. The output of the joint simulator is a warping field ϕ that is applied to the input X to derive the simulated $\hat{X}$.

$$\alpha_k = r_k(f, t) := \texttt{sigmoid}([\texttt{GlobalAvgPool}(f), t] * R_k), \tag{4}$$

where R_k are the learnable parameters to be multiplied with the concatenation of the pooled feature and the task label. In doing so, the behavior of the convolution can adapt to subject-specific brain appearance encoded in f and the specific task.

3.3 Learning Warping Fields

In principle, the two simulators can generate any patterns that separate the healthy and diseased cohorts (intensity difference, shape change, etc.). In scenarios where the disease is known to impact brain morphometry, we can enforce the simulators to only learn the shape patterns that differentiate cohorts. To do so, we let the output of the simulators be 3D warping fields $\phi_1 := \mathbb{G}_1(X)$ and $\phi_2 := \mathbb{G}_2(X)$, which are then applied to the input images to derive the warped images $\hat{X} = X \circ \phi_1$, $\hat{Y} = Y \circ \phi_2$. The warping layer is implemented the same as in [14], which uses linear interpolation to compute the intensity of a sub-voxel defined at non-integer locations. As also adopted in [14], a diffusion regularizer is added to the warping field ϕ to preserve the smoothness of ϕ. Let $\mathbf{V}$ be the voxels in the image space. The smoothness loss is

$$E_\phi := \lambda_\phi \sum_{\mathbf{v} \in \mathbf{V}} ||\nabla\phi(\mathbf{v})||^2 \text{ , where } \nabla\phi(\mathbf{v}) = (\frac{\partial\phi(\mathbf{v})}{\partial x}, \frac{\partial\phi(\mathbf{v})}{\partial y}, \frac{\partial\phi(\mathbf{v})}{\partial z}). \tag{5}$$

The final objective function is $E := E_{logit} + E_{cycle} + E_\phi$.

4 Experiments

To showcase the concept of our cycle-consistent image simulation, we first evaluated the method on a synthetic dataset by only considering E_{logit} and E_{cycle} during training. We then incorporated E_ϕ in the training to show the advantage of warping-field visualization over existing visualization techniques in the context of analyzing Alzheimer's Disease. Lastly, we applied the proposed approach to identify regional atrophy linked to alcohol dependence.

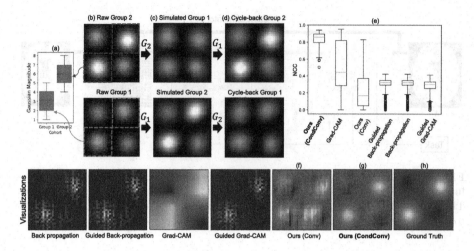

Fig. 3. (a) The group-separating pattern was the magnitude of two off-diagonal Gaussians. (b, c, d) The learned simulators could reduce and increase the intensity of off-diagonal Gaussians of a given image in a cycle-consistent fashion; (e) Normalized cross-correlation (NCC) between the ground-truth pattern and the pattern derived by different approaches. Bottom: visualizations of the group-separating patterns.

4.1 Synthetic Experiments

Dataset: We generated a synthetic dataset comprising two groups of data, each containing 512 images of resolution 32×32 pixels. Each image was generated by 4 Gaussians, whose locations randomly varied within each of the 4 blocks (Fig. 3(b)). We assume the magnitude of the two off-diagonal Gaussians defined the differential pattern between the two cohorts. Specifically, the magnitude was sampled from a uniform distribution $\mathcal{U}(1,5)$ for each image from Group 1 and from $\mathcal{U}(4,8)$ (with stronger intensities) for Group 2 (Fig. 3(a)). On the other hand, the magnitude of the two diagonal Gaussians was sampled from $\mathcal{U}(1,6)$ and regarded as subject-specific information impartial to group assignment. Gaussian noise was added to the images with standard deviation 0.002.

Classification: We first trained a classifier to distinguish the two groups on 80% of the data. The classifier network ($\mathbb{P}$) comprised of 3 stacks of 2D convolution (feature dimension = $\{2, 4, 8\}$), ReLU, and max-pooling layers. The resulting 128 features were fed to a multi-layer perceptron with one hidden layer of dimension 16 and ReLU activation. Training the classifier resulted in a classification accuracy of 87.5% on the remaining 20% testing images.

Visualization: To visualize the group-separating pattern learned by the classifier, we designed the simulator as a U-net structure with skip connections (Fig. 2). The encoder was 4 stacks of 2D CondConv (feature dimension = $\{1, 2, 4, 8\}$), BatchNorm, LeakyReLu, and max-pooling layers. Each CondConv operation used 3 experts ($K = 3$) as adopted in the original implementation of [13].

The resulting 64 features were fed into a fully connected layer of dimension 64 and ReLU activation. The decoder had an inverse structure of the encoder by replacing the pooling layers with up-sampling layers. The warping field was not used in this experiment, so the networks directly generated simulated images. The logit shift threshold was set to $\delta = 5$. For each test image, we then computed the intensity difference between the raw and simulated images $(X - \hat{X})$.

Baseline: We also generated visualizations through 4 baseline approaches: back-propagation (BP), guided BP [6], Grad-CAM, and guided Grad-CAM [7]. To show the importance of using conditional convolution for our model, we also generated the pattern using our model trained with two separate encoders using conventional convolution. As the results of different approaches had different scales, each estimated pattern was compared with the ground-truth using normalized cross-correlation (NCC), where the ground-truth was defined as the magnitude difference associated with the two off-diagonal Gaussians (Fig. 3(h)).

Results: Figure 3 shows two examples of the learned simulation. For a training image from Group 2 (Fig. 3(b)), the simulator reduced the intensity of off-diagonal Gaussians, indicating that the model successfully captured the group-separating patterns (Fig. 3(c)). Meanwhile, the model preserved subject-specific information including the location and magnitude of the two diagonal Gaussians. Through cycle-consistent simulation, the model also accurately recovered the input image (Fig. 3(d)). In line with the visual comparison, the pattern generated by our model (Fig. 3(g)) only focused on the off-diagonal Gaussians and closely resembled the ground-truth (Fig. 3(h)). Note, when replacing the CondConv with conventional convolution, the pattern became less robust (Fig. 3(f)). On the other hand, the visualizations derived by BP, guided BP and guided Grad-CAM were noisy as the saliency values frequently switched signs. This behavior was inconsistent with our data construction, where the magnitude change of the Gaussians had the same sign at each voxel. The pattern associated with Grad-CAM was too smooth to accurately locate the object of interest. Lastly, this qualitative analysis was supported by the NCC metric (Fig. 3(e)) indicating our model with CondConv was the most accurate approach for defining the pattern.

4.2 Visualizing the Effect of Alzheimer's Disease

Dataset: We evaluated the proposed model on 1344 T1-weighted MRIs from the Alzheimer's Disease Neuroimaging Initiative (ADNI1). The dataset consisted of images from 229 Normal Control (NC) subjects (age: 76 ± 5.0 years) and 185 subjects with Alzheimer's Disease (75.3 ± 7.6 years). Each subject had 1 to 8 longitudinal scans within a 4 year study period and only contained MRIs that were successfully preprocessed. The preprocessing consisted of denoising, bias field correction, skull stripping, affine registration to a template, re-scaling to a $64 \times 64 \times 64$ volume, and transforming image intensities within the brain mask to z-scores. This dataset was randomly split into 80% training and 20% testing on the subject level.

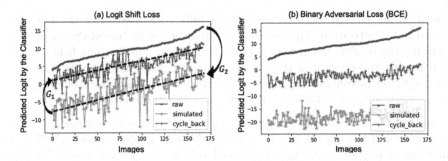

Fig. 4. Predicted logic values by the classifier of all raw AD images (blue) in the test set, simulated images after removing disease patterns (orange), and cycle-back simulations (green). Images are re-ordered based on the raw logic values. The simulator is learned based on (a) the proposed logit loss or (b) the binary cross-entropy loss. (Color figure online)

Implementation:[1] We first trained a classifier $\mathbb{P}$ containing 4 stacks of $3 \times 3 \times 3$ convolutional layers (feature dimension $\{16, 32, 64, 16\}$), ReLU, and max-pooling layers. The resulting 512 features were fed into a multi-layer perceptron with one hidden layer of dimension 64 and ReLU activation. Based on this architecture, the classifier achieved 88% NC/AD classification accuracy (balanced accuracy) on the testing set. Note, as the goal of our work was to visualize a trained classifier as opposed to optimizing the classification accuracy on a particular dataset, we did not consider the dependency of longitudinal scans for simplicity. To interpret this trained classifier, we adopted a similar simulator architecture as in the synthetic experiment while using 5 convolutional stacks with 3D CondConv (feature dimension $= \{16, 32, 64, 16, 16\}$), a fully connected layer of dimension 512, and a 3-channel output (warping field ϕ). We set $\lambda_\phi = 0.02$ and the logit shift threshold $\delta = 12.5$. The simulators were trained on all the NC and AD subjects by an Adam optimizer for 45 epochs with a learning rate of 1e−4.

Results: We first show the impact of the logit shift loss on the cycle-consistency of the simulation. Figure 4(a) displays the logit values of all raw testing images predicted by the classifier $\mathbb{P}$ (blue curve). After removing and injecting disease patterns through the cycle-consistent simulators, the logit values consistently decreased and increased while preserving their relative positions. However, if we replaced the logit shift loss by the binary cross-entropy loss [12] (BCE, Fig. 4(b)), the logit values of the simulated and cycle-back images became all uniform. This was undesirable as the goal of the simulator was to uncover the pattern that correlated with the severity of the brain disorder, which was encoded by the magnitude of the logit values. Using the BCE loss simply 'fooled' the classifier but lost this important information.

---

[1] Source code can be found at https://github.com/ZucksLiu/DeepInterpret.

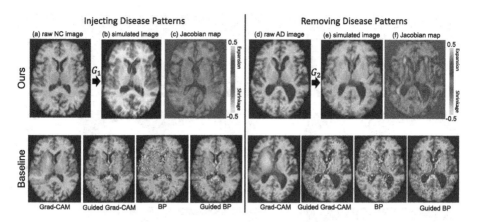

Fig. 5. Example visualization of our proposed approach and the baselines. Color scales were omitted for baseline approaches as they are arbitrary across models and subjects. All the computation was performed in the down-sampled space and resized to the original resolution for easy visualization. (Color figure online)

Figure 5(b) shows a simulated image after injecting the AD pattern into the raw image of an NC subject. By directly comparing the two grayscale images, we observe enlargement of the ventricles and cerebrospinal fluid (CSF) and atrophy of brain tissue. This pattern comported with the effects of AD reported in prior literature [15]. Moreover, the morphological change captured by the simulator can be quantitatively measured by the log of Jacobian determinant of the warping field ϕ (Fig. 5(c)). We used this Jacobian map as the visualization produced by our method, which was then compared with the visualization of the same subject produced by the baseline approaches. In line with the synthetic experiment, the Grad-CAM saliency map was smooth and did not locate meaningful regions with respect to the AD effect. Other saliency maps by BP, guided BP, and guided Grad-CAM were noisy and contained frequent sign changes in the saliency values. As a second example, we also visualize the simulated image (Fig. 5(e)) after removing the disease pattern from an AD subject and the corresponding Jacobian map (Fig. 5(f)). The patterns were similar to Fig. 5(c) except for the change of direction (regions with shrinkage now showed expansion), indicating the cycle-consistent nature of the two coupled simulators.

Beyond the subject-level visualization, we also produced the Jacobian visualization on the group level by non-rigidly registering the structural maps of all NC subjects to a template and computing the average Jacobian map in the template space (Fig. 6). This procedure was also used to produce the group-level visualization of baseline approaches. We also generated a group-level visualization based on the occlusion method [8] (this method cannot be applied to generate subject-level visualization), which first used a sliding window of $8 \times 8 \times 8$ with stride 4 to mask the test images and then re-computed the testing accuracy as the saliency score associated with the center voxel of the sliding window.

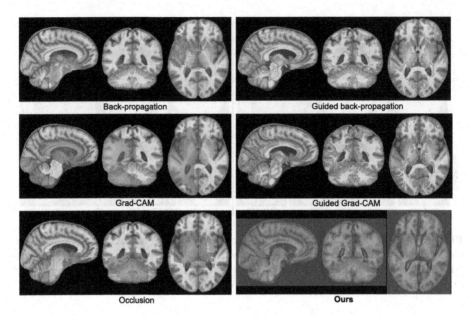

Fig. 6. Group-level visualization for the ADNI dataset. Color scale is defined according to the subject-level visualization in Fig. 5. (Color figure online)

After inspecting the subject-level and group-level visualizations, we now summarize 4 advantages of the Jacobian-based visualization: (1) Our Jacobian maps accurately located the disease pattern while avoided generating overly smooth or noisy visualizations; (2) The Jacobian values had real morphological meanings (tissue volume change) while the baseline visualizations only informed the location of the disease pattern; (3) The Jacobian values were signed (shrinkage or expansion) informing the direction of changes, while the sign of the saliency values by baseline methods was less meaningful in the context of MR analysis; (4) The Jacobian values had a deterministic scale (percentage of volume change) while the saliency values of the baseline approaches are meaningless and highly variant across models and subjects.

4.3   Visualizing the Effect of Alcohol Dependence

The dataset comprised 1225 T1-weighted MRIs of 274 NC subjects (age: 47.3 ± 17.6) and 329 participants with alcohol dependence (age: 49.3 ± 10.5) according to DSM-IV criteria [16]. 74 of the alcohol dependent group were also human immunodeficiency virus (HIV) positive. All experimental settings replicated the ADNI experiment. Based on an 80%–20% training and testing split on the subject level, the classifier resulted in a 76.2% accuracy for classifying alcohol-dependent subjects. After training the simulators on all images, we computed the group-level Jacobian visualization for all NC subjects in the testing set. Figure 7 indicates that regions with the most severe atrophy were

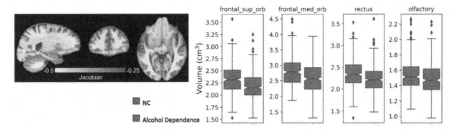

Fig. 7. Left: Jacobian visualization of the effect of alcohol dependence; Right: gray matter volume of 4 brain regions from the orbitofrontal cortex measured for all NC and alcohol-dependent subjects. The volumes scores were corrected for age and sex.

located in the orbitofrontal cortex. This converges with recent studies that frequently suggested the disruption in the structural and functional properties of the orbitofrontal cortex associated with alcohol dependence [17].

To confirm this finding, we tested the group difference in the volumetric measures of 4 regions of interest: the superior and medical fronto-orbital gyri, the rectus, and the olfactory gyrus. Only the baseline MR of each subject was used in this analysis. The volumetric measures were extracted by segmenting the brain tissue into gray matter, white matter, and CSF via Atropos and parcellating the regions by the SRI24 atlas. With age and gender being the covariates, a general linear model tested the group difference between NC and alcohol-dependent subjects in the gray matter volume of the 4 regions. All tests resulted in significant group differences based on two-tailed t-statistics ($p < 0.001$, see boxplots in Fig. 7), which confirmed the validity of our visualization result. These results indicate that our data-driven visualization can be readily combined with *a priori* regional analysis (e.g., Fig. 7), which allows neuroscientists to cross-validate findings from data-driven and hypothesis-driven analyses.

5   Conclusion

In this work, we have proposed a novel interpretation/visualization technique based on the image-to-image translation scheme. By learning simulators that could inject and remove disease patterns from a given image, our approach permitted human-understandable and robust visualization on both the subject level and group level. While the experiment focused on identifying morphological changes associated with a disease, the proposed framework has the potential to study generic disease effects, e.g., intensity changes induced by lesions. Moreover, our method also has great generalizability as it is independent of the classifier's architecture. In summary, our work marks an important step towards the application of deep learning in neuroimaging studies.

Acknowledgements. This work was supported by NIH Grants MH113406, AA005965, AA010723, and AA017347, and by Stanford HAI AWS Cloud Credit.

References

1. Zhu, G., Jiang, B., Tong, L., Xie, Y., Zaharchuk, G., Wintermark, M.: Applications of deep learning to neuro-imaging techniques. Front. Neurol. **10**, 1–13 (2019)
2. Lee, G., Nho, K., Kang, B., Sohn, K.A., Kim, D.: Predicting Alzheimer's disease progression using multi-modal deep learning approach. Sci. Rep. **9**, 1–12 (2019)
3. Willemink, M., et al.: Preparing medical imaging data for machine learning. Radiology **295**, 4–15 (2020)
4. Brammer, M.: The role of neuroimaging in diagnosis and personalized medicine-current position and likely future directions. Dialogues Clin. Neurosci. **11**, 389–96 (2009)
5. Ouyang, J., et al.: Longitudinal pooling & consistency regularization to model disease progression from MRIs. IEEE J. Biomed. Health Inform. (2020, in press)
6. Springenberg, J.T., Dosovitskiy, A., Brox, T., Riedmiller, M.: Striving for simplicity: the all convolutional net. arXiv preprint arXiv:1412.6806 (2014)
7. Selvaraju, R.R., Cogswell, M., Das, A., Vedantam, R., Parikh, D., Batra, D.: Grad-CAM: visual explanations from deep networks via gradient-based localization. In: Proceedings of the IEEE ICCV, pp. 618–626 (2017)
8. Zeiler, M.D., Fergus, R.: Visualizing and understanding convolutional networks. In: Fleet, D., Pajdla, T., Schiele, B., Tuytelaars, T. (eds.) ECCV 2014. LNCS, vol. 8689, pp. 818–833. Springer, Cham (2014). https://doi.org/10.1007/978-3-319-10590-1_53
9. Ghorbani, A., Wexler, J., Zou, J.Y., Kim, B.: Towards automatic concept-based explanations. In: NeurIPS, vol. 32 (2019)
10. Kaji, S., Kida, S.: Overview of image-to-image translation by use of deep neural networks: denoising, super-resolution, modality conversion, and reconstruction in medical imaging. Radiol. Phys. Technol. **12**, 235–248 (2019). https://doi.org/10.1007/s12194-019-00520-y
11. Qin, C., Shi, B., Liao, R., Mansi, T., Rueckert, D., Kamen, A.: Unsupervised deformable registration for multi-modal images via disentangled representations. In: Chung, A.C.S., Gee, J.C., Yushkevich, P.A., Bao, S. (eds.) IPMI 2019. LNCS, vol. 11492, pp. 249–261. Springer, Cham (2019). https://doi.org/10.1007/978-3-030-20351-1_19
12. Zhu, J.Y., Park, T., Isola, P., Efros, A.A.: Unpaired image-to-image translation using cycle-consistent adversarial networks. In: ICCV, pp. 2242–2251 (2017)
13. Yang, B., Bender, G., Le, Q.V., Ngiam, J.: CondConv: conditionally parameterized convolutions for efficient inference. In: Advances in Neural Information Processing Systems, pp. 1307–1318 (2019)
14. Balakrishnan, G., Zhao, A., Sabuncu, M., Guttag, J., Dalca, A.: VoxelMorph: a learning framework for deformable medical image registration. IEEE Trans. Med. Imaging **38**, 1788–1800 (2019)
15. Pini, L., et al.: Brain atrophy in Alzheimer's disease and aging. Ageing Res. Rev. **30**, 25–48 (2016)
16. Sullivan, E., et al.: The role of aging, drug dependence, and hepatitis C comorbidity in alcoholism cortical compromise. JAMA Psychiatry **75**, 474–483 (2018)
17. Moorman, D.: The role of the orbitofrontal cortex in alcohol use, abuse, and dependence. Prog. Neuro-Psychopharmacol. Biol. Psychiatry **87**, 85–107 (2018)

Generative Modelling

Enabling Data Diversity: Efficient Automatic Augmentation via Regularized Adversarial Training

Yunhe Gao[1], Zhiqiang Tang[1(✉)], Mu Zhou[1,2(✉)], and Dimitris Metaxas[1(✉)]

[1] Department of Computer Science, Rutgers University, Piscataway, USA
{zhiqiang.tang,dnm}@cs.rutgers.edu
[2] SenseBrain and Shanghai AI Laboratory and Centre for Perceptual and Interactive Intelligence, Hong Kong, Hong Kong SAR

Abstract. Data augmentation has proved extremely useful by increasing training data variance to alleviate overfitting and improve deep neural networks' generalization performance. In medical image analysis, a well-designed augmentation policy usually requires much expert knowledge and is difficult to generalize to multiple tasks due to the vast discrepancies among pixel intensities, image appearances, and object shapes in different medical tasks. To automate medical data augmentation, we propose a regularized adversarial training framework via two min-max objectives and three differentiable augmentation models covering affine transformation, deformation, and appearance changes. Our method is more automatic and efficient than previous automatic augmentation methods, which still rely on pre-defined operations with human-specified ranges and costly bi-level optimization. Extensive experiments demonstrated that our approach, with less training overhead, achieves superior performance over state-of-the-art auto-augmentation methods on both tasks of 2D skin cancer classification and 3D organs-at-risk segmentation.

Keywords: Data augmentation · AutoML · Adversarial training · Medical image analysis

1 Introduction

Data augmentation is a crucial technique for deep neural network training and model optimization [6,14–16]. The basic idea is to improve data amount and diversity through a set of transformations, such as image rotation, scale, deformation, and random noise [15]. The increased amount of training samples are valuable for the performance of computer-assisted medical systems and tasks such as skin cancer diagnosis [2] and organs-at-risk segmentation [8].

This research was supported in part by NSF: IIS 1703883, NSF IUCRC CNS-1747778 and funding from SenseBrain, CCF-1733843, IIS-1763523, IIS-1849238, MURI-Z8424104 -440149 and NIH: 1R01HL127661-01 and R01HL127661-05. and in part by Centre for Perceptual and Interactive Intelligence (CPII) Limited, Hong Kong SAR.

© Springer Nature Switzerland AG 2021
A. Feragen et al. (Eds.): IPMI 2021, LNCS 12729, pp. 85–97, 2021.
https://doi.org/10.1007/978-3-030-78191-0_7

However, there are wide variations in image intensity, appearance, and object shape for different medical tasks. A hand-crafted augmentation policy requires expert knowledge and is unlikely to generalize across multiple tasks. Furthermore, an augmentation policy usually comes with random sampling, which is not adaptive to the target model's state during training. The isolation from model training impairs the effectiveness of data augmentation. Therefore, medical image analysis faces a vital problem: *How to effectively augment medical data with more diversity and less human effort?*

The recent works on automatic data augmentation (i.e., AutoAugment) [5,26] are at the forefront to address the above challenge. Nevertheless, the formulation of AutoAugment has restricted its scope of usability in terms of automation and efficiency. First, it still relies on a set of human-specified transformation functions. Designing useful search space, i.e., defining the transformations with proper boundaries, may require domain knowledge on new tasks, leading to reduced automation and increased user burdens. Second, it uses validation data to evaluate data augmentation performance, resulting in an inefficient bi-level optimization problem, despite using proxy techniques (e.g., smaller models) [5]. Moreover, the quantized parameters (probability and magnitude) in AutoAugment are not differentiable, causing additional optimization difficulty.

To address the automation and efficiency issues, we propose a data augmentation framework via regularized adversarial training. To improve automation, we establish a new search space consisting of three components: global affine transformation, local deformation, and appearance perturbation, each of which is parameterized by a conditional generative network. Towards efficient training, we propose two min-max objectives, where the augmentation generators compete with both the discriminator and target learner to generate realistic (for discriminator) and challenging (for target learner) augmentations. The generators, discriminator, and target learner are optimized jointly in an end-to-end manner without using any validation data. The intuition is that automatically controlled adversarial training can reduce the target learner's overfitting and enhance its generalization power. Overall, our major contributions are:[1]

- We propose a new search space parameterized by three differentiable conditional generative networks that generate global and local geometric transformations as well as appearance perturbation with little domain knowledge.
- To boost training efficiency, we avoid using validation data and switch the bilevel optimization objective in AutoAugment to two min-max games [9,10], which are carefully formulated within a triplet: an augmentation generator, a discriminator, and a target network.
- Our data augmentation framework is automatic, generalizable, and computationally efficient for a variety of data-driven tasks. Extensive experiments demonstrated its superior performance and efficiency on both 2D skin cancer classification and 3D organ-at-risk segmentation tasks.

---

[1] Project page: https://github.com/yhygao/Efficient_Data_Augmentation.

2   Related Work

Our analysis is conceptually related to previous data augmentation approaches, techniques to automate data augmentation, and adversarial training on pixel perturbation and image transformation.

Data augmentation applies transformations to the training samples to facilitate model training and reducing overfitting in machine learning. Previously, there were limited augmentation operations available such as random crop, scaling, flipping and rotation prepared for network training [15]. In the medical image field, random elastic local deformation was used for simulating anatomical variations [12]. Random perturbation on color or intensity values was also used to diversify the training data [14]. However, all of these methods are based on human-designed heuristics requiring substantial domain knowledge that are unable to extend well in unseen datasets.

Automatic data augmentation is emerging to search the optimal composition of transformations to improve machine learning model performance. AutoAugment [5] explores policies and validates their effectiveness by repeatedly training models from scratch. Due to the large search space and bi-level optimization using reinforcement learning, AutoAugment suffers from extremely high computational demand. Subsequent works [6,16] aim at reducing the computational complexity of the searching. In the medical image field, Yang et al. [26] proposed an automated searching approach for both data augmentation and other training strategies for 3D medical image segmentation. [25] propose a differentiable way to update augmentation parameters by means of stochastic relaxation and Monte-Carlo method. However, they all followed the formulation of AutoAugment and used pre-defined transformations (e.g. rotation or contrast enhancement) and search for the optimal magnitude. These randomly sampled transformations can be insufficient for capturing subtle variations in medical images and have not fully exploited the capabilities of augmentation space.

To automatically explore the transformation, researchers used spatial and appearance transform model [27] to learn the registration field and additive mask between two MR images. During model training, they considered the two models to augment training samples by matching external unlabeled data. Also, a deformation model and an intensity model [3] were considered to generate realistic augmentation images. However, these methods are more complicated to use as they require multi-stage training.

Adversarial training is designed to train networks using samples with a small perturbation in the adversarial direction to improve the model's robustness to adversarial attack [10,17]. Most existing works choose to add small pixel-wise perturbation to the input by adding gradient-based adversarial noise [18,21]. Some works use GAN to approximate the distribution of adversarial examples and generate adversarial perturbations [23]. Recent findings suggested that spatial transformations, such as affine transformations [7], elastic deformations [1], can help produce adversarial examples. Our study draws inspiration from adversarial training, but we focus on increasing the generalization capability and improving the performance of clean data instead of adversarial samples.

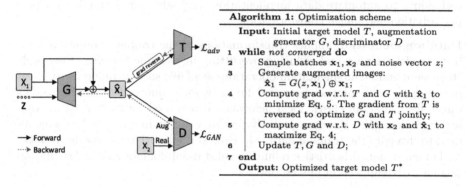

Algorithm 1: Optimization scheme

Input: Initial target model T, augmentation generator G, discriminator D

1   **while** *not converged* **do**
2   Sample batches x_1, x_2 and noise vector z;
3   Generate augmented images:
       $\hat{x}_1 = G(z, x_1) \oplus x_1$;
4   Compute grad w.r.t. T and G with $\hat{x}_1$ to minimize Eq. 5. The gradient from T is reversed to optimize G and T jointly;
5   Compute grad w.r.t. D with x_2 and $\hat{x}_1$ to maximize Eq. 4;
6   Update T, G and D;
7   **end**

Output: Optimized target model T^*

Fig. 1. The regularized adversarial data augmentation framework (**Left**) and its training algorithm (**Right**). Augmentation generator G plays two min-max games with target model T and discriminator D simultaneously to generate challenging and realistic augmented images, hence reduced overfitting and improved generalization.

3 Method

3.1 Preliminaries

In the vanilla supervised training setting with data augmentation, the objective function is

$$\underset{T}{\arg\min} \; \mathbb{E}_{x,y \in \Omega} \; \mathcal{L}(\phi(x), y; T) \tag{1}$$

where $\mathcal{L}(\cdot, \cdot; \cdot)$ is the loss function, T and ϕ are the target and augmentation models; x is a sample from the training dataset Ω; and y is its corresponding ground-truth label. For example, in the skin lesion diagnosis task, x, y are dermoscopic images and the corresponding lesion categories; and T is a classifier with cross-entropy loss $\mathcal{L}$. Note that for some tasks like segmentation, a spatial transformation should be applied to x and y simultaneously.

In hand-crafted data augmentation, ϕ includes a set of pre-defined transformation operations with manually designed boundaries and sampling probabilities. AutoAugment [5] moves one step further by searching for the transformation magnitudes, probabilities, and combinations. However, it still depends on the pre-defined operations and human-specified boundaries. In our approach, ϕ are learnable generative neural networks, with broad, differentiable, and continuous search space.

3.2   Regularized Adversarial Data Augmentation

The key idea of our approach is to use adversarial training to automate data augmentation. In Fig. 1, we propose the regularized adversarial training framework including three networks: an augmentation generator G, a target network T, and a discriminator D and two min-max objectives. In the spirit of adversarial training, augmentation generator G competes with target network T:

$$\mathcal{L}_{adv} = \min_T \max_G \ \mathbb{E}_{x,y \in \Omega} \ [\mathcal{L}(G(z,x) \oplus x, y; T)], \tag{2}$$

where G is a conditional generative network that generates augmentation transformations based on the original image x and the Gaussian noise vector z. The wrapping operation $\oplus$ varies for different augmentation models, whose details will be introduced in Sect. 3.3. The above objective Eq. 2 allows the augmentation model to search along the adversarial direction, such that it generates challenging augmentations to let the target model learn robust features, thus alleviate the potential overfitting issue.

Without proper constraint, adversarial training probably leads to excessive augmentations that hurt the model generalization on clean data [11,22]. To avoid this, we offer two regularization terms that work in the augmentation and image spaces, respectively. First, we regularize the augmentation magnitude by:

$$\mathcal{L}_{reg} = \min_G \ \mathbb{E}_{x \in \Omega} \mathcal{R}(G(z,x)), \tag{3}$$

which aims to penalize large augmentations since they probably move the original data out of distribution. We will elaborate $\mathcal{L}_{reg}$ in Sect. 3.3 as it is related to concrete augmentation models. To further improve the augmentation quality, we use discriminator D to encourage augmented data to look realistic. Thus, we propose the second adversarial objective:

$$\mathcal{L}_{GAN} = \min_G \ \max_D \ \mathbb{E}_{x \in \Omega} \left[\log D(x) \right] + \mathbb{E}_{x \in \Omega} \left[\log(1 - D(G(z,x) \oplus x)) \right] \tag{4}$$

Combining Eq. 2, 3, and 4 gives the overall objective:

$$\mathcal{L}_{overall} = \mathcal{L}_{adv} + \lambda \mathcal{L}_{GAN} + \gamma \mathcal{L}_{reg}, \tag{5}$$

where λ and γ represent loss weights.

Our regularized adversarial data augmentation plays two min-max games within a triplet of G, D, and T. Augmentation generator G, considering both input data and target network T's training state, aims to generate challenging augmentations for target learner T. Simultaneously, it still needs to ensure that the augmented data are in-distribution and achievable by regularizing the augmentation magnitude and forcing the augmented data to be realistic by discriminator D. Using the discriminator is beneficial because small transformations may still make augmented data look fake. By competing with T and D, G can automatically learn data augmentation and thus require little human effort.

The optimization of the triplet is efficient in an end-to-end manner. In each iteration of Algorithm 1, we sample two mini-batches x_1 and x_2 from the training data. x_1 and the sampled Gaussian noises z will go through augmentation generator G to become augmented $\hat{x}_1$, which is then fed into target learner T and discriminator D. Note that we reverse the gradient from T before it flows into G, such that we can compute the gradient with respect to T and G at the same time to minimize Eq. 5 through one backward call. Then $\hat{x}_1$ and x_2 are used to compute the gradient of D to maximize Eq. 4. Thus we can update the triplet with only one pair of forward and backward flow. The steps of training the triplet are given in Algorithm 1.

3.3   Data Augmentation Space and Models

We characterize the medical image variations by three types of transformations: affine transformation, local deformation, and appearance perturbations. These transformations commonly exist for a wide range of medical tasks [2,12,26]. Instead of relying on expert knowledge to specify the transformation ranges, we use three convolutional neural networks (G_A, G_D, and G_I) to learn to generate transformations adaptively. The learning is fully automatic when plugging them into the above regularized adversarial data augmentation framework. Each transformation generator, conditioned on an input image x and a Gaussian noise vector z, produces an affine field, deformation field, or additive appearance mask. Figure 2 illustrates the three transformations and we introduce details below.

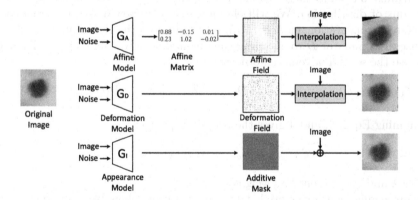

Fig. 2. Illustration of the three augmentation models which perform affine transformation (**Top**), local deformation (**Middle**), and appearance transformation (**Bottom**). Each model is conditioned on an input image and a Gaussian noise vector and generates an affine matrix, a deformation field, or additive appearance mask.

We use affine transformation to approximate the global geometric transformation of an image. In the case of 2D images, our affine model G_A can generate a 2×3 affine matrix A, representing an affine transformation. To make the affine transformation differentiable, we turn to the spatial transformer module [13] that first converts affine matrix A to a flow field denoted as $G_A(z, x)$, and then conducts differentiable image sampling $\oplus$ to generate a transformed image $\hat{x} = G_A(z, x) \oplus x$. We regularize the magnitude of flow field $G_A(z, x)$ as follows:

$$\mathcal{L}_{reg}^A = ||G_A(z, x) - f_{id}||_2, \qquad (6)$$

where the f_{id} is the identity flow field indicating no transformation.

Complementary to global affine transformation, deformation can characterize local geometric transformations. Deformation model G_D directly generates a residual flow field $G_D(z, x)$ including pixel-wise displacements. Then we add identity flow field f_{id} on $G_D(z, x)$ to obtain the deformation field and then use the differentiable sampling $\oplus$ to obtain the deformed image $\hat{x} = (G_D(z, x) + f_{id}) \oplus x$. Here we encourage the deformation smoothness by the following regularization:

$$\mathcal{L}_{reg}^D = ||\nabla G_D(z, x)||_2, \qquad (7)$$

where ∇ is the spatial gradient operator to calculate the differences between neighbor elements in the deformation field $G_D(z, x)$.

Orthogonal to geometric transformations, appearance transformation perturbs the pixel intensity. For simplicity, we transform image appearance by pixel-wise addition. Appearance transformation model G_I outputs the appearance mask $G_I(z, x)$ to generate the perturbed image $\hat{x} = G_I(z, x) + x$. We use the following regularization loss:

$$\mathcal{L}_{reg}^I = ||G_I(z, x)||_2, \qquad (8)$$

which can constrain the perturbation magnitude of $G_I(z, x)$.

To combine the three augmentation models, we draw inspirations from AdvProp [24] to use three groups of auxiliary batch normalizations (BNs) in the target network to capture three augmentation distributions separately, and a main group of BNs for the clean data. In mini-batch training, we split a batch into four parts, three of which are processed by the three augmentation models to generate augmented data. They are fed into the target learner T using their corresponding BNs, and then we update the triplet, as illustrated in Algorithm 1. When testing the trained target network, we only use the main BNs.

4 Experiments

4.1 Experiments Setup

Datasets. We performed experiments on a 2D image classification task and a 3D image segmentation task.

- Skin lesion diagnosis. We used the public ISIC 2018 challenge dataset [4] to make automated predictions of 7 categories of skin lesion within 2D dermoscopic images. The training dataset consists of 10,015 skin lesion images with a fix size of 450×600 pixels.
- Organ-at-risk (OAR) segmentation. We used OARs dataset in MICCAI 2015 challenge to segment 9 OARs in head-and-neck region from 3D CT images. It consists of 38 CT scans for training and 10 scans for testing.

Implementation Details. The three augmentation generators share similar architectures, which take an image and a 128-dimension Gaussian noise vector as inputs, but with different outputs. They are similar to the generator in DCGAN [19] but consist of two branches to process the inputs. The Gaussian noise vector is reshaped to a feature map and processed by six convolutional layers, interleaved with upsampling layers and is finally upsampled to the same size as the image. The image branch also outputs a feature map with the same size through 4 convolutional layers. The two feature maps are concatenated together and then is further processed with 4 convolutional layers to the output layer. G_A first global average pool the feature map and use a fully-connected layer to output the affine matrix. The output layer of G_D and G_I are convolutional layers followed the tanh activation function. All convolutional layers are followed by BN and ReLU except for the output layer. The three generator shares a discriminator, which consists of a series of convolutional layers, BN, and LeakyReLU with slope 0.2, and outputs the final probability through a Sigmoid activation function. For 3D tasks, all networks are modified to theirs 3D counterpart. We set $\lambda = 1$ and $\gamma = 0.1$ in Eq. 5 in the experiments.

Comparison Methods. For 2D classification, we considered multiple classification backbones, including Efficientnet B0-B2 [20], ResNet34-50 and DenseNet121, to compare the effectiveness of data augmentation methods. First, we trained the classification network without data augmentation, named "no-aug" as the lower bound. We applied three strong auto-augmentation methods as comparison methods. RandAug [6] applies a simplified search space for efficient data augmentation containing only two hyper-parameters. Fast-AutoAug [16] searches effective augmentation policies based on density matching without back-propagation for network training. *cGAN* [3] is a task-driven data augmentation approach. All methods train the target network using the same setting for 70 epochs.

For 3D segmentation, we used the 3D ResUNet as the backbone network. The baseline method was trained without any data augmentation except for random cropping. We compared our method with a commonly used manually designed augmentation policies used in the nnUNet framework [12], which is wrapped as a Python image library for network training[2]. It consists of scaling, rotation, elastic deformation, gamma transformation, and additive noise. We used all the transformation with the default parameters defined in the library (named as *nnUNet Full*). We also tried to remove the gamma transformation and train the network (named as *nnUNet Reduce*). The approach in [3] was also extended to 3D as a comparison method (named as *cGAN*).

---

[2] https://github.com/MIC-DKFZ/batchgenerators.

4.2 Skin Lesion Diagnosis Result

We evaluated each method's performance using the average recall score (also known as balanced multi-class accuracy (BMCA)) and reported the accuracy of 5-fold cross-validation in the following sections.

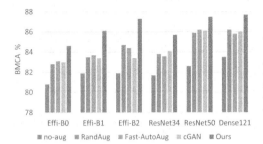

	W/o image condition	W/o discriminator	W/ both
Affine	0.837	0.833	0.844
Deform.	0.830	0.824	0.832
Appear.	0.827	0.819	0.831
Comb.	0.864	0.859	0.873

Fig. 3. Comparisons of different data augmentation methods with multiple target classifiers in the skin lesion task (**Left**) and ablation studies on image condition and discriminator usage in our method using the Efficientnet-B2 classifier (**Right**). Our data augmentation can notably outperform other methods in increasing classification accuracy. Additionally, the image condition and discriminator usage are beneficial because they can help produce customized transformations and realistic augmented images.

Results. Figure 3 shows the results of different classification backbones with data augmentation methods. Our method achieved leading performance across all backbones, especially in the Efficientnet series. Also, all automatic data augmentation methods had a large performance gain compared with no augmentation. Among Efficientnet backbones, the model complexity goes up from B0 to B2, but the increase of complexity did not always improve performance. Without data augmentation, Efficientnet-B2 resulted in similar performance with Efficientnet-B1. We found that data augmentation can further release the large models' potential, and our model obtained more improvement to Efficientnet-B2 compared to the results of RandAug and Fast AutoAug.

Figure 4 highlighted representative augmented images from our augmentation models. Strikingly, we observed that the deformation and appearance transformations are highly centered around the lesion region, which is valuable for boosting performance of deep-learning classifiers. As opposed to traditional random deformation, the strength of our models is that they were adversarially trained with the target model and conditioned upon the input image. Therefore, our approach can generate semantically hard examples for the target model, enabling rich information extraction for the region-of-interest.

Ablation Study. Figure 3 (right) presented the ablation study of each component of our proposed method on Efficientnet-B2 backbone. Among the three

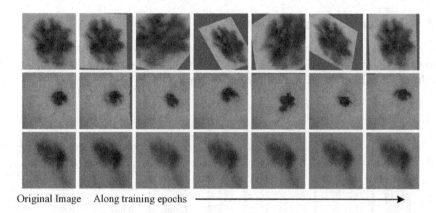

Original Image   Along training epochs ⟶

Fig. 4. Visualization of augmented skin lesion images along six sampled training epochs. Our affine transformation (**Top**), deformation (**Middle**), and appearance perturbation (**Bottom**) models can generate diverse augmentations. For better visualization quality, please see the GIF in the project page.

proposed augmentation models, the affine model performed the best when they were applied separately. After combining them, the performance was further boosted. We also conducted experiments on the input to see if the generator conditioned on the image is useful, see the results in *'W/o image condition'*. The generator's architecture was the same as the previous one, except that the image branch was removed. The results showed that conditioning on image can let the generator samples more meaningful image transformations. *'W/o discriminator'* presented the results without the discriminator. Although regularization loss can constrain the magnitude of augmentation, the discriminator make the generated data more realistic from the image space and therefore have better performance.

Efficiency Analysis. Table 1 exhibited the GPU hours that each method consumed to search augmentation policy for the ResNet-50 backbone. The efficiency of our approach was exemplified by the joint optimization with the target model, where no retraining is needed. Our single model only took approximately 1.57x time than the original 'no-aug' training, while using the combination of three models only takes up to 2.07x time. By comparison, Fast-AutoAug searched the augmentation policies (5.5 h) and continued to retrain the target network

Table 1. Training hours when using different augmentation methods with ResNet-50 in the skin lesions diagnosis. We use the NVIDIA RTX8000 GPUs and report the total training time, including updating both ResNet-50 and augmentation networks/policies.

Method	no-aug	Fast AA	RandAug	cGAN [3]	Ours single	Ours combined
GPU hours	3	8.5	36	18.7	4.7	6.2

(3 h). RandAug reduced the search space to two parameters, but required to train the target network 12 times. cGAN [3] had two transformation models via pre-training (about 4.5 h respectively) and then were fixed to retrain the target network using both original and augmentation data (about 9.7 h).

4.3   Organ-at-Risk Segmentation Result

We extended to conduct experiments on a different OAR segmentation task using 3D CT images to reaffirm the high-level performance of our approach. We used the average Dice score over all organs as the evaluation metric.

Table 2. Comparison to previous data augmentation methods on the OAR segmentation. Our three individual models obtain comparable performance as the strong baseline nnUNet and more advanced cGAN. Combining them brings the highest Dice score.

Method	3D UNet baseline	nnUNet full	nnUNet reduce	cGAN [3]	Ours			
					Affine	Deform	Appear	Comb
AVG Dice	0.784	0.786	0.798	0.803	0.809	0.808	0.792	0.814

Results. Table 2 showed that combination of our transformation models outperformed other competing methods. Even our single affine transformation model achieved higher performance than the cGAN [3] which used pre-training to facilitate the augmentation. Notably, all of our single models demonstrated competitive performance comparing to the manually-designed *nnUNet* methods. Such

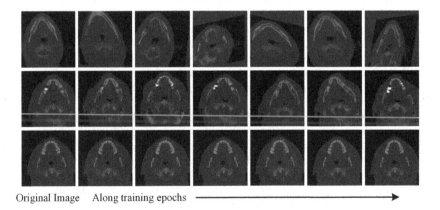

Original Image   Along training epochs ⟶

Fig. 5. Visualization of augmented images of the affine model (**Top**), deformation model (**Middle**) and appearance model (**Bottom**) in OAR segmentation. The augmented images present diverse variations and also preserve details of organ anatomy.

advance can be probably attributed to the capability of adversarial training allowing us to augment diverse training samples. Furthermore, the higher result of *nnUNet Reduce* over *nnUNet Full* reflected the inherent complexity of medical image tasks, suggesting that one good setting of data augmentation parameters in a task (i.e., *nnUNet Full*) is unlikely to generalize well in different tasks. Figure 5 presented the diverse variations of the intermediate slices from our augmentation models.

5   Conclusion

In this paper, we have proposed an efficient automatic data augmentation framework via regularized adversarial training. Three augmentation models were designed to learn the comprehensive distribution of augmentation for improving medical image analysis. The regularized adversarial training is crucial for boosting neural network performance and the joint optimization brings computational efficiency. We showed that the augmentation model can generate meaningful transformations that produce hard yet realistic augmented images. Extensive experiments demonstrated that our method outperformed state-of-the-art augmentation methods in both performance and efficiency. This approach could aid in many image-based clinical applications, especially when limited annotated examples are available.

References

1. Alaifari, R., Alberti, G.S., Gauksson, T.: ADef: an iterative algorithm to construct adversarial deformations. arXiv preprint arXiv:1804.07729 (2018)
2. Brinker, T.J., et al.: Skin cancer classification using convolutional neural networks: systematic review. J. Med. Internet Res. **20**, e11936 (2018)
3. Chaitanya, K., Karani, N., Baumgartner, C.F., Becker, A., Donati, O., Konukoglu, E.: Semi-supervised and task-driven data augmentation. In: Chung, A.C.S., Gee, J.C., Yushkevich, P.A., Bao, S. (eds.) IPMI 2019. LNCS, vol. 11492, pp. 29–41. Springer, Cham (2019). https://doi.org/10.1007/978-3-030-20351-1_3
4. Codella, N., et al.: Skin lesion analysis toward melanoma detection 2018: a challenge hosted by the international skin imaging collaboration (ISIC). arXiv preprint arXiv:1902.03368 (2019)
5. Cubuk, E.D., Zoph, B., Mane, D., Vasudevan, V., Le, Q.V.: AutoAugment: learning augmentation policies from data. arXiv preprint arXiv:1805.09501 (2018)
6. Cubuk, E.D., Zoph, B., Shlens, J., Le, Q.V.: RandAugment: practical automated data augmentation with a reduced search space. In: Proceedings of the IEEE/CVF Conference on CVPR Workshops, pp. 702–703 (2020)
7. Engstrom, L., Tran, B., Tsipras, D., Schmidt, L., Madry, A.: Exploring the landscape of spatial robustness. In: ICML, pp. 1802–1811 (2019)
8. Gao, Y., et al.: FocusNet: imbalanced large and small organ segmentation with an end-to-end deep neural network for head and neck CT images. In: Shen, D., et al. (eds.) MICCAI 2019. LNCS, vol. 11766, pp. 829–838. Springer, Cham (2019). https://doi.org/10.1007/978-3-030-32248-9_92

9. Goodfellow, I., et al.: Generative adversarial nets. In: Advances in Neural Information Processing Systems pp. 2672–2680 (2014)
10. Goodfellow, I.J., Shlens, J., Szegedy, C.: Explaining and harnessing adversarial examples. arXiv preprint arXiv:1412.6572 (2014)
11. Ilyas, A., Santurkar, S., Tsipras, D., Engstrom, L., Tran, B., Madry, A.: Adversarial examples are not bugs, they are features. In: Advances in NIPS, pp. 125–136 (2019)
12. Isensee, F., et al.: nnU-Net: self-adapting framework for U-Net-based medical image segmentation. arXiv:1809.10486 (2018)
13. Jaderberg, M., Simonyan, K., Zisserman, A., et al.: Spatial transformer networks. In: Advances in Neural Information Processing Systems, pp. 2017–2025 (2015)
14. Krizhevsky, A., Sutskever, I., Hinton, G.E.: ImageNet classification with deep convolutional neural networks. In: Advances in NIPS, pp. 1097–1105 (2012)
15. LeCun, Y., Bottou, L., Bengio, Y., Haffner, P.: Gradient-based learning applied to document recognition. Proc. IEEE **86**(11), 2278–2324 (1998)
16. Lim, S., Kim, I., Kim, T., Kim, C., Kim, S.: Fast AutoAugment. In: Advances in Neural Information Processing Systems, pp. 6665–6675 (2019)
17. Madry, A., Makelov, A., Schmidt, L., Tsipras, D., Vladu, A.: Towards deep learning models resistant to adversarial attacks. arXiv preprint arXiv:1706.06083 (2017)
18. Paschali, M., Conjeti, S., Navarro, F., Navab, N.: Generalizability vs. robustness: adversarial examples for medical imaging. arXiv preprint arXiv:1804.00504 (2018)
19. Radford, A., Metz, L., Chintala, S.: Unsupervised representation learning with deep convolutional generative adversarial networks. arXiv:1511.06434 (2015)
20. Tan, M., Le, Q.V.: EfficientNet: rethinking model scaling for convolutional neural networks. arXiv preprint arXiv:1905.11946 (2019)
21. Tramèr, F., Boneh, D.: Adversarial training and robustness for multiple perturbations. In: Advances in NIPS, pp. 5866–5876 (2019)
22. Tsipras, D., Santurkar, S., Engstrom, L., Turner, A., Madry, A.: Robustness may be at odds with accuracy. arXiv preprint arXiv:1805.12152 (2018)
23. Xiao, C., Li, B., Zhu, J.Y., He, W., Liu, M., Song, D.: Generating adversarial examples with adversarial networks. arXiv preprint arXiv:1801.02610 (2018)
24. Xie, C., Tan, M., Gong, B., Wang, J., Yuille, A.L., Le, Q.V.: Adversarial examples improve image recognition. In: Proceedings of the IEEE/CVF Conference on Computer Vision and Pattern Recognition, pp. 819–828 (2020)
25. Xu, J., Li, M., Zhu, Z.: Automatic data augmentation for 3D medical image segmentation. In: Martel, A.L., et al. (eds.) MICCAI 2020. LNCS, vol. 12261, pp. 378–387. Springer, Cham (2020). https://doi.org/10.1007/978-3-030-59710-8_37
26. Yang, D., Roth, H., Xu, Z., Milletari, F., Zhang, L., Xu, D.: Searching learning strategy with reinforcement learning for 3D medical image segmentation. In: Shen, D., et al. (eds.) MICCAI 2019. LNCS, vol. 11765, pp. 3–11. Springer, Cham (2019). https://doi.org/10.1007/978-3-030-32245-8_1
27. Zhao, A., Balakrishnan, G., Durand, F., Guttag, J.V., Dalca, A.V.: Data augmentation using learned transformations for one-shot medical image segmentation. In: Proceedings of the IEEE Conference on CVPR, pp. 8543–8553 (2019)

Blind Stain Separation Using Model-Aware Generative Learning and Its Applications on Fluorescence Microscopy Images

Xingyu Li(✉)(iD)

University of Alberta, Edmonton, AB, Canada
`xingyu@ualberta.ca`

Abstract. Multiple stains are usually used to highlight biological substances in biomedical image analysis. To decompose multiple stains for co-localization quantification, blind source separation is usually performed. Prior model-based stain separation methods usually rely on stains' spatial distributions over an image and may fail to solve the co-localization problem. With the advantage of machine learning, deep generative models are used for this purpose. Since prior knowledge of imaging models is ignored in purely data-driven solutions, these methods may be sub-optimal. In this study, a novel learning-based blind source separation framework is proposed, where the physical model of biomedical imaging is incorporated to regularize the learning process. The introduced model-relevant adversarial loss couples all generators in the framework and limits the capacities of the generative models. Further more, a training algorithm is innovated for the proposed framework to avoid inter-generator confusion during learning. This paper particularly takes fluorescence unmixing in fluorescence microscopy images as an application example of the proposed framework. Qualitative and quantitative experimentation on a public fluorescence microscopy image set demonstrates the superiority of the proposed method over both prior model-based approaches and learning-based methods.

Keywords: Blind source separation · Model-aware generative learning · Fluorescence microscopy image

1 Introduction

In biomedical image analysis, multiple stains are usually used to highlight biological substances of interest and their interactions in tissue samples for quantitative and qualitative analysis. Fluorescence staining and histopathology staining are the representative staining protocols widely adopted in tissue sample analysis. One issue in stained images is mixing/blurred colors due to co-localization of stained biological substances. To regain the information provided by the contrast

© Springer Nature Switzerland AG 2021
A. Feragen et al. (Eds.): IPMI 2021, LNCS 12729, pp. 98–107, 2021.
https://doi.org/10.1007/978-3-030-78191-0_8

of individual stains, stain separation that facilitates the quantitative evaluation of degree of co-localization is highly desired in biological research.

Stain unmixing, or stain separation, is a specific source separation process that separates the mixing stains in a biomedical image into a collection of single-stained planes/images. Model-based unmixing algorithms rely on specific mixing models, which can be formulated as either linear or nonlinear. For instance, fluorescence imaging follows a linear mixing model [1] and H&E stained histopathology imaging is characterized by the non-linear Beer–Lambert law [2]. In early literature, stain unmixing is usually formulated as a model-based inverse problem and many classic matrix decomposition techniques, for instance, independent component analysis (ICA) [3] and singular value decomposition (SVD) [4], were deployed. Later, to address such an underdetermined source separation problem, various regularization terms such as sparsity [7] and non-negative constraint [5,6] are introduced in model-based methods. Since the non-negative constraint is in accordance with stains' physical properties, methods with this constraint, for example, non-negative matrix factorization (NMF), achieve top performance in model-based image stain separation. In NMF, both the stain vectors and stain depths are modeled by low-rank matrices of the original image matrix, with non-negative matrix elements. However, all above statistics approaches heavily rely on stains' distributions in an image and usually fail for weak stained instances.

With the advance of deep learning, blind source separation (BSS) problems are now tackled by generative models [8,9]. Particularly for stain separation, the special case of BSS, deep models (such as U-Net [10] and generative adversary networks (GAN) [11,12]) can be built based on a set of training samples that consists of pairs of multi-color biomedical images and their decompositions. Different from the model-based methods relying on the statistics of stains in an image, deep generative models learn the decomposition function from the training set and thus are less sensitive to stains' distribution in a specific image.

In this work, a novel model-aware GAN-based BSS framework is proposed for stain separation in biomedical images. Unlike the previous deep learning BSS works which are only data-driven, the specific imaging model is incorporated in the proposed scheme. Briefly, in the proposed framework, multiple deep nets are trained to generate single-stained images. By exploiting the imaging model, a model-relevant adversarial loss is used to couple individual generator nets in the learning process. Additionally, a new training algorithm is innovated, where the model-relevant adversarial loss is involved in training and a learning strategy is investigate to avoid inter-generator error propagation. Experimentation on fluorescence separation in biomedical images demonstrates that prior knowledge of imaging model improves the learning performance and outperforms prior arts. In summary, the contribution of the paper are as follows:

- To our best of knowledge, it is the first time in literature to innovate a model-aware deep learning framework for biomedical image stain separation.
- We incorporate generative learning and physical imaging models within the proposed framework. The solution is robust to variations in stains' statistics in an image. Compared to prior deep models, the proposed method generates decomposition results in higher quality.

– A novel training algorithm is proposed to optimize the learning efficiency. The model-relevant loss is incorporated in training to couple individual generators toward the optimal solution and accelerate the learning process in the late training phase.

2   Methodology

Framework Overview: Stain separation decomposes a multi-stained image I into multiple images I_i, each containing biological substances of interest stained by one stain. Figure 1 depicts the overview system architecture. In the framework, N generator nets are used for single-stained image generation. After the image syntheses module which takes the corresponding physical imaging model as the basis, a discriminator net is incorporated to yield a model-relevant adversarial loss. Note that the generator $G_i : I \rightarrow I_i$ and discriminator D are trainable and that the synthesis module $S : \{I_1, ..., I_N\} \rightarrow I$ adopts a specific imaging model of the on-hand problem to couple the N generators.

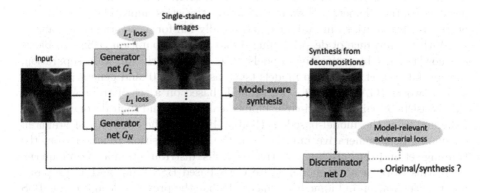

Fig. 1. Overview of the model-aware stain separation learning architecture, where the orange modules represent learning models with trainable parameters and the blue module is defined by the deterministic imaging model. During training, each G_i first targets to minimize the L_1 loss between the ground-truth and its generated single-stained image only; when L_1 losses are small, the model-relevant adversarial loss is incorporated to accelerate generators' optimization. During test, G_i are used for stain separation. (Color figure online)

It is noteworthy that though the proposed framework adopts the adversarial loss, it is distinct from the classical GAN scheme. Instead of using multiple GAN nets to generate individual single-stained images, only one discriminator D is used to couple all generators in the learning processing. The model-aware adversarial loss drives all generators to work hard together to compete against the discriminator. Consider the subsystem between the input I and its synthesis $\hat{I}$, let's denote it as $F \circ S$ where $F = \{G_1, ..., G_N\} : I \rightarrow \{I_1, ..., I_N\}$ is the decomposition function contributed by all generator nets and $\circ$ represents module concatenation. Then the proposed model-aware scheme can be rephrased as to find the decomposition function F such that $F \circ S$ is an identity function, i.e. $F \circ S : I \rightarrow I$. To this end, the proposed model-aware adversarial loss is designed as a function of $F \circ S$, uniting all generators in training.

One may notice that error associated with G_i may propagate to other generators G_j for $j \neq i$ through the model-aware adversarial loss, consequently causing failure. To avoid such inter-generator confusion in learning, a novel training algorithm is proposed to decouple generators at the early training phase.

Loss Functions: As illustrated in Fig. 1, there are two categories of loss functions in the proposed scheme. For each generator G_i, an L_1 loss is used to quantify the difference between the generated single-stained image $\hat{I}_i$ and its ground truth I_i, i.e.

$$\mathcal{L}_{L_1}^i(G_i) = \mathbf{E}[|I_i - \hat{(I_i)}|_1] = \mathbf{E}[|I_i - G_i(I)|_1]. \tag{1}$$

The reason that L_1 loss is preferred over the common L_2 loss is that L_2 loss tends to generate smooth/blue images.

For the proposed architecture, we innovate a model-aware adversarial loss that couples all G_is. Based on the design, $F \circ S : I \rightarrow I$ is equivalent to an autoencoder with specific intermediate representations defined by the decomposition ground truth. Then $F \circ S$ and D compose a conditional GAN, where $F \circ S$ targets to fool the discriminator D and D tries to improve its classification performance. Hence, the model-aware adversarial loss is

$$\mathcal{L}_{cGAN}(D, F \circ S) = \mathbf{E}[\log D(I, I)] + \mathbf{E}[\log(1 - D(I, F \circ S(I)))]. \tag{2}$$

Note that since the synthesis module S is deterministic and well-defined by a specific imaging model, all trainable parameters in the subsystem $F \circ S$ originate from $F = \{G_1, ..., G_N\}$. This suggests that each generator G_i ties to minimize the adversarial loss in Eq. (3) while the discriminator D tries to maximize it.

The advantage of the model-aware adversarial loss is to couple all generators for learning augmentation. But it also brings in a risk that the inter-generator confusion collapses the whole BSS system. Specifically, stain decomposition is an under-determined problem as there may be numerous sets of $\{\hat{I}_i, ..., \hat{I}_N\}$ satisfying the imaging model S. Hence, if the single-stained image $\hat{I}_i$ generated by G_i greatly deviates from its true value I_i, the corresponding error may propagate to other generators through the adversarial loss. To address this issue, rather than directly training $F \circ S$ towards the identity function via the adversarial loss, we enforce the generators G_i focusing on estimation of decomposition ground-truth by L_1 loss in Eq. (2); G_is are coupled through the model-aware adversarial loss only after generators have converged to the region that is close to the ground truth I_i. In this way, the learning process will be accelerated even at the late phase of training. In sum, the overall loss function is

$$\mathcal{L}(D, F \circ S) = \sum_{i=1}^{N} \mathcal{L}_{L_1}^i + \lambda \mathcal{L}_{cGAN}(D, F \circ S), \tag{3}$$

where λ is a hyper-parameter to weight the adversarial loss in the overall target function. In the early training phase, $\lambda = 0$ to enable the generators to learn from the decomposition ground truth I_i. In the late phase of training when L_1 loss is small, $\lambda > 0$ to couple all generators for parameter optimization. Therefore, the optimal solution to the problem is

$$F^* = \arg\min_F \max_D \mathcal{L}(D, F \circ S) = \arg\min_F \max_D \left[\sum_{i=1}^{N} \mathcal{L}_{L_1}^i + \lambda \mathcal{L}_{cGAN}(D, F \circ S) \right].$$

Training Algorithm: In this work, the standard procedures in GAN update [11] is followed - we alternate between one gradient descent step on discriminator D and then one step on generators G_i. The specific training procedure is described in Algorithm 1.

Algorithm 1: Minibatch stochastic gradient descent training of the proposed model-aware BBS learning

---

Input: Training data set: multi-color images Is and its BBS ground truth $I_i, i = 1, ..., N$, the number of sourse N, adversarial loss weight λ, and adversarial loss involvement parameter α

Output: Parameters of generators θ_{G_i} and deccriminator θ_D

for *number of training iterations* **do**

    Sample minibatch of m training data $\{I^1, ..., I^m\}$;

    Update the discriminator D by ascending the stochastic gradient:

    $\nabla_{\theta_D} \frac{1}{m} \sum_{j=1}^{m} \left[\log D(I^j, I^j) + \log(1 - D(I^j, F \circ S(I^j))) \right]$;

    Sample minibatch of m training data $\{I^1, ..., I^m\}$ and $\{I_i^1, ..., I_i^m\}$;

    if *first $100 - \alpha$ percent iterations* **then**

        Update the generators G_i by ascending the stochastic gradients:

        $\nabla_{\theta_{G_i}} \frac{1}{m} \sum_{j=1}^{m} |I_i^j - G_i(I_i^j)|_1$;

    else

        Update the generators G_i by ascending the stochastic gradients:

        $\nabla_{\theta_{G_i}} \frac{1}{m} \sum_{j=1}^{m} \left[|I_i^j - G_i(I_i^j)|_1 + \lambda \log(1 - D(I^j, F \circ S(I^j))) \right]$;

    end

end

---

3   Fluorescence Unmixing

Fluorescence microscopy is a technique used to visualize and identify the distribution of proteins or other molecules of interest stained with fluorescent stains. Because fluorescence microscopy is able to precisely distinguish individual antigens, it is the most popular cell and molecular biological research tool to study dynamical changes in the cell. To highlight multiple molecules of interest within a sample and analyze their interactions, multi-color fluorescence microscopy is used.

Fluorescence unmixing aims to decompose a multi-color fluorescence microscopy image into multiple images, each containing proteins or other molecules of interest stained with one fluorescent stain only. Mathematically, given that there are N types of fluorescent stains in an image and let V_i and D_i represent the ith fluorescent stain's spectrum vector and staining density map that consists of stain proportions over all pixels, a fluorescence microscopy image can be formulated as a linear combination of the N staining density maps [1]:

$$I = V \times D = [V_1, ..., V_N] \times [D_1, ..., D_N]^T = \sum_{i=1}^{N} V_i D_i = \sum_{i=1}^{N} I_i, \qquad (4)$$

where I and I_i are the observed multi-color fluorescence microscopy image and its ith decomposed instance, i.e. the single-stained image associated with the ith fluorescent stain, respectively. $[.]^T$ represents matrix transpose.

To achieve fluorescent stain separation, model-based approaches in literature exploit the imaging model in Eq. (4) and estimate stains' spectrum matrix V from a query image. Then staining density maps D is obtained by matrix inverse operation, and single-stained image I_i is derived by $I_i = V_i D_i$. Among matrix inverse methods, NMF based approaches achieves top performance [5], where non-negative properties of D and V physically are considered during matrix factorization. However, NMF-based solutions usually have weak ability to handle molecules' co-localization.

In this paper, we use fluorescence separation as the application of the proposed framework. Different from model-based approaches that searches optimal V and D first, the proposed method takes Eq. (4) as the image synthesis model $S : \{I_1, ..., I_N\} \rightarrow I$ and directly generates a set of separation results $\{I_i\}$. Note that the fluorescence imaging model formulated in Eq. (4) is differentiable and thereby easy to integrate into the learning strategy in Algorithm 1. In the next section, we evaluate the proposed stain separation framework on fluorescence images and compare its performance with prior arts.

4 Experimental Evaluation

4.1 Experimental Setup

Dataset: We use image set BBBC020 from the Broad Bioimage Benchmark Collection [14] in this study. In the high-resolution RGB-format fluorescence microscopy images of murine bone-marrow derived macrophages from C57BL/6 mice, nuclei were labeled by DAPI in blue and cell surface was stained by CD11b/APC in yellow [15]. In addition to multicolor images containing two fluorescent stains, single-stained images (i.e. DAPI images and CD22b/APC images) are provided in the image set. Since the cells possess an irregular shape and some of the macrophages touch or overlap each other, this dataset can be used to assess an algorithm's ability to deal with co-localization cell data [14]. In this study, each high-resolution image is divided into 30 256×256 patches. In this way, we collect 2250 image patches coming from 750 decomposition patch pairs, each pair containing one multi-color image and its source separation ground truth (i.e. one DAPI image and one CD11b/APC image). Then we randomly picked 10% image pairs as test cases and the rest are used to train the proposed BBS model.

Network Architectures & Hyperparameter Setting: In this study, we adopt the generators and discriminator from those in [12]. Specifically, U-Net256 [13] is used to realize the generators, where the input tensor has a size of 256×256. Compared to the encoder-decoder structure, the skip path in U-Net helps to maintain cell/molecule structures in images. Regarding to the discriminator, a 70×70 PatchGAN which aim to classify whether 70×70 overlapping image patches are real or fake is adopted. It is noteworthy that the U-Net and the PatchGAN are applicable on any color images whose resolution is larger than 256×256. To train the model, minibatch SGD realized by Adam [16] is applied, with a learning rate of 0.0002, and momentum parameters $\beta_1 = 0.5, \beta_2 = 0.999$. For hyperparameters relevant to model-aware adversarial loss, $\alpha = 75, \lambda = 0.01$.

Comparison with State-of-the-Art Methods: NMF based methods achieved top performance in model-based fluorescence microscopy image separation. Hence, we include the NMF based method [5] in this comparison evaluation and use it as the baseline. Since there is no existing learning based approaches proposed for biomedical image stain separation, two common generative learning models are evaluated. In specific, since we have two fluorescence stains in the image set, either 2 U-Nets [13] with the L_1 loss or 2 pix2pix GAN [12] are used.

Evaluation Metrics: Both qualitative and quantitative evaluations are conducted. In qualitative comparison, spectral separation results generated by different methods are visually examined. We also compute three major image quality metrics (MSE, PSNR, and SSIM [17]) between the decomposition results and the ground truth for quantitative comparison.

4.2   Results and Discussions

Figure 2 presents examples of stain separation obtained by different methods. As illustrated in the figure, the NMF-based method [5] and U-nets [13] fail to separate co-localized fluorescent stains in the images. Though the pix2pix GAN [12] obtains better results, block-check artifacts which usually occur in GAN models are observed, especially along image boundaries. Compared to prior arts, the proposed method yields the top source separation results.

Table 1 records the quantitative evaluation of the examined methods. For the first column which corresponds to MSE, smaller values suggest better decomposition results. For PSNR and SSIM, the large the values are, the better the performance is. From the table, all three metrics advocates to the superiority

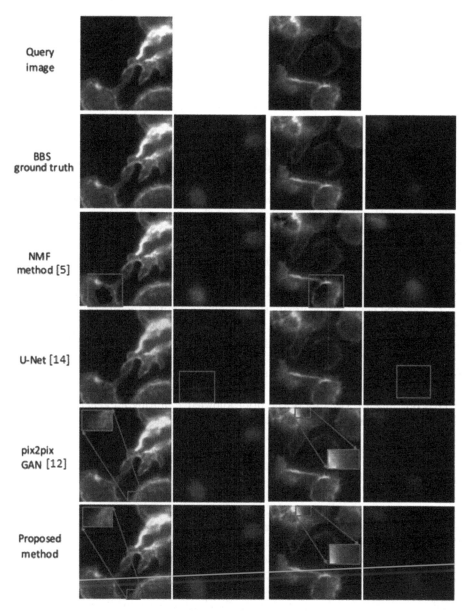

Fig. 2. Samples of fluorescence separation using different methods. Images in the second row correspond to BSS ground truth. The NMF method [5] and U-Net [13] may fail to handle co-localization; Images generated by the pix2pix GAN [12] appears with noticeable check-block effects, while the proposed method generates smooth results as shown in the figure (It is recommended to compare the results between pix2pix GAN and the proposed method by enlarging the figure in PDF). (Color figure online)

Table 1. Quantitative evaluation of BBS via major image quality metrics, where the best values are marked black.

	NMF method [5]	U-nets [13]	pix2pix GAN [12]	proposed method
MSE	73.65	88.13	8.86	**5.85**
PSNR	30.67	32.97	39.13	**41.10**
SSIM	0.92	0.89	0.95	**0.97**

of the proposed method, and the pix2pix GAN ranks the second despite of its check-block artifact. This quantitative comparison is consistent with our qualitative visual examination.

The good performance of the proposed method is due to two reasons. First, let's compare the U-Net based method and the proposed method. It should be noted that both approaches adopt the U-Net as the generators. The major difference is that the proposed method introduces a model-aware adversarial loss in training. Inherent from GAN, the discriminator always tries to find a better objective function that distinguishes the reconstruction and the original input. As a result, instead of passively approaching the decomposition ground truth by L_1 loss, the generator works hard to compete against the discriminator. Second, let's focus on the pix2pix GAN [12] and the proposed method. Since both approaches adopt the adversarial game in training, they outperform the U-Net based model. But different from the model that needs 2 independent pix2pix GAN to generate the spectral decomposition results, the proposed method innovates the use of one discriminator to couple all generators via the fluorescence microscopy images. Because of the prior knowledge uniting all generators in the scheme, the proposed method has less freedom in image generation compared to the pix2pix GAN method.

5   Conclusions

This study proposed a novel deep learning based framework for BSS in biomedical images. In particular, it utilized the physical imaging model to augment the generative learning. In addition, the learning scheme was further empowered and regularized by a model-aware loss. Both qualitative and quantitative experiments had validated the efficiency of the proposed method by public fluorescence microscopy image set. Future work would aim at evaluating the proposed stain unmixing scheme on other BSS scenarios such as multi-stained histo-pathology images.

References

1. Yi, H.J., et al.: Multilevel, hybrid regularization method for reconstruction of fluorescent molecular tomography. Appl. Opt. **51**(7), 975–986 (2012)

2. Ruifrok, A., Johnston, D.: Quantification of histochemical staining by color deconcolution. Anal. Quant. Cytol. Histol. Int. Acad. Cytol. Amer. Soc. Cytol. **23**(4), 291–299 (2001)
3. Cardoso, J.F.: Blind signal separation: statistical principles. Proc. IEEE **86**(10), 2009–2025 (1998)
4. Macenko, M., et al.: A method for normalizing histology slides for quantitative analysis. In: IEEE International Symposium on Biomedical Imaging: From Nano to Macro (ISBI), pp. 1107–1110 (2009)
5. Montcuquet, A.S., et al.: Nonnegative matrix factorization: a blind spectra separation method for in vivo fluorescent optical imaging. J. Biomed. Opt. **15**(5), 056009 (2010)
6. Li, X., et al.: Circular mixture modeling of color distribution for blind stain separation in pathology images. IEEE J. Biomed. Health Inform. **21**(1), 150–161 (2017)
7. Kopriva, I., et al.: Blind decomposition of low-dimensional multi-spectral image by sparse component analysis. J. Chemom. **23**(11), 590–597 (2009)
8. Subakan, C., et al.: Generative adversarial source separation. arVix (2017)
9. Kong, Q.K., et al.: Single-channel signal separation and deconvolution with generative adversarial networks. In: 28th International Joint Conference on Artificial Intelligence, pp. 2747–2753 (2019)
10. Ronneberger, O., Fischer, P., Brox, T.: U-Net: convolutional networks for biomedical image segmentation. In: Navab, N., Hornegger, J., Wells, W.M., Frangi, A.F. (eds.) MICCAI 2015. LNCS, vol. 9351, pp. 234–241. Springer, Cham (2015)
11. Goodfellow, I.J., et al.: Generative adversarial Nets. In: 28th Conference on Neural Information Processing Systems (NIPS) (2014)
12. Isola, F., et al.: Image-to-image translation with generative adversarial networks. In: Conference on Computer Vision and Pattern Recognition (CVPR) (2017)
13. Johnson, J., Alahi, A., Fei-Fei, L.: Perceptual losses for real-time style transfer and super-resolution. In: Leibe, B., Matas, J., Sebe, N., Welling, M. (eds.) ECCV 2016. LNCS, vol. 9906, pp. 694–711. Springer, Cham (2016)
14. Lyosa, V., et al.: Annotated high-throughput microscopy image sets for validation. Nat. Methods **9**, 637 (2012)
15. Wenzel, J., et al.: Measurement of TLR-induced macrophage spreading by automated image analysis: differential role of Myd88 and MAPK in early and late responses. Front. Physiol. **2**, 71 (2011)
16. Kingma, D., et al.: Adam: a method for stochastic optimization. In: International Conference on Learning Representations (ICLR) (2015)
17. Wang, Z., et al.: Image quality assessment: from error visibility to structural similarity. IEEE Trans. Image Process. **13**(4), 600–612 (2004)

MR Slice Profile Estimation by Learning to Match Internal Patch Distributions

Shuo Han[1]([⊠]) [iD], Samuel Remedios[2] [iD], Aaron Carass[3] [iD], Michael Schär[4] [iD], and Jerry L. Prince[3] [iD]

[1] Department of Biomedical Engineering, Johns Hopkins University, Baltimore, MD 21218, USA
shan50@jhu.edu
[2] Department of Computer Science, Johns Hopkins University, Baltimore, MD 21218, USA
sremedi1@jhu.edu
[3] Department of Electrical and Computer Engineering, Johns Hopkins University, Baltimore, MD 21218, USA
{aaron_carass,prince}@jhu.edu
[4] Department of Radiology, Johns Hopkins University, Baltimore, MD 21205, USA
mschar3@jhu.edu

Abstract. To super-resolve the through-plane direction of a multi-slice 2D magnetic resonance (MR) image, its slice selection profile can be used as the degeneration model from high resolution (HR) to low resolution (LR) to create paired data when training a supervised algorithm. Existing super-resolution algorithms make assumptions about the slice selection profile since it is not readily known for a given image. In this work, we estimate a slice selection profile given a specific image by learning to match its internal patch distributions. Specifically, we assume that after applying the correct slice selection profile, the image patch distribution along HR in-plane directions should match the distribution along the LR through-plane direction. Therefore, we incorporate the estimation of a slice selection profile as part of learning a generator in a generative adversarial network (GAN). In this way, the slice selection profile can be learned without any external data. Our algorithm was tested using simulations from isotropic MR images, incorporated in a through-plane super-resolution algorithm to demonstrate its benefits, and also used as a tool to measure image resolution. Our code is at https://github.com/shuohan/espreso2.

Keywords: Slice profile · Super resolution · MRI · GAN

1 Introduction

To reduce scan time and maintain adequate signal-to-noise ratio, magnetic resonance (MR) images of multi-slice 2D acquisitions often have a lower through-plane resolution than in-plane resolution. This is particularly the case in

A. Feragen et al. (Eds.): IPMI 2021, LNCS 12729, pp. 108–119, 2021.
https://doi.org/10.1007/978-3-030-78191-0_9

clinical applications, where cost and patient throughput are important considerations. Therefore, there has recently been increased interest in the use of super-resolution algorithms as a post-processing step to improve the through-plane resolution of such images [15,16,18]. Doing so can improve image visualization as well as improve subsequent analysis and processing of medical images, i.e., registration and segmentation [19].

Supervised super-resolution algorithms conventionally require a degeneration model converting high-resolution (HR) images into low-resolution (LR) to help create paired training data. In multi-slice 2D MR images, this model is often expressed by the slice profile; indeed, when exciting MR signals using radio frequency (RF) pulses within an imaging slice, the slice profile describes the transverse magnetization of spins along the through-plane direction [12]. It acts as a 1D point-spread function (PSF) convolved with the object to be imaged, whose full width at half maximum (FWHM) is interpreted as the slice thickness. That is to say, if the slice profile is known, we can then convolve it with HR images and downsample the resultant volume to match the through-plane resolution when creating paired training data. Even some unsupervised super-resolution algorithms [3] require learning a degeneration model in order to simulate training data from available images.

Previous methods to estimate the slice profile either require a simulation using the Bloch equation [10] or measurement on an MR image of a physical phantom [1,9]. When imaging an object, the effective slice profile can be different from what was originally designed using the pulse sequence. It has been reported that a phantom test can allow the slice thickness—represented by the FWHM of the slice profile—to deviate by as much as 20% in a *calibrated* scanner [1]. Without knowing the true slice profile, some super-resolution algorithms [18] assume that it can be approximated by a 1D Gaussian function whose FWHM is equal to the slice separation. Xuan et al. [16], which takes an alternative approach, does not take the slice profile into account and reduces the slice separation without altering the slice thickness. Given the potential slice thickness error of 20% in a calibrated scanner and even possible slice gaps (the slice thickness is designed to be smaller than slice separation) or overlaps (the slice thickness is designed to be larger than slice separation), we anticipate that being able to estimate an image-specific slice profile would help improve the results of previously proposed super-resolution works. Moreover, accurate estimation of the slice profile, without any external knowledge, could be fundamental in calibrating scanners, determining the exact spatial resolution of acquired MR data, and measuring the resolution improvement achieved by super-resolution algorithms.

Motivated by previous super-resolution work [15,18], we note that, in medical imaging, the texture patterns along different axes of the underlying object can be assumed to follow the same distributions. In particular, for multi-slice 2D MR images, this principle indicates that if we use the correct slice profile, we can degrade patches extracted from the HR in-plane directions such that the distribution of these patches will match the distribution of those LR through-plane patches that are directly extracted from the MR volume. In other words, the slice profile can be estimated by learning to match patch distributions from

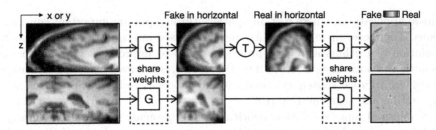

Fig. 1. Flowchart of our algorithm. The generator blurs and downsamples the *horizontal direction* of an extracted image patch, and the discriminator determines whether the *horizontal direction* of the input is fake or real LR and outputs a "pixel-wise" probability map. **G**: generator; **D**: discriminator; **T**: transpose.

these different directions. Generative adversarial networks (GANs) [6] have been used to perform image translation tasks, where they learn to match the distribution of generated images to the distribution of true images. This motivates us to use a GAN framework to match internal patch distributions of an image volume from a multi-slice 2D MR acquisition, where the slice profile is learned as a part of the generator.

Our work shares a similarity with several recent super-resolution algorithms. In [3,5], GANs are also used to learn the degeneration models. However, they do not explicitly impose the form of a PSF. Although their algorithms are capable of learning other image artifacts, these generators are not guaranteed to obey the physical process of resolution degradation. Our work is more similar to [2], as they also explicitly learn a resolution degradation PSF using a GAN. However, they assume patch recurrence across downsampling scales, while we base our algorithm upon the similarity along different directions within the MR image. The contributions of this work are: **1)** we propose an analysis to tie the slice profile estimation to the matching of the patch distributions in the HR and LR orientations; **2)** we realize this theoretical analysis in a GAN to learn the slice profile as part of the generator; **3)** we test our algorithm with numerical simulations and incorporate it into a recent super-resolution algorithm in [18] to demonstrate its benefits for improving super-resolution results; **4)** we show that the proposed algorithm is capable of measuring the resultant image resolution of super-resolution algorithms.

2   Methods

2.1   Slice Profile

We regard the 3D object, f, imaged in a MR scanner, as being represented by the continuous function $f(x, y, z)$. We model the slice selections and signal excitation in a multi-slice 2D acquisition as a convolution between f and the 1D PSF $p_l(z)$,

$$f(x, y, z) *_z p_l(z).$$

We use $*_z$ to denote the 1D convolution along the z-axis, since the symbol $*$ generally represents the 3D convolution along x-, y-, and z-axes. We assume that the truncated k-space sampling imposes two 1D PSFs $p_h(x)$ and $p_h(y)$, which are identical to each other but operate on different axes, onto the xy-plane,

$$f(x, y, z) *_z p_l(z) *_x p_h(x) *_y p_h(y),$$

where $*_x$ and $*_y$ denote the 1D convolutions along the x- and y-axes, respectively. In general, the in-plane—the xy-plane in this case—resolution is higher than the through-plane—the z-axis—resolution. This indicates that p_h (usually) has a smaller FWHM than p_l. Additionally, the acquisition of an image also includes sampling or digitization. In this work, we represent this as,

$$\{f *_z p_l *_x p_h *_y p_h\} \downarrow_{(s_z, s_x, s_y)}, \tag{1}$$

where s_x, s_y, and s_z are sampling step sizes along the x-, y-, and z-axes, respectively. We further assume that $s_x = s_y < s_z$, which is the situation in a typical multi-slice 2D acquisition.

2.2 Slice Profile and Internal Patch Distributions

In medical imaging, we observe that f can express similar patterns (without any blurring) along the x, y, and z axes [15,18]. We use the following notations,

$$I_{xz} = f(x, y, z) |_{(x,y,z) \in \Omega_{xz}} \quad \text{and} \quad I_{zx} = f(x, y, z) |_{(x,y,z) \in \Omega_{zx}},$$

to denote 2D patches extracted from the xz- and zx-planes, respectively, where Ω_{xz} and Ω_{zx} are the corresponding coordinate domains of these 2D patches. It should be self-evident that the patches I_{xz} and their transposes I_{zx} can be assumed to follow the same distribution $\mathcal{F}$. That is,

$$I_{xz} \sim \mathcal{F} \quad \text{and} \quad I_{zx} = I_{xz}^T \sim \mathcal{F}.$$

The self-similar phenomenon implies that the patches extracted from the yz- and zy-planes can also be assumed to follow $\mathcal{F}$. Without loss of generality, we restrict our exposition to the patches I_{xz} and I_{zx}.

In a multi-slice 2D MR image, we cannot directly extract patches from f. Indeed, as noted in Eq. (1), the continuous f is blurred by PSFs then sampled to form a digital image. Instead, we think of the *sampled* patches as,

$$I_{hl} = \{I_{xz} *_1 p_h *_2 p_l\} \downarrow_{(s_x, s_z)} \quad \text{and} \quad I_{lh} = \{I_{zx} *_1 p_l *_2 p_h\} \downarrow_{(s_z, s_x)}, \tag{2}$$

where $*_1$ and $*_2$ are 1D convolutions along the first and second dimensions of these patches, respectively, and $\downarrow_{(s_x, s_z)}$ represents the sampling along the first and second dimensions with factors s_x and s_z, respectively. This can be summarized as saying that I_{lh} is blurrier in its first dimension than its second dimension since $s_z > s_x$, and p_l has a wider FHWM than p_h; in contrast, in I_{hl}, the second dimension is blurrier than its first dimension. Therefore, these two patches, I_{lh} and I_{hl}, cannot be assumed to follow the same distribution anymore.

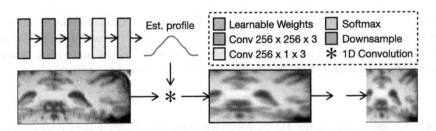

Fig. 2. Architecture of our generator. A series of 1D convolutions, followed by softmax, outputs the estimated slice profile. An image patch is convoled with this slice profile then downsampled. **Conv $C_{in} \times C_{out} \times W$**: 1D convolution along the horizontal dimension with the number of input channels C_{in}, the number of output channels C_{out}, and the size of the kernel W; **Est. profile**: the estimated slice profile. (Color figure online)

All is not lost, however. Suppose that we know the difference between p_h and p_l, which we express as another 1D function k, such that $p_h * k = p_l$, and the difference between the sampling rates s_x and s_z, defined as $s = s_z/s_x$. In this case, we can use the self-similar phenomenon and make the following statements:

$$\{I_{hl} *_1 k\} \downarrow_{(s,1)} \sim \mathcal{F}' \quad \text{and} \quad \{I_{lh} *_2 k\} \downarrow_{(1,s)} \sim \mathcal{F}', \tag{3}$$

where $\mathcal{F}'$ is the resultant patch distribution. This indicates that after *correctly* blurring then downsampling each patch, these new patches should follow the same distribution, namely $\mathcal{F}'$. We note that Eq. (3) only holds approximately; in general, convolution and downsampling operations do not commute.

Since k is the difference of the through-plane slice profile p_l from the in-plane HR PSF p_h, we call k a *"relative"* slice profile. We argue that estimating k should be sufficient for the task of improving supervised super-resolution since we only want to create training pairs from the HR image or patches that have already been blurred by p_h, and p_h may or may not be known. Based on Eq. (3), we formulate the estimation of k as a problem of internal patch distribution matching. This points us to using a GAN, which is capable of learning an image distribution during an image translation task.

2.3   Slice Profile and GAN

According to our analysis in Sect. 2.2, we can estimate the *relative* slice profile k by learning to match the internal patch distributions of a given image volume. In this work, we use a GAN to facilitate this process. In the following discussion, we directly use the term "slice profile" to refer to k for simplicity.

The flowchart of our proposed algorithm is shown in Fig. 1. Suppose that the xy-axes are HR directions and the z-axis is LR. xz or yz patches are randomly extracted from the given image volume with sampling probabilities proportional to the image gradients. As shown in Fig. 1, our generator blurs and downsamples an input image patch only along the horizontal direction. If the generator output is transposed, its horizontal direction is the real LR from the image volume; if not

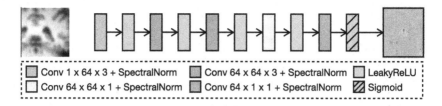

Fig. 3. Architecture of our discriminator. This discriminator has a *1D horizontal* receptive field and determines whether each pixel location *horizontally* corresponds to the real LR or is degraded by the generator. **Conv** $C_{in} \times C_{out} \times W$: 1D convolution along the horizontal dimension with the number of input channels C_{in}, the number of output channels C_{out}, and the size of the kernel W; **SpectralNorm**: Spectral normalization.

transposed, it means that its horizontal direction is degraded by the generator. Therefore, we restrict the receptive field of our discriminator to be 1D, so it can only learn to distinguish the horizontal direction of the image patch.

Loss Function. We updated the conventional GAN value function of the min-max equation [6] to accommodate our model in Eq. (3) as,

$$\min_{G} \max_{D} \left\{ \mathbb{E}_I[\log D(G(I)^T)] + \mathbb{E}_I[\log(1 - D(G(I)))] \right\}, \qquad (4)$$

where G is the generator, D is the discriminator, I is a 2D patch extracted from the image volume, and the superscript T represents transpose. Since the first term in Eq. (4) includes the generator G, we include it in the generator loss function:

$$L_{adv} = \log D(G(I_1)^T) + \log(1 - D(G(I_2))) \qquad (5)$$

to learn the generator, where I_1 and I_2 are two patches independently sampled from the image. In practice, since our D outputs a pixel-wise probability map (see Fig. 3), we calculate L_{adv} as the average across all pixels of a patch.

Generator Architecture. The architecture of our GAN generator is shown in Fig. 2. Different from previous methods [2,3,5], we do not take the image patch as the input to the generator network. Instead, we use the network to learn a 1D slice profile and convolve it with the patch (without padding). In this way, we can enforce the model in Eq. (3) and impose positivity and the property of sum-to-one for the slice profile using softmax. Similar to [2], we do not have non-linearity between convolutions. Additionally, we want the slice profile to be smooth. Inspired by the deep image prior [4,13,14], we note that this smoothness can be regarded as local correlations within the slice profile. We then use a learnable tensor (the green box in Fig. 2) as input to the generator network and simultaneously learn a series of convolution weights on top of it. In other words, we can capture the smoothness of the slice profile using only the network architecture. For this to work, we additionally incorporate an l^2 weight decay during the learning of this architecture, as suggested by [4].

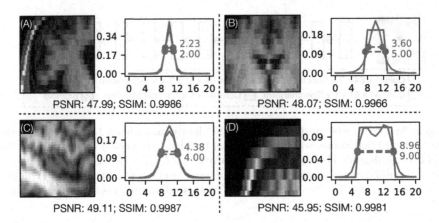

Fig. 4. Example estimated slice profiles of the simulations. Image slices are shown partially with nearest neighbor upsampling for display purposes. True (red) and estimated (blue) slice profiles are shown with their corresponding FWHMs. (**A**): FWHM = 2 mm, scale factor = 4; (**B**): FWHM = 5 mm, scale factor = 4; (**C**): FWHM = 4 mm, scale factor = 2; (**D**): FWHM = 9, scale factor = 8. (Color figure online)

Discriminator Architecture. The architecture of the discriminator is shown in Fig. 3. To restrict its receptive field, we only use 1D convolutions (without padding) along the horizontal direction. The first three convolutions have kernel size 3, and the last two have kernel size 1. This is equivalent to a receptive field of 7, so the discriminator is forced to learn from local information. To stabilize GAN training, we adjust the convolution weights using spectral normalization [11] and use leaky ReLU with a negative slope equal to 0.1 in-between. This discriminator learns to distinguish whether the horizontal direction at each pixel is from the real LR or degraded by the generator; it outputs a "pixel-wise" probability map.

2.4 Regularization Functions and Other Details

In addition to our adversarial loss in Eq. (5), we use the following losses to regularize the slice profile k:

$$L_c = \left(\sum_{i=0}^{K-1} ik_i - \lfloor K/2 \rfloor \right)^2 \quad \text{and} \quad L_b = k_0 + k_1 + k_{K-1} + k_{K-2},$$

where K is the length of k and $\lfloor . \rfloor$ is the floor operation. L_c encourages the centroid of k to align with the central coordinate, and L_b encourages its borders to be zero [2]. Note that our k is guaranteed to be positive and sum to one due to the use of softmax (Fig. 2). Therefore, our total loss for the generator is

$$L = L_{adv} + \lambda_c L_c + \lambda_b L_b + \lambda_w WD,$$

where WD is l^2 weight decay, and $\lambda_c = 1$, $\lambda_b = 10$, and $\lambda_w = 0.05$ are the corresponding loss weights, determined empirically. Inspired by [17], we further use exponential moving average $\bar{k}$ as our result to stabilize the estimation,

Table 1. Errors between true and estimated profiles in the simulations with Gaussian and rect profiles. The mean values across five subjects are shown for each metric. F. err.: absolute error between FWHMs; P. err.: sum of absolute errors between profiles.

Gaussian profile									
FWHM	2 mm			4 mm			8 mm		
Scale	2	4	8	2	4	8	2	4	8
F. Err.	0.32	0.41	0.69	0.36	0.26	0.52	0.97	0.23	1.33
P. Err.	0.20	0.23	0.33	0.11	0.11	0.13	0.10	0.09	0.23
PSNR	46.68	45.80	42.81	50.34	51.45	51.46	50.26	55.43	46.93
SSIM	0.9976	0.9974	0.9957	0.9987	0.9991	0.9993	0.9982	0.9994	0.9975
Rect profile									
FWHM	3 mm			5 mm			9 mm		
Scale	2	4	8	2	4	8	2	4	8
F. Err	0.55	0.62	0.35	0.06	1.54	1.98	0.18	0.53	0.46
P. Err	0.44	0.44	0.47	0.28	0.41	0.45	0.25	0.24	0.23
PSNR	45.89	46.01	43.43	47.02	46.25	45.19	46.92	50.47	48.77
SSIM	0.9971	0.9976	0.9963	0.9973	0.9972	0.9971	0.9960	0.9987	0.9986

$$\bar{k}^{(t)} = \beta \bar{k}^{(t-1)} + (1 - \beta)k^{(t)},$$

where t is the index of the current iteration, and $\beta = 0.99$. We use two separate Adam optimizers [7] for the generator and the discriminator, respectively, with parameters learning rate $= 2 \times 10^{-4}$, $\beta_1 = 0.5$, and $\beta_2 = 0.999$. Unlike the generator, the optimizer of the discriminator does not have weight decay, and the generator optimizer also has gradient clipping. The number of iterations is 15,000 with a mini-batch size of 64. The size of an image patch is 16 along the LR direction, and we make sure that after the generator, the HR direction also has size 16. We initialize the slice profile to be an impulse function before training.

3   Experiments and Results

3.1   Simulations from Isotropic Images

In the first experiment to test the proposed algorithm, we simulated LR images from isotropic brain scans of five subjects from the OASIS-3 dataset [8]. These images are scanned using the magnetization prepared rapid acquisition gradient echo (MPRAGE) sequence with a resolution of 1 mm. We generated two types of 1D functions, Gaussian and rect, to blur the through-plane direction of these images. The Gaussian functions have FWHMs of 2, 4, and 8 mm, and the rect functions have FWHMs of 3, 5, and 9 mm. After blurring, we downsampled these images with scale factors of 2, 4, and 8. As a result, we generated $2 \times 3 \times 3 = 18$ types of simulations for each of the five subjects. We then ran our algorithm on all

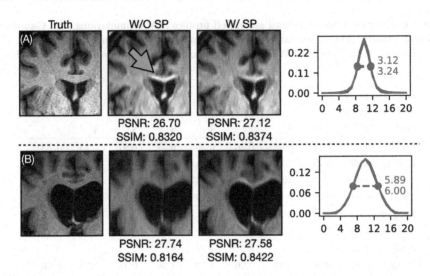

Fig. 5. SMORE results. Image slices are shown partially for display purposes. True (red) and estimated (blue) profiles are shown with their corresponding FWHMs. The arrow points to an artifact. Row **(A)**: FWHM = 3.2 mm, scale factor = 4; Row **(B)**: FWHM = 6.0 mm, scale factor = 4. **W/O SP**, **W/SP**: without and with incorporating our estimate of the profile into SMORE, respectively. (Color figure online)

Table 2. SSIM and PSNR between SMORE results and the true HR images with and without using the estimated slice profiles. Each metric is shown as the mean across five subjects. **W/SP**: incorporating our estimate of slice profile.

FWHM	2.0 mm		3.2 mm		4.8 mm		6.0 mm	
W/SP	False	True	False	True	False	True	False	True
PSNR	26.11	**27.81**	27.57	27.86	**28.57**	27.78	**28.15**	27.79
SSIM	0.8223	**0.8517**	0.8523	**0.8558**	**0.8570**	0.8565	0.8343	**0.8540**

these simulated images. Four metrics were used to evaluate the estimated profiles: the absolute error between the FWHMs of true and estimated profiles (FHWM error), the sum of absolute errors between the true and estimated profiles (profile error), and peak signal-to-noise ratio (PSNR) and structural similarity (SSIM) between the images degraded by the true and estimated profiles. Note that we calculate SSIM and PSNR within a head mask. We show these results in Table 1. Example images and slice profiles are shown in Fig. 4. Despite high FHWM and profile errors, we observe that the PSNR and SSIM results are very good. We attribute this disparity to the ill-posed nature of the problem, as different slice profiles can generate very similar LR images.

3.2 Incorporating Slice Profile Estimation into SMORE

SMORE [18] is a self-supervised (without external training data) super-resolution algorithm to improve the through-plane resolution of multi-slice 2D MR images. It does not know the slice profile and assumes it is a 1D Gaussian function with FWHM equal to the slice separation. In this experiment, we incorporated our algorithm into SMORE and compared the performance difference with and without our estimated slice profiles. Throughout this work, we trained SMORE from scratch for 8,000 iterations. We simulated low through-plane resolution images from our five OASIS-3 scans. We used only Gaussian functions to blur these images with a scale factor of 4. The Gaussian functions have FWHMs of 2, 3.2, 4.8, and 6 mm. Therefore, we generated 4 simulations for each of the five scans. When not knowing the slice profile, we assume it is a Gaussian function with FWHM = 4 mm (which is the slice separation in our simulations). After running SMORE, we calculated the PSNR and SSIM between the SMORE results and the true HR images as shown in Table 2. Example SMORE results with and without knowing the estimated slice profiles are shown in Fig. 5. Table 2 shows better PSNR and SSIM, if our estimated profiles are used, for simulations with FWHMs of 2 and 3.2 mm. The PSNR are worse for 4.8 and 6.0 mm, but SSIM is better for FWHM 6.0 mm.

3.3 Measuring Through-Plane Resolution After Applying SMORE

In this experiment, we use the FWHMs of our estimated slice profiles to measure the resultant resolution after applying SMORE to an image. We used Gaussian functions to blur the five OASIS-3 scans. The first type (Type 1) of simulations has a FWHM of 2 mm and a scale factor of 2, while the second type (Type 2) has FWHM of 4 mm and a slice factor of 4. We first used SMORE to super-resolve these images then applied our slice profile estimation to measure resultant through-plane resolution. Type 1 has mean FWHM = 1.9273 mm with standard deviation (SD) = 0.0583 mm across the five subjects. Type 2 has mean FWHM = 2.9044 mm with SD = 0.1553 mm. Example SMORE results and resolution measurements are shown in Fig. 6.

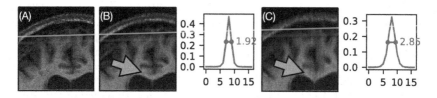

Fig. 6. Resolution measurements of super-resolved images. SMORE results and the corresponding slice profile estimates from the *resultant* images of SMORE are shown in (B) and (C). The FWHMs of estimated profiles are marked on the side. The arrows point to the differences. **(A)**: truth HR image; **(B)**: SMORE result from a simulation with FWHM = 2 mm; **(C)**: SMORE result from a simulation with FWHM = 4 mm.

4   Discussion and Conclusions

In this work, we proposed to estimate slice profiles of multi-slice 2D MR images by learning to match the internal patch distributions. Specifically, we argue that if an HR in-plane direction is degraded by the correct slice profile, the distribution of patches extracted from this direction should match the distribution of patches extracted from the LR through-plane direction. We then proposed to use a GAN to learn the slice profile as a part of the generator. Our algorithm is validated using numerical simulations and incorporated into SMORE to improve its super-resolution results. We further show that our algorithm is also capable of measuring through-plane resolution.

The first limitation of our algorithm is that it is unable to learn a slice profile with a flexible shape as shown in Fig. 4, where the true profiles are rect functions. This is because we used a similar generator architecture as the deep image prior to encourage smoothness. We found that the value of λ_w for weight decay greatly affected the performance. Specifically, with a small λ_w, the shape of the learned slice profile is more flexible, but the training is very unstable and can even diverge. A better way to regularize the slice profile should be investigated in the future.

The second limitation is our inconclusive improvement to the SMORE algorithm. Indeed, we have better PSNR and SSIM when the slice thickness is smaller than the slice separation (resulting in slice gaps when FWHMs are 2 and 3.2 mm in Table 2); this does not seem to be the case when the slice thickness is larger (resulting in slice overlaps when FWHMs are 4.8 and 6.0 mm in Table 2). We regard this as a counter-intuitive result and plan to conduct more experiments with SMORE, such as train with more iterations, and testing other super-resolution algorithms.

Acknowledgments. This work was supported by a 2019 Johns Hopkins Discovery Award and NMSS Grant RG-1907-34570.

References

1. American College of Radiology Magnetic Resonance Imaging Accreditation Program: Phantom Test guidance for use of the large MRI phantom for the ACR MRI accreditation program, p. 16 (2018). https://www.acraccreditation.org/-/media/ACRAccreditation/Documents/MRI/LargePhantomGuidance.pdf
2. Bell-Kligler, S., Shocher, A., Irani, M.: Blind super-resolution kernel estimation using an internal-GAN. In: Advances in Neural Information Processing Systems 32, pp. 284–293. Curran Associates, Inc. (2019)
3. Chen, S., et al.: Unsupervised image super-resolution with an indirect supervised path. In: Proceedings of the IEEE/CVF Conference on Computer Vision and Pattern Recognition Workshops (2020)
4. Cheng, Z., Gadelha, M., Maji, S., Sheldon, D.: A Bayesian perspective on the deep image prior. In: Proceedings of the IEEE/CVF Conference on Computer Vision and Pattern Recognition (2019)

5. Deng, S., et al.: Isotropic reconstruction of 3D EM images with unsupervised degradation learning. In: Martel, A.L., et al. (eds.) MICCAI 2020. LNCS, vol. 12265, pp. 163–173. Springer, Cham (2020). https://doi.org/10.1007/978-3-030-59722-1_16

6. Goodfellow, I., et al.: Generative adversarial nets. In: Advances in Neural Information Processing Systems 27, pp. 2672–2680. Curran Associates, Inc. (2014)

7. Kingma, D.P., Ba, J.: Adam: a method for stochastic optimization. arXiv preprint: 1412.6980 (2017)

8. LaMontagne, P.J., et al.: OASIS-3: Longitudinal neuroimaging, clinical, and cognitive dataset for normal aging and Alzheimer disease. medRxiv (2019)

9. Lerski, R.A.: An evaluation using computer simulation of two methods of slice profile determination in MRI. Phys. Med. Biol. **34**(12), 1931–1937 (1989)

10. Liu, H., Michel, E., Casey, S.O., Truwit, C.L.: Actual imaging slice profile of 2D MRI. In: Medical Imaging 2002: Physics of Medical Imaging, vol. 4682, pp. 767–773. SPIE (2002)

11. Miyato, T., Kataoka, T., Koyama, M., Yoshida, Y.: Spectral normalization for generative adversarial networks. In: International Conference on Learning Representations (2018)

12. Prince, J.L., Links, J.M.: Medical Imaging Signals and Systems. Pearson Prentice Hall, Upper Saddle River (2006)

13. Ren, D., Zhang, K., Wang, Q., Hu, Q., Zuo, W.: Neural blind deconvolution using deep priors. In: Proceedings of the IEEE/CVF Conference on Computer Vision and Pattern Recognition (2020)

14. Ulyanov, D., Vedaldi, A., Lempitsky, V.: Deep image prior. In: Proceedings of the IEEE/CVF Conference on Computer Vision and Pattern Recognition (2018)

15. Weigert, M., Royer, L., Jug, F., Myers, G.: Isotropic reconstruction of 3D fluorescence microscopy images using convolutional neural networks. In: Descoteaux, M., Maier-Hein, L., Franz, A., Jannin, P., Collins, D.L., Duchesne, S. (eds.) MICCAI 2017. LNCS, vol. 10434, pp. 126–134. Springer, Cham (2017). https://doi.org/10.1007/978-3-319-66185-8_15

16. Xuan, K., et al.: Reduce slice spacing of MR images by super-resolution learned without ground-truth. arXiv preprint: arXiv:2003.12627 (2020)

17. Yazıcı, Y., Foo, C., Winkler, S., Yap, K., Piliouras, G., Chandrasekhar, V.: The unusual effectiveness of averaging in GAN training. In: International Conference on Learning Representations (2019)

18. Zhao, C., et al.: A deep learning based anti-aliasing self super-resolution algorithm for MRI. In: Frangi, A.F., Schnabel, J.A., Davatzikos, C., Alberola-López, C., Fichtinger, G. (eds.) MICCAI 2018. LNCS, vol. 11070, pp. 100–108. Springer, Cham (2018). https://doi.org/10.1007/978-3-030-00928-1_12

19. Zhao, C., et al.: Applications of a deep learning method for anti-aliasing and super-resolution in MRI. Magn. Reson. Imaging **64**, 132–141 (2019)

Shape

Partial Matching in the Space of Varifolds

Pierre-Louis Antonsanti[1,2]([✉]) [iD], Joan Glaunès[2] [iD], Thomas Benseghir[1] [iD],
Vincent Jugnon[1] [iD], and Irène Kaltenmark[2] [iD]

[1] GE Healthcare, 78530 Buc, France
{pierrelouis.antonsanti,thomas.benseghir,vincent.jugnon}@ge.com
[2] MAP5, Universite de Paris, 75006 Paris, France
{alexis.glaunes,irene.kaltenmark}@u-paris.fr

Abstract. In computer vision and medical imaging, the problem of matching structures finds numerous applications from automatic annotation to data reconstruction. The data however, while corresponding to the same anatomy, are often very different in topology or shape and might only partially match each other. We introduce a new asymmetric data dissimilarity term for various geometric shapes like sets of curves or surfaces. This term is based on the Varifold shape representation and assesses the embedding of a shape into another one without relying on correspondences between points. It is designed as data attachment for the Large Deformation Diffeomorphic Metric Mapping (LDDMM) framework, allowing to compute meaningful deformation of one shape onto a subset of the other. Registrations are illustrated on sets of synthetic 3D curves, real vascular trees and livers' surfaces from two different modalities: Computed Tomography (CT) and Cone Beam Computed Tomography (CBCT). All experiments show that this data dissimilarity term leads to coherent partial matching despite the topological differences.

1 Introduction

Finding shape correspondences is a standard problem in computer vision that has numerous applications such as pattern recognition [5,6,17], annotation [4,12] and reconstruction [16]. In particular, in the field of medical imaging, matching an atlas and a patient's anatomy [12], or comparing exams of the same patient acquired with different imaging techniques [2,27], provide critical information to physicians for both planning and decision making.

In medical imaging, this problem has been tackled by numerous authors [26] by registering directly the images, most of the time assuming that both images contains the entire object of interest. But in practice, it often happens that only part of an object is visible in one of the two modalities: in CBCT for instance, the imaged organs can be larger than the field of view, when the whole organ can be acquired in CT. In order to make the best of the two modalities, one needs to find a partial matching between them. This work is focused on sparse segmented structures registration where only part of these structures can be matched.

© Springer Nature Switzerland AG 2021
A. Feragen et al. (Eds.): IPMI 2021, LNCS 12729, pp. 123–135, 2021.
https://doi.org/10.1007/978-3-030-78191-0_10

Previous Works. The problem of matching shapes has been widely addressed in the literature in the past decades [18]. In the specific case of partial matching, one can find two main approaches to such problem: either by finding correspondences, sparse or dense, between structures from descriptors that are invariant to different transformations [1,15,24], or by looking for a deformation aligning the shapes with respect to a given metric [1,4,12,16].

The early works on partial shape correspondence as reviewed in [18] rely on **correspondences** between points computed from geometric descriptors extracted from an isotropic local region around the selected points. The method is refined in [17] by selecting pairs of points to better fit the local geometry using bilateral map. The features extracted can also be invariant to different transformation, as in [25] where the descriptors extracted are scale invariant. Such sparse correspondences are naturally adapted to partial matching, yet they cannot take the whole shapes into account in the matching process.

Using a different approach, functional maps were introduced in [22] allowing dense correspondences between shapes by transferring the problem to linear functions between spaces of functions defined over the shapes. In [24] the non-rigid partial shape correspondence is based on the Laplace-Beltrami eigenfunctions used as prior in the spectral representation of the shapes. Recently in [15], such functional map models were adapted in a deep unsupervised framework by finding correspondences minimizing the distortion between shapes. Such methods are yet limited to surface correspondences.

The second kind of approaches relies on the **deformations** that can be generated to align the shapes with each other. It usually involves minimizing a function called data attachment that quantifies the alignment error between the shapes. A deformation cost is sometimes added to regularize these deformations. The sparse correspondences being naturally suited to partial matching, they are notably used in Iterative Closest Point (ICP) methods and their derivatives to guide a registration of one shape onto the other. In [1] a regularized version of the ICP selects the sets of four co-planar points in the points cloud. In [4] the ICP is adapted to the specific case of vascular trees and compute curves' correspondences through an Iterative Closest Curve method. Working on trees of 3D curves as well, [12] hierarchically selects the overall curves correspondences minimizing the tree space geodesic distance between the trees. This latter method although specific to tree-structures, allows topological changes in the deformation.

On the other hand some authors compute the deformation guided by a dense data attachment term. In [6] isometry-invariant minimum distortion deformations are applied to 2D Riemannian manifolds thanks to a multiscale framework using partial matching derived from Gromov's theory. This work is extended in [5] by finding the optimal trade-off between partial shape matching and similarity between these shapes embedded in the same metric space. Recently in [16] a partial correspondence is performed through a non-rigid alignment of one shape and its partial scan seen as points clouds embedded in the same representation space. The non-rigid alignment is done with a Siamese architecture network.

This approach seems promising and is part of a completion framework, however it requires a huge amount of data to train the network.

Interestingly, the regularization cost can be seen as a distance between shapes itself (as in [12]) by quantifying the deformation amount necessary to register one shape onto the other. This provides a complementary tool to the metrics used to quantify the shapes dissimilarities.

A well established and versatile framework to compute meaningful deformations is the Large Deformation Diffeomorphic Metric Mapping. It allows to see the difference between shapes through the optimal deformations to register a source shape S onto a target shape T. However, the data attachment metrics proposed so far aim to compare the source and target shapes in their entirety [9], or look for explicit correspondences between subparts of these shapes [13]. In [20] the growth model presented introduces a first notion of partial matching incorporated to the LDDMM framework, yet no explicit partial dissimilarity term was proposed.

We propose a new asymmetric dissimilarity term adapted as data attachment in the LDDMM framework derived from the Varifold shape representation [10] to quantify the partial shape matching. This term can be used in both continuous and discrete settings, and applied to many discrete shape representations without requiring any point correspondences. When combined with LDDMM, this approach allows to build meaningful deformations while being adapted to the partial matching between shapes.

2   Partial Matching

We are interested in the problem of finding an optimal deformation to register a source shape S onto an unknown subset of a target shape T, where S, T are assumed to be finite unions of m-dimensional submanifolds of $E = \mathbb{R}^d$, with either $m = 1$ (curves) or $m = d - 1$ (hypersurfaces).

2.1   The Varifold Framework for Shape Matching

In this section we will quickly review the oriented varifold framework introduced in [19], of which the varifold framework [10] is a particular case.

Let $E = \mathbb{R}^d$, with $d \geq 2$ the ambient space. Shapes S and T are assumed to be compact m-rectifiable subsets of $\mathbb{R}^d$. In particular at almost every point $x \in S$ (resp. $y \in T$) is defined a unit tangent - for curves - or normal - for hypersurfaces - vector $\tau_x S \in \mathbb{S}^{d-1}$ (resp. $\tau_y T$).

Let W be a Reproducing Kernel Hilbert Space (RKHS) of functions defined over $\mathbb{R}^d \times \mathbb{S}^{d-1}$, continuously embedded in $C_0(\mathbb{R}^d \times \mathbb{S}^{d-1})$. Its dual space W' is a space of varifolds. The following proposition gives a practical way to define such a space:

Proposition 1 ([10], Lemma 4.1).   *Assume that we are given a positive-definite real kernel k_e on the space $\mathbb{R}^d$ such that k_e is continuous, bounded and* *for all $x \in \mathbb{R}^d$, the function $k_e(x,.)$ vanishes at infinity. Assume that a second positive-definite real kernel k_t is defined on the manifold $\mathbb{S}^{d-1}$ and is also continuous. Then the RKHS W associated to the positive-definite kernel $k_e \otimes k_t$ is continuously embedded into the space $C_0(\mathbb{R}^d \times \mathbb{S}^{d-1})$.*

In the following we assume that the reproducing kernel of W is of the form $k_e \otimes k_t$, with the assumptions of Proposition 1. We also assume that k_e and k_t are non negative functions. In practice, we will use for $k_e : (\mathbb{R}^d)^2 \rightarrow \mathbb{R}$ a gaussian kernel $k_e(x,y) = e^{-\|x-y\|^2/\sigma_W^2}$, where σ_W is a scale parameter, and for $k_t : (\mathbb{S}^{d-1})^2 \rightarrow \mathbb{R}$ the kernel $k_t(u,v) = e^{\langle u,v \rangle_{\mathbb{R}^d}}$.

We associate with shape S the canonical function $\omega_S \in W$ defined for all $y \in \mathbb{R}^d$ and $\tau \in \mathbb{S}^{d-1}$ as follows:

$$\omega_S(y,\tau) = \int_S k_e(y,x)k_t(\tau,\tau_x S)dx.$$

This function corresponds to the unique representer of the varifold $\mu_S \in W'$ via the Riesz representation theorem. Similarly, we define the canonical function ω_T associated with shape T. Via this representation of shapes, one may express the scalar product between the varifolds μ_S, μ_T, or equivalently between the canonical functions ω_S, ω_T as follows:

$$\langle \mu_S, \mu_T \rangle_{W'} = \langle \omega_S, \omega_T \rangle_W = \int_S \int_T k_e(x,y)k_t(\tau_x S, \tau_y T)dx\,dy.$$

Finally, the shape matching distance as defined in [10] is the following:

$$d_{W'}(S,T)^2 = \|\omega_S - \omega_T\|_W^2 = \|\mu_S - \mu_T\|_{W'}^2$$
$$= \langle \mu_S, \mu_S \rangle_{W'} - 2\langle \mu_S, \mu_T \rangle_{W'} + \langle \mu_T, \mu_T \rangle_{W'}.$$

In order to adapt this distance for partial matching, a first and intuitive way could be to use half of the expression as follows:

$$\Delta(S,T) = \langle \mu_S, \mu_T - \mu_S \rangle_{W'}^2 = \langle \mu_S, \mu_S - \mu_T \rangle_{W'}^2.$$

The intuition behind this definition is that if S is a subset of T, then $\mu_T - \mu_S$ is the varifold corresponding to $T \setminus S$, which is disjoint from shape S and thus roughly orthogonal to it from the varifold metric viewpoint.

Yet, if $S = S_1 \sqcup S_2$, a mismatch of S_1 into T, characterized by $\langle \mu_{S_2}, \mu_S - \mu_T \rangle_{W'} > 0$, can be compensated by an overrated characterization of the inclusion $S_2 \subset T$ with $\langle \mu_{S_2}, \mu_S - \mu_T \rangle_{W'} < 0$, which happens if the mass of T around S_2 is larger than the mass of S_2. Hence, we introduce in this paper a localized characterization of the inclusion.

2.2   Definition of the Partial Matching Dissimilarity

To simplify the notation, we denote for $x, x' \in S$, $\mathbf{x} = (x, \tau_x S)$, $\omega_S(\mathbf{x}) = \omega_S(x, \tau_x S)$ and $k(\mathbf{x}, \mathbf{x}') = k_e(x, x')k_t(\tau_x S, \tau_{x'} S)$.

Definition 1. Let $g : \mathbb{R} \mapsto \mathbb{R}$ defined as $g(s) = (\max(0, s))^2$. We define the partial matching dissimilarity as follows:

$$\Delta(S, T) = \int_S g\left(\omega_S(\mathbf{x}) - \omega_T(\mathbf{x})\right) dx$$

$$= \int_S g\left(\int_S k(\mathbf{x}, \mathbf{x}')dx' - \int_T k(\mathbf{x}, \mathbf{y})dy\right) dx.$$

With $g(s) = s$, we would retrieve $\langle \mu_S, \mu_S - \mu_T \rangle_{W'}$. The threshold $\max(0, \cdot)$ prevents the compensation of a local mismatch by an overrated match in another area.

Proposition 2. *If* $S \subset T$, $\Delta(S, T) = 0$.

Since k_e and k_t are assumed to be non negative functions, we have

$$\Delta(S, T) = \int_S g\left(\int_S k(\mathbf{x}, \mathbf{y})dy - \int_T k(\mathbf{x}, \mathbf{y})dy\right) dx$$

$$= \int_S g\left(-\int_{T \setminus S} k(\mathbf{x}, \mathbf{y})dy\right) dx = 0. \quad \square \tag{1}$$

The next proposition highlights the local nature of the dissimilarity function Δ.

Proposition 3. *If* $S' \subset S$, *then* $\Delta(S', T) \leq \Delta(S, T)$. *In particular, if* $\Delta(S, T) = 0$ *then for any subset* S' *of* S, $\Delta(S', T) = 0$.

Since $k \geq 0$, we have for any $S' \subset S$ and any $\mathbf{y} \in \mathbb{R}^d \times \mathbb{S}^{d-1}$

$$\omega_{S'}(\mathbf{y}) = \int_{S'} k(\mathbf{x}, \mathbf{y})dx \leq \int_S k(\mathbf{x}, \mathbf{y})dx = \omega_S(\mathbf{y}).$$

Hence, since g is an increasing function

$$g\left(\omega_{S'}(\mathbf{y}) - \omega_T(\mathbf{y})\right) \leq g\left(\omega_S(\mathbf{y}) - \omega_T(\mathbf{y})\right)$$

and thus $\Delta(S', T) \leq \int_S g\left(\omega_S(\mathbf{x}) - \omega_T(\mathbf{x})\right) dx = \Delta(S, T)$. $\quad \square$

In the next proposition, we show that Δ does not satisfies the property $\Delta(S, T) = 0 \Rightarrow S \subseteq T$.

Proposition 4. *Consider the two following shapes. The source is a segment* $S_\epsilon = \{(s, \epsilon) \mid s \in [-\alpha, \alpha]\}$ *slightly shifted by a step* $\epsilon > 0$ *above a larger target* $T = \{(t, 0) \mid t \in [-\beta, \beta]\}$, *with* $0 < \alpha < \beta$. *Since the tangent vectors are almost all equal, we can ignore* k_t *and consider a kernel* k_e *defined by a decreasing function* $\rho : \mathbb{R}^+ \to \mathbb{R}^+$ *as follows* $k_e(x, x') = \rho(|x - x'|^2)$. *Then for any such* ρ, *there exists* $(\epsilon, \alpha, \beta)$ *such that* $\Delta(S_\epsilon, T) = 0$ *and* $S_\epsilon \cap T = \emptyset$.

We need to show that for any $x_0 \in S_\epsilon$, $w_{S_\epsilon}(x_0) \leq w_T(x_0)$ where $w_{S_\epsilon}(x_0) = \int_{S_\epsilon} k_e(x_0, x) dx$ and $w_T(x_0) = \int_T k_e(x_0, x') dx'$. Denote $x = (s, \epsilon) \in S_\epsilon$, $x_0 = (s_0, \epsilon) \in S_\epsilon$ and $x' = (t, 0) \in T$ then $\|x - x_0\|^2 = \|(s, \epsilon) - (s_0, \epsilon)\|^2 = (s - s_0)^2$ and $\|x' - x_0\|^2 = \|(t, \epsilon) - (s_0, \epsilon)\|^2 = (t - s_0)^2 + \epsilon^2$. We then obtain

$$w_{S_\epsilon}(x_0) = \int_{-\alpha}^{\alpha} \rho((s - s_0)^2) ds, \qquad w_T(x_0) = \int_{-\beta}^{\beta} \rho((s - s_0)^2 + \epsilon^2) ds.$$

Denote these integrals $I_\alpha(s_0) = \int_{-\alpha}^{\alpha} \rho((s - s_0)^2) ds$ and $I_\beta(s_0, \epsilon) = \int_{-\beta}^{\beta} \rho((s - s_0)^2 + \epsilon^2) ds$. The integrals are symmetric with respect to $s = s_0$ and since ρ is decreasing, we have the following inequalities:

$$\text{for any } s_0 \in [-\alpha, \alpha], \qquad I_\alpha(\alpha) \leq I_\alpha(s_0) \leq I_\alpha(0), \tag{2}$$

$$\text{for any } s_0 \in [-\alpha, \alpha], \text{for any } \epsilon > 0, \qquad I_\beta(\alpha, \epsilon) \leq I_\beta(s_0, \epsilon) \leq I_\beta(0, \epsilon). \tag{3}$$

Let us now show that there exist $(\epsilon, \alpha, \beta)$ such that $I_\alpha(0) \leq I_\beta(\alpha, \epsilon)$ that is $\int_{-\alpha}^{\alpha} \rho(s^2) ds \leq \int_{-\beta}^{\beta} \rho((s - \alpha)^2 + \epsilon^2) ds$.

For α small enough and β large enough, $\int_{-\beta}^{\beta} \rho((s - \alpha)^2 + \epsilon^2) ds \geq \int_{-2\alpha}^{2\alpha} \rho(s^2 + \epsilon^2) ds$. This last integral tends to $\int_{-2\alpha}^{2\alpha} \rho(s^2) ds$ when ϵ tends to 0 and this limit is strictly larger than $I_\alpha(0)$ (with α small enough, $\rho(\alpha) > 0$). Thus, for ϵ small enough, we have $I_\alpha(0) < I_\beta(\alpha, \epsilon)$.

Thanks to Eq. (2) and (3), we deduce that for any $x_0 \in S$, $w_S(x_0) \leq w_T(x_0)$. $\square$

This example shows that if the mass of the target is larger than the mass of the source then this excess of mass can compensate the lack of alignment between the shapes. For this reason, we introduce a normalized dissimilarity term.

2.3   Normalized Partial Matching Dissimilarity

Assume that $x_0 \in S$ and $y_0 \in T$ are two close points. If around these points, the mass of T is twice the mass of S, i.e. $w_S(\mathbf{x}_0) \approx \frac{1}{2} w_T(\mathbf{y}_0)$, then the local embedding of S in T is characterized by $w_S(\mathbf{x}_0) \leq \frac{1}{2} w_T(\mathbf{x}_0)$ and more generally by $w_S(\mathbf{x}_0) \leq \frac{w_S(\mathbf{x}_0)}{w_T(\mathbf{y}_0)} w_T(\mathbf{x}_0)$. Conversely, if the mass of S is twice the mass of T, then we consider that locally $S \not\subseteq T$ (e.g. two branches of a tree should not match the same branch of a target). Hence, the criterion of Definition 1 that should be preserved : $w_S(\mathbf{x}_0) \leq w_T(\mathbf{x}_0)$ is not satisfied. These observations lead to a new dissimilarity term that encompasses these two cases.

Definition 2. Using the same threshold function g as in Definition 1, we define the **normalized** partial matching dissimilarity as follows:

$$\underline{\Delta}(S, T) = \int_S g\left(w_S(\mathbf{x}) - \int_T \min_\epsilon\left(1, \frac{w_S(\mathbf{x})}{w_T(\mathbf{y})}\right) k(\mathbf{x}, \mathbf{y}) dy\right) dx$$

where $\min_\epsilon(1, s) = \frac{s + 1 - \sqrt{\epsilon + (s-1)^2}}{2}$ with $\epsilon > 0$ small, is used as a smooth approximation of the $\min(1, \cdot)$ function.

2.4   Use in the LDDMM Setting

The framework we propose is sufficiently flexible to be embedded in a variety of inexact registration methods; in this paper, we focus on the LDDMM model described in [3]. In this model, diffeomorphisms are constructed as flows of time-dependent square integrable velocity fields $t \in [0,1] \mapsto v_t$, each v_t belonging to a predefined Hilbert space V of smooth vector fields. In the following we will denote ϕ_1^v the diffeomorphism of $\mathbb{R}^d$, solution at $t = 1$ of the flow equation $\partial_t \phi_t^v = v_t \circ \phi_t^v$ with initial condition $\phi_0^v = id$.

Proposition 5. *Let $\lambda > 0$ be a fixed parameter. The partial matching problem, which consists in minimizing over L_V^2 the function:*

$$J(v) = \lambda \int_0^1 \|v_t\|_V^2 dt + \underline{\Delta}(\phi_1^v(S), T),$$

has a solution.

From [14], theorem 7, the proof boils down to showing that the mapping $v \mapsto A(v) = \underline{\Delta}(\phi_1^v(S), T)$, is weakly continuous on L_V^2. Let (v_n) be a sequence in L_V^2, weakly converging to some $v \in L_V^2$. We need to show that $\underline{\Delta}(\phi_1^{v_n}(S), T) \longrightarrow \underline{\Delta}(\phi_1^v(S), T)$.

To simplify we denote $S_n = \phi_1^{v_n}(S)$, $S_* = \phi_1^v(S)$ and for any $\mathbf{x} \in \mathbb{R}^d \times \mathbb{S}^{d-1}$,
$$f_n(\mathbf{x}) = \omega_{S_n}(\mathbf{x}) - \int_T \min_\epsilon \left(1, \frac{\omega_{S_n}(\mathbf{x})}{\omega_T(\mathbf{y})}\right) k(\mathbf{x}, \mathbf{y}) dy \text{ and } f_*(\mathbf{x}) \text{ likewise for } S_*.$$
We then have

$$\underline{\Delta}(S_n, T) - \underline{\Delta}(S_*, T) = \mu_{S_n}(g \circ f_n) - \mu_{S_*}(g \circ f_*). \tag{4}$$

The area formula

$$\mu_{\phi(S)}(\omega) = \int_S \omega(\phi(x), d_x\phi(\tau_x S)) \left| d_x\phi_{|\tau_x S} \right| dx,$$

leads to

$$\left| \mu_{S_n}(g \circ f_n) - \mu_{S_*}(g \circ f_*) \right| \leq \int_S \left| g \circ f_n(\phi^n(x), d_x\phi^n(\tau_x S)) \cdot \left| d_x\phi^n_{|\tau_x S} \right| \right.$$
$$\left. - g \circ f_*(\phi(x), d_x\phi(\tau_x S)) \cdot \left| d_x\phi_{|\tau_x S} \right| \right| dx$$

$$\leq \int_S \left| g \circ f_n(\phi^n(x), d_x\phi^n(\tau_x S)) \cdot \left| d_x\phi^n_{|\tau_x S} \right| - g \circ f_n(\phi(x), d_x\phi(\tau_x S)) \cdot \left| d_x\phi_{|\tau_x S} \right| \right.$$
$$\left. + g \circ f_n(\phi(x), d_x\phi(\tau_x S)) \cdot \left| d_x\phi_{|\tau_x S} \right| - g \circ f_*(\phi(x), d_x\phi(\tau_x S)) \cdot \left| d_x\phi_{|\tau_x S} \right| \right| dx$$

$$\leq \int_S |g \circ f_n|_\infty \cdot \left| \left| d_x\phi^n_{|\tau_x S} \right| - \left| d_x\phi_{|\tau_x S} \right| \right| + |d_x\phi|_\infty |g \circ f_n - g \circ f_*|_\infty dx.$$

Since $d_x\phi^n$ converge to $d_x\phi$, uniformly on $x \in S$ [14], we only need to show that $|g \circ f_n - g \circ f_*|_\infty \to 0$. We first show that $|f_n - f_*|_\infty \to 0$. For any $\mathbf{x} \in \mathbb{R}^d \times \mathbb{S}^{d-1}$

$$f_n(\mathbf{x}) - f_*(\mathbf{x}) = \omega_{S_n}(\mathbf{x}) - \omega_{S_*}(\mathbf{x})$$
$$+ \int_T k(\mathbf{x}, \mathbf{y}) \left[\min_\epsilon \left(1, \frac{\omega_{S_n}(\mathbf{x})}{\omega_T(\mathbf{y})} \right) - \min_\epsilon \left(1, \frac{\omega_{S_*}(\mathbf{x})}{\omega_T(\mathbf{y})} \right) \right] dy .$$
(5)

Since W is continuously embedded in $C_0^2(\mathbb{R}^d \times \mathbb{S}^{d-1})$, there exists c_W such that for any n, $|\omega_{S_n} - \omega_{S_*}|_\infty \leq c_W |\omega_{S_n} - \omega_{S_*}|_W$. Moreover, since v_n weakly converges to v, Corollary 1 from [7] ensures that $|\omega_{S_n} - \omega_{S_*}|_W \to 0$.

Regarding the integral, since $\mathbb{R} \ni s \mapsto \min_\epsilon(1, s)$ is Lipschitz, there exists $c_\epsilon > 0$ such that

$$\left| \int_T k(\mathbf{x}, \mathbf{y}) \left[\min_\epsilon \left(1, \frac{\omega_{S_n}(\mathbf{x})}{\omega_T(\mathbf{y})} \right) - \min_\epsilon \left(1, \frac{\omega_{S_*}(\mathbf{x})}{\omega_T(\mathbf{y})} \right) \right] dy \right|$$
$$\leq \int_T \frac{k(\mathbf{x}, \mathbf{y})}{|\omega_T(\mathbf{y})|} c_\epsilon |\omega_{S_n}(\mathbf{x}) - \omega_{S_*}(\mathbf{x})| dy \leq c_\epsilon c_W |\omega_{S_n} - \omega_{S_*}|_W \int_T \frac{k(\mathbf{x}, \mathbf{y})}{\omega_T(\mathbf{y})} dy \quad (6)$$

Since T is compact and ω_T is continuous and strictly positive on $\mathbf{T} = \{(y, \tau_y T) \mid y \in T\}$, we have $c_T = \inf_{\mathbf{T}} \omega_T(\mathbf{y}) > 0$ so that $\int_T \frac{k(\mathbf{x}, \mathbf{y})}{\omega_T(\mathbf{y})} dy \leq \frac{\omega_T(\mathbf{x})}{c_T} \leq \frac{c_W |\omega_T|_W}{c_T} < +\infty$. This shows that $|f_n - f_*|_\infty \to 0$. Now, since f_* is bounded, there exists $M > 0$ such that for any n, $|f_*|_\infty + |f_n|_\infty \leq M$ and since g is locally Lipschitz, we deduce that $|g \circ f_n - g \circ f_*|_\infty \to 0$.   □

Discrete Formulation. The discrete versions of the partial matching dissimilarities can be derived very straightforwardly, following the same discrete setting described in [9] for varifold matching. We omit its complete description here. The LDDMM registration procedure is numerically solved via a geodesic shooting algorithm [21], optimizing on a set of initial momentum vectors located at the discretization points of the source shape. Implementations of the dissimilarity terms are available on our github repository[1].

3   Experiments

In order to evaluate the proposed dissimilarity terms, we conducted three experiments on two different types of data : two on sets of 3D-curves (one synthetic and one real) and one on surfaces. In all the following experiments, we initialize the registration by aligning objects barycenters since no prior positioning is known in our applications. To model non-rigid deformations, we define the reproducing kernel K_V of V to be a sum of Gaussian kernels

---

[1] https://github.com/plantonsanti/PartialMatchingVarifolds.

$K_V(x,y) = \sum_s \exp\left(-\|x-y\|^2 / (\sigma_0/s)^2\right)$, where $s \in [1,4,8,16]$ and σ_0 is about half the size of the shapes bounding boxes. For each set of experiments we use the same hyperparameters $(\sigma_0, \sigma_W, \lambda)$ to compare the influence of the data attachment terms. Our Python implementation makes use of the libraries PyTorch [23] and KeOps [8], to benefit from automatic differentiation and GPU acceleration of kernel convolutions.

Synthetic Experiment

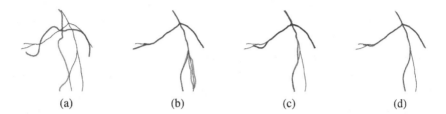

Fig. 1. Diffeomorphic registrations of a trimmed tree (blue) onto a richer one (red). (a) Initial Positions; (b) Varifold registration; (c) Partial matching registration (Eq. 1); (d) Normalized partial matching registration (Eq. 2). (Color figure online)

A first experiment was conducted to validate our approach on synthetic trees of 3D-curves. The target is composed of six 3D-curves (red tree in Fig. 1(a)), while the source (blue colored tree in Fig. 1(a)) is a trimmed version of the target. Then we apply to the source a random diffeomorphic deformation ψ that we will try to retrieve by registration.

We have shown in Fig. 1 that the classic distance aims at registering the entire source onto the entire target. This leads to abnormal distortions of the source curves that can be observed in the light blue stretched curve in Fig. 1(b). On the contrary, both partial dissimilarity terms successfully guide the registration of the source onto a subset of the target. The main difference between these two terms can be seen in the bifurcations' neighborhoods: the partial matching dissimilarity fails to register the source curves when the normalized partial matching doesn't fall into a flat local minima. The excess of mass in the target at the bifurcation has no negative effect with the normalization.

Registration of a Template onto a Real Vascular Tree. Now that we have illustrated the potential of our method on a toy example, we continue on entire vascular trees extracted from real patients datasets. Finding correspondences between the annotated template and a raw target is of great interest in clinical applications such as interventional radiology, and could provide automatic partial annotation of the imaged vascular tree. Because of the high topological variability of the vasculature, there is no perfect template of all the patients, and a simpler template seems suited. The target trees (Fig. 2(b), (e)) are obtained by automatic centerlines extraction from an injected CBCT inspired from the fast

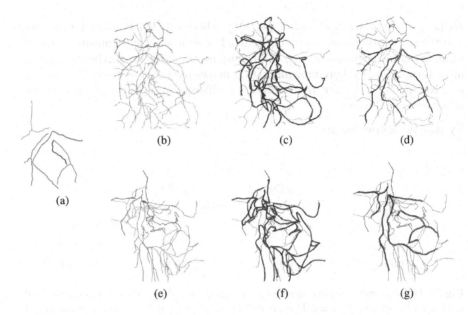

Fig. 2. (a) Template composed of different arteries of interest. (b), (e) Real vascular trees. (c), (f) Varifold registrations. (d), (g) Normalized partial matching registrations (Eq. 2).

marching method [11] that have been labeled by a clinical expert. The source tree (Fig. 2(a)) is a manually simplified template in which arteries of interest have been selected. This experiment is particularly difficult in the classic LDDMM framework, and the partial normalized dissimilarity term introduces a meaningful deformation of the simple template onto a subset of the target despite the wide topological difference.

Liver Surface Registration with Truncation. In the third experiment, we register a truncated liver surface manually segmented from a CBCT onto a complete liver surface manually segmented from a CT scan. In CBCT exams, the livers are usually larger than the field of view, causing the truncation of the surface. Both acquisitions come from the same patient and are separated in time by one month.

We show in Fig. 3 the registrations results of the LDDMM associated to the distance in the space of Varifolds and to the normalized partial dissimilarity term. The deformed shapes are colored by the determinant of the Jacobian of the deformation, that can be seen as its intensity. As expected the Varifold distance leads to unrealistic deformation that tends to fill the holes in the source shape to cover the entire target. From the anatomical and medical point of view this is misleading. On the contrary the partial matching allows a coherent deformation of the source.

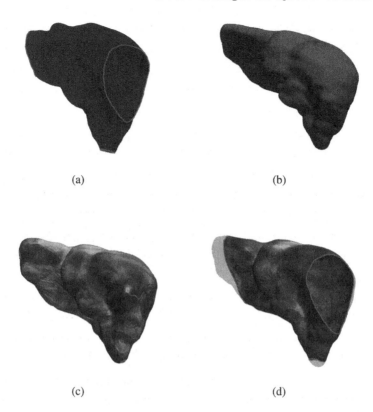

(a)   (b)

(c)   (d)

Fig. 3. Registration of a truncated liver's surface from a CBCT (a) onto a complete liver's surface from a CT (b). The deformed surfaces are colored by the determinant of the Jacobian. (c) Varifold registration; (d) Partial normalized registration (2) (d).

4   Conclusion

In this paper we adapted dissimilarity metrics in the space of Varifolds to guide partial shape matching and registration. We applied this new data attachment term to the registration of a template vascular tree onto real cases. We also showed that it is suitable for the registration of a truncated surface onto a complete one. This data term is suited to different shapes comparison such as unions of curves or surfaces.

The main bottleneck of our approach is the risk of shrinkage when no easy registration is possible. A promising lead to tackle this issue would be to also find a subset of the target to include in the source, such as [5]. The dissimilarity term introduced can be modified to fit the problem of registering a complete shape onto a truncated one. In further work we would also like to extend this dissimilarity term to other space of representations such as the Normal Cycles or the functional Varifolds.

134   P.-L. Antonsanti et al.

Acknowledgements. The authors would like to thank Perrine Chassat for her early work on the partial matching, allowing us to easily adapt the new data fidelity terms to the real case of liver surfaces registrations.

References

1. Aiger, D., Mitra, N., Cohen-Or, D.: 4-points congruent sets for robust pairwise surface registration. In: 35th International Conference on Computer Graphics and Interactive Techniques (SIGGRAPH 2008), vol. 27, August 2008. https://doi.org/10.1145/1399504.1360684
2. Bashiri, F.S., Baghaie, A., Rostami, R., Yu, Z., D'Souza, R.: Multi-modal medical image registration with full or partial data: a manifold learning approach. J. Imaging **5**, 5 (2018). https://doi.org/10.3390/jimaging5010005
3. Beg, M.F., Miller, M., Trouvé, A., Younes, L.: Computing large deformation metric mappings via geodesic flows of diffeomorphisms. Int. J. Comput. Vis. **61**, 139–157 (2005). https://doi.org/10.1023/B:VISI.0000043755.93987.aa
4. Benseghir, T., Malandain, G., Vaillant, R.: Iterative closest curve: a framework for curvilinear structure registration application to 2D/3D coronary arteries registration. In: Mori, K., Sakuma, I., Sato, Y., Barillot, C., Navab, N. (eds.) MICCAI 2013. LNCS, vol. 8149, pp. 179–186. Springer, Heidelberg (2013). https://doi.org/10.1007/978-3-642-40811-3_23
5. Bronstein, A., Bronstein, M., Bruckstein, A., Kimmel, R.: Partial similarity of objects, or how to compare a centaur to a horse. Int. J. Comput. Vis. **84**, 163–183 (2009). https://doi.org/10.1007/s11263-008-0147-3
6. Bronstein, A.M., Bronstein, M.M., Kimmel, R.: Generalized multidimensional scaling: a framework for isometry-invariant partial surface matching. Proc. Natl. Acad. Sci. **103**(5), 1168–1172 (2006). https://doi.org/10.1073/pnas.0508601103
7. Charlier, B., Charon, N., Trouvé, A.: The Fshape framework for the variability analysis of functional shapes. Found. Comput. Math. **17**(2), 287–357 (2015). https://doi.org/10.1007/s10208-015-9288-2
8. Charlier, B., Feydy, J., Glaunès, J.A., Collin, F.D., Durif, G.: Kernel operations on the GPU, with Autodiff, without memory overflows. J. Mach. Learn. Res. **22**(74), 1–6 (2021). http://jmlr.org/papers/v22/20-275.html
9. Charon, N., Charlier, B., Glaunèss, J., Gori, P., Roussillon, P.: 12 - fidelity metrics between curves and surfaces: currents, varifolds, and normal cycles, pp. 441–477 (2020). https://doi.org/10.1016/B978-0-12-814725-2.00021-2
10. Charon, N., Trouvé, A.: The varifold representation of nonoriented shapes for diffeomorphic registration. SIAM J. Imaging Sci. **6**(4), 2547–2580 (2013). https://doi.org/10.1137/130918885
11. Deschamps, T., Cohen, L.D.: Fast extraction of minimal paths in 3D images and applications to virtual endoscopy. Med. Image Anal. **5**(4), 281–99 (2001)
12. Feragen, A., Petersen, J., de Bruijne, M., et al.: Geodesic atlas-based labeling of anatomical trees: application and evaluation on airways extracted from CT. IEEE Trans. Med. Imaging **34**, 1212–1226 (2015)
13. Feydy, J., Charlier, B., Vialard, F.-X., Peyré, G.: Optimal transport for diffeomorphic registration. In: Descoteaux, M., Maier-Hein, L., Franz, A., Jannin, P., Collins, D.L., Duchesne, S. (eds.) MICCAI 2017. LNCS, vol. 10433, pp. 291–299. Springer, Cham (2017). https://doi.org/10.1007/978-3-319-66182-7_34
14. Glaunès, J.: Transport par difféomorphismes de points, demesures et de courants pour la comparaison de formes et l'anatomie numérique (2005)

15. Halimi, O., Litany, O., Rodolà, E.R., Bronstein, A.M., Kimmel, R.: Unsupervised learning of dense shape correspondence, pp. 4365–4374 (2019). https://doi.org/10.1109/CVPR.2019.00450
16. Halimi, O., et al.: The whole is greater than the sum of its nonrigid parts. CoRR abs/2001.09650 (2020)
17. van Kaick, O., Zhang, H., Hamarneh, G.: Bilateral maps for partial matching. In: Computer Graphics Forum (CGF), September 2013. https://doi.org/10.1111/cgf.12084
18. van Kaick, O., Zhang, H., Hamarneh, G., Cohen-Or, D.: A survey on shape correspondence. Comput. Graph. Forum **30**(6), 1681–1707 (2011). https://doi.org/10.1111/j.1467-8659.2011.01884.x
19. Kaltenmark, I., Charlier, B., Charon, N.: A general framework for curve and surface comparison and registration with oriented varifolds July 2017
20. Kaltenmark, I., Trouvé, A.: Estimation of a growth development with partial diffeomorphic mappings. Q. Appl. Math. **77**, 227–267 (2018)
21. Miller, M.I., Trouvé, A., Younes, L.: Geodesic shooting for computational anatomy. J. Math. Imaging Vis. **24**(2), 209–228 (2006)
22. Ovsjanikov, M., Ben-Chen, M., Solomon, J., Butscher, A., Guibas, L.: Functional maps: a flexible representation of maps between shapes. ACM Trans. Graph. **31**(4) (2012). https://doi.org/10.1145/2185520.2185526
23. Paszke, A., et al.: Automatic differentiation in PyTorch. In: NIPS Autodiff Workshop (2017)
24. Rodolà, E., Cosmo, L., Bronstein, M.M., Torsello, A., Cremers, D.: Partial functional correspondence. Comput. Graph. Forum **36**(1), 222–236 (2017). https://doi.org/10.1111/cgf.12797
25. Rodolà, E., Albarelli, A., Bergamasco, F., Torsello, A.: A scale independent selection process for 3D object recognition in cluttered scenes. Int. J. Comput. Vis. **102**, 129–145 (2013). https://doi.org/10.1007/s11263-012-0568-x
26. Sotiras, A., Davatzikos, C., Paragios, N.: Deformable medical image registration: a survey. IEEE Trans. Med. Imaging **32**(7), 1153–1190 (2013). https://doi.org/10.1109/TMI.2013.2265603
27. Zhen, X., Gu, X., Yan, H., Zhou, L., Jia, X., Jiang, S.B.: **57**(21), 6807–6826 (2012). https://doi.org/10.1088/0031-9155/57/21/6807

Nested Grassmanns for Dimensionality Reduction with Applications to Shape Analysis

Chun-Hao Yang[1] and Baba C. Vemuri[2(✉)]

[1] Department of Statistics, University of Florida, Gainesville, FL, USA
[2] Department of CISE, University of Florida, Gainesville, FL, USA
vemuri@ufl.edu

Abstract. Grassmann manifolds have been widely used to represent the geometry of feature spaces in a variety of problems in medical imaging and computer vision including but not limited to shape analysis, action recognition, subspace clustering and motion segmentation. For these problems, the features usually lie in a very high-dimensional Grassmann manifold and hence an appropriate dimensionality reduction technique is called for in order to curtail the computational burden. To this end, the Principal Geodesic Analysis (PGA), a nonlinear extension of the well known principal component analysis, is applicable as a general tool to many Riemannian manifolds. In this paper, we propose a novel framework for dimensionality reduction of data in Riemannian homogeneous spaces and then focus on the Grassman manifold which is an example of a homogeneous space. Our framework explicitly exploits the geometry of the homogeneous space yielding reduced dimensional nested sub-manifolds that need not be geodesic submanifolds and thus are more expressive. Specifically, we project points in a Grassmann manifold to an embedded lower dimensional Grassmann manifold. A salient feature of our method is that it leads to higher expressed variance compared to PGA which we demonstrate via synthetic and real data experiments.

Keywords: Grassmann manifolds · Dimensionality reduction · Shape analysis

1 Introduction

In medical imaging, non-Euclidean spaces are commonly used to model descriptive features extracted from the raw data. For example, diffusion tensor imaging (DTI) [5] uses symmetric positive-definite (SPD) matrices to characterize the local diffusivity of the water molecules within each voxel of the DTI scan. The ensemble average propagator (EAP) [6], which captures the distribution of the diffusion of the water molecules in the tissue being imaged and is much more

This research was in part funded by NSF the grant IIS-1724174 to Vemuri.

A. Feragen et al. (Eds.): IPMI 2021, LNCS 12729, pp. 136–149, 2021.
https://doi.org/10.1007/978-3-030-78191-0_11

expressive than the diffusion tensors, can be parameterized as a point on a Hilbert sphere which is a constant curvature manifold. Another example is the Kendall's shape space (Procrustes shape space) [18] which is a manifold used to model shapes in computational anatomy. In the examples described above, the dataset is a collection of DTI scans, EAP fields, or the shapes of a segmented region of the brain. The data lie in a high-dimensional space: a DTI scan contains hundreds of thousands of diffusion tensors (DTs), which are 3×3 SPD matrices; an EAP field contains hundreds of thousands of EAPs and each EAP can be represented as a high-dimensional probability vector; the shape of the Corpus Callosum (which is used in our experiments) is represented by a several hundreds of boundary points in $\mathbb{R}^2$. Thus, in these cases, dimensionality reduction techniques, if applied appropriately, can benefit the subsequent statistical analysis.

Principal component analysis (PCA) is the simplest and most well-known (unsupervised) dimensionality reduction technique for data in $\mathbb{R}^n$. Using PCA, the data in $\mathbb{R}^n$ is projected to a vector subspace of dimension $k \ll n$ such that maximal variance in the original data is captured in the projected data. There are different generalizations of PCA to Riemannian manifolds. Authors in [11] proposed an expression for exact PGA, but due to the computational challenges they resorted to the tangent PCA (tPCA) approximation. Exact PGA (EPGA) was later proposed by [23] which does not use the tPCA approximation. However, EPGA is computationally expensive since it involves two non-linear optimizations steps per iteration (projection to the geodesic submanifold and finding the new geodesic direction such that the loss of information is minimized). Authors in [7] improved upon EPGA by deriving the closed-form expressions for the projection in the case of constant curvature manifolds, e.g. hyperspheres and hyperbolic spaces. There are several other variants of PGA, see [3,15,16,26]. Instead of projecting data to a geodesic submanifold, one may also find a curve on the manifold, called the principal curve [14] (this is a generalization of the principal curve in the Euclidean space by [13]), to represent the data using a lower dimensional submanifold.

PGA and its variants provided a dimensionality reduction technique for general Riemannian manifolds. Nonetheless, different Riemannian manifolds possess different geometric structures, e.g. curvature and symmetry. Therefore, by exploiting the geometry and/or other properties, one may design a more efficient and better dimensionality reduction method for specific Riemannian manifolds. For example, by utilizing the fact that S^q embedded inside S^p with $q < p$ is a geodesic submanifold of S^p, authors in [17] proposed a method called the *principal nested spheres* to perform dimensionality reduction on S^p. By translating the nested spheres, PGA on S^p can be seen as a special case of principal nested spheres. Another example is that of the manifold of SPD matrices, P_n. In [12], authors proposed to project data on P_n to P_m where $m \ll n$ by designing a projection map from P_n to P_m that maximized the projected variance or inter-class discrimination in the case of supervised dimensionality reduction. Although in this case, P_m is not a geodesic submanifold of P_n which makes it different from

PGA, such an algorithm has the ability to handle supervised dimensionality reduction which PGA lacks. Indeed, considering only the geodesic submanifolds is certainly not sufficient in many applications. In [9], authors consider nested sequence of relations which lead to a nested sequence of submanifolds that are not necessarily geodesic. This works for most submanifolds of the Euclidean space, for example the n-sphere, as they are characterized by the set of solutions to some equations. However, for manifolds other than Euclidean spaces and spheres, the sequence of relations is not known and is probably nontrivial. Recently, Pennec proposed the exponential barycentric subspace (EBS) as a generalization of PGA [22]. A k-dimensional EBS is defined as the locus of weighted exponential barycenters of $(k+1)$ affinely independent reference points. The nested structure of EBS can be achieved by adding or removing points. However, the choice of the $(k+1)$ reference points can be computationally inefficient for high-dimensional spaces. Additional analysis is required to mitigate this problem.

Motivated by the expressiveness of the nested representations as observed in the earlier work described above, in this paper, we propose to develop a nested structure for Riemannian homogeneous spaces (under some mild conditions). Specifically, we will focus our attention on unsupervised and supervised dimensionality reduction for data on the Grassmann manifold $\mathrm{Gr}(p, V)$ which is a homogeneous space of all p-dimensional linear subspaces of the vector space V where $1 \leq p \leq \dim V$. We will assume that V is either $\mathbb{R}^n$ or $\mathbb{C}^n$. In shape analysis, the space of planar shapes, i.e., shapes that are represented by k ordered points in $\mathbb{R}^2$, is a complex projective space $\mathbb{C}P^{k-2} \cong \mathrm{Gr}(1, \mathbb{C}^{k-1})$. The number of points k is usually a few hundred and dimension of the underlying manifold $\mathrm{Gr}(1, \mathbb{C}^{k-1})$ is also large. Hence the core idea of our dimensionality reduction is to approximate $\mathcal{X} \in \mathrm{Gr}(p, V)$ by $\hat{\mathcal{X}} \in \mathrm{Gr}(p, \tilde{V})$ where $\dim \tilde{V} \ll \dim V$. Thus, the main contributions of our work here are: (i) We propose a nested structure for Riemannian homogeneous spaces (under some mild conditions) unifying the recently proposed nested structures for spheres [17] and SPD manifolds [12]. (ii) We present novel dimensionality reduction techniques based on the concept of nested geometric structures for the Grassmann manifold case. (iii) Synthetic and real data experiments demonstrate higher expressed variance captured by our lower dimensional nested submanifold representation scheme.

The rest of the paper is organized as follows. In Sect. 2, we review the geometry of the Grassmann manifold and present the nested structure of homogeneous spaces. Then, by using this nested structure, we describe algorithms for our unsupervised and supervised dimensionality reduction techniques for data on the Grassmann. In Sect. 3, we present experimental results. Finally, we draw conclusions in Sect. 4.

2   Nested Grassmannians

We will first review the Riemannian geometry of the Grassmann manifold in Sect. 2.1 and then the nested Grassmann model will be derived in Sect. 2.2. In Sect. 2.3 and 2.4, we describe the unsupervised and supervised dimensionality reduction using the nested Grassmann model. In Sect. 2.5, we will present some technical details required for implementation. A technique for the choosing the dimension of the 'reduced' model is then presented in Sect. 2.6.

2.1 The Riemannian Geometry of Grassmann Manifolds

For the sake of simplicity, we assume $V = \mathbb{R}^n$. For the case of $V = \mathbb{C}^n$, the results hold by replacing real matrices with complex matrices, $\boldsymbol{M}^T$ with the conjugate transpose $\boldsymbol{M}^H$, and the orthogonal group $O(n)$ with the unitary group $U(n)$. The *Grassmann manifold* $\mathrm{Gr}(p,n) := \mathrm{Gr}(p, \mathbb{R}^n)$ is the space of all p-dimensional subspaces in $\mathbb{R}^n$. The dimension of $\mathrm{Gr}(p,n)$ is $p(n-p)$. In this paper, for elements $\mathcal{X} \in \mathrm{Gr}(p,n)$, we write $\mathcal{X} = \mathrm{span}(\boldsymbol{X})$ where, $\boldsymbol{X} = [\boldsymbol{x}_1, \ldots, \boldsymbol{x}_p]$ is an orthonormal basis (o.n.b) for $\mathcal{X}$. The *Stiefel manifold* $\mathrm{St}(p,n)$ is the space of all orthonormal p-frames in $\mathbb{R}^n$. Let $O(n) := \mathrm{St}(n,n)$ be the set of $n \times n$ orthogonal matrices. The Stiefel manifold can be identified as a *homogeneous space* $\mathrm{St}(p,n) \cong O(n)/O(n-p)$ and so is the Grassmann manifold $\mathrm{Gr}(p,n) \cong \mathrm{St}(p,n)/O(p) \cong O(n)/(O(n) \times O(n-p))$ [10]. There are other ways to represent the Grassmann manifolds, see [19, Table 2] and we choose this particular one as it is the most widely used and easy to interpret. Since $\mathrm{St}(p,n)$ is a submanifold of $\mathbb{R}^{n \times p}$, a natural Riemannian metric for $\mathrm{St}(p,n)$ is induced from the Euclidean metric on $\mathbb{R}^{n \times p}$, i.e. for $\boldsymbol{U}, \boldsymbol{V} \in T_{\boldsymbol{X}} \mathrm{St}(p,n)$, $\langle \boldsymbol{U}, \boldsymbol{V} \rangle_{\boldsymbol{X}} = \mathrm{tr}(\boldsymbol{U}^T \boldsymbol{V})$. The canonical Riemannian metric on the Grassmann manifold is then inherited from the metric on $\mathrm{St}(p,n)$ as it is invariant to the left multiplication by elements of $O(n)$ [1,10]. We now state a few important geometric concepts that are relevant to our work.

With the canonical metric on the Grassmann manifolds, the geodesic can be expressed in closed form. Let $\mathcal{X} = \mathrm{span}(\boldsymbol{X}) \in \mathrm{Gr}(p,n)$ where $\boldsymbol{X} \in \mathrm{St}(p,n)$ and $\boldsymbol{H}$ be an $n \times p$ matrix. The geodesic $\gamma(t)$ with $\gamma(0) = \mathcal{X}$ and $\gamma'(0) = \boldsymbol{H}$ is given by $\gamma_{\mathcal{X},\boldsymbol{H}}(t) = \mathrm{span}(\boldsymbol{X}\boldsymbol{V}\cos\boldsymbol{\Sigma}t + \boldsymbol{U}\sin\boldsymbol{\Sigma}t)$ where, $\boldsymbol{U}\boldsymbol{\Sigma}\boldsymbol{V}^T$ is the compact singular value decomposition of $\boldsymbol{H}$ [10, Theorem 2.3]. The *exponential map* at $\mathcal{X}$ is a map from $T_{\mathcal{X}}\mathrm{Gr}(p,n)$ to $\mathrm{Gr}(p,n)$ defined by $\mathrm{Exp}_{\mathcal{X}}\boldsymbol{H} = \gamma_{\mathcal{X},\boldsymbol{H}}(1) = \mathrm{span}(\boldsymbol{X}\boldsymbol{V}\cos\boldsymbol{\Sigma} + \boldsymbol{U}\sin\boldsymbol{\Sigma})$. If $\boldsymbol{X}^T\boldsymbol{Y}$ is invertible, the geodesic distance between $\mathcal{X} = \mathrm{span}(\boldsymbol{X})$ and $\mathcal{Y} = \mathrm{span}(\boldsymbol{Y})$ is given by $d_g^2(\mathcal{X},\mathcal{Y}) = \mathrm{tr}\boldsymbol{\Theta}^2 = \sum_{i=1}^p \theta_i^2$ where $(\boldsymbol{I} - \boldsymbol{X}\boldsymbol{X}^T)\boldsymbol{Y}(\boldsymbol{X}^T\boldsymbol{Y})^{-1} = \boldsymbol{U}\boldsymbol{\Sigma}\boldsymbol{V}^T$, $\boldsymbol{U} \in \mathrm{St}(p,n)$, $\boldsymbol{V} \in O(p)$, and $\boldsymbol{\Theta} = \tan^{-1}\boldsymbol{\Sigma}$. The diagonal entries $\theta_1, \ldots, \theta_k$ of $\boldsymbol{\Theta}$ are known as the principal angles.

2.2 Embedding of $\mathrm{Gr}(p,m)$ in $\mathrm{Gr}(p,n)$

Let $\mathcal{X} = \mathrm{span}(\boldsymbol{X}) \in \mathrm{Gr}(p,m)$, $\boldsymbol{X} \in \mathrm{St}(p,m)$. The map $\iota : \mathrm{Gr}(p,m) \to \mathrm{Gr}(p,n)$, for $m < n$, defined by, $\iota(\mathcal{X}) = \mathrm{span}\left(\begin{bmatrix} \boldsymbol{X} \\ \boldsymbol{0}_{(n-m)\times p} \end{bmatrix}\right)$ is an embedding and it is easy to check that this embedding is isometric [25, Eq. (8)]. However, for the dimensionality reduction problem, the above embedding is insufficient as it is not flexible enough to encompass other possible embeddings. To design flexible embeddings, we propose a general framework for Riemannian homogeneous spaces $M \cong G/H$ e.g., the Grassmann manifold, see Fig. 1. Note that in Fig. 1,

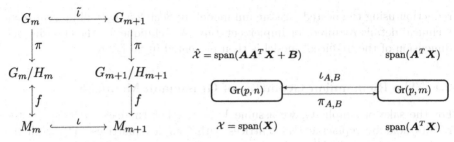

Fig. 1. Commutative diagram of the induced embedding for homogeneous spaces.

Fig. 2. Illustration of the embedding of $\mathrm{Gr}(p,m)$ in $\mathrm{Gr}(p,n)$ parameterized by $A \in \mathrm{St}(m,n)$ and $B \in \mathbb{R}^{n \times p}$ such that $A^T B = 0$.

we impose the following **mild conditions:** *(i) the groups G_m and G_{m+1} are of the same "type", i.e., $G_m = \mathrm{GL}(m)$ or $G_m = \mathrm{O}(m)$, and so are H_m and H_{m+1}, and (ii) the diagram commutes.*

The idea is to define an embedding $\tilde{\iota} : G_m \to G_{m+1}$. This embedding $\tilde{\iota}$, together with the submersion $\pi : G_m \to G_m/H_m$ and the identification map $f : G_m/H_m \to M_m$, induces an embedding $\iota : M_m \to M_{m+1}$ provided that *the diagram commutes.* For the Grassmann manifolds, $G_m = \mathrm{O}(m)$ and $H_m = \mathrm{O}(m) \times \mathrm{O}(m-p)$. We consider the embedding $\tilde{\iota}_m : \mathrm{O}(m) \to \mathrm{O}(m+1)$ given by,

$$\tilde{\iota}_m(O) = \mathrm{GS}\left(R \begin{bmatrix} O & a \\ b^T & c \end{bmatrix} \right) \tag{1}$$

where $O \in \mathrm{O}(m)$, $R \in \mathrm{O}(m+1)$, $a, b \in \mathbb{R}^m$, $c \in \mathbb{R}$, $c \neq b^T O^{-1} a$, and $\mathrm{GS}(\cdot)$ is the Gram-Schmidt process. Hence the induced embedding $\iota_m : \mathrm{Gr}(p,m) \to \mathrm{Gr}(p, m+1)$ is given by,

$$\iota_m(\mathcal{X}) = \mathrm{span}\left(R \begin{bmatrix} X \\ b^T \end{bmatrix} \right) = \mathrm{span}(\tilde{R} X + v b^T),$$

where $b \in \mathbb{R}^p$, $R \in \mathrm{O}(m+1)$, $\tilde{R}$ contains the first m columns of R (which means $\tilde{R} \in \mathrm{St}(m, m+1)$), v is the last column of R, and $\mathcal{X} = \mathrm{span}(X) \in \mathrm{Gr}(p,m)$. It is easy to see that for $R = I$ and $b = 0$, this gives the natural embedding described at the beginning of this section.

Proposition 1. *If $b = 0$, then ι_m is an isometric embedding.*

Proof. Let $\tilde{X} = \tilde{R} X$ and $\tilde{Y} = \tilde{R} Y$. We first compute the principal angles between $\mathrm{span}(\tilde{X})$ and $\mathrm{span}(\tilde{Y})$. Since $\tilde{R} \in \mathrm{St}(m, m+1)$, we have $(I - \tilde{X}\tilde{X}^T)\tilde{Y}(\tilde{X}^T \tilde{Y})^{-1} = \tilde{R}(I - XX^T)Y(X^T Y)^{-1}$. Hence the principal angles between $\mathrm{span}(\tilde{X})$ and $\mathrm{span}(\tilde{Y})$ are the same as those of $\mathrm{span}(X)$ and $\mathrm{span}(Y)$. By the Myers-Steenrod theorem [21, Theorem 1], ι_m is an isometric embedding.

With the embedding ι_m, we can construct the corresponding projection $\pi_m : \mathrm{Gr}(p, m+1) \to \mathrm{Gr}(p,m)$ using the following proposition.

Proposition 2. *The projection* $\pi_m : Gr(p, m + 1) \to Gr(p, m)$ *corresponding to* ι_m *is given by* $\pi_m(\mathcal{X}) = \mathrm{span}(\tilde{\boldsymbol{R}}^T \boldsymbol{X})$.

Proof. First, let $\mathcal{Y} = \mathrm{span}(\boldsymbol{Y}) \in Gr(p, m)$ and $\mathcal{X} = \mathrm{span}(\boldsymbol{X}) \in Gr(p, m + 1)$ be such that $\mathcal{X} = \mathrm{span}(\tilde{\boldsymbol{R}}\boldsymbol{Y} + \boldsymbol{v}\boldsymbol{b}^T)$. Then $\boldsymbol{X}\boldsymbol{L} = \tilde{\boldsymbol{R}}\boldsymbol{Y} + \boldsymbol{v}\boldsymbol{b}^T$ for some $\boldsymbol{L} \in \mathrm{GL}(p)$. Therefore, $\boldsymbol{Y} = \tilde{\boldsymbol{R}}^T(\boldsymbol{X}\boldsymbol{L} - \boldsymbol{v}\boldsymbol{b}^T) = \tilde{\boldsymbol{R}}^T\boldsymbol{X}\boldsymbol{L}$ and $\mathcal{Y} = \mathrm{span}(\boldsymbol{Y}) = \mathrm{span}(\tilde{\boldsymbol{R}}^T\boldsymbol{X}\boldsymbol{L}) = \mathrm{span}(\tilde{\boldsymbol{R}}^T\boldsymbol{X})$. Hence, the projection is given by $\pi_m(\mathcal{X}) = \mathrm{span}(\tilde{\boldsymbol{R}}^T\boldsymbol{X})$. This completes the proof. ∎

The nested relation can be extended inductively and we refer to this construction as the *nested Grassmann structure*:

$$\mathrm{Gr}(p, m) \overset{\iota_m}{\hookrightarrow} \mathrm{Gr}(p, m + 1) \overset{\iota_{m+1}}{\hookrightarrow} \dots \overset{\iota_{n-2}}{\hookrightarrow} \mathrm{Gr}(p, n - 1) \overset{\iota_{n-1}}{\hookrightarrow} \mathrm{Gr}(p, n).$$

Thus the embedding from $\mathrm{Gr}(p, m)$ into $\mathrm{Gr}(p, n)$ can be constructed inductively by $\iota := \iota_{n-1} \circ \dots \circ \iota_{m-1} \circ \iota_m$ and similarly for the corresponding projection. The explicit forms of the embedding and the projection are given in the following proposition.

Proposition 3. *The embedding of* $Gr(p, m)$ *into* $Gr(p, n)$ *for* $m < n$ *is given by* $\iota_{A,B}(\mathcal{X}) = \mathrm{span}(\boldsymbol{AX} + \boldsymbol{B})$ *where* $\boldsymbol{A} \in St(m, n)$ *and* $\boldsymbol{B} \in \mathbb{R}^{n \times p}$ *such that* $\boldsymbol{A}^T\boldsymbol{B} = 0$. *The corresponding projection from* $Gr(p, n)$ *to* $Gr(p, m)$ *is given by* $\pi_A = \mathrm{span}(\boldsymbol{A}^T\boldsymbol{X})$.

Proof. By the definition, $\iota := \iota_{n-1} \circ \dots \circ \iota_{m-1} \circ \iota_m$ and thus the embedding $\iota : \mathrm{Gr}(p, m) \to \mathrm{Gr}(p, n)$ can be simplified as

$$\iota_{A,B}(\mathcal{X}) = \mathrm{span}\left(\left(\prod_{i=m}^{n-1} \boldsymbol{R}_i\right)\boldsymbol{X} + \sum_{i=m}^{n-1}\left(\prod_{j=i+1}^{n-1} \boldsymbol{R}_j\right)\boldsymbol{v}_i\boldsymbol{b}_i^T\right) = \mathrm{span}(\boldsymbol{AX} + \boldsymbol{B})$$

where $\boldsymbol{R}_i \in St(i, i + 1)$, $\boldsymbol{v}_i$ is such that $[\boldsymbol{R}_i \; \boldsymbol{v}_i] \in O(i + 1)$, $\boldsymbol{b}_i \in \mathbb{R}^p$, $\boldsymbol{A} = \boldsymbol{R}_{n-1}\boldsymbol{R}_{n-2} \dots \boldsymbol{R}_m \in St(m, n)$, and $\boldsymbol{B} = \sum_{i=m}^{n-1}\left(\prod_{j=i+1}^{n-1} \boldsymbol{R}_j\right)\boldsymbol{v}_i\boldsymbol{b}_i^T$ is an $n \times p$ matrix. It is easy to see that $\boldsymbol{A}^T\boldsymbol{B} = 0$. Similar to Proposition 2, the projection $\pi_A : \mathrm{Gr}(p, n) \to \mathrm{Gr}(p, m)$ is then given by $\pi_A(\mathcal{X}) = \mathrm{span}(\boldsymbol{A}^T\boldsymbol{X})$. This completes the proof. ∎

From Proposition 1, if $\boldsymbol{B} = 0$ then ι_A is an isometric embedding. *Hence, our nested Grassmann structure is more flexible than PGA as it allows one to project the data onto a non-geodesic submanifold.* An illustration is shown in Fig. 2.

Connections to Other Nested Structures. The nested homogeneous spaces proposed in this work (see Fig. 1) is actually a unifying framework for the nested spheres [17] and the nested SPD manifolds [12]. Since the n-sphere can be identified with a homogeneous space $S^{n-1} \cong O(n)/O(n-1)$, with the embedding (1), the induced embedding of S^{n-1} into S^n is

$$\iota(\boldsymbol{x}) = \mathrm{GS}\left(\boldsymbol{R}\begin{bmatrix}\boldsymbol{x} \\ b\end{bmatrix}\right) = \frac{1}{\sqrt{1 + b^2}}\boldsymbol{R}\begin{bmatrix}\boldsymbol{x} \\ b\end{bmatrix} = \boldsymbol{R}\begin{bmatrix}\sin(r)\boldsymbol{x} \\ \cos(r)\end{bmatrix}$$

where $x \in S^{n-1}$, $b \in \mathbb{R}$, and $r = \cos^{-1}\left(\frac{b}{\sqrt{1+b^2}}\right)$. This is precisely the nested sphere proposed in [17, Eq. (2)]. For the SPD manifold $P_n \cong \mathrm{GL}(n)/\mathrm{O}(n)$, a carefully chosen embedding of $\mathrm{GL}(n)$ into $\mathrm{GL}(n+1)$ gives the nested SPD manifolds in [12].

2.3 Unsupervised Dimensionality Reduction

We can now apply the nested Grassmann (NG) structure to the problem of unsupervised dimensionality reduction. Suppose that we are given the points, $\mathcal{X}_1, \ldots, \mathcal{X}_N \in \mathrm{Gr}(p, n)$. We would like to have lower dimensional representations in $\mathrm{Gr}(p, m)$ for $\mathcal{X}_1, \ldots, \mathcal{X}_N$ with $m \ll n$. The desired projection map π_A that we seek is obtained by the minimizing the reconstruction error, i.e. $L_u(A, B) = \frac{1}{N}\sum_{i=1}^{N} d^2(\mathcal{X}_i, \hat{\mathcal{X}}_i)$ where d is a distance metric on $\mathrm{Gr}(p, n)$. It is clear that L_u has a $\mathrm{O}(m)$-symmetry in the first argument, i.e. $L_u(AO, B) = L_u(A, B)$ for $O \in \mathrm{O}(m)$. Hence, the optimization is performed over the space $\mathrm{St}(m, n)/\mathrm{O}(m) \cong \mathrm{Gr}(m, n)$ when optimizing with respect to this particular loss function. Now we can apply the Riemannian gradient descent algorithm [10] to obtain A and B by optimizing $L_u(A, B)$ over $\mathrm{span}(A) \in \mathrm{Gr}(m, n)$ and $B \in \mathbb{R}^{n \times p}$ such that $A^T B = 0$. Note that the restriction $A^T B = 0$ simply means that the columns of B are in the nullspace of A^T, denoted $N(A^T)$. Hence in practice this restriction can be handled as follows: For arbitrary $\tilde{B} \in \mathbb{R}^{n \times p}$, project $\tilde{B}$ on to $N(A^T)$, i.e. $B = P_{N(A^T)}\tilde{B}$ where $P_{N(A^T)} = I - AA^T$ is the projection from $\mathbb{R}^n$ to $N(A^T)$. Thus, the loss function can be written as

$$L_u(A, B) = \frac{1}{N}\sum_{i=1}^{N} d^2(\mathrm{span}(X_i), \mathrm{span}(AA^T X_i + (I - AA^T)B))$$

and it is optimized over $\mathrm{Gr}(m, n) \times \mathbb{R}^{n \times p}$.

2.4 Supervised Dimensionality Reduction

If in addition to $\mathcal{X}_1, \ldots, \mathcal{X}_N \in \mathrm{Gr}(p, n)$, we are given the associated labels $y_1, \ldots, y_N \in \{1, \ldots, k\}$, then we would like to utilize this extra information to sharpen the result of dimensionality reduction. Specifically, we expect that after reducing the dimension, points from the same class are still close to each other while points from different classes are well separated. We use an *affinity function* $a : \mathrm{Gr}(p, n) \times \mathrm{Gr}(p, n) \to \mathbb{R}$ to encode the structure of the data as suggested by [12, Sect 3.1, Eq. (14)–(16)]. The desired projection map π_A that we seek is obtained by the minimizing the following loss function

$$L_s(A) = \frac{1}{N^2}\sum_{i,j=1}^{N} a(\mathcal{X}_i, \mathcal{X}_j) d^2(\mathrm{span}(A^T X_i), \mathrm{span}(A^T X_j))$$

where d is a distance metric on $\mathrm{Gr}(p, m)$. Note that if the distance metric d has $\mathrm{O}(m)$-symmetry, e.g. the geodesic distance, so does L_s. In this case the optimization can be done on $\mathrm{St}(m, n)/\mathrm{O}(m) \cong \mathrm{Gr}(m, n)$. Otherwise it is on $\mathrm{St}(m, n)$. This supervised dimensionality reduction is termed as, supervised nested Grassmann (sNG).

2.5   Choice of the Distance d

The loss functions L_u and L_s depend on the choice of the distance $d : \mathrm{Gr}(p, n) \times \mathrm{Gr}(p, n) \to \mathbb{R}_{\geq 0}$. Besides the geodesic distance, there are many widely used distances on the Grassmann manifold, see for example [10, p. 337] and [25, Table 2]. In this work, we use two different distance metrics: (1) the geodesic distance d_g and (2) the projection distance, which is also called the chordal distance in [25] and the projection F-norm in [10]. The geodesic distance was defined in Sect. 2.1 and the projection distance is defined as follows. For $\mathcal{X}, \mathcal{Y} \in \mathrm{Gr}(p, n)$, denote the projection matrices onto $\mathcal{X}$ and $\mathcal{Y}$ by $P_\mathcal{X}$ and $P_\mathcal{Y}$ respectively. Then, the distance between $\mathcal{X}$ and $\mathcal{Y}$ is given by $d_p(\mathcal{X}, \mathcal{Y}) = \|P_\mathcal{X} - P_\mathcal{Y}\|_F / \sqrt{2} = \left(\sum_{i=1}^{p} \sin^2 \theta_i \right)^{1/2}$ where $\theta_1, \ldots, \theta_p$ are the principal angles of $\mathcal{X}$ and $\mathcal{Y}$. If $\mathcal{X} = \mathrm{span}(X)$, then $P_\mathcal{X} = X(X^T X)^{-1} X^T$. It is also easy to see the projection distance has $\mathrm{O}(n)$-symmetry. We choose the projection distance mainly for its computational efficiency as it involves only matrix multiplication which has a time complexity $O(n^2)$ while the geodesic distance requires SVD which has a time complexity of $O(n^3)$.

2.6   Analysis of Principal Nested Grassmanns

In practice, we might not have prior knowledge about m. So one can choose $p < m_1 < \ldots < m_k < n$ and construct a sequence of Grassmann manifolds. Then, for each nested Grassmann, we compute the percentage of variance explained. Suppose $\mathcal{X}_1 = \mathrm{span}(X_1), \ldots, \mathcal{X}_N = \mathrm{span}(X_N) \in \mathrm{Gr}(p, n)$ and A_i and B_i are obtained for $\mathrm{Gr}(p, m_i)$ from the algorithm described in the previous section. The percentage of variance explained in $\mathrm{Gr}(p, m_i)$ is given by the ratio of variance of the $\hat{\mathcal{X}}_j$'s where $\hat{\mathcal{X}}_j = \mathrm{span}(A_i^T X_j)$ and the variance of the $\mathcal{X}_j$'s. The desired dimension m can be chosen according to the desired percentage of variance explained somewhat similar to the way one chooses the number of principal components.

3   Experiments

In this section, we will demonstrate the performance of the proposed dimensionality reduction technique, i.e. NG and sNG, via experiments on synthetic and real data. The implementation[1] is based on the python library pymanopt [24] and we use the conjugate gradient descent algorithm for the optimization (with default parameters in pymanopt). The optimization was performed on a desktop with 3.6 GHz Intel i7 processors and took about 30 s to converge.

---

[1] The code is available at https://github.com/cvgmi/NestedGrassmann.

3.1 Synthetic Data

In this subsection, we compare the performance of the projection and the geodesic distances respectively. The questions we will answer are the following: (1) From Sect. 2.5, we see that using projection distance is more efficient than using the geodesic distance. But how do they perform compared to each other under varying dimension n and variance level σ^2? (2) Is our method of dimensionality reduction better than PGA? Under what conditions does our method outperform PGA?

Comparison of Projection and Geodesic Distances. The procedure we used to generate random points on $\mathrm{Gr}(p,n)$ for the synthetic experiments is the following. First, we generate N points from a uniform distribution on $\mathrm{St}(p,m)$ [8, Ch. 2.5], generate A from the uniform distribution on $\mathrm{St}(m,n)$, and generate B as an $n \times p$ matrix with i.i.d entries from $N(0, 0.1)$. Then we compute $\tilde{\mathcal{X}}_i = \mathrm{span}(AX_i + (I - AA^T)B) \in \mathrm{Gr}(p,n)$. Finally, we compute $\mathcal{X}_i = \mathrm{Exp}_{\tilde{\mathcal{X}}_i}(\sigma U_i)$, where $U_i = \tilde{U}_i/\|\tilde{U}_i\|$ and $\tilde{U}_i \in T_{\tilde{\mathcal{X}}_i}\mathrm{Gr}(p,n)$, to include some perturbation.

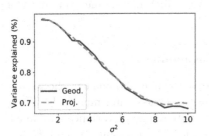

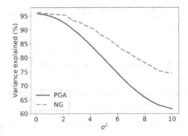

Fig. 3. Comparison of the NG representations based on the projection and geodesic distances using the ratio of expressed variance.

Fig. 4. Comparison of NG and PGA algorithms via percentage of explained variance.

This experiment involves comparing the performance of the NG representation in terms of the ratio of the variance explained, under different levels of data variance. In this experiment, we set $N = 50$, $n = 10$, $m = 3$, and $p = 1$ and σ is ranging from 1 to 10. The results are averaged over 100 repetitions and are shown in Fig. 3. From these results, we can see that the ratios of variance explained for the projection distance and the geodesic distance are indistinguishable but the one using projection distance is much faster than the one using the geodesic distance. The reason is that when two points on the Grassmann manifold are close, the geodesic distance can be well-approximated by the projection distance. When the algorithm converges, the original point $\mathcal{X}_i$ and the reconstructed point $\hat{\mathcal{X}}_i$ should be close and the geodesic distance can thus be well-approximated by the projection distance. Therefore, for the experiments in the next section, we use the projection distance for the sake of efficiency.

Table 1. The percentage of explained variance by PGA and NG representations respectively.

	$\tilde{m}$ (dim. of submanifold)				
	2	4	6	8	10
NG	33.12%	50.49%	59.98%	67.85%	73.77%
PGA	16.36%	29.41%	40.81%	50.63%	59.29%

Fig. 5. Example Corpus Callosi shapes from three distinct age groups, each depicted using the boundary point sets.

Comparison of NG and PGA. Now we compare our NG representation to PGA. Similar to the previous experiment, we set $N = 50$, $n = 30$, $m = 20$, $p = 2$, and $\sigma = 0.1$ and apply the same procedure to generate synthetic data. There is a subtle difference between PGA and NG, that is, in order to project the points on $\mathrm{Gr}(p, n) = \mathrm{Gr}(2, 30)$ to a $\tilde{m}$-dimensional submanifold, for PGA we need to choose $\tilde{m}$ principal components and for NG we need to project them to $\mathrm{Gr}(2, \tilde{m}/2 + 2)$ (since $\dim \mathrm{Gr}(2, \tilde{m}/2 + 2) = \tilde{m}$). The results are averaged over 100 repetitions and are shown in Table 1.

From Table 1, we can see that our method outperforms PGA by virtue of the fact that it is able to capture a larger amount of variance contained in the data. Next, we will investigate the conditions under which our method and PGA perform equally well and when our method outperforms PGA. To answer this question, we set $N = 50$, $n = 10$, $m = 5$, $p = 2$, and σ is ranging from 0.01 to 2. We then apply PGA and NG to reduce the dimension to 2 (i.e. choosing 2 principal components in PGA and project to $\mathrm{Gr}(2, 3)$ in NG). The results are averaged over 100 repetitions and are shown in Fig. 4. We can see that when the variance is small, our method produces almost the same result as PGA, whereas, our method is significantly better for the large data variance case. Note that when the variance in the data is small, i.e. the data are tightly clustered around the FM and PGA captures the essence of the data well. However, the requirement in PGA on the geodesic submanifold to pass through the anchor point, namely the FM, is not meaningful for data with large variance as explained through the following simple example. Consider, a few data points spread out on the equator of a sphere. The FM in this case is likely to be the north pole of the sphere if we restrict ourselves to the upper hemisphere. Thus, the geodesic submanifold computed by PGA will pass through this FM. However, what is more meaningful is a submanifold corresponding to the equator, which is what a nested spheres representation [17] in this case yields. In similar vein, for data with large variance on a Grassmann manifold, our NG representation will yield a more meaningful representation than PGA.

3.2 Application to Planar Shape Analysis

We now apply our method to planar (2-dimensional) shape analysis. A planar shape σ can be represented as an ordered set of $k > 2$ points in $\mathbb{R}^2$, called k-ads. Here we assume that these k points are not all identical. The space of all planar shapes (after removing the effect of translations, rotations, and scaling)

Table 2. Percentage of explained variance by PGA and NG representations respectively.

	m				
	1	5	10	15	20
NG	26.38%	68.56%	84.18%	90.63%	94.04%
PGA	7.33%	43.74%	73.48%	76.63%	79.9%

Table 3. Classification accuracies and explained variances for sPGA and sNG.

	Accuracy	Explained Var.
gKNN	33.33%	N/A
gKNN + sPGA	38.89%	3.27%
gKNN + sNG	66.67%	98.7%
gKNN + PGA	30.56%	46.61%
gKNN + NG	30.56%	84.28%

is denoted by $\Sigma_2^k = (\mathbb{R}^{k \times 2}/\mathrm{Sim}(2)) \setminus \{0\}$ where $\mathrm{Sim}(2)$ is the group of similarity transformations of $\mathbb{R}^2$, i.e. if $g \in \mathrm{Sim}(2)$, then $g \cdot \boldsymbol{x} = s\boldsymbol{R}\boldsymbol{x} + \boldsymbol{t}$ for some $s > 0$, $\boldsymbol{R} \in O(2)$, and $\boldsymbol{t} \in \mathbb{R}^2$. $\{0\}$ is excluded because we assume the k points are not all identical. It was shown in [18] that Σ_2^k is a smooth manifold and, when equipped with the Procrustean metric, is isometric to the complex projective space $\mathbb{C}P^{k-2}$ equipped with the Fubini-Study metric which is a special case of the complex Grassmannians, i.e. $\mathbb{C}P^{k-2} \cong \mathrm{Gr}(1, \mathbb{C}^{k-1})$. In practice, we need to preprocess the k-ads as follows to make it lie in $\mathrm{Gr}(1, \mathbb{C}^{k-1})$. Let $\boldsymbol{X}$ be the $k \times 2$ matrix containing the k points in $\mathbb{R}^2$. First, the effect of translation is removed by subtracting the first point. Then all these points are mapped to the complex vector space and take the span of the resulting vector to remove the effect of rotation and scaling.

OASIS Corpus Callosum Data Experiment. The OASIS database [20] is a publicly available database that contains T1-MR brain scans of subjects of age ranging from 18 to 96. In particular, it includes subjects that are clinically diagnosed with mild to moderate Alzheimer's disease. We further classify them into three groups: *young* (aged between 10 and 40), *middle-aged* (aged between 40 and 70), and *old* (aged above 70). For demonstration, we randomly choose 4 brain scans within each decade, totalling 36 brain scans. From each scan, the Corpus Callosum (CC) region is segmented and 250 points are taken on the boundary of the CC region. See Fig. 5 for samples of the segmented corpus callosi. In this case, the shape space is $\Sigma_2^{248} \cong \mathbb{C}P^{248} \cong \mathrm{Gr}(1, \mathbb{C}^{249})$. Results are shown in Table 2. Note that in Table 2, m is the dimension of the submanifold, i.e. for NG, we project to $\mathrm{Gr}(1, \mathbb{C}^{m+1})$ and for PGA, we take first m principal components.

Since the data are divided into three groups (young, middle-aged, and old), we can apply the sNG described in Sect. 2.4 to reduce the dimension. *The purpose of this experiment is not to demonstrate state-of-the-art classification accuracy for this dataset. Instead, our goal here is to demonstrate that the proposed nested Grassmann representation in a supervised setting is much more discriminative than the competition, namely the supervised PGA.* Hence, we choose a naive and impoverished classifier such as the geodesic kNN (gKNN) to highlight the aforementioned discriminative power of the nested Grassmann over PGA.

For comparison, the PGA can be easily extended to *supervised PGA* (sPGA) by first diffeomorphically mapping all the data to the tangent space anchored at the FM and then performing supervised PCA [2,4] on the tangent space. In this demonstration, we apply a gKNN classifier with $k = 5$ to the data before and after reducing the dimension (with and without supervision). Specifically, *the classification here is using a leave-one-out technique*, i.e. the prediction of $\mathcal{X}_j$ is determined by the geodesic k nearest neighbors of the $\mathcal{X}_i$'s excluding $\mathcal{X}_j$. In this experiment, we choose $m = 10$, i.e. $\mathrm{Gr}(1, \mathbb{C}^{249}) \to \mathrm{Gr}(1, \mathbb{C}^{11})$ (for PGA/sPGA, the number of principal components would be $m = 10$). The results are shown in Table 3. These results are in accordance with our expectation since in both sNG and sPGA, we seek a projection that minimizes the within-group variance while maximizing the between-group variance. However, as we observed earlier, the constraint of requiring the geodesic submanifold to pass through the FM is not well suited for this dataset which has a large variance across the data. This accounts for why the sNG exhibits far superior performance compared to sPGA in accuracy as well as in explained variance.

4   Conclusion

In this work, we proposed a nested structure for homogeneous spaces and applied this structure to the dimensionality reduction problems of data in Grassmann manifolds. We also discuss how this nested structure served as a generalization of other existing nested structures for spheres and the manifold of SPD matrices. Specifically, we showed that a lower dimensional Grassmann manifold can be embedded into a higher dimensional Grassmann manifold and via this embedding we constructed a sequence of nested Grassmann manifolds. Compared to the PGA, which is designed for general Riemannian manifolds, the proposed method can capture a higher percentage of data variance after reducing the dimensionality. This is primarily because our method unlike the PGA does not require the reduced dimensional submanifold to be a geodesic submanifold. To sum up, the nested Grassmann structure allows us to fit the data to a larger class of submanifolds than PGA. We also proposed a supervised dimensionality reduction technique which simultaneously differentiates data classes while reducing dimensionality. Efficacy of our method was demonstrated on the OASIS Corpus Callosi data for dimensionality reduction and classification. We showed that our method outperforms the widely used PGA significantly.

References

1. Absil, P.A., Mahony, R., Sepulchre, R.: Riemannian geometry of Grassmann manifolds with a view on algorithmic computation. Acta Applicandae Mathematica **80**(2), 199–220 (2004)
2. Bair, E., Hastie, T., Paul, D., Tibshirani, R.: Prediction by supervised principal components. J. Am. Stat. Assoc. **101**(473), 119–137 (2006)
3. Banerjee, M., Chakraborty, R., Vemuri, B.C.: Sparse exact PGA on Riemannian manifolds. In: Proceedings of the IEEE International Conference on Computer Vision, pp. 5010–5018 (2017)

4. Barshan, E., Ghodsi, A., Azimifar, Z., Jahromi, M.Z.: Supervised principal component analysis: visualization, classification and regression on subspaces and submanifolds. Pattern Recogn. **44**(7), 1357–1371 (2011)
5. Basser, P.J., Mattiello, J., LeBihan, D.: MR diffusion tensor spectroscopy and imaging. Biophys. J. **66**(1), 259–267 (1994)
6. Callaghan, P.T.: Principles of Nuclear Magnetic Resonance Microscopy. Oxford University Press on Demand (1993)
7. Chakraborty, R., Seo, D., Vemuri, B.C.: An efficient exact-PGA algorithm for constant curvature manifolds. In: Proceedings of the IEEE Conference on Computer Vision and Pattern Recognition, pp. 3976–3984 (2016)
8. Chikuse, Y.: Statistics on Special Manifolds. LNS, vol. 174. Springer, New York (2003). https://doi.org/10.1007/978-0-387-21540-2
9. Damon, J., Marron, J.: Backwards principal component analysis and principal nested relations. J. Math. Imaging Vis. **50**(1–2), 107–114 (2014)
10. Edelman, A., Arias, T.A., Smith, S.T.: The geometry of algorithms with orthogonality constraints. SIAM J. Matrix Anal. Appl. **20**(2), 303–353 (1998)
11. Fletcher, P.T., Lu, C., Pizer, S.M., Joshi, S.: Principal geodesic analysis for the study of nonlinear statistics of shape. IEEE Trans. Med. Imaging **23**(8), 995–1005 (2004)
12. Harandi, M., Salzmann, M., Hartley, R.: Dimensionality reduction on SPD manifolds: the emergence of geometry-aware methods. IEEE Trans. Pattern Anal. Mach. Intell. **40**(1), 48–62 (2018)
13. Hastie, T., Stuetzle, W.: Principal curves. J. Am. Stat. Assoc. **84**(406), 502–516 (1989)
14. Hauberg, S.: Principal curves on Riemannian manifolds. IEEE Trans. Pattern Anal. Mach. Intell. **38**(9), 1915–1921 (2016)
15. Huckemann, S., Hotz, T., Munk, A.: Intrinsic shape analysis: geodesic PCA for Riemannian manifolds modulo isometric Lie group actions. Statistica Sinica **20**, 1–58 (2010)
16. Huckemann, S., Ziezold, H.: Principal component analysis for Riemannian manifolds, with an application to triangular shape spaces. Adv. Appl. Probab. **38**(2), 299–319 (2006)
17. Jung, S., Dryden, I.L., Marron, J.: Analysis of principal nested spheres. Biometrika **99**(3), 551–568 (2012)
18. Kendall, D.G.: Shape manifolds, Procrustean metrics, and complex projective spaces. Bull. London Math. Soc. **16**(2), 81–121 (1984)
19. Lai, Z., Lim, L.H., Ye, K.: Simpler Grassmannian optimization. arXiv preprint arXiv:2009.13502 (2020)
20. Marcus, D.S., Wang, T.H., Parker, J., Csernansky, J.G., Morris, J.C., Buckner, R.L.: Open Access Series of Imaging Studies (OASIS): cross-sectional MRI data in young, middle aged, nondemented, and demented older adults. J. Cogn. Neurosci. **19**(9), 1498–1507 (2007)
21. Myers, S.B., Steenrod, N.E.: The group of isometries of a Riemannian manifold. Ann. Math. **40**, 400–416 (1939)
22. Pennec, X., et al.: Barycentric subspace analysis on manifolds. Ann. Stat. **46**(6A), 2711–2746 (2018)
23. Sommer, S., Lauze, F., Hauberg, S., Nielsen, M.: Manifold valued statistics, exact principal geodesic analysis and the effect of linear approximations. In: Daniilidis, K., Maragos, P., Paragios, N. (eds.) ECCV 2010. LNCS, vol. 6316, pp. 43–56. Springer, Heidelberg (2010). https://doi.org/10.1007/978-3-642-15567-3_4

24. Townsend, J., Koep, N., Weichwald, S.: Pymanopt: a Python toolbox for optimization on manifolds using automatic differentiation. J. Mach. Learn. Res. **17**(137),
1–5 (2016). http://jmlr.org/papers/v17/16-177.html
25. Ye, K., Lim, L.H.: Schubert varieties and distances between subspaces of different
dimensions. SIAM J. Matrix Anal. Appl. **37**(3), 1176–1197 (2016)
26. Zhang, M., Fletcher, T.: Probabilistic principal geodesic analysis. In: Advances in
Neural Information Processing Systems, pp. 1178–1186 (2013)

Hierarchical Morphology-Guided Tooth Instance Segmentation from CBCT Images

Zhiming Cui[1,6,7], Bojun Zhang[2], Chunfeng Lian[3], Changjian Li[4(✉)],
Lei Yang[1], Wenping Wang[1,5], Min Zhu[2(✉)], and Dinggang Shen[6,7(✉)]

[1] Department of Computer Science, The University of Hong Kong, Hong Kong, China
[2] Shanghai Ninth People's Hospital, Shanghai JiaoTong University, Shanghai, China
ZHUM1612@sh9hospital.org.cn
[3] School of Mathematics and Statistics, Xi'an Jiaotong University, Xi'an, China
[4] Department of Computer Science, University College London, London, UK
changjian.li@ucl.ac.uk
[5] Department of Visualization, Texas A&M University, College Station, TX, USA
[6] School of Biomedical Engineering, ShanghaiTech University, Shanghai, China
dgshen@shanghaitech.edu.cn
[7] Shanghai United Imaging Intelligence Co., Ltd., Shanghai, China

Abstract. Automatic and accurate segmentation of individual teeth, i.e., tooth instance segmentation, from CBCT images is an essential step for computer-aided dentistry. Previous works typically overlooked rich morphological features of teeth, such as tooth root apices, critical for successful treatment outcomes. This paper presents a two-stage learning-based framework that explicitly leverages the comprehensive geometric guidance provided by a hierarchical tooth morphological representation for tooth instance segmentation. Given a 3D input CBCT image, our method first learns to extract the tooth centroids and skeletons for identifying each tooth's rough position and topological structures, respectively. Based on the outputs of the first step, a multi-task learning mechanism is further designed to estimate each tooth's volumetric mask by simultaneously regressing boundary and root apices as auxiliary tasks. Extensive evaluations, ablation studies, and comparisons with existing methods show that our approach achieved state-of-the-art segmentation performance, especially around the challenging dental parts (i.e., tooth roots and boundaries). These results suggest the potential applicability of our framework in real-world clinical scenarios.

1 Introduction

Computer-aided design (CAD) has been widely used in digital dentistry for diagnosis, restoration, and orthodontic treatment planning. In these processes, 3D tooth models, typically segmented from cone beam computed tomography

---

Z. Cui and B. Zhang–Equal contribution.

© Springer Nature Switzerland AG 2021
A. Feragen et al. (Eds.): IPMI 2021, LNCS 12729, pp. 150–162, 2021.
https://doi.org/10.1007/978-3-030-78191-0_12

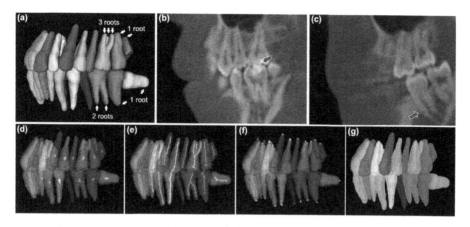

Fig. 1. The first row shows three typical examples, including (a) teeth with large shape variations; (b) touching boundaries of maxillary and mandibular teeth during close bite; (c) blurred signals between tooth roots and the surrounding alveolar bones. The second row illustrates different components of the hierarchical morphological representations, including the points (i.e., the tooth centroid (d) and the root landmarks at root apices (f)), the tooth skeleton (e), and the tooth boundary surface (g).

(CBCT) images [4,5], are essential to assist dentists in extracting, implanting, or rearranging teeth. In clinical practice, dentists need to manually label each tooth slice-by-slice from the CBCT images, which is laborious and time-consuming, and also highly depends on an operator's experience. Thus, it is practically demanded of accurate and fully automatic methods to segment individual teeth from dental CBCT images.

However, automatic segmentation of individual teeth is still a challenging task as teeth exhibit large variations in their geometry. For example, maxillary molars usually have three roots, while mandibular molars usually have two roots [8] (see Fig. 1(a)). Beyond the general rules, special cases where molars have one root can also be found (Fig. 1(a)) and such disparities are fairly commonplace in the real-world clinics. Even state-of-the-art learning-based methods [4,5,14] often fail to handle such complicated cases. This is mainly because such methods employ only simple representations (e.g., the tooth centroid or the bounding box) for teeth and thus cannot capture detailed shape variations in each tooth. This is even worse at the regions where image contrast is low, such as the common boundary of touching teeth during close bite (Fig. 1(b)) and the interface between tooth roots and their surrounding alveolar bone (Fig. 1(c)). Without any prior knowledge of the tooth structure, either traditional methods [1,2,6,7,9,11,15] or learning-based networks [4,5,14] cannot properly segment the tooth from the background tissue at these regions, although the tooth root information is critical in orthodontic treatment to ensure apices cannot penetrate the surrounding alveolar bone during tooth movement.

In this paper, we propose a hierarchical morphological representation for capturing the complicated tooth shapes and important tooth features. Specifically, this hierarchical morphological representation consists of the tooth centroid and root apices (i.e., points), skeleton, boundary surface, and volume (Fig. 1(d)–(g), (a)). Based on this hierarchical representation, we design a coarse-to-fine learning-based framework for automatic and accurate tooth instance segmentation. Given a 3D input CBCT image, to capture the positions and varying topological structures of all individual teeth, especially at the multi-root areas, a neural network at the 1st-stage (at the coarse level) is designed to predict tooth centroids and skeletons, respectively. Then, a multi-task network is further proposed at the 2nd-stage to simultaneously predict the detailed geometric features, i.e., root landmarks (or apices), boundary surface, and volumetric mask of each tooth using the tooth skeletons estimated at the 1st-stage as guidance. Since the three tasks are intrinsically related from a geometric perspective, regressing the root landmarks and boundary surface of each tooth can intuitively boost the segmentation performance at the important and challenging regions (e.g., the tooth boundary and root apices). The performance of our method was evaluated through extensive experiments on a CBCT dataset collected from real-world clinics. The corresponding results showed that our method significantly outperformed other state-of-the-art approaches, suggesting the efficacy of the hierarchical morphological representations designed in this study for tooth instance segmentation.

2   Methods

The proposed framework consists of two stages. At the 1st-stage, a prediction network is designed to extract the coarse-level morphological representations, i.e., the centroid and skeleton of each tooth, to represent the tooth structure. At the 2nd-stage, a segmentation network with the coarse-level morphological guidance (the tooth skeleton) is trained with a multi-task learning mechanism to generate a detailed tooth volume, boundary, and root landmarks. The schematic diagrams of these two steps are shown in Figs. 2 and 3, respectively, with the details elaborated below.

2.1   Tooth Centroid and Skeleton Extraction Network

As the centroid and skeleton of a tooth define its spatial location and topological structure, respectively, the network in this step aims to achieve the following goals: 1) localize individual teeth by identifying their centroids, and then 2) capture their topological structures by predicting their skeletons.

Given the 3D input CBCT image I, two sub-networks are designed to this end, as shown in Fig. 3. Each sub-network contains two output branches to produce a binary segmentation map B and a 3D offset map O. Specifically, the binary segmentation map B indicates whether a voxel of the input CBCT image belongs to a foreground tooth object or the background tissue (denoted as B_c

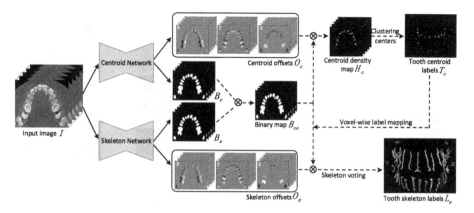

Fig. 2. The pipeline of our 1st-stage network for tooth skeleton extraction. The CBCT scan is first fed into both the centroid network and the skeleton network to generate the offsets and binary maps, respectively. Then, the tooth centroids and skeletons are detected and predicted by the later steps (dotted lines).

and B_s of the centroid sub-network and the skeleton sub-network, respectively). The 3D offset map O indicates the 3D vector pointing from each foreground voxel to its target point. Here, for each voxel, its target point in centroid offset map O_c refers to a vector pointing to the centroid of the corresponding tooth, while in skeleton offset map O_s the target point is defined as a vector pointing to the nearest point on the skeleton of the corresponding tooth.

With the outputs of the two sub-networks, we detect the tooth centroids and skeletons as follows. First, the common binary map B_{cs} is produced by the element-wise product of B_c and B_s, which masks out the foreground voxels shared by both centroid and skeleton offsets. Then, we generate a tooth centroid density map H_c by counting the frequency of a voxel being pointed by other voxels according to the 3D centroid offset map. Finally, we adopt a fast search clustering method [13] to localize the peaks in H_c as the predicted tooth centroids, denoted as T_c. The rationale is that the clustering centers usually have relatively high density values (i.e., frequency) and large distance to the nearest point with a higher density value, defined as:

$$T_c = (H_c^i > \delta) \cap (DT_c^i > \lambda), \tag{1}$$

where DT_c^i refers to the distance between voxel i and its nearest voxel with higher density value than H_c^i. The scalars $\delta = 20$ and $\lambda = 10$ are the density and distance thresholds, respectively. Moreover, we assign each foreground voxel in B_{cs} with different instance labels based on the minimum distance from its predicted candidate tooth centroid to the clustered tooth centroids in T_c.

Although a tooth centroid is stable to distinguish and localize a tooth, a single point is insufficient to capture its geometric and topological properties, compared to the skeletal representation. To obtain the tooth skeleton, we add the skeleton offsets on the coordinates of corresponding foreground voxels in B_{cs}.

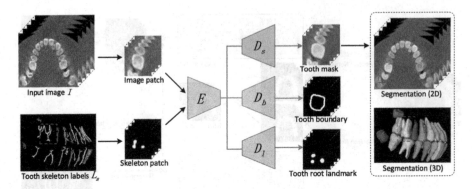

Fig. 3. The pipeline of our $2nd$-stage multi-task network for tooth instance segmentation guided by skeletons. The inputs are the cropped input image and skeleton patches cropped from the 3D input image and tooth skeleton label map, and the outputs are the tooth segmentation volume, boundary, and root landmarks.

After frequency counting, the skeleton density map H_l is obtained in the same process as the generation of H_c. Finally, we filter voxels in H_l with the lower frequency to produce the target tooth skeleton map. Notably, as the foreground voxels already have the instance labels after the centroid clustering, we can generate the instance-level tooth skeleton label map L_s in a straightforward manner, as shown in Fig. 3.

The two sub-networks are trained independently with the same loss functions.

$$\mathcal{L}_{CS} = \mathcal{L}_{seg}^b + \eta \mathcal{L}_{reg}^{smoothL1}, \tag{2}$$

where η is the balancing weight empirically set as 10 in our experiments. Specifically, the smooth L1 loss is employed to calculate the offset regression error ($\mathcal{L}_{reg}^{smoothL1}$) on the voxels belonging to tooth objects. And the binary cross-entropy loss is utilized to compute the binary segmentation error ($\mathcal{L}_{seg}^b$).

2.2   Multi-task Learning for Tooth Segmentation

Guided by the instance-level tooth skeleton label map L_s, we further extract individual teeth. To improve the segmentation accuracy, especially near the tooth boundary and root areas, we introduce a multi-task learning mechanism that can efficiently employ the intrinsic relatedness between the tooth volume, boundary, and root landmarks.

To train the multi-task learning network, we process the 3D CBCT image I and tooth skeleton label map L_s at a finer scale where individual tooth patches are extracted and processed. In Step one, we select a tooth skeleton instance and crop two patches (with the same size, and centered at the mass of the skeleton) from the original image I (the image patch) and the skeleton instance label map L_s, respectively. In Step two, the selected tooth skeleton instance is further converted to a Gaussian map centered at the skeleton voxels with a small standard deviation $\delta_1 = 3$ voxel-size, serving as one of the inputs (the skeleton patch). As shown in Fig. 3, the skeleton patch is concatenated with the original image patch, yielding a two-channel input of the tooth segmentation network.

Using the two-channel input, we design the segmentation network by leveraging a multi-task learning mechanism, i.e., simultaneously predicting the tooth volume, boundary, and corresponding root landmarks. Figure 3 presents an overview of the network that consists of a shared encoder (E) and three task-specific decoders $(D_s, D_b$ and $D_l)$ with the skip connections combining features of different levels. The three individual branches output the tooth segmentation, boundary, and root landmarks, respectively. Notably, each tooth's ground-truth boundary and root landmark are defined as the 3D Gaussian heatmaps centered at the surface and point location with a standard deviation δ_2 set as 3 voxel-size in our experiments. The loss function $\mathcal{L}_{MT}$ of this multi-task network is defined as:

$$\mathcal{L}_{MT} = \mathcal{L}_{seg} + \lambda(\mathcal{L}_b + \mathcal{L}_l), \qquad (3)$$

where $\mathcal{L}_{seg}$, $\mathcal{L}_b$ and $\mathcal{L}_l$ refer to the tooth volume segmentation, boundary, and landmark prediction losses, respectively. For $\mathcal{L}_{seg}$, we combine the Dice loss and binary cross-entropy loss in our experiment, while for $\mathcal{L}_b$ and $\mathcal{L}_l$, we use the L2 error. The hyper-parameter λ is empirically fixed as 0.2 to balance the loss terms.

2.3 Implementation Details

We employed 3D V-Net [12] as the network backbone of our two-stage framework. All CBCT images were converted to have the same input size of $256 \times 256 \times 256$ in the $1st$-stage. The cropped patch size of the $2nd$-stage was set as $96 \times 96 \times 96$ to ensure that the whole foreground tooth object is included. The framework was implemented in PyTorch, which was trained using Adam optimizer with a fixed learning rate of $1e^{-4}$. The networks were trained in $50K$ iterations in both two stages. Generally, the training time was around 5 h ($1st$-stage) and 8 h ($2nd$-stage) on a Linux server with one Nvidia GeForce 1080Ti GPU.

3   Experimental Results

3.1   Dataset and Evaluation Metrics

We have extensively evaluated the proposed framework on 100 CBCT scans collected from patients before or after orthodontic treatments in dental clinics. The dataset contains many abnormal cases with teeth crowding, missing or malocclusion problems. The resolution of the dataset is 0.4 mm. We manually crop the tooth area on the 3D CBCT image, resize it to $256 \times 256 \times 256$, and then normalize the CBCT image intensity to the range of $[0, 1]$. To obtain the ground truth, the segmentation labels and tooth root landmarks are manually annotated by dentists. The corresponding tooth skeletons and boundaries are generated using morphological operations [10] based on the annotated segmentation labels, and

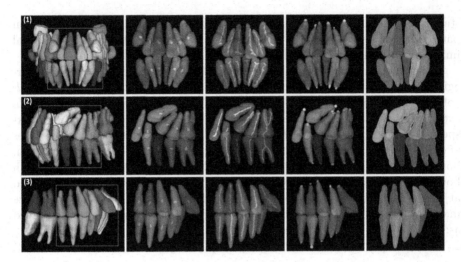

Fig. 4. Typical results of the hierarchical tooth morphological representation. From left to right: 3D segmentation results, predicted tooth centroids, skeletons, root apices, and boundaries. The last four columns are the partial results of the first column within the red boxes. (Color figure online)

the tooth centroids are directly computed based on the labelled mask. To train the network, the dataset is randomly split into three subsets, i.e., 50 scans for training, 10 scans for validation, and the remaining 40 scans for testing.

To quantitatively evaluate the performance of our framework, we employ different metrics to measure the tooth detection and segmentation accuracy. Specifically, we measure the tooth detection accuracy (DA) by $DA = \frac{|GT \cap P|}{|P|}$, where GT and P refer to two sets of the ground-truth and the predicted teeth. For the tooth segmentation, four metrics, including Dice, Jaccard, the average surface distance (ASD), and Hausdorff distance (HD), are utilized to evaluate the performance. Since the Hausdorff distance is the maximum of the minimum distances between the predicted and the ground-truth tooth surfaces, it is the key metric to especially measure the segmentation error around the tooth root area with only a tiny percentage of foreground voxels.

3.2   Evaluation and Comparison

We conduct extensive experiments to demonstrate the effectiveness of our tooth instance segmentation framework guided by hierarchical morphological components, including skeleton representation, and multi-task learning for joint prediction of tooth boundary and root landmarks. In Table 1, we present segmentation results of four configurations: (1) we build our baseline network (bNet) by directly utilizing the tooth centroid to detect and represent each tooth in the 1st-stage network, and also a single-task segmentation network without tooth boundary and root landmark predictions in the 2nd-stage network; (2) we add

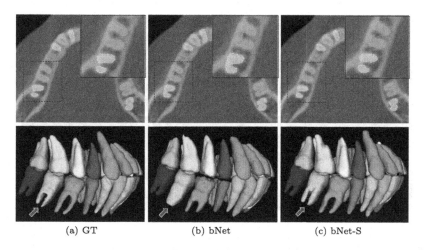

(a) GT   (b) bNet   (c) bNet-S

Fig. 5. The qualitative comparison of tooth segmentation with (c) or without (b) tooth skeleton representation. bNet-S achieves better results especially near the tooth root area highlighted by red boxes and arrows, compared to the ground truth (a). (Color figure online)

Table 1. Quantitative results of ablation analysis of different morphological components.

Methods	Dice [%]	Jaccard [%]	ASD [mm]	HD [mm]
bNet	92.1 ± 1.5	84.7 ± 2.4	0.33 ± 0.10	2.42 ± 0.88
bNet-S	93.1 ± 1.1	85.3 ± 1.7	0.31 ± 0.05	2.30 ± 0.77
bNet-S-L	94.3 ± 0.6	88.4 ± 1.0	0.26 ± 0.02	1.63 ± 0.45
FullNet	$\mathbf{94.8 \pm 0.4}$	$\mathbf{89.1 \pm 0.9}$	$\mathbf{0.18 \pm 0.02}$	$\mathbf{1.52 \pm 0.28}$

only one tooth morphological information, i.e., the tooth skeleton, to the baseline network to better represent each tooth object, which is denoted as bNet-S; (3) compared to bNet-S, we add the tooth root landmark detection as a separate branch in the $2nd$-stage network for multi-task learning, denoted as bNet-S-L; (4) we further argument bNet-S-L with tooth boundary prediction branch in our $2nd$-stage network as the final network (FullNet). Note that all of the four configurations utilize the tooth centroid point to detect the tooth object in the 3D CBCT image, thus the detection accuracy is the same and not listed in Table 1.

Benefits of Tooth Skeleton Representation. Compared with the tooth centroid, the tooth skeleton provides richer and more faithful geometric and topological information to guide the subsequent tooth segmentation, especially for handling the molars with multi-roots. To validate its effectiveness, we add the tooth skeleton detection component (bNet-S) to the baseline network (bNet) in the $1st$-stage, and show the quantitative results in Table 1. It can be seen that bNet-S consistently improves the segmentation performance in terms of all

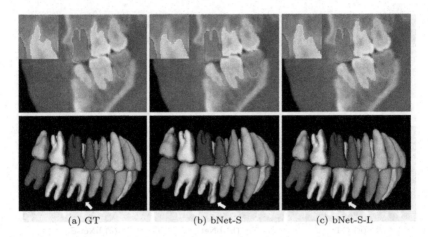

(a) GT   (b) bNet-S   (c) bNet-S-L

Fig. 6. The qualitative comparison of tooth segmentation with (c) or without (b) tooth root landmark detection branch. Compared to the ground truth (a), bNet-S-L avoids under- or over-segmentation around the tooth root apices highlighted by red boxes and arrows. (Color figure online)

metrics (e.g., 1.0% Dice improvement and 0.02 mm ASD improvement, respectively). Additionally, a typical visual comparison is shown in Fig. 5, which indicates that, with the guidance of tooth skeleton, the 2nd-stage segmentation network can accurately separate different roots of a molar. This demonstrates that the tooth skeleton, with clear tooth shape information, brings significant benefits to capture complicated tooth shapes.

Benefits of Tooth Root Landmark Detection. In our 2nd-stage network, instead of only generating the segmentation mask, bNet-S-L adds another branch to predict the tooth root landmarks by a multi-task learning mechanism. As shown in Table 1, compared with bNet-S, the Hausdorff distance of bNet-S-L significantly drops from 2.30 mm to 1.63 mm. Note that the HD metric measures the maximum of the minimum surface distances between the ground-truth and predicted tooth surfaces, such that the under- or over-segmentation near the tooth root apices usually leads to the large error. This indicates the multi-task learning of tooth segmentation prediction and landmark detection assists the network to capture the intrinsic relatedness from a geometric perspective and then benefits the segmentation task. To further analyze the effectiveness, we also provide a visual example in Fig. 6, where bNet-S-L efficiently addresses the under- or over-segmentation problem of the tooth roots (highlighted by the red boxes) even with limited intensity contrast.

Benefits of Tooth Boundary Prediction. In our FullNet, a third branch, tooth boundary prediction, is added in the 2nd-stage network, which encourages the network to pay more attention to the tooth boundary area with limited intensity contrast. Statistically, the FullNet obtains the best segmentation

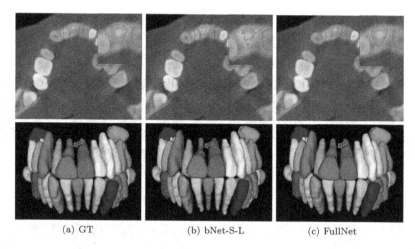

(a) GT   (b) bNet-S-L   (c) FullNet

Fig. 7. The qualitative comparison of tooth segmentation with (c) or without (b) tooth boundary prediction branch. Compared to the ground truth (a), FullNet produces more accurate segmentation results especially on the boundaries with metal-artifacts.

Table 2. Quantitative comparison with the state-of-the-art methods in terms of the segmentation and detection accuracy.

Methods	Dice [%]	Jaccard [%]	ASD [mm]	HD [mm]	DA [%]
MWTNet [3]	89.6 ± 1.3	82.5 ± 1.9	0.36 ± 0.14	4.82 ± 1.68	98.1 ± 0.8
ToothNet [5]	91.6 ± 1.4	84.2 ± 1.8	0.30 ± 0.11	2.82 ± 1.02	98.6 ± 1.1
CGDNet [14]	92.5 ± 1.1	85.2 ± 1.6	0.27 ± 0.03	2.21 ± 0.69	98.9 ± 1.5
Ours	**94.8 ± 0.4**	**89.1 ± 0.9**	**0.18 ± 0.02**	**1.52 ± 0.28**	**99.7 ± 0.6**

performance and boosts the average Dice score and the ASD error to 94.8% and 0.18 mm, respectively. The qualitative results in Fig. 7 also show that the FullNet can segment more accurate tooth boundaries even with metal artifacts in CBCT images. More representative segmentation results of the FullNet are presented in Fig. 4 and Fig. 8.

3.3   Comparison with the State-of-the-Art Methods

We implement and compare our framework with several state-of-the-art deep learning based tooth segmentation methods, including the region proposal based network (ToothNet) [5], the center-guided network (CGDNet) [14], and the semantic-based method (MWTNet) [3]. Note that we utilized the same network backbone (V-Net) in all methods for fair comparison. As shown in Table 2, compared with MWTNet [3] that directly utilizes tooth boundaries to simultaneously detect and segment individual teeth in a single step, our method leads to remarkable improvement of 5.2% Dice score and 3.30 mm HD error, demonstrating the advantage of the two-stage detect-then-segment framework. Although

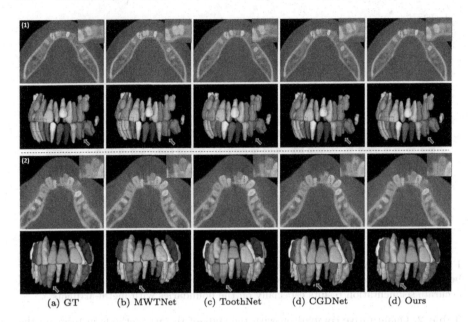

(a) GT   (b) MWTNet   (c) ToothNet   (d) CGDNet   (d) Ours

Fig. 8. The visual comparison of tooth segmentation results by four different methods. Two typical examples are presented, each being shown by two rows with 2D segmentation masks and corresponding 3D reconstruction results, respectively.

ToothNet [5] is a two-stage network, it only utilizes bounding boxes to represent individual teeth and our method still outperforms it in terms of segmentation and detection performances by a large margin. At last, it is also observed that our approach consistently achieves higher accuracy than CGDNet [14], which achieves the state-of-the-art performance in this specific task. Particularly, the segmentation accuracy (Dice) is increased from 92.5% to 94.8%, and the detection accuracy (DA) is improved from 98.9% to 99.7%. It is worth noting that all these competing methods pay little attention to the segmentation around tooth root apices with limited intensity contrast, which usually leads to under- or over-segmentation of the tooth roots and a higher HD error, even if the root information is an important consideration in orthodontic treatment.

To further demonstrate the advantage of our method, we provide a quantitative comparison of two typical examples in Fig. 8. It can be found that the segmentation results generated by our approach (in the last column) match better with the ground truth (in the 1st column), especially near the tooth root apices and occlusion planes with blurred boundary signals. Notably, MWTNet (the 2nd column) is more likely to lead to failure in tooth separation. For example, two incisors are regarded as the same object in the 1st case, and a cuspid is broken into two parts in the 2nd case. This shows that the tooth boundaries alone are not stable signals for segmenting adjacent teeth due to limited intensity contrast between these teeth. Besides, ToothNet [5] (the 3nd column) and CDGNet [14] (the 4th column), respectively representing each tooth by a bounding box or a center point, produce lots of artifacts near the tooth boundary and root areas, since most tooth topological features are overlooked by the simple representation of the bounding box or the center point. The visual results shown in Fig. 8 are consistent with the quantitative comparison, indicating the effectiveness and advantages of the hierarchical morphology-guided tooth instance segmentation framework.

4   Conclusion

In this paper, we present a novel tooth instance segmentation network from CBCT images guided by the hierarchical morphological representations of each tooth, including its centroid and root landmarks at apices (i.e., points), skeleton, boundary surface, and volumetric mask. Specifically, the tooth centroid and skeleton are first utilized to detect and represent each tooth. Then, a multi-task learning mechanism is presented to achieve high segmentation accuracy especially around tooth boundaries and tooth root apices. Comprehensive experiments have validated the effectiveness of our method, showing it can outperform the state-of-the-art methods. This gives the potential of our method to be widely used in the real-world clinics.

References

1. Akhoondali, H., Zoroofi, R.A., Shirani, G.: Rapid automatic segmentation and visualization of teeth in CT-scan data. J. Appl. Sci. **9**(11) (2009)
2. Barone, S., Paoli, A., Razionale, A.V.: CT segmentation of dental shapes by anatomy-driven reformation imaging and B-spline modelling. Int. J. Numer. Methods Biomed. Eng. (2015)
3. Chen, Y., et al.: Automatic segmentation of individual tooth in dental CBCT images from tooth surface map by a multi-task FCN. IEEE Access **8**, 97296–97309 (2020)
4. Chung, M., Lee, M., Hong, J., Park, S., Shin, Y.G.: Pose-aware instance segmentation framework from cone beam CT images for tooth segmentation. Comput. Biol. Med. **120**, 103720 (2020)
5. Cui, Z., Li, C., Wang, W.: ToothNet: automatic tooth instance segmentation and identification from cone beam CT images. In: Proceedings of the IEEE Conference on Computer Vision and Pattern Recognition, pp. 6368–6377 (2019)
6. Gan, Y., Xia, Z., Xiong, J., Li, G., Zhao, Q.: Tooth and alveolar bone segmentation from dental computed tomography images. IEEE J. Biomed. Health Inform. **22**(1), 196–204 (2018)
7. Gao, H., Chae, O.: Individual tooth segmentation from CT images using level set method with shape and intensity prior. Pattern Recogn. **43**(7), 2406–2417 (2010)
8. Ibsen, O., Phelan, J.: Oral Pathology for the Dental Hygienist. Saunders/Elsevier
9. Keyhaninejad, S., Zoroofi, R.A., Setarehdan, S.K., Shirani, G.: Automated segmentation of teeth in multi-slice CT images. In: IET International Conference on Visual Information Engineering. VIE 2006 (2006)
10. Lee, T.C.: Building skeleton models via 3-D medial surface/axis thinning algorithms. Graph. Models Image Process. **56**(6), 462–478 (1994)

11. Li, W., et al.: Automated segmentation of dental CBCT image with prior-guided sequential random forests. Med. Phys. **43**, 336–346 (2015)
12. Milletari, F., Navab, N., Ahmadi, S.A.: V-Net: fully convolutional neural networks for volumetric medical image segmentation. In: 2016 Fourth International Conference on 3D Vision (3DV), pp. 565–571. IEEE (2016)
13. Rodriguez, A., Laio, A.: Clustering by fast search and find of density peaks. Science **344**(6191), 1492–1496 (2014)
14. Wu, X., Chen, H., Huang, Y., Guo, H., Qiu, T., Wang, L.: Center-sensitive and boundary-aware tooth instance segmentation and classification from cone-beam CT. In: 2020 IEEE 17th International Symposium on Biomedical Imaging (ISBI), pp. 939–942. IEEE (2020)
15. Xia, Z.: Towards accurate tooth segmentation from computer tomography images using a hybrid active contour model. Med. Phys. (2014)

Cortical Morphometry Analysis Based on Worst Transportation Theory

Min Zhang[1], Dongsheng An[2], Na Lei[3(✉)], Jianfeng Wu[4], Tong Zhao[5], Xiaoyin Xu[6], Yalin Wang[4], and Xianfeng Gu[2]

[1] Zhejiang University, Hangzhou, China
min_zhang@zju.edu.cn
[2] Department of Computer Science, Stony Brook University, Stony Brook, USA
{doan,gu}@cs.stonybrook.edu
[3] DUT-RU ISE, Dalian University of Technology, Dalian, China
nalei@dlut.edu.cn
[4] School of Computing, Informatics, and Decision Systems Engineering,
Arizona State University, Tempe, AZ, USA
{jianfen6,ylwang}@asu.edu
[5] Université Côte d'Azur, Inria, Nice, France
tong.zhao@inria.fr
[6] Brigham and Women's Hospital, Harvard Medical School, Boston, USA
xxu@bwh.harvard.edu

Abstract. Biomarkers play an important role in early detection and intervention in Alzheimer's disease (AD). However, obtaining effective biomarkers for AD is still a big challenge. In this work, we propose to use the worst transportation cost as a univariate biomarker to index cortical morphometry for tracking AD progression. The worst transportation (WT) aims to find the least economical way to transport one measure to the other, which contrasts to the optimal transportation (OT) that finds the most economical way between measures. To compute the WT cost, we generalize the Brenier theorem for the OT map to the WT map, and show that the WT map is the gradient of a concave function satisfying the Monge-Ampere equation. We also develop an efficient algorithm to compute the WT map based on computational geometry. We apply the algorithm to analyze cortical shape difference between dementia due to AD and normal aging individuals. The experimental results reveal the effectiveness of our proposed method which yields better statistical performance than other competing methods including the OT.

Keywords: Alzheimer's disease · Shape analysis · Worst transportation

1 Introduction

As the population living longer, Alzheimer's disease (AD) is now a major public health concern with the number of patients expected to reach 13.8 million

---

M. Zhang and D. An—The two authors contributed equally to this paper.

© Springer Nature Switzerland AG 2021
A. Feragen et al. (Eds.): IPMI 2021, LNCS 12729, pp. 163–176, 2021.
https://doi.org/10.1007/978-3-030-78191-0_13

by the year 2050 in the U.S. alone [7]. However, the late interventions or the targets with secondary effects and less relevant to the disease initiation often make the current therapeutic failures in patients with dementia due to AD [11]. The accumulation of beta-amyloid plaques ($A\beta$) in human brains is one of the hallmarks of AD, and preclinical AD is now viewed as a gradual process before the onset of the clinical symptoms. The $A\beta$ positivity is treated as the precursor of anatomical abnormalities such as atrophy and functional changes such as hypometabolism/hypoperfusion.

It is generally agreed that accurate presymptomatic diagnosis and preventative treatment of AD could have enormous public health benefits. Brain $A\beta$ pathology can be measured using positron emission tomography (PET) with amyloid-sensitive radiotracers, or in cerebrospinal fluid (CSF). However, these invasive and expensive measurements are less attractive to subjects in preclinical stage and PET scanning is also not widely available in clinics. Therefore, there is strong interest to develop structural magnetic resonance imaging (MRI) biomarkers, which are largely accessible, cost-effective and widely used in AD clinical research, to predict brain amyloid burden [3]. Tosun et al. [16] combine MRI-based measures of cortical shape and cerebral blood flow to predict amyloid status for early-MCI individuals. Pekkala et al. [13] use the brain MRI measures like volumes of the cortical gray matter, hippocampus, accumbens, thalamus and putamen to identify the $A\beta$ positivity in cognitively unimpaired (CU) subjects. Meanwhile, a univariate imaging biomarker would be highly desirable for clinical use and randomized clinical trials (RCT) [14,17]. Though a variety of research studies univariate biomarkers with sMRI analysis, there is limited research to develop univariate biomarker to predict brain amyloid burden, which will enrich our understanding of the relationship between brain atrophy and AD pathology and thus benefit assessing disease burden, progression and effects of treatments.

In this paper, we propose to use the worst transportation (WT) cost as a univariate biomarker to predict brain amyloid burden. Specifically, we compare the population statistics of WT costs between the $A\beta+$ AD and the $A\beta-$ CU subjects. The new proposed WT transports one measure to the other in the least economical way, which contrasts to the optimal transportation (OT) map that finds the most economical way to transport from one measure to the other. Similar to the OT map, the WT map is the gradient of a strictly concave function, which also satisfies the Monge-Ampere equation. Furthermore, the WT map can be computed by convex optimization with the geometric variational approach like the OT map [10,15]. Intuitively, the OT/WT maps are solely determined by the Riemannian metric of the cortical surface, and they reflect the intrinsic geometric properties of the brain. Therefore, they tend to serve as continuous and refined shape difference measures.

Contributions. The contribution of the paper includes: (i) In this work, we generalize the Brenier theorem from the OT map to the newly proposed WT map, and rigorously show that the WT map is the gradient of a concave function that satisfies the Monge-Ampere equation. To the best of our knowledge, it is the first WT work in medical imaging research; (ii) We propose an efficient and robust computational algorithm to compute the WT map based on computational geometry. We further validate it with geometrically complicated human cerebral cortical surfaces; (iii) Our extensive experimental results show that the proposed WT cost performs better than the OT cost when discriminating Aβ+ AD patients from Aβ− CU subjects. This surprising result may help broaden univariate imaging biomarker research by opening up and addressing a new theme.

2 Theoretic Results

In this section, we briefly review the theoretical foundation of optimal transportation, then generalize the Brenier theorem and Yau's theorem to the worst transportation.

2.1 Optimal Transportation Map

Suppose $\Omega, \Omega^* \subset \mathbb{R}^d$ are domains in Euclidean space, with probability measures μ and ν respectively satisfying the equal total mass condition: $\mu(\Omega) = \nu(\Omega^*)$. The density functions are $d\mu = f(x)dx$ and $d\nu = g(y)dy$. The transportation map $T : \Omega \to \Omega^*$ is *measure preserving* if for any Borel set $B \subset \Omega^*$, $\int_{T^{-1}(B)} d\mu(x) = \int_B d\nu(y)$, denoted as $T_\# \mu = \nu$.

Monge raised the *optimal transportation map problem* [18]: given a *transportation cost function* $c : \Omega \times \Omega^* \to \mathbb{R}^+$, find a transportation map $T : \Omega \to \Omega^*$ that minimizes the *total transportation cost*,

$$(MP) \quad \min_T \left\{ \int_\Omega c(x, T(x)) : T : \Omega \to \Omega^*, T_\# \mu = \nu \right\}.$$

The minimizer is called the *optimal transportation map* (OT map). The total transportation cost of the OT map is called the *OT cost*.

Theorem 1 (Brenier [6]). *Given the measures μ and ν with compact supports $\Omega, \Omega^* \subset \mathbb{R}^d$ with equal total mass $\mu(\Omega) = \nu(\Omega^*)$, the corresponding density functions $f, g \in L^1(\mathbb{R}^d)$, and the cost function $c(x, y) = \frac{1}{2}|x - y|^2$, then the optimal transportation map T from μ to ν exists and is unique. It is the gradient of a convex function $u : \Omega \to \mathbb{R}$, the so-called Brenier potential. u is unique up to adding a constant, and $T = \nabla u$.*

If the Brenier potential is C^2, then by the measure preserving condition, it satisfies the Monge-Ampère equation,

$$\det D^2 u(x) = \frac{f(x)}{g \circ \nabla u(x)}. \tag{1}$$

where $D^2 u$ is the Hessian matrix of u.

2.2 Worst Transportation Map

With the same setup, the worst transportation problem can be formulated as follows: given the transportation cost function $c : \Omega \times \Omega^* \to \mathbb{R}^+$, find a measure preserving map $T : \Omega \to \Omega^*$ that maximizes the total transportation cost,

$$(WP) \quad \max_{T} \left\{ \int_{\Omega} c(x, T(x)) : T : \Omega \to \Omega^*, T_{\#}\mu = \nu \right\}.$$

The maximizer is called the *worst transportation map*. The transportation cost of the WT map is called the *worst transportation cost* between the measures. In the following, we generalize the Brenier theorem to the WT map.

Theorem 2 (Worst Transportation Map). *Given the probability measures μ and ν with compact supports $\Omega, \Omega^* \subset \mathbb{R}^d$ respectively with equal total mass $\mu(\Omega) = \nu(\Omega^*)$, and assume the corresponding density functions $f, g \in L^1(\mathbb{R}^d)$, the cost function $c(x, y) = \frac{1}{2}|x - y|^2$, then the **worst** transportation map exists and is unique. It is the gradient of a **concave** function $u : \Omega \to \mathbb{R}$, where u is the worst Brenier potential function, unique up to adding a constant. The WT map is given by $T = \nabla u$. Furthermore, if u is C^2, then it satisfies the Monge-Ampère equation in Eq. (1).*

Proof. Suppose $T : \Omega \to \Omega^*$ is a measure-preserving map, $T_{\#}\mu = \nu$. Consider the total transportation cost,

$$\int_{\Omega} |x - T(x)|^2 d\mu = \int_{\Omega} |x|^2 d\mu + \int_{\Omega} |T(x)|^2 d\mu - 2 \int_{\Omega} \langle x, T(x) \rangle d\mu$$

$$= \int_{\Omega} |x|^2 d\mu + \int_{\Omega^*} |y|^2 d\nu - 2 \int_{\Omega} \langle x, T(x) \rangle d\mu, \quad \text{with } y = T(x).$$

Therefore, maximizing the transportation cost is equivalent to $\min_{T_{\#}\mu = \nu} \int_{\Omega} \langle x, T(x) \rangle d\mu$. With the Kantorovich formula, this is equivalent to finding the following transportation plan $\gamma : \Omega \times \Omega^* \to \mathbb{R}$,

$$\min_{\gamma} \left\{ \int_{\Omega \times \Omega^*} \langle x, y \rangle d\gamma, (\pi_x)_{\#}\gamma = \mu, (\pi_y)_{\#}\gamma = \nu \right\},$$

where π_x, π_y are the projections from $\Omega \times \Omega^*$ to Ω and Ω^* respectively. By duality, this is equivalent to $\max\{J(u, v), (u, v) \in K\}$, where the energy $J(u, v) := \int_{\Omega} u(x)f(x)dx + \int_{\Omega^*} v(y)g(y)dy$, and the functional space $K := \{(u, v) : u(x) + v(y) \leq \langle x, y \rangle\}$. Now we define the c-transform,

$$u^c(y) := \inf_{x \in \bar{\Omega}} \langle x, y \rangle - u(x). \tag{2}$$

Fixing x, $\langle x, y \rangle - u(x)$ is a linear function, hence $u^c(y)$ is the lower envelope of a group of linear functions, and thus is a concave function with Lipschitz condition (since the gradient of each linear function is $x \in \bar{\Omega}$, $\bar{\Omega}$ is bounded). We construct a sequence of function pairs $\{(u_k, v_k)\}$, where $u_k = v^c_{k-1}, v_k = u^c_k$. Then $J(u_k, v_k)$ increases monotonously, and the Lipschitz function pairs (u_k, v_k)

converge to (u, v), which is the maximizer of J. Since u and v are c-transforms of each other, we have

$$u(x) + v(T(x)) = \langle x, T(x) \rangle. \tag{3}$$

This shows the existence of the solution.

From the definition of c-transform in Eq. (2), we obtain $v(y) = \inf_{x \in \bar{\Omega}} \langle x, y \rangle - u(x)$. Since $u(x)$ is concave and almost everywhere differentiable, we have $\nabla_x \langle x, y \rangle - \nabla u(x) = 0$, which implies that $y = T(x) = \nabla u(x)$. Therefore, the WT map is the gradient of the worst Brenier potential u.

Next, we show the uniqueness of the WT map. Suppose there are two maximizers $(\varphi, \psi) \in K$ and $(u, v) \in K$, because $J(u, v)$ is linear, therefore $\frac{1}{2}(\varphi + u, \psi + v) \in K$ is also a maximizer. Assume

$$\varphi(x_0) + \psi(y_0) = \langle x_0, y_0 \rangle, \varphi(x_0) + \psi(y) < \langle x_0, y \rangle, \forall y \neq y_0$$
$$u(x_0) + v(z_0) = \langle x_0, z_0 \rangle, u(x_0) + v(z) < \langle x_0, z \rangle, \forall z \neq z_0.$$

If $y_0 \neq z_0$, then $\forall y$, $1/2(\varphi + u)(x_0) + 1/2(\psi + v)(y) < \langle x_0, y \rangle$. But $(\frac{1}{2}(\varphi + u), \frac{1}{2}(\psi + v))$ is also a maximizer, this contradicts to the Eq. (3). This shows the uniqueness of the WT map.

Finally, u is concave and piecewise linear, therefore by Alexandrov's theorem [2], it is almost everywhere C^2. Moreover, the WT map $T = \nabla u$ is measure-preserving and $T_{\#}\mu = \nu$, thus we have

$$\det(DT)(x) = \frac{f(x)}{g \circ T(x)} \implies \det(D^2 u)(x) = \frac{f(x)}{g \circ \nabla u(x)}$$

This completes the proof. □

2.3   Geometric Variational Method

If u is not smooth, we can still define the Alexandrov solution. The sub-gradient of a convex function u at x is defined as

$$\partial u(x) := \left\{ p \in \mathbb{R}^d : u(z) \geq \langle p, z - x \rangle + u(x), \forall z \in \Omega \right\}$$

The sub-gradient defines a set-valued map: $\partial u : \Omega \to 2^{\Omega^*}$, $x \mapsto \partial u(x)$. We can use the sub-gradient to replace the gradient map in Eq. (1), and define

Definition 1 (Alexandrov Solution). *A convex function* $u : \Omega \to \mathbb{R}$ *satisfies the equation* $(\partial u)_{\#}\mu = \nu$, *or* $\mu((\partial u)^{-1}(B)) = \nu(B)$, $\forall Borel$ *set* $B \subset \Omega^*$, *then* u *is called an Alexandrov solution to the Monge-Ampère equation Eq. (1).*

The work of [10] proves a geometric variational approach for computing the Alexandrov solution of the optimal transportation problem.

Semi-discrete OT/WT Maps. Suppose the source measure is (Ω, μ), Ω is a compact convex domain with non-empty interior in $\mathbb{R}^d$ and the density function $f(x)$ is continuous (Fig. 1(a) gives an example). The target discrete measure (Ω^*, ν) is defined as $\nu = \sum_{i=1}^{n} \nu_i \delta(y - p_i)$, where $p_i \subset \mathbb{R}^d$ are distinct n points with $\nu_i > 0$ and $\sum_{i=1}^{n} \nu_i = \mu(\Omega)$ (Fig. 1(c) shows an example with the discrete measure coming from the 3D surface of Fig. 1(b)). Alexandrov [2] claims that there exists a *height vector* $\mathbf{h} = (h_1, \ldots, h_n) \in \mathbb{R}^n$, so that the upper envelope $u_{\mathbf{h}}$ of the hyper-planes $\{\pi_i(x) := \langle x, p_i \rangle + h_i\}_{i=1}^{n}$ gives an open convex polytope $P(\mathbf{h})$, the volume of the projection of the i-th facet of $P(\mathbf{h})$ in Ω equals to $\nu_i \; \forall i = 1, 2, \ldots, n$. Furthermore, this convex polytope is unique up to a vertical translation. In fact, Yau's work [10] pointed out that the Alexandrov convex polytope $P(\mathbf{h})$, or equivalently the upper envelop $u_{\mathbf{h}}$ is exactly the Brenier potential, whose gradient gives the OT map shown in Fig. 1(d).

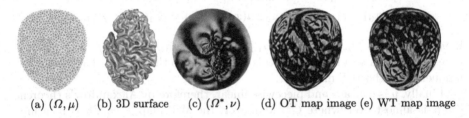

(a) (Ω, μ) (b) 3D surface   (c) (Ω^*, ν) (d) OT map image (e) WT map image

Fig. 1. The OT map and WT map from the source measure to the target measure given by the 3D surface.

Theorem 3 (Yau et al. [10]). *Let $\Omega \in \mathbb{R}^d$ be a compact convex domain, $\{p_1, ..., p_n\}$ be a set of distinct points in $\mathbb{R}^d$ and $f : \Omega \to \mathbb{R}$ be a positive continuous function. Then for any $\nu_1, \ldots, \nu_n > 0$ with $\sum_{i=1}^{n} \nu_i = \int_{\Omega} f(x)dx$, there exists $\mathbf{h} = (h_1, h_2, \ldots, h_n) \in \mathbb{R}^n$, unique up to adding a constant $(c, c, \ldots, c)$, so that $\mu(W_i(\mathbf{h}) \cap \Omega) = \int_{W_i(\mathbf{h}) \cap \Omega} f(x)dx = \nu_i, \; \forall \; i = 1, 2, \ldots, n$. The height vector $\mathbf{h}$ is exactly the minimum of the following convex function*

$$E(\mathbf{h}) = \int_0^h \sum_{i=1}^{n} \mu(W_i(h) \cap \Omega) dh_i - \sum_{i=1}^{n} h_i \nu_i \qquad (4)$$

on the open convex set (admissible solution space)

$$\mathcal{H} = \{\mathbf{h} \in \mathbb{R}^n | \mu(W_i(\mathbf{h}) \cap \Omega) > 0 \; \forall i = 1, 2, \ldots, n\} \bigcap \left\{ \mathbf{h} \in \mathbb{R}^n | \sum_{i=1}^{n} h_i = 0 \right\}. \quad (5)$$

Furthermore, the gradient map $\nabla u_{\mathbf{h}}$ minimizes the quadratic cost $\frac{1}{2} \int_{\Omega} |x - T(x)|^2 f(x)dx$ among all the measure preserving maps $T : (\Omega, \mu) \to (\mathbb{R}^d, \nu = \sum_{i=1}^{n} \nu_i \delta_{p_i}), T_{\#}\mu = \nu$.

Theorem 4 (Semi-Discrete Worst Transportation Map). *Let $\Omega \in \mathbb{R}^d$ be a compact convex domain, $\{p_1, ..., p_n\}$ be a set of distinct points in $\mathbb{R}^d$ and $f : \Omega \to \mathbb{R}$ be a positive continuous function. Then for any $\nu_1, \ldots, \nu_n > 0$ with $\sum_{i=1}^{n} \nu_i = \int_\Omega f(x)dx$, there exists $\mathbf{h} = (h_1, h_2, \ldots, h_n) \in \mathbb{R}^n$, unique up to adding a constant $(c, c, \ldots, c)$, so that $\mu(W_i(\mathbf{h}) \cap \Omega) = \int_{W_i(\mathbf{h}) \cap \Omega} f(x)dx = \nu_i, \forall i$. The height vector $\mathbf{h}$ is exactly the **maximum** of the following concave function*

$$E(\mathbf{h}) = \int_0^h \sum_{i=1}^n \mu(W_i(\mathbf{h}) \cap \Omega)dh_i - \sum_{i=1}^n h_i \nu_i \tag{6}$$

*on the open convex set (admissible solution space) defined on Eq. (5). Furthermore, the gradient map $\nabla u_{\mathbf{h}}$ **maximizes** the quadratic cost $\frac{1}{2}\int_\Omega |x - T(x)|^2 f(x)dx$ among all the measure preserving maps $T : (\Omega, \mu) \to (\mathbb{R}^d, \nu = \sum_{i=1}^n \nu_i \delta_{p_i})$, $T_{\#}\mu = \nu$.*

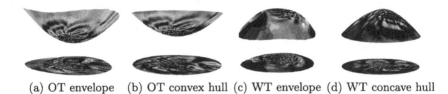

(a) OT envelope   (b) OT convex hull (c) WT envelope (d) WT concave hull

Fig. 2. The Brenier potential for OT map and WT map, equivalently the upper (a) and lower (c) envelopes. The Legendre dual of the potential of the OT map and WT map, equivalently the lower (b) and upper (d) convex hulls.

Proof. Given the height vector $\mathbf{h} = (h_1, h_2, \cdots, h_n)$, $\mathbf{h} \in \mathcal{H}$, we construct the upper convex hull of $v_i(\mathbf{h}) = (p_i, -h_i)$'s (see Fig. 2(d)), each vertex corresponds to a plane $\pi_i(\mathbf{h}, x) := \langle p_i, x \rangle + h_i$. The convex hull is dual to the lower envelope of the plane $\pi_i(\mathbf{h}, \cdot)$ (see Fig. 2(c)), which is the graph of the concave function $u_{\mathbf{h}}(x) := \min_{i=1}^n \{\langle p_i, x \rangle + h_i\}$. The projection of the lower envelope induces a farthest power diagram $\mathcal{D}(\mathbf{h})$ (see Fig. 2(c)) with $\Omega = \bigcup_{i=1}^n W_i(\mathbf{h}) \cap \Omega$, $W_i(\mathbf{h}) := \{x \in \mathbb{R}^d$ and $\nabla u_{\mathbf{h}}(x) = p_i\}$.

The μ-volume of each cell is defined as

$$w_i(\mathbf{h}) := \mu(W_i(\mathbf{h}) \cap \Omega) = \int_{W_i(\mathbf{h}) \cap \Omega} f(x)dx. \tag{7}$$

Similar to Lemma 2.5 in [10], by direct computation we can show the symmetric relation holds:

$$\frac{\partial w_i(\mathbf{h})}{\partial h_j} = \frac{\partial w_j(\mathbf{h})}{\partial h_i} = \frac{1}{|p_i - p_j|} \int_{W_i(\mathbf{h}) \cap W_j(\mathbf{h}) \cap \Omega} f(x)ds. \tag{8}$$

This shows the differential form $\omega = \sum_{i=1}^n w_i(\mathbf{h})dh_i$ is a closed one-form. As in [10], by Brunn-Minkowski inequality, one can show that the admissible height space $\mathcal{H}$ in Eq. (5) is convex and simply connected. Hence ω is exact. So the energy $E(\mathbf{h}) := \int_0^{\mathbf{h}} \omega$ is well defined and its Hessian matrix is given by

$$\frac{\partial^2 E(\mathbf{h})}{\partial h_i \partial h_j} = \frac{w_i(\mathbf{h})}{\partial h_j} \geq 0, \tag{9}$$

Since the total volume of all the cells is the constant $\mu(\Omega)$, we obtain

$$\frac{\partial^2 E(\mathbf{h})}{\partial h_i^2} = -\sum_{j \neq i} \frac{w_i(\mathbf{h})}{\partial h_j} < 0. \tag{10}$$

Therefore, the Hessian matrix is negative definite in $\mathcal{H}$ and the energy is strictly concave in $\mathcal{H}$. By adding a linear term, the following energy is still strictly concave,

$$E(\mathbf{h}) = \int_0^{\mathbf{h}} \sum_{i=1}^n w_i(\mathbf{h}) dh_i - \sum_{i=1}^n \nu_i h_i.$$

The gradient of $E(\mathbf{h})$ is given by

$$\nabla E(\mathbf{h}) = (w_1(\mathbf{h}) - \nu_1, w_2(\mathbf{h}) - \nu_2, \cdots, w_n(\mathbf{h}) - \nu_n). \tag{11}$$

On the boundary of $\mathcal{H}$, there is an empty cell $W_k(\mathbf{h})$, and the k-th component of the gradient is $-\nu_k$, which points to the interior of $\mathcal{H}$. This shows that the global unique maximum of the energy is in the interior of $\mathcal{H}$. At the maximum point $\mathbf{h}^*$, $\nabla E(\mathbf{h}^*)$ is zero and $w_i(\mathbf{h}^*) = \nu_i$. Thus, $\mathbf{h}^*$ is the unique solution to the semi-discrete worst transportation problem, as shown in Fig. 1(e).   □

3   Computational Algorithms

This section gives a unified algorithm to compute both the optimal and the worst transportation maps based on convex geometry [5].

3.1   Basic Concepts from Computational Geometry

A hyperplane in $\mathbb{R}^{d+1}$ is represented as $\pi(x) := \langle p, x \rangle + h$. Given a family of hyperplanes $\{\pi_i(x) = \langle p_i, x \rangle + h_i\}_{i=1}^n$, their *upper envelope* of $\{\pi_i\}_{i=1}^n$ is the graph of the function $u(x) := \max_{i=1}^n \{\langle p_i, x \rangle + h_i\}$; the *lower envelope* is the graph of the function $u(x) := \min_{i=1}^n \{\langle p_i, x \rangle + h_i\}$; the *Legendre dual* of u is defined as $u^*(y) := \max_{x \in \mathbb{R}^d} \langle x, y \rangle - u(x)$. The c-transform of u is defined as

$$u^c(y) := \min_{x \in \mathbb{R}^d} \langle x, y \rangle - u(x). \tag{12}$$

Each hyperplane $\pi_i(x)$ has a dual point in $\mathbb{R}^{d+1}$, namely $\pi_i^* := (p_i, -h_i)$. The graph of u^* is the *lower convex hull* of the dual points $\{\pi_i^*\}_{i=1}^n$. And the graph of u^c is the *upper convex hull* of the dual points $\{\pi_i^*\}_{i=1}^n$. (i) The projection of the upper envelope induces a *nearest power diagram* $\mathcal{D}(\Omega)$ of Ω with

$\Omega = \bigcup_{i=1}^{n} W_i(\mathbf{h})$ and $W_i(\mathbf{h}) := \{x \in \Omega | \nabla u(x) = p_i\}$. And the projection of the lower convex hull u^* induces a *nearest weighted Delaunay triangulation* $T(\Omega^*)$ of Ω^*. (*ii*) The projection of the lower envelope induces a *farthest power diagram* $\mathcal{D}^c$ of Ω. And the projection of the upper convex hull u^c induces a *farthest weighted Delaunay triangulation* $T^c(\Omega^*)$. $\mathcal{D}(\Omega)$ and $T(\Omega^*)$ are dual to each other, namely p_i connects p_j in $T(\Omega^*)$ if and only if $W_i(\mathbf{h})$ is adjacent to $W_j(\mathbf{h})$. Similarly, $\mathcal{D}^c$ and T^c are also dual to each other. Figure 2 shows these basic concepts.

3.2   Algorithms Based on Computational Geometry

Pipeline. The algorithm in Algorithm 1 mainly optimizes the energy $E(\mathbf{h})$ in the admissible solution space $\mathcal{H}$ using Newton's method. At the beginning, for the OT (WT) map, the height vector $\mathbf{h}_0$ is initialized as $h_i = -\frac{1}{2}|p_i|^2$ ($h_i = \frac{1}{2}|p_i|^2$). At each step, the convex hull of $\{(p_i, -h_i)\}_{i=1}^{n}$ is constructed. For the OT (WT) map, the lower (upper) convex hull is projected to induce a nearest (farthest) weighted Delaunay triangulation T of $\{p_i\}$'s. Each vertex $v_i(\mathbf{h}) = (p_i, -h_i)$ on the convex hull corresponds to a supporting plane $\pi_i(\mathbf{h}, x) = \langle p_i, x \rangle + h_i$, each face $[v_i, v_j, v_k]$ in the convex hull is dual to the vertex in the envelope, which is the intersection point of π_i, π_j and π_k. For the OT (WT) map, the lower (upper) convex hull is dual to the upper (lower) envelope, and the upper (lower) envelope induces the nearest (farthest) power diagram. The relationship of the convex hulls and the envelopes are shown in Fig. 2.

   Then we compute the μ-volume of each power cell using Eq. (7), the gradient of the energy Eq. (6) is given by Eq. (11). The Hessian matrix $\text{Hess}(E(\mathbf{h}))$ can be constructed using Eq. (9) for off diagonal elements and Eq. (10) for diagonal elements. The Hessian matrices of the OT map and the WT map differ by a sign. Then we solve the following linear system to find the update direction,

$$\text{Hess}(E(\mathbf{h}))\mathbf{d} = \nabla E(\mathbf{h}). \tag{13}$$

Next we need to determine the step length λ, such that $\mathbf{h} + \lambda\mathbf{d}$ is still in the admissible solution space $\mathcal{H}$ in Eq. (5). Firstly, we set $\lambda = -1$ for OT map and $\lambda = +1$ for WT map. Then we compute the power diagram $\mathcal{D}(\mathbf{h} + \lambda\mathbf{d})$. If some cells disappear in $\mathcal{D}(\mathbf{h} + \lambda\mathbf{d})$, then it means $\mathbf{h} + \lambda\mathbf{d}$ exceeds the admissible space. In this case, we shrink λ by half, $\lambda \leftarrow \frac{1}{2}\lambda$, and recompute the power diagram with $\mathbf{h} + \lambda\mathbf{d}$. We repeat this process to find an appropriate step length λ and update $\mathbf{h} = \mathbf{h} + \lambda\mathbf{d}$. We repeat the above procedures until the norm of the gradient $\|\nabla E(\mathbf{h})\|$ is less than a prescribed threshold ε. As a result, the upper (lower) envelope is the Brenier potential, the desired OT(WT) mapping maps each nearest (farthest) power cell $W_i(\mathbf{h})$ to the corresponding point p_i.

Convex Hull. In order to compute the power diagram, we need to compute the convex hull [5]. The conventional method [15] computes the convex hull from the scratch at each iteration, which is the most time-consuming step in the algorithm

---

Algorithm 1: Worst/Optimal Transportation Map

Input: (Ω, μ), $\{(p_i, \nu_i)\}_{i=1}^n$
Output: The optimizer $\mathbf{h}$ of the Brenier potential $u_{\mathbf{h}}$
Normalize $\{p_1, p_2, \ldots, p_n\}$ to be inside Ω by translation and scaling;
Initialize $h_i = \pm\langle p_i, p_i\rangle/2$ for WT/OT;
while *true* **do**

    Compute the upper (lower) convex hull of $\{(p_i, -h_i)\}_{i=1}^n$ for WT/OT map;

    Compute the lower (upper) envelope of the planes $\{\langle p_i, x\rangle + h_i\}_{i=1}^n$ for WT/OT map;

    Project the lower (upper) envelope to Ω to get the farthest (nearest) power diagram $\Omega = \bigcup_{i=1}^n W_i(\mathbf{h})$ for WT/OT map ;

    Compute the μ-volume of each cell $w_i(\mathbf{h}) = \mu(W_i(\mathbf{h}))$ using Eqn. (7);

    Compute the gradient of the energy $E(\mathbf{h})$, $\nabla E(\mathbf{h}) = (w_i(\mathbf{h}) - \nu_i)$;

    if $\|\nabla E(\mathbf{h})\| < \varepsilon$ **then**

        | return $\mathbf{h}$;

    end

    Compute the μ-lengths of the power Voronoi edges $W_i(\mathbf{h}) \cap W_j(\mathbf{h}) \cap \Omega$ using Eqn. (8);

    Construct the Hessian matrix of the energy $E(\mathbf{h})$ for WT/OT map:

$$\text{Hess}(E(\mathbf{h})) := \frac{\partial^2 E(\mathbf{h})}{\partial h_i \partial h_j} = \pm\frac{\mu(W_i(\mathbf{h}) \cap W_j(\mathbf{h}))}{|y_i - y_j|}$$

    Solve the linear system: $\text{Hess}(E(\mathbf{h}))\mathbf{d} = \nabla E(\mathbf{h})$;

    $\lambda \leftarrow \pm 1$ for WT/OT map;

    repeat

        | Compute the farthest (nearest) power diagram $\mathcal{D}(\mathbf{h} + \lambda\mathbf{d})$ for WT/OT map;

        | $\lambda \leftarrow \frac{1}{2}\lambda$;

    until *no empty power cell*;

    Update the height vector $\mathbf{h} \leftarrow \mathbf{h} + \lambda\mathbf{d}$;

end

---

pipeline. Actually, at the later stages of the optimization, the combinatorial structure of the convex hull does not change much. Therefore, in the proposed method, we only locally update the connectivity of the convex hull. Basically, we check the local power Delaunay property of each edge, and push the non-Delaunay edges to a stack. While the stack is non-empty, we pop the top edge and check whether it is local power Delaunay, if it is then we continue, otherwise we flip it. Furthermore, if the flipping causes some overlapped triangles, we flip it back. By repeating this procedure, we will finally update the convex hull and project it to the weighted Delaunay triangulation. If in the end, the stack is empty, but there are still non-local power Delaunay edges, then it means that the height vector $\mathbf{h}$ is outside the admissible space $\mathcal{H}$ and some power cells are empty. In this scenario, we reduce the step length λ by half and try again.

Subdivision. With a piecewise linear source density, we need to compute the μ-area of the power cells and the μ-length of the power diagram edges. The source measure is represented by a piecewise linear density function, defined on a triangulation, as shown in Fig. 3(a). Therefore, we need to compute the overlay (Fig. 3(c)) of the triangulation (Fig. 3(a)) and the power diagram (Fig. 3(b)) in each iteration. This step is technically challenging. If we use a naive approach to compute the intersection between each triangle and each power cell, the complexity is very high. Therefore, we use a Bentley-Ottmann type sweep line approach [4] to improve the efficiency. Basically, all the planar points are sorted, such that the left-lower points are less than the right-upper ones. Then for each cell we find the minimal vertex and maximal vertex. A sweep line goes from left to right. When the sweep line hits the minimal vertex of a cell, the cell is born; when the sweep line passes the maximal vertex, the cell dies. We also keep the data structure to store all the alive triangles and cells, and compute the intersections among them. This greatly improves the computation efficiency.

4 Experiments

To show the practicality of our framework for structural MR images as well as the robustness over large brain image datasets, we aim to use the WT cost to statistically discriminate $A\beta+$ AD patients and $A\beta-$ CU subjects.

Data Preparation. Brain sMRI data are obtained from the Alzheimer's Disease Neuroimaging Initiative (ADNI) database [1], from which we use 81 $A\beta+$ AD patients and 110 $A\beta-$ CU subjects. The ADNI florbetapir PET data is processed using AVID pipeline [12] and later converted to centiloid scales. A centiloid cutoff of 37.1 is used to determine amyloid positivity [9]. The sMRIs are preprocessed using FreeSurfer [8] to reconstruct the pial cortical surfaces and we only use the left cerebral surfaces. For each surface, we remove the corpus callosum region which has little morphometry information related to AD, so that the final surface becomes a topological disk. Further, we compute the conformal mapping ϕ from the surface S to the planar disk $\mathbb{D}$ with the discrete

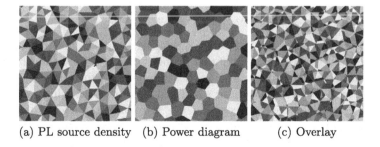

(a) PL source density   (b) Power diagram   (c) Overlay

Fig. 3. The subdivision algorithm computes the subdivision of the source triangulation, where the density function is defined, and the power diagram.

surface Ricci flow [19]. To eliminate the Mobius ambiguity, we map the vertex
with the largest z coordinate on S to the origin of the disk, and the vertex with
the largest z coordinate on the boundary ∂S to $(0,1)$ coordinate of $\mathbb{D}$.

Computation Process. In the experiment, we randomly select one subject
from the $A\beta-$ CU subjects as the template, and then compute both the OT
costs and WT costs from the template to all other cortical surfaces. The source
measure is piecewisely defined on the parameter space of the template, namely
the planar disk. The measure of each triangle $[\phi(v_i), \phi(v_j), \phi(v_k)]$ on the disk is
equal to the corresponding area of the triangle $[v_i, v_j, v_k]$ on S. Then the total
source measure is normalized to be 1. For the target surface M, the measure is
defined on the planar points $y_i = \phi(v_i)$ with $v_i \in M$. The discrete measure ν_i
corresponding to both v_i and y_i is given by $\nu_i = \frac{1}{3}\sum_{[v_i,v_j,v_k]\in M} area([v_i, v_j, v_k])$,
where $[v_i, v_j, v_k]$ represents a face adjacent to v_i on M in R^3. After normalization, the summation of the discrete measures will be equal to the measure of the
planar disk, namely 1. Then we compute both the OT cost and the WT cost
from the planar source measure induced by the template surface to the target
discrete measures given by the ADs and CUs. Finally, we run a permutation test
with 50,000 random assignments of subjects to groups to estimate the statistical
significance of both measurements. Furthermore, we also compute surface areas
and cortical volumes as the measurements for comparison and the same permutation test is applied. The p-value for the WT cost is 2e−5, which indicates
that the WT-based univariate biomarkers are statistically significant between
two groups and they may be used as a reliable indicator to separate two groups.
It is worth noting that it is also far better than that of the surface area, cortical
volume and OT cost, which are given by 0.7859, 0.5033 and 0.7783, respectively,
as shown in Table 1.

Table 1. The permutation test results with surface area, surface volume, OT cost and
WT cost for group difference between those of $A\beta+$ ADs and $A\beta-$ CUs.

Method	Surface area	Cortical volume	OT Cost	WT Cost
p-value	0.7859	0.5033	0.7783	**2e-5**

Our results show that the WT cost is promising as an AD imaging biomarker.
It is unexpected to see that it performs far better than OT. A plausible explanation is that although human brain cortical shapes are generally homogeneous,
the AD-induced atrophy may have some common patterns which are consistently exaggerated in the WT cost but OT is robust to these changes. More
experiments and theoretical study are warranted to validate our observation.

5   Conclusion

In this work, we propose a new algorithm to compute the WT cost and validate its potential as a new AD imaging biomarker. In the future, we will validate our framework with more brain images and offer more theoretical interpretation to its improved statistical power.

References

1. Adni database. http://adni.loni.usc.edu/
2. Alexandrov, A.D.: Convex polyhedra Translated from the 1950 Russian edition by N. S. Dairbekov, S. S. Kutateladze and A. B. Sossinsky. Springer Monographs in Mathematics. Springer, Heidelberg (2005). https://doi.org/10.1007/b137434
3. Ansart, M., et al.: Reduction of recruitment costs in preclinical AD trials: validation of automatic pre-screening algorithm for brain amyloidosis. Stat. Methods Med. Res. **29**(1), 151–164 (2020)
4. Bentley, J.L., Ottmann, T.A.: Algorithms for reporting and counting geometric intersections. IEEE Trans. Comput. **28**, 643–647 (1979)
5. de Berg, M., Cheong, O., van Kreveld, M., Overmars, M.: Computational Geometry: Algorithms and Applications, 3rd edn. Springer, Heidelberg (2008). https://doi.org/10.1007/978-3-540-77974-2
6. Brenier, Y.: Polar factorization and monotone rearrangement of vector-valued functions. Commun. Pure Appl. Math. **44**(4), 375–417 (1991)
7. Brookmeyer, R., Johnson, E., Ziegler-Graham, K., Arrighi, H.M.: Forecasting the global burden of Alzheimer's disease. Alzheimers Dement. **3**(3), 186–91 (2007)
8. Fischl, B., Sereno, M.I., Dale, A.M.: Cortical surface-based analysis. II: inflation, flattening, and a surface-based coordinate system. Neuroimage **9**(2), 195–207 (1999)
9. Fleisher, A.S., et al.: Using positron emission tomography and florbetapir F18 to image cortical amyloid in patients with mild cognitive impairment or dementia due to Alzheimer disease. Arch. Neurol. **68**, 1404–1411 (2011)
10. Gu, D.X., Luo, F., Sun, J., Yau, S.-T.: Variational principles for Minkowski type problems, discrete optimal transport, and discrete Monge-Ampère equations. Asian J. Math. **20**, 383–398 (2016)
11. Hyman, B.T.: Amyloid-dependent and amyloid-independent stages of Alzheimer disease. Arch. Neurol. **68**(8), 1062–4 (2011)
12. Navitsky, M., et al.: Standardization of amyloid quantitation with florbetapir standardized uptake value ratios to the Centiloid scale. Alzheimers Dement **14**(12), 1565–1571 (2018)
13. Pekkala, T., et al.: Detecting amyloid positivity in elderly with increased risk of cognitive decline. Front. Aging Neurosci. **12**, 228 (2020)
14. Shi, J., Wang, Y.: Hyperbolic Wasserstein distance for shape indexing. IEEE Trans. Pattern Anal. Mach. Intell. **42**(6), 1362–1376 (2020)
15. Su, Z., et al.: Optimal mass transport for shape matching and comparison. IEEE Trans. Pattern Anal. Mach. Intell. **37**, 2246–2259 (2015)
16. Tosun, D., Joshi, S., Weiner, M.W.: Multimodal MRI-based imputation of the aβ+ in early mild cognitive impairment. Ann. Clin. Transl. Neurol. **1**, 160–170 (2014)
17. Tu, Y., et al.: Computing univariate neurodegenerative biomarkers with volumetric optimal transportation: a pilot study. Neuroinformatics **18**(4), 531–548 (2020). https://doi.org/10.1007/s12021-020-09459-7

18. Villani, C.: Optimal Transport: Old and New, 1st edn. Grundlehren der mathematischen Wissenschaften, vol. 338. Springer, Heidelberg (2008). https://doi.org/10.1007/978-3-540-71050-9
19. Wang, Y., et al.: Brain surface conformal parameterization with the Ricci flow. IEEE Trans. Med. Imaging **31**(2), 251–264 (2012)

Geodesic B-score for Improved Assessment of Knee Osteoarthritis

Felix Ambellan$^{(\boxtimes)}$ (ID), Stefan Zachow (ID), and Christoph von Tycowicz (ID)

Visual and Data-Centric Computing, Zuse Institute Berlin, Berlin, Germany
{ambellan,zachow,vontycowicz}@zib.de

Abstract. Three-dimensional medical imaging enables detailed under-standing of osteoarthritis structural status. However, there remains a vast need for automatic, thus, reader-independent measures that provide reliable assessment of subject-specific clinical outcomes. To this end, we derive a consistent generalization of the recently proposed B-score to Riemannian shape spaces. We further present an algorithmic treatment yielding simple, yet efficient computations allowing for analysis of large shape populations with several thousand samples. Our intrinsic formulation exhibits improved discrimination ability over its Euclidean counterpart, which we demonstrate for predictive validity on assessing risks of total knee replacement. This result highlights the potential of the geodesic B-score to enable improved personalized assessment and stratification for interventions.

Keywords: Statistical shape analysis · Osteoarthritis · Geometric statistics · Riemannian manifolds

1 Introduction

Osteoarthritis (OA) is a highly prevalent, degenerative joint disease with a considerable societal and economic impact, in addition to the physical and psychological sequelae it causes in affected individuals. The pathophysiology of OA involves several tissues and is primarily associated with a deterioration of articular cartilage as well as related changes in the underlying bone and at the joint margins. While OA can affect any joint, knee OA accounts for more than 80% of the global disease burden [33]. There exist various ways of characterizing OA in the literature ranging from subjective assessment to clinical and radiographic ones, albeit with a limited degree of concordance between them. In practice, plain radiography remains a mainstay for the diagnosis of OA with the Kellgren and Lawrence (KL) grading system [19] posing the de-facto standard classification scheme. However, due to its sensitivity on acquisition method and rater reliability, which is reflected in the high number of disagreements between the readers (cf. [6]), there is a dire need for accurate and reliable assessment of OA status.

Whereas plain radiography only provides 2-dimensional projections, advances in imaging technologies, especially in magnetic resonance imaging (MRI), have

© Springer Nature Switzerland AG 2021
A. Feragen et al. (Eds.): IPMI 2021, LNCS 12729, pp. 177–188, 2021.
https://doi.org/10.1007/978-3-030-78191-0_14

enabled the understanding of 3-dimensional (3D) OA structural pathology. In particular, bone shape derived from MRI has been found to be associated with radiographic structural progression [16], to predict radiographic onset of OA [23], and to discriminate knees w.r.t. osteophyte formation [31] and OA status [30]. These findings suggest that bone morphology validly relates to a broader construct of OA pathology. Furthermore, shape-based assessment holds the promise of reduced sensitivity on image appearance and data acquisition set-ups; e.g., systematic changes due to regular technology upgrades with full hardware replacements every 5 to 10 years. In this light, Bowes et al. [6] recently introduced a novel, geometrically derived measure to quantify knee OA from bone morphology termed *B-score*. Contrary to the semi-quantitative KL grade, the B-score is determined fully automatically from femur bone shape and, thus, does not suffer from the subjectivity of the practitioner. Being a continuous score it enables fine-grained stratification of OA-related structural changes and increases discrimination of risk for clinically important outcomes such as total knee replacement (TKR) surgery.

Despite these recent advances, the formulation of B-score builds upon the popular *active shape model* (ASM) [11] that treats shapes as elements of Euclidean spaces. However, such linearity assumptions are often inadequate for capturing the high, natural variability in biological shapes (see [1] and the references therein). In particular, sizable empirical improvements can be observed when taking the inherent, geometric structure of shape spaces into account [4, 12, 31, 34].

Since the pioneering work of Kendall [20], which introduced a rigorous mathematical foundation for shape spaces and statistics thereon, numerous approaches employing geometric as well as physical concepts such as Hausdorff distance [10], elasticity [27, 32, 34], and viscous flows [7, 15, 17] were devised. An overview of the various concepts can be found in the chapter by Rumpf and Wirth [28]. Another string of contributions–mainly within the field of computational anatomy–studies shapes in terms of deformations of the ambient space and we refer to [22] for a comprehensive survey. In general, these methods suffer from high computational costs and, hence, lack fast response rates limiting their practical applicability especially in large-scale morphological studies. To address these challenges, one line of work models shapes by a collection of elementary building blocks called primitives (e.g., triangles, M-reps etc.) [3, 13, 14, 30] with natural, geometric structure that effectively encodes local changes in shape. Performing intrinsic calculus on the uncoupled primitives allows for fast computations while, at the same time, accounting for the nonlinearity in shape variation. Within this category, Ambellan et al. [4] recently proposed a surface-theoretic approach that is invariant under Euclidean motion and, thus, is not susceptible to any bias due to misalignment.

Contributions. In this work, we derive a generalization of the recently proposed B-score to manifold shape spaces that adheres to the rich geometric structure thereof and at the same time is consistent with its Euclidean counterpart. To this end, we build upon a solid mathematical foundation employing concepts from differential geometry and geometric statistics. We further present an original Newton-type fixed point iteration for projection onto geodesics that is both simple to implement and computationally efficient. To the best of our knowledge, previous algorithms restrict to first-order descent schemes [29] or are tailored to special manifolds [9,18]. On the application side, we show that the derived geodesic B-score features improved predictive performance on assessing the risk of TKR surgery within 8 years using a single time point. This result highlights the potential of the Riemannian generalization to enable improved personalized assessment and stratification for interventions.

2   Background

2.1   Shape Space

Before we summarize the employed shape representation, we would like to emphasize that the derived concepts and algorithms provided in this work are not tailored towards a particular choice and are indeed applicable to general Riemannian shape spaces.

For experimental evaluation, we opt for the recently introduced fundamental coordinates model (FCM) [4]. This model is formulated within the commonly employed deformation-based morphometric framework in which shapes are expressed as deformations of a common reference surface. More precisely, a digital surface S is encoded via the orientation preserving deformation ϕ of a triangular surface mesh $\bar{S}$. For simplicial ϕ, the deformation gradient $\nabla\phi$ (also known as Jacobian matrix) is a 3×3 matrix of partial derivatives and constant on each triangle of $\bar{S}$. In analogy to surface theory, discrete first and second fundamental forms can be derived from $\nabla\phi$ that furnish a complete description of the intrinsic and extrinsic geometry of S. While the former takes the form of a piece-wise constant (one per triangle) field of 2×2 symmetric positive-definite matrices ($\text{Sym}^+(2)$), the latter is given by 3D rotations ($\text{SO}(3)$) associated with the edges. In particular, let m, n be the number of triangles and inner edges, then the resulting shape space is given as the product $\Sigma := \text{SO}(3)^n \times \text{Sym}^+(2)^m$. Remarkably, Σ can be equipped with a bi-invariant Lie group structure (by virtue of the log-Euclidean framework for $\text{Sym}^+(2)$ [5,25]) that lends itself for efficient computations of Riemannian operations. Furthermore, the FCM provides a Euclidean motion invariant–hence alignment-free–shape representation that assures valid shape instances even in presence of strong nonlinear variability.

2.2   Geometric Statistics

The nonlinear nature of shape spaces implies that there are no such familiar properties as vector space structure or global system of coordinates (that is, linear combinations of shapes do not generally lie in the space again and shape variations w.r.t. to different base shapes are not directly comparable). Consequently, core operations pervasive in machine learning and statistics often have to be generalized based on the geometry and specifics of the data at hand. Approaches that generalize statistical tools to non-Euclidean domains in order to leverage the intrinsic structure belong to the field of geometric statistics and we refer to [25] for an overview.

The simplest–yet also perhaps most fundamentally important–statistic is the sample mean, which estimates the center of a data set. Because a Riemannian manifold $\mathcal{M}$ has a distance $\text{dist}_{\mathcal{M}}$ (length of the shortest path connecting two points), we can characterize the mean as the point closest to the data points $x_1, \ldots, x_N \in \mathcal{M}$. This leads to the notion of (sample) Fréchet mean that is the minimizer of the sum-of-squared geodesic distances to the data:

$$\mu = \arg \min_{x \in \mathcal{M}} \sum_{i=1}^{N} \text{dist}_{\mathcal{M}}^2 (x, x_i).$$

While closed-form solutions exist in flat spaces, solving this least-squares problem in general requires iterative optimization routines. For geodesic manifolds, solutions always exist and are unique for well-localized data [25, Theorem 2.1–2.2].

Another fundamental problem is the (statistical) normalization of shape trajectories, i.e., smooth curves in shape space encoding e.g., soft-body motion of anatomical structures. Normalization of such trajectories into a common reference frame is a challenging task in curved spaces (due to holonomy). The aim is to preserve as much as possible of the structural variability, while allowing a precise comparison in a common geometric space. To this end, *parallel transport* [8] provides a promising approach with a strong mathematical foundation. Parallel transport allows to propagate a tangent vector (i.e., an infinitesimal shape change) along a path by preserving its properties w.r.t. the space geometry, such as a notion of parallelism.

3 Geodesic B-score

In this section, we derive a generalization of the recently proposed B-score [6] to Riemannian shape spaces and present a simple, yet effective computational scheme for the determination thereof. In doing so, our guiding principle is to obtain expressions that take the rich geometric structure of shape space into account (e.g., refraining from linearization) and at the same time are consistent with its Euclidean counterpart (i.e., agree with the original definition for the special case of flat vector spaces). We term the resulting quantity *geodesic B-score* and will refer to the original definition (respectively, its application in linear spaces) as *Euclidean B-score* whenever this distinction is necessary.

3.1 Generalization

At the core of the construction in [6] lies the projection to an *OA-vector* that is defined as the line passing through the mean shapes of populations with and

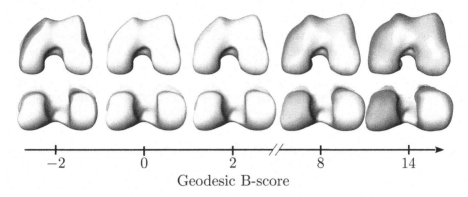

Fig. 1. Signed vertex deviation from mean shape of mixed-sex non-OA group along the OA-geodesic. Color-coding: $-1\,\text{mm}$ ▄▄▄▄▄▄▄▄ $5\,\text{mm}$, with neutral window (i.e., yellowish bone color) from $-0.3\,\text{mm}$ to $0.4\,\text{mm}$. (Color figure online)

without OA as determined by KL grades ≥ 2 and ≤ 1, respectively. While we can readily rely on the Fréchet mean, differential geometry provides us with a consistent notion of straight lines known as geodesics [8]. In particular, we define the OA-geodesic γ as the length minimizing geodesic between the Fréchet means of the two populations (which will be unique under the assumptions for the means and the observed overlap of both distributions [6,23]). A visualization of the OA-geodesic is provided in Fig. 1 (details on the underlying data are provided in Sect. 4.1). In order to determine the B-score for a shape $\sigma \in \Sigma$, we first perform an (intrinsic) projection onto the OA-geodesic:

$$\pi_\gamma(\sigma) := \arg\min_{x \in \gamma} \text{dist}_\Sigma^2(x, \sigma). \tag{1}$$

The signed distance of $\pi_\gamma(\sigma)$ along the OA-geodesic w.r.t. the non-OA mean (with positive values in direction of the OA mean) then yields the desired notion of geodesic B-score, i.e.,

$$B_{\gamma,\lambda}(\sigma) = \lambda\, g_{\gamma(0)} \left(\dot{\gamma}(0)/\|\dot{\gamma}(0)\|, \text{Log}_{\gamma(0)} \circ \pi_\gamma(\sigma) \right), \tag{2}$$

where λ is a positive weighting factor and g, Log denote the Riemannian metric, logarithmic map. In order to increase interpretability, we take a statistical approach that weights the distances in terms of their distribution within the non-OA population. More precisely, we employ the Mahalanobis distance such that λ is determined as the inverse of the standard deviation $\text{std}(\{B_{\gamma,1}(\sigma)|\sigma \in \mathcal{H}\})$ for the non-OA group $\mathcal{H}$. In fact, this statistical re-weighting relates the score to the natural morphological inter-subject variability and renders it unitless and scale-invariant.

3.2   Sex-Specific Reference

Females and males have systematically different bone shape [6] introducing a bias during estimation of the B-score. In line with the Euclidean B-score, we correct for this bias using sex-specific OA-geodesics determined by translating γ s.t. it passes through the separately computed non-OA mean shapes for each sex. As a geodesic is uniquely determined by a point and a direction (viz. tangent vector at that point), we perform parallel transport of the defining vector along the geodesic connecting the mixed-sex and the sex-specific mean of the respective non-OA group. Given sex-specific OA geodesics $\gamma^{\male}, \gamma^{\female}$ we also estimate weighting factors $\lambda^{\male}, \lambda^{\female}$ for each sex and define the B-score as

$$B(\sigma) = \begin{cases} B_{\gamma^{\female}, \lambda^{\female}}(\sigma), & \sigma \text{ female} \\ B_{\gamma^{\male}, \lambda^{\male}}(\sigma), & \sigma \text{ male.} \end{cases}$$

3.3 Algorithmic Treatment

Determining solutions to the projection problem in Eq. (1) does not admit closed-form expressions (except for the special case of constant curvature manifolds [9]), thus, requiring iterative optimization. However, this step is an essential ingredient for the computation of the geodesic B-score. In order to derive an efficient numerical scheme we assume (without loss of generality) $\gamma : t \mapsto \gamma(t) \in \Sigma$ to be an arc-length parameterized geodesic and express the projection problem as an unconstrained optimization over t with objective function $F(t) = \text{dist}_\Sigma^2(\gamma(t), \sigma)$. A well-established scheme for this type of problem is Newton's method that employs second-order approximations to gain greatly in convergence speed, achieving quadratic convergence rate when close enough to the optimum. Analogously, a quadratic approximation for the objective F is given by

$$F(t + \delta) \approx F(t) + \frac{\mathrm{d}}{\mathrm{d}t} F(t) \cdot \delta + \frac{1}{2} \frac{\mathrm{d}^2}{\mathrm{d}t^2} F(t) \cdot \delta^2, \text{ with}$$

$$\frac{\mathrm{d}}{\mathrm{d}t} F(t) = -2g_{\gamma(t)} \left(\text{Log}_{\gamma(t)}(\sigma), \dot{\gamma}(t) \right), \text{ and}$$

$$\frac{\mathrm{d}^2}{\mathrm{d}t^2} F(t) = -2g_{\gamma(t)} \left(\mathrm{d}_{\gamma(t)} \text{Log}_{\gamma(t)}(\sigma)(\dot{\gamma}(t)), \dot{\gamma}(t) \right).$$

Additionally, employing the first-order approximation for the differential of the logarithm $\mathrm{d}_{\gamma(t)} \text{Log}_{\gamma(t)}(\sigma) \approx -Id$ [24, Eq. (5)] (Id denoting the identity) we can obtain an optimal step size δ^* for this quadratic model as

$$\delta^* = g_{\gamma(t)} \left(\text{Log}_{\gamma(t)}(\sigma), \dot{\gamma}(t) \right). \tag{3}$$

Indeed, verifiable by direct calculation, this step agrees with the explicit solution for the case of flat spaces. Eventually, we derive the Newton-type fixed point iteration

$$\pi_{i+1} = \text{Exp}_{\pi_i}(\delta_i^* \dot{\gamma}_i), \tag{4}$$

where Exp denotes the Riemannian exponential map. In our setting, the choice $\pi_0 = \gamma(0)$ as initial guess is reasonable, since it is the healthy mean.

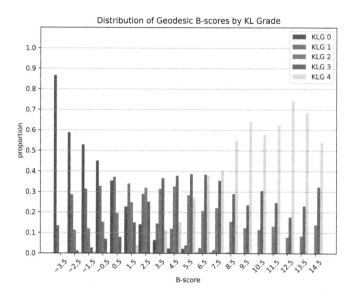

Fig. 2. Distribution of B-scores by KL grades normalized w.r.t. KL grade imbalance.

4   Results and Discussion

4.1   Data Description

Within this practical evaluation we rely on 3D sagittal Double Echo Steady-State MRI acquired at baseline as part of the Osteoarthritis Initiative (OAI) database[1] [26]. We segmented the distal femur bone for 9290 (of 9345) scans and established pointwise correspondence employing a fully automatic method combining convolutional neural networks with statistical shape knowledge achieving state-of-the art accuracy [2]. The 55 cases not taken into consideration were omitted due to imaging artifacts or failure of the segmentation pipeline. All reconstructed distal femur shapes are taken as left femurs, i.e., all right shapes were mirrored suitably and every shape consists of 8614 vertices and 17024 faces. Apart from image data the OAI database also provides clinical scores as KL and information about clinical outcomes such as TKR surgery. An overview on the employed data is given in Table 1. Note that the list of unique MRI scan IDs defining the study population is publicly available as supplementary file[2].

Since the shape space we employ is not scale invariant (as well as the ASM) this leaves the option to factor it out. However, since femoral osteoarthritis, among others, leads to flattening and widening of the condyle region that at least partially appears as deviation in scale w.r.t. a healthy configuration we forego scale alignment to preserve sensitivity for scale. Based on the geodesic B-score as derived in Sect. 3.1, we restrict our study population to the B-score

---

[1] nda.nih.gov/oai.

[2] urn:nbn:de:0297-zib-81930.

Table 1. Demographic information for the data under study.

No. of shapes	9290
Laterality (left, right)	4678, 4612
Sex (male, female)	3825, 5465
Age [years]	61.1 ± 9.2
BMI [k/m^2]	$28,6 \pm 4.8$
KL 0, 1, 2, 3, 4	3382, 1557, 2313, 1198, 282
TKR within 8 years	508

percentile range from 0.75 to 99.25 (in terms of B-score: -3.12, 14.65) in order to exclude outliers. The resulting distribution of geodesic B-scores per KL grade is shown in Fig. 2, visualizing the positive correlation of both grading schemes. Note that the depicted distribution is normalized to account for imbalance within the OAI database of KL grade frequencies , i.e., re-weighted as if KL groups were of equal cardinality.

4.2   Efficiency of Projection Algorithm

We empirically evaluate the performance of the derived Newton-type iteration listed in Eq. (4) using a python-based prototype implementation without parallelization , publicly available as part of the Morphomatics[3] library. To this end, we computed projections of 100 randomly selected femur shapes. We were able to observe quadratic convergence of the algorithm for all cases with 0.97 s and three iterations per case in average.

4.3   Predictive Validity

We assess the value of the geodesic B-score as a measure of OA status by examining its relationship with risk of TKR surgery—an important clinical outcome. Here and throughout, we refer to the risk of an outcome as the proportion w.r.t. a population. Additionally, we perform a comparison of the predictive performance between the geodesic and Euclidean B-score. To this end, we follow the proposed setup from [6] by modeling the predictor of TKR (within the follow-up period of 8 years) against B-score using logistic regression.

   The determination of Euclidean B-scores is based on the space of vertex coordinates. To reduce confounding effects due to misalignment of the input shapes we employed generalized Procrustes analysis [11] (adding a certain degree of nonlinearity over the approach in [6]). No such considerations apply for the FCM-based geodesic B-score as it inherits the invariance to rigid motions. For both scores, computations were performed on the same input meshes using a modular software design sharing all routines that are not specific to the respective shape

---

[3] morphomatics.github.io.

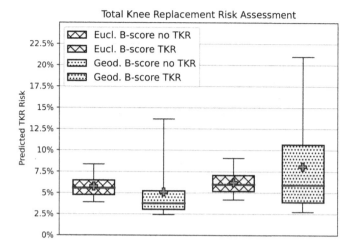

Fig. 3. Comparison of TKR risk assessment for patient groups with TKR and No TKR clinical outcome respectively. Orange plus: mean, red line: median, box range: 25th to 75th percentile, whisker range: 5th to 95th percentile (Color figure online).

space. To compare the predictive performance of the derived models we grouped the study population into a TKR cohort that did receive TKR and a non-TKR cohort that did not. In Fig. 3, we provide box plots for the resulting risk distributions that show clear differences in median risk between non-TKR and TKR. Furthermore, for the non-TKR cohort the geodesic B-score model validly yields median risks that are half of those for the Euclidean model. All these differences are statistically significant as determined using Mann–Whitney U tests. While both approaches yield the same median risk for the TKR cohort, the distribution of the geodesic B-score model is skewed towards higher risks. These findings substantiate an improved predictive power for the geodesic B-score.

5   Conclusion and Future Work

We introduced a consistent generalization of the recently presented B-score to Riemannian shape spaces. We showed that the obtained formulation features superior predictive power in an experiment on TKR risk assessment, thus, suggesting improved discrimination of morphological status across the range of OA severity. These advances foster the potential of B-score to replace imprecise and insensitive measures for the assessment of OA status based on plain radiography. Moreover, we further presented an original algorithm for the projection of points in a Riemannian manifold onto a geodesic. In particular, the obtained iteration exposes fast, quadratic convergence and is simple to implement.

We chose FCM because–due to its deep foundation in differential geometry and link to thin elastic shells–it faithfully captures nonlinear shape variability, while offering fast processing of large-scale shape collections. On the theoretical side, the price to pay is that there is no guarantee that the projection is diffeomorphic. However, we would like to remark that the estimated OA-geodesic contains only diffeomorphic deformations within the confidence interval, guaranteeing valid instances even if the input shapes are not. Furthermore, contrary to shape spaces based on diffeomorphic metric mapping, the FCM is invariant under Euclidean motion and, thus, not susceptible to any bias due to misalignment.

In this work, we carefully generalized the B-score mimicking the geometric construction of the Euclidean counterpart. However, there are various statistical approaches that allow to estimate submanifolds based on separation or regression considerations, e.g., geodesic discriminant analysis [21] or higher-order regression [16], respectively. An interesting direction for future work is to investigate to which extend such geometric statistics can serve as a foundation for advanced notions of an intrinsic B-score. From a medical perspective, it will be most interesting to explore the relationship of the geodesic B-score with further clinically important outcomes such as pain and loss of function. In particular, we will investigate to which degree the geodesic B-score can improve the related risk assessment. Since the presented statistical approach can directly be extended to multiple connected components, another line of work will aim on extension to multi-structure B-scores, e.g., for Femur and Tibia. Moreover, for the future we envision a longitudinal characterization beyond the static B-score that takes subject-specific shape developments into account.[4]

Acknowledgments. F. Ambellan is funded by the Deutsche Forschungsgemeinschaft (DFG, German Research Foundation) under Germany's Excellence Strategy – The Berlin Mathematics Research Center MATH+ (EXC-2046/1, project ID: 390685689). This work was supported by the Bundesministerium fuer Bildung und Forschung (BMBF) through BIFOLD - The Berlin Institute for the Foundations of Learning and Data (ref. 01IS18025A and ref 01IS18037A). Furthermore, we are grateful for the open-access dataset of the Osteoarthritis Initiative[4].

References

1. Ambellan, F., Lamecker, H., von Tycowicz, C., Zachow, S.: Statistical shape models: understanding and mastering variation in anatomy. In: Rea, P.M. (ed.) Biomedical Visualisation. AEMB, vol. 1156, pp. 67–84. Springer, Cham (2019). https://doi.org/10.1007/978-3-030-19385-0_5

---

[4] Osteoarthritis Initiative is a public-private partnership comprised of five contracts (N01-AR-2-2258; N01-AR-2-2259; N01-AR-2-2260; N01-AR-2-2261; N01-AR-2-2262) funded by the National Institutes of Health, a branch of the Department of Health and Human Services, and conducted by the OAI Study Investigators. Private funding partners include Merck Research Laboratories; Novartis Pharmaceuticals Corporation, GlaxoSmithKline; and Pfizer, Inc. Private sector funding for the OAI is managed by the Foundation for the National Institutes of Health. This manuscript was prepared using an OAI public use data set and does not necessarily reflect the opinions or views of the OAI investigators, the NIH, or the private funding partners.

2. Ambellan, F., Tack, A., Ehlke, M., Zachow, S.: Automated segmentation of knee bone and cartilage combining statistical shape knowledge and convolutional neural networks: data from the osteoarthritis initiative. Med. Image Anal. **52**(2), 109–118 (2019)
3. Ambellan, F., Zachow, S., von Tycowicz, C.: An as-invariant-as-possible $GL^+(3)$-based statistical shape model. In: Zhu, D., et al. (eds.) MBIA/MFCA-2019. LNCS, vol. 11846, pp. 219–228. Springer, Cham (2019). https://doi.org/10.1007/978-3-030-33226-6_23
4. Ambellan, F., Zachow, S., von Tycowicz, C.: A surface-theoretic approach for statistical shape modeling. In: Shen, D., et al. (eds.) MICCAI 2019. LNCS, vol. 11767, pp. 21–29. Springer, Cham (2019). https://doi.org/10.1007/978-3-030-32251-9_3
5. Arsigny, V., Fillard, P., Pennec, X., Ayache, N.: Log-Euclidean metrics for fast and simple calculus on diffusion tensors. Magn. Reson. Med. **56**(2), 411–421 (2006)
6. Bowes, M.A., et al.: Machine-learning, MRI bone shape and important clinical outcomes in osteoarthritis: data from the osteoarthritis initiative. Ann. Rheum. Dis. **80**(4), 502–508 (2020). Published online first: 13 November 2020
7. Brandt, C., von Tycowicz, C., Hildebrandt, K.: Geometric flows of curves in shape space for processing motion of deformable objects. Comput. Graph. Forum **35**(2), 295–305 (2016)
8. do Carmo, M.P.: Riemannian Geometry (Mathematics: Theory and Applications), 2nd edn. Birkhäuser, Boston, MA (1992)
9. Chakraborty, R., Seo, D., Vemuri, B.C.: An efficient exact-PGA algorithm for constant curvature manifolds. In: Proceedings of the Computer Vision and Pattern Recognition, pp. 3976–3984 (2016)
10. Charpiat, G., Faugeras, O., Keriven, R., Maurel, P.: Distance-based shape statistics. In: Proceedings of the International Conference on Acoustics, Speech, and Signal Processing, pp. V925–V928 (2006)
11. Cootes, T.F., Taylor, C.J., Cooper, D.H., Graham, J.: Active shape models-their training and application. Comput. Vis. Image Underst. **61**(1), 38–59 (1995)
12. Davis, B.C., Fletcher, P.T., Bullitt, E., Joshi, S.: Population shape regression from random design data. Int. J. Comput. Vis. **90**(2), 255–266 (2010)
13. Fletcher, P.T., Lu, C., Joshi, S.: Statistics of shape via principal geodesic analysis on Lie groups. In: Proceedings of the Computer Vision and Pattern Recognition, vol. 1, p. I-95 (2003)
14. Freifeld, O., Black, M.J.: Lie bodies: a manifold representation of 3D human shape. In: Fitzgibbon, A., Lazebnik, S., Perona, P., Sato, Y., Schmid, C. (eds.) ECCV 2012. LNCS, vol. 7572, pp. 1–14. Springer, Heidelberg (2012). https://doi.org/10.1007/978-3-642-33718-5_1
15. Fuchs, M., Jüttler, B., Scherzer, O., Yang, H.: Shape metrics based on elastic deformations. J. Math. Imaging Vis. **35**(1), 86–102 (2009)
16. Hanik, M., Hege, H.-C., Hennemuth, A., von Tycowicz, C.: Nonlinear regression on manifolds for shape analysis using intrinsic Bézier splines. In: Martel, A.L., et al. (eds.) MICCAI 2020. LNCS, vol. 12264, pp. 617–626. Springer, Cham (2020). https://doi.org/10.1007/978-3-030-59719-1_60
17. Heeren, B., Zhang, C., Rumpf, M., Smith, W.: Principal geodesic analysis in the space of discrete shells. Comput. Graph. Forum **37**(5), 173–184 (2018)
18. Huckemann, S., Hotz, T.: Principal component geodesics for planar shape spaces. J. Multivar. Anal. **100**(4), 699–714 (2009)
19. Kellgren, J., Lawrence, J.: Radiological assessment of osteo-arthrosis. Ann. Rheum. Dis. **16**(4), 494 (1957)

20. Kendall, D.G.: A survey of the statistical theory of shape. Stat. Sci. **4**(2), 87–99 (1989)
21. Louis, M., Charlier, B., Durrleman, S.: Geodesic discriminant analysis for manifold-valued data. In: Proceedings of the Workshops at Computer Vision and Pattern Recognition, pp. 332–340 (2018)
22. Miller, M.I., Trouvé, A., Younes, L.: Hamiltonian systems and optimal control in computational anatomy: 100 years since D'Arcy Thompson. Annu. Rev. Biomed. Eng. **17**, 447–509 (2015)
23. Neogi, T., et al.: Magnetic resonance imaging-based three-dimensional bone shape of the knee predicts onset of knee osteoarthritis. Arthritis Rheum. **65**(8), 2048–2058 (2013)
24. Pennec, X.: Hessian of the Riemannian squared distance. Université Côte d'Azur and Inria Sophia-Antipolis Méditerranée, Technical report (2017)
25. Pennec, X., Sommer, S., Fletcher, T.: Riemannian Geometric Statistics in Medical Image Analysis. Academic Press (2019)
26. Peterfy, C., Gold, G., Eckstein, F., Cicuttini, F., Dardzinski, B., Stevens, R.: MRI protocols for whole-organ assessment of the knee in osteoarthritis. Osteoarthritis Cartilage **14**, 95–111 (2006)
27. Rumpf, M., Wirth, B.: An elasticity-based covariance analysis of shapes. Int. J. Comput. Vis. **92**(3), 281–295 (2011)
28. Rumpf, M., Wirth, B.: Variational methods in shape analysis. In: Scherzer, O. (eds.) Handbook of Mathematical Methods in Imaging. Springer, New York, NY (2015). https://doi.org/10.1007/978-1-4939-0790-8_56
29. Sommer, S., Lauze, F., Nielsen, M.: Optimization over geodesics for exact principal geodesic analysis. Adv. Comput. Math. **40**(2), 283–313 (2013). https://doi.org/10.1007/s10444-013-9308-1
30. von Tycowicz, C., Ambellan, F., Mukhopadhyay, A., Zachow, S.: An efficient Riemannian statistical shape model using differential coordinates. Med. Image Anal. **43**, 1–9 (2018)
31. von Tycowicz, C.: Towards shape-based knee osteoarthritis classification using graph convolutional networks. In: Proceedings of the International Symposium on Biomedical Imaging, pp. 750–753 (2020)
32. von Tycowicz, C., Schulz, C., Seidel, H.P., Hildebrandt, K.: Real-time nonlinear shape interpolation. Trans. Graph. **34**(3), 34:1–34:10 (2015)
33. Vos, T., et al.: Years lived with disability (YLDs) for 1160 sequelae of 289 diseases and injuries 1990–2010: a systematic analysis for the global burden of disease study 2010. Lancet **380**(9859), 2163–2196 (2012)
34. Zhang, C., Heeren, B., Rumpf, M., Smith, W.A.: Shell PCA: satistical shape modelling in shell space. In: Proceedings of the International Conference on Computer Vision, pp. 1671–1679 (2015)

Brain Connectivity

Cytoarchitecture Measurements in Brain Gray Matter Using Likelihood-Free Inference

Maëliss Jallais$^{(\boxtimes)}$ ⓘ, Pedro L. C. Rodrigues$^{(\boxtimes)}$ ⓘ, Alexandre Gramfort$^{(\boxtimes)}$ ⓘ, and Demian Wassermann$^{(\boxtimes)}$ ⓘ

Université Paris-Saclay, Inria, CEA, 91120 Palaiseau, France
{maeliss.jallais,pedro.rodrigues,alexandre.gramfort,
demian.wassermann}@inria.fr

Abstract. Effective characterisation of the brain grey matter cytoarchitecture with quantitative sensitivity to soma density and volume remains an unsolved challenge in diffusion MRI (dMRI). Solving the problem of relating the dMRI signal with cytoarchitectural characteristics calls for the definition of a mathematical model that describes brain tissue via a handful of physiologically-relevant parameters and an algorithm for inverting the model. To address this issue, we propose a new forward model, specifically a new system of equations, requiring six relatively sparse b-shells. These requirements are a drastic reduction of those used in current proposals to estimate grey matter cytoarchitecture. We then apply current tools from Bayesian analysis known as likelihood-free inference (LFI) to invert our proposed model. As opposed to other approaches from the literature, our LFI-based algorithm yields not only an estimation of the parameter vector $\boldsymbol{\theta}$ that best describes a given observed data point $\boldsymbol{x}_o$, but also a full posterior distribution $p(\boldsymbol{\theta}|\boldsymbol{x}_o)$ over the parameter space. This enables a richer description of the model inversion results providing indicators such as confidence intervals for the estimations, and better understanding of the parameter regions where the model may present indeterminacies. We approximate the posterior distribution using deep neural density estimators, known as normalizing flows, and fit them using a set of repeated simulations from the forward model. We validate our approach on simulations using `dmipy` and then apply the whole pipeline to the HCP MGH dataset.

Keywords: Diffusion MRI · Brain microstructure · Likelihood-free inference

1 Introduction

Obtaining quantitative measurements of brain grey matter microstructure with a dedicated soma representation is a growing field of interest in the diffusion MRI (dMRI) community [13,18]. However, current methods require demanding

© Springer Nature Switzerland AG 2021
A. Feragen et al. (Eds.): IPMI 2021, LNCS 12729, pp. 191–202, 2021.
https://doi.org/10.1007/978-3-030-78191-0_15

acquisitions and stabilise parameter fitting by enforcing constraints which are not valid across all brain tissue. Yet, these still encounter large indetermination areas in the solution space making the results unstable [12]. To overcome these limitations, we propose a new model based on diffusion signal summary measurements, computed from boundary approximations. Our model has the benefit of reducing acquisition requirements while retaining microstructure sensitivity. Combining it with a likelihood-free inference (LFI) method from Bayesian analysis, we readily compute the posterior distribution of the model fitting at each voxel. Real asset to this method, it describes the quality of the fit. Notably, it provides confidence intervals and better understanding of the parameter regions where the model may present indeterminacies.

Accessing cortical cytoarchitecture *in vivo* is a sought step to understand diseases such as Alzheimer's. Unlike histology, diffusion MRI enables to quantify brain tissue characteristics non-invasively. Our method could, for example, help understanding dementia and cognitive deficits, which appear to be mostly related to neuronal loss and synaptic pathology. Relationships between cellular microstructure and cognition could also be established [9]. A major asset brought by the proposed method is its reliance on only a few relatively sparse q-shells, equivalently b-shells, along with confidence intervals that help to guarantee the good fitting of the parameters.

Current microstructure models are predominantly based on the two compartment Standard Model (SM) [11,18]. Recent evidence shows that the SM, mainly used in white matter, does not hold for grey matter microstructure analysis [17]. Several assumptions aim at explaining this issue such as increased permeability in neurite membranes [17], or curvy projections along with longer pulse duration [11]. We follow the hypothesis that the SM doesn't hold due to an abundance of cell bodies in gray matter [13]. Our proposed biophysical model is then based on three compartments [13]: neurites; somas; and extra-cellular space (ECS). Despite its increased complexity, the main advantage of such model is the possibility to jointly estimate the characteristic features of each compartment.

By proposing a forward model for grey matter using three-compartments, we are able to simulate the dMRI signal for known tissue parameters. However, using it to quantify microstructure from the signal remains tricky. Several approaches have tried to tackle this non-linear inverse problem. Still, most popular solutions to date, such as NODDI [e.g., 18], stabilise this inverse problem by imposing constraints on model parameters which are not biologically plausible [12]. This biases parameter estimation and the inverse problem remains largely degenerate. Our proposal tackles these limitations based on three contributions. First, we introduce a new parameter that jointly encodes soma radius and inner diffusivity without imposing constraints on these values. This new parameter reduces indeterminacies in the model and has relevant physiological interpretations. Second, we present a new method to fit the model through summary features of the dMRI signal based on a large and small q-value analysis. These rotationally-invariant features relate directly to the tissue parameters, and enable us to invert the model without manipulating the raw dMRI signals. These summary statistics allow to have a stable solution of the parameter estimations, as opposed to the indeterminate models used in [13,18]. Third, we employ modern tools from Bayesian analysis known as likelihood-free inference (LFI) to determine the posterior distribution of the fitted parameters. This posterior offers a full description of the solution landscape and can point out degeneracies.

The likelihood function of complex simulators is often very hard to obtain and, therefore, determining the posterior distribution via Bayes's formula is hopeless. LFI bypasses this bottleneck by recurring to several simulations of the model using different parameters and learning the posterior distribution from these examples. The first works on LFI are also known as approximate Bayesian computation (ABC) and have been applied to invert models from ecology, population genetics, and epidemiology [16]. Recently, there has been a growing interest in the machine learning community in improving the limitations of ABC methods. These limitations include the large number of simulations required for the posterior estimations or the need of defining a distance function to compare the results of two simulations. A special class of neural networks called normalizing flows has been used to approximate the posterior distribution of simulator models and has demonstrated promising results in different research fields [8].

In what follows, we present our three contributions and validate our workflow for inverting dMRI signals on a set of physiologically relevant situations using the dmipy simulator. Then, we apply our method on the HCP MGH dataset, which contains in-vivo human brain acquisitions, and present the results of parameter estimations in grey matter along with an assessment of their variances.

2   Methods

2.1   Modeling the Brain Gray Matter with a 3-Compartment Model

To characterize cortical cytoarchitecture, we propose a method to relate the diffusion MRI signal to specific tissue parameters. To that aim, we first need to define a model of the grey matter tissue. Histology teaches us that grey matter is composed of neurons embedded in a fluid environment. Each neuron is composed of a soma, corresponding to the cellular body, surrounded by neurites connecting neurons together. Following this tissue biophysical composition, we model the grey matter tissue as three-compartmental [13], moving away from the SM designed for white matter. We are assuming that our acquisition protocol is not sensitive to exchanges between those compartments, i.e., molecules moving from one compartment to another have a negligible influence on the signal [13]. The acquired signal is then considered as resulting from a convex mixture of signals arising from somas, neurites, and extra-cellular space (ECS). Unlike white matter-centric methods, we are not interested in the fiber orientation and only estimate orientation-independent parameters. This enables us to work on the direction-averaged dMRI signal, denoted $\bar{S}(q)$, known as the powder averaged signal. This consideration mainly matters for neurites, as their signal is not isotropic, as opposed to the proposed model for somas and ECS. Our direction-averaged grey matter signal model is then:

$$\frac{\bar{S}(q)}{S(0)} = f_n \bar{S}_{\text{neurites}}(q, D_a) + f_s \bar{S}_{\text{somas}}(q, D_s, r_s) + f_{\text{ECS}} \bar{S}_{\text{ECS}}(q, D_e). \quad (1)$$

In this equation, f_n; f_s; and f_{ECS} represent signal fractions for neurites; somas; and ECS respectively ($f_n + f_s + f_{ECS} = 1$). Note that the relative signal fractions do not correspond to the relative volume fractions of the tissue compartments as they are also modulated by a difference in T2 values [11]. D_a corresponds to axial diffusivity inside neurites, while D_s and D_e correspond to somas and extra-cellular diffusivities. r_s is the average soma radius within a voxel. We use q-values for more readability and harmonization throughout the paper, but a direct conversion to b-values is also possible, using $b = (2\pi q)^2 \tau$ with $\tau = \Delta - \delta/3$.

We now review the model for each compartment, to make explicit the impact of each parameter on the diffusion MRI signal.

Neurite Compartment. Neurites, as in the SM, are modeled as 0-radius impermeable cylinders ("sticks"), with effective diffusion along the parallel axis, and a negligible radial intra-neurite diffusivity. In our acquisition setting, this model has been shown to hold [17]. Its direction averaged signal is [17]:

$$\bar{S}_{\text{neurites}}(q) \simeq \frac{1}{4\sqrt{\pi\tau D_a}} \cdot q^{-1} \quad (2)$$

Soma Compartment. Somas are modeled as spheres, whose signal can be computed using the GPD approximation [3]:

$$- \log \bar{S}_{\text{somas}}(q) = C(r_s, D_s) \cdot q^2 \quad (3)$$

We exploit this relation here to extract a parameter $C_s = C(r_s, D_s)[m^2]$ which, at fixed diffusivity D_s, is modulated by the radius of the soma r_s:

$$C(r_s, D_s) = \frac{2}{D_s \delta^2} \sum_{m=1}^{\infty} \frac{\alpha_m^{-4}}{\alpha_m^2 r_s^2 - 2}$$
$$\cdot \left(2\delta - \frac{2 + e^{-\alpha_m^2 D_s(\Delta-\delta)} - e^{-\alpha_m^2 D_s \delta} - e^{-\alpha_m^2 D_s \Delta} + e^{-\alpha_m^2 D_s(\Delta+\delta)}}{\alpha_m^2 D_s} \right)$$

where α_m is the mth root of $(\alpha r_s)^{-1} J_{\frac{3}{2}}(\alpha r_s) = J_{\frac{5}{2}}(\alpha r_s)$, with $J_n(x)$ the Bessel functions of the first kind.

Extra-cellular Space Compartment. The extra-cellular space is approximated as isotropic Gaussian diffusion, i.e., a mono-exponential diffusion signal with a scalar diffusion constant D_e, which reflects the molecular viscosity of the fluid. This approximation assumes that the ECS is fully connected. The approximation is therefore:

$$- \log(\bar{S}_{\text{ECS}}(q)) = (2\pi q)^2 \tau D_e \quad (4)$$

We are estimating D_e from the ventricles, given the same metabolic composition of the extracellular space and ventricles: cerebrospinal fluid.

2.2   An Invertible 3-Compartment Model: dMRI Summary Statistics

The tissue model presented in Sect. 2.1 enables to relate the dMRI signal with parameters representing grey matter tissue microstructure. However, solving the inverse problem directly from Eq. (1) is a difficult task, leading to indeterminacies and bad parameter estimations. Current methods addressing this issue have not studied its stability [13] but simpler models with only two compartments have been shown to be indeterminate [11].

To produce a method which addresses this indeterminacy, we introduce rotationally invariant summary statistics to describe the dMRI signal. Furthermore, we solve the inverse problem efficiently reducing indeterminacies and we develop a method to detect them in Sect. 2.3. These dMRI-based summary statistics are extracted from our proposed model presented in Sect. 2.1 via the following analysis of the dMRI signal on the boundaries of large and small q-value cases.

Large q -value Approximation: RTOP. We compute a q-bounded RTOP, a direct measure of the restrictions of the diffusing fluid molecule motion that gives us information about the structure of the media [10]:

$$\mathrm{RTOP}(q) = 4\pi \int_0^q \frac{\bar{S}(\eta)}{S(0)} \eta^2 d\eta \qquad (5)$$

For q large enough, RTOP on our 3-compartment model in Eq. (1), yields a soma and extra-cellular signal which converges towards a constant value in q, while the neurites' contribution becomes quadratic in q. In this case, RTOP becomes:

$$\mathrm{RTOP}(q) = \underbrace{f_s \left(\frac{\pi}{C_s}\right)^{3/2} + \frac{f_{\mathrm{ECS}}}{8(\pi\tau D_e)^{3/2}}}_{a_{\mathrm{fit}}} + \underbrace{\frac{f_n}{2} \cdot \sqrt{\frac{\pi}{\tau D_a}}}_{b_{\mathrm{fit}}} \cdot q^2 \qquad (6)$$

By accurately estimating the second derivative of RTOP(q) at q large enough, we can solve the coefficients of the polynomial in Eq. (6): a_{fit} and b_{fit}. We do this efficiently by casting it as an overdetermined ordinary least squares problem which has a unique solution.

Small q-value Approximation: Spiked LEMONADE. We propose a second approximation, based on a moment decomposition for small q-values [12]:

$$\frac{S_{\hat{\mathbf{g}}}(q)}{S(0)} = 1 - b(q)M_{i_1 i_2}^{(2)} g_1 g_2 + \frac{b(q)^2}{2!}M_{i_1...i_4}^{(4)} g_1 \cdots g_4 - \ldots, \quad b(q) = (2\pi q)^2 \tau \quad (7)$$

where i_k are the directional basis of the tensors M, $g_k = i_k \cdot \hat{\mathbf{g}} \in \mathbb{R}^3$, and $\hat{\mathbf{g}}$ the unit direction of the dMRI acquisition. From the moment tensors of this decomposition, LEMONADE [12] extracts rotational invariant scalar indices $M^{(i),j}$, $i, j \in \{0, 2, 4, \ldots\}$. These quantify white matter microstructure by plugging the 2-compartment SM into Eq. (7) [see [12], App. C].

In this work, we extended LEMONADE to our 3-compartment model presented in Sect. 2.1 by plugging Eq. (1) into Eq. (7) and performing tedious arithmetic. This results in the following equation system, which now includes the soma parameter C_s, relating the dMRI signal to gray matter microstructure:

$$\begin{cases} M^{(2),0} = f_n D_a + 3f_s \frac{C_s}{(2\pi)^2 \tau} + 3f_{\text{ECS}} D_e \\ M^{(2),2} = f_n D_a p_2 \\ M^{(4),0} = f_n D_a^2 + 5f_s \left(\frac{C_s}{(2\pi)^2 \tau}\right)^2 + 5f_{\text{ECS}} D_e^2 \\ M^{(4),2} = f_n D_a^2 p_2 \end{cases} \tag{8}$$

where p_2 is a scalar measure of neurite orientation dispersion [12].

Note that only the shells with $b(q) \leq 3$ ms μm^{-2} are used, to get an unbiased estimation of the rotational invariant moments $M^{(2),0}$, $M^{(2),2}$, $M^{(4),0}$ and $M^{(4),2}$.

Complete System. Combining Eqs. (6) and (8) and adding the constraint that the fractions for the three compartments sum to one, we obtain a system of 7 equations and 7 unknowns. Following Menon et al. [9], we assume D_e nearly-constant per subject acquisition and that it can be estimated as the mean diffusivity in the subject's ventricles. This assumption allows us to drop an unknown from the system, use D_e as a reference diffusivity and render our variables unitless as $D_a^u = \frac{D_a}{D_e}$ and $C_s^u = \frac{C_s}{(2\pi)^2 \tau D_e}$, obtaining:

Spiked LEMONADE Small q-values	RTOP Large q-values
$\begin{cases} \frac{M^{(2),0}}{D_e} = f_n D_a^u + 3f_s C_s^u + 3f_{\text{ECS}} \\ \frac{M^{(2),2}}{D_e} = f_n D_a^u \cdot p_2 \\ \frac{M^{(4),0}}{D_e^2} = f_n D_a^{u2} + 5f_s C_s^{u2} + 5f_{\text{ECS}} \\ \frac{M^{(4),2}}{D_e^2} = f_n D_a^{u2} \cdot p_2 \end{cases}$	$\begin{cases} a_{\text{fit}} (\tau D_e)^{3/2} = \frac{f_s}{8(\pi C_s^u)^{3/2}} + \frac{f_{\text{ECS}}}{8\pi^{3/2}} \\ b_{\text{fit}} (\tau D_e)^{1/2} = \frac{f_n}{2} \sqrt{\frac{\pi}{D_a^u}} \end{cases}$
$f_n + f_s + f_{\text{ECS}} = 1$	

2.3   Solving the Inverse Problem via Likelihood Free Inference

The Bayesian Formalism. The system of equations presented in Sect. 2.2 describes how the tissue parameters $\boldsymbol{\theta} = (D_a^u, C_s^u, p_2, f_s, f_n, f_{\text{ECS}}) \in \mathbb{R}^6$ are related to the vector of summary statistics obtained from the raw dMRI signal

$$\boldsymbol{x} = \left(\frac{M^{(2),0}}{D_e}, \frac{M^{(2),2}}{D_e}, \frac{M^{(4),0}}{D_e^2}, \frac{M^{(4),2}}{D_e^2}, a_{\text{fit}}(\tau D_e)^{3/2}, b_{\text{fit}}\sqrt{\tau D_e} \right) \in \mathbb{R}^7 .$$

We denote this relation by $\mathcal{M} : \mathbb{R}^6 \rightarrow \mathbb{R}^7$ such that $\boldsymbol{x} = \mathcal{M}(\boldsymbol{\theta})$. We interpret the inverse problem of inferring the parameters $\boldsymbol{\theta}_o$ that best describe a given observed summary feature vector $\boldsymbol{x}_o$ as that of determining the posterior distribution of $\boldsymbol{\theta}$ given an observation $\boldsymbol{x}_o$. By first choosing a prior distribution $p(\boldsymbol{\theta})$

describing our initial knowledge of the parameter values, we may use Bayes' theorem to write

$$p(\boldsymbol{\theta}|\boldsymbol{x}_o) = \frac{p(\boldsymbol{x}_o|\boldsymbol{\theta})p(\boldsymbol{\theta})}{p(\boldsymbol{x}_o)} \ , \tag{9}$$

where $p(\boldsymbol{x}_o|\boldsymbol{\theta})$ is the likelihood of the observed data point and $p(\boldsymbol{x}_o)$ is a normalizing constant. Note that such probabilistic approach returns not only which $\boldsymbol{\theta}$ best fits the observed data (i.e., the parameter that maximizes the posterior distribution) but also describes the variance of the parameters being estimated. Furthermore, it provides a full description of which regions of the parameter space may generate the same vector of observed summary features.

Bypassing the Likelihood Function. Despite its apparent simplicity, it is usually difficult to use Eq. (9) to determine the posterior distribution, since the likelihood function for data points generated by complex non-linear models is often hard to write. To avoid such difficulty, we directly approximate the posterior distribution using a class of neural networks called normalizing flows [14]. These flows are invertible functions capable of transforming vectors generated by a simple base distribution (e.g., the standard multivariate Gaussian distribution) into an approximation of the true posterior distribution. We denote a normalizing flow by $q_\phi^N(\boldsymbol{\theta}|\boldsymbol{x})$, where ϕ parametrizes the neural network, N indicates how many data points were available when training the neural density estimator, and $\boldsymbol{\theta}$ and $\boldsymbol{x}$ are input arguments. In this work, we use normalizing flows with an autoregressive architecture implemented via the masked autoencoder for distribution estimation (MADE) [6]. We follow the same setup from [8] for LFI problems, stackings five MADEs, each with two hidden layers of 50 units, and a standard normal base distribution. This choice provides a sufficiently flexible function capable of approximating complex posterior distributions. We refer the reader to [14] for more information on the different types of normalizing flows.

Our setup for approximating $p(\boldsymbol{\theta}|\boldsymbol{x}_o)$ with a normalizing flow is the following: first, generate a set of N paired samples $(\boldsymbol{\theta}_i, \boldsymbol{x}_i)$, where $\boldsymbol{\theta}_i \sim p(\boldsymbol{\theta})$ and $\boldsymbol{x}_i = \mathcal{M}(\boldsymbol{\theta}_i)$. The parameters ϕ are then obtained via stochastic gradient descent to minimize the loss function

$$\mathcal{L}(\phi) = -\sum_{i=1}^{N} \log\left(q_\phi^N(\boldsymbol{\theta}_i|\boldsymbol{x}_i)\right) \ . \tag{10}$$

Note that (10) is a Monte-Carlo approximation to the Kullback-Leibler (KL) divergence between $q_\phi^N(\boldsymbol{\theta}|\boldsymbol{x})$ and $p(\boldsymbol{\theta}|\boldsymbol{x})$, so the parameter ϕ that minimizes it yields a normalizing flow which is the closest to the true posterior distribution in the KL-sense. Moreover, it is possible to show that the minimizer of Eq. (10) converges to $p(\boldsymbol{\theta}|\boldsymbol{y})$ when $N \to \infty$ [8]. We obtain the posterior distribution for observation $\boldsymbol{x}_o$ by simply writing $p(\boldsymbol{\theta}|\boldsymbol{x}_o) \approx q_\phi^N(\boldsymbol{\theta}|\boldsymbol{x}_o)$.

3   Results and Discussion

3.1   Simulations

Validating LFI on a Base Case. In this experiment, our goal was to validate the use of the LFI procedure described in Sect. 2.3 to approximate the posterior distribution of the tissue parameters in a simple setting, where their ground truth values are known. We report the results with a single choice of ground truth parameters, but our actual complete validation was performed on a set of physiologically relevant choices of parameters.

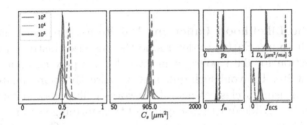

Fig. 1. Histograms of 10^4 samples of the approximate posterior distribution with observed dMRI signals generated under two acquisition setups, $\mathcal{A}$ and $\mathcal{B}$ (see text for details). Vertical black dashed lines represent ground truth values of θ_o which generated the observed signals. Different colors show how the posterior distribution gets sharper as the number N of simulations in the training dataset increases. Solid curves indicate results for setup $\mathcal{A}$, which are very close to the true values, and dashed curves for setup $\mathcal{B}$, which present a bias.

Experimental Setup. We simulated the three-compartment model described in Sect. 2.1 using the dmipy simulator [5]. Somas have been modeled as spheres with a 35 μm diameter and 2.3 μm²ms⁻¹ diffusivity; neurites as tubes with 1 μm diameter and 1.7 μm²ms⁻¹ axial diffusivity; and extra-cellular space as isotropic Gaussian diffusion with a diffusivity of 2.6 μm²ms⁻¹. These values have been selected to mimic existing neurons available from the NeuroMorpho database (neuromorpho.org). In what follows, we denote this choice of tissue parameters θ_o. We have considered two acquisition setups for generating diffusion signals, with $\delta = 12.9$ ms and $\Delta = 21.8$ ms. These values correspond to the acquisition parameters used in the HCP MGH dataset. Both setups have b-shells with 128 uniformly distributed directions, but they differ in their b-values. Setup $\mathcal{A}$ corresponds to an "ideal" case with 10 b-values between 0 and 10 ms μm⁻². Setup $\mathcal{B}$ reproduces the more challenging setup from the HCP dataset, with only 5 b-values: 0, 1, 3, 5 and 10 ms μm⁻². We simulated a diffusion signal for each setup and computed their summary statistics, obtaining $x_o^{\mathcal{A}}$ and $x_o^{\mathcal{B}}$. Note that in setup $\mathcal{B}$ we have added an extra step when extracting the summary features: we used MAPL [4] to interpolate an additional b-value to the simulations at 0.1 ms μm⁻², aiming to improve the close-to-zero approximation of the moments (as presented in Sect. 2.2), which requires 3 b-values inferior to 2.5 ms μm⁻².

We trained a neural density estimator $q_\phi^N(\boldsymbol{\theta}|\boldsymbol{x})$ using the procedure described in Sect. 2.3 with N simulations from the three-compartment model and an uniform prior distribution defined on physiologically relevant intervals:

$$D_a \in [10^{-5}, 3.5], \ C_s \in [50, 2500], \text{and } p_2, f_s, f_n, f_{ECS} \in [0,1] \ . \tag{11}$$

By the end of the optimization procedure that minimizes Eq. (10), we obtain approximations $q_\phi^N(\boldsymbol{\theta}|\boldsymbol{x}_o^{\mathcal{A}}) \approx p(\boldsymbol{\theta}|\boldsymbol{x}_o^{\mathcal{A}})$ and $q_\phi^N(\boldsymbol{\theta}|\boldsymbol{x}_o^{\mathcal{B}}) \approx p(\boldsymbol{\theta}|\boldsymbol{x}_o^{\mathcal{B}})$.

The Estimated Posterior Distribution. Figure 1 portrays the marginal posterior distributions for each tissue parameter in setup $\mathcal{A}$ with $N \in \{10^3, 10^4, 10^5\}$ and setup $\mathcal{B}$ with $N = 10^5$. We see that the marginals of $q_\phi^N(\boldsymbol{\theta}|\boldsymbol{x}_o^{\mathcal{A}})$ become sharper around the ground truth values $\boldsymbol{\theta}_o$ when N increases. This indicates that the LFI method is able to correctly inverse the proposed model in Eq. (1) based on the summary statistics presented in Sect. 2.1 when enough b-values are available. The posterior marginals of $q_\phi^N(\boldsymbol{\theta}|\boldsymbol{x}_o^{\mathcal{B}})$ present a bias with respect to the ground truth parameters, most likely due to the reduced number of b-values available in this setup. Note, however, that the bias is relatively low for the C_s estimation, indicating that our procedure can still be useful for describing the somas sizes in the HCP MGH dataset, as we show in Sect. 3.2.

C_s Avoids Model Indeterminacy. In Sect. 2.1, we introduce the parameter C_s, which serves as a proxy of the soma radius and provides key information on the soma compartment. Estimating this parameter instead of the soma radius (r_s) and diffusivity (D_s) separately avoids falling into model indeterminacy problems, such as those observed in the literature [13]. Indeed, Fig. 2 presents the marginal posterior distributions of r_s and D_s as well as their joint distribution in the $\mathcal{A}$ setup; we extend the prior distribution intervals from Eq. 11 to include $r_s \in [10^{-5}, 30]$ and $D_s \in [1,3]$ with the ground truth parameters $r_s = 17.5$ and $D_s = 2.3$. In addition to larger marginal posterior distributions for each parameter, the joint posterior shows a valley of values for the (r_s, D_s) pair, including

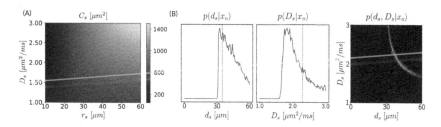

Fig. 2. (A) C_s dependence on soma radius r_s and diffusivity D_s. We see that there are several values of (d_s, D_s) that yield the same C_s. (B) Histograms of 10^4 samples from the marginal and joint posterior distributions of $d_s = 2r_s$ and D_s. The ridge in the joint distribution indicates that there are several possible values for the pair (d_s, D_s) with high probability, which are those yielding the same C_s. Estimating C_s directly bypasses this indeterminacy.

the ground truth parameters, with high probability. In this situation the LFI procedure is unable to determine among all the possible solutions which one is the ground truth. Using C_s instead of r_s and D_s separately, we avoid such indeterminacy, as seen in Fig. 1. Note that such behavior derives naturally from the way we define our model and inference procedure. As such, similar results can be expected when applying our method to the HCP dataset.

Assessing the Quality of the Posterior Estimations. Deriving the posterior distributions of the parameter vectors allows us to report the values of the most likely tissue parameters for a given observation, along with our certitude regarding our inference. Figure 3 presents the logarithm of the standard deviation of the marginal posterior samples for different ground truth parameter choices (varying f_s and f_n) under setup $\mathcal{A}$. These values indicate how sharp a posterior distribution is and, therefore, quantify the quality of the fit. We observe larger standard deviations in the absence (or weak presence) of soma compartments in the mixture signal, e.g., the standard deviation of C_s is large when few or no somas are present ($f_s \approx 0$). This is to be expected, the lack of contribution from the somas in diffusion signal making it difficult to estimate parameters related to them. Conversely, a low standard deviation is observed for signals generated in grey matter tissue conditions, where a soma predominance is expected.

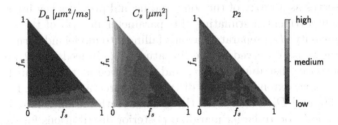

Fig. 3. Logarithm of the standard deviations for the marginal posterior distribution of D_a, C_s, and p_2 with different choices of ground truth parameters (varying f_s and f_n). We see that when the signal fraction of somas decreases ($f_s \to 0$) the standard deviation of the C_s-estimation increases; and when less neurites are present ($f_n \to 0$) the standard deviation of p_2 and D_a increase.

3.2   HCP MGH Results

We used the open data set HCP MGH Adult Diffusion [15] to study the variation of all the parameters on the human brain grey matter. It is composed of 35 subjects with $\delta/\Delta = 12.9/21.8$ ms and $b = 1, 3, 5, 10$ ms μm^{-2}. We used the 3, 5 and 10 ms μm^{-2} b-values for the RTOP approximation. For the Spiked LEMONADE approximation, we fitted MAPL on the 0, 1 and 3 ms μm^{-2} b-values and interpolated a point at 0.1 ms μm^{-2} to reduce noise and improve the estimation. D_e was estimated as the mean diffusivity in the ventricles. Our results are shown in Fig. 4. Overlay colormaps are masked showing only areas where parameters are stable. We deemed

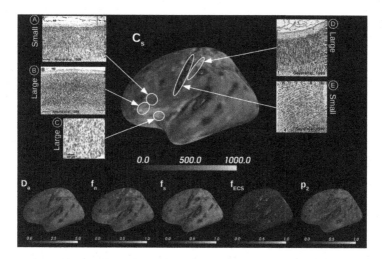

Fig. 4. Microstructural measurements averaged over 31 HCP MGH subjects. We deemed stable measurements with a z-score larger than 2, where the standard deviation on the posterior estimates was estimated through our LFI fitting approach. In comparing with Nissl-stained cytoarchitectural studies we can qualitatively evaluate our parameter C_s: Broadmann area 44 (A) has smaller soma size in average than area 45 (B) [2]; large von Economo neurons predominate the superior anterior insula (C) [1]; precentral gyrus (E) shows very small somas while post-central (D) larger ones [7].

parameters stable when their value was larger than 2 times the LFI-obtained standard deviations of the fitted posterior. This results in a lack of stability on small sections including the auditory cortex and the precentral gyrus fundus. Our figure assesses qualitatively the results on soma size by comparing with nissl-stained histological studies [1, 2, 7]. This comparison shows good agreement between different cortical areas and our parameter C_s which, under nearly-constant intra-soma diffusion D_s, is modulated by soma size.

4   Conclusion

Quantifying grey matter tissue composition is challenging. In this work, we have presented a methodology to estimate the parameters of a model that best fit an observed data point, and also their full posterior distribution. This rich description provides many useful tools, such as assessing the quality of the parameter estimation or characterizing regions in the parameter space where it is harder to invert the model. Moreover, our proposal alleviates limitations from current methods in the literature by not requiring physiologically unrealistic constraints on the parameters and avoiding indeterminacies when estimating them.

Acknowledgements. This work was supported by the ERC-StG NeuroLang ID:757672 and the ANR BrAIN grants.

References

1. Allman, J.M., et al.: The von Economo neurons in frontoinsular and anterior cingulate cortex in great apes and humans. Brain Struct. Funct. **214**, 495–517 (2010)
2. Amunts, K., Schleicher, A., Bürgel, U., Mohlberg, H., Uylings, H.B., Zilles, K.: Broca's region revisited: cytoarchitecture and intersubject variability. J. Comp. Neurol. **412**(2), 319–341 (1999)
3. Balinov, B., Jönsson, B., Linse, P., Söderman, O.: The NMR self-diffusion method applied to restricted diffusion. Simulation of echo attenuation form molecules in spheres and between planes. J. Magn. Reson. Ser. A **104**(1), 17–25 (1993)
4. Fick, R.H., Wassermann, D., Caruyer, E., Deriche, R.: MAPL: tissue microstructure estimation using Laplacian-regularized MAP-MRI and its application to HCP data. Neuroimage **134**, 365–385 (2016)
5. Fick, R.H.J., Wassermann, D., Deriche, R.: The Dmipy toolbox: diffusion MRI multi-compartment modeling and microstructure recovery made easy. Front. Neuroinform. **13**, 64 (2019)
6. Germain, M., Gregor, K., Murray, I., Larochelle, H.: Made: masked autoencoder for distribution estimation. In: Proceedings of the 32nd International Conference on Machine Learning, vol. 37, pp. 881–889. PMLR (2015)
7. Geyer, S., Schleicher, A., Zilles, K.: Areas 3a, 3b, and 1 of human primary somatosensory cortex. NeuroImage **10**(1), 63–83 (1999)
8. Greenberg, D., Nonnenmacher, M., Macke, J.: Automatic posterior transformation for likelihood-free inference. In: Proceedings of the 36th International Conference on Machine Learning, vol. 97, pp. 2404–2414. PMLR (2019)
9. Menon, V., et al.: Microstructural organization of human insula is linked to its macrofunctional circuitry and predicts cognitive control. eLife **9**, e53470 (2020)
10. Mitra, P.P., Latour, L.L., Kleinberg, R.L., Sotak, C.H.: Pulsed-field-gradient NMR measurements of restricted diffusion and the return-to-origin probability. J. Magn. Reson. **114**, 47–58 (1995)
11. Novikov, D.S., Fieremans, E., Jespersen, S.N., Kiselev, V.G.: Quantifying brain microstructure with diffusion MRI: theory and parameter estimation. NMR in Biomed. **32**, e3998 (2018)
12. Novikov, D.S., Veraart, J., Jelescu, I.O., Fieremans, E.: Rotationally-invariant mapping of scalar and orientational metrics of neuronal microstructure with diffusion MRI. NeuroImage **174**, 518–538 (2018)
13. Palombo, M., et al.: SANDI: a compartment-based model for non-invasive apparent soma and neurite imaging by diffusion MRI. NeuroImage **215**, 116835 (2020)
14. Papamakarios, G., Nalisnick, E.T., Rezende, D.J., Mohamed, S., Lakshminarayanan, B.: Normalizing flows for probabilistic modeling and inference. arXiv arXiv:1912.02762 (2019)
15. Setsompop, K., et al.: Pushing the limits of in vivo diffusion MRI for the human connectome project. Neuroimage **80**, 220–233 (2013)
16. Sisson, S.A.: Handbook of Approximate Bayesian Computation. Chapman and Hall/CRC (September 2018)
17. Veraart, J., et al.: Noninvasive quantification of axon radii using diffusion MRI. eLife **9**, e49855 (2020)
18. Zhang, H., Schneider, T., Wheeler-Kingshott, C.A., Alexander, D.C.: NODDI: practical in vivo neurite orientation dispersion and density imaging of the human brain. Neuroimage **61**(4), 1000–1016 (2012)

Non-isomorphic Inter-modality Graph Alignment and Synthesis for Holistic Brain Mapping

Islem Mhiri[1,2], Ahmed Nebli[1,2], Mohamed Ali Mahjoub[1],
and Islem Rekik[2(✉)]

[1] Université de Sousse, Ecole Nationale d'Ingénieurs de Sousse, LATIS- Laboratory of
Advanced Technology and Intelligent Systems, 4023 Sousse, Tunisie
[2] BASIRA Lab, Faculty of Computer and Informatics Engineering,
Istanbul Technical University, Istanbul, Turkey
irekik@itu.edu.tr
http://basira-lab.com/

Abstract. Brain graph synthesis marked a new era for predicting a target brain graph from a source one without incurring the high acquisition cost and processing time of neuroimaging data. However, works on recovering a brain graph in one modality (e.g., functional brain imaging) from a brain graph in another (e.g., structural brain imaging) remain largely scarce. Besides, existing *multimodal* graph synthesis frameworks have several limitations. *First*, they mainly focus on generating graphs from the same domain (intra-modality), overlooking the rich multimodal representations of brain connectivity (inter-modality). *Second*, they can only handle *isomorphic* graph generation tasks, limiting their generalizability to synthesizing target graphs with a different node size and topological structure from those of the source one. More importantly, both target and source domains might have different distributions, which causes a domain fracture between them (i.e., distribution misalignment). To address such challenges, we propose an inter-modality aligner of non-isomorphic graphs (IMANGraphNet) framework to infer a target graph modality based on a given modality. Our three core contributions lie in (i) predicting a target graph (e.g., functional) from a source graph (e.g., morphological) based on a novel graph generative adversarial network (gGAN); (ii) using non-isomorphic graphs for both source and target domains with a different number of nodes, edges and structure; and (iii) enforcing the source distribution to match that of the ground truth graphs using a graph aligner to relax the loss function to optimize. Furthermore, to handle the unstable behavior of gGAN, we design a new Ground Truth-Preserving (GT-P) loss function to guide the non-isomorphic generator in learning the topological structure of ground truth brain graphs more effectively. Our comprehensive experiments on predicting target functional brain graphs from source morphological graphs demonstrate the outperformance of IMANGraphNet in comparison with its variants. IMANGraphNet presents the first framework for brain graph synthesis based on aligned non-isomorphic inter-modality brain graphs which handles variations

This project has been funded by the TUBITAK 2232 Fellowship (No: 118C288). GitHub: https://github.com/basiralab/IMANGraphNet.

A. Feragen et al. (Eds.): IPMI 2021, LNCS 12729, pp. 203–215, 2021.
https://doi.org/10.1007/978-3-030-78191-0_16

in graph size, distribution and structure. This can be further leveraged for integrative and holistic brain mapping as well as developing multimodal neurological disorder diagnosis frameworks.

Keywords: Inter-modality graph alignment · Non-isomorphic graph generator

1 Introduction

Multimodal brain imaging spinned several medical image analysis applications thanks to the rich multimodal information it provides [1,2]. Multiple data sources such as magnetic resonance imaging (MRI), computed tomography (CT), and positron emission tomography (PET) offer the possibility of learning more holistic and informative data representations. However, such modalities introduce challenges including high acquisition cost and processing time across different clinical facilities.

Following the exponential growth of deep learning applications using MRI data, recently, such end-to-end frameworks have been investigated for multimodal MR image synthesis [3,4]. These methods either synthesize one modality from another (i.e., cross-modality) or map both modalities to a commonly shared domain. Specifically, generative adversarial networks (GANs) have held great promise in predicting medical images of different brain image modalities from a given modality [5–7]. For instance, [5] suggested a joint neuroimage synthesis and representation learning (JSRL) framework with transfer learning for subjective cognitive decline conversion prediction where they imputed missing PET images using MRI scans. In addition, [6] proposed a unified GAN to train only a single generator and a single discriminator to learn the mappings among images of four different modalities. Furthermore, [7] translated a T1-weighted magnetic resonance imaging (MRI) to T2-weighted MRI using GAN. Although significant clinical representations were obtained from the latter studies, more substantial challenges still exist [2]. As the reader may recognize, the brain connectome is a complex non-linear structure, which makes it difficult to be captured by linear models [8,9]. Besides, many methods do not make good use of or even fail to treat non-euclidean structured data (i.e., geometric data) types such as graphs and manifolds [10]. Hence a deep learning model that preserves the topology of graph-based data representations for the target learning task presents a pertinent research direction to explore.

Recently, deep learning techniques have achieved great success on graph-structured data which provides a new way to model the non-linear cross-modality relationship. Specifically, deep graph convolutional networks (GCNs) have permeated the field of brain graph research [11–13] via diverse tasks such as learning the mapping between human connectome and disease diagnosis. Recently, landmark studies used GCNs to predict a target brain graph from a source brain graph. For instance, [11] proposed a novel GCN model for multimodal brain networks analysis to generate a functional connectome from a structural connectome. Moreover, [14] presented a multi-GCN based generative adversarial network (MGCN-GAN) to infer individual structural connectome from a functional connectome. Another recent work [15] introduced MultiGraph-GAN architecture, which predicts multiple brain graphs from a single brain graph while preserving the topological structure of each target predicted graph. However, all these works use *isomorphic* graphs which means that the source graphs and the ground-truth graphs have the same number of edges, nodes, and are topologically identical. Therefore, using *non-isomorphic* graphs remains a significant challenge in designing generalizable and scalable brain graph synthesis. Moreover, inferring a target domain from a source domain introduces the problem of *domain fracture* resulting in the difference in distribution between the source and target domains. Remarkably, domain alignment is strikingly lacking in brain graph synthesis tasks [11, 14, 15] (Fig. 1).

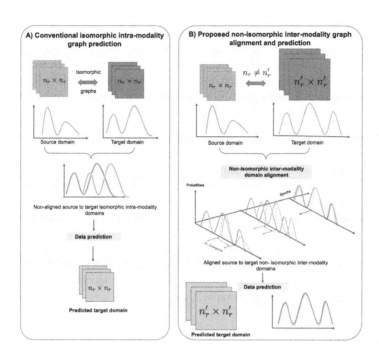

Fig. 1. *Conventional isomorphic intra-modality graph prediction versus proposed non-isomorphic inter-modality graph alignment and prediction framework.* **A)** Conventional brain graph synthesis works focus on predicting *isomorphic intra-modality* target graphs without alignment. **B)** To overcome the limitations of such models, we design a simple but effective *non-isomorphic inter-modality* graph alignment and prediction framework with the following contributions. *First,* we propose a KL divergence-based graph aligner to align the distribution of the training source graphs (from a source modality) to that of the target graphs (from a target modality). *Second,* we design a graph GAN to synthesize a target modality graph from a source one while handling shifts in graph resolution (i.e., node size). *Third,* we design a new Ground Truth-Preserving (GT-P) loss function to guide the *non-isomorphic* generator in learning the topological structure of ground truth target brain graphs more effectively.

To address such unsolved challenges and motivated by the recent development of geometric deep neural network-based solutions, we propose an inter-modality aligner of non-isomorphic brain graphs (IMANGraphNet) framework based on generative adversarial learning. To do so, prior to the prediction block, we propose a graph aligner network to align the training graphs of the source modality to that of the target one. Second, given the aligned source graph, we design a non-isomorphic graph GAN (gGAN) to map the *aligned* source graph from one modality (e.g., morphological) to the target graph modality (e.g., functional). Note that the alignment step facilitates the training of our non-isomorphic gGAN since both source and target domains have been aligned by the aligner network (i.e., shared mode) (Fig. 2–A). Besides, in order to capture the complex relationship in both direct and indirect brain connections [14], we design the generator and discriminator of our GAN using GCNs. Moreover, to resolve the inherent instability of GAN, we propose a novel ground-truth-preserving (GT-P) loss function to force our *non-isomorphic* generator to learn the ground-truth brain graph more efficiently. More importantly, by comparing the strongest connectivities of the ground-truth graphs with those of the predicted brain graphs for the same subjects, we investigate the *reproducible* power of our IMANGraphNet which not only predicts reliable brain graphs but also captures the delicate difference across subjects. The compelling aspects of our method can be summarized as follows:

1. *On a methodological level.* IMANGraphNet presents the first work on inter-modality non-isomorphic graph alignment and synthesis, which can be also leveraged for developing precision medicine using network neuroscience [8].
2. *On a clinical level.* Learning brain connectivity inter-modality synthesis can provide holistic brain maps that capture multimodal interactions (functional, structural, and morphological) between brain regions, thereby charting brain dysconnectivity patterns in disordered populations [9].
3. *On a generic level.* Our framework is a generic method as it can be applied to predict brain graphs derived from any neuroimaging modalities with complex nonlinear distributions even when they are non-isomorphic. IMANGraphNet can also be applied to other types of non-biological graphs.

2   Methodology

In this section, we detail our non-isomorphic inter-modality graph alignment and prediction framework (Fig. 2). In the first stage, we propose a Kullback-Leibler (KL) divergence-based graph aligner which maps the distribution of the ground truth domain to the source domain. In the second stage, we design a non-isomorphic gGAN to synthesize one modality graph from another while handling graph resolution shifts. Moreover, to handle the unstable behavior of gGAN, we propose a new ground truth-preserving (GT-P) loss function to guide the non-isomorphic generator in learning the topological structure of ground truth brain graphs more effectively.

- **Problem statement.** Let $G_i(V_i, E_i)$ denote a brain graph where each node in V_i denotes a brain region of interest (ROI) and each edge in E_i connecting two ROIs k and l denotes the strength of their connectivity. Each training subject i in our dataset is represented by two brain graphs $\{G_{s_i}(V_{s_i}, E_{s_i}), G_{t_i}(V_{t_i}, E_{t_i})\}$, where G_s represents the source brain graph with n_r nodes and G_t is the target brain graph with $n_{r'}$ nodes with $n_r \neq n_{r'}$. Specifically, these two graphs are considered as non-isomorphic with no correspondence between nodes and edges across source and target graphs – i.e., they are topologically different (Fig. 1). Formally, graph isomorphism can be defined as follows.

Definition 1. *Two graphs* **G** *and* **H** *are isomorphic if there is a bijection* $f : V(\mathbf{G}) \rightarrow V(\mathbf{H})$ *so that, for any* $v, w \in V(\mathbf{G})$, *the number of edges connecting* v *to* w *is the same as the number of edges* $f(v)$ *to* $f(w)$. *The function* f *is called an isomorphism from* **G** *to* **H**.

Definition 2. *Two graphs* **G** *and* **H** *are* non-isomorphic *if they do not satisfy at least one of the following conditions: (i) equal number of nodes, (ii) equal number of edges, and (iii) topologically identical (i.e., preservation of the local neighborhood of each node).*

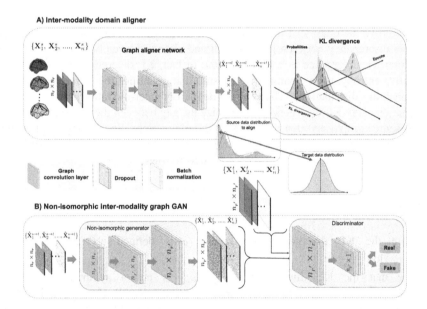

Fig. 2. *Illustration of the proposed non-isomorphic inter-modality brain graph alignment and synthesis using IMANGraphNet.* **A) Graph aligner for inter-modality domain alignment.** We aim to align the training graphs of the source modality $\mathbf{X}^s$ to that of the target one $\mathbf{X}^t$. Therefore, we design a KL divergence-based graph aligner to bridge the gap between the distributions of the source and target graphs. **B) Non-isomorphic inter-modality graph GAN.** Next, we propose a non-isomorphic graph GAN to transform the aligned source brain graph $\hat{\mathbf{X}}^{s \rightarrow t}$ (e.g., morphological) into the target graph (e.g., functional) with different structural and topological properties. Both aligner and generator networks are trained in an end-to-end manner by optimizing a novel Ground Truth-Preserving (GT-P) loss function which guides the non-isomorphic generator in learning the topology of the target ground truth brain graphs more effectively.

- **Graph-based inter-modality aligner block.** The first block of IMANGraphNet (Fig. 2-A) comprises a graph-based inter-modality aligner that constrains the distribution of the mapped source brain graphs to match that of the ground-truth target brain graphs. Inspired by the dynamic edge convolution proposed in [16] and the U-net architecture [17] with skip connections, we propose an aligner network which is composed of three-layer graph convolutional neural network (GCN) (Fig. 2-A). Given a set of n training source brain networks (e.g., morphological connectomes) $\mathbf{X}_{tr}^s$ and a set of n training ground-truth brain networks (e.g., functional connectomes) $\mathbf{X}_{tr}^t$, for each subject i, our aligner takes $\mathbf{X}_i^s$ as input and outputs $\hat{\mathbf{X}}_i^{s \to t}$ which shares the same distribution of $\mathbf{X}_i^t$. Our model consists of three GCN layers adjusted by adding batch normalization and dropout to the output of each layer. Specifically, batch normalization efficiently accelerates the network training through a fast convergence of the loss function and dropout eliminates the risk of overfitting. Hence, these two operations help optimize and simplify the network training.

To improve the quality of the inter-modality aligner network, we propose to minimize the discrepancy between ground-truth and aligned source brain graph distributions using KL divergence as a loss function. In fact, KL divergence, also known as the relative entropy, is an asymmetric measure that quantifies the difference between two probability distributions. Thereby, we define our inter-modality graph alignment loss function using KL divergence to minimize the gap between the distributions of the aligned source graphs and that of ground-truth target graphs. Specifically, we compute the KL divergence between the ground truth distribution q_{tr} and aligned distribution p_{tr} for the training subjects which is expressed as follows:

$$\mathcal{L}_{KL} = \sum_{i=1}^{n} KL\left(q_i \| p_i\right) \tag{1}$$

where the KL divergence for subject i is defined as: $KL\left(q_i \| p_i\right) = \int_{-\infty}^{+\infty} q_i(x) \log \frac{q_i(x)}{p_i(x)} dx$

Note that the KL divergence $KL\left(q_i \| p_i\right)$ is not a symmetrical function $KL\left(q_i \| p_i\right) \neq KL\left(p_i \| q_i\right)$ and defines the information gained by changing beliefs from a prior probability distribution p to the posterior probability distribution q (i.e., moving the prior distribution towards the posterior one). Intuitively, q is the true distribution and p is the aligned.

- **Adversarial non-isomorphic graph generator block.** Following the alignment step, we design a *non-isomorphic* generator architecture that handles shifts in graph resolution (i.e., node size variation) coupled with an adversarial discriminator.

Non-isomorphic Brain Graph Generator. Our non-isomorphic graph generator G is composed of three GCN layers regularized using batch normalization and dropout to the output of each layer (Fig. 2-B), taking as input the aligned source graphs to the target distribution $\hat{\mathbf{X}}_i^{s \to t}$ of size $n_r \times n_r$ and outputting the predicted target brain graphs $\hat{\mathbf{X}}_i^t$ of size $n_{r'} \times n_{r'}$ where $n_r \neq n_{r'}$. Specifically, owing to dynamic graph-based edge convolution operation [16], each GCN layer includes a unique dynamic filter that outputs edge-specific weight matrix which dictates the information flow between nodes k and l to learn a comprehensive vector representation for each node. Next, to learn our inter-modality non-isomorphic mapping, we define a mapping function $\mathcal{T}_r : \mathbb{R}^{n_r \times n_{r'}} \mapsto \mathbb{R}^{n_{r'} \times n_{r'}}$ that takes as input the embedded matrix of the whole graph in the latest GCN layer of size $n_r \times n_{r'}$ and outputs the generated target graph of size $n_{r'} \times n_{r'}$ (see subsection: *Graph resolution shift based on dynamic edge convolution*).

Graph Discriminator Based on Adversarial Training. Our non-isomorphic generator G is trained in an adversarial manner against a discriminator network D (Fig. 2-B). In order to discriminate between the predicted and ground truth target graph data, we design a two-layer graph neural network [16]. Our discriminator D takes as input the real connectome $\mathbf{X}_i^t$ and the generator's output $\hat{\mathbf{X}}_i^t$. The discriminator outputs a value between 0 and 1 measuring the realness of the generator's output. To enhance our discriminator's ability to distinguish between the target predicted and ground truth brain graphs, we adopt the adversarial loss function so that it maximizes the discriminator's output value for the $\mathbf{X}_i^t$ and minimizes it for $\hat{\mathbf{X}}_i^t$.

Graph Resolution Shift Based on Dynamic Edge Convolution. In all network blocks of IMANGraphNet, each proposed GCN layer uses a dynamic graph-based edge convolution process [16]. Specifically, let h be the layer index in the neural network and d_h denote the output dimension of the corresponding layer. Each layer h includes a filter generating network $F^h : \mathbb{R} \mapsto \mathbb{R}^{d_h \times d_{h-1}}$ that dynamically generates a weight matrix for filtering message passing between ROIs k and l given the edge weight e_{kl}. Here e_{kl} is edge feature (i.e., connectivity weight) that quantifies the relationship between ROIs k and l. The purpose of each layer in our IMANGraphNet is to produce the graph convolution result which can be observed as a filtered signal $\mathbf{z}^h(k) \in \mathbb{R}^{d_h \times 1}$ at node k. The overall edge-conditioned convolution operation is defined as follows:

$$\mathbf{z}_k^h = \boldsymbol{\Theta}^h . \mathbf{z}_k^{h-1} + \frac{1}{|N(k)|} \sum_{l \in N(k)} F^h(e_{kl}; \mathbf{W}^h)\mathbf{z}_l^{h-1} + \mathbf{b}^h \tag{2}$$

where $\mathbf{z}_k^h \in \mathbb{R}^{d_h \times 1}$ is the embedding of node k in layer h, $\Theta_{lk}^h = F^h(\mathbf{e}_{kl}; \mathbf{W}^h)$ represents the dynamically generated edge-specific weights by F^h. $\mathbf{b}^h \in \mathbb{R}^{d_h}$ denotes a network bias and $N(k)$ denotes the neighbors of node k.

Given the learned embedding $\mathbf{z}_k^h \in \mathbb{R}^{d_h}$ for node k in layer h, we define the embedding of the whole graph in layer h as $\mathbf{Z}^h \in \mathbb{R}^{n_r \times d_h}$ where n_r is the number of nodes. We draw to the attention of the reader that any resolution shift can be easily expressed as a transformation $\mathcal{T}_r : \mathbb{R}^{n_r \times d_h} \mapsto \mathbb{R}^{d_h \times d_h}$ where $\mathcal{T}_r$ is formulated as follows: $\mathcal{T}_r = (\mathbf{Z}^h)^T \mathbf{Z}^h$. As such, shifting resolution is only defined by fixing the desired target graph resolution d_h. In our case, we set d_h of the latest layer in the generator to $n_{r'}$ to output the predicted target brain graph $\hat{\mathbf{X}}^t$ of size $n_{r'} \times n_{r'}$ (Fig. 2).

Ground Truth-Preserving Loss Function. GAN generators are conventionally optimized according to the response of their corresponding discriminators. However, within a few training epochs, we note that the discriminator can easily distinguish real graphs from predicted graphs and the adversarial loss would be close to 0. In this case, the generator cannot provide good results and will keep producing bad quality graphs. To overcome this issue, we need to enforce a synchrony between the generator and the discriminator learning throughout the whole training process. Thus, we propose a new ground truth-preserving (GT-P) loss function composed of four sub-losses: adversarial loss, $L1$ loss, Pearson correlation coefficient (PCC) loss and topological loss, which we detail below. We define our GT-P loss function as follows:

$$\mathcal{L}_{\text{GT-P}} = \lambda_1 \mathcal{L}_{adv} + \lambda_2 \mathcal{L}_{L1} + \lambda_3 \mathcal{L}_{PCC} + \lambda_4 \mathcal{L}_{top} \tag{3}$$

where $\mathcal{L}_{adv}$ represents the adversarial loss which quantifies the difference between the generated and ground truth target graphs as both non-isomorphic generator and discriminator are iteratively optimized through the adversarial loss:

$$\arg\min_G \max_D \mathcal{L}_{adv} = \mathbb{E}_{G(\mathbf{X}^t)} \left[\log \left(D \left(G \left(\mathbf{X}^t \right) \right) \right) \right] + \mathbb{E}_{G(\hat{\mathbf{X}}^t)} \left[\log \left(1 - D \left(G \left(\hat{\mathbf{X}}^t \right) \right) \right) \right] \tag{4}$$

To improve the quality of the predicted target brain graphs, we propose to add an $l1$ loss term that minimizes the distance between each predicted subject $\hat{\mathbf{X}}^t$ and its related ground truth $\mathbf{X}^t$. The $l1$ loss function is expressed as follows: $\mathcal{L}_{l1} = \left\| \mathbf{X}^t - \hat{\mathbf{X}}^t \right\|_1$.

Even robust to outliers, the $l1$ loss only focuses on the element-wise similarity in edge weights between the predicted and real brain graphs and ignores the overall correlation between both graphs. Hence, we include the Pearson correlation coefficient (PCC) in our loss which measures the overall correlation between the predicted and real brain graphs. Since (i) the non-isomorphic generator aims to minimize its loss function and (ii) higher PCC indicates a higher correlation between the ground-truth and the predicted graphs, we propose to minimize the PCC loss function as follows: $\mathcal{L}_{PCC} = 1 - PCC$.

We further note that each brain graph has its unique topology which should be preserved when generating the target brain graphs. Therefore, we introduce a topological loss function that forces the non-isomorphic generator to maintain the nodes' topological profiles while learning the global graph structure. To do so, we first compute eigenvector centrality (capturing the centralities of a node's neighbors) of each node for both predicted and real brain graphs. Then, we define the $l1$ loss between the real and predicted eigenvector centralities in order to minimize the discrepancy between them. Hence, we define our topology loss as $\mathcal{L}_{top} = \|\mathbf{c}^t - \hat{\mathbf{c}}^t\|_1$, where $\hat{\mathbf{c}}^t$ denotes the eigenvector centrality vector of the predicted brain graph and $\mathbf{c}^t$ is the eigenvector centrality vector of the real one.

3   Experimental Results and Discussion

Evaluation Dataset. We used three-fold cross-validation to evaluate the proposed IMANGrahNet framework on 150 subjects from the Southwest University Longitudinal Imaging Multimodal (SLIM) public dataset[1] where each subject has T1-w, T2-w MRI and resting-state fMRI (rsfMRI) scans. Our IMANGraphNet is implemented using PyTorch-Geometric library [18].

---

[1] http://fcon_1000.projects.nitrc.org/.

Morphological Brain Networks (Source). We used FreeSurfer [19] to reconstruct the cortical morphological network for each subject from structural T1-w MRI. Specifically, we parcellated each cortical hemisphere into 35 cortical regions using Desikan-Killiany cortical atlas. Finally, by computing the pairwise absolute difference in cortical thickness between pairs of regions of interest, we generated a 35×35 morphological connectivity matrix for each subject denoted as $\mathbf{X}^s$.

Functional Brain Networks (Target). Following several preprocessing steps of each resting-state fMRI using preprocessed connectomes project quality assessment protocol, brain graphs (connectomes) were produced using a whole-brain parcellation approach as proposed in [20]. Each brain rfMRI was partitioned into 160 ROIs. Functional connectivity weights were computed using the Pearson correlation coefficient between two average fMRI signals of pairs of ROIs. These denote our target brain graphs $\mathbf{X}^t$.

Parameter Setting. For the hyperparameters of the aligner network, we set $\lambda_{KL} = 0.001$. Also, we set the non-isomorphic generator's hyperparameters as follows: $\lambda_1 = 1$, $\lambda_2 = 1$, $\lambda_3 = 0.1$, and $\lambda_4 = 2$. Moreover, we chose AdamW [21] as our default optimizer and set the learning rate at 0.025 for both the aligner and the non-isomorphic gen-

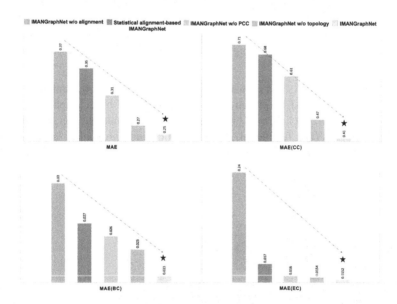

Fig. 3. *Prediction results using different evaluation metrics.* Evaluation of alignment and prediction brain graph synthesis by our framework IMANGraphNet against four comparison methods: (1) IMANGraphNet w/o alignment, (2) Statistical alignment-based IMANGraphNet, (3) IMANGraphNet w/o PCC and (4) IMANGraphNet w/o topology. As evaluation metrics, we used the mean absolute error (MAE) between the target ground truth and predicted brain graphs as well as their mean absolute difference in three topological measures (CC: closeness centrality, BC: betweenness centrality and EC: eigenvector centrality). w/o: without. ⋆: Our method IMANGraphNet *significantly* outperformed all benchmark methods using two-tailed paired t-test ($p < 0.05$) – excluding the statistical alignment-based IMANGraphNet using MAE(EC).

erator networks and 0.01 for the discriminator. Finally, we trained our IMANGraphNet for 400 epochs using a single Tesla V100 GPU (NVIDIA GeForce GTX TITAN with 32 GB memory). The feature dimensions of GCNs in the aligner are: GCN1 = (35, 35), GCN2 = (35, 1), GCN3 = (35, 35). The feature dimensions of GCNs in the non-isomorphic generator are: GCN1 = (35, 35), GCN2 = (35, 160), GCN3 = (160, 160). Similarly, feature dimensions of GCNs in the discriminator are set to GCN1 = (160, 160) and GCN2 = (160, 1).

Evaluation and Comparison Methods. To evaluate the effectiveness of our proposed method for predicting one modality from another, we carried out four major comparisons: (1) IMANGraphNet wøalignment which considers only the prediction task without aligning the distribution of the source graph to the ground truth graph. (2) Statistical alignment-based IMANGraphNet where we used a statistical alignment instead of the learned alignment when matching the distribution of the source graphs to the ground truth graphs. (3) IMANGraphNet wøPCC where we used our proposed framework without the Pearson correlation coefficient based loss. (4) IMANGraphNet wøtopology where we used our proposed framework without any topological loss. As illustrated in Fig. 3, we computed the mean absolute error between the target predicted brain graphs and the real brain graphs. Clearly, our IMANGraphNet *significantly* ($p - value < 0.05$ using two-tailed paired t-test) outperformed comparison methods by achieving the lowest error between the predicted and real brain graphs across all evaluation metrics including topological properties using closeness centrality, betweenness centrality and eigenvector centrality.

Brain Graph Alignment. As it is shown in Fig. 3, IMANGraphNet wøalignment method achieved the highest (MAE) between the real and predicted brain graphs. This shows that the domain alignment improves the quality of the generated brain graphs in the target modality domain (i.e., functional). We also notice an improvement in performance

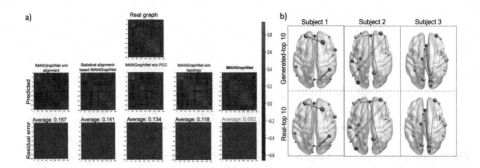

Fig. 4. *Visual comparison between the real and the predicted target brain graphs.* a) Comparison between the ground truth and predicted brain graphs by IMANGraphNet and four baseline methods (IMANGraphNet w/o alignment, Statistical alignment-basedIMANGraphNet, IMANGraphNet w/o PCC, IMANGraphNet w/o topology) using a representative testing subject. We display the residual matrices computed using the absolute difference between ground truth and predicted brain graph connectivity matrices. b) The top 15 strongest connectivities of real and predicted functional brain networks of 3 randomly selected testing subjects.

when using a simple statistical alignment strategy (statistical alignment-based IMAN-GraphNet) despite the inherent assumption that both source and target distributions are normal (a bell-shaped curve). Hence, when using a complex non-linear distribution (as our source morphological distribution in Fig. 2), the statistical aligner cannot align to the target distribution properly. Undeniably, a *learning-based* aligner has the ability to better adapt to any kind of distribution, thereby achieving the best inter-modality graph synthesis results.

Insights into Topological Measures. To investigate the fidelity of the predicted brain graphs to the real brain graphs in topology and structure, we evaluated our method using different topological measures (eigenvector, closeness, and betweenness). As shown in Fig. 3, our framework produced the smallest MAE between the functional ground truth and predicted brain graphs across all topological measurements. This shows that our IMANGraphNet is able to well preserve the most central and important nodes (i.e., hub nodes) in the synthesized functional connectomes.

Insights into the Proposed Loss Objective. To prove the superiority of the proposed GT-P loss function, we trained our IMANGraphNet with different loss functions. As illustrated in Fig. 3, our GT-P loss function outperforms its ablated versions. These results can be explained by the fact that the $l1$ loss focuses only on minimizing the distance between two brain graphs at the local level. Besides, PCC captures the strength of the correlation between both brain graphs. It aims to maximize the similarity of global connectivity patterns between the predicted and real brain graphs. However, both losses overlook the topological properties of brain graphs (e.g., node centrality). For this reason, we introduced the eigenvector centrality in our topological loss which quantifies the influence of a node on information flow in a network. The combination of these complementary losses achieved the best functional connectivity prediction results from morphological connectivity while relaxing the graph isomorphism (Definition 1) assumption between source and target domains.

Reproducibility. In addition to generating realistic functional brain graphs, our framework could also capture the delicate differences in connectivity patterns across subjects. Specifically, we display in Fig. 4-a the real, predicted, and residual brain graphs for a representative testing subject using five different methods. The residual graph is calculated by taking the absolute difference between the real and predicted brain graphs. An average difference value of the residual is displayed on top of each residual graph. We observe that the residual was noticeably reduced by our IMANGraphNet method.

Clinical Interest. Figure 4-b displays the top 10 strongest connectivities of real and predicted functional brain graphs of 3 randomly selected testing subjects. Since brain connectivity patterns vary across different individuals [22], we notice that the top 10 connectivities are not identical. However, our model can reliably predict such variations as well as individual trends in functional connectivity based solely on morphological brain graphs derived from T1-w MRI. This result further confirms that our approach is trustworthy for predicting *multimodal* brain dysconnectivity patterns in disordered populations [9] from limited neuroimaging resources.

4 Conclusion

In this paper, we introduced the first geometric deep learning architecture, namely IMANGraphNet, for *inter-modality non-isomorphic* brain graph synthesis, which nicely handles variations in graph distribution, size and structure. Our key contributions consist in designing: (1) a graph aligner network to align the training graphs of the source modality to that of the target one and (2) a non-isomorphic generator architecture that handles shifts in graph resolution (i.e., node size variation) coupled with an adversarial discriminator using GCNs. Furthermore, we proposed a new ground truth-preserving loss function which guides the non-isomorphic generator in learning the topology of the target ground truth brain graphs more effectively. Our framework outperforms the baseline methods in terms of alignment and prediction results. IMAN-GraphNet not only predicts reliable functional brain graphs from morphological ones but also preserves the topology of the target domain. In our future work, we will extend our architecture to predict *multiple* modality graphs from a single source one.

References

1. Shen, L., Liu, T., Yap, P.-T., Huang, H., Shen, D., Westin, C.-F. (eds.): MBIA 2013. LNCS, vol. 8159. Springer, Cham (2013). https://doi.org/10.1007/978-3-319-02126-3
2. Zhang, Y., Huang, H.: New graph-blind convolutional network for brain connectome data analysis. In: Chung, A.C.S., Gee, J.C., Yushkevich, P.A., Bao, S. (eds.) IPMI 2019. LNCS, vol. 11492, pp. 669–681. Springer, Cham (2019). https://doi.org/10.1007/978-3-030-20351-1_52
3. Yu, B., Wang, Y., Wang, L., Shen, D., Zhou, L.: Medical image synthesis via deep learning. In: Deep Learning in Medical Image Analysis, pp. 23–44 (2020)
4. Zhou, T., Fu, H., Chen, G., Shen, J., Shao, L.: Hi-Net: hybrid-fusion network for multi-modal MR image synthesis. IEEE Trans. Med. Imaging **39**, 2772–2781 (2020)
5. Liu, Y., et al.: Joint neuroimage synthesis and representation learning for conversion prediction of subjective cognitive decline. In: International Conference on Medical Image Computing and Computer-Assisted Intervention, pp. 583–592 (2020)
6. Dai, X., et al.: Multimodal MRI synthesis using unified generative adversarial networks. Med. Phys. **47**, 6343–6354 (2020)
7. Yang, Q., et al.: MRI cross-modality image-to-image translation. Sci. Rep. **10**, 1–18 (2020)
8. Bassett, D.S., Sporns, O.: Network neuroscience. Nat. Neurosci. **20**, 353–364 (2017)
9. van den Heuvel, M.P., Sporns, O.: A cross-disorder connectome landscape of brain dysconnectivity. Nat. Rev. Neurosci. **20**, 435–446 (2019)
10. Bronstein, M.M., Bruna, J., LeCun, Y., Szlam, A., Vandergheynst, P.: Geometric deep learning: going beyond Euclidean data. IEEE Sig. Process. Mag. **34**, 18–42 (2017)
11. Zhang, W., Zhan, L., Thompson, P., Wang, Y.: Deep representation learning for multimodal brain networks. In: Martel, A.L., et al. (eds.) MICCAI 2020. LNCS, vol. 12267, pp. 613–624. Springer, Cham (2020). https://doi.org/10.1007/978-3-030-59728-3_60
12. Nebli, A., Kaplan, U.A., Rekik, I.: Deep EvoGraphNet architecture for time-dependent brain graph data synthesis from a single timepoint. In: Rekik, I., Adeli, E., Park, S.H., Valdés Hernández, M.C. (eds.) PRIME 2020. LNCS, vol. 12329, pp. 144–155. Springer, Cham (2020). https://doi.org/10.1007/978-3-030-59354-4_14
13. Bessadok, A., Mahjoub, M.A., Rekik, I.: Brain graph synthesis by dual adversarial domain alignment and target graph prediction from a source graph. Med. Image Anal. **68**, 101902 (2021)

14. Zhang, L., Wang, L., Zhu, D.: Recovering brain structural connectivity from functional connectivity via multi-GCN based generative adversarial network. In: International Conference on Medical Image Computing and Computer-Assisted Intervention, pp. 53–61 (2020)
15. Bessadok, A., Mahjoub, M.A., Rekik, I.: Topology-aware generative adversarial network for joint prediction of multiple brain graphs from a single brain graph. In: International Conference on Medical Image Computing and Computer-Assisted Intervention, pp. 551–561 (2020)
16. Simonovsky, M., Komodakis, N.: Dynamic edge-conditioned filters in convolutional neural networks on graphs. In: Proceedings of the IEEE Conference on Computer Vision and Pattern Recognition, pp. 3693–3702 (2017)
17. Ronneberger, O., Fischer, P., Brox, T.: U-net: convolutional networks for biomedical image segmentation. In: International Conference on Medical Image Computing and Computer-Assisted Intervention, pp. 234–241 (2015)
18. Fey, M., Lenssen, J.E.: Fast graph representation learning with PyTorch geometric. arXiv preprint arXiv:1903.02428 (2019)
19. Fischl, B.: Freesurfer. Neuroimage **62**, 774–781 (2012)
20. Dosenbach, N.U., et al.: Prediction of individual brain maturity using fMRI. Science **329**, 1358–1361 (2010)
21. Loshchilov, I., Hutter, F.: Fixing weight decay regularization in Adam (2018)
22. Glasser, M., Coalson, T., Robinson, E., Hacker, C.D., et al.: A multi-modal parcellation of human cerebral cortex. Nature **536**, 171–178 (2016)

Knowledge Transfer for Few-Shot Segmentation of Novel White Matter Tracts

Qi Lu[ID] and Chuyang Ye[✉][ID]

School of Information and Electronics, Beijing Institute of Technology, Beijing, China
chuyang.ye@bit.edu.cn

Abstract. *Convolutional neural networks* (CNNs) have achieved state-of-the-art performance for *white matter* (WM) tract segmentation based on *diffusion magnetic resonance imaging* (dMRI). These CNNs require a large number of manual delineations of the WM tracts of interest for training, which are generally labor-intensive and costly. The expensive manual delineation can be a particular disadvantage when novel WM tracts, i.e., tracts that have not been included in existing manual delineations, are to be analyzed. To accurately segment novel WM tracts, it is desirable to transfer the knowledge learned about existing WM tracts, so that even with only a few delineations of the novel WM tracts, CNNs can learn adequately for the segmentation. In this paper, we explore the transfer of such knowledge to the segmentation of novel WM tracts in the few-shot setting. Although a classic fine-tuning strategy can be used for the purpose, the information in the last task-specific layer for segmenting existing WM tracts is completely discarded. We hypothesize that the weights of this last layer can bear valuable information for segmenting the novel WM tracts and thus completely discarding the information is not optimal. In particular, we assume that the novel WM tracts can correlate with existing WM tracts and the segmentation of novel WM tracts can be predicted with the logits of existing WM tracts. In this way, better initialization of the last layer than random initialization can be achieved for fine-tuning. Further, we show that a more adaptive use of the knowledge in the last layer for segmenting existing WM tracts can be conveniently achieved by simply inserting a warmup stage before classic fine-tuning. The proposed method was evaluated on a publicly available dMRI dataset, where we demonstrate the benefit of our method for few-shot segmentation of novel WM tracts.

Keywords: White matter tract · Few-shot segmentation · Convolutional neural network

1 Introduction

White matter (WM) tract segmentation based on *diffusion magnetic resonance imaging* (dMRI) allows identification of specific WM pathways [16], which are

A. Feragen et al. (Eds.): IPMI 2021, LNCS 12729, pp. 216–227, 2021.
https://doi.org/10.1007/978-3-030-78191-0_17

linked to brain development, function, and disease [18]. To achieve automated and accurate WM tract segmentation, *convolutional neural networks* (CNNs) have been applied to the segmentation task, and they have achieved state-of-the-art performance. For example, CNNs can be used to label fiber streamlines, which represent WM pathways and are computed with tractography [4], based on the feature maps extracted for each fiber streamline [18]. The labeled streamlines form the representation of specific WM tracts. It is also possible to perform volumetric WM tract segmentation that directly labels each voxel in a dMRI scan according to the WM tracts it belongs to based on diffusion feature maps [8] or fiber orientation maps [9,16]. Since volumetric segmentation assigns labels to voxels instead of fiber streamlines, the tractography step is not necessarily needed for this type of methods.

CNN-based methods of WM tract segmentation generally require a large number of manual delineations of WM tracts for training. These delineations can be very labor-intensive and costly. Although there can be existing delineations of certain WM tracts that are accumulated throughout time, the expensive delineation can be a particular disadvantage when novel WM tracts—i.e., WM tracts that have not been included in existing manual delineations—are to be analyzed. It is desirable to perform accurate segmentation of these novel WM tracts with only a few delineations, and this can be achieved by exploiting the knowledge learned about existing WM tracts. For example, the classic fine-tuning strategy [14] can be used for this few-shot setting, where knowledge about existing WM tracts is transferred to the novel WM tracts by replacing the last layer of the network for segmenting existing WM tracts with a randomly initialized output layer for the novel WM tracts. Then, all network parameters are jointly learned from the limited number of annotations of novel WM tracts.

Although classic fine-tuning can be effective for few-shot segmentation of novel WM tracts, it completely discards the information in the last task-specific layer for segmenting existing WM tracts. Since different WM tracts can be correlated, the discarded layer may bear valuable information that is relevant to the novel WM tracts, and thus classic fine-tuning may be suboptimal. Therefore, in this paper, we further explore the transfer of knowledge learned from abundant annotations of existing WM tracts to the segmentation of novel WM tracts in the few-shot setting. In particular, we focus on the scenario where only the model trained for segmenting existing WM tracts is available and the training data for existing WM tracts is inaccessible. This scenario is common for medical imaging due to privacy or other practical concerns [1]. Also, this work focuses on methods of volumetric segmentation because they do not require the step of tractography that could be sensitive to the choice of algorithms and hyperparameters, although the proposed idea may be extended to those methods based on fiber streamlines as well.

We assume that knowledge about segmenting existing WM tracts can inform the segmentation of novel WM tracts, and this can be achieved from the logits—the unnormalized predictions before the final activation function—of existing WM tracts. For simplicity, a logistic regression model is used for the prediction, which is then combined with the last layer for segmenting existing WM tracts to provide better network initialization for segmenting the novel WM tracts.

In this way, all knowledge learned for segmenting existing WM tracts, including the information in the last layer, is transferred to the segmentation of novel WM tracts. Further, we show that this problem formulation motivates a more adaptive transfer of the knowledge, and it turns out that this adaptive knowledge transfer is simply equivalent to the insertion of a warmup stage before classic fine-tuning. We evaluated the proposed method using the publicly available *Human Connectome Project* (HCP) dataset [15]. Experimental results show that our method improves the performance of few-shot segmentation of novel WM tracts.

2   Methods

2.1   Problem Formulation and Classic Fine-Tuning

Suppose we have a CNN-based segmentation model trained with abundant annotations for a set of WM tracts, and the annotations may not be accessible. We are interested in the segmentation of a novel set of WM tracts that are not considered during the training of the given model. Only a few manual annotations are available for these novel WM tracts, and our goal is to achieve decent segmentation performance for the novel WM tracts given the scarce annotations. To achieve such a goal, a common practice is to transfer the knowledge in the model learned for segmenting existing WM tracts to the segmentation of novel WM tracts. Intuitively, the knowledge transfer can be performed with the classic fine-tuning strategy [14], which we formulate mathematically as follows.

For convenience, we denote the network models for segmenting existing and novel WM tracts by $\mathcal{M}_e$ and $\mathcal{M}_n$, respectively. In classic fine-tuning, $\mathcal{M}_e$ and $\mathcal{M}_n$ share the same network structure except for the last layer, which is task-specific. Suppose the input image is $\mathbf{X}$, the task-specific weights in the last layer L_e of $\mathcal{M}_e$ and the last layer L_n of $\mathcal{M}_n$ are denoted by $\boldsymbol{\theta}_e$ and $\boldsymbol{\theta}_n$, respectively, and the other weights in $\mathcal{M}_e$ or $\mathcal{M}_n$ are denoted by $\boldsymbol{\theta}$. From $\mathbf{X}$ a multi-channel feature map $\mathbf{F}$ is computed with a mapping $f(\mathbf{X}; \boldsymbol{\theta})$ parameterized by $\boldsymbol{\theta}$:

$$\mathbf{F} = f(\mathbf{X}; \boldsymbol{\theta}), \tag{1}$$

and the segmentation probability map $\mathbf{P}_e$ or $\mathbf{P}_n$ for existing or novel WM tracts is computed from $\mathbf{F}$ with L_e or L_n using another mapping $g_e(\mathbf{F}; \boldsymbol{\theta}_e)$ or $g_n(\mathbf{F}; \boldsymbol{\theta}_n)$ parameterized by $\boldsymbol{\theta}_e$ or $\boldsymbol{\theta}_n$, respectively:

$$\mathbf{P}_e = g_e(\mathbf{F}; \boldsymbol{\theta}_e) = g_e(f(\mathbf{X}; \boldsymbol{\theta}); \boldsymbol{\theta}_e) \quad \text{and} \quad \mathbf{P}_n = g_n(\mathbf{F}; \boldsymbol{\theta}_n) = g_n(f(\mathbf{X}; \boldsymbol{\theta}); \boldsymbol{\theta}_n). \tag{2}$$

Instead of directly training $\mathcal{M}_n$ from scratch—i.e., $\boldsymbol{\theta}$ and $\boldsymbol{\theta}_n$ are randomly initialized—using the scarce annotations of novel WM tracts, in classic fine-tuning the information in $\mathcal{M}_e$ is exploited. Because $\mathcal{M}_e$ is trained by minimizing the difference between $\mathbf{P}_e$ and the abundant annotations of existing WM tracts, the learned values $\tilde{\boldsymbol{\theta}}$ of the weights $\boldsymbol{\theta}$ for segmenting existing WM tracts can provide useful information about feature extraction. Thus, $\tilde{\boldsymbol{\theta}}$ is used to initialize $\boldsymbol{\theta}$ for training $\mathcal{M}_n$, and only $\boldsymbol{\theta}_n$ is randomly initialized. In this way, the knowledge learned for segmenting existing WM tracts can be transferred to the segmentation of novel WM tracts, and this classic fine-tuning strategy has been proved successful in a variety of image processing applications [14].

2.2 Knowledge Transfer for Few-Shot Segmentation of Novel WM Tracts

Although the classic fine-tuning strategy can be used for the few-shot segmentation of novel WM tracts, it completely discards the information about θ_e in the last layer L_e learned for existing WM tracts. We hypothesize that the information in these discarded weights could also bear information relevant to the segmentation of novel WM tracts. For example, in a considerable number of voxels, WM tracts are known to co-occur as crossing fiber tracts [2]. Thus, it is reasonable to assume that existing and novel WM tracts can be correlated and novel WM tracts could be predicted from existing WM tracts, and this assumption allows us to explore the discarded information in L_e as well for training $\mathcal{M}_n$.

Suppose $\mathbf{P}_e^v$ and $\mathbf{P}_n^v$ are the vectors of segmentation probabilities at the v-th voxel of $\mathbf{P}_e$ and $\mathbf{P}_n$, respectively, where $v \in \{1, 2, \ldots, V\}$ and V is the total number of voxels. In existing segmentation networks, L_e and L_n generally use a convolution with a kernel size of one to classify each voxel (e.g., see [16]), which is equivalent to matrix multiplication (plus a bias vector) at each voxel. Therefore, we rewrite the task-specific weights as $\theta_e = \{\mathbf{W}_e, \boldsymbol{b}_e\}$ and $\theta_n = \{\mathbf{W}_n, \boldsymbol{b}_n\}$, so that the segmentation probabilities can be explicitly expressed as

$$\mathbf{P}_e^v = \sigma\left(\mathbf{W}_e \mathbf{F}^v + \boldsymbol{b}_e\right) \quad \text{and} \quad \mathbf{P}_n^v = \sigma\left(\mathbf{W}_n \mathbf{F}^v + \boldsymbol{b}_n\right), \tag{3}$$

where $\mathbf{F}^v$ represents the feature vector at the v-th voxel of the feature map $\mathbf{F}$, and $\sigma(\cdot)$ is the sigmoid activation because there can be multiple WM tracts in a single voxel.

In classic fine-tuning the information about $\mathbf{W}_e$ and $\boldsymbol{b}_e$ is completely discarded. However, according to our assumption, it is possible to exploit $\mathbf{W}_e$ and $\boldsymbol{b}_e$ to provide better initialization for $\mathbf{W}_n$ and $\boldsymbol{b}_n$. To this end, we investigate the prediction of novel WM tracts with the logits $\mathbf{H}_e$ of existing WM tracts given by the trained $\mathcal{M}_e$. For simplicity, this prediction is achieved with a logistic regression. We denote the logit vector at voxel v given by the trained $\mathcal{M}_e$ by $\mathbf{H}_e^v = (h_{e,1}^v, \ldots, h_{e,M}^v)^\mathsf{T}$, where M is the number of existing WM tracts. Then, the prediction $p_{e \to n,j}^v$ of the j-th novel WM tract at voxel v from the information of existing WM tracts is given by

$$p_{e \to n,j}^v = \frac{1}{1 + \exp\left(-(b_j + \sum_{i=1}^{M} w_{ij} h_{e,i}^v)\right)}, \tag{4}$$

where w_{ij} and b_j are the regression parameters to be determined.

Suppose the total number of novel WM tracts is N. Combining the prediction of all novel WM tracts into $\mathbf{P}_{e \to n}^v$, we simply have

$$\mathbf{P}_{e \to n}^v = \sigma\left(\mathbf{W} \mathbf{H}_e^v + \boldsymbol{b}\right), \tag{5}$$

where

$$\mathbf{W} = \begin{bmatrix} w_{11} & \cdots & w_{1M} \\ \vdots & \ddots & \vdots \\ w_{N1} & \cdots & w_{NM} \end{bmatrix} \text{ and } \boldsymbol{b} = [b_1, \ldots, b_N]^\mathsf{T}. \tag{6}$$

Note that $\mathbf{H}_e^v = \widetilde{\mathbf{W}}_e\widetilde{\mathbf{F}}^v + \tilde{b}_e$, where $\widetilde{\mathbf{F}}^v$ corresponds to the v-th voxel of $\widetilde{\mathbf{F}} = f(\mathbf{X}; \tilde{\theta})$ that is computed with the weights $\tilde{\theta}$ learned for existing WM tracts, and $\widetilde{\mathbf{W}}_e$ and $\tilde{b}_e$ are the values of $\mathbf{W}_e$ and b_e learned for existing WM tracts, respectively. Then, we have

$$\mathbf{P}_{e\to n}^v = \sigma\left(\mathbf{W}\left(\widetilde{\mathbf{W}}_e\widetilde{\mathbf{F}}^v + \tilde{b}_e\right) + b\right) = \sigma\left(\mathbf{W}\widetilde{\mathbf{W}}_e\widetilde{\mathbf{F}}^v + \mathbf{W}\tilde{b}_e + b\right). \qquad (7)$$

Comparing Eqs. (3) and (7), we notice that instead of being randomly initialized, θ_n may be better initialized using the information in $\theta_e = \{\mathbf{W}_e, b_e\}$. Here, $\mathbf{W}$ and b still need to be computed for initializing θ_n, and they can be computed by minimizing the difference between $\mathbf{P}_{e\to n}^v$ and the annotation of novel WM tracts. Note that although there are only a few annotations of novel WM tracts, they are sufficient for the computation of $\mathbf{W}$ and b because the number of unknown parameters is also drastically reduced. Then, suppose the estimates of $\mathbf{W}$ and b are $\widetilde{\mathbf{W}}$ and $\tilde{b}$, respectively; $\mathbf{W}_n$ and b_n are initialized as

$$\mathbf{W}_n \leftarrow \widetilde{\mathbf{W}}\widetilde{\mathbf{W}}_e \quad \text{and} \quad b_n \leftarrow \widetilde{\mathbf{W}}\tilde{b}_e + \tilde{b}. \qquad (8)$$

Finally, with θ initialized by $\tilde{\theta}$ like in classic fine-tuning, all network weights are learned jointly for $\mathcal{M}_n$ using the scarce annotations of novel WM tracts.

2.3 A Better Implementation with Warmup

The derivation above suggests a possible way of using all information in $\mathcal{M}_e$. However, it is possible to have a more convenient implementation. If we let $\mathbf{W}' = \mathbf{W}\widetilde{\mathbf{W}}_e$ and $b' = \mathbf{W}\tilde{b}_e + b$, Eq. (7) becomes

$$\mathbf{P}_{e\to n}^v = \sigma\left(\mathbf{W}'\widetilde{\mathbf{F}}^v + b'\right). \qquad (9)$$

This suggests that we can directly estimate $\mathbf{W}'$ and b' and use the estimated values to initialize θ_n. This is equivalent to inserting a warmup stage before the classic fine-tuning, and the information in θ_e becomes redundant with such a fine-tuning strategy (but not with classic fine-tuning). Specifically, given the trained model $\mathcal{M}_e$, for $\mathcal{M}_n$ we first set $\theta \leftarrow \tilde{\theta}$, fix θ, and learn θ_n (randomly initialized) from the scarce annotations of novel WM tracts. With the values of θ_n learned in the first stage, we then jointly fine-tune the weights θ and θ_n using the annotated novel WM tracts.

This implementation not only is more convenient than the derivation in Sect. 2.2, but also could lead to better performance for the following reasons. First, the warmup strategy is not restricted to the decomposition in Eq. (8) and allows a more adaptive use of the information in θ_e. It can find the initialization corresponding to the decomposition as well as possibly better initialization that may not be decomposed as Eq. (8). Second, even for the case where the decomposed form allows the best initialization, the separate computation of $\{\widetilde{\mathbf{W}}, \tilde{b}\}$ and $\{\widetilde{\mathbf{W}}_e, \tilde{b}_e\}$ could accumulate the error of each computation and slightly degrade the initialization, whereas directly estimating $\mathbf{W}'$ and b' avoids the problem.

Table 1. A list of the 12 novel WM tracts and their abbreviations.

	WM tract name	Abbreviation		WM tract name	Abbreviation
1	Corticospinal tract left	CST_left	7	Optic radiation left	OR_left
2	Corticospinal tract right	CST_right	8	Optic radiation right	OR_right
3	Fronto-pontine tract left	FPT_left	9	Inferior longitudinal fascicle left	ILF_left
4	Fronto-pontine tract right	FPT_right	10	Inferior longitudinal fascicle right	ILF_right
5	Parieto-occipital pontine left	POPT_left	11	Uncinate fascicle left	UF_left
6	Parieto-occipital pontine right	POPT_right	12	Uncinate fascicle right	UF_right

2.4 Implementation Details

We use the state-of-the-art TractSeg architecture proposed in [16] as our backbone network.[1] TractSeg is inspired by the U-net architecture [11], and it performs 2D processing for each orientation separately. For test scans, the results of each orientation are fused by averaging for the final 3D WM tract segmentation.

In TractSeg, the network inputs are fiber orientation maps computed with multi-shell multi-tissue constrained spherical deconvolution [5]. A maximum number of three fiber orientations is used at each voxel, and thus the input has nine channels. For voxels with fewer than three fiber orientations, the values in the corresponding empty channels are set to zero. The outputs of TractSeg are probability maps of WM tracts.

We have implemented the proposed method using PyTorch [10]. Like [16], for all network training the cross-entropy loss is minimized using Adamax [6] with a learning rate of 0.001 and a batch size of 47 [17]; we also use dropout [13] with a probability of 0.4 [16]. 200 training epochs are used to ensure training convergence. Model selection is performed according to the epoch with the best Dice score on a validation set.

3 Results

3.1 Data Description and Experimental Settings

We used the preprocessed dMRI scans in the HCP dataset [3,15] for evaluation, which were acquired with 270 diffusion gradients (b = 1000, 2000, and 3000 s/mm^2) and 18 $b0$ images [12]. The image resolution is 1.25 mm isotropic.

We selected 60 and 12 tracts as the existing and novel WM tracts, respectively, i.e., $M = 60$ and $N = 12$. These 72 WM tracts in total are the same WM tracts considered in [16]. The list of the novel WM tracts is shown in Table 1, and they were randomly selected from the bilateral WM tracts. The existing WM tracts correspond to the remaining WM tracts in [16].[2] A segmentation model

---

[1] Our method can also be integrated with other networks for volumetric WM tract segmentation.

[2] Refer to [16] for the list of these remaining WM tracts.

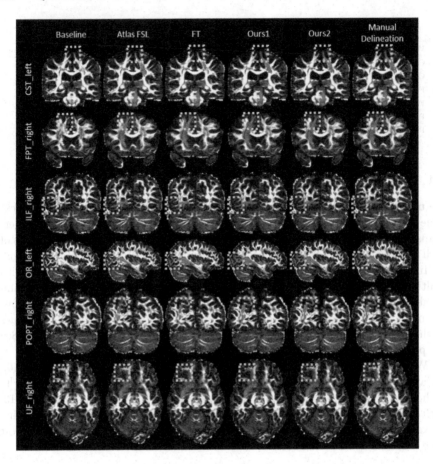

Fig. 1. Cross-sectional views of the segmentation results (red) overlaid on the fractional anisotropy maps for representative test subjects and novel WM tracts. The manual delineations are also shown for reference. Note the highlighted regions for comparison. (Color figure online)

was trained for the existing WM tracts using 65 dMRI scans, which were split into a training set comprising 52 dMRI scans and a validation set comprising 13 dMRI scans. For segmenting the novel WM tracts, we selected four other dMRI scans for network fine-tuning, where three dMRI scans were used as the training set and one dMRI scan was used as the validation set. For evaluation, the proposed method was applied to 30 test scans that were different from all the training and validation scans described above. The annotations of all training, validation, and test scans are provided by [16].

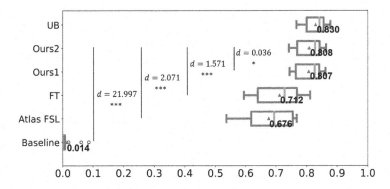

Fig. 2. Boxplots of the average Dice coefficient for each tract. The means of the average Dice coefficients are indicated. The effect sizes (Cohen's d) between Ours2 and the other methods are also listed. Asterisks indicate that the difference between Ours2 and the other method is significant using a paired Student's t-test. ($^{*}p < 0.05$, $^{***}p < 0.001$.)

3.2 Evaluation of Segmentation Accuracy

We first evaluated the accuracy of the proposed method, where the segmentation model for existing WM tracts was fine-tuned with the annotations of novel WM tracts using either the initialization strategy proposed in Sect. 2.2 or the more convenient implementation in Sect. 2.3. These two approaches are referred to as Ours1 and Ours2, respectively. We compared our methodology with three competing methods. The first one is the baseline TractSeg network that was trained from scratch with the annotations of novel WM tracts. The second one is a representative conventional registration-based method Atlas FSL described in [17], where an atlas is created from the available annotated scans and registered to test scans for segmentation. The third one is the classic fine-tuning method based on the segmentation model for existing WM tracts, which is referred to as FT.

The proposed method was first evaluated qualitatively. Cross-sectional views of the segmentation results for representative test subjects and novel WM tracts are shown in Fig. 1. The manual delineations are also shown for reference. It can be seen that the results of both of our strategies better resemble the manual delineations than the competing methods.

Next, we evaluated the proposed method quantitatively. The Dice coefficient between the segmentation result and manual delineation was used as the evaluation metric. For reference, we also computed the *upper bound* (UB) performance, where abundant annotations were available for the novel WM tracts and the segmentation network was trained from scratch using these annotated scans. Specifically, the annotations of novel WM tracts on the 65 dMRI scans for training the network for existing WM tracts were also given, and they were used in conjunction with the other four scans annotated for the novel WM tracts to train a network that segments the novel WM tracts.

We computed the average Dice coefficient for each tract, and the results are summarized in Fig. 2. In addition, we compared Ours2 (which has slightly higher

Table 2. The means of the average Dice coefficients of the 12 novel WM tracts achieved with different numbers of annotated training scans. Our results are highlighted in bold. The effect sizes (Cohen's d) between Ours2 and the other methods are also listed. Asterisks indicate that the difference between Ours2 and the other method is significant using a paired Student's t-test. ($^{**}p < 0.01$, $^{***}p < 0.001$, n.s. $p \geq 0.05$.)

Annotated training scans		Baseline	Atlas FSL	FT	Ours1	Ours2	UB
1	Dice	0	0.645	0.590	**0.777**	**0.784**	0.828
	d	20.444	1.919	1.944	0.131	-	-
	p	***	***	***	**	-	-
5	Dice	0.052	0.683	0.757	**0.811**	**0.812**	0.830
	d	10.362	2.004	1.000	0.021	-	-
	p	***	***	***	n.s	-	-

average Dice coefficients than Ours1) with the other methods (including Ours1) using paired Student's t-tests and measured the effect sizes (Cohen's d). The results are also shown in Fig. 2. We can see that our method (either Ours1 or Ours2) achieved higher Dice coefficients than the baseline, Atlas FSL, and FT, and the performance of our method is much closer to the upper bound than those of the competing methods. Also, Ours2 highly significantly ($p < 0.001$) outperforms the baseline method, Atlas FSL, and FT with large effect sizes ($d > 0.8$). The performances of Ours1 and Ours2 are quite similar, which is indicated by the close average Dice coefficients and small effect size. Combined with the significant difference between them, these results show that Ours2 is consistently better than Ours1 with a very small margin, and this is consistent with our derivation and expectation in Sect. 2.3.

3.3   Impact of the Number of Annotated Training Scans

In addition to the experimental setting above, to investigate the impact of the number of training scans annotated for the novel WM tracts on the segmentation accuracy, we considered two additional experimental settings, where additional annotated dMRI scans were included in the training and validation sets, or some of the annotated dMRI scans in the training and validation sets were excluded. Specifically, in the two cases, the numbers of annotated scans in the training/validation set were 1/0 and 5/2, respectively. The first case corresponds to a one-shot setting, and in this case model selection was performed based on the training data. The test set was not changed in these cases.

We computed the average Dice coefficient for each tract and each method under these two settings, and the means of the average Dice coefficients are shown in Table 2. Here, we compared Ours2 with the other methods using paired Student's t-tests and measured the effect sizes. The UB performance was also computed. Under these two settings, our method (either Ours1 or Ours2) still outperforms the competing methods. In particular, the performance of Ours2

Table 3. The means of the average RVDs of the 12 novel WM tracts. Our results are highlighted in bold. The effect sizes (Cohen's d) between Ours2 and the other methods are also listed. Asterisks indicate that the difference between Ours2 and the other method is significant using a paired Student's t-test. ($^*p < 0.05$, $^{**}p < 0.01$, $^{***}p < 0.001$, n.s. $p \geq 0.05$.)

Annotated training scans		Baseline	Atlas FSL	FT	Ours1	Ours2	UB
1	RVD	1	0.182	0.392	**0.156**	**0.151**	0.105
	d	17.458	0.403	1.854	0.067	-	-
	p	***	*	***	n.s	-	-
3	RVD	0.986	0.175	0.207	**0.130**	**0.129**	0.107
	d	20.566	0.671	0.901	0.009	-	-
	p	***	*	*	n.s	-	-
5	RVD	0.955	0.199	0.158	**0.129**	**0.131**	0.105
	d	11.234	0.815	0.372	0.036	-	-
	p	***	*	*	n.s	-	-

is very close to the UB with five annotated training scans, and with only one annotated training scan for the novel WM tracts, the performance of either Ours1 or Ours2 is better than that of classic fine-tuning with five annotated training scans. In addition, Ours2 highly significantly outperforms the baseline, Atlas FSL, and FT with large effect sizes, and it is slightly better than Ours1.

3.4   Evaluation of Volume Difference

In addition to segmentation accuracy, we considered an additional evaluation metric, the *relative volume difference* (RVD) between the segmented novel WM tracts and the manual delineations, for all the experimental settings in Sects. 3.2 and 3.3. This metric was considered because tract volume is an important biomarker [7] that is often used to indicate structural alterations. A smaller RVD is desired as it indicates a smaller bias in the structural analysis.

For each experimental setting, where the number of scans annotated for the novel WM tracts in the training set was one, three, or five, we computed the average RVD for each novel WM tract, and the means of these average RVDs are reported in Table 3. Again, Ours2 was compared with the other methods using paired Student's t-tests and the effect sizes were computed. Also, the UB performance is listed for reference. Either Ours1 or Ours2 has better RVD values than the competing methods, and Ours2 is significantly better than these competing methods with mostly large ($d > 0.8$) or medium (d close to 0.5) effect sizes. The performances of Ours1 and Ours2 are still comparable, and they are much closer to the UB than the performances of the competing methods are.

4 Discussion

Classic fine-tuning discards the information in the task-specific layer of an existing model, whereas we propose to also incorporate the information in this task-specific layer during knowledge transfer for the segmentation of novel WM tracts. We have derived that in this way the task-specific layer for segmenting the novel WM tracts can be better initialized than the random initialization in classic fine-tuning. In addition, we have derived that the use of the information can be achieved more adaptively by inserting a warmup stage before classic fine-tuning. From a different perspective, this derivation also explains that warmup is beneficial to the transfer of knowledge about WM tracts because it implicitly allows a more comprehensive use of existing knowledge. Our derivations are consistent with the experimental results under different settings.

Our method may be extended to deep networks [18] that classify fiber streamlines as well. Those networks also comprise feature extraction and task-specific classification layers, and the knowledge transfer can incorporate the task-specific layers using the proposed method for classifying novel fiber streamlines.

5 Conclusion

We have explored the transfer of knowledge learned from the segmentation of existing WM tracts for few-shot segmentation of novel WM tracts. Unlike classic fine-tuning, we seek to also exploit the information in the task-specific layer. The incorporation of this knowledge allows better initialization for the network that segments novel WM tracts. Experimental results on the HCP dataset indicate the benefit of our method for the segmentation of novel WM tracts.

Acknowledgements. This work is supported by Beijing Natural Science Foundation (L192058 & 7192108) and Beijing Institute of Technology Research Fund Program for Young Scholars. The HCP dataset was provided by the Human Connectome Project, WU-Minn Consortium and the McDonnell Center for Systems Neuroscience at Washington University.

References

1. Burton, P.R., et al.: Data safe havens in health research and healthcare. Bioinformatics **31**(20), 3241–3248 (2015)
2. Ginsburger, K., Matuschke, F., Poupon, F., Mangin, J.F., Axer, M., Poupon, C.: Medusa: a GPU-based tool to create realistic phantoms of the brain microstructure using tiny spheres. Neuroimage **193**, 10–24 (2019)
3. Glasser, M.F., et al.: The minimal preprocessing pipelines for the human connectome project. Neuroimage **80**, 105–124 (2013)
4. Jeurissen, B., Descoteaux, M., Mori, S., Leemans, A.: Diffusion MRI fiber tractography of the brain. NMR in Biomed. **32**, e3785 (2017)
5. Jeurissen, B., Tournier, J.D., Dhollander, T., Connelly, A., Sijbers, J.: Multi-tissue constrained spherical deconvolution for improved analysis of multi-shell diffusion MRI data. Neuroimage **103**, 411–426 (2014)

6. Kingma, D.P., Ba, J.: Adam: a method for stochastic optimization. arXiv preprint arXiv:1412.6980 (2014)
7. Lebel, C., Treit, S., Beaulieu, C.: A review of diffusion MRI of typical white matter development from early childhood to young adulthood. NMR Biomed. **32**(4), e3778 (2019)
8. Li, B., et al.: Neuro4Neuro: a neural network approach for neural tract segmentation using large-scale population-based diffusion imaging. Neuroimage **218**, 116993 (2020)
9. Lu, Q., Li, Y., Ye, C.: White matter tract segmentation with self-supervised learning. In: Martel, A.L., et al. (eds.) MICCAI 2020. LNCS, vol. 12267, pp. 270–279. Springer, Cham (2020). https://doi.org/10.1007/978-3-030-59728-3_27
10. Paszke, A., et al.: PyTorch: an imperative style, high-performance deep learning library. In: Advances in Neural Information Processing Systems, pp. 8024–8035 (2019)
11. Ronneberger, O., Fischer, P., Brox, T.: U-Net: convolutional networks for biomedical image segmentation. In: Navab, N., Hornegger, J., Wells, W.M., Frangi, A.F. (eds.) MICCAI 2015. LNCS, vol. 9351, pp. 234–241. Springer, Cham (2015). https://doi.org/10.1007/978-3-319-24574-4_28
12. Sotiropoulos, S.N., et al.: Advances in diffusion MRI acquisition and processing in the human connectome project. Neuroimage **80**, 125–143 (2013)
13. Srivastava, N., Hinton, G., Krizhevsky, A., Sutskever, I., Salakhutdinov, R.: Dropout: a simple way to prevent neural networks from overfitting. J. Mach. Learn. Res. **15**(1), 1929–1958 (2014)
14. Tajbakhsh, N., et al.: Convolutional neural networks for medical image analysis: full training or fine tuning? IEEE Trans. Med. Imaging **35**(5), 1299–1312 (2016)
15. Van Essen, D.C., Smith, S.M., Barch, D.M., Behrens, T.E., Yacoub, E., Ugurbil, K.: WU-Minn HCP consortium: the WU-Minn human connectome project: an overview. Neuroimage **80**, 62–79 (2013)
16. Wasserthal, J., Neher, P., Maier-Hein, K.H.: TractSeg - fast and accurate white matter tract segmentation. Neuroimage **183**, 239–253 (2018)
17. Wasserthal, J., Neher, P.F., Hirjak, D., Maier-Hein, K.H.: Combined tract segmentation and orientation mapping for bundle-specific tractography. Med. Image Anal. **58**, 101559 (2019)
18. Zhang, F., Karayumak, S.C., Hoffmann, N., Rathi, Y., Golby, A.J., O'Donnell, L.J.: Deep white matter analysis (DeepWMA): fast and consistent tractography segmentation. Medical Image Analysis **65**, 101761 (2020)

Discovering Spreading Pathways of Neuropathological Events in Alzheimer's Disease Using Harmonic Wavelets

Jiazhou Chen[1], Defu Yang[2], Hongmin Cai[1(✉)], Martin Styner[2], and Guorong Wu[2]

[1] School of Computer Science and Engineering, South China University of Technology,
Guangzhou, China
hmcai@scut.edu.cn

[2] Department of Psychiatry, University of North Carolina at Chapel Hill, Chapel Hill, USA

Abstract. A plethora of neuroscience studies show that neurodegenerative diseases such as Alzheimer's disease (AD) manifest network dysfunction much earlier before the onset of clinical symptoms, where neuropathological burdens often propagate across brain networks in a prion-like manner. In this context, characterizing the *in-vivo* spreading pathway of neuropathological events provides a new window to understand the pathophysiological mechanism of AD progression. However, little attention has been paid to the intrinsic geometry associated with the spreading pathway of neuropathological events, which indeed requires a network-specific algebra to quantify the associated propagation profile across individuals. To address this challenge, we propose a novel manifold harmonic approach to construct a set of region-adaptive harmonic wavelets, which allow us to capture diverse local network geometry in the aging population using the "swiss army knife" of the network topology. The learned common harmonic wavelets constitute the most representative spreading pathways that can be used to characterize the local propagation patterns of neuropathology on an individual basis. We have evaluated the power of our novel harmonic wavelets in identifying AD-related spreading pathways that lead to cognitive decline. Compared with other popular empirical biomarkers, the harmonic-based propagation patterns show much high sensitivity and specificity in stratifying cognitive normal (CN), early-stage mild cognitive impairment (MCI), and late-stage MCI, which indicates the great potential of being a putative biomarker in predicting the risk of developing AD at the pre-clinical stage.

Keywords: Biomarkers · Brain network · Harmonic wavelets · Manifold optimization · Alzheimer's disease

1 Introduction

Modern neuroimaging technology allows us to investigate the connection of two brain regions *in vivo*, where we used to study each region separately. For example, we can measure the diffusion of water molecules at each voxel using the diffusion-weighted

A. Feragen et al. (Eds.): IPMI 2021, LNCS 12729, pp. 228–240, 2021.
https://doi.org/10.1007/978-3-030-78191-0_18

imaging (DWI) technique and generate tissue-specific contrast in MR (magnetic resonance) images. Since white matter is composed of fiber bundles that connect various grey matter areas of the brain to each other, DWI has been widely used to map white matter tractography. Then, the structural brain network is constructed by counting the number of white matter fibers that connect two underlying ROIs (regions of interest).

There is a wide consensus that neurodegenerative disease such as AD can be understood as a disconnection syndrome, where the connectivity of large-scale brain networks are progressively disrupted by molecular pathomechanism [1]. For example, amyloid plaques and neurofibrillary tangles are two neuropathological hallmarks of AD. Many neuroimaging studies show that abnormal depositions of AD pathologies are found not randomly appear but instead show unique spatial patterns that follow the existing large-scale brain networks [2–4]. Furthermore, multiple threads of evidence converge to suggest that the pathological events are steered by the prion-like transmission of the abnormal pathological burden from one donor neuron to a recipient neuron adjoined through the white matter pathways [5, 6]. Since the network topology varies significantly across individuals, it is of high necessity to quantify the spreading pathway and interpret the propagation pattern of neuropathological burdens in a common space.

Striking efforts have been made to characterize how neuropathological events spread across brain networks. In [7], a network diffusion model is presented to predict the longitudinal trajectory of atrophy and metabolism in AD, where the subject-specific propagation is modeled by the eigenvectors derived from the graph Laplacian matrix of the underlying brain network. Furthermore, Atasoy et al. [8] proposed the concept of network harmonics to carry on statistical inference in the graph spectrum domain spanned by the graph eigenvectors. Recently, a manifold group-mean method has been proposed in [9] to unify the individual eigenvectors and construct the common harmonic bases that can be used for group comparison, where oscillation pattern (Fig. 1(a)) in each harmonic basis characterizes the whole-brain spreading pathway under a certain harmonic frequency. Although promising results have been demonstrated in identifying harmonic-like biomarkers in AD, the global nature of harmonic bases limits the application in identifying harmonic frequency alteration only, despite that most neuroimaging studies are more interested in investigating the altered nodes in the brain network.

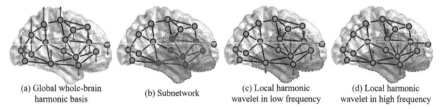

(a) Global whole-brain harmonic basis   (b) Subnetwork   (c) Local harmonic wavelet in low frequency   (d) Local harmonic wavelet in high frequency

Fig. 1. (a) The global nature of whole-brain harmonics precludes the identification of oscillation-like alterations that occurred at each brain region. Since we derive the region-adaptive harmonic wavelets within the associated subnetwork (b), our harmonic wavelets (c–d) depict the local network alterations, which allows us to capture spatial-harmonic patterns in brain network inference.

To overcome this limitation, we propose a novel manifold harmonic localization approach to discover a set of region-adaptive harmonic wavelets (Fig. 1(c–d)) in the spatial domain of a subnetwork (Fig. 1(b)), which (1) capture the local network topology and (2) provide complementary information to the existing whole-brain harmonic bases. As a result, the oscillation patterns in each harmonic wavelet characterize the spreading pathway that can be used to investigate the local propagation pattern of neuropathological events in AD. Since each harmonic wavelet exhibits the localized oscillation patterns across the localized brain network, the identified harmonic wavelets provide a new window to investigate the localized harmonic-based network alterations, which is more attractive in AD studies. We have evaluated the effectiveness of our method on synthetic data and neuroimaging data from the ADNI database. Compared to other popular empirical biomarkers, our proposed method achieves enhanced statistical power and representation capability for CN, EMCI, and LMCI classification.

2   Methods

2.1   Manifold Harmonics

Network-Specific Harmonic Bases. The brain network is often encapsulated in a $N \times N$ adjacency matrix, where N denotes the number of nodes. Each element in the adjacency matrix reflects the strength of node-to-node connection. To obtain the population-wise topological structure of all brain networks, we first generate an average adjacency matrix $W = [w_{ij}]_{i,j=1}^{N} \in \mathbb{R}^{N \times N}$ across all individual brain networks. Since the estimation of group-mean brain network is beyond the interest of this work, we simply apply element-wise average to yield the average adjacency matrix W. Interested readers can refer to manifold group-mean and parallel transportation techniques [10].

As stated in [8], a set of global harmonic bases $\Psi \in \mathbb{R}^{N \times P}$ ($P \leq N$) can be derived from the eigen-system of the underlying Laplacian matrix $L = D - W$, where D is a diagonal matrix with each element being equal to the total connectivity degree at the underlying node. Specifically, the global harmonics Ψ are estimated by minimizing:

$$\arg \min_{\Psi} tr\left(\Psi^T L \Psi\right), \quad s.t., \quad \Psi^T \Psi = I_{P \times P}, \tag{1}$$

where $tr(\cdot)$ is the trace norm operator. The optimal $\Psi = [\psi_p]_{p=1}^{P}$ eventually consists of the eigenvectors of L that associated with the first P smallest eigenvalues $\{\lambda_p | p = 1, \ldots, P, \lambda_1 \leq \lambda_2 \leq \cdots \leq \lambda_P\}$ [11]. As shown in Fig. 1(a), harmonic basis in higher frequency (larger eigenvalue) tend to exhibit faster oscillations than lower frequency counterparts. Since Ψ is estimated from the group-mean adjacency matrix W, it is reasonable to consider Ψ as the common harmonic bases [8, 12] that can be used to characterize the frequency-like feature representations for each instance of neuropathology measurements (such as amyloid) $f = [f_i]_{i=1}^{N}$, where each element in the data array f corresponds to the exact node in the underlying brain network.

Laplace-Beltrami Operator: The Backbone of Harmonic Analysis. Conventional approaches simply treat f as a data array. However, since f is associated with the nodes in the brain network that might be closely connected, it is more reasonable to consider f residing on the network-specific Riemannian manifold, i.e., $f \in \mathcal{M}$. In this context, the geometry of f is manifested through the pairwise relationship between f_i and f_j that is characterized by the underlying connection w_{ij} in the network.

Recall the key to quantify the spreading pathway is to have a quantitative measurement of the influx and outflux of neuropathological burdens across brain networks. Thus, a set of network-specific algebra is of necessity to analyze f on the associated Riemannian manifold $\mathcal{M}$. As shown in [11], graph Laplacian L is eventually analogous to the *Laplace-Beltrami* operator $\mathcal{L}f \overset{\text{def}}{=} -div_{\mathcal{M}}(\nabla_{\mathcal{M}}f)$, where $div_{\mathcal{M}}$ and $\nabla_{\mathcal{M}}$ denote for divergence operator and intrinsic gradient on the manifold $\mathcal{M}$. Considering f consists of the amyloid level on each node, the *Laplace-Beltrami* operator $\mathcal{L}$ can be interpreted as the normalized difference between the amyloid burden on each node v_i and average amyloid burden of all neighboring nodes that connected to v_i. Since $\mathcal{L}$ is self-adjoint, the Laplacian eigen-vectors Ψ (Eq. 1) form orthonormal bases for $\mathcal{M}$, called *manifold harmonics*. Therefore, each f can be expressed as the Fourier series: $f = \Psi \hat{h} = \Psi(\Psi^T f)$ if $P = N$. Following the notation in [8], we call $\hat{h} = \left[\hat{h}_p\right]_{p=1}^{P} = \Psi^T f$ the attribute of harmonic power, where each element $\hat{h}_p$ in $\hat{h}$ characterizes the frequency response (aka. Fourier coefficient) associated with ψ_p.

Revisit the Construction of Harmonic Bases. Suppose the Riemannian structure of manifold $\mathcal{M}$ is spanned by $\Psi = \{\psi_1, \psi_2, \ldots, \psi_P\}$. Thus, $\nabla_{\mathcal{M}}\psi$ become a vector field on $\mathcal{M}$. Smoothness on the manifold demands points near x being mapped to points near $\psi(x)$. That is, for a small δx in a local coordinate chart, $\|\psi(x + \delta x) - \psi(x)\| \approx \|\langle\nabla_{\mathcal{M}}\psi(x), \delta x\rangle\| \leq \|\nabla_{\mathcal{M}}\psi(x)\|\|\delta x\|$. To preserve the locality, $\|\nabla_{\mathcal{M}}\psi(x)\|$ is required to be small by minimizing $\int_{\mathcal{M}} \|\nabla_{\mathcal{M}}\psi(x)\|^2$. Following the Stokes theorem, we have:

$$\int_{\mathcal{M}} \|\nabla_{\mathcal{M}}\psi\|^2 = \int_{\mathcal{M}} \nabla_{\mathcal{M}}\psi, \nabla_{\mathcal{M}}\psi = \int_{\mathcal{M}} -div(\nabla_{\mathcal{M}}\psi)\psi = \int_{\mathcal{M}} \psi^T \mathcal{L}\psi \quad (2)$$

To that end, the calculation of bases Ψ can be formulated as:

$$\arg\min_{\Psi} \sum_{p=1}^{P} \psi_p^T \mathcal{L}\psi_p \Leftrightarrow \arg\min_{\Psi} \frac{1}{2}tr(\Psi^T L\Psi) \quad (3)$$

The solution to Eq. (3) is eventually equivalent to finding eigenvectors of the graph Laplacian L, as shown in Eq. (1).

It is clear that Eq. (2) offers a new window to understand harmonic bases through manifold optimization, which allows us further to extend global harmonic bases to localized harmonic wavelets as follows.

2.2 Construction of Region-Adaptive Harmonic Wavelets

Optimization of Region-Adaptive Harmonic Wavelets. To alleviate the limitation of whole-brain harmonic bases Ψ, we present the following energy function to optimize the localized harmonic wavelets $\Phi_i = [\varphi_{i,q}]_{q=1}^{Q}$ $(\varphi_{i,q} \in \mathbb{R}^N, Q < N)$ for each node v_i, which consists of three criteria.

First, we expect the localized harmonic wavelets Φ_i to preserve the locality of manifold geometry by minimizing the manifold smoothness term $E_s(\Phi_i) = tr(\Phi_i^T L \Phi_i)$, which can be derived from Eq. (2). Additionally, we require Φ_i be orthogonal bases, i.e., $\Phi_i^T \Phi_i = I_{Q \times Q}$.

Second, we require the support of each harmonic wavelets Φ_i no further than a subnetwork (shown in Fig. 1(b)) that is centered at the underlying node v_i. To do so, we generate a binary mask vector $u_i = [u_i(j)]_{j=1}^{N}$, where $u_i(j) = 1$ if the node v_j can be reached by v_i within k hops and $u_i(j) = 0$ otherwise. Note, we use the shortest path to measure the distance between two nodes v_i and v_j, base on a binarized edge map via thresholding on W. We define the harmonic localization term $E_l(\Phi_i) = tr(\Phi_i^T diag(1 - u_i)\Phi_i)$, where the minimizing $E_l(\Phi_i)$ is equivalent to encourage $\|\Phi_i\|^2$ to be zero out of the subnetwork. Thus, E_l is used to suppress the waves (oscillations) far from v_i while perverse the waves nearby v_i, since $diag(1 - u_i)$ is zero for the nodes closely connected to v_i within k hops and has no effect in minimizing E_l.

Third, notice that we have global harmonic bases Ψ from Eq. (1). To reduce the redundancy between Ψ and each Φ_i, we further require local harmonic wavelets Φ_i to be orthogonal to global harmonic bases Ψ by enforcing $\Phi_i^T \Psi = 0$. Since it is not trivial to optimize Φ_i with the hard constraint $\Phi_i^T \Psi = 0$, we relax it by minimizing $E_p = tr(\Phi_i^T \Psi \Psi^T \Phi_i)$, which promotes the orthogonality to the subspace spanned by Ψ.

Thus, the overall energy function of localized harmonic wavelets Φ_i is given by:

$$\arg\min_{\Phi_i} E_s(\Phi_i) + \mu_1 E_l(\Phi_i) + \mu_2 E_p(\Phi_i), \quad s.t., \quad \Phi_i^T \Phi_i = I_{Q \times Q}, \tag{4}$$

where μ_1 and μ_2 are two scalars that control the strength of subnetwork localization and orthogonality to the global harmonic bases Ψ, respectively.

Optimization. It is apparent that three trace norms in Eq. (4) can be unified into a matrix $\Theta_i = L + \mu_1 diag(1 - u_i) + \mu_2 \Psi \Psi^T$. Thus, the optimization of Eq. (4) is boiled down to the eigen-decomposition of the matrix Θ:

$$\underset{\Phi_i}{argmin} tr\left(\Phi_i^T \Theta_i \Phi_i\right) s.t. \Phi_i^T \Phi_i = I_{Q \times Q} \tag{5}$$

Since Θ is symmetric and positive semi-definite, it is computationally efficient to obtain Φ_i for each node v_i.

Discussion. There are several limitations regarding the optimization of our harmonic wavelets. *First*, considering the computation complexity, our approach does not add orthogonality to the harmonic wavelets across network nodes. As a result, there might be an overlap between the subspaces spanned by the harmonic wavelets at two neighboring nodes. *Second*, since we optimize Φ_i for each node separately, it is difficult to establish the correspondence of the associated eigenvalues between Φ_i and Φ_j. Neither is the correspondence between Φ_i and Ψ. *Third*, our localized harmonic wavelets depend on the topology of the underlying subnetwork (encoded in u_i). Different network distance metric might result in different harmonic wavelets.

Despite these limitations, we present the novel network-specific manifold algebra to characterize the propagation of neuropathology events across brain networks by investigating the localized harmonic power (called *harmonic wavelet fingerprint*) per node v_i and per harmonic frequency q:

$$\hat{h}_{i,q} = \sum_{j=1}^{N} f(j)\varphi_{i,q}(j) \tag{6}$$

In Sect. 3, we will demonstrate the enhanced sensitivity and specificity by our novel harmonic wavelets fingerprint (HWF in short) in neuroimaging studies than current empirical features.

3   Experiments

In the following experiments, we evaluate the statistical power of our harmonic wavelet fingerprint on both synthetic and real datasets. Specifically, the evaluation metrics include (1) the representation power after projecting the simulated data to the harmonic spectral space and reconstructing it back to the signal domain, and (2) the sensitivity and specificity of stratifying aging subjects in the pre-clinical stage of AD.

Data Description. We calculate the group-mean adjacency matrix W from 138 structural brain networks, where each network is obtained by the following image processing on the T1-weighted MR and DWI images from the ADNI database (http://adni.loni. usc.edu/). First, we parcellate the cortical surface into 148 cortical regions based on T1-weighted MRI according to a Destrieux atlas [13] and then apply tractography technique [13] on DWI images to construct a 148×148 anatomical connectivity matrix. After we optimize the harmonic wavelets $\{\Phi_i | i = 1, \ldots, N\}$ based on W, we perform group comparison analysis on a different dataset from ADNI, where the imaging modalities include amyloid-PET, tau-PET, and FDG-PET imaging data. The demographic information is shown in Table 1. For each neuroimaging scan, we parcellate the cortical surface into 148 Destrieux regions and then calculate the standard update value ratio (SUVR) of PET imaging for each region, where the cerebellum is used as the reference in calculating SUVR. We stack the SUVR in each region into a data array f of whole-brain pathological burden.

Parameter Setting. In our objective function Eq. 4, the parameter P controls the dimension of global harmonic bases Ψ, which can be determined by calculating the distribution reconstruction loss between the original Laplacian matrix and the reconstructed Laplacian matrix using only the top P smallest eigenvalues and eigenvectors. The number of harmonic wavelets Q is empirically set based on the average node degree on the adjacency matrix W. After that, we use the line search to determine the optimal parameters μ_1 and μ_2 based on the reconstruction loss on simulated data which is presented in Sect. 3.1. In our experiments, P and Q are set to 60 and 10, respectively. In addition, we select $\mu_1 = 110$ and $\mu_2 = 170$ as the optimal parameters, which achieve the lowest reconstruction loss.

Table 1. Demographic information of multi-modal neuroimaging data in our experiments.

Data	Gender	Number	Range of age	Average age	CN	EMCI	LMCI
Amyloid	Male	450	55.0–91.4	73.4	136	184	130
	Female	389	55.0–89.6	71.7	148	145	96
	Total	**839**	**55.0–91.4**	**72.6**	**284**	**329**	**226**
Tau	Male	255	55.0–90.1	72.4	124	69	62
	Female	269	55.0–89.9	70.3	177	44	48
	Total	**524**	**55.0–90.1**	**71.3**	**301**	**113**	**110**
FDG	Male	592	55.0–91.4	73.9	169	182	241
	Female	472	55.0–89.6	72.2	166	148	158
	Total	**1064**	**55.0–91.4**	**73.1**	**335**	**330**	**399**

3.1 Evaluate the Representation Power on Harmonic Wavelets

Synthetic Data. As shown in Fig. 2(a), we synthesize a brain network with 30 nodes and then randomly generate a set of 30-element data array f along with the network nodes with each element ranging from -1 and $+1$. Then, we measure the reconstruction loss $(f - \Psi\Psi^T f)$ by using whole-brain harmonic bases Ψ. Note, since we only use the first P eigenvectors, $\Psi\Psi^T \neq I$. In Fig. 2(b), we display the reconstruction loss at each node and the loss histogram, where red and blue arrows indicate positive and negative losses, respectively. Note, we use 20 out of harmonic bases, i.e., $P = 20$.

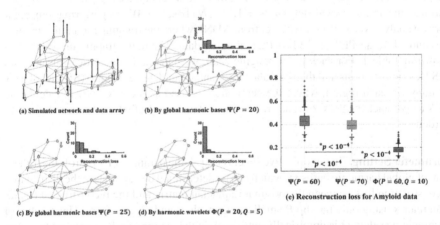

(a) Simulated network and data array   (b) By global harmonic bases $\Psi(P = 20)$

(c) By global harmonic bases $\Psi(P = 25)$ (d) By harmonic wavelets $\Phi(P = 20, Q = 5)$

$\Psi(P = 60)$ $\Psi(P = 70)$ $\Phi(P = 60, Q = 10)$

(e) Reconstruction loss for Amyloid data

Fig. 2. (a) The simulated brain network and one example of data array along with the network nodes. The reconstruction loss on simulated data by using global harmonic bases Ψ ($P = 20$), global harmonic bases Ψ ($P = 25$), and our harmonic wavelets Φ ($P = 20$ and $Q = 5$). (e) The reconstruction loss on amyloid data on the brain network with 148 nodes by global harmonic bases Ψ ($P = 60$) in red, global harmonic bases Ψ ($P = 70$) in green, and our harmonic wavelets Φ ($P = 60, Q = 10$) in blue, where '*' denote statistical significance ($p < 0.01$).

Recall that our harmonic wavelets Φ_i at each node v_i is the complementary bases to the global harmonic bases Ψ (in Eq. (4)). In the context, we evaluate the reconstructed loss at each node v_i by $\Psi\Psi^T(f \odot u_i) + \Phi_i\Phi_i^T f$, where $\odot$ is the Hadamard product and u_i is the subnetwork mask vector used to optimize Φ_i. The first term quantifies the global reconstruction loss of truncated signal $f \odot u_i$, where we set $P = 20$. In addition, the second term measures the local reconstruction loss, where we set $Q = 5$. We show the node-wise reconstruction loss and its histogram in Fig. 2(d). It is apparent that our harmonic wavelets have significantly reduced the reconstruction loss than using global harmonic bases only. Since the reconstruction result by our harmonic wavelets uses more bases than that by global harmonic based in Fig. 2(b), we further show the reconstruction result of using the same amount of global harmonic bases ($P = 25$) in Fig. 2(c). However, the reconstruction loss is still worse than our harmonic wavelets even we increase the number of bases to 25.

Real Data. We evaluate the reconstruction of amyloid data, where the average reconstruction loss by using 60 global harmonics, 70 global harmonics, and our localized harmonic wavelets ($P = 60$ and $Q = 10$) are displayed in red, green, and blue, respectively, in Fig. 2(e). Our harmonic wavelets achieve better performance than global harmonic bases, where the improvement is statistically significant under t-test ($p < 0.05$).

3.2   Evaluate the Statistic Power of Harmonic Wavelet Fingerprint

In what follows, we evaluate the statistical power of our HWF (in Eq. 6) in stratifying clinical cohorts in the pre-clinical stage of AD. Since the region-wise SUVR from amyloid-PET, tau-PET, and FDG-PET have been widely used in many neuroimaging studies, we compare our harmonic wavelets fingerprint with these empirical features.

First, we perform the group comparison (across CN, EMCI, and LMCI) for each modality to identify node alterations using empirical SUVR and HWF. For each node, we apply the conventional permutation t-test on the SUVR data between two cohorts. Since each node is associated with $Q = 10$ HWF values, we apply the multivariate Hotelling's T-squared test [14], instead of the permutation t-test, to identify whether the underlying node exhibits significant group difference on HWF. In both statistical tests, all the p values are corrected using the Benjamini-Hochberg (BH) procedure [15] since we assume each node in the brain network has a certain degree of dependence on all other nodes. *Second*, we compare the diagnostic value of empirical SUVR and HWF by evaluating the accuracy of early diagnosis of AD in the pre-clinical stage. Specifically, we train the linear support vector machine (SVM) based on SUVR and HWF separately. Then we evaluate the classification accuracy (as well as sensitivity, specificity, and F score) using 10-fold cross validation.

Region-Wise Amyloid SUVR vs. Harmonic-Based Amyloid HWF. First, 98 nodes exhibit CN/EMCI difference on amyloid SUVR, compared to 113 nodes identified by amyloid HWF. In addition, 98 nodes show EMCI/LMCI difference, and 143 nodes show CN/LMCI difference using amyloid SUVR. However, we find all of the 148 nodes show a significant difference in EMCI/LMCI and CN/LMCI comparison by our amyloid HWF.

Note, all the above statistical tests have been corrected with FDR-adjusted $p < 0.01$. These results suggest that not only the concentration of amyloid but also the spreading of amyloid on the brain cortex could be the sign of cognitive decline in the pre-clinical stage of AD.

Since our amyloid HWF shows more statistical power in identifying disrupted regions than the empirical neuroimaging features, it is worthy of investigating more in-depth understating the role of the cortical spreading pathway in AD progression. To do so, we run the permutation t-test for each harmonic wavelet associated with the identified altered network node. As shown in Fig. 3, we visualize the harmonic wavelets with the top three strongest statistical differences (smallest p-values), where the red dot denotes the underlying node, and the red/blue arrows indicate the positive/negative oscillations in each harmonic wavelet.

Furthermore, we evaluate the diagnostic value of identified significant amyloid SUVR and amyloid HWF by training a linear SVM model for CN/EMCI/LMCI classification using SUVR and HWF separately. We use 10-fold cross-validation to evaluate the classification results, as displayed in Table 2, where the '*' indicates that the SVM trained using our HWF is significantly better ($p < 0.01$) than SVM trained using SUVR. It is apparent that our harmonic-based amyloid HWF feature consistently achieves significantly higher performance in classification accuracy, sensitivity, specificity, and F-score, compared with empirical amyloid SUVR. These results demonstrate the great potential of applying our proposed localized harmonic wavelets technique in early diagnosis for AD.

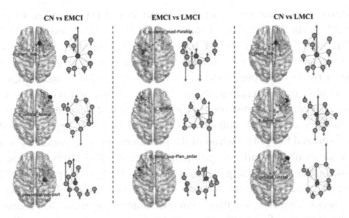

Fig. 3. The visualization of the top three significant local harmonic wavelets associated with amyloid-PET in CM/EMCI (left), EMCI/LMCI (middle), and CN/LMCI (right) comparison. The underlying center node of the harmonic wavelet is designated with a red dot. The up/down oscillation pattern in each wavelet is displayed by red/blue arrows. (Color figure online)

Region-Wise Tau SUVR vs. Harmonic-Based Tau HWF. Similarly, we find that 14, 123, and 145 nodes exhibit a significant difference in CN/EMCI, EMCI/LMCI, and CN/LCMI comparison, based on the SUVR from tau-PET. In contrast, 30, 85, and 148

Table 2. CN/EMCI/LMCI classification results of using amyloid SUVR and amyloid HWF

Data	Methods	Accuracy	Sensitivity	Specificity	F-score
CN vs EMCI	Amyloid SUVR	0.561 ± 0.017	0.558 ± 0.016	0.567 ± 0.019	0.574 ± 0.017
	Amyloid HWF	$0.586 \pm 0.014^*$	$0.576 \pm 0.013^*$	$0.605 \pm 0.019^*$	$0.617 \pm 0.015^*$
EMCI vs LMCI	Amyloid SUVR	0.550 ± 0.021	0.550 ± 0.022	0.554 ± 0.023	0.558 ± 0.023
	Amyloid HWF	$0.587 \pm 0.020^*$	$0.582 \pm 0.020^*$	$0.598 \pm 0.022^*$	$0.601 \pm 0.021^*$
CN vs LMCI	Amyloid SUVR	0.653 ± 0.015	0.639 ± 0.014	0.678 ± 0.018	0.671 ± 0.015
	Amyloid HWF	$0.661 \pm 0.014^*$	$0.652 \pm 0.013^*$	0.679 ± 0.018	0.672 ± 0.015

nodes are found significantly different between CN/EMCI, EMCI/LMCI, and CN/LMCI cohorts, using our HWF of tau-PET (FDR-adjusted $p < 0.01$). We only observe our tau HWF has identified less number of altered nodes in EMCI and LMCI group comparison than using tau SUVR. We reckon the possible reason is that it is more difficult to survive from Hotelling's test than the univariate permutation test, as evidenced by the fact that the top 10 nodes identified by our tau HWF (average $= 2.51 \times 10^{-5}$) have stronger group-to-group separation than using empirical tau SUVR (average $p = 4.99 \times 10^{-5}$). Next, we also map the top three significant harmonic wavelets on the cortical surface in Fig. 4 for CN/EMCI, EMCI/LMCI, and CN/LMCI, respectively. Furthermore, the classification results of CN/EMCI, EMCI/LMCI, and CN/LMCI using tau-SUVR and tau-HWF are shown in Table 3, where our tau-HWF significantly outperforms tau-SUVR in most of the classification scores ($p < 0.01$).

Region-Wise FDG-PET SUVR vs. Harmonic-Based FDG-PET HWF. Here, we evaluate the statistical power of FDG-PET, which is one of the AD neurodegeneration biomarkers. Using empirical SUVR from FDG-PET, we find 13 network nodes showing a significant difference between CN and EMCI cohorts, 68 nodes showing the difference between EMCI and LMCI, and 98 nodes showing the difference between CN and LMCI (FDR-adjusted $p < 0.01$). Using our HWF on FDG-PET, we find 96 nodes having significant differences in CN/EMCI comparison, 142 nodes in EMCI/LMCI comparison, and 130 nodes in CN/LMCI comparison (FDR-adjusted $p < 0.01$). The top three significant harmonic wavelets in each group comparison are displayed in Fig. 5. In addition, the classification results using either SUVR or HWF features in CN/EMCI, EMCI/LMCI, and CN/LMCI classifications are shown in Table 4, where our harmonic-based HWF features consistently achieve higher accuracy (under t-test with $p < 0.01$) than empirical SUVR features.

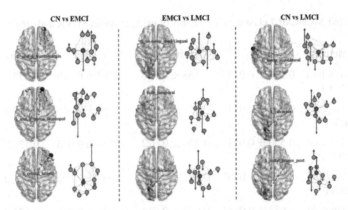

Fig. 4. The visualization of the top three significant harmonic wavelets in Tau-PET. We use the same symbols as Fig. 3 for the illustration of harmonic wavelets.

Table 3. CN/EMCI/LMCI classification results of using tau SUVR and tau HWF.

Data	Methods	Accuracy	Sensitivity	Specificity	F-score
CN vs. EMCI	Tau SUVR	0.514 ± 0.032	0.513 ± 0.031	0.517 ± 0.037	0.532 ± 0.035
	Tau HWF	$0.591 \pm 0.035^*$	$0.586 \pm 0.032^*$	$0.604 \pm 0.041^*$	$0.607 \pm 0.036^*$
EMCI vs. LMCI	Tau SUVR	0.590 ± 0.021	0.567 ± 0.016	0.649 ± 0.035	0.652 ± 0.018
	Tau HWF	$0.629 \pm 0.024^*$	$0.601 \pm 0.020^*$	$0.692 \pm 0.035^*$	$0.677 \pm 0.022^*$
CN vs. LMCI	Tau SUVR	0.681 ± 0.029	$0.661 \pm 0.027^*$	0.732 ± 0.040	0.704 ± 0.028
	Tau HWF	0.686 ± 0.024	0.643 ± 0.021	$0.798 \pm 0.038^*$	$0.733 \pm 0.021^*$

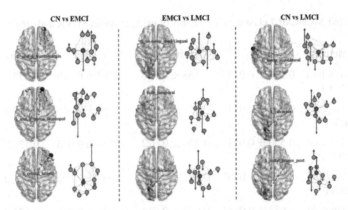

Fig. 5. The visualization of the top three significant harmonic wavelets in FDG-PET. We use the same symbols as Fig. 3 for the illustration of harmonic wavelets.

Table 4. CN/EMCI/LMCI classification results of using SUVR and HWF on FDG-PET.

Data	Methods	Accuracy	Sensitivity	Specificity	F-score
CN vs. EMCI	FDG-PET SUVR	0.595 ± 0.011	0.605 ± 0.013	0.589 ± 0.011	0.576 ± 0.013
	FDG-PET HWF	$0.619 \pm 0.010^*$	$0.651 \pm 0.014^*$	$0.601 \pm 0.008^*$	0.574 ± 0.012
EMCI vs. LMCI	FDG-PET SUVR	0.633 ± 0.015	0.626 ± 0.014	0.645 ± 0.018	0.644 ± 0.016
	FDG-PET HWF	$0.678 \pm 0.013^*$	$0.666 \pm 0.013^*$	$0.698 \pm 0.016^*$	$0.691 \pm 0.013^*$
CN vs. LMCI	FDG-PET SUVR	0.618 ± 0.016	0.614 ± 0.015	0.625 ± 0.018	0.624 ± 0.016
	FDG-PET HWF	$0.636 \pm 0.016^*$	$0.644 \pm 0.016^*$	$0.632 \pm 0.016^*$	0.625 ± 0.018

4 Conclusions

In this paper, we present a novel Riemannian manifold algebra to discover network alterations presented in the critical spreading pathways of neuropathology burden that lead to cognitive decline in AD. The backbone of our approach is a set of localized harmonic wavelets that are driven by the *Laplace-Beltrami* operator on the network-specific Riemannian manifold. In light of this, our manifold harmonic technique offers a new window to capture the ubiquitous oscillation patterns at each brain region with greater mathematics insight, as evidence by the enhanced statistical power in group comparison than the empirical features. In the future, we plan to apply our harmonic wavelets to other neurological disorders that show network dysfunction syndrome.

References

1. Stam, C.J.: Modern network science of neurological disorders. Nat. Rev. Neurosci. **15**(10), 683–695 (2014)
2. Sepulcre, J., et al.: Neurogenetic contributions to amyloid beta and tau spreading in the human cortex. Nat. Med. **24**(12), 1910–1918 (2018)
3. Braak, H., Braak, E.: Evolution of the neuropathology of Alzheimer's disease. Acta Neurol. Scand. Suppl. **165**, 3–12 (1996)
4. Wu, J.W., et al.: Neuronal activity enhances tau propagation and tau pathology in vivo. Nat. Neurosci. **19**, 1085 (2016)
5. Braak, H., Del Tredici, K.: Neuroanatomy and pathology of sporadic Alzheimer's disease. Adv. Anat. Embryol. Cell Biol. **215**, 1–162 (2015)
6. Braak, H., Del Tredici, K.: Alzheimer's pathogenesis: is there neuron-to-neuron propagation? Acta Neuropathol. **121**(5), 589–595 (2011)
7. Raj, A., Kuceyeski, A., Weiner, M.: A network diffusion model of disease progression in dementia. Neuron **73**(6), 1204–1215 (2012)

8. Atasoy, S., Donnelly, I., Pearson, J.: Human brain networks function in connectome-specific harmonic waves. Nat. Commun. **7**(1), 10340 (2016)
9. Chen, J., et al.: Estimating common harmonic waves of Brain networks on Stiefel Manifold. In: Martel, A.L., et al. (eds.) MICCAI 2020. LNCS, vol. 12267, pp. 367–376. Springer, Cham (2020). https://doi.org/10.1007/978-3-030-59728-3_36
10. Yair, O., Ben-Chen, M., Talmon, R.: Parallel transport on the cone manifold of SPD matrices for domain adaptation. IEEE Trans. Sig. Process. **67**(7), 1797–1811 (2019)
11. Chavel, I.: Eigenvalues in Riemannian Geometry, vol. 115. Academic Press (1984)
12. Atasoy, S., Roseman, L., Kaelen, M., Kringelbach, M.L., Deco, G., Carhart-Harris, R.L.: Connectome-harmonic decomposition of human brain activity reveals dynamical repertoire re-organization under LSD. Sci. Rep. **7**(1), 17661 (2017)
13. Destrieux, C., Fischl, B., Dale, A., Halgren, E.: Automatic parcellation of human cortical gyri and sulci using standard anatomical nomenclature. Neuroimage **53**(1), 1–15 (2010)
14. Hotelling, H.: The generalization of student's ratio. In: Kotz, S., Johnson, N.L. (eds.) Breakthroughs in statistics, pp. 54–65. Springer, New York (1992). https://doi.org/10.1007/978-1-4612-0919-5_4
15. Benjamini, Y., Hochberg, Y.: Controlling the false discovery rate: a practical and powerful approach to multiple testing. J. Roy. Stat. Soc. Ser. B (Methodol.) **57**(1), 289–300 (1995)

A Multi-scale Spatial and Temporal Attention Network on Dynamic Connectivity to Localize the Eloquent Cortex in Brain Tumor Patients

Naresh Nandakumar[1](✉), Komal Manzoor[2], Shruti Agarwal[2], Jay J. Pillai[2],
Sachin K. Gujar[2], Haris I. Sair[2], and Archana Venkataraman[1]

[1] Department of Electrical and Computer Engineering, Johns Hopkins University,
Baltimore, USA
nnandak1@jhu.edu
[2] Department of Neuroradiology, Johns Hopkins School of Medicine, Baltimore, USA

Abstract. We present a deep neural network architecture that combines multi-scale spatial attention with temporal attention to simultaneously localize the language and motor areas of the eloquent cortex from dynamic functional connectivity data. Our multi-scale spatial attention operates on graph-based features extracted from the connectivity matrices, thus honing in on the inter-regional interactions that collectively define the eloquent cortex. At the same time, our temporal attention model selects the intervals during which these interactions are most pronounced. The final stage of our model employs multi-task learning to differentiate between the eloquent subsystems. Our training strategy enables us to handle missing eloquent class labels by freezing the weights in those branches while updating the rest of the network weights. We evaluate our method on resting-state fMRI data from one synthetic dataset and one in-house brain tumor dataset while using task fMRI activations as ground-truth labels for the eloquent cortex. Our model achieves higher localization accuracies than conventional deep learning approaches. It also produces interpretable spatial and temporal attention features which can provide further insights for presurgical planning. Thus, our model shows translational promise for improving the safety of brain tumor resections.

Keywords: Brain Tumor rs-fMRI · CNN · Eloquent cortex localization

1 Introduction

The eloquent cortex consists of regions in the brain that are responsible for language and motor functionality. Neurosurgical procedures are carefully planned to avoid these regions in order to minimize postoperative deficits [1]. However,

© Springer Nature Switzerland AG 2021
A. Feragen et al. (Eds.): IPMI 2021, LNCS 12729, pp. 241–252, 2021.
https://doi.org/10.1007/978-3-030-78191-0_19

it can be difficult to accurately localize the eloquent cortex due to its varying anatomical boundaries across people [2]. The language network has especially high interindividual variability and can appear on one or both hemispheres [3]. The gold standard for preoperative mapping of the eloquent areas is intraoperative electrocortical stimulation (ECS) [1]. While reliable, ECS requires the patient to be awake and responsive during surgery and it carries much greater risk when performed on obese patients or individuals with respiratory problems [4]. For these reasons, task-fMRI (t-fMRI) has emerged as a noninvasive complement to ECS [5]. However, t-fMRI activations are unavailable for certain populations, like young children, the cognitively impaired, or aphasic patients, due to excessive head motion or an inability to perform the task protocol [6]. Resting-state fMRI (rs-fMRI) is an alternative modality that captures spontaneous fluctuations in the brain when the subject is awake and at rest. In contrast to t-fMRI paradigms, which are designed to activate an isolated cognitive region, rs-fMRI correlations can be used to simultaneously identify multiple cognitive systems [7]. Thus, rs-fMRI is an exciting alternative to t-fMRI activations for localizing sub-regions associated with the eloquent cortex [6,8,9].

Prior work that uses rs-fMRI for eloquent cortex localization can be broadly divided into three categories [10]. In the simplest case, a seed region of interest (ROI) is used to identify highly-correlated voxels in the eloquent cortex [11,12]. A more sophisticated method uses independent component analysis (ICA) to delineate functionally coherent systems in the brain, from which the eloquent networks can be identified [13,14]. While promising, these methods require expert intervention, either via the choice of seed ROI or the component selection. Furthermore, early studies are limited by the tremendous variability of rs-fMRI data. In fact, the works of [13,14] reveal highly variable accuracies across a large patient cohort (N > 50), particularly when mapping the language network.

The use of deep learning has fueled interest in end-to-end methods for eloquent cortex localization. For example, the work of [15] has proposed a multilayer perceptron that classifies voxels of the rs-fMRI data into one of seven functional systems based on seed correlation maps; this method was extended in [16] to handle tumor cases. While the perceptron has high sensitivity across several patients, its specificity is not quantified. Also, since the perceptron is trained on healthy subjects, it cannot account for neural plasticity effects from to the tumor. The authors of [8] propose the first end-to-end graph neural network (GNN) that leverages functional connectivity to localize a single eloquent subsystem. While the GNN outperforms a perceptron architecture, separate GNNs must be trained and evaluated for each eloquent area, which requires more data and longer training times. In addition, the GNN specificity is quite low, particularly for language. Finally, the work of [9] extends the original GNN to track dynamic connectivity changes associated with the eloquent cortex. However, the language localization accuracy and specificity are too low for clinical practice.

Recent work in the deep learning literature has introduced the idea of *spatial attention*, which mimics information processing in the human visual system. For example, a 2D spatial attention model learns where in the image to focus, thus improving the quality of the learned representations [17]. The notion of attention has been extended to the time domain in applications such as video

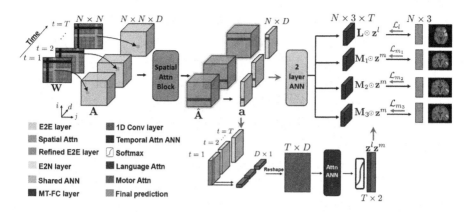

Fig. 1. Top: Convolutional features extracted from dynamic connectivity are refined using a multi-scale spatial attention block. **Bottom**: The dynamic features are input to an ANN temporal attention network to learn weights $\mathbf{z}^l$ (language) and $\mathbf{z}^m$ (motor). **Right**: Multi-task learning to classify language (**L**), finger (**M$_1$**), tongue (**M$_2$**), and foot (**M$_3$**) subnetworks, where each subnetwork is a 3-class classification which is shown in red, white, and blue respectively on segmentation maps.

processing [18]. In line with these works, we develop a spatiotemporal attention model to localize eloquent cortex from dynamic whole-brain rs-fMRI connectivity matrices. Unlike a 2D image, our "spatial" field corresponds to salient interactions in connectivity data, captured via graph-based convolutional filters. Our multi-scale spatial attention model pools three levels of granularity to amplify important interactions and suppress unnecessary ones. Then, our temporal attention mechanism selects key intervals of the dynamic input that are most relevant for either language or motor localization. Our model operates on a fine resolution parcellation and can handle missing training labels. We use t-fMRI activations as ground truth labels and validate our framework on rs-fMRI data from 100 subjects in the publicly available Human Connectome Project (HCP) [19] with artificially-inserted tumors as well as 60 subjects from an in-house dataset. Our model uniformly achieves higher localization accuracies than competing baselines. Our attention mechanisms learn interpretable feature maps, thus demonstrating the promise of our model for preoperative mapping.

2   A Multi-scale Spatial and Temporal Attention Network to Localize the Eloquent Cortex

Our framework assumes that while the anatomical boundaries of the eloquent cortex may shift across individuals, its resting-state functional connectivity with the rest of the brain will be preserved [14]. Adding a layer of complexity, the eloquent cortex represents a relatively small portion of the brain. This is the motivation for our spatial attention mechanism, i.e., to zone in on the key connectivity patterns. Furthermore, the networks associated with the eloquent

Multi-Scale Spatial Attention Model

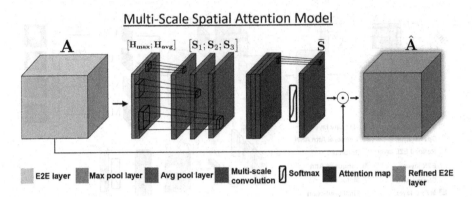

Fig. 2. Our multi-scale spatial attention model extracts features from max pool and average pool features along the channel dimension. We use separate convolutional filters with increasing receptive field size to extract multi-scale features, and use a 1×1 convolution and softmax to obtain our spatial attention map $\bar{S}$. This map is element-wise multiplied along the channel dimension of the original E2E features.

cortex will likely phase in and out of synchrony across the rs-fMRI scan [9]. Our temporal attention mechanism will track these changes. Figure 1 shows our over-all framework. As seen, we explictly model the tumor in our dynamic similarity graph construction and feed this input into a deep neural network which uses specialized convolutional layers designed to handle connectome data [20].

2.1 Input Dynamic Connectivity Matrices

We use the sliding window technique to construct our dynamic inputs [21]. Let N be the number of brain regions in our parcellation, T be the total number of sliding windows (i.e., time points in our model), and $\{\mathbf{W}^t\}_{t=1}^T \in \mathbb{R}^{N \times N}$ be the dynamic similarity matrices. $\mathbf{W}^t$ is constructed from the normalized input time courses $\{\mathbf{X}^t\}_{t=1}^T \in \mathbb{R}^{G \times N}$, where each $\mathbf{X}^t$ is a segment of the rs-fMRI obtained with window size G. Formally, the input $\mathbf{W}^t \in \mathbb{R}^{N \times N}$ is

$$\mathbf{W}^t = \exp\left[(\mathbf{X}^t)^T \mathbf{X}^t - 1\right]. \tag{1}$$

Our setup must also accomodate for the presence of brain tumors that vary across patients and are generally believed to represent non-functioning areas of the brain. Therefore, we follow the approach of [8,9] and treat the corresponding rows and columns of the simlarity matrix as "missing data" and fixing them to zero (shown by black bars in LHS of Fig. 1).

2.2 Multi-scale Spatial Attention on Convolutional Features

Our network leverages the specialized convolutional layers developed in [20] for feature extraction on each of the dynamic inputs. The edge-to-edge (E2E) filter (pink in Fig. 1) acts across rows and columns of the input matrix $\mathbf{W}^t$. This cross-shaped receptive field can accommodate node reordering, and it mimics the computation of graph theoretic measures. Mathematically, let $d \in \{1, \cdots, D\}$ be the E2E filter index, $\mathbf{r}^d \in \mathbb{R}^{1 \times N}$ be the row filter d, $\mathbf{c}^d \in \mathbb{R}^{N \times 1}$ be the column filter d, $\mathbf{b} \in \mathbb{R}^{D \times 1}$ be the E2E bias, and $\phi(.)$ be the activation function. For each time point t the feature map $\mathbf{A}^{d,t} \in \mathbb{R}^{N \times N}$ is computed as follows:

$$\mathbf{A}^{d,t}_{i,j} = \phi\left(\mathbf{W}^t_{i,:}(\mathbf{r}^d)^T + (\mathbf{c}^d)^T \mathbf{W}^t_{:,j} + \mathbf{b}_d\right). \tag{2}$$

The E2E filter output $\mathbf{A}^{d,t}_{ij}$ for edge (i,j) extracts information associated with the connectivity of node i and node j with the rest of the graph. We use the same D E2E filters $\{\mathbf{r}^d, \mathbf{c}^d\}$ for each time point to standardize the feature computation.

Figure 2 illustrates our multi-scale spatial attention model. The attention model acts on the E2E features and implicitly learns "where" informative connectivity hubs are located for maximum downstream class separation. The multi-scale setup uses filters of different receptive field sizes to capture various levels of connectivity profiles within the E2E features [22]. Following [17], we apply an average pooling and max pooling operation along the feature map axis and concatenate them to generate an efficient feature descriptor. Mathematically,

$$\mathbf{H_{avg}} = \frac{1}{DT} \sum_{d=1}^{D} \sum_{t=1}^{T} \mathbf{A}^{d,t} \tag{3}$$

is the $N \times N$ average pool features and

$$\mathbf{H}^{i,j}_{\mathbf{max}} = \max_{d,t} \mathbf{A}^{d,t}_{i,j} \tag{4}$$

is the $N \times N$ max pool features. Note that we extract the maximum and average activations across all feature maps and time points simultaneously. We then apply a multi-scale convolution to this feature descriptor, which implicitly identifies the deviation of the maximum activation from the neighborhood average, thus highlighting informative regions to aid in downstream tasks [23].

We apply three separate convolutions with increasing filter sizes to the concatenated feature descriptor to obtain different scales of resolution of our analysis. The convolution outputs $\mathbf{S}_1, \mathbf{S}_2$ and $\mathbf{S}_3 \in \mathbb{R}^{N \times N}$ are computed using a 3×3, 7×7, and 11×11 kernel, respectively, on the concatenated maps $[\mathbf{H_{avg}}; \mathbf{H_{max}}]$. The convolutions include zero padding to maintain dimensionality. Each successive convolutional filter has an increasing receptive field size to help identify various connectivity hubs within the E2E layer. We obtain our spatial attention map $\bar{\mathbf{S}} \in \mathbb{R}^{N \times N}$ with an element-wise softmax operation on the weighted summation, derived using a 1×1 convolution with bias b, across the three scales;

$$\bar{\mathbf{S}} = \mathrm{Softmax}\left(\sum_{i=1}^{3} w_i \mathbf{S}_i + b\right). \tag{5}$$

This weighted combination is designed to highlight salient hubs in the network which appear across different spatial scales. The softmax transforms our attention into a gating operation, which we use to refine our convolutional features

$\mathbf{A}^{d,t}$ by element-wise multiplication with $\bar{\mathbf{S}}$. Let $\odot$ denote the Hadamard product. The refined features $\hat{\mathbf{A}}^{d,t} \in \mathbb{R}^{N \times N}$ are computed as

$$\hat{\mathbf{A}}^{d,t} = \mathbf{A}^{d,t} \odot \bar{\mathbf{S}}. \tag{6}$$

Finally, we condense our representation along the column dimension by using the edge-to-node (E2N) filter [20]. Our E2N filter (brown in Fig. 1) performs a 1D convolution along the columns of each refined feature map to obtain region-wise representations. Mathematically, let $\mathbf{g}^d \in \mathbb{R}^{N \times 1}$ be E2N filter d and $\mathbf{p} \in \mathbb{R}^{D \times 1}$ be the E2N bias. The E2N output $\mathbf{a}^{d,t} \in \mathbb{R}^{N \times 1}$ from input $\hat{\mathbf{A}}^{d,t}$ is computed as

$$\mathbf{a}_i^{d,t} = \phi\Big(\hat{\mathbf{A}}_{i,:}^{d,t}\mathbf{g}_n^d + \mathbf{p}_d\Big). \tag{7}$$

Again, we apply the same E2N filters to each time point. At a high level, the E2N computation is similar to that of graph-theoretic features, such as node degree. The E2N outputs are fed into both the temporal attention model (bottom branch of Fig. 1) and the multi-task node classifier (right branch of Fig. 1).

2.3   Temporal Attention Model and Multi-task Learning

We use a 1D convolution to collapse the region-wise information into a low dimensional vector for our temporal attention network. Let $\mathbf{k}^d \in \mathbb{R}^{N \times 1}$ be the weight vector for filter d and $\mathbf{j} \in \mathbb{R}^{D \times 1}$ be the bias across all filters. A scalar output $q^{d,t}$ for each input $\mathbf{a}^{d,t}$ is obtained

$$q^{d,t} = \phi\Big((\mathbf{k}^d)^T \mathbf{a}^{d,t} + \mathbf{j}_d\Big). \tag{8}$$

The resulting $T \times D$ matrix $[q^{d,t}]^T$ is fed into a fully-connected layer of two perceptrons with size D to extract our temporal attention weights. We obtain one language network attention vector $\mathbf{z}^l \in \mathbb{R}^{T \times 1}$ and one motor network attention vector $\mathbf{z}^m \in \mathbb{R}^{T \times 1}$, which learn the time intervals during which the corresponding eloquent subnetwork is more identifiable. The FC attention model is more flexible than a recurrent architecture and can be easily trained on small clinical datasets (<100 subjects). We observed that the FC attention shows a good trade-off between representation and robustness to training with a limited sample size.

In parallel, the top branch of Fig. 1 applies a cascade of two FC layers to the E2N topological features for our downstream multi-task classification. In this work, we are interested in identifying four separate sub-regions of the eloquent cortex, as depicted by the multi-task FC (MT-FC) layers in Fig. 1. Let $\mathbf{L}^t, \mathbf{M}_1^t, \mathbf{M}_2^t$, and $\mathbf{M}_3^t \in \mathbb{R}^{N \times 3}$ be the output of the language, finger, foot, and tongue MT-FC layers, respectively, at time t. We consolidate information along the time axis using an element-wise multiplication with our temporal attention vectors, as shown in our loss function below. The $N \times 3$ matrix represents the region-wise assignment into one of three classes; eloquent, tumor, and background, where the tumor class is introduced to disentangle the effect that the zero entries have on learning the eloquent class.

We use a weighted cross-entropy loss function which is designed to handle membership imbalance in multi-class problems. Let δ_c be the risk factor associated with class c. If δ_c is small, then we pay a smaller penalty for misclassifying samples that belong to class c ($c = 1, 2, 3$). Since the language network is generally smaller than the motor network, we set different values for the language class $\{\delta_c^l\}$ and motor classes $\{\delta_c^m\}$ respectively. Let $\mathbf{Y}^l, \mathbf{Y}^{m_1}, \mathbf{Y}^{m_1}$, and $\mathbf{Y}^{m_3} \in \mathbb{R}^{N \times 3}$ be one-hot encoding matrices for the ground-truth class labels of the language and motor subnetworks. Our loss function is the sum of four terms:

$$\mathcal{L}_\Theta(\{\mathbf{W}^t\}_{t=1}^T, \mathbf{Y}) = \sum_{n=1}^N \sum_{c=1}^3 \underbrace{\left[-\delta_c^l \log\left(\sigma\left(\sum_{t=1}^T \mathbf{L}_{n,c}^t \cdot \mathbf{z}^{l,t}\right)\right)\mathbf{Y}_{n,c}^l \right.}_{\text{Language Loss } \mathcal{L}_l}$$

$$\underbrace{-\delta_c^m \log\left(\sigma\left(\sum_{t=1}^T \mathbf{M}_{1n,c}^t \cdot \mathbf{z}^{m,t}\right)\right)\mathbf{Y}_{n,c}^{m_1}}_{\text{Finger Loss } \mathcal{L}_{m_1}} \underbrace{-\delta_c^m \log\left(\sigma\left(\sum_{t=1}^T \mathbf{M}_{2n,c}^t \cdot \mathbf{z}^{m,t}\right)\right)\mathbf{Y}_{n,c}^{m_2}}_{\text{Foot Loss } \mathcal{L}_{m_2}} \quad (9)$$

$$\underbrace{-\delta_c^m \log\left(\sigma\left(\sum_{t=1}^T \mathbf{M}_{3n,c}^t \cdot \mathbf{z}^{m,t}\right)\right)\mathbf{Y}_{n,c}^{m_3} \right]}_{\text{Tongue Loss } \mathcal{L}_{m_3}}$$

where $\sigma(\cdot)$ is the sigmoid function. Our loss in Eq. (9) allows us to handle missing patient training labels for the eloquent subsystems across patients. Specifically, we freeze the branches corresponding to missing data and backpropagate the known loss terms. This backpropagation technique will refine the shared layers prior to the MT-FC layer, thus maximizing the information used from our training data. Our model is flexible to handle any number of functional systems by changing the number of MT-FC layers and kernels in the temporal attention.

Implementation Details. We implement our network in PyTorch using the SGD optimizer with weight decay $= 5 \times 10^{-5}$ for parameter stability, and momentum $= 0.9$ to improve convergence. We train our model with learning rate $= 0.005$ and 140 epochs, which provides for reliable performance without overfitting. We specified $D = 50$ feature maps in the convolutional branch. The LeakyReLU with slope $= -0.1$ was used for $\phi(.)$.

We compare the performance of our model against three baselines:

1. Random forest on dynamic connectivity matrices (RF)
2. A fully-connected network with temporal attention (FC-tANN)
3. Same as proposed without spatial attention (w/o sp. attn.)

The first baseline is a traditional machine learning RF approach to our problem. The FC-tANN maintains the same number of parameters as our model but has fully-connected layers instead of convolutional layers. Finally, we compare against our same architecture without spatial attention to observe the performance gain of focusing on different neighborhoods. To avoid biasing performance, we selected the hyperparameters using a development set

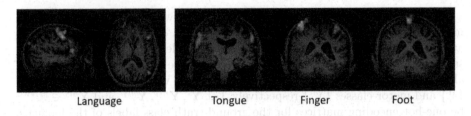

Language   Tongue   Finger   Foot

Fig. 3. Left: One sagital and axial view of a language network. **Right**: Coronal views of the motor sub-networks for one patient.

of 100 subjects downloaded from the Human Connectome Project (HCP). The final settings are: $\delta^m = (1.48, 0.44, 0.18), \delta^l = (2.16, 0.44, 0.18)$ for proposed, $\delta^m = (1.57, 0.42, 0.22), \delta^l = (2.31, 0.42, 0.22)$ for FC-tANN and $\delta^m = (1.51, 0.46, 0.19), \delta^l = (2.22, 0.46, 0.19)$ for w/o sp. attn.

3   Experimental Results

3.1   Dataset and Preprocessing

We evaluate the methods on rs-fMRI data from an additional HCP cohort [19] in which we artificially insert "fake tumors" by zeroing out entries of the connectivity matrix, and an in-house brain tumor dataset. All subjects underwent t-fMRI scanning, which we use to derive pseudo ground-truth labels for the language, finger, tongue and foot subnetworks. Figure 3 shows each of the cognitive networks of interest. Details on the acquisition paramters, sequencing, and preprocessing of the HCP dataset can be found in [19].

Our in-house tumor dataset contains 60 patients. Since the t-fMRI data was acquired for clinical purposes, not all patients in the in-house dataset performed each task. The number of subjects that performed the tasks are displayed in the left column of Table 1. The fMRI data was acquired using a 3.0 T Siemens Trio Tim (TR = 2000 ms, TE = 30 ms, FOV = 24 cm, res = 3.59 × 3.59 × 5 mm). Preprocessing steps include slice timing correction, motion correction and registration to the MNI-152 template. The rs-fMRI was further bandpass filtered from 0.01 to 0.1 Hz, spatially smoothed with a 6 mm FWHM Gaussian kernel, scrubbed using the ArtRepair toolbox [24] in SPM8, linearly detrended, and underwent nuisance regression using the CompCor package [25]. A general linear model implemented in SPM8 was used to obtain t-fMRI activation maps.

We used the Schaefer atlas to obtain $N = 1000$ brain regions [26], which is on par with the resolution of eloquent areas we are trying to detect. Tumor boundaries for each patient were manually delineated by a medical fellow using the MIPAV software package [27]. The fake tumors added to the HCP dataset are randomly positioned but created to be spatially continuous with the same size as the real tumor segmentations we obtained from the in-house dataset. An ROI was determined as belonging to the eloquent class if a majority of its voxel

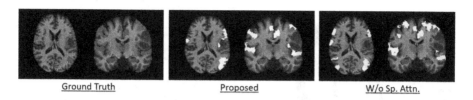

Ground Truth   Proposed   W/o Sp. Attn.

Fig. 4. Ground truth (blue) and predicted (yellow) for a bilateral language subject. (Color figure online)

Table 1. Overall accuracy, and ROC statistics. The number in the second column indicates number of patients who performed the task.

Dataset	Task	Method	Accuracy	Sens	Spec	F1	AUC
HCP	Language (100)	RF	0.58	0.32	0.55	0.42	0.5
		FC-tANN	0.65	0.61	0.58	0.59	0.64
		W/o Sp. Attn	0.77	0.73	0.68	0.69	0.72
		Proposed	**0.83**	**0.79**	**0.81**	**0.82**	**0.80**
	Finger (100)	RF	0.70	0.53	0.67	0.64	0.56
		FC-tANN	0.76	0.70	0.72	0.73	0.72
		W/o Sp. Attn	0.87	0.83	0.78	0.80	0.86
		Proposed	**0.91**	**0.86**	**0.85**	**0.85**	**0.88**
	Foot (100)	RF	0.67	0.48	0.65	0.62	0.53
		FC-tANN	0.79	0.77	0.69	0.73	0.76
		W/o Sp. Attn	0.86	<u>0.86</u>	0.83	0.84	0.85
		Proposed	**0.90**	**0.87**	**0.86**	**0.86**	**0.88**
	Tongue (100)	RF	0.70	0.46	0.68	0.63	0.53
		FC-tANN	0.75	0.72	0.68	0.72	0.73
		W/o Sp. Attn	0.81	0.83	0.80	0.81	0.81
		Proposed	**0.89**	**0.87**	**0.85**	**0.85**	**0.86**
In-house	Language (60)	RF	0.65	0.40	0.66	0.59	0.53
		FC-tANN	0.78	0.76	0.70	0.71	0.73
		W/o Sp. Attn	0.84	0.85	0.74	0.79	0.82
		Proposed	**0.93**	**0.91**	**0.85**	**0.87**	**0.91**
	Finger (36)	RF	0.67	0.43	0.67	0.61	0.55
		FC-tANN	0.76	0.75	0.69	0.71	0.77
		W/o Sp. Attn	0.88	**0.88**	0.79	0.82	0.85
		Proposed	**0.91**	**0.88**	**0.85**	**0.84**	**0.89**
	Foot (17)	RF	0.68	0.49	0.65	0.60	0.56
		FC-tANN	0.79	0.73	0.68	0.72	0.75
		W/o Sp. Attn	0.86	<u>0.86</u>	0.78	0.80	0.82
		Proposed	**0.89**	**0.87**	**0.83**	**0.84**	**0.86**
	Tongue (39)	RF	0.69	0.38	0.70	0.64	0.52
		FC-tANN	0.79	0.78	0.71	0.74	0.76
		W/o Sp. Attn	0.86	0.85	0.77	0.81	0.84
		Proposed	**0.90**	**0.87**	**0.82**	**0.84**	**0.87**

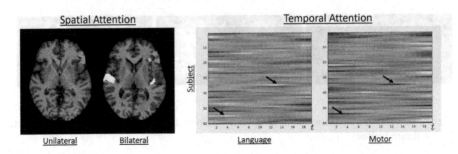

Fig. 5. Left: Heat map for the nodes with highest total spatial attention for a unilateral and a bilateral language subject. **Right:** Temporal attention weights for language and motor networks. The black arrows indicate networks phasing in and out with each other.

membership coincided with that of the t-fMRI activation map. Tumor labels were determined in a similar fashion according to the MIPAV segmentations.

3.2   Localization Results

We use 10-fold cross-validation to evaluate each method. Table 1 shows the performance metrics for detecting the eloquent class. In the second column, the number next to the task refers to the number of subjects whom we have training labels. As highlighted in bold, our proposed method outperforms the baseline algorithms in nearly all cases. We observe that the spatial attention model improves the specificity by improving the ratio of true negatives to false positives. Our performance gains are most notable regarding the language network, which is arguably the most challenging rea to localize during preoperative mapping. Figure 4 shows the ground truth (blue) and predicted (yellow) for all four systems in a challenging bilateral language subject, with both the proposed and w/o spatial attention methods. The model without spatial attention overpredicts the right-hemisphere language nodes, and misses various parts of the motor strip. Our model can localize functional regions right on the tumor boundary that the baseline method misses as well, which is relevant for clinical practice.

3.3   Feature Analysis

To better understand how the attention models improve the localization performance, Fig. 5 illustrates the spatial attention (left) and temporal attention weights (right) for our in-house dataset. These plots are generated by summing across the rows of the attention map $\bar{\mathbf{S}}$ and plotting the top ten nodes in one unilateral language and one bilateral language case. The spatial attention model is accurately able to capture right hemisphere activation in the bilateral case while correctly omitting this region in the unilateral case. This lateralization ability may be why localization performance increases for the language network. On the right-hand side of Fig. 5, we show the temporal attention weights for both language and motor networks across all patients and time. The language and motor networks phase in and out at different times, which improves localization by identifying important time intervals within the scan for each network.

4   Conclusion

We present a novel deep learning framework that leverages specialized convolutional layers, multi-scale spatial attention, temporal attention, and multi-task learning to identify critical regions of the eloquent cortex in tumor patients using dynamic resting-state connectivity. We validate our method on a real in-house dataset and a synthetic dataset to show generalizability of our method. We outperform machine and deep learning baselines by a large margin. Finally, we show the spatial and temporal attention features, which can be important biomarkers for simultaneous language and motor network identification. Future work includes exploring different pooling operations to improve atlas selection. Taken together, our results show promise for using rs-fMRI for presurgical planning of resection procedures.

Acknowledgements. This work was supported by the National Science Foundation CAREER award 1845430 (PI: Venkataraman) and the Research & Education Foundation Carestream Health RSNA Research Scholar Grant RSCH1420.

References

1. Gupta, D.K., et al.: Awake craniotomy versus surgery under general anesthesia for resection of intrinsic lesions of eloquent cortex-a prospective randomised study. Clin. Neurol. Neurosurg. **109**(4), 335–343 (2007)
2. Tomasi, D., Volkow, N.: Language network: segregation, laterality and connectivity. Mol. Psychiatry **17**(8), 759 (2012)
3. Tzourio-Mazoyer, N., et al.: Interindividual variability in the hemispheric organization for speech. Neuroimage **21**(1), 422–435 (2004)
4. Yang, I., Prashant, G.N.: Advances in the surgical resection of temporo-parieto-occipital junction gliomas. In: New Techniques for Management of 'Inoperable' Gliomas, pp. 73–87. Elsevier (2019)
5. Suarez, R.O., et al.: Threshold-independent functional MRI determination of language dominance: a validation study against clinical gold standards. Epilepsy Behav. **16**(2), 288–297 (2009)
6. Lee, M.H., et al.: Clinical resting-state fMRI in the preoperative setting: are we ready for prime time? Top. Magn. Reson. Imaging (TMRI) **25**(1), 11 (2016)
7. Biswal, B., et al.: Functional connectivity in the motor cortex of resting human brain using echo-planar MRI. Magn. Reson. Med. **34**(4), 537–541 (1995)
8. Nandakumar, N., Manzoor, K., Pillai, J.J., Gujar, S.K., Sair, H.I., Venkataraman, A.: A novel graph neural network to localize eloquent cortex in brain tumor patients from resting-state fMRI connectivity. In: Schirmer, M.D., Venkataraman, A., Rekik, I., Kim, M., Chung, A.W. (eds.) CNI 2019. LNCS, vol. 11848, pp. 10–20. Springer, Cham (2019). https://doi.org/10.1007/978-3-030-32391-2_2

9. Nandakumar, N., et al.: A multi-task deep learning framework to localize the eloquent cortex in brain tumor patients using dynamic functional connectivity. arXiv preprint arXiv:2011.08813 (2020)

10. Hart, M.G., et al.: Functional connectivity networks for preoperative brain mapping in neurosurgery. J. Neurosurg. 126(6), 1941–1950 (2016)

11. Qiu, T.-M., et al.: Localizing hand motor area using resting-state fMRI: validated with direct cortical stimulation. Acta Neurochir. 156(12), 2295–2302 (2014)

12. Zhang, D., et al.: Preoperative sensorimotor mapping in brain tumor patients using spontaneous fluctuations in neuronal activity imaged with functional magnetic resonance imaging: initial experience. Operative Neurosurg. 65(Suppl. 6), ons226–ons236 (2009)

13. Cochereau, J., et al.: Comparison between resting state fMRI networks and responsive cortical stimulations in glioma patients. Hum. Brain Mapp. 37(11), 3721–3732 (2016)

14. Sair, H.I., et al.: Presurgical brain mapping of the language network in patients with brain tumors using resting-state fMRI: comparison with task fMRI. Hum. Brain Mapp. 37(3), 913–923 (2016)

15. Mitchell, T.J., et al.: A novel data-driven approach to preoperative mapping of functional cortex using resting-state functional magnetic resonance imaging. Neurosurgery 73(6), 969–983 (2013)

16. Leuthardt, E.C., et al.: Integration of resting state functional MRI into clinical practice-a large single institution experience. PLOS ONE 13(6), e0198349 (2018)

17. Woo, S., Park, J., Lee, J.-Y., Kweon, I.S.: CBAM: convolutional block attention module. In: Ferrari, V., Hebert, M., Sminchisescu, C., Weiss, Y. (eds.) ECCV 2018. LNCS, vol. 11211, pp. 3–19. Springer, Cham (2018). https://doi.org/10.1007/978-3-030-01234-2_1

18. Li, D., et al.: Unified spatio-temporal attention networks for action recognition in videos. IEEE Trans. Multimedia 21(2), 416–428 (2018)

19. Van Essen, D.C., et al.: The WU-Minn human connectome project: an overview. Neuroimage 80, 62–79 (2013)

20. Kawahara, J., et al.: BrainNetCNN: convolutional neural networks for brain networks; towards predicting neurodevelopment. NeuroImage 146, 1038–1049 (2017)

21. Hutchison, R.M., et al.: Dynamic functional connectivity: promise, issues, and interpretations. Neuroimage 80, 360–378 (2013)

22. Chen, J., et al.: Multi-scale spatial and channel-wise attention for improving object detection in remote sensing imagery. IEEE Geosci. Remote Sens. Lett. 17(4), 681–685 (2019)

23. Zagoruyko, S., Komodakis, N.: Paying more attention to attention: improving the performance of convolutional neural networks via attention transfer. arXiv preprint arXiv:1612.03928 (2016)

24. Mazaika, P.K., et al.: Methods and software for fMRI analysis of clinical subjects. Neuroimage 47(Suppl. 1), S58 (2009)

25. Behzadi, Y., et al.: A component based noise correction method (CompCor) for bold and perfusion based fMRI. Neuroimage 37(1), 90–101 (2007)

26. Schaefer, A., et al.: Local-global parcellation of the human cerebral cortex from intrinsic functional connectivity MRI. Cereb. Cortex 28, 3095–3114 (2018)

27. McAuliffe, M.J., et al.: Medical image processing, analysis and visualization in clinical research. In: Proceedings 14th IEEE Symposium on Computer-Based Medical Systems, CBMS 2001, pp. 381–386. IEEE (2001)

Learning Multi-resolution Graph Edge Embedding for Discovering Brain Network Dysfunction in Neurological Disorders

Xin Ma[1]([✉]), Guorong Wu[2], Seong Jae Hwang[3], and Won Hwa Kim[1,4]

[1] University of Texas at Arlington, Arlington, USA
xin.ma@mavs.uta.edu
[2] University of North Carolina at Chapel Hill, Chapel Hill, USA
[3] University of Pittsburgh, Pittsburgh, USA
[4] POSTECH, Pohang-si, South Korea

Abstract. Tremendous recent literature show that associations between different brain regions, i.e., brain connectivity, provide early symptoms of neurological disorders. Despite significant efforts made for graph neural network (GNN) techniques, their focus on graph nodes makes the state-of-the-art GNN methods not suitable for classifying brain connectivity as graphs where the objective is to characterize disease-relevant network dysfunction patterns on graph links. To address this issue, we propose Multi-resolution Edge Network (MENET) to detect disease-specific connectomic benchmarks with high discrimination power across diagnostic categories. The core of MENET is a novel graph edge-wise transform that we propose, which allows us to capture multi-resolution "connectomic" features. Using a rich set of the connectomic features, we devise a graph learning framework to jointly select discriminative edges and assign diagnostic labels for graphs. Experiments on two real datasets show that MENET accurately predicts diagnostic labels and identify brain connectivities highly associated with neurological disorders such as Alzheimer's Disease and Attention-Deficit/Hyperactivity Disorder.

1 Introduction

Many neuroimaging studies operate with data from a population of cohort that can be stratified into two or more groups (e.g., diseased vs. control). Given registered imaging measures acquired from participants, contrasting the different groups at each pixel/voxel over the whole brain identifies those regions that are affected by the variable of interest (e.g., disease or risk factors) [8]. However, due to poor correlation between cognitive changes and pathological features from images, recent studies motivate that characterizing changes in the *brain connectivity* or *network* that comprise several affected regions yield a better understanding of the brain over traditional spatial analyses [3,11,21].

In brain connectivity studies, an individual brain is divided into registered regions of interests (ROIs) and associations across the ROIs are defined via

© Springer Nature Switzerland AG 2021
A. Feragen et al. (Eds.): IPMI 2021, LNCS 12729, pp. 253–266, 2021.
https://doi.org/10.1007/978-3-030-78191-0_20

functional/structural images, formulated as a "graph" that consists of nodes and edges. Changes in individual connectivity have shown strong implication of neurological diseases with evidence such as Parkinson's [27] and Alzheimer's disease (AD) [6]. Still, few frameworks exist for traditional prediction tasks for registered but topologically variant graphs *without node-specific features*.

Existing techniques including Graph Neural Network (GNN) methods mainly focus on analyzing features defined on graph nodes, where the graph is given as the domain of the signal [18,34]. GNNs for point clouds may work but their nodes are merely arbitrarily sampled points over surfaces of non-rigid shapes [19]. Notice that such settings are not in the interest of this study where we deal with alternations in the "connectivity", i.e., edges, instead of measures at each node. Graph kernels that compare local substructures [28,31] are often inadequate for training, and alternative deep learning methods for graph such as [32,37] lose interpretability in space particularly with dense graphs. For brain connectivity analysis, the method must be able to investigate local edge-wise variation and predict global diagnostic labels to identify disease-specific symptoms. Hence, it is critical to develop a framework that can *adaptively* transform graph "edges" with graphs' inherent *structure* of the graphs to increase *sensitivity* but maintain location-wise *interpretability* even with small sample sizes.

To achieve the objectives above, we propose a new convolution neural network (CNN) framework for graph edges that derives flexible multi-resolution features sensitive to topological variations in graphs (example shown in Fig. 1). The key of our method is at the adaptive graph edge transform— adopting ideas from spectral graph wavelet transform [12], we define a novel *multi-resolution edge trans-*

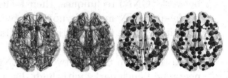

Fig. 1. Example of multi-resolution representation of brain connectivity. 1) original network, 2)-4) filtered network at $s = 0.3, 0.8, 1.8$. Sparsity of the network increases and nodal degree decreases (red to blue) as the scale changes. (Color figure online)

form that deals with a positive semi-definite (p.s.d.) matrix. Defining a graph specific orthonormal tensor as a surrogate to transform a p.s.d. matrix, we obtain its multi-resolution representation with trainable kernel functions in a dual space. Such an *edge-wise* analysis is at the core of brain connectivity analysis identifying which of the brain connectivities are significantly related to disease-specific variables. The **contributions** of our work are, 1) defining a novel graph edge transform that derives flexible representation of graph edges, 2) proposing a framework that can efficiently train and classify diagnostic labels for graphs as well as identify disease-specific brain connectivity, 3) extensive empirical results on two independent real brain connectivity data for AD and Attention-Deficit/Hyperactivity Disorder (ADHD) to validate our framework. Our discoveries identifying subtle variations in brain connectivity align with other on-going studies, suggesting that our framework has potential for various brain disorder analyses.

1.1 Related Work

Graph Kernels (GK): GK methods map graphs into a Hilbert space, which can be fed to downstream classifiers (e.g., Support Vector Machine (SVM)) to perform graph classification [10]. The designs of kernels include neighborhood aggregation (e.g., Weisfeiler-Lehman [30]), extraction of subgraph patterns (e.g., Graphlet [31], and walks/paths (e.g., shortest-path [1] and random walk [14]).

GNN: Graph Convolution Network (GCN) methods transform "node features" into informative node embeddings by aggregating and propagating node features via graph convolution. Such node embeddings have shown to excel at node classification [18] and graph classifications [34] with specific pooling mechanisms, e.g., Dynamic Graph CNN (DGCNN), one of the state-of-the-art methods, uses a specialized SortPooling layer for graph classification [35]. Despite their success, GCNs and their variants rely heavily on the node features provided by the data which, in fact, may not even be provided in certain datasets. In other words, graphs may *only* come with edge features, leading to sub-optimal use of GCN by reluctantly utilizing weak node features such as nodal degrees.

Benefits of Our Work. Unlike the two approaches above, we use parametric kernels can adaptively derive beneficial representations for graph classification that can be directly applied to edge measures instead of node features. Different from the methods that define multi-resolution in the native graph space with hops on nodes [36] or thresholds on edges [13], we use a dual space and smooth kernels that can be described by the theory of traditional wavelet transform.

2 Proposed Method

The key in our approach is to derive the multi-resolution representation of *edges* by developing a novel graph edge transform, which we introduce below.

2.1 Multi-resolution Graph Edge Transform

Consider a set of graphs with registered nodes with label y assigned for each graph G. Each graph with N nodes is represented as its adjacency matrix $A_{N \times N}$, whose non-negative element a_{ij} denotes edge weight (i.e., measure of association) between the i-th and j-th nodes. Given an adjacency matrix A (e.g., a brain connectivity), one can derive a degree matrix $D_{N \times N}$ as a diagonal matrix whose i-th diagonal is the sum of edge weights connected to the i-th node (i.e., volume). Its graph Laplacian $\mathcal{L}$ is defined as $D - A$, and a normalized one is defined as $\mathcal{L}_{norm} = D^{-1/2} \mathcal{L} D^{-1/2}$. Both Laplacians, $\mathcal{L}$ and $\mathcal{L}_{norm}$, are symmetric and p.s.d. with non-negative eigenvalues λ_ℓ and orthonormal eigenvectors u_ℓ. Previous works used the λ_ℓ and u_ℓ to define a wavelet transform on node signals and constructed GCNs for signals defined on the nodes n, i.e., $f(n)$ [12,18]. However, notice that $f(n)$ is not of our interest but we define a transform for $f(e)$, i.e., weights on the edges e, to derive "multi-resolution" views.

Let us first decompose a graph Laplacian $\mathcal{L} = \sum_{l=0}^{N-1} \lambda_l u_l u_l^T = U\Lambda U^T$ where $U = [u_0, u_1, \cdots, u_{N-1}]$ and Λ is a diagonal matrix whose $(l+1)$-th diagonal is λ_l. Traditional continuous wavelet transform suggests that derive multi-resolution representation of signals can be derived using an orthogonal transform and defining scales in a dual space [12,17,22]. Hence, we define an orthonormal basis for a "matrix" using an outer product of u_l, together with a kernel $k(\cdot)$ as $\psi_{l,s}(i,j) = k(s\lambda_l)u_l(i)u_l(j)$ and a transform using the $\psi_{l,s}(i,j)$ is defined as

$$\beta_{\mathcal{L},l}(s) = \langle \mathcal{L}, \psi_l \rangle = \sum_i \sum_j k(s\lambda_l)u_l(i)u_l(j) \sum_{l'=0}^{N-1} \lambda_{l'} u_{l'}(i)u_{l'}(j) = \lambda_l k(s\lambda_l) \quad (1)$$

which yields a resultant coefficient $\beta_{\mathcal{L},\ell}(s)$. Note that its inverse is

$$\mathcal{L}(i,j) = \frac{1}{C_k} \int_0^\infty \sum_{l=0}^{N-1} \beta_{\mathcal{L},l}(s)\psi_{s,l}(i,j) \frac{ds}{s} \quad (2)$$

which reconstructs $\mathcal{L}$ with a kernel normalization constant $C_k = \int_0^\infty \frac{k(x)^2}{x} dx$.

Lemma 1 *(Graph Laplacian Admissibility Condition). Given a kernel dependent normalization constant $C_k = \int_0^\infty \frac{k(x)^2}{x} dx < \infty$, the original graph Laplacian $\mathcal{L}$ can be perfectly reconstructed via the inverse transformation.*

Proof. Projecting the coefficients $\beta_{\mathcal{L},l}(s)$ back to the original domain with $\psi_{l,s}$,

$$\frac{1}{C_k} \int_0^\infty \sum_{l=0}^{N-1} \beta_{\mathcal{L},l}(s)\psi_{l,s}(i,j) \frac{ds}{s} = \frac{1}{C_k} \int_0^\infty \sum_{l=0}^{N-1} \lambda_l k(s\lambda_l)^2 u_l(i)u_l(j) \frac{ds}{s}$$

$$= \sum_{l=0}^{N-1} \lambda_l \left[\frac{1}{C_k} \int_0^\infty \frac{k(s\lambda_l)^2}{s} ds\right] u_l(i)u_l(j) = \mathcal{L}(i,j)$$

and $\mathcal{L}(i,j)$ is obtained by substituting $s\lambda_l = x$.

The Lemma above follows the traditional admissibility condition in wavelet transform [22], i.e., a superposition of multi-resolution representation of $\mathcal{L}$ over scales s. It lets us to define new representation $\mathcal{L}_s$ at different scales **s**:

$$\mathcal{L}_s(i,j) = \sum_{l=0}^{N-1} \lambda_l k(s\lambda_l)^2 u_l(i)u_l(j) \quad (3)$$

by focusing at a specific scale s. It is given as a matrix operation as

$$\mathcal{L}_s = U k(s\Lambda)^2 \Lambda U^T \quad (4)$$

where $k(s\Lambda)^2$ is a diagonal matrix with the $k(\cdot)$ applied at each λ. The shape of $k(\cdot)$ determines the shape of wavelet-like basis and multi-resolution views of $\mathcal{L}$. For regular images, this yields filtered images (e.g., band-pass filtered signal), and our framework extracts similar representations of edges $f(e)$ as in Fig. 1.

2.2   Efficient Graph Matrix Transform

The transform (3) requires eigendecomposition of a graph Laplacian (or estimating a partial set of eigenvectors) which can be computationally burdening,
especially with a large number of nodes or graph samples. We therefore suggest
an approximation of (3) that significantly reduces computation with marginal
error, which extends the approximation in [12] to our graph matrix transform.

For this, let us assume $g(\Lambda) = \Lambda k(s\Lambda)^2$ from (4) and $\tilde{\Lambda} = \frac{2}{\lambda_{max}}\Lambda - I_N$ since
the largest eigenvalue of a normalized graph Laplacian is bounded by 2. Then,
$\tilde{\Lambda} = \Lambda - I_N$ and $g(\tilde{\Lambda}) = g(\Lambda - I_N)$. If we expand $g(\Lambda)$ with I_N then,

$$g(\Lambda) = \sum_{n=0}^{\infty} \frac{g^{(n)}(I_N)}{n!}(\Lambda - I_N)^n = \sum_{n=0}^{\infty} \frac{g^{(n)}(0_N)}{n!}\tilde{\Lambda}^n. \tag{5}$$

Considering that the elements of $\tilde{\Lambda}$ are in $[-1, 1]$, we assume there exists a
positive K where if $n > K$, $\tilde{\Lambda}^n \to 0$. Here, $g(\Lambda)$ can be approximated as

$$g(\Lambda) \approx \sum_{n=0}^{K} \frac{g^{(n)}(0_N)}{n!}\tilde{\Lambda}^n. \tag{6}$$

Since $U\Lambda^m U^T = (U\Lambda U^T)^m$, $\mathcal{L}_s$ now can be written as

$$\mathcal{L}_s = Ug(\Lambda)U^T \approx \sum_{n=0}^{K} \frac{g^{(n)}(0_N)}{n!}U\tilde{\Lambda}^n U^T \approx \sum_{n=0}^{K} \frac{g^{(n)}(0_N)}{n!}\tilde{\mathcal{L}}^n \tag{7}$$

where $\tilde{\mathcal{L}} = \mathcal{L} - I_{N \times N}$. This approximation lets our overall framework more
practical to handle large scale graph data.

2.3   Network Architecture

Based on the matrix transform (3) as a convolution, we propose *Multi-resolution
Edge Network (MENET)* which is a novel CNN framework that utilizes multi-
resolution representations of graph edges for classification. Figure 2 illustrates
the overall pipeline with the following components:

Convolution Layer: Taking a graph as an input, it returns multi-resolution
representation $\mathcal{L}_s$ of its graph Laplacian using the transform in (4) as a tensor,
i.e., $|s| \times N \times N$ where $|s|$ is the total number of scales. It maps $\mathcal{L}$ to a high-
dimensional space of filtered graph edges with $|s|$.

FC Layer: This component is a fully connected Deep Neural Network (DNN)
classifier that takes the multi-resolution features of a graph as an input and
predicts its class label. It has L output units where L is the number of available
classes. The values o_l computed at each output unit, when normalized, become
the pseudo-probability of an input belong to a specific class.

MENET learns two sets of parameters: 1) scale s that define the resolutions
of graph edges, and 2) weight $\mathbf{W}^h$ within the FC for prediction. Notice that there

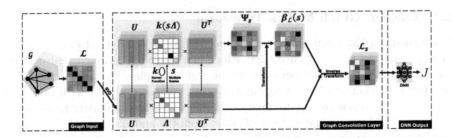

Fig. 2. Overall architecture of MENET. A graph matrix is transformed to yield multi-resolution representations, and then fully connected (FC) DNN is applied at the end. Error is backpropagated to train the weights $\mathbf{W^h}$ and update the scales s to obtain the optimal representations.

is no pooling; while it is important to increase the efficiency of the algorithm, without an invertible method for pooling on edges, we want to keep *spatial interpretability* for neuroimaging applications. Also, the pooling in conventional methods are required for multi-scale analysis with fixed window size, but our framework inherits such behavior within the matrix transform.

2.4 Training MENET

Given a training set with N_G number of individual graphs G with corresponding labels y, the learning process consists of feedforward and backpropagation steps. In the feedforward propagation of MENET, a graph G is inputted to the framework as a graph Laplacian, and the probability that the G belongs to a particular class is computed at the output. Suppose we are given an input graph G with N vertices and a set of initial scales $\mathbf{s}$. First, using the operation in (4), the input G is transformed to $\mathcal{L}_s$. Since each $\mathcal{L}_s$ is represented as a matrix and there are $|\mathbf{s}|$ of them, $\mathcal{L}_s$ are combined to consist a feature map M as a tensor:

$$M = \mathcal{L}_{s_0} \cup \mathcal{L}_{s_1} \cup \cdots \cup \mathcal{L}_{s_{|\mathbf{s}|}} \tag{8}$$

Given T hidden units in the hidden layers of the DNN module, at each t-th hidden unit, the learned features in hidden units are linearly combined with corresponding weights in the first layer of DNN as

$$z_t = \sum_{s,p,q}^{|\mathbf{s}|,N,N} w_{t,spq}^h m_{spq}, \tag{9}$$

where m_{spq} represents a feature element in M (i.e., an element at (p,q) in s-th scale) and $w_{t,spq}^h$ denotes the weight on a connection between a hidden unit m_{spq} to the t-th hidden unit of the following layer. A non-linear activation function $\sigma()$ (e.g., sigmoid or rectified linear function) is applied on z_t and is then fed to the next layer. At the output of the DNN, a soft-max function is used to get the final outcome o_l for the l-th output unit as a pseudo probability from which a prediction is made as $\hat{y} = \arg\max_l o_l$.

Once the output o_l is obtained from the feedforward system above, an error can be computed between the o_l and the target value y_l, i.e., a label with one-hot-encoding for the input graph. We use focal loss [20] to measure the error:

$$J(\mathbf{s}, \mathbf{W}^h) = -\frac{1}{N_G} \sum_{i=1}^{N_G} \sum_{l=1}^{L} -\alpha_{il}(1 - p_{il})^\gamma \log(p_{il}) \tag{10}$$

where $p_{il} = o_{il}$ if target value $y_{il} = 1$ at l-th output unit with i-th sample, otherwise $p_{il} = 1 - o_{il}$, N_G and L are the total number of graphs in a batch and the total number of available classes respectively, α and γ are balanced variants. Our framework "adaptively" learns scale parameters $\mathbf{s}$ for novel graph representations and $\mathbf{W}^h$ in the FC layer (embedded in o_l) by primarily minimizing the classification error in (10) via backpropagation. In traditional wavelet transform, the $\mathbf{s}$ is fixed to yield theoretical guarantees, however, we freely explore different aspects of $\mathbf{s}$ to find the optimal resolutions that yield the least loss.

Regularization. To avoid overfitting (especially with small sample size) and achieve desirable properties in the learned parameters, we impose the following constraints to our model. We first assume that only a few edges in the graphs are highly associated with the variable of interest. This is a natural assumption as changes due to a brain disorder do not manifest over the whole brain but sparsely appear in different ROIs. We therefore impose an ℓ_1-norm constraint to the first layer of $\mathbf{W}^h$ which includes the fully connected weights. We expect that this constraint will set many elements in the first layer of $\mathbf{W}^h$ to zeros and identify the edges that are highly related to the prediction of labels. Second, we expect $\mathbf{s}$ to be smooth with an ℓ_2-norm constraint. This lets us obtain a smoothly transiting multi-resolution representation, i.e., avoid $\mathbf{s}$ from diverging.

With these assumptions and (10), we minimize our final objective function

$$\tilde{J}(\mathbf{s}, \mathbf{W}^h) = J(\mathbf{s}, \mathbf{W}^h) + \frac{\theta_1}{N_G}|\mathbf{W}_1^h|_1 + \frac{\theta_2}{N_G}||\mathbf{s}||_2 \tag{11}$$

where $\mathbf{W}_1^h$ represents the weights of the first layer of DNN module, θ_1 and θ_2 are the regularization parameters for ℓ_1-norm and ℓ_2-norm respectively.

The MENET is trained based on the partial derivatives of the objective function (11) with respect to the trainable parameters, i.e., $\frac{\partial \tilde{J}(\mathbf{s}, \mathbf{W}^h)}{\partial w_{t,spq}^h}$ and $\frac{\partial \tilde{J}(\mathbf{s}, \mathbf{W}^h)}{\partial s}$. These parameters $\mathbf{W}^h$ and $\mathbf{s}$ are then updated using gradient descent with different learning rates r_W and r_s respectively.

3   Experiments

In this section, we demonstrate experiments on two independent real datasets: structural brain connectivity from Diffusion Tensor Images (DTI) in Alzheimer's Disease Neuroimaging Initiative (ADNI) and functional connectivity from resting-state functional magnetic resonance images (rs-fMRI) in ADHD-200.

3.1   Datasets

ADNI. From the initiative, individual DTIs were processed by our in-house tractography pipeline to extract structural brain networks using Destrieux atlas [7] with 148 ROIs. Each brain network is given as an adjacency matrix whose elements denote *number of neuron fiber tracts* connecting two different ROIs. The dataset included $N = 506$ subjects and we merged control (CN) and Early Mild Cognitive Impairment (EMCI) groups as *Pre-clinical AD* group and combined Late Mild Cognitive Impairment (LMCI) and AD groups as *Prodromal AD* group to ensure sufficient sample size and compare their subtle differences.

ADHD-200. We adopted rs-fMRI data which were registered to Automated Anatomical Labeling (AAL) atlas with 116 ROIs [33]. We computed Pearson's correlation coefficients (without threshold) between 116 different ROIs to construct functional brain connectivity for each participant. Taking the samples without artifact and removing groups with few subjects, we ended up with total of $N = 756$ samples labeled as 1) Typically Developing Children (TDC), 2) ADHD-Combined (ADHD-C), and 3) ADHD-Inattentive (ADHD-I). Our result may vary from [2] as the experimental settings are different (Table 1).

Table 1. Demographics of ADNI and ADHD-200 Datasets

Category	ADNI		ADHD-200		
	Preclinical AD (CN,EMCI)	Prodromal AD (LMCI,AD)	TDC	ADHD-C	ADHD-I
# of Subjects	276 (109,167)	171 (94,77)	487	159	110
Age (mean, std)	72.7(73.8,72.0), 6.9(5.8,7.5)	74.2(72.6,76.1), 6.9(6.4,7.0)	12.2(3.3)	11.2(3.0)	12.0(2.6)
Gender (M/F)	163/113 (57/52, 106/61)	98/73 (51/43, 47/30)	258/229	130/29	85/25

3.2   Experimental Settings

Evaluation Measures. We used 3-fold cross validation (CV) to evaluate our model and baselines with unbiased results. Evaluation measures were accuracy, precision, recall and F1-score averaged across the folds.

Parameters. The kernel was defined as $k_s(x) = sxe^{-sx}$ to ensure that the $k()$ behaves as a band-pass filter (i.e., it achieves 0 at the origin), and the total number of scales to derive multi-resolution representation was $|\mathbf{s}| = 5$. Weights were randomly initialized with Xavier initialization and the scales were uniformly selected between $[0.01, 2.5]$. The input to DL methods was the flattened $\mathcal{L}_s$ and the number of hidden units was set to 256. LeakyReLU activation function with negative slope 0.2 and batch normalization were applied to hidden units. ℓ_1-norm was applied on the first layer of DNN with hyper-parameter $\theta_1 = 0.0001$ to achieve sparsity. ℓ_2-norm was adopted on scales with hyper-parameter $\theta_2 = 0.001$.

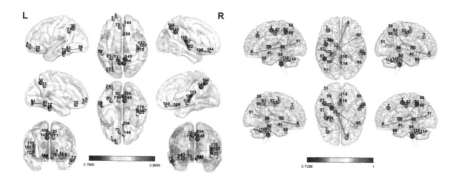

Fig. 3. Top-10 Connectivities from ADNI (Left) and ADHD-200 (Right) Analyses. Edge thickness denotes average trained edge weight and node color denotes its degree.

The learning rate of scale parameters was set to $r_s = 0.01$, and that of weight parameters was set to $r_W = 0.001$. The γ for focal loss was set to 2.

Baselines. We used SVM with RBF kernel, Logistic regression (LR), DNN, graph kernel (Shortest Path (SP)) with SVM, and several state-of-the-art graph learning frameworks (i.e., graph2vec [26] and DGCNN [35], and GCN [18]) as baselines for comparisons. For SVMs, we used Principal Component Analysis (PCA) with the rank of 10 to perform dimension reduction otherwise the models predicted all test samples as a single class with poor precision and recall. Node degree was used as node feature if a method required one.

3.3 Structural Brain Connectivity Analysis on ADNI

Result. Analysis on structural connectivity for Preclinical AD was performed. Binary classification task was designed to identify differences between the Preclinical (N=276) and Prodromal AD (N=171) groups instead of classifying four groups. As there is no effective treatment for AD, predicting the risk of developing dementia in the preclinical stage which is critical to enable disease-modifying interventions. Moreover, this task is particularly challenging since the physiological distinction between EMCI and LMCI, which lie along the decision boundary between Preclinical and Prodromal AD, is known to be especially subtle [4,24].

The classification results of all baselines and MENET across four evaluation measures (accuracy, precision, recall, and F1-score) averaged across the folds are shown in Table 3. We show that MENET outperforms *all* other baselines. First, we see that SVM and graph kernel SVM achieved accuracy around ~60%, close to 61.7% which is the random prediction would yield in this dataset, with poor precision and recall. GNNs (i.e., DGCNN and GCN) did not perform well either; this may be due to both GCN and DGCNN emphasizing nodes instead of edges that better characterize these particular graphs. While graph2vec with SVM showed higher performance than GNNs, its graph embedding is characterized by node and not edges, hence not interpretable at the connectivity level. Interestingly, directly applying LR on these $\mathcal{L}$ outperforms most of the previously mentioned baselines. This further demonstrates that the existing graph-based deep models may be *sub-optimal* for the current task; instead, the key is to effectively operate on $\mathcal{L}$ as we observe next.

Ablation Study ($\mathcal{L}$ vs. $\mathcal{L}_s$). DNN directly applied on $\mathcal{L}$ immediately improves over LR. Although this gain is somewhat expected, we point out the significance of the multi-resolution graph transform $\mathcal{L}_s$: MENET, which is essentially DNN on $\mathcal{L}_s$ with the *same* network classifier, shows significant improvements. MENET improves over DNN (*second best* model) in *all* evaluations by 10.9% in accuracy, 9.1% in precision, 14.6% in recall, and 14.0% in F1-score.

Clinical Validation. To help clinical interpretation of our findings, we investigate the trained edge weights that are connected to the trained $\mathcal{L}_s$, and visualize them as a brain network in Fig. 3. Only top-10 connectivities with the largest average weights are shown for sparsity—the most discriminative connectivities for Preclinical and Prodromal AD. The edge thickness and the node color respectively correspond to the edge weight and nodal degree of each ROI based on the trained weights. The list of the 10 connections is given along the figure that span across 17 ROIs (full ROI labels are in [7]). We observed several temporal regions (i.e., inferior temporal gyrus (37), inferior temporal sulcus (72), superior temporal gyrus (107)) [9,16], precuneus (30, 104) [15], subparietal regions (71, 145) [5], and many others, all of which are corroborated by various AD literature.

3.4 Functional Brain Connectivity Analysis on ADHD

Result. Our results on multi-class classification on ADHD-200 are summarized in Table 3. We note that identifying the differences among these groups is innately challenging in ADHD-200 dataset consisting of adolescents with actively developing brains, inducing high variation. Further, compared to the previous AD experiment, this *multi-class* classification is particularly difficult especially with the severe class imbalance (64.4% random test set prediction accuracy). Thus, it is crucial that a method benefits all four evaluations in this analysis. In fact, throughout our experiments, we often observed undesirable behaviors

Table 2. List of Top-10 Significant Brain Connectivities from Fig. 3.

ADNI			ADHD-200		
Index	Row (ROI label [7])	Col (ROI label)	Index	Row(ROI label [33])	Col(ROI label)
1	115 (rLat_Fis-post)	107 (rG_temp_sup-G_T_transv)	1	114 (Vermis_8)	116 (Vermis_10)
2	122 (rS_circular_insula_inf)	115 (rLat_Fis-post)	2	6 (Frontal_Sup_Orb_R)	51 (Occipital_Mid_L)
3	106 (rG_subcallosal)	144 (rS_suborbital)	3	41 (Amygdala_L)	73 (Putamen_L)
4	51 (lS_collat_transv_post)	2 (lG_and_S_occipital_inf)	4	59 (Parietal_Sup_L)	107 (Cerebelum_10_L)
5	72 (lS_temporal_inf)	37 (lG_temporal_inf)	5	1 (Precentral_L)	57 (Postcentral_L)
6	51 (lS_collat_transv_post)	61 (lS_oc-temp_med_and_Lingual)	6	41 (Amygdala_L)	75 (Pallidum_L)
7	1 (lG_and_S_frontomargin)	5 (lG_and_S_transv_frontopol)	7	33 (Cingulum_Mid_L)	66 (Angular_R)
8	30 (lG_precuneus)	71 (lS_subparietal)	8	61 (Parietal_Inf_L)	88 (Tem_Pole_Mid_R)
9	145 (rS_subparietal)	104 (rG_precuneus)	9	86 (Temporal_Mid_R)	90 (Temporal_Inf_R)
10	5 (lG_and_S_transv_frontopol)	70 (lS_suborbital)	10	7 (Frontal_Mid_L)	88 (Tem_Pole_Mid_R)

Table 3. Classification Performances on ADNI and ADHD-200 Datasets.

Model	ADNI				ADHD-200			
	Accuracy	Precision	Recall	F1-score	Accuracy	Precision	Recall	F1-score
SVM	62.19 ± 5.86%	57.67 ± 8.90%	56.93 ± 7.17%	56.21 ± 8.49%	52.06 ± 4.39%	31.95 ± 3.11%	32.56 ± 2.28%	31.75 ± 1.98%
LR	74.27 ± 2.70%	74.47 ± 1.91%	69.60 ± 4.15%	70.08 ± 4.63%	45.29 ± 8.36%	27.18 ± 4.56%	28.74 ± 3.50%	27.21 ± 3.53%
SP-SVM	58.61 ± 1.14%	42.02 ± 4.58%	48.13 ± 1.14%	39.77 ± 1.50%	51.13 ± 4.25%	31.84 ± 1.06%	32.36 ± 1.00%	31.63 ± 0.68%
DNN	78.65 ± 0.92%	80.24 ± 1.15%	74.49 ± 2.35%	75.45 ± 2.13%	56.04 ± 7.17%	41.94 ± 9.23%	34.63 ± 0.96%	31.91 ± 3.45%
Graph2vec	74.83 ± 5.93%	75.06 ± 5.56%	71.89 ± 7.25%	71.69 ± 7.64%	61.62 ± 1.79%	21.36 ± 0.08%	31.82 ± 0.93%	25.56 ± 0.35%
DGCNN	65.77 ± 2.90%	73.20 ± 11.48%	62.20 ± 3.31%	61.89 ± 4.03%	62.27 ± 3.12%	37.47 ± 13.34%	35.20 ± 1.95%	29.94 ± 4.06%
GCN	67.79 ± 3.71%	67.67 ± 7.30%	62.34 ± 3.33%	62.21 ± 3.44%	59.76 ± 6.23%	39.68 ± 10.91%	33.66 ± 0.37%	29.49 ± 3.08%
MENET	**87.27 ± 3.71%**	**87.56 ± 2.90%**	**85.39 ± 5.06%**	**86.02 ± 4.41%**	**62.82 ± 1.60%**	**44.95 ± 4.46%**	**35.48 ± 1.82%**	**32.41 ± 3.38%**

from these algorithms biasing towards predicting all testing instances as TDC for maximal high accuracy while sacrificing precision and recall. For instance, graph2vec+SVM achieved the third-highest accuracy with nearly the worst precision, recall and F1-score even with our best effort to alleviate this issue. Therefore, all the models were carefully tuned to prevent such cases as much as possible. Again, MENET achieved higher performance than all baseline models in *all* evaluation metrics by achieving the highest average accuracy at 62.82% while also improving precision, recall and F1-score. DNN, DGCNN and GCN suffered from large standard deviations, indicating unstable learning across the CV folds (Table 2).

Clinical Validation. To help clinical interpretation of our findings, we similarly derived the top-10 functional connectivities that are associated with the classification of ADHD stages. The top-10 connectivities with the highest average weights are shown in Fig. 3, whose edge thickness and node color correspond to the edge weight and degree of each ROI respectively. The list of the 10 connections, that span across 18 ROIs, is given along the figure (full ROI names in [33]). We observed several ROIs in temporal regions (mid-temporal pole (86, 88), inferior temporal cortex (90)) [29], frontal regions (frontal superior orbital (6), mid-frontal (7)) [25], and Amygdala (41) [23]; these results along with other identified ROIs are already well documented in many ADHD literature.

3.5   Discussions on Convergence of Scales

Figure 4 shows the convergence of scales for AD (top) and ADHD (bottom) experiments. The scale parameters of our model converge very fast; the low-pass filter (i.e., Scale 0) of the ADNI experiment tends to increase while ADHD tends to decrease in the experiments. One possible reason is that the ADHD classification requires the model to involve more local context information as the problem is more difficult than the AD experiment.

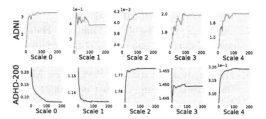

Fig. 4. Convergence of scales w.r.t. training epoch. Top: ADNI, Bottom: ADHD-200.

4   Conclusion

We developed a novel graph transform-based CNN framework designed to perform classification tasks with a population of registered graphs. The transform derives multi-resolution representations of a graph matrix, i.e., edges, that serve as effective features suited to perform classification on graphs. Using a parametric kernel, our framework, i.e., MENET, can train well with relatively small sample size and was validated with extensive experiments on two independent connectivity datasets, yielding clinically sound results on AD and ADHD supported by existing literature. We believe that MENET has significant potential to domains with graph data practically challenged by small sample sizes.

Acknowledgments. This research was supported by NSF IIS CRII 1948510, NSF IIS 2008602, NIH R01 AG059312, IITP-2020-2015-0-00742, and IITP-2019-0-01906 funded by MSIT (AI Graduate School Program at POSTECH).

References

1. Borgwardt, K.M., Kriegel, H.P.: Shortest-path kernels on graphs. In: ICDM (2005)
2. Brown, M.R., Sidhu, G.S., Greiner, R., et al.: ADHD-200 global competition: diagnosing ADHD using personal characteristic data can outperform resting state fMRI measurements. Front. Syst. Neurosci. **6**, 69 (2012). https://doi.org/10.3389/fnsys.2012.0006
3. Bullmore, E., Sporns, O.: Complex brain networks: graph theoretical analysis of structural and functional systems. Nat. Rev. Neurosci. **10**(3), 186 (2009)
4. Chincarini, A., Bosco, P., Calvini, P., et al.: Local MRI analysis approach in the diagnosis of early and prodromal Alzheimer's disease. Neuroimage **58**(2), 469–480 (2011). https://doi.org/10.1016/j.neuroimage.2011.05.083
5. Choo, I.H., Lee, D.Y., Oh, J.S., et al.: Posterior cingulate cortex atrophy and regional cingulum disruption in mild cognitive impairment and Alzheimer's disease. Neurobiol. Aging **31**(5), 772–779 (2010). https://doi.org/10.1016/j.neurobiolaging.2008.06.015
6. Dennis, E.L., Thompson, P.M.: Functional brain connectivity using fMRI in aging and Alzheimer's disease. Neuropsychol. Rev. **24**(1), 49–62 (2014). https://doi.org/10.1007/s11065-014-9249-6
7. Destrieux, C., Fischl, B., Dale, A., Halgren, E.: Automatic parcellation of human cortical gyri and sulci using standard anatomical nomenclature. Neuroimage **53**(1), 1–15 (2010). https://doi.org/10.1016/j.neuroimage.2010.06.010
8. Friston, K.J.: Statistical Parametric Mapping. In: Kötter, R. (eds.) Neuroscience Databases. Springer, Boston (2003). https://doi.org/10.1007/978-1-4615-1079-6_16
9. Galton, C.J., Patterson, K., Graham, K., et al.: Differing patterns of temporal atrophy in Alzheimer's disease and semantic dementia. Neurology **57**(2), 216–225 (2001). https://doi.org/10.1212/wnl.57.2.216
10. Gärtner, T., Flach, P., Wrobel, S.: On graph kernels: hardness results and efficient alternatives. In: Schölkopf, B., Warmuth, M.K. (eds.) COLT-Kernel 2003. LNCS (LNAI), vol. 2777, pp. 129–143. Springer, Heidelberg (2003). https://doi.org/10.1007/978-3-540-45167-9_11

11. Greicius, M.D., Krasnow, B., Reiss, A.L., Menon, V.: Functional connectivity in the resting brain: a network analysis of the default mode hypothesis. Proc. Natl. Acad. Sci. **100**(1), 253–258 (2003). https://doi.org/10.1073/pnas.0135058100
12. Hammond, D., Vandergheynst, P., Gribonval, R.: Wavelets on graphs via spectral graph theory. Appl. Comput. Harmon. Anal. **30**(2), 129–150 (2011). https://doi.org/10.1016/j.acha.2010.04.005
13. Jie, B., Zhang, D., Wee, C.Y., Shen, D.: Topological graph kernel on multiple thresholded functional connectivity networks for mild cognitive impairment classification. Hum. Brain Mapp. **35**(7), 2876–2897 (2014). https://doi.org/10.1002/hbm.22353
14. Kang, U., Tong, H., Sun, J.: Fast random walk graph kernel. In: ICDM (2012)
15. Karas, G., Scheltens, P., Rombouts, S., et al.: Precuneus atrophy in early-onset Alzheimer's disease: a morphometric structural MRI study. Neuroradiology **49**(12), 967–976 (2007). https://doi.org/10.1007/s00234-007-0269-2
16. Kim, W.H., Pachauri, D., Hatt, C., et al.: Wavelet based multi-scale shape features on arbitrary surfaces for cortical thickness discrimination. Adv. Neural Inf. Process. Syst. **2012**, 1241–1249 (2012)
17. Kim, W.H., Kim, H.J., Adluru, N., Singh, V.: Latent variable graphical model selection using harmonic analysis: applications to the human connectome project (hcp). In: CVPR, pp. 2443–2451 (2016)
18. Kipf, T.N., Welling, M.: Semi-supervised classification with graph convolutional networks. In: ICLR (2017)
19. Landrieu, L., Simonovsky, M.: Large-scale point cloud semantic segmentation with superpoint graphs. In: CVPR, pp. 4558–4567 (2018)
20. Lin, T.Y., Goyal, P., Girshick, R., He, K., Dollár, P.: Focal loss for dense object detection. In: ICCV, pp. 2980–2988 (2017)
21. Ma, X., Wu, G., Kim, W.H.: Enriching statistical inferences on brain connectivity for Alzheimer's disease analysis via latent space graph embedding. In: ISBI, pp. 1685–1689. IEEE (2020)
22. Mallat, S.: A Wavelet Tour of Signal Processing. Academic Press (1999)
23. Marsh, A.A., Finger, E.C., Mitchell, D.G., et al.: Reduced amygdala response to fearful expressions in children and adolescents with callous-unemotional traits and disruptive behavior disorders. Am. J. Psychiatry **165**(6), 712–20 (2008). https://doi.org/10.1176/appi.ajp.2007.07071145
24. Moradi, E., Pepe, A., Gaser, C., Huttunen, H., Tohka, J., Initiative, A.D.N.: Machine learning framework for early MRI-based Alzheimer's conversion prediction in MCI subjects. Neuroimage **104**, 398–412 (2015). https://doi.org/10.1016/j.neuroimage.2014.10.002
25. Murias, M., Swanson, J.M., Srinivasan, R.: Functional connectivity of frontal cortex in healthy and ADHD children reflected in EEG coherence. Cereb. Cortex **17**(8), 1788–1799 (2006)
26. Narayanan, A., Chandramohan, M., Venkatesan, R., et al.: graph2vec: learning distributed representations of graphs. arXiv preprint arXiv:1707.05005 (2017)
27. Ng, B., Varoquaux, G., Poline, J.B., Thirion, B., Greicius, M.D., Poston, K.L.: Distinct alterations in Parkinson's medication-state and disease-state connectivity. NeuroImage Clin. **16**, 575–585 (2017)
28. Riesen, K., Bunke, H.: Graph classification based on vector space embedding. Int. J. Pattern Recognit. Artif. Intell. **23**(06), 1053–1081 (2009). https://doi.org/10.1142/7731

29. Rubia, K., Smith, A.B., Brammer, M.J., Taylor, E.: Temporal lobe dysfunction in medication-Naive boys with attention-deficit/hyperactivity disorder during attention allocation and its relation to response variability. Biol. Psychiat. **62**(9), 999–1006 (2007). https://doi.org/10.1016/j.biopsych.2007.02.024

30. Shervashidze, N., Schweitzer, P., Van Leeuwen, E.J., Mehlhorn, K., Borgwardt, K.M.: Weisfeiler-Lehman graph kernels. JMLR **12**(9), 2539–2561 (2011)

31. Shervashidze, N., Vishwanathan, S., Petri, T., Mehlhorn, K., Borgwardt, K.: Efficient graphlet kernels for large graph comparison. In: AISTATS (2009)

32. Simonovsky, M., Komodakis, N.: Dynamic edge-conditioned filters in convolutional neural networks on graphs. In: CVPR, pp. 3693–3702 (2017)

33. Tzourio-Mazoyer, N., Landeau, B., Papathanassiou, D., et al.: Automated anatomical labeling of activations in SPM using a macroscopic anatomical parcellation of the MNI MRI single-subject brain. Neuroimage **15**(1), 273–289 (2002). https://doi.org/10.1006/nimg.2001.0978

34. Veličković, P., Cucurull, G., Casanova, A., Romero, A., Lio, P., Bengio, Y.: Graph attention networks. arXiv preprint arXiv:1710.10903 (2017)

35. Wang, Y., Sun, Y., Liu, Z., Sarma, S.E., Bronstein, M.M., Solomon, J.M.: Dynamic graph CNN for learning on point clouds. ACM Trans. Graph. **38**, 146 (2019)

36. Xu, N., Wang, P., Chen, L., Tao, J., Zhao, J.: MR-GNN: multi-resolution and dual graph neural network for predicting structured entity interactions. arXiv preprint arXiv:1905.09558 (2019)

37. Zhang, M., Cui, Z., Neumann, M., Chen, Y.: An end-to-end deep learning architecture for graph classification. In: AAAI (2018)

Equivariant Spherical Deconvolution: Learning Sparse Orientation Distribution Functions from Spherical Data

Axel Elaldi$^{(\boxtimes)}$ (ID), Neel Dey (ID), Heejong Kim (ID), and Guido Gerig (ID)

Department of Computer Science and Engineering,
New York University, New York, USA
{axel.elaldi,neel.dey,heejong.kim,gerig}@nyu.edu

Abstract. We present a rotation-equivariant self-supervised learning framework for the sparse deconvolution of non-negative scalar fields on the unit sphere. Spherical signals with multiple peaks naturally arise in Diffusion MRI (dMRI), where each voxel consists of one or more signal sources corresponding to anisotropic tissue structure such as white matter. Due to spatial and spectral partial voluming, clinically-feasible dMRI struggles to resolve crossing-fiber white matter configurations, leading to extensive development in spherical deconvolution methodology to recover underlying fiber directions. However, these methods are typically linear and struggle with small crossing-angles and partial volume fraction estimation. In this work, we improve on current methodologies by nonlinearly estimating fiber structures via self-supervised spherical convolutional networks with guaranteed equivariance to spherical rotation. We perform validation via extensive single and multi-shell synthetic benchmarks demonstrating competitive performance against common baselines. We further show improved downstream performance on fiber tractography measures on the Tractometer benchmark dataset. Finally, we show downstream improvements in terms of tractography and partial volume estimation on a multi-shell dataset of human subjects.

1 Introduction

Diffusion-weighted MRI (dMRI) measures voxel-wise molecular diffusivity and enables the in vivo investigation of tissue microstructure via analysis of white matter fiber configurations and tractography. Localized profiles of water diffusion can be constructed via multiple directional magnetic excitations, with each excitation direction corresponding to an image volume. Due to partial voluming, voxels with two or more crossing fibers require increased directional sampling [20] for reliable resolution of multiple fiber directions. However, higher numbers of directions (also referred to as diffusion gradients) lead to clinically infeasible scanning times. Consequently, a series of reconstruction models [4] characterizing voxel-specific diffusivity and enabling fewer gradients have been proposed.

A. Elaldi and N. Dey—these authors contributed equally.

© Springer Nature Switzerland AG 2021
A. Feragen et al. (Eds.): IPMI 2021, LNCS 12729, pp. 267–278, 2021.
https://doi.org/10.1007/978-3-030-78191-0_21

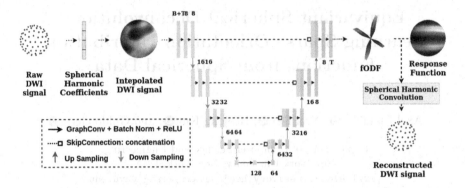

Fig. 1. Framework overview. The raw DWI signal is interpolated onto a spherical Healpix grid [5] and fed into a rotation-equivariant spherical U-Net which predicts sparse fiber orientation distribution functions. The architecture is trained under a regularized reconstruction objective.

In particular, these reconstruction models seek to estimate a *fiber orientation distribution function* (fODF) [18]: a function on the unit sphere $\mathcal{S}^2$ providing fiber orientation/direction and intensity. The fODF can be obtained via spherical deconvolution of the dMRI signal with a tissue *response function* (analogous to a point spread function for planar images). The fODF model represents tissue micro-structure as a sparse non-negative signal, giving higher precision to fiber estimation. The constrained spherical deconvolution (CSD) model [18] has been extended to handle multiple tissue types (e.g., white and grey matter, cerebrospinal fluid) with multiple excitation shells (MSMT-CSD) [6]. Recent works aim to recover a sparser fODF, either via dictionary-learning [1] or by using specialized basis functions [21]. However, these methods may fail to recover difficult micro-structures such as crossing-fibers with small crossing angles.

Emerging literature demonstrates the utility of deep networks towards learning fODFs. Patel et al. use an autoencoder pretrained for fODF reconstruction as a regularizer for the MSMT-CSD optimization problem [14]. Nath et al. train a regression network on ground truth fiber orientations acquired via ex-vivo confocal microscopy images of animal histology sections co-registered with dMRI volumes [13]. Such an approach is typically impracticable due to the need for ex vivo histological training data. More recently, a series of work [7,8,10,16] proposes to train supervised deep regression networks directly on pairs of input dMRI signals and their corresponding MSMT-CSD model fits. We argue that such approaches are inherently limited by the quality of the MSMT-CSD solution and show that the underlying deconvolution itself can be improved via a self-supervised deep learning approach. Moreover, none of these learning approaches (with the exception of [16]) are equivariant to spherical rotation.

In these inverse problems aiming to recover the fODF model, we argue that as the DWI signal lives on the unit sphere, planar convolutional layers may not have the appropriate inductive bias. Standard convolutional layers are constructed for equivariance to planar translation, whereas the analogous operation for spherical signals is rotation. Designing the appropriate form of equivariance for a given network and task is key, as it enables a higher degree of weight sharing, parameter efficiency, and generalization to poses not seen in training data [2]. Fortunately, rotation-equivariant spherical convolutional layers for data on $\mathcal{S}^2$ have been proposed [3,15] with natural applicability to dMRI data[1].

In this work, we tackle sparse self-supervised fODF estimation via rotation-equivariant spherical convolutional networks. This reformulation is trained under a regularized reconstruction objective and allows for the nonlinear estimation of sparse non-negative fiber structures with incorporation of relevant symmetries and leads to improved performance on a variety of fODF estimation settings for both single-shell and multi-shell data. When ground truth is available via benchmark datasets, we obtain more accurate fiber detection and downstream fiber tractography. For real-world application to humans without ground truth, we show downstream improvements in terms of tractography and partial volume estimation on a real-world multi-shell dataset. Our learning framework is flexible and amenable to various regularizers and inductive priors and is applicable to generic spherical deconvolution tasks. Our code is publicly available at https:// github.com/AxelElaldi/equivariant-spherical-deconvolution.

2 Methods

2.1 Background and Preliminaries

dMRI Deconvolution. The dMRI signal is a function $S : \mathcal{S}^2 \to \mathbb{R}^B$, where B is the number of gradients strengths/sampling shells, with the fODF given as $F : \mathcal{S}^2 \to \mathbb{R}$ such that $S = \mathcal{A}(F)$, where $\mathcal{A}$ is the spherical convolution of the fODF with a response function (RF) $R : \mathcal{S}^2 \to \mathbb{R}^B$. The RF can be seen as the dMRI signal containing only one fiber in the **y**-axis direction. The spherical convolution is defined as $S(p) = (R * F)(p) = \int_{\mathcal{S}^2} R(P_p^{-1}q)F(q)dq$, where $p, q \in \mathcal{S}^2$ are spherical coordinates and P_p is the rotation associated to the spherical angles of coordinate p. We note that the fODF is voxel-dependent and shell-independent with antipodal symmetry and that the RF is voxel-independent, shell-dependent, and rotationally symmetric about the **y**-axis. Typically, convolution between two $\mathcal{S}^2$ signals yields a signal on $\mathbf{SO}(3)$ (the group of 3D rotations) as the rotation matrix $P_p \in \mathbf{SO}(3)$ is a 3D rotation [3]. Specific to spherical deconvolution, as the RF is symmetric about the y-axis, all rotations which differ only by rotation around the **y**-axis give the same convolution result. Therefore, P_p can be expressed with two angles and the output of the convolution lives on $\mathcal{S}^2$.

Spherical Harmonics. We utilize the orthonormal Spherical Harmonics (SH) basis $\{Y_l^m\}_{l \in \mathbb{N}, m \in \{-l,...,l\}} : \mathcal{S}^2 \to \mathbb{R}$ to express square-integrable $f : \mathcal{S}^2 \to \mathbb{R}$ as $f(p) = \sum_{l=0}^{\infty} \sum_{m=-l}^{l} f_{l,m} Y_l^m(p)$, where $p \in \mathcal{S}^2$, $\{f_{l,m}\}_{l \in \mathbb{N}, m \in \{-l,...,l\}} \in \mathbb{R}$ are

---

[1] Contemporaneously to our work, [12] presents networks equivariant to spatial roto-translations and voxel-wise rotations with applications to dMRI lesion segmentation.

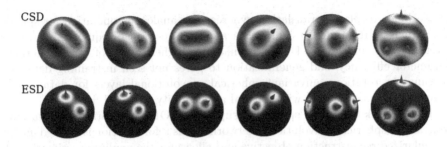

Fig. 2. Qualitative synthetic (Sect. 3.1) results showing fODF estimation on 128-gradient 2 and 3-fiber samples with violet arrows representing ground truth fibers and the heatmap showing model prediction. Row 1: CSD [6], Row 2: ESD (ours).

the spherical harmonic coefficients (SHC) of f. We assume f to be bandwidth limited such that $0 \leq l \leq 2l_{max}$. As even degree SH functions are antipodally symmetric and odd degree SH functions are antipodally anti-symmetric, the odd degree SHC of both RF and fODF are null. Moreover, the m order SH functions are azimuthal symmetric only for $m = 0$. Thus, RF has only 0-order SHC. Therefore, the dMRI signal S^b for the b-th shell is $S^b(p) = \sum_{l=0}^{l_{max}} \sum_{m=-2l}^{2l} \sqrt{\frac{4\pi}{4l+1}} r_{2l}^b f_{2l,m} Y_{2l}^m(p)$ for $l \in \{0, ..., l_{max}\}, m \in \{-2l, ..., 2l\}$ where $p \in \mathcal{S}^2$, $L = (2l_{max} + 1)(l_{max} + 1)$ is the number of coefficients, and $\{r_{2l,0}^b\}$ and $\{f_{2l,m}\}$ are the SHC of the RF and fODF, respectively.

Matrix Formulation. Let the dMRI signal be sampled over B shells for V voxels. For a specific b-shell, a set of n^b gradient directions $\{(\theta_i^b, \phi_i^b)\}_{1 \leq i \leq n^b}$ is chosen, where θ_i^b and ϕ_i^b are angular coordinates of the ith gradient direction. This set gives n^b values $\{S_i^{b,v}\}_{1 \leq i \leq n^b}$ for each voxel v, where $S_i^{b,v} = S^{b,v}(\theta_i^b, \phi_i^b)$. Let $\mathbf{S}^b \in \mathcal{M}_{V,n^b}(\mathbb{R})$ be the sampling of the vth voxel of the b-shell, with the vth row being $\{S_i^{b,v}\}_{1 \leq i \leq n}$. Let $\mathbf{Y}^b \in \mathcal{M}_{L,n}(\mathbb{R})$ be the SH sampled on the ith gradient of the b-shell $\{(\theta_i^b, \phi_i^b)\}$ with its ith column being $\{Y_{2l}^m(\theta_i^b, \phi_i^b)\}_{l,m}$. Let $\mathbf{F} \in \mathcal{M}_{V,L}(\mathbb{R})$ be the matrix of the fODF SH coefficients with the vth row being the coefficients $\{f_{2l,m}^v\}_{l,m}$ of the vth voxel. Finally, let $\mathbf{R}^b \in \mathcal{M}_{L,L}(\mathbb{R})$ be a diagonal matrix, with diagonal elements $\sqrt{\frac{4\pi}{4l+1}} r_{2l}^b$ in blocks of length $4l + 1$ for $l \in \{0, ..., l_{max}\}$. The diffusion signal can now be written as $\mathbf{S}^b = \mathbf{F} \mathbf{R}^b \mathbf{Y}^b$, with $\mathbf{F}\mathbf{R}^b$ giving the SHC of S and $\mathbf{Y}^b$ transforming SHC into spatial data.

Multi-tissue Decomposition. So far, formalism has been presented for voxels with a single tissue type. In reality, brain tissue comprises multiple components, e.g., white matter (WM), grey matter (GM), and cerebrospinal fluid (CSF). To this end, [6] presents a diffusion signal decomposition between WM/GM/CSF such that $S(p) = S_{wm}(p) + S_{gm} + S_{csf}$. GM and CSF are assumed to have isotropic diffusion limiting their spherical harmonic bandwidth to $l_{max} = 0$. Thus, $\mathbf{S}^b = \mathbf{F}_{wm} \mathbf{R}_{wm}^b \mathbf{Y}_{wm}^b + (\mathbf{F}_{gm} \mathbf{R}_{gm}^b + \mathbf{F}_{csf} \mathbf{R}_{csf}^b) \mathbf{Y}_{iso}^b$, where $\mathbf{F}_{gm}, \mathbf{F}_{csd} \in$

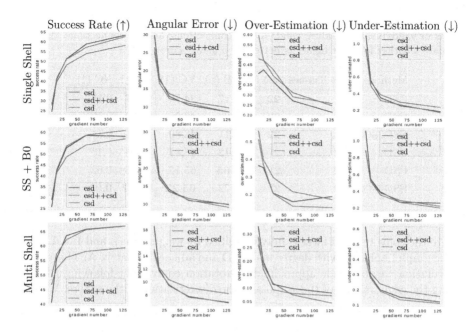

Fig. 3. Synthetic results relative to the number of gradients on 3 dMRI settings in terms of Success Rate, Angular Error, Over-estimation, and Under-estimation. Arrows indicate whether lower or higher is better for a given score.

$\mathcal{M}_{V,1}(\mathbb{R})$, $\mathbf{R}_{gm}, \mathbf{R}_{csd} \in \mathcal{M}_{1,1}(\mathbb{R})$, and $\mathbf{Y}_{iso} \in \mathcal{M}_{1,n}(\mathbb{R})$. Simplifying notation, we finally aim to solve the spherical deconvolution optimization problem to find SH coefficients of the V fODFs. Deconvolution methods typically assume the SH coefficients of the RF $\mathbf{R}$ to be known. Thus, the estimated fODF is:

$$\hat{\mathbf{F}} = \text{argmin}_{\mathbf{F}, \mathbf{FY} \geq 0} ||\mathbf{S} - \mathbf{FRY}||^2 + \lambda Reg(\mathbf{F}) \tag{1}$$

where Reg is a sparsity regularizer on the fODF and $FY \geq 0$ implies a non negativity constraint on the fODF intensities used in [18] with a threshold of 0.

2.2 Equivariant Spherical Deconvolution

Here, we outline how to take a self-supervised deep spherical network towards sparse non-negative fODF estimation, with an overview shown in Fig. 1 and applicability to single-shell single-tissue (SSST), single-shell multi-tissue (SSMT), and multi-shell multi-tissue (MSMT) deconvolution.

Graph Convolution. We utilize the rotation-equivariant graph convolution developed in [15] due to its improved time complexity over harmonic methods such as [3]. The sphere is discretized into a graph $\mathcal{G}$, such that $f : \mathcal{S}^2 \to \mathbb{R}^B$ is sampled on the N vertices of $\mathcal{G}$ such that the signal becomes a matrix $\mathbf{f} \in \mathcal{M}_{N,B}(\mathbb{R})$. A graph convolution can now be written as $h(\mathbf{L})\mathbf{f} = \sum_{i=0}^{P} w_i \mathbf{L}^i \mathbf{f}$,

Table 1. Downstream post-deconvolution tractography results on Tractometer in terms of valid/invalid bundles, valid/invalid connections, and no connections. Arrows indicate whether lower or higher is better for a given score.

Method	# Tissues	VB (↑)	IB (↓)	VC (↑)	IC (↓)	NC (↓)
CSD	1	**22**	117	34.79	65.07	0.15
ESD	1	**22**	123	48.06	51.82	0.12
ESD+CSD	1	**22**	111	48.80	51.06	0.14
CSD	2	21	112	46.81	53.06	0.13
ESD	2	21	**65**	65.12	34.86	0.02
ESD+CSD	2	21	72	**65.22**	**34.77**	**0.01**

where the convolutional filter is fully described by weights $\{w_i\}$, and $\mathbf{L} = \mathbf{D} - \mathbf{A}$ is the graph Laplacian with degree matrix $\mathbf{D}$ and adjacency matrix $\mathbf{A}$. This graph convolution can be made approximately rotation equivariant following [15] by fixing the edge weights of the graph and the discretization of the sphere. We use exponential weighting $d_{i,j} = e^{-\frac{||x_i - x_j||_2^2}{\rho^2}}$ if i and j are neighbors and $d_{i,j} = 0$ otherwise, where i and j are vertex indices of the graph, x_i is the coordinate of the i-th vertex, and ρ is the average distance between two neighbors. We use hierarchical Healpix sampling [5] of the sphere to construct our graph.

Spherical Harmonics Resampling. Real-world DWI acquisition protocols sample diffusion signals over a few dozen to at most a few hundred points with these points not corresponding to Healpix sampling. Therefore, to construct the deconvolution network input, we resample the diffusion signal onto the Healpix grid using spherical harmonics interpolation as illustrated in Fig. 1. We thus obtain $\mathbf{S}_{input} \in \mathcal{M}_{V,B,N}(\mathbb{R})$, where V is the number of voxels in a batch, B is the number of shells and N is the number of vertices. In the case the sampling and the frequency bandwidth of the DWI signal are not consistent, this step introduces a non-rotation equivariant operation. However, the model is still equivariant to the set of rotations that permute the sampling gradients.

Sparsity. Typically CSD methods represent the fODF with spherical harmonics up to degree 8, implying that the fODF representation cannot approximate a Dirac-like function and thus two close fibers cannot be distinguished. We maintain the spherical harmonic basis, but increase their degree to 20 for better representation with the ability to separate small crossing-fibers. To ensure the sparsity of the predicted fODF, we forgo L_1 regularization as in other sparse reconstruction work [9] and assume that the fODF follows a heavy-tailed Cauchy distribution and regularize towards it as $Reg(\mathbf{F}) = \sum_{i=1}^{N} log(1 + \frac{f_i^2}{2\sigma_c^2})$, where N is the number of points we estimate the fODF on, f_i is the fODF value on the ith sphere pixel and σ_c controls the sparsity level of the fODF.

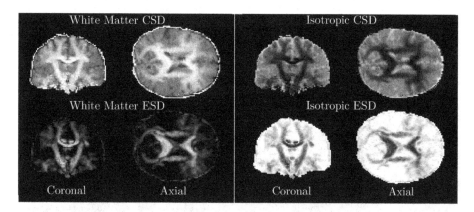

Fig. 4. Tractometer partial volume fractions estimated from CSD (row 1) and ESD (row 2), for the WM compartment (col. 1–2) and the isotropic GM and CSF compartments (col. 3–4). ESD returns more accurate localized tissue maps.

Learning Framework. An overview of the overall network architecture is described in Fig. 1. Response functions for the tissue compartments are precalculated with MRTrix3 [19]. We input the Healpix-resampled signal into a rotation-equivariant graph convolutional network, following a U-net style architecture. We use max pooling and unpooling over the Healpix grid for down and upsampling, with batch normalization and ReLU nonlinearities following every convolution except for the last layer. For the final pre-fODF layer, we use the Softplus activation for MSMT and ReLU for SSST for increased stability.

The fODF outputs are T signals $\mathbf{O} \in \mathcal{M}_{V,T,N}(\mathbb{R})$ each corresponding to a tissue compartment. The SHCs of the WM fODF are the even SHC degrees of the first output signal. For the isotropic GM and CSF, we take the maximum values of the second and third output signal and use them as the GM and CSF fODF SHC. Finally, the predicted fODF is convolved with the RF to reconstruct the signal S, training the network under a regularized reconstruction objective as below. For simplicity, we omit the indices for the multiple tissue compartments.

$$\mathcal{L}(fODF) = ||S - fODF * RF||_2^2 + \lambda \sum_{i=1}^{N} log(1 + \frac{fODF_i^2}{2\sigma_c^2}) + ||fODF_{fODF<0}||_2^2$$

where the first term represents signal reconstruction, the second corresponds to sparsity as described before, and the third term encouraging non-negativity. As we use a ReLU or Softplus nonlinearity on the network output, the initially estimated fODF is entirely non-negative. However, as we use only the even-order SHC of the fODF for convolution with the RF for reconstruction (the fODF is symmetric), eliminating the odd-order SHC may introduce negative values to the fODF which we suppress using an L_2 regularizer on only its negative elements $fODF_{fODF<0}$. We use a batch size of 32 and Adam for minimization with a 10^{-2}

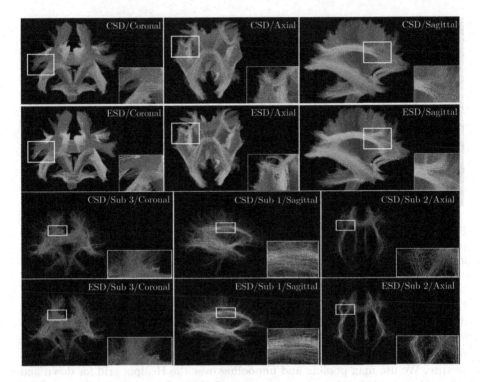

Fig. 5. Post-deconvolution tractography for Tractometer (rows 1–2; single-shell) and a human subject (rows 3–4; multi-shell). For both datasets, ESD (rows 2 and 4) demonstrates clearer streamlines with lower noise as opposed to CSD (rows 1 and 3). Readers are encouraged to zoom-in for visual inspection.

step size, step-decayed on loss plateau. Depending on the dataset, all networks are found to rapidly converge within 20–30 epochs.

3   Experiments

We benchmark our methodologies across diverse datasets and deconvolution settings including: (1) synthetic data generated from a noisy multi-tensor model where we evaluate SSST, SSMT, and MSMT; (2) the Tractometer dMRI benchmark for SSST and SSMT; (3) an *in-vivo* human multi-shell dataset (MSMT). We compare our methods against the widely-used CSD implementation available in MRTrix3 [19]. Ground truth fODFs are not available for Tractometer and the human dataset, thus motivating our use of surrogate evaluations in terms of downstream utility via tractography and partial volume estimation. For completeness, we test whether concatenating CSD deconvolutions to the network input for feature engineering (ESD+CSD) would improve performance.

3.1 Noisy Synthetic Benchmark

Dataset. We use the multi-tissue diffusion model from [6] to generate a multi-shell multi-tissue dataset. Representative response functions are estimated from a human subject (subject 1, center 1 from [17]) using MRTrix. We add Rician noise to the simulated signal corresponding to real MR noise. To assess the robustness of the method against the number of gradients and shells, we generate five single-shell datasets with b-value $3000\,\mathrm{s/mm^2}$ and $\{8, 16, 32, 64, 128\}$ diffusion gradients per method. We also generate five multi-shell datasets ($b = \{1000, 2000, 3000\}\ \mathrm{s/mm^2}$) corresponding to $\{8, 16, 32, 64, 128\}$ diffusion gradients per shell. Finally, we generate a single $b = 0$ signal. We simulate 1e5 samples, split into $\{7e4, 1e4, 2e4\}$ for training, validation and testing.

Evaluation Scores. As ground truth microstructure is known, performance evaluation is performed via five scores: (1) The *success rate* measures the ability to correctly estimate the number and location of white matter fibers via the number of voxels corrected processed. A voxel is successfully processed by the model if each ground truth fiber can be match to a predicted fiber and the number of predicted fibers is the same as ground truth fibers. Following [1], a ground truth fiber is matched to a predicted fiber if it is no further than 25° away; (2) The *angular error* measures angular distance between a ground truth fiber and the closest predicted fiber; (3) The *overestimatation error* estimates the number of predicted fibers outside of the 25-degree cone of the ground truth fibers; (4) The *underestimation error* measures the number of ground-truth fibers without predicted fibers in their 25-degree cone; (5) Finally, we measure the estimated fractional volume of each tissue component (a probability mass function) per voxel in terms of the KL-divergence to the ground truth. For scores 1–4, we use the peak detection algorithm from [1] to predict fiber directions, where the amplitude threshold selection is done on each validation set.

Results. Evaluation scores are presented in Fig. 3. Our models consistently improve success rate, angular error and under-estimation over all gradients, shells, and number of tissue decompositions, save for 8 gradients. These results suggest that sharp fODFs returned by our methods allow for better localization and detection of fibers, decreased undetected fibers, while reducing the number of spurious fibers detected. Figure 2 shows the better capacity of ESD to detect small-angle crossing fibers over CSD. Table 2 demonstrates better partial volume fraction estimation with our models, leading to better tissue component estimation and better localization of white matter fibers.

Table 2. Partial volume fraction estimation in terms of KL divergence to ground truth. **Left:** synthetic performance relative to the number of gradients. **Right:** performance on a multi-shell Human dataset for individual subjects (S1–3).

Method	#Tissues	Number of gradients				
		8	16	32	64	128
CSD	2	0.46	**0.40**	0.39	0.39	0.38
ESD	2	0.39	0.61	0.14	**0.13**	0.15
ESD+CSD	2	**0.31**	0.66	**0.12**	0.15	**0.13**
CSD	3	0.54	0.44	0.38	0.36	0.35
ESD	3	**0.09**	**0.07**	**0.06**	**0.06**	**0.06**
ESD+CSD	3	0.10	**0.07**	**0.06**	**0.06**	0.07

Method	S.1	S.2	S.3
CSD	3.46	3.10	3.42
ESD	1.23	0.98	**0.93**
ESD+CSD	**0.83**	**0.82**	0.99

3.2   The Tractometer Benchmark

Dataset. To assess downstream deconvolution utility, we utilize the ISMRM 2015 Tractometer challenge [11] which provides a realistic single-shell multi-tissue brain phantom with 25 ground truth fiber-bundles, 32 diffusion gradients and one b0 image. We apply basic dMRI motion-correction and use probabilistic tractography algorithm from DiPy on the deconvolved fODF to estimate the fiber tracks. For tractography, we use the brain mask as the seed region, with density 1, we use a maximum angle of 75° and a stopping criterion threshold of 0.25 on the FA map and delete short tracks from the output.

Evaluation Scores. We follow Tractometer evaluation scores using Valid Bundles (**VB**/True Positives), Invalid Bundles (**IB**/False Positives), Valid Connections (**VC**/fraction of predicted streamlines part of a valid bundle), Invalid Connections (**IC**/fraction of predicted streamlines part of an invalid bundle), and No Connections (**NC**/fraction of predicted streamlines not part of any bundle).

Results. Tractometer results are shown in Table 1, where our proposed models increase the fraction of valid connections while decreasing the fraction of invalid and non-connected streamlines. This suggests that our models allow for more accurate downstream fiber tracking. While the proposed model does not impact on the number of valid bundles, it halves the number of invalid bundles in a 2-tissue decomposition setting. We show the partial volume maps on that specific setting on Fig. 4, where ESD shows a clear separation between the two compartments while CSD overestimates the white matter volume fraction in the isotropic part of the phantom. A qualitative view of the tractography in the 2-tissue decomposition setting is presented in Fig. 5. We see that the streamlines are less noisy with ESD than CSD with better trajectory coherence.

3.3   Real-World Multi-shell Human Dataset

Here, we use the preprocessed multishell human dataset from [17]. The dataset has three different subjects and we use scans of all three subjects from the first center. The protocol has three b-values {1000, 2000, 3000} each with 98 gradients and 27 $B0$ images. We use a 3-tissue decomposition for fODF estimation.

Evaluation Scores. Assessing deconvolution performance on a real brain is non-trivial due to the lack of micro-structural ground-truth. Therefore, we follow a downstream utility based evaluation similar to Sect. 3.2. We estimate the ground-truth partial volume from the T1 images of each subject using FSL FAST [22]. We also analyze qualitative tractograms, computed with the same probabilistic tractography algorithm as the tractometer dataset.

Results. Quantitative results are shown in Table 2. The KL-divergence is consistently improved for the three subjects, suggesting a better estimation of the overall partial volume fractions. Moreover, we show qualitative tractography views of the three subjects in the Fig. 5. Again, with ESD, we observe less noise and more streamline consistency.

4   Discussion

We present a self-supervised rotation-equivariant spherical CNN for the nonlinear estimation of the fiber orientation distribution function from diffusion MRI signals. The framework is applicable with or without multi-shell data and with an arbitrary number of DWI gradients. Our experiments demonstrate improved micro and macro-structure estimation over state-of-the-art deconvolution frameworks in terms of the detection of smaller crossing-angle fibers, better fiber localization, and better partial-volume estimation. Finally, improved local performances have a positive impact on global white matter fiber tracking in terms of noise and streamline coherence. Our model generically applies to a wide variety of settings, including natural image spherical deconvolution.

Acknowledgements. Supported by NIH 1R01DA038215-01A1, R01-HD055741-12, 1R01HD088125-01A1, 1R01MH118362-01, R01ES032294, R01MH122447, and 1R34DA050287.

References

1. Canales-Rodríguez, E.J., Legarreta, J.H., Pizzolato, M., Rensonnet, G., Girard, G., et al.: Sparse wars: a survey and comparative study of spherical deconvolution algorithms for diffusion MRI. NeuroImage **184**, 140–160 (2019)
2. Cohen, T., Welling, M.: Group equivariant convolutional networks. In: International Conference on Machine Learning, pp. 2990–2999 (2016)
3. Cohen, T.S., Geiger, M., Köhler, J., Welling, M.: Spherical CNNs. In: International Conference on Learning Representations (2018)
4. Daducci, A., Canales-Rodriguez, E.J., Descoteaux, M., Garyfallidis, E., Gur, Y., et al.: Quantitative comparison of reconstruction methods for intra-voxel fiber recovery from diffusion MRI. IEEE Trans. Med. Imaging **33**(2), 384–399 (2013)
5. Gorski, K.M., Wandelt, B.D., Hansen, F.K., Hivon, E., Banday, A.J.: The HEALPix primer. arXiv preprint arXiv:astro-ph/9905275 (1999)

6. Jeurissen, B., Tournier, J.D., Dhollander, T., Connelly, A., Sijbers, J.: Multi-tissue constrained spherical deconvolution for improved analysis of multi-shell diffusion MRI data. NeuroImage **103**, 411–426 (2014)

7. Karimi, D., Vasung, L., Jaimes, C., Machado-Rivas, F., Khan, S., et al.: A machine learning-based method for estimating the number and orientations of major fascicles in diffusion-weighted magnetic resonance imaging (2020)

8. Lin, Z., et al.: Fast learning of fiber orientation distribution function for MR tractography using convolutional neural network. Med. Phys. **46**(7), 3101–3116 (2019)

9. Liu, C., Wang, D., Wang, T., Feng, F., Wang, Y.: Multichannel sparse deconvolution of seismic data with shearlet-Cauchy constrained inversion. J. Geophys. Eng. **14**(5), 1275–1282 (2017)

10. Lucena, O., Vos, S.B., Vakharia, V., Duncan, J., Ashkan, K., et al.: Using convolution neural networks to learn enhanced fiber orientation distribution models from commercially available diffusion magnetic resonance imaging (2020)

11. Maier-Hein, K.H., Neher, P.F., Houde, J.C., Côté, M.A., Garyfallidis, E., et al.: The challenge of mapping the human connectome based on diffusion tractography. Nat. Commun. **8**(1), 1–13 (2017)

12. Müller, P., Golkov, V., Tomassini, V., Cremers, D.: Rotation-equivariant deep learning for diffusion MRI. arXiv preprint arXiv:2102.06942 (2021)

13. Nath, V., Schilling, K.G., Parvathaneni, P., Hansen, C.B., Hainline, A.E., et al.: Deep learning reveals untapped information for local white-matter fiber reconstruction in diffusion-weighted MRI. Magn. Reson. Imaging **62**, 220–227 (2019)

14. Patel, K., Groeschel, S., Schultz, T.: Better fiber ODFs from suboptimal data with autoencoder based regularization. In: Frangi, A.F., Schnabel, J.A., Davatzikos, C., Alberola-López, C., Fichtinger, G. (eds.) MICCAI 2018. LNCS, vol. 11072, pp. 55–62. Springer, Cham (2018). https://doi.org/10.1007/978-3-030-00931-1_7

15. Perraudin, N., Defferrard, M., Kacprzak, T., Sgier, R.: DeepSphere: efficient spherical convolutional neural network with HEALPix sampling for cosmological applications. Astron. Comput. **27**, 130–146 (2019)

16. Sedlar, S., Papadopoulo, T., Deriche, R., Deslauriers-Gauthier, S.: Diffusion MRI fiber orientation distribution function estimation using voxel-wise spherical U-net. In: Computational Diffusion MRI, MICCAI Workshop (2020)

17. Tong, Q., He, H., Gong, T., Li, C., et al.: Multicenter dataset of multi-shell diffusion MRI in healthy traveling adults with identical settings. Sci. Data **7**, 157 (2020)

18. Tournier, J.D., Calamante, F., Connelly, A.: Robust determination of the fibre orientation distribution in diffusion MRI: non-negativity constrained super-resolved spherical deconvolution. Neuroimage **35**(4), 1459–1472 (2007)

19. Tournier, J.D., Smith, R., Raffelt, D., Tabbara, R., Dhollander, T., et al.: Mrtrix3: a fast, flexible and open software framework for medical image processing and visualisation. NeuroImage **202**, 116137 (2019)

20. Wedeen, V., et al.: Mapping fiber orientation spectra in cerebral white matter with Fourier-transform diffusion MRI. In: Proceedings of the 8th Annual Meeting of ISMRM (2000)

21. Yan, H., Carmichael, O., Paul, D., Peng, J., et al.: Estimating fiber orientation distribution from diffusion MRI with spherical needlets. Med. Image Anal. **46**, 57–72 (2018)

22. Zhang, Y., Brady, M., Smith, S.: Segmentation of brain MR images through a hidden Markov random field model and the expectation-maximization algorithm. IEEE Trans. Med. imaging **20**(1), 45–57 (2001)

Geodesic Tubes for Uncertainty Quantification in Diffusion MRI

Rick Sengers$^{(\boxtimes)}$, Luc Florack, and Andrea Fuster

Eindhoven University of Technology, Eindhoven, The Netherlands
{H.J.C.E.Sengers,L.M.J.Florack,A.Fuster}@tue.nl

Abstract. Based on diffusion tensor imaging (DTI), one can construct a Riemannian manifold in which the dual metric is proportional to the DTI tensor. Geodesic tractography then amounts to solving a coupled system of nonlinear differential equations, either as initial value problem (given seed location and initial direction) or as boundary value problem (given seed and target location). We propose to furnish the tractography framework with an uncertainty quantification paradigm that captures the behaviour of geodesics under small perturbations in (both types of) boundary conditions. For any given geodesic this yields a coupled system of linear differential equations, for which we derive an exact solution. This solution can be used to construct a *geodesic tube*, a volumetric region around the fiducial geodesic that captures the behaviour of perturbed geodesics in the vicinity of the original one.

Keywords: Diffusion tensor imaging · Uncertainty quantification · Geodesic tractography · Geodesic deviation · Riemannian geometry

1 Introduction

Geodesic tractography for diffusion weighted magnetic resonance imaging (DWI) asserts that neuronal tracts are geodesics relative to some data induced metric. In the case of diffusion tensor imaging (DTI) a Riemannian metric presents itself, since its tensorial type matches that of the diffusion tensor. Indeed, from a heuristic point of view a connection between DTI and Riemannian geometry is intuitive if one stipulates the *dual* metric to be proportional to the diffusion tensor [13,15], for in that case short paths are tantamount to high diffusivity pathways, reflecting the preferred orientation of white matter tracts in line with the vestigial idea of classical streamline tractography. Finally, the Hopf-Rinow theorem [12] guarantees the existence of at least one tentative geodesic tract between any given pair of points, which may contribute to efforts of minimising false negatives. Clearly this compels us to furnish the method with an explicit criterion for pruning false positives. We will refer to the comprehensive framework accounting for all these observations as the *Riemann-DTI paradigm*[1].

---

[1] The manifest inclusion of a geodesic pruning criterion actually requires a coupling to Euclidean geometry, so a more accurate designation would be 'Riemann-Euclidean-DTI paradigm'.

© Springer Nature Switzerland AG 2021
A. Feragen et al. (Eds.): IPMI 2021, LNCS 12729, pp. 279–290, 2021.
https://doi.org/10.1007/978-3-030-78191-0_22

The qualitative plausibility of the Riemann-DTI paradigm has been confirmed in numerous experiments on real and synthetic data. However, despite adaptations proposed to overcome shortcomings [4,8,11], state of the art geodesic tractography does not, in general, produce quantitative results. This is not surprising, since complex fiber configurations induce articulated diffusivity profiles that cannot be captured by DTI and, a fortiori, by any Riemann-DTI paradigm, due to insufficient degrees of freedom. But even in the restricted case of 'single fiber coherence', with neatly aligned axons forming smooth bundles, the stipulation of an unambiguous correspondence between DTI data and Riemannian metric consistent with white matter organisation may be too much to hope for. Water diffusion and axon geometry are, albeit correlated, entirely different things.

Nevertheless, by virtue of its non-invasive nature, intuitive appeal and relative simplicity, DTI does have clinical potential. In this article we explore avenues to make the Riemann-DTI paradigm amenable for use in the neurosurgical workflow [16]. One crucial aspect, highlighted in this endeavour, is the quantitative effect of *perturbations* of seed and target regions in tractography. In this article we adopt a generic approach, applicable to any Riemann-DTI paradigm. The precise form of the metric is immaterial for our analysis, although we will illustrate results for a particular instance.

We stress that our goal is not overly ambitious. Inevitable model errors (such as the inadequacy of DTI or of a particular Riemann-DTI paradigm) are not considered. What we aim to accomplish is to avoid conveying a false sense of faith in crisp tractography results towards the clinician, an inherent risk of any deterministic method. We do so by furnishing the Riemann-DTI paradigm with a rigorous uncertainty analysis detailed in the next section. The uncertainty alluded to is of a *fundamental* nature and cannot be removed or diminished without data-extrinsic knowledge.

2   Theory

We address the stability of geodesic tractography in the sense of robustness to generic perturbations of initial or boundary conditions. We focus on how such perturbations affect a tractogram in terms of a conservative estimate of uncertainty that prevails regardless of additional sources of uncertainty along a tractography pipeline, such as DTI data noise. This 'intrinsic' uncertainty enables a fair comparison between different tractography results, since geometrical differences can only be meaningfully quantified if one accounts for the empirical margins of uncertainty.

We depart from a metric tensor field $g_{ij}(x)$ on an n-dimension manifold $\mathcal{M}$ and a pair of unperturbed initial or boundary conditions,

$$(x(0), \dot{x}(0)) \doteq (x_0, v_0), \quad \text{or} \tag{1a}$$

$$(x(0), x(T)) \doteq (x_0, x_T), \tag{1b}$$

for a fiducial geodesic path $x = x(t)$, $t \in [0, T]$, with $\dot{x}(t) \doteq dx(t)/dt$. By virtue of the second order nature of geodesic tractography and the geodesic completeness theorem, recall Sect. 1, there are no a priori constraints on the components of each pair. We then consider two types of perturbations, representing variations of (1a) or (1b):

$$(\overline{x}_0, \overline{v}_0) = (x_0, v_0) + \eta(z_0, w_0) + \mathcal{O}(\eta^2) , \tag{2a}$$

$$(\overline{x}_0, \overline{x}_T) = (x_0, x_T) + \eta(z_0, z_T) + \mathcal{O}(\eta^2) . \tag{2b}$$

The parameter $0 \leq \eta \ll 1$ is dimensionless. Terms of order $\mathcal{O}(\eta^2)$ are considered negligible and will be suppressed henceforth.

The geodesic equation for $x = x(t)$ is given, component-wise relative to some coordinate basis, by

$$\ddot{x}^i + \Gamma^i_{jk}(x)\dot{x}^j \dot{x}^k = 0 , \tag{3}$$

assuming arclength parametrization relative to the metric $g_{ij}(x)$ and employing summation convention [14, 17]. The Christoffel symbols in (3) are given by

$$\Gamma^i_{jk} = \frac{1}{2} g^{i\ell} \left(\partial_j g_{\ell k} + \partial_k g_{j\ell} - \partial_\ell g_{jk} \right) . \tag{4}$$

As usual, g^{ij} indicates the components of the Gram matrix of the dual metric, i.e., $g^{ik} g_{kj} = \delta^i_j$. We furnish (3) with either (1a) or (1b), and consider a perturbed path

$$\overline{x}^i(t; \eta) = x^i(t) + \eta z^i(t) , \tag{5}$$

induced by (2). Each boundary condition, either (1a) or (1b), guarantees the existence of a unique solution to (3) within a sufficiently small tubular neighbourhood of the unperturbed trajectory $x(t)$. The requirement that the perturbed path (5) represents itself a geodesic for any sufficiently small η imposes constraints on the function $z = z(t)$. Technically, it is, unlike the coordinate path $x = x(t)$, vector-valued. From a geometric point of view this is rigorously justified if one regards (5) as the first order expansion of a parametrized geodesic congruence with parameter η (keeping t fixed), induced by the tangent vector

$$z(t) \doteq \left. \frac{\partial}{\partial \eta} \overline{x}^i(t; \eta) \right|_{\eta = 0} . \tag{6}$$

We will refer to $z(t)$ as the *deviation vector*, as it measures the first order difference between the geodesics $x(t)$ and $\overline{x}(t, \eta)$.

Inserting (5) into (3) the function $z = z(t)$ can be seen to satisfy the geodesic deviation equation [14, 17]:

$$\frac{D^2 z^i}{dt^2} + \mathrm{R}^i_{jk\ell} \dot{x}^j z^k \dot{x}^\ell = 0 , \tag{7}$$

in which $\mathrm{R}^i_{jk\ell}$ is the Riemann tensor :

$$\mathrm{R}^i_{jk\ell} = \partial_k \Gamma^i_{j\ell} - \partial_\ell \Gamma^i_{jk} + \Gamma^i_{km} \Gamma^m_{j\ell} - \Gamma^i_{\ell m} \Gamma^m_{jk} . \tag{8}$$

The operator D/dt in (7) represents a *covariant* derivative [14,17] along $x(t)$. For the components v^i of a vector field v it is given in terms of the ordinary t-derivative and Γ-correction terms by $Dv^i/dt = dv^i/dt + \Gamma^i_{jk}v^j\dot{x}^k$.

We may rewrite (7) as a first order system:

$$\begin{cases} \dfrac{Dz^i}{dt} = w^i\,, \\ \dfrac{Dw^i}{dt} = -R^i_{jk\ell}\dot{x}^j z^k \dot{x}^\ell\,. \end{cases} \tag{9}$$

Resolving covariant derivatives in terms of ordinary derivatives and Γ-correction terms leads to

$$\begin{cases} \dfrac{dz^i}{dt} = w^i - \Gamma^i_{jk}z^j\dot{x}^k\,, \\ \dfrac{dw^i}{dt} = -R^i_{jk\ell}\dot{x}^j z^k \dot{x}^\ell - \Gamma^i_{jk}w^j\dot{x}^k\,. \end{cases} \tag{10}$$

This system can in turn be written as a homogeneous vector-valued first order ordinary differential equation of dimension $2n$:

$$\frac{d}{dt}\begin{bmatrix} z \\ w \end{bmatrix} = \begin{bmatrix} A & I_n \\ B & A \end{bmatrix}\begin{bmatrix} z \\ w \end{bmatrix}\,, \tag{11}$$

in which A, B and I_n are $n \times n$-matrices with entries

$$A^i_j \doteq -\Gamma^i_{jk}\dot{x}^k \qquad (I_n)^i_j \doteq \delta^i_j \qquad B^i_j \doteq -R^i_{kj\ell}\dot{x}^k\dot{x}^\ell\,. \tag{12}$$

The solution may be conveniently written in terms of product integrals from multiplicative calculus, cf. Gill and Johansen [9] for a survey, and Florack and Van Assen [7] for the non-commutative case at hand. Abbreviating (11) as

$$\frac{d}{dt}Z = MZ\,, \tag{13}$$

with $Z(t) = (z(t), w(t))$ and initial condition $Z_0 \doteq Z(0)$, the closed-form solution is given by

$$Z(t) = \prod_0^t \exp\left(M(s)ds\right) Z_0\,, \tag{14}$$

in which exp is the matrix exponential function, and

$$\prod_0^t \exp\left(M(s)ds\right) \doteq \lim_{N\to\infty} \exp\left(M(s_N^*)\Delta s_N\right)\dots\exp\left(M(s_1^*)\Delta s_1\right)\,, \tag{15}$$

for any partitioning of the integration interval $[0, t]$, with interval widths $\Delta s_i = s_i - s_{i-1}$ and sample points $s_i^* \in [s_{i-1}, s_i]$, $i = 1, \dots, N$, such that $s_0 = 0$, $s_N = t$. We may write (14) as $Z(t) = \Pi(t)Z_0$, with $2n \times 2n$ block matrix

$$\varPi(t) \doteq \prod_{0}^{t} \exp\left(M(s)ds\right) \doteq \begin{bmatrix} \varPi_{11}(t) & \varPi_{12}(t) \\ \varPi_{21}(t) & \varPi_{22}(t) \end{bmatrix} . \tag{16}$$

Using this notation, the solution $z(t)$ to the system (7) furnished with initial conditions (2a) may be succinctly expressed as

$$z(t) = \varPi_{11}(t)z_0 + \varPi_{12}(t)w_0 . \tag{17}$$

If, instead of (2a), we consider endpoint perturbations of type (2b), then we must treat $w_0 \doteq w(0)$ as an unknown, such that upon setting $t = T$ in (17) we have $z(T) = z_T$. By making this substitution we obtain a relation between the unknown constant w_0 and the pair (z_0, z_T). Solving this relation for w_0 in terms of (z_0, z_T) and substituting it into (17), the solution of the boundary value problem, i.e., (7) and (2b), can be written as

$$z(t) = \left(\varPi_{11}(t) - \varPi_{12}(t)\varPi_{12}(T)^{-1}\varPi_{11}(T)\right) z_0 + \varPi_{12}(t)\varPi_{12}(T)^{-1}z_T . \tag{18}$$

Equations (17) and (18) are the closed-form solutions for our deviation vector $z(t)$ along the fiducial geodesic $x(t)$ in terms of initial, respectively endpoint perturbations, (z_0, w_0) and (z_0, z_T), recall (2). Also recall that, given $x(t)$, these closed-form expressions for $z(t)$ imply a closed-form expression for any perturbed path $\overline{x}(t)$ via (5), valid up to first order in η.

To further investigate the perturbations (2), we note that the deviation vector $z(t)$ in (5) is found to be bilinear in (z_0, w_0), respectively (z_0, z_T), recall (17) and (18). Hence we may generically write

$$z(t) = P(t)z_0 + Q(t)y. \tag{19}$$

for matrices $P(t), Q(t) \in \mathbb{R}^{n \times n}$, with either $y \doteq w_0$ or $y \doteq z_T$.

Instead of regarding the perturbation (z_0, y) as fixed, it is instructive to view it as a realization of some random variable, rendering $z(t)$ stochastic as well. In this way we are able to capture the behaviour of $z(t)$ for different perturbations (z_0, y) all at once. Let f_{z_0}, f_y be the probability density functions of the random variables z_0 and y, assuming a zero mean for both. Assuming z_0 and y to be independent of each other, the probability density $f_{z(t)}$ of $z(t)$ is given by a convolution of the densities of each of the terms in (19):

$$f_{z(t)} = \frac{1}{\det(P(t))}\frac{1}{\det(Q(t))}(f_{z_0} \circ P^{-1}(t)) * (f_y \circ Q^{-1}(t)) . \tag{20}$$

This may be restated in terms of Fourier transforms[2] [10]:

$$f_{z(t)} = \mathcal{F}^{-1}\left(\left(\mathcal{F}(f_{z_0}) \circ P^{\mathrm{T}}(t)\right)\left(\mathcal{F}(f_y) \circ Q^{\mathrm{T}}(t)\right)\right) , \tag{21}$$

---

[2] The Fourier transform of a probability density function, $\mathcal{F}(f)$, is also known as the *characteristic function*. It always exists and, like the density function, it completely characterizes the random variable.

in which the superscript T denotes matrix transposition. Note that (21) is valid even for singular $P(t)$ and/or $Q(t)$, unlike (20). The level sets of $f_{z(t)}$ may be used to visualize the distribution of $z(t)$ for each parameter value t. In general, however, these sets are curved surfaces embedded in $n = 3$ dimensional space and thus likely to overlap and intersect for different values of t, obfuscating the visualization. To avoid this we note that components of the deviation vectors $z(t)$ parallel to $\dot{x}(t)$ are geometrically irrelevant and may be absorbed into a reparameterization of the curve. Therefore we consider the Euclidean projection of $z(t)$ onto the plane orthogonal to the tangent vector $\dot{x}(t)$:

$$z_\perp(t) = \left(I_3 - \frac{\dot{x}(t)\dot{x}^T(t)}{\|\dot{x}(t)\|^2} \right) z(t) . \tag{22}$$

The corresponding probability density $f_{z_\perp(t)}$ is obtained by the formal replacement in (21)

$$P(t) \mapsto P_\perp(t) \doteq \left(I_3 - \frac{\dot{x}(t)\dot{x}^T(t)}{\|\dot{x}(t)\|^2} \right) P(t) , \quad Q(t) \mapsto Q_\perp(t) \doteq \left(I_3 - \frac{\dot{x}(t)\dot{x}^T(t)}{\|\dot{x}(t)\|^2} \right) Q(t) , \tag{23}$$

Instead of representing tractograms as a collection of 'naked' curves, we propose the concept of *geodesic tubes*, constructed by inflating these curves to tubes with local cross sections given by the level sets of $f_{z_\perp(t)}$, see Fig. 1. More precisely, the tube around geodesic curve $x(t)$ is given by

$$\text{Tube}(x, \beta) = \bigcup_{t \in [0,T]} \{ x(t) + \eta z : f_{z_\perp(t)}(z) = \beta \} , \tag{24}$$

for some parameter $\beta > 0$ controlling the extent of the level sets. By constructing geodesic tubes in this way, a non-vanishing geodesic deviation is tantamount to an inflated tube, whose volume reflects the first order geodesic path corrections induced by the stochastic perturbations at hand. Thus a geodesic tube provides an estimation of the uncertainty for any computed geodesic.

Last, we note that the visualization of geodesic tubes may be challenging in case geodesics are not sufficiently far from each other, since their tubes are likely to cause clutter. This difficulty can be overcome by constructing a probability density f from (20) or (21), by summing over x, integrating over t and suitable renormalization, so that

$$f(\xi) \propto \sum_x \int_t f_{z(t)} \left(\frac{\xi - x(t)}{\eta} \right) dt . \tag{25}$$

Recall that $f_{z(t)}$ itself, and not only through its argument, depends on x (not indicated for simplicity of notation). Equation (25) may be seen as a generalization of (20), (21) for multiple geodesics, representing the probability to find a perturbed trajectory induced by *any* of the unperturbed geodesics. The level set $\{ f(\xi) = \beta \}$ represents the uncertainty arising from a collection of geodesics due to perturbations in initial or boundary conditions, and it is the generalization of (24).

3   Experiments

We perform experiments on two clinical DWI datasets, acquired with a Philips Achieva 3T MRI scanner ($b = 1500$, 50 diffusion-weighting directions, six $b = 0$ images, 2 mm isotropic voxel size). Note that throughout our experiments the dimension of space is $n = 3$ and the defining Gram matrix for our Riemann-DTI paradigm is the adjugate of the DTI matrix D, $g_{ij} = \det D\, D_{ij}^{\mathrm{inv}}$, cf. Fuster et al. [8] for a geometric motivation. In the experiments we restrict ourselves to perturbations of type (2b), so that $y \doteq z_T$ in (19). Perturbations of type (2a) will induce tubes with ever growing cross sections, corresponding to the accumulation of errors when solving (7) as an initial value problem; in this case we cannot expect the first order approximation (5) to hold along the entire geodesic. By restricting ourselves to perturbations of type (2b) we ensure that, at least near the two endpoints, the perturbations are sufficiently small.

We assume variables z_0, z_T to follow normal distributions $\mathcal{N}(0, I_3)$, in which case $z_\perp(t)$ is also normally distributed with covariance matrix

$$\Sigma_\perp(t) = P_\perp(t)P_\perp^{\mathrm{T}}(t) + Q_\perp(t)Q_\perp^{\mathrm{T}}(t). \tag{26}$$

From the expression

$$f_{z_\perp(t)}(\xi) = \frac{1}{\sqrt{(2\pi)^2 \det(\Sigma_\perp(t))}} \exp\left(-\frac{1}{2}\xi^{\mathrm{T}}\Sigma_\perp^{-1}(t)\xi\right) \tag{27}$$

it is clear that the level sets are determined by the quadratic form $\xi \mapsto \xi^{\mathrm{T}}\Sigma_\perp^{-1}(t)\xi$ and thus will be elliptical. We set the parameters in (24) to $\eta = 1.0$ and $\beta = 0.1/\sqrt{(2\pi)^2 \det(\Sigma_\perp(t))}$. Parameter β is chosen such that the integral of $f_{z_\perp(t)}$ over the superlevel set $\{\xi : f_{z_\perp(t)}(\xi) \geq \beta\}$ is 0.9, i.e., so that the tube covers 90% of the probability distribution $f_{z_\perp(t)}$.

Figure 1 illustrates the construction of geodesic tubes for two arbitrarily chosen, unperturbed geodesics, in relation to explicitly computed neighbouring geodesics (from explicitly perturbed endpoints). The geodesic tubes enclose most of the perturbed geodesics, except for a few in the bottom right illustration. In both cases, the ellipses representing the level sets become almost degenerate indicating a unidirectional deviation, which is in agreement with the perturbed geodesics. Although we do not satisfy the 'usual' constraint for linear perturbation theory[3], viz. $\eta \ll 1$, we still obtain plausible results. In the bottom right illustration we notice perturbed geodesic curves running (partly) outside the interior of the tube, but upon closer inspection we find that these curves have boundary values z_0, z_T, fairly distant from x_0, x_T. It no surprise then, that the first order approximation underlying the geodesic tube ceases to be valid.

---

[3] The role of η is confounded with the widths of the probability distributions for z_0 and z_T by virtue of (2). If these are sufficiently narrow, then η is a formal parameter that may be set to 1 without loss of generality.

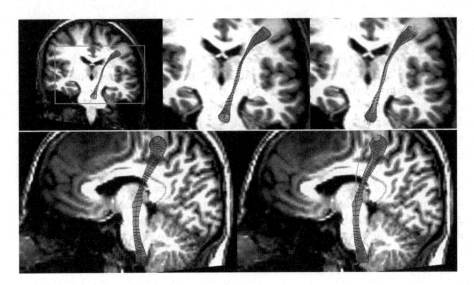

Fig. 1. Left: In red, two arbitrarily chosen geodesics between a seedpoint in the brain stem and a target in the precentral gyrus. In translucent blue, the associated geodesic tubes, cf. Eq. (24). **Right**: In green, 40 perturbed geodesics in the vicinity of the original, unperturbed geodesics. Note that the perturbed boundary values do not need to be confined to the plane perpendicular to $\dot{x}(0)$, respectively $\dot{x}(T)$. (Color figure online)

Figure 2 presents a qualitative comparison of the Cortico Spinal Tract (CST). We generated 5000 geodesics and their associated densities $f_{z(t)}$. Every unperturbed geodesic gives rise to 40 perturbed ones, yielding a total of 2×10^5 geodesics, which are explicitly computed for the sake of this experiment by repeatedly solving (3) with boundary conditions (2b). Our proposed alternative avoids solving—in principle arbitrarily many—nonlinear differential equations for neighbouring geodesics via (3), solving instead a single linear differential equation for a representative geodesic tube, recall (7). Our experiments indicate that the computation of geodesic tubes may indeed be a feasible strategy as long as the perturbations remain sufficiently small. To ensure that we only illustrate geodesics having this property, we compute from the densities in (27) the pointwise expectation value $\mathbb{E}[\|z_\perp(t)\|_2]$, and subsequently the tractwise quantity

$$M = \max_{t \in [0,T]} \mathbb{E}[\|z_\perp(t)\|_2]. \tag{28}$$

Of the 5000 computed tracts, only 2352 (resp. 2170) are used in determining the density f in (25), viz. those for which $M \leq 3\,\mathbb{E}[\|z_\perp(0)\|_2] = 3\sqrt{\pi/2} \approx 3.75$. Although in no way rigourous, this ad-hoc threshold allows us to impose the condition that deviations are sufficiently small, ensuring validity of (5). The images on the left show the 90% level set of the densities f and the ones on the right illustrate the empirical densities of the perturbed geodesics, obtained by counting how many of them pass through each voxel.

Figure 3 presents a comparison between the geodesic tubes and the iFOD2 probabilistic fiber tracking algorithm of MRtrix3 [18]. In both the geodesic and the probabilistic MRtrix3 tracking, we have constrained the tracts of the right Inferior Fronto-Occipital Fasciculus (IFOF) to pass through the capsula externa. This criterion is induced by anatomical prior knowledge and not by the usage of geodesic deviation. Results in Fig. 3 show a good qualitative agreement between probabilistic and geodesic tracking.

4 Discussion

We have addressed the stability of geodesic tractography in the sense of its robustness to perturbations of initial or boundary conditions. By perturbing such conditions for a fiducial geodesic, the first order effect on the considered geodesic is analytically computed for the first time (for a general metric), using the well-known geometric concept of geodesic deviation. Based on this, we have proposed the idea of *geodesic tubes* to visually capture the collective behaviour of perturbed tracts in the vicinity of the original geodesic.

Our experiments indicate that the computation of geodesic tubes (for a relatively sparse set of geodesics with uncertain boundary conditions) may indeed be a feasible strategy, providing both an estimation of the uncertainty for any computed geodesic as well as a dimensionality reduction principle for handling massive bundles of geodesics, as long as perturbations remain sufficiently small. Such reduction is gained by solving a single linear differential equation instead of, in principle, arbitrarily many, non-linear differential equations. This leads to a computational efficiency which favours our analytical approach over practical methods, e.g., brute force Monte Carlo simulations. At the same time the experiments reveal the need for an operational definition of what 'sufficiently small' means in this context. The appropriate length scales must somehow be induced by the local data structure, which we will address in future work.

Our framework can be extended in several ways. Firstly, instead of perturbed boundary conditions we may consider perturbations of the metric tensor field g_{ij} induced by DTI noise. This leads to an inhomogeneous geodesic deviation equation, generalizing (7), in which an additional force term is active along the entire geodesic path. This extension will be studied in future work.

Secondly, we may consider the more general Finsler-DWI paradigm [1–3,5,6], stipulated as a 'canonical' extension of the Riemann-DTI paradigm. Such a Finslerian extension offers the advantages that (i) an analogous geometric description of geodesic tractography and perturbative effects applies, albeit mathematically more cumbersome, and (ii) the descriptive power is greatly enhanced by the removal of the quadratic restriction underlying the Riemann-DTI paradigm (i.e., the limitation to DTI, respectively to inner product induced norms), making it the natural choice for an unconstrained DWI (HARDI) representation. Thus our perturbative analysis is potentially relevant beyond the scope of Riemann-DTI.

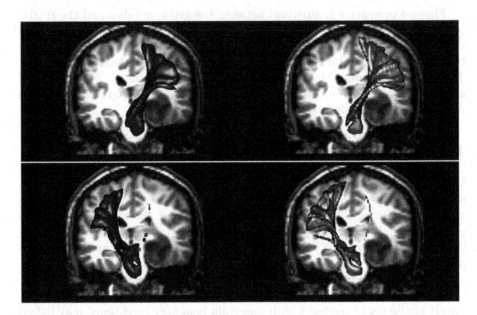

Fig. 2. Anterior view of a coronal cross section of a DWI scan with a tumor on the left side of the brain. **Left:** Density of the geodesic deviation, as per (25). Such accumulated density over all unperturbed geodesics prevents clutter arising from geodesics and corresponding tubes being too close to each other. **Right:** Empirical density of the perturbed geodesics obtained by counting how many of them pass through each voxel. Every one of the 5000 unperturbed geodesics generates 40 perturbed geodesics. In total we have solved nonlinear differential equation (3) 2×10^5 times, in contrast to the construction of the densities in (20) or (21), which requires both (3) and (7) to be solved just 5000 times, illustrating the computational profit gained from the use of geodesic tubes.

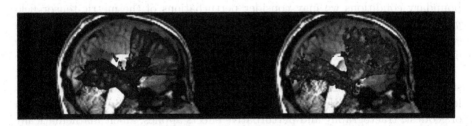

Fig. 3. Sagittal cross section of the same DWI scan as in Fig. 2. **Left:** Density induced by tracts from the right Inferior Fronto-Occipital Fasciculus (IFOF), as per (25). Of the 5000 computed tracts, only 1264 have been used in (25), viz. those which pass through the capsula externa and satisfy $M \leq 3\sqrt{\pi/2}$. **Right:** 2514 tracts generated by MRtrix3 FOD-based probabilistic fiber tracking of the right IFOF, again including only tracts that pass through the capsula externa.

Acknowledgements. This work is part of the research programme "Diffusion MRI Tractography with Uncertainty Propagation for the Neurosurgical Workflow" with project number 16338, which is (partly) financed by the Netherlands Organisation for Scientific Research (NWO). The work of A. Fuster is part of the research program of the Foundation for Fundamental Research on Matter (FOM), which is financially supported by the Netherlands Organisation for Scientific Research (NWO). We would like to thank neurosurgeon Geert-Jan Rutten for sharing the two clinical datasets used in our experiments at the Elisabeth TweeSteden Hospital (ETZ) in Tilburg, The Netherlands, and for fruitful discussions.

References

1. Astola, L.J., Florack, L.M.J.: Finsler geometry on higher order tensor fields and applications to high angular resolution diffusion imaging. Int. J. Comput. Vision **92**(3), 325–336 (2011). https://doi.org/10.1007/s11263-010-0377-z
2. Dela Haije, T., et al.: Structural connectivity analysis using Finsler geometry. SIAM J. Imag. Sci. **12**(1), 551–575 (2019). https://doi.org/10.1137/18M1209428
3. Dela Haije, T.C.J.: Geometry in Diffusion Weighted MRI. Ph.D. thesis, Eindhoven University of Technology, Eindhoven, The Netherlands (16 May 2017)
4. Dong, X., Zhang, Z., Srivastava, A.: Bayesian tractography using geometric shape priors. Front. Neurosci. **11** (2017). https://doi.org/10.3389/fnins.2017.00483
5. Hotz, I., Schultz, T. (eds.): Visualization and Processing of Higher Order Descriptors for Multi-Valued Data. MV. Springer, Cham (2015). https://doi.org/10.1007/978-3-319-15090-1
6. Westin, C.-F., Vilanova, A., Burgeth, B. (eds.): Visualization and Processing of Tensors and Higher Order Descriptors for Multi-Valued Data. MV. Springer, Heidelberg (2014). https://doi.org/10.1007/978-3-642-54301-2
7. Florack, L., van Assen, H.: Multiplicative calculus in biomedical image analysis. J. Math. Imaging Vis. **42**(1), 64–75 (2012)
8. Fuster, A., Dela Haije, T., Tristán-Vega, A., Plantinga, B., Westin, C.-F., Florack, L.: Adjugate diffusion tensors for geodesic tractography in white matter. J. Math. Imaging Vis. **54**(1), 1–14 (2015). https://doi.org/10.1007/s10851-015-0586-8
9. Gill, R.D., Johansen, S.: A survey of product-integration with a view toward application in survival analysis. Ann. Stat. **18**, 1501–1555 (1990)
10. Grimmett, G.R., Stirzaker, D.R.: Probability and Random Processes, 4th edn. Oxford University Press (2020)
11. Hao, X., Zygmunt, K., Whitaker, R.T., Fletcher, P.T.: Improved segmentation of white matter tracts with adaptive Riemannian metrics. Med. Image Anal. **18**, 161–175 (2014). https://doi.org/10.1016/j.media.2013.10.007
12. Hopf, H., Rinow, W.: Ueber den Begriff der vollständigen differentialgeometrischen Fläche. Commentarii Mathematici Helvetici **3**(1), 209–225 (1931). https://doi.org/10.1112/blms/7.3.261
13. Lenglet, C., Deriche, R., Faugeras, O.: Inferring white matter geometry from diffusion tensor mri: application to connectivity mapping. In: Pajdla, T., Matas, J. (eds.) ECCV 2004. LNCS, vol. 3024, pp. 127–140. Springer, Heidelberg (2004). https://doi.org/10.1007/978-3-540-24673-2_11
14. Lovelock, D., Rund, H. (eds.): Tensors, Differential Forms, and Variational Principles. Dover Publications Inc., Mineola (1988)

15. O'Donnell, L., Haker, S., Westin, C.-F.: New approaches to estimation of white matter connectivity in diffusion tensor MRI: elliptic pdes and geodesics in a tensor-warped space. In: Dohi, T., Kikinis, R. (eds.) MICCAI 2002. LNCS, vol. 2488, pp. 459–466. Springer, Heidelberg (2002). https://doi.org/10.1007/3-540-45786-0_57
16. Rutten, G.J.M., Kristo, G., Pigmans, W., Peluso, J., Verheul, H.B.: Het gebruik van MR-tractografie in de dagelijkse neurochirurgische praktijk. Tijdschrift voor Neurologie Neurochirurgie **115**(4), 204–211 (2014). With English abstract
17. Tu, L.W.: Principal bundles and characteristic classes. Differential Geometry. GTM, vol. 275, pp. 241–291. Springer, Cham (2017). https://doi.org/10.1007/978-3-319-55084-8_6
18. Tournier, J.D., et al.: MRtrix3: a fast, flexible and open software framework for medical image processing and visualisation. Neuroimage **202** (2019). https://doi.org/10.1016/j.neuroimage.2019.116137

Structural Connectome Atlas Construction in the Space of Riemannian Metrics

Kristen M. Campbell[1]($\boxtimes$), Haocheng Dai[1], Zhe Su[2], Martin Bauer[3], P. Thomas Fletcher[4], and Sarang C. Joshi[1,5]

[1] Scientific Computing and Imaging Institute, University of Utah, Salt Lake City, UT, USA
kris@sci.utah.edu
[2] Department of Neurology, University of California Los Angeles, Los Angeles, CA, USA
[3] Department of Mathematics, Florida State University, Tallahassee, FL, USA
[4] Electrical and Computer Engineering, University of Virginia, Charlottesville, VA, USA
[5] Department of Bioengineering, University of Utah, Salt Lake City, UT, USA

Abstract. The structural connectome is often represented by fiber bundles generated from various types of tractography. We propose a method of analyzing connectomes by representing them as a Riemannian metric, thereby viewing them as points in an infinite-dimensional manifold. After equipping this space with a natural metric structure, the Ebin metric, we apply object-oriented statistical analysis to define an atlas as the Fréchet mean of a population of Riemannian metrics. We demonstrate connectome registration and atlas formation using connectomes derived from diffusion tensors estimated from a subset of subjects from the Human Connectome Project.

1 Introduction

In this paper we develop for the first time statistical techniques on the infinite-dimensional space of Riemannian metrics for analyzing the variability of the architecture of the human brain. Diffusion-weighted MRI (DWMRI) allows us to model an individual human brain as a Riemannian manifold with axonal connections that are geodesic curves of an appropriate metric. A Riemannian manifold is a topological manifold with an inner product defined on the tangent space at each point, the Riemannian metric. The Riemannian metric fundamentally

M. Bauer was supported by NSF grants DMS-1912037, DMS-1953244. K. Campbell, H. Dai, S. Joshi and P. Fletcher were supported by NSF grant DMS-1912030. Z. Su was supported by NSF grant DMS-1912037, NIH/NIAAA award R01-AA026834. Data were provided in part by the Human Connectome Project, WU-Minn Consortium (Principal Investigators: David Van Essen and Kamil Ugurbil; 1U54MH091657) funded by the 16 NIH Institutes and Centers that support the NIH Blueprint for Neuroscience Research; and by the McDonnell Center for Systems Neuroscience at Washington University.

© Springer Nature Switzerland AG 2021
A. Feragen et al. (Eds.): IPMI 2021, LNCS 12729, pp. 291–303, 2021.
https://doi.org/10.1007/978-3-030-78191-0_23

defines the "shape" of the manifold and defines the distance measured intrinsically on the manifold via geodesic curves. It is our fundamental assumption that the topology of the normal human brain is consistent across individuals, but the difference in the connectomics is because of the individual variation in the local Riemannian metric.

Several strategies have been used in previous work to construct white matter atlases from a population of diffusion MRI. Mori et al. [21] construct a diffusion tensor imaging (DTI) atlas by registering the diffusion-weighted MRI of multiple subjects to a standardized anatomical template. They build the DTI atlas by transforming the diffusion tensors for each subject [1] and then taking the Euclidean average of the transformed diffusion tensors at each voxel. This approach does not use the white matter directionality information encoded in the diffusion images during the registration. It also suffers from the fact that the Euclidean average of diffusion tensors does not take into account the directionality and tends to be fatter (i.e., less anisotropic) than the input tensors [11]. Another approach by Yeh et al. [25] is to register q-space diffusion images into an anatomical template and estimate the spin distribution function (SDF) at each voxel in the template. Then the SDFs are averaged on a per-voxel basis. While this method does take into account the directionality of the white matter in a local neighborhood, it does not take into account consistency of long-range white matter connections.

In this paper we develop a statistical groupwise atlas estimation algorithm for structural connectomes. The proposed algorithm uses not only local diffusion data but also long-range connectomics of the subjects as inferred by tractography [6]. We do this by estimating a Riemannian metric of the brain manifold whose geodesic curves coincide with the tractography.

2   Structural Connectomes as Riemannian Metrics

In the white matter of the brain, the diffusion of water is restricted perpendicular to the direction of the axons. Diffusion-weighted MRI measures the microscopic diffusion of water in multiple directions at every voxel in a 3D volume. Thus, the directionality of connections in the brain can be locally inferred. Traditionally, global connections of the white matter have been estimated by a procedure called *tractography*, which numerically computes integral curves of the vector field formed by the most likely direction of fiber tracts at each point. DTI models connection directions with a tensor, $D(x)$, at each voxel whose principal eigenvector is aligned with the direction of the strongest diffusion.

Riemannian metrics that represent connectomics of a subject have been developed in diffusion imaging [23] and include the inverse-tensor metric $\tilde{g} = D(x)^{-1}$. However, the geodesics associated with the inverse-tensor metric tend to deviate from the principal eigenvector directions and take straighter paths through areas of high curvature.

In this work we build on the algorithm developed by [16], which estimates a spatially-varying function, $\alpha(x)$, that modulates the inverse-tensor metric to create a locally-adaptive Riemannian metric, $g_\alpha = e^{\alpha(x)}\tilde{g}$. We briefly describe the method here for completeness but refer the reader to [16] for details. This adaptive *connectome metric*, g_α, is conformally equivalent to the inverse-tensor metric and is better at capturing the global connectomics, particularly through regions of high curvature. Figure 1 shows how well the geodesics of each metric match the integral curve of the vector field. The connectome metric geodesics are very closely aligned with the integral curves.

The geodesic between two end-points, p, q, associated with the inverse-tensor metric, $\tilde{g}(x) = D(x)^{-1}$, minimizes the energy functional, $\tilde{E}$. While the geodesic associated with the connectome metric, $g_\alpha(x) = e^{\alpha(x)}D(x)^{-1}$, minimizes the energy functional, E_α:

$$\tilde{E}(\gamma) = \int_0^1 \langle T(t), T(t) \rangle_{\tilde{g}} dt, \qquad E_\alpha(\gamma) = \int_0^1 e^{\alpha(x)} \langle T(t), T(t) \rangle_{\tilde{g}} dt, \qquad (1)$$

where $\gamma : [0, 1] \rightarrow M$, $\gamma(0) = p$, $\gamma(1) = q$, $T = \frac{d\gamma}{dt}$.

Analyzing the variation of E_α leads to the geodesic equation, $\text{grad}\,\alpha = 2\nabla_T T$, where the Riemannian gradient of α, $\text{grad}\,\alpha = \tilde{g}^{-1}\left(\frac{\partial\alpha}{\partial x^1}, \frac{\partial\alpha}{\partial x^2}, \cdots, \frac{\partial\alpha}{\partial x^n}\right)$, and $\nabla_T T$ is the covariant derivative of T along its integral curve.

To enforce the desired condition where the tangent vectors, T, of the geodesic match the vector field, V, of the unit principal eigenvectors of $D(x)$, we minimize the functional, $F(\alpha) = \int_M \|\text{grad}\,\alpha - 2\nabla_V V\|^2 dx$. The equation for α that minimizes $F(\alpha)$ is

$$\Delta\alpha = 2\,\text{div}(\nabla_V V), \qquad (2)$$

where div and Δ are the Riemannian divergence and Laplace-Beltrami operator. We discretize the Poisson equation in Eq. (2) using a second-order finite difference scheme that satisfies both the Neumann boundary conditions $\frac{\partial\alpha}{\partial\vec{n}} = \langle\text{grad}\,\alpha, \vec{n}\rangle = \langle 2\nabla_V V, \vec{n}\rangle$ and the governing equation on the boundary. We then solve for α.

Note that we can use this method to match the geodesics of the connectome metric to other vector fields defining the tractogram, e.g., from higher-order diffusion models that can represent multiple fiber crossings in a voxel. In particular, for tractography based on fiber orientation distributions (FODs), we can use the techniques presented in [22] to generate the vector field V.

3   The Geometry of the Manifold of All Metrics

Once we have estimated a Riemannian metric for a human connectome, it is a point in the infinite-dimensional manifold, Met(M), where M is the domain of the image. We will equip the infinite-dimensional space of all Riemannian metrics with a diffeomorphism-invariant Riemannian metric, called the Ebin or DeWitt metric [9,10]. We base the statistical framework on this infinite-dimensional geometric structure. The invariance of the infinite-dimensional metric under the group of diffeomorphisms Diff(M) is a crucial property, as it guarantees the

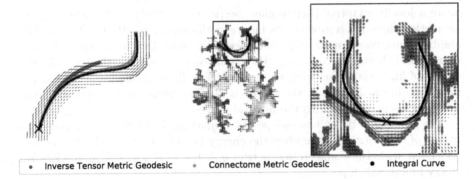

• Inverse Tensor Metric Geodesic   • Connectome Metric Geodesic   • Integral Curve

Fig. 1. A geodesic of the inverse-tensor metric (blue) and adaptive metric (orange), along with an integral curve (black) associated with the principal eigenvectors for a synthetic tensor field (left) and a subject's connectome metric from the Human Connectome Project (center). Right shows a detailed view of the metric in the corpus callosum. (Color figure online)

independence of an initial choice of coordinate system on the brain manifold. In the following we will describe the details of our mathematical framework.

Let M be a smooth n-dimensional manifold; for our targeted applications n will be two or three. We denote by $\mathrm{Met}(M)$ the space of all smooth Riemannian metrics on M, i.e., each element g of the space $\mathrm{Met}(M)$ is a symmetric, positive-definite $\binom{0}{2}$ tensor field on M. It is convenient to think of the elements of M as being point-wise positive-definite sections of the bundle of symmetric two-tensors $S^2 T^* M$, i.e., smooth maps from M with values in $S^2_+ T^* M$. Thus, the space $\mathrm{Met}(M)$ is an open subset of the linear space $\Gamma(S^2 T^* M)$ of all smooth symmetric $\binom{0}{2}$ tensor fields and hence itself a smooth Fréchet-manifold [10]. Furthermore, let $\mathrm{Diff}(M)$ denote the infinite-dimensional Lie group of all smooth diffeomorphisms of the manifold M. Elements of $\mathrm{Diff}(M)$ act as coordinate changes on the manifold M. This group acts on the space of metrics via pullback

$$\mathrm{Met}(M) \times \mathrm{Diff}(M) \to \mathrm{Met}(M), \qquad (g, \varphi) \mapsto \varphi^* g = g(T\varphi \cdot, T\varphi \cdot). \qquad (3)$$

It is important to note that the geometries of the metrics g and $\varphi^* g$ are also related via φ. In particular, geodesics with respect to g are mapped via φ to geodesics with respect to $\varphi^* g$.

On the infinite-dimensional manifold $\mathrm{Met}(M)$, there exists a natural Riemannian metric: the reparameterization-invariant L^2-metric. To define the metric, we need to first characterize the tangent space of the manifold of all metrics: $\mathrm{Met}(M)$ is an open subset of $\Gamma(S^2 T^* M)$. Thus, every tangent vector h is a smooth bilinear form $h : TM \times_M TM \to \mathbb{R}$ that can be equivalently interpreted as a map $TM \to T^* M$. The L^2-metric is given by

$$G_g^E(h, k) = \int_M \mathrm{Tr}\left(g^{-1} h g^{-1} k\right) \mathrm{vol}(g), \qquad (4)$$

with $g \in \mathrm{Met}(M)$, $h, k \in T_g \mathrm{Met}(M)$ and $\mathrm{vol}(g)$ the induced volume density of the metric g. This metric, introduced in [10], is also known as the Ebin metric. We call the metric *natural* as it requires no additional background structure and is consequently invariant under the action of the diffeomorphism group, i.e.,

$$G_g(h, k) = G_{\varphi^* g}(\varphi^* h, \varphi^* k) \tag{5}$$

for all $\varphi \in \mathrm{Diff}(M)$, $g \in \mathrm{Met}(M)$ and $h, k \in T_g \mathrm{Met}(M)$. Note that the invariance of the metric follows directly from the substitution formula for multi-dimensional integrals.

The Ebin metric induces a particularly simple geometry on the space $\mathrm{Met}(M)$, with explicit formulas for geodesics, geodesic distance and curvature. In the following we will present the most important of these formulas, which will be of importance for our proposed metric matching framework.

First we note that a metric $g \in \mathrm{Met}(M)$, in local coordinates, can be represented as a field of symmetric, positive-definite $n \times n$ matrices that vary smoothly over M. Similarly, each tangent vector at g can be represented as a field of symmetric $n \times n$ matrices. By the results of [8,12,13], one can reduce the investigations of the space of all Riemannian metrics to the study of the geometry of the finite-dimensional space of symmetric, positive-definite $n \times n$ matrices: the point wise nature of the Ebin metric allows one to solve the geodesic initial and boundary value problem on $\mathrm{Met}(M)$ for each $x \in M$ separately and thus the formulas for geodesics, geodesic distance and curvature on the finite-dimensional matrix space can be translated directly to results for the Ebin metric on the infinite-dimensional space of Riemannian metrics.

Note that the space of Riemannian metrics, $\mathrm{Met}(M)$ with the Ebin metric, is not metrically complete and not geodesically convex. Thus the minimal geodesic between two Riemannian metrics may not exist in $\mathrm{Met}(M)$, but only in a larger space; the metric completion $\overline{\mathrm{Met}}(M)$, which consists of all possibly degenerate Riemannian metrics. This construction has been worked out in detail by Clarke [7] – including the existence of minimizing paths in $\overline{\mathrm{Met}}(M)$. In the following we will omit these details and refer the interested reader to the article [7] for a more in-depth discussion. In the following theorem, we present an explicit formula for the minimizing geodesic in $\overline{\mathrm{Met}}(M)$ that connects two given Riemannian metrics.

Theorem 1. *For $g_0, g_1 \in \mathrm{Met}(M)$ we define*

$$k(x) = \log\left(g_0^{-1}(x)g_1(x)\right), \quad k_0(x) = k(x) - \frac{\mathrm{Tr}(k(x))}{n}\,\mathrm{Id} \tag{6}$$

$$a(x) = \sqrt[4]{\det(g_0(x))}, \quad b(x) = \sqrt[4]{\det(g_1(x))}, \quad \kappa(x) = \frac{\sqrt{n}\,\mathrm{Tr}(k_0(x)^2)}{4} \tag{7}$$

$$q(t, x) = 1 + t\left(\frac{b(x)\cos(\kappa(x)) - a(x)}{a(x)}\right), \quad r(t, x) = \frac{t b(x)\sin(\kappa(x))}{a(x)}, \tag{8}$$

Then the minimal path $g(t, x)$ with respect to the Ebin metric in $\overline{\mathrm{Met}}(M)$ that connects g_0 to g_1 is given by

$$g = \begin{cases} \left(q^2 + r^2\right)^{\frac{2}{n}} g_0 \exp\left(\frac{\arctan(r/q)}{\kappa} k_0\right) & 0 < \kappa < \pi, \\ q^{\frac{4}{n}} g_0 & \kappa = 0, \\ \left(1 - \frac{a+b}{a} t\right)^{\frac{4}{n}} g_0 \mathbb{1}_{[0, \frac{a}{a+b}]} + \left(\frac{a+b}{b} t - \frac{a}{b}\right)^{\frac{4}{n}} g_1 \mathbb{1}_{[\frac{a}{a+b}, 1]} & \kappa \geq \pi, \end{cases} \tag{9}$$

where $\mathbb{1}$ denotes the indicator function in the variable t. We suppressed the functions' dependence on t and x for better readability.

Proof. This theorem is essentially a reformulation of the minimal geodesic formula given in [8, Theorem 4.16]. We obtain it by combining formulas for the exponential mapping, inverse exponential mapping, and minimal geodesic in [8, Theorem 4.4, 4.5, 4.16]. As these calculations are rather tedious we refrain from presenting them.

We now recall that the geodesic distance of a Riemannian metric is defined as the infimum of all paths connecting two given points,

$$\mathrm{dist}_{\mathrm{Met}}(g_0, g_1) = \inf \int_0^1 \sqrt{G_g(\partial_t g, \partial_t g)} \, dt, \tag{10}$$

where the infimum is taken over all paths $g : [0, 1] \to \mathrm{Met}(M)$ with $g(0) = g_0$ and $g(1) = g_1$. As a direct consequence of Theorem 1 we obtain an explicit formula for this distance function:

Corollary 1. *Let $g_0, g_1 \in \mathrm{Met}(M)$ and let k, k_0, a, b and κ be as in Theorem 1. Let $\theta(x) = \min\{\pi, \kappa(x)\}$. Then the squared geodesic distance of the Ebin metric is given by:*

$$\mathrm{dist}_{\mathrm{Met}}(g_0, g_1)^2 = \frac{16}{n} \int_M \left(a(x)^2 - 2a(x)b(x)\cos(\theta(x)) + b(x)^2\right) dx. \tag{11}$$

Having equipped the space of Riemannian metric with the distance function (11), we can consider the Fréchet mean $\hat{g}$ of a collection of metrics $g_1, \ldots g_N$, which is defined as a minimizer of the sum of squared distances:

$$\hat{g} = \operatorname*{argmin}_g \sum_{i=1}^N \mathrm{dist}^2_{\mathrm{Met}}(g, g_i). \tag{12}$$

One could directly minimize this functional using a gradient-based optimization procedure. As our distance function is the geodesic distance function of a Riemannian metric and since we have access to an explicit formula for the minimizing geodesics, we will instead use the iterative geodesic marching algorithm, see e.g., [17], to approximate the Fréchet mean. Given N Riemannian metrics g_i, we approximate the Fréchet mean via $\hat{g} = \hat{g}_N$, where $\hat{g}_i$ is recursively defined as $\hat{g}_0 = g_0$, $\hat{g}_i(x) = g(1/(i+1), x)$ and where $g(t, x)$ is the minimal path, as given in Theorem 1, connecting $\hat{g}_{i-1}$ to the i-th data point g_i. Thus one only has to calculate N geodesics *in total* in the space of Riemannian metrics, whereas a gradient-based algorithm would require one to calculate N geodesic distances *in each step* of the gradient descent.

3.1   The Induced Distance Function on the Diffeomorphism Group

We can use the geodesic distance function of the Ebin metric to induce a right-invariant distance function on the group of diffeomorphisms. As we will be using this distance function as a regularization term in our matching functional, we will briefly describe this construction here. We fix a Riemannian metric $g \in \mathrm{Met}(M)$ and define the "distance" of a diffeomorphism φ to the identity via

$$\mathrm{dist}^2_{\mathrm{Diff}}(\mathrm{id}, \varphi) = \mathrm{dist}^2_{\mathrm{Met}}(g, \varphi^* g). \tag{13}$$

To be more precise, this distance can be degenerate on the full diffeomorphism group since the isometries of the Riemannian metric g form the kernel of $\mathrm{dist}_{\mathrm{Diff}}$. For our purposes we will consider the Euclidean metric for the definition of $\mathrm{dist}_{\mathrm{Diff}}$. Thus the only elements in the kernel are translations and rotations. The right invariance of $\mathrm{dist}_{\mathrm{Diff}}$ follows directly from the $\mathrm{Diff}(M)$-invariance of the Ebin metric. We note, however, that $\mathrm{dist}_{\mathrm{Diff}}$ is not directly associated with a Riemanian structure on the diffeomorphism group: the orbits of the diffeomorphism group in the space of metrics are not totally geodesic and thus $\mathrm{dist}_{\mathrm{Diff}}$ is not the geodesic distance of the pullback of the Ebin metric to the space of diffeomorphisms. See also [20] where this construction has been studied in more detail.

4   Computational Anatomy of the Human Connectome

Fundamental to the precise characterization and comparison of the human connectome of an individual subject or a population as a whole is the ability to map or register two different human connectomes. The framework of Large Deformation Diffeomorphic Metric Mapping (LDDMM) is well developed for registering points [19] curves [15] and surfaces [24] all modeled as sub-manifolds of $\mathbb{R}^3$ as well as images modeled as an L^2 function [5]. This framework has also been extended to densities [4] modeled as volume forms. We now extend the diffeomorphic mapping framework to the connectome modeled as Riemannian metrics. The diffeomorphisms group acts naturally on the space of metrics, see Eq. (3). With this action and a reparameterization-invariant metric, the problem of registering two connectomes fits naturally into the framework of computational anatomy. We register two connectomes by solving the following minimization problem:

$$E(\varphi) = \inf_{\varphi \in \mathrm{Diff}(M)} \mathrm{dist}^2_{\mathrm{Diff}}(\mathrm{id}, \varphi) + \lambda \, \mathrm{dist}^2_{\mathrm{Met}}(g_0, \varphi^* g_1) \tag{14}$$

where $\mathrm{dist}_{\mathrm{Diff}}$ is a right invariant distance on Diff and $\mathrm{dist}_{\mathrm{Met}}$ is a reparameterization-invariant distance on the space of all Riemannian metrics, e.g., the geodesic distance of the metrics studied above. The first term measures the deformation cost and the second term is a similarity measure between the target and the deformed source connectome. The invariance of the two distances is essential for the minimization problem to be independent of the choice of coordinate system on the brain manifold.

We use the distance function as introduced in Sect. 3.1 to measure the deformation cost, i.e., $\text{dist}_{\text{Diff}}(\text{id}, \varphi) = \text{dist}_{\text{Met}}(g, \varphi^* g)$ where g is the restriction of the euclidean metric to the brain domain. This choice greatly increases computational efficiency since we can now use the formulas from Sect. 3 as explicit formulas for both terms of the energy functional. To minimize the energy functional, we use a gradient flow approach described in Algorithm 1, where the gradient on $\text{Diff}(M)$ is calculated with respect to a right invariant Sobolev metric of order one, called the information metric [4]. We choose this specific gradient because of the relation of the information metric to both the Ebin metric on the space of metrics and the Fisher-Rao metric on the space of probability densities. See [4, 20] for a precise description of the underlying geometric picture.

Note, that our framework allows for the immediate inclusion of points, curves, surfaces and images in the registration problem, which we plan to incorporate in future work. Image intensity information, for example, can be easily incorporated in the registration problem by simply adding an appropriate similarity measure for the image term (e.g., the standard L^2 metric between the deformed source image and the target image) to the energy functional.

Algorithm 1. Inexact Metric Matching Algorithm

Inputs:
    source and target metric g_0, g_1
Initialize:
    learning rate ϵ; weight parameter λ; max iteration times MaxIter
$\varphi, E \leftarrow \text{id}, 0$
for iteration $= 0 : \text{MaxIter}$ **do**
    $\varphi^* g_1 \leftarrow (d\varphi)^T (g_1 \circ \varphi)(d\varphi)$ $\triangleright$ Pullback of φ
    $E \leftarrow \text{EbinEnergy}(\varphi^* g_1, g_0, \lambda)$ $\triangleright$ Calculate energy by Eq. (14)
    $v \leftarrow -\Delta^{-1}(E.\,\text{grad})$ $\triangleright$ Transfer gradient w.r.t. information metric to L^2
    $\psi \leftarrow \text{id} + \epsilon v$ $\triangleright$ Construct the approximation
    $\varphi \leftarrow \psi \circ \varphi$ $\triangleright$ Update the diffeomorphism
end for
return φ

4.1 Estimating the Atlas for a Population of Connectomes

Given a collection of connectomes modeled as points on an abstract Riemannian manifold, we can directly apply least squared estimation to define the average connectome. Thus the template estimation problem can be formulated as a joint minimization problem:

$$\hat{g} = \underset{g, \varphi_i}{\text{argmin}} \sum_{i=1}^{N} \text{dist}_{\text{Diff}}^2(\text{id}, \varphi_i) + \lambda \, \text{dist}_{\text{Met}}^2(g, \varphi_i^* g_i) \tag{15}$$

We use the iterative alternating algorithm proposed in [18] for solving the above optimization problem: we alternate gradient steps between optimizing with respect to each diffeomorphism, $\varphi_i^{-1}, i = 1, \cdots, N$, and minimizing with respect to the metric average $\hat{g}$. In the metric optimization step we use the Fréchet mean algorithm described in Sect. 3. See Algorithm 2 for details of this process.

Algorithm 2. Atlas Building Algorithm

Inputs:
    sample metric fields list G
Initialize:
    max iteration times MaxIter
for iteration = 0 : MaxIter **do**
    $g_{\text{mean}} \leftarrow \text{FrechetMean}(G)$ ▷ Sect. 3
    for $i = 0 : \text{len}(G)$ **do**
        $\varphi \leftarrow \text{MetricMatching}(g_{\text{mean}}, G[i])$ ▷ Algorithm 1
        $G[i] \leftarrow \varphi^* G[i]$ ▷ Update $G[i]$ by pullback of φ
    end for
end for
return g_{mean}

4.2 Implementation Details

As done in [16], we apply a mask to both the connectome metric estimation process and the atlas building algorithm for two reasons. First, it is important that we constrain the problem to biologically realistic white matter tracts by not allowing tractography to flow through regions of CSF. Second, we avoid numeric issues associated with processing air and other noisy regions outside the skull. This also speeds up computation, as we only need to look at voxels inside the masked region instead of the entire image volume. For the atlas building algorithm, we deform each individual mask into atlas space at each outer iteration, and apply the union of these deformed masks when computing the current atlas estimate. For each iteration of the atlas building algorithm, we perform only 2 iterations inside the metric matching function to avoid overfitting the individual metrics to early estimates of the Fréchet mean. In practice, we find the algorithm behaves well when we update ϵ in Algorithm 1 such that $1/\epsilon$ is approximately equal to the energy (14).

5 Results

Simulated Data: We verified our method by generating vector fields whose central integral curves are a family of parameterized cubic functions. We used the method of parallel curves to add vectors for additional integral curves parallel to the central curve with a distance $k \in [-0.2, 0.2]$ from the central curve. We then constructed tensors whose principal eigenvectors align with the generated vector fields and that have a specified major axis to minor axis ratio of 6:1.

We first estimated the adaptive metric conformal to the inverse-tensor metric such that the geodesics of the adaptive metrics align with the integral curves of the simulated vector fields. After finding the connectome metric for each subject, we ran 400 iterations of the atlas building Algorithm 2 to estimate the atlas in Fig. 2. To help the diffeomorphisms update smoothly, we set $\lambda = 100$ in Eq. (14) and the learning rate $\epsilon = 5$ in Algorithm 1.

We compared a geodesic of the atlas starting from a particular seed point with geodesics of the 4 connectome metrics starting from the atlas seed point mapped into individual space. Figure 2 shows these individual geodesics in atlas space before and after applying the diffeomorphisms. We see that the atlas geodesic is nicely centered in the middle of the undeformed individual geodesics as expected. Also, the deformed individual geodesics align well with the atlas geodesic.

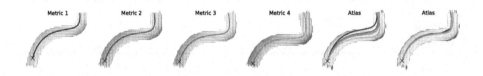

Fig. 2. Left: geodesics of 4 synthetic metrics starting from the atlas seed point (X) mapped into each metric's space. Second from right: estimated atlas with geodesic (orange) starting from the seed point (X) overlaid on non-deformed geodesics from each of the 4 metrics. Right: estimated atlas with geodesic (orange) overlaid on geodesics from the 4 metrics deformed into atlas space. (Color figure online)

Real Data: We used a subset of subjects from the Human Connectome Project Young Adult (HCP) dataset [14]. For each subject, we fit a diffusion tensor model to the images with a b-value of 1000 using `dtifit` from FSL [2] and generated a white-matter mask based on fractional isotropy values. We estimated the adaptive connectome metric from the inverse-tensor metric associated with the diffusion tensors.

To generate the atlas shown in Fig. 3, we ran atlas building for 5000 iterations with $\lambda = 100$, $\epsilon = 1$, which took 50 min on an Intel Xeon Silver 4108 CPU. The regularization term, λ, balances the magnitudes of the diffeomorphisms from each subject's connectome metric to the atlas. To ensure that the final geodesics in the atlas also follow the major eigenvectors of the atlas tensors, we solve for the α conformal factor for the atlas as described in Sect. 2.

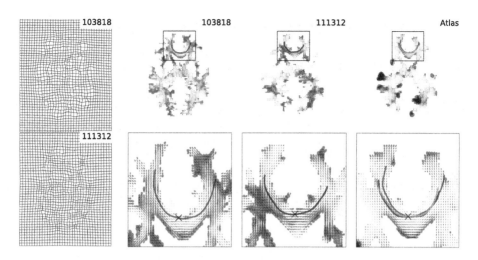

Fig. 3. Left: diffeomorphism from HCP subjects (103818, 111312) to the atlas. Center: each subject's connectome metric and a geodesic (blue, red) starting from the atlas seed (X) mapped to subject space. Right: atlas and a geodesic (orange) starting at the seed (X). Subject geodesics are mapped to atlas space (blue, red). Bottom: detailed view of corpus callosum. (Color figure online)

6   Conclusions

In this paper, we introduce a novel framework for statistically analyzing structural connectomes by representing them as a point on the manifold of Riemannian metrics, enabling us to perform geometric statistics. Using this representation, we build a framework for connectome atlas construction based on the action of the diffeomorphism group and the natural Ebin metric on the space of all Riemannian metrics. Although the Ebin metric is canonical, it is not the only diffeomorphism-invariant metric available on the space of all Riemannian metrics, c.f. [3]. Our framework allows for other choices of metrics and regularization terms, which we will explore more fully in future work. We also plan to investigate in more detail the convergence properties of the proposed algorithms, the impact of the parameter choice on results, and comparisons to other existing methods. We expect this new methodology to open up opportunities for a deeper understanding of structural connectomes and their variabilities.

References

1. Alexander, D.C., Pierpaoli, C., Basser, P.J., Gee, J.C.: Spatial transformations of diffusion tensor magnetic resonance images. IEEE Trans. Med. Imaging **20**(11), 1131–1139 (2001)
2. Basser, P.J., Mattiello, J., LeBihan, D.: Estimation of the effective self-diffusion tensor from the NMR spin echo. J. Magn. Reson. Ser. B **103**(3), 247–254 (1994)

3. Bauer, M., Harms, P., Michor, P.W.: Sobolev metrics on the manifold of all Riemannian metrics. J. Differ. Geom. **94**(2), 187–208 (2013)
4. Bauer, M., Joshi, S., Modin, K.: Diffeomorphic density matching by optimal information transport. SIAM J. Imag. Sci. **8**(3), 1718–1751 (2015)
5. Beg, M.F., Miller, M.I., Trouvé, A., Younes, L.: Computing large deformation metric mappings via geodesic flows of diffeomorphisms. Int. J. Comput. Vis. **61**(2), 139–157 (2005)
6. Cheng, G., Salehian, H., Forder, J.R., Vemuri, B.C.: Tractography from HARDI using an intrinsic unscented Kalman filter. IEEE Trans. Med. Imaging **34**(1), 298–305 (2015)
7. Clarke, B.: The completion of the manifold of Riemannian metrics. J. Differ. Geom. **93**(2), 203–268 (2013)
8. Clarke, B.: Geodesics, distance, and the CAT(0) property for the manifold of Riemannian metrics. Math. Z. **273**(1–2), 55–93 (2013)
9. DeWitt, B.S.: Quantum theory of gravity. I. The canonical theory. Phys. Rev. **160**(5), 1113–1148 (1967)
10. Ebin, D.G.: The manifold of Riemannian metrics. In: Global Analysis (Proceedings of Symposia in Pure Mathematics, vol. XV, Berkeley, California, 1968), pp. 11–40. American Mathematical Society, Providence (1970)
11. Fletcher, P.T., Joshi, S.: Riemannian geometry for the statistical analysis of diffusion tensor data. Sig. Process. **87**(2), 250–262 (2007)
12. Freed, D.S., Groisser, D., et al.: The basic geometry of the manifold of Riemannian metrics and of its quotient by the diffeomorphism group. Michigan Math. J. **36**(3), 323–344 (1989)
13. Gil-Medrano, O., Michor, P.W.: The Riemannian manifold of all Riemannian metrics. Q. J. Math. (Oxford) **42**, 183–202 (1991)
14. Glasser, M.F., et al.: The minimal preprocessing pipelines for the human connectome project. Neuroimage **80**, 105–124 (2013)
15. Glaunès, J., Qiu, A., Miller, M.I., Younes, L.: Large deformation diffeomorphic metric curve mapping. Int. J. Comput. Vis. **80**(3), 317 (2008)
16. Hao, X., Zygmunt, K., Whitaker, R.T., Fletcher, P.T.: Improved segmentation of white matter tracts with adaptive Riemannian metrics. Med. Image Anal. **18**(1), 161–175 (2014)
17. Ho, J., Cheng, G., Salehian, H., Vemuri, B.: Recursive Karcher expectation estimators and geometric law of large numbers. In: Artificial Intelligence and Statistics, pp. 325–332 (2013)
18. Joshi, S., Davis, B., Jomier, M., Gerig, G.: Unbiased diffeomorphic atlas construction for computational anatomy. Neuroimage **23**, S151–S160 (2004)
19. Joshi, S.C., Miller, M.I.: Landmark matching via large deformation diffeomorphisms. IEEE Trans. Image Process. **9**(8), 1357–1370 (2000)
20. Khesin, B., Lenells, J., Misiolek, G., Preston, S.C.: Geometry of diffeomorphism groups, complete integrability and geometric statistics. Geom. Funct. Anal. **23**(1), 334–366 (2013)
21. Mori, S., et al.: Stereotaxic white matter atlas based on diffusion tensor imaging in an ICBM template. Neuroimage **40**(2), 570–582 (2008)
22. Nie, X., Shi, Y.: Topographic filtering of Tractograms as vector field flows. In: Shen, D., et al. (eds.) MICCAI 2019. LNCS, vol. 11766, pp. 564–572. Springer, Cham (2019). https://doi.org/10.1007/978-3-030-32248-9_63

23. O'Donnell, L., Haker, S., Westin, C.-F.: New approaches to estimation of white matter connectivity in diffusion tensor MRI: elliptic pdes and geodesics in a tensor-warped space. In: Dohi, T., Kikinis, R. (eds.) MICCAI 2002. LNCS, vol. 2488, pp. 459–466. Springer, Heidelberg (2002). https://doi.org/10.1007/3-540-45786-0_57
24. Vaillant, M., Glaunès, J.: Surface matching via currents. In: Christensen, G.E., Sonka, M. (eds.) IPMI 2005. LNCS, vol. 3565, pp. 381–392. Springer, Heidelberg (2005). https://doi.org/10.1007/11505730_32
25. Yeh, F.C., et al.: Population-averaged atlas of the macroscale human structural connectome and its network topology. Neuroimage **178**, 57–68 (2018)

A Higher Order Manifold-Valued Convolutional Neural Network with Applications to Diffusion MRI Processing

Jose J. Bouza[1], Chun-Hao Yang[1] (ORCID), David Vaillancourt[2],
and Baba C. Vemuri[1](✉)

[1] University of Florida CISE, Gainesville, FL 32611, USA
vemuri@ufl.edu
[2] University of Florida Applied Physiology and Kinesiology,
Gainesville, FL 32611, USA

Abstract. In this paper, we present a novel generalization of the Volterra Series, which can be viewed as a higher-order convolution, to manifold-valued functions. A special case of the manifold-valued Volterra Series (MVVS) gives us a natural extension of the ordinary convolution to manifold-valued functions that we call, the manifold-valued convolution (MVC). We prove that these generalizations preserve the equivariance properties of the Euclidean Volterra Series and the traditional convolution operator. We present novel deep network architectures using the MVVS and the MVC operations which are then validated via two experiments. These include, (i) movement disorder classification from diffusion magnetic resonance images (dMRI), and (ii) fiber orientation distribution function (fODF) reconstruction from compressed sensed dMRIs. In both the experiments, MVVS and MVC networks outperform the state-of-the-art.

Keywords: Riemannian manifolds · Volterra series · Convolutional neural network · Diffusion MRI · fODF reconstruction · Geometric deep learning

1 Introduction

Theory. In the recent past, there has been a surge in medical imaging and computer vision research to develop deep neural networks(DNNs) that can cope with manifold-valued data e.g., the manifold of $(n \times n)$ symmetric positive-definite (SPD) matrices, P_n, the special orthogonal group, $SO(n)$, the Grassmann

---

J.J. Bouza and C.H. Yang—Contributed equally to the work presented here.
This research was in part funded by the NSF grant IIS-1724174 to BCV.

Electronic supplementary material The online version of this chapter (https://doi.org/10.1007/978-3-030-78191-0_24) contains supplementary material, which is available to authorized users.

A. Feragen et al. (Eds.): IPMI 2021, LNCS 12729, pp. 304–317, 2021.
https://doi.org/10.1007/978-3-030-78191-0_24

manifold, $\mathsf{Gr}(p, n)$, and the n-sphere, S^n. At the outset, it will be useful to categorize two types of problems concerning data in non-Euclidean spaces. These are: (i) data that are samples of functions defined on smooth manifolds, i.e. $f : M \rightarrow R$ and (ii) data that are samples of manifold-valued functions whose domain is Euclidean i.e., $f : Z^d \rightarrow M$ where M is a Riemannian manifold and Z^d is a Euclidean sample lattice. *In this paper we address the problem of developing DNNs for the data type defined in (ii).*

For methods suited to data in category (i) described above, we refer the reader to a recent survey [5]. In the context of data described in (ii) above, authors in [15] presented a DNN that consists of layers which explicitly utilize the structure of SPD matrices. In [16] authors presented a DNN for classification of hand-crafted features residing in a Grassmann manifold. However, the above architectures do not attempt to develop a counterpart of the classical convolutional layer in the traditional convolutional neural network (CNN) which is viewed as one of the key components to the success of CNNs. Besides convolutional layers, batch normalization is also a useful trick used in CNNs to smooth the loss surface, and authors in [6] recently proposed such a technique for data in the manifold of SPD matrices. In this paper, we focus our attention to data represented on a grid where each grid point is associated with a value in a manifold, M, with known geometry, i.e., $f : Z^d \rightarrow M$. The lack of a consistent framework for designing DNN architectures for data residing in a general Riemannian manifold was partly due to the fact that unlike for functions defined on manifolds, there was no natural analog of the convolution operation for manifold-valued functions until recently. In [24] authors defined the weighted Fréchet mean (wFM) [23] as an analog to the classical (Euclidean space) convolution operation for manifold-valued data and recently, the use of wFM operation to build a CNN for manifold-valued data was pioneered by authors of [7,8]. Note that although their definition of wFM as a "plug-in" operation for convolutions is valid for any Riemannian manifold, the convexity constraints in the definition used for wFM restricts the range of values of the wFM leading to model capacity limitations of their network.

In this paper, we propose the idea that for *complete Riemannian manifolds*, it is possible to map the manifold-valued data points within a convolution window defined over the manifold-valued image to the tangent space anchored at the FM of these points using the Riemannian **Log** map. Then, perform the linear combination operation in the tangent space (which is isomorphic to the Euclidean space) and map it back to the manifold using the Riemannian **Exp** map. We provide the details of this operation called the manifold-valued convolution (MVC) in the next section. To increase the expressiveness and hence the capacity of the network, we introduce the novel concept of higher order manifold-valued convolutions via Volterra series representation [26]. The traditional convolution is indeed the first order term of the Volterra Series, which will be briefly reviewed in Sect. 2. In [18], authors empirically showed that replacing a convolution filter with a higher order Volterra series filter increased model accuracy. The Volterra Series was also used recently to design DNNs for data in category (i) [3]. In this paper, we generalize the Volterra Series for real-valued functions to manifold-valued functions and call it the manifold-valued Volterra Series (MVVS). We show that the MVVS (MVC) is equivariant to translation in the domain which allows for weight sharing. The MVVS (MVC) can be used as an alternative to the wFM-based convolutions presented in [7,8] and we call the network based on MVVS (MVC) the MVVS (MVC)-Net. In addition to the translation equivariance, the MVC is also equivariant to the isometry group actions admitted by the manifold. This latter equivariance however does not hold for the MVVS. Hence, by considering only the first-order term of the MVVS, we lose some expressiveness, but we gain the isometry equivariance and computational efficiency. Note that the MVC and the wFM-based convolution are different by construction and a key difference is that for wFM the associated weights need to be positive while such restriction is not required by the MVC. In practice, this restriction limits the output of a wFM layer to the convex cone of the input data points and hence greatly reduces the capacity of the network.

Applications. To demonstrate the performance of the MVVS (MVC)-Net, we test the proposed network on classification and reconstruction problems encountered in diffusion magnetic resonance image (dMRI) processing. In the context of classification, we apply MVVS and MVC networks to classify dMRI brain scans of patients with movement disorders from controls. In the context of reconstruction, we will reconstruct the fiber orientation distribution function (fODF) field [29] from highly undersampled dMRI data. There is a vast body of literature on fODF reconstruction from dMRI data and we refer the reader to a recent comprehensive survey [11] and references therein. Here, we limit ourselves to the review of DNNs for fODF reconstruction from compressed sensed dMRI data. Recently, authors in [27] proposed a novel deep spherical U-Net for the fODF reconstruction but did not enforce non-negativity constraint on the reconstructed fODFs. They represent the fODF in terms of the spherical harmonics (SH) and the reconstruction thus involves estimating the SH coefficients. In [20,21] 3D-CNN networks were explored for fODF reconstruction, but these networks do not guarantee the non-negativity of the reconstructed fODFs. We choose to use the square-root parametrization of the fODF which maps fODFs to a hypersphere. *Since all operations in our network are intrinsic, the output is automatically a valid (non-negative) fODF.* In fODF reconstruction networks, we would like to point out a distinction between *inter*-voxel models and *intra*-voxel models. We define inter-voxel models as combining (macro-structural) features *between* voxels in the brain, while intra-voxel models extract (micro-structural) features from *within each* voxel. Prior work in [27] focused primarily on building intra-voxel models. The primary novelty of the architecture we present here is a layer which acts as an inter-voxel model. We expected and have found empirically that combining intra- and inter-voxel models within one network significantly improves performance over using just one of the two. Thus the empirical results presented here should be viewed as complementary to prior work [27] on intra-voxel fODF reconstruction.

Contributions. Thus, the main contributions of our work in this paper are: (i) We define the manifold-valued Volterra Series representation for general (complete) Riemannian manifolds and prove that the MVVS is equivariant to translation. Additionally, we prove that the MVC, which is the first-order term of the MVVS, is equivariant to isometry group actions admitted by the manifold. (ii) We present a DNN architecture based on MVVS (MVC), called MVVS(MVC)-Net, for **any** complete Riemannian manifold. (iii) Further, we experimentally demonstrate the performance of the MVVS (MVC)-Net on dMRI classification and fODF reconstruction problems along with comparisons to the state-of-the-art (SOTA). Our results demonstrate significant improvement in accuracy and time efficiency over the SOTA.

The rest of this paper is organized as follows. In Sect. 2, we review background material in Riemannian geometry and the Euclidean Volterra Series. In Sect. 3, we present a novel generalization, the MVVS, of the Volterra Series to manifold-valued functions and prove its equivariance properties. Then, we present a DNN architecture based on MVVS, called the MVVS-Net. In Sect. 4, we present the experimental results and draw conclusions in Sect. 5.

2   Preliminary

In this section, we review some basic material from Riemannian geometry that is necessary in our work and the Volterra Series expansion of nonlinear functions. We briefly review how the Volterra Series is utilized in the deep learning literature as a higher order alternative to the convolution in CNNs.

Riemannian Geometry. Let (M, g) be a d-dimensional complete Riemannian manifold. The *tangent space* at $p \in M$ is denoted T_pM, which is a d-dimensional vector space. For $p \in M$ and $v \in T_pM$, the geodesic emanating from p with initial direction v is denoted by $\gamma_v(t)$ where $\gamma_v(0) = p$ and $\gamma'_v = v$. The *Exponential map* $\mathbf{Exp}_p : D(p) \subset T_pM \to M$ is defined by $\mathbf{Exp}_p(v) = \gamma_v(1)$ where $D(p) = \{v \in T_pM : \gamma_v(1)$ is defined and $\gamma_v(t)$ is a minimizing geodesic for $0 < t < 1\}$. The exponential map is a diffeomorphism from $D(p)$ to its image, and its inverse is denoted $\mathbf{Log}_p = \mathbf{Exp}_p^{-1}$. These two maps will be of fundamental importance for the construction of the MVVS which will be discussed subsequently.

The Riemannian metric g induces a distance between any two points $p \in M$ and $q \in M$ given by $d_g(p,q) = \inf\{\int_0^1 \sqrt{g(\gamma'_{p,q}(t), \gamma'_{p,q}(t))}dt$: for all $\gamma_{p,q}\}$. Let $x_1, \dots, x_n \in M$. The Fréchet mean (FM) of $x_1, \dots, x_n$ is $\bar{x} = \operatorname{argmin}_{m \in M} \sum_{i=1}^n d_g^2(x_i, m)$. This is a generalization of the mean of points in a vector space. For the existence and uniqueness of the FM we refer the reader to [1]. Very briefly, the FM is unique if $x_1, \dots, x_N$ lie in a open ball of radius r_{cvx}, where r_{cvx} is the *convexity radius* of M [13]. This is often the case in practice and in all our experiments presented subsequently.

For a Riemannian manifold, a metric-preserving diffeomorphism is an isometry. For a smooth map $f : M \to M$, a desired property would be the *isometry equivariance*, i.e. $\phi \circ f = f \circ \phi$ where ϕ is an isometry map. Another similar concept is the *isometry invariance*, i.e. $f \circ \phi = f$.

Volterra Series. As is well-known, the traditional convolution is linear shift-invariant. A non-linear shift-invariant system can be approximated by the Volterra Series [26], which is given by $h(x) = \sum_{n=1}^{N} \int \cdots \int g(\tau_1, \ldots, \tau_n) \prod_{i=1}^{n} f(x - \tau_i) d\tau_i$, where g is the Volterra kernel. For the case of $N = 1$, $h(x) = \int g(\tau) f(x - \tau) d\tau = (g \star f)(x)$ is the usual convolution.

3 Manifold-Valued Volterra Series and Convolution

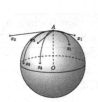 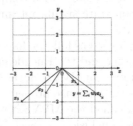 

(a) Log map all of the data in the window onto the tangent space, i.e. $x_i = \mathbf{Log}_A(z_i)$.

(b) Perform a weighted sum in the tangent space $T_A \mathcal{M}$ to get $y = \sum_i w_i x_i$

(c) Project the resulting vector down using the Riemannian exponential map, i.e. the output is $\mathbf{Exp}_A(y)$.

Fig. 1. Manifold-valued convolution operation within a window.

We now present a novel extension of the Volterra series to manifold-valued functions. We show the first order approximation of the proposed MVVS gives a natural extension of the convolution operation to manifold-valued functions. Further, we show that this MVC is equivariant to the isometry group action admitted by the manifold and discuss how to use the MVVS/MVC as basic building blocks to design efficient networks for different tasks.

3.1 Manifold-Valued Volterra Series

For manifold-valued data, we can define an analog of the traditional Volterra series. Let $\odot$ be the Hadamard product, i.e. $x_1 \odot x_2 = [x_{11}x_{21}, \ldots, x_{1n}x_{2n}]$ and $\bigodot_{i=1}^{k} x_i = \left[\prod_{i=1}^{k} x_{i1}, \ldots, \prod_{i=1}^{k} x_{in} \right]$. Hadamard product depends on the tangent vector representation and we use the coordinates induced by the **Log** maps, which are given for the sphere and SPD manifold in Sect. 3.3. Then the MVVS is defined as follows.

Definition 1. *Let (M, g) be a complete Riemannian manifold and $f : Z^d \to M$ be a function defined on Z^d. Let $\{w^{(j)} : (Z^d)^j \to \mathbb{R}\}$ be a collection of kernels. Then*

$$MVVS(f, w^{(1)}, \ldots, w^{(N)})(\mathbf{y}) :=$$

$$\mathbf{Exp}_{m(\mathbf{y})} \left(\sum_{j=1}^{N} \sum_{z_1, \ldots, z_j} w^{(j)}(z_1 - \mathbf{y}, \ldots, z_j - \mathbf{y}) \bigodot_{i=1}^{j} \mathbf{Log}_{m(\mathbf{y})} f(z_i) \right)$$

for $\mathbf{y} \in Z^d$ *where* $m(\mathbf{y}) = FM(f(\mathbf{z}))$ *where* $\mathbf{z}$ *ranges over the support of the Volterra masks* $w^{(j)}$ *centered at* $\mathbf{y}$.

Note that the FM is computed locally in each window centered at the point $\mathbf{y}$. The most prominent feature of the convolution in Euclidean spaces is translation equivariance (in the domain), which allows weight sharing. Similar to the equivariance to translations (in the domain) of the Volterra series in Euclidean space, the following theorem states that MVVS possesses a similar property.

Theorem 1 (Equivariance to Translation). *Let* $h = MVVS(f, w^{(1)}, \dots, w^{(N)})$, *then* $h_t = MVVS(f_t, w^{(1)}, \dots, w^{(N)})$ *for all* $t \in Z^d$, *where,* $f_t(z) = f(z - t)$ *and* $h_t(y) = h(y - t)$.

The proof follows trivially from the definition of the MVVS through a change of variables and hence we will skip it here. For $N = 1$, we write the MVVS as $MVC(f, w)(y) = \mathbf{Exp}_m \left(\sum_{z \in Z^d} w(z - y) \mathbf{Log}_m f(z) \right)$ which gives us a natural generalization of convolution to manifold-valued functions. An illustration of the MVC operations are depicted in Fig. 1. In this work, we also consider the second-order MVVS as a more expressive alternative to the MVC. In the situation with only finite observations at the grid points $z_1, \dots, z_n \in Z^d$, i.e. we have $x_i = f(z_i)$, $w_i^{(1)} = w^{(1)}(z_i)$, and $w_i^{(2)} = w^{(2)}(z_i)$ for $i = 1, \dots, n$, we write $MVC(\{x_i\}_{i=1}^n, \{w_i\}_{i=1}^n) = \mathbf{Exp}_m \left(\sum_{i=1}^n w_i \mathbf{Log}_m x_i \right)$ and

$$MVVS(\{x_i\}_{i=1}^n, \{w_i^{(1)}\}_{i=1}^n, \{w_{i,j}^{(2)}\}_{1 \le i, j \le n}) =$$

$$\mathbf{Exp}_{\bar{x}} \left(\sum_{i=1}^n w_i^{(1)} \mathbf{Log}_{\bar{x}} x_i + \sum_{i,j} w_{i,j}^{(2)} \mathbf{Log}_{\bar{x}} x_i \odot \mathbf{Log}_{\bar{x}} x_j \right).$$

The MVC and the MVVS can be used to generalize CNN and its variants to manifold-valued data. Due to the symmetry of the Hadamard product, we can assume $w_{i,j}^{(2)} = 0$ for $i > j$ to reduce the number of parameters.

Besides the translation equivariance in the domain, the Euclidean convolution is also equivariant to the translation in the range. The translation equivariance in the range leads to, for example, the invariance to changes in brightness by a constant. For the case of MVC, the range (of the input function) is however the manifold M and hence the analogous result would be the equivariance to isometry group action admitted by the manifold. The following theorem states that the proposed MVC is equivariant to the isometry group action admitted by the manifold M. From the proof, it is also obvious that this equivariance is not satisfied by the MVVS for $N > 1$.

Theorem 2. *The MVC is equivariant to the isometry group action admitted by* M, *i.e.* $\phi \circ MVC(f, w) = MVC(\phi \circ f, w)$ *where* $\phi : M \to M$ *is an isometry.*

Proof. The proof relies on the fact that the exponential map commutes with the isometry, i.e., $\phi \circ \mathbf{Exp}_p = \mathbf{Exp}_{\phi(p)} \circ d\phi_p$ [19, Prop. 5.9]. Therefore, when the inverse of $\mathbf{Exp}_p$ exists, $\mathbf{Log}_{\phi(p)} = d\phi_p \circ \mathbf{Log}_p \circ \phi^{-1}$. By the invariance of the intrinsic distance metric, the FM is equivariant to the isometry. Since the MVC is a composition of the exponential map, the log map, and the FM, it is equivariant to the isometry group action.

3.2 Manifold-Valued Deep Network Based on MVVS/MVC

The key components of a CNN are the convolutional layers, the non-linear activation function, and the full-connected (FC) layer. To build an analogous manifold-valued deep network, we need equivalent operations in the context of manifold-valued inputs. We propose to replace the convolution by the MVVS. For the non-linear activation function, the most widely used one is ReLU and we suggest a similar operation called the tangent ReLU (tReLU), which is defined as follows. For $x_1, \ldots, x_n \in M$, $\text{tReLU}(x_i) = \mathbf{Exp}_{\bar{x}}(\text{ReLU}(\mathbf{Log}_{\bar{x}}(x_i)))$ where $\bar{x}$ is the FM of $x_1, \ldots, x_n$ and $\text{ReLU}(x) = \max(x, 0)$ is applied component-wise to its argument. Note that a similar operation was proposed by [9] but they restricted it to the hyperbolic spaces while ours is valid for general complete Riemannian manifolds. Finally, to design a deep network that is invariant to isometry group actions, we need the FC layers to be invariant to the isometry (since the MVC layers are equivariant to the isometry by Theorem 2). In this work, we consider the invariant FC layer proposed in [8] which is constructed by first transforming x_i to $d_i = d_g(x_i, \bar{x})$ and then feeding the d_i's to the usual FC layers. Replacing the MVC with the MVVS, we have a higher order manifold-valued deep network.

Another concern is the extra parameters, i.e. the weights, required by the MVVS compared to the MVC. Note that for a fixed filter size d the number of weights in the MVC is d^2 and for the second-order MVVS is $d^2 + d^2(d^2 + 1)/2$ which is a substantial increase. A way to mitigate this problem is to assume that the kernel $w^{(2)}(z_1, z_2)$ is *separable*, that is, $w^{(2)}(z_1, z_2) = w_1(z_1)w_2(z_2)$. Under this assumption, the number of weights is $3d^2$, which is in the same order as the MVC. The separability of the kernel is assumed in all of our experiments.

We like to emphasize that the proposed MVC/MVVS and the tReLU operations are substitutions for the Euclidean space convolution and the ReLU operations respectively. In the next section, we present closed form Riemannian Exp and Log operations for the manifolds we use in the experiments.

3.3 The Cases of S^n and SPD(n)

Here we specify concrete versions of the building blocks (Exp and Log maps) presented above for particular application domains in dMRI processing. We will tackle two fundamental problems in dMRI processing using this framework: 1) diffusion tensor imaging classification and 2) fODF reconstruction from severely undersampled data.

Diffusion Tensor Image Classification. Diffusion tensor imaging (DTI) is a simple and popular model in dMRI processing. Diffusion tensors (DTs) are 3×3 SPD matrices [4]. A dMRI scan processed using the DTI model will output a 3D field of DTs $f : \mathbb{Z}^3 \to \text{SPD}(3)$. Closed form expressions of the Riemannian **Log** and **Exp** maps for the SPD(3) manifold with the GL(n)-invariant metric are given by

$$\mathbf{Exp}_Y(X) = Y^{1/2} \exp(Y^{-1/2} X Y^{-1/2}) Y^{1/2} \text{ and } \mathbf{Log}_Y(X) = Y^{1/2} \log(Y^{-1/2} X Y^{-1/2}) Y^{1/2}$$

where exp, log are the matrix exponential and logarithmic maps, respectively.

fODF Reconstruction. Accurate reconstruction of the fODF from under-sampled $S(k, q)$ data has the potential to significantly accelerate dMRI acquisition. Here we present a framework for achieving this. Our fODF reconstruction method performs convolutions on the unit hypersphere S^n. The closed form expressions for the **Log** and **Exp** maps on the sphere are given by the following expression, where $U = X - \langle X, Y \rangle Y$ [28].

$$\mathbf{Exp}_Y(X) = \cos(\|X\|)Y + \sin(\|X\|)\frac{X}{\|X\|} \text{ and } \mathbf{Log}_Y(X) = U \cos^{-1}(\langle X, Y \rangle)/\langle U, U \rangle$$

4 Experiments

In this section we present several real data experiments demonstrating the performances of MVC-net and MVVS-net respectively.

4.1 Parkinson's Disease vs. Controls Classification

We now present an application of the MVC-Net and the MVVS-Net to the problem of classification of Parkinson's disease (PD) patients vs controls. The dataset consists of dMRI scans acquired from 355 PD patients and 356 controls. The acquisition parameters were, # of gradient directions = 64, $b = 0, 1000 \text{ s/mm}^2$, repetition time = 7748 ms, echo time = 86 ms, field of view = (224, 224) mm, slice thickness of 2 mm, matrix size of (112, 112).

From each of these dMRIs, 12 regions of interest (ROIs) – six on each hemisphere of the brain – in the sensorimotor tract are segmented by registering to the sensorimotor area tract template (SMATT) [2]. These tracts are known to be affected by PD. For this experiment, we adopt the most widely used representation of dMRI in the clinic namely, the DTI and also to demonstrate that our methods work well for the SPD manifold. DTs are 3×3 SPD matrices [4]. Each of the ROIs (12 in total) contain 26 voxels. For each patient (control), all the ROIs are concatenated together to form a $12 \times 26 \times 3 \times 3$ input tensor to the network. The output is a binary class label specifying whether the input image came from a PD or control.

Table 1. Comparison results for PD vs. Controls classification.

Model	Non-linearity	# params.	time (s) / sample	Accuracy Test accuracy (60/40)	Test accuracy (90/10)
MVVS-net	tReLU	~23K	~0.34	**0.966**	**0.973**
MVC-net	tReLU	~14K	~0.13	0.942	**0.973**
DTI-ManifoldNet [7]	None	~30K	~0.3	0.934	0.948
ODF-ManifoldNet [7]	tReLU	~153K	~0.02	0.941	0.942
ResNet-34 [14]	ReLU	~30M	~0.008	0.708	0.713
CapsuleNet [25]	ReLU	~30M	~0.009	0.618	0.622

Architecture. The MVC-Net architecture is obtained from the traditional CNN by replacing the convolution operations with MVC (and MVVS) operations and the ReLU with **tReLU**. For this experiment, the MVC-net consists of five **MVC + tReLU** layers. Each of the MVC (MVVS) layers has a window size of 4 and a stride of 1. We use the closed form exponential and log maps for the SPD(n) manifold presented in Sect. 3.3.

Experimental Results. In this experiment on PD vs. Control classification from DTI brain scans, we compared the performance of MVC-Net and MVVS-Net with several deep net architectures including the ManifoldNet [7,8] the ResNet-34 architecture [14] and a CapsuleNet architecture [25] with dynamic routing. To perform the comparison, we applied each of the aforementioned deep net architectures to the above described diffusion tensor image data sets. For the ResNET-34 and CapsuleNet, we vectorize the diffusion tensors as these networks are applicable only to vector space data.

We train our MVC-net architecture for 200 epochs using the cross-entropy loss and an Adam opti-

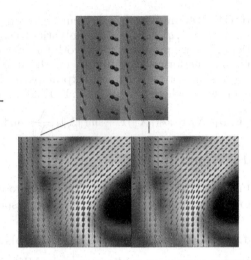

Fig. 2. Left: HCP sample patch from centrum semiovale ground truth/gold standard fODF. Right: Network reconstruction from 7% sampled data. Zoomed-in figures display a particularly hard crossing-fiber ROI.

mizer with the learning rate set to 0.005. We report two different results for each architecture. One is obtained on a 90/10 training to test split. Since the results for the top performing architectures in this category were all high, we also report a more challenging 60/40 training to test split to obtain more differentiation between the methods.

As is evident from the Table 1, MVC-net and MVVS-Net outperform all other methods on both training and test accuracy while simultaneously keeping the lowest parameter count. MVVS-net either is equal (90/10 split) or outperforms (60/40 split) MVC-net, as expected from the increased model capacity of the MVVS. The inference speeds under-perform ResNet-34 and CapsuleNet, but these architectures utilize operations that were optimized heavily for inference speed over the years. Further, in terms of the possible application domain of automated PD diagnosis, the inference speeds we have achieved are more than sufficient in practice.

4.2 fODF Reconstruction

In this experiment, we consider the problem of reconstructing fODFs from compressed sensed (CS) dMRI data. Specifically, given sub-Nyquist sampled (compressed sensed in the 6-dimensional $(\mathbf{k}, \mathbf{q})$ Fourier space) dMRI data, we seek to reconstruct a field of fODF that characterize the diffusional properties of tissue being imaged. The goal of the network will be to learn the highly non-linear mapping between an under-sampled (aliased) reconstruction of the fODF field to the fully-sampled reconstruction of the fODF field.

The fODF can be obtained from fully sampled data using a constrained spherical deconvolution [29]. The fODF is a real-valued positive function on the sphere $f : \mathbb{S}^2 \to \mathbb{R}^+$ and after normalization can be represented as a square-root density, i.e. a point on the unit Hilbert sphere. For sampled fODFs, this representation reduces to a point on the unit hypersphere, $\mathbb{S}^{n-1}$. This unit hypersphere representation will be used in the inter-voxel layers, while the sampled $f : \mathbb{S}^2 \to \mathbb{R}^+$ representation will be used in the intra-voxel layers, leveraging a recent architecture introduced in [10]. that will be elaborated on below. For the inter-voxel layers, we will use MVC and MVVS convolution layers on the unit hypersphere manifold, with closed form expressions for the **Exp** and **Log** maps respectively as presented in Sect. 3.3.

Data Description. We test our fODF reconstruction network on real data from the Human Connectome Project (HCP) [31]. Since the HCP data is acquired with extremely dense sampling, we consider the fODF reconstructions from these HCP scans as the ground truth/gold standard. fODFs in this case are generated using MSMT-CSD [17]. implemented in the *mrtrix3* library [30] which guarantees positivity of the fODF amplitudes. fODFs are represented by sampling on a consistent spherical grid consisting of 768 points in the Healpix sampling [12].

For under-sampling, we apply an inverse power-law under-sampling scheme (see [22]) in the $(\mathbf{k}, \mathbf{q})$ space, which is the data acquisition space.

The training data sets consist of pairs of aliased (under-sampled) and ground-truth (fully sampled) fODF field reconstructions. The goal of the network is to learn to reconstruct the fully sampled fODF field from the input aliased fODF field reconstruction. Due to limited computational resources, in this experiment, we only consider patches of size 21×21 in a slice, i.e., one training sample is a pair consisting of an under-sampled 21×21 patch reconstruction and a fully sampled reconstruction of the same patch. This patch-based approach is quite common in CS-based reconstruction algorithms.

For the real data, we extract the 21×21 voxel ROI from a large subset of HCP scans (432 in total) in the centrum semiovale where projection, commissural and association tracts cross and pose a great challenge for under-sampled reconstruction. We use 40 random samples for testing and train on the remaining 392 samples.

Architecture. As explained previously, the network consists of two components: an *intra-voxel* component which operates individually inside each voxel and an *inter-voxel*

Method	HCP Data					
	MAE (7 %)	MAE (11 %)	MAE (20 %)	bNMSE (7 %)	bNMSE (11 %)	bNMSE (20 %)
MVVS + SphereConv	9.31	9.29	7.41	0.24	0.40	0.38
MVC + SphereConv	10.12	9.43	7.42	0.28	0.41	0.43
SphereConv [10]	13.92	12.61	10.76	0.34	0.64	0.65
$\mathbb{S}^2$ U-net [27]	11.04	10.93	8.03	0.31	0.57	0.59
3D CNN [20]	11.88	11.60	8.77	0.35	0.61	0.65
MSMT-CSD (baseline)	16.81	16.32	12.14	1	1	1

Fig. 3. Comparison results on dMRI fODF reconstruction. The number in parenthesis indicates the sampling rate of the under-sampled reconstruction input.

component which combines features across voxels. The inter-voxel component consists of a series of **MVC** → **tReLU** or **MVVS** → **tReLU** blocks. The input to these blocks is a $H \times W \times C \times N$ tensor representing a patch within a slice of the dMRI scan, where N is the number of sample points of the fODF spherical function and C the number of channels. For example, in the real data experiments, we have an initial input size of $21 \times 21 \times 1 \times 768$. The intra-voxel model needs to process the data within voxels, i.e., the individual fODFs. We design and implement a novel intra-voxel layer using a spherical convolution layer that we denote by **SphereConv** presented in the recent DeepSphere paper [10]. This layer represent the spherical signal of the fODF as a graph with node weights equal to the fODF value at the sample points, and applies spectral graph convolutions to transform the signal. There are approximate rotational equivariance guarantees for **SphereConv** that fit the fODF reconstruction problem well. We would like to stress that the choice of intra-voxel layer is orthogonal to the novelty of this work, namely the inter-voxel **MVC** and **MVVS** convolutions.

In summary, the inter-voxel component combines features between voxels by using the **MVC** layer, while the intra-voxel component shares weights between all voxels but has the capacity to learn within the voxel. We found that applying the inter-voxel layers first, followed by intra-voxel layers later gives optimal performance. With these details in mind, we used the following architecture for real data fODF reconstruction.

$$\textbf{MVVS}(1,8) \rightarrow \textbf{MVVS}(8,16) \rightarrow \textbf{MVVS}(16,32) \rightarrow \textbf{MVVS}(32,32) \rightarrow 7 \times (\textbf{SphereConv})$$

where, $\textbf{MVVS}(C_i, C_o)$ represents an MVVS layer with C_i input and C_o output channels respectively. All layers use a kernel size of 3 and a stride of 1. The **SphereConv** layers have feature channels $32 \rightarrow 64 \rightarrow 128 \rightarrow 256 \rightarrow 256 \rightarrow 128 \rightarrow 48 \rightarrow 1$ and use a U-net style architecture, i.e., with channel concatenation between encoder and decoder layers. All **MVVS** and **SphereConv** layers are followed by a **tReLU** and **ReLU** operation respectively. Results for the same architecture but using **MVC** layers instead of **MVVS** are also presented. For training, the Adam optimizer with an initial learning rate of 0.03 is used. We use an MSE function *weighted by the fractional anisotropy of the undersampled ground truth image* as the reconstruction loss function during training. This FA-weighted MSE encourages the network to focus more on reconstruction of highly anisotropic voxels which in some cases was found to improve visual results substantially. It is possible that this loss could give low weight to crossing fiber voxels (which will appear as low FA regions), but no visual degradation was observed in these regions.

Experimental Results. We quantitatively measure the model performance using mean-angular error (MAE) and baseline normalized MSE (bNMSE). The MAE is computed for only crossing fiber voxels using the method presented in the experiments of [27]. In summary, a threshold of 0.1 of the largest peak is used to eliminate spurious fibers, and all corresponding two-peak voxels from the network output and ground truth are compared using the angular error in degrees. The bNMSE is defined as $\text{MSE}(F_g, F_o)/\text{MSE}(F_g, F_i)$, where F_g, F_o and F_i are the ground truth fODF, the network output and the under-sampled (aliased) fODF respectively. Thus the bNMSE compares the accuracy of the network output to the accuracy of the baseline method (MSMT-CSD in this case), where lower values indicate more improvement relative to the baseline method. This metric was used in place of $\text{MSE}(F_g, F_o)$ to allow more robust comparisons with competing methods, given that results reported in competing methods were most likely obtained from different ROIs and hence difficult to compare to without knowing the precise ROI localization, thus a direct MSE comparison may bias results.

All models are trained for 1000 epochs on a single Quadro RTX 6000 GPU (about 64 h total training time). Figure 3 reports the results for HCP data experiments. As evident, for all sampling rates, our method outperforms other deep learning and the baseline (MSMT-CSD) methods in terms of both MAE and bNMSE. Visualization results shown in Fig. 2 are similarly compelling. The zoomed in area shows a difficult crossing fiber pattern which the network has reconstructed quite well. These results constitute improvements that can reduce dMRI scan acquisition time by orders of magnitude while retaining image quality. Moreover, from an ablation view point, we see that the **MVC** layers (the inter-voxel component) improves accuracy substantially over just the intra-voxel **SphereConv** layers, and **MVVS** further improves the accuracy. Note that our chosen intra-voxel layer actually performs worse in all cases than the intra-voxel layer presented in [27]. This suggests that further improvements could be made by combining our novel inter-voxel **MVVS/MVS** layers with [27] which will be explored in our future work.

5 Conclusion

In this paper, we presented a novel higher order CNN for manifold-valued images. We defined the the analog of the traditional convolutions for manifold-valued images and proved powerful equivariance properties. Finally, we presented experiments demonstrating the superior performance of the MVC (MVVS)-Net in comparison to other SOTA methods on important problems in dMRI.

References

1. Afsari, B.: Riemannian L^p center of mass: existence, uniqueness, and convexity. Proc. Am. Math. Soc. **139**(02), 655 (2011). https://doi.org/10.1090/S0002-9939-2010-10541-5
2. Archer, D., Vaillancourt, D., Coombes, S.: A template and probabilistic atlas of the human sensorimotor tracts using diffusion MRI. Cereb. Cortex **28**, 1–15 (2017). https://doi.org/10.1093/cercor/bhx066
3. Banerjee, M., Chakraborty, R., Bouza, J., Vemuri, B.C.: A higher order convolutional network with group equivariance for homogeneous manifolds. IEEE Trans. Pattern Anal. Mach. Intell. **1**, 1 (2020). https://doi.org/10.1109/TPAMI.2020.3035130

4. Basser, P.J., Mattiello, J., LeBihan, D.: MR diffusion tensor spectroscopy and imaging. Biophys. J. **66**(1), 259–267 (1994)

5. Bronstein, M.M., Bruna, J., LeCun, Y., Szlam, A., Vandergheynst, P.: Geometric deep learning: going beyond Euclidean data. IEEE Signal Process. Mag. **34**(4), 18–42 (2017)

6. Brooks, D., Schwander, O., Barbaresco, F., Schneider, J.Y., Cord, M.: Riemannian batch normalization for SPD neural networks. In: Advances in NeurIPS, pp. 15463–15474 (2019)

7. Chakraborty, R., Bouza, J., Manton, J., Vemuri, B.C.: Manifoldnet: a deep neural network for manifold-valued data with applications. IEEE Trans. Pattern Anal. Mach. Intell. **1**, 1 (2020)

8. Chakraborty, R., Bouza, J., Manton, J., Vemuri, B.C.: A deep neural network for manifold-valued data with applications to neuroimaging. In: Chung, A.C.S., Gee, J.C., Yushkevich, P.A., Bao, S. (eds.) IPMI 2019. LNCS, vol. 11492, pp. 112–124. Springer, Cham (2019). https://doi.org/10.1007/978-3-030-20351-1_9

9. Chami, I., Ying, Z., Ré, C., Leskovec, J.: Hyperbolic graph convolutional neural networks. In: Advances in NeurIPS, pp. 4869–4880 (2019)

10. Defferrard, M., Milani, M., Gusset, F., Perraudin, N.: Deepsphere: a graph-based spherical CNN. In: ICLR (2019)

11. Dell'Acqua, F., Tournier, J.D.: Modelling white matter with spherical deconvolution: How and why? NMR Biomed. **32**, e3945 (2017). https://doi.org/10.1002/nbm.394518

12. Gorski, K.M., et al.: Healpix: a framework for high-resolution discretization and fast analysis of data distributed on the sphere. Astrophys. J. **622**(2), 759 (2005)

13. Groisser, D.: Newton's method, zeroes of vector fields, and the Riemannian center of mass. Adv. Appl. Math. **33**(1), 95–135 (2004). https://doi.org/10.1016/j.aam.2003.08.003

14. He, K., Zhang, X., Ren, S., Sun, J.: Deep residual learning for image recognition. In: Proceedings of the IEEE CVPR, pp. 770–778 (2016)

15. Huang, Z., Van Gool, L.J.: A Riemannian network for SPD matrix learning. In: AAAI, vol. 1, p. 3 (2017)

16. Huang, Z., Wu, J., Van Gool, L.: Building deep networks on Grassmann manifolds. In: 32 AAAI Conference on Artificial Intelligence (2018)

17. Jeurissen, B., Tournier, J.D., Dhollander, T., Connelly, A., Sijbers, J.: Multi-tissue constrained spherical deconvolution for improved analysis of multi-shell diffusion MRI data. Neuroimage **103**, 411–426 (2014)

18. Kumar, R., Banerjee, A., Vemuri, B.C., Pfister, H.: Trainable convolution filters and their application to face recognition. IEEE Trans. Pattern Anal. Mach. Intell. **34**(7), 1423–1436 (2011)

19. Lee, J.M.: Riemannian Manifolds. GTM, vol. 176. Springer, New York (1997). https://doi.org/10.1007/b98852

20. Lin, Z., et al.: Fast learning of fiber orientation distribution function for MR tractography using convolutional neural network. Med. Phys. **46**(7), 3101–3116 (2019)

21. Lucena, O., Vos, S.B., Vakharia, V., Duncan, J., Ourselin, S., Sparks, R.: Convolutional neural networks for fiber orientation distribution enhancement to improve single-shell diffusion MRI tractography. In: Bonet-Carne, E., Hutter, J., Palombo, M., Pizzolato, M., Sepehrband, F., Zhang, F. (eds.) Computational Diffusion MRI. MV, pp. 101–112. Springer, Cham (2020). https://doi.org/10.1007/978-3-030-52893-5_9

22. Lustig, M., Donoho, D., Pauly, J.: Sparse MRI: the application of compressed sensing for rapid MR imaging. Magn. Reson. Med. **58**(6), 1182–1195 (2007)

23. Fréchet, M.: Les éléments aléatoires de nature quelconque dans un espace distancié. Annales de l'I. H. P., **10**(4), 215–310 (1948)

24. Pennec, X., Fillard, P., Ayache, N.: A Riemannian framework for tensor computing. Int. J. Comput. Vis. **66**(1), 41–66 (2006). https://doi.org/10.1007/s11263-005-3222-z

25. Sabour, S., Frosst, N., Hinton, G.E.: Dynamic routing between capsules. In: Advances in NeurIPS, pp. 3856–3866 (2017)

26. Schetzen, M.: The Volterra and Wiener Theories of Nonlinear Systems (1980)

27. Sedlar, S., Papadopoulo, T., Deriche, R., Deslauriers-Gauthier, S.: Diffusion MRI fiber orientation distribution function estimation using voxel-wise spherical U-net. In: Computational Diffusion MRI, MICCAI Workshop (2020)

28. Srivastava, A., Jermyn, I., Joshi, S.: Riemannian analysis of probability density functions with applications in vision. In: 2007 IEEE CVPR, pp. 1–8. IEEE (2007)

29. Tournier, J.D., Calamante, F., Connelly, A.: Robust determination of the fibre orientation distribution in diffusion MRI: non-negativity constrained super-resolved spherical deconvolution. Neuroimage **35**(4), 1459–1472 (2007)

30. Tournier, J.D., et al.: Mrtrix3: a fast,flexible and open software framework for medical image processing and visualisation. Neuroimage **202**, 116137 (2019)

31. Van Essen, D.C., et al.: The WU-Minn human connectome project: an overview. Neuroimage **80**, 62–79 (2013)

Representation Learning

Representation Disentanglement for Multi-modal Brain MRI Analysis

Jiahong Ouyang[1]([✉])[iD], Ehsan Adeli[1][iD], Kilian M. Pohl[1,2][iD], Qingyu Zhao[1][iD],
and Greg Zaharchuk[1][iD]

[1] Stanford University, Stanford, CA, USA
{jiahongo,eadeli,kilian.pohl,qingyuz,gregz}@stanford.edu
[2] SRI International, Menlo Park, CA, USA

Abstract. Multi-modal MRIs are widely used in neuroimaging applications since different MR sequences provide complementary information about brain structures. Recent works have suggested that multi-modal deep learning analysis can benefit from explicitly disentangling anatomical (shape) and modality (appearance) information into separate image presentations. In this work, we challenge mainstream strategies by showing that they do not naturally lead to representation disentanglement both in theory and in practice. To address this issue, we propose a margin loss that regularizes the similarity in relationships of the representations across subjects and modalities. To enable robust training, we further use a conditional convolution to design a single model for encoding images of all modalities. Lastly, we propose a fusion function to combine the disentangled anatomical representations as a set of modality-invariant features for downstream tasks. We evaluate the proposed method on three multi-modal neuroimaging datasets. Experiments show that our proposed method can achieve superior disentangled representations compared to existing disentanglement strategies. Results also indicate that the fused anatomical representation has potential in the downstream task of zero-dose PET reconstruction and brain tumor segmentation. The code is available at https://github.com/ouyangjiahong/representation-disentanglement.

1 Introduction

Multi-modal MRIs using different pulse sequences (e.g., T1-weighted and T2 Fluid Attenuated Inversion Recovery) are widely used to probe complementary and mutually informative aspects of the brain structure, thereby playing a pivotal role in improving the understanding of neurodevelopment across the life span and diagnosis of neuropsychiatric disorders [15]. However, compared to uni-modal image analysis, models that operate on multi-modal data are more likely to encounter the issue of incomplete inputs (some cases have missing modalities) due to data corruption, when applied to larger MRI datasets [7].

To tackle these challenges, recent works [15,17] have suggested to explicitly disentangle anatomical and modality-specific information from multi-modal

© Springer Nature Switzerland AG 2021
A. Feragen et al. (Eds.): IPMI 2021, LNCS 12729, pp. 321–333, 2021.
https://doi.org/10.1007/978-3-030-78191-0_25

MRIs. Specifically, each image is encoded into two representations: an *anatomical representation* that encodes the morphological shape of brain anatomies and is mostly shared across all modalities of the same subject, and a *modality representation* that encodes image appearance information specific to the modality. Such disentanglement is typically derived based on *cross-reconstruction* [8], i.e., by examining the quality of images synthesized from anatomical and modality representations from mixed sources. The resulting disentangled representations are shown to be useful for downstream tasks including cross-modality deformable registration [14], multi-modal segmentation [17], image harmonization [4], multi-domain image synthesis, and imputation of missing modalities [15].

All the above studies focused on evaluating the results of the downstream tasks. It remains *unclear* whether the learned representations are truly disentangled or not. In this work, we show that the cross-reconstruction strategies can easily lead to information leakage between representations, i.e., representations are still partly coupled after disentanglement. To address this issue, we propose a margin loss that regularizes the within-subject across-modality similarity between representations with respect to the across-subject within-modality similarity. Such regularization encourages the anatomical and modality information to fully disentangle in the representation space. Further, to obtain a robust training scheme, we use a modified conditional convolution to combine separate encoders associated with the modalities into a single coherent model. Lastly, we introduce a fusion function to combine the disentangled anatomical representations as a set of modality-invariant features, which can be used to solve various downstream tasks. We evaluate our method on three multi-modal neuroimaging datasets, including T1- and T2-weighted MRIs of 692 adolescents from the National Consortium on Alcohol and Neurodevelopment in Adolescence (NCANDA) [19], T1-weighted and T2-FLAIR MRIs of 173 adults for zero-dose PET reconstruction, and multi-modal MRIs (T1, post-contrast T1, T2, and T2 Fluid Attenuated Inversion Recovery) from 369 subjects of the BraTS 2020 dataset [10]. Results indicate that our method achieves better disentanglement between anatomical and modality representations compared to several baseline methods. The fused modality-invariant representation shows potential in the downstream task of PET reconstruction and brain tumor segmentation (BraTS).

2   Related Works

Representation disentanglement is an active topic in image-to-image translation tasks lately [8]. The goal of these tasks is to disentangle the content (e.g., anatomical information) and style (e.g., modality, texture, appearance) information from an image so that images of the same content can be translated between different styles. The disentanglement is learned by optimizing a cross reconstruction loss on synthesized images, with content and style sampled from different training images [2,6]. A major issue is that these methods do not explicitly enforce the disentanglement, and hence the learned representations still suffer from information leakage.

Based on this observation, methods based on adversarial training [1,3,8,9] further regularize the content representations to be independent of the source style domain. For example, DRIT [8] couples adversarial training with a cross-cycle consistency loss to achieve between-domain translation based on unpaired data. MTAN [9] uses a multi-class adversarial loss for the style labels. DRNet [3] leverages the adversarial loss to disentangle the stationary and temporal components. Sagie et al. [1] proposed a zero loss to force the style encoder to capture information relevant to the specific domain. However, adversarial training can be unstable and easily stuck in a local optimum. In addition, only one of the two representations (usually the content representation) can be adversarially regularized, which can easily cause information leakage into the other representation. As an extreme scenario, the style representation can contain all the information about the input, while the content representation may carry little or random information, just enough to fool the discriminator.

Lastly, a common issue of the above methods is that they utilize a separate decoder for each domain. It means that regardless of being disentangled or not, the learned content representations can always produce satisfying results for domain translation or downstream tasks as long as they carry task-related information from the input. In conclusion, in the absence of visualization or evaluation of the disentangled representations, it is unclear if the representations learned by the above methods are still coupled or not.

3 Proposed Method

To address this ambiguity, we first introduce a robust model for disentangling the anatomical and modality representations for multi-modal MRI based on image-to-image translation in Sect. 3.1. Next, we introduce a strategy for fusing the disentangled anatomical representations from all available modalities of a subject into a modality-invariant representation, which can be used as the input for any downstream model.

3.1 Representation Disentanglement by Image-to-image Translation

We assume each subject in the training set has MRIs of m modalities (sequences) and let $x_i \in \mathcal{X}_i$ denote the input image of the i-th modality. As shown in Fig. 1a, we aim to disentangle x_i into an anatomical representation s_i by an anatomical encoder $s_i = E_i^A(x_i)$ and a modality representation z_i by a modality encoder $z_i = E_i^M(x_i)$. We assume that the anatomical representation s_i encodes the morphological information of brain structures that is mostly impartial to the imaging modality, while z_i provides image appearance information specific to a modality. The decoder D then reconstructs x_i from a pair of anatomical and modality representations. Prior works [2] have suggested that such disentangled representations can be learned by optimizing the *self-reconstruction* and *cross-reconstruction* losses; Given a pair of s_i and z_j derived from images of any two

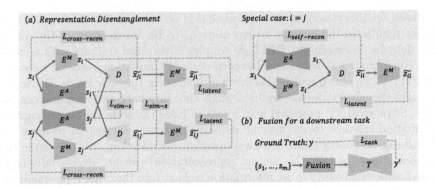

Fig. 1. Overview: (a) An image x_i is disentangled into an anatomical representation s_i and a modality representation z_i by E_A and E_M. The decoder D reconstructs the input from the two representations. These networks are trained by the reconstruction and latent consistency losses. We propose to add a similarity regularization L_{sim} that models the relationships between the representations from different images; (b) The disentangled anatomical representations of a subject are fused into one modality-invariant encoding that can be used as an input to a downstream model T.

modalities, D is supposed to synthesize an image that is similar to the input image $x_j \in \mathcal{X}_j$, whose synthesized domain corresponds to the j-th modality.

$$L_{self-recon} = \frac{1}{m} \sum_{i=1}^{m} \mathbf{E}_{x_i \sim \mathcal{X}_i} [\| \widetilde{x_{ii}} - x_i \|_1],$$

$$L_{cross-recon} = \frac{\lambda_c}{m^2 - m} \sum_{i=1}^{m} \sum_{j=1, j \neq i}^{m} \mathbf{E}_{x_i \sim \mathcal{X}_i, x_j \sim \mathcal{X}_j} [\| \widetilde{x_{ij}} - x_j \|_1],$$

where $\widetilde{x_{ij}} = D(E_i^A(x_i), E_j^M(x_j))$. In addition to these reconstruction losses, another loss function commonly used for training image-to-image translation [14] is the *latent consistency* loss, which encourages the representations derived from raw inputs to be similar to the ones from the synthesized images.

$$L_{latent} = \frac{\lambda_l}{m^2} \sum_{i=1}^{m} \sum_{j=1}^{m} \mathbf{E}_{x_i \sim \mathcal{X}_i, x_j \sim \mathcal{X}_j} [\| \widetilde{z_{ji}} - z_i \|_1], \tag{1}$$

where $\widetilde{z_{ji}} = E_i^M(D(E_j^A(x_j), E_i^M(x_i)))$ is the modality representation derived from a synthesized image.

Enforcing Disentanglement by Similarity Regularization. Although prior works have leveraged the above concept of disentanglement for several multi-modal downstream tasks, there is no theoretical guarantee that the cross reconstruction can encourage the encoder to disentangle anatomical and modality representations. In fact, information can freely leak between representations. As a naive example, both s_i and z_i can be an exact copy of x_i so that the decoder D can easily reconstruct the input.

We resolve this problem by exploring the similarity relationships between representations. As the brain's morphological shape is highly heterogeneous across subjects, we assume the anatomical representations s from the same subject but different modalities should be more similar than those from the same modality but different subjects. Note, s_i of the same subject are not necessary to be exactly the same, as multi-modal imaging is designed to capture distinct characteristics of brain anatomies. For instance, the brain tumor itself is more visible on T1-weighted MR with contrast (T1c) compared to T1 without contrast due to the injected contrast medium. On the other hand, modality representations z from the same modality but different subjects should be more similar than those from the same subject but different modalities. We propose to model such relationships using a similarity loss inspired by the margin-based hinge loss [5].

$$L_{sim} = \frac{\lambda_s}{m^2} \sum_{i=1}^{m} \sum_{j=1}^{m} \mathbf{E}[\max(0, \alpha_s - \cos(f(s_i^p), f(s_j^p)) + \cos(f(s_i^p), f(s_i^q)))] +$$

$$\frac{\lambda_z}{m^2} \sum_{i=1}^{m} \sum_{j=1}^{m} \mathbf{E}[\max(0, \alpha_z - \cos(z_i^p, z_i^q) + \cos(z_i^p, z_j^p))] \tag{2}$$

where p and q correspond to a pair of subjects randomly sampled in a mini-batch, $\cos(\cdot, \cdot)$ denotes the cosine distance between two vectors, and f denotes a MaxPooling and flattening operation. Unlike the L_2-based similarity loss, Eq. (2) encourages the within-subject and across-subject distances to differ by the margins α_s and α_z and thereby avoids deriving identical representations.

Conditional Convolution. Another drawback of traditional multi-modal image translation methods is that each modality is associated with a pair of anatomical and modality encoders that are independently learned. However, these encoding tasks are highly dependent across modalities. Hence, each convolutional operation at a certain layer should function similarly across networks. To enable robust multi-modal translation, we couple the set of independent anatomical encoders $\{E_i^A(x_i)\}$ into one coherent encoder model $E^A(x; i)$ and likewise couple all modality encoders $\{E_i^M(x_i)\}$ into $E^M(x; i)$ with i being an additional input to the model. We construct these two unified models using Conditional Convolution (CondConv) [16] as the fundamental building blocks. As inspired by [16], parameters of a convolutional kernel is conditioned on the input modality i using a mixture-of-experts model $CondConv(x; i) = \sigma((\beta_1^i \cdot W_1 + ... + \beta_n^i \cdot W_n) \circledast x)$, where $\sigma(\cdot)$ is the sigmoid activation function, $\circledast$ denotes regular convolution, $\{W_1, ..., W_n\}$ are the learnable kernels associated with n experts, and $\{\beta_1^i, ... \beta_n^i\}$ are the modality-specific mixture weights. As such, the convolutional kernel exhibits correlated behavior across modalities as the n experts are jointly trained on data of all modalities.

3.2   Fusing Disentangled Representations for Downstream Tasks

As shown in Fig. 1b, after obtaining the disentangled representations, the anatomical representations from all available modalities of a subject are fused into one fixed-size encoding as the input for a downstream model T, which can be any state-of-the-art model for the downstream task. Note that the fusion function here should pool features of a various number of channels to a fixed number of channels. Let s be the concatenation of anatomical representations from the available modalities $Concat(s_i, ..., s_j)$. Then the fusion is the concatenation of several pooling functions: $Concat(MaxPool(s), MeanPool(s), MinPool(s))$. With this fusion operation, one can use two strategies to train the downstream model T. We can either solely train T based on the frozen s derived by the self-supervised learning of the encoders (Sect. 3.1), or fine-tune the encoders jointly with the downstream task model T. Though the joint training can potentially result in representations that better suit the downstream task, we confine our analysis to the first strategy (fixing encoders) in this work to emphasize the impact of representation disentanglement.

4   Experiments

We first describe the dataset and the experimental settings in Sect. 4.1 and 4.2. We then show in Sect. 4.3 that our proposed approach (Sect. 3.1) can effectively disentangle anatomical and modality representations on three neuroimaging datasets. We further show in Sect. 4.4 that the disentangled representations in combination with the fusion strategy (Sect. 3.2) can alleviate the missing modality problem in two downstream tasks.

4.1   Datasets

ZeroDose. The dataset comprised brain FDG-PET and two MR modalities (T1-weighted and T2 FLAIR) from 171 subjects with multiple diagnosis types including tumor, epilepsy, and dementia. The FLAIR and PET images were first registered to T1, and then all modalities were normalized to a standard template and resized to 192×160 in the axial plane. Intensities in the brain region of each image were converted to z-scores. The top and bottom 20 slices in each image were omitted from analysis. Each 3 adjacent axial slices were converted to a 3-channel image as the input to the encoder models. Random flipping of brain hemispheres was used as augmentation during training. Five-fold cross-validation was conducted with 10% training cases used for validation. The downstream task was zero-dose PET reconstruction, i.e., to synthesize high quality FDG-PET from multi-modal MRIs. This is useful in practice as the injected radiotracer in current PET imaging protocols can lead to the risk of primary or secondary cancer in scanned subjects. Moreover, PET is more expensive than MRI and not offered in the majority of medical centers worldwide.

NCANDA. Based on the public data release[1], we used the T1 and T2 MRIs of 692 adolescents with no-to-low alcohol drinking from the NCANDA dataset [19]. The images were preprocessed by a pipeline [18] composed of denoising, bias field correction, skull stripping, aligning T1 and T2 to a template, and resizing to 192×160. Other settings were the same as the ZeroDose dataset. As this dataset only contained healthy individuals, we used it solely for evaluating the representation disentanglement based on the middle 40 slices in each image.

BraTS. Multimodal Brain Tumor Segmentation Challenge 2020 [10] provides multi-modal brain MRI of 369 subjects with four modalities: T1, post-contrast T1 (T1Gd), T2, and T2-FLAIR (FLAIR). Three categories were labeled for brain tumor segmentation, i.e., Gd-enhancing tumor (ET), peritumoral edema (ED), and necrotic and non-enhancing tumor core (NCR/NET). We used the 55 middle axial slices and cropped the image size to 192×160. Other preprocessing steps and settings were kept the same.

4.2 Experimental Settings

Implementation Details. The anatomical encoder E^A was a U-Net type model. Let C_k denote a Convolution-BatchNorm-ReLU block with k filters (4×4 spatial filters with stride 2), and CD_k an Upsample-Convolution-BatchNorm-ReLU block. The architecture was designed as C_{32}-C_{64}-C_{128}-C_{256}-C_{256}-CD_{256}-CD_{128}-CD_{64}-CD_{32}. A convolution then mapped the resulting representations to 4 channels with softmax activation as the anatomical representation. The modality encoder E^M consisted of 5 convolution layers of 3×3 filters and stride 2 with LeakyReLU of a 0.2 slope. Numbers of filters were 16-32-64-128-128. A fully connected layer mapped the resulting features to a 16-D representation. The decoder D was based on SPADE [13] with the architecture used in [2]. The networks were trained for 50 epochs by the Adam optimizer with learning rate of 2×10^{-4} and weight decay of 10^{-5}. The regularization rates were set to $\lambda_c = 2.0$, $\lambda_l = 0.1$, $\lambda_s = 10.0$, $\lambda_z = 2.0$. The margins in the similarity loss were set to $\alpha_s = \alpha_z = 0.1$. For the downstream model T in the zero-dose PET reconstruction, a U-Net based model with attention modules [12] was adopted. The downstream model for BraTS brain tumor segmentation was the BraTS 2018 challenge's winner NVNet [11].

Competing Methods. We first implemented the encoders using traditional convolution (training separate encoders), denoted as **Conv**. Based on this implementation, our disentanglement approach incorporating the similarity losses is denoted as **+Sim**. We then compared our approach with two types of methods. We term the first type [2,6] that regularized the disentanglement merely using cross-reconstruction and latent consistency loss as **+NA**. The other type

---

[1] NCANDA_PUBLIC_4Y_STRUCTURAL_V01 (DOI: https://doi.org/10.7303/ syn22216457); collection was supported by NIH grants AA021697, AA021695, AA021692, AA021696, AA021681, AA021690, and AA02169.

[1,3,8,9,14,15,17] that utilized adversarial training on the anatomical representations are termed as **+Adv**. To make fair comparison on the disentanglement strategies, all comparison methods used the same network structure for the encoder and decoder. Finally, we replaced **Conv** with **CondConv** (training a single encoder) to show the advantage of using conditional convolution.

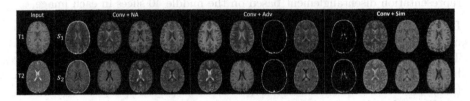

Fig. 2. Visualization of s_1 and s_2 of one NCANDA subject. Only our approach (+Sim) resulted in visually similar anatomical representations from T1 and T2.

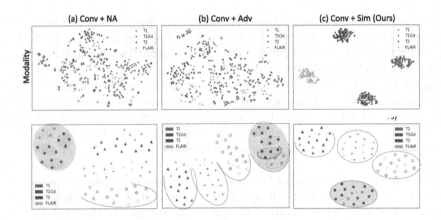

Fig. 3. t-SNE visualization of the z space (a,b,c) and the s space (d,e,f) for BraTS dataset in 2D spaces. Fully disentangled z should cluster by modality (denoted by color); Fully disentangled s should cluster by subjects (denoted by marker style) with no modality bias (sub-clusters by modality).

4.3   Evaluation on Disentangled Representation

We first evaluated the methods on representation disentanglement and image cross reconstruction based on 5-fold cross-validation. We derived the anatomical and modality representations of the test subjects learned by the approaches. Figure 2 visualizes the 4-channel anatomical representations of one subject from NCANDA. We observe that s_1 and s_2 (extracted from T1 and T2) learned by the two baselines (Conv+NA and Conv+Adv) were *substantially different*, indicating that they might still contain modality-specific information. On the other hand, our approach (Conv+Sim) produced visually more similar anatomical representations than the baselines. This indicates that the proposed similarity regularization can decouple the modality-specific appearance features from the structural information shared between modalities.

This result is also supported by the visualization of the learned representation spaces. As shown in Fig. 3a–c, we randomly selected 200 modality representations in the test set of the BraTS dataset and projected them into a 2D space by t-SNE. Only our approach clearly separated the representations of different modalities into 4 distinct clusters (Fig. 3c), which was in line with the regularization on z in Eq. (2). The clustering with respect to modalities was not evident for the projections of the baseline approaches (Fig. 3a,b), indicating that complimentary information had leaked into the modalities representations. Moreover, the baseline approaches failed to disentangle T1 and T1Gd, two contrasts with high visual resemblance, as the red and blue dots were coupled in the representation space. Likewise, we visualized the space of anatomical representations in Fig. 3d–f. We randomly selected 4 subjects in the BraTS test set and projected the pooled anatomical representation $f(s_i)$ of 4 consecutive slices into a 2D space. Now the 4 distinct clusters of our approach were defined with respect to subjects as opposed to modalities, and there was no apparent bias of modality in each subject's cluster (Fig. 3f), indicating the representations solely encoded subject-specific yet modality-invariant information. The representation spaces learned by the two baselines contained both subject-specific anatomical and modality information (Fig. 3d,e); that is, although the projections could be separated by subjects (black circles), each subject-specific cluster could be further stratified by modalities (color of the markers).

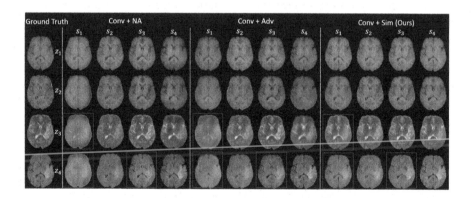

Fig. 4. Cross reconstruction results for one test subject from the BraTS dataset.

The improved disentanglement also resulted in better cross-reconstruction. Figure 4 shows the results of a test subject from the BraTS dataset. In each panel, $\widetilde{x_{ij}}$ is displayed on the jth row and i^{th} column; Diagonal images correspond to self-reconstruction and off-diagonal ones are cross-reconstruction.

Table 1. 5-fold cross-validation for quantitative cross-reconstruction evaluation.

(a) ZeroDose

Methods	T1	FLAIR
	PSNR/SSIM	PSNR/SSIM
Conv+NA	25.603/0.682	24.435/0.612
Conv+Adv	27.131/**0.742**	25.846/0.674
Conv+ Sim(Ours)	27.222/0.735	25.970/0.667
CondConv+ Sim(Ours)	**27.231/0.742**	**25.978/0.681**

(b) NCANDA

Methods	T1	T2
	PSNR/SSIM	PSNR/SSIM
Conv+NA	29.719/0.849	28.077/0.808
Conv+Adv	**30.421/0.866**	27.950/0.807
Conv+ Sim(Ours)	30.266/0.863	28.367/0.825
CondConv+ Sim(Ours)	30.331/0.865	**28.451/0.832**

(c) BraTS

Methods	T1	T1Gd	T2	FLAIR
	PSNR/SSIM	PSNR/SSIM	PSNR/SSIM	PSNR/SSIM
Conv+NA	27.304/0.717	24.897/0.638	25.148/0.621	25.166/0.617
Conv+Adv	27.485/0.717	25.385/0.656	25.951/0.658	26.135/0.642
Conv+Sim(Ours)	27.892/0.756	26.114/0.723	**26.479/0.744**	**26.588/0.692**
CondConv+Sim(Ours)	**27.916/0.752**	**26.221/0.731**	26.445/0.735	26.489/0.687

The proposed Conv+Sim achieved the best visual quality (accurate structural details), especially the FLAIR reconstruction highlighted in red boxes, where the tumor area was more precisely reconstructed. This improvement was quantitatively supported by the higher similarity between ground-truth and synthesized images in terms of peak-signal-noise ratio (PSNR) and structural similarity index (SSIM) (Table 1). For each image of a specific modality, we synthesized it based on its own modality representation and the anatomical representation from another modality (For each image in the BraTS dataset, we computed the average metrics over all three cross reconstruction results). According to Table 1, Conv+NA achieved the lowest reconstruction quality for both SSIM and PSNR on all three datasets. The quality improved when adding adversarial training on the anatomical representations (Conv+Adv) but was still lower than the two implementations with the proposed similarity loss (except for T1 reconstruction in NCANDA). Of the two models with +Sim, CondConv+Sim recorded better performance on the ZeroDose and NCANDA datasets. This indicates that CondConv enabled more stable reconstruction results by coupling highly dependent modality-specific encoders. However, on the BraTS dataset, Conv+Sim achieved better cross-reconstruction for T2 and FLAIR. The reason could be that CondConv shared anatomical and modality encoders across modalities at the expense of model capacity, especially when more than two modalities were involved. It is also worth mentioning that all methods achieved higher performance on NCANDA because it was the only dataset of healthy controls. Taken all together, only our approach resulted in true disentanglement between anatomical and modality representations, which was not guaranteed by the baselines.

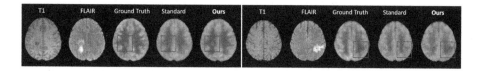

Fig. 5. ZeroDose PET reconstruction from T1 and FLAIR for two test subjects.

4.4 Evaluation on Downstream Tasks

Deep learning models that rely on multi-modal input often suffer from the missing input problem. When a model is trained on data with complete inputs and tested on data with one modality missing, standard approaches either fill in all zero values (**Standard+Zero**) or use the average image of that modality over the entire cohort (**Standard+Avg**). Here, we demonstrate that an alternative solution is to train and test the model on the fusion of disentangled anatomical representations from all available modalities (**Ours**, CondConv+Sim). We show that this strategy can largely alleviate the impact of missing inputs.

In each run of the cross-validation, we first learned the disentangled representations and then trained the downstream models (based on the raw multi-modal images for the standard methods or fused anatomical representations for our proposed method) for zero-dose PET reconstruction. Then, the downstream model was tested on data with or without missing modalities. When all modalities were used for testing, the standard and proposed approaches achieved comparable reconstruction accuracy in terms of both PSNR and SSIM (N/A in Table 2), but we observe that our approach could generally result in more accurate tumor reconstruction (Fig. 5), which could not be reflected in the whole-brain similarity measure. The improvement of our approach became evident when one of the modalities was missing (Table 2). In particular, missing FLAIR induced larger performance drop for all approaches, as ZeroDose contained a large number of images with tumor, which was more pronounced in FLAIR than T1.

Table 2. Performance of two downstream tasks with incomplete input. Left: zero-dose PET reconstruction; Right: brain tumor segmentation.

Methods	ZeroDose			BraTS				
	N/A	T1	FLAIR	N/A	T1	T1Gd	T2	FLAIR
	PSNR/SSIM	PSNR/SSIM	PSNR/SSIM	DICE				
Standard+Zero	**25.475/0.739**	18.122/0.436	18.8863/0.435	**0.826**	0.364	0.240	0.616	0.298
Standard+Avg		24.425/0.676	23.137/0.631		0.724	0.279	0.733	0.452
Ours	25.386/0.729	**24.610/0.682**	**24.193/0.674**	0.821	**0.782**	**0.779**	**0.758**	**0.772**

Next, we replicated this experiment for the downstream task of brain tumor segmentation on the BraTS dataset and measured the performance using the dice coefficient (DICE; Each cell in Table 2 records the average DICE across three categories: ET, ED, and NCR/NET). In line with the results of the Zero-Dose experiment, the standard and proposed methods both obtained similar DICE scores, when complete inputs were used during testing. Standard+Zero recorded the lowest accuracy when missing any modality. Standard+Avg was less impacted when T1 or T2 was missing, but more impacted by T1Gd and FLAIR as the standard model relied mostly on those two modalities for localizing the tumor. The proposed method achieved the highest DICE score in all scenarios, among which the missing T2 recorded the largest drop on DICE. This might be because T2 had the most distinct appearance compared to other modalities, thus having the largest impact on the fused representation.

5 Conclusion

In this paper, we first proposed a novel margin loss to regularize the within-subject across-modality similarity between representations with respect to the across-subject within-modality similarity. It alleviates the information leakage problem in existing disentanglement methods. We further introduced a modified conditional convolution layer to enable training a single model for multiple modalities. Lastly, we proposed a fusion function to combine the disentangled anatomical representations from available modalities as a set of modality-invariant features for downstream tasks. Experiments on three brain MR datasets and two downstream tasks demonstrated that the proposed method achieved meaningful and robust disentangled representations compared with the existing methods. Though we only evaluated on brain images, the method is likely to generalize to other organs as long as the assumption on the within-subject across-modality and across-subject within-modality similarity holds.

Acknowledgement. This work was supported by NIH funding AA021697 and by the Stanford HAI AWS Cloud Credit.

References

1. Benaim, S., Khaitov, M., Galanti, T., Wolf, L.: Domain intersection and domain difference. In: ICCV, pp. 3445–3453 (2019)
2. Chartsias, A., et al.: Disentangle, align and fuse for multimodal and zero-shot image segmentation. IEEE Trans. Med. Imaging (2020)
3. Denton, E.L., et al.: Unsupervised learning of disentangled representations from video. NeurIPS **30**, 4414–4423 (2017)
4. Dewey, B.E., et al.: A disentangled latent space for cross-site MRI harmonization. In: Martel, A.L., et al. (eds.) MICCAI 2020. LNCS, vol. 12267, pp. 720–729. Springer, Cham (2020). https://doi.org/10.1007/978-3-030-59728-3_70
5. Frome, A., et al.: Devise: a deep visual-semantic embedding model. In: NeurIPS, pp. 2121–2129 (2013)
6. Huang, X., Liu, M.Y., Belongie, S., Kautz, J.: Multimodal unsupervised image-to-image translation. In: ECCV, pp. 172–189 (2018)

7. Lee, D., Kim, J., Moon, W.J., Ye, J.C.: Collagan: collaborative GAN for missing image data imputation. In: Proceedings of the IEEE/CVF Conference on Computer Vision and Pattern Recognition, pp. 2487–2496 (2019)
8. Lee, H.Y., Tseng, H.Y., Huang, J.B., Singh, M., Yang, M.H.: Diverse image-to-image translation via disentangled representations. In: ECCV, pp. 35–51 (2018)
9. Liu, Y., Wang, Z., Jin, H., Wassell, I.: Multi-task adversarial network for disentangled feature learning. In: CVPR, pp. 3743–3751 (2018)
10. Menze, B.H., et al.: The multimodal brain tumor image segmentation benchmark (brats). IEEE Trans. Med. Imaging **34**(10), 1993–2024 (2014)
11. Myronenko, A.: 3D MRI brain tumor segmentation using autoencoder regularization. In: Crimi, A., Bakas, S., Kuijf, H., Keyvan, F., Reyes, M., van Walsum, T. (eds.) BrainLes 2018. LNCS, vol. 11384, pp. 311–320. Springer, Cham (2019). https://doi.org/10.1007/978-3-030-11726-9_28
12. Ouyang, J., Chen, K., Zaharchuk, G.: Zero-dose pet reconstruction with missing input by U-net with attention modules. In: Medical Imaging Meets NeurIPS (2020)
13. Park, T., Liu, M.Y., Wang, T.C., Zhu, J.Y.: Semantic image synthesis with spatially-adaptive normalization. In: CVPR, pp. 2337–2346 (2019)
14. Qin, C., Shi, B., Liao, R., Mansi, T., Rueckert, D., Kamen, A.: Unsupervised deformable registration for multi-modal images via disentangled representations. In: Chung, A.C.S., Gee, J.C., Yushkevich, P.A., Bao, S. (eds.) IPMI 2019. LNCS, vol. 11492, pp. 249–261. Springer, Cham (2019). https://doi.org/10.1007/978-3-030-20351-1_19
15. Shen, L., et al.: Multi-domain image completion for random missing input data. arXiv preprint arXiv:2007.05534 (2020)
16. Yang, B., Bender, G., Le, Q.V., Ngiam, J.: Condconv: conditionally parameterized convolutions for efficient inference. In: NeurIPS, pp. 1307–1318 (2019)
17. Yang, J., et al.: Cross-modality segmentation by self-supervised semantic alignment in disentangled content space. In: Albarqouni, S., et al. (eds.) DART/DCL -2020. LNCS, vol. 12444, pp. 52–61. Springer, Cham (2020). https://doi.org/10.1007/978-3-030-60548-3_6
18. Zhao, Q., Adeli, E., Pfefferbaum, A., Sullivan, E.V., Pohl, K.M.: Confounder-aware visualization of ConvNets. In: Suk, H.-I., Liu, M., Yan, P., Lian, C. (eds.) MLMI 2019. LNCS, vol. 11861, pp. 328–336. Springer, Cham (2019). https://doi.org/10.1007/978-3-030-32692-0_38
19. Zhao, Q., et al.: Association of heavy drinking with deviant fiber tract development in frontal brain systems in adolescents. JAMA psychiatry **78**(4), 407–415 (2020)

Variational Knowledge Distillation for Disease Classification in Chest X-Rays

Tom van Sonsbeek[1]([⊠]), Xiantong Zhen[1,2], Marcel Worring[1], and Ling Shao[2]

[1] University of Amsterdam, Amsterdam, The Netherlands
{t.j.vansonsbeek,x.zhen,m.worring}@uva.nl
[2] Inception Institute of Artificial Intelligence, Abu Dhabi, UAE
ling.shao@ieee.org

Abstract. Disease classification relying solely on imaging data attracts great interest in medical image analysis. Current models could be further improved, however, by also employing Electronic Health Records (EHRs), which contain rich information on patients and findings from clinicians. It is challenging to incorporate this information into disease classification due to the high reliance on clinician input in EHRs, limiting thepossibility for automated diagnosis. In this paper, we propose *variational knowledge distillation* (VKD), which is a new probabilistic inference framework for disease classification based on X-rays that leverages knowledge from EHRs. Specifically, we introduce a conditional latent variable model, where we infer the latent representation of the X-ray image with the variational posterior conditioning on the associated EHR text. By doing so, the model acquires the ability to extract the visual features relevant to the disease during learning and can therefore perform more accurate classification for unseen patients at inference based solely on their X-ray scans. We demonstrate the effectiveness of our method on three public benchmark datasets with paired X-ray images and EHRs. The results show that the proposed variational knowledge distillation can consistently improve the performance of medical image classification and significantly surpasses current methods.

Keywords: Multi-modal learning · Medical image classification · Electronic health records · Knowledge distillation · Variational inference

1 Introduction

Advances in deep learning for medical imaging have been shown to perform on par or better than clinicians on an increasing number of tasks [17]. The expansion of data and computational resources has played a large role in this. In fact, while deep learning models and clinicians may seem very different at first, their underlying prediction process is similar, as they both acquire experience through data. However, clinicians currently have an advantage; their decision making is not only based on medical images. In addition to their own knowledge and experience, information on the patient can also provide important guidance when

© Springer Nature Switzerland AG 2021
A. Feragen et al. (Eds.): IPMI 2021, LNCS 12729, pp. 334–345, 2021.
https://doi.org/10.1007/978-3-030-78191-0_26

making a diagnosis. Thus, there is an opportunity for deep learning methods to be even further improved if they could also incorporate this information.

EHRs contain rich information about the patients, which could be explored for disease classification based on X-ray scans. Besides important patient information, e.g., disease history, sex and reason for hospital admission, they record observations and findings that are usually provided by clinicians from reading the scans in combination with their professional knowledge and clinical experiences. It has been demonstrated that (longitudinal) EHR data can be used as a diagnosis predictor [2,7,28,35]. Thus it would be greatly helpful to if we can leverage EHRs to support clinicians by improving the performance of various automated medical imaging tasks.

However, it is a challenging problem to incorporate information from EHRs into medical image analysis due to several reasons. Firstly, representing EHR in models is complicated by the large variety in content, structure, language, noise, random errors, and sparseness [2,28]. Secondly, there are privacy concerns in using medical images associated with (longitudinal) EHR data, as their combined use limits the extent of possible anonymization [33]. However the major limiting factor is that combining visual and textual modalities adds complexity, because it requires methods that span both vision and language processing fields.

From a clinical point of view, the usage of EHR data available during testing or model deployment should be approached with caution, because EHR data is not always available coupled to the patient at the time of diagnosis. It is important to keep in mind that tasks performed on medical data are only relevant in a clinical setting. Requiring EHR data as input for a model would prevent this model from being completely automated, because the EHR still needs to be created by a clinician. However, this is not a problem during training when access to large databases of medical images and EHRs is possible. Therefore, to effectively utilize EHRs in combination with medical images, they should be optimally utilized during training time, with minimum reliance on them during testing. In a clinical setting, this would make most sense, because we would like the model to assist clinicians rather than relying on them.

It is particularly appealing to leverage information in EHRs for disease classification of X-ray scans. This is because chest X-rays are one of the most common scans in clinical routines due to their ease of acquiring and low cost, offering an effective and efficient tool for screening various diseases. A consequence of this is a large quantity of scans, the bulk of which will fall under a frequent set of diagnoses. Both the potential usefulness of EHRs and importance of automated diagnosis in clinical setting make X-rays an excellent application domain.

In this work, we tackle the challenging scenario where the EHRs are only available in the learning stage but not at inference time. We propose variational knowledge distillation, a new probabilistic inference framework to leverage knowledge in EHRs for medical image classification. We make three-fold contributions: i) We propose the first probabilistic inference framework for joint learning from EHRs and medical images, which enables us to explore multimodal data during training and perform disease classification relying only on images during testing. ii) We introduce variational knowledge distillation, which enables the model to extract visual features relevant to disease by transferring useful information from EHRs to images. *iii*) We demonstrate the effectiveness of the proposed method in X-ray disease classification and achieve consistently better performance than counterpart methods.

2   Related Work

In recent years there has been an increase in methods exploring automated diagnosis from radiology images. This can be linked to the increasing availability of public chest X-ray datasets, such as ChestX-ray14 [31], CheXpert [11], OpenI [20] and MIMIC-CXR [12], where the latter two also contain associated EHR.

The most notable image-based approach for chest X-ray classification is ChexNet [22]. Rajpurkar *et al.* showed that diagnosis using a deep architecture based on DensetNet-121 [9] can exceed radiologist performance. Wang *et al.* [31] also reached high performance using pre-trained convolutional neural network (CNN). Recently, Chen *et al.* [3] introduced a graph based model which exceeds the performance of the prior methods in this classification task.

Current multi-modal approaches for chest X-ray classification rely on EHR inputs during both training and testing. A common denominator in these methods is that image and EHR features are joined through an attention mechanism. Nunes *et al.* [19] proposed a method which requires a chest X-ray and its associated EHR to generate a diagnosis. Wang *et al.* [32] require a similar input but use an auxiliary EHR generation task in an end-to-end CNN-recurrent neural network (RNN) architecture to improve classification. Related to this, Xue *et al.* [36] generate EHRs to enhanced image-based classification. No EHR input is required or used during both training and testing. Where our approach uses both image and EHR during training, but only images during testing, their approach only requires images in both training and testing.

Recent advances in the general non-medical vision-language field have been accelerated by the emergence of contextual Transformer [29] based language models such as BERT [5]. Moreover in visual-question-answering (VQA), models such as LXMERT [27], VL-BERT [26], VILBERT [18] and Uniter [4] vastly outperform traditional state-of-the-art models. The Transformer architecture has proven to be highly effective in multi-modal settings. Recently, Li *et al.* [16] showed how these vision-language models can be applied to the medical domain. Specifically, they showed that Transformer-based vision-language models result in high performance on medical datasets containing chest X-ray images and paired EHRs, requiring both modalities as input during training and testing.

3   Methodology

We formulate the disease classification from medical images as a conditional variational inference problem. We introduce a conditional latent variable model that infers the latent representations of X-Ray images. The knowledge is transferred from the EHR to X-rays scans by making the variational posterior conditioned on the associated EHR text. The model learns the ability to extract visual features that are relevant to the disease guided by the associated EHR in the learning stage. At inference time it is able to make accurate predictions relying solely on X-ray scans. We start with preliminaries on variational auto-encoders [15,23], based on which we derive our probabilistic modeling of disease classification on X-rays and variational knowledge distillation from EHRs.

3.1   Preliminaries

The variational auto-encoder (VAE) [15,23] is a powerful generative model that combines graphical models and deep learning. Given an input $\mathbf{x}$ from a data distribution $p(\mathbf{x})$, we aim to find its representation $\mathbf{z}$ in a latent space, from which we can generate new images that are similar to $\mathbf{x}$. The objective of the VAE is to maximize what is called the evidence lower bound (ELBO), as follows:

$$\mathcal{L}_{\text{VAE}} = \mathbb{E}[\log p(\mathbf{x}|\mathbf{z})] - D_{\text{KL}}[q(\mathbf{z}|\mathbf{x})||p(\mathbf{z})], \tag{1}$$

where $q(\mathbf{z}|\mathbf{x})$ is the variational posterior for approximating the exact posterior $p(\mathbf{z}|\mathbf{x})$ and $p(\mathbf{z})$ is the prior distribution over $\mathbf{z}$, which is usually set to an isotropic Gaussian distribution $\mathcal{N}(0, I)$. The VAE offers an effective probabilistic inference framework to learn latent representations in a unsupervised way, which we explore for the supervised, disease classification task by introducing conditioning into the probabilistic framework.

3.2   Disease Classification by Conditional Variational Inference

Since disease classification based on X-rays is a supervised learning problem, we resort to conditional variational inference, which has shown great effectiveness in structure prediction tasks [25]. Given an input X-ray image $\mathbf{x}_I$ associated with its class label $\mathbf{y}$, we introduce the latent variable $\mathbf{z}_I$ as the representation of $\mathbf{x}_I$. From a probabilistic perspective, predicting of the class label $\mathbf{y}$ amounts to maximizing the following conditional log-likelihood:

$$\log p(\mathbf{y}|\mathbf{x}_I) = \log \int p(\mathbf{y}|\mathbf{x}_I, \mathbf{z}_I) p(\mathbf{z}_I|\mathbf{x}_I) d\mathbf{z}_I, \tag{2}$$

where $p(\mathbf{z}_I|\mathbf{x}_I)$ is the conditional prior over the latent representation $\mathbf{z}_I$ (See Fig. 1). To find the posterior $p(\mathbf{z}_I|\mathbf{x}_I, \mathbf{y})$ over $\mathbf{z}_I$, we usually resort to a variational distribution $q(\mathbf{z}_I)$ by minimizing the Kullback-Leibler (KL) divergence

$$D_{\text{KL}}[q(\mathbf{z}_I)||p(\mathbf{z}_I|\mathbf{x}_I, \mathbf{y})]. \tag{3}$$

By applying Bayes' rule, we obtain

$$\mathcal{L}_{\text{CVI}} = \mathbb{E}[\log p(\mathbf{y}|\mathbf{x}_I, \mathbf{z}_I)] - D_{\text{KL}}[q(\mathbf{z}_I)||p(\mathbf{z}_I|\mathbf{x}_I)], \tag{4}$$

which is the ELBO of the conditionally predictive log-likelihood in Eq. (2) and can be directly maximized to learn the model parameters. Note that maximizing the ELBO is equivalent to minimizing the KL divergence in Eq. (3). Actually, we are free to design the variational posterior $q(\mathbf{z})$. In this work, we incorporate the information from EHRs into the inference of latent representation by making the variational posterior dependent on the associated EHRs during learning.

3.3   Knowledge Distillation from EHRs

We introduce a new variational posterior that depends on the corresponding EHR text $\mathbf{x}_T$, which enables us to distill knowledge from EHRs to the representations of images in the latent space. To be more specific, we design the variational posterior as $q(\mathbf{z}_T|\mathbf{x}_T)$, shown in Fig. 1, which gives rise to a new ELBO, as follows:

$$\mathcal{L}_{\text{VKD}} = \mathbb{E}\big[\log p(\mathbf{y}|\mathbf{x}_I, \mathbf{z}_I)\big] - D_{\text{KL}}\big[q(\mathbf{z}_T|\mathbf{x}_T)||p(\mathbf{z}_I|\mathbf{x}_I)\big]. \tag{5}$$

By maximizing the above ELBO, the distributional distance in terms of KL divergence between the latent representations of the X-ray image and its associated EHR text is minimized. This encourages the rich knowledge contained in the EHR to be transferred to the image representations.

In order to extract from the EHR the most relevant information for accurate disease classification, the latent representation $\mathbf{z}_T$ should also be maximally predictive of the disease. This can be achieved by maximizing the mutual information $I(Z_T, Y)$ between Z_T and Y, which is intractable. Instead, we can maximize its variational lower bound inspired by [1], as follows:

$$I(Z_T, Y) \geq \int p(\mathbf{x}_T)p(\mathbf{y}|\mathbf{x}_T)p(\mathbf{z}_T|\mathbf{x}_T)\log q(\mathbf{y}|\mathbf{z}_T)d\mathbf{x}_T d\mathbf{y} d\mathbf{z}_T = \mathcal{L}_{\text{MI}}, \tag{6}$$

where $q(\mathbf{y}|\mathbf{z}_T)$ is the variational approximation of the true predictive distribution $p(\mathbf{y}|\mathbf{z}_T)$. Likewise, we can calculate the empirical approximation of the term on the right hand side in Eq. (6) by following [1]:

$$\mathcal{L}_{\text{MI}} \approx \frac{1}{N}\sum_{n=1}^{N}\int p(\mathbf{z}_T|\mathbf{x}_T^n)\log q(\mathbf{y}^n|\mathbf{z}_T)d\mathbf{z}_T, \tag{7}$$

where n is the number of the X-ray image and EHR text pairs. In practice, $\mathcal{L}_{\text{MI}}$ is implemented as a cross entropy loss.

3.4   Empirical Objective Function

By combining Eqs. (5) and (6), we obtain the following empirical objective function for optimization:

$$\tilde{\mathcal{L}}_{\text{VKD}} = -\frac{1}{N}\sum_{n=1}^{N}\Big[\frac{1}{M}\sum_{m=1}^{M}\log p(\mathbf{y}^n|\mathbf{x}_I, \mathbf{z}_I^{(m)}) - \frac{1}{L}\sum_{\ell=1}^{L}\log q(\mathbf{y}^n|\mathbf{z}_T^{(\ell)})$$
$$+ D_{\text{KL}}\big[q(\mathbf{z}_T|\mathbf{x}_T^n)||p(\mathbf{z}_I|\mathbf{x}_I^n)\big]\Big], \tag{8}$$

where $\mathbf{z}_I^{(m)} \sim p(\mathbf{z}_I|\mathbf{x}_I)$, $\mathbf{z}_T^{(\ell)} \sim q(\mathbf{z}_T|\mathbf{x}_T)$, and L and M are the number of Monte Carlo samples. Note that we take the variational posterior $q(\mathbf{z}_T|\mathbf{x}_T)$ in Eq. (5) as the posterior $p(\mathbf{z}_T|\mathbf{x}_T)$ in Eq. (7). The resultant objective combines the strengths

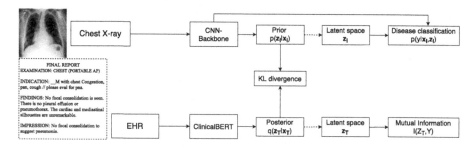

Fig. 1. Illustration of the proposed variational knowledge distillation from EHR texts to X-ray images.

of the conditional variational auto-encoder and the variational information bottleneck, resulting in a new variational objective for knowledge distribution from EHR texts to X-rays for disease classification. Optimization with $\tilde{\mathcal{L}}_{\mathrm{VKD}}$ is a process through which the model learns to read X-ray scans like a radiologist to find the relevant visual features to diseases.

3.5 Implementation with Neural Networks

We implement the optimization objective with deep neural networks (see Fig. 1) by adopting the amortization technique [15]. Both the variational posterior $q(\mathbf{z}_T|\mathbf{x}_T)$ and the prior $p(\mathbf{z}_I|\mathbf{x}_I)$ are parameterized as diagonal Gaussian distributions. To enable back propagation, we adopt the reparameterization trick [15] for sampling $\mathbf{z}$: $\mathbf{z}^{(\ell)} = f(\mathbf{x}, \epsilon^{(\ell)})$ with $\epsilon^{(\ell)} \sim \mathcal{N}(0, I)$, where $f(\cdot)$ is a deterministic differentiable function.

In prior $p(\mathbf{z}_I|\mathbf{x}_I)$, $\mathbf{x}_I$ is taken as the representation of the X-ray image from a CNN. The inference network of the distribution parameters is implemented by a multi-layer perceptron (MLP). $\mathbf{x}_T$ in the variational posterior $q(\mathbf{z}_T|\mathbf{x}_T)$ is generated through the use of deep contextualized word embeddings. The successful BERT [5] language model based on the Transformer [29] is used. More specifically, we use a pre-trained version of this model fine-tuned on a database with over two million EHRs [13]: ClinicalBERT [10]. To avoid computationally costly fine-tuning, the weights of ClinicalBERT are frozen and a brief fine-tuning step is applied by passing the embeddings through a single trainable Transformer encoder block ($\sim 1/12$ the size of ClinicalBERT). Similar to $p(\mathbf{z}_I|\mathbf{x}_I)$, the posterior $q(\mathbf{z}_T|\mathbf{x}_T)$ is also generated by an MLP.

Algorithm 1: Learning

Input: Training data: $(\mathbf{x}_I^n, \mathbf{x}_T^n, \mathbf{y}^n)$, $n = 1, ..., N$,
Output: Latent space distributions $p(\mathbf{z}_I|\mathbf{x})$, $q(\mathbf{z}_T|\mathbf{x}_T)$,

1 **while** *not converged:* **do**
2   Draw Monte Carlo samples $\mathbf{z}_I^{(m)}$ and $\mathbf{z}_T^{(\ell)}$ from $p(\mathbf{z}_I|\mathbf{x}_I^n)$ and $q(\mathbf{z}_T|\mathbf{x}_T^n)$, respectively
3   Estimate the prediction distributions: $p(\mathbf{y}|\mathbf{x}_I^n, \mathbf{z}_I^{(m)})$ and $q(\mathbf{y}|\mathbf{z}_T^{(\ell)})$
4   Compute $\tilde{\mathcal{L}}_{\mathrm{VKD}}$ in Eq. (8)
5   Update models weights via gradient descent on $\tilde{\mathcal{L}}_{\mathrm{VKD}}$

Algorithm 2: Inference

Input: Testing data with only the X-Ray images $\mathbf{x}_I^j$.
Output: Prediction class label $\mathbf{y}$
1 Draw Monte Carlo samples $\mathbf{z}_I^{(\ell)}$ from the conditional prior $p(\mathbf{z}_I|\mathbf{x}_I^j)$
2 Estimate the prediction distribution $p(\mathbf{y}|\mathbf{x}_I^j, \mathbf{z}_I^{(\ell)})$

Algorithm 1 demonstrates the learning process, when the model requires a multi-modal input: an image and the associated EHR. Once trained, the model performs disease classification based on new X-ray scans without the need of an EHR input at inference time, as can be seen in Algorithm 2.

4 Experiments

4.1 Datasets

Three public chest X-ray datasets are used: 1) **MIMIC-CXR** [12] is the largest publicly available dataset containing full-text structured EHR and accompanying annotated chest X-rays [12]. The dataset contains $377,110$ chest x-rays associated with $227,827$ anonymized EHRs. Each EHR is associated with (multiple) frontal and/or saggital X-ray views, each labelled according to specific classes (e.g. atelectasis, pneumothorax and pneumonia). 2) **OpenI**[20] is a similar public dataset with $7,470$ chest X-rays associated with $3,955$ anonymized EHRs. 3) **Chest X-ray14** [31] contains $112,120$ chest X-rays, without associated EHRs. Paired EHRs exist for this dataset but they are not publicly available. Therefore, we use this dataset for testing but not for training.

Each image-EHR pair in these datasets is labelled according to a rule-based labelling procedure based on the EHR for fourteen distinct classes. MIMIC-CXR is labelled according to a different labeller [11] than Chest X-ray14 [31]. These different labelling procedures have an overlap in seven out of fourteen label classes. In this paper the classification labels in MIMIC-CXR are followed.

4.2 Experimental Settings

X-ray images are normalized and standardized to grayscale with dimensions of 224×224, to align them with the DenseNet-121 CNN backbone, pre-trained on ImageNet [8]. Pre-trained CNN backbones have been proven effective in similar medical applications [21], and DenseNet-121 specifically has been proven ideal for X-ray images [22,36]. Each EHR is tokenized according to WordPiece [34] tokenization, which has a library of around 30000 tokens. Each tokenized EHR is preceded by a $[CLS]$ classification token and ended with a $[SEP]$ token, following the methodology used in [5,10]. The maximum number of tokens is set to 256. Shorter EHRs are zero padded to obtain text embeddings of the same sizes. The size of latent spaces $\mathbf{z}_I$ and $\mathbf{z}_T$ is set to an empirically determined value of 512. Two-layer MLPs with layer sizes $\{512, 512\}$ are used for the amortized inference of the prior and variational posterior. A dropout rate of 0.5 is applied to all layers, except the CNN backbone and the final layer in the generation of latent space **z**, to which no dropout is applied. These architectures are trained on an NVIDIA RTX 2080ti GPU, using Adam [14] optimization for a duration defined by early stopping with a tolerance of 1%.

A common problem in optimizing variational architectures is KL vanishing. To prevent this, cyclical KL annealing [6] is applied according to Eq. 9, where the KL loss is multiplied with β_t. $g(\tau)$ is a monotonically increasing function, T is the number of batch iterations, t the current iteration, R ($= 0.5$) determines the annealing grade and C ($= 4$) is the number of annealing cycles per epoch:

$$\beta_t = \begin{Bmatrix} g(\tau), & \tau \leq R \\ 1, & \tau > R \end{Bmatrix}, \quad \text{where} \quad \tau = \frac{\mod(t-1, [T/C])}{T/C} \tag{9}$$

4.3 Results

State-of-the-Art Comparison. The performance of our architecture in comparison with earlier works on image-based chest X-ray classification [19,22,31,32,36] is shown in Table 1. We report the results of the proposed method with and without variational knowledge distillation (i.e., no EHR). Results of our proposed method on the Chest X-ray14 dataset are obtained by fine-tuning a model pre-trained on MIMIC-CXR. Note that the fine-tuning step is necessary to alleviate domain shift between different datasets. Results on the OpenI and MIMIC-CXR datasets are obtained without any specific pre-training on radiology images from other datasets.

Results on the OpenI and MIMIC-CXR datasets show the performance gain due to knowledge distillation, where the performance improvement is consistent on the latter vastly larger dataset. It is worth mentioning that the high performance on Chest X-ray14 further indicates that the proposed variational

Table 1. Comparison of AUC values per class for NIH chest X-ray14 (partial), OpenI and MIMIC-CXR datasets.

	Chest X-ray14					Open-I				MIMIC-CXR	
	[22]	[36]	[31]	[3]	Ours	[31]	[19]	Ours (no EHR)	Ours	Ours (no EHR)	Ours
No Finding	–	–	–	–	–	–	–	0.711	**0.720**	0.825	**0.827**
Enlarged cardiomediastinum	–	–	–	–	–	–	–	–	–	0.589	**0.838**
Cardiomegaly	0.889	0.892	0.810	0.893	**0.899**	0.803	–	0.837	**0.851**	0.739	**0.758**
Lung opacity	–	–	–	–	–	–	–	0.720	**0.698**	0.698	**0.695**
Lung lesion	–	–	–	–	–	–	–	0.539	**0.710**	0.663	**0.690**
Edema	0.888	**0.898**	0.805	0.850	**0.893**	0.799	–	0.897	**0.923**	0.832	**0.861**
Consolidation	0.790	0.813	0.703	0.751	**0.819**	0.790	–	**0.859**	0.652	0.731	**0.783**
Pneumonia	0.768	0.767	0.658	0.739	**0.781**	0.642	–	0.610	**0.619**	0.618	**0.627**
Atelectasis	0.809	0.822	0.700	0.786	**0.825**	0.702	–	0.771	**0.797**	0.725	**0.749**
Pneumothorax	0.889	0.870	0.799	0.876	**0.903**	0.631	–	**0.784**	0.637	0.721	**0.758**
Pleural effusion	0.864	**0.881**	0.759	0.832	0.871	0.890	–	**0.904**	0.858	0.864	**0.892**
Pleural other	–	–	–	–	–	–	–	0.637	**0.876**	0.731	**0.776**
Fracture	–	–	–	–	–	–	–	0.486	**0.532**	0.557	**0.698**
Support devices	–	–	–	–	–	–	–	0.553	**0.581**	0.854	**0.897**
Average	–	0.842	0.722	0.826	**0.872**	0.719	0.621	0.837	**0.885**	0.807	**0.839**

Table 2. AUC scores for varying architecture compositions.

	OpenI	MIMIC-CXR
Full architecture	**0.885**	**0.839**
w/o $\mathcal{L}_{MI}$ (Eq. 7)	0.873	0.832
w/o VKD (no EHR)	0.837	0.807

Table 3. AUC scores for varying size of latent space **z**.

Size of **z**	OpenI	MIMIC-CXR
64	0.814	0.775
128	0.870	0.829
512 - default	0.885	0.839
1024	**0.891**	**0.842**

knowledge distillation is transferable between datasets, even when the new target dataset does not contain EHRs. Note that our approach outperforms all previous approaches for chest X-ray classification.

Ablation Studies. To verify the effectiveness of all elements in the proposed architecture two ablation studies are conducted. In the first ablation study, $\mathcal{L}_{MI}$ (Eq. (7)) is left out of the objective function, thus there is no specific requirement for z_T. Moreover, only the classification objective from the image branch is taken into account, removing the KL term, which results in a regular image-based classifier. This first ablation study (Table 2) reveals that the major contributing factor to the performance of our method shows to be variational knowledge distillation, whereas the addition of the objective function in the EHR branch ($\mathcal{L}_{MI}$) has a relatively smaller, yet considerable effect. Secondly, we test the effect of the size of latent space **z** on the performance (Table 3). It appears that increasing the size of **z** can improve model performance, while this effect tends to be smaller with larger values of **z**. The current value of **z** was chosen to be 512, which maximizes performance against computational cost.

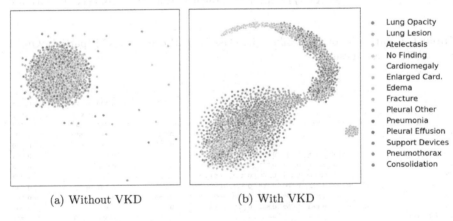

(a) Without VKD	(b) With VKD	

- Lung Opacity
- Lung Lesion
- Atelectasis
- No Finding
- Cardiomegaly
- Enlarged Card.
- Edema
- Fracture
- Pleural Other
- Pneumonia
- Pleural Effusion
- Support Devices
- Pneumothorax
- Consolidation

Fig. 2. t-SNE embeddings of latent space z_I with and without VKD, overlayed with class labels, showing that VKD causes structuring of z_I.

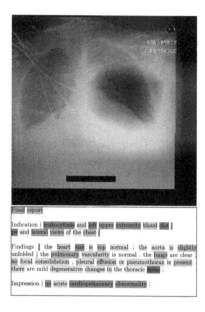 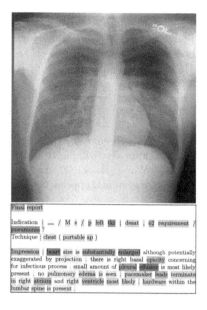

Fig. 3. Importance of words and image regions for two image-EHR pairs. WordPiece tokens of the EHRs are averaged if needed to form full words. Darker red means higher importance.

Visualizations. The difference between $\mathbf{z}_I$ with and without variational knowledge distillation is shown in Fig. 2. With variational knowledge distillation a structurenedness in classes within $\mathbf{z}_I$ can be observed, whereas without it there seems to be more reliance on image tokens directly passed to the classification head, consequently resulting in a less structured $\mathbf{z}_I$. In Fig. 3 weight visualizations for the final CNN-layer with Grad-cam [24] and the final Transformer layer with BertViz [30] are shown for images and EHRs respectively. As can clearly be seen the visual focus is correctly on the lung region. Weights of the EHR tokens show a clear emphasis on important nouns and adjectives in the EHR. Verbs and prepositions show lower weights. These visualizations provide an intuitive illustration that our model is able to extract visual features relevant to the disease due to the proposed variational knowledge distillation.

5 Conclusion

In this paper, we propose a new probabilistic inference framework of multi-modal learning for disease classification based on X-rays by leveraging EHRs. We developed a latent variable model to learn latent representations of X-ray images. We introduce variational knowledge distillation that enables the model to acquire the ability to extract visual features relevant to the disease. This strategy enables us to incorporate the knowledge in EHRs during training, without relying on them in the testing stage. We conduct experiments on the current largest and most widely used chest X-ray - EHR datasets: MIMIC-CXR and OpenI, showing the benefit of variational knowledge distillation. Moreover we demonstrate our method performs well on Chest X-ray14 with only images by pre-training on MIMIC-CXR, which indicates its strong transfer ability across datasets.

References

1. Alemi, A.A., Fischer, I., Dillon, J.V., Murphy, K.: Deep variational information bottleneck. arXiv:1612.00410 (2016)
2. Cai, Q., Wang, H., Li, Z., Liu, X.: A survey on multimodal data-driven smart healthcare systems: approaches and applications. IEEE Access **7**, 133583–133599 (2019)
3. Chen, B., Li, J., Lu, G., Yu, H., Zhang, D.: Label co-occurrence learning with graph convolutional networks for multi-label chest x-ray image classification. IEEE J. Biomed. Health Inform. **24**, 2292–2302 (2020)
4. Chen, Y.C., et al.: UNITER: learning universal image-text representations. arXiv:1909.11740 (2019)
5. Devlin, J., Chang, M.W., Lee, K., Toutanova, K.: BERT: pre-training of deep bidirectional transformers for language understanding. arXiv:1810.04805 (2018)
6. Fu, H., Li, C., Liu, X., Gao, J., Celikyilmaz, A., Carin, L.: Cyclical annealing schedule: a simple approach to mitigating kl vanishing. arXiv:1903.10145 (2019)
7. Harerimana, G., Kim, J.W., Yoo, H., Jang, B.: Deep learning for electronic health records analytics. IEEE Access **7**, 101245–101259 (2019)
8. He, K., Zhang, X., Ren, S., Sun, J.: Deep residual learning for image recognition. In: IEEE CVPR, June 2016
9. Huang, G., Liu, Z., Van Der Maaten, L., Weinberger, K.Q.: Densely connected convolutional networks. In: Proceedings of the IEEE CVPR, pp. 4700–4708 (2017)
10. Huang, K., Altosaar, J., Ranganath, R.: ClinicalBERT: modeling clinical notes and predicting hospital readmission. arXiv:1904.05342 (2019)
11. Irvin, J., et al.: CheXpert: a large chest radiograph dataset with uncertainty labels and expert comparison. In: Proceedings of the AAAI Conference on Artificial Intelligence, vol. 33, pp. 590–597 (2019)
12. Johnson, A.E., et al.: MIMIC-CXR: a large publicly available database of labeled chest radiographs. arXiv:1901.07042 (2019)
13. Johnson, A.E., et al.: MIMIC-III, a freely accessible critical care database. Sci. Data **3**, 160035 (2016)
14. Kingma, D.P., Ba, J.: Adam: A method for stochastic optimization. arXiv:1412.6980 (2014)
15. Kingma, D.P., Welling, M.: Auto-encoding variational Bayes. In: International conference on learning representations (2014)
16. Li, Y., Wang, H., Luo, Y.: A comparison of pre-trained vision-and-language models for multimodal representation learning across medical images and reports. arXiv:2009.01523 (2020)
17. Liu, X., et al.: A comparison of deep learning performance against health-care professionals in detecting diseases from medical imaging: a systematic review and meta-analysis. Lancet Digital Health **1**(6), e271–e297 (2019)
18. Lu, J., Batra, D., Parikh, D., Lee, S.: ViLBERT: pretraining task-agnostic visiolinguistic representations for vision-and-language tasks. In: Advances in Neural Information Processing Systems, pp. 13–23 (2019)

19. Nunes, N., Martins, B., André da Silva, N., Leite, F., J. Silva, M.: A multi-modal deep learning method for classifying chest radiology exams. In: Moura Oliveira, P., Novais, P., Reis, L.P. (eds.) EPIA 2019. LNCS (LNAI), vol. 11804, pp. 323–335. Springer, Cham (2019). https://doi.org/10.1007/978-3-030-30241-2_28
20. OpenI: Indiana university - chest X-rays (PNG images) https://openi.nlm.nih.gov/faq.php
21. Raghu, M., Zhang, C., Kleinberg, J., Bengio, S.: Transfusion: understanding transfer learning for medical imaging. In: Advances in Neural Information Processing Systems, vol. 32. Curran Associates, Inc. (2019)
22. Rajpurkar, P., et al.: CheXNet: radiologist-level pneumonia detection on chest X-rays with deep learning. arXiv:1711.05225 (2017)
23. Rezende, D.J., Mohamed, S., Wierstra, D.: Stochastic backpropagation and approximate inference in deep generative models. arXiv:1401.4082 (2014)
24. Selvaraju, R.R., Cogswell, M., Das, A., Vedantam, R., Parikh, D., Batra, D.: Grad-CAM: visual explanations from deep networks via gradient-based localization. In: Proceedings of the IEEE ICCV, pp. 618–626 (2017)
25. Sohn, K., Lee, H., Yan, X.: Learning structured output representation using deep conditional generative models. In: Advances in Neural Information Processing Systems, pp. 3483–3491 (2015)
26. Su, W., et al.: VL-BERT: pre-training of generic visual-linguistic representations. arXiv:1908.08530 (2019)
27. Tan, H., Bansal, M.: LXMERT: learning cross-modality encoder representations from transformers. arXiv:1908.07490 (2019)
28. Tobore, I., et al.: Deep learning intervention for health care challenges: some biomedical domain considerations (2019)
29. Vaswani, A., et al.: Attention is all you need. In: Advances in Neural Information Processing Systems, pp. 5998–6008 (2017)
30. Vig, J.: A multiscale visualization of attention in the transformer model. arXiv:1906.05714 (2019)
31. Wang, X., Peng, Y., Lu, L., Lu, Z., Bagheri, M., Summers, R.M.: ChestX-ray8: hospital-scale chest x-ray database and benchmarks on weakly-supervised classification and localization of common thorax diseases. In: Proceedings of the IEEE CVPR, pp. 2097–2106 (2017)
32. Wang, X., Peng, Y., Lu, L., Lu, Z., Summers, R.M.: TieNet: text-image embedding network for common thorax disease classification and reporting in chest X-rays. In: Proceedings of the IEEE CVPR, pp. 9049–9058 (2018)
33. Weiskopf, N.G., Hripcsak, G., Swaminathan, S., Weng, C.: Defining and measuring completeness of electronic health records for secondary use. J. Biomed. Inform. 46(5), 830–836 (2013)
34. Wu, Y., et al.: Google's neural machine translation system: bridging the gap between human and machine translation. arXiv:1609.08144 (2016)
35. Xiao, C., Choi, E., Sun, J.: Opportunities and challenges in developing deep learning models using electronic health records data: a systematic review. J. Am. Med. Inform. Assoc. 25(10), 1419–1428 (2018)
36. Xue, Y., Huang, X.: Improved disease classification in chest X-Rays with transferred features from report generation. In: Chung, A.C.S., Gee, J.C., Yushkevich, P.A., Bao, S. (eds.) IPMI 2019. LNCS, vol. 11492, pp. 125–138. Springer, Cham (2019). https://doi.org/10.1007/978-3-030-20351-1_10

Information-Based Disentangled Representation Learning for Unsupervised MR Harmonization

Lianrui Zuo[1,2]([✉]) [iD], Blake E. Dewey[1] [iD], Aaron Carass[1] [iD], Yihao Liu[1] [iD], Yufan He[1] [iD], Peter A. Calabresi[3] [iD], and Jerry L. Prince[1] [iD]

[1] Department of Electrical and Computer Engineering, Johns Hopkins University, Baltimore, MD 21218, USA
{lr_zuo,blake.dewey,aaron_carass,yliu236,heyufan,prince}@jhu.edu
[2] Laboratory of Behavioral Neuroscience, National Institute on Aging, National Institute of Health, Baltimore, MD 20892, USA
[3] Department of Neurology, Johns Hopkins School of Medicine, Baltimore, MD 21287, USA
pcalabr1@jhmi.edu

Abstract. Accuracy and consistency are two key factors in computer-assisted magnetic resonance (MR) image analysis. However, contrast variation from site to site caused by lack of standardization in MR acquisition impedes consistent measurements. In recent years, image harmonization approaches have been proposed to compensate for contrast variation in MR images. Current harmonization approaches either require cross-site traveling subjects for supervised training or heavily rely on site-specific harmonization models to encourage harmonization accuracy. These requirements potentially limit the application of current harmonization methods in large-scale multi-site studies. In this work, we propose an unsupervised MR harmonization framework, CALAMITI (Contrast Anatomy Learning and Analysis for MR Intensity Translation and Integration), based on information bottleneck theory. CALAMITI learns a disentangled latent space using a unified structure for multi-site harmonization without the need for traveling subjects. Our model is also able to adapt itself to harmonize MR images from a new site with fine tuning solely on images from the new site. Both qualitative and quantitative results show that the proposed method achieves superior performance compared with other unsupervised harmonization approaches.

Keywords: Harmonization · Unsupervised · Image to image translation · Disentangle · Synthesis

1 Introduction

Magnetic resonance (MR) imaging is a commonly used non-invasive imaging modality due to its flexibility and good tissue contrast. For the purposes of

A. Feragen et al. (Eds.): IPMI 2021, LNCS 12729, pp. 346–359, 2021.
https://doi.org/10.1007/978-3-030-78191-0_27

describing MR imaging analytically, we can think of an MR image as a function (i.e., imaging equation) of the anatomy being imaged and the associated acquisition parameters [3]. By changing the acquisition parameters or underlying imaging equations, MR images with different contrasts can be generated. To take advantage of this flexibility, MR images of the same anatomy with different contrasts are often acquired in a single session. For example, T_1-weighted (T_1-w) images are typically used to achieve balanced contrast between T_2-weighted (T_2-w) images [3]. However, a consequence of this flexibility is that there is no standardization when it comes to MR contrasts. For example, both magnetization-prepared rapid gradient echo (MPRAGE) and spoiled gradient echo (SPGR) are commonly used T_1-w images with very different visual appearances. This lack of standardization makes machine learning (ML) models trained on MPRAGE images often fail on SPGR images and underperform on MPRAGE images acquired by different scanners or with slightly different parameters [19]. Scanner software and calibration differences can also contribute to this effect.

The issue of contrast variation is commonly seen in multi-site studies, where a trained model degrades in performance when tested on data from another site (i.e., the *domain shift* problem). This is because ML based methods assume the training and testing are conducted on data drawn from the same distribution (domain). This is not the case for MR images acquired from different sites, scanners, or with differing imaging parameters. For example, T_1-w images acquired from two scanners with different configurations should obviously be treated as two domains. However, T_1-w and T_2-w images acquired from the same scanner should also be considered as coming from two domains.

MR image harmonization [6] alleviates domain shift by treating the problem as an *image-to-image translation* (IIT) (or synthesis) task, where the goal is to translate image contrasts between domains (e.g., T_1-w images acquired from different scanners). MR harmonization can be separated into two categories: supervised and unsupervised. In the supervised setting, MR images of the same anatomy across multiple sites are available; these are known as *traveling subjects* or *inter*-site paired data. These images are used to train intensity transformations between sites. However, traveling subjects are impractical in large-scale multi-site harmonization tasks. Unsupervised harmonization methods do not require inter-site paired data. Instead, these methods often rely on domain-specific models (e.g., intensity transformations and discriminators). We outline recent related work in IIT and unsupervised domain adaptation (UDA), below.

IIT learns a transformation of images between different domains, e.g., MR to CT [24,26] or T_1-w to T_2-w [28]. In both supervised and unsupervised IIT, the goal is to approximate the joint distribution drawn from the (two) domains. Supervised IIT methods use pixel-to-pixel reconstruction error during model training. Recent unsupervised IIT work has explored learning disentangled representations [10,14,25], the idea being to tease apart the domain-invariant and domain-specific information in the representation. As an unsupervised IIT method, unsupervised harmonization faces four challenges. First, the

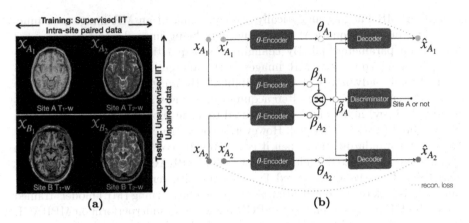

Fig. 1. (a) Given T_1-w and T_2-w images from Sites A and B, our method solves intra-site supervised IIT (T_1–T_2 synthesis) and inter-site unsupervised IIT (harmonization), where an alphabetical index indicates site and a numerical index indicate MR contrast. (b) The proposed method consists of a *single* θ-encoder, a β-encoder, a decoder, and a β-discriminator that work on all domains. x and x' share the same contrast but have different anatomy. The same networks work on all sites.

lack of inter-site paired data along with the coupling theory [15] tells us there are infinitely many possible joint distributions given the two marginal distributions. Therefore, to learn a meaningful harmonization model (joint distribution), further constraints are required. Cycle-consistency is commonly assumed in unsupervised IIT [10,16,27]. However, there is no theory that supports the validity of this assumption. Second, the lack of inter-site paired data means that pixel-to-pixel regularization cannot be easily achieved. Domain-specific discriminators are commonly used in many unsupervised IIT methods [10,16,27]. For harmonization, performance will heavily rely on the discriminators' "judgement" during training, and geometry shift is a common drawback in unsupervised harmonization. Third, the use of site specific-models means that the size of the harmonization model grows with the number of sites. Lastly, most existing harmonization approaches are not able to work on domains not seen in the training data. When testing and training domains differ, most methods require retraining with images from all domains, which is not practical.

In general, the goal of UDA is to learn a model from a source domain with labeled data and apply it to a target domain with unlabeled data during testing [9,12,20,23]. Without special design, domain shifts between training and testing can cause a performance drop. Different from IIT, which aims at mapping image data across domains, a UDA tries to adjust the model during testing. A UDA allows the model to detect a domain and then provide self-supervision for model adjustment during testing. UDAs are especially helpful in medical imaging, where training and testing data are likely to come from different sources.

We propose an unsupervised harmonization approach, CALAMITI (contrast anatomy learning and analysis for MR intensity translation and integration), which integrates the merits of both IIT and UDA. Building upon the recent work in [7], we use the routinely acquired multi-contrast MR images *within* each site (called *intra*-site paired data) during the same imaging session. However, as we discuss in Sect. 2.2, this technique alone does not provide a globally disentangled latent space and cannot be easily generalized to data from a new site. CALAMITI is an improved, theoretically grounded, unsupervised harmonization approach based on an information bottleneck (IB) [22] that learns a global, disentangled latent space of anatomical and contrast information and can be easily adapted to a new testing site using only the new data. To our knowledge, this is the first work that overcomes the four challenges in unsupervised harmonization. **First**, by taking advantage of the intra-site paired data, the proposed method solves an unsupervised IIT problem in a supervised way, avoiding introducing any extra constraint (e.g., cycle-consistency) on the model and achieving better pixel-to-pixel regularization. **Second**, it has a unified structure for multi-site harmonization, which means that model size does not grow with the number of sites. **Third**, it provides a global latent space for all training data by encouraging a consistent description of the anatomy. **Finally**, it is able to adapt to a new site without any retraining on the original data. For all of this work, we also provide a theoretical explanation of the disentangled latent space using IB theory.

2 Method

2.1 The Disentangling Framework

Our method uses multi-contrast MR images of the same subject *within* each site (intra-site paired data) to train a cross-site harmonization model. Here, we emphasize the relationship between "site", "domain", and "MR contrast". As shown in Fig. 1(a), given T_1-w and T_2-w images from Sites A and B, there are four domains $\mathcal{X}_{A_1}$, $\mathcal{X}_{A_2}$, $\mathcal{X}_{B_1}$, and $\mathcal{X}_{B_2}$, where an alphabetical index indicates site and a numerical index represents contrast. Our goal is to learn a disentangled representation that captures anatomical and contrast information from the input images. Following the notation in [7], the anatomical representation (β) is domain-invariant and the contrast representation (θ) has some domain-specific information. Thus, combining the β from one site with the θ from another allows harmonization across sites. To learn the disentangled representation, we solve the inter-site unsupervised IIT problem based on training from intra-site supervised data.

Figure 1(b) outlines our framework, which consists of a θ-encoder, a β-encoder, a decoder, and a β-discriminator that work on all domains. Here, we outline the high-level training strategy using the proposed framework, and we highlight the role of our β-discriminator in Sect. 2.2. Each site has paired T_1-w and T_2-w images—with different imaging parameters at each site—which train a disentangled network in a supervised IIT way. For example, intra-site paired images x_{A_1} and x_{A_2} of the same subject imaged at Site A (in our case T_1-w and T_2-w images from Site A) are sent to a β-encoder to extract anatomical information. These images have the same anatomy, so the extracted anatomical representations β_{A_1} and β_{A_2} should be the same. To encourage similarity of β, we randomly shuffle between β_{A_1} and β_{A_2} before decoding as well as introduce a small l_1 loss between the two β's. To prevent contrast representation θ from capturing anatomical information, we provide the θ-encoder with an image of different anatomy (but the same contrast), x'_{A_1}. This is achieved by selecting a different slice from the same volume as x_{A_1}. The decoder takes the randomly selected anatomical representation $(\tilde{\beta}_A)$, concatenated with a θ to generate a synthetic image. The contrast of the synthetic image depends on which θ has been chosen. The *same* β-encoder, θ-encoder, decoder, and β-discriminator are used for all training sites to achieve a unified structure.

Our β-encoder and decoder both have a U-Net like architecture with four downsampling layers, while the θ-encoder is four convolutional layers followed by three fully connected layers. β is one-hot encoded with multiple channels and the same spatial extents as the input image. For gradients to backpropagate through the one-hot encoded β, we adopt and implement the trick introduced in [7,18], wherein β's are calculated using a Gumbel-softmax layer. One-hot encoding β restricts its capacity, encouraging β to capture only anatomical information.

2.2   Creating a Consistent Anatomical Space

To learn a consistent anatomical space for all sites, we introduce a β-discriminator to our framework. Because our training strategy only uses supervised IIT *within* each site—with no supervision *between* sites—the β-encoder could possibly learn a *distinct* β space for each site. In this case, the β's and θ's are disentangled within each site, and we refer to it as a locally disentangled latent space. This is not desirable in harmonization, as combining these β's and θ's across sites would not be ideal. To avoid this, we must encourage the learned β's of all sites to be from the same distribution (i.e., β's and θ's are globally disentangled). This leads us to use a one-class discriminator on β space to encourage distribution similarity. No matter which site an input β comes from, the β-discriminator learns to distinguish whether the β is from Site A or not, further pushing θ to describe the difference between sites as well as different MR contrasts.

The proposed framework solves a number of outstanding problems. First, it performs unsupervised IIT by using supervised IIT during training. This avoids geometry issues inherent in unsupervised IIT by penalizing pixel-to-pixel error during training our framework. This is more effective than introducing a cycle consistency constraint, as cycle consistency still allows a model to learn "circle–square–circle". Second, our unified harmonization structure means we have one β-encoder, one θ-encoder, one decoder, and one β-discriminator that work on all domains; Sect. 3 includes an 8-site experiment using this structure. This saves a significant number of parameters when there are many sites—e.g., the Cycle-GAN [27] requires $O(N^2)$ image translation models and N discriminators, for N sites. Third, our discriminator functions on the latent variables β instead of the harmonized images. This encourages our decoder to act like a *universal* imaging equation, generating synthetic MR images based on any β and θ within the distribution of the training data. This strategy combined with the unified structure, makes our model more robust when there are more sites involved during

Table 1. Features of recent unsupervised IIT and UDA approaches.

	Bidirection	Multiple domains	Unified structure	Disentangle	Global latent space	Domain adaptation
CycleGAN [27]	✓	–	–	–	–	–
UNIT [17]	✓	–	–	–	–	–
MUNIT [10]	✓	✓	–	✓	–	–
DCMIT [25]	✓	✓	–	✓	✓	–
SDAnet [9]	–	–	✓	–	–	✓
Dewey et al. [7]	✓	✓	✓	✓	–	–
CALAMITI	✓	✓	✓	✓	✓	✓

training. Lastly, our discriminator makes a one-class decision: whether an input β is from Site A or not. We show in Sect. 2.4, that this allows our model to adapt to a new testing site after fine tuning. Table 1 provides a summary comparison of the proposed method with other unsupervised IIT approaches.

2.3 Learning from an Information Bottleneck

By providing the θ-encoder with an image of a different anatomy (but the same contrast) as provided to the β-encoder, we create a conditional variational autoencoder (CVAE) [21] even though the condition variable β is not connected to the θ-encoder. All of these strategies help us to limit the information that can be passed through each of the β and θ channels, which we now show theoretically forms an IB given the model design.

IB theory [22] describes a constrained optimization problem with the goal of learning a compressed latent representation Z such that the mutual information (MI) between Z and the task variable Y is maximized while Z captures minimum information about the input variable X. Mathematically, this can be formulated as $Z^* = \arg\min_Z I(Z; X) - \lambda I(Z; Y)$, where $I(\cdot; \cdot)$ is the MI and λ is a hyper-parameter. IB theory is closely related to the variational autoencoders (VAEs) and disentangled representation learning (cf. [4,5]). [2] showed that IB is a more general case of the VAE objective.

Our network structure forms a CVAE. To better illustrate the IB in a general setting, we slightly modify the notation (i.e., remove site index), and highlight the CVAE structure.

Theorem 1. *It can be shown that optimizing our network structure is equivalent to solving a conditional IB problem, i.e.,*

$$\theta^* = \arg\min_\theta I(X'; \theta) - \lambda I(X; \theta|\tilde{\beta}). \tag{1}$$

The proof of Theorem 1 is similar to that in [2], despite the fact that we are solving a CVAE problem with condition $\tilde{\beta}$. The reason why the first term of Eq. 1 is free from condition $\tilde{\beta}$ is because $\tilde{\beta}$ is disentangled from θ and will be ignored in calculating θ. An intuitive understanding of Eq. 1 is that the proposed method learns a contrast representation θ that captures minimum information about the input variable X', while the (conditional) MI between θ and the target variable X is maximized. Since the shared information between variables X and X' is the contrast, we would expect θ to capture only contrast information about X' after training. Equation 1 can be re-organized as a KL divergence term and a reconstruction term (similar to the CVAE loss [21]), and directly optimized as network loss functions, i.e.,

$$\theta^* = \arg \min_{\theta} \mathcal{D}_{\mathrm{KL}} \left[p(\theta|x')||p(\theta) \right] - \lambda \mathbb{E}_{p(\theta|x')} \left[\log p(x|\theta, \tilde{\beta}) \right], \tag{2}$$

where $p(\theta)$ is a zero mean unit variance Gaussian distribution. $p(\theta|x')$ and $p(x|\theta, \tilde{\beta})$ can be modeled by a probabilistic θ-encoder and decoder, respectively. This KL divergence term encourages a bounded value for θ, which even if lightly weighted restricts its possible expression. Accordingly, our network loss functions include a reconstruction loss for supervised IIT (l_1 and perceptual loss [11]), a KL divergence term on θ, an adversarial loss between β-discriminator and β-encoder, and a similarity loss on β between contrasts[1].

2.4   Domain Adaptation

Suppose the proposed model was pretrained on Sites A and B, and the goal is to harmonize a new site, Site C, to Site A or B without a retraining that includes data from all sites. As in regular CALAMITI training, the supervised IIT is conducted on images from Site C. However, the decoder and β-discriminator weights are frozen, and only the last few layers of the β- and θ-encoders are updated. We rely on the assumption that our decoder is well-generalized in previous training to produce a variety of contrast images. Our β-discriminator guides the β-encoder to generate β's that follow the previously learned distribution of β; avoiding a Site C specific β space. Thus our β-discriminator acts as a domain shift detector on β space like other UDA methods [9,23]. Until the β-encoder generates β for Site C that is less distinguishable from previously learned β, the β-discriminator will produce a loss for mismatching β's. As the decoder weights are frozen in fine tuning, once β's from Site C match previously learned β distribution, we are able to harmonize images between new and previous sites. Thus by combining β_{C_1} with θ_{A_1}, we can harmonize anatomy imaged at Site C with the corresponding contrast from Site A. Thus Site C can be harmonized to any site included in the original training.

3   Experiments and Results

3.1   Datasets and Preprocessing

MR images, both T_1-w and T_2-w, acquired from eight different sites (scanners) were used to evaluate the proposed method. Data source, scanner details, and

---

[1] Code is available at https://iacl.ece.jhu.edu/index.php?title=CALAMITI.

Table 2. Scanner make, image sequence and parameters (TE, TR, TI if necessary), and acquisition extent. T_1-w sequence key: M - MPRAGE; ME - MEMPRAGE.

	Site *A* (IXI [1])	Site *B* (IXI)	Site *C* (OASIS3 [13])	Site *D* (OASIS3)
	Philips Intera 1.5T	Philips Gyroscan 3.0T	Siemens Sonata 1.5T	Siemens TimTrio 3.0T
T_1-w	M: 4.6 ms, unknown, unknown	M: 4.6 ms, unknown, unknown	M: 3.93 ms, 1.9s, 1.1s	M: 3.16 ms, 2.4s, 1s
	1.2 × 0.94 × 0.94 mm	1.2 × 0.94 × 0.94 mm	1 × 1 × 1 mm	1 × 1 × 1 mm
T_2-w	TSE: 100 ms, 8.2s	TSE: 100 ms, 8.2s	TSE: 116 ms, 6s	TSE: 455ms, 3.2s
	0.94 × 0.94 × 1.25 mm	0.94 × 0.94 × 1.25 mm	0.9 × 0.9 × 5 mm	1 × 1 × 1mm
	Site *E* (OASIS3)	Site *F* (OASIS3)	Site *G* (Private)	Site *H* (Private)
	Siemens TimTrio 3.0T	Siemens BioGraph 3.0T	Philips Achieva 3.0T	Philips Achieva 3.0T
T_1-w	M: 2.4s, 1s	M: 2.95 ms, 2.3s, 0.9s	ME: 6.2 ms, 2.5s, 0.9s	M: 3.16 ms, 2.4s, 1s
	1 × 1 × 1 mm	1.05 × 1.05 × 1.2 mm	1 × 1 × 1mm	1.1 × 1.1 × 1.18mm
T_2-w	TSE: 455 ms, 3.2s	TSE: 454 ms, 3.2s	TSE: 240 ms, 2.5s	TSE: 80 ms, 4.2s
	1 × 1 × 1 mm	1 × 1 × 1 mm	1 × 1 × 1 mm	1.1 × 1.1 × 2.2 mm

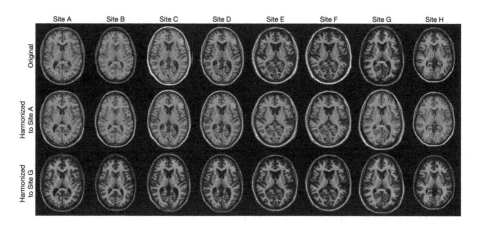

Fig. 2. Harmonization results of the proposed method. T_1-w MR images from eight sites with different manufacturer and imaging parameters are harmonized to Site *A* (middle row) and Site *G* (bottom row). The contrast of harmonized images is determined by the mean θ value over all testing images at a site.

imaging parameters are provided in Table 2. Sites *A* thru *F* are healthy controls, Sites *G* and *H* imaged multiple sclerosis (MS) subjects. Sites *D* and *E* have similar scanners and sequences and thus similar contrast. Images underwent preprocessing including N4 inhomogeneity correction, super-resolution for 2D acquired scans, registration to 1 mm^3 MNI space, and white matter (WM) peak normalization. The center 60 axial slices with spatial dimension of 224 × 192 were extracted for each subject.

3.2 Qualitative and Quantitative Evaluation

For Sites *C*, *D*, *E*, and *F*, there are 10 subjects (600 axial slices) used from each site for training. For the remaining sites, 20 subjects from each site are used in training. There are longitudinal scans in the OASIS3 [13] dataset acquired by different scanners with a short period between visits. These scans are held-out

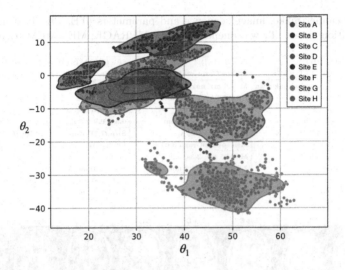

Fig. 3. Visualization of θ space on testing T_1-w images. Contours are fitted to the θ clusters for visualization purpose.

and used as traveling subjects for quantitative evaluation in testing. Specifically, there are seven traveling subjects between Site C and D, and ten traveling subjects between Site E and Site F. The average days between two visits for Sites C/D and Sites E/F are 162 d and 13 d, respectively. In our experiments, β is a four-channel one-hot encoded map, with spatial dimension the same as the image, while θ is a two-dimensional vector. Figure 2 shows harmonized MR images from the eight sites. The mean θ value of all testing images at each site was used to harmonize images between sites. Our analysis has focused on the T_1-w images, as these represent the images with the greatest disparity across the imaging sites and the primary contrast for neuroimaging analysis. With regard to the T_2-w images, we achieve similar image quality as the T_1-w images. Figure 3 shows θ values of the held-out T_1-w testing images. We observe that Sites D and E overlap, which is good as the sites have identical scanner configurations. Second, images acquired using different methods (MPRAGE, and MEMPRAGE) are separated. Third, the distance in θ space corresponds to human perception; sites with visually similar contrast have closer clusters in θ space. For example, although images in Sites D, E, F, and H are all MPRAGE images, θ points are more closely clustered in Sites D, E and F, than Site H.

In Table 3 and Fig. 4, we show qualitative and quantitative comparison of different unsupervised IIT methods. The traveling subjects are used in the quantitative comparison. Specifically, our baseline is the MR images without harmonization (No har), and we compare the structural similarity index measurement (SSIM) and peak signal-to-noise ratio (PSNR) of histogram matching (Hist), CycleGAN [27], Dewey et al. [7], and CALAMITI. Histogram matching is a non-training method, while the other approaches are ML-based. To select a reference image for histogram matching, we first randomly chose a volume, then

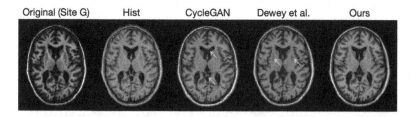

Fig. 4. Visual comparison of different harmonization approaches. An MR image from Site G is harmonized to Site A (see Fig. 2 for reference images). Yellow arrows indicate geometry change. (Color figure online)

Table 3. Numerical comparison (Mean±Std. Dev.) of unsupervised IIT approaches. From left to right: no harmonization (No har), histogram matching (Hist), CycleGAN [27], Dewey et al. [7], and the proposed method (Ours). The proposed method shows significant improvements over all comparison methods based on paired Wilcoxon signed rank tests, with an exception of PSNR of Site $D \to C$. Bold numbers indicate the best mean performance.

		No har	Hist	CycleGAN	Dewey et al.	Ours (2 sites)	Ours (8 sites)
Site C→D	SSIM	0.8034 ± 0.0184	0.8349 ± 0.0456	0.8729 ± 0.0346	0.8637 ± 0.0345	0.8811 ± 0.0292	**0.8814 ± 0.0254**
	PSNR	26.81 ± 1.07	28.03 ± 1.45	29.60 ± 1.62	29.35 ± 1.06	29.80 ± 0.98	**29.82 ± 0.80**
Site D→C	SSIM	0.8034 ± 0.0184	0.7983 ± 0.0297	0.8583 ± 0.0264	0.8554 ± 0.0300	0.8617 ± 0.0245	**0.8663 ± 0.0233**
	PSNR	26.81 ± 1.07	27.53 ± 1.21	28.63 ± 1.52	28.31 ± 1.30	28.50 ± 1.20	**28.68 ± 1.28**
Site E→F	SSIM	0.8706 ± 0.0447	0.8255 ± 0.0375	0.8737 ± 0.0404	0.8748 ± 0.0400	0.8815 ± 0.0366	**0.8834 ± 0.0374**
	PSNR	29.74 ± 1.72	27.46 ± 1.04	29.70 ± 2.16	29.66 ± 1.82	30.05 ± 1.72	**30.17 ± 1.82**
Site F→E	SSIM	0.8706 ± 0.0447	0.7935 ± 0.0596	0.8719 ± 0.0537	0.8719 ± 0.0482	0.8817 ± 0.0402	**0.8843 ± 0.0464**
	PSNR	29.74 ± 1.72	27.75 ± 1.26	29.79 ± 1.92	29.54 ± 1.57	30.28 ± 1.55	**30.36 ± 1.68**

selected the same slice number as our source image. For a fair comparison, we consider two training scenarios for CALAMITI: only include two sites (the source and target site in harmonization) or include all eight sites during training. Paired Wilcoxon signed rank tests were conducted between CALAMITI (two sites) and each comparison method under each performance measurement. Results show that CALAMITI has significantly ($p < 0.001$, $N = 420$ for Sites C and D, $N = 600$ for Sites E and F) better performance over all comparison methods, except for the PSNR of Site $D \to C$. The null hypothesis is that the difference of SSIM or PSNR between the two sites is from a distribution with zero median. Interestingly, CALAMITI has slightly better performance when more sites are used in training. We suggest two possible reasons for this. First, CALAMITI has a unified structure, which makes the whole model less likely to overfit. Second, our β-discriminator is a single class discriminator, so more sites should improve the robustness of the discriminator.

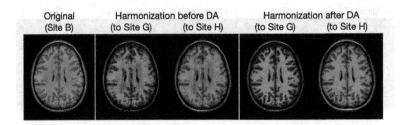

Fig. 5. Visual comparison of fine tuning. Harmonization model is trained on Sites G and H, and tested on Site B. The task is to harmonize Site B images to Site G or Site H. Fine tuning is conducted only on Site B.

Table 4. Demonstration of domain adaptation feature of our method. Paired Wilcoxon signed rank tests show that the proposed method achieves significant ($p < 0.001$, $N = 420$) improvements after DA.

	Site C→D		Site D→C	
	Before DA	After DA	Before DA	After DA
SSIM	0.8729 ± 0.0301	0.8743 ± 0.0291	0.8028 ± 0.0309	0.8486 ± 0.0253
PSNR	29.01 ± 1.07	29.41 ± 0.98	25.37 ± 1.31	27.82 ± 0.82

3.3 Domain Adaptation

We provide both qualitative and quantitative results to test domain adaptation (DA). For qualitative comparison, we trained our harmonization model using Sites G and H and applied the trained model on Site B in testing. The task is to harmonize Site B to Site G or Site H without using data from Sites G or H. As shown in Fig. 5, after fine tuning only on a subset of Site B images, the model is able to adjust itself to produce reasonable harmonization results. Table 4 shows quantitative DA results. In each experiment, the proposed method was trained on the corresponding target site and Site G, while testing and fine tuning were conducted solely on the source site. For example, when evaluating DA in Site $C \rightarrow D$, the model was trained on Site D and G, and Site C was used as a previously unseen site for testing and fine tuning. Results show that the proposed method achieves significant ($p < 0.001$, $N = 420$) improvements after DA.

4 Discussion and Conclusion

Both qualitative and quantitative results from our eight-site experiment show the potential of the proposed method in large-scale multi-site studies. There are some limitations. First, the requirement of intra-site paired images in training could potentially restrict some applications—pediatric data for example—where acquiring multi-contrast images is not practical. Second, in our experiments, we only used paired T_1-w and T_2-w images. However, the proposed method can be extended to include more contrast MR images such as fluid-attenuated inversion recovery (FLAIR) images to achieve a better disentanglement. Third, our experiments on MS patients show that the proposed method does not produce a satisfactory harmonization result on WM lesion areas. We hypothesize that inclusion of FLAIR images would improve this. Fourth, although satisfactory results have been observed in Sect. 3.3, the way we used our β-discriminator to update the β-encoder during domain adaptation is theoretically flawed. According to Goodfellow et al. [8], the generator and discriminator must be updated jointly to achieve optimal performance. We view all these limitations as opportunities for future improvements.

In conclusion, we propose an unsupervised MR harmonization approach, CALAMITI, which integrates merits from both unsupervised IIT and UDA, and is grounded in information bottleneck theory. Our model learns a *universal* imaging equation and a disentangled latent space without inter-site paired data. In contrast to many unsupervised harmonization methods, our model takes advantages of the intra-site paired data to prevent the geometry shift problem. Experiments show that the proposed approach achieves state-of-the-art harmonization performance both visually and in terms of SSIM and PSNR.

Acknowledgments. This research was supported by the TREAT-MS study funded by the Patient-Centered Outcomes Research Institute PCORI/MS-1610-37115, the Intramural Research Program of the NIH, National Institute on Aging, and NIH grant R01-NS082347.

References

1. IXI Brain Development Dataset. https://brain-development.org/ixi-dataset/. Accessed 10 Dec 2019
2. Alemi, A., et al.: Deep variational information bottleneck. In: International Conference on Learning Representations (2017)
3. Brown, R.W., et al.: Magnetic Resonance Imaging: Physical Principles and Sequence Design, 2nd edn. Wiley, Hoboken (2014)
4. Burgess, C.P., et al.: Understanding disentangling in beta-VAE. In: Advances in Neural Information Processing Systems (2017)
5. Dai, B., et al.: Compressing Neural Networks using the Variational Information Bottleneck. In: International Conference on Machine Learning, pp. 1135–1144 (2018)
6. Dewey, B.E., et al.: DeepHarmony: a deep learning approach to contrast harmonization across scanner changes. Magn. Reson. Imaging **64**, 160–170 (2019)
7. Dewey, B.E., et al.: A disentangled latent space for cross-site MRI harmonization. In: Martel, A.L., et al. (eds.) MICCAI 2020. LNCS, vol. 12267, pp. 720–729. Springer, Cham (2020). https://doi.org/10.1007/978-3-030-59728-3_70
8. Goodfellow, I., et al.: Generative adversarial networks. Commun. ACM **63**(11), 139–144 (2020)

9. He, Y., Carass, A., Zuo, L., Dewey, B.E., Prince, J.L.: Self domain adapted network. In: Martel, A.L., et al. (eds.) MICCAI 2020. LNCS, vol. 12261, pp. 437–446. Springer, Cham (2020). https://doi.org/10.1007/978-3-030-59710-8_43

10. Huang, X., et al.: Multimodal unsupervised image-to-image translation. In: Proceedings of the European Conference on Computer Vision, pp. 172–189 (2018)

11. Johnson, J., et al.: Perceptual losses for real-time style transfer and super-resolution. In: European Conference on Computer Vision, pp. 694–711 (2016)

12. Kamnitsas, K., et al.: Unsupervised domain adaptation in brain lesion segmentation with adversarial networks. In: Niethammer, M., et al. (eds.) IPMI 2017. LNCS, vol. 10265, pp. 597–609. Springer, Cham (2017). https://doi.org/10.1007/978-3-319-59050-9_47

13. LaMontagne, P.J., et al.: OASIS-3: Longitudinal Neuroimaging, Clinical, and Cognitive Dataset for Normal Aging and Alzheimer Disease. medRxiv (2019)

14. Lee, H.Y., et al.: Diverse image-to-image translation via disentangled representations. In: Proceedings of the European Conference on Computer Vision, pp. 35–51 (2018)

15. Lindvall, T.: Lectures on the Coupling Method. Courier Corporation, Mineola (2002)

16. Liu, A.H., et al.: A unified feature disentangler for multi-domain image translation and manipulation. In: Advances in Neural Information Processing Systems, pp. 2590–2599 (2018)

17. Liu, M.Y., et al.: Unsupervised image-to-image translation networks. In: Advances in Neural Information Processing Systems, pp. 700–708 (2017)

18. Liu, Y., et al.: Variational intensity cross channel encoder for unsupervised vessel segmentation on OCT angiography. In: Medical Imaging 2020: Image Processing. vol. 11313, p. 113130Y. International Society for Optics and Photonics (2020)

19. Pham, D.L., et al.: Contrast adaptive tissue classification by alternating segmentation and synthesis. In: International Workshop on Simulation and Synthesis in Medical Imaging, pp. 1–10 (2020)

20. Saito, K., et al.: Maximum classifier discrepancy for unsupervised domain adaptation. In: Proceedings of the IEEE Conference on Computer Vision and Pattern Recognition, pp. 3723–3732 (2018)

21. Sohn, K., et al.: Learning structured output representation using deep conditional generative models. In: Advances in Neural Information Processing Systems, pp. 3483–3491 (2015)

22. Tishby, N., et al.: The information bottleneck method. In: The 37th Annual Allerton Conference on Communication, Control, and Computing, pp. 368–377 (1999)

23. Varsavsky, T., Orbes-Arteaga, M., Sudre, C.H., Graham, M.S., Nachev, P., Cardoso, M.J.: Test-time unsupervised domain adaptation. In: Martel, A.L., et al. (eds.) MICCAI 2020. LNCS, vol. 12261, pp. 428–436. Springer, Cham (2020). https://doi.org/10.1007/978-3-030-59710-8_42

24. Wolterink, J.M., et al.: Deep MR to CT synthesis using unpaired data. In: International Workshop on Simulation and Synthesis in Medical Imaging, pp. 14–23 (2017)

25. Xia, W., et al.: Unsupervised multi-domain multimodal image-to-image translation with explicit domain-constrained disentanglement. Neural Netw. **131**, 50–63 (2020)

26. Zhao, C., Carass, A., Lee, J., Jog, A., Prince, J.L.: A supervoxel based random forest synthesis framework for bidirectional MR/CT synthesis. In: Tsaftaris, S.A., Gooya, A., Frangi, A.F., Prince, J.L. (eds.) SASHIMI 2017. LNCS, vol. 10557, pp. 33–40. Springer, Cham (2017). https://doi.org/10.1007/978-3-319-68127-6_4
27. Zhu, J.Y., et al.: Unpaired image-to-image translation using cycle-consistent adversarial networks. In: Proceedings of the IEEE International Conference on Computer Vision, pp. 2223–2232 (2017)
28. Zuo, L., et al.: Synthesizing realistic brain MR images with noise control. In: Burgos, N., Svoboda, D., Wolterink, J.M., Zhao, C. (eds.) SASHIMI 2020. LNCS, vol. 12417, pp. 21–31. Springer, Cham (2020). https://doi.org/10.1007/978-3-030-59520-3_3

A³DSegNet: Anatomy-Aware Artifact Disentanglement and Segmentation Network for Unpaired Segmentation, Artifact Reduction, and Modality Translation

Yuanyuan Lyu[1], Haofu Liao[2], Heqin Zhu[3,5], and S. Kevin Zhou[3,4,5(✉)]

[1] Z²Sky Technologies Inc., Suzhou, China
[2] Medical Imaging, Robotics, and Analytic Computing Laboratory and Engineering (MIRACLE) Group, Beijing, China
[3] Medical Imaging, Robotics, and Analytic Computing Laboratory and Engineering (MIRACLE) Group, Shenzhen, China
[4] School of Biomedical Engineering and Suzhou Institute for Advance Research, University of Science and Technology of China, Suzhou 215123, China
[5] Key Lab of Intelligent Information Processing of Chinese Academy of Sciences (CAS), Institute of Computing Technology, CAS, Beijing 100190, China

Abstract. Spinal surgery planning necessitates automatic segmentation of vertebrae in cone-beam computed tomography (CBCT), an intraoperative imaging modality that is widely used in intervention. However, CBCT images are of low-quality and artifact-laden due to noise, poor tissue contrast, and the presence of metallic objects, causing vertebra segmentation, even manually, a demanding task. In contrast, there exists a wealth of artifact-free, high quality CT images with vertebra annotations. This motivates us to build a CBCT vertebra segmentation model using unpaired CT images with annotations. To overcome the *domain and artifact gaps* between CBCT and CT, it is a must to address the *three heterogeneous tasks* of vertebra segmentation, artifact reduction and modality translation all together. To this, we propose a novel *anatomy-aware artifact disentanglement and segmentation network* (**A³DSegNet**) that intensively leverages knowledge sharing of these three tasks to promote learning. Specifically, it takes a random pair of CBCT and CT images as the input and manipulates the synthesis and segmentation via different decoding combinations from the disentangled latent layers. Then, by proposing various forms of consistency among the synthesized images and among segmented vertebrae, the learning is achieved without paired (i.e., anatomically identical) data. Finally, we stack 2D slices together and build 3D networks on top to obtain final 3D segmentation result. Extensive experiments on a large number of clinical CBCT (21,364) and CT (17,089) images show that the proposed **A³DSegNet** performs significantly better than state-of-the-art competing methods trained independently for each task and, remarkably, it achieves an average Dice coefficient of 0.926 for unpaired 3D CBCT vertebra segmentation.

© Springer Nature Switzerland AG 2021
A. Feragen et al. (Eds.): IPMI 2021, LNCS 12729, pp. 360–372, 2021.
https://doi.org/10.1007/978-3-030-78191-0_28

Keywords: Modality translation · Unpaired segmentation · Metal artifact reduction · Disentanglement learning

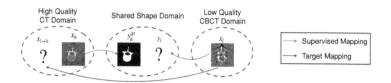

Fig. 1. Sample images x_l from the CBCT domain, x_h from the CT domain and the paired vertebra segmentation y_l^{gt}. Due to the lack of high-quality, artifact-free CBCT images with vertebra annotations, it is challenging to directly learn a reliable CBCT vertebra segmentation model. We propose to leverage the knowledge from CT (both image and shape) to address this challenge under an unpaired setting.

1 Introduction

Cone-beam computed tomography (CBCT) has been widely used in spinal surgery as an intraoperative imaging modality to guide the intervention [19,20]. However, compared with conventional CT, intraoperative CBCT images have pronounced noise and poor tissue contrast [13,15]. Moreover, it is common to have metallic objects (such as pedicle screws) present during operation, which cause metal artifacts and degrade the quality of CBCT images [12]. To facilitate spinal surgery planning and guidance, it is of great importance to accurately identify the vertebrae [1]; yet the poor CBCT image quality makes it challenging to delineate the vertebra shape even manually.

This paper aims to design a computational method to automatically segment vertebrae from clinical CBCT images, not from cadaver images as in [12]. Since it is challenging to create a large number of CBCT images with annotations and yet high quality (artifact-free and high contrast) spinal CT datasets with vertebra delineations are easy to access [17], we investigate the feasibility of learning a CBCT vertebra segmentation model using unpaired CT images with annotations as in Fig. 1. Such learning has to overcome two obvious gaps: (i) the **modality gap** between CT and CBCT, that is, the image appearances look different even for the same content; and (ii) the **artifact gap** as the CT image is artifact-free and the CBCT is artifact-laden. In other words, we have to address *three heterogeneous tasks of vertebra segmentation, artifact reduction, and modality translation* all together in order to derive a good solution.

There are existing methods that deal with modality translation [4,8,10,21], or modality translation and artifact reduction [9], or modality translation and unpaired segmentation [7,16,18]. However, none of them can tackle all three. In this paper, we propose **for the first time** a unified framework that jointly addresses the three tasks, building on top of artifact disentanglement network (ADN) [9]. Specifically, we propose a novel *anatomy-aware artifact disentanglement and segmentation network* ($\mathbf{A^3DSegNet}$) that 1) supports different forms

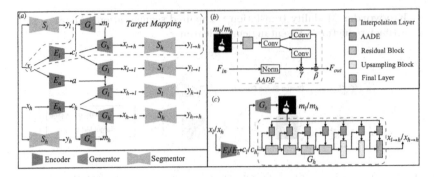

Fig. 2. (a) The architecture of anatomy-aware artifact disentanglement & segmentation network (A^3DSegNet). (b) The proposed anatomy-aware de-normalization (AADE) layer. (c) The detail of anatomy-aware generator G_h.

of image synthesis and vertebra segmentation with joint learning, 2) utilizes an *anatomy-aware de-normalization (AADE) layer* to boost the image translation performance by explicitly fusing anatomical information into the generator, and 3) induces different forms of consistency between the inputs and outputs to guide learning. Given unpaired CBCT and CT images, the proposed framework encodes disentangled representations and manipulates the synthesis and segmentation via different combinations of the decodings. Then, by discovering various forms of consistency among the synthesized images and among segmented vertebrae, self-learning from images and CT annotations is achieved without paired data for CBCT. Furthermore, to increase the segmentation performance, we utilize the anatomy-aware image translation to guide unpaired 3D segmentation for better inter-slice continuity by inducing more 3D shape consistencies.

In summary, the contributions of this work are as follows:

- By utilizing disentangled representations and anatomical knowledge from the target domain, we introduce a unified framework for tackling unpaired vertebra segmentation, artifact reduction, and modality translation, building on top of ADN. The three tasks benefit from each other via joint learning.
- We propose a novel A^3DSegNet that supports different forms of image synthesis and vertebra segmentation and discovers different forms of consistency to enable disentanglement learning. Also, we utilize an AADE layer to explicitly fuse the anatomical information, learned through shape consistency, into the generator and therefore boost the image synthesis performance.
- We embed the anatomy-aware disentanglement network as image translator into a final 3D segmentation network, which retains the spatial continuity between slices. Ultimately, it achieves an average Dice coefficient of 0.926 for unsupervised 3D vertebra segmentation from CBCT.

2   Methodology

Let $\mathbb{X}_l$ be the domain of low-quality, artifact-laden CBCT images, $\mathbb{X}_h$ be the domain of high-quality, artifact-free CT images, and $\mathbb{Y}$ be the domain of vertebra shapes. A CBCT image $x_l \in \mathbb{X}_l$ is usually noisy and may contain streak artifacts while a CT image $x_h \in \mathbb{X}_h$ is artifact-free and provides more anatomical details. A vertebra shape $y \in \mathbb{Y}$ can be presented as a binary segmentation mask where $y(k) \in \{0,1\}$ indicates whether a pixel at location k belongs to a vertebra.

The proposed approach aims to learn a translator $\mathcal{F} : \mathbb{X}_l \rightarrow \mathbb{X}_h \times \mathbb{Y}$ that maps x_l to its corresponding high-quality image $x_h \in \mathbb{X}_h$ and vertebra shape $y_l \in \mathbb{Y}$ without paired, anatomically identical groundtruth data x_l and y_l^{gt} available for supervision. To facilitate this unpaired learning, we assume the availability of a high-quality image dataset of $\{(x_h, y_h^{gt}) \mid x_h \in \mathbb{X}_h, y_h^{gt} \in \mathbb{Y}\}$. Figure 1 shows sample images from these three domains. Note that $\mathbb{X}_l$ and $\mathbb{X}_h$ are independent, *i.e.*, they are collected from different patients.

2.1   Network Architecture

An overview of the proposed network architecture is shown in Fig. 2(a). Inspired by recent progress in disentangled image-to-image translation [4,8,9], we assume that the content c_l (*i.e.*, bones, soft tissues, etc.) and artifact a (*i.e.*, noises, streaks, etc.) of a low-quality image x_l is disentangled in the latent space, see Fig. 2(a). For a high-quality image x_h, there is no artifact and therefore only the content c_h is encoded.

Our network takes two unpaired images $x_l \in \mathbb{X}_l$ and $x_h \in \mathbb{X}_h$ as inputs. For x_l, we use a content encoder E_l and an artifact encoder E_a to encode its content and artifact components, respectively. As x_h does not contain artifacts, we only use a content encoder E_h to encode its content. The latent codes are written as, $c_l = E_l(x_l), c_h = E_h(x_h), a = E_a(x_l)$.

This disentanglement allows decodings among the different combinations of the artifact and content components of $\mathbb{X}_l$ and $\mathbb{X}_h$, which enable four generators $x_{l \rightarrow l}$, $x_{l \rightarrow h}$, $x_{h \rightarrow l}$, and $x_{h \rightarrow h}$. $x_{i \rightarrow j}$ means that the output is encoded with the content of $x_i, i \in \{l, h\}$ and intended to look like a sample from $\mathbb{X}_j, j \in \{l, h\}$. We use two different generators G_l and G_h for each image domain. The low-quality image generator G_l takes a content code $c_i, i \in \{l, h\}$ and an artifact code a as inputs and outputs a low-quality image $x_{i \rightarrow l}$:

$$x_{l \rightarrow l} = G_l(c_l, a), x_{h \rightarrow l} = G_l(c_h, a). \tag{1}$$

The high-quality image generator G_h takes a content code $c_i, i \in \{l, h\}$ and a shape attention map m_i as inputs and outputs a high-quality image $x_{i \rightarrow h}$:

$$x_{l \rightarrow h} = G_h(c_l, m_l), x_{h \rightarrow h} = G_h(c_h, m_h), \tag{2}$$

where the shape attention map $m_i = G_s(c_i)$ is generated by a shape generator G_s. We use m_i to explicitly fuse the vertebra shape information into the decoding such that G_h (Fig. 2(c)) generates better the vertebra region, which is critical in clinical practice. We will also show later (Sect. 2.2) that learning m_i can be achieved using the vertebra shapes y_h^{gt} from G_h.

One goal of this work is to segment vertebra shapes $\mathbb{Y}$ from $\mathbb{X}_l$. Hence, we use a low-quality image segmentor S_l and a high-quality image segmentor S_h to map images from domain $\mathbb{X}_l$ and domain $\mathbb{X}_h$ to space $\mathbb{Y}$, respectively:

$$y_l = S_l(x_l), y_{l \to l} = S_l(x_{l \to l}), y_{h \to l} = S_l(x_{h \to l}),$$
$$y_h = S_h(x_h), y_{h \to h} = S_h(x_{h \to h}), y_{l \to h} = S_h(x_{l \to h}). \tag{3}$$

2.2   Network Learning and Loss Functions

To promote network learning, we design image- and shape-domain losses that leverage the adversarial costs as well as various forms of consistency between the inputs and outputs to obviate the need for the groundtruth data of x_l.

Image domain losses encourage the network to generate the four outputs $\{x_{i \to j} \mid i \in \{l, h\}, j \in \{l, h\}\}$ as intended, i.e., $x_{i \to j}$ should match the content of x_i and look like a sample from $\mathbb{X}_j$. We use L_1 loss to regularize in-domain reconstruction and adversarial losses to encourage cross-domain translation,

$$\mathcal{L}_{recon} = \mathbb{E}_{\mathbb{X}_l, \mathbb{X}_h}[||x_l - x_{l \to l}||_1 + ||x_h - x_{h \to h}||_1], \tag{4}$$

$$\mathcal{L}_{adv} = \mathbb{E}_{\mathbb{X}_l}[\log D_l(x_l)] + \mathbb{E}_{\mathbb{X}_l, \mathbb{X}_h}[1 - \log D_l(x_{h \to l})]$$
$$+ \mathbb{E}_{\mathbb{X}_h}[\log D_h(x_h)] + \mathbb{E}_{\mathbb{X}_l, \mathbb{X}_h}[1 - \log D_h(x_{l \to h})]. \tag{5}$$

To ensure the artifacts generated in $x_{h \to l}$ can also be removable by our model, we apply the cycle consistency loss [4,21] for $x_h \to x_{h \to l} \to x_{h \to l \to h}$:

$$\mathcal{L}_{cycle} = \mathbb{E}_{\mathbb{X}_l, \mathbb{X}_h}[||G_h(E_l(x_{h \to l}), G_s(E_l(x_{h \to l}))) - x_h||_1]. \tag{6}$$

To further impose the anatomy preciseness, we employ an *artifact consistency loss* [9], ensuring that the same artifact is removed from x_l and added to $x_{h \to l}$:

$$\mathcal{L}_{arti} = \mathbb{E}_{\mathbb{X}_l, \mathbb{X}_h}[||(x_l - x_{l \to h}) - (x_{h \to l} - x_h)||_1]. \tag{7}$$

Shape domain losses leverage the ground truth vertebra shape y_h^{gt} in CT domain and shape consistencies for the learning of two segmentors S_l and S_h. Based on Dice loss δ against y_h^{gt}, explicit shape constraints can be applied on the segmentation maps $\{y_h, y_{h \to l}, y_{h \to h}\}$ and the decoded attention map m_h of the image x_h:

$$\mathcal{L}_{segm} = \mathbb{E}_{\mathbb{X}_l, \mathbb{X}_h}[\delta(y_h) + \delta(y_{h \to l}) + \delta(y_{h \to h})]; \quad \mathcal{L}_{segm}^m = \mathbb{E}_{\mathbb{X}_h}[\delta(m_h)]. \tag{8}$$

As the anatomical information is supposed to be retained during image reconstruction and translation, we employ *anatomy consistency* losses to minimize the distance of their segmentation results,

$$\mathcal{L}_{anat} = \mathbb{E}_{\mathbb{X}_l, \mathbb{X}_h}[||y_l - y_{l \to l}||_1 + ||y_h - y_{h \to h}||_1 + ||y_l - y_{l \to h}||_1 + ||y_h - y_{h \to l}||_1]. \tag{9}$$

The overall objective function is the weighted sum of all the above losses, we set the weight of $\mathcal{L}_{adv}$ to 1, and all the other weights to 5. We set the weights of losses based on the importance of each component and experimental experience.

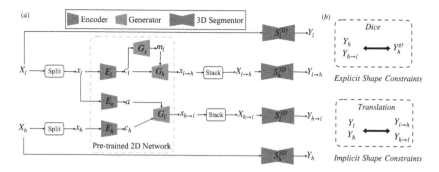

Fig. 3. (a) Anatomy-aware 3D segmentation pipeline. (b) Shape constraints.

2.3 Anatomy-Aware Modality Translation

To better retain the anatomical structure in the synthetic CT image, we integrate the anatomy knowledge into the idea of SPADE [11] and form an **anatomy-aware de-normalization (AADE) layer** (see Fig. 2(b)). AADE first normalizes the input feature F_{in} with a scale σ and a shift μ using a parameter-free batch-normalization (Norm) layer, and then denormalizes it based on a shape attention map $m_i, i \in \{l, h\}$ through learn-able parameters γ and β:

$$F_{out} = \frac{F_{in} - \mu(F_{in})}{\sigma(F_{in})} \times \gamma(\mathcal{R}(m_i)) + \beta(\mathcal{R}(m_i)). \tag{10}$$

where $\mathcal{R}$ resamples m_i to the spatial dimension of F_{in}, and F_{out} denotes the output feature map. γ and β are learned from m_i by three Conv layers. The first Conv layer encodes $\mathcal{R}(m_i)$ to a hidden space and then the other two Conv layers learn spatially related parameter γ and β, respectively. All the Norm layers in residual, upsampling and final blocks of G_h are replaced by the AADE layer. Our model benefits from the new structure in two aspects. First, the learned shape representation guides the synthesis, which prevents washing away the anatomical information. Second, the soft mask allows the gradients to be back-propagated through disentanglement learning, which encourages the encoding of content code to be more accurate.

2.4 3D Segmentation

As the above network is designed for 2D images, it is difficult to keep inter-slice spatial continuity. As in Fig. 3(a), we design a 3D segmentation network. A 3D CBCT volume X_l and a CT volume X_h are first split to 2D images x_l and x_h, then the pre-trained A³DSegNet network serves as an online translator and generates synthetic images $x_{l \to h}$ and $x_{h \to l}$. We recombine $x_{l \to h}$ and $x_{h \to l}$ to $X_{l \to h}$ and $X_{h \to l}$ by stacking them along the slice dimension. Finally, we use a low-quality 3D segmentor S_l^{3D} and a high-quality 3D segmentor S_h^{3D} to map a volume from image domain to shape domain:

$$Y_l = S_l^{3D}(X_l), Y_{h \to l} = S_l^{3D}(X_{h \to l}), Y_h = S_h^{3D}(X_h), Y_{l \to h} = S_h^{3D}(X_{l \to h}). \tag{11}$$

Since the groundtruth segmentation of CBCT image is not available, we apply explicit shape constraints on CT segmentation and implicit shape constraints between raw and translated segmentation results (Fig. 3(b)):

$$\mathcal{L}_{segm}^{3D} = \mathbb{E}_{\mathbb{X}_h}[\delta(Y_h) + \delta(Y_{h\rightarrow l})], \tag{12}$$

$$\mathcal{L}_{anat}^{3D} = \mathbb{E}_{\mathbb{X}_l,\mathbb{X}_h}[||Y_l - Y_{l\rightarrow h}||_1 + ||Y_h - Y_{h\rightarrow l}||_1]. \tag{13}$$

3   Experiments

3.1   Dataset and Experiment Setup

CBCT Data. The CBCT data were collected by a Siemens Arcadis Orbic 3D system during spinal intervention. The dataset contains 109 CBCT scans and all of the scans cover two or three lumbar vertebrae. The size of CBCT volumes is $256 \times 256 \times 256$. The isotropic voxel size is 0.5 mm. Due to the severe cone-beam geometry distortion at the two ends of the sagittal axis, we only keep 196 slices in the middle for each volume. We use 97 volumes for training and 12 volumes for testing, resulting in 19,012 slices in the training set and 2,352 slices in the testing set. To evaluate the segmentation performance, the vertebra masks for the testing set only were manually labeled by an expert.

CT Data. We include four public datasets as high-quality CT images: Dataset 13 and Dataset 15 of SpineWeb [3,5,17], VerSe 19 [14], UL dataset [6]. In total, we include 125 CT scans with corresponding segmentation masks for the vertebrae. The in-plane resolution is [0.31,1.0] mm and the slice thickness is [0.7,3.0] mm. We only include the CT slices of the lumbar vertebrae in the experiment. To match the resolution and spatial dimension of CBCT image, all the CT images are resampled to a spacing of $0.5 \times 0.5 \times 1\,\mathrm{mm}^3$. We use 105 scans for training and 20 scans for testing with the same training/testing ratio for every dataset, resulting in 14,737 images for training and 2,352 images for testing.

Implementation Details. We implement our model using the PyTorch framework. For 2D disentanglement network, we train it for 15 epochs using the Adam optimizer with a learning rate of 1×10^{-4} and a batch size of 1. For 3D segmentation network, the size of the input patch is $96 \times 256 \times 256$ and we downsample the patch to a spacing of $1 \times 1 \times 1\,\mathrm{mm}^3$ after translation to save GPU memory. We train the 3D segmentation network for 78,386 iterations.

Metrics. We evaluate the performance of vertebra segmentation using the Dice score and the average symmetric surface distance (ASD). We obtain the segmentation mask from shape prediction by applying a threshold of 0.5. A higher Dice and a lower ASD mean a better segmentation performance.

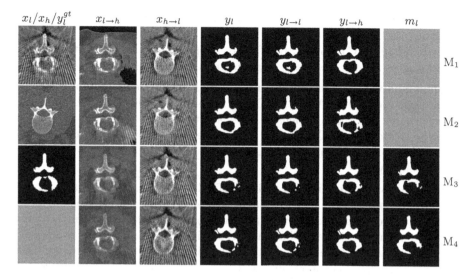

Fig. 4. Visual comparison for synthetic image and segmentation of different models. M_4 (full) produces the least amount of artifact and the most complete segmentation. (Color figure online)

Table 1. Quantitative evaluation segmentation performance for different models.

Dice/ ASD(mm)	m_l	y_l	$y_{l\to l}$	$y_{l\to h}$	m_h	y_h	$y_{h\to h}$	$y_{h\to l}$
M_1	n.a./n.a	.802/2.16	.801/2.17	.806/2.12	n.a./n.a	.925/0.89	.918/0.98	.911/1.11
M_2	n.a./n.a	.806/1.94	.805/1.96	.806/2.04	n.a./n.a	.930/0.80	.928/0.83	.923/**0.89**
M_3	.774/2.58	.828/1.68	.828/1.69	.836/1.64	**.918/1.14**	.930/0.79	.929/0.80	.923/1.00
M_4	**.829/2.01**	**.843/1.57**	**.843/1.56**	**.847/1.54**	.915/1.18	**.932/0.79**	**.932/0.79**	**.925**/0.94

3.2 Ablation Study

In this section, we investigate the effectiveness of different modules and objectives of the proposed architecture. Here we focus on the A^3DSegNet network using E_l, E_h, E_a, G_l, G_h, G_s and learning with image domain losses ($\mathcal{L}_{adv}$, $\mathcal{L}_{recon}$, $\mathcal{L}_{cycle}$, and $\mathcal{L}_{arti}$) and shape domain losses ($\mathcal{L}_{segm}$, $\mathcal{L}_{segm}^m$, and $\mathcal{L}_{anat}$). The configurations of different models are as follows:

- M_1: $\{E_l, E_h, E_a, G_l, G_h\} + \{S_l, S_h\}$, using $\mathcal{L}_{recon}$, $\mathcal{L}_{adv}$, $\mathcal{L}_{cycle}$, and $\mathcal{L}_{segm}$;
- M_2: M_1 but using $\mathcal{L}_{anat}$ as an additional loss;
- M_3: $M_2 + \{G_s\}$, using AADE and $\mathcal{L}_{segm}^m$ as an additional loss;
- M_4 (full): M_3 without using $\mathcal{L}_{arti}$.

Disentanglement and Explicit Shape Constraints. As shown in Fig. 4, we can see streak metal artifacts nearly everywhere in x_l. M_1 can roughly disentangle artifacts and anatomical information but strong vertical artifacts and strange air area appear in $x_{l \to h}$ (see red arrows of M_1 in Fig. 4). For the anatomical structure, M_1 learns to segment vertebrae with fully supervised S_h and S_l applied on various CT images, but fails to suppress the false bony structure in y_l and $y_{l \to l}$ as S_l may misclassify some metal artifacts as bone.

Implicit Shape Constraints. With $\mathcal{L}_{anat}$, all segmentations are improved with higher Dices and smaller ASDs, see Table 1. As shown in Fig. 4, y_l, $y_{l \to l}$ and $y_{l \to h}$ become similar but the high density bone is not correctly segmented in $y_{l \to h}$ as it maybe treated as metal artifacts. Comparing $x_{l \to h}$ between M_2 and M_1, the abnormal air region disappears but metal artifact reduction performance is still not satisfactory.

Anatomy-Aware Generation. With AADE layer in M_3, y_l, $y_{l \to l}$ and $y_{l \to h}$ are substantially improved as shown in Table 1. Note, m_l is used as attention map, so we do not expect it to be identical to y_l^{gt}. In $x_{l \to h}$, metal artifacts are further suppressed comparing with M_2. Thus, AADE is critical to our anatomy-aware artifact disentanglement framework. With the special structure, G_s can be punished in the image translation and reconstruction processes and the other encoders and generators receive more guidance. However, as shown by blue arrows in Fig. 4, we observe a shadow of vertebra edge of x_l appears in $y_{l \to h}$ of M_3 and the vertebra boundaries get smoothed out in $y_{h \to l}$. It may be because sharp edges are encoded as metal artifacts and forced to be added to $y_{h \to l}$ by artifact consistency loss $\mathcal{L}_{arti}$.

Removal of $\mathcal{L}_{arti}$. To mitigate vertebrae shadows, we remove $\mathcal{L}_{arti}$. The segmentation performance of most images in M_4 gets improved because of better synthetic images. Overall, $y_{l \to h}$ in M_4 yields the best segmentation performance for CBCT images with an average Dice of 0.847 and an average ASD of 1.54 mm. For the synthetic images, M_4 generates $x_{l \to h}$ with the best quality and least metal artifacts among all the models. M_4 also outputs $x_{h \to l}$ without vertebra shadows. The results indicate our shape-aware network could preserve anatomical details and transfer the metal artifacts precisely without $\mathcal{L}_{arti}$.

3.3   Comparison with State-of-the-Art

We compare our model with competing methods to show the benefits of joint learning of segmentation, artifact reduction, and modality translation tasks.

2D Segmentation. Our model is compared with two methods based on domain adaptation: AdaptSegNet [16] and SIFA [2]. AdaptSegNet and SIFA are trained with the officially released codes. AdaptSegNet is trained with Dice loss as we only have one class here. The results are summarized in Fig. 5 and Table 2(a). AdaptSegNet invokes DeeplabV2 as the segmentor and cannot capture the vertebra especially when metal artifacts exist. SIFA outputs plausible predictions but the performance is heavily affected by the metal artifacts. Also, the segmentations predicted by SIFA can not capture vertebrae precisely and show false positive bones and enlarged masks (see red arrows in Fig. 5). With joint learning, our model achieves the best segmentation performance with an average Dice of 0.847 and an average ASD of 1.54 mm.

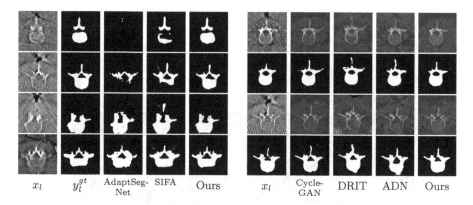

| x_l | y_l^{gt} | AdaptSeg-Net | SIFA | Ours |

| x_l | Cycle-GAN | DRIT | ADN | Ours |

Fig. 5. Visualization for x_l and segmentation results of competing methods on two cases. (Color figure online)

Fig. 6. Visualization for modality translation of two cases. Odd rows are $x_{l \to h}$, and even rows are segmentations outputed by a pre-trained UNet on CT images. (Color figure online)

Table 2. Quantitative comparison of different competing methods for (a) segmentation, (b) modality translation.

(a) Dice/ASD (mm)	Segmentation perf.
AdaptSeg [16]	.508/5.06
SIFA [2]	.825/1.93
A^3DSegNet (ours)	**.847/1.54**

(b) Dice/ASD (mm)	Segmentation perf.
CycleGAN [21]	.828/2.02
DRIT [8]	.659/3.79
ADN [9]	.739/2.89
A^3DSegNet (ours)	**.846/1.72**

Modality Translation and Artifact Reduction. Here we compare our model with other methods: CycleGAN [21], DRIT [8], ADN [9]. All the models are trained with our data using their officially released codes. Further, we train a UNet segmentation network using annotated CT data and apply it to synthesized CT images as an anatomy-invariant segmentation evaluator. As shown in Table 2(b), our model achieves the best performance with a much larger average Dice compared with other methods. Figure 6 shows the synthetic images and segmentation results. CycleGAN and DRIT tend to output plausible and realistic CT images but are not able to preserve the anatomical information precisely. As shown by the red arrows in Fig. 6, the bony structures appear distorted and noisy. ADN can retain most of the anatomical information but not for the bone pixels with high intensity, which might be classified into metal artifacts. With anatomical knowledge learned from the CT domain, our model outputs high-quality synthetic CT images while keeping anatomical consistency.

For artifact reduction, ADN and DRIT [8] could not successfully recover the clean images and streak artifacts remain in the synthetic image (see blue arrows in Fig. 6). CycleGAN [21] could output clean images but the distorted bones

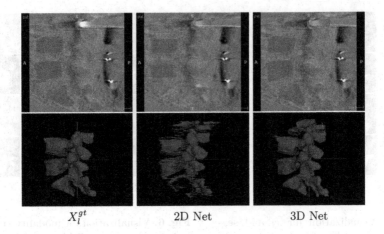

$$X_l^{gt} \qquad\qquad \text{2D Net} \qquad\qquad \text{3D Net}$$

Fig. 7. Segmentation performance for 2D and 3D Nets. (Row 1): sagittal view and (2): rendering of 3D segmentation mask. The inter-slice discontinuity is fixed using 3D Net.

make them less valuable. Our model can suppress all the artifacts and keep the bone edges sharp, which outperforms all the other methods.

To further improve the segmentation performance, we introduce the 3D segmentation network as in Fig. 3. Our 3D model increases the Dice score from 0.819 to 0.926 and reduces the average ASD by **44%** (from 1.47 mm to 0.82 mm). As shown in Fig. 7, the typical inter-slice discontinuous problem happening in 2D segmentation is fixed with our 3D model, which also runs **over 100 times** (0.38 s vs. 42.33 s) faster than slice-by slice 2D segmentation as measured on a PC with an Intel Xeon E5-2678 and a Nvidia GeForce GTX 2080 Ti.

4   Conclusions

To learn a vertebra segmentation model for low-quality, artifact-laden CBCT images from unpaired high-quality, artifact-free CT images with annotations, it is a must to bridge the domain and artifact gaps. To this, we present for the first time a unified framework to address three heterogeneous tasks of unpaired modality translation, vertebra segmentation, and artifact reduction. The proposed A^{3}DSegNet jointly learns content/artifact encoders, generators, and segmentors, together with an anatomy-aware de-normalization layer, through the utilization of vertebra appearance and shape knowledge across domains. Extensive results on a large number of CBCT/CT images demonstrate the effectiveness of our A^{3}DSegNet, outperforming various competing methods. In the future, we plan to conduct a clinical evaluation at multiple spinal surgery sites.

References

1. Burström, G., Buerger, C., et al.: Machine learning for automated 3-dimensional segmentation of the spine and suggested placement of pedicle screws based on intraoperative cone-beam computer tomography. J. Neurosurg. Spine **31**(1), 147–154 (2019)
2. Chen, C., Dou, Q., Chen, H., Qin, J., Heng, P.A.: Unsupervised bidirectional cross-modality adaptation via deeply synergistic image and feature alignment for medical image segmentation. IEEE Trans. Med. Imaging **39**, 2494–2505 (2020)
3. Glocker, B., Zikic, D., Konukoglu, E., Haynor, D.R., Criminisi, A.: Vertebrae localization in pathological spine CT via dense classification from sparse annotations. In: Mori, K., Sakuma, I., Sato, Y., Barillot, C., Navab, N. (eds.) MICCAI 2013. LNCS, vol. 8150, pp. 262–270. Springer, Heidelberg (2013). https://doi.org/10.1007/978-3-642-40763-5_33
4. Huang, X., Liu, M.Y., Belongie, S., Kautz, J.: Multimodal unsupervised image-to-image translation. In: ECCV, pp. 172–189 (2018)
5. Ibragimov, B., Korez, R., Likar, B., Pernuš, F., Xing, L., Vrtovec, T.: Segmentation of pathological structures by landmark-assisted deformable models. IEEE Trans. Med. Imaging **36**(7), 1457–1469 (2017)
6. Ibragimov, B., Korez, R., et al.: Interpolation-based detection of lumbar vertebrae in CT spine images. In: Recent Advances in Computational Methods and Clinical Applications for Spine Imaging, pp. 73–84. Springer (2015). https://doi.org/10.1007/978-3-319-14148-0_7
7. Kamnitsas, K., Baumgartner, C., et al.: Unsupervised domain adaptation in brain lesion segmentation with adversarial networks. In: MICCAI. pp. 597–609. Springer (2017). https://doi.org/10.1007/978-3-319-59050-9_47
8. Lee, H.Y., Tseng, H.Y., Huang, J.B., Singh, M., Yang, M.H.: Diverse image-to-image translation via disentangled representations. In: ECCV, pp. 35–51 (2018)
9. Liao, H., Lin, W.A., Zhou, S.K., Luo, J.: ADN: artifact disentanglement network for unsupervised metal artifact reduction. IEEE Trans. Med. Imaging **39**(3), 634–643 (2019)
10. Liu, M.Y., Breuel, T., Kautz, J.: Unsupervised image-to-image translation networks. In: Advances in Neural Information Processing Systems, pp. 700–708 (2017)
11. Park, T., Liu, M.Y., Wang, T.C., Zhu, J.Y.: Semantic image synthesis with spatially-adaptive normalization. In: CVPR, pp. 2337–2346 (2019)
12. Pauwels, R., et al.: Quantification of metal artifacts on cone beam computed tomography images. Clinical Oral Implants Res. **24**, 94–99 (2013)
13. Schafer, S., et al.: Mobile C-arm cone-beam CT for guidance of spine surgery: image quality, radiation dose, and integration with interventional guidance. Med. Phys. **38**(8), 4563–4574 (2011)
14. Sekuboyina, A., Bayat, A., et al.: VerSe: a vertebrae labelling and segmentation benchmark. arXiv preprint arXiv:2001.09193 (2020)
15. Siewerdsen, J.H.: Cone-beam CT with a flat-panel detector: from image science to image-guided surgery. Nucl. Instrum. Meth. Phys. Res. Sect. A: Accelerators, Spectrometers, Detectors and Associated Equipment **648**, S241–S250 (2011)
16. Tsai, Y.H., Hung, W.C., et al.: Learning to adapt structured output space for semantic segmentation. In: Proceedings of the IEEE Conference on Computer Vision and Pattern Recognition, pp. 7472–7481 (2018)
17. Yao, J., Burns, J.E., et al.: A multi-center milestone study of clinical vertebral CT segmentation. Comput. Med. Imaging Graph. **49**, 16–28 (2016)

18. Zhang, Z., Yang, L., Zheng, Y.: Translating and segmenting multimodal medical volumes with cycle-and shape-consistency generative adversarial network. In: CVPR, pp. 9242–9251 (2018)
19. Zhou, S.K., et al.: A review of deep learning in medical imaging: imaging traits, technology trends, case studies with progress highlights, and future promises. In: Proceedings of the IEEE (2021)
20. Zhou, S.K., Rueckert, D., Fichtinger, G.: Handbook of medical image computing and computer assisted intervention. Academic Press, Cambridge (2019)
21. Zhu, J.Y., Park, T., Isola, P., Efros, A.A.: Unpaired image-to-image translation using cycle-consistent adversarial networks. In: ICCV, pp. 2223–2232 (2017)

Unsupervised Learning of Local Discriminative Representation for Medical Images

Huai Chen[1]⬤, Jieyu Li[1], Renzhen Wang[2], Yijie Huang[1], Fanrui Meng[1],
Deyu Meng[2], Qing Peng[3], and Lisheng Wang[1(✉)]⬤

[1] Institute of Image Processing and Pattern Recognition, Department of Automation,
Shanghai Jiao Tong University, Shanghai 200240, People's Republic of China
`lswang@sjtu.edu.cn`
[2] Xi'an Jiaotong University, Xi'an, People's Republic of China
[3] Department of Ophthalmology, Shanghai Tenth People's Hospital,
Tongji University, Shanghai, People's Republic of China

Abstract. Local discriminative representation is needed in many medical image analysis tasks such as identifying sub-types of lesion or segmenting detailed components of anatomical structures. However, the commonly applied supervised representation learning methods require a large amount of annotated data, and unsupervised discriminative representation learning distinguishes different images by learning a global feature, both of which are not suitable for localized medical image analysis tasks. In order to avoid the limitations of these two methods, we introduce local discrimination into unsupervised representation learning in this work. The model contains two branches: one is an embedding branch which learns an embedding function to disperse dissimilar pixels over a low-dimensional hypersphere; and the other is a clustering branch which learns a clustering function to classify similar pixels into the same cluster. These two branches are trained simultaneously in a mutually beneficial pattern, and the learnt local discriminative representations are able to well measure the similarity of local image regions. These representations can be transferred to enhance various downstream tasks. Meanwhile, they can also be applied to cluster anatomical structures from unlabeled medical images under the guidance of topological priors from simulation or other structures with similar topological characteristics. The effectiveness and usefulness of the proposed method are demonstrated by enhancing various downstream tasks and clustering anatomical structures in retinal images and chest X-ray images.

Keywords: Unsupervised representation learning · Local discrimination · Topological priors

1 Introduction

In medical image analysis, transferring pre-trained encoders as initial models is an effective practice, and supervised representation learning is widely applied,

A. Feragen et al. (Eds.): IPMI 2021, LNCS 12729, pp. 373–385, 2021.
https://doi.org/10.1007/978-3-030-78191-0_29

while it usually depends on a large amount of annotated data and the learnt features might be less efficient for new tasks differing from original training task [4]. Thus, some researchers turn to study unsupervised representation learning [9,17], and particularly unsupervised discriminative representation learning was proposed to measure similarity of different images [7,16,18]. However, these methods mainly learn the instance-wise discrimination based on global semantics, and cannot characterize the similarities of local regions in image. Hence, they are less efficient for many medical image analysis tasks, such as lesion detection, structure segmentation, identifying distinctions between different structures, in which local discriminative features are needed to be captured. In order to make unsupervised representation learning suitable for these tasks, we introduce local discrimination into unsupervised representation learning in this work.

It is known that medical images of humans contain similar anatomical structures, and thus pixels can be classifying into several clusters based on their context. Based on such observations, a local discriminative embedding space can be learnt, in which pixels with similar context will distribute closely and dissimilar pixels can be dispersed. In this work, a model containing two branches is constructed following a backbone network, in which an embedding branch is used to generate pixel-wise embedding features and a clustering branch is used to generate pseudo segmentations. Through jointly updating these two branches, pixels belonging to the same cluster will have similar embedding features and different clusters will have dissimilar ones. In this way, local discriminative features can be learnt in an unsupervised way, which can be used for evaluating similarity of local image regions.

The proposed method is further applied to several typical medical image analysis tasks respectively in fundus images and chest X-ray images: (1) The learnt features are utilized in 9 different downstream tasks via transfer learning, including segmentations of retinal vessel, optic disk (OD) and lungs, detection of haemorrhages and hard exudates, etc., to enhance the performances of these tasks. (2) Inspired by specialists' ability of recognizing anatomical structures based on prior knowledge, we utilize the learnt features to cluster local regions of the same anatomical structure under the guidance of topological priors, which are generated by simulation or from other structures with similar topology.

2   Related Work

Instance discrimination learning method [1,7,16,18] is an unsupervised representation learning framework providing a good initialization for downstream tasks and it can be considered as an extension of exemplar convolution neural network (CNN) [4]. The main conception of instance discrimination is to build an encoder to dispersedly embed training samples over a hypersphere [16]. Specifically speaking, a CNN is trained to project each image onto a low-dimensional unit hypersphere, in which the similarity between images can be evaluated by cosine similarity. In this embedding space, dissimilar images are forced to be separately distributed and similar images are forced to be closely distributed. Thus, the encoder can make instance-level discrimination. Wu et al. [16] introduce a memory bank to store historical feature vectors for each image. Then the probability of image being recognized as i-th example can be expressed by inner product of the embedding vector and vectors stored in the memory bank. And the discrimination ability of encoder is obtained by learning to correctly classify image instance into the corresponding record in the memory bank. However, the vectors stored in the memory bank are usually outdated caused by discontinuous updating. To address this problem, Ye et al. [18] propose a framework with siamese network which introduces augmentation invariant into the embedding space to cluster similar images to realize real-time comparison.

The ingenious design enables instance discrimination effectively utilize unlabeled images to train a generalized feature extractor for downstream tasks and shrink the gap between unsupervised and supervised representation learning [7]. However, summarizing a global feature for image instance miss local details, which are crucial for medical image tasks, and the high similarity of global semantics between images of same body part makes instance-wise discrimination less practical. Therefore, it is more convinced to focus on local discrimination of medical images. Meanwhile, medical images of the same body part can be divided into several clusters due to the similar anatomical structures, which inspires us to propose a framework to cluster similar pixels to learn local discrimination.

3 Methods

The illustration of our unsupervised framework is shown in Fig. 1. This model has two main components. The first is learning a local discriminative representation, which aims to project pixels into a l_2-normalized low-dimensional space, i.e. a K-D unit hypersphere, and pixels with similar context should be closely distributed and dissimilar pixels should be far away from each other on this embedding space. The learnt local discriminative representation can be taken as a good feature extractor for downstream tasks. The second is introducing prior

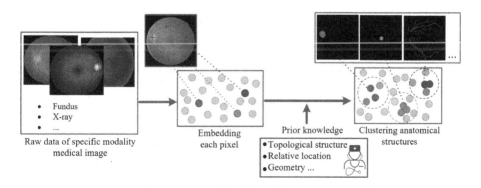

Fig. 1. Illustration of our proposed learning model.

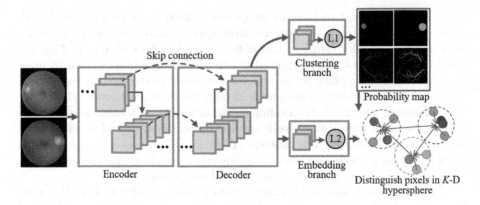

Fig. 2. Illustration of local discrimination learning.

knowledge of topological structure and relative location into local discrimination, where the prior knowledge will be fused into the model to make the distribution of pseudo segmentations closer to the distribution of priors. By combining priors of structures with local discrimination, regions of the expected anatomical structure can be clustered.

3.1   Local Discrimination Learning

As medical images of the same body region contain same anatomical structures, image pixels can be classified into several clusters, each of which corresponds to a specific kind of structure. Therefore, local discrimination learning is proposed to train representations to embed each pixel onto a hypersphere, on which pixels with similar context will be encoded closely. To achieve this, two branches, including an embedding branch to encode each pixel and a clustering branch to generate pseudo segmentations to cluster pixels, are built following a backbone network and trained in a mutually beneficial manner (Fig. 2).

Notation: We denote f_θ as the deep neural network, where θ is the parameters of network. The unlabeled image examples are denoted as $X = \{x_1, ..., x_N\}$ where $x_i \in \mathbb{R}^{H,W}$. After feeding x_i into the network, we can get embedding features v_i and probability map r_i, i.e., $v_i, r_i = f_\theta(x_i)$, where $v_i(h, w) \in \mathbb{R}^K$ is the K-dimensional encoded vector for position (h, w) of image x_i and $r_i(h, w) \in \mathbb{R}^M$ is a vector representing the probability of classifying pixel $x_i(h, w)$ into M clusters. And $r_{mi}(h, w)$ denotes the probability of classifying pixel $x_i(h, w)$ into the m-th cluster. We force $||r_i(h, w)||_1 = 1$ and $||v_i(h, w)||_2 = 1$ by respectively setting l_1 and l_2 normalization in clustering branch and embedding branch.

Jointly Train Clustering Branch and Embedding Branch: After getting embedding features and pseudo segmentations, the center embedding feature c_m

of m-th cluster can be formulated as followed:

$$c_m = \frac{\sum_{i,h,w} r_{mi}(h,w)v_i(h,w)}{||\sum_{i,h,w} r_{mi}(h,w)v_i(h,w)||_2} \tag{1}$$

Where l_2 normalization is used to make c_m on the hypersphere. Thus, the similarity between c_m and $v_i(w,h)$ can be evaluated by cosine similarity as followed:

$$t(c_m, v_i(w,h)) = c_m^T v_i(w,h) \tag{2}$$

To make pixels of same cluster closely distributed and pixels of different clusters dispersedly distributed, there should be high similarity between $v_i(w,h)$ and corresponding center embedding features c_m, and low similarity between c_m and $c_n (m \neq n)$ as well. Thus, the loss function can be formulated as followed:

$$loss_{ld} = -\frac{1}{MNHW} \sum_{m,i,h,w} r_{mi}(h,w)t(c_m, v_i(w,h)) + \frac{1}{M(M-1)} \sum_{m,n \neq m} c_m^T c_n \tag{3}$$

More Constraints: We also add entropy loss and area loss to make high confidence of predictions and avoid blank outputs for some clusters. The losses are as followed:

$$loss_{entropy} = -\frac{1}{MNHW} \sum_{m,i,h,w} r_{mi}(h,w)log r_{mi}(h,w) \tag{4}$$

$$area_{mi} = \sum_{h,w} r_{mi}(h,w) \tag{5}$$

$$loss_{area} = \frac{1}{NM} \sum_{m,i} relu(\frac{1}{4M}HW - area_{mi}) \tag{6}$$

where $relu$ is rectified linear units [5], $loss_{area}$ will impose punishment if the area of pseudo segmentation is smaller than $\frac{1}{4M}HW$.

3.2 Prior-Guided Anatomical Structure Clustering

Commonly, specialists can easily identify anatomical structures based on corresponding prior knowledge, including relative location, topological structure, and even based on knowledge of similar structures. Therefore, DNN's ability of recognizing structures based on local discrimination and topological priors is studied in this part. Reference images, which are binary masks of similar structures, real data or simulation and show knowledge of location and topological structure, is introduced to the network to force the clustering branch to obtain corresponding structures as shown in Fig. 3.

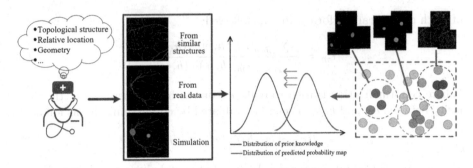

Fig. 3. Based on prior knowledge and local discrimination to recognize structures.

We denote the distribution of m-th cluster as P_m and the distribution of corresponding references as Q_m. The goal of optimization is to minimize Kullback-Leibler (KL) divergence between them, and it can be formulated as followed:

$$\min_{f_\theta} KL(P_m||Q_m) = \sum_i P_m(r_{mi})log\frac{P_m(r_{mi})}{Q_m(r_{mi})} \tag{7}$$

To minimize the KL divergence between P_m and Q_m, adversarial learning [6] is utilized to encourage the produced pseudo segmentation to be similar as the reference mask. During training, a discriminator D is set to discriminate pseudo segmentation r_m and reference mask s_m, while f_θ aims to cheat D. The loss function for D and adversarial loss for f_θ are defined as followed:

$$loss_D = loss_{bce}(D(s_m), 1) + loss_{bce}(D(r_m), 0) \tag{8}$$

$$loss_{bce}(\hat{y}, y) = -\frac{1}{N}\sum_i(y_i log\hat{y}_i + (1 - y_i)log(1 - \hat{y}_i)) \tag{9}$$

$$loss_{adv} = loss_{bce}(D(r_m), 1) \tag{10}$$

Reference Masks: (1) From similar structures: Similar structures share similar geometry and topology. Therefore, we can utilize segmentation annotations from similar structures to guide the segmentation of target, e.g., annotations of vessel in OCTA can be utilized for the clustering of retinal vessel in fundus images. (2) From real data: Corresponding annotations of target structure can be directly set as the prior knowledge. (3) Simulation: Based on the comprehension, experts can draw the pseudo masks to show the information of relative location, topology, etc. For example, based on retinal vessel mask, the approximate location of OD and fovea can be identified. Then, ellipses can be placed at these positions to represent OD and fovea based on their geometry priors.

4 Experiments and Discussion

The experiments can be divided into two parts to show the effectiveness of our proposed unsupervised local discrimination learning and prove the feasibility of combining local discrimination and topological priors to cluster target structures.

4.1 Network Architectures and Initialization

The backbone is a U-net consisted with a VGG-liked encoder and a decoder. The encoder is a tiny version of VGG-16 without fully connection layers (FCs), whose channel number is quarter of VGG-16. The decoder is composed with 4 convolution blocks, each of which is made up of two convolution layers. The final features of decoder will be concatenated with the features generated by the first convolution block of encoder for the further processing of the clustering branch and the embedding branch. Embedding branch is formed of 2 convolution layers with 32 channels and a l_2 normalization layer to project each pixel onto a 32-D hypersphere. Clustering branch is consisted with 2 convolution layers with 8 channels followed by a l_1 normalization layer.

To minimize the KL divergence between the pseudo segmentation distribution and the references distribution, a discriminator is created. The discriminator is a simple classifier with 7 convolution layers and 2 FCs. The channel numbers of convolution layers are 16, 32, 32, 32, 32, 64, 64 and the first 5 layers are followed by a max-pooling layer to halve the image size. FCs' channels are 32 and 1, and the final FC is followed by a Sigmoid layer.

Patch Discrimination to Initialize the Network: It is hard to simultaneously train the clustering branch and the embedding branch from scratch. Thus, we firstly jointly pre-train the backbone and the embedding branch by patch discrimination, which is an improvement of instance discrimination [18]. The main idea is that the embedding branch should project similar patches (patches under various augmentations) onto close positions on the hypersphere. The embedding features v_i will be firstly processed by an adaptive average pooling layer (APP) to generate spatial features, each of which represents feature of corresponding patches of image x_i. We denote $s_i(j)$ as the embedding vector for $x_i(j)$ (j-th patch of x_i), where $||s_i(j)||_2 = 1$ by applying a l_2 normalization. $\hat{s}_i(j)$ denotes the embedding vector of corresponding augmentation patch $\hat{x}_i(j)$. The probability of region $\hat{x}_i(j)$ being recognized as region $x_i(j)$ can be defined as followed:

$$P(ij|\hat{x}_i(j)) = \frac{\exp(s_i^T(j)\hat{s}_i(j)/\tau)}{\sum_{k,l} \exp(s_k^T(l)\hat{s}_i(j)/\tau)}, \quad (11)$$

Assuming all patches being recognized as $x_i(j)$ is independent, then the joint probability of $\hat{x}_i(j)$ being recognized as $x_i(j)$ and $x_k(l)(k \neq i \text{ or } l \neq j)$ not being recognized as $x_i(j)$ is as followed:

$$P_{ij} = P(ij|\hat{x}_i(j)) \prod_{k \neq i \text{ or } l \neq j} (1 - P(ij|\hat{x}_k(l))). \quad (12)$$

The negative log likelihood and loss function are formulated as followed:

$$J_{ij} = -\log P(ij|\hat{x}_i(j)) - \sum_{k \neq i \ or \ l \neq j} \log(1 - P(ij|\hat{x}_k(l))).$$ (13)

$$loss_{pd} = \sum_{i,j} J_{ij}$$ (14)

We also introduce mixup [19] to make the representations more robust. Based on mixup, virtual sample $\tilde{x}_i = \lambda x_a + (1 - \lambda)x_b$ is firstly generated by linear interpolation of x_a and x_b, where $\lambda \in (0,1)$. The embedded representation for patch $\tilde{x}_i(j)$ is $\tilde{s}_i(j)$, and we expect it is similar to the mixup feature $z_i(j)$. The loss is defined as followed:

$$z_i(j) = \frac{\lambda s_a(j) + (1 - \lambda)s_b(j)}{||\lambda s_a(j) + (1 - \lambda)s_b(j)||_2}.$$ (15)

$$\tilde{P}(ij|\tilde{s}_i(j)) = \frac{\exp(z_i^T(j)\tilde{s}_i(j)/\tau)}{\sum_{k,l} \exp(z_k^T(l)\tilde{s}_i(j)/\tau)}.$$ (16)

$$\tilde{J}_{ij} = -\log \tilde{P}(ij|\tilde{s}_i(j)) - \sum_{k \neq i \ or \ l \neq j} \log(1 - \tilde{P}(ij|\tilde{s}_k(l))),$$ (17)

$$loss_{mixup} = \sum_{i,j} \tilde{J}_{ij}$$ (18)

When pre-training this model, we set the training loss as $loss_{pd} + loss_{mixup}$. The output size of APP is set as 4×4 to split each image into 16 patches. And each batch contains 16 groups of images and 8 corresponding mixup images, and each of group contains 2 augmentations of one image. The augmentation methods contain $RandomResizedCrop$, $RandomGrayscale$, $ColorJitter$, $RandomHorizontalFlip$, $Rotation90$ in pytorch. The optimizer is Adam with initial learning rate (lr) of 0.001, which will be half if the validation loss does not decrease over 3 epochs. The maximum training epoch is 20.

4.2   Experiments for Learning Local Discrimination

Datasets and Preprocessing: Our method is evaluated in two medical scenes. **Fundus images**: The model will be firstly trained on diabetic retinopathy (DR) detection dataset of kaggle [3][1] ($30k$ for training, $5k$ for validation). Then, the pre-trained encoder is transferred to 8 segmentation tasks: (1) Retinal vessel: DRIVE [13] (20 for training, 20 for testing), STARE [8] (10 for training, 10 for testing) and CHASEDB1 [10] (20 training, 8 testing). (2) OD and cup: Drishti-GS [12] (50 for training, 50 for testing). ID (OD) [11] (54 for training, 27 for testing). (3) Lesions: Haemorrhages dataset (Hae) and hard exudates dataset (HE) from IDRID [11]. **Chest X-ray:** The encoder is pre-trained on ChestX-ray8 [15] ($100k$ for training and $12k$ for validation) and transferred to lung segmentation [2] (69 for training, 69 for testing). All images of above datasets are resized to 512×512.

---

[1] https://www.kaggle.com/c/diabetic-retinopathy-detection/data.

Table 1. Comparison of results of downstream segmentation tasks.

Encoder	Retinal vessel			Optic disc and cup			Lesions		X-ray
	DRIVE	STARE	CHASE	GS(cup)	GS(OD)	ID(OD)	Hae	HE	Lung
Random	80.76	76.26	78.30	77.76	95.41	89.11	37.76	57.44	96.34
Supervised	81.06	80.59	78.56	86.94	96.40	93.56	**51.11**	61.34	–
Wu et al.	74.98	66.15	68.31	84.59	94.58	88.70	26.34	48.67	96.27
Ye et al.	80.87	81.22	79.85	87.30	**97.40**	94.68	46.79	59.40	96.63
LD	**82.15**	**83.42**	**80.35**	**89.30**	96.53	**95.59**	46.72	**65.77**	**97.51**

Implementation Details:

(1) Local discriminative representation learning: The model is firstly initialized by pre-trained model of patch discrimination. Then the training loss is set as $loss_{pd} + loss_{mixup} + 10loss_{ld} + loss_{entropy} + 5loss_{area}$. Each batch has 6 groups of images, each of which contains 2 augmentations of one image, and 3 mixup images. The maximum training epoch is 80 and the optimizer is Adam with $lr = 0.001$.

(2) Transferring: The encoder of downstream tasks is initialized by the learnt feature extractor of local discrimination. The decoder is composed with 5 convolution blocks, each of which contains 2 convolution layers and is followed by a up-pooling layer. The loss is set as $loss_{dsc} = \frac{2|p \times g|}{|g| + |p|}$. This model will be firstly trained in 100 epochs in frozen pattern with Adam with $lr = 0.001$, and then be trained in fine-tune pattern with $lr = 0.0001$ in the following 100 epochs.

(3) Comparative methods: **Random:** The network is trained from scratch. **Supervised:** Supervised by the manual score of DR, the encoder will be firstly trained by making classification. **Wu et al.** [16] and **Ye et al.** [18]: Instance discrimination methods proposed in [16] and [18]. **LD:** The proposed method.

Results: The evaluation metric is mean Dice-Sørensen coefficient (DSC): $DSC = \frac{2|P \times G|}{|P| + |G|}$, where P is the binary results of predictions and G is the ground truth. Quantitative evaluations for downstream tasks are shown in Table 1, and we can have following observations:

1) The generalization ability of the trained local discriminative representation is demonstrated by the leading performance in the 6 fundus tasks and lung segmentation. Compared with models trained from scratch, models initialized by our pre-trained encoder can respectively gain improvements of 1.39%, 7.16%, 2.05%, 11.54%, 1.12%, 6.48%, 8.96%, 8.33% and 1.17% in DSC for all 9 tasks.

2) Compared with instance discrimination methods by Wu et al. [16] and Ye et al. [18], the proposed local discrimination is capable to learn finer features

and is more suitable for unsupervised representation learning of medical images.

3) The proposed unsupervised method is free from labeled images and the learnt representation is more generalized, while supervised representation learning relies on expensive manual annotations and learns specialized representations. As shown in Table 1, our method shows better performance than supervised representation learning, whose target is to classification DR, and the only exception is on segmenting haemorrhages which is the key evidence for DR.

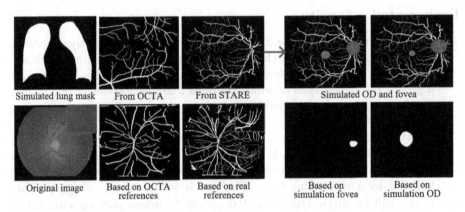

Fig. 4. Some examples of reference masks and predicted results: The first row show some reference images and the second row show the predictions.

4.3 Experiments for Clustering Structures Based on Prior Knowledge

Implementation Details: In this part, we respectively fuse reference images from real data, similar structures and simulations into local discrimination to investigate the ability of clustering anatomical structures. A dataset with 3110 high-quality fundus images from [14] and 1482 frontal X-rays from [15] are utilized as the training data. The reference images can be constructed in 3 ways: (1) From real references: ALL 40 retinal vessel masks of DRIVE are utilized as the references for clustering pixels of vessel. (2) From similar structures: Similar structures share similar priors, thus, 10 OCTA vessel masks are utilized as the references for retinal vessel of fundus. (3) Simulation: We directly draw 20 simulated lung masks to guide lung segmentation. Meanwhile, based on vessel masks of DRIVE, we place ellipses at approximate center location of OD and fovea to generate pseudo masks. Some reference masks are shown in Fig. 4.

f_θ needs to jointly learn local discrimination and cheat D, thus, it will be updated by minimizing the following loss:

$$loss_{f_\theta} = loss_{pd} + loss_{mixup} + 10loss_{ld} + loss_{entropy} + 5loss_{area} + 2loss_{adv} \quad (19)$$

The optimizer for f_θ is Adam with $lr = 0.001$. The discriminator is optimized by minimizing $loss_D$ and the optimizer is Adam with $lr = 0.0005$. It is worth noting that during the clustering training of OD and fovea, all masks of real vessel, fovea and OD are concatenated and fed into D to provide enough information and f_θ is firstly pre-trained to cluster retinal vessel. The maximum training epoch is 80.

Results: Visualization examples are shown in Fig. 4. Quantitative evaluations are as followed: (1) Retinal vessel segmentation is evaluated in the test data of STARE. And the DSC are respectively 66.25% and 57.35% for models based on real references and based on OCTA annotations. (2) The segmentation of OD is evaluated in the test data of Drishti-GS and gains DSC of 83.60%. (3) The segmentation of fovea is evaluated in the test data of STARE. Because the region of fovea is fuzzy, we measure the mean distance between the real center of fovea and the predicted center. The mean distance is $7.63pixels$. (4) The segmentation of lung is evaluated in NLM [2] and the DSC is 81.20%.

Based on above results, we can have following observations:

1) In general, topological priors generated from simulation or similar structures in a different modality is effective to guide the clustering of target regions.
2) However, real masks contain more detailed information and are able to provide more precise guidance. For example, compared with vessel segmentations based on OCTA annotations, which missing the thin blood vessels due to the great thickness of OCTA mask, segmentations based on real masks can recognize thin vessels due to the details provided and the constraint of clustering pixels with similar context.
3) For anatomical structures with fuzzy intensity pattern, such as fovea, combining local similarity and structure priors is able to guide precise recognition.

5   Conclusion

In this paper, we propose an unsupervised framework to learn local discriminative representation for medical images. By transferring the learnt feature extractor, downstream tasks can be improved to decrease the demand for expensive annotations. Furthermore, similar structures can be clustered by fusing prior knowledge into the learning framework. The experimental results show that our methods have best performance on 7 out of 9 tasks in fundus and chest X-ray images, demonstrating the great generalization of the learnt representation. Meanwhile, the feasibility of clustering structures based on prior knowledge and unlabeled images is demonstrated by combining local discrimination and topological priors from real data, similar structures or even simulations to segment anatomical structures including retinal vessel, OD, fovea and lung.

References

1. Bachman, P., Hjelm, R.D., Buchwalter, W.: Learning representations by maximizing mutual information across views. In: Advances in Neural Information Processing Systems, pp. 15535–15545 (2019)
2. Candemir, S., et al.: Lung segmentation in chest radiographs using anatomical atlases with nonrigid registration. IEEE Trans. Med. Imaging 33(2), 577–590 (2013)
3. Cuadros, J., Bresnick, G.: Eyepacs: an adaptable telemedicine system for diabetic retinopathy screening. J. Diabetes Sci. Technol. 3(3), 509–516 (2009)
4. Dosovitskiy, A., Fischer, P., Springenberg, J.T., Riedmiller, M., Brox, T.: Discriminative unsupervised feature learning with exemplar convolutional neural networks. IEEE Trans. Pattern Anal. Mach. Intell. 38(9), 1734–1747 (2015)
5. Glorot, X., Bordes, A., Bengio, Y.: Deep sparse rectifier neural networks. In: Proceedings of the Fourteenth International Conference on Artificial Intelligence and Statistics. pp. 315–323 (2011)
6. Goodfellow, I., et al.: Generative adversarial nets. In: Advances in Neural Information Processing Systems, pp. 2672–2680 (2014)
7. He, K., Fan, H., Wu, Y., Xie, S., Girshick, R.: Momentum contrast for unsupervised visual representation learning. In: Proceedings of the IEEE/CVF Conference on Computer Vision and Pattern Recognition, pp. 9729–9738 (2020)
8. Hoover, A., Kouznetsova, V., Goldbaum, M.: Locating blood vessels in retinal images by piecewise threshold probing of a matched filter response. IEEE Trans. Med. Imaging 19(3), 203–210 (2000)
9. Mahmood, U., et al.: Whole MILC: generalizing learned dynamics across tasks, datasets, and populations. In: Martel, A.L., et al. (eds.) MICCAI 2020. LNCS, vol. 12267, pp. 407–417. Springer, Cham (2020). https://doi.org/10.1007/978-3-030-59728-3_40
10. Owen, C.G., et al.: Measuring retinal vessel tortuosity in 10-year-old children: validation of the computer-assisted image analysis of the retina (caiar) program. Invest. Ophthalmol. Vis. Sci. 50(5), 2004–2010 (2009)
11. Porwal, P., et al.: Indian diabetic retinopathy image dataset (idrid): a database for diabetic retinopathy screening research. Data 3(3), 25 (2018)
12. Sivaswamy, J., Krishnadas, S., Joshi, G.D., Jain, M., Tabish, A.U.S.: Drishti-gs: Retinal image dataset for optic nerve head (onh) segmentation. In: 2014 IEEE 11th International Symposium on Biomedical Imaging (ISBI), pp. 53–56. IEEE (2014)
13. Staal, J., Abràmoff, M.D., Niemeijer, M., Viergever, M.A., Van Ginneken, B.: Ridge-based vessel segmentation in color images of the retina. IEEE Trans. Med. Imaging 23(4), 501–509 (2004)
14. Wang, R., Chen, B., Meng, D., Wang, L.: Weakly-supervised lesion detection from fundus images. IEEE Trans. Med. Imaging 38, 1501–1512 (2018)
15. Wang, X., Peng, Y., Lu, L., Lu, Z., Bagheri, M., Summers, R.M.: Chestx-ray8: Hospital-scale chest x-ray database and benchmarks on weakly-supervised classification and localization of common thorax diseases. In: Proceedings of the IEEE Conference on Computer Vision and Pattern Recognition, pp. 2097–2106 (2017)
16. Wu, Z., Xiong, Y., Yu, X.S., Lin, D.: Unsupervised feature learning via nonparametric instance discrimination. In: Proceedings of the IEEE Conference on Computer Vision and Pattern Recognition, pp. 3733–3742 (2018)

17. Xie, X., Chen, J., Li, Y., Shen, L., Ma, K., Zheng, Y.: Instance-aware self-supervised learning for nuclei segmentation. In: Martel, A.L., et al. (eds.) MICCAI 2020. LNCS, vol. 12265, pp. 341–350. Springer, Cham (2020). https://doi.org/10.1007/978-3-030-59722-1_33
18. Ye, M., Zhang, X., Yuen, P.C., Chang, S.F.: Unsupervised embedding learning via invariant and spreading instance feature. In: Proceedings of the IEEE Conference on Computer Vision and Pattern Recognition, pp. 6210–6219 (2019)
19. Zhang, H., Cisse, M., Dauphin, Y.N., Lopez-Paz, D.: Mixup: beyond empirical risk minimization. In: International Conference on Learning Representations (2018)

TopoTxR: A Topological Biomarker for Predicting Treatment Response in Breast Cancer

Fan Wang$^{(\boxtimes)}$, Saarthak Kapse, Steven Liu, Prateek Prasanna,
and Chao Chen

Stony Brook University, Stony Brook, NY 11794, USA
fanwang1@cs.stonybrook.edu,
{saarthak.kapse,steven.h.liu,prateek.prasanna,
chao.chen.1}@stonybrook.edu

Abstract. Characterization of breast parenchyma on dynamic contrast-enhanced magnetic resonance imaging (DCE-MRI) is a challenging task owing to the complexity of underlying tissue structures. Current quantitative approaches, including radiomics and deep learning models, do not explicitly capture the complex and subtle parenchymal structures, such as fibroglandular tissue. In this paper, we propose a novel method to direct a neural network's attention to a dedicated set of voxels surrounding biologically relevant tissue structures. By extracting multi-dimensional topological structures with high saliency, we build a topology-derived biomarker, *TopoTxR*. We demonstrate the efficacy of *TopoTxR* in predicting response to neoadjuvant chemotherapy in breast cancer. Our qualitative and quantitative results suggest differential topological behavior of breast tissue on treatment-naïve imaging, in patients who respond favorably to therapy versus those who do not.

Keywords: Topology · Persistent homology · Breast cancer · Neoadjuvant chemotherapy

1 Introduction

Traditional cancer imaging biomarker studies have mostly been focused on texture and shape-based analysis of the lesion, often ignoring valuable information harbored in the tumor microenvironment. There is an overwhelming evidence of diagnostic and prognostic information in the tumor periphery, such as the peritumoral stroma and parenchyma [4]. In breast cancer, the phenotypic heterogenity in the extra-tumoral regions stems from factors such as stromal immune infiltration, vascularity, and a combination of fatty and scattered fibroglandular tissue.

This work was partially supported by grants NSF IIS-1909038, CCF-1855760, and NCI 1R01CA253368-01. This work used the Extreme Science and Engineering Discovery Environment (XSEDE) [27] Bridges-2 at the Pittsburgh Supercomputing Center through allocation TG-CIS210012, which is supported by NSF ACI-1548562.

© Springer Nature Switzerland AG 2021
A. Feragen et al. (Eds.): IPMI 2021, LNCS 12729, pp. 386–397, 2021.
https://doi.org/10.1007/978-3-030-78191-0_30

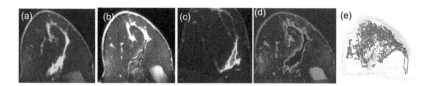

Fig. 1. An example MRI image (a) and different radiomics features such as (b) tumor 3D shape, (c) intratumoral texture (Haralick entropy), and (d) whole breast texture (Haralick energy). In (e), we show topological structures from *TopoTxR*, capturing the density of fibroglandular tissue.

Breast density, composition of fibroglandular tissue, and background parenchymal enhancement have been shown to be associated with breast cancer risk and are also implicated in differential response to therapy [16]. There is hence a need for novel interpretable quantitative approaches to comprehensively characterize breast cancer biology by interrogating the tumor microenvironment and the surrounding parenchyma as observed on routine imaging scans.

Radiomic approaches have been recently used to learn diagnostic and prognostic signatures from breast tumor and surrounding peritumoral regions. Although promising, radiomic features cannot explicitly model the complex and subtle parenchymal tissue structures. Therefore, the learning outcome lacks sufficient interpretability; one cannot derive actionable knowledge regarding the tissue structures from the learnt diagnostic/prognostic models. Convolutional neural networks (CNNs), on the other hand, have shown great promise in various domains, as they learn feature representations in an end-to-end manner. For breast cancer, CNN models trained on mammography images have shown very strong diagnostic efficacy [1]. However, mammograms are of relatively low resolution and are only 2D projections of 3D tissue structures. The loss of true topology and geometry of the 3D tissue structures fundamentally limits the power of mammography-based models. CNN models have been proposed for MRIs, which can characterize the true 3D tissue structures [20]. Such models are capable of learning features that combine lower level abstractions and high order details which maximally discriminate between different classes. While promising, these methods take whole breast MRI as direct input; a large portion of the input volume may be biologically irrelevant and even noisy enough to significantly bias the prediction task. Besides, 3D CNNs have millions of parameters, and require a large amount of training data which is often unavailable for controlled clinical trials such as the I-SPY1 trial (less than 250 cases) [24]. CNNs also suffer from the limitation of feature interpretability as they lack direct grounding with the breast tissue structures.

We present a novel topological biomarker for breast DCE-MRI. Our method bridges the two extremes (hand-crafted imaging features vs. completely data-driven CNNs). The key idea is to **direct the model's attention to a much smaller set of voxels surrounding tissue structures with high biological relevance**. This way, the deep convolutional network can be efficiently trained with limited MRI data. Meanwhile, the learning outcome has the potential of connecting to the biological cause manifested on the tissue structure topology. As shown in Fig. 1, our topological descriptor (e) directly models the breast parenchymal tissue structures, whereas other features (b-d) do not.

To explicitly extract tissue structure is a challenging task. Training a segmentation model may not be always feasible due to the lack of ground truth. Instead, we propose an unsupervised approach to extract the tissue structures using the theory of persistent homology [10]. Our method extracts 1D and 2D topological structures (loops and bubbles) with high saliency. These structures correspond to curvelinear tissue structures (e.g., ducts, vessels, etc.) and voids enclosed by tissues and glands in their proximity. We consider these topological structures a reasonable approximation of the tissue structures and combine them with the original MRI image as the input to train 3D CNNs. By focusing on such tissue structures and their periphery, we can effectively train a 3D CNN even with small datasets. Additionally, the tissue-centric representation can be effectively visualized for better interpretation.

Although our approach is domain-agnostic, as a use case we focus on predicting treatment response (TxR) in breast cancer treated with neoadjuvant chemotherapy (NAC). Correct prediction of pathological complete response (pCR) prior to NAC administration can help avoid ineffective treatment that introduces unnecessary suffering and costs. However, reliably predicting pCR using treatment-naive DCE-MRI still remains a challenge with current clinical metrics and techniques. Our method, called *TopoTxR*, significantly outperforms existing methods, including radiomics and image-only CNNs, on the I-SPY1 dataset [24].

Persistent homology has been used in various biomedical image analysis tasks [7,8,14,15,29,30]. However, most existing approaches focus on only using the persistence diagrams as direct features. Meanwhile, the topological structures uncovered through the algorithm carry rich geometric information that has not been explicitly utilized. **Our approach leverages topological structures based on the persistent homology to explicitly direct the attention of convolutional neural networks.** The topology-driven attention enables the CNNs to learn efficiently. Our method outperforms various baselines, including ones that use persistence diagram features. A Python implementation of TopoTxR can be found at our GitHub repository: https://github.com/TopoXLab/TopoTxR.

1.1   Related Work

Quantitative imaging features have been used in conjunction with machine learning classifiers for prediction of pCR [5,21]. Radiomics approaches, involving analysis of quantitative attributes of tumor texture and shape, have shown promise in assessment of treatment response. In particular, such features capture appearance of the tumors and, more recently, peritumor regions [3,11]. Such approaches are often limited by their predefined nature, lack of generalizability, dependency on accurate lesion segmentation, and inability to explain phenotypic differences

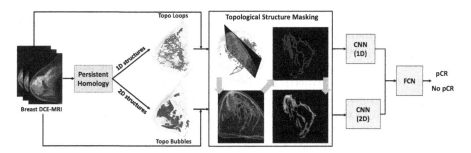

Fig. 2. Our proposed TopoTxR pipeline. We extract 1D and 2D topological structures from breast MRI with persistent homology. We create new images in which voxels belonging to these structures have their intensity value from the original breast MRI, and zero otherwise. We create two images corresponding to 1D and 2D topological structures. We use two 3D CNNs and a fully connected network for pCR prediction.

beyond the peritumoral margin. CNNs have been previously applied to breast DCE-MRI for pCR prediction [12,19,25]. Owing to the sub-optimal performance of image-only models, image based CNN approaches have been fused with non-imaging clinical variables in order to bolster prediction [9].

Topological information, in particular, persistent homology, has been used in various image analysis tasks, such as cardiac image analysis [30], brain network analysis [18], and neuron image segmentation [14]. In recent years, it has been combined with deep neural networks to enforce topological constraints in image segmentation tasks [7,14]. Abundant work has been done to learn from information represented by persistence diagrams, e.g., via vectorization [2], kernel machines [6,17,26], or deep neural networks [13]. However, the topological structures associated with the diagrams, e.g., cycles and bubbles, have not been explored. These structures describe geometric details of the breast tissue (e.g. fibroglandular tissue) and can be mapped to the original breast volume to provide an explicit attention mechanism for CNNs.

2   Methodology

We propose a topological approach to (1) extract topological structures with high saliency as an approximation of the tissue structures, and (2) use the extracted topological structures as explicit attention to train a deep convolutional network. Our method is summarized in Fig. 2.

We first compute salient topological structures from the input image based on the theory of persistent homology [10]. Topological structures of dimensions 1 and 2, i.e., loops and bubbles, can both correspond to important tissue structures. 1D topological structures capture curvelinear structures such as ducts, vessels, etc. 2D topological structures represent voids enclosed by the tissue structures and their attached glands. These topological structures directly delineate the critical tissue structure with high biological relevance. Thus we hypothesize that by focusing on these tissue structures and their affinity, we will have relevant contextual information for prediction.

Next, we propose a topological-cycle-driven CNN to learn from MRIs and the discovered topological structures. We explicitly mask the input MRI image so that only voxels of the extracted topological structures and their vicinity regions are visible. We then train a 3D CNN on this masked image. By focusing on the tissue structure vicinity region, we can train the CNN effectively even with a limited training set. We note that there are two types of relevant topological structures, loops and bubbles. Our network consists of two separate 3D CNNs, treating the two types of topological structures separately. The feature representation from the two convolutional networks are concatenated and are provided to fully connected layers for the prediction (pCR vs. no pCR). As will be shown empirically, both types of topology capture complementary structural signatures and are necessary to achieve the best predictive performance.

In this section, we will first explain the background knowledge about persistent homology. Next, we introduce cycles representing the topological structures. Finally, we will describe our topological-cycle-driven CNN.

2.1   Background: Persistent Homology

We review basics of persistent homology in this section. Interested readers may refer to [10] for more details. Persistent homology extracts the topological information of data observed via a scalar function. Given an image domain, X, and a real-valued function $f : X \rightarrow \mathbb{R}$, we can construct a sublevel set $X_t = \{x \in X : f(x) \leq t\}$ where t is a threshold controlling the "progress" of sublevel sets. The family of sublevel sets $\mathcal{X} = \{X_t\}_{t \in \mathbb{R}}$ defines a filtration, i.e., a family of subsets of X nested with respect to the inclusion: $X_\alpha \subseteq X_\beta$ if $\alpha \leq \beta$. As the threshold t increases from $-\infty$ to $+\infty$, topological structures such as connected components, handles, and voids appear and disappear. The birth time of a topological structure is the threshold t at which the structure appears in the filtration. Similarly, the death time is the threshold at which the structure disappears. Persistent homology tracks the topological changes of sublevel sets X_t and encodes them in a *persistence diagram*, i.e., a point set in which each point (b, d) represents a topological structure born at b and killed at d.

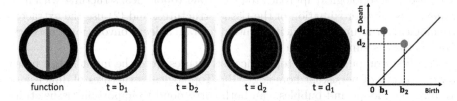

Fig. 3. From left to right: a synthetic image f, sublevel sets at thresholds $b_1 < b_2 < d_2 < d_1$ (in black), and the persistence diagram of dimension 1. The red loop represents a 1D structure born at b_1 and killed at d_1. The green loop represents a 1D structure born at b_2 and killed at d_2. They correspond to the red and green dots in the diagram. (Color figure online)

See Fig. 3 for an example function f and its sublevel sets at different thresholds. At time b_1, a new handle (delineated by the red cycle c_1) is created. This handle is later destroyed at time d_1. Another handle delineated by the green cycle c_2 is created and killed at b_2 and d_2 respectively. The topological changes are summarized in a persistence diagram on the right. Each handle corresponds to a 2D dot in $\mathbb{R}^2$, whose x and y coordinates are birth and death times. The difference between a dot's birth and death times is called its *persistence*.

2.2   Persistence Cycles and Their Computation

In this section, we introduce cycles that represent topological structures discovered by persistent homology. We also present an algorithm to compute these cycles. Intuitively, a topological cycle of dimension p is a p-manifold without boundary. A 1-dimensional (1D) cycle is a loop (or a union of a set of loops). A 2-dimensional (2D) cycle is a bubble (or a union of a set of bubbles). A cycle z represents a persistent homology structure if it delineates the structure at its birth. For example, in Fig. 3, the red and the green loops represent the handles born at time b_1 and b_2, respectively.

We assume a discretization of the image domain into distinct elements, i.e., vertices (corresponding to voxels), edges connecting adjacent vertices, squares, and cubes. These elements are 0-, 1-, 2-, and 3-dimensional cells. Any set of p-cells is called a p-*chain*. We define the *boundary operator* of a p-cell, σ, as the set of its $(p-1)$ faces. The boundary of an edge is its two vertices. The boundary of a square consists of the 4 edges enclosing it. The boundary of a cube consists of the 6 squares enclosing it. For any p-chain, c, its boundary is $\partial(c) = \sum_{\sigma \in c} \partial(\sigma)$, under mod-2 sum. For a set of edges forming a path, its boundary are the two end vertices. For any set of squares forming a patch, its boundary is the loop enclosing the patch. The boundary of a set of cubes is the bubble enclosing them.

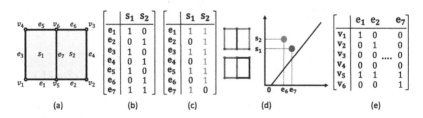

Fig. 4. (a) Example of a cubical complex whose cells are sorted according to the function values. (b) 2D Boundary matrix ∂. (c) Reduced boundary matrix. (d) Persistence diagram and resulting cycles corresponding to ∂. (e) 1D boundary matrix.

A p-chain is a p-*cycle* if its boundary is empty. All p-cycles form the null space of the boundary operator, i.e. $\{c : \partial(c) = \emptyset\}$. Any topological structure, formally defined as a *homology class*, can be delineated by different cycles, which are equivalent to each other in terms of topology. We can choose any of them to represent this class. In persistent homology, for each dot in the persistence diagram, we can represent it with one representative cycle at its birth. In Fig. 3, the red and green cycles represent the two corresponding handles. Note that the choice of representative cycle is not unique. A relevant question is to choose the shortest representative cycle (i.e., one with the least number of edges) for each dot in the diagram [30,31]. In this paper, we focus on choosing a standard representative cycle, leaving the optimal cycle for future work.

Computation of Persistent Homology and Representative Cycles. We assume a filtration function on a discretization of the image domain. An example discretization of a 2D image is given in Fig. 4(a). We first sort all cells in increasing order according to their function values. The computation of persistence diagrams is then performed by encoding the p-dimensional boundary operator in binary matrices named *boundary matrices*, ∂_p. ∂_p maps p-cells to their boundaries. Figure 4 shows the 1D and 2D boundary matrices of the given complex and its filtration. The 1D boundary matrix is essentially the incidence matrix of the underlying graph (Fig. 4(e)). High dimensional boundary matrices are defined similarly (e.g., a 2D boundary matrix in Fig. 4(b)).

Persistence diagram is computed by reducing the boundary matrix similar to Gaussian elimination, but without row or column perturbation. We reduce through column operations performed on ∂ from left to right. Figure 4(c) shows the reduced 2D boundary matrix. Once the boundary matrices are reduced. Each non-zero column corresponds to a persistent dot in the diagram. The reduced column itself is the cycle representing the corresponding topological structure. In this paper, we pay attention to both 1D and 2D cycles, corresponding to loops and bubbles. The extracted cycles will be used to explicitly guide 3D CNNs for analysis. The computation of topological cycles is of the same complexity as the computation of persistent homology. In theory, it takes $O(n^\omega)$ time ($\omega \approx 2.37$ is the exponent in the matrix multiplication time, i.e., time to multiply two $n \times n$ matrices) [23]. Here n is the number of voxels in an image. In practice, to compute all cycles of an input image (256^3), it takes approximately 5 min.

2.3 Topological-Cycle-Driven 3D CNN

An overview of our topological-cycle-driven 3D CNN has been provided in the beginning of Sect. 2. Here we describe the technical details.

To compute persistence and topological cycles, we invert the MRI image $f = -I$ so that the tissue structures correspond to low intensity. After the computation, we select topological cycles representing dots of the diagram with high persistence. The general belief is that low-persistence dots tend to be due to noise. Thus we only select high-persistence cycles, which are considered more salient structures, and more likely to represent true tissue structures. The threshold is a hyperparamter tuned in practice.

Next, we create two binary 3D masks representing 1D and 2D topological cycles, respectively. Both masks are dilated slightly in order to cover both the structures and their vicinity. Instead of directly using these binary masks for

Table 1. Comparisons of proposed method against baseline methods on four metrics: accuracy, AUC, specificity, and sensitivity. The p-values in the last row are computed between baseline MRI and TopoTxR.

	Accuracy	AUC	Specificity	Sensitivity
	Without feature selection			
Radiomics	0.517 ± 0.086	0.536 ± 0.098	0.557 ± 0.058	0.477 ± 0.176
PD	0.529 ± 0.071	0.537 ± 0.078	0.543 ± 0.075	0.515 ± 0.151
Radiomics+PD	0.533 ± 0.080	0.538 ± 0.095	0.567 ± 0.065	0.5 ± 0.175
	With feature selection			
Radiomics	0.563 ± 0.085	0.593 ± 0.098	0.552 ± 0.180	0.575 ± 0.081
PD	0.549 ± 0.081	0.567 ± 0.097	0.551 ± 0.167	0.547 ± 0.071
Radiomics+PD	0.563 ± 0.093	0.587 ± 0.099	0.592 ± 0.178	0.534 ± 0.087
	3D CNN			
MRI	0.633 ± 0.200	0.621 ± 0.102	0.570 ± 0.322	0.673 ± 0.354
TopoTxR (MRI+Topo)	$\mathbf{0.851} \pm \mathbf{0.045}$	$\mathbf{0.820} \pm \mathbf{0.035}$	$\mathbf{0.736} \pm \mathbf{0.086}$	$\mathbf{0.904} \pm \mathbf{0.068}$
p-value	0.0625	0.0625	0.3750	0.1875

pCR prediction, we fill the foreground voxels with their original image intensity values. In other words, we mask the input image with the complement of the cycle mask. See *Topological Structure Masking* step in Fig. 2 for the masked MRI image. We generate masked images for both 1D and 2D, and provide them to two CNNs. All masked MRIs are padded to the same size of $256 \times 256 \times 256$.

We use separate networks with the same architecture for cycles and bubbles. The CNN consists of 5 3D convolution layers, each followed by a batch normalization layer and a LeakyReLU. The output feature maps from these two 3D CNNs are reshaped and concatenated into a feature vector. This feature vector is sent into a fully connected (FC) network with three FC layers for final pCR prediction. Besides ReLU and batch normalization, a dropout layer is added to the second FC layer. The final output is a vector of size 2. All three networks are trained together in an end-to-end fashion with stochastic gradient descent (SGD) as the optimizer and cross-entropy as loss.

3   Experimental Results

We validate our method on the task of pCR prediction with ISPY-1 post-contrast DCE-MRI data [24]. A total of 162 patients are considered - 47 achieving pCR (mean age = 48.8 years), 115 non-pCR (mean age = 48.5 years). All experiments were performed in a 5-fold cross-validation setting. The performance was evaluated with accuracy, area under curve (AUC), specificity, and sensitivity. Both mean and standard deviation are reported. For all methods, hyperparameters (learning rate, momentum, weight decay factor, batch size, and dropout rate for the dropout layer) are tuned using a grid search, and are selected from a 3-fold cross validation on a small set held out for validation.

Table 2. Ablation study results. All numbers are reported from 5-fold cross validations.

	Accuracy	AUC	Specificity	Sensitivity
Persistence threshold				
90% Remain	0.826 ± 0.069	0.783 ± 0.063	0.675 ± 0.1115	0.891 ± 0.084
60% Remain	$\mathbf{0.851} \pm 0.021$	0.793 ± 0.028	0.647 ± 0.073	$\mathbf{0.939} \pm 0.017$
Dimension				
Dimension 1	0.718 ± 0.068	0.697 ± 0.025	0.639 ± 0.149	0.754 ± 0.161
Dimension 2	0.756 ± 0.036	0.691 ± 0.013	0.520 ± 0.116	0.863 ± 0.103
Dilation radius				
Radius 2	0.721 ± 0.036	0.673 ± 0.024	0.569 ± 0.037	0.777 ± 0.055
Radius 4	0.677 ± 0.023	0.603 ± 0.007	0.442 ± 0.063	0.764 ± 0.054
Radius 8	0.646 ± 0.034	0.569 ± 0.040	0.399 ± 0.057	0.737 ± 0.033

We compare with various baseline methods. **Radiomics**: We compute a 92 dimensional radiomic signature [28] and train a classifier on it. Features are extracted solely from the tumor region. **PD**: We train a classifier using persistence-diagram-based features, i.e., features extracted from persistence diagrams (PDs) of the input MRI images. While various classifier options are available and behave similarly, we use the sliced Wasserstein kernel distance for PDs as a feature vector [6]. **Radiomics+PD**: We combine both radiomics and PD features and train a classifier on them. **With feature selection**: We apply feature selection to all aforementioned methods, using Mutual Information Difference (MID) and Mutual Information Quotient (MIQ). For all baseline features, we search exhaustively among all combinations of feature selection schemes and a set of classifiers (Random Forests, Linear Discriminant Analysis, Quadratic Discriminant Analysis and SVM). We report the best results. **MRI**: we directly apply a 3D CNN to the original DCE-MRIs.

Quantitative Results. Radiomics and PD features yielded better performance when used together with a Random Forest classifier (Table 1). We observe that direct application of a 3D CNN (method MRI) does not perform well, presumably due to the lack of sufficient amount of data. Our proposed approach (*TopoTxR*: MRI+Topo) outperforms all baseline methods. Due to the imbalance in the dataset, we also report the classifier specificity and sensitivity. Further evaluation, to address data imbalance, will be carried out in future work.

Ablation Study. Recall that the persistence of a topological structure is defined as the difference between its birth and death times. We threshold out topological structures with low persistence, as they are generally caused by noise and could negatively influence the results. We explore the impact of persistence thresholding by choosing 3 different thresholds so that 90%, 60%, and 30% of the structures remain. According to Table 2, retaining 30% structures (refer to TopoTxR's results in Table 1) yielded an optimal trade-off between the

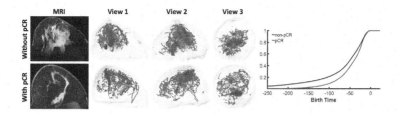

Fig. 5. Qualitative comparison of patients with and without pCR. First column: Slices of breast DCE-MRI with tumor masked in orange (tumor masks are not used in building TopoTxR). Columns 2–4: 3D renderings of topological structures from three different views. 1-D structures (loops) are rendered in blue and 2-D structures (bubbles) in red. Top row: no pCR, Bottow row: pCR. Right: cumulative density function of topological structures' birth times. (Color figure online)

quantity and quality of the topological structures. We also tested the method using 1D structures (loops) only and 2D structures (bubbles) only. Both are better than baseline methods, but still inferior to *TopoTxR*. This shows that the 1D and 2D structures provide complementary predictive information. Finally, the topology structures are dilated to form a mask. We ran an ablation study with regard to the dilation radius and obtain the best performance when no dilation is performed. The results of *TopoTxR* in Table 1 is reported with 30% structures remaining using combined 1 and 2D structures without dilation.

3.1 Discussion and TopoTxR Feature Interpretation

The topological structures extracted by TopoTxR capture the breast tissue structures. Learning directly on these structures and their vicinity provides the opportunity for interpreting the learning outcomes and drawing novel biological insights. Here we provide some visual analysis as a proof of concept.

Figure 5 shows the TopoTxR topographical structures from different views for a representative DCE-MRI scan from each group. We observe that the structures (1D and 2D) are sparse for the case exhibiting pCR, and are relatively dense for the non-pCR case. In the corresponding MRI images, we note that the pCR breast has scattered fibroglandular breast density with minimal background parenchymal enhancement. The non-pCR breast has a more heterogenous fibroglandular breast density with moderate background parenchymal enhancement. This possibly suggests that the *TopoTxR* features capture the complex fibrogladular structure which can be a potential indicator of treatment response.

We also compare the topological behavior of the two populations. Recall the birth time of a topological structure is the threshold at which a cycle appears. In our experiments, since we use the inverse image $f = -I$, the birth time essentially captures -1 times the brightness of a structure. In Fig. 5 (right), we plot the cumulative density function (CDF) of the birth time of topological structures for pCR (red) and non-pCR (blue) patients. The CDFs suggest that pCR patients' tissue structures are generally less bright (or less visible) compared with that of non-pCR patients. This is consistent with our observation on qualitative examples. A Kolmogorov-Smirnov test [22] is performed to compare these CDFs. The computed *p-value* is 0.0002, indicating a significant difference between the distributions of birth times of the pCR and non-pCR patient groups.

4   Conclusion

This paper presents a novel topological biomarker, *TopoTxR*, that leverages the rich geometric information embedded in structural MRI and enables improvement in downstream CNN processing. In particular, we compute 1D cycles and 2D bubbles from breast DCE-MRIs with the theory of persistent homology; these structures are then used to direct the attention of neural networks. We further demonstrate that *TopoTxR* on treatment-naive imaging is predictive of pCR.

References

1. Abdelhafiz, D., Yang, C., Ammar, R., Nabavi, S.: Deep CNN for mammography: advances, challenges and applications. BMC Bioinform. **20**, 281(2019). https:// doi.org/10.1186/s12859-019-2823-4
2. Adams, H., et al.: Persistence images: a stable vector representation of persistent homology. J. Mach. **18**, 1–35 (2017)
3. Braman, N., et al.: Association of peritumoral radiomics with tumor biology and pathologic response to preoperative targeted therapy for HER2 (ERBB2)–positive breast cancer. JAMA Netw. Open **2**(4), e192561–e192561 (2019)
4. Braman, N.M., et al.: Intratumoral and peritumoral radiomics for the pretreatment prediction of pathological complete response to neoadjuvant chemotherapy based on breast DCE-MRI. Breast Cancer Res. **19**, 1–14 (2017)
5. Cain, E., Saha, A., Harowicz, M., Marks, J., Marcom, P., Mazurowski, M.: Multivariate ML models for prediction of pCR to NAC in BCa using MRI features: a study using an independent validation set. BCa Res. Treat. **173**, 455–463 (2019)
6. Carriere, M., Cuturi, M., Oudot, S.: Sliced Wasserstein Kernel for persistence diagrams. In: ICML. JMLR. org (2017)
7. Clough, J., Byrne, N., Oksuz, I., Zimmer, V.A., Schnabel, J.A., King, A.: A topological loss function for deep-learning based image segmentation using persistent homology. In: TPAMI (2020)
8. Dey, T.K., Wang, J., Wang, Y.: Road network reconstruction from satellite images with machine learning supported by topological methods. In: Proceedings of the 27th ACM SIGSPATIAL (2019)
9. Duanmu, H.: Prediction of pCR to NAC in BCa using deep learning with integrative imaging, molecular and demographic data. In: MICCAI (2020)
10. Edelsbrunner, H., Harer, J.: Computational topology: an introduction. Am. Math. Soc. (2010)
11. Grimm, L.: Breast MRI radiogenomics: current status and research implications. J. Magn. Reson. Imaging **43**, 1269–1278 (2015)
12. Ha, R.: Prior to initiation of chemotherapy, can we predict breast tumor response? Deep learning convolutional neural networks approach using a breast MRI tumor dataset. J. Digital Imaging (2018). https://doi.org/10.1007/s10278-018-0144-1

13. Hofer, C., Kwitt, R., Niethammer, M., Uhl, A.: Deep learning with topological signatures. In: Advances in Neural Information Processing Systems (2017)
14. Hu, X., Li, F., Samaras, D., Chen, C.: Topology-preserving deep image segmentation. In: NeurIPS (2019)
15. Hu, X., Wang, Y., Fuxin, L., Samaras, D., Chen, C.: Topology-aware segmentation using discrete Morse theory. In: ICLR (2021)
16. King, V., Brooks, J.D., Bernstein, J.L., Reiner, A.S., Pike, M.C., Morris, E.A.: Background paren. enhancement at breast MRI and BCa risk. Radiology 260, 50–60 (2011)
17. Kusano, G., Hiraoka, Y., Fukumizu, K.: Persistence weighted Gaussian Kernel for topological data analysis. In: ICML (2016)
18. Lee, H., Kang, H., Chung, M.K., Kim, B.-N., Lee, D.S.: Persistent brain network homology from the perspective of dendrogram. IEEE Trans. Med. Imaging 31, 2267–2277 (2012)
19. Liu, M.Z., Mutasa, S., Chang, P., Siddique, M., Jambawalikar, S., Ha, R.: A novel CNN algorithm for pathological complete response prediction using an i-SPY TRIAL breast MRI database. Magn. Reson. Imaging 73, 148–151 (2020)
20. Lundervold, A.S., Lundervold, A.: An overview of deep learning in medical imaging focusing on MRI. Zeitschrift für Medizinische Physik 29(2), 102–127 (2019)
21. Mani, S.: Machine learning for predicting the response of breast cancer to neoadjuvant chemotherapy. JAMIA 20, 688–695 (2013)
22. Massey Jr, F.J.: The Kolmogorov-Smirnov test for goodness of fit. J. Am. Stat. Assoc. 46, 68–78 (1951)
23. Milosavljević, N., Morozov, D., Skraba, P.: Zigzag persistent homology in matrix multiplication time. In: SoCG, pp. 216–225 (2011)
24. Newitt, D., Hylton, N.: Multi-center breast DCE-MRI data and segmentations from patients in the I-SPY 1/ACRIN 6657 trials. Cancer Imaging Arch. (2016)
25. Qu, Y., Zhu, H., Cao, K., Li, X., Ye, M., Sun, Y.: Prediction of pathological complete response to neoadjuvant chemotherapy in breast cancer using a deep learning (dl) method. Thoracic Cancer (2020)
26. Reininghaus, J., Huber, S., Bauer, U., Kwitt, R.: A stable multi-scale Kernel for topological machine learning. In: CVPR (2015)
27. Towns, J., et al.: XSEDE: accelerating scientific discovery. Comput. Sci. Eng. 16(5), 62–74 (2014)
28. Van Griethuysen, J.J., et al.: Computational radiomics system to decode the radiographic phenotype. Cancer Res. 77, e104–e107 (2017)
29. Wang, F., Liu, H., Samaras, D., Chen, C.: TopoGAN: a topology-aware generative adversarial network. In: ECCV, vol. 2 (2020)
30. Wu, P., et al.: Optimal topological cycles and their application in cardiac trabeculae restoration. In: IPMI (2017)
31. Zhang, X., Wu, P., Yuan, C., Wang, Y., Metaxas, D.N., Chen, C.: Heuristic search for homology localization problem and its application in cardiac trabeculae reconstruction. In: IJCAI, pp. 1312–1318 (2019)

Segmentation

Segmenting Two-Dimensional Structures with Strided Tensor Networks

Raghavendra Selvan[1,2(✉)] , Erik B. Dam[1] , and Jens Petersen[1,3]

[1] Department of Computer Science, University of Copenhagen,
Copenhagen, Denmark
{raghav,erikdam,phup}@di.ku.dk
[2] Department of Neuroscience, University of Copenhagen, Copenhagen, Denmark
[3] Department of Oncology, Rigshospitalet, Glostrup, Denmark

Abstract. Tensor networks provide an efficient approximation of operations involving high dimensional tensors and have been extensively used in modelling quantum many-body systems. More recently, supervised learning has been attempted with tensor networks, primarily focused on tasks such as image classification. In this work, we propose a novel formulation of tensor networks for supervised image segmentation which allows them to operate on high resolution medical images. We use the matrix product state (MPS) tensor network on non-overlapping patches of a given input image to predict the segmentation mask by learning a pixel-wise *linear* classification rule in a high dimensional space. The proposed model is end-to-end trainable using backpropagation. It is implemented as a *strided tensor network* to reduce the parameter complexity. The performance of the proposed method is evaluated on two public medical imaging datasets and compared to relevant baselines. The evaluation shows that the strided tensor network yields competitive performance compared to CNN-based models while using fewer resources. Additionally, based on the experiments we discuss the feasibility of using fully linear models for segmentation tasks.(Source code: https://github.com/raghavian/strided-tenet)

Keywords: Tensor networks · Linear models · Image segmentation

1 Introduction

Large strides made in the quality of computer vision in the last decade can be attributed to deep learning based methods [10]; in particular, to the auxiliary developments (powerful hardware, better optimisers, tricks such as dropout, skip connections etc.) that have made convolutional neural networks (CNNs) more effective. This has also influenced biomedical image segmentation with models such as the U-net [22] which have become widely popular[1].

---

[1] First author of [22] noted their U-net work was cited more than once every hour in 2020. https://bit.ly/unet2020.

© Springer Nature Switzerland AG 2021
A. Feragen et al. (Eds.): IPMI 2021, LNCS 12729, pp. 401–414, 2021.
https://doi.org/10.1007/978-3-030-78191-0_31

Tensor networks are factorisations of high dimensional tensors, and have been widely used to study quantum many-body systems [16]. Conceptually, they can be interpreted as linear models operating in high dimensional spaces, in contrast to neural networks which are highly non-linear models operating in lower dimensional spaces. Tensor networks have been used as feature extractors [2], predictors operating in very high dimensional spaces [13] and to compress neural networks [15]. More recently, they are also being studied in the context of supervised learning with growing success [5,23,25]. They have been primarily used for image classification [5,25] and most recently to classify medical images [23]. Tensor networks have not been studied for image segmentation to the best of the authors' knowledge.

In this work, we propose the strided tensor network: a tensor network based image segmentation method. Tensor network operations are performed on image patches to learn a hyper-plane that classifies pixels into foreground and background classes in a high dimensional space. This is similar to classical pixel classification methods operating in some expressive feature space [24,26]. The key difference with tensor networks is that they do not require designed features that encode domain specific knowledge, and still are able to learn *linear* models that are competitive with state-of-the-art CNN-based models, as has been shown for tasks such as image classification [5,23]. Further, the proposed model can be trained in an end-to-end manner in a supervised learning set-up by backpropagating a relevant loss function. We experiment on two biomedical imaging datasets: to segment nuclei from microscopy images of multi-organ tissues, and to segment lungs from chest X-rays (CXR). We compare the strided tensor network with relevant baselines, including deep learning models, and demonstrate that the tensor network based model can yield similar performance compared to CNN-based models with fewer resources.

2   Methods

2.1   Overview

In this work, we propose a tensor network based model to perform image segmentation. This is performed by approximating the segmentation decision as a *linear* model in an exponentially high dimensional space. That is, we are interested in deriving a hyper-plane in a high dimensional space such that it is able to classify pixels into foreground and background classes across all images in the dataset.

We consider non-overlapping image patches, flatten them into 1D vectors and apply simple sinusoidal feature transformations resulting in *local* feature maps. By taking tensor product of these local feature maps, we obtain *global* feature maps which in effect lift the input image patch into an exponentially high dimensional space. Weights for the linear model that operate on the global feature maps, resulting in segmentation predictions, are approximated using the matrix product state (MPS) tensor network[2] [17,19]. The same trainable MPS

---

[2] Matrix product states are also known as Tensor Trains in literature.

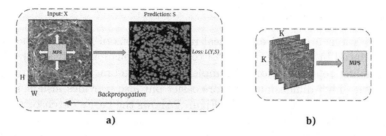

Fig. 1. a) High level overview of the proposed strided tensor network model. Matrix product state (MPS) operations are performed on non-overlapping regions of the input image, X, of size H × W resulting in the predicted segmentation, S. Loss computed between prediction, S, and the ground truth, Y, are backpropagated during training. Arrows on MPS block are used to indicate that the same MPS block is applied across the image. **b)** In practice, the strided tensor network operations can be accelerated using batch processing by creating non-overlapping patches (size K × K) on the fly as input to MPS, and tiling these batched predictions to reconstruct the full image segmentation.

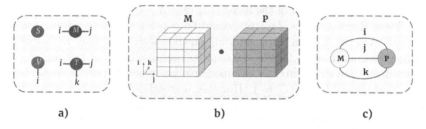

Fig. 2. a) Graphical tensor notation depicting an order-0 tensor (scalar S), order-1 tensor (vector V^i), order-2 tensor (matrix M^{ij}) and an order-3 tensor T^{ijk}. Tensor indices – seen as the dangling edges – are written as superscripts by convention. **b)** Illustration of $< M, P >$: the dot product of two order-3 tensors of dimensions $i = 4, j = 3, k = 2$. **c)** Tensor notation depicting the same dot product between the tensors M_{ijk} and P_{ijk}. Indices that are summed over (tensor contraction) are written as subscripts. Tensor notations can capture operations involving higher order tensors succinctly.

is used on non-overlapping image patches from the entire image resulting in our strided tensor network model for image segmentation. Predicted segmentations are compared with ground truth labels in the training set to obtain a suitable loss which is backpropagated to optimise the weights of our model. A high level overview of the proposed model is illustrated in Fig. 1.

In the remainder of this section, we present a brief introduction to tensor notation, describe the choice of local feature maps, going from local to global feature maps and details on approximating the segmentation rule with MPS, in order to fully describe the proposed strided tensor network for image segmentation.

2.2   Tensor Notation

Tensor notations are concise graphical representations of high dimensional tensors introduced in [18]. A grammar of tensor notations has evolved through the years enabling representation of complex tensor algebra. This not only makes working with high dimensional tensors easier but also provides insight into how they can be efficiently manipulated. Figure 2 shows the basics of tensor notations and one important operation – tensor contraction (in sub-figures b & c). We build upon the ideas of tensor contractions to understand tensor networks such as the MPS, which is used extensively in this work. For more detailed introduction to tensor notations we refer to [3].

2.3   Image Segmentation Using Linear Models

In order to motivate the need for using patches, we first describe the model at the full image level.

Consider a 2 dimensional image, $X \in \mathbb{R}^{H \times W \times C}$ with $N = H \times W$ pixels and C channels. The task of obtaining an M–class segmentation, $Y \in \{0,1\}^{H \times W \times M}$ is to learn the decision rule of the form $f(\cdot \; ; \; \Theta) : X \mapsto Y$, which is parameterised by Θ. These decision rules, $f(\cdot \; ; \; \Theta)$, could be non-linear transfer functions such as neural networks. In this work, building on the success of tensor networks used for supervised learning [5,23,25], we explore the possibility of learning $f(\cdot \; ; \; \Theta)$ that are linear. For simplicity, we assume two class segmentation of single channel images, implying $M = 1$, $C = 1$. However, extending this work to multi-class segmentation of inputs with multiple channels is straightforward.

Before applying the linear decision rule, the input data is first lifted to an exponentially high dimensional space. This is based on the insight that non-linearly separable data in low dimensions could possibly become linearly separable when lifted to a sufficiently high dimensional space [4]. The lift in this work is accomplished in two steps.

First, the image is flattened into a 1-dimensional vector $\mathbf{x} \in \mathbb{R}^N$. Simple transformations are applied to each pixel to increase the number of features per pixel. These increased features are termed local feature maps. Pixel intensity-based local feature maps have been explored in recent machine learning applications of tensor networks [5,21,23]. We use a general sinusoidal local feature map from [25], which increases local features of a pixel from 1 to d:

$$\psi^{i_j}(x_j) = \sqrt{\binom{d-1}{i_j-1}} \left(\cos(\frac{\pi}{2}x_j)\right)^{(d-i_j)} \left(\sin(\frac{\pi}{2}x_j)\right)^{(i_j-1)} \forall \, i_j = 1 \ldots d. \quad (1)$$

The intensity values of individual pixels, x_j, are assumed to be normalised to be in $[0,1]$. Further, the local feature maps are constrained to have unit norm so that the global feature map in the next step also has unit norm.

In the second step, a global feature map is obtained by taking the tensor product[3] of the local feature maps. This operation takes N order-1 tensors and

---

[3] Tensor product is the generalisation of matrix outer product to higher order tensors.

outputs an order-N tensor, $\Phi^{i_1\cdots i_N}(\mathbf{x}) \in [0,1]^{d^N}$ given by

$$\Phi^{i_1\cdots i_N}(\mathbf{x}) = \psi^{i_1}(x_1) \otimes \psi^{i_2}(x_2) \otimes \cdots \otimes \psi^{i_N}(x_N). \qquad (2)$$

Note that after this operation each image can be treated as a vector in the d^N dimensional Hilbert space [16,25].

Given the d^N global feature map in Eq. (2), a linear decision function $f(\cdot;\Theta)$ can be estimated by simply taking the tensor dot product of the global feature map with an order-(N+1) weight tensor, $\Theta^m_{i_1\ldots i_N}$:

$$f^m(\mathbf{x}\;;\;\Theta) = \Theta^m_{i_1\ldots i_N} \cdot \Phi_{i_1\ldots i_N}(\mathbf{x}). \qquad (3)$$

The additional superscript index m on the weight tensor and the prediction is the output index of dimension N. That is, the resulting order-1 tensor from Eq. (3) has N entries corresponding to the pixel level segmentations. Equation (3) is depicted in tensor notation in Fig. 3-a.

2.4 Strided Tensor Networks

While the dot product in Eq. (3) looks easy enough conceptually, on closer inspection its intractability comes to light. The approach used to overcome this intractability leads us to the proposed strided tensor network model.

1. **Intractability of the Dot Product:** The sheer scale of the number of parameters in the weight tensor Θ in Eq. (3) can be mind boggling. For instance, the weight tensor required to operate on an tiny input image of size 16×16 with local feature map $d = 2$ is $N \cdot d^N = 1024 \cdot 2^{1024} \approx 10^{79}$ which is close to the number of atoms in the observable universe[4] (estimated to be about 10^{80}).

2. **Loss of Spatial Correlation:** The assumption in Eqs. (1), (2) and (3) is that the input is a 1D vector. Meaning, the 2D image is flattened into a 1D vector. For tasks like image segmentation, spatial structure of the images can be informative in making improved segmentation decisions. Loss of spatial pixel correlation can be detrimental to downstream tasks; more so when dealing with complex structures encountered in medical images.

We overcome these two constraints by approximating the linear model in Eq. (3) using MPS tensor network and by operating on strides of smaller non-overlapping image patches.

Matrix Product State. Computing the inner product in Eq. (3) becomes infeasible with increasing N [25]. It also turns out that only a small number of degrees of freedom in these exponentially high dimensional Hilbert spaces are relevant [16,20]. These relevant degrees of freedom can be efficiently accessed using tensor networks such as the MPS [17,19]. In image analysis, accessing this

---

[4] https://en.wikipedia.org/wiki/Observable_universe.

smaller sub-space of the high dimensional Hilbert space corresponds to accessing interactions between pixels that are local either in spatial- or in some feature-space sense that is relevant for the task.

MPS is a tensor factorisation method that can approximate any order-N tensor with a chain of order-3 tensors. This is visualized using tensor notation in Fig. 3-b for approximating $\Theta^{ij}_{i_1...i_N}$ using $A^{ij}_{\alpha_j\alpha_{j+1}} \forall j = 1...N$ which are of order-3 (except on the borders where they are order-2). The dimension of subscript indices of α_j which are contracted can be varied to yield better approximations. These variable dimensions of the intermediate tensors in MPS are known as bond dimension β. MPS approximation of $\Theta^m_{i_1...i_N}$ depicted in Fig. 3-b is given by

$$\Theta^m_{i_1...i_N} = \sum_{\alpha_1,\alpha_2,...\alpha_N} A^{i_1}_{\alpha_1} A^{i_2}_{\alpha_1\alpha_2} A^{i_3}_{\alpha_2\alpha_3} \cdots A^{m,i_j}_{\alpha_j\alpha_{j+1}} \cdots A^{i_N}_{\alpha_N}. \tag{4}$$

The components of these intermediate lower-order tensors $A^{ij}_{\alpha_j\alpha_{j+1}} \forall j = 1...N$ form the tunable parameters of the MPS tensor network. This MPS factorisation in Eq. (4) reduces the number of parameters to represent Θ from $N \cdot d^N$ to $\{N \cdot d \cdot N \cdot \beta^2\}$ with β controlling the quality of these approximations[5]. Note that when $\beta = d^{N/2}$ the MPS approximation is exact [16,25].

Various implementations of MPS perform the sequence of tensor contractions in different ways for efficiency. We use the TorchMPS implementation in this work, which first contracts the horizontal edges and performs tensor contractions along the vertical edges [12, 23].

MPS on Non-overlapping Patches. The issue of loss in spatial pixel correlation is not alleviated with MPS as it operates on flattened input images. MPS with higher bond dimensions could possibly allow interactions between all pixels but, due to the quadratic increase in number of parameters with the bond dimension β, working with higher bond dimensions can be prohibitive.

To address this issue, we apply MPS on small non-overlapping image regions. These smaller patches can be flattened

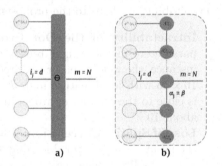

Fig. 3.   a) Linear decision rule in Eq. 3 depicted in tensor notation. Note that Θ has N+1 edges as it is an order-(N+1) tensor. The d-dimensional local feature maps are the gray nodes marked $\psi^{i_j}(x_j)$. b) Matrix product state (MPS) approximation of Θ in Eq. 4 into a tensor train comprising up to order-3 tensors, $A^{ij}_{\alpha_j\alpha_{j+1}}$.

without severe degradation of spatial correlation. Similar strategy of using MPS on small image regions has been used for image classification using tensor networks in [23]. This is also in the same spirit of using convolutional filter kernels

---

[5] Tensor indices are dropped for brevity in the remainder of the manuscript.

in CNNs when the kernel width is set to be equal to the stride length. This formulation of using MPS on regions of size $K \times K$ with a stride equal to K in both dimensions results in the strided tensor network formulation, given as

$$f(\mathbf{x}; \Theta_K) = \{\Theta_K \cdot \Phi(\mathbf{x}_{(i,j)})\} \quad \forall\, i = 1, \ldots, H/K,\; j = 1, \ldots, W/K \qquad (5)$$

where (i, j) are used to index the patch from row i and column j of the image grid with patches of size $K \times K$. The weight matrix in Eq. (5), Θ_K is subscripted with K to indicate that MPS operations are performed on $K \times K$ patches.

In summary, with the proposed strided tensor network formulation, linear segmentation decisions in Eq. (3) are approximated at the patch level using MPS. The resulting patch level predictions are tiled back to obtain the $H \times W$ segmentation mask.

2.5 Optimisation

The weight tensor, Θ_K, in Eq. (5) and in turn the lower order tensors in Eq. (4) which are the model parameters can be learned in a supervised setting. For a given labelled training set with T data points, $\mathcal{D} : \{(\mathbf{x}_1, \mathbf{y}_1), \ldots (\mathbf{x}_T, \mathbf{y}_T)\}$, the training loss to be minimised is

$$\mathcal{L}_{tr} = \frac{1}{T} \sum_{t=1}^{T} L(f(\mathbf{x}_i), \mathbf{y}_i), \qquad (6)$$

where $\mathbf{y}_i$ are the binary ground truth masks and $L(\cdot)$ can be a suitable loss function suitable for segmentation tasks. In this work, as both datasets were largely balanced (between foreground and background classes) we use binary cross entropy loss.

3 Data and Experiments

Segmentation performance of the proposed strided tensor network is evaluated on two datasets and compared with relevant baseline methods. Description of the data and the experiments are presented in this section.

3.1 Data

MO-NuSeg Dataset. The first dataset we use in our experiments is the multi-organ nuclei segmentation (MO-NuSeg) challenge dataset[6] [8]. This dataset consists 44 Hematoxylin and eosin (H&E) stained tissue images, of size 1000×1000, with about 29,000 manually annotated nuclear boundaries. The dataset has tissues from seven different organs and is a challenging one due to the variations across different organs. The challenge organizers provide a split of 30 training/validation images and 14 testing images which we also follow to allow for

---

[6] https://monuseg.grand-challenge.org/.

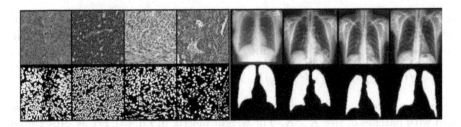

Fig. 4. (First four columns) Sample images from the MO-Nuseg dataset comprising histopathology slides from multiple organs (top row) and the corresponding binary masks (bottom row). (Last four columns) Sample chest X-ray images from the Lung-CXR dataset with corresponding binary masks.

comparisons with other reported methods. Four training tissue images and the corresponding binary nuclei masks are shown in the first four columns of Fig. 4.

Lung-CXR Dataset. We also use the lung chest X-ray dataset collected from the Shenzhen and Montgomery hospitals with posterio-anterior views for tuberculosis diagnosis [7]. The CXR images used in this work are of size 128×128 with corresponding binary lung masks for a total of 704 cases which is split into training (352), validation (176) and test (176) sets. Four sample CXRs and the corresponding binary lung masks are shown in the last four columns of Fig. 4.

3.2   Experiments

Experimental Set-Up. The proposed strided tensor network model was compared with a convolutional neural network (U-net [22]), a modified tensor network (MPS TeNet) that uses one large MPS operation similar to the binary classification model in [5], and a multi-layered perceptron (MLP). Batch size of 1 and 32 were used for the MO-NuSeg and Lung-CXR datasets, respectively, which was the maximum batch size usable with the baseline U-net; all other models were trained with the same batch size for a fairer comparison. The models were trained with the Adam optimizer and an initial learning rate of 5×10^{-4}, except for the MPS TeNet which required smaller learning rate of 1×10^{-5} for convergence; they were trained until there was no improvement in validation accuracy for 10 consecutive epochs. The model based on the best validation performance was used to predict on the test set. All models were implemented in PyTorch and trained on a single GTX 1080 graphics processing unit (GPU) with 8 GB memory. The development and training of all models in this work was estimated to produce 61.9 kg of CO2eq, equivalent to 514.6 km travelled by car as measured by Carbontracker[7] [1].

Metrics. Performance of the different methods for both datasets are compared using Dice score based on binary predictions, $\hat{y}_i \in \{0, 1\}$ obtained by thresholding soft segmentations at 0.5 which we recognise is an arbitrary threshold.

---

[7] https://github.com/lfwa/carbontracker/.

A more balanced comparison is provided using the area under the precision-recall curve (PRAUC or equivalently the average precision) using the soft segmentation predictions, $s_i \in [0, 1]$.

Model Hyperparameters. The initial number of filters for the U-net model was tuned from $[8, 16, 32, 64]$ and a reasonable choice based on validation performance and training time was found to be 8 for MO-NuSeg dataset and 16 for Lung-CXR dataset. The MLP consists of 6 levels, 64 hidden units per layer and ReLU activation functions and was designed to match the strided tensor network in number of parameters. The strided tensor network has two critical hyperparameters: the bond dimension (β) and the stride length (K), which were tuned using the validation set performance. The bond dimension controls the quality of the MPS approximations and was tuned from the range $\beta = [2, 4, 8, 12, 16, 20, 24]$. The stride length controls the field of view of the MPS and was tuned from the range $K = [2, 4, 8, 16, 32, 64, 128]$. For MO-NuSeg dataset, the best validation performance was stable for any $\beta \geq 4$, so we used the smallest with $\beta = 4$ and the best performing stride parameter was $K = 8$. For the Lung-CXR dataset similar performance was observed with $\beta \geq 20$, so we set $\beta = 20$ and obtained $K = 32$. The local feature dimension (d) was set to 4 (see Sect. 4 for additional discussion on local feature maps).

Table 1. Test set performance comparison for segmenting nuclei from the stained tissue images (MO-NuSeg) and segmenting lungs from chest CT (Lung-CXR). For all models, we report the number of parameters $|\Theta|$, computation time per training epoch, area under the curve of the precision-recall curve (PRAUC) and average Dice accuracy (with standard deviation over the test set). The representation (Repr.) used by each of the methods at input is also mentioned.

Dataset	Models	Repr.	$|\Theta|$	t(s)	PRAUC	Dice
MO-NuSeg	Strided TeNet (ours)	1D	$5.1K$	21.2	0.78	0.70 ± 0.10
	U-net [22]	2D	$500K$	24.5	0.81	0.70 ± 0.08
	MPS TeNet [5]	1D	$58.9M$	240.1	0.55	0.52 ± 0.09
	CNN	2D	–	510	–	0.69 ± 0.10
Lung-CXR	Strided TeNet (ours)	1D	$2.0M$	6.1	0.97	0.93 ± 0.06
	U-net [22]	2D	$4.2M$	4.5	0.98	0.95 ± 0.02
	MPS TeNet [5]	1D	$8.2M$	35.7	0.67	0.57 ± 0.09
	MLP	1D	$2.1M$	4.1	0.95	0.89 ± 0.05

3.3 Results

MO-NuSeg. Performance of the strided tensor network compared to the baseline methods on the MO-NuSeg dataset are presented in Table 1 where we report the PRAUC, Dice accuracy, number of parameters and the average training time per epoch for all the methods. Based on both PRAUC and Dice accuracy, we see

that the proposed strided tensor network (PRAUC = 0.78, Dice = 0.70) and the
U-net (PRAUC = 0.81, Dice = 0.70) obtain similar performance. There was no
significant difference between the two methods based on paired sample t-tests.
The Dice accuracy reported in the paper that introduced the dataset[8] in [8]
(0.69) is also in the same range as the reported numbers for the strided tensor network. A clear performance difference is seen in comparison to the MPS
tensor network (PRAUC = 0.55, Dice = 0.52); the low metrics for this method
is expected as it is primarily a classification model [5] modified to perform segmentation to compare with the most relevant tensor network.

Lung-CXR Dataset. Segmentation accuracy of the strided tensor network is
compared to U-net, MPS tensor network and MLP on the Lung-CXR dataset in
Table 1. U-net (0.98) and the proposed strided tensor network (0.97) attain very
high PRAUC, and the Dice accuracy for strided tensor network is 0.93 and for
U-net it is 0.95; there was no significant difference based on paired sample t-test.
Two test set predictions where the strided tensor network had high false positive
(top row) and high false negative (bottom row), along with the predictions from
other methods and the input CXR are shown in Fig. 5.

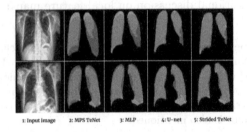

1: Input image   2: MPS TeNet   3: MLP   4: U-net   5: Strided TeNet

Fig. 5. Two test set CXRs from Lung-CXR dataset along with the predicted segmen-
tations from the different models. All images are upsampled for better visualisation.
(Prediction Legend – Green: True Positive, Grey: False Negative, Pink: False Positive)
(Color figure online)

4   Discussion and Conclusions

Results from Table 1 show that the proposed strided tensor network compares
favourably to other baseline models across both datasets. In particular, to the
U-net where there is no significant difference in Dice accuracy and PRAUC. The
computation cost per training epoch of strided tensor network is also reported in
Table 1. The training time per epoch for both datasets for the proposed strided
tensor network is in the same range of those for U-net. In multiple runs of
experiments we noticed that U-net converged faster ($\approx$50 epochs) whereas the

---

[8] These numbers are reported from [8] for their CNN2 model used for binary segmentation. Run time in Table 1 for CNN2 model could be lower with more recent
hardware.

tensor network model converged around 80 epochs. Overall, the training time for tensor network models on both datasets was under one hour. A point also to be noted is that operations for CNNs are highly optimised in frameworks such as PyTorch. More efficient implementations of tensor network operations are being addressed in recent works [6,14] and the computation cost is expected to reduce further.

An additional observation in the experiments on MO-NuSeg data, reported in Table 1 is the number of parameters used by the strided tensor network (5.1 K) which is about two orders of magnitude smaller than that of the U-net (500 K), without a substantial difference in segmentation accuracy. As a consequence, the maximum GPU memory utilised by the proposed tensor network was 0.8 GB and it was 6.5 GB for U-net. This difference in GPU memory utilisation can have ramifications as the strided tensor network can handle larger batch sizes (resulting in more stable, faster training). This could be most useful when dealing with large medical images which can be processed without patching them for processing. In general, tensor network models require lesser GPU memory as they do not have intermediate feature maps and do not store the corresponding computation graphs in memory, similar to MLPs [23].

The predicted lung masks in Fig. 5 show some interesting underlying behaviours of the different methods. MPS TeNet, MLP and the strided tensor network all operate on 1D representations of the data (flattened 2D images). The influence of loss of spatial correlation due to flattening is clearly noticeable with the predicted segmentations from MPS TeNet (column 2) and MLP (column 3), where both models predict lung masks which resemble highly regularised lung representations learned from the training data. The predictions from strided tensor network (column 5) are able to capture the true shape with more fidelity and are closer to the U-net (column 4). This behaviour could be attributed to the input representations used by each of these models. U-net operates on 2D images and does not suffer from this loss of spatial correlation between pixels. The proposed strided tensor network also operates on flattened 1D vectors but only on smaller regions due to the patch-based striding. Loss of spatial correlation in patches is lower when compared to flattening full images.

Influence of Local Feature Maps. Local feature map in Eq. (1) used to increase the local dimension (d) are also commonly used in many kernel based methods and these connections have been explored in earlier works [25]. We also point out that the local maps are similar to *warping* in Gaussian processes which are used to obtain non-stationary covariance functions from stationary ones [11]. While in this work we used simple sinusoidal transformations, it has been speculated that more expressive features could improve the tensor network performance [25]. To test this, we explored the use of jet-based features [9] which can summarise pixel neighbourhoods using first and second order derivatives at multiple scales, and have previously shown promising results. However, our experiments on the Lung-CXR dataset showed no substantial difference in the segmentation performance compared to when simply using the sinusoidal feature map in Eq. (1). We plan on exploring a more comprehensive analysis of local feature maps on other datasets in possible future work.

Learning a Single Filter? CNNs like the U-net thrive by learning banks of filters at multiple scales, which learn distinctive features and textures, making them effective in computer vision tasks. The proposed strided tensor network operates on small image patches at the input resolution. Using the CNN framework, this is analogous to learning a single filter that can be applied to the entire image. We illustrate this behaviour in Fig. 6, where the strided tensor network operates on 32×32 image regions. We initially see block effects due to the large stride and within a few epochs the model is able to adapt to the local pixel information. This we find to be quite an interesting behaviour. A framework that utilises multiple such tensor network based *filters* could make these classes of models more versatile and powerful.

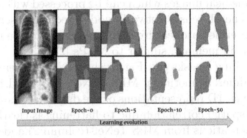

Fig. 6. Progression of learning for the strided tensor network, for the task of segmenting lung regions. Two *validation* set input chest CT images (column 1) and the corresponding predictions at different training epochs are visualized overlaid with the ground truth segmentation. Images are of size 128×128 and the stride is over 32×32 regions. All images are upsampled for better visualisation. (Prediction Legend – Green: True Positive, Grey: False Negative, Pink: False Positive) (Color figure online)

Conclusions. In this work, we presented a novel tensor network based image segmentation method. We proposed the strided tensor network which uses MPS to approximate hyper-planes in high dimensional spaces, to predict pixel classification into foreground and background classes. In order to alleviate the loss of spatial correlation, and to reduce the exponential increase in number of parameters, the strided tensor network operates on small image patches. We have demonstrated promising segmentation performance on two biomedical imaging tasks. The experiments revealed interesting insights into the possibility of applying linear models based on tensor networks for image segmentation tasks. This is a different paradigm compared to the CNNs, and could have the potential to introduce a different class of supervised learning methods to perform image segmentation.

Acknowledgements. Jens Petersen is partly funded by a research grants from the Danish Cancer Society (grant no. R231-A13976) and Varian Medical Systems.

References

1. Anthony, L.F.W., Kanding, B., Selvan, R.: Carbontracker: tracking and predicting the carbon footprint of training deep learning models. In: ICML Workshop on Challenges in Deploying and monitoring Machine Learning Systems, July 2020. arXiv:2007.03051
2. Bengua, J.A., Phien, H.N., Tuan, H.D., Do, M.N.: Matrix product state for feature extraction of higher-order tensors. arXiv preprint arXiv:1503.00516 (2015)
3. Bridgeman, J.C., Chubb, C.T.: Hand-waving and interpretive dance: an introductory course on tensor networks. J. Phys. **50**(22), 223001 (2017)
4. Cortes, C., Vapnik, V.: Support-vector networks. Mach. Learn. **20**(3), 273–297 (1995)
5. Efthymiou, S., Hidary, J., Leichenauer, S.: Tensornetwork for Machine Learning. arXiv preprint arXiv:1906.06329 (2019)
6. Fishman, M., White, S.R., Stoudenmire, E.M.: The ITensor software library for tensor network calculations. arXiv preprint arXiv:2007.14822 (2020)
7. Jaeger, S., Candemir, S., Antani, S., Wáng, Y.X.J., Lu, P.X., Thoma, G.: Two public chest x-ray datasets for computer-aided screening of pulmonary diseases. Quant. Imaging Med. Surg. **4**(6), 475 (2014)
8. Kumar, N., Verma, R., Sharma, S., Bhargava, S., Vahadane, A., Sethi, A.: A dataset and a technique for generalized nuclear segmentation for computational pathology. IEEE Trans. Med. Imaging **36**(7), 1550–1560 (2017)
9. Larsen, A.B.L., Darkner, S., Dahl, A.L., Pedersen, K.S.: Jet-based local image descriptors. In: Fitzgibbon, A., Lazebnik, S., Perona, P., Sato, Y., Schmid, C. (eds.) ECCV 2012. LNCS, vol. 7574, pp. 638–650. Springer, Heidelberg (2012). https://doi.org/10.1007/978-3-642-33712-3_46
10. LeCun, Y., Bengio, Y., Hinton, G.: Deep learning. Nature **521**(7553), 436–444 (2015)
11. MacKay, D.J.: Introduction to Gaussian processes. NATO ASI Series F Computer and Systems Sciences **168**, 133–166 (1998)
12. Miller, J.: Torchmps. https://github.com/jemisjoky/torchmps (2019)
13. Novikov, A., Trofimov, M., Oseledets, I.: Exponential machines. Bull. Polish Acad. Sci. Tech. Sci. **66**(6), 789–797 (2018)
14. Novikov, A., Izmailov, P., Khrulkov, V., Figurnov, M., Oseledets, I.V.: Tensor train decomposition on tensorflow (t3f). J. Mach. Learn. Res. **21**(30), 1–7 (2020)
15. Novikov, A., Podoprikhin, D., Osokin, A., Vetrov, D.P.: Tensorizing neural networks. In: Advances in Neural Information Processing Systems, pp. 442–450 (2015)
16. Orús, R.: A practical introduction to tensor networks: matrix product states and projected entangled pair states. Ann. Phys. **349**, 117–158 (2014)
17. Oseledets, I.V.: Tensor-train decomposition. SIAM J. Sci. Comput. **33**(5), 2295–2317 (2011)
18. Penrose, R.: Applications of negative dimensional tensors. Comb. Math. Appl. **1**, 221–244 (1971)
19. Perez-Garcia, D., Verstraete, F., Wolf, M.M., Cirac, J.I.: Matrix product state representations. arXiv preprint quant-ph/0608197 (2006)
20. Poulin, D., Qarry, A., Somma, R., Verstraete, F.: Quantum simulation of time-dependent Hamiltonians and the convenient illusion of Hilbert space. Phys. Rev. Lett. **106**(17), 170501 (2011)
21. Reyes, J., Stoudenmire, M.: A multi-scale tensor network architecture for classification and regression. arXiv preprint arXiv:2001.08286 (2020)

22. Ronneberger, O., Fischer, P., Brox, T.: U-Net: convolutional networks for biomedical image segmentation. In: Navab, N., Hornegger, J., Wells, W.M., Frangi, A.F. (eds.) MICCAI 2015. LNCS, vol. 9351, pp. 234–241. Springer, Cham (2015). https://doi.org/10.1007/978-3-319-24574-4_28

23. Selvan, R., Dam, E.B.: Tensor networks for medical image classification. In: International Conference on Medical Imaging with Deep Learning - Full Paper Track. Proceedings of Machine Learning Research, vol. 121, pp. 721–732. PMLR (06–08 Jul 2020)

24. Soares, J.V., Leandro, J.J., Cesar, R.M., Jelinek, H.F., Cree, M.J.: Retinal vessel segmentation using the 2-D Gabor wavelet and supervised classification. IEEE Trans. Med. Imaging 25(9), 1214–1222 (2006)

25. Stoudenmire, E., Schwab, D.J.: Supervised learning with tensor networks. In: Advances in Neural Information Processing Systems, pp. 4799–4807 (2016)

26. Vermeer, K., Van der Schoot, J., Lemij, H., De Boer, J.: Automated segmentation by pixel classification of retinal layers in ophthalmic OCT images. Biomed. Opt. Express 2(6), 1743–1756 (2011)

Distributional Gaussian Process Layers for Outlier Detection in Image Segmentation

Sebastian G. Popescu[1]([✉]), David J. Sharp[1], James H. Cole[2],
Konstantinos Kamnitsas[1], and Ben Glocker[1]

[1] Imperial College London, London, UK
s.popescu16@imperial.ac.uk
[2] University College London, London, UK

Abstract. We propose a parameter efficient Bayesian layer for hierarchical convolutional Gaussian Processes that incorporates Gaussian Processes operating in Wasserstein-2 space to reliably propagate uncertainty. This directly replaces convolving Gaussian Processes with a distance-preserving affine operator on distributions. Our experiments on brain tissue-segmentation show that the resulting architecture approaches the performance of well-established deterministic segmentation algorithms (U-Net), which has never been achieved with previous hierarchical Gaussian Processes. Moreover, by applying the same segmentation model to out-of-distribution data (i.e., images with pathology such as brain tumors), we show that our uncertainty estimates result in out-of-distribution detection that outperforms the capabilities of previous Bayesian networks and reconstruction-based approaches that learn normative distributions.

1 Introduction

Deep learning methods have achieved state-of-the-art results on a plethora of medical image segmentation tasks [15]. However, their application in clinical settings is very limited due to issues pertaining to lack of reliability and miscalibration of estimated confidence in predictions. Most research into incorporating uncertainty into medical image segmentation has gravitated around modelling inter-rater variability and the inherent aleatoric uncertainty associated to the dataset, which can be caused by noise or inter-class ambiguities. However, not much focus has been placed on how models behave when processing unexpected input, which differ from what has been processed during training, often called anomalies, outliers or out-of-distribution samples.

Out-of-distribution detection (OOD) in medical imaging has been mostly approached through the lens of reconstruction-based techniques involving some

Electronic supplementary material The online version of this chapter (https:// doi.org/10.1007/978-3-030-78191-0_32) contains supplementary material, which is available to authorized users.

A. Feragen et al. (Eds.): IPMI 2021, LNCS 12729, pp. 415–427, 2021.
https://doi.org/10.1007/978-3-030-78191-0_32

form of encoder-decoder network trained on normative datasets [5]. Conversely, we focus on enhancing task-specific models (e.g. a segmentation model) with reliable uncertainty quantification that enables outlier detection. Standard deep neural networks (DNNs), despite their high predictive performance, often show poor calibration between confidence estimates and prediction accuracy when processing unseen samples that are not from the data manifold of training set (e.g. in the presence of pathology). To alleviate this, Bayesian approaches that assign posteriors over both weights and function space have been proposed [14]. In this paper we follow an alternative approach, using Gaussian Processes (GP) as the building block for deep Bayesian networks. The usage of GP for image classification has garnered interest in the past years. Convolutional GP were stacked on feed forward GP layers applied in a convolutional manner, with promising improvements in accuracy compared to their shallow counterpart [4]. We expand on the latter work, by introducing a simpler convolutional mechanism, which does not require convolving GP at each layer and hence alleviates the computational cost of optimizing over inducing points' locations residing in high dimensional spaces. We propose a plug-in Bayesian layer more amenable to CNN architectures, which replaces the convolved filter followed by parametric activation function with a distance-preserving affine operator on stochastic layers for convolving the Gaussian measures from the previous layer of a hierarchical GP, and subsequently using Distributional Gaussian Processes (DistGP) [13] as a one-to-one mapping, essentially acting as a non-parametric activation function. DistGP were shown to be better at propagating outliers, as given by high variance, compared to standard GP due to their kernel design.

1.1 Related Work

Research into Bayesian models has focused on a separation of uncertainty into two different types, aleatoric (data intrinsic) and epistemic (model parameter uncertainty). The former is irreducible, given by noise in the data acquisition process and has been extensively used for medical image segmentation [10], whereas the latter can be reduced by giving the model more data. It has also found itself used in segmentation tasks [11]. However, none of these works test how their models behave in the presence of outliers. Another type of uncertainty is introduced in [13], where Sparse Gaussian Processes (SGP) [8] are decomposed into components that separate within-data manifold uncertainty from distributional uncertainty. The latter increases away from the training data manifold, which we use here as a measure of OOD. To find similar metrics of OOD we explored general OOD literature for models which we can adapt for image segmentation. Variations of classical one-versus-all models have been adapted to neural networks [6,12]. The closest work that we could find to our proposed approach uses a deep network as a feature extractor for an RBF network [2]. The authors quantify epistemic uncertainty as the L2 distance between a given data point and centroids corresponding to different classes, much alike the RBF kernels and the inducing point approach seen in SGP.

1.2 Contributions

This work makes the following main contributions:

- We introduce a Bayesian layer that combines convolved affine operators that are upper bounded in Wasserstein-2 space and DistGP as "activation functions", which results in an expressive non-parametric convolutional layer with Lipschitz continuity and reliable uncertainty quantification.
- We show for the first time that a GP-based convolutional architecture achieves competitive results in segmentation tasks in comparison to a U-Net.
- We demonstrate improved OOD results compared to Bayesian models and reconstruction-based models.

2 Hierarchical GP with Wasserstein-2 Kernels

We denote input points $X = (x_1, ..., x_n)$ and the output vector $Y = (y_1, ..., y_n)$. We consider a Deep GP (DGP), which is a composition of functions $p_L = p_L \circ ... \circ p_1$. Each p_l is given by a $GP(m, k)$ prior on the stochastic function F_l, where under standard Gaussian identities we have: $p(Y|F_L) = \mathcal{N}(Y|F_L, \beta)$, $p(F_l|U_l; F_{l-1}, Z_{l-1}) = \mathcal{N}(F_l|K_{nm}K_{mm}^{-1}U_l, K_{nn} - K_{nm}K_{mm}^{-1}K_{mn}; X, Z)$ and $p(U_l; Z_l) = \mathcal{N}(U_l|0, K_{mm})$, Z_l and U_l are the locations and values respectively of the GP's inducing points. β represents the likelihood noise and $K_{\cdot, \cdot}$ represents the kernel. A DGP is then defined as a stack of shallow SGP operating in Euclidean space with the prior being:

$$p(Y) = \underbrace{p(Y|F_L)}_{\text{likelihood}} \underbrace{\prod_{l=1}^{L} p(F_l|U_l; F_{l-1}, Z_{l-1})p(U_l)}_{\text{Euclidean prior}} \tag{1}$$

where for brevity of notation we denote $Z_0 = X$. Differently from DGP, in a Hierarchical DistGP [13] all layers except the last one are deterministic operations on Gaussian measures. Concretely, it has the following joint density prior:

$$p(Y, \{F_l, U_l\}_{l=1}^{L}) = \underbrace{p(Y|F_L)}_{\text{likelihood}} \underbrace{\prod_{l=2}^{L} p(F_l|F_{l-1}, U_l; Z_{l-1})p(U_l)}_{\text{Wasserstein space prior}} \underbrace{p(F_1|U_1; X)p(U_1)}_{\text{Euclidean space prior}} \tag{2}$$

A factorized posterior between layers and dimensions is introduced $q(F_L, \{U_l\}_{l=1}^{L}) = p(F_L|U_L; Z_{L-1}) \prod_{l=1}^{L} q(U_l)$, where for $1 \leq l \leq L$ the approximate posterior over is $U_l \sim \mathbb{N}(m_l, \Sigma_l)$ and $Z_l \sim \mathbb{N}(z_{m_l}, Z_{\Sigma_l})$. Z_0 is optimized in standard Euclidean space. Using Jensen's inequality we arrive at the evidence lower bound (ELBO):

$$L = \mathbb{E}_{q(F_L, \{U_l\}_{l=1}^{L})} \frac{p(Y, F_L, \{U_l\}_{l=1}^{L})}{q(F_L, \{U_l\}_{l=1}^{L})} = \mathbb{E}_{q(F_L, \{U_l\}_{l=1}^{L})} p(Y|F_L) - \sum_{l=1}^{L} KL(q(U_l)|p(U_l)) \tag{3}$$

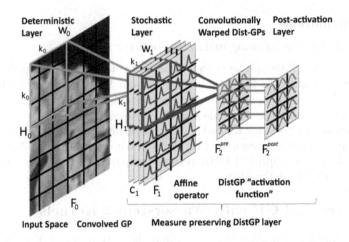

Fig. 1. Schematic of measure-preserving DistGP layer.

3 Convolutionally Warped DistGP and Activation Function

For ease of notation and graphical representation we describe the case of the input being a 2D image, with no loss of generality. We denote the image's representation $F_l \in \mathbb{R}^{H_l, W_l, C_l}$ with width W_l, height H_l and C_l channels at the l-th layer of a multi-layer model. F_0 is the image. Consider a square kernel of size $k_l \times k_l$. We denote with $F_l^{[p,k_l]} \in \mathbb{R}^{k_l, k_l, C_l}$ the p-th patch of F_l, which is the area of F_l that the kernel covers when overlaid at position p during convolution (e.g. orange square for a 3×3 kernel in Fig. 1). We introduce the convolved $GP_0 : F_0^{[p,k_0]} \to \mathcal{N}(m,k)$ with $Z_0 \in \mathbb{R}^{k_0,k_0,C_0}$ to be the SGP operating on the Euclidean space of patches of the input image in a similar fashion to the layers introduced in [4]. For $1 \leq l \leq L$ we introduce affine embeddings $A_l \in \mathbb{R}^{k_l,k_l,C_{l-1},C_{l,pre}}$, where $C_{l,pre}$ denotes the number of channels in the pre-activation (e.g. F_2^{pre} in Fig. 1), which are convolved on the previous stochastic layer in the following manner:

$$m(F_l^{pre}) = Conv_{2D}(m(F_{l-1}), A_l) \tag{4}$$

$$var(F_l^{pre}) = Conv_{2D}(var(F_{l-1}), A_l^2) \tag{5}$$

The affine operator is sequentially applied on the mean, respectively variance components of the previous layer F_{l-1} so as to propagate the Gaussian measures to the next pre-activation layer F_l^{pre}. To obtain the post-activation layer, we apply a $DistGP_l : F_l^{pre,[p,1]} \to \mathcal{N}(m,k)$ in a many-to-one manner on the pre-activation patches to arrive at F_l^{post}. Figure 1 depicts this new module, entitled "Measure preserving DistGP" layer. In [4] the convolved GP is used across the entire hierarchy, thereby inducing points are in high-dimensional space ($k_l^2 * C_l$). In our case, the convolutional process is replaced by an inducing points free affine operator, with inducing points in low-dimensional space $(C_{l,pre})$ for the DistGP activation functions. The affine operator outputs $C_{l,pre}$, which is taken to be higher than the associated output space of DistGP activation functions C_l. Hence, the affine operator can cheaply expand the channels, in constrast to the layers in [4] which would require high-dimensional multi-output GP. We motivate the preservation of distance in Wasserstein-2 space in the following section.

4 Imposing Lipschitz Conditions in Convolutionally Warped DistGP

If a sample is identified as an outlier at certain layer, respectively being flagged with high variance, in an ideal scenario we would like to preserve that status throughout the remainder of the network. As the kernels operate in Wasserstein-2 space, the distance of a data point's first two moments with respect to inducing points is vital. Hence, we would like our network to vary smoothly between layers, so that similar objects in previous layers get mapped into similar spaces in the Wasserstein-2 domain. In this section, we accomplish this by quantifying the *"Lipschitzness"* of our "Measure preserving DistGP" layer and by imposing constraints on the affine operators so that they preserve distances in Wasserstein-2 space.

Definition. We define the Wasserstein-2 distance as $W_2(\mu, \nu) = (\inf_{\pi \in \Pi(\mu,\nu)} \int [x-y]^2 d\pi(x, y))^{1/2}$, where $\Pi(\mu, \nu)$ the set of all probability measures Π over the product set $\mathbb{R} \times \mathbb{R}$ with marginals μ and ν. The squared Wasserstein-2 distance between two multivariate Gaussian distributions $\mathbb{N}(m_1, \Sigma_1)$ and $\mathbb{N}(m_2, \Sigma_2)$ with diagonal covariances is : $\|m_1 - m_2\|_2^2 + \|\Sigma_1^{1/2} - \Sigma_2^{1/2}\|_F^2$, where $\|\cdot\|_F$ represents the Frobenius norm.

Proposition 1. *For a given DistGP F and a Gaussian measure $\mu \sim \mathcal{N}(m_1, \Sigma_1)$ to be the centre of an annulus $B(x) = \{\nu \sim \mathcal{N}(m_2, \Sigma_2 | 0.125 \leq \frac{W_2(\mu,\nu)}{l^2} \leq 1.0$ and choosing any ν inside the ball we have the following Lipschitz bounds: $W_2 (F(\mu), F(\nu)) \leq LW_2(\mu, \nu)$, where $L = (\frac{4\sigma^2}{l})^2 [\|K_z^{-1}m\|_2^2 + \|K_z^{-1}(K_z - S) K_z^{-1}\|_2]$ and l, σ^2 are the lengthscales and variance of the kernel.*

Proof is given in Sect. 4.1. This theoretical result shows that the *DistGP activation functions* have Lipschitz constants with respect to the Wasserstein-2 metric in both output and input domain. It is of vital importance to ensure the hidden layers F_l^{pre} preserve the distance in Wasserstein-2 space in relation to the one at F_{l-1}^{post}, especially taking into consideration that we apply convolutional affine operators (Eq. 4, 5), which could break the smoothness of DistGP activations. This will ensure that the distance between previously identified outliers and inliers will stay constant.

Proposition 2. *We consider the affine operator $A \in \mathbb{R}^{C,1}$ operating in the space of multivariate Gaussian measures of size C. Consider two distributions $\mu \sim \mathcal{N}(m_1, \sigma_1^2)$ and $\nu \sim \mathcal{N}(m_2, \sigma_2^2)$, which can be thought of as elements of a hidden layer patch, then for the affine operator function $f(\mu) = \mathbb{N}(m_1 A, \sigma_1^2 A^2)$ we have the following Lipschitz bound: $W_2(f(\mu), f(\nu)) \leq LW_2(\mu, \nu))$, where $L = \sqrt{C}\|W\|_2^2$.*

Proof is given in Sect. 4.1. We denote the l-th layer weight matrix, computing the c-th channel by column matrix $A_{l,c}$. We can impose the Lipschitz condition to Eq. 4, 5 by having constrained weight matrices with elements of the form

$$A_{l,c} = \frac{A_{l,1}}{C^{\frac{1}{4}}\sqrt{\sum_{c=1}^{C} W_{l,c}^2}}.$$

4.1 Proving Lipschitz Bounds in a DistGP Layer

We here prove Propositions 1 and 2 of Sect. 4.

Definition. The Wasserstein-2 distance between two multivariate Gaussian distributions $\mathbb{N}(m_1, \Sigma_1)$ and $\mathbb{N}(m_2, \Sigma_2)$ with diagonal covariances is : $\|m_1 - m_2\|_2^2 + \|\sigma_1^{1/2} - \sigma_2^{1/2}\|_F^2$, where $\|\cdot\|_F$ represents the Frobenius norm.

Lemmas on p-norms. We have the following relations between norms : $\|x\|_2 \leq \|x\|_1$ and $\|x\|_1 \leq \sqrt{D}\|x\|_2$. Will be used for the proof of Proposition 2.

Proof of Proposition 1. Throughout this subsection we shall refer to the first two moments of a Gaussian measure by $m(\cdot)$, $v(\cdot)$. Explicitly writing the Wasserstein-2 distances of the inequality we get: $|m(F(\mu)) - m(F(\nu))|^2 + |v(F(\mu)) - v(F(\nu))|^2 \leq L|m_1 - m_2|^2 + |\Sigma_1 - \Sigma_2|^2$. We focus on the mean part and applying Cauchy–Schwarz we get the following inequality $|[K_{\mu,Z} - K_{\nu,Z}]K_Z^{-1}m|^2 \leq \|K_{\mu,Z} - K_{\nu,Z}\|_2^2\|K_Z^{-1}m\|_2^2$.

To simplify the problem and without loss of generality we consider U_z to be a sufficient statistic for the set of inducing points Z. Expanding the first term of the r.h.s. we get $\left[\sigma^2 \exp\frac{-W_2(\mu,U_z)}{l^2} - \sigma^2 \exp\frac{-W_2(\nu,U_z)}{l^2}\right]$.

We assume $\nu = \mu + h$, where $h \sim \mathcal{N}(|m_1 - m_2|, |\Sigma_1 - \Sigma_2|)$ and μ is a high density point in the data manifold, hence $W_2(\mu - U_z) = 0$. We denote $m(h)^2 + var(h)^2 = \lambda$. Considering the general equality $\log(x - y) = \log(x) + \log(y) + \log(\frac{1}{y} - \frac{1}{x})$ and applying it to our case we get $\log|m(F(\mu)) - m(F(\nu))|^2 \leq \log\left[\sigma^2 - \sigma^2 \exp\frac{-\lambda}{l^2}\right]^2 = 2\log\sigma^2 - 2\frac{\lambda}{l^2} + 2\log\left[\exp\frac{\lambda}{l^2} - 1\right] \leq 2\log\left[\sigma^2 \exp\frac{\lambda}{l^2}\right]$.

We have the general inequality $\exp x \leq 1 + x + x^2$ for $x \leq 1.79$, which for $0 \leq x \leq 1$ can be modified as $\exp x \leq 1 + 2x$. Applying this new inequality, $|m(F(\mu)) - m(F(\nu))|^2 \leq \left[\sigma^2 + 2\sigma^2\frac{\lambda}{l^2}\right]^2 = \sigma^4 + \sigma^4\frac{\lambda}{l^2} + 4\sigma^4\frac{(\lambda)^2}{l^4} \leq 16\sigma^4\frac{\lambda}{l^2}$, where the last inequality follows from the ball constrains.

We now move to the variance components of the Lipschitz bound, we notice that $|v(F(\mu))^{\frac{1}{2}} - v(F(\nu))^{\frac{1}{2}}|^2 \leq |v(F(\mu))^{\frac{1}{2}} - v(F(\nu))^{\frac{1}{2}}||v(F(\mu))^{\frac{1}{2}} + v(F(\nu))^{\frac{1}{2}}| = |v(F(\mu)) - v(F(\nu))|$, which after applying Cauchy–Schwarz results in an upper bound of the form $\|K_{\mu,U_z} - K_{\nu,U_z}\|_2^2\|K_{U_z}^{-1}(K_{U_z} - S)K_{U_z}^{-1}\|_2$. Using that $\|K_{\mu,U_z} - K_{\nu,U_z}\|_2^2 \leq \frac{16\sigma^4\lambda}{l^2}$ we obtain that $|v(F(\mu)) - v(F(\nu))| \leq \frac{16\sigma^4\lambda}{l^2}\|K_{U_z}^{-1}(K_{U_z} - S)K_{U_z}^{-1}\|_2$. Now taking into consideration both the upper bounds on the mean and variance components we arrive at the desired Lipschitz constant.

Proof of Proposition 2. Using the definition for Wasserstein-2 distances and taking the l.h.s of the inequality, we obtain $\|m_1A - m_2A\|_2^2 + \|(\sigma_1^2A^2)^{1/2} - (\sigma_2^2A^2)^{1/2}\|_F^2$, which after rearranging terms and noticing that inside the Frobenius norm we have scalars, becomes $\|(m_1 - m_2)A\|_2^2 + [\sigma_1^2A^2)^{1/2} - (\sigma_2^2A^2)^{1/2}]^2$.

We can now apply the Cauchy–Schwarz inequality for the part involving means and multiplying the right hand side with $\sqrt{C}$, which represents the number of channels, we get: $\|(m_1 - m_2)A\|_2^2 + [\sigma_1^2 A^2)^{1/2} - (\sigma_2^2 A^2)^{1/2}]^2 \leq \|m_1 - m_2\|_2^2 \sqrt{C}\|A\|_2^2 + \sqrt{C}[\sigma_1^2 A^2)^{1/2} - (\sigma_2^2 A^2)^{1/2}]^2$. We can notice that the Lipschitz constant for the component involving mean terms is $\sqrt{C}\|A\|_2^2$. Hence, we try to prove that the same L is also available for the variance terms component. Hence, $L = \sqrt{C}\|A\|_2^2 \leftrightarrow \sqrt{C}[\sigma_1^2 A^2)^{1/2} - (\sigma_2^2 A^2)^{1/2}]^2 \leq [\sigma_1 - \sigma_2]^2 \sqrt{C}\|A\|_2^2$. By virtue of Cauchy–Schwarz we have the following inequality $\sqrt{C}[\sigma_1 A - \sigma_2 A]^2 \leq [\sigma_1 - \sigma_2]^2 \sqrt{C}\|A\|_2^2$.

Hence the aforementioned if and only if statement will hold if we prove that $\sqrt{C}\left[(\sigma_1^2 A^2)^{\frac{1}{2}} - (\sigma_2^2 A^2)^{\frac{1}{2}}\right]^2 \leq \sqrt{C}[\sigma_1 A - \sigma_2 A]^2$, which after expressing in terms of norms becomes $\sqrt{C}\left[\|\sigma_1 A\|_2 - \|\sigma_2 A\|_2\right]^2 \leq \sqrt{C}\left[\|\sigma_1 A\|_1 - \|\sigma_2 A\|_1\right]^2$. Expanding the square brackets gives $\sqrt{C}\left[\|\sigma_1 A\|_2^2 + \|\sigma_2 A\|_2^2 - 2\|\sigma_1 A\|_2\|\sigma_2 A\|_2\right] \leq \sqrt{C}\left[\|\sigma_1 A\|_1^2 + \|\sigma_2 A\|_1^2 - 2\|\sigma_1 A\|_1\|\sigma_2 A\|_1\right]$

This inequality holds by applying the p-norm lemmas, thereby the if and only if statement is satisfied. Consequently, the Lipschitz constant is $\sqrt{C}\|A\|_2^2$.

5   DistGP-Based Segmentation Network and OOD Detection

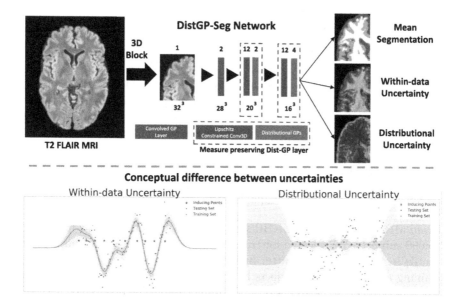

Fig. 2. Top: Schematic of proposed DistGP activated segmentation net. Above and below each layer we show the number of channels and their dimension respectively. **Bottom**: Visual depiction of the two uncertainties in DistGP after fitting a toy regression manifold. Distributional uncertainty increases outside the manifold of training data and is therefore useful for OOD detection.

The above introduced modules in Sect. 4 can be used to construct a convolutional network that benefits from properties of DistGP. Specifically, we construct a 3D network for segmenting volumetric medical images, which is depicted in Fig. 2 (top). It consists of a convolved GP layer, followed by two measure-preserving DistGP layers. Each hidden layer uses filters of size 5×5×5. To increase the model's receptive field, in the second layer we use convolution dilated by 2. We use 250 inducing points and 2 channels for the DistGP "activation functions". The affine operators project the stochastic patches into a 12 dimensional space. The size of the network is limited by computational requirements for GP-based layers, which is an active research area. Like regular convolutional nets, this model can process input of arbitrary size but GPU memory requirement increases with input size. We here provide input of size 32^3 to the model, which then segments the central 16^3 voxels. To segment a whole scan we divide it into tiles and stitch together the segmentations.

While prediction uncertainty can be computed for standard neural networks by using the softmax probability, these uncertainty estimates are often over-confident [7,9], and are less reliable than those obtained by Bayesian networks [11]. For our model we decompose the model uncertainty into two components by splitting the last DistGP layer in two parts: $h(\cdot) = \mathcal{N}(h|0, K_{nn} - K_{nm}K_{mm}^{-1}K_{mn})$ and $g(\cdot) = \mathcal{N}(g|K_{nm}K_{mm}^{-1}m, K_{nm}K_{mm}^{-1}SK_{mm}^{-1}K_{mn})$. The $h(\cdot)$ variance captures the shift from within to outside the data manifold and will be denoted as *distributional uncertainty*. The variance $g(\cdot)$ is termed here as *within-data uncertainty* and encapsulates uncertainty present inside the data manifold. A visual depiction of the two is provided in Fig. 2 (bottom).

6   Evaluation on Brain MRI

In this section we evaluate our method alongside recent OOD models [2,6,12], assessing their capabilities to reach segmentation performance comparable to well-established deterministic models and whether they can accurately detect outliers.

6.1   Data and Pre-processing

For evaluation we use publicly available datasets:

1) Brain MRI scans from the UKBB study [1], which contains scans from nearly 15,000 subjects. We selected for training and evaluation the bottom 10% percentile in terms of white matter hypointensities with an equal split between training and testing. All subjects have been confirmed to be normal by radiological assessment. Segmentation of brain tissue (CSF,GM,WM) has been obtained with SPM12.

2) MRI scans of 285 patients with gliomas from BraTS 2017 [3]. All classes are fused into a *tumor* class, which we will use to quantify OOD detection performance.

In what follows, we use only the FLAIR sequence to perform the brain tissue segmentation task and OOD detection of tumors, as this MRI sequence is available for both UKBB and BraTS. All FLAIR images are pre-processed with skull-stripping, N4 bias correction, rigid registration to MNI152 space and histogram matching between UKBB and BraTS. Finally, we normalize intensities of each scan via linear scaling of its minimum and maximum intensities to the $[-1,1]$ range.

6.2   Brain Tissue Segmentation on Normal MRI Scans

Table 1. Performance on UK Biobank in terms of Dice scores per tissue.

Model	Hidden layers	DICE CSF	DICE GM	DICE WM
OVA-DM [12]	3	0.72	0.79	0.77
OVNNI [6]	3	0.66	0.77	0.73
DUQ [2]	3	0.745	0.825	0.781
DistGP-Seg (ours)	3	0.829	0.823	0.867
U-Net	3 scales	0.85	0.89	0.86

Task: We train and test our model on segmentation of brain tissue of healthy UKBB subjects. This corresponds to the within-data manifold in our setup.

Baselines: We compare our model with recent Bayesian approaches for enabling task-specific models (such as image segmentation) to perform uncertainty-based OOD detection [2,6,12]. For fair comparison, we use these methods in an architecture similar to ours (Fig. 2), except that each layer is replaced by standard convolutional layer, each with 256 channels, LeakyRelu activations, and dilation rates as in ours. We also compare these Bayesian methods with a well-established deterministic baseline, a U-Net with 3 scales (down/up-sampling) and 2 convolution layers per scale in encoder and 2 in decoder (total 12 layers).

Results: Table 1 shows that DistGP-Seg surpasses other Bayesian methods with respect to Dice score for all tissue classes. Our method approaches the performance of the deterministic U-Net, which has a much larger architecture and receptive field. We emphasize this has not been previously achieved with GP-based architectures, as their size (e.g. number of layers) is limited due to computational requirements. This supports the potential of DistGP, which is bound to be further unlocked by advances in scaling GP-based models.

6.3   Outlier Detection in MRI Scans with Tumors

Task: The previous task of brain tissue segmentation on UKBB serves as a proxy task for learning normative patterns with our network. Here, we apply this pre-trained network on BRATS scans with tumors. We expect the region surrounding the tumor and other related pathologies, such as squeezed brain parts or shifted ventricles, to be highlighted with higher distributional uncertainty, which is the OOD measure for the Bayesian deep learning models. To evaluate quality of OOD detection at a pixel level, we follow the procedure in [5], for example to get the 5.0% False Positive Ratio threshold value we compute the 95% percentile of distributional variance on the testing set of UKBB, taking into consideration that there is no outlier tissue there. Subsequently, using this value we threshold the distributional variance heatmaps on BraTS, with tissue having a value above the threshold being flagged as an outlier. We then quantify the overlap of the pixels detected as outliers (over the threshold) with the ground-truth tumor labels by computing the Dice score between them.

Table 2. Performance comparison of Dice for detecting outliers on BraTS for different thresholds obtained from UKBB.

Model	DICE FPR = 0.1	DICE FPR = 0.5	DICE FPR = 1.0	DICE FPR = 5.0
OVA-DM [12]	0.382	0.428	0.457	0.410
OVNNI [6]	≤ 0.001	≤ 0.001	≤ 0.001	≤ 0.001
DUQ [2]	0.068	0.121	0.169	0.182
DistGP-Seg (ours)	0.512	0.571	0.532	0.489
VAE-LG [5]	0.259	0.407	0.448	0.303
AAE-LG [5]	0.220	0.395	0.418	0.302

Results: Table 2 shows the results from our experiments with DistGP and compared Bayesian deep learning baselines. We also provide performance of reconstruction-based OOD detection models as reported in [5] for similar experimental setup. DistGP-Seg surpasses its Bayesian deep learning counterparts, as well as reconstructed-based models. In Fig. 3 we provide representative results from the methods we implemented for qualitative assessment. Moreover, although BRATS does not provide labels for WM/GM/CSF tissues hence we cannot quantify how well these tissues are segmented, visual assessment shows our method compares favorably to compared counterparts.

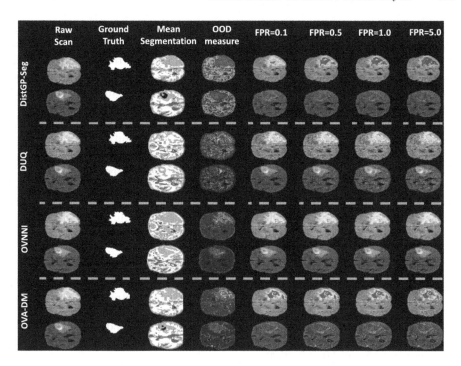

Fig. 3. Comparison between models in terms of voxel-level outlier detection of tumors on BRATS scans. Mean segmentation represents the hard segmentation of brain tissues. OOD measure is the quantification of uncertainty for each model, using their own procedure. Higher values translate to appartenance to outlier status, whereas for OVNNI it is the converse.

7   Discussion

We have introduced a novel Bayesian convolutional layer with Lipschitz continuity that is capable of reliably propagating uncertainty . General criticism surrounding deep and convolutional GP involves the issue of under-performance compared to other Bayesian deep learning techniques, and especially compared to deterministic networks. Our experiments demonstrate that our 3-layers model, size limited due to computational cost, is capable of approaching the performance of a U-Net, an architecture with a much larger receptive field. Further advances in computational efficient GP-based models, an active area of research, will enable our model to scale further and unlock its full potential. Importantly, we showed that our DistGP-Seg network offers better uncertainty estimates for OOD detection than the state-of-the-art Bayesian approaches, and also surpasses recent unsupervised reconstruction-based deep learning models for identifying outliers corresponding to pathology on brain scans. Our results indicate that OOD methods that do not take into account distances in latent space, such as OVNNI, tend to fail in detecting outliers, whereas OVA-DM and DUQ that make predictions based on distances in the last layer perform better. Our model utilises distances at every hidden layer, thus allowing the notion of outlier to evolve gradually through the depth of our network. This difference can be noticed in the smoothness of OOD measure for our model in comparison to other methods in Fig. 3. A drawback of our study resides in the small architecture used. Extending our "measure preserving DistGP" module to larger architectures such as U-Net for segmentation or modern CNNs for whole-image prediction tasks remains a prospective research avenue fuelled by advances in scalability of SGP. In conclusion, our work shows that incorporating DistGP in convolutional architectures provides both competitive performance and reliable uncertainty quantification in medical image analysis, opening up a new direction of research.

Acknowledgements. SGP is funded by an EPSRC Centre for Doctoral Training studentship award to Imperial College London. KK is funded by the UKRI London Medical Imaging & Artificial Intelligence Centre for Value Based Healthcare.

References

1. Alfaro-Almagro, F., et al.: Image processing and quality control for the first 10,000 brain imaging datasets from UK Biobank. Neuroimage **166**, 400–424 (2018)
2. van Amersfoort, J., Smith, L., Teh, Y.W., Gal, Y.: Simple and scalable epistemic uncertainty estimation using a single deep deterministic neural network. arXiv preprint arXiv:2003.02037 (2020)
3. Bakas, S., et al.: Advancing the cancer genome atlas Glioma MRI collections with expert segmentation labels and radiomic features. Sci. Data **4**, 170117 (2017)
4. Blomqvist, K., Kaski, S., Heinonen, M.: Deep convolutional gaussian processes. arXiv preprint arXiv:1810.03052 (2018)
5. Chen, X., Pawlowski, N., Glocker, B., Konukoglu, E.: Unsupervised lesion detection with locally Gaussian approximation. In: Suk, H.-I., Liu, M., Yan, P., Lian, C. (eds.) MLMI 2019. LNCS, vol. 11861, pp. 355–363. Springer, Cham (2019). https://doi.org/10.1007/978-3-030-32692-0_41
6. Franchi, G., Bursuc, A., Aldea, E., Dubuisson, S., Bloch, I.: One versus all for deep neural network incertitude (OVNNI) quantification. preprint arXiv:2006.00954 (2020)
7. Guo, C., Pleiss, G., Sun, Y., Weinberger, K.Q.: On calibration of modern neural networks. arXiv preprint arXiv:1706.04599 (2017)
8. Hensman, J., Fusi, N., Lawrence, N.D.: Gaussian processes for big data. arXiv preprint arXiv:1309.6835 (2013)
9. McClure, P., et al.: Knowing what you know in brain segmentation using Bayesian deep neural networks. Front. Neuroinform. **13**, 67 (2019)
10. Monteiro, M., et al.: Stochastic segmentation networks: modelling spatially correlated aleatoric uncertainty. arXiv preprint arXiv:2006.06015 (2020)
11. Nair, T., Precup, D., Arnold, D.L., Arbel, T.: Exploring uncertainty measures in deep networks for multiple sclerosis lesion detection and segmentation. Med. Image Anal. **59**, 101557 (2020)
12. Padhy, S., Nado, Z., Ren, J., Liu, J., Snoek, J., Lakshminarayanan, B.: Revisiting One-vs-All classifiers for predictive uncertainty and out-of-distribution detection in neural networks. arXiv preprint arXiv:2007.05134 (2020)
13. Popescu, S., Sharp, D., Cole, J., Glocker, B.: Hierarchical Gaussian processes with Wasserstein-2 Kernels. arXiv preprint arXiv:2010.14877 (2020)

14. Wilson, A.G., Izmailov, P.: Bayesian deep learning and a probabilistic perspective of generalization. arXiv preprint arXiv:2002.08791 (2020)
15. Zhou, S.K., et al.: A review of deep learning in medical imaging: image traits, technology trends, case studies with progress highlights, and future promises. arXiv preprint arXiv:2008.09104 (2020)

Deep Label Fusion: A 3D End-To-End Hybrid Multi-atlas Segmentation and Deep Learning Pipeline

Long Xie[1]([envelope]), Laura E. M. Wisse[2], Jiancong Wang[1], Sadhana Ravikumar[1],
Trevor Glenn[1], Anica Luther[2], Sydney Lim[1], David A. Wolk[3,4],
and Paul A. Yushkevich[1]

[1] Penn Image Computing and Science Laboratory (PICSL), Department of Radiology,
University of Pennsylvania, Philadelphia, USA
long.xie@uphs.upenn.edu
[2] Department of Diagnostic Radiology, Lund University, Lund, Sweden
[3] Penn Memory Center, University of Pennsylvania, Philadelphia, USA
[4] Department of Neurology, University of Pennsylvania, Philadelphia, USA

Abstract. Deep learning (DL) is the state-of-the-art methodology in various medical image segmentation tasks. However, it requires relatively large amounts of manually labeled training data, which may be infeasible to generate in some applications. In addition, DL methods have relatively poor generalizability to out-of-sample data. Multi-atlas segmentation (MAS), on the other hand, has promising performance using limited amounts of training data and good generalizability. A hybrid method that integrates the high accuracy of DL and good generalizability of MAS is highly desired and could play an important role in segmentation problems where manually labeled data is hard to generate. Most of the prior work focuses on improving single components of MAS using DL rather than directly optimizing the final segmentation accuracy via an end-to-end pipeline. Only one study explored this idea in binary segmentation of 2D images, but it remains unknown whether it generalizes well to multi-class 3D segmentation problems. In this study, we propose a 3D end-to-end hybrid pipeline, named deep label fusion (DLF), that takes advantage of the strengths of MAS and DL. Experimental results demonstrate that DLF yields significant improvements over conventional label fusion methods and U-Net, a direct DL approach, in the context of segmenting medial temporal lobe subregions using 3T T1-weighted and T2-weighted MRI. Further, when applied to an unseen similar dataset acquired in 7T, DLF maintains its superior performance, which demonstrates its good generalizability.

1 Introduction

Deep learning (DL) algorithms generate state-of-the-art performance in segmenting anatomical structures in medical images. However, to reach their full potential, they require relatively large amounts of manually labeled training data, which may not be practical in some applications, such as hippocampal subfield segmentation. In addition, the generalizability of DL methods to data that is not well represented in the training

© Springer Nature Switzerland AG 2021
A. Feragen et al. (Eds.): IPMI 2021, LNCS 12729, pp. 428–439, 2021.
https://doi.org/10.1007/978-3-030-78191-0_33

sample is poor. On the other hand, multi-atlas segmentation (MAS) has been shown to generate promising segmentation using relatively small amounts of training data and generalize well on unseen data due to its intrinsic strong spatial constraints and robustness to variability of anatomical structures and image intensity. MAS has two main components: (1) non-linearly registering and warping a set of atlases, i.e. images with the structure of interest manually labeled, to the target image and (2) performing label fusion to derive a consensus segmentation of the target image by combining the warped atlas segmentations (candidate segmentations), typically via weighted voting [1]. Majority voting (MV) [2], the simplest multi-atlas segmentation scheme, gives equal weights to all the atlases at each spatial location. Segmentation accuracy can be improved by assigning spatially varying weights based on local similarity between atlas and target patches, referred to as spatially varying weighted voting (SVWV) [3, 4]. Instead of treating each atlas independently as in SVWV, joint label fusion (JLF) [5] takes correlated errors among atlases into account when estimating weights and yields better label fusion accuracy.

A hybrid algorithm taking advantage of the high accuracy of DL and better generalizability of MAS is desirable, especially in applications that have limited training data. Indeed, there have been a number of attempts to integrate MAS and DL. Some recent studies have used DL to improve the detection of similar (or dissimilar) patches between the target and atlas, for deriving weights in SVWV. Sanroma et al. [6] and Ding et al. [7] uses neural network to learn a nonlinear embedding to transform the patches to a feature space in which the discriminability of the sum of squared difference (SSD) metric is maximized and generates weight maps for SVWV using SSD in this feature space. Ding et al. [8] and Xie et al. [9] directly apply DL to estimate the probability of an atlas having an erroneous vote either at a patch level [9] or the whole image level [8]. SVWV or JLF are then integrated with the probability estimation to generate the final segmentation. A common limitation of the above approaches is that improving the ability to estimate the probability of an atlas having an erroneous vote does not directly translate to the label fusion accuracy. Indeed, as found in [8], a 2% improvement in discriminating erroneous votes translates to only 0.4% improvement in the final segmentation accuracy, similarly seen in [7] and [9]. In the current study, we hypothesize that greater improvement in segmentation accuracy can be realized by incorporating label fusion into an *end-to-end hybrid MAS-DL segmentation pipeline* with a loss function that directly reflects segmentation accuracy. The most relevant prior work is [10], in which authors propose an end-to-end label fusion pipeline consisting of feature extraction and label fusion subnets. Only the feature extraction subnet has learnable parameters, while the label fusion subnet has a fixed structure mimicking the conventional label fusion procedure. Since the label fusion subnet is designed to be differentiable, the network can be trained end-to-end. However, it is only evaluated on binary segmentation of 2D images, which limits its application.

In this work, we propose deep label fusion (DLF, Fig. 1) with the following contributions: (1) This is the first 3D hybrid MAS-DL pipeline that can be trained end-to-end. (2) Promising experimental results show improvements compared to conventional label fusion and direct DL methods in a difficult real-world multi-label problem of segmenting medial temporal lobe (MTL) subregions on multi-modality 3T MRI. (3) When applying to an unseen 7T MRI dataset, we demonstrate that the proposed DLF inherits the good generalizability of MAS. (4) The network is designed to accept a variable number of atlases in testing, which is a unique feature for an end-to-end pipeline.

2 Materials

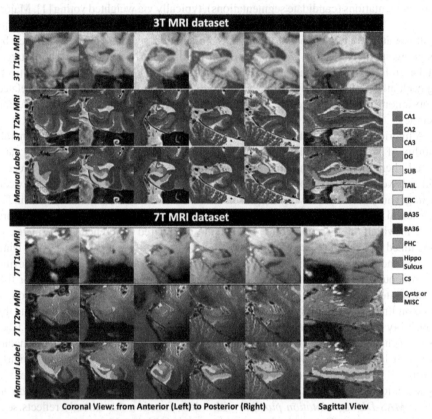

Fig. 1. Examples T1w and T2w MRI images and manual segmentation of the 3T (top) and 7T datasets (bottom).

A multimodal structural 3T MRI dataset (3T MRI dataset) from the University of Pennsylvania was used in this study to develop and validate the proposed DLF algorithm. It consists of T1-weighted (T1w, $0.8 \times 0.8 \times 0.8$ mm^3) and T2-weighted (T2w, $0.4 \times 0.4 \times 1.2$ mm^3) MRI scans of 23 subjects [12 with mild cognitive impairment (MCI) and 11 cognitively normal controls (NC)] together with the corresponding manual segmentations of the bilateral MTL subregions in the space of the T2w MRI (example in Fig. 1). There are $N_{label} = 15$ labels in total including background, 10 Gy matter (GM) labels [cornu ammonis (CA) 1 to 3, dentate gyrus (DG), subiculum (SUB), the tail of hippocampus (TAIL), entorhinal cortex (ERC), Brodmann areas 35 and 36 (BA35/36) and parahippocampal cortex (PHC)] and 4 supporting non-GM labels [hippocampal sulcus, collateral sulcus (CS), cysts in the hippocampus and miscellaneous (MISC) voxels around the cortex]. Labeling MTL subregions requires exquisite understanding of neuroanatomy, is done in consultation with multiple histological references, and takes many hours per individual. Since the number of available labeled datasets is small, we utilize cross-validation experimental design, with the dataset randomly divided into 4 folds (6 subjects in each of the first 3 folds and 5 subjects in the last fold) keeping the proportion of MCI and NC subjects in each fold similar. A unique aspect of this dataset is that there is no perceivable difference in contrast between most adjacent GM subregions, and boundaries are defined based on anatomical landmarks and geometric rules. Spatial context is required to correctly determine the extent of CA2, CA3, TAIL and the cortex subregions. These factors make the segmentation problem more challenging and well-suited to compare the proposed work to general DL frameworks, such as the U-Net [11].

In addition, a similar MRI dataset (7T MRI dataset) acquired from a 7T rather than 3T MTI was used to serve as an independent out-of-sample dataset to evaluate the generalizability of the proposed approach. Similar to the 3T dataset, the 7T one also consists of T1w ($0.7 \times 0.7 \times 0.7$ mm^3) and T2w ($0.4 \times 0.4 \times 1.0$ mm^3) MRI scans of 24 subjects. The two datasets differ in the tissue contrast and image resolution. In addition, although the manual segmentations were generated according to the same segmentation protocol, subtle difference in placement of tissue boundaries is expected because they are segmented by different persons. Figure 1 shows examples from the two datasets.

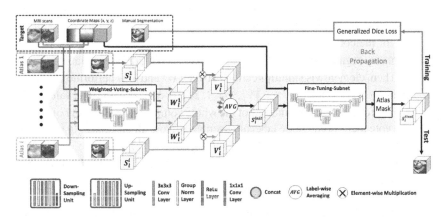

Fig. 2. Network architecture of the proposed deep label fusion network.

3 Method

3.1 Deep Label Fusion

Figure 2 summarizes the two-step structure of the proposed DLF network: (1) *Weighted-voting-subnet*: takes in a pair of target-atlas images to generate label-specific weight maps for each candidate segmentation, i.e. the registered atlas manual segmentation, and performs weighted averaging to produce an initial segmentation and (2) *Fine-tuning-subnet*: corrects errors of the initial segmentation to improve segmentation accuracy. Both subnets adopt a U-Net architecture [11]. Details are described below.

3.1.1 Network Architecture

Weighted-Voting-Subnet: The weighted-voting-subnet takes T1w and T2w target and atlas MRI patches (i.e., 4 channels of dimension $N_x \times N_y \times N_z$) as well as the coordinate-maps with coordinates in the whole target image (3 channels for coordinates in x, y and z directions) as input and generates a 15-channel feature map with the same dimension of $N_x \times N_y \times N_z$, serving as the label-specific weight maps (one for each label). This is different from conventional weighted voting methods, which only compute one weight map for all the labels. The subnet adapts the U-Net architecture that consists of three consecutive down-sampling units (two repetitions of $3 \times 3 \times 3$ convolutional, batch normalization [12] and ReLu layers [13], then follow by one $2 \times 2 \times 2$ pooling layer) followed by three consecutive up-sampling units (one $3 \times 3 \times 3$ transpose convolutional layer with $2 \times 2 \times 2$ stripe, two repetitions of $3 \times 3 \times 3$ convolutional, batch normalization and ReLu layers). The padding is set to $1 \times 1 \times 1$ to preserve the size of the feature maps. The number of feature maps is doubled at each level and the initial number of feature maps is set to 32. Skipped connections are established between each level of up/down sampling. A $1 \times 1 \times 1$ convolutional layer is applied in the end to generate the label-specific weight maps. For the ith atlas-target pair ($i = 1, 2, \ldots N_{atlas}$), the weighted-voting-subnet (the same network for all the atlases) is applied to generate label-specific weight maps [denoted as $W^i = \{W^i_l, l = 1, 2, \ldots, N_{label}\}$ with voxel value w^i_{ln}] for the corresponding candidate segmentation (S^i) [which can be converted to a set of binary segmentations $S^i = \{S^i_l, l = 1, 2, \ldots, N_{label}\}$ for each label with voxel value s^i_{ln}]. Then, elementwise multiplication between W^i and S^i is performed to generate the vote-maps for all the labels [$V^i = \{V^i_l, l = 1, 2, \ldots, N_{label}\}$ with voxel value v^i_{ln}], i.e. $v^i_{ln} = w^i_{ln} \times s^i_{ln}$ for each location index n of the whole volume and each label l of the N_{label} labels. The vote maps of the same label are averaged across all the atlases to generate the 15-channel output of the weighted-voting-subnet [$S^{init} = \{S^{init}_l, l = 1, 2, \ldots, N_{label}\}$ with voxel value s^{init}_{ln}], i.e. $s^{init}_{ln} = (\sum_{i=1}^{N_{atlas}} v^i_{ln})/N_{atlas}$ for each n and l. Importantly, the average operation allows the network to take any number of atlases as inputs, i.e. the number of atlases in training can be different from those in the testing phase.

Fine-Tuning-Subnet and Atlas Mask: The fine-tuning-subnet gives the network flexibility to adjust the output generated by the weighted-voting-subnet. It employs the same U-Net structure as the weighted-voting-subnet, with the only exception of having four levels of down/up sampling instead of three. It takes S^{init} and the coordinate maps as inputs and generate output feature maps that are the same size of S^{init} (15 channels for the 15 labels). Then, each channel of the feature map is multiplied by a mask generated by thresholding the mean votes of the corresponding label of all the atlases (threshold is set to 0.2 empirically). This is based on the assumption that final segmentation of each label should be inside the region of most of the atlas votes of that label. The final segmentation is generated by performing the *arg-max* operation across the 15 channels of the masked feature maps.

3.1.2   Implementation Details

Obtaining the Patch-Level Training and Test Sets. Limited by the GPU memory capacity, we trained the proposed network using image patches. Each patch of the training set consists of patches of the target image and all the registered atlases (both images and candidate segmentations) at the same location. To obtain such a training set, we perform leave-one-out cross-validation among the training subjects, i.e. image and manual segmentation of one subject is left out as the target subject and the remaining subjects are treated as atlases in each experiment. To be noted, this cross-validation experiment is performed to train the network and it is different from the top-level 4-fold cross-validation mentioned in Sect. 2. Since each subject has bilateral MTL segmentations available, to maximize the number of atlases, we include the left-right flipped atlases in the training, i.e. each subject provides both left and right MTL as atlases. For each bilateral MTL, the atlases are registered to the target following these steps: (1) the atlases and target T2w MRI scans are cropped around the MTL using the preprocessing pipeline described in [14]; (2) the cropped T2w MRI scans are up-sampled to $0.4 \times 0.4 \times 0.4$ mm^3; (3) T1w MRI is affinely registered and resampled to the cropped T2w MRI; (4) cropped atlases images are registered (multimodal deformable registration) to the cropped target image; (5) the atlases and the manual labels are warped to the space of the cropped target image. All the registrations are done using the Greedy registration toolbox (github.com/pyushkevich/greedy).

Twelve patches (10 centered on voxels with foreground and 2 on background) with size $72 \times 72 \times 72$ voxels are sampled for the target image and all the registered atlases. T1w and T2w patches are normalized by subtracting the mean and dividing by the standard deviation. The same strategy was used to generate the patch-level test set by treating the test subject as the target and all the training subjects as the atlases.

Augmentation Strategies. When generating the training samples, the most straightforward way is to use all the atlases and have their sequence fixed. However, this may result in a network that is not robust to different atlas combinations or different atlas sequences and, thus, will not generalize well in the test phase. This is important because the number of atlases in the test phase may be different from training (e.g. there will be one more atlas available in the test phase using the leave-one-out strategy). In order to overcome this limitation, when sampling each patch, we randomly selected (with replacement) N_{atlas} out of all the available atlases (N_{atlas} can be bigger than the number of available atlases). This sampling strategy may result in repeated presentation of some atlases, which is desired as it may teach the network to deal with correlated errors among the atlases, similar to the core idea of JLF [5]. In addition, random elastic deformation augmentation [15] is applied to all the training patches to double the size of the training set. In our experiment, random flipping and random rotation ($\leq 10°$) did not improve segmentation accuracy and thus was not performed in the interest of time.

Other Implementation Details. The model was implemented in PyTorch and trained using a NVidia Tesla P100 GPU available in the Google Cloud Platform using generalized Dice loss [16]. The model converged after 10 epochs when trained using Adam optimizer (initial learning rate was set to 0.0005 and was reduced by a factor of 0.2 every 2 epochs beginning at the 4th epoch). The batch size was set to 1, constrained by GPU memory. The deep-supervision scheme [17] (4 levels with weights of 1, 0.5, 0.2, 0.1) was adopted to in the fine-tuning-subnet to train DLF, which was found to be beneficial. In testing, we sampled the test images with dense Cartesian grid ($36 \times 36 \times 36$ voxels spacing) to generate patches, which were fed to the trained DLF network to generate the final segmentation.

3.2 Alternative Methods for Comparisons

3.2.1 Conventional Label Fusion Methods

Conventional label fusion methods, including MV, SVWV and JLF, were performed together with a neighborhood search scheme [18] to obtain benchmark performance. In addition, we also performed corrective learning (CL) [19], which is commonly used together with JLF, to get the best performance of conventional MAS methods. A grid search was performed for each approach to determine the optimal set of hyper-parameters that yields the best generalized Dice similarity coefficient (GDSC) [20] of all the GM labels between the automatic and manual segmentations.

3.2.2 Direct U-Net

A 3D U-Net [11] was trained to generate benchmark performance of direct DL method. Its architecture is almost the same as the fine-tuning-subnet. The U-Net was trained on patches of the multimodal images (20 foreground and 8 background patches per hemisphere per subject) sampled from the aligned cropped T1w and T2w MRI generated in Sect. 3.1.2. and augmented using the random elastic deformation augmentation [15]. The patch size was set to $72 \times 72 \times 72$ voxels for fair comparisons. The U-Net was trained over 20 epochs using generalized Dice loss and Adam optimizer (initial learning rate was set to 0.0005 and was reduced by a factor of 0.2 every 4 epochs beginning at the 9th epoch) with a batch size equal to 7. The dense-sampling approach described in Sect. 3.1.2 was used to generate segmentations of the test images. The same deep-supervision scheme was adopted to train the 3D U-Net.

We observed that the direct U-Net generates a lot of erroneous foreground labels at the edge of the cropped image, which could be due to training on patches. An additional post-processing step is required to generate reasonable final segmentation. This is done by multiplying the initial segmentation with a binary mask generated by taking the largest connected component of the foreground label. Interestingly, the proposed DLF framework does not have this issue which may be the benefit of the intrinsic spatial constraints of the MAS-based framework.

4 Experiments and Results

Validation on the 3T MRI Dataset. Segmentation accuracy is evaluated using the Dice similarity coefficient (DSC) (GDSC for GM labels together) between the automatic and manual segmentations. For the 3T dataset, we use the 1st fold as the test set and the other

3 folds as the training set to search for the optimal sets of hyper-parameters that yield the best GDSC of all the GM labels for each method. Then, the same set of optimal parameters is applied in the other three cross-validation experiments (excluding the one using the first fold as the test set to reduce potential bias) to generate the evaluation results, reported in Table 1. Paired-sample t-test (2-sided) was performed between DLF and each of the other methods to evaluate the significance of the improvement. In addition, to visualize the locations where each method makes errors, we warped the errormaps (binary map with label 1 indicating disagreement between the automatic and manual segmentations) to an unbiased population template, built using the manual segmentations as in [21]. Mean errormaps of all the methods were generated by averaging the corresponding errormaps of all the test subjects, reported in Fig. 2.

Table 1. Mean (±standard deviation) DSC and generalized DSC (GDSC) of all subregions between automatic and manual segmentations in the test folds of the 3T MRI dataset. Volume of each label is provided for better interpretation DSC scores. For better interpretation, background color of each cell indicates the relative performance compared to the best (most red) and worst (most blue) performance in each row (the more red/blue, the closer to the best/worst performance respectively).

	Volume (cm³)	MV	SVWV	JLF + CL	U-Net	DLF
GDSC	-	70.8±4.3*	75.8±3.8*	77.9±3.8*	77.1±4.8*	**80.1± 3.2**
Hippo	2.84±0.46	88.5±2.1*	91.5±1.2*	92.9±1.3	91.5±3.5*	**93.1±1.1**
CA1	0.67±0.14	68.4±6.0*	73.3±3.9*	75.4±4.2*	77.6±4.1	**78.0±2.8**
CA2	0.07±0.01	54.2±9.6*	61.3±7.4*	69.0±5.1*	**72.3±3.9**	72.2±4.0
CA3	0.16±0.03	63.5±5.2*	68.1±4.5*	71.3±3.5*	73.7±4.5*	**75.6±4.2**
DG	0.52±0.11	75.1±4.1*	79.9±2.8*	82.1±2.4*	82.5±3.1	**83.3±1.5**
SUB	1.02±0.20	75.2±7.7*	78.3±7.1*	83.1±2.9*	81.4±5.4*	**84.0±2.2**
TAIL	0.40±0.13	79.9±3.2*	**81.8±3.0**	80.1±7.1	77.3±8.3	78.8±6.7
ERC	0.87±0.24	75.0±3.9*	78.6±3.7*	80.8±3.7*	80.3±6.0*	**84.4±3.3**
BA35	0.63±0.14	56.8±10.1*	64.4±9.4*	66.4±8.9*	69.4±8.2*	**72.2±6.9**
BA36	1.74±0.58	68.7±6.4*	76.3±5.6*	78.2±5.3*	74.6±7.2*	**80.0±6.0**
PHC	0.60±0.19	67.8±9.1*	71.2±7.9*	74.6±8.0	75.5±7.8	**76.4±6.1**

Note: *: p < 0.05 compared to DLF. Hyper-parameters: SVWV: β = 0.05; JLF + CL: β = 2.0. The optimal patch size is 3 × 3 × 1voxels for both SVWV and JLF + CL. The optimal search radius is 4 × 4 × 1 voxels for SVWV and 3 × 3 × 1 voxels for JLF + CL

Overall, DLF significantly improves segmentation accuracy in most of the subregions compared to label fusion methods with the biggest improvement in CA1–3, ERC and BA35, which are the most important subregions in Alzheimer's disease research. On the other hand, U-Net performs significantly worse than DLF in majority of the subregions (except CA1–2, DG, TAIL and PHC) with whole hippocampus, ERC, BA35 and BA36 being the worst. Notably, judging from the difference in errormaps in Fig. 3 (top), the improvements of DLF over JLF + CL and U-Net are not the same. Smaller error is observed in anterior and posterior BA35 as well as the anterior TAIL boundary compared to JLF + CL (white arrows) while medial ERC and lateral BA36 are the hotspots compared to U-Net (yellow arrows). This suggests that DLF is able to integrate the differential strong aspects of MAS and DL to improve segmentation accuracy.

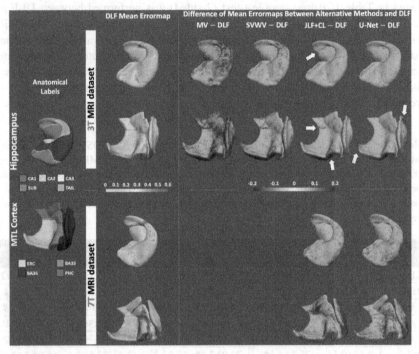

Fig. 3. Mean errormap of DLF and anatomical labels of the 3T (top) and 7T (bottom) MRI datasets. Difference in mean errormaps between alternative methods and DLF are shown on the right with red or blue indicating the alternative methods having more or less mean errors respectively. (Color figure online)

Testing the Generalizability on the 7T MRI Dataset. To test whether the proposed DLF can generalize better to unseen data of a similar task, we directly apply DLF as well as JFL + CL (the best conventional label fusion method in Table 1) and U-Net that are trained on the 3T to the 7T dataset and evaluate the segmentation accuracy in terms of DSC/GDSC between the generated segmentations and the manual ones of the 7T dataset. As shown in Table 2 and Fig. 3 (bottom), DLF significantly outperforms JLF + CL and U-Net in most of the subregions (except for SUB and TAIL compared to JLF + CL and PHC compared to U-Net). In general, JLF + CL and U-Net perform better in segmenting hippocampal subfields (CA1–2, DG, SUB, TAIL) and MTL cordial subregions (BA35, BA36, PHC) respectively. Interestingly, DLF is able to take advantage of both approaches and generalizes the best in the unseen 7T dataset. One thing to be noted is that the performance in the 7T dataset is worse compared to the 3T dataset in terms of smaller DSC scores, which is expected given that the manual segmentations were generated by different raters on images with different contrast. Indeed, the segmentation errors (bottom second column in Fig. 3) are mainly concentrated at tissue boundaries between neighborhood GM subregions, where the highest inter-rater variability is expected, rather than gray/white matter or gray matter/cerebral spinal fluid boundaries.

Table 2. Mean (±standard deviation) DSC and generalized DSC (GDSC) of all subregions between automatic and manual segmentations in the 7T MRI dataset. Volume of each label is provided for better interpretation of the DSC scores. Background color of each cell follow the same rule in Table 1.

	Volume (cm^3)	JLF+CL	U-Net	DLF
GDSC	-	66.7±5.8*	65.3±7.6*	**70.7±5.6**
Hippo	2.74±0.44	89.0±2.1*	80.2±7.7*	**89.4±2.2**
CA1	0.64±0.16	71.5±4.1*	61.6±9.9*	**74.2±5.6**
CA2	0.06±0.01	62.1±9.4*	58.0±15.5*	**65.3±10.7**
CA3	0.13±0.03	58.7±7.9*	58.9±11.8*	**64.6±7.6**
DG	0.47±0.09	77.7±4.4*	71.3±10.6*	**79.2±4.9**
SUB	0.97±0.14	78.4±3.2	68.1±7.8*	**78.7±4.6**
TAIL	0.46±0.17	71.4±5.8	67.1±8.0*	**72.0±5.5**
ERC	0.72±0.17	69.1±9.3*	68.3±12.5*	**73.8±8.2**
BA35	0.53±0.09	52.5±10.3*	60.0±8.5*	**62.3±8.8**
BA36	1.44±0.42	56.7±10.5*	60.8±10.0*	**64.6±8.3**
PHC	0.53±0.17	61.1±13.7*	**70.5±8.9***	67.7±10.0

Note: *: p < 0.05 compared to DLF. Hyper-parameters are the same as that in Table 1

Evaluate the Contributions of Sub-Components of DLF. To demonstrate the importance of the contribution of the important or unique sub-components of DLF, i.e. weighted-voting-subnet, fine-tunning-subnet and atlas mask, we also report in Table 3 the performance of DLF in the training fold (the first fold, rather than the other three folds as in Table 1 and Table 2) with each of them taken out. The results show that the fine-tuning-subnet contributes most (+6.2 in GDSC). Although the atlas mask brings small improvement (+0.5 in GDSC), it may be important in constraining spatial location of the final segmentation, potentially contributing to better generalizability.

5   Conclusion

In this work, we proposed an end-to-end 3D hybrid multi-atlas segmentation and deep learning segmentation pipeline. Experimental results on MTL subregion segmentation in the 3T dataset demonstrate significant improvement compared to both conventional multi-atlas segmentation approaches and U-Net, a direct DL method. Further, results on the unseen 7T dataset highlight the better generalizability of the proposed DLF approach. Future work includes investigating the relative contribution of T1w and T2w MRI, evaluating the proposed pipeline in other tissue segmentation tasks, speeding up registration

Table 3. Mean (±standard deviation) DSC and generalized DSC (GDSC) of all subregions between automatic and manual segmentations in the training fold (the first fold) of the 3T MRI dataset with components of DLF taken out. No statistical test was performed because of the limited sample size. Note: w/o = without. Background color of each cell follow the same rule in Table 1.

	w/o fine-tuning-subnet	w/o atlas mask	w/o weighted-voting-subnet	DLF
GDSC	72.9±6.0	77.6±4.2	75.7±4.5	78.1±4.7
Hippo	88.2±3.8	93.4±1.2	93.3±1.4	93.6±1.3
CA1	66.0±8.1	74.6±4.8	76.0±4.8	75.6±5.2
CA2	55.3±15.5	71.2±5.9	72.9±2.4	71.6±4.7
CA3	66.9±7.5	74.0±5.6	73.5±4.9	73.4±6.7
DG	81.7±2.6	81.8±2.5	82.2±2.3	83.2±2.8
SUB	79.7±3.1	81.6±3.2	81.8±3.4	82.4±3.2
TAIL	71.5±9.8	79.3±3.6	78.7±5.8	79.4±4.2
ERC	77.9±4.3	84.2±2.8	81.7±4.3	83.7±3.3
BA35	66.0±12.6	71.8±7.7	69.7±8.1	72.0±9.5
BA36	70.6±10.8	77.1±5.3	71.1±7.7	77.4±5.7
PHC	69.7±10.7	69.0±9.6	67.9±8.8	70.4±10.3

using learning-based methods, and performing more comprehensive comparisons with other learning-based label fusion approaches.[1]

References

1. Iglesias, J.E., Sabuncu, M.R.: Multi-atlas segmentation of biomedical images: a survey. Med. Image Anal. **24**, 205–219 (2015)
2. Heckemann, R.A., Hajnal, J.V., Aljabar, P., Rueckert, D., Hammers, A.: Automatic anatomical brain MRI segmentation combining label propagation and decision fusion. Neuroimage **33**, 115–126 (2006)
3. Coupé, P., Manjón, J.V., Fonov, V., Pruessner, J., Robles, M., Collins, D.L.: Patch-based segmentation using expert priors: application to hippocampus and ventricle segmentation. Neuroimage **54**, 940–954 (2011)
4. Sanroma, G., Benkarim, O.M., Piella, G., Wu, G., Zhu, X., Shen, D., Ballester, M.Á.G.: Discriminative Dimensionality Reduction for Patch-Based Label Fusion. Presented at the (2015)
5. Wang, H., Suh, J.W., Das, S.R., Pluta, J., Craige, C., Yushkevich, P.A.: Multi-atlas segmentation with joint label fusion. IEEE Trans. Pattern Anal. Mach. Intell. **35**, 611–623 (2012)
6. Sanroma, G., et al.: Learning non-linear patch embeddings with neural networks for label fusion. Med. Image Anal. **44**, 143–155 (2018)
7. Ding, W., Li, L., Zhuang, X., Huang, L.: Cross-modality multi-atlas segmentation using deep neural networks. In: Martel, A.L., et al. (eds.) MICCAI 2020. LNCS, vol. 12263, pp. 233–242. Springer, Cham (2020). https://doi.org/10.1007/978-3-030-59716-0_23

[1] This work was supported by NIH (grant numbers R01-AG056014, R01-AG040271, P30-AG010124, R01-EB017255, R01-AG055005) and Google Cloud.

8. Ding, Z., Han, X., Niethammer, M.: VoteNet+ : An improved deep learning label fusion method for multi-atlas segmentation. Lecture Notes in Computer Science (including Subseries Lecture Notes in Artificial Intelligence Lecture Notes in Bioinformatics), vol. 11766 LNCS, pp. 202–210 (2019).
9. Xie, L., Wang, J., Dong, M., Wolk, D.A., Yushkevich, P.A.: Improving multi-atlas segmentation by convolutional neural network based patch error estimation. In: Shen, D., et al. (eds.) MICCAI 2019. LNCS, vol. 11766, pp. 347–355. Springer, Cham (2019). https://doi.org/10.1007/978-3-030-32248-9_39
10. Yang, H., Sun, J., Li, H., Wang, L., Xu, Z.: Neural multi-atlas label fusion: application to cardiac MR images. Med. Image Anal. 49, 60–75 (2018)
11. Ronneberger, O., Fischer, P., Brox, T.: U-Net: convolutional networks for biomedical image segmentation. In: Navab, N., Hornegger, J., Wells, W.M., Frangi, A.F. (eds.) MICCAI 2015. LNCS, vol. 9351, pp. 234–241. Springer, Cham (2015). https://doi.org/10.1007/978-3-319-24574-4_28
12. Ioffe, S., Szegedy, C.: Batch normalization: Accelerating deep network training by reducing internal covariate shift. In: 32nd International Conference on Machine Learning, ICML 2015. pp. 448–456. International Machine Learning Society (IMLS) (2015).
13. Nair, V., Hinton, G.E.: Rectified Linear Units Improve Restricted Boltzmann Machines (2010)
14. Yushkevich, P.A., et al.: Automated volumetry and regional thickness analysis of hippocampal subfields and medial temporal cortical structures in mild cognitive impairment. Hum. Brain Mapp. 36, 258–287 (2015)
15. Lin, M., Chen, Q., Yan, S.: Best practices for ConvNets applied to object recognition. arXiv Prepr. 1, 10 (2013)
16. Sudre, C.H., Li, W., Vercauteren, T., Ourselin, S., Cardoso, M.J.: Generalised Dice overlap as a deep learning loss function for highly unbalanced segmentations. Lecture Notes in Computer Science (including Subseries Lecture Notes in Artificial Intelligence Lecture Notes in Bioinformatics), vol. 10553 LNCS, pp. 240–248 (2017)
17. Dou, Q., Chen, H., Jin, Y., Yu, L., Qin, J., Heng, P.-A.: 3D deeply supervised network for automatic liver segmentation from CT volumes. In: Ourselin, S., Joskowicz, L., Sabuncu, M.R., Unal, G., Wells, W. (eds.) MICCAI 2016. LNCS, vol. 9901, pp. 149–157. Springer, Cham (2016). https://doi.org/10.1007/978-3-319-46723-8_18
18. Wang, H., Suh, J.W., Das, S., Pluta, J., Altinay, M., Yushkevich, P.: Regression-Based Label Fusion for Multi-Atlas Segmentation. Conf. Comput. Vis. Pattern Recognit. Work. IEEE Comput. Soc. Conf. Comput. Vis. Pattern Recognition. Work, pp. 1113–1120 (2011)
19. Wang, H., et al.: A learning-based wrapper method to correct systematic errors in automatic image segmentation: consistently improved performance in hippocampus, cortex and brain segmentation. Neuroimage 55, 968–985 (2011)
20. Crum, W.R., Camara, O., Hill, D.L.G.: Generalized overlap measures for evaluation and validation in medical image analysis. IEEE Trans. Med. Imaging 25, 1451–1461 (2006)
21. Xie, L., et al.: Multi-template analysis of human perirhinal cortex in brain MRI: explicitly accounting for anatomical variability. Neuroimage 144, 183–202 (2017)

Feature Library: A Benchmark
for Cervical Lesion Segmentation

Yuexiang Li, Jiawei Chen, Kai Ma, and Yefeng Zheng[✉]

Tencent Jarvis Lab, Shenzhen, China
yefengzheng@tencent.com

Abstract. Cervical cancer causes the fourth most cancer-related deaths of women worldwide. One of the most commonly-used clinical tools for the diagnosis of cervical intraepithelial neoplasia (CIN) and cervical cancer is colposcopy examination. However, due to the challenging imaging conditions such as light reflection on the cervix surface, the clinical accuracy of colposcopy examination is relatively low. In this paper, we propose a computer-aided diagnosis (CAD) system to accurately segment the lesion areas (i.e., CIN and cancer) from colposcopic images, which can not only assist colposcopists for clinical decision, but also provide the guideline for the location of biopsy sites. In clinical practice, colposcopists often need to zoom in the potential lesion area for clearer observation. The colposcopic images with multi-scale views result in a difficulty for current straight-forward deep learning networks to process. To address the problem, we propose a novel attention mechanism, namely feature library, which treats the whole backbone network as a pool of features and extract the useful features on different scales from the pool to recalibrate the most informative representation. Furthermore, to well-train and evaluate our deep learning network, we collect a large-scale colposcopic image dataset for CervIcal lesioN sEgMentAtion (**CINEMA**), consisting of 34,337 images from 9,652 patients. The lesion areas in the colposcopic images are manually annotated by experienced colposcopists. Extensive experiments are conducted on the CINEMA dataset, which demonstrate the effectiveness of our feature library dealing with cervical lesions of varying sizes.

Keywords: Attention mechanism · Lesion segmentation · Colposcopy

1 Introduction

Cervical cancer contributes the fourth highest number of deaths in female cancers, carrying high risks of morbidity and mortality [18]. Over 88% of deaths from cervical cancer occur in low- and middle-income countries (LMICs), where gender discrimination and extreme poverty severely limit a woman's choice to seek care [6]. Due to the long period from precancerous cervical stage (i.e., cervical intraepithelial neoplasia (CIN)) to invasive cancer, the early identification

© Springer Nature Switzerland AG 2021
A. Feragen et al. (Eds.): IPMI 2021, LNCS 12729, pp. 440–451, 2021.
https://doi.org/10.1007/978-3-030-78191-0_34

of CIN can significantly decrease the number of deaths caused by cervical cancer. To this end, a low-cost and effective diagnosis tool for cervical cancer needs to be promoted. As one of the potential solutions, colposcopy with biopsy is widely-used for the diagnosis of CIN and cervical cancer worldwide. If a patient potentially having CIN or cancer is identified by the colposcopist, a colposcopy-directed biopsy is required to perform for the confirmation. However, due to the large population of patients and the limited number of skilled colposcopists, the accuracy of colposcopy examination in low-resource areas is relatively low [10]. Underwood et al. [22] reported that the average test positivity rate of colposcopic biopsy was 63.3% in some LMICs, resulting in over- or under-diagnosis.

Witnessing the recent development of machine learning, researchers tried to develop computer-aided diagnosis (CAD) systems to assist colposcopists and improve their clinical performance. Thorough reviews can be found in [4,12]. For examples, Song et al. [21] developed a data-driven algorithm to interpret colposcopic images based on color and texture, and integrated the results of human papillomavirus (HPV) and Pap tests for the final prediction of cervical dysplasia. Xu et al. [23] constructed a feature pyramid, consisting of multiple pyramid histograms generated from different feature spaces, for automated dysplasia classification. Recently, some researchers made the efforts to adopt deep learning networks to the development of CAD systems [13,20]. However, most of the existing frameworks tackled the task of abnormality identification, i.e., telling whether the patient has the risk of CIN or cancer, but could not provide the guideline (potential lesion areas) for the following biopsy. Therefore, if the colposcopists perform biopsy on the wrong sites, the patient may still be misdiagnosed as false-negative.

In this paper, we propose a deep-learning-based CAD system for the diagnosis of CIN and cervical cancer. The proposed system can not only identify the abnormal patients, but also segment the cervical lesion areas to guide the accurate location of biopsy sites for colposcopists. In clinical practice, colposcopists used to zoom in the potential lesion areas for clearer observation, as shown in Figs. 1 (a) and (b). The lesion size widely varies in such images, which results in a high requirement of multi-scale feature extraction for a CAD system to perform accurate cervical lesion segmentation. Although some solutions have been proposed, such as U-Net [19], PSPNet [25] and DeepLab [3], there remains spaces for improvement. In this regard, a novel global attention mechanism, namely feature library,[1] is proposed, which treats the whole backbone network as a feature pool and adaptively selects the features on different scales to recalibrate the most informative representation. Furthermore, we notice that there are few of existing frameworks proposed for the task of cervical lesion segmentation, due to the difficulty of data collection and annotation. To this end, we collect a large-scale annotated colposcopic image dataset, namely CINEMA, which consists of 34,337 images captured from 9,652 patients, for the training and evaluation of deep learning networks. The experimental results illustrate that the proposed feature library achieves a robust segmentation performance for cervical lesion areas.

---

[1] The backbone network is seen as a library containing various books (features) on different topics (scales).

2   Related Works

In this section, we introduce the existing studies on automated cervical lesion segmentation and publicly available colposcopic image datasets, respectively.

2.1   Automated Cervical Lesion Segmentation

Due to the importance of accurate cervical lesion segmentation for the subsequent biopsy, several studies focusing on cervical lesion segmentation have been recently proposed. Bai et al. [2] developed a squeeze-excitation convolutional neural network and a region proposal network to generate proposal boxes locating the cervical lesion regions and classify them into specific dysplasia. Compared to the rough detection with bounding boxes, Liu et al. [16] implemented a U-Net for the pixel-wise segmentation of cervical lesions in colposcopic images. The network was trained with about 2,500 labeled data. The colposcopist was required to label the contour of lesion regardless of dysplasia in this study. In a more recent study, Yuan et al. [24] trained a U-Net with a larger dataset consisting of 11,198 colposcopic images, which significantly boosted the segmentation accuracy. However, the pixel-wise annotations are still lack of dysplasia information. Different from the existing studies, our CINEMA dataset is much larger, which consists of 34,337 images captured from 9,652 patients, and the annotated lesion areas are categorized to CIN and cancer, respectively.

2.2   Colposcopic Image Datasets

Although numerous works proposed CAD systems based on colposcopic images, most of them reported the performance on their private datasets, which leads to the difficulty for the fair comparison between existing methods, and suggests the potential direction for further improvement. Facing this dilemma, Intel and MobileODT released a Kaggle challenge[2] to encourage researchers to develop robust algorithms for the cervical cancer screening. The competition aimed at developing a computer aided system to accurately identify a woman's cervix type based on images. The released dataset consists of 1,481 colposcopic images, which can be categorized to three cervix types (type 1, type 2 and type 3). These different types of cervix are all considered normal (non-cancerous), but since the cervical transformation zones are not always visible, some of the patients require further testing (types 2 and 3) while others do not (type 1). This decision is important for the treatment of patients. Deep learning models had been applied to address this challenge in several studies [1,9].

Another publicly available colposcopic image dataset (Quality Assessment of Digital Colposcopies) was released by Central University of Venezuela [5].[3] The dataset explores the subjective quality assessment of digital colposcopies. There are 284 colposcopic images contained in the dataset. Pixel-wise annotations for

---

[2] https://www.kaggle.com/c/intel-mobileodt-cervical-cancer-screening.

[3] https://archive.ics.uci.edu/ml/datasets.

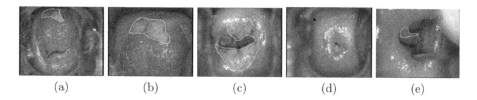

(a)   (b)   (c)   (d)   (e)

Fig. 1. Examplar colposcopic images in our CINEMA dataset. The lesion areas of CIN and cervical cancer are annotated with green and blue contours, respectively. (a) CIN patient under colposcopy. (b) Zoom-in view of the potential lesion areas of (a). (c) The patient may have the CIN and cancer areas at the same time. There are some difficulties for accurate segmentation of cervical lesion areas, such as the false-positive caused by the light reflection on normal cervix surface (d) and the occlusion caused by artifacts (e).

categories, such as artifacts, cervix, speculum and vaginal walls, and image-level labels on image quality are provided. One common drawback of both public datasets is the lack of pathological report, which results in the difficulty to use them for the development of computer aided diagnosis systems for cervical cancer screening and diagnosis.

3   CINEMA Dataset

The CINEMA dataset consists of 34,337 colposcopic images from 9,652 patients (63 normal, 9,227 CIN, and 362 cancer cases), which are collected by the collaborative hospital. The colposcopic images have a uniform size 640×480 pixels. The cervical lesions, which can be categorized to CIN and cancer according to the pathological reports, are annotated by the experienced colposcopists. As shown in Fig. 1 (c), a colposcopic image may contain lesion areas of different categories. We randomly separate the dataset to training, validation and test sets, according to the ratio of 70:10:20. To our best knowledge, this is currently the largest dataset for cervical lesion segmentation, which will be publicly available soon.

Challenge. By analyzing the dataset, we find several challenges for automatically segmenting the cervical lesions in the colposcopic images from our CINEMA dataset. First, as aforementioned, in clinical practice, colposcopists often need to zoom in the potential lesion area for clearer observation. The colposcopic images with multi-scale views (see Fig. 1 (a) and (b)) result in a difficulty for current straight-forward deep learning networks to process. Second, the cervical lesion areas on different dysplasia levels (CIN and cancer) may have similar appearances (see Fig. 1 (c)). Third, in the colposcopy exams, noises (see Fig. 1 (d)) and artifacts (see Fig. 1 (e)) may be introduced into the colposcopic images.

4   Benchmark Method

In this section, we present the proposed global attention mechanism (i.e., feature library) in details. The features on different stages of conventional convolution

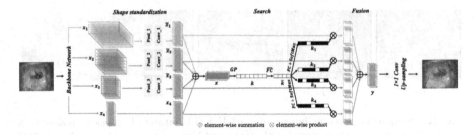

Fig. 2. The pipline of the library searching module (Conv_1: Conv 1 × 1, in_channel 256, out_channel 2048; Conv_2: Conv 1 × 1, in_channel 512, out_channel 2048; Conv_3: Conv 1 × 1, in_channel 1024, out_channel 2048; Pool_1: MaxPool 8 × 8; Pool_2: Max-Pool 4 × 4; Pool_3: MaxPool 2 × 2).

neural networks (CNNs) contain different information—the shallow layers are responsible for the extraction of low-level features (e.g., texture and boundary), while the deep layers aim to extract the semantic features. To this end, we propose a global attention mechanism, namely feature library, which collects all the features from different stages as a feature pool and globally selects meaningful features to constitute the robust representation for cervical lesion segmentation. The proposed feature library is a plug-in module; hence the backbone network can be any prevalent CNN such as ResNet [7]. Henceforward, we use ResNet-50 as an example. Figure 2 shows the pipeline of our feature library, which involves three components—*Shape standardization, Search* and *Fusion*.

Shape Standardization. The colored volumes (x_1, x_2, x_3, x_4) in Fig. 2 are the sets of feature maps yielded by different stages of ResNet-50 (i.e., *conv2_3, conv3_4, conv4_6* and *conv5_3* according to [7]). Since those feature maps have different sizes and numbers of channels, we first need to transform them to a uniform shape for the following search module, which consists of element-wise summation. The max pooling and 1 × 1 convolution are adopted for this purpose. The detailed information of max pooling and convolutional layers used for shape standardization is listed in Table 1.

Table 1. The detailed information of max pooling and convolutional layers used by the shape standardization module. The kernel size of max pooling and convolutional layers is listed. H, W and C are the height, width and number of channels, respectively.

Input size	Max pooling	Convolution	Output
$x_1 \in \mathbb{R}^{H_1 \times W_1 \times C_1}$	$\left(\frac{H_1}{H_4}, \frac{W_1}{W_4}\right)$	$(1, 1, C_4)$	$\tilde{x}_1 \in \mathbb{R}^{H_4 \times W_4 \times C_4}$
$x_2 \in \mathbb{R}^{H_2 \times W_2 \times C_2}$	$\left(\frac{H_2}{H_4}, \frac{W_2}{W_4}\right)$	$(1, 1, C_4)$	$\tilde{x}_2 \in \mathbb{R}^{H_4 \times W_4 \times C_4}$
$x_3 \in \mathbb{R}^{H_3 \times W_3 \times C_3}$	$\left(\frac{H_3}{H_4}, \frac{W_3}{W_4}\right)$	$(1, 1, C_4)$	$\tilde{x}_3 \in \mathbb{R}^{H_4 \times W_4 \times C_4}$

Search and Fusion. Several studies [8] have demonstrated that self-gating attention mechanism is an effective and lightweight solution to regulate the information flow of feature maps. In this regard, we integrate the self-gating approach into our search module to globally select the useful features among backbone network and adaptively construct the robust feature representation for cervical lesion segmentation. First, to integrate information from multi-scale features, our search module fuses the standardized feature maps via an element-wise summation: $x = \tilde{x}_1 + \tilde{x}_2 + \tilde{x}_3 + x_4$, where $\{\tilde{x}_1, \tilde{x}_2, \tilde{x}_3\}$ are the unified features from different stages. Then, the global information x is aggregated across the spatial dimensions $(H \times W)$ by using a global average pooling (depicted as GP in Fig. 2) and a channel-wise statistic $k \in \mathbb{R}^C$ (C is the number of channels) is thereby yielded. Formally, the c-th element of k is calculated by:

$$k_c = GP\left(x_c\right) = \frac{1}{H \times W} \sum_{i=1}^{H} \sum_{j=1}^{W} x_c(i, j). \tag{1}$$

To achieve more accurate guidance for feature selection, the channel-wise statistic k is further compacted to a feature $\tilde{k}$ via a fully-connected layer $\tilde{FC}$, which can be written as:

$$\tilde{k} = \tilde{FC}(k) = \delta(\beta(\tilde{W}k)) \tag{2}$$

where $\tilde{W} \in \mathbb{R}^{d \times C}$, $\tilde{k} \in \mathbb{R}^d$, δ and β are the ReLU activation function and the batch normalization, respectively. Here, d is a hyper-parameter ($d = C/2$ in our experiments). The compacted feature $\tilde{k}$ is then fed to four identical branches, which consist of fully connected and softmax layers, depicted as FC and $SoftMax$ in Fig. 2, respectively, for the generation of adaptive feature weights

$$k_i = SoftMax(FC(\tilde{k})) = \sigma_i(W\tilde{k}) \quad \text{for } i = [1, 2, 3, 4] \tag{3}$$

where $W \in R^{C' \times d}$ and $\sigma(.)$ is defined as follows:

$$\sigma(\mathbf{z})_n = \frac{e^{z_n}}{\sum_{m=1}^{C'} e^{z_m}} \quad \text{for } n = [1, \ldots, C'] \tag{4}$$

where C' denotes the number of channels of k_i (i.e., $C' = C_4$) and $\mathbf{z} = W\tilde{k}$.

The generated weights $\{k_1, k_2, k_3, k_4\}$ can adaptively assign network attentions to features on different scales, i.e., enhancing the informative features and suppressing the useless ones. The final feature map $\mathbf{y}$ is obtained by weighted summation of features on different scales:

$$\mathbf{y} = \sum_{i=1}^{L} k_i \cdot \tilde{x}_i \tag{5}$$

where L is the number of feature scales, i.e., $L = 4$ in our experiments.

Up-Sampling. The fused feature representation $\mathbf{y}$ contains the information of multi-scale features, which is robust to segment the cervical lesion areas with multi-scale views. We upsample the fused representation to the size of input image [25] and yield the segmentation result—a 1×1 convolution reduces the number of channels of **y** to 1 and an upsampling layer interpolates **y** to the original image size.

5 Experiments

The proposed feature library framework is evaluated on our large-scale CINEMA colposcopic dataset, collected from the collaborative hospital, to demonstrate its effectiveness on the segmentation of cervical lesions. As aforementioned, the CINEMA dataset is randomly separated to training, validation and test sets. In this section, we mainly use the validation and test sets for performance evaluation.

Evaluation Criterion. The widely-used Dice coefficient (DSC) [15,17], which measures the spatial overlap ratio between the segmentation result and ground truth, is adopted as the metric to assess the segmentation accuracy. For the multi-class task (e.g., CIN and cancer), we calculate the DSC for each class and average them to yield a mean DSC (mDSC) for performance evaluation.

Implementation Details. The proposed feature library is implemented using PyTorch. The widely used ResNet-50 [7] is used as the backbone of the framework. The initial learning rate is set to 0.001. The network is trained with a mini-batch size of 16. The Adam solver [11] is adopted for network optimization. For fair comparison, all the baselines are trained according to the same protocol.

Baselines. Our feature library aims to extract multi-scale features from colposcopic images to better tackle the segmentation of cervical lesions with varying sizes. Therefore, network architectures widely used for multi-scale feature extraction and their variants are adopted as baselines for performance evaluation. A brief description is given in the following:

U-Net [19] is a network architecture widely-accepted in the area of medical image processing, which consists of an encoder and a decoder. The encoder is responsible for feature extraction, while the decoder aims to reconstruct the feature maps to the original resolution of the input image. There are shortcut connections between each stage of the encoder and decoder, which enable the information flow of multi-scale features. Since our feature library adopts the ResNet-50 [7] as backbone, a ResU-Net using ResNet-50 as the encoder is implemented for fair comparison. Furthermore, an attention-based variant, i.e., SE-ResU-Net, which utilizes the SE-ResNet [8] as the encoder, is also involved for comparison.

PSPNet [25] is another widely used architecture for multi-scale feature extraction. A pyramid pooling module is proposed to exploit and fuse features on four different scales, which can be added to the end of any CNN for context aggregation. The global prior representation yielded by PSPNet produces good quality results on the natural image processing tasks, e.g., scene parsing. To be consistent with our feature library, the ResNet-50 is used as backbone of PSPNet and a variant with attention mechanism, i.e., SE-PSPNet, is also implemented.

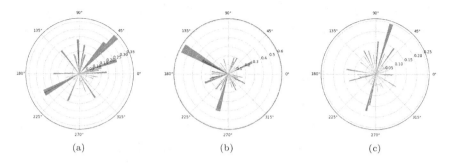

Fig. 3. Network attentions on different stages. Our feature library with three stages (x_2, x_3, x_4), which yields the best performance in Table 2, is taken as an example. (a)-(c) are the activation pattern of x_2, x_3, and x_4, respectively. The polar histogram presents the 2048-d activation pattern in a circle, where $0°$ is the first element. Note that the listed three circles have different scales.

DeepLab-v3 [3] has a similar architecture to PSPNet, which replaces the pyramid pooling module with atrous spatial pyramin pooling (ASPP). The ASPP module extracts multi-scale features from high level semantic features using atrous convolutions with different atrous rates. Consistently, DeepLab-v3 using ResNet-50 as backbone and its variant SE-DeepLab-v3 are included.

SKNet [14] is a convolutional neural network proposed for image classification, which does not involve the decoder part. Compared to SENet, SKNet has an attention-based multi-scale module (i.e., selective kernel unit), which neutralizes the performance improvements yielded by the decoder (e.g., short-cut connections in ResU-Net and pyramid pooling module in PSPNet). Therefore, the hybrid methods, such as SK-ResU-Net and SK-PSPNet, result in a difficulty to determine the source boosting the performance. In this regard, we use a convolutional and a upsampling layer, similar to our feature library, to compact the number of channels and generate the segmentation result of the same size to the input image.

5.1   Ablation Study

To evaluate the importance of features on different scales, we implement two variants of feature library by reducing the number of stages for feature selection, denoted as Feature Library w/ (x_3, x_4) and w/ (x_2, x_3, x_4) in Table 2. It can be observed that the segmentation accuracy for CIN and cancer slightly increases by removing the features of x_1. The underlying reason may be that the shallow layers of a neural network mainly extract the low-level information, such as texture, from images. Due to the element-wise summation adopted for feature fusion in the very beginning of our feature library, those low-level features may dilute the information contained in semantic features and thereby influence the segmentation accuracy.

Table 2. Comparison of different frameworks in terms of DSC (%) and network parameters (Params). (F. L.—Feature Library)

	Validation			Test			Params
	CIN	Cancer	mDSC	CIN	Cancer	mDSC	(million)
ResNet-50 [7]	–	–	–	–	–	–	25
ResU-Net [7,19]	70.79	84.26	77.53	68.12	82.92	75.52	48
SE-ResU-Net [7,8,19]	71.10	85.17	78.14	69.44	84.42	76.93	51
PSPNet [25]	67.37	83.51	75.44	64.48	80.43	72.46	89
SE-PSPNet [8,25]	69.03	84.42	76.73	66.21	83.48	74.85	92
DeepLab-v3 [3]	68.65	83.99	76.32	65.36	81.50	73.43	64
SE-DeepLab-v3 [3,8]	70.14	85.02	77.58	67.88	83.24	75.56	67
SKNet + Upsampling [14]	67.77	88.84	77.81	67.22	83.69	75.45	28
F. L. w/ (x_3, x_4) (Ours)	73.93	87.05	80.49	71.35	84.80	78.08	31
F. L. w/ (x_2, x_3, x_4) (Ours)	**74.82**	**88.75**	**81.79**	**72.97**	**86.12**	**79.55**	35
F. L. w/ (x_1, x_2, x_3, x_4) (Ours)	74.19	88.21	81.20	71.85	85.28	78.57	37
w/o Attention Mechanism*							
F. L. w/ (x_3, x_4)	70.69	84.19	77.44	68.49	81.86	75.18	25
F. L. w/ (x_2, x_3, x_4)	72.30	85.76	79.03	70.88	83.34	77.11	26
F. L. w/ (x_1, x_2, x_3, x_4)	71.02	84.86	77.94	69.52	82.07	75.80	27

* Using element-wise summation directly for feature fusion.

Attention of Feature Library. To provide an in-depth investigation on the attention of our feature library while segmenting cervical lesions, we visualize the activation pattern, i.e., the *Weights* after FC + SoftMax, of each stage, as illustrated in Fig. 3. It can be observed that the proposed feature library prefers to assign nearly equal attention to the elements of x_4, as they contain the most semantic information related to the lesion segmentation. Different from that, some of the elements of x_2 and x_3 gain relatively higher attention than the others, which demonstrates that our feature library really learns to select features beneficial for cervical lesion segmentation from early stages.

5.2   Comparison with Baselines

To validate the effectiveness of our feature library module, we evaluate the performance of different frameworks on the validation and test sets. The evaluation results are presented in Table 2.

It can be observed from Table 2 that our feature library achieves the best segmentation accuracy for CIN and cervical cancer lesions on both validation and test sets, which are +3.65% and +2.62% higher than the mean DSC of the runner-up (i.e., SE-ResU-Net). The PSPNet and DeepLab-v3, and their variants (SE-PSPNet and SE-DeepLab-v3) achieve relatively lower accuracy—mean DSCs of 72.46%, 73.43%, 74.85%, and 75.56% on the test set, respectively, since

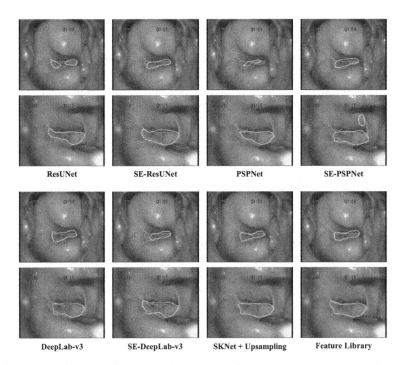

Fig. 4. Comparison of segmentation results yielded by different frameworks (U. L.–upsampling layers). The colposcopist zooms in the lesion area (i.e., the second row) for clearer observation during the colposcopy examination. The lesion areas predicted by algorithms are marked with yellow contours, while the ground-truth annotations are marked with green ones. Compared to the baselines, the proposed feature library produces more accurate segmentation for cervical lesions under different views (original and zoom in).

they extract the multi-scale features by the end of backbone network, i.e., the feature extracted by the early stages are not directly exploited. The attention-based multi-scale framework (i.e., SKNet + Upsampling) achieves a mean DSC of 75.45% (i.e., -4.1% lower than our feature library), which demonstrates the effectiveness of our feature library strategy—fusing information across the whole backbone network. A consistent increase of DSC is observed by integrating the attention module (SE module) into the baseline frameworks. To further evaluate the segmentation performance, the segmentation results yielded by benchmarking algorithms and our feature library are presented in Fig. 4. Compared to the baselines, the proposed feature library produces more accurate segmentation for cervical lesions under different views (original and zoom in).

Model Complexity. Since the feature library is a plug-in module, which can be easily integrated to any CNN, the extra model complexity caused by the module is one of the most concerns for practical applications. The numbers of parameters of different network architectures are listed in Table 2. With the same backbone, ResNet-50, the feature library, which achieves the best DSC on the test set, introduces the least extra parameters (i.e., 10 million) to ResNet-50, compared to the benchmarking algorithms, which demonstrates the efficiency and effectiveness of the proposed module. We also evaluate the computational complexity of our feature library (i.e., 22.33 GFlops), which is just slightly higher than original ResNet-50 (i.e., 21.51 GFlops).

6 Conclusion

In this paper, we proposed a global attention mechanism, namely feature library, to effectively segment cervical lesions of varying sizes. The proposed framework can not only assist colposcopists for clinical decision, i.e., identifying the CIN and cancer lesions, but also provide the guideline for the location of biopsy sites, i.e., segmenting the lesion areas. To train and evaluate deep learning networks on the task of cervical lesion segmentation, we collected a large-scale annotated dataset, namely CINEMA, from the collaborative hospital. The experimental results on the test set demonstrated the efficiency and effectiveness of our feature library.

Acknowledgment. This work was founded by the Key-Area Research and Development Program of Guangdong Province, China (No. 2018B010111001), National Key R&D Program of China (2018YFC2000702) and the Scientific and Technical Innovation 2030-'New Generation Artificial Intelligence' Project (No. 2020AAA0104100).

References

1. Arora, M., Dhawan, S., Singh, K.: Deep neural network for transformation zone classification. In: International Conference on Secure Cyber Computing and Communication (2018)
2. Bai, B., Du, Y., Liu, P., Sun, P., Li, P., Lv, Y.: Detection of cervical lesion region from colposcopic images based on feature reselection. Biomed. Signal Process. Control **57**, 101785 (2020)
3. Chen, L.C., Papandreou, G., Schroff, F., Adam, H.: Rethinking atrous convolution for semantic image segmentation. arXiv preprint arXiv:1706.05587 (2017)
4. Fernandes, K., Cardoso, J.S., Fernandes, J.: Automated methods for the decision support of cervical cancer screening using digital colposcopies. IEEE Access **6**, 33910–33927 (2018)
5. Fernandes, K., Cardoso, J.S., Fernandes, J.: Transfer learning with partial observability applied to cervical cancer screening. In: Iberian Conference on Pattern Recognition and Image Analysis (2017)
6. Ginsburg, O.M.: Breast and cervical cancer control in low and middle-income countries: Human rights meet sound health policy. J. Cancer Policy **1**(3-4), e35-e41 (2013)
7. He, K., Zhang, X., Ren, S., Sun, J.: Deep residual learning for image recognition. In: IEEE Conference on Computer Vision and Pattern Recognition, pp. 770–778 (2016)
8. Hu, J., Shen, L., Sun, G.: Squeeze-and-excitation networks. In: IEEE Conference on Computer Vision and Pattern Recognition (2018)

9. Kaur, N., Panigrahi, N., Mittal, A.K.: Automated cervical cancer screening using transfer learning. In: International Conference on Recent Advances in Engineering Science and Management (2017)
10. Khan, M.J., Werner, C.L., Darragh, T.M., Guido, R.S., Mathews, C., Moscicki, A.B., et al.: ASCCP colposcopy standards: role of colposcopy, benefits, potential harms, and terminology for colposcopic practice. J. Lower Genital Tract Dis. **21**(4), 223–229 (2017)
11. Kingma, D.P., Ba, J.: Adam: A method for stochastic optimization. arXiv preprint arXiv:1412.6980 (2014)
12. Kudva, V., Prasad, K.: Pattern classification of images from acetic acid-based cervical cancer screening: a review. Crit. Rev. Biomed. Eng. **46**(2), 117–133 (2018)
13. Kudva, V., Prasad, K., Shyamala, G.: Automation of detection of cervical cancer using convolutional neural networks. Crit. Rev. Biomed. Eng. **46**(2), 135–145 (2018)
14. Li, X., Wang, W., Hu, X., Yang, J.: Selective kernel networks. In: IEEE Conference on Computer Vision and Pattern Recognition, pp. 510–519 (2019)
15. Li, Y., Shen, L.: Skin lesion analysis towards melanoma detection using deep learning network. Sensors **18**(2), 556 (2018)
16. Liu, Y., Bai, B., Chen, H., Liu, P., Feng, H.: Cervical image segmentation using U-Net model. In: International Symposium on Intelligent Signal Processing and Communication Systems (2019)
17. Luna, M., Kwon, M., Park, S.H.: Precise separation of adjacent nuclei using a Siamese neural network. In: International Conference On Medical Image Computing & Computer Assisted Intervention, pp. 577–585 (2019)
18. Peng, L., Yuan, X., Jiang, B., Tang, Z., Li, G.C.: LncRNAs: key players and novel insights into cervical cancer. Tumour Biol. **37**(3), 2779–2788 (2016)
19. Ronneberger, O., Fischer, P., Brox, T.: U-Net: Convolutional networks for biomedical image segmentation. In: International Conference on Medical Image Computing & Computer Assisted Intervention (2015)
20. Sato, M., Horie, K., Hara, A., Miyamoto, Y., Kurihara, K., Tomio, K.: Application of deep learning to the classification of images from colposcopy. Oncol. Lett. **15**(3), 3518–3523 (2018)
21. Song, D., Kim, E., Huang, X., Patruno, J., Munozavila, H., Heflin, J., et al.: Multimodal entity coreference for cervical dysplasia diagnosis. IEEE Trans. Med. Imaging **34**(1), 229–245 (2015)
22. Underwood, M., Arbyn, M., Parry-Smith, W.P., Bellis-Ayres, S.D., Moss, E.: Accuracy of colposcopy-directed punch biopsies: a systematic review and meta-analysis. BJOG: Int. J. Obstet. Gynaecol. **119**(11), 1293–1301 (2012)
23. Xu, T., Zhang, H., Xin, C., Kim, E., Huang, X.: Multi-feature based benchmark for cervical dysplasia classification evaluation. Pattern Recogn. **63**, 468–475 (2017)
24. Yuan, C., et al.: The application of deep learning based diagnostic system to cervical squamous intraepithelial lesions recognition in colposcopy images. Sci. Rep. **10**, 11639 (2020)
25. Zhao, H., Shi, J., Qi, X., Wang, X., Jia, J.: Pyramid scene parsing network. In: IEEE Conference on Computer Vision and Pattern Recognition (2017)

Generalized Organ Segmentation by Imitating One-Shot Reasoning Using Anatomical Correlation

Hong-Yu Zhou[1], Hualuo Liu[2], Shilei Cao[2], Dong Wei[2(✉)], Chixiang Lu[3], Yizhou Yu[1], Kai Ma[2], and Yefeng Zheng[2]

[1] The University of Hong Kong, Pok Fu Lam, Hong Kong
yizhouy@acm.org
[2] Tencent, Shenzhen, China
lhl18@mails.jlu.edu.cn, {donwei,kylekma,yefengzheng}@tencent.com
[3] Huazhong University of Science and Technology, Wuhan, China

Abstract. Learning by imitation is one of the most significant abilities of human beings and plays a vital role in human's computational neural system. In medical image analysis, given several exemplars (anchors), experienced radiologist has the ability to delineate unfamiliar organs by imitating the reasoning process learned from existing types of organs. Inspired by this observation, we propose *OrganNet* which learns a generalized organ concept from a set of annotated organ classes and then transfer this concept to unseen classes. In this paper, we show that such process can be integrated into the one-shot segmentation task which is a very challenging but meaningful topic. We propose pyramid reasoning modules (PRMs) to model the anatomical correlation between anchor and target volumes. In practice, the proposed module first computes a correlation matrix between target and anchor computerized tomography (CT) volumes. Then, this matrix is used to transform the feature representations of both anchor volume and its segmentation mask. Finally, OrganNet learns to fuse the representations from various inputs and predicts segmentation results for target volume. Extensive experiments show that OrganNet can effectively resist the wide variations in organ morphology and produce state-of-the-art results in one-shot segmentation task. Moreover, even when compared with fully-supervised segmentation models, OrganNet is still able to produce satisfying segmentation results.

Keywords: One-shot learning · Image segmentation · Anatomical similarity

1 Introduction

Organ segmentation has wide applications in disease diagnosis, treatment planning, intervention, radiation therapy and other clinical workflows [9]. Thanks to deep learning, remarkable progress has been achieved in organ segmentation tasks. However, existing deep models usually focus on a predefined set of organs given abundant annotations for training (e.g., heart, aorta, trachea, and esophagus in [22]) but fail to generalize

---

H.Y. Zhou, H. Liu and S. Cao—First three authors contributed equally. Work done at Tencent.

© Springer Nature Switzerland AG 2021
A. Feragen et al. (Eds.): IPMI 2021, LNCS 12729, pp. 452–464, 2021.
https://doi.org/10.1007/978-3-030-78191-0_35

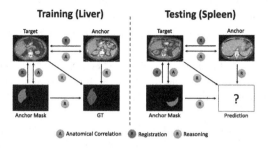

Fig. 1. Conceptual overview of proposed one-shot reasoning process. During the training stage, given a target image and paired anchor image with its annotation mask, we first conduct registration between anchor and target images. Then, the proposed reasoning module tries to model the anatomical correlation between anchor and target images. The correlation matrix is further used to transform the feature representations of both anchor image and its corresponding mask, which are jointly learned with target image features to produce final predictions. We argue that the generalized organ concept can be learned from a set of sufficiently annotated organs in such process (left). In the test stage, the learned knowledge generalize to unseen abdominal organs whose segmentation results can be easily inferred (right). Note that in practice, the inputs are 3D volumes instead of 2D images.

to unseen abdominal organ with only limited annotations (in the extreme case, only one annotation is available), which limits their clinical usage in practice.

A potential solution to this problem is the one-shot segmentation methodology [23, 25], which attempts to learn knowledge from only one labeled sample. Nonetheless, these approaches lack the ability to handle large variations among different organ types and thus cannot be directly applied to one-shot organ segmentation. On the other hand, we find that human radiologists naturally maintain the ability to effectively learn unfamiliar organ concepts given limited annotated data, which we think can be attributed to their usage of anatomical similarity to segment both seen and unseen organs. Meanwhile, it is also a reasonable setting to transfer the learned knowledge from richly annotated organs to less annotated ones. Inspired by these observations, we propose a new one-shot segmentation paradigm where we assume that a *generalized* organ concept can be learned from a set of sufficiently annotated organs and applied for effective one-shot learning to segment some previously unseen abdominal organs. We illustrate the proposed method in Fig. 1 where we call it ONE-SHOT REASONING as it imitates the reasoning process of human radiologists by making use of anatomical similarity.

Anatomical similarity have been widely used in medical image segmentation [7, 15]. Compared to these methods, our work mainly exploits using anatomical similarity within each one-shot pair of images to perform reasoning. In this sense, our work provides a new segmentation paradigm by utilizing learned organ priors, with a focus on the one-shot scenario. In this paper, we propose OrganNet to implement the concept of generalized organ learning for one-shot organ segmentation in medical images. Our contributions can be summarized as follows:

1. We propose a new organ segmentation paradigm which learns a generalized organ concept from seen organ classes and then generalize to unseen classes using one-shot pairs as supervision.
2. A reasoning module is developed to exploit the anatomical correlation between adjacent spatial regions of anchor and target computerized tomography (CT) volumes, which can be utilized to enhance the representations of anchor volume and its segmentation annotation.
3. We introduce OrganNet, which includes two additional encoders to basic 3D U-Net architecture to jointly learn representations from target volume, anchor volume and its corresponding segmentation mask.
4. We conduct comprehensive experiments to evaluate OrganNet. The experimental results on both organ and non-organ segmentation tasks demonstrate the effectiveness of OrganNet.

2   Related Work

Utilizing the anatomical correlation is one of the key designs of proposed OrganNet. In this section, we first review existing works related to the utilization of anatomical priors and then list the most related works in one-shot medical segmentation.

Anatomical Correlation in Medical Image Segmentation. A large body of literature [1,19,20] exploits anatomical correlation for medical image segmentation within the deep learning framework. The anatomical correlation also serves as the foundation of atlas-based segmentation [12,15], where one or several labeled reference images (i.e., atlases) are non-rigidly registered to a target image based on the anatomical similarity, and the labels of the atlases are propagated to the target image as the segmentation output. Different from these methods, OrganNet has the ability to learn anatomical similarity between images by employing the reasoning process. With this design, the proposed approach is able to learn a generalized organ concept for one-shot organ segmentation.

One-Shot Medical Segmentation. Zhao *et al.* [25] presented an automated data augmentation method for synthesizing labeled medical images on resonance imaging (MRI) brain scans. However, DataAug is strictly restricted to segmenting objects when only small changes exist between anchor and target images. Based on DataAug, Dalca *et al.* [6] further extended it to an alternative strategy that combines a conventional probabilistic atlas-based segmentation with deep learning. Roy *et al.* [21] proposed a few-shot volumetric segmenter by optimally pairing a few slices of the support volume to all the slices of the query volume. Similar to DataAug, Wang *et al.* [23] introduced cycle consistency to learn reversible voxel-wise correspondences for one-shot medical image segmentation. Lu *et al.* [17] proposed a one-shot anatomy segmentor which is based on a naturally built-in human-in-the-loop mechanism. Different from these approaches, this paper focuses on a more realistic setting: we use richly annotated organs to assist the segmentation of less annotated ones. Also, our method is partially related to the siamese learning [2,26–28] which often takes a pair of images as inputs.

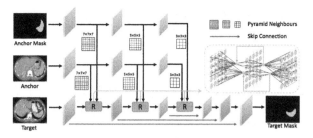

Fig. 2. Network structure of proposed OrganNet. It augments the classic U-Net structure with two additional encoders to learn to perform one-shot reasoning from an anchor image and its corresponding segmentation annotation. Pyramid reasoning modules (PRMs, denoted as **R**) are proposed to model the anatomical similarity between target and anchor volumes. Note that all operations, and the input and output of OrganNet are 3D; here we use 2D slices of the 3D volumes for the purpose of idea illustration.

3   Proposed Method

In this section, we introduce OrganNet, which is able to perform one-shot reasoning by exploiting anatomical correlation within input pairs. Particularly, we propose to explore such correlation from multiple scales where we use different sizes of neighbour regions as shown in Fig. 2. More details will be presented in the following.

Before we send anchor and target images (in practice, CT volumes) to OrganNet, it is suggested that registration should be conducted in order to align their image space. Since most of data come from abdomen, we apply DEEDS (DEnsE Displacement Sampling) [10] as it yielded the best performance in most CT-based datasets [24]. Note that the organ mask is also aligned according to its corresponding anchor image.

3.1   One-Shot Reasoning Using OrganNet

As shown in Fig. 2, OrganNet has three encoders which learn representations for target volume, anchor volume and anchor mask, respectively. Moreover, we propose pyramid reasoning modules (PRMs) to connect different encoders which decouples Organ-Net into two parts: one part for learning representations from anchor volume and its paired organ mask (top two branches) and the other for exploiting anatomical similarity between the anchor and the target volumes (bottom two branches). We argue that the motivation behind can be summarized as: the generalized organ concept can be learned from a set of sufficiently annotated organs, and then generalize to previously unseen abdominal organs by utilizing only a single one-shot pair.

The OrganNet is built upon the classic 3D U-Net structure [4] and we extend it to a tri-encoder version to include extra supervision from anchor image and its annotation. In practice, we ddesign OrganNet to be light-weight in order to alleviate the overfitting problem caused by small datasets in medical image analysis. Specifically, for each layer, we only employ two bottlenecks for both encoders and only one bottleneck for the decoder branch. Since all operations are in 3D, we use a relatively small number of channels for each convolutional kernel to reduce computational cost.

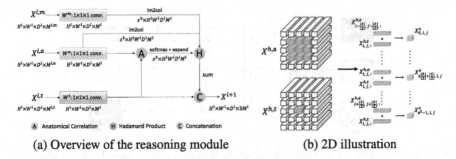

(a) Overview of the reasoning module   (b) 2D illustration

Fig. 3. Main architecture of the reasoning module. (a) $X^{l,t}$, $X^{l,a}$ and $X^{l,m}$ represent layer l's input tensors for target volume, anchor volume and anchor mask, respectively. We apply *softmax* to tensor's first dimension where *sum* operation is also conducted after Hadamard product. In (b), we provide a simplified 2D illustration of the reasoning module.

Imitation is a powerful cognitive mechanism that humans use to make inferences and learn new abstractions [8]. We propose to model the anatomical similarity between images to provide strong knowledge prior for learning one-shot segmentation. However, the variations in organ location, shape, size, and appearance among individuals can be regarded as an obstacle for a network to make reasonable decisions. To address these challenges, we propose PRMs to effectively encapsulate representations from multiple encoders.

3.2 Pyramid Reasoning Modules

These modules are designed to address the situation in which the organ morphologies and structures of target and anchor volumes show different levels of variations. Since features in different feature pyramids capture multi-scale information, we propose to aggregate information at each pyramid level with a reasoning function. To account for the displacement between the two images, large sizes of neighbour regions are employed in shallow layers, whereas small region sizes are employed in deep layers. The underlying reason of such allocation is that the receptive fields of shallow layers are smaller than those of deep ones. Concretely, we first compute the correlation matrix between feature maps of target and anchor volumes. Then, we apply this matrix to transform feature representations of anchor input and its segmentation mask, respectively. Finally, we concatenate representations of three inputs and treat them as the input to next layer.

As shown in Fig. 3, at layer l, each reasoning module has three input tensors $X^{l,t}$, $X^{l,a}$ and $X^{l,m}$, corresponding to target volume, anchor volume and anchor mask, respectively. We first apply three $3 \times 3 \times 3$ convolutional operators to above three input tensors in order to normalize them to the same scale. The outputs of such operations are $X^{h,t}$, $X^{h,a}$ and $X^{h,m}$, and the size of each is $H^l \times W^l \times D^l \times M^l$.

To model the anatomical correlation between $X^{h,t}$ and $X^{h,a}$, we apply inner product operation to neighbour regions from both tensors. Particularly, given a specific vector $X^{h,t}_{i,j,k,:}$ in tensor $X^{h,t}$ with $0 \le i < H^l$, $0 \le j < W^l$ and $0 \le k < D^l$, we compute the inner product based on its neighbour regions in $X^{h,a}$ which can be summarized as:

$$X^o_{n,i,j,k} = (X^{h,a}_{i+i',j+j',k+k',:})^T X^{h,t}_{i,j,k,:}$$ (1)

where $\{i',j',k'\} \in \{-\lfloor \frac{s}{2} \rfloor, ..., \lfloor \frac{s}{2} \rfloor\}$. s stands for the size of neighbour region which changes with layer depth. And n stands for the total index which can be computed as:

$$n = (i' + \lfloor \frac{s}{2} \rfloor) + (j' + \lfloor \frac{s}{2} \rfloor) \times s + (k' + \lfloor \frac{s}{2} \rfloor) \times s^2.$$ (2)

$X^o \in \mathcal{R}^{s^3 \times H^l \times W^l \times D^l}$. For better understanding,, we provide an illustration of the computation process of anatomical correlation in 2D network, which can be found in the supplementary material.

Now X^o represents the anatomical similarity between $X^{h,t}$ and $X^{h,a}$. Then, we apply *softmax* normalization along with the first dimension of X^o and *expand* its dimension to $s^3 \times H^l W^l D^l M^l$, which can be summarized as:

$$X^w = expand(softmax(X^o)).$$ (3)

Considering the efficiency of matrix multiplication, we introduce *im2col* operation to convert $X^{h,a}$ and $X^{h,m}$ to tensors sized $s^3 \times H^l W^l D^l M^l$. In this way, we can multiply them with X^w using Hadamard product and apply summation to aggregate the contribution of adjacent filters. Formally, the computation process can be formalized as:

$$X^p = sum(X^w \odot im2col\,(X^{h,a}))$$ (4)

$$X^q = sum(X^w \odot im2col\,(X^{h,m})),$$ (5)

where $\odot$ denotes Hadamard product and $\{X^p, X^q\} \in \mathcal{R}^{H^l \times W^l \times D^l \times M^l}$. *sum* is applied to the first dimension. Finally, we concatenate three outputs to form next layer's input X^{l+1}:

$$X^{l+1} = concat(X^{h,t}, X^p, X^q)$$ (6)

Generally speaking, the reasoning module learns how to align the semantic representations of anchor and target volumes from seen organs. During the inference stage, the learned rule can be well applied to unseen classes using one-shot pair as supervision signals.

Training and Inference. During the training stage, we first build a pool of annotated images for each organ class. In each training iteration, we randomly pick anchor and target samples from the same class pool (thus it is a binary segmentation task). The anchor input is fed to the top two encoders together with its annotation. Meanwhile, the target image is passed to the bottom encoder after registration, and its annotation is used as the ground truth for training. In practice, we use image batches as inputs considering the training efficiency. Particularly, we manually make each batch to have different class annotations which help to produce better segmentation results in our experiments. We train OrganNet with a combination of Dice and cross entropy losses with equal weights. With the large training pool, the organ concept is learned under full supervision. In the inference phase, when a previously unseen abdominal organ needs to be segmented, only one anchor image and its annotation are needed. It is worth noting that we pick the most similar example to the anatomical average computed for each organ class as the anchor image during the inference stage following the instruction from [25].

4   Experiments and Results

In this section, we conduct experiments together with ablation studies to demonstrate the strength of OrganNet. First, we briefly introduce the dataset and evaluation metric used for experiments. Then, we present the implementation details of OrganNet and display the experimental results under various settings.

4.1   Dataset and Evaluation Metric

We evaluate our method on 90 abdominal CT images collected from two publicly available datasets: 43 subjects from The Cancer Image Archive (TCIA) Pancreas CT dataset [5] and 47 subjects from the Beyond the Cranial Vault (BTCV) Abdomen dataset [14] with segmentations of 14 classes which include spleen, left/right kidneys, gallbladder, esophagus, liver, stomach, aorta, inferior vena cava, portal vein and splenic vein, pancreas, and left/right adrenal glands[1]. In practice, we test the effectiveness of the Organ-Net on 5 kinds of unseen abdominal organs (spleen, right kidney, aorta, pancreas and stomach), which present great challenges because of their variations in size and shape, and use the rest 9 organs for training. We employ the Dice coefficient as our evaluation metric.

4.2   Implementation Details

We build OrganNet based on 3D U-Net. To be specific, each encoder branch and the decoder (cf. Fig. 2) share the same architecture as those of 3D U-Net. The initial channel number of the encoder is 8 which is doubled after features maps are downsampled. Moreover, as mentioned in Sect. 3.1 and Fig. 2, we use different neighbour sizes in PRMs, which are $7 \times 7 \times 7$, $5 \times 5 \times 5$ and $3 \times 3 \times 3$ from shallow layers to deep layers, respectively. Following [25], for each organ class, we pick the most similar example to the anatomical average computed for each organ class from the test set, and treat it as the anchor image during the inference stage. Moreover, we repeat each experiments for three times and report their standard deviation. We conduct all experiments with the PyTorch framework [18]. We use the Adam optimizer [13] and train our model for fifty epochs. The batch size is 8 (one per GPU) with 8 NVIDIA GTX 1080 Ti GPUs. The cosine annealing technique [16] is adopted to adjust the learning rate from 10^{-3} to 10^{-6} with a weight decay of 10^{-4}. For organs used to train the OrganNet, we use 80%

---

[1] https://zenodo.org/record/1169361.

Table 1. Comparing OrganNet with DataAug [25], squeeze & excitation [21] and LT-Net [23]. "*" denotes that we **pretrain the segmentation network with 9 seen organ classes so that all approaches (including OrganNet) access the same set of labeled data which helps to guarantee the fairness of comparison.**

Method	Dice					
	Spleen	Right kidney	Aorta	Pancreas	Stomach	Mean
DataAug	$69.9_{\pm0.8}$	$73.6_{\pm0.7}$	$45.2_{\pm0.9}$	$48.8_{\pm0.9}$	$55.1_{\pm0.8}$	$58.5_{\pm0.8}$
Squeeze & Excitation	$70.6_{\pm0.6}$	$75.2_{\pm0.4}$	$47.7_{\pm0.6}$	$52.3_{\pm0.7}$	$57.5_{\pm0.8}$	$60.7_{\pm0.6}$
LT-Net	$73.5_{\pm0.7}$	$76.4_{\pm0.5}$	$52.1_{\pm0.5}$	$54.8_{\pm0.6}$	$60.2_{\pm0.7}$	$63.4_{\pm0.6}$
DataAug*	$79.6_{\pm0.6}$	$78.7_{\pm0.6}$	$63.8_{\pm0.7}$	$64.2_{\pm0.8}$	$77.3_{\pm0.6}$	$72.7_{\pm0.7}$
Squeeze & Excitation*	$79.2_{\pm0.5}$	$80.7_{\pm0.4}$	$67.4_{\pm0.7}$	$67.8_{\pm0.6}$	$78.1_{\pm0.5}$	$74.6_{\pm0.5}$
LT-Net*	$82.6_{\pm0.5}$	$82.9_{\pm0.5}$	$72.2_{\pm0.6}$	$70.7_{\pm0.5}$	$80.2_{\pm0.4}$	$77.7_{\pm0.5}$
OrganNet	$\mathbf{89.1}_{\pm0.6}$	$\mathbf{86.0}_{\pm0.6}$	$\mathbf{77.0}_{\pm0.7}$	$\mathbf{72.8}_{\pm0.5}$	$\mathbf{82.6}_{\pm0.7}$	$\mathbf{81.5}_{\pm0.6}$

Table 2. Comparison with 3D U-Net trained with different number of unseen class samples. "*" denotes the fully-supervised upper bound.

Method	Number of training samples for each unseen class	Mean dice
3D U-Net	1	$20.9_{\pm11.8}$
3D U-Net	30%	$79.3_{\pm0.4}$
OrganNet	1	$81.5_{\pm0.6}$
3D U-Net*	100%	$87.4_{\pm0.3}$

of data for training, and the remaining 20% are used for validation. For organs used to test the OrganNet, we randomly select 20% data for evaluation. The other 80% are used to train a fully-supervised 3D U-Net.

4.3 Comparison with One-Shot Segmentation Methods: Better Performance

We compare our OrganNet against DataAug [25], Squeeze & Excitation [21] and LT-Net [23]. We do not compare with CTN [17] as it is based on human intervention. As we have mentioned above, a prerequisite of using atlas-based method is that the differences between anchor and target inputs should be small enough to learn appropriate transformation matrix. To enable DataAug and LT-Net to segment all 5 test organs, we propose two settings. The first setting is to use the original implementations which are based on only one annotated sample for each class. The second setting is to pretrain DataAug and LT-Net using 9 seen organ classes and then retrain *5 independent* models using a number of each unseen class (denoted as * in Table 1). In contrast, our OrganNet only needs

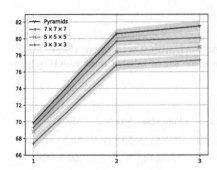

Fig. 4. Mean Dice scores for varying number of reasoning modules and different sizes of neighbour regions. The shaded region represents the standard deviation of each experiment setting.

Table 3. Influence of employing weight sharing across different encoders. For simplicity, we denote the encoder for target volume as **1**, the encoder for anchor volume as **2** and the encoder for anchor mask as **3**, respectively. Bracketed numbers mean that these encoders share the same model weights.

Method	Mean dice (%)
[1, 2, 3]	$79.6_{\pm0.5}$
[1, 2] + 3	$80.1_{\pm0.7}$
1 + 2 + 3	$81.2_{\pm1.2}$
1 + [2, 3]	$81.5_{\pm0.6}$

one network to be trained once to segment all 5 organs. We report the results in Table 1, from which we observe that our OrganNet outperforms the naive DataAug, Squeeze & Excitation and LT-Net (without "*") by a significant margin. Even after these three models are pretrained using the other 9 classes' data, OrganNet is still able to surpass them by at least 3.8%. We believe the poor performance of DataAug and LT-Net may be explained by the fact that explicit transformation functions are difficult to learn in abdominal CT images, where large displacements usually happen. For Squeeze & Excitation, we believe it may achieve better performance after adding its human-in-the-loop mechanism.

4.4 Comparison with Supervised 3D U-Nets: Less Labeling Cost

Lastly, we compare our OrganNet with 3D U-Net [4] which follows a supervised training manner. For the sake of fairness, we first pretrain 3D U-Net on 9 seen organs which are used to train OrganNet, and then fine-tune the 3D U-Net for each unseen class using different amount of labeled samples. Results are displayed in Table 2.

One obvious observation is that using one training sample for unseen classes is far not enough for supervised baseline because the supervised training process may lead to severe overfitting problem. Even if we add more labeled samples to 30%, our OrganNet can still achieve competitive results compared with supervised baseline. It is worth noting that annotating CT volumes is an intensive work which may cost several days of several well-trained radiologists. Thus, our OrganNet can greatly reduce the annotation cost. Finally, we offer a fully-supervised model which utilizes all training samples of unseen abdominal organs.

4.5 Ablation Study on Network Design

Number of Reasoning Modules and Different Sizes of Neighbour Regions. In Fig. 4, we display the experimental results of using different numbers of PRMs and

Anchor Slices   Target Slice   Anchor Slices

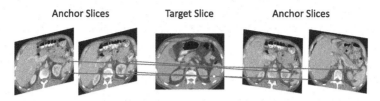

Fig. 5. Given a specific position (white dot with a red border) in the target slice, we visualize the most related regions in adjacent slices (discovered by OrganNet) of the anchor image. The green contour denotes the spleen. The white dots in the target slice stand for two randomly selected positions. (Color figure online)

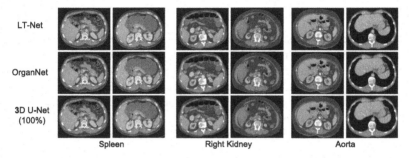

LT-Net

OrganNet

3D U-Net (100%)

Spleen   Right Kidney   Aorta

Fig. 6. Visualization of segmentation results. The red contours denote the ground truths while the blue ones represent model predictions. (Color figure online)

sizes of neighbour regions. We can find that adding more reasoning modules can consistently improve the model results and different sizes of neighbour regions behave similarly. If we compare the results of using different sizes of neighbour regions, it is easy to find that the proposed pyramid strategies works the best (red curve), even surpassing using $7 \times 7 \times 7$ which considers more adjacent regions. Such comparison verifies our hypothesis that deep layers require smaller neighbour sizes because their receptive fields are much larger while large kernel sizes may import additional noise. Interestingly, we can find that increasing the number from 2 to 3 would bring obvious improvements, suggesting adding more PRMs may not benefit a lot.

Shared Encoders or Not? Since the encoder of normal 3D U-Net is heavy, we study if it is possible to perform weight sharing across three different encoders. In Table 3, we report the experimental results of using different weight sharing strategies. It is obvious that sharing weights across all three encoders performs the worst. This phenomenon implies that different inputs may need different encoders. When making the bottom encoder (1) and the middle encoder (2) share weights, the average performance is slightly improve by approximate 0.5%. Somewhat surprisingly, building independent encoders $(1+2+3)$ helps to improve the overall performance a lot, showing that learning specific features for each input is workable. Finally, when the top encoder shares the same weights with the middle encoder, our OrganNet is able to achieve the best average performance. Such results suggest that the top two encoders may complement each other.

Table 4. Comparison of OrganNet and 3D U-Net in tumor segmentation, both of which are pre-trained with LiTS. "*" stands for the fully-supervised upper bound.

Method	Number of training samples for kidney tumor	Kidney tumor dice (%)
3D U-Net	30%	$77.1_{\pm 0.9}$
OrganNet	1	$78.5_{\pm 1.2}$
3D U-Net*	100%	$84.5_{\pm 0.6}$

4.6 Visual Analysis

In this part, we conduct visual analyses on proposed OrganNet. Firstly, in Fig. 5, we visualize the most related regions learned by OrganNet. We can find that, given a specific position in the target slice, OrganNet can automatically discover most related regions in the anchor image based on computed anatomical similarity scores. In practice, OrganNet incorporates segmentation labels from these regions and produces a final prediction for the target region. From Fig. 6, we can see that OrganNet is able to produce comparable results with 3D U-Net trained with 100% labeled data.

4.7 Generalization to Non-organ Segmentation

To better demonstrate the effectiveness of OrganNet, we conduct experiments on LiTS [3] and KiTS [11], where we use LiTS to train OrganNet and test it on KiTS with only one labeled sample (following the one-shot segmentation scenario. From Table 4, we can see that OrganNet still maintains its advantages over 3D U-Net trained with 30% labeled data, demonstrating the generalization ability of OrganNet to non-organ segmentation problems.

5 Conclusions and Future Work

In this paper, we present a novel one-shot medical segmentation approach that enables us to learn a generalized organ concept by employing a reasoning process between anchor and target CT volumes. The proposed OrganNet models the key components, i.e., the anatomical similarity between images, within a single deep learning framework. Extensive experiments demonstrate the effectiveness of proposed OrganNet.

References

1. BenTaieb, A., Hamarneh, G.: Topology aware fully convolutional networks for histology gland segmentation. In: MICCAI, pp. 460–468 (2016)
2. Bertinetto, L., Valmadre, J., Henriques, J.F., Vedaldi, A., Torr, P.H.: Fully-convolutional siamese networks for object tracking. In: ECCV, pp. 850–865 (2016)
3. Bilic, P., Christ, P.F., et al.: The Liver Tumor Segmentation Benchmark (LiTS). arXiv preprint arXiv:1901.04056 (2019)

4. Çiçek, Ö., Abdulkadir, A., Lienkamp, S.S., Brox, T., Ronneberger, O.: 3D U-net: learning dense volumetric segmentation from sparse annotation. In: MICCAI, pp. 424–432 (2016)
5. Clark, K., et al.: The cancer imaging archive (TCIA): maintaining and operating a public information repository. J. Digit. Imaging **26**(6), 1045–1057 (2013). https://doi.org/10.1007/s10278-013-9622-7
6. Dalca, A.V., Yu, E., Golland, P., Fischl, B., Sabuncu, M.R., Eugenio Iglesias, J.: Unsupervised deep learning for Bayesian brain MRI segmentation. In: Shen, D., et al. (eds.) MICCAI 2019. LNCS, vol. 11766, pp. 356–365. Springer, Cham (2019). https://doi.org/10.1007/978-3-030-32248-9_40
7. Dinsdale, N.K., Jenkinson, M., Namburete, A.I.: Spatial warping network for 3D segmentation of the hippocampus in MR images. In: MICCAI, pp. 284–291 (2019)
8. Gentner, D., Holyoak, K.J.: Reasoning and learning by analogy: introduction. Am. Psychol. **52**(1), 32 (1997)
9. Gibson, E., et al.: Automatic multi-organ segmentation on abdominal CT With dense v-networks. IEEE Trans. Med. Imaging **37**(8), 1822–1834 (2018)
10. Heinrich, M.P., Jenkinson, M., Brady, M., Schnabel, J.A.: MRF-based deformable registration and ventilation estimation of lung CT. IEEE Trans. Med. Imaging **32**(7), 1239–1248 (2013)
11. Heller, N., Sathianathen, N., Kalapara, A., et al.: The KiTS19 Challenge Data: 300 Kidney Tumor Cases with Clinical Context, CT Semantic Segmentations, and Surgical Outcomes. arXiv preprint arXiv:1904.00445 (2019)
12. Iglesias, J.E., Sabuncu, M.R.: Multi-atlas segmentation of biomedical images: a survey. Med. Image Anal. **24**(1), 205–219 (2015)
13. Kingma, D.P., Ba, J.: Adam: A Method for Stochastic Optimization. arXiv preprint arXiv:1412.6980 (2014)
14. Landman, B., Xu, Z., Eugenio, I.J., et al.: MICCAI multi-atlas labeling beyond the cranial vault-workshop and challenge (2015)
15. Liang, Y., Song, W., Dym, J., Wang, K., He, L.: CompareNet: anatomical segmentation network with deep non-local label fusion. In: MICCAI, pp. 292–300 (2019)
16. Loshchilov, I., Hutter, F.: SGDR: Stochastic Gradient Descent with Warm Restarts. arXiv preprint arXiv:1608.03983 (2016)
17. Lu, Y., et al.: Learning to segment anatomical structures accurately from one exemplar. In: MICCAI (2020)
18. Paszke, A., Gross, S., Massa, F., et al.: PyTorch: an imperative style, high-performance deep learning library. In: NeurIPS, pp. 8024–8035 (2019)
19. Ravishankar, H., Thiruvenkadam, S., Venkataramani, R., Vaidya, V.: Joint deep learning of foreground, background and shape for robust contextual segmentation. In: IPMI, pp. 622–632 (2017)
20. Ravishankar, H., Venkataramani, R., Thiruvenkadam, S., Sudhakar, P., Vaidya, V.: Learning and incorporating shape models for semantic segmentation. In: MICCAI, pp. 203–211 (2017)
21. Roy, A.G., Siddiqui, S., Pölsterl, S., Navab, N., Wachinger, C.: 'Squeeze & Excite' guided few-shot segmentation of volumetric images. Med. Image Anal. **59**, 101587 (2020)
22. Trullo, R., Petitjean, C., Dubray, B., Ruan, S.: Multiorgan segmentation using distance-aware adversarial networks. J. Med. Imaging **6**(1), 014001 (2019)
23. Wang, S., et al.: LT-net: label transfer by learning reversible voxel-wise correspondence for one-shot medical image segmentation. In: CVPR, pp. 9162–9171 (2020)
24. Xu, Z., et al.: Evaluation of six registration methods for the human abdomen on clinically acquired CT. IEEE Trans. Biomed. Eng. **63**(8), 1563–1572 (2016)

25. Zhao, A., Balakrishnan, G., Durand, F., Guttag, J.V., Dalca, A.V.: Data augmentation using learned transformations for one-shot medical image segmentation. In: CVPR, pp. 8543–8553 (2019)
26. Zhou, H.Y., Gao, B.B., Wu, J.: Sunrise or Sunset: Selective Comparison Learning for Subtle Attribute Recognition. arXiv preprint arXiv:1707.06335 (2017)
27. Zhou, H.Y., Oliver, A., Wu, J., Zheng, Y.: When Semi-supervised Learning Meets Transfer Learning: Training strategies, Models and Datasets. arXiv preprint arXiv:1812.05313 (2018)
28. Zhou, H.-Y., Yu, S., Bian, C., Hu, Y., Ma, K., Zheng, Y.: Comparing to learn: surpassing ImageNet pretraining on radiographs by comparing image representations. In: Martel, A.L., et al. (eds.) MICCAI 2020. LNCS, vol. 12261, pp. 398–407. Springer, Cham (2020). https://doi.org/10.1007/978-3-030-59710-8_39

EnMcGAN: Adversarial Ensemble Learning for 3D Complete Renal Structures Segmentation

Yuting He[1], Rongjun Ge[1], Xiaoming Qi[1], Guanyu Yang[1,3(✉)], Yang Chen[1,3], Youyong Kong[1,3], Huazhong Shu[1,3], Jean-Louis Coatrieux[2], and Shuo Li[4]

[1] LIST, Key Laboratory of Computer Network and Information Integration (Southeast University), Ministry of Education, Nanjing, China
yang.list@seu.edu.cn
[2] Univ Rennes, Inserm, LTSI - UMR1099, 35000 Rennes, France
[3] Centre de Recherche en Information Biomédicale
Sino-Français (CRIBs), Rennes, France
[4] Department of Medical Biophysics, University of Western Ontario, London, ON, Canada

Abstract. 3D complete renal structures (CRS) segmentation targets on segmenting the kidneys, tumors, renal arteries and veins in one inference. Once successful, it will provide preoperative plans and intraoperative guidance for laparoscopic partial nephrectomy(LPN), playing a key role in the renal cancer treatment. However, no success has been reported in 3D CRS segmentation due to the complex shapes of renal structures, low contrast and large anatomical variation. In this study, we utilize the adversarial ensemble learning and propose *Ensemble Multi-condition GAN* (EnMcGAN) for 3D CRS segmentation for the first time. Its contribution is three-fold. 1) Inspired by windowing [4], we propose the multi-windowing committee which divides CTA image into multiple narrow windows with different window centers and widths enhancing the contrast for salient boundaries and soft tissues. And then, it builds an ensemble segmentation model on these narrow windows to fuse the segmentation superiorities and improve whole segmentation quality. 2) We propose the multi-condition GAN which equips the segmentation model with multiple discriminators to encourage the segmented structures meeting their real shape conditions, thus improving the shape feature extraction ability. 3) We propose the adversarial weighted ensemble module which uses the trained discriminators to evaluate the quality of segmented structures, and normalizes these evaluation scores for the ensemble weights directed at the input image, thus enhancing the ensemble results. 122 patients are enrolled in this study and the mean Dice coefficient of the renal structures achieves 84.6%. Extensive experiments with promising results on renal structures reveal powerful segmentation accuracy and great clinical significance in renal cancer treatment.

© Springer Nature Switzerland AG 2021
A. Feragen et al. (Eds.): IPMI 2021, LNCS 12729, pp. 465–477, 2021.
https://doi.org/10.1007/978-3-030-78191-0_36

1   Introduction

3D complete renal structures(CRS) segmentation on CTA image targets on segmenting the kidneys, tumors, renal arteries and veins in one inference. Once successful, it will provide preoperative plans and intraoperative guidance for laparoscopic partial nephrectomy (LPN) [20,21], playing a key role in renal cancer treatment [19]. *Preoperatively*, the renal artery reaching the interlobar arteries will guide the estimation of perfusion regions to select the tumor-feeding branches and locate the arterial clamping position [20]. The kidney and tumor will show the lesions' location to pre-plan the tumor resection surface [25]. *Intraoperatively*, the veins outside the hilum will help the clinicians exclude the unconcerned vessels thus clamping the accurate arterial positions quickly. Besides, the 3D CRS visual model will also be fused with the laparoscopic videos bringing the augmented reality [15], so that the invisible regions will be supplemented to guide the operation smoothly. With the assistance of 3D CRS segmentation, the safety of renal surgery is improved, the pain of patients is relieved and the cost of the treatment is reduced.

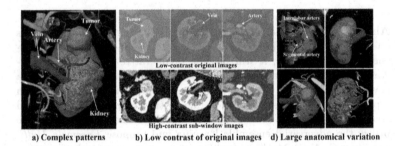

a) Complex patterns   b) Low contrast of original images   d) Large anatomical variation

Fig. 1. The challenges of the 3D CRS segmentation. a) The renal structures has complex shapes making difficult feature extraction. b) The original CTA images has low contrast bringing low segmentation quality on boundaries. c) The renal structures has large anatomical variation in different cases causing weak generalization ability.

However, there is no effective solution for 3D CRS segmentation. Taha et al. [23] utilized a Kid-Net achieving the renal vessels segmentation. He et al. [6] proposed a semi-supervised framework and achieved the fine renal artery segmentation. Li et al. [9] designed a Residual U-Net for renal structures segmentation. The related works are limited in our task: **1)** On one hand, some works [6,23] only focused on partial renal structures lacking the countermeasures to the complete structures in one-inference segmentation. The one-by-one segmentation also will make overlap of different structures especially on low-contrast boundaries. **2)** On the other, some works [9,23] lack the fine detail of the segmented structures limiting the clinical downstream tasks. For example, their arteries only reaches the segmental arteries losing the ability of perfusion regions estimation.

Formidable challenges of 3D CRS segmentation are limiting its further applications: **1)** Complex shapes of renal structures. These structures have complex shapes, for example, the arteries have tree-like shape while the tumors have ball-like shape (Fig. 1 (a)). The model has to represent their features simultaneously resulting in a difficult feature extraction process and limiting its generalization ability. **2) Coarse-grained pattern and low contrast.** CT image has a large gray range (4096), and the structures of interests in our task are only in a narrow range. This makes the contrast of soft tissues and the boundary regions are low in original images (Fig. 1(b)) such as the tumors and veins, making coarse-grained pattern. Therefore, the segmentation network will difficult to perceive the fine-grained pattern in such a narrow distribution limiting the integrity of the structures and the quality of boundaries. **3) Large anatomical variation.** Renal vessels have uncertain branch numbers and growth topology [6,17], and the location of the tumors and their damage to the kidneys are uncertain(Fig. 1(c)). These anatomical variation makes it difficult to cover all variation, limiting the model's generalization.

The windowing [4] removes irrelevant gray ranges and expands the interested distribution making the network focus on the wider distribution to perceive fine-grained pattern. Inspired by the radiologist delineating the renal structures in different window widths and centers (sub-windows) via windowing, we propose the *multi-windowing committee (MWC)*. We select the sub-windows which of superiority in renal structures on CTA images, and divide the CTA image into these sub-windows thus expanding our task-interested distribution and making fine-grained pattern such as boundaries (Fig. 2(a)). We train multiple learners on these sub-window images for the fine-grained representations on their covered distributions making segmentation superiorities. Finally, these superiorities will be fused [18] improving the integrated segmentation quality.

The shape regularisation utilizes the shape knowledge learned by an additional model to encourage the CNN extracting higher-order shape features [10,13,16]. We propose the *Multi-condition GAN (McGAN)* which equips the segmentation model with multiple discriminators for global shape constraints (Fig. 2(b)). During adversarial training, the discriminators learn to evaluate the similarity between the segmented structures' shapes and real shapes, thus learning the higher-order shape knowledge of the renal structures via the min-max game of the adversarial training [5]. Then, these knowledge are made as the conditions that the segmented renal structures have to meet when optimizing the segmentation models, improving the shape feature extraction ability.

Fusing the segmentation superiorities of the learners will bridge their representation preferences caused by large anatomical variations [3,18]. These preferences will make the learners have better segmentation quality in their advantageous regions and poor quality in vulnerable regions, if being fused, the whole accuracy will be improved. Therefore, we propose the *adversarial weighted Ensemble (AWE)* (Fig. 2(c)) which utilizes the trained discriminators to evaluate the pixel-wise segmentation quality of the results, thus giving higher weights to better quality regions and making the ensemble direct at the segmentation quality dynamically. So, the fusion of the advantageous regions in the results will balance the representation preferences and bring personalized ensemble process.

We propose an adversarial ensemble learning framework, EnMcGAN, for 3D CRS segmentation for the first time. Our detailed contributions are as follow:

- We propose the adversarial ensemble learning which equips the ensemble segmentation model with adversarial learning for the first time, and propose the *EnMcGAN* for 3D CRS segmentation which will play an important role in accurate preoperative planning and intraoperative guidance of LPN. Our complete experiments demonstrate its excellent performance.
- We propose the *multi-windowing committee (MWC)* which divides CTA image into the sub-windows which of superiority in renal structures, making fine-grained pattern. Then the learners trained on these sub-windows are constructed as an ensemble framework to fuse the fine-grained representations on the covered distributions of these sub-windows, thus improving integrated segmentation quality.
- We present the *multi-condition GAN (McGAN)* which embeds the shape knowledge in segmentation model via multiple discriminators, thus encouraging the segmented results being consistent with their shape prior knowledge and improving the shape features extraction ability.
- We propose the *adversarial weighted Ensemble (AWE)* which utilizes segmentation quality evaluation ability of the trained discriminators to fuse the advantageous regions in the segmented results, thus bringing personalized fine ensemble process and balancing the representation preferences.

2   Methodology

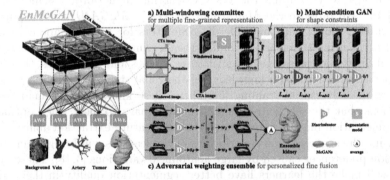

Fig. 2. The illustration of our EnMcGAN: a) MWC enhances the contrast on windowed images bringing salient boundaries and soft tissues (Sect. 2.1); b) McGAN utilizes multiple discriminators for shape constraints (Sect. 2.2) and c) AWE module utilizes the trained discriminators for dynamic ensemble weights (Sect. 2.3).

As shown in Fig. 2, our proposed EnMcGAN takes adversarial ensemble learning for high quality 3D CRS segmentation. It has three cooperative elements:

1) Multi-windowing committee (MWC, Sect. 2.1) thresholds and normalizes the CTA image enhancing the contrast and making the fine-grained pattern, and fuses the segmentation superiorities of multiple segmentation learners trained in different covered distributions improving the integrated segmentation quality. 2) Multi-condition GAN (McGAN, Sect. 2.2) utilizes shape constraints from the discriminator to encourage the segmented renal structures meeting their real shape conditions, thus improving the shape features extraction ability. 3) Adversarial weighted Ensemble (AWE, Sect. 2.3) utilizes the trained discriminator for dynamic ensemble weights, thus and balancing the representation preferences and providing the personalized ensemble results.

2.1 Multi-windowing Committee for Multiple Fine-Grained Representation

Our MWC (Fig. 2(a)) divides CTA image to multiple narrow windows [4] and expends their distributions making the significant region and fine-grained pattern. And then it fuse the segmentation superiorities from the distributions covered by multiple sub-windows, thus improving integrated segmentation quality.

Windowing for Fine-Grained Pattern. The CTA image x is divided to multiple narrow windows with different window centers and widths. Firstly, nine different windows are selected. We segment CTA images via k-means clustering [14] for c categories, in our experiment $c = 5$. Then, the mean CT values of these categories in our dataset are calculated and selected for three window centers c, in our experiment, $\{c_0 = 1032.7834, c_1 = 1150.0825, c_2 = 1332.1959\}$. We also define three default window widths $\{w_0 = 256, w_1 = 512, w_2 = 768\}$, thus combining for nine sub-windows. Then, the CTA image x is thresholded to remove irrelevant gray range and normalized to expand the interested distribution via windowing, thus making nine windowed images $\{x_0, x_1, ..., x_8\}$: $x_i = \frac{max(min(x, c_j - \frac{w_k}{2}), c_j + \frac{w_k}{2}) - (c_j - \frac{w_k}{2})}{w_k}$. Finally, these images are used to train nine segmentation learners $S()$ which will learn the fine-grained representations on the distributions covered by these sub-windows.

Summary of the Advantages. 1) The CTA image is thresholded with different window centers and widths for small gray ranges and normalized to $[0, 1]$, thus the irrelevant gray range will be removed and the interested distribution will be expended. Therefore, these sub-windows will have significant regions and fine-grained patterns improving the segmentation quality. **2)** The image in different narrow windows will have different significant regions, so our multiple learners trained on these sub-window images will learn the fine-grained representations on their covered distributions making segmentation superiorities. These superiorities are fused improving the final segmentation quality.

2.2 Multi-condition GAN for Shape Constraints

Our McGAN (Fig. 2(b)) utilizes multiple discriminators to provide the segmentation model shape constraints, thus encouraging the segmented structures meeting their real shape conditions, improving the shape feature extraction ability.

McGAN for Adversarial Segmentation. In training stage, our McGAN inputs the real or segmented renal structures together with the CTA image into five discriminators resulting in a conditional GAN [12] for shape constraints of renal structures. The segmentation model S takes the DenseBiasNet [6] which fuses the multi-receptive field features for the multi-scale feature representation ability. The discriminators $\{D_0, ..., D_4\}$ follow the 3D version of the VGG-A [22] and activated by sigmoid function. As shown in Fig. 2 (b), it takes the original image x and the segmented $S(x_i)_n$ or ground truth y_n mask of each structure are input to discriminator to learn the shape constraint of each renal structure and the evaluation ability of segmentation quality. The binary cross-entropy loss $\mathcal{L}_{bce}$ is calculated as the adversarial loss $\mathcal{L}_{adv_n}$ of each structure:

$$\mathcal{L}_{adv_n}(\theta_{D_n}) = \mathcal{L}_{bce}(D_n(x, y_n), 1) + \mathcal{L}_{bce}(D_n(x, S(x_i)_n), 0). \tag{1}$$

The segmentation model takes the windowed images x_i as input and is optimized by the multi-class cross-entropy loss $\mathcal{L}_{mce}$ from the segmented results $S(x)$ and labels y, together with the adversarial losses corresponding to renal structures from the discriminator. Therefore, the hybrid segmentation loss is:

$$\mathcal{L}_{seg}(\theta_S) = \mathcal{L}_{mce}(S(x_i), y) + \lambda \sum_{n=0}^{N} \mathcal{L}_{bce}(D_n(x, S(x_i)_n), 1), \tag{2}$$

where the λ is the weight to balance loss functions in this hybrid loss. In our experiment, it is 0.01. The θ_S and θ_{D_n} is the parameters of the segmentation model and discriminators. As an ensemble model, narrow-window images are used to train nine McGANs which share their discriminators iteratively.

Summary of the Advantages. During adversarial training, the discriminators learn to evaluate the similarity between the segmented structures' shapes and real shapes. When optimizing the segmentation model, the real shapes will become the conditions encoded by the discriminators, so the adversarial loss will encourage the segmented structures to meet them improving the shape feature extraction ability of the segmentation model.

2.3   Adversarial Weighted Ensemble for Personalized Fine Fusion

Our AWE module (Fig. 2(c)) utilizes the trained discriminators from our McGAN to evaluate the segmentation quality of renal structures and generate the dynamic ensemble weights directed at the input image, thus bringing personalized fine ensemble process and balancing the representation preferences.

Ensemble Process of AWE. In testing stage, our AWE module fuses the results based on their segmentation quality, improving the ensemble results. Figure 2 (c) illustrates the ensemble process of this module taking the kidney as an example. The segmented kidneys $\{kidney_0, ..., kidney_8\}$ from the segmentation learners together with the original image x are putted into the trained discriminators for evaluation scores $\{s_0, .., s_8\}$. Then, these scores are normalized via $w_i = \frac{s_i}{\sum_{n=0}^{8} s_n}$ for the ensemble weights directed at the input image. Finally, these weights are used to weight the average ensemble enhancing the results: $y_{kid\hat{n}ey} = \frac{1}{9} \sum_{i=0}^{9} kidney_i * w_i$.

Summary of the Advantages. The trained discriminators evaluate the segmentation qualities of renal structures, so we utilize them for dynamic ensemble weights directed at input images. Therefore, the incorrect weights are avoided, and the ensemble results are effectively enhanced.

3   Materials and Configurations

Dataset. 122 patients with renal cancer treated with LPN are enrolled in this study. The kidney region of interests (ROIs) with tumors on their CTA images were extracted as the dataset in our experiments. Their pixel sizes are between 0.47 mm and 0.74 mm, the slice thickness is 0.5 mm and the image size is $150 \times 150 \times 200$. Five kidney tumor subtypes including clear renal cell carcinomas, papillary, chromophobe, angiomyolipoma and eosinophilic adenoma are included in this dataset resulting in large heterogeneity and anatomical variation, and the tumor volume is vary up to 300 times. The kidney, tumor, vein and artery on these images are fine labeled.

Comparison Settings. To evaluate the superiority of our framework, we perform extensive experiments. The V-Net [11], 3D U-Net [2], Res-U-Net [9], Kid-Net [23], DenseBiasNet [6] and the ensemble model, VFN [24], are trained as the comparison models. For fair comparison, VFN also takes DenseBiasNet as the segmentation learners. The Dice coefficient (DSC) [%], mean surface voxel distance (MSD) are used to evaluate the coincidence of the region and surface. Besides, the mean centerline voxel distance (MCD) is used to evaluate the coincidence of the artery topology following [7].

Implementation. During training, $150 \times 150 \times 128$ patches are cropped in the z-axis so that the dataset is enlarged and the GPU memory is saved. Each model is optimized by Adam [8] with the batch size of 1, learning rate of 1×10^{-4} and iterations of 40000. The 5-fold cross-validation is performed for comprehensive evaluation. All methods are implemented with PyTorch and trained on NVIDIA TITAN Xp GPUs.

4   Results and Analysis

Our EnMcGAN brings the fine-grained pattern and significant regions, embeds shape priori knowledge into segmentation model and bridge the representation preferences caused by large anatomical variations thus achieving the excellent 3D complete renal structures segmentation. In this part, we will thoroughly evaluate and analyze the effectiveness of our proposed EnMcGAN: 1) The quantitative evaluation, qualitative evaluation and the ROC and PR curves in comparative study (Sect. 4.1) will show the superiorities of our framework compared with other models. **2)** The ablation study (Sect. 4.2) will demonstrate the contribution of each our innovation in our framework. **3)** The the performances of each segmentation learner and the number of fused learners will be analysed in framework analysis (Sect. 4.3).

4.1   Comparative Study Shows Superiority

Quantitative Evaluation. As shown in Table 1, our proposed framework achieves the state-of-the-art performance. In our EnMcGAN, the artery achieves 89.0% DSC, 1.66 MCD and 0.69 MSD which will strongly support the perfusion regions estimation and the arterial clamping position selection. The kidney gets 95.2% DSC and 0.94 MSD, the tumor gets 76.5% DSC and 5.18 MSD, and the vein gets 77.7% DSC and 1.38 MSD which will provide operation guidance. The ensemble model, VFN, fuses the 2D information in different perspectives, achieving good performance on artery. However, similar to the V-Net, 3D U-Net, Res-U-Net, DenseBiasNet, it has poor performance on veins and tumors owing to the low contrast and the complex shapes.

Table 1. Evaluation on renal structures reveal powerful performance of our framework. The 'En' means the method is the ensemble learning model.

Method	Kidney		Tumor		Vein		Artery			Mean DSC
	DSC	MSD	DSC	MSD	DSC	MSD	DSC	MCD	MSD	±std
V-Net [11]	94.1±2.3	1.17±0.72	67.5±26.8	7.01±6.36	66.9±14.8	4.57±6.35	83.0±8.2	3.21±2.66	2.03±2.81	77.9±7.8
3D U-Net [2]	91.9±10.9	1.11±0.60	72.1±26.3	5.22±6.12	65.4±20.8	2.41±1.60	80.5±9.9	1.93±1.06±	1.30±1.28	77.5±12.2
Res-U-Net [9]	92.5±3.8	1.63±0.95	51.2±29.7	13.02±16.73	63.4±17.7	3.00±1.73	81.9±6.1	2.95±2.00	1.91±2.00	72.2±7.9
Kid-Net [23]	91.0±11.5	1.49±1.14	69.4±23.2	7.63±7.07	57.2±21.8	3.70±2.71	73.9±12.9	3.76±2.35	1.91±1.94	72.9±11.1
DenseBiasNet [6]	94.1±2.4	1.31±0.87	67.0±26.9	8.51±8.70	71.8±14.8	2.13±1.81	87.1±6.5	2.00±1.18	0.97±0.85	80.0±7.1
VFN (En) [24]	94.3±2.2	1.47±0.76	66.2±27.0	8.50±12.16	70.3±16.3	3.07±2.39	88.5±5.6	**1.36±0.64**	**0.53±0.46**	80.0±8.5
Ours (En)	**95.2±1.9**	**0.94±0.55**	**76.5±22.9**	**5.18±7.11**	**77.7±12.1**	**1.38±0.95**	**89.0±6.8**	1.66±0.89	0.69±0.66	**84.6±6.7**

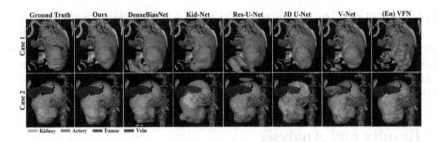

Fig. 3. Our proposed framework has powerful visual superiority which will provide visual guidance for surgery. Case 1 is a left kidney with angiomyolipoma and the case 2 is a right kidney with clear renal cell carcinomas.

Qualitative Evaluation. As demonstrated in Fig. 3, our proposed framework has great visual superiority which will provide visual guidance for surgery. Compared with the ground truth, our EnMcGAN enhances the contrast and utilizes the shape constraints from discriminator improving the integrity of tumors and the segmentation quality of veins. The Kid-Net and 3D U-Net have blur segmentation on small artery branches, and the DenseBiasNet, Res-U-Net, V-Net and VFN have serious under-segmentation because of the low contrast, complex shape and large anatomical variation in our CRS segmentation task.

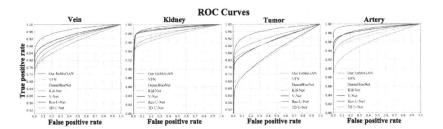

Fig. 4. The ROCs show that our EnMcGAN has higher segmentation accuracy than other comparison methods in our renal structures.

ROC Curves. As shown in Fig. 4, the ROC curve of our EnMcGAN covers the other comparison methods which means our proposed method has more powerful performance in each segmented renal structure. Due to the class imbalance in our task, the true positive rate will rise rapidly when plotting the ROC curve. For better demonstration, we show the ROC curves with a true positive rate between 0.8 and 1 in artery and kidney, and between 0.5 and 1 in vein and tumor.

4.2 Ablation Study Shows Improvements of the Innovations

Table 2. The ablation study analyses the contributions of our innovations.

McGAN	MWC	AWE	DSC(%)±std				
			Kidney	Tumor	Vein	Artery	AVG
			94.1±2.4	67.0±26.9	71.8±14.8	87.1±6.5	80.0±7.1
✓			94.7±2.4	75.0±22.7	72.8±12.8	87.6±8.1	82.5±7.1
✓	✓		94.8±2.2	75.8±21.1	75.3±12.9	**89.3±4.7**	83.8±6.7
✓	✓	✓	**95.2±1.9**	**76.5±22.9**	**77.7±12.1**	89.0±6.8	**84.6±6.7**

The innovations in our framework brings significant enhancements. Our McGAN takes the shape constraints and improves 8.0% DSC on tumor compared with the basic segmentation network (DenseBiasNet). When taking our MWC with the majority voting [1], the vein and artery achieve 2.5% and 1.7% additional DSC improvement owing the fine-grained pattern in narrow windows. When adding our AWE module, the DSC of the tumor and vein are increased by 0.7% and 2.4% due to its dynamic ensemble weights directed at the input image. Totally, compared with the basic network, our EnMcGAN enhances the 1.1%, 9.5%, 5.9% and 1.9% DSC in kidney, tumor, vein and artery (Table 2).

4.3 Framework Analysis

Segmentation Learners Analysis. As illustrated in Fig. 5, two conclusions will be summarized: **1)** The learners have segmentation superiorities in different narrow-window images which have different salient regions. For example, when c_1w_2, the learner achieves significant performance on artery (88.0%), but it has poor performance on tumor (72.3%). The c_0w_2 has ordinary performance (85.4%) on artery, but it achieves the highest DSC (77.4%) on tumor. **2)** Fusing the segmentation superiorities of the learners will improve the whole segmentation quality which higher than the quality of each learner. Our EnMcGAN achieves 95.2%, 76.5%, 77.7% and 89.0% DSC on kidney, tumor, vein and artery which are higher than the best learners of renal structures (94.9%, 77.4%, 74.9% and 88.0%).

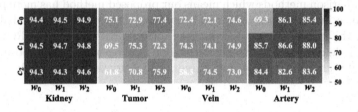

Fig. 5. The learners have segmentation superiorities in different narrow-window images. The heatmaps show the DSC of the learners on the renal structures.

Amount of Fused Learners Analysis. As shown in Fig. 6, our with the amount of the fused learners trained in different sub-windows increasing, the ensemble accuracy will increase. We rank the trained segmentation learners in different sub-windows, and fuse them start from the best via our AWE strategy. It illustrate the characteristic in two aspect: 1) Overall, with the amount of the fused learners increasing, the average ensemble performance is increasing because more segmentation preferences are integrated into the model. 2) The renal structures

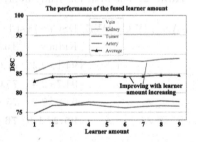

Fig. 6. With the amount of the fused learners increasing, the ensemble DSC will increase, and the structures have different sensitivity to the increasing of the learners.

has different sensitivity to the increasing of the learners. The performance of the kidney is almost unchanged because it has relatively large volume and wide gray range. The performance of tumor is increasing and decreasing, because it is sensitive to variation of window width and center. When the learner trained in the bad sub-window of tumor fused into the ensemble model, it will become the noise which will weaken the performance.

5   Conclusion

In this paper, we equips adversarial learning with ensemble segmentation models, and propose the EnMcGAN, the first 3D CRS segmentation model, for technical support of LPN. 1) Our multi-window committee divides CTA image into narrow windows with different window centers and widths enhancing the contrast and making fine-grained pattern, and constructs the ensemble model based on these narrow windows fusing the segmentation superiorities on different covered distributions. 2) Our multi-condition GAN utilizes the shape constraints of adversarial losses to encourage the segmented renal structures being consistent with their real shape, thus segmentation will tend to extract the features that matches the priori shape. 3) Our adversarial weighted ensemble module uses the trained discriminator to score the quality of each structure from each learner for dynamic ensemble weights, enhancing the ensemble results. Extensive experiments with promising results reveal powerful 3D CRS segmentation performance and significance in renal cancer treatment.

Acknowledgements. This research was supported by the National Natural Science Foundation under grants (31571001, 61828101, 31800825), Southeast University-Nanjing Medical University Cooperative Research Project (2242019K3DN08) and Excellence Project Funds of Southeast University. We thank the Big Data Computing Center of Southeast University for providing the facility support on the numerical calculations in this paper.

References

1. Breiman, L.: Bagging predictors. Mach. Learn. **24**(2), 123–140 (1996)
2. Çiçek, Ö., Abdulkadir, A., Lienkamp, S.S., Brox, T., Ronneberger, O.: 3D U-net: learning dense volumetric segmentation from sparse annotation. In: Ourselin, S., Joskowicz, L., Sabuncu, M.R., Unal, G., Wells, W. (eds.) MICCAI 2016. LNCS, vol. 9901, pp. 424–432. Springer, Cham (2016). https://doi.org/10.1007/978-3-319-46723-8_49
3. Dietterich, T.G., et al.: Ensemble learning. Handb. Brain Theor. Neural Netw. **2**, 110–125 (2002)
4. Goldman, L.W.: Principles of CT and CT technology. J. Nucl. Med. Technol. **35**(3), 115–128 (2007)
5. Goodfellow, I., et al.: Generative adversarial nets. In: Advances in Neural Information Processing Systems, pp. 2672–2680 (2014)

6. He, Y., et al.: DPA-DenseBiasNet: semi-supervised 3d fine renal artery segmentation with dense biased network and deep priori anatomy. In: Shen, D., et al. (eds.) MICCAI 2019. LNCS, vol. 11769, pp. 139–147. Springer, Cham (2019). https://doi.org/10.1007/978-3-030-32226-7_16

7. He, Y., et al.: Dense biased networks with deep priori anatomy and hard region adaptation: semi-supervised learning for fine renal artery segmentation. Med. Image Anal. **63**, 101722 (2020)

8. Kingma, D.P., Ba, J.L.: Adam: a method for stochastic optimization. In: ICLR 2015: International Conference on Learning Representations 2015 (2015)

9. Li, J., Lo, P., Taha, A., Wu, H., Zhao, T.: Segmentation of renal structures for image-guided surgery. In: Frangi, A.F., Schnabel, J.A., Davatzikos, C., Alberola-López, C., Fichtinger, G. (eds.) MICCAI 2018. LNCS, vol. 11073, pp. 454–462. Springer, Cham (2018). https://doi.org/10.1007/978-3-030-00937-3_52

10. Luc, P., Couprie, C., Chintala, S., Verbeek, J.: Semantic segmentation using adversarial networks. In: NIPS Workshop on Adversarial Training (2016)

11. Milletari, F., Navab, N., Ahmadi, S.A.: V-net: fully convolutional neural networks for volumetric medical image segmentation. In: 2016 Fourth International Conference on 3D Vision (3DV), pp. 565–571 (2016)

12. Mirza, M., Osindero, S.: Conditional generative adversarial nets. arXiv preprint arXiv:1411.1784 (2014)

13. Mosinska, A., Marquez-Neila, P., Koziński, M., Fua, P.: Beyond the pixel-wise loss for topology-aware delineation. In: Proceedings of the IEEE Conference on Computer Vision and Pattern Recognition, pp. 3136–3145 (2018)

14. Ng, H., Ong, S., Foong, K., Goh, P., Nowinski, W.: Medical image segmentation using k-means clustering and improved watershed algorithm. In: 2006 IEEE Southwest Symposium on Image Analysis and Interpretation, pp. 61–65. IEEE (2006)

15. Nicolau, S., Soler, L., Mutter, D., Marescaux, J.: Augmented reality in laparoscopic surgical oncology. Surg. Oncol. **20**(3), 189–201 (2011)

16. Oktay, O., et al.: Anatomically constrained neural networks (ACNNs): application to cardiac image enhancement and segmentation. IEEE Trans. Med. Imaging **37**(2), 384–395 (2017)

17. Petru, B., Elena, Ş., Dan, I., Klara, B., Radu, B., Constantin, D.: Morphological assessments on the arteries of the superior renal segment. Surg. Radiol. Anat. **34**(2), 137–144 (2012)

18. Polikar, R.: Ensemble learning. In: Zhang, C., Ma, Y. (eds.) Ensemble Machine Learning. Springer, Boston (2012) https://doi.org/10.1007/978-1-4419-9326-7_1

19. Porpiglia, F., Fiori, C., Checcucci, E., Amparore, D., Bertolo, R.: Hyper accuracy three-dimensional reconstruction is able to maximize the efficacy of selective clamping during robot-assisted partial nephrectomy for complex renal masses. Eur. Urol. **74**(5), 651–660 (2018)

20. Shao, P., et al.: Laparoscopic partial nephrectomy with segmental renal artery clamping: technique and clinical outcomes. Eur. Urol. **59**(5), 849–855 (2011)

21. Shao, P., et al.: Precise segmental renal artery clamping under the guidance of dual-source computed tomography angiography during laparoscopic partial nephrectomy. Eur. Urol. **62**(6), 1001–1008 (2012)

22. Simonyan, K., Zisserman, A.: Very deep convolutional networks for large-scale image recognition. In: ICLR 2015: International Conference on Learning Representations 2015 (2015)

23. Taha, A., Lo, P., Li, J., Zhao, T.: Kid-net: convolution networks for kidney vessels segmentation from CT-volumes. In: Frangi, A.F., Schnabel, J.A., Davatzikos, C., Alberola-López, C., Fichtinger, G. (eds.) MICCAI 2018. LNCS, vol. 11073, pp. 463–471. Springer, Cham (2018). https://doi.org/10.1007/978-3-030-00937-3_53
24. Xia, Y., Xie, L., Liu, F., Zhu, Z., Fishman, E.K., Yuille, A.L.: Bridging the gap between 2D and 3D organ segmentation with volumetric fusion net. In: Frangi, A.F., Schnabel, J.A., Davatzikos, C., Alberola-López, C., Fichtinger, G. (eds.) MICCAI 2018. LNCS, vol. 11073, pp. 445–453. Springer, Cham (2018). https://doi.org/10.1007/978-3-030-00937-3_51
25. Zhang, S., et al.: Application of a functional3-dimensional perfusion model in laparoscopic partial nephrectomy with precise segmental renal artery clamping. Urology **125**, 98–103 (2019)

Segmentation with Multiple Acceptable Annotations: A Case Study of Myocardial Segmentation in Contrast Echocardiography

Dewen Zeng[1(✉)], Mingqi Li[2], Yukun Ding[1], Xiaowei Xu[2], Qiu Xie[2], Ruixue Xu[2], Hongwen Fei[2], Meiping Huang[2], Jian Zhuang[2], and Yiyu Shi[1]

[1] University of Notre Dame, Notre Dame, USA
dzeng2@nd.edu
[2] Guangdong Provincial People's Hospital, Guangzhou, China

Abstract. Most existing deep learning-based frameworks for image segmentation assume that a unique ground truth is known and can be used for performance evaluation. This is true for many applications, but not all. Myocardial segmentation of Myocardial Contrast Echocardiography (MCE), a critical task in automatic myocardial perfusion analysis, is an example. Due to the low resolution and serious artifacts in MCE data, annotations from different cardiologists can vary significantly, and it is hard to tell which one is the best. In this case, how can we find a good way to evaluate segmentation performance and how do we train the neural network? In this paper, we address the first problem by proposing a new extended Dice to effectively evaluate the segmentation performance when multiple accepted ground truth is available. Then based on our proposed metric, we solve the second problem by further incorporating the new metric into a loss function that enables neural networks to flexibly learn general features of myocardium. Experiment results on our clinical MCE data set demonstrate that the neural network trained with the proposed loss function outperforms those existing ones that try to obtain a unique ground truth from multiple annotations, both quantitatively and qualitatively. Finally, our grading study shows that using extended Dice as an evaluation metric can better identify segmentation results that need manual correction compared with using Dice.

1 Introduction

Deep Neural Networks (DNNs) have been widely used in supervised image segmentation tasks, which rely on manual annotations to provide ground truth in training and evaluation [7,8,11,17]. However, in many cases there exist large variations among different annotators due to various reasons including human factors and image qualities. For variations caused by human factors such as differences in annotators' training, expertise and consistency over time, [12] and

© Springer Nature Switzerland AG 2021
A. Feragen et al. (Eds.): IPMI 2021, LNCS 12729, pp. 478–491, 2021.
https://doi.org/10.1007/978-3-030-78191-0_37

[14] present methods to train DNNs to learn the behaviour of individual annotators as well as their consensus. As such, the resulting performance is much better than that can be achieved by learning from one annotator alone. An important assumption in these methods is that a unique ground truth is known in the evaluation process and can be obtained by the majority vote of the experienced annotators, which is true for human-factor induced variations.

For variations caused by low quality images such as those of low resolution or significant artifacts, however, the unique ground truth may not be available. Take the myocardial segmentation task of Myocardial Contrast Echocardiography (MCE) as an example. An inter-observer experiment was conducted among five experienced cardiologists, and Fig. 1(a)(b) visualize the annotations of two images from three of these cardiologists. It can be seen that the labels by different cardiologists vary significantly, especially in locations where the intensity information of myocardium is very similar to the background. Table 1 shows the average Dice of the annotation of each cardiologist, using one of the others' as the ground truth, over 180 images. We can observe that none of the Dice is above 0.9, some even under 0.8, confirming significant variations among the annotations. In this case, as the variations are caused by the image quality, even these cardiologists cannot tell which annotation is better than others, and a majority vote for ground truth would not make sense sometimes as can be seen in Fig. 1(c)(d). For this reason, we cannot obtain a unique ground truth in the evaluation process and the traditional metrics such as Dice and IoU cannot be used.

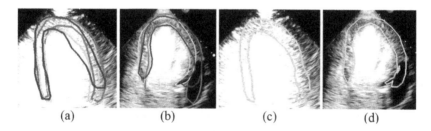

(a)   (b)   (c)   (d)

Fig. 1. Visualization of annotations from three experienced cardiologists marked with red, blue and green in (a) (b), and the corresponding pixel-wise majority vote (c) (d). (Color figure online)

This leads to our key motivation, in this paper, we propose a new extended Dice metric to effectively evaluate the quality of segmentation performance when multiple accepted ground truths are available in the evaluation process. We further incorporate the new metric into a loss function to train our segmentation network, which can help the networks better learn the general features of myocardium and ignore variations caused by individual annotators. To evaluate our proposed method, we collect an MCE data set of decent size with annotations from multiple experienced cardiologists. Experimental results on the data

Table 1. Average dice of the annotations of each cardiologist using one of the others' as ground truth (calculated from 180 annotated images).

	Cardiologist 1	Cardiologist 2	Cardiologist 3	Cardiologist 4	Cardiologist 5
Cardiologist 1	1	–	–	–	–
Cardiologist 2	0.898	1	–	–	–
Cardiologist 3	0.844	0.849	1	–	–
Cardiologist 4	0.783	0.790	0.800	1	–
Cardiologist 5	0.803	0.807	0.814	0.787	1

set show that compared with existing methods that try to create a unique ground truth in evaluation through multiple annotations, our method can achieve a higher extended Dice. Furthermore, even if we assume that the ground truth is one of the cardiologists' annotation or the majority voting of all cardiologists' annotations, our proposed method always outperforms the existing methods consistently in terms of conventional metrics such as Dice, Intersection over Union (IoU) and Hausdorff distance, showing stronger robustness. In addition, in terms of clinical value, our method also performs the best on the extraction of frame-intensity curve, commonly used in myocardial perfusion analysis [5,10], as well as in a visual grading study of the segmentation results. Finally, our result shows that the proposed extended Dice can better identify segmentation results that need manual correction compared with using Dice. In view of the lack of MCE data set available in the public domain, we will make ours available [1].

2   Related Work

Currently the analysis of MCE data heavily relies on human visual system. The assessment of coronary artery disease (CAD) through MCE data is based on the observation and knowledge of cardiologists, which is time consuming and hardly replicable. Therefore, automatic myocardial segmentation of MCE can help reduce the workload of cardiologists and improve productivity. Compared to traditional B-mode echocardiopraphy, MCE data have a few unique challenges: a) The signal-to-noise ratio is low and the contrast changes a lot over time because of the movement of microbubbles; b) The shape and pose of myocardium vary with heart motion, body physical difference, and scan setting [13]. Different chamber views have different myocardial structure feature; and c) Misleading structures such as papillary muscle have the same intensity and grayscale information as myocardium, which makes it harder to find the myocardium border accurately.

There exist some works that focus on training neural networks with noisy labels assuming independence between samples and noise [12,14–16]. [16] proposed an algorithm to estimate the underlying true segmentation from a collection of segmentations generated by human raters or automatic algorithms. However, information about the original image is completely neglected. [14] proposed a method to simultaneously learn the individual annotator model and the underlying true label distribution through the confusion matrices of annotators. [12] demonstrated that jointly modeling both individual and consensus estimates can lead to significant improvements in performance. Although these methods deal with classification problems where multiple annotators exist, the variations were caused by human factors and a unique ground truth can still be obtained in the evaluation process by the majority vote of multiple experienced annotators. Such an approach, however, may not work well in myocardial segmentation of MCE data as the variations are caused by the image quality. It is hard to tell the best one among multiple annotations from experienced cardiologists or to perform pixel-wise majority vote which may lead to irregular boundaries. In other words, even in the evaluation process, it is impossible to obtain the ground truth.

3   Method

In this section, we introduce a new metric for image segmentation tasks where multiple acceptable annotations exist in the evaluation process. According to our observation on the MCE data, the annotation from each cardiologist is acceptable clinically, i.e., it can be directly used in myocardial perfusion analysis. Such an observation is also true in many other medical applications such as CT measurement [9] and MRI interpretation [2]. Note that this is fundamentally different from human-factor caused variations, which may lead to noisy or error-prone annotations. They can be addressed using methods discussed in [12,14] and thus are not included in our discussion.

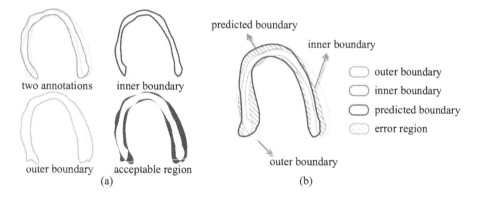

Fig. 2. (a) Visual illustration of two different boundary annotations, inner boundary, outer boundary and acceptable region, respectively. (b) Illustration of the computation of extended Dice, a toy example.

For simplicity of discussion, we use myocardial boundary annotations from two cardiologists as an example. The same concept can be readily extended to more cardiologists. We first obtain an inner boundary and an outer boundary based on these two annotations, as shown in Fig. 2(a). The inner boundary is defined by that of the intersection of the two regions enclosed by the annotated boundaries. In other words, every pixel inside the inner boundary is labeled as myocardium by both of the cardiologists. The outer boundary is that of the union of the two regions, i.e., every pixel inside the outer boundary is labeled as myocardium by at least one cardiologist. As both annotations are accept-able based on our assumption, we can obtain an acceptable region, which is the region between the inner boundary and outer boundary. The pixels inside the acceptable region can be classified as either myocardium or background; any boundary that completely falls inside the acceptable region shall be considered acceptable. Intuitively, in light of the existence of multiple acceptable annota-tions, the introduction of acceptable region can allow the prediction boundary to have some flexibility in regions where significant large inter-observer variabil-ity exists. Such flexibility will potentially lead to better overall segmentation quality.

Based on the observation above, we can extend the traditional Dice metric which is based on a single ground truth. Denote the region enclosed by the inner boundary and the outer boundary as I and O, respectively. The region inside the predicted boundary is P. Then our metric can be calculated as

$$Metric(P, I, O) = 1 - \frac{(P - P \cap O) + (I - P \cap I)}{P + I}. \tag{1}$$

A simple illustration is shown in Fig. 2(b). We can easily see that the metric is penalizing the total segmented region outside the outer boundary $P - P \cap O$ and inside the inner boundary $I - P \cap I$. The denominator $P + I$ helps scale the final result to range $[0, 1]$. We can see that if the predicted boundary is completely inside the acceptable region, the metric is 1. Otherwise, if it has no overlap with the acceptable region, the metric is 0.

Relationship to Dice: Notice that our metric can be simplified into

$$Metric(P, I, O) = \frac{(P \cap O) + (P \cap I)}{P + I}. \tag{2}$$

When multiple annotators give the same annotation results, which means the ground truth annotation is known and the inner boundary and the outer bound-ary completely overlap, the proposed metric will become the conventional Dice. Therefore, it can be viewed as extended Dice.

Once we have the proposed metric, we can further use it as a loss function to train a neural network to help the model focus more on the general features of myocardium and ignore variations from the individual cardiologist for better performance. We denote the pixel-wise annotation of the regions enclosed by the inner boundary and the outer boundary as I_n and O_n, and the prediction for the myocardium region in the training process as $P_n \in [0, 1]$, respectively. n is the index of pixel space N. Then our extended Dice loss function is then defined as follows:

$$\mathcal{L} = \frac{\sum_{n=1}^{N}(P_n - (P_n \times O_n)) + \sum_{n=1}^{N}(I_n - (I_n \times P_n))}{\sum_{n=1}^{N}(P_n + I_n)}. \tag{3}$$

The idea of the introduced loss function is that, for pixels inside the acceptable region, any prediction result is reasonable and should not contribute to the loss function. For pixels outside the acceptable region, any misclassification should be penalized.

4 Experiment

4.1 Dataset

Our dataset consists of 100 subjects in total, 40 of which were diagnosed with coronary artery diseases (CAD) and the rest were not. MCE sequence data was collected from these subjects by an ultrasonography system (Philips 7C or iE ELITE, Philips Medical Systems, Best, Netherlands) equipped with a broadband transducer, and SonoVue (Bracco Research SA, Geneva, Switzerland) as the contrast agent. For each of the subjects, an MCE sequence in the apical of 4-chamber view was acquired, and we randomly selected 10 images from the MCE sequence, which result in an MCE dataset with 1000 images in total. We split our data into training and test set with a ratio of 7:3, i.e., 700 images from 70 subjects were used for training and 300 images from 30 subjects were used for validation. The manual annotations of myocardium in MCE images were performed by five experienced cardiologists, and the time for labeling each image is around 1–2 minutes per cardiologist. Our dataset is available online at [1].

4.2 Training DNN with Extended Dice Loss

Experiment Setup. We base our experiments on two segmentation networks, U-Net and DeepLab, using Pytorch based implementations in [6] and [4], respectively. The initial MCE images were cropped into 512×512. For data augmentation during training, we randomly scale all the images by $[0.8, 1.2]$ and rotate them by $[-30°, 30°]$. We also shifted the image brightness, contrast and saturation by $[-0.1, 0.1]$. During test, we do not employ any augmentations. Batch size is set to 5 and the training epoch is 20. The learning rate is 0.0002 for the first half of epochs, and then 0.00002 for the rest.

We train U-Net and DeepLab using the proposed loss function and compare it with the following methods. For training with a single annotation as the ground truth, we include the following (a) one of the cardiologists, (b) the inner boundary, (c) the outer boundary and (d) the consensus boundary of all cardiologists through pixel-wise majority vote, which are referred to as Single Cardiologist (SC), Inner Boundary (IB), Outer Boundary (OB), and Consensus, respectively. Cross-entropy loss is used in these methods. For training with multiple annotations, we adopt the average cross-entropy of all cardiologists referred as Average Cross Entropy (ACE) and three state-of-the-art approaches refered as Confusion Matrix (CM) [12], Consistency [14] and STAPLE [3]. For STAPLE, we use the fast implementation from [18]. Note that these four methods, while taking multiple annotations into consideration in the training, still assume that a unique ground truth is known in the evaluation through majority voting. For example, in [14] ground truth is acquired by choosing the samples where the three most experienced sonographers agreed in a given label in their cardiac view classification experiments. However, in our problem the unique ground truth is unknown.

Quantitative Analysis. As discussed earlier, because a unique ground truth cannot be obtained through either majority vote or best of annotations, in order to evaluate the performance of our proposed method, we conduct comparisons from the following three aspects. (a) we treat one of the cardiologists' annotation as well as the majority vote of the annotations as the ground truth of the test images (which is again not necessarily the "real" ground truth), and evaluate the conventional metrics (e.g., Dice) of different methods. (b) we compare the extended Dice across all the test images of all the methods in Table 3. (c) we use an important method named frame-intensity curve, which is commonly used for myocardial perfusion analysis in MCE [10], along with visual grading study by an experienced cardiologist to further show the clinical efficacy of our method.

Evaluation Using Conventional Metrics: Note that in our experiment we cannot obtain the unique ground truth. So in order to use traditional evaluation metric to assess the model performance, we assume that one of the cardiologists' annotations or the majority vote of the annotations is the ground truth in the test set and compute the conventional Dice, IoU and Hausdorff distance of the segmentation result of different methods. U-net is used as the network architecture. The results can be seen in Table 2. Note that only the best result among the five cardiologists is reported for the "single cardiologist" method. We can observe that among all the methods, our method performs best consistently (i.e., with highest Dice/IoU, lowest Hausdorff distance and the smallest standard deviation) when any of the cardiologists' annotation is used as the ground truth. The conclusion also holds if we use the majority voting of all cardiologists' annotations as the ground truth. As such, our method shows stronger robustness over other methods. Notice that when using cardiologist 4 as the ground truth, the Single cardiologist method performs best in terms of Dice coefficient and IoU. This is because in this particular method the model is trained with cardiologist 4's annotation as the ground truth. However, the method's performance drops significantly when other cardiologists' annotations are used as the ground truth.

Evaluation Using Extended Dice: We then evaluate these methods using the proposed extended Dice metric, which does not require the unique ground truth to be known. Specifically, the mean/standard deviation of the extended Dice of all methods are calculated. U-net and Deeplab architecture are used, we use the same experimental setup as discussed in Sect. 4.2. From Table 3 we can see that

Table 2. Performance evaluation of different methods using Dice, IoU and Hausdorff distance (pixel point), respectively. Ground truth (GT) is assumed to be one of the cardiologists' annotations (cardiologist 1 to cardiologist 5) or the majority vote of five cardiologists' annotations. Results are reported in the form of mean(standard deviation) of all test images.

Method	GT: cardiologist 1			GT: cardiologist 2			GT: cardiologist 3		
	Dice	IoU	HD	Dice	IoU	HD	Dice	IoU	HD
Single Cardiologist	0.760(.09)	0.623(.10)	35.4(15)	0.809(.13)	0.694(.12)	32.8(17)	0.818(.11)	0.707(.13)	30.5(16)
Inner Boundary	0.732(.10)	0.589(.10)	37.1(18)	0.741(.11)	0.601(.11)	37.9(17)	0.744(.11)	0.605(.11)	36.0(17)
Outer Boundary	0.729(.07)	0.581(.09)	40.1(12)	0.782(.10)	0.654(.12)	36.4(13)	0.790(.10)	0.665(.12)	36.1(12)
Consensus	0.765(.10)	0.632(.11)	35.3(18)	0.824(.13)	0.719(.14)	31.7(19)	0.833(.13)	0.732(.14)	30.0(18)
Average Cross Entropy	0.765(.09)	0.631(.11)	33.2(14)	0.819(.12)	0.709(.13)	29.4(15)	0.827(.12)	0.722(.13)	28.0(14)
Confusion Matrix [14]	0.752(.10)	0.614(.11)	45.2(21)	0.808(.13)	0.695(.14)	40.4(21)	0.817(.13)	0.708(.14)	39.0(21)
Consistency [12]	0.770(.08)	0.635(.10)	37.2(15)	0.826(.11)	0.719(.13)	32.3(16)	0.831(.11)	0.726(.13)	31.7(16)
STAPLE [16]	0.743(.07)	0.598(.09)	39.6(13)	0.810(.10)	0.694(.12)	33.0(17)	0.816(.11)	0.703(.13)	32.7(17)
Our method	**0.780(.08)**	**0.649(.10)**	**31.5(12)**	**0.829(.10)**	**0.721(.12)**	**28.9(14)**	**0.836(.10)**	**0.732(.12)**	**27.7(14)**

Method	GT: cardiologist 4			GT: cardiologist 5			GT: majority vote		
	Dice	IoU	HD	Dice	IoU	HD	Dice	IoU	HD
Single Cardiologist	**0.824(.10)**	**0.716(.13)**	35.4(15)	0.791(.08)	0.665(.10)	29.4(17)	0.838(.11)	0.735(.12)	28.4(17)
Inner Boundary	0.766(.11)	0.634(.12)	36.6(17)	0.734(.08)	0.590(.09)	36.6(17)	0.770(.11)	0.638(.11)	34.2(17)
Outer Boundary	0.749(.08)	0.608(.10)	35.5(12)	0.800(.05)	0.672(.07)	35.5(12)	0.785(.09)	0.656(.11)	34.0(12)
Consensus	0.818(.12)	0.710(.14)	31.5(19)	0.806(.08)	0.686(.10)	31.5(19)	0.847(.12)	0.753(.14)	28.0(19)
Average Cross Entropy	0.816(.11)	0.704(.13)	29.4(15)	0.806(.07)	0.685(.09)	29.4(15)	0.844(.11)	0.745(.13)	26.4(15)
Confusion Matrix [14]	0.795(.11)	0.675(.13)	39.7(22)	0.805(.07)	0.682(.09)	39.7(22)	0.826(.12)	0.719(.13)	37.9(22)
Consistency [12]	0.816(.10)	0.704(.13)	31.5(15)	0.815(.07)	0.696(.09)	31.5(15)	0.847(.10)	0.749(.13)	29.8(16)
STAPLE [16]	0.779(.09)	0.647(.11)	33.8(15)	0.810(.04)	0.686(.06)	33.8(15)	0.814(.09)	0.695(.11)	31.8(16)
Our method	0.822(.09)	0.710(.12)	28.6(13)	**0.817(.07)**	**0.699(.09)**	**28.6(13)**	**0.855(.10)**	**0.759(.12)**	**25.4(14)**

Table 3. Performance comparison in terms of extended dice using different methods. Results are reported as mean(standard deviation) across all test images. SC, IB, OB, ACE and CM refer to single cardiologist, inner boundary, outer boundary, average cross entropy and confusion matrix, respectively.

Method	SC	IB	OB	Consensus	ACE	CM	Consistency	STAPLE	Ours
U-Net	0.929(.06)	0.947(.05)	0.848(.07)	0.940(.06)	0.919(.06)	0.951(.06)	0.947(.06)	0.912(.06)	**0.958(.05)**
DeepLab	0.942(.07)	0.906(.08)	0.891(.07)	0.946(.08)	0.945(.07)	0.924(.08)	0.944(.07)	0.921(.07)	**0.954(.06)**

our method always achieves the highest extended Dice among all the methods on both U-Net and DeepLab. The standard deviation of our method is also lower than the others, which shows our method outperforms the others statistically. This is because, in our training approach, the acceptable region allows neural networks some flexibility to learn more general texture and structure features of myocardium. Notice that Confusion Matrix and Consistency methods target classification problems originally, so their performance in the segmentation task may not be as good.

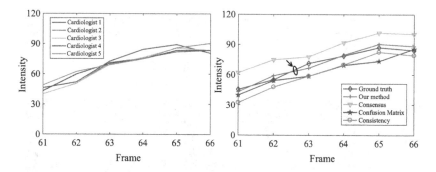

Fig. 3. Quantitative analysis of different methods. Left: frame-intensity curves from the annotations of five different cardiologists, which are very close to each other. Right: frame-intensity curves of different methods and the ground truth obtained by averaging the curves on the left. Ours is the closest to the ground truth.

Evaluation Using Frame-Intensity Curve: In order to show that the proposed extended Dice and loss function are indeed superior from the clinical application perspective, we also use the frame-intensity curve of segmented myocardium, which is commonly used in myocardial perfusion analysis [5,10], to evaluate the segmentation performance. Frame-intensity curve, also known as the time-intensity curve, can be used to reflect the relative microvascular blood volume after microbubbles infusion, thus help estimate myocardial ischemia. Figure 3 shows the frame-intensity curves of six frames of a subject (Frame 61–66) using the annotations from each of the five cardiologists (left), and from the top four methods in Table 3, namely our method, Consensus, Confusion Matrix and Consistency (right). U-Net is used as the segmentation framework. Although the annotations from the five cardiologists are very different as shown in Table 1, from the left figure we can see that the resulting frame-intensity curve from each of them are very similar to each other. Based on this observation, we obtain a ground truth frame-intensity curve through averaging. It can be seen in the right figure that among all the four methods compared, the curve generated by our method is the closest to the ground truth curve. This convincingly shows that our method can better help myocardial perfusion analysis.

Table 4. Visual grading study of different methods by an independent and experienced cardiologist without knowing which method is applied on each image.

Grading level	Consensus	Confusion matrix	Consistency	Our method
Level 4 (Highest)	58	71	69	**72**
Level 3	56	39	42	50
Level 2	11	17	22	20
Level 1 (Lowest)	25	23	17	**8**

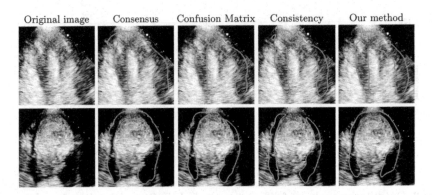

| Original image | Consensus | Confusion Matrix | Consistency | Our method |

Fig. 4. Visualization of myocardial segmentation results of two examples using U-Net as the backbone with different methods.

Qualitative Analysis. A visual grading study is conducted to further demonstrate the efficacy of our proposed metric and the loss function. In this experiment, an independent and experienced cardiologist is asked to grade the myocardial segmentation result in a blind setting (i.e., without knowing which method was used). We randomly select 5 frames for each subject in the test set for grading, resulting in 30×5 frames in total. Grading is based on the segmentation accuracy which can be classified into 4 levels: Level 4, excellent - no manual correction needed; Level 3, slight yet observable shape deviation; Level 2, obviously irregular shapes; Level 1, severe disconnection/mistakes. Similar to the frame-intensity curve study, we compare our method with the three best methods in Table 3. Table 4 demonstrates the grading results for each method. It can be seen that compared with other methods, our proposed method has the most number of frames in the highest quality level (level 4), and fewest in the lowest level (level 1), which means that out method is less likely to made a segmentation which has severe disconnections or mistakes.

Visualization of myocardial segmentation from these methods is also shown in Fig. 4. We can see that for the Consensus, Confusion Matrix and Consistency methods, some unregulated shapes or discontinuity exist because the model cannot discriminate the actual myocardial from the artifacts which have the same intensity and texture information. However, the results of our method can alleviate the problem and accurately segment myocardium in MCE images.

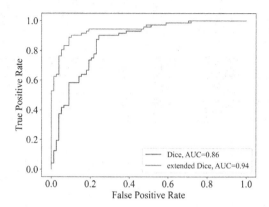

Fig. 5. ROC curve of using dice and extended dice as the segmentation evaluation metric in classifying segmentations based on whether manual correction is needed.

4.3   Extended Dice as a Superior Evaluation Metric

In order to demonstrate the advantage of extended Dice over Dice as an evaluation metric, we use these two metrics to evaluate the prediction generated by our training method in the grading study in Sect. 4.2. The objective is to identify the segmentation results that need manual correction, which can be viewed as a binary classification problem. The segmentations in the grading Level 1, Level 2 and Level 3 are defined as the class 0 that need manual correction. The segmentations in Level 4 are defined as class 1 which do not need manual correction. Figure 5 shows the Receiver Operating Characteristic (ROC) curve of using Dice and extended Dice as the metric for the classification problem. It can be seen that using extended Dice, we can improve the classification AUC from 0.86 to 0.94, suggesting that compared to Dice, extended Dice is better in distinguishing segmentations that need manual correction from those that do not.

In Fig. 6, we show the evaluation comparison of four images using Dice and extended Dice. Images in each group represent the Dice evaluated by cardiologist 2, Dice evaluated by cardiologist 5 and extended Dice. It can be seen that there exist large variations in Dice when using different cardiologists' annotations as the ground truth, which may lead to misjudgment during evaluation. For example, we may think the segmentation quality is low (Dice<0.77) based on the annotation from one of the cardiologists, but the quality is actually pretty good based on the annotation from another one (Dice>0.86). However, using extended Dice will alleviate the problem because all these images are considered good (extended Dice>0.96).

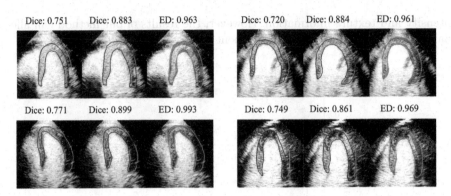

Fig. 6. Evaluation comparison of four images using dice and extended dice (denoted as ED). Images from left to right in one group represent the Dice evaluated by cardiologist 2, dice evaluated by cardiologist 5, and extended dice evaluated by all cardiologists, respectively. Green boundary is the prediction, blue boundary is the ground truth, and blue area is the acceptable region.

5   Conclusion

In this paper, we proposed an extended Dice metric for evaluating the performance of image segmentation where multiple annotations exist and unique ground truth is unknown due to low image qualities. Based on the metric, we further use it as a loss function for training DNN to help the network better learn the general features of myocardium and ignore variations caused by individual annotators. Experiments on MCE data set demonstrate that the proposed loss function can improve the segmentation performance evaluated by conventional metrics, by the proposed metric, by the extraction of frame-intensity curve used in myocardial perfusion analysis, and by a visual grading study of the segmentation results in a blind setting. Comparing Dice and extended Dice as segmentation evaluation metrics, extended Dice performs better in identifying images that need manual correction. While we only demonstrate the efficacy of the proposed method on myocardial segmentation, it is likely that it can be applied to other problems where multiple acceptable annotations are available.

References

1. Mce dataset. https://github.com/dewenzeng/MCE_dataset
2. Beresford, M.J., Padhani, A.R., et al.: Inter-and intraobserver variability in the evaluation of dynamic breast cancer MRI. J. Magn. Reson. Imaging Official J. Int. Soc. Magn. Reson. Med. **24**(6), 1316–1325 (2006)
3. Butakoff, C., Balocco, S., Ordas, S.: Simulated 3d ultrasound lv cardiac images for active shape model training. In: Medical Imaging 2007: Image Processing, vol. 6512, p. 65123U. International Society for Optics and Photonics (2007)

4. Chen, L.C., Zhu, Y., Papandreou, G., Schroff, F., Adam, H.: Encoder-decoder with atrous separable convolution for semantic image segmentation. In: Proceedings of the European Conference on Computer Vision (ECCV), pp. 801–818 (2018)

5. Dewey, M., et al.: Clinical quantitative cardiac imaging for the assessment of myocardial ischaemia. Nat. Rev. Cardiol. **17**(7), 427–450 (2020)

6. Isensee, F., Petersen, J., et al.: nnu-net: Self-adapting framework for u-net-based medical image segmentation. arXiv preprint arXiv:1809.10486 (2018)

7. Litjens, G., et al.: A survey on deep learning in medical image analysis. Med. Image Anal. **42**, 60–88 (2017)

8. Liu, Z., et al.: Machine vision guided 3d medical image compression for efficient transmission and accurate segmentation in the clouds. In: Proceedings of the IEEE Conference on Computer Vision and Pattern Recognition, pp. 12687–12696 (2019)

9. McErlean, A., et al.: Intra-and interobserver variability in CT measurements in oncology. Radiology **269**(2), 451–459 (2013)

10. Porter, T.R., Mulvagh, S.L., Abdelmoneim, S.S., Becher, H., et al.: Clinical applications of ultrasonic enhancing agents in echocardiography: 2018 American society of echocardiography guidelines update. J. Am. Soc. Echocardiogr. **31**(3), 241–274 (2018)

11. Ronneberger, O., Fischer, P., Brox, T.: U-net: convolutional networks for biomedical image segmentation. In: Navab, N., Hornegger, J., Wells, W.M., Frangi, A.F. (eds.) MICCAI 2015. LNCS, vol. 9351, pp. 234–241. Springer, Cham (2015). https://doi.org/10.1007/978-3-319-24574-4_28

12. Sudre, C.H., et al.: Let's agree to disagree: learning highly debatable multirater labelling. In: Shen, D., et al. (eds.) MICCAI 2019. LNCS, vol. 11767, pp. 665–673. Springer, Cham (2019). https://doi.org/10.1007/978-3-030-32251-9_73

13. Tang, M.X., et al.: Quantitative contrast-enhanced ultrasound imaging: a review of sources of variability. Interface Focus **1**(4), 520–539 (2011)

14. Tanno, R., Saeedi, A., Sankaranarayanan, S., Alexander, D.C., Silberman, N.: Learning from noisy labels by regularized estimation of annotator confusion. In: Proceedings of the IEEE Conference on Computer Vision and Pattern Recognition, pp. 11244–11253 (2019)

15. Wang, H., Suh, J.W., Das, S.R., Pluta, J.B., Craige, C., Yushkevich, P.A.: Multiatlas segmentation with joint label fusion. IEEE Trans. Pattern Anal. Mach. Intell. **35**(3), 611–623 (2012)

16. Warfield, S.K., Zou, K.H., Wells, W.M.: Simultaneous truth and performance level estimation (staple): an algorithm for the validation of image segmentation. IEEE Trans. Med. Imaging **23**(7), 903–921 (2004)

17. Xu, X., et al.: Whole heart and great vessel segmentation in congenital heart disease using deep neural networks and graph matching. In: Shen, D., et al. (eds.) MICCAI 2019. LNCS, vol. 11765, pp. 477–485. Springer, Cham (2019). https://doi.org/10.1007/978-3-030-32245-8_53

18. Yaniv, Z., Lowekamp, B.C., Johnson, H.J., Beare, R.: Simpleitk image-analysis notebooks: a collaborative environment for education and reproducible research. J. Digit. Imaging **31**(3), 290–303 (2018)

A New Bidirectional Unsupervised Domain Adaptation Segmentation Framework

Munan Ning[1,2], Cheng Bian[1(✉)], Dong Wei[1], Shuang Yu[1], Chenglang Yuan[1], Yaohua Wang[2], Yang Guo[2], Kai Ma[1], and Yefeng Zheng[1]

[1] Tencent Jarvis Lab, Shenzhen, China
tronbian@tencent.com
[2] National University of Defense Technology, Changsha, China

Abstract. Domain shift happens in cross-domain scenarios commonly because of the wide gaps between different domains: when applying a deep learning model well-trained in one domain to another target domain, the model usually performs poorly. To tackle this problem, unsupervised domain adaptation (UDA) techniques are proposed to bridge the gap between different domains, for the purpose of improving model performance without annotation in the target domain. Particularly, UDA has a great value for multimodal medical image analysis, where annotation difficulty is a practical concern. However, most existing UDA methods can only achieve satisfactory improvements in one adaptation direction (e.g., MRI to CT), but often perform poorly in the other (CT to MRI), limiting their practical usage. In this paper, we propose a bidirectional UDA (BiUDA) framework based on disentangled representation learning for equally competent two-way UDA performances. This framework employs a unified domain-aware pattern encoder which not only can adaptively encode images in different domains through a domain controller, but also improve model efficiency by eliminating redundant parameters. Furthermore, to avoid distortion of contents and patterns of input images during the adaptation process, a content-pattern consistency loss is introduced. Additionally, for better UDA segmentation performance, a label consistency strategy is proposed to provide extra supervision by recomposing target-domain-styled images and corresponding source-domain annotations. Comparison experiments and ablation studies conducted on two public datasets demonstrate the superiority of our BiUDA framework to current state-of-the-art UDA methods and the effectiveness of its novel designs. By successfully addressing two-way adaptations, our BiUDA framework offers a flexible solution of UDA techniques to the real-world scenario.

Keywords: Domain adaptation · Multi-modality · Segmentation

M. Ning and C. Bian—Contributed equally to this work.

A. Feragen et al. (Eds.): IPMI 2021, LNCS 12729, pp. 492–503, 2021.
https://doi.org/10.1007/978-3-030-78191-0_38

1 Introduction

Deep learning based models have become dominant for computer-aided automated analysis of medical images and achieved great success in recent years [1,2,6,13,17,19]. Usually, a great quantity of manual annotations are required for training deep learning models, yet the annotation process is known to be expertise-demanding, labor-intensive, and time-consuming. Multimodal imaging—which plays an important role and provides valuable complementary information in disease diagnosis, prognosis, and treatment planning in clinical practice nowadays—may further increase the demand for annotations, as a model well-trained with data of one specific modality often performs poorly on another due to domain shift [20]. Unsupervised domain adaptation (UDA) [7,8] is a quickly rising technique which aims to tackle the domain shift problem by adapting models trained in one domain (the *source* domain) to another (the *target* domain) without manual annotations in the latter [3,16,18,20]. The concept of UDA is readily applicable to the lack-of-annotation problem in multimodal medical imaging [4,5]. For example, Chen *et al.* [4] applied UDA for model adaptation from cardiac magnetic resonance imaging (MRI) to cardiac computed tomography (CT) based on image-level alignment. In spite of impressive results obtained for adapting MRI-trained models for CT data [4,5], few existing methods simultaneously concern the opposite, i.e., CT to MRI. In practice, situations may arise in which the CT data have already been annotated while the MRI data are not, and the adaptation of CT-trained models for MRI becomes useful. Therefore, a comprehensive UDA method that is able to effectively accomplish bidirectional adaptations (termed *BiUDA* in this work) is of great clinical value.

Given the importance of BiUDA, we conducted experiments to examine the capabilities of several state-of-the-art (SOTA) UDA methods [3–5,16,18,20] for bidirectional adaptations between MRI and CT using the Multi-Modality Whole Heart Segmentation (MMWHS) challenge dataset [24] and the Multi-Modality Abdominal Segmentation (MMAS) dataset [12,14]. Taking MMWHS dataset as an example, we show the bidirectional adaptation results in Fig. 2. In general, these methods worked effectively for adapting MRI-trained models for CT data. When reversing the adaptation direction, however, most of them suffered a dramatic drop in performance and failed to produce comparable results. Similar results can also be found on the MMAS dataset. We call this phenomenon *domain drop*, which intuitively reflects the substantial performance gap between the bidirectional adaptations in BiUDA. Recently, Dou *et al.* [5] improved performance of the CT-MRI BiUDA by switching the early layers of the two encoders to fit individual modality and sharing the higher layers between two modalities. It is presumed that the improvement was due to the isolation of low-level features of each modality. Motivated by the presumption, we propose a novel framework based on the concept of disentangled representation learning (DRPL) [11,15], to address the domain drop problem in BiUDA. Specifically, our framework decomposes an input image into a content code and a pattern code, with the former representing domain-invariant characteristics shared by different modalities (e.g., shape) and the latter representing domain-specific features isolated from each other (e.g., appearance).

Our main contributions include:

1) We propose a novel BiUDA framework based on DRPL, which effectively mitigates the domain drop problem and achieves SOTA results for both adaptation directions in experiments on the MMWHS and MMAS datasets.
2) Unlike existing works [3,11,15] that adopted a separate pattern encoder for each modality, we design a domain-aware pattern encoder to unify the encoding process of different domains in a single module with a domain controller. This design not only reduces parameters but also improves performance of the network. In addition, a content-pattern consistency loss is proposed to avoid the distortion of the content and pattern codes.
3) For better performance in the UDA segmentation task, we propose a label consistency loss, utilizing the target-domain-styled images and corresponding source-domain annotations for auxiliary training.

2   Method

2.1   Problem Definition

In the UDA segmentation problem, there is an annotated dataset $\left\{\left(x_s^i, a_s^i\right)\right\}_{i=1}^{N_s}$ in the source domain $\mathcal{X}_s$, where each image x_s^i has a unique pixel-wise annotation a_s^i. Meanwhile, there exists an unannotated dataset $\left\{x_t^i\right\}_{i=1}^{N_t}$ in the target domain $\mathcal{X}_t$. The goal of our framework is to utilize the annotated source-domain data to obtain a model that is able to perform well on the unannotated target-domain data. We shall omit the superscript index i and superscript domain indicators s and t for simplicity in case of no confusion.

Figure 1(a) shows the diagram of our DRPL-based BiUDA framework equipped with the domain-aware pattern encoder, which will be elaborated in Sect. 2.2. Figure 1(b) illustrates the information flow and corresponding loss computations within the proposed framework, which will be elaborated in Sect. 2.3.

2.2   DRPL Framework with Domain-Aware Pattern Encoder

Compared to the existing UDA methods that attempted to align the features extracted in different domains, we argue that a better solution is to explicitly make the model aware of the cross-domain commonalities and differences. For this reason, we adopt the DRPL [11,15] framework to disentangle the image space into a domain-sharing content space $\mathcal{C}$ (implying anatomical structures) and a domain-specific pattern space $\mathcal{P}$ (implying appearances), using a content encoder E_c and a pattern encoder E_p (see Fig. 1(a)), respectively. Concretely, $E_c : \mathcal{X} \to \mathcal{C}$ maps an input image to its content code: $c = E_c(x)$, and $E_p : \mathcal{X} \to \mathcal{P}$ maps the image to its pattern code. It is worth mentioning that as the pattern codes are domain-specific, a common strategy is to employ dual pattern encoders—one for each domain [3,11,15]. On the contrary, we propose a unified domain-aware pattern encoder for both domains, which is controlled by a domain

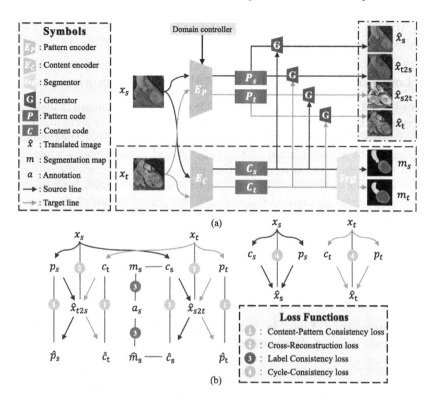

Fig. 1. (a) Framework diagram; (b) Data flow and corresponding loss functions.

controller $d \in \{0,1\}$, where 0 and 1 indicate the source and target domains, respectively. Hence, by specifying d, E_p adaptively encodes images from different domains into representative pattern codes: $\boldsymbol{p}_s = E_p(x|0)$ and $\boldsymbol{p}_t = E_p(x|1)$. The proposed $E_p(x|d)$ simplifies our network design, greatly reducing the number of parameters to learn during training. Moreover, the proposed domain controller improves the encoding ability since it forces the pattern encoder to learn the differences between two domains by providing additional pattern information.

After being extracted from the input images, the content and pattern codes in different domains are permuted and recombined, and the resulting pairs are input to a generator $G : (\mathcal{C}, \mathcal{P}) \rightarrow \hat{\mathcal{X}}$ to recompose images with the anatomical structures specified by $\boldsymbol{c}$ and appearance specified by $\boldsymbol{p}$: $\hat{x} = G(\boldsymbol{c}, \boldsymbol{p})$. Here, $\hat{\cdot}$ indicates the variable is within or resulted from the recomposed image space. Four types of images can be recomposed based on the permutation of $\boldsymbol{c}$ and $\boldsymbol{p}$, i.e., reconstructed source image $\hat{x}_s$ (both $\boldsymbol{c}$ and $\boldsymbol{p}$ from the source domain), reconstructed target image $\hat{x}_t$ (both $\boldsymbol{c}$ and $\boldsymbol{p}$ from the target domain), and translated images $\hat{x}_{s2t}$ ($\boldsymbol{c}$ from the source and $\boldsymbol{p}$ from the target domain) and $\hat{x}_{t2s}$ ($\boldsymbol{c}$ from the target and $\boldsymbol{p}$ from the source domain); here, 's2t' stands for 'source to target', and vice versa. Note that a single generator is used for the recomposition of the four types of images. See the generator and recomposed images in Fig. 1(a). Lastly, a segmenter S is employed to decode the content codes c to semantic segmentation masks m: $m = S(c)$.

2.3   Loss Functions for DRPL-based BiUDA Framework

Content-Pattern Consistency Loss. When performing domain transfer with many existing DRPL methods (e.g., [11] and [15]), we notice apparent anatomical and/or texture distortions in the recomposed images. We assume the fundamental reason to be the distortion of the content and pattern codes while going through the decomposition-recomposition process. To avoid such distortion, we propose a content-pattern consistency loss to penalize potential distortions of c and p in the workflow. Let $\hat{c} = E_c(\hat{x})$ and $\hat{p} = E_p(\hat{x}, d)$ denote the content and pattern codes for the *reconstructed* image $\hat{x}$ (i.e., $\hat{x}_s$ or $\hat{x}_t$), and $c = E_c(x)$ and $p = E_p(x, d)$ for the input image x. Then, the content-pattern consistency loss $\mathcal{L}^{cpc}$ (represented by ① in Fig. 1(b)) is formulated as:

$$\mathcal{L}^{cpc} = \mathbb{E}_{\hat{c}\sim\hat{C},c\sim C}\left[\|\hat{c} - c\|_1\right] + \mathbb{E}_{\hat{p}\sim\hat{P},p\sim P}\left[\|\hat{p} - p\|_1\right], \qquad (1)$$

where $\|\cdot\|_1$ represents the L1 norm.

Label Consistency Loss. In our proposed DRPL framework, ideally, the source-domain image x_s and source-to-target transferred image $\hat{x}_{s2t}$ should contain the same anatomical structures, since the latter is recomposed with the content code of the former. In addition, their anatomical consistency is further enhanced by the content consistency loss described above. Therefore, a label consistency loss is introduced to supervise the segmentation of both x_s and $\hat{x}_{s2t}$ with the same annotation a_s. Let $m_s = S(c_s)$ and $\hat{m}_s = S(\hat{c}_s)$ denote the segmentation masks of x_s and $\hat{x}_{s2t}$, respectively, where $c_s = E_c(x_s)$ and $\hat{c}_s = E_c(\hat{x}_{s2t})$. Then, the segmentation masks can be supervised by a_s using a combination of the cross-entropy and Dice losses:

$$\mathcal{L}^{seg}(a_s, m) = 1 - \frac{1}{N}\sum_j a_s(j)\log m(j) - \sum_j \frac{2a_s(j)m(j)}{a_s^2(j) + m^2(j)}, \qquad (2)$$

where j iterates over all locations and channels in a_s and m, and N is the total number of iterations. Accordingly, the proposed label consistency loss (represented by ③ in Fig. 1(b)) is defined as:

$$\mathcal{L}^{lc} = \mathcal{L}^{seg}(a_s, m_s) + \mathcal{L}^{seg}(a_s, \hat{m}_s). \qquad (3)$$

It is worth noting that $\mathcal{L}^{seg}(a_s, \hat{m}_s)$ in Eq. (3) can be viewed as providing supplementary target-domain training data to make up the vacancy of annotation in the target domain. Therefore, it is expected to help relieve the domain drop.

Cycle-Consistency and Cross-reconstruction Losses. Following the intuition in CycleGAN [23], the input images and their reconstructions are constrained to be close with a cycle-consistency loss (represented by ④ in Fig. 1(b)):

$$\mathcal{L}^{cycle} = \mathbb{E}_{\hat{x}\sim\hat{X},x\sim X}\left[\|\hat{x} - x\|_1\right]. \qquad (4)$$

Note that $\hat{x}$ in Eq. (4) should only be reconstructed images, i.e., either $\hat{x}_s$ or $\hat{x}_t$. In addition, the translated images $\hat{x}_{s2t}$ should be indistinguishable from the real target-domain images x_t, to provide $\mathcal{L}^{seg}(a_s, \hat{m}_s)$ with high-quality recomposed target-domain data. Following the generative adversarial network (GAN) [9], a discriminator D is introduced and the cross-reconstruction loss (represented by ② in Fig. 1(b)) is defined as:

$$\mathcal{L}_{\hat{x}_{s2t}}^{GAN} = \mathbb{E}_{\hat{x}_{s2t} \sim \hat{\mathcal{X}}_{s2t}} \left[\log \left(1 - D\left(\hat{x}_{s2t}\right) \right) \right] + \mathbb{E}_{x_t \sim \mathcal{X}_t} \left[\log D\left(x_t\right) \right]. \qquad (5)$$

Likewise, a cross-reconstruction loss $\mathcal{L}_{\hat{x}_{t2s}}^{GAN}$ is also proposed for the target-to-source transferred images $\hat{x}_{t2s}$ as:

$$\mathcal{L}_{\hat{x}_{t2s}}^{GAN} = \mathbb{E}_{\hat{x}_{t2s} \sim \hat{\mathcal{X}}_{t2s}} \left[\log \left(1 - D\left(\hat{x}_{t2s}\right) \right) \right] + \mathbb{E}_{x_s \sim \mathcal{X}_s} \left[\log D\left(x_s\right) \right]. \qquad (6)$$

Overall Loss Function. The overall loss function of our BiUDA framework is a weighted summation of the above-described losses ($\mathcal{L}^{cpc}$ and $\mathcal{L}^{cycle}$ are computed in both the source and target domains):

$$\mathcal{L} = \lambda_1(\mathcal{L}_s^{cpc} + \mathcal{L}_t^{cpc}) + \lambda_2 \mathcal{L}^{lc} + \lambda_3(\mathcal{L}_s^{cycle} + \mathcal{L}_t^{cycle}) + \lambda_4(\mathcal{L}_{\hat{x}_{s2t}}^{GAN} + \mathcal{L}_{\hat{x}_{t2s}}^{GAN}). \qquad (7)$$

3   Experiments

Datasets. The proposed BiUDA framework is evaluated using the MMWHS challenge dataset [24] and the MMAS dataset. The MMWHS dataset includes 20 MRI (47–127 slices per scan) and 20 CT (142–251 slices per scan) cardiac scans. Four cardiac anatomic structures, including ascending aorta (AA), left atrium blood cavity (LABC), left ventricle blood cavity (LVBC), and left ventricle myocardium (LVM), are annotated. The MMAS dataset includes 20 MRI scans (21–33 slices per scan) from the CHAOS Challenge [12] and 30 CT scans (35–117 slices per scan) from [14]. Multiple organs are manually annotated, including liver, right kidney (R-Kid), left kidney (L-Kid), and spleen. For a fair comparison, every input slice is resized to 256 × 256 pixels and augmented in the same way as SIFA [4], including random crop, flip and rotation. A 5-fold cross-validation strategy is employed to test our framework.

Evaluation Metrics. The Dice coefficient (Dice) and F1 score are used as the basic evaluation metrics. The performance upper-bounds are established by separately training and testing two segmentation networks (one for each modality) using data of the same modality, and denoted by 'M2M' (MRI to MRI) and 'C2C' (CT to CT), respectively. Followed by the same adaptation direction reported in [4], we define the adaptation from MRI (as suorce domain) to CT (as target domain) as the forward adaptation, and vice versa. Since the levels of difficulty are markedly different for MRI- and CT-based cardiac segmentation due to distinct modal characteristics (see the rows for M2M and C2C in Table 1), it would be difficult to directly compare Dice or F1 scores obtained via the forward and backward adaptations. Instead, we resort to the performance drop, which

Table 1. Performance comparison of our proposed BiUDA framework with SOTA UDA algorithms on the MMWHS dataset using the average performance drops (lower is better) in Dice and F1 score.

Method	AA		LABC		LVBC		LVM		Mean	
	Dice$^\downarrow$	F1$^\downarrow$	Dice$^\downarrow$	F1$^\downarrow$	Dice$^\downarrow$	F1$^\downarrow$	Dice$^\downarrow$	F1$^\downarrow$	Dice$^\downarrow$	F1$^\downarrow$
M2M*	81.68	82.11	85.25	85.39	93.01	93.07	84.68	84.71	86.16	86.39
C2C*	96.17	96.21	93.25	93.28	89.67	89.92	84.26	84.54	90.84	91.07
AdaptSegNet [20]	55.80	52.50	48.94	48.67	23.20	19.62	34.14	33.41	40.52	37.62
BDL [16]	55.31	48.06	48.91	47.88	32.33	25.42	44.47	44.15	45.25	40.15
CLAN [18]	56.90	51.46	49.17	47.47	23.18	19.58	33.49	32.76	40.68	36.68
DISE [3]	38.48	34.89	43.70	34.39	12.61	10.66	32.62	27.31	31.85	25.19
SIFA [4]	16.29	15.02	22.72	21.58	20.61	19.42	27.74	27.05	21.84	20.49
ACE [21]	13.39	11.48	11.43	10.81	5.08	4.76	24.00	23.31	13.47	12.44
Ours	**8.70**	**8.54**	**6.68**	**6.37**	**3.50**	**3.48**	**15.07**	**14.76**	**8.49**	**8.29**

*Upper-bound performances are reported as the original Dice and F1 scores.

Table 2. Performance comparison of our proposed BiUDA framework with SOTA UDA algorithms on the MMAS dataset. Dice$^\downarrow$: average performance drop in Dice; F1$^\downarrow$: average performance drop in F1 score.

Method	Liver		R.kidney		L.kidney		Spleen		Mean	
	Dice$^\downarrow$	F1$^\downarrow$	Dice$^\downarrow$	F1$^\downarrow$	Dice$^\downarrow$	F1$^\downarrow$	Dice$^\downarrow$	F1$^\downarrow$	Dice$^\downarrow$	F1$^\downarrow$
M2M*	93.89	93.98	93.34	93.16	92.30	92.13	91.95	92.6	92.87	92.97
C2C*	96.25	96.06	90.99	90.68	91.86	92.27	93.72	92.96	93.21	92.99
AdaptSegNet [20]	14.29	17.87	27.33	32.58	39.52	43.36	27.36	32.46	27.12	31.57
BDL [16]	21.94	26.81	27.93	32.59	44.18	48.79	27.29	30.91	30.33	34.77
CLAN [18]	19.90	24.80	27.63	32.61	40.37	44.07	27.37	32.57	28.82	33.51
DISE [3]	8.00	10.04	9.38	11.24	10.01	12.34	8.27	10.71	8.92	11.08
SIFA [4]	5.84	5.93	5.75	5.93	9.94	10.94	8.55	8.96	7.52	7.94
ACE [21]	5.36	5.90	5.82	7.16	5.02	5.99	4.89	5.57	5.27	6.15
Ours	**5.04**	**5.79**	**4.44**	**5.13**	**3.69**	**4.42**	**4.38**	**5.42**	**4.39**	**5.19**

*Upper-bound performances are reported as the original Dice and F1 scores.

is computed by subtracting the UDA performance from the corresponding target domain upper-bound, e.g., subtracting MRI-to-CT UDA performance from C2C. Lastly, to intuitively reflect the quality of BiUDA using a single metric, we further calculate the average performance drop by averaging the bidirectional performance drops.

Implementation. The content encoder E_c is based on PSP-101 [22], accompanied by a fully convolutional network as the segmenter S. The domain-aware pattern encoder E_p comprises several downsampling units followed by a global average pooling layer and a 1×1 convolution layer. Each unit contains a convolution layer with $stride = 2$, followed by a batch normalization layer and a ReLU layer. The discriminator D has a similar structure to E_p, with its units consisting of a convolution layer with $stride = 2$, an instance normalization layer and a leaky-ReLU layer. The generator G is composed of a set of residual blocks with

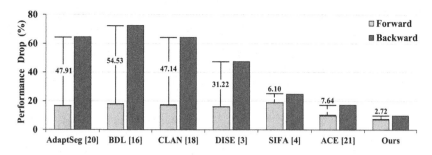

Fig. 2. MMWHS: the visualizaiton of the performance drops in Dice in the forward (yellow bars) and backward (red bars) adaptation directions (lower is better), and the gap between the bidirectional performance drops for each method (narrower is better) on the MMWHS dataset. It proves that our method achieved SOTA results for both adaptation directions and comparable performance gap. (Color figure online)

adaptive instance normalization (AdaIN) [10] layers and several upsampling and convolution layers. During the inference stage, only E_c and S are used to obtain the segmentation results. The whole framework is implemented with PyTorch on an NVIDIA Tesla P40 GPU. We use a mini-batch size of 8 for training, and train the framework for 30,000 iterations. We use the SGD optimizer with an initial learning rate of 2.5×10^{-4} for E_c, and the Adam optimizer with an initial learning rate of 1.0×10^{-3} for E_p and G. The alternating training scheme [9] is adopted to train the discriminator D using the Adam optimizer with an initial learning rate of 1.0×10^{-4}. The polynomial decay policy is adopted to adjust all learning rates. The hyper-parameters $\lambda_1, \lambda_2, \lambda_3$ and λ_4 in Eq. (7) are empirically set to 0.01, 1.0, 0.5, and 0.01, respectively, although we find in our experiments that the results are not very sensitive with respect to the exact values of these parameters. The upper-bound networks for M2M and C2C are implemented using the standard PSP101 backbone and trained with the same settings as E_c.

Quantitative and Qualitative Analyses. To validate the efficacy of our framework in addressing the domain drop problem, extensive experiments are conducted on the two datasets. The competing algorithms include several SOTA UDA methods [3–5,16,18,20] in both the computer vision and medical image fields. We reimplement all compared methods with the origin released codes and apply with the default configurations. Table 1 presents the average performance drops in Dice and F1 score for the four cardiac structures as well as the mean values across structures on the MMWHS dataset. Table 2 presents the average performance drops for four abdominal structures and the mean values across them on the MMAS dataset. As can be seen, our framework outperforms all competing methods by large margins for all structures on these datasets. In addition, Fig. 2 visualizes the forward and backward performance drops and corresponding gaps between the bidirectional drops on the MMWHS dataset. For most competing UDA methods, there exist considerable gaps between the performances of the forward and backward adaptations. In contrast, our method

Table 3. Ablation studies of our proposed modules on the MMWHS dataset. The bidirectional average performance drop in Dice is used for evaluation.

Methods	Combination				Dice↓(%)				
	DRPL	CPC	LC	DAE	AA	LABC	LVBC	LVM	Mean
Source Only					74.51	67.57	37.30	62.97	60.59
DRPL	✓				44.56	39.05	15.75	46.12	36.37
DRPL+CPC	✓	✓			27.15	30.08	13.41	32.26	25.73
DRPL+CPC+LC	✓	✓	✓		14.90	11.53	5.66	19.83	12.98
Ours	✓	✓	✓	✓	**8.70**	**6.68**	**3.50**	**15.07**	**8.49**

Source Only: Baseline model trained with only source domain data. **DRPL**: Disentangled representation learning.
CPC: Content-pattern consistency loss. **LC**: Label consistency loss. **DAE**: Domain-aware pattern encoder.

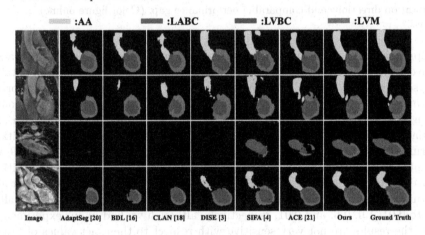

Fig. 3. Illustration of the BiUDA segmentation results by different methods on the MMWHS dataset [24]. The top two rows show the forward adaptation, while the bottom rows are the backward adaptations, respectively.

significantly narrows this gap, and achieves the lowest performance drops in both adaptation directions. To further show the effectiveness of our method, we visualize the segmentation results by ours and competing methods in Fig. 3 and Fig. 4 for qualitative comparisons. As we can see, the segmentations by our method are much closer to the ground truth, especially for the backward adaptation. To summarise, the comparative experiments indicate that our framework can effectively address the domain drop problem, which has been overlooked by other UDA methods. Accordingly, our proposed framework presents new SOTA results for BiUDA segmentation on both the MMWHS and MMAS datasets.

Ablation Study. We conduct ablation studies with incremental evaluations to validate the effectiveness of our novel modules, including the content-pattern consistency loss, the label consistency loss, and the domain-aware pattern encoder. The results on the MMWHS dataset are shown in Table 3. As we can

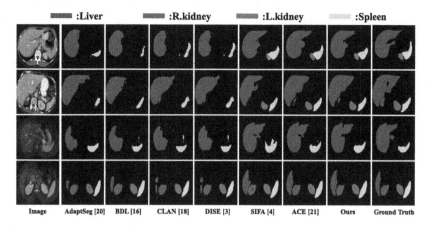

Fig. 4. Illustration of the BiUDA segmentation results by different methods on the MMAS dataset [12,14]. The top two rows show the forward adaptation, while the bottom rows are the backward adaptations, respectively.

see, after adding the content-pattern consistency loss, the average performance drop in Dice is reduced to 25.73%. In addition, the introduction of the label consistency loss further reduces the average drop to 12.98%, benefiting from pseudo training pairs in the target domain. Lastly, with the domain controller, the unified domain-aware pattern encoder learns pattern information from different modalities simultaneously, further reducing the average drop to 8.49%.

4   Discussion

In this section, we summarize existing SOTA UDA methods and discuss the differences of our proposed framework with them. The core idea of AdaptSegNet [20], BDL [16], and CLAN [18] is to align the source domain with the target domain in feature space. These approaches work effectively on data of similar patterns and contents (e.g., natural images), since it is easy to align features from domains closer to each other. However, for our multi-modal medical image data, the difference between modalities presents a sharp change. This sharp change makes the source domain far away from the target domain, and makes these feature-aligning methods fail to deliver a decent performance. In contrast, SIFA [4] was tailored for medical scenarios and proposed additional alignments in the image and annotation spaces. Nonetheless, it only works effectively in the easier UDA direction (i.e., MRI to CT on the MMWHS dataset) but yields restricted performance in the reverse, more difficult direction (i.e., CT to MRI on the MMWHS dataset), as shown in Fig. 2.

Making the model insensitive to different patterns for better UDA is a more elegant way. Specifically, we can explicitly make the model aware of the content and pattern of a given image, and then apply the pattern from the target domain to the content from the source domain for training the UDA model. For example, ACE [21] utilizes a VGG net to extract the pattern code from the target-domain image and then integrates it into the source-domain image for UDA training. In contrast, DISE [3] leverages DRPL to extract the content and pattern codes from input of two domains, and adopts the decompose-recompose training strategy for these codes to realize UDA. This method has been verified effective on the BiUDA problem thus has a great potential in medical imaging UDA application. Different from DISE with separated pattern encoders, we propose a unified encoder that helps the model better understand the pattern difference. As shown in Table 3, with the unified pattern encoder, the framework achieves about 4% reduction in Dice drop. In addition, under the supervision of the CPC and LC losses, the pattern codes extracted by our method are more effective than those extracted from the VGG net. For this reason, the proposed method outperforms DISE and ACE, as shown in Table 1 and Table 2.

5   Conclusion

This work presented a novel, DRPL-based BiUDA framework to address the domain drop problem. The domain-aware pattern encoder was proposed for obtaining representative pattern codes from both the source and target domains and meanwhile simplifying the network complexity. To minimize potential data distortion in the process of domain adaptation, the content-pattern consistency loss was devised. In addition, the label consistency loss was proposed to achieve higher UDA segmentation performance. The comparative experiments indicates that our framework achieves new SOTA results for the challenging BiUDA segmentation tasks on both MMWHS and MMAS datasets.

References

1. Avendi, M., Kheradvar, A., Jafarkhani, H.: A combined deep-learning and deformable-model approach to fully automatic segmentation of the left ventricle in cardiac MRI. Med. Image Anal. **30**, 108–119 (2016)
2. Bernard, O., et al.: Deep learning techniques for automatic MRI cardiac multi-structures segmentation and diagnosis: is the problem solved? IEEE Trans. Med. Imaging **37**(11), 2514–2525 (2018)
3. Chang, W.L., Wang, H.P., Peng, W.H., Chiu, W.C.: All about structure: adapting structural information across domains for boosting semantic segmentation. In: IEEE Conference on Computer Vision and Pattern Recognition, pp. 1900–1909 (2019)
4. Chen, C., Dou, Q., Chen, H., Qin, J., Heng, P.A.: Unsupervised bidirectional cross-modality adaptation via deeply synergistic image and feature alignment for medical image segmentation. IEEE Trans. Med. Imaging **39**(7), 2494–2505 (2020)
5. Dou, Q., et al.: PnP-AdaNet: plug-and-play adversarial domain adaptation network with a benchmark at cross-modality cardiac segmentation. arXiv preprint arXiv:1812.07907 (2018)
6. Fritscher, K., Raudaschl, P., Zaffino, P., Spadea, M.F., Sharp, G.C., Schubert, R.: Deep neural networks for fast segmentation of 3D medical images. In: Ourselin, S., Joskowicz, L., Sabuncu, M.R., Unal, G., Wells, W. (eds.) MICCAI 2016. LNCS, vol. 9901, pp. 158–165. Springer, Cham (2016). https://doi.org/10.1007/978-3-319-46723-8_19

7. Ganin, Y., Lempitsky, V.: Unsupervised domain adaptation by backpropagation. arXiv preprint arXiv:1409.7495 (2014)
8. Gong, B., Grauman, K., Sha, F.: Connecting the dots with landmarks: discriminatively learning domain-invariant features for unsupervised domain adaptation. In: International Conference on Machine Learning, pp. 222–230 (2013)
9. Goodfellow, I., et al.: Generative adversarial nets. In: Advances in Neural Information Processing Systems, pp. 2672–2680 (2014)
10. Huang, X., Belongie, S.: Arbitrary style transfer in real-time with adaptive instance normalization. In: IEEE International Conference on Computer Vision, pp. 1501–1510 (2017)
11. Huang, X., Liu, M.Y., Belongie, S., Kautz, J.: Multimodal unsupervised image-to-image translation. In: European Conference on Computer Vision, pp. 172–189 (2018)
12. Kavur, A.E., et al.: CHAOS challenge-combined (CT-MR) healthy abdominal organ segmentation. arXiv preprint arXiv:2001.06535 (2020)
13. Kermany, D.S., et al.: Identifying medical diagnoses and treatable diseases by image-based deep learning. Cell 172(5), 1122–1131 (2018)
14. Landman, B., Xu, Z., Igelsias, J., Styner, M., Langerak, T., Klein, A.: Multi-atlas labeling beyond the cranial vault. https://www.synapse.org (2015)
15. Lee, H.Y., Tseng, H.Y., Huang, J.B., Singh, M., Yang, M.H.: Diverse image-to-image translation via disentangled representations. In: European Conference on Computer Vision, pp. 35–51 (2018)
16. Li, Y., Yuan, L., Vasconcelos, N.: Bidirectional learning for domain adaptation of semantic segmentation. In: IEEE Conference on Computer Vision and Pattern Recognition, pp. 6936–6945 (2019)
17. Litjens, G., et al.: A survey on deep learning in medical image analysis. Med. Image Anal. 42, 60–88 (2017)
18. Luo, Y., Zheng, L., Guan, T., Yu, J., Yang, Y.: Taking a closer look at domain shift: category-level adversaries for semantics consistent domain adaptation. In: IEEE Conference on Computer Vision and Pattern Recognition, pp. 2507–2516 (2019)
19. Ronneberger, O., Fischer, P., Brox, T.: U-net: convolutional networks for biomedical image segmentation. In: Navab, N., Hornegger, J., Wells, W.M., Frangi, A.F. (eds.) MICCAI 2015. LNCS, vol. 9351, pp. 234–241. Springer, Cham (2015). https://doi.org/10.1007/978-3-319-24574-4_28
20. Tsai, Y.H., Hung, W.C., Schulter, S., Sohn, K., Yang, M.H., Chandraker, M.: Learning to adapt structured output space for semantic segmentation. In: IEEE Conference on Computer Vision and Pattern Recognition, pp. 7472–7481 (2018)
21. Wu, Z., Wang, X., Gonzalez, J.E., Goldstein, T., Davis, L.S.: ACE: adapting to changing environments for semantic segmentation. In: IEEE International Conference on Computer Vision, pp. 2121–2130 (2019)
22. Zhao, H., Shi, J., Qi, X., Wang, X., Jia, J.: Pyramid scene parsing network. In: IEEE Conference on Computer Vision and Pattern Recognition, pp. 2881–2890 (2017)
23. Zhu, J.Y., Park, T., Isola, P., Efros, A.A.: Unpaired image-to-image translation using cycle-consistent adversarial networks. In: IEEE International Conference on Computer Vision, pp. 2223–2232 (2017)
24. Zhuang, X., Shen, J.: Multi-scale patch and multi-modality atlases for whole heart segmentation of MRI. Med. Image Anal. 100(31), 77–87 (2016)

3D Nucleus Instance Segmentation
for Whole-Brain Microscopy Images

Junbo Ma[1], Oleh Krupa[2,3], Madison Rose Glass[2,3], Carolyn M. McCormick[2,3],
David Borland[4], Minjeong Kim[5], Jason L. Stein[2,3], and Guorong Wu[1,6(✉)]

[1] Department of Psychiatry, The University of North Carolina At Chapel Hill, Chapel Hill,
NC 27514, USA
guorong_wu@med.unc.edu
[2] UNC Neuroscience Center, The University of North Carolina At Chapel Hill, Chapel Hill, NC
27599, USA
[3] Department of Genetics, The University of North Carolina At Chapel Hill, Chapel Hill,
NC 27599, USA
[4] RENCI, The University of North Carolina At Chapel Hill, Chapel Hill, NC 27599, USA
[5] Department of Computer Science, The University of North Carolina At Greensboro,
Greensboro, NC 27412, USA
[6] Department of Computer Science, The University of North Carolina
At Chapel Hill, Chapel Hill, NC 27514, USA

Abstract. Tissue clearing and light-sheet microscopy technologies offer new
opportunities to quantify the three-dimensional (3D) neural structure at a cellular or even sub-cellular resolution. Although many efforts have been made to
recognize nuclei in 3D using deep learning techniques, current state-of-the-art
approaches often work in a two-step manner, i.e., first segment nucleus regions
within a 2D optical slice and then assemble the regions into the 3D instance of
a nucleus. Due to the poor inter-slice resolution in many volumetric microscopy
images and lack of contextual information across image slices, the current two-
step approaches yield less accurate instance segmentation results. To address these
limitations, a novel neural network for 3D nucleus *instance* segmentation (NIS) is
proposed, called NIS-Net, which jointly segments and assembles the 3D instances
of nuclei. Specifically, a pretext task is designed to predict the image appearance of
the to-be-processed slice using the learned context from the processed slices, where
the well-characterized contextual information is leveraged to guide the assembly
of 3D nuclei instances. Since our NIS-Net progressively identifies nuclei instances
by sliding over the entire image stack, our method is capable of segmenting nuclei
instances for the whole mouse brain. Experimental results show that our proposed
NIS-Net achieves higher accuracy and more reasonable nuclei instances than the
current counterpart methods.

Keywords: Nucleus instance segmentation · Light-sheet microscopy images ·
Self-supervised learning · Variational autoencoder · Deep learning

© Springer Nature Switzerland AG 2021
A. Feragen et al. (Eds.): IPMI 2021, LNCS 12729, pp. 504–516, 2021.
https://doi.org/10.1007/978-3-030-78191-0_39

1 Introduction

Recent advances in tissue clearing and light-sheet microscopy (TCLSM) technologies enable the acquisition of cellular resolution images of intact whole brain samples [12]. This is a great boon to brain structure studies since TCLSM enables us to characterize the three-dimensional (3D) arrangement of immunolabeled cells rather than slices limited to specific brain regions [16]. However, quantitatively analyzing these large-scale microscopy images has lagged behind the ability to acquire them, resulting in their most common use as visualizations rather than quantified results.

The most basic step in the quantification of brain structure involves counting nuclei in defined brain regions, co-localization with immunolabeled cell-type-specific markers, and comparison between groups defined by a biological condition, such as genotype [9, 14]. In this regard, a high-throughput computational method to delineate each nucleus in large-scale microscopy images is of high demand in the neuroscience field. This process includes two key steps: (1) segmentation of nucleus regions in each slice and (2) assembly of nucleus regions into the instance of the nucleus in 3D.

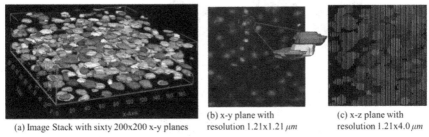

(a) Image Stack with sixty 200x200 x-y planes

(b) x-y plane with resolution 1.21x1.21 μm

(c) x-z plane with resolution 1.21x4.0 μm

Fig. 1. Typical tissue clearing and light-sheet microscopy images. Nucleus instance segmentation (NIS) aims to detecting and delineating each distinct 3D nucleus at the voxel level. (a) shows the 3D view of an image stack with manually annotated 3D nuclei masks. It has 60 image slices (z-axis), and each slice is a 200 × 200 pixel (x-y plane) gray-scale image. The color in (a) implies the unique identity of each nucleus. The image resolution is 1.21 × 1.21 × 4.0 μm. (b) shows a typical image slice (x-y plane) from the 3D image stack. The red circle shows an example of touching nuclei. (c) shows the slice-by-slice nature of the image stack in the x-z plane, where image artifacts across slices create challenges for 3D nucleus instance segmentation.

Regarding nucleus region segmentation, a plethora of efforts has been made to improve the accuracy and scalability of segmentation results, from classic deformable models [11] to recent deep learning techniques such as convolutional neural network (CNN) based approaches [7, 15, 18]. Since it is time-consuming and extremely laborious to have a large pool of manual annotations of 3D nuclei, the majority of current methods segment nucleus regions using 2D methods. To alleviate this issue, some works proposed to train the neural network with synthetic 3D nuclei samples [2]. However, the synthetic samples are biased on the synthetizing dataset and may not generalize well in real applications.

Although state-of-the-art deep learning techniques, such as 3D U-Net [15] and 3D Mask R-CNN [4], achieve great success in computer vision and medical imaging areas, they often yield less-accurate nucleus instance segmentation results in microscopy images due to the following two reasons. **(1) Anisotropic Image Resolution.** Since light-sheet microscopy images are acquired slice by slice, the intra-slice resolution (the x-y plane in Fig. 1(b)) is usually 2–10 times higher than the inter-slice resolution (the x-z plane in Fig. 1(c)), which leads to a significant amount of image artifacts such as discontinuous appearance and spurious boundaries. As shown in Fig. 1(a)(b) and Fig. 3(a), the large inter-slice gap leads to irregular and highly distorted 3D shapes of the nuclei. Since conventional deep neural networks for 3D nucleus region segmentation work under the assumption that image appearance is spatially smooth and image resolution is isotropic, their segmentation results are often sub-optimal. **(2) Densely Packed Nuclei.** As shown in Fig. 1(b), it is common that nuclei touch each other in certain cell-dense regions of the brain, such as the hippocampus. Disentangling individual nuclei within cell-dense regions is important in many neuroscience applications. However, it is very challenging to address this issue, partially due to the lack of 3D manual annotations of touching nuclei.

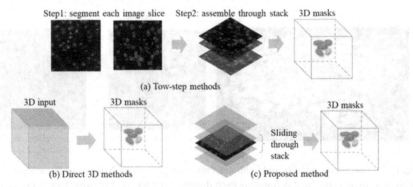

Fig. 2. A high-level sketch of various solutions for 3D nuclei instance segmentation. (a) Two-step methods first segment the 2D nucleus regions in each image slice, then assemble the 2D regions into 3D masks. (b) The end-to-end solution directly predicts 3D masks of all possible nucleus instances. (c) Our proposed method jointly segments nuclear regions and assembles the nuclear voxels into individual 3D nuclei instances by sliding over the image stack.

Regarding nucleus instance assembly, most of the current methods first segment the 2D masks of nuclei in each slice, then deploy a post hoc image processing algorithm such as watershed or region growing to delineate the 3D contour for each nucleus from the segmented 2D masks [7, 18]. However, due to the challenges shown in Fig. 3, it is difficult to assemble the nucleus regions into the 3D instance of nuclei without knowing the 3D context of the nuclei-to-nuclei relationship.

Figure 2 illustrates a high-level sketch of different strategies for 3D nuclei instance segmentation. Due to the large inter-slice gap and complex layout of nuclei in the 3D environment, conventional two-step methods Fig. 2(a) have very limited power to accurately assemble all identified nucleus regions at the voxel level to the nuclei instances. End-to-end direct 3D methods Fig. 2(b) seem like the ultimate solution for recognizing nuclei instances from a given image stack. However, the spatial relationships between nuclei in the image stack are highly complicated, not to mention the scenario of densely packed nuclei. Such challenges make the learning complexity in the end-to-end approach grow exponentially as the size of the image stack increases.

In contrast, our NIS-Net Fig. 2(c) segments 3D nucleus instances by progressively considering part of the 3D image stack in a sliding window manner and jointly segments and assembles 3D masks of nucleus instances throughout the sliding process. In this way, our NIS-Net avoids the limitations of either two-step or end-to-end methods and achieves comparable performance to human experts with very limited annotated training samples. Furthermore, our NIS-Net provides a flexible end-to-end 3D solution that is less demanding on 3D manual annotations but can be scaled up to whole-brain ($> 10^5$ voxels in each dimension) nucleus instance segmentation. We have evaluated the nucleus instance segmentation results from our NIS-Net on light-sheet microscopy images of the mouse brain. Compared to current state-of-the-art methods in Sect. 4, our NIS-Net achieves more accurate and reasonable 3D nuclei identification results, which indicates its applicability for neuroscience applications.

2   Problem Formulation

The 3D nucleus instance segmentation problem can be formally defined as follows: Given a 3D TCLSM image stack V that has T slices, $V = \{S_1, \ldots, S_T\}$, S_t is the t-th slice in the image stack V. The aim of NIS is to segment all the nucleus instances at the voxel level in the image stack. Suppose there are N nucleus instances in the image stack V. In an image slice S_t, we denote the 2D segmentation masks $M_t = \{m_{n,t}\}$ and their corresponding bounding boxes $B_t = \{b_{n,t}\}$. Segmentation mask $m_{n,t}$ is a binary representation of the nuclear regions in each image slice, where 1 means the corresponding pixel belonging to nucleus instance n. $id_{n,t}$ is the unique identity corresponding to $m_{n,t}$. Then, the segmentation masks in M with the same identity across the image stack can be assembled as the 3D mask of a nucleus.

There are three major challenges to this problem. The first one is the issue of the appearance gap between two consecutive slices. For example, in Fig. 3(a), the appearance gap leads to a significant shape change of the 2D masks from the same nucleus between adjacent slices. Also, from Fig. 3(a), we can see that the masks of the same nucleus only appear in very few slices. This is because the size of the nucleus is small compared to the physical distance between two image slices when acquiring the image stack. In our dataset, one nucleus usually lies across 5.4 slices on average, making the appearance gap issue much more challenging to solve. The second challenge is how to identify the segmentation mask belonging to the same nucleus at the voxel level. As shown in Fig. 3(b), there are 68 nucleus instances in this 200×200 image slice. Moreover, the instances crowded and touched each other in some areas, which makes it much harder to determine the mask boundaries between the touching nuclei instances, such as the red rectangle in Fig. 3(b) shows. The third challenge is that 3D shapes are highly diverse in the image stack, as the nuclei are flexible to change shape when crowding together. As shown in Fig. 3(c), these nuclei not only crowd within a slice but also across slices. Thus, the 3D shape of nuclei can change dramatically between slices when crowding together, which leads to more complex 3D structures and makes NIS more challenging to solve. An additional possible complication is a rare situation where one nucleus may have two or more non-connected segmentation masks in one image slice. Such a rare case may happen when a nucleus bends in 3D like a banana while the plane of an image slice coincidentally cuts the nucleus through its two ends without cutting the "body." In our current implementation, we assume one nucleus only has one segmentation mask in an image slice.

All these challenges make 3D NIS a unique problem. To address these challenges, a novel NIS-Net model is proposed in the next section.

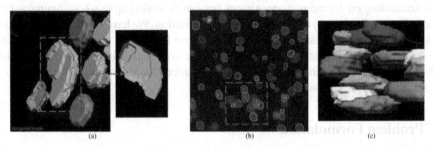

(a)   (b)   (c)

Fig. 3. Three challenging scenarios. (a) shows a nucleus's 2D mask shape changing dramatically through consecutive image slices. Also, we can see that nuclei only lie across very few slices. (b) shows the density of nuclei in one image slice. In the red rectangle area, nuclei crowded together. (c) shows the nuclei crowding and touching each other in 3D, making the NIS more challenging to solve.

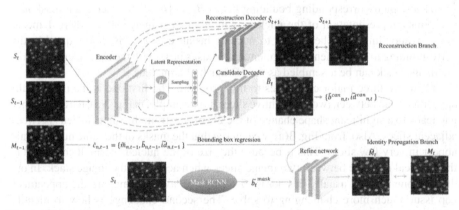

Fig. 4. The architecture of the proposed NIS-Net. It consists of two branches, the reconstruction branch and the identity propagation branch. The reconstruction branch aims to reconstruct the next image slice S_{t+1}, from the previous image slice S_{t-1} and current image slice S_t. This will force the model to encode the 3D context information in the adjacent slices. The identity propagation branch will first propagate the identities of existing nuclei in the previous slice to the current slice, then refine the masks and assign new identities to the newly arising nuclei. Masks with the same identity will be considered as coming from the same nucleus.

3   Proposed Model

As discussed in the previous sections, because of the high density of the instances, the large appearance gap, and the complex 3D structure, the 3D NIS problem is very challenging. To address these challenges, our approach fully explores the 3D context information between adjacent slices. Inspired by the self-supervised learning technique [5, 6, 10], a pretext task is specifically designed to ensure the model learns the 3D context information. The proposed model follows a Variational Autoencoder (VAE) architecture [8] with two branches, the reconstruction branch, and the identity propagation branch, as shown in Fig. 4. We will introduce them in detail in the following sections.

3.1   Encoder

The encoder of NIS-Net utilizes the Residual Neural Network (Res-Net) as the backbone to extract image features. It takes the previous image slice S_{t-1} and current image slice S_t as inputs and encodes them into a latent representation vector. Following the VAE's architecture, instead of producing a latent representation vector with actual values, the encoder produces a vector of means μ and a vector of standard derivations σ. Then, each element in the latent representation vector is sampled from the (μ, σ) pair. In this way, the generalization ability of the NIS-Net is expanded, and the requirement of a large amount of annotated samples is partially relaxed through the sampling process. However, the VAE itself cannot guarantee to focus on encoding the 3D successive information between slices. Thus, a specially designed pretext learning task is introduced into VAE in the reconstruction branch.

3.2   Reconstruction Branch

A pretext learning task is introduced into this branch, which aims to reconstruct the next image slice S_{t+1} based on the successive information learned from the previous slice S_{t-1} and current slice S_t. To ensure the reconstruction decoder successfully decode the latent representation into the next image slice S_{t+1}, the latent representation must have encoded enough successive 3D information between slices throughout the image stack.

   The reconstruction decoder is also implemented with residual blocks. Subpixel convolution [13] is utilized to perform up-sampling between residual blocks. However, in practice, because of the aliasing effect of up-sampling, the reconstructed images are usually very "blurry." To avoid this, we enhance the reconstruction branch by the spatial information extracted and preserved during the encoding process, which follows the implementation of the U-Net. The latent connections, as the dashed lines show in Fig. 4, can reduce the aliasing effect of up-sampling and enrich the texture details, thus, resulting in sharper reconstructed images. The mean square error (MSE) between the reconstructed image and the ground truth image is used as the loss function for this branch, which means we do not need extra annotation for this task, and this task learns from itself.

   By solving this pretext learning task, the proposed NIS-Net can focus on encoding more successive information into the latent representation, and the backbone Res-Net in Encoder can extract more spatially informative features passing through the latent connections. All this information is used to process the identities propagating between two adjacent slices throughout the image stack.

3.3 Identity Propagation Branch

The identity propagation branch has two steps. The first step aims to propagate existing identities $\left\{ \tilde{id}_{n,t-1} \right\}$ from the previous image slice S_{t-1} to the current slice S_t, which is performed by the candidate decoder, as shown in Fig. 4. The second step aims to deal with the newly arising nuclei in the current slice that do not exist in previous slices, which is performed by the refine network.

The candidate decoder has a similar implementation to the reconstruction decoder. It first decodes the latent representation learned by the encoder into a latent feature map. Then, following the bounding box regression implementation of Fast-RCNN [3], a Region of Interest Alignment (RoIAlign) network is used to find the most relevant areas. However, instead of relying on the region proposal network to generate the regions of interest (RoIs) on the latent feature map, we use the bounding boxes from the previous slice $B_{t-1} = \{b_{n,t-1}\}$ as the RoI. If a bounding box $\tilde{b}_{n,t}^{can}$ is detected with the region of the bounding box $b_{n,t-1}$, the identity of the detected bounding box $\tilde{id}_{n,t}^{can}$ will inherit the identity of $b_{n,t-1}$. Finally, the candidate decoder will produce a list of predicted bounding boxes and their corresponding identities $\left\{ \tilde{b}_{n,t}^{can}, \tilde{id}_{n,t}^{can} \right\}$.

As there may be newly arising nuclei in the current slice, a refine network is designed to solve this case. The first question is how to find these newly arisen nuclei. As Mask-RCNN has already achieved great success in the 2D nuclei segmentation task [18], we first run Mask-RCNN on the current slice S_t to produce another list of bounding boxes $\tilde{b}_t^{mask}$. Note that, since Mask-RCNN works solely on one 2D image slice, there will be no identities associated with these bounding boxes. With these two bounding box lists, $\left\{ \tilde{b}_{n,t}^{can}, \tilde{id}_{n,t}^{can} \right\}$ and $\left\{ \tilde{b}_{m,t}^{mask} \right\}$, the refine network first performs a matching between the two lists. The matching is based on the intersection over union (IoU) ratio between two boxes. Two boxes are considered as a match only if their IoU ratio is greater than a threshold τ. The optimal matching pairs set is obtained by the Hungarian algorithm. For the matched pairs, a new bounding box is created by the union of two boxes, and the same identity is assigned as the $\tilde{id}_{n,t}^{can}$. For the unmatched $\tilde{b}_{n,t}^{can}$, it will keep its identity $\tilde{id}_{n,t}^{can}$. For the unmatched $\tilde{b}_{m,t}^{mask}$, a new identity will be assigned to it, and this one is considered as the newly arisen nucleus. Finally, based on these bounding boxes, the pixel-level instance masks are produced following the implementation of the mask branch in Mask-RCNN [4].

The whole NIS-Net is jointly trained, which means that NIS-Net is backpropagated based on the sum of the three loss functions: (1) the MSE of the reconstruction loss, (2) the bounding box regression loss of the candidate decoder, and (3) the mask loss of the refine network. After all the instances are detected in the image stack, a list of masks and their corresponding identities are produced. Then, the 3D masks of the nuclei instances can be automatically assembled based on the instance identities of the 2D masks.

4 Experiments

As there are no publicly available annotated 3D TCLSM image stacks for the 3D NIS problem, we manually annotated 5 image stacks for our experiments. We use the tool proposed in [1] for annotation and 3D visualization. The details of the 5 image stacks can be found in the following section. The 2D quantitative metric follows the traditional mAP@IoU score from the computer vision field, which is the mean of the average precision (mAP) scores for all the segmentation categories above different levels of the Intersection over Union (IoU) value. The IoU value is calculated as the area of overlap divided by the area of union between the predicted masks and the ground truth masks.

4.1 Dataset

Table 1. The details of our manually annotated dataset.

	Stack1	Stack2	Stack3	Stack4	Stack5
2D Masks	4398	4522	2753	3728	3832
Nuclei	786	816	510	729	707

The dataset we are using in this paper is split from a TCLSM image stack of a whole mouse brain. For the acquisition of the TCLSM image stack, 1 mm paraformaldehyde (PFA) fixed sections of adult mice were processed according to the iDISCO + protocol. Sections were stained with nuclei dye To-Pro3 (1:400; Thermo Fisher), washed, and embedded in agarose blocks to maintain structural integrity during mounting. Light-sheet imaging was performed using a LaVision Ultramicroscope II equipped with a 2X MVPLAPO (0.5NA) objective. The light-sheet thickness was set to 4 μm, and the physical resolution of each voxel in the image stack is $1.21 \times 1.21 \times 4$ μm. We chose 5 sub-image stacks from the top and side of the cortex area and manually annotated the 3D nuclei masks. Each image stack has 60 image slices. Each image slice is a 200×200 pixels image. 2D masks and nuclei counts for the 5 annotated image stacks are listed in Table 1.

4.2 Experiment Setup

With only 5 annotated image stacks, it is impossible to train a complex 3D U-net or 3D Mask-RCNN, both of which require a larger dataset. Thus, in this paper, we focus only on comparing the proposed method with the two-step methods. For the 2D semantic segmentation step in each image slice, we specifically compare with the Mask-RCNN, as our proposed model already needs a fine-tuned Mask-RCNN. For the assembling step, we used the solutions of the top 3 winners in the CVPR 2020 multiple objects tracking challenge [19] and reported the best one to compare with our NIS-Net.

The metric for the 2D segmentation step follows the traditional mean average precision score (mAP). However, for the tracking step and the 3D nuclei segmentation, traditional evaluation metrics, such as the soft multi-object tracking and segmentation accuracy (sMOTSA) [17], do not work well. This is because these metrics are designed for relatively high frame-rate videos. As one instance may stay in the video for dozens of frames, the miss prediction in several frames will not decrease the metric score too much. However, in our dataset, one nucleus only lies in 5.4 consecutive image slices on average. Any miss prediction will significantly decrease the metric score. Furthermore, these metrics are designed with potential occlusions in mind. However, occlusion cannot happen in the NIS problem. If a nucleus stops appearing in one image slice, there will be no other part of this nucleus in future slices. Thus, in our paper, we use the Dice score to evaluate the 3D nuclei masks evaluation.

The Res-Net101 is used as the backbone for both Mask-RCNN and NIS-Net and initialized with the pre-trained weights on ImageNet. The convolution stride is set to 2, and the size of the convolution kernels is set to 3. 5-fold cross-validation is applied to all methods. In each fold, one image stack is left out for validation, and the other 4 image stacks are used for training. The average score is reported in the next section.

4.3 Results

The proposed NIS-Net itself needs a thoroughly fine-tuned Mask-RCNN to help refine the candidate masks. Thus, the first comparison is the mAP score of the predicted 2D masks between the proposed NIS-Net and Mask RCNN, as shown in Table 2. The mAP score of the proposed NIS-Net is consistently better than Mask-RCNN because the refinement network in the NIS-Net can reduce the miss predictions of Mask-RCNN by keeping the unmatched $\tilde{b}_{n,t}^{can}$. The unmatched $\tilde{b}_{n,t}^{can}$ originally come from the bounding box regression based on the bounding box regions in the previous slice. In other words, this advantage comes from the 3D information successively propagating between adjacent slices. The high mAP score at the lower IoU thresholds indicates the correct detection of nuclei. However, the mAP is significantly dropped at IoU 90%. In some image slices, only several predictions can get through the 90% IoU threshold. This is because it is much harder to exactly match the manual annotation at every voxel.

Figure 5 shows the 2D segmentation results of NIS-Net and the Mask-RCNN in the same area comparing with the manually annotated ground truth. In this area, Fig. 5 both NIS-Net and the Mask-RCNN work well in general Fig. 5(a)(c). In the more detailed comparison shown in Fig. 5(d)(e), our NIS-Net works better than Mask-RCNN in terms of IoU with ground truth. This is because our NIS-Net refines the results produced from both Mask-RCNN and our candidate decoder. In the heavily crowded area, Mask-RCNN mis-predicted the three nuclei as one nucleus, whereas our NIS-Net predicted three nuclei correctly. This may because our NIS-Net can utilize the 3D information successively from the previous slice to untangle the touching pixels.

Figure 6 shows the 3D segmentation results of NIS-Net, the ground truth, and the two-step method in the same area. As we can see, our NIS-Net did a better job matching the ground truth, even in the area exhibiting touching nuclei. As discussed in the previous sections, multiple object tracking methods are designed ideally for high framerate video data and with occlusions in mind; thus, these methods tend to aggressively connect the masks across the image stack. This is why the two-step methods have a low 3D Dice score.

Table 2. The quantitative comparison of the methods

mAP@IoU	50%	60%	70%	80%	90%	3D Dice
Mask-RCNN	0.9486 ± 0.0196	0.9230 ± 0.0234	0.8746 ± 0.0296	0.7592 ± 0.0541	0.3275 ± 0.1052	0.6095 ± 0.0714
NIS-Net	**0.9615 ± 0.0129**	**0.9443 ± 0.0140**	**0.9170 ± 0.0183**	**0.8392 ± 0.0316**	**0.4866 ± 0.0675**	**0.8184 ± 0.0397**
NIS-Net (no pretext)	0.9523 ± 0.0168	0.9269 ± 0.0213	0.8848 ± 0.0248	0.7733 ± 0.0435	0.4327 ± 0.0950	0.7349 ± 0.0641

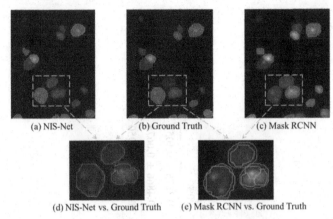

(a) NIS-Net   (b) Ground Truth   (c) Mask RCNN

(d) NIS-Net vs. Ground Truth   (e) Mask RCNN vs. Ground Truth

Fig. 5. Sample results of 2D segmentation. (a) (b) (c) shows the sample results of NIS-Net, Ground Truth, and Mask RCNN in the same area, respectively. The colors of masks are randomly generated. (d) (e) shows the detailed comparison. The green contour is the manually annotated ground truth. The red contour is the prediction of NIS-Net. The orange contour is the prediction of Mask-RCNN. It is clear that our NIS-Net works better than Mask RCNN in this area in terms of IoU. Also, Mask RCNN miss-predicted the three crowding nuclei as one.

(a) NIS-Net   (b) Ground Truth   (c) Two-step method

Fig. 6. The 3D results of the same area. Although the proposed method missed predicting one nucleus at the right-above corner, it did a much better job than the two-step method, which tends to connect more masks across the image stack.

Furthermore, we wanted to know how the pretext self-supervised learning task impacts the NIS-Net. Thus, we tested the NIS-Net without the reconstruction decoder. The 2D mAP score and 3D Dice score are reported in Table 2. The quantitative comparison of the methods Without the pretext learning task, the mAP score lies between the full NIS-Net and the Mask-RCNN, while nearer to the results of Mask-RCNN. This result implies that, without the pretext self-supervised learning task, the NIS-Net cannot fully exploit the successive 3D information, and the 2D segmentation power comes more from the Mask-RCNN rather than from the 3D successive information. The significant drop of the 3D Dice score also demonstrates the importance of the pretext self-supervised learning task in the 3D NIS problem.

5   Conclusion

3D nuclei instance segmentation (NIS) for tissue clearing and light-sheet microscopy (TCLSM) image stacks is a challenging problem due to the anisotropic resolution of the TCLSM image stacks, the irregular and highly diverse 3D shapes of the nuclei, and nuclei crowding. In this paper, a novel NIS-Net is proposed to solve this challenging problem via a sliding window methodology, significantly reducing the requirement of annotated 3D samples. Moreover, to fully explore the coherent 3D context information between two successive slices, a pretext learning task designed in a self-supervised learning manner is introduced into the NIS-Net, which enhanced the NIS-Net, focusing on encoding the successive information between adjacent slices. Experimental results demonstrated the effectiveness and efficiency of the proposed NIS-Net. Furthermore, our NIS-Net can be easily scaled up to solve the 3D NIS problem for whole-brain datasets, which we plan to address in our future work.

References

1. Borland, D., et al.: Segmentor: a tool for manual refinement of 3D microscopy annotations. bioRxiv (2021). https://doi.org/10.1101/2021.01.25.428119
2. Dunn, K.W., et al.: Deepsynth: three-dimensional nuclear segmentation of biological images using neural networks trained with synthetic data. Sci. Rep. **9**(1), 1–15 (2019)
3. Girshick, R.: Fast r-cnn. In: Proceedings of the IEEE International Conference on Computer Vision, pp. 1440–1448 (2015)
4. He, K., Gkioxari, G., Doll´ar, P., Girshick, R.: Mask r-cnn. In: Proceedings of the IEEE International Conference on Computer Vision, pp. 2961–2969 (2017)
5. Hendrycks, D., Mazeika, M., Kadavath, S., Song, D.: Using self-supervised learning can improve model robustness and uncertainty. In: Advances in Neural Information Processing Systems, pp. 15663–15674 (2019)
6. Jing, L., Tian, Y.: Self-supervised visual feature learning with deep neural networks: a survey. IEEE Trans. Pattern Anal. Mach. Intell. (2020)
7. Jung, H., Lodhi, B., Kang, J.: An automatic nuclei segmentation method based on deep convolutional neural networks for histopathology images. BMC Biomed. Eng. **1**(1), 24 (2019)
8. Kingma, D.P., Welling, M.: Auto-encoding variational bayes. In: 2nd International Conference on Learning Representations, ICLR2014, Banff, AB, Canada, April 14–16, 2014, Conference Track Proceedings (2014)
9. Lindsey, B.W., Douek, A.M., Loosli, F., Kaslin, J.: A whole brain staining, embedding, and clearing pipeline for adult zebrafish to visualize cell proliferation and morphology in 3-dimensions. Frontiers Neurosci. **11**, 750 (2018)
10. Misra, I., Maaten, L.v.d.: Self-supervised learning of pretext-invariant representations. In: Proceedings of the IEEE/CVF Conference on Computer Vision and Pattern Recognition, pp. 6707–6717 (2020)
11. Plissiti, M.E., Nikou, C.: Cell nuclei segmentation by learning a physically based deformable model. In: 2011 17th International Conference on Digital Signal Processing (DSP), pp. 1–6. IEEE (2011)
12. Richardson, D.S., Lichtman, J.W.: Clarifying tissue clearing. Cell **162**(2), 246–257 (2015)
13. Shi, W., et al.: Real-time single image and video super-resolution using an efficient subpixel convolutional neural network. In: Proceedings of the IEEE Conference on Computer Vision and Pattern Recognition, pp. 1874–1883 (2016)

14. Susaki, E.A., et al.: Whole-brain imaging with single-cell resolution using chemical cocktails and computational analysis. Cell **157**(3), 726–739 (2014)
15. Tokuoka, Y., et al.: 3D convolutional neural networks-based segmentation to acquire quantitative criteria of the nucleus during mouse embryogenesis. NPJ Syst. Biol. Appl. **6**(1), 1–12 (2020)
16. Vigouroux, R.J., Belle, M., Chédotal, A.: Neuroscience in the third dimension: shedding new light on the brain with tissue clearing. Mol. Brain **10**, 33 (2017)
17. Voigtlaender, P., Krause, M., Osep, A., Luiten, J., Sekar, B.B.G., Geiger, A.,Leibe, B.: Mots: Multi-object tracking and segmentation. In: Proceedings of theIEEE/CVF Conference on Computer Vision and Pattern Recognition, pp. 7942–7951 (2019)
18. Zaki, G., et al.: A deep learning pipeline for nucleus segmentation. Cytometry Part A **97**(12), 1248–1264 (2020)
19. CVPR 2020 MOTS Challenge. https://motchallenge.net/results/CVPR_2020_MOTS_Challenge/

Teach Me to Segment with Mixed Supervision: Confident Students Become Masters

Jose Dolz[1,2]([✉]), Christian Desrosiers[1], and Ismail Ben Ayed[1,2]([✉])

[1] ETS Montreal, Montreal, Canada
{jose.dolz,ismail.benayed}@etsmtl.ca
[2] CRCHUM Montreal, Montreal, Canada

Abstract. Deep neural networks have achieved promising results in a breadth of medical image segmentation tasks. Nevertheless, they require large training datasets with pixel-wise segmentations, which are expensive to obtain in practice. Mixed supervision could mitigate this difficulty, with a small fraction of the data containing complete pixel-wise annotations, while the rest being less supervised, e.g., only a handful of pixels are labeled. In this work, we propose a dual-branch architecture, where the upper branch (teacher) receives strong annotations, while the bottom one (student) is driven by limited supervision and guided by the upper branch. In conjunction with a standard cross-entropy over the labeled pixels, our novel formulation integrates two important terms: (i) a Shannon entropy loss defined over the less-supervised images, which encourages confident student predictions at the bottom branch; and (ii) a Kullback-Leibler (KL) divergence, which transfers the knowledge from the predictions generated by the strongly supervised branch to the less-supervised branch, and guides the entropy (student-confidence) term to avoid trivial solutions. Very interestingly, we show that the synergy between the entropy and KL divergence yields substantial improvements in performances. Furthermore, we discuss an interesting link between Shannon-entropy minimization and standard pseudo-mask generation, and argue that the former should be preferred over the latter for leveraging information from unlabeled pixels. Through a series of quantitative and qualitative experiments, we show the effectiveness of the proposed formulation in segmenting the left-ventricle endocardium in MRI images. We demonstrate that our method significantly outperforms other strategies to tackle semantic segmentation within a mixed-supervision framework. More interestingly, and in line with recent observations in classification, we show that the branch trained with reduced supervision and guided by the top branch largely outperforms the latter.

Keywords: Mixed supervision · Segmentation · Deep learning

1 Introduction

The advent of deep learning has led to the emergence of high-performance algorithms, which have achieved a remarkable success in a wide span of medical image

© Springer Nature Switzerland AG 2021
A. Feragen et al. (Eds.): IPMI 2021, LNCS 12729, pp. 517–529, 2021.
https://doi.org/10.1007/978-3-030-78191-0_40

segmentation tasks [10, 22, 29]. One key factor for these advances is the access to large training datasets with high-quality, fully-labeled segmentations. Nevertheless, obtaining such annotations is a cumbersome process, which is prone to observer variability and, in the case of medical images, requires additional expertise. To alleviate the need for large labeled datasets, weakly supervised learning has recently emerged as an appealing alternative. In this scenario, one has access to a large amount of weakly labeled data, which can come in the form of bounding boxes [17, 28], scribbles [21], image tags [20] or anatomical priors [16, 26]. However, even though numerous attempts have been done to train segmentation models from weak supervision, most of them still fall behind their supervised counterparts, limiting their applicability in real-world settings.

Another promising learning scenario is mixed supervision, where only a small fraction of data is densely annotated, and a larger dataset contains less-supervised images. In this setting, which enables to keep the annotation budget under control, strongly-labeled data –where all pixels are annotated– can be combined with images presenting weaker forms of supervision. Prior literature [20, 28] has focused mainly on leveraging weak annotations to generate accurate initial pixel-wise annotations, or *pseudo-masks*, which are then combined with strong supervisions to augment the training dataset. The resulting dataset is employed to train a segmentation network, mimicking fully supervised training. Nevertheless, we argue that treating both equally in a single branch may result in limited improvements, as the less-supervised data is underused. Other approaches resort to multi-task learning [24, 31, 33], where the mainstream task (i.e., segmentation) is assisted by auxiliary objectives that are typically integrated in the form of localization or classification losses. While multi-task learning might enhance the common representation for both tasks in the feature space, this strategy has some drawbacks. First, the learning of relevant features is driven by commonalities between the multiple tasks, which may generate suboptimal representations for the mainstream task. Secondly, the specific task objectives do not enable direct interactions between the multi-stream outputs. This impedes, for example, explicitly enforcing consistency on the predictions between multiple branches, which, as we show in our experiments, significantly improves the results.

Motivated by these observations, we propose a novel formulation for learning with mixed supervision in medical image segmentation. Particularly, our dual-branch network imposes separate processing of the strong and weak annotations, which prevents direct interference of different supervision cues. As the uncertainty of the predictions at the unlabeled pixels remains high, we enhance our loss with the Shannon entropy, which enforces high-confidence predictions. Furthermore, in contrast to prior works [24, 31, 33], which have overlooked the co-operation between multiple branches' predictions by considering independent multi-task objectives, we introduce a Kullback-Leibler (KL) divergence term. The benefits of the latter are two-fold. First, it transfers the knowledge from the predictions generated by the strongly supervised branch (teacher) to the less-supervised branch (student). Second, it guides the entropy (student-confidence) term to avoid trivial solutions. Very interestingly, we show that the synergy between the entropy and KL term yields substantial improvements in performances. Furthermore, we discuss an interesting link between Shannon-entropy minimization and pseudo-mask generation, and argue that the former should be preferred over the latter for leveraging information from unlabeled pixels. We report comprehensive experiments and comparisons with other strategies for learning with mixed supervision, which show the effectiveness of our novel formulation. An interesting finding is that the branch receiving weaker supervision considerably outperforms the strongly supervised branch. This phenomenon, where **the student surpasses the teacher's performance**, is in line with recent observations in the context of image classification.

2   Related Work

Mixed-Supervised Segmentation. An appealing alternative to training CNNs with large labeled datasets is to combine a reduced number of fully-labeled images with a larger set of images with reduced annotations. These annotations can come in the form of bounding boxes, scribbles or image tags, for example[1]. A large body of the literature in this learning paradigm addresses the problem from a multi-task objective perspective [5,13,24,31,33], which might hinder their capabilities to fully leverage joint information for the mainstream objective. Furthermore, these methods typically require carefully-designed task-specific architectures, which also integrate task-dependent auxiliary losses, limiting the applicability to a wider range of annotations. For example, the architecture designed in [31] requires, among others, landmark annotations, which might be difficult to obtain in many applications. More recently, Luo et al. [23] promoted the use of a dual-branch architecture to deal separately with strongly and weakly labeled data. Particularly, while the strongly supervised branch is governed by available fully annotated masks, the weakly supervised branch receives supervision from a proxy ground-truth generator, which requires some extra information, such as class labels. While we advocate the use of independent branches to process naturally different kinds of supervision, we believe that this alone is insufficient, and may lead to suboptimal results. Thus, our work differs from [23] in several aspects. First, we make a better use of the labeled images by enforcing consistent segmentations between the strongly and weakly supervised branches on these images. Furthermore, we enforce confident predictions at the weakly supervised branch by minimizing the Shannon entropy of the softmax predictions.

Distilling Knowledge in Semantic Segmentation. Transferring knowledge from one model to another has recently gained attention in segmentation tasks. For example, the teacher-student strategy has been employed in model compression [1], to distil knowledge from multi-modal to mono-modal segmentation networks [14], or in domain adaptation [34]. Semi-supervised segmentation has also benefited from teacher-student architectures [8,30]. In these approaches,

---

[1] Note that this type of supervision differs from semi-supervised methods, which leverage a small set of labeled images and a much larger set of unlabeled images.

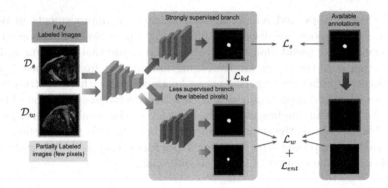

Fig. 1. Overview of the proposed method. Both fully and partial labeled images are fed to the network. The top branch generates predictions for fully labeled images, whereas the bottom branch generates the outputs for partially labeled images. Furthermore, the bottom branch also generates segmentations for the fully labeled images, which are guided by the KL term between the two branches.

however, the segmentation loss evaluating the consistency between the teacher and student models is computed on the unannotated data. A common practice, for example, is to add additive Gaussian noise to the unlabeled images, and enforce similar predictions for the original and noised images. This contrasts with our method, which enforces consistency only on the strongly labeled data, thereby requiring less additional images to close the gap with full supervision.

3   Methodology

Let us denote the set of training images as $\mathcal{D} = \{(\mathbf{X}_n, \mathbf{Y}_n)\}_n$, where $\mathbf{X}_i \in \mathbb{R}^{\Omega_i}$ represents the ith image and $\mathbf{Y}_i \in \{0,1\}^{\Omega_i \times C}$ its corresponding ground-truth segmentation mask. Ω_i denotes the spatial image domain and C the number of segmentation classes (or regions). We assume the dataset has two subsets: $\mathcal{D}_s = \{(\mathbf{X}_1, \mathbf{Y}_1), ..., (\mathbf{X}_m, \mathbf{Y}_m)\}$, which contains complete pixel-level annotations of the associated C categories, and $\mathcal{D}_w = \{(\mathbf{X}_{m+1}, \mathbf{Y}_{m+1}), ..., (\mathbf{X}_n, \mathbf{Y}_n)\}$, whose labels can take the form of semi- or weakly-supervised annotations. Furthermore, for each image $\mathbf{X}_i$ in $\mathcal{D} = \mathcal{D}_s \cup \mathcal{D}_w$, $\mathbf{P}_i \in [0,1]^{\Omega_i \times C}$ denotes the softmax probability outputs of the network, i.e., the matrix containing a simplex column vector $\mathbf{p}_i^l = \left(p_i^{l,1}, ..., p_i^{l,C}\right)^T \in [0,1]^C$ for each pixel $l \in \Omega_i$. Note that we omit the parameters of the network here to simplify notation.

3.1   Multi-branch Architecture

The proposed architecture is composed of multiple branches, each dedicated to a specific type of supervision (see Fig. 1). It can be divided in two components: a shared feature extractor and independent but identical decoding networks (one per type of supervision), which differ in the type of annotations received. Even though the proposed multi-branch architecture has similarities with the recent work in [23], there exist significant differences, particularly in the loss functions, which leads to different optimization scenarios.

3.2 Supervised Learning

The top-branch is trained under the fully-supervised paradigm, where a set of training images containing pixel-level annotations for all the pixels is given, i.e., $\mathcal{D}_s$. The problem amounts to minimizing with respect to the network parameters a standard full-supervision loss, which typically takes the form of a cross-entropy:

$$\mathcal{L}_s = -\sum_{i=1}^{m} \sum_{l \in \Omega_i} (\mathbf{y}_i^l)^T \log \left(\mathbf{p}_i^l\right)_{\text{top}} \tag{1}$$

where row vector $\mathbf{y}_i^l = \left(y_i^{l,1}, \ldots, y_i^{l,C}\right) \in \{0,1\}^C$ describes the ground-truth annotation for pixel $l \in \Omega_i$. Here, notation $(.)_{\text{top}}$ refers to the softmax outputs of the top branch of the network.

3.3 Not So-Supervised Branch

We consider the scenario where only the labels for a handful of pixels are known, i.e., scribbles or points. Particularly, we use the dataset $\mathcal{D}_w$ whose pixel-level labels are partially provided. Furthermore, for each image on the labeled training set, $\mathcal{D}_s$, we generate partially supervised labels (more details in the experiments' section), which are added to augment the dataset $\mathcal{D}_w$. Then, for the partially-labeled set of pixels, which we denote $\Omega_i^{\text{partial}}$ for each image $i \in \{1, \ldots n\}$, we can resort to the following partial-supervision loss, which takes the form of a cross-entropy on the fraction of labeled pixels:

$$\mathcal{L}_w = -\sum_{i=1}^{n} \sum_{l \in \Omega_i^{\text{partial}}} (\mathbf{y}_i^l)^T \log \left(\mathbf{p}_i^l\right)_{\text{bottom}} \tag{2}$$

where notation $(.)_{\text{bottom}}$ refers to the softmax outputs of the bottom branch of the network.

3.4 Distilling Strong Knowledge

In addition to the specific supervision available at each branch, we transfer the knowledge from the teacher (top branch) to the student (bottom branch). This is done by forcing the softmax distributions from the bottom branch to mimic the probability predictions generated by the top branch for the fully labeled images in $\mathcal{D}_s$. This knowledge-distillation regularizer takes the form of a Kullback-Leibler divergence ($\mathcal{D}_{KL}$) between both distributions:

$$\mathcal{L}_{kd} = \sum_{i=1}^{m} \sum_{l \in \Omega_i} \mathcal{D}_{KL} \left(\left(\mathbf{p}_i^l \right)_{\text{top}} \| \left(\mathbf{p}_i^l \right)_{\text{bottom}} \right) \tag{3}$$

where $\mathcal{D}_{KL}(\mathbf{p}\|\mathbf{q}) = \mathbf{p}^T \log \frac{\mathbf{p}}{\mathbf{q}}$, with T denoting the transpose operator.

3.5 Shannon-Entropy Minimization

Finally, we encourage high confidence in the student softmax predictions for the partially labeled images by minimizing the Shannon entropy of the predictions on the bottom branch:

$$\mathcal{L}_{ent} = \sum_{i=m+1}^{n} \sum_{l \in \Omega_i} \mathcal{H}\left(\mathbf{p}_i^l\right) \tag{4}$$

where $\mathcal{H}(\mathbf{p}) = -\mathbf{p}^T \log \mathbf{p}$ denotes the Shannon entropy of distribution $\mathbf{p}$.

Entropy minimization is widely used in semi-supervised learning (SSL) and transductive classification [4,6,9,12] to encourage confident predictions at unlabeled data points. Figure 2 plots the entropy in the case of a two-class distribution $(p, 1 - p)$, showing how the minimum is reached at the vertices of the simplex, i.e., when $p = 0$ or $p = 1$. However, surprisingly, in segmentation, entropy is not commonly used, except a few recent works in the different contexts of SSL and domain adaptation [2,27,32]. As we will see in our experiments, we found that the synergy between the entropy term for confident students, $\mathcal{L}_{ent}$, and the student-

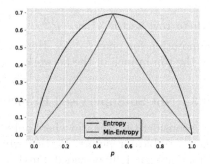

Fig. 2. Shannon entropy (blue) and min-entropy (red) for a two-class distribution $(p, 1-p)$, with $p \in [0, 1]$. (Color figure online)

teacher knowledge transfer term, $\mathcal{L}_{kd}$, yield substantial increases in performances. Furthermore, in the following, we discuss an interesting link between *pseudo-mask generation*, common in the segmentation literature, and entropy minimization, showing that the former could be viewed as a proxy for minimizing the latter. We further provide insights as to why entropy minimization should be preferred for leveraging information from the set of unlabeled pixels.

3.6 Link Between Entropy and Pseudo-mask Supervision

In the weakly- and semi-supervised segmentation literature, a very dominant technique to leverage information from unlabeled pixels is to generate pseudo-masks and use these as supervision in a cross-entropy training, in an alternating way [18,21,25]. This self-supervision principle is also well known in classification [19]. Given pixel-wise predictions $\mathbf{p}_i^l = (p_i^{l,1}, \dots, p_i^{l,C})$, pseudo-masks $q_i^{l,k}$ are generated as follows: $q_i^{l,k} = 1$ if $p_i^{l,k} = \max_c p_i^{l,c}$ and 0 otherwise. By plugging these pseudo-labels in a cross-entropy loss, it is easy to see that this corresponds to minimizing the *min-entropy*, $\mathcal{H}_{\min}(\mathbf{p}_i^l) = -\log(\max_c p_i^{l,c})$, which is a lower bound on the Shannon entropy; see the red curve in Fig. 2. Figure 2 provides a good insight as to why entropy should be preferred over min-entropy (pseudo-masks) as a training loss for unlabeled data points, and our experiments confirm this. With entropy, the gradients of un-confident predictions at the middle of the simplex are small and, therefore, dominated by the other terms at the beginning of training. However, with min-entropy, the inaccuracies resulting from un-confident predictions are re-inforced (pushed towards the simplex vertices), yielding early/unrecoverable errors in the predictions, which might mislead training. This is a well-known limitation of self-supervision in the SSL literature [7].

3.7 Joint Objective

Our final loss function takes the following form:

$$\mathcal{L}_t = \mathcal{L}_s + \lambda_w \mathcal{L}_w + \lambda_{kd} \mathcal{L}_{kd} + \lambda_{ent} \mathcal{L}_{ent}$$

where λ_w, λ_{kd} and λ_{ent} balance the importance of each term.

4   Experimental Setting

Benchmark Dataset. We focused on the task of left ventricular (LV) endocardium segmentation on cine MRI images. Particularly, we used the training set from the publicly available data of the 2017 ACDC Challenge [3], which consists of 100 cine magnetic resonance (MR) exams covering several well defined pathologies, each exam containing acquisitions only at the diastolic and systolic phases. We split this dataset into 80 exams for training, 5 for validation and the remaining 15 for testing.

Generating Partially Labeled Images. The training exams are divided into a small set of fully labeled images, $\mathcal{D}_s$, and a larger set of images with reduced supervision, $\mathcal{D}_w$, where only a handful of pixels are labeled. Concretely, we employ the same partial labels as in [15,16]. To evaluate how increasing the amount of both fully and partially labeled affects the performance, we evaluated the proposed models in three settings, referred to as *Set-3*, *Set-5*, and *Set-10*. In these settings, the number of fully labeled images is 3, 5 and 10, respectively, while the number of images with partial labels is ×5 times the number of labeled images.

Evaluation Metrics. For evaluation purposes, we employ two well-known metrics in medical image segmentation: the Dice similarity score (DSC) and the modified Hausdorff-Distance (MHD). Particularly, the MHD represents the $95th$ percentile of the symmetric HD between the binary objects in two images.

Baseline Methods. To demonstrate the efficiency of the proposed model, we compared to several baselines. First, we include fully-supervised baselines that will act as lower and upper bounds. The lower bound employs only a small set of fully labeled images (either 3, 5 or 10, depending on the setting), whereas the upper bound considers all the available training images. Then, we consider a single-branch network, referred to as *Single*, which receives both fully and partially labeled images without making distinction between them. To assess the impact of decoupling the branches without further supervision, similar to [23], we modify the baseline network by integrating two independent decoders, while the encoder remains the same. This model, which we refer to as *Decoupled*, is governed by different types of supervision at each branch. Then, our first model, which we refer to as *KL*, integrates the KL divergence term presented in Eq. (3). Last, *KL+Ent* corresponds to the whole proposed model, which couples the two important terms in Eqs. (3) and (4) in the formulation.

Implementation Details. We employed UNet as backbone architecture for the single branch models. Regarding the dual-branch architectures, we modified the decoding path of the standard UNet to accommodate two separate branches. All the networks are trained during 500 epochs by using Adam optimizer, with a batch size equal to 8. We empirically set the values of λ_w, λ_{kd} and λ_{ent} to 0.1, 50 and 1, respectively. We found that our formulation provided the best results when the input distributions to the KL term in Eq. (3) were very smooth, which was achieved by applying softmax over the softmax predictions. All the hyper-parameters were fixed by using the independent validation set. Furthermore, we perform 3 runs for each model and report the average values. The code was implemented in PyTorch, and all the experiments were performed in a server equipped with an NVIDIA Titan RTX.

4.1   Results

Main Results. Table 1 reports the quantitative evaluation of the proposed method compared to the different baselines.

First, we observe that across all the settings, simply adding partial annotations to the training set does not considerably improve the segmentation performance. Nevertheless, by integrating the guidance from the upper branch, the network is capable of leveraging additional partially-labeled images more efficiently, through the bottom branch. Furthermore, if we couple the KL divergence term with an objective based on minimizing the entropy of the predictions on the partially labeled images, the segmentation performance substantially increases. Particularly, the gain obtained by the complete model is consistent across the several settings, improving the DSC by 6–12% compared to the *KL* model, and reducing the MHD by nearly 30%. Compared to the baseline dual-branch model, i.e., *Decoupled*, our approach brings improvements of 10–20% in terms of DSC and reduces the MHD values by 30–40%. These results demonstrate the strong capabilities of the proposed model to leverage fully and partially labeled images during training. It is noteworthy to mention that findings on these results, where **the student surpasses the teacher**, aligns with recent observations in classification [11,35].

Table 1. Results on the testing set for the *top* and *bottom* branches (when applicable). Results are averaged over three runs.

Setting	Model	FS	PS	Top DSC	Top HD-95	Bottom DSC	Bottom HD-95
Set-3	Lower bound	✓	–	54.66	80.05	–	–
	Single	✓	✓	57.42	78.80	–	–
	Decoupled [23]	✓	✓	56.61	74.95	5.01	120.06
	Ours (KL)	✓	✓	56.39	63.27	63.98	67.67
	Ours (KL+Ent)	✓	✓	69.25	49.93	**75.92**	**30.12**
Set-5	Lower bound	✓	–	69.71	51.75	–	–
	Single	✓	✓	70.73	51.34	–	–
	Decoupled [23]	✓	✓	70.96	54.42	4.29	127.68
	Ours (KL)	✓	✓	67.96	44.01	72.69	40.75
	Ours (KL+Ent)	✓	✓	67.10	45.28	**78.77**	**23.29**
Set-10	Lower bound	✓	–	78.28	44.16	–	–
	Single	✓	✓	78.17	42.99	–	–
	Decoupled [23]	✓	✓	77.53	32.23	4.58	125.36
	Ours (KL)	✓	✓	80.60	27.19	82.21	33.96
	Ours (KL+Ent)	✓	✓	83.96	30.71	**88.07**	**4.37**
All images	Upper bound	✓	–	93.31	3.46	–	–

FS and PS indicate full or partial supervised images.

Comparison with Proposals. As mentioned previously, a popular paradigm in weakly and semi-supervised segmentation is to resort to pseudo-masks generated by a trained model, which are used to re-train the network, thereby mimicking full supervision. To demonstrate that our model leverages more efficiently the available data, we train a network with the proposals generated by the *Lower bound* and *KL* models, whose results are reported in Table 2. We can observe that, despite improving the base model, minimizing the cross-entropy over proposals does not outperform directly minimizing the entropy of the predictions of the partially labeled images.

Ablation Study on the Importance of the KL Term. The objective of this ablation study is to assess the effect of balancing the importance of the KL term in our formulation. Particularly, the KL term plays a crucial role in the proposed formulation, as it guides the Shannon entropy term during training to avoid degenerate solutions. We note that the value of the KL term is typically 2 orders of magnitude smaller than the entropy objective. Therefore, by setting its weight (λ_{kl}) to 1, we demonstrate empirically its crucial role during training

Table 2. Results obtained by training on an augmented dataset composed by fully labeled images and proposals generated from the *Lower bound* and *KL* models (Results obtained by both are reported in Table 1).

	Proposals (Lower bound)		Proposals (KL)		Ours (KL+Ent)	
Setting	DSC	HD-95	DSC	HD-95	DSC	HD-95
Set-3	63.11	49.99	70.94	45.32	**75.92**	**30.12**
Set-5	73.91	45.54	75.06	40.62	**78.77**	**23.29**
Set-10	81.31	29.95	82.78	24.36	**88.07**	**4.37**

when coupled with the entropy term. In this setting ($\lambda_{kl} = 1$), the entropy term strongly dominates the training, impacting negatively the model, particularly when fully-labeled images are scarce, i.e., *Set-3*. This confirms our hypothesis that minimizing the entropy alone results in degenerated solutions. Increasing the weight of the KL term typically alleviates this issue. However, when much importance is given to this objective, the performance also degrades. This is likely due to the fact that the bottom branch is strongly encouraged to follow the behaviour of the top branch, and to the effect of the entropy term being diminished (Table 3).

Table 3. Impact of λ_{kl} on the proposed formulation.

	Set-3		Set-5		Set-10	
	DSC	HD-95	DSC	HD-95	DSC	HD-95
$\lambda_K = 1$	24.89	117.52	46.30	82.89	73.88	38.23
$\lambda_K = 10$	64.42	67.47	59.16	58.01	78.66	31.79
$\lambda_K = 20$	72.30	47.52	70.47	37.84	83.47	16.97
$\lambda_K = 50$	**75.92**	**30.12**	**78.77**	**23.29**	**88.07**	**4.37**
$\lambda_K = 100$	60.64	71.62	66.01	43.83	84.34	16.60

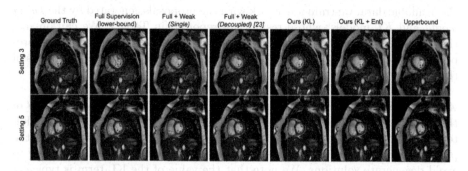

Fig. 3. Qualitative results for the analyzed models under two different settings.

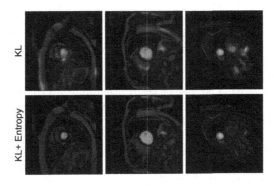

Fig. 4. Probability maps obtained by the proposed KL and $KL + Ent$ models.

Qualitative Results. In addition to the numerical results presented, we also depict qualitative results in Fig. 3 and Fig. 4. Particularly, Fig. 3 depicts the segmentation results for the models evaluated in Table 1. We can observe that segmentation results obtained by models with a single network typically undersegment the object of interest (*first row*) or generate many false positives (*second row*). Decoupling the decoding branches might reduce the false positive rate, however, it also tends to undersegment the target. Finally, we observe that both of our formulations achieve qualitatively better segmentation results, with the $KL+Ent$ model yielding segmentations similar to those generated by the upper bound model. Furthermore, in Fig. 4, we illustrate additional qualitative results of our models. We observe that, without the entropy term, our model produces less confident predictions.

References

1. Bar, A., Huger, F., Schlicht, P., Fingscheidt, T.: On the robustness of redundant teacher-student frameworks for semantic segmentation. In: CVPRW (2019)
2. Bateson, M., Kervadec, H., Dolz, J., Lombaert, H., Ben Ayed, I.: Source-relaxed domain adaptation for image segmentation. In: Martel, A.L., et al. (eds.) MICCAI 2020. LNCS, vol. 12261, pp. 490–499. Springer, Cham (2020). https://doi.org/10.1007/978-3-030-59710-8_48
3. Bernard, O., et al.: Deep learning techniques for automatic MRI cardiac multi-structures segmentation and diagnosis: is the problem solved? IEEE TMI **37**(11), 2514–2525 (2018)
4. Berthelot, D., Carlini, N., Goodfellow, I., Papernot, N., Oliver, A., Raffel, C.A.: Mixmatch: a holistic approach to semi-supervised learning. In: NeurIPS (2019)
5. Bhalgat, Y., Shah, M., Awate, S.: Annotation-cost minimization for medical image segmentation using suggestive mixed supervision fully convolutional networks. In: Medical Imaging Meets NeurIPS Workshop (2018)
6. Boudiaf, M., Ziko, I., Rony, J., Dolz, J., Piantanida, P., Ben Ayed, I.: Information maximization for few-shot learning. NeurIPS (2020)
7. Chapelle, O., Scholkopf, B., Zien, A.: Semi-supervised learning. IEEE Trans. Neural Networks **20**(3), 542–542 (2009)

8. Cui, W., et al.: Semi-supervised brain lesion segmentation with an adapted mean teacher model. In: IPMI, pp. 554–565 (2019)
9. Dhillon, G.S., Chaudhari, P., Ravichandran, A., Soatto, S.: A baseline for few-shot image classification. In: ICLR (2019)
10. Dolz, J., Desrosiers, C., Ayed, I.B.: 3D fully convolutional networks for subcortical segmentation in MRI: a large-scale study. NeuroImage **170**, 456–470 (2018)
11. Furlanello, T., Lipton, Z., Tschannen, M., Itti, L., Anandkumar, A.: Born again neural networks. In: ICML (2018)
12. Grandvalet, Y., Bengio, Y.: Semi-supervised learning by entropy minimization. In: NeurIPS (2005)
13. Hong, S., Noh, H., Han, B.: Decoupled deep neural network for semi-supervised semantic segmentation. In: NeurIPS (2015)
14. Hu, M., et al.: Knowledge distillation from multi-modal to mono-modal segmentation networks. In: Martel, A.L., et al. (eds.) MICCAI 2020. LNCS, vol. 12261, pp. 772–781. Springer, Cham (2020). https://doi.org/10.1007/978-3-030-59710-8_75
15. Kervadec, H., Dolz, J., Granger, É., Ben Ayed, I.: Curriculum semi-supervised segmentation. In: Shen, D.D., et al. (eds.) MICCAI 2019. LNCS, vol. 11765, pp. 568–576. Springer, Cham (2019). https://doi.org/10.1007/978-3-030-32245-8_63
16. Kervadec, H., Dolz, J., Tang, M., Granger, E., Boykov, Y., Ayed, I.B.: Constrained-CNN losses for weakly supervised segmentation. MedIA **54**, 88–99 (2019)
17. Kervadec, H., Dolz, J., Wang, S., Granger, E., Ben Ayed, I.: Bounding boxes for weakly supervised segmentation: Global constraints get close to full supervision. In: MIDL (2020)
18. Khoreva, A., Benenson, R., Hosang, J., Hein, M., Schiele, B.: Simple does it: Weakly supervised instance and semantic segmentation. In: CVPR (2017)
19. Lee, D.H.: Pseudo-label: the simple and efficient semi-supervised learning method for deep neural networks. In: Workshop on Challenges in Representation Learning, ICML (2013)
20. Lee, J., Kim, E., Lee, S., Lee, J., Yoon, S.: Ficklenet: weakly and semi-supervised semantic image segmentation using stochastic inference. In: CVPR (2019)
21. Lin, D., Dai, J., Jia, J., He, K., Sun, J.: Scribblesup: scribble-supervised convolutional networks for semantic segmentation. In: CVPR (2016)
22. Litjens, G., et al.: A survey on deep learning in medical image analysis. MedIA **42**, 60–88 (2017)
23. Luo, W., Yang, M.: Semi-supervised semantic segmentation via strong-weak dual-branch network. In: Vedaldi, A., Bischof, H., Brox, T., Frahm, J.-M. (eds.) ECCV 2020. LNCS, vol. 12350, pp. 784–800. Springer, Cham (2020). https://doi.org/10.1007/978-3-030-58558-7_46
24. Mlynarski, P., Delingette, H., Criminisi, A., Ayache, N.: Deep learning with mixed supervision for brain tumor segmentation. J. Med. Imaging **6**, 034002 (2019)
25. Papandreou, G., Chen, L.C., Murphy, K.P., Yuille, A.L.: Weakly-and semi-supervised learning of a deep convolutional network for semantic image segmentation. In: ICCV (2015)
26. Peng, J., Kervadec, H., Dolz, J., Ben Ayed, I., Pedersoli, M., Desrosiers, C.: Discretely-constrained deep network for weakly supervised segmentation. Neural Networks **130**, 297–308 (2020)
27. Peng, J., Pedersoli, M., Desrosiers, C.: Mutual information deep regularization for semi-supervised segmentation. In: MIDL (2020)
28. Rajchl, M., et al.: Deepcut: object segmentation from bounding box annotations using convolutional neural networks. IEEE TMI **36**(2), 674–683 (2016)

29. Ronneberger, O., Fischer, P., Brox, T.: U-Net: convolutional networks for biomedical image segmentation. In: Navab, N., Hornegger, J., Wells, W.M., Frangi, A.F. (eds.) MICCAI 2015. LNCS, vol. 9351, pp. 234–241. Springer, Cham (2015). https://doi.org/10.1007/978-3-319-24574-4_28

30. Sedai, S., et al.: Uncertainty guided semi-supervised segmentation of retinal layers in OCT images. In: Shen, D., et al. (eds.) MICCAI 2019. LNCS, vol. 11764, pp. 282–290. Springer, Cham (2019). https://doi.org/10.1007/978-3-030-32239-7_32

31. Shah, M.P., Merchant, S.N., Awate, S.P.: MS-net: mixed-supervision fully-convolutional networks for full-resolution segmentation. In: Frangi, A.F., Schnabel, J.A., Davatzikos, C., Alberola-López, C., Fichtinger, G. (eds.) MICCAI 2018. LNCS, vol. 11073, pp. 379–387. Springer, Cham (2018). https://doi.org/10.1007/978-3-030-00937-3_44

32. Vu, T.H., Jain, H., Bucher, M., Cord, M., Pérez, P.: Advent: adversarial entropy minimization for domain adaptation in semantic segmentation. In: CVPR (2019)

33. Wang, D., et al.: Mixed-supervised dual-network for medical image segmentation. In: Shen, D., et al. (eds.) MICCAI 2019. LNCS, vol. 11765, pp. 192–200. Springer, Cham (2019). https://doi.org/10.1007/978-3-030-32245-8_22

34. Xu, Y., Du, B., Zhang, L., Zhang, Q., Wang, G., Zhang, L.: Self-ensembling attention networks: addressing domain shift for semantic segmentation. In: AAAI (2019)

35. Yim, J., Joo, D., Bae, J., Kim, J.: A gift from knowledge distillation: fast optimization, network minimization and transfer learning. In: CVPR (2017)

Sequential Modelling

Future Frame Prediction
for Robot-Assisted Surgery

Xiaojie Gao[1], Yueming Jin[1], Zixu Zhao[1], Qi Dou[1,2(✉)],
and Pheng-Ann Heng[1,2]

[1] Department of Computer Science and Engineering,
The Chinese University of Hong Kong, Hong Kong, China
{xjgao,ymjin,zxzhao,qdou,pheng}@cse.cuhk.edu.hk
[2] T Stone Robotics Institute, CUHK, Hong Kong, China

Abstract. Predicting future frames for robotic surgical video is an interesting, important yet extremely challenging problem, given that the operative tasks may have complex dynamics. Existing approaches on future
prediction of natural videos were based on either deterministic models
or stochastic models, including deep recurrent neural networks, optical
flow, and latent space modeling. However, the potential in predicting
meaningful movements of robots with dual arms in surgical scenarios
has not been tapped so far, which is typically more challenging than
forecasting independent motions of one arm robots in natural scenarios.
In this paper, we propose a ternary prior guided variational autoencoder (TPG-VAE) model for future frame prediction in robotic surgical
video sequences. Besides content distribution, our model learns motion
distribution, which is novel to handle the small movements of surgical
tools. Furthermore, we add the invariant prior information from the gesture class into the generation process to constrain the latent space of
our model. To our best knowledge, this is the first time that the future
frames of dual arm robots are predicted considering their unique characteristics relative to general robotic videos. Experiments demonstrate
that our model gains more stable and realistic future frame prediction
scenes with the suturing task on the public JIGSAWS dataset.

Keywords: Video prediction for medical robotics · Deep learning for
visual perception · Medical robots and systems

1 Introduction

With advancements in robot-assisted surgeries, visual data are crucial for surgical context awareness that promotes operation reliability and patient safety.
Owing to their rich representations and direct perceptibility, surgical videos
have been playing an essential role on driving automation process on tasks
with obvious clinical significance such as surgical process monitoring [3,4], gesture and workflow recognition [10,11,18], and surgical instrument detection and

© Springer Nature Switzerland AG 2021
A. Feragen et al. (Eds.): IPMI 2021, LNCS 12729, pp. 533–544, 2021.
https://doi.org/10.1007/978-3-030-78191-0_41

segmentation [5,14,16,25]. However, these methods either only focus on providing semantic descriptions of current situations or directly assume that future information is available, thus developing future scene prediction models for surgeries should be investigated. With only happened events available, future prediction will serve as a crucial prerequisite procedure to facilitate advanced tasks including generating alerts [3], boosting online recognition with additional information [33], and supporting decision making of reinforcement learning agents [11,24]. Besides supplying an extra source of references, predicted frames could also be converted into an entity demonstration in an imitation style [31], which will indeed accelerate the training of surgeons.

Recently, deep learning techniques have been applied to solve nature video prediction problems. To model the temporal dependencies, early methods used the Long Short Term Memory (LSTM) [13] or convolutional LSTM, [28] to capture the temporal dynamics in videos [30,35]. Villegas et al. utilized the predicted high-level structures in videos to help generate long-term future frames [36]. Methods based on explicit decomposition or multi-frequency analysis were also explored [6,15,35]. Action-conditional video prediction methods were developed for reinforcement learning agents [8,27]. However, these deterministic methods might yield blurry generations due to the missing considerations of multiple moving tendencies [7]. Thus, stochastic video prediction models are proposed to capture the full distributions of uncertain future frames, which are mainly divided into three types: autoregressive models [19], flow-based generative models [23], generative adversarial networks [32], and VAE based approaches [2,7]. As a famous VAE method, Denton and Fergus proposed SVG-LP that uses learned prior from content information rather than standard Gaussian prior [7]. Diverse future frames could also be generated based on stochastic high-level keypoints [20,26]. Although these approaches gain favorable results on general robotic videos [2,7,8,23], the domain knowledge in dual arm robotic surgical videos, such as the limited inter-class variance and class-dependent movements, are not considered.

Contrast to general robotic videos, a complete surgical video consists of several sub-phases with limited inter-class variances, meaningful movements of specific sub-tasks, and more than one moving instruments, which make this task extremely challenging. Another challenge in surgical robotic videos is that some actions have more complicated motion trajectories rather than repeated or random patterns in general videos. Although predicting one-arm robotic videos were investigated in [2,8], robots with more than one arm will lead to more diverse frames and make the task even more difficult. Targeting at the intricate movements of robotic arms, we utilize the content and motion information jointly to assist in predicting the future frames of dual arm robots. In addition, experienced surgeons will refer to the classes of current gestures as prior knowledge constantly to forecast future operations. How to incorporate content, motion, and class information into the generation model is of great importance to boosting the predicting outcomes of robotic surgery videos.

In this paper, we propose a novel approach named Ternary Prior Guided Variational Autoencoder (TPG-VAE) for generating the future frames of dual arm robot-assisted surgical videos. Our method combines the learned content and motion prior together with the constant class label prior to constrain the latent space of the generation model, which is consistent with the forecasting procedure of humans by referring to various prior. Notably, while the diversity of future tendencies is represented as distribution, the class label prior, a specific high-level target, will maintain invariant until the end of this phase, which is highly different from general robotic videos. Our main contributions are summarized as follows. **1)**. A ternary prior guided variational autoencoder model is tailored for robot-assisted surgical videos. To our best knowledge, this is the first time that future scene prediction is devised for dual arm medical robots. **2)**. Given the tangled gestures of the two arms, the changeable prior from content and motion is combined with the constant prior from the class of the current action to constrain the latent space of our model. **3)**. We have extensively evaluated our approach on the suturing task of the public JIGSAWS dataset. Our model outperforms baseline methods in general videos in both quantitative and qualitative evaluations, especially for the long-term future.

2   Method

2.1   Problem Formulation

Given a video clip $\mathbf{x}_{1:t_p}$, we aim to generate a sequence $\hat{\mathbf{x}}_{t_p+1:T}$ to represent the future frames, where $\mathbf{x}_t \in \mathbb{R}^{w \times h \times c}$ is the t-th frame with w, h, and c denoting the width, height, and number of channels, respectively. As shown in Fig. 1, we assume that $\mathbf{x}_t$ is generated by some random process, involving its previous frame $\mathbf{x}_{t-1}$ and a ternary latent variable $\mathbf{z}_t$. This process is denoted using a conditional distribution $p_\theta(\mathbf{x}_t | \mathbf{z}_{1:t}, \mathbf{x}_{1:t-1})$, which can be realized via an LSTM. The posterior distributions of $\mathbf{z}_t$ can also be encoded using LSTM. Then, after obtaining $\mathbf{z}_t$ by sampling from the posterior distributions, the modeled generation process is realized and the output $\hat{\mathbf{x}}_t$ from the neural network is adjusted to fit $\mathbf{x}_t$. At the meanwhile, the posterior distribution is fitted by a prior network to learn the diversity of the future frames.

2.2   Decomposed Video Encoding Network

Exacting spatial and temporal features from videos is essential for modeling the dynamics of future trends. In this regard, we design encoders using Convolutional Neural Network (CNN) for spatial information which is followed by an LSTM to model the temporal dependency. The content encoder Enc_c, which is realized by a CNN based on VGG net [29], takes the input as the last observed frame and extracts content features as a one-dimensional hidden vector $\mathbf{h}_t$. We use $\mathbf{C}_t$ to denote the latent code sampled from the content distribution, which is part of $\mathbf{z}_t$. To preserve dependency, we use LSTM_{φ^c} to model the conditional distribution

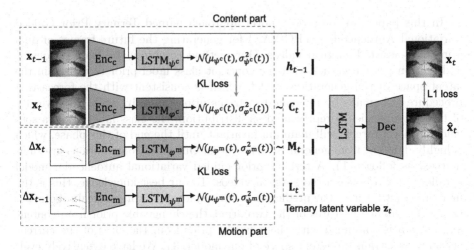

Fig. 1. Illustration of the training process of the proposed model. The posterior latent variables of content and motion at time step t together with the class label prior L_t try to reconstruct the original frame x_t conditioning on previous frames. And the prior distributions from content and motion at time step $t - 1$ are optimized to fit the posterior distributions at time step t.

of the video content. And the posterior distribution of C_t is estimated as a Gaussian distribution $\mathcal{N}_{\varphi^c}$ with its expectation and variance as

$$
\begin{aligned}
\mathbf{h}_t &= \text{Enc}_c(\mathbf{x}_t), \\
\mu_{\varphi^c}(t), \sigma^2_{\varphi^c}(t) &= \text{LSTM}_{\varphi^c}(\mathbf{h}_t).
\end{aligned}
\tag{1}
$$

To further obtain an overall distribution of videos, a motion encoder is adopted to capture the changeable movements of surgical tools. With a similar structure to the content encoder, the motion encoder Enc_m observes the frame difference $\Delta\mathbf{x}_t$ computed by $\mathbf{x}_t - \mathbf{x}_{t-1}$ and outputs motion features as a one-dimensional hidden vector $\mathbf{h}'_t$. Note that $\Delta\mathbf{x}_t$ is calculated directly using the element-wise subtraction between the two frames that are converted to gray images in advance. As another part of $\mathbf{z}_t$, we denote the random latent code from motion as M_t. And LSTM_{φ^m} is utilized to calculate the posterior distribution of M_t as a Gaussian distribution $\mathcal{N}_{\varphi^m}$ with its expectation and variance as

$$
\begin{aligned}
\mathbf{h}'_t &= \text{Enc}_m(\Delta\mathbf{x}_t), \\
\mu_{\varphi^m}(t), \sigma^2_{\varphi^m}(t) &= \text{LSTM}_{\varphi^m}(\mathbf{h}'_t).
\end{aligned}
\tag{2}
$$

It is worth to mention that our motion encoder also play a role as attention mechanism since the minor movements of instruments are caught by the difference between frames. The motion encoder helps alleviate the problem of limited inter-class variance which is caused by the huge proportion of unchanged parts of surgical frames. Although our method also explicitly separates the content and motion information in a video as [35], we consider the comprehensive distribution rather than deterministic features.

For prior distributions of $\mathbf{C}_t$ and $\mathbf{M}_t$, two LSTMs with the same structure are applied to model them as normal distribution $\mathcal{N}_{\psi^c}$ and $\mathcal{N}_{\psi^m}$, respectively, as

$$
\begin{aligned}
\mu_{\psi^c}(t), \sigma_{\psi^c}^2(t) &= \text{LSTM}_{\psi^c}(\mathbf{h}_{t-1}), \\
\mu_{\psi^m}(t), \sigma_{\psi^m}^2(t) &= \text{LSTM}_{\psi^m}(\mathbf{h}'_{t-1}).
\end{aligned}
\tag{3}
$$

The objective of prior networks is to estimate the posterior distribution of time step t with information up to $t-1$.

2.3   Ternary Latent Variable

Anticipating the future development based on some inherent information can reduce the uncertainty, which also holds for the robotic video scenario. Here, we apply the class label information of the video to be predicted as the non-learned part of the latent variable $\mathbf{z}_t$, which is the available ground truth label. Even if there are not ground truth labels, they could be predicted since the gesture recognition problem have been solved with a relatively high accuracy [17], for example, 84.3% [10] in robotic video dataset JIGSAWS [1,12]. With the obtained surgical gesture label, we encode it as a one-hot vector $\mathbf{L}_t \in \{0,1\}^{n_l}$, where n_l is the number of gesture classes. For each video clip, $\mathbf{L}_t$ is directly applied as a part of the ternary latent variable to the generation process by setting the current gesture class as 1 and all others 0. Thus, the complete ternary latent variable of our method is written as

$$
\mathbf{z}_t = [\mathbf{C}_t, \mathbf{M}_t, \mathbf{L}_t],
\tag{4}
$$

where $\mathbf{C}_t$ and $\mathbf{M}_t$ are sampled from $\mathcal{N}_{\varphi^c}$ and $\mathcal{N}_{\varphi^m}$ during training, respectively. Note that $\mathbf{L}_t$ will keep unchanged for frames with the same class label.

After acquiring $\mathbf{z}_t$, we can perform the future frame prediction using an LSTM to keep the temporal dependencies and a decoder to generate images. The features go through the two neural networks to produce the next frame $\hat{\mathbf{x}}_t$ as

$$
\begin{aligned}
\mathbf{g}_t &= \text{LSTM}_\theta(\mathbf{h}_{t-1}, \mathbf{z}_t), \\
\hat{\mathbf{x}}_t &= \text{Dec}(\mathbf{g}_t).
\end{aligned}
\tag{5}
$$

To provide features of the static background, skip connections are employed from content encoder at the last ground truth frame to the decoder like [7].

During inference, the posterior information of the ternary latent variable $\mathbf{z}_t$ is not available and a prior estimation is needed to generate latent codes at time step t. A general way to define the prior distribution is to let the posterior distribution get close to a standard normal distribution where prior latent code is then sampled. However, this sampling strategy tends to lose the temporal dependencies between video frames. Employing a recurrent structure, the conditional relationship can also be learned by a prior neural network [7]. And we directly use the expectation of the prior distribution rather than the sampled latent code to produce the most likely prediction under the Gaussian latent distribution assumption. Another reason is that choosing the best generation after sampling several times is not practical for online prediction scenarios. Hence, we directly use the outputs of Eq. (3) and $\mathbf{z}_t$ is replaced of the ternary prior $\mathbf{z}'_t$ as

$$\mathbf{z}'_t = [\mu_{\psi^c}(t), \mu_{\psi^m}(t), \mathbf{L}_t]. \tag{6}$$

It is worth noting that our method considers the stochasticity during training for an overall learning, while produces the most possible generation during testing.

2.4   Learning Process

In order to deal with the intractable distribution of latent variables, we train our neural networks by maximizing the following variational lower bound using the re-parametrization trick [22]:

$$\sum_{t=1}^{T} [\mathbb{E}_{q_\varphi(\mathbf{z}_{1:T}|\mathbf{x}_{1:T})} \log p_\theta(\mathbf{x}_t|\mathbf{z}_{1:t}, \mathbf{x}_{1:t-1})$$
$$- \beta D_{\mathrm{KL}}\left(q_{\varphi^c}(\mathbf{C}_t|\mathbf{x}_{1:t}) \| p_{\psi^c}(\mathbf{C}_t|\mathbf{x}_{1:t-1})\right) \tag{7}$$
$$- \beta D_{\mathrm{KL}}\left(q_{\varphi^m}(\mathbf{M}_t|\mathbf{x}_{1:t}) \| p_{\psi^m}(\mathbf{M}_t|\mathbf{x}_{1:t-1}))\right],$$

where β is used to balance the frame prediction error and the prior fitting error. As shown in Fig. 1, we use reconstruction loss to replace the likelihood term [34] and the loss function to minimize is

$$\mathcal{L} = \sum_{t=1}^{T} [\|\mathbf{x}_t - \hat{\mathbf{x}}_t\|_1 + \beta D_{\mathrm{KL}}(\mathcal{N}_{\varphi^c}(t)\|\mathcal{N}_{\psi^c}(t)) \quad + \beta D_{\mathrm{KL}}(\mathcal{N}_{\varphi^m}(t)\|\mathcal{N}_{\psi^m}(t))], \tag{8}$$

where $\|\cdot\|_1$ represents the ℓ_1 loss.

3   Experimental Results

We evaluate our model for predicting surgical robotic motions on the dual arm *da Vinci* robot system [9]. We design experiments to investigate: 1) whether the complicated movements of the two robotic arms could be well predicted, 2) the effectiveness of the content and motion latent variables in our proposed video prediction model, and 3) the usefulness of the constant label prior in producing the future motions of the dual arm robots.

3.1   Dataset and Evaluation Metrics

We validate our method with the suturing task of the JIGSAWS dataset [1,12], a public dataset recorded using *da Vinci* surgical system. The gesture class labels are composed of a set of 11 sub-tasks annotated by experts. We only choose gestures with a sufficient amount of video clips (~100), i.e. positioning needle

(G2), pushing needle through tissue (G3), transferring needle from left to right (G4), and pulling suture with left hand (G6). The records of the first 6 users are used as training dataset (470 sequences) and the rest 2 users for testing (142 sequences), which is consistent with the leave-one-user-out (LOUO) setting in [12]. Every other frame in the dataset is chosen as the input $\mathbf{x}_t$.

We show quantitative comparisons by calculating VGG Cosine Similarity, Peak Signal-to-Noise Ratio (PSNR) and structural similarity (SSIM) scores [34] between ground truth and generated frames. VGG Cosine Similarity uses the output vector of the last fully connected layer of a pre-trained VGG neural network. PSNR generally indicates the quality of reconstruction while SSIM is a method for measuring the perceived quality.

3.2   Implementation Details

The encoder for content and decoder use the same architecture as VGG-based encoder in [7], while the motion encoder utilizes only one convolutional layer after each pooling layer with one eighth channel numbers. The dimensions of outputs from the two encoders are both 128. All LSTMs have 256 cells with a single layer except LSTM_θ with two layers. A linear embedding layer is employed for each LSTM. The hidden output of LSTM_θ is followed by a fully connected layer activated using a tanh function before going into the decoder, while the hidden outputs of the rest LSTMs are followed by two separate fully connected layers indicating expectation and the logarithm of variance.

Following the previous study [7], we set the resolution of the videos as 64×64 from 640×480 to save time and storage. The dimensionalities of the $\mathbf{g}_t$ and the Gaussian distributions are 128 and 16, respectively. We train all the components of our method using the Adam optimizer [21] in an end-to-end fashion, with a learning rate of $1e - 4$. We set $\beta = 1e - 4$ and $T = 20$, i.e., the max length of video frames to train. For all the experiments, we train each model on predicting 10 time steps into the future conditioning on 10 observed frames, i.e. $t_p = 10$. All models are trained with 200 epochs.

Based on their released codes, we re-implement MCnet [35] and SVG-LP [7] on the robotic dataset, which are the typical methods of deterministic and stochastic predictions. We also show the results of two ablation settings: 1) SVG-LP*: SVG-LP trained using ℓ_1 loss and tested without sampling; 2) ML-VAE: our full model without latent variables of content. We randomly choose 100 video clips from the testing dataset with the number of different gestures equal. Then, we test each model by predicting 20 subsequent frames conditioning on 10 observed frames. The longer testing period than training demonstrates the generalization capability of each model. For SVG-LP, we draw 10 samples from the model for each test sequence and choose the best one given each metric. Other VAE based methods directly use the expectation of the latent distribution without sampling for inference.

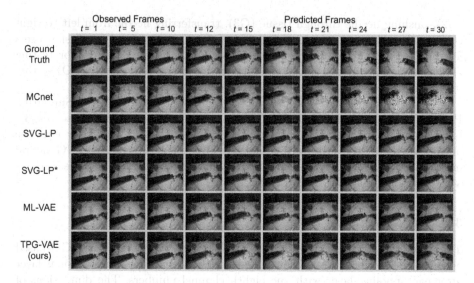

Fig. 2. Qualitative results showing the gesture of G2 among different models. Compared to other VAE-based methods, our model captures the moving tendency of the left hand while other methods only copy the last ground truth frame. Frames with blue edging indicate the ground truth while the rest are generated by each model. (Color figure online)

3.3   Results

Qualitative Evaluation. Figure 2 shows some of the outcomes denoting the gesture G2 from each model. Generations from MCnet are sharp for initial time steps, but the results rapidly distort in later time steps. Although MCnet also utilizes skip connections, it cannot produce a crisp background in a longer time span, which implies that the back and forth moving patterns of the two arms can hardly be learned the deterministic model. SVG-LP and SVG-LP* tend to predict static images of the indicated gesture, which implies that the two misunderstand the purpose of the current gesture. ML-VAE also tends to lose the movement of the left hand, which confirms the importance of content encoder. Capturing the movements of the two arms, our TPG-VAE model gives the closest predictions towards the ground truth.

Quantitative Evaluation. We compute VGG cosine similarity, PSNR, and SSIM for earlier mentioned models on the 100 unseen test sequences. Figure 3 plots the average of all three metrics on the testing set. Concerning VGG Cosine Similarity, MCnet shows the worst curve because of the lowest generation quality, while other methods behaves similarly. The reason might be that the frames with good quality are similar to each other on a perceptual level. For PSNR and SSIM, all methods maintain a relatively high level at the beginning while deteriorate as going further into the future. SVG-LP* shows better performance than the

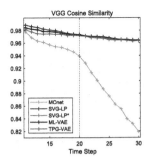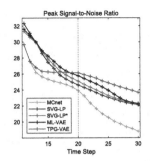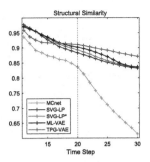

Fig. 3. Quantitative evaluation on the average of the three metrics towards the 100 testing clips. The dotted line indicates the frame number the models are trained to predict up to; further results beyond this line display their generalization ability. For the reported metrics, **higher is better**.

Table 1. Comparison of predicted results at different time step (mean±std).

Methods	PSNR				SSIM			
	t = 15	t = 20	t = 25	t = 30	t = 15	t = 20	t = 25	t = 30
MCnet [35]	25.34 ± 2.58	23.92 ± 2.46	20.53 ± 2.06	18.79 ± 1.83	0.874 ± 0.053	0.836 ± 0.058	0.712 ± 0.074	0.614 ± 0.073
SVG-LP [7]	27.47 ± 3.82	24.62 ± 4.21	23.06 ± 4.20	22.14 ± 4.09	0.927 ± 0.054	0.883 ± 0.080	0.852 ± 0.089	0.832 ± 0.088
SVG-LP*	27.85 ± 3.57	25.09 ± 4.13	23.30 ± 4.30	22.30 ± 4.21	0.933 ± 0.046	0.893 ± 0.072	0.857 ± 0.087	0.836 ± 0.088
M-VAE	27.74 ± 3.67	25.14 ± 4.09	23.24 ± 4.30	22.15 ± 4.10	0.932 ± 0.050	0.894 ± 0.072	0.857 ± 0.088	0.834 ± 0.087
CM-VAE	27.44 ± 3.83	25.09 ± 4.07	23.02 ± 4.19	22.16 ± 4.16	0.927 ± 0.056	0.893 ± 0.075	0.853 ± 0.087	0.834 ± 0.088
CL-VAE	28.00 ± 3.73	25.32 ± 4.15	23.49 ± 4.34	22.24 ± 4.28	0.935 ± 0.042	0.897 ± 0.073	0.862 ± 0.087	0.835 ± 0.088
ML-VAE	**28.24 ± 3.51**	25.77 ± 4.02	23.95 ± 4.26	22.28 ± 4.26	**0.936 ± 0.046**	0.903 ± 0.071	0.870 ± 0.084	0.836 ± 0.088
TPG-VAE (ours)	26.26 ± 3.17	**26.13 ± 3.85**	**24.88 ± 3.68**	**23.67 ± 3.50**	0.917 ± 0.048	**0.911 ± 0.060**	**0.892 ± 0.067**	**0.871 ± 0.071**

SVG-LP, which indicates the ℓ_1 loss is more appropriate than MSE in this task. Both ML-VAE and TPG-VAE demonstrate better outcomes than the two published methods, i.e., MCnet and SVG-LP, particularly in later time steps. Interestingly, MCnet demonstrates a poor generalization capacity that its performance curves on three metrics deteriorate faster after going through the dotted lines in Fig. 3. Our full model exhibits a stronger capability to retain image quality in longer time span. Note that methods without sampling random variables when testing also gain favorable results, which suggests that the movements in the JIGSAWS dataset have relatively clear objectives.

Table 1 lists the average and standard deviation of the performances of each method on the 100 testing clips. VGG Cosine Similarity is not shown because it cannot distinguish the results of VAE based models. All methods tend to degrade as the time step goes on. ML-VAE also exhibits superior outcomes than the other compared methods, which verifies the effectiveness of the proposed motion encoder and class prior. With the ternary prior as high-level guidance, our TPG-VAE maintains high generation quality while showing stable performances with the smallest standard deviation.

Further Ablations. Table 1 also shows additional ablations of our TPG-VAE. Each of the following settings is applied to justify the necessity: 1) M-VAE: our

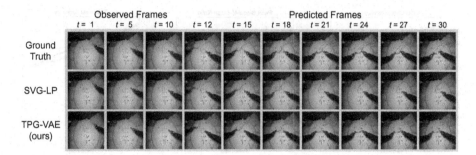

Fig. 4. Qualitative comparison indicating the gesture of G4. Our method generates images with high quality and predicts the actual location of the left arm, while other methods tend to lose the left arm. Frames with blue edging indicate the ground truth while the rest are generated by each model. (Color figure online)

full model without latent variables of content and class labels; 2) CM-VAE: our full model without latent variables of class labels; 3) CL-VAE: our full model without latent variables of motion. All three ablation models give better outcomes than SVG-LP. Comparing CM-VAE with CL-VAE, we find that class labels contribute more than motion latent variables since class information helps the model remove more uncertainty, which suggests that recognizing before predicting is a recommended choice. To be mentioned, we do not consider the ablation setting with the only label prior since it degenerates into a deterministic model that cannot interpret the diversities of videos.

Discussion on Dual Arm Cases. The two arms of the *da Vinci* robot cooperate mutually to achieve a certain task, thus the movements are highly entangled, which makes prediction very challenging. Without enough prior information, the predicted frames might lead to unreasonable outcomes due to the loss of temporal consistency. Figure 4 shows the results of gesture G4, where the left arm is gradually getting into the visual field. As for the first 10 predicted frames, all models realize the temporal images that the left hand is moving to the center. For the rest 10 predictions, SVG-LP tend to lose the left hand due misunderstanding the current phase. Owning to more complete guidance, i.e., the ternary prior, our TPG-VAE predicts the movements of the two arms successfully while shows crisp outcomes, which verifies our assumption that additional references help for prediction of the dual arm movements.

4   Conclusion and Future Work

In this work, we present a novel method based on VAE for conditional robotic video prediction, which is the first work for dual arm robots. The suggested model employs learned and intrinsic prior information as guidance to help generate future scenes conditioning on the observed frames. The stochastic VAE based method is adapted as a deterministic approach by directly using the expectation of the distribution without sampling. Our method outperforms the baseline methods on the challenging dual arm robotic surgical video dataset. Future work can be made to explore higher resolution generation and apply the predicted future frames to other advanced tasks.

Acknowledgements. This work was supported by Key-Area Research and Development Program of Guangdong Province, China (2020B010165004), Hong Kong RGC TRS Project No. T42-409/18-R, National Natural Science Foundation of China with Project No. U1813204, and CUHK Shun Hing Institute of Advanced Engineering (project MMT-p5-20).

References

1. Ahmidi, N., et al.: A dataset and benchmarks for segmentation and recognition of gestures in robotic surgery. IEEE. Trans. Biomed. Eng. **64**(9), 2025–2041 (2017)
2. Babaeizadeh, M., Finn, C., Erhan, D., Campbell, R.H., Levine, S.: Stochastic variational video prediction. In: ICLR (2018)
3. Bhatia, B., Oates, T., Xiao, Y., Hu, P.: Real-time identification of operating room state from video. In: AAAI (2007)
4. Bricon-Souf, N., Newman, C.R.: Context awareness in health care: a review. Int. J. Med. Inform. **76**(1), 2–12 (2007)
5. Colleoni, E., Moccia, S., Du, X., De Momi, E., Stoyanov, D.: Deep learning based robotic tool detection and articulation estimation with spatio-temporal layers. RA-L (2019)
6. Denton, E., Birodkar, V.: Unsupervised learning of disentangled representations from video. In: NurIPS (2017)
7. Denton, E., Fergus, R.: Stochastic video generation with a learned prior. In: ICML (2018)
8. Finn, C., Goodfellow, I., Levine, S.: Unsupervised learning for physical interaction through video prediction. In: NurIPS (2016)
9. Freschi, C., Ferrari, V., Melfi, F., Ferrari, M., Mosca, F., Cuschieri, A.: Technical review of the da Vinci surgical telemanipulator. Int. J. Med. Robot. **9**(4), 396–406 (2013)
10. Funke, I., Bodenstedt, S., Oehme, F., von Bechtolsheim, F., Weitz, J., Speidel, S.: Using 3D convolutional neural networks to learn spatiotemporal features for automatic surgical gesture recognition in video. In: Shen, D., et al. (eds.) MICCAI 2019. LNCS, vol. 11768, pp. 467–475. Springer, Cham (2019). https://doi.org/10.1007/978-3-030-32254-0_52
11. Gao, X., Jin, Y., Dou, Q., Heng, P.A.: Automatic gesture recognition in robot-assisted surgery with reinforcement learning and tree search. In: ICRA (2020)
12. Gao, Y., et al.: JHU-ISI gesture and skill assessment working set (JIGSAWS): a surgical activity dataset for human motion modeling. In: MICCAI Workshop: M2CAI (2014)
13. Hochreiter, S., Schmidhuber, J.: Long short-term memory. Neural Computation (1997)
14. Islam, M., Atputharuban, D.A., Ramesh, R., Ren, H.: Real-time instrument segmentation in robotic surgery using auxiliary supervised deep adversarial learning. RA-L (2019)

15. Jin, B., et al.: Exploring spatial-temporal multi-frequency analysis for high-fidelity and temporal-consistency video prediction. In: CVPR (2020)
16. Jin, Y., Cheng, K., Dou, Q., Heng, P.-A.: Incorporating temporal prior from motion flow for instrument segmentation in minimally invasive surgery video. In: Shen, D., et al. (eds.) MICCAI 2019. LNCS, vol. 11768, pp. 440–448. Springer, Cham (2019). https://doi.org/10.1007/978-3-030-32254-0_49
17. Jin, Y., et al.: SV-RCNet: workflow recognition from surgical videos using recurrent convolutional network. IEEE Trans. Med, Imaging **37**, 1114–1126 (2017)
18. Jin, Y., et al.: Multi-task recurrent convolutional network with correlation loss for surgical video analysis. Med. Image Anal. **59**, 101572 (2020)
19. Kalchbrenner, N., et al.: Video pixel networks. In: ICML (2017)
20. Kim, Y., Nam, S., Cho, I., Kim, S.J.: Unsupervised keypoint learning for guiding class-conditional video prediction. In: NurIPS (2019)
21. Kingma, D.P., Ba, J.: Adam: a method for stochastic optimization. arXiv preprint arXiv:1412.6980 (2014)
22. Kingma, D.P., Welling, M.: Auto-encoding variational bayes. In: ICLR (2014)
23. Kumar, M., et al.: VideoFlow: A Conditional Flow-Based Model for Stochastic Video Generation. In: ICLR (2020)
24. Liu, D., Jiang, T.: Deep reinforcement learning for surgical gesture segmentation and classification. In: Frangi, A.F., Schnabel, J.A., Davatzikos, C., Alberola-López, C., Fichtinger, G. (eds.) MICCAI 2018. LNCS, vol. 11073, pp. 247–255. Springer, Cham (2018). https://doi.org/10.1007/978-3-030-00937-3_29
25. Milletari, F., Rieke, N., Baust, M., Esposito, M., Navab, N.: CFCM: segmentation via coarse to fine context memory. In: Frangi, A.F., Schnabel, J.A., Davatzikos, C., Alberola-López, C., Fichtinger, G. (eds.) MICCAI 2018. LNCS, vol. 11073, pp. 667–674. Springer, Cham (2018). https://doi.org/10.1007/978-3-030-00937-3_76
26. Minderer, M., Sun, C., Villegas, R., Cole, F., Murphy, K.P., Lee, H.: Unsupervised learning of object structure and dynamics from videos. In: NurIPS (2019)
27. Oh, J., Guo, X., Lee, H., Lewis, R.L., Singh, S.: Action-conditional video prediction using deep networks in Atari games. In: NurIPS (2015)
28. Shi, X., Chen, Z., Wang, H., Yeung, D.Y., Wong, W.K., Woo, W.C.: Convolutional lstm network: a machine learning approach for precipitation nowcasting. In: NurIPS (2015)
29. Simonyan, K., Zisserman, A.: Very deep convolutional networks for large-scale image recognition. In: ICLR (2015)
30. Srivastava, N., Mansimov, E., Salakhudinov, R.: Unsupervised learning of video representations using LSTMs. In: ICML (2015)
31. Tanwani, A.K., Sermanet, P., Yan, A., Anand, R., Phielipp, M., Goldberg, K.: Motion2Vec: semi-Supervised Representation Learning from Surgical Videos. In: ICRA (2020)
32. Tulyakov, S., Liu, M.Y., Yang, X., Kautz, J.: MoCoGAN: decomposing motion and content for video generation. In: CVPR (2018)
33. Twinanda, A.P., Shehata, S., Mutter, D., Marescaux, J., De Mathelin, M., Padoy, N.: EndoNet: a deep architecture for recognition tasks on laparoscopic videos. IEEE Trans. Med, Imaging (2016)
34. Villegas, R., Pathak, A., Kannan, H., Erhan, D., Le, Q.V., Lee, H.: High fidelity video prediction with large stochastic recurrent neural networks. In: NurIPS (2019)
35. Villegas, R., Yang, J., Hong, S., Lin, X., Lee, H.: Decomposing motion and content for natural video sequence prediction. In: ICLR (2017)
36. Villegas, R., Yang, J., Zou, Y., Sohn, S., Lin, X., Lee, H.: Learning to generate long-term future via hierarchical prediction. In: ICML (2017)

Velocity-To-Pressure (V2P) - Net: Inferring Relative Pressures from Time-Varying 3D Fluid Flow Velocities

Suprosanna Shit[1]([✉]), Dhritiman Das[1,2], Ivan Ezhov[1], Johannes C. Paetzold[1], Augusto F. Sanches[1,3], Nils Thuerey[1], and Bjoern H. Menze[1,4]

[1] Department of Informatics, Technical University of Munich, Munich, Germany
`{suprosanna.shit,ivan.ezhov,johannes.paetzold,nils.thuerey}@tum.de`
[2] McGovern Institute for Brain Research, MIT, Cambridge, MA, USA
`dasd@mit.edu`
[3] Institute of Neuroradiology, University Hospital LMU, Munich, Germany
`augusto.sanches@med.uni-muenchen.de`
[4] Department of Quantitative Biomedicine, University of Zurich, Zürich, Switzerland
`bjoern.menze@uzh.ch`

Abstract. Pressure inference from a series of velocity fields is a common problem arising in medical imaging when analyzing 4D data. Traditional approaches primarily rely on a numerical scheme to solve the pressure-Poisson equation to obtain a dense pressure inference. This involves heavy expert intervention at each stage and requires significant computational resources. Concurrently, the application of current machine learning algorithms for solving partial differential equations is limited to domains with simple boundary conditions. We address these challenges in this paper and present V2P-Net: a novel, neural-network-based approach as an alternative method for inferring pressure from the observed velocity fields. We design an end-to-end hybrid-network architecture motivated by the conventional Navier-Stokes solver, which encapsulates the complex boundary conditions. It achieves accurate pressure estimation compared to the reference numerical solver for simulated flow data in multiple complex geometries of human in-vivo vessels.

1 Introduction

Imaging modalities such as 3D phase-contrast magnetic resonance imaging [14] or particle imaging velocimetry [23] enable us to get an in-vivo measurement of blood flow velocity. Relative pressure fields, inferred from the measured velocity fields, serve as a clinical biomarker for various cardiovascular diseases such as aortic valve stenosis, aortic coarctation, and aortic aneurysm. Additionally, the spatio-temporal distribution of pressure fields within a vessel segment is often used for clinical intervention and therapeutic planning in neurovascular diseases, such as cerebral angioma and intracranial aneurysm.

Given the velocity measurements, solving pressure fields simplifies the Navier-Stokes equation to the Pressure-Poisson Equation (PPE). [22] used an iterative

© Springer Nature Switzerland AG 2021
A. Feragen et al. (Eds.): IPMI 2021, LNCS 12729, pp. 545–558, 2021.
https://doi.org/10.1007/978-3-030-78191-0_42

scheme to solve the PPE. Heuristics-based attempts to compute a robust line integral have been proposed by [18]. [4] proposed an alternate method to the conventional PPE solution by using the work-energy conservation principle. [10] introduced a finite-element method (FEM) to solve the PPE and [15] improved upon this by incorporating flow-aware boundary tagging. A detailed analysis of the pressure estimation methods, in particular has been presented in [1].

In medical imaging, although mesh-based solutions are popular, they are computationally intensive. Recent machine learning-based solutions [9] are also compute-costly. Moreover, these methods demand expert intervention to accurately take care of patient-specific simulation domain and spatiotemporal discretization. Moving towards a fundamentally different direction from the prior literature, the goal of this paper is to propose an alternate, fast, and accurate pressure inference scheme without requiring the computationally expensive mesh-based analysis. In this paper, we mainly focus on neural network (NN)-based methods which can provide a good approximation of costly numerical schemes, such as the Navier-Stokes, for Partial Differential Equations (PDE).

Differential Equations (DE) have been studied in physics and engineering for quite a few decades. However, a strong connection between the NN and the DE has only been established very recently. While numerical schemes for solving DE can be exploited to design efficient network architectures, enforcing physics in an NN could also accelerate the numerical solutions of DE [3]. Recent methods based on a fully supervised training regime have shown promising results to learn the unknown physics model from conditional latent variables [8] and using a fully convolutional neural network (FCN) [5,20]. However, these methods are only favorable to solve the forward simulation problem. On the other hand, explicit prior information about the underlying physics can help an NN to solve forward and inverse problems in the PDE system. Two main categories of methods have emerged in recent times to incorporate physics in the network:

1. **Physics constraints in the architecture of the NN:** Classical approaches to solving a PDE system can be substituted by an approximation model that can be learned from the observed data. This formulation relies on a specific spatio-temporal discretization of a continuous-time process that offers the ability to generalize well over a variety of domains. [12] proposed one such generic network architecture (PDE-Net), which is parameterized by a learnable coefficient and constrained convolutional kernel to discover the underlying PDE from observed data. [21] has shown that an FCN can approximate well an intermediate step of the Euler velocity update rule for the inviscous Navier-Stokes equation by solving the Poisson equation.

2. **Physics constraints in the loss of the NN:** An alternate approach to obeying a PDE equation is to include it as a standalone loss or as an additional regularizer along with a data-fidelity loss. [16] show that prior knowledge about the form of a PDE in a loss function can help in exploiting differentiable programming (deep learning), to simulate a PDE and use the learned system to infer unknown system parameters. While this helps to obtain a robust fitting of a parameterized continuous-time generative model, the inclusion

of PDE system parameters in a domain-specific boundary loss restricts its generalization. Note that we refer to the coefficients of the PDE equation as the system parameters to differentiate it from the learnable NN parameters.

[21]'s method achieves significant acceleration for inviscid fluid flow simulation by using a semi-implicit Lagrangian convection scheme coupled with an FCN to approximate the traditional Jacobi iteration-based Poisson's equation solver. While this method shares our goal to infer pressure fields, they do not account for the change in velocity at the boundary (inflow-outflow) and the pressure drop from the viscous energy loss. Their proposed FCN assumes zero Neumann BC whereas, on the contrary, this is non-zero at the inlet and outlet boundaries of the flow as shown by [6]. Hence, it is not readily applicable for inferring pressure in the case of transient viscous fluid flow such as blood.

Our Contribution: In this paper, we present a proof-of-concept study of **V2P-Net** - a novel NN-based framework for inferring pressure from time-varying 3D velocity fields (Fig. 1). The two key properties of V2P-Net are: 1) inclusion of diffusion in an end-to-end trainable network that emulates the Navier-Stokes equation solver, and 2) decoupling the relative pressure into: a) convection induced pressure p_G, and b) inlet-outlet boundary driven pressure p_B. We show that p_G and p_B can be estimated using two separate neural networks dedicated to solving the Poisson's and Laplace's equations (Eqs. 3 & 4), respectively. p_G is modeled by solving the zero Neumann BC using a FCN, while a fully-connected NN (MLP) is used to map a geometry specific p_B conditioned on the non-zero Neumann BC. The FCN leverages the physics constraint in the network architecture, which enables it to generalize well over a different domain, while the MLP learns a domain-specific function by satisfying the non-zero Neumann BC as the loss function. Both of them are optimized by exploiting the underlying physics of the Navier-Stokes equation in an unsupervised way, thus obviating any need for ground-truth training data of the pressure distribution. We demonstrate the efficiency of the V2P-Net architecture on simulated cerebral blood flow geometries.

2   Methodology

2.1   Background

The Navier-Stokes equation for incompressible fluid in 3D volume is described by the following momentum-balance equation:

$$\underbrace{\frac{\partial \mathbf{u}}{\partial t}}_{\text{Transient}} + \underbrace{\nabla \mathbf{u} \cdot \mathbf{u}}_{\text{Convection}} = \underbrace{\nu \Delta \mathbf{u}}_{\text{Diffusion}} - \frac{1}{\rho}\nabla p + \mathbf{f}; \text{ subject to } \nabla \cdot \mathbf{u} = 0 \qquad (1)$$

In a bounded domain Ω with Dirichlet BC, $\mathbf{u} = \mathbf{u}_b(\mathbf{x}, t)$ on boundary $\delta\Omega$; subject to $\int_{\delta\Omega} \boldsymbol{\eta} \cdot \mathbf{u}_b = 0$, ∇ and Δ represent the gradient and Laplacian operations

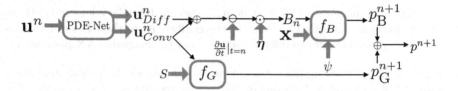

Fig. 1. Overview of V2P-Net. PDE-Net, f_G and f_B represent constrained convolutions, an FCN and an MLP respectively. Individual architecture of PDE-Net, f_G, and f_B are defined in detail in Fig. 2. S and B_n denote the vessel segmentation and BC respectively. $\mathbf{u}_{Conv}^n$ has a non-zero divergence field which is subsequently corrected using the convective induced pressure p_G^{n+1}.

respectively and $\boldsymbol{\eta}$ is the normal on $\delta\Omega$. In Eq. 1, $\mathbf{u}, p, \nu, \rho$ and, $\mathbf{f}$ denote velocity, pressure, kinematic viscosity, density of the fluid and external force respectively.

In our case, velocity ($\mathbf{u}$) is known and the pressure (p) is unknown. For a divergence-free flow, taking divergence of 1, we have to solve

$$\Delta p^{n+1} = \nabla \cdot (-\nabla \mathbf{u}^n \cdot \mathbf{u}^n), \text{ subject to } \frac{\partial p^{n+1}}{\partial \eta} = B_n \qquad (2)$$

where the boundary condition (BC) $B_n = \boldsymbol{\eta} \cdot (\nu \Delta \mathbf{u}^n - \nabla \mathbf{u}^n \cdot \mathbf{u}^n - \frac{\partial \mathbf{u}}{\partial t}|_{t=n})$. In the following, we show that this equation can be modelled in a feed-forward NN, the V2P-Net (c.f. Fig. 1).

2.2   V2P-Net:

Here, we formulate the pressure estimation problem (Eq. 2) in the context of PDE approximation using an NN and describe our proposed *hybrid* NN architecture, V2P-Net, which consists of: 1) constrained convolution operations as **PDE-Net** [12], 2) an **FCN**, and 3) an **MLP** module. Parallels can be drawn between the proposed network and a recurrent neural network (RNN), where each time step update of the Navier-Stokes equation can be viewed as an unrolled step of the recurrence scheme. However, a conventional RNN would need explicit supervision for training, and therefore we use our hybrid network, which is unsupervised.

Convection-Diffusion Modelling (PDE-Net): The convection-diffusion ($\nabla \mathbf{u}^n \cdot \mathbf{u}^n, \Delta \mathbf{u}^n$) operation is commonly solved in semi-implicit form for better numerical stability. However, semi-Lagrangian semi-implicit schemes lose the end-to-end trainability over multiple time-steps [21]. Therefore, we opt for an explicit convection-diffusion operation modeled as a *constrained convolution kernel* [12]. The constrained convolution represents a particular differential operator (in this case, convection and diffusion) as a learnable parameter in the explicit scheme. Thus, the network becomes end-to-end trainable even in the presence of viscosity over multiple time steps. We denote the resultant convection-diffusion

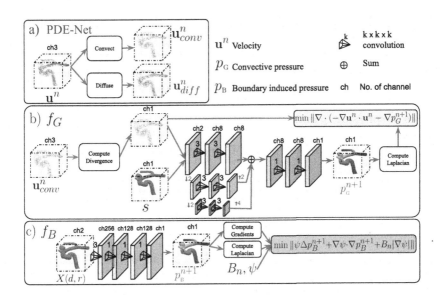

Fig. 2. Building blocks of our proposed method: a) The explicit convection-diffusion step is modeled using constrained convolution shown as *PDE-Net*, which enables an end-to-end differentiability. The resultant convective term ($\mathbf{u}_{conv}^n$) acts as a source for f_G, while the diffused term ($\mathbf{u}_{diff}^n$) contributes to the boundary condition B_n. b) f_G is a *FCN*, with ReLU activation, which takes the divergence of the convective velocity and segmentation mask S as input and produces the convective pressure, p_G. c) f_B is an *MLP* on channel dimension with *tanh* activation, which takes a domain descriptor $\mathbf{X}$ (Fig. 5) as input and maps it to a spatial function p_B. f_B is optimized for a specific geometry with their corresponding phase-field function ψ and specific boundary condition B_n.

operation ($\nabla \mathbf{u}^n \cdot \mathbf{u}^n$, $\Delta \mathbf{u}^n$) as ($\mathbf{u}_{Diff}^n$, $\mathbf{u}_{Conv}^n$). This part of the network is detailed as PDE-Net in Fig. 2a.

Pressure Decoupling (p_G, p_B): The resultant diffused and convective velocity from the PDE-Net ($\mathbf{u}_{Diff}^n$ and $\mathbf{u}_{Conv}^n$) in Fig. 2a contributes to the source of the pressure gradient. We make a few observations here: 1) $\nabla \cdot (-\nabla \mathbf{u}^n \cdot \mathbf{u}^n)$ causes a pressure gradient due to the geometric variation within the control volume. Additionally, the BC is non-zero at the inlet-outlet boundary and zero elsewhere. Thus, the pressure drop due to BC is global in nature for a particular computational domain. 2) One may question as to why we do not use an end-to-end FCN to infer pressure from velocity directly? To infer pressure from velocity, the computational domain plays an important role through the BC (Dirichlet for velocity and Neumann for pressure generally). Although FCNs are good for learning generalizable feature aggregates (from low-level edges to high-level objects in a hierarchical manner), we need to solve a volumetric non-local operation such as a boundary-conditioned volume integral to solve the pure Neumann BC. This requires the whole domain information at once, which is nontrivial for an FCN to learn with a finite receptive field. 3) Similarly, we do not design an MLP-only model with the Navier-Stokes equation embedded in the loss [17] because, if the contribution in the pressure from the local geometric variation and global BC are not balanced, the MLP often overlooks the weaker contribution.

To overcome the above problems, we propose to decouple the total pressure, p^{n+1}, as a sum of two components, i.e. $p^{n+1} = p_G^{n+1} + p_B^{n+1}$ (Fig. 1), where p_G^{n+1} denotes the pressure quantity induced by the convection due to variation in local geometric shape and p_B^{n+1} represents the pressure distribution coming from the inflow-outflow BC. Henceforth, the PPE needs to solve two separate equations,

$$\text{Poisson's Equation: } \Delta p_G^{n+1} = \nabla \cdot (-\nabla \mathbf{u}^n \cdot \mathbf{u}^n); \text{s.t. } \frac{\partial p_G^{n+1}}{\partial \eta} = 0 \qquad (3)$$

$$\text{Laplace's Equation: } \Delta p_B^{n+1} = 0; \text{s.t. } \frac{\partial p_B^{n+1}}{\partial \eta} = B_n \qquad (4)$$

For complex blood vessel geometries, the handling of BC is difficult due to: a) discretization error, b) error in the boundary estimate, and c) implementation of finite difference schemes for non-trivial BC, i.e., non-zero Neumann. [11] have shown a practical approximation for complex geometry by using a phase-field function for the Neumann BC in Eq. 4.

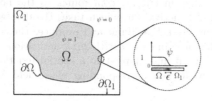

Fig. 3. An illustration of the phase-field function on a complex boundary. The original BC was Neumann at the boundary $\partial\Omega$. Diffused domain approximation transforms it into a Dirichlet BC at the modified simpler boundary $\partial\Omega_1$. The smoothness factor (ϵ) controls the approximation error vs robustness to noisy boundary trade-off.

As shown in Fig. 3, the computational domain can be realized as a phase-field function ψ, where $\psi = 1$ inside the domain and $\psi = 0$ outside the domain. At the boundary, this creates a smooth transition from $1 \rightarrow 0$ and therefore improves the handling of complex geometries.

We solve the following approximated PDE problem,

$$\psi \Delta p_B^{n+1} + \nabla \psi \cdot \nabla p_B^{n+1} + B_n |\nabla \psi| = 0 \qquad (5)$$

This formulation transforms the Neumann BC into a source term in the modified advection-diffusion equation (Eq. 5) with spatially varying coefficients. Additionally, this alleviates the Lagrange multiplier tuning between the energy of the Laplacian of the predicted field inside the domain and the energy mismatch at the boundary as used in [13].

FCN & MLP Share the Burden: To predict the convective induced pressure p_G^{n+1}, we need to learn a relationship between the divergence source term to a compensating scalar field. Since the divergence occurs locally in nature, an FCN is an ideal candidate for this task. We incorporate the multi-resolution FCN proposed by [21] to solve Eq. 3. Let's denote this network as f_G parameterized by θ (as described in Fig. 2b). The predicted pressure, p_G^{n+1}, is given by,

$$p_G^{n+1} = f_G \left(\nabla \cdot (-\nabla \mathbf{u}^n \cdot \mathbf{u}^n), S; \theta \right) \tag{6}$$

where S is the binary segmentation mask of the vessel. We train f_G by minimizing the cumulative divergence of the predicted velocities over T time steps,

$$\mathcal{L}_G = \frac{1}{T} \sum_{i=1}^{T} \int_{\Omega} \left\| \nabla \cdot \left(-\nabla \mathbf{u}^n \cdot \mathbf{u}^n - \frac{\delta t}{\rho} \nabla p_G^{i+1} \right) \right\| dv \tag{7}$$

As shown earlier, Eq. 4 ensures a smooth BC even for complex geometries. We, therefore, leverage the universal approximator property of the MLP to parameterize the functional form of the solution of Eq. 4 by f_B with a set of parameters ϕ. As shown in the MLP module in Fig. 2.c, f_b takes a description of the domain (Fig. 5) as input and maps it to a continuous spatial functional field. While in a simpler geometry, the Cartesian coordinate system is a good domain descriptor, a manifold aware descriptor is essential for the f_B to learn unctions, which are specific to geometries, such as blood vessels. To encode the manifold information in the domain discriminator, we employ a local cylindrical coordinate system as shown in Fig. 5. The f_B network architecture is explained in Fig. 2.c. Now, p_B^{n+1} is computed as follows

$$p_B^{n+1} = f_B(\mathbf{x}, B_n, \psi; \phi) \tag{8}$$

We adopt the phase-field approximation as described in the previous section to easily handle complex geometry and increase robustness against noisy BC. We train this network by minimizing the Laplacian energy over the control volume while obeying the BC.

$$\mathcal{L}_B = \underbrace{\int_{\Omega} \| \psi \Delta p_B^{n+1} + \nabla \psi \cdot \nabla p_B^{n+1} + B_n |\nabla \psi| \| dv}_{\text{volume integral}} \tag{9}$$

Appropriate discretization is employed to numerically evaluate the volume and surface integral in Eq. 9. Note that both Eqs. 7 and 9 are trained in an unsupervised manner. Initial conditions, the BC and segmented vessel mask are sufficient inputs for training.

3   Experiments

In the following, we introduce a proof-of-concept study for validating our proposed method on a simulated blood flow for brain aneurysms. We aim to estimate the pressure within a blood vessel from the velocity fields for a viscous and transient fluid such as blood. As we do not have the ground truth pressure to compare within the case of in-vivo 3D phase-contrast MRI, we rely on patient-specific simulated flow models to validate our method. Furthermore, due to the unavailability of standard datasets, it is a common practice [7,16,19] to validate the learning-based method by comparing it to a numerical reference solution. Therefore, given these constraints, we adopt a similar approach in our work to validate our proposed pressure estimation model against the solution of a numerical solver. Moreover, the unavailability of open-source codes posed a critical bottleneck for us to benchmark against competing methods.

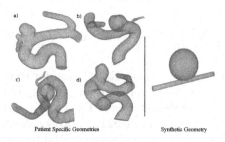

Patient Specific Geometries   Synthetic Geometry

Fig. 4. (**Left**) Four patient-specific geometries $(a \rightarrow d)$ are used for simulation of the flow segmented from 3D rotational angiogram images. These are the internal carotid arteries with aneurysms, which makes the data representative of complex blood vessel structures. After voxelization, the average size is $85 \times 110 \times 106$ voxels. (**Right**) Synthetic aneurysm geometry used for simulation of the flow. The spherical structure of the aneurysm induces vortex and complex flow which is used to train f_G

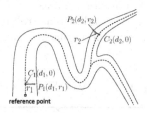

Fig. 5. Local cylindrical co-ordinates capture better domain topology than global Cartesian co-ordinates in case of blood vessel geometry as illustrated in the figure above. Points P_1 and P_2 are far apart to each other in the computational domain than the Euclidean distance between them. An efficient alternative way to describe the relative position is with respect to its distance from the nearest center-line points. Thus P_1 or P_2 can be represented with a pair of a) the distance from its closest centerline point, and b) the distance between its closest centerline point and the reference point along the centerline.

Flow Simulation: We use four patient-specific geometries with cerebral aneurysm (Fig. 4) to simulate 3D PC MRI sequences for one cardiac cycle, each with 24 time-points with temporal resolution of 36 ms and spatial resolution of 0.2 mm. We also have one synthetic geometry emulating an aneurysm in a uniform cylindrical vessel. We obtain two simulated flow sequences using the synthetic geometry, each with 100-time points and with a time step of 16 ms. The blood flow for each geometry was modeled as an unsteady Newtonian incompressible fluid with the following parameters: viscosity $= 0.0032\,\text{Pa·s}$; density $= 1050\,\text{kg/m}^3$. The Navier-Stokes equations were solved using the finite volume-based open-source platform OpenFOAM.V3.0. A second-order upwind scheme for the convective terms and a semi-implicit method for the pressure linked equations is used. The inlet patient-specific flow BC was extracted from 2D PC-MRI, and a zero pressure condition was used at the outlet. All the vascular walls were assumed rigid.

Training and Inference: Although the ground truth pressure is available at our disposal, we use them only for evaluation purposes. f_G is trained for direct inference of p_G (while ignoring p_B as it has no contribution in the inference of p_G due to the decoupling). We select a point for each geometry to use it as a reference point for quantitative and qualitative comparison. We only use two simulated sequences from the synthetic geometry for training f_G. Since f_B is a parameterized function conditioned by the specific BC, it is optimized on-the-fly during inference. Experimentally, the optimization of f_B converges after 40 iterations.

4   Results and Discussion:

Individual Performance of f_G and f_B (Ablation Study): For quantitative evaluation, we compare the predicted pressure, $p_G + p_B$, with the reference pressure for all four test geometries. Furthermore, we find that the contribution of p_B is more than that of p_G which is an expected behavior for highly viscous flow, such as blood, under transient acceleration. The total pressure is the only reference that is available from the CFD simulation and, therefore, we resort to additionally solving f_G using the Jacobi iteration and compare it with the prediction of f_G. This also serves as the ablation study of our approach since it evaluates f_G and f_B separately. Figure 8 shows box plots for the absolute error in total pressure $(p_G + p_B)$ and p_G with respect to the CFD simulated reference pressure and reference p_G obtained from Jacobi method respectively. We observe that the highest error occurs at the most complex structure of geometry d.

From Fig. 6, we observe that the pressure estimation at the aneurysm boundary has a higher absolute error than the areas with high flow. The outliers observed in the Bland-Altman plot (Fig. 9) originate from this region. We hypothesize that the local-cylindrical coordinate is optimal for a healthy vessel-like structure but sub-optimal for degenerated cases as in aneurysm (which does not have any active inflow or outflow rather than turbulent vortex). Our future

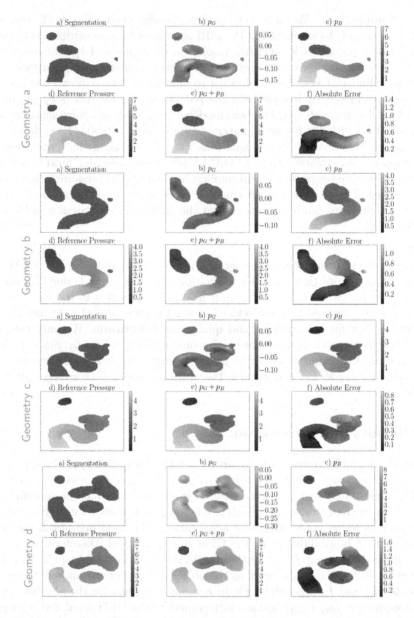

Fig. 6. An example qualitative comparison from the test sequence at a time instant (at t = 288 ms) from our experiment for all four geometries. All views are a 2D slice taken from the mid-section of the geometry. The unit for pressure is in mm Hg and the reference pressure at the primary outlet is set zero for the ground-truth, p_G, and p_B. a) shows the segmented mask. b) shows that f_G accurately captures the convective local pressure variation and c) shows that f_B infers a rather global pressure distribution induced by BC. d) shows simulated reference pressure. f) shows the absolute difference between $p_G + p_B$ (shown in e) and the reference pressure.

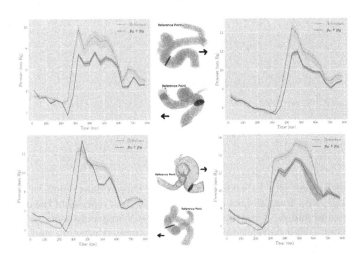

Fig. 7. Comparison between the mean reference and the mean estimated pressure for four different geometries at the slice locations shown in the middle. The banded curves indicate the 25% and 75% percentile of the distribution. The predicted pressure shows a good agreement in dynamic behaviour as the simulated reference.

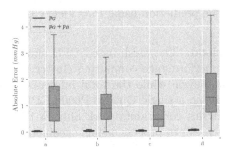

Fig. 8. Box plot for the absolute error in estimate of p_G and $p_G + p_B$ for four different geometries over one cardiac cycle. The median error for $p_G + p_B$ is consistently less than 1.5 mm Hg for all four geometries. Since, the contribution from p_B is higher compared to p_G, the error in $p_G + p_B$ mainly comes from p_B.

work will focus on learning a more general domain descriptor using geometric deep learning [2] suitable for a larger class of geometries than using hard-coded coordinates. This will facilitate the extension of our approach to arbitrary structures in multiple applications.

Distribution of Slice Dynamics: We examine the dynamic behavior of the predicted pressure at a particular plane over one cardiac cycle. The comparison depicted in Fig. 7 shows a good agreement between the simulated reference and the estimated pressure in terms of mean value and the distribution at the selected slice. We observe that our proposed method underestimates when the reference

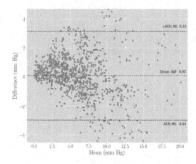

Fig. 9. Bland-Altman plot between 500 randomly chosen data points of the reference pressure and $p_G + p_B$ from all four geometry. The X-Axis represents the average of the reference pressure and $p_G + p_B$ estimates while the Y-axis represents their difference. This plot shows a high correlation between the estimated $p_G + p_B$ and the reference pressure with very few outliers.

pressure is high. We attribute this to be a performance trade-off as a consequence of the increased robustness offered by the phase-field approximation against the uncertainty in the BC values. The slice-wise processing is done as a post-processing step after the prediction using ParaView v5.6.0 software.

Run-Time Comparison: The mesh-based CFD simulation to generate reference data in a high performance computing cluster takes circa **10 h** for one subject per one cardiac cycle while the total inference time for out proposed method is circa **20 min** on a single Quadro P6000 GPU. A recent study based on an MLP where physics constraints work only in the loss function [9] has reported several hours (~ 7) to process a single geometry on a Tesla P100 GPU on the geometry of an aorta. Since they learn the convective source and the BC for every time points altogether, it takes a longer time for the network to learn the spatial distribution of pressure. On the contrary, our method leverages time discretization through network architecture and the splitting of pressure facilitates fast inference of p_G and spends most of its computing time only to infer p_B.

5   Conclusion

We introduce an end-to-end neural network approximating the traditional Navier-Stokes solver for incompressible Newtonian fluid flow with non-zero Neumann boundary conditions. Furthermore, in the context of pressure inference from the time-varying velocity field, we propose a novel approach for pressure decoupling and validate this using a generalizable FCN and an anatomy specific MLP-regressor based on the convection and boundary condition of the fluid. We evaluate the proposed method on simulated patient-specific blood flow data and find that our estimation closely approximates the simulated ground truth.

Acknowledgment. S. Shit and I. Ezhov are supported by the TRABIT Network under the EU Marie Curie Grant ID: 765148. D. Das is supported by the National Institute of Health (NIH) through the Nobrainer Project under the grant number: 1RF1MH121885-01A1. We thank NVIDIA for granting a Quadro P6000.

References

1. Bertoglio, C., et al.: Relative pressure estimation from velocity measurements in blood flows: SOTA and new approaches. Int. J. Numer. Meth. Bio. 34(2) (2018)
2. Bronstein, M.M., et al.: Geometric deep learning: going beyond euclidean data. IEEE Signal Process. Mag. **34**(4), 18–42 (2017)
3. Chen, T.Q., et al.: Neural ordinary differential equations. In: Proceedings of the NeurIPS. pp. 6571–6583 (2018)
4. Donati, F., et al.: Non-invasive pressure difference estimation from PC-MRI using the work-energy equation. Med. Image Anal. **26**(1), 159–172 (2015)
5. Ezhov, I., et al.: Geometry-aware neural solver for fast bayesian calibration of brain tumor models. arXiv preprint arXiv:2009.04240 (2020)
6. Gresho, P.M., Sani, R.L.: On pressure boundary conditions for the incompressible Navier-Stokes equations. Int. J. Numer. Methods Fluids. **7**(10), 1111–1145 (1987)
7. Hsieh, J.T., et al.: Learning neural PDE solvers with convergence guarantees. In: Proceedings of the ICLR (2019)
8. Kim, B., et al.: Deep fluids: a generative network for parameterized fluid simulations. In: Computer Graphics Forum, vol. 38, pp. 59–70. Wiley Online Library (2019)
9. Kissas, G., et al.: Machine learning in cardiovascular flows modeling: Predicting arterial blood pressure from non-invasive 4d flow MRI data using physics-informed neural networks. Comput. Methods. Appl. Mech. Eng. **358**, (2020)
10. Krittian, S.B., et al.: A finite-element approach to the direct computation of relative cardiovascular pressure from time-resolved MR velocity data. Med. Image Anal. **16**(5), 1029–1037 (2012)
11. Li, X., et al.: Solving PDEs in complex geometries: a diffuse domain approach. Commun. Math. Sci. **7**(1), 81 (2009)
12. Long, Z., et al.: PDE-net: learning PDEs from data. In: Proceedings of the 35th ICML, vol. 80, pp. 3208–3216. PMLR (2018)
13. Magill, M., et al.: Neural networks trained to solve differential equations learn general representations. In: Proceedings of the NeurIPS, pp. 4071–4081 (2018)
14. Markl, M., et al.: 4D flow MRI. JMRI **36**(5), 1015–1036 (2012)
15. Mihalef, V., et al.: Model-based estimation of 4D relative pressure map from 4D flow MR images. In: STACOM. pp. 236–243. Springer (2013)
16. Raissi, M., et al.: Physics-informed neural networks: a deep learning framework for solving forward and inverse problems involving nonlinear partial differential equations. J. Comput. Phys. **378**, 686–707 (2019)
17. Raissi, M., et al.: Hidden fluid mechanics: learning velocity and pressure fields from flow visualizations. Science (2020)
18. Rengier, F., et al.: Noninvasive pressure difference mapping derived from 4D flow MRI in patients with unrepaired and repaired aortic coarctation. Cardiovascular Diagnosis Therapy **4**(2), 97 (2014)
19. Shit, S., et al.: Implicit neural solver for time-dependent linear pdes with convergence guarantee. arXiv preprint arXiv:1910.03452 (2019)

20. Thuerey, N., et al.: Deep learning methods for reynolds-averaged navier-stokes simulations of airfoil flows. AIAA Journal pp. 1–12 (2019)
21. Tompson, J., et al.: Accelerating Eulerian fluid simulation with convolutional networks. In: Proceedings of the 34th ICML, vol. 70, pp. 3424–3433. PMLR (2017)
22. Tyszka, J.M., et al.: Three-dimensional, time-resolved (4D) relative pressure mapping using magnetic resonance imaging. JMRI **12**(2), 321–329 (2000)
23. Van Oudheusden, B.: PIV-based pressure measurement. Measur. Sci. Technol. **24**(3), 1–32 (2013)

Lighting Enhancement Aids Reconstruction of Colonoscopic Surfaces

Yubo Zhang[1]([✉]) [iD], Shuxian Wang[1] [iD], Ruibin Ma[1] [iD], Sarah K. McGill[2] [iD], Julian G. Rosenman[3] [iD], and Stephen M. Pizer[1] [iD]

[1] Department of Computer Science, University of North Carolina at Chapel Hill, Chapel Hill, USA
{zhangyb,shuxian,ruibinma,pizer}@cs.unc.edu
[2] Department of Medicine, University of North Carolina at Chapel Hill, Chapel Hill, USA
mcgills@email.unc.edu
[3] Department of Radiation Oncology, University of North Carolina at Chapel Hill, Chapel Hill, USA
rosenmju@med.unc.edu

Abstract. High screening coverage during colonoscopy is crucial to effectively prevent colon cancer. Previous work has allowed alerting the doctor to unsurveyed regions by reconstructing the 3D colonoscopic surface from colonoscopy videos in real-time. However, the lighting inconsistency of colonoscopy videos can cause a key component of the colonoscopic reconstruction system, the SLAM optimization, to fail. In this work we focus on the lighting problem in colonoscopy videos. To successfully improve the lighting consistency of colonoscopy videos, we have found necessary a lighting correction that adapts to the intensity distribution of recent video frames. To achieve this in real-time, we have designed and trained an RNN network. This network adapts the gamma value in a gamma-correction process. Applied in the colonoscopic surface reconstruction system, our light-weight model significantly boosts the reconstruction success rate, making a larger proportion of colonoscopy video segments reconstructable and improving the reconstruction quality of the already reconstructed segments.

Keywords: Colonoscopy · Image enhancement · 3D reconstruction

1 Introduction

Colonoscopy is an effective examination to prevent colon (large intestine) cancer by screening for lesions. During a colonoscopy a flexible tube called a colonoscope is inserted up to the distal end of the patient's colon, and then it is withdrawn through the colon while producing a video by a camera that is attached at the tip of the colonoscope. A point light attached to the colonoscope tip moves with the camera to provide the lighting source. During a colonoscopy the camera sends back live images of the colon wall to the doctor, who watches, detects

© Springer Nature Switzerland AG 2021
A. Feragen et al. (Eds.): IPMI 2021, LNCS 12729, pp. 559–570, 2021.
https://doi.org/10.1007/978-3-030-78191-0_43

and removes cancerous or pre-cancerous lesions with a surgical knife inside the colonoscope.

Fig. 1. The lighting in the colonoscopy video can change rapidly from frame to frame, and a large part of the colon interior can be poorly lit due to the complicated colon terrain. This lighting issue can bring troubles to the diagnosis and the colon surface reconstruction system.

Due to time limitations, colonoscopy is a one-pass exam, but high coverage of screening and high polyp detection rate are crucial. Previous work tried to aid the colonoscopy process by alerting the doctor to unsurveyed colon regions ("blind spots") revealed by reconstructing the already screened surfaces in real-time from colonoscopy videos [11]. However, as shown in Fig. 1, the complex topography makes a notable proportion of the colon surface be poorly lit; also, it causes brightness and contrast to change rapidly from frame to frame. The poor lighting situation challenges 1) lesion detection by the doctor and 2) successful reconstruction of the surfaces, thereby allowing alerts as to blind spots.

In this work we focus on this lighting issue in colonoscopy. We aim to make the lighting of colonoscopy videos consistent between consecutive frames and also to brighten the dark regions in colonoscopy video frames. Such image enhancement is commonly carried out by curve adjustment approaches [6,7] such as gamma correction, and recent deep learning methods can apply a more sophisticated adjustment to each image pixel with CNN- [5,19] or GAN-based models [1,8]. Considering that our inputs are video frames, we adopt the learning-based approach and develop an RNN-based network for adaptive curve adjustment. Our network is trained in an unsupervised fashion using a loss measuring the lighting consistency among nearby frames and will produce well-lit frame sequences at test time. Applying our model as a pre-processing step to the frames for reconstruction leads to significant improvement of both the number of reconstructable colonoscopy video segments and the quality of reconstructions, with time overhead small enough to be ignored.

Overall, the contributions of this work are

- To our knowledge, our work is the first one to focus on the lighting consistency issue in the colonoscopy video.
- We propose a light-weight RNN model for lighting enhancement of an image sequence, which can be trained without ground-truth. Tested on real colonoscopy images, our model can effectively brighten the poorly lit regions in each frame, and make the lighting consistent from frame to frame.

- Most importantly, applied in the colonoscopic surface reconstruction system, our model effectively boosts the reconstruction success rate and improves the reconstruction quality without sacrificing the time efficiency of the system.

2   Background: SLAM and Colonoscopic Reconstruction

Here, we review the mechanism behind the 3D reconstruction technique SLAM, which is a key component in colonoscopic reconstruction systems. We then analyze why the lighting issue in colonoscopy can cause the SLAM system to fail.

2.1   SLAM Mechanism

3D reconstruction is a challenging task in computer vision. One of the most successful methods for this task is Simultaneous Localization And Mapping (SLAM). SLAM systems have achieved tremendous success in indoor and outdoor-scene reconstruction [4,17]. Recently, with the development of deep learning, neural networks have been applied to aid SLAM for better reconstruction [18,20,24], especially in the more challenging scenarios such as reconstruction from colonoscopy video [11].

SLAM is an algorithm that can achieve real-time dense reconstruction from a sequence of monocular images [2,3,12,13]. As the name suggests, SLAM has a localization component and a mapping component; the two components operate cooperatively. The localization (tracking) component predicts the camera poses from each incoming image frame. Based on the visual clues extracted from the images, the mapping component optimizes especially the pose predictions but also the keypoints' depth estimates. The objective function used in the optimization of the SLAM of [2], which is applied in colonoscopic reconstruction [11], is

$$E_{ij} = \sum_{p \in \mathcal{P}_j} \omega_p \left\| (I_j[p'] - b_j) - \frac{e^{a_j}}{e^{a_i}} (I_i[p] - b_i) \right\|_\gamma \tag{1}$$

$$p' = \Pi(T\Pi^{-1}(p, d_p)) \tag{2}$$

Sampled from a source image I_i, each keypoint p in the keypoint set $\mathcal{P}_j$ can be projected to a location p' in a target image I_j, based on its predicted depth d_p and the predicted camera transformation T. Π denotes the projection. Supposing the transformation and depth predictions are correct, p of image I_i and p' of image I_j come from the same surface point, so $I_i[p]$ and $I_j[p']$ should have the same intensity. This assumption is the mechanism behind the energy function E_{ij} which is the photometric error between two frames I_i and I_j in Eq. 1, where $\|*\|_\gamma$ denotes the Huber norm. The a_k and b_k values are discussed below.

2.2   The Lighting Problem in Colonoscopic Surface Reconstruction

The photometric-based optimization in SLAM depends on the light consistency between frames, that assuming the same physical location in the environment is shown in similar intensities in different frames. This is a prerequisite that can be mostly fulfilled in an indoor or outdoor scenario with the steady lighting source, e.g., sunlight. When it comes to colonoscopy, this lighting consistency assumption can often be violated since the point light is moving with the camera and can change rapidly due to motion and occlusion. Although the SLAM algorithm also optimizes an additional brightness transformation as a compensation, denoted as $e^{-a}(I-b)$ in Eq. 1, it just fixes each frame's exposure and cannot handle the more complicated lighting changes in colonoscopy videos such as contrast difference (bright regions become brighter and dark regions become darker). So without specific brightness adjustment, this kind of rapid lighting change in colonoscopy makes the SLAM system unstable, often leading to tracking failure.

We want to alleviate the failures caused by lighting changes. In this work we accomplished this by explicitly adjusting the brightness of the image sequence to make them more consistent. This requires solving an adaptive image enhancement problem that each image in the sequence is enhanced in relation to adjacent frames. We develop a deep learning method for this task, which will be discussed in detail in the next section.

3   Method

In this work we apply an adaptive intensity mapping to enhance the colonoscopy frame sequence with the help of an RNN network, whose implementation and unsupervised training strategy will be introduced in this section.

3.1   Adaptive Gamma Correction

Image enhancement is a classical topic in computer vision. Multiple directions have been proposed to resolve the issue, such as histogram equalization and its variants [14,22], unsharp masking [10,15] and more recently deep learning pixel-wise prediction approaches [5,8,9].

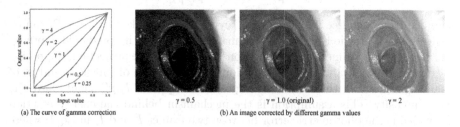

(a) The curve of gamma correction   (b) An image corrected by different gamma values

Fig. 2. The gamma correction: (a) Gamma correction's effect on image intensity; (b) The figure in the middle is been adjusted by different gamma values.

Our driving problem of the reconstruction from colonoscopy video requires real-time execution, so our lighting enhancement must be accomplished at the video frame rate. This requires that only a handful of parameters be adjusted from frame to frame in an enhancement method. An example approach that meets this requirement is gamma correction [6,7]. In gamma correction, for every pixel in an image, its input value I_{in} is adjusted by the power γ, then multiplied by a constant A to get the enhanced value I_{out}:

$$I_{out} = AI_{in}^{\gamma} \tag{3}$$

In practice, the input intensities will be normalized to $[0,1]$, so the constant A will be set to 1 and γ is the only parameter controlling the adjustment. By applying a different γ value, the same image can be brightened or darkened to a different extent, as the example shown in (b) of Fig. 2.

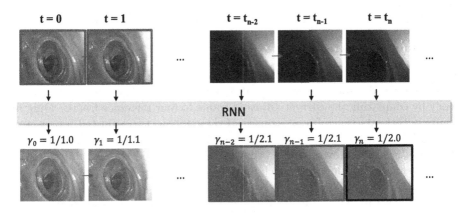

Fig. 3. At each time step, the RNN takes an input image and predicts its γ value to enhance the image. The network is trained by contrasting the current corrected image with two previous corrected images and the first two input images of the sequence.

Our goal is to improve the lighting consistency of an image sequence. Adjusting the way in which each frame is enhanced requires an adaptive version. To model this adaptation, we specifically design a recurrent neural network (RNN) to capture the temporal information needed in the enhancement and to predict the γ value for each image. The overall pipeline of our RNN-based adaptive gamma correction is shown in Fig. 3. The details of the RNN network will be discussed next.

3.2 RNN Network

Although the gamma correction is cheap in computation, our enhancement RNN network also needs to be light-weight in order to serve as an additional preprocessing step for the current real-time colonoscopic surface reconstruction system. Thus, we build our RNN network on the ConvLSTM unit [23], with only two additional convolution layers:

$$x_1 = \text{ReLU}(\text{Conv}(I_i)) \tag{4}$$

$$[x_2, h_i] = \text{ConvLSTM}([x_1, h_{i-1}]) \tag{5}$$

$$x_3 = \text{ReLU}(\text{Conv}(x_2)) \tag{6}$$

$$f = \text{AvgPool}(x_3) \tag{7}$$

$$\gamma_i = \text{ReLU}(Af + b) \tag{8}$$

At test time, at each time step the network takes the current image frame I_i as the input, includes latent information of the previous frames h_{i-1} into the computation, and predicts the gamma correction value γ_i for the current frame. The prediction happens recurrently, enhancing the entire sequence as shown in Fig. 3.

3.3   Training Strategy

With no ground-truth to supervise the network training, our RNN is trained in an unsupervised fashion to achieve lighting consistency. We achieve this consistency by comparing the current adjusted frame to four reference frames. Only in training, these reference frames consist of the previous two adjusted frames and the first two images of the entire sequence, which serve as the "seed" images to stabilize the training by setting a brightness baseline. For example in Fig. 3, the target frame is surrounded in black and all the reference frames are surrounded in red.

The loss we are optimizing utilizes the structural similarity measurement [21]:

$$L_{ssim} = \text{mean}(1 - \text{SSIM}(I_r, I_t)) \tag{9}$$

$$= \text{mean}(1 - \frac{(2\mu_{I_r}\mu_{I_t} + c_1)(2\sigma_{I_r I_t} + c_2)}{(\mu_{I_r}^2 + \mu_{I_t}^2 + c_1)(\sigma_{I_r}^2 + \sigma_{I_t}^2 + c_2)}) \tag{10}$$

where at each pixel location, μ_I is the local average, σ_I^2 is the local variance and $\sigma_{I_r I_t}$ is the covariance of two images. c_1 and c_2 are small constants to avoid dividing by zero. The SSIM function is composed of three comparisons: luminance, contrast and structure. When applying to training, the luminance and contrast comparisons will force the network to produce adjusted images with similar lighting to the reference frames.

Specular regions have very high intensities that inordinately influence the lighting estimation in a frame. Therefore, in training when computing the L_{ssim}, we mask out the pixels with input intensity larger than 0.7. Each training sequence contains 10 sequential frames, with the first two as seeds, and the loss of each target frame is computed as the average L_{ssim} of its four reference frames.

4   Experiments

4.1   Implementation Details

To build the dataset of our task, we collected 105 colonoscopy video snippets, each containing 50 to 150 frames. 60 snippets were used as the training data, 1 was used for validation, and the rest were reserved for evaluation. Among the 44 evaluation sequences, 12 of them could be successfully reconstructed using the colonoscopic surface reconstruction system in previous work [11], while 32 of them could not.

For the training and validation snippets, we divided them into 10-frame overlapping sub-sequences. In this way we created about 1800 training sequences. We used the Adam optimizer with a fixed learning rate of 5×10^{-5} to train the RNN network for 10 epochs. A batch size of 4 was used. We implemented our method using the PyTorch framework on a single Nvidia Quadro RTX5000 GPU.

At test time our network enhances the entire snippet from start to end with an average image enhancement run time of less than a millisecond. Considering the frame rate we use to extract images from video is 18 frames per second, the overhead brought by our method is small enough and does not violate the real-time execution when added to the colonoscopic reconstruction system.

4.2   Visual Effect

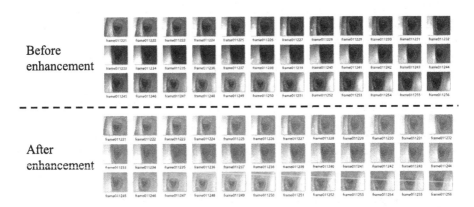

Fig. 4. The visual comparison of the same sequence before (top) and after (bottom) the RNN enhancement. After enhancement, the extreme dark regions have been brightened up and the lighting consistency improves.

In Fig. 4 we show a snippet that is been enhanced using our trained RNN network, where the original frames are shown on the top and the enhanced ones on the bottom. The overall brightness of the sequence has been largely improved and the "down the barrel" regions are brightened up and clearly revealed after enhancement. Moreover, the lighting consistency is significantly improved. The image contrast changes rapidly in the original sequence, due to a haustral ridge blocking much of the light. After enhancement, these changes across frames from bright on average to dark on average and then back to bright on average are far less obvious: the lighting of the sequence becomes much more consistent.

4.3   Application in Colonoscopic Surface Reconstruction

In the colonoscopic surface reconstruction system RNNSLAM [11], a deep learning RNN network runs in parallel with a standard SLAM system. The RNN component predicts the depths and pose of each camera frame to initialize their SLAM optimization, and the SLAM outputs the improved values of poses and depths and updates the hidden states of RNN. This combination leads to low tracking error. Our RNN lighting enhancement network can also run in parallel with the RNNSLAM. The enhanced images produced by our method are given to its SLAM component as the image inputs.

Success on the Cases that Fail with Original Images. To prove the validity of our method, we tested the RNNSLAM system with enhanced images on 32 cases which cannot be reconstructed with the original images. A case is categorized as a failure when RNNSLAM predicts obvious discontinuous camera poses, or the system aborts automatically when it cannot give reasonable pose prediction. We noticed that most of the previous failure cases include significant lighting changes or large camera motion that leads to lighting occlusion. When testing them with our enhancement module inserted, 21 of 32 succeeded without tracking failure: the reconstruction success rate significantly increased. We also tested these 32 cases with the images enhanced by histogram equalization [14] and by a neural-network method Zero-DCE [6][1]; only 8 and 12, respectively succeeded, showing our method outperforms the traditional and deep-learning single-image enhancement approaches on improving the reconstruction success rate.

In Fig. 5 we illustrate a case of improved tracking using our lighting correction, where the predicted camera trajectory without enhancement is shown in red, and the trajectory after enhancement is shown in blue. In each case the camera is predicted to start from the top right position and to move along the respective trajectory to the bottom left position. Particularly in the figure, we show the positions predicted for two successive keyframes t and $t+1$. Although it is clear to the human eye that the motion between these two images is subtle, due to a lighting change, the camera pose prediction changes by a dramatic distance of 2.63 when using the original frames, clearly indicating an error comparing to the 0.03 median camera translation of this trajectory. This issue of discontinuity in predicted poses does not occur after we enhance the input images, where the

---

[1] We implemented the training in [6] without color constancy loss using the colonoscopy images from our training set.

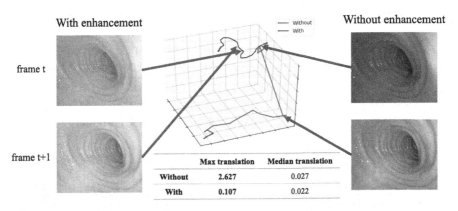

Fig. 5. The comparison of pose trajectories for the same sequence without (red) and with (blue) the RNN lighting enhancement. The pose discontinuity issue indicated by large camera translation does not occur after using enhanced images.

predicted camera poses move smoothly and the maximum camera translation of this trajectory is 0.11.

Pose Improvement of Previously Reconstructable Sequences. Not only does our lighting enhancement allow previously un-reconstructable sequences to be reconstructed, but as demonstrated in the following, it improves the pose trajectories produced from sequences that were previously reconstructable. To quantitatively measure the pose improvement, we adopt the evaluation method in [11], using COLMAP [16] on the un-enhanced images to generate a high-quality baseline trajectory as the virtual "ground-truth" for each video sequence. As the evaluation metric we compute the absolute pose error (APE) of each timestamp in the generated trajectory compared to its "ground-truth". For each trajectory, the RMSE of the APE statistics of all timestamps is computed. We tested 12 colonoscopic sequences that were already reconstructable without our enhancement strategy. We computed the RMSE and other APE statistics (mean, std, etc.) of each sequence respectively, and in Table 1 we list the summary statistics across these 12 sequences. For better reference, we also show the errors of the trajectories produced by COLMAP when using enhanced images. Since we are measuring the error, the lower the result is, the better.

For every sample in these 12 sequences, even though the original lighting is consistent enough for the SLAM to produce decent pose predictions, our enhancement method brought further improvement, decreasing their pose errors. This result shows that besides significantly increasing the reconstruction success rate, our method can also bring minor improvement to the reconstruction quality in cases that can be reconstructed successfully without lighting enhancement.

Table 1. The average APE statistics of 12 colonoscopic sequences

Method	Mean RMSE	Mean APE	Std APE	Min APE	Median APE	Max APE
COLMAP w/Enhanced img	0.329	0.295	0.143	0.077	0.278	0.736
RNNSLAM w/Original img	0.840	0.752	0.371	0.203	0.694	1.666
RNNSLAM w/Enhanced img	**0.680**	**0.606**	**0.302**	**0.105**	**0.554**	**1.388**

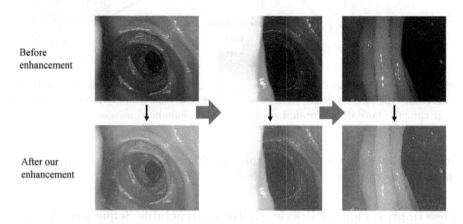

Before
enhancement

After our
enhancement

Fig. 6. An extreme tracking condition, the "close occluder". Its complicated lighting situation is beyond our enhancement method's capacity.

5   Discussion and Conclusion

Due to the complexity of colon geometry, the lighting in colonoscopy videos tends to have rapid changes that lead to failures in the colonoscopic surface reconstruction system. In this work we focused on improving the lighting consistency in colonoscopy videos. We proposed a light-weight RNN network for an adaptive lighting enhancement method to enhance the colonoscopy image sequence, which brightens the dark regions and makes lighting consistent from frame to frame. With the help of our enhancement module, a larger portion of colonoscopy videos can now be successfully reconstructed and the reconstruction quality is improved.

Future Work.

1. Our method is initially designed to improve the lighting consistency of colonoscopy sequences, but it is also applicable for other video modalities. For example, for other types of endoscopy videos and outdoor driving sequences with large lighting changes, our network can be trained on these data to improve their lighting consistency for better reconstruction.

2. Although our method successfully increases the reconstruction success rate, there is still a notable fraction of colonoscopy sequences that cannot be reconstructed after the lighting fix. They usually contain some extreme tracking conditions, and one of them is what we call the "close occluder". In this case, as the colonoscope moving behind a haustral ridge, or moving side-way and being really close to the colon surface, the image foreground occupies a large portion of an image frame, as shown in the last two images of Fig. 6. The lighting in these images is usually extremely bright in the foreground and extremely dark in the background. Moreover, when using these frames, the SLAM system will choose keypoints for optimization not only from the "down the barrel" portion of the image, as it usually does with the normal frames, but also from the bright foreground. Therefore, in order for these cases to succeed, the bright and the dark regions both need to be more elaborately adjusted to achieve global lighting consistency. Currently our method cannot handle this complicated scenario and a more sophisticated image enhancement technique is needed; we leave it to future work.

Acknowledgement. We thank Prof. Jan-Michael Frahm for useful consultations. This work was carried out with financial support from the Olympus Corporation, the UNC Kenan Professorship Fund, and the UNC Lineberger Cancer Center.

References

1. Chen, Y.S., Wang, Y.C., Kao, M.H., Chuang, Y.Y.: Deep photo enhancer: Unpaired learning for image enhancement from photographs with GANs. In: Proceedings of the IEEE Conference on Computer Vision and Pattern Recognition, pp. 6306–6314 (2018)
2. Engel, J., Koltun, V., Cremers, D.: Direct sparse odometry. IEEE Trans. Pattern Anal. Mach. Intell. **40**(3), 611–625 (2017)
3. Engel, J., Sturm, J., Cremers, D.: Semi-dense visual odometry for a monocular camera. In: Proceedings of the IEEE International Conference on Computer Vision, pp. 1449–1456 (2013)
4. Geiger, A., Lenz, P., Stiller, C., Urtasun, R.: Vision meets robotics: The kitti dataset. Int. J. Robot. Res. **32**(11), 1231–1237 (2013)
5. Gharbi, M., Chen, J., Barron, J.T., Hasinoff, S.W., Durand, F.: Deep bilateral learning for real-time image enhancement. ACM Trans. Graph. (TOG) **36**(4), 1–12 (2017)
6. Guo, C., et al.: Zero-reference deep curve estimation for low-light image enhancement. In: Proceedings of the IEEE/CVF Conference on Computer Vision and Pattern Recognition, pp. 1780–1789 (2020)
7. Huang, S.C., Cheng, F.C., Chiu, Y.S.: Efficient contrast enhancement using adaptive gamma correction with weighting distribution. IEEE Trans. Image Process. **22**(3), 1032–1041 (2012)
8. Jiang, Y., et al.: Enlightengan: deep light enhancement without paired supervision. In: Proceedings of the IEEE Conference on Computer Vision and Pattern Recognition (2019)

570   Y. Zhang et al.

9. Ke, Z., Qiu, D., Li, K., Yan, Q., Lau, R.W.: Guided collaborative training for pixel-wise semi-supervised learning. In: European Conference on Computer Vision (ECCV) (August 2020)
10. Luft, T., Colditz, C., Deussen, O.: Image enhancement by un sharp masking the depth buffer. ACM Trans. Graph. (TOG) 25(3), 1206–1213 (2006)
11. Ma, R., Wang, R., Pizer, S., Rosenman, J., McGill, S.K., Frahm, J.-M.: Real-Time 3D reconstruction of colonoscopic surfaces for determining missing regions. In: Shen, D., et al. (eds.) MICCAI 2019. LNCS, vol. 11768, pp. 573–582. Springer, Cham (2019). https://doi.org/10.1007/978-3-030-32254-0_64
12. Mur-Artal, R., Montiel, J.M.M., Tardos, J.D.: Orb-slam: a versatile and accurate monocular slam system. IEEE Trans. Robot. 31(5), 1147–1163 (2015)
13. Newcombe, R.A., Lovegrove, S.J., Davison, A.J.: Dtam: dense tracking and mapping in real-time. In: 2011 International Conference on Computer Vision, pp. 2320–2327. IEEE (2011)
14. Pizer, S.M., et al.: Adaptive histogram equalization and its variations. Comput. Vis. Graph. Image Process. 39(3), 355–368 (1987)
15. Polesel, A., Ramponi, G., Mathews, V.J.: Image enhancement via adaptive unsharp masking. IEEE Trans. Image Process. 9(3), 505–510 (2000)
16. Schönberger, J.L., Frahm, J.M.: Structure-from-motion revisited. In: Conference on Computer Vision and Pattern Recognition (CVPR) (2016)
17. Sturm, J., Engelhard, N., Endres, F., Burgard, W., Cremers, D.: A benchmark for the evaluation of RGB-d slam systems. In: Proceedings of the International Conference on Intelligent Robot Systems (IROS) (October 2012)
18. Tateno, K., Tombari, F., Laina, I., Navab, N.: CNN-slam: Real-time dense monocular slam with learned depth prediction. In: Proceedings of the IEEE Conference on Computer Vision and Pattern Recognition, pp. 6243–6252 (2017)
19. Wang, R., Zhang, Q., Fu, C.W., Shen, X., Zheng, W.S., Jia, J.: Underexposed photo enhancement using deep illumination estimation. In: Proceedings of the IEEE Conference on Computer Vision and Pattern Recognition, pp. 6849–6857 (2019)
20. Wang, S., Clark, R., Wen, H., Trigoni, N.: Deepvo: towards end-to-end visual odometry with deep recurrent convolutional neural networks. In: 2017 IEEE International Conference on Robotics and Automation (ICRA), pp. 2043–2050. IEEE (2017)
21. Wang, Z., Bovik, A.C., Sheikh, H.R., Simoncelli, E.P.: Image quality assessment: from error visibility to structural similarity. IEEE Trans. Image Process. 13(4), 600–612 (2004)
22. Xiao, B., Xu, Y., Tang, H., Bi, X., Li, W.: Histogram learning in image contrast enhancement. In: Proceedings of the IEEE Conference on Computer Vision and Pattern Recognition Workshops (2019)
23. Xingjian, S., Chen, Z., Wang, H., Yeung, D.Y., Wong, W.K., Woo, W.C.: Convolutional LSTM network: a machine learning approach for precipitation nowcasting. In: Advances in Neural Information Processing Systems, pp. 802–810 (2015)
24. Yang, N., Wang, R., Stuckler, J., Cremers, D.: Deep virtual stereo odometry: leveraging deep depth prediction for monocular direct sparse odometry. In: Proceedings of the European Conference on Computer Vision (ECCV), pp. 817–833 (2018)

Mixture Modeling for Identifying Subtypes in Disease Course Mapping

Pierre-Emmanuel Poulet$^{(\boxtimes)}$ ⓘ and Stanley Durrleman ⓘ

Inria, Aramis Project-team, Paris Brain Institute, Inserm U 1127, CNRS UMR 7225, Sorbonne Université, 75013 Paris, France
{pierre-emmanuel.poulet,stanley.durrleman}@inria.fr

Abstract. Disease modeling techniques summarize the possible trajectories of progression from multimodal and longitudinal data. These techniques often assume that individuals form a homogeneous cluster, thus ignoring possible disease subtypes within the population. We extend a non-linear mixed-effect model used for disease course mapping with a mixture framework. We jointly estimate model parameters and subtypes with a tempered version of a stochastic approximation of the Expectation Maximisation algorithm. We show that our model recovers the ground truth parameters from synthetic data, in contrast to the naive solution consisting in *post hoc* clustering of individual parameters from a one-class model. Applications to Alzheimer's disease data allows the unsupervised identification of disease subtypes associated with distinct relationship between cognitive decline and progression of imaging and biological biomarkers.

Keywords: Mixture model · Non-linear mixed-effect model · Disease course mapping · Alzheimer's disease subtypes

1 Introduction

In the wake of medical progress and general increase of life expectancy, neurodegenerative diseases have seen a dramatic surge in the population. In order to better understand these diseases, our goal is to build digital models of their progression, which may span decades in the life of the patients. Such models may be estimated from longitudinal data sets of several patients at different disease stages. Data may include cognitive or behavioral assessments, biological biomarkers or image-based biomarkers such as regional brain volumes.

The statistical analysis of longitudinal data is often done in the framework of mixed-effects models [1]. Linear mixed-effects models (LMEM) are widely

S. Durrleman—This research has received funding from the program "Investissements d'avenir" ANR-10-IAIHU-06. This work was also funded in part by the French government under management of Agence Nationale de la Recherche as part of the "Investissements d'avenir" program, reference ANR-19-P3IA-0001 (PRAIRIE 3IA Institute), for the Alzheimer's Disease Neuroimaging Initiative.

A. Feragen et al. (Eds.): IPMI 2021, LNCS 12729, pp. 571–582, 2021.
https://doi.org/10.1007/978-3-030-78191-0_44

used, yet their application to medical observations is not adapted because of the non-linearity of the disease progression over large periods of time [2]. Nonlinear mixed-effects models (NLMEM) have been proposed in recent years [3,4]. Mixed-effects models separate fixed effects, assumed to be common to the population, and individual effects, which are random variables describing how the model should change to accommodate for inter-individual differences. They are often assumed to follow a unimodal distribution, thus assuming the homogeneity of the population. However, this is often not the case as neurodegenerative diseases are known to be heterogeneous, with various subtypes that are difficult to characterize. Uncovering the underlying clusters of population is a complex task to perform in addition to an already complex NLMEM.

Our work contribution is a framework allowing for both unsupervised clustering and estimation of an NLMEM for each cluster. We propose a mixture model based on a nonlinear Riemannian mixed-effect model which we will refer to as a disease course mapping model [5]. The joint estimation of clusters and model parameters is performed using a mixture Monte-Carlo Markov chain stochastic approximation Expectation Maximisation (M-MCMC SAEM) algorithm [6]. This end-to-end approach differs from a more naive approach based on *a posteriori* clustering the parameters of the individual effects after the estimation of an NLMEM. We applied the proposed mixture model to the Alzheimer's disease neuroimaging initiative (ADNI) cohort. Our main focus is the separation of two obvious clusters: controls and patients diagnosed with Alzheimer. We then included the mild cognitive impaired (MCI) patients to understand their position relatively to the two previously found clusters.

2   Related Work

Analysis of longitudinal data can be performed with various types of models. Discrete models include event-based models which estimate the temporal ordering of sequence of pathological events [7–9]. This approach has been extended with the SuStaIn model [10] to identify clusters in the population.

Continuous models include the linear mixed-effects model [1]. Several NLMEM have been proposed, one being the generalized linear framework [11] where the observations result of simple non-linear transformation of an LMEM. Typically the link function can be the logit, allowing for a sigmoid-shaped model. NLMEM include univariate models with time-reparameterizing functions [12]. Multivariate approaches include DIVE [4], a voxel-based model which also clusters disease trajectories, and disease course mapping which combines variations in progression dynamics with phenotypic differences [5,13–15]. In this approach, the observations belong to a Riemannian manifold and each individual trajectory in time is a parallel to a geodesic curve representing the population trajectory. Other models are also based on differential equation models [3]. Non parametric models using deep learning were also explored [16].

Estimation of complex parametric models such as NLMEM corresponds to the maximization of the likelihood. Such optimization can be performed with the

Expectation Maximization (EM) and more especially its stochastic approximation variant with Monte-Carlo Markov chain (MCMC SAEM) which has been
proven to have good theoretical properties [17–19]. Moreover the EM algorithm
is also a staple for mixture model estimation. Combining the estimation of the
mixture model and the NLMEM has already been studied [6]. However the theoretical properties are often not enough as the MCMC SAEM tends, in practice,
to suffer from local maxima attraction. In particular, changing cluster assignments is known to be challenging in such methods; it is a problem referred to
as trapping states. Adding a tempering scheme has been shown to alleviate this
issue by flattening the target distribution and thus easing the exploration of the
parameter space [20]. A mixture model on top of a disease progression model was
also proposed in [21], the clustering during estimation was handled with hard
labels and a probability for individuals to switch from one cluster to another.

3   Method

3.1   Disease Course Mapping Model

We present here the disease course mapping model first mentioned in [5] and
improved in [13,15]. We introduce the notations and essential equations for the
rest of the article. In this work we focus on the particular case where the model
takes the form of a series of logistic curves for each biomarker.

We assume a longitudinal dataset $(y_{ijk})_{1 \leq i \leq n, 1 \leq j \leq N_i, 1 \leq k \leq d}$ where each
patient i has N_i visits, at time t_{ij}, and d features observed at each visit. The
number of visits N_i may vary from one patient to another. Data y_{ijk} are assumed
to be points on a Riemannian manifold $\mathcal{M}$. This model is a mixed effect model
in the following sense: we define the population parameters or fixed effects as a
set of parameters describing an average population trajectory as a geodesic γ_0
in the Riemannian manifold, with $\gamma_0(t_0) = \mathbf{p}$ and $\dot{\gamma}_0(t_0) = \mathbf{v}$. The individual
effects take into account a temporal effect with an individual reparametrization
of time and space-shifts, also called inter-marker spacing parameters. Following
the hypothesis of sigmoids for neurodegenerative disease biomarkers [2], we use
the logistic variant of the disease course mapping model:

$$y_{ijk} = \left(1 + (\frac{1}{p_k} - 1)exp(-\frac{v_k(e^{\xi_i}(t_{ij} - t_0 - \tau_i) + t_0) + w_{ik}}{p_k(1 - p_k)})\right)^{-1} + \epsilon_{ijk} \quad (1)$$

with the noise $\epsilon_{ij} \sim \mathcal{N}(\mathbf{0}_d, \sigma^2 \mathbf{I}_d)$. The individual time reparametrization takes
the following form: $\psi_i(t) = \alpha_i(t - t_0 - \tau_i) + t_0$, where τ_i is called the time-
shift and models a straight delay or advance one individual can have on the
average trajectory, and $\alpha_i = e^{\xi_i}$ is called the acceleration factor. This time
reparametrization captures two phenomena: the fact that a patient can have an
early or late disease onset, and the fact that a patient can be a slow or fast
progressor. The space-shifts $(\mathbf{w}_i)_i$ have the same dimension as the observations,
but for more interpretability the model uses an ICA decomposition with N_s
independent sources $(\mathbf{s}_i)_{1 \leq i \leq N_s}$. This leads to a formulation $\mathbf{w}_i = A\mathbf{s}_i$ such that

the columns $A_l = \sum_{k=1}^{d-1} \beta_{lk} B_k$ are a linear combination of an orthonormal basis $(B_k)_{1 \leq k \leq d-1}$ of the orthogonal hyperplane to $Span(\mathbf{v})$.

The hierarchical statistical model assumes that the population and individual parameters are latent, and follow Gaussian distributions directly or after transformation: $\xi_i \sim \mathcal{N}(0, \sigma_\xi^2)$, $\tau_i \sim \mathcal{N}(0, \sigma_\tau^2)$ and $\mathbf{s}_i \sim \mathcal{N}(\mathbf{0}_{N_s}, \mathbf{I}_{N_s})$; $g_k = \frac{1}{p_k} - 1$ and $\mathbf{g} \sim \mathcal{N}(\bar{\mathbf{g}}, \sigma_g^2 \mathbf{I}_d)$, $v_k = e^{\tilde{v}_k}$ and $\tilde{\mathbf{v}} \sim \mathcal{N}(\bar{\mathbf{v}}, \sigma_v^2 \mathbf{I}_d)$, $t_0 \sim \mathcal{N}(\bar{t_0}, \sigma_t^2)$, $\beta_{lk} \sim \mathcal{N}(\bar{\beta}_{lk}, \sigma_\beta^2)$. The individual parameters are noted $z_i = (\xi_i, \tau_i, \mathbf{w}_i)$. The population parameters, i.e. the fixed effects, are noted $z_{pop} = (\mathbf{g}, \mathbf{v}, t_0, A)$. All the latent variables are noted $\mathbf{z} = (z_{pop}, (z_i)_{1 \leq i \leq n})$. Finally the statistical model parameters are $\theta = (\sigma_\xi, \sigma_\tau, \bar{\mathbf{g}}, \bar{\mathbf{v}}, \bar{t_0}, \bar{\beta}_{lk})$, while $\sigma_g, \sigma_t, \sigma_v, \sigma_\beta$ are fixed.

MCMC-SAEM. The estimation of the parameters in the disease course mapping model is performed with the Monte Carlo Markov chain stochastic approximation variant of the Expectation Maximization algorithm. The convergence of the MCMC-SAEM has been proven [18] for the curved exponential family, which is the family of distributions for which the log-likelihood can be written as: $\forall \theta \in \Theta, \log q(\mathbf{y}, \mathbf{z}, \theta) = -\Phi(\theta) + \langle S(\mathbf{y}, \mathbf{z}), g(\theta) \rangle$ where Φ and g are smooth functions, S are called the sufficient statistics. The sufficient statistics are to be understood as a summary of the required information from the latent variables $\mathbf{z}$ and the observations $\mathbf{y}$. The algorithm alternates between two steps:

- **Expectation**: latent parameters are estimated by a Metropolis-Hastings within Gibbs sampler algorithm. First new values $\mathbf{z}^*$ are sampled from a proposal law. Proposal value $\mathbf{z}^*$ is accepted over current value $\mathbf{z}_K$ with probability $1 \wedge \frac{q(\mathbf{y}, \mathbf{z}^* | \theta)}{q(\mathbf{y}, \mathbf{z}_K | \theta)}$. This Metropolis-Hastings scheme guarantees that the new value z_{K+1} is asymptotically sampled from the target distribution $q(\mathbf{y}, \cdot | \theta_K)$. The Gibbs sampler is used to sequentially estimate the population parameters z_{pop} and the individual parameters z_i. Based on the latent variables z_{K+1}, the sufficient statistics are computed, giving an approximation of $\log q$
- **Maximization**: the model parameters θ_K are updated by maximizing the expectation of the log-likelihood $\theta_{K+1} = \underset{\theta \in \Theta}{argmax} \ \log(q(\mathbf{y}, \mathbf{z}_{K+1}, \theta))$, which is computed in closed form as a function of the sufficient statistics only

3.2   Mixture of Disease Course Mapping Models

The improvement we brought to the disease course mapping model is a new layer atop of the hierarchical structure already built. If we write $q(\mathbf{y}, \mathbf{z}, \theta)$ the likelihood of the model parametrized by θ, with latent variables $\mathbf{z}$ and observations $\mathbf{y}$, then the likelihood of a mixture model with L clusters is: $Q_{\theta_1, \dots, \theta_L}(\mathbf{y}, \mathbf{z}) = \sum_{c=1}^{L} \pi^c q(\mathbf{y}, \mathbf{z}, \theta_c)$ where π^c denotes the probability of cluster c. Then each cluster c has its own set of parameters θ_c. We assume that each individual has a true latent class π_i and a set of individual parameters $\mathbf{z}_i^{\pi_i}$ corresponding to the model attached to the cluster π_i. The estimation algorithm is described in Algorithm 1. It is a mixture version of the MCMC-SAEM, where we add the latent variables π_i^c for the probability of each individual i to be in each cluster c, and $(z_i^c)_i$ are the individual parameters for an individual i in cluster c. Contrarily to [21] where the latent variable is directly π_i, forcing individuals to attach to a cluster, our use of soft cluster labelling avoids cluster freeze and trapping states. By conditioning, we rewrite the likelihood of individual i in cluster c $q(y_i, z_i^c|\theta^c, z_{pop}^c)$ as the product of $q(y_i|\theta^c, z_{pop}^c, z_i^c)$ the likelihood of the observations and $p(z_i^c|\theta^c, z_{pop}^c)$ the likelihood of the individual parameters. These two terms are akin to the classical terms of the L2 loss (resulting from the choice of the Gaussian noise) and the regularization respectively.

Algorithm 1: M-MCMC-SAEM estimation

Initialization: π_0, (θ_0^c), $(\mathbf{z}_{0,i}^c)$

for $K = 0...N$ **do**

  Compute probability of individual i to belong to cluster c:

  $$\pi_{K+1,i}^c = \frac{\pi_K^c q(y_i|\theta_K^c, z_{K,i}^c, z_{K,pop}^c))p(z_{K,i}^c|\theta_K^c, z_{K,pop}^c))}{\sum_j \pi_K^j q(y_i|\theta_K^j, z_{K,i}^j, z_{K,pop}^j))p(z_{K,i}^j|\theta_K^j, z_{K,pop}^j))}$$

  for $c = 1...L$ **do**

    • **E step**

    Population parameters estimation

    Sample $z_{*,pop}^c$ and compute acceptance ratio

    $$\alpha = 1 \wedge \frac{q(\mathbf{y}|\theta_K^c, (z_{K,i}^c)_i, z_{*,pop}^c)p((z_{K,i}^c)_i|\theta_K^c, z_{*,pop}^c)}{q(\mathbf{y}|\theta_K^c, (z_{K,i}^c)_i, z_{K,pop}^c)p((z_{K,i}^c)_i|\theta_K^c, z_{K,pop}^c)}$$

    Set $z_{K+1,pop}^c = z_{*,pop}^c$ with probability α else $z_{K+1,pop}^c = z_{K,pop}^c$

    Individual parameters estimation

    Sample $(z_{*,i}^c)_i$ and compute acceptance ratios

    $$\alpha_i = 1 \wedge \frac{q(y_i|\theta_K^c, z_{*,i}^c, z_{K+1,pop}^c))p(z_{*,i}^c|\theta_K^c, z_{K+1,pop}^c)}{q(y_i|\theta_K^c, z_{K,i}^c, z_{K+1,pop}^c))p(z_{K,i}^c|\theta_K^c, z_{K+1,pop}^c)}$$

    $\forall i$, set $z_{K+1,i}^c = z_{*,i}^c$ with probability α_i else $z_{K+1,i}^c = z_{K,i}^c$

    Compute sufficient statistics $(S^c(y_i, \mathbf{z}_{K+1}))_i$

    • **M step**

    Update $\theta_{K+1}^c = \underset{\theta \in \Theta}{argmax} \, log \, q(\mathbf{y}, z_{K+1,pop}^c, (z_{K+1,i}^c)_i, \theta)$

    Compute $\pi_K^c = \frac{1}{n}\sum_i \pi_{K,i}^c$

  end

end

The challenging part is the update of model parameters within each cluster. In the case of a single model, the updates of the parameters θ of the model are computed in a closed form and are only a function of the total sufficient statistic, which writes $S(\mathbf{y}, \mathbf{z}_{K+1}) = \sum_i S(y_i, \mathbf{z}_{K+1})$ since the observations $(y_i)_i$ are supposed independent. When mixtures are involved, the log-likelihood changes to $log \, q(\mathbf{y}, \mathbf{z}^c, \theta^c) = \sum_i log \left(\sum_c \pi_i^c q(y_i, z_i^c, z_{pop}^c, \theta^c) \right)$. However since the EM computes an expectation of the log-likelihood, we can condition on the true latent class π_i of each individual i such that $\pi_i^c = \mathbf{P}(\pi_i = c)$:

$$\mathbf{E}_\mathbf{z}\left(log \left(\sum_c \pi_i^c q(y_i, z_i^c, z_{pop}^c, \theta^c) \right) \right) = \mathbf{E}_\pi\left(\mathbf{E}_\mathbf{z}\left(log \left(\sum_c \mathbf{1}_{\pi_i=c} q(y_i, z_i^c, z_{pop}^c, \theta^c) \right) | \pi_i \right) \right)$$

$$= \mathbf{E}_\pi\left(\mathbf{E}_\mathbf{z}\left(\sum_c \mathbf{1}_{\pi_i=c} log \left(q(y_i, z_i^c, z_{pop}^c, \theta^c) \right) | \pi_i \right) \right)$$

$$= \mathbf{E_z} \Big(\sum_c \pi_i^c \log \left(q(y_i, z_i^c, z_{pop}^c, \theta^c) \right) \Big)$$

Thus we obtain the total sufficient statistics for each cluster $S^c(\mathbf{y}, \mathbf{z}_{K+1}) = \sum_i \pi_i^c S(y_i, \mathbf{z}_{K+1})$ which can be used to update θ^c. This formula is intuitive: each sufficient statistic for each cluster weights the contribution of the individual data by the probability of this individual being in the cluster. This result also proves that the mixture model still belongs to the curved exponential family. Therefore, the convergence of this algorithm is guaranteed by the MCMC-SAEM proof [18].

3.3   Tempered Scheme

Even with theoretical guarantees, the convergence might be very slow in practice. The estimation of individual parameters in a non-linear single model may be challenging. Building a mixture on top of it further adds to the difficulty. Practical experiences show a high reliability on initialization. One of the bottleneck is the amount of cluster regularization contained in the term $p(z_i^c | \theta^c, z_{pop}^c)$ in the likelihood. Until the cluster population parameters stabilize, we do not want to restrict the exploration of the individual parameters space.

We thus propose to use a tempered scheme for the Gibbs sampler, mimicking simulated annealing. Tempered MCMC-SAEM has been shown to converge [20]. In a tempered scheme, inverse temperature comes as a multiplier of the log-likelihood of the model. We realized our model had overly constraining regularization, outweighing the data term in the likelihood. Thus we applied temperature only to the regularization term of the log-likelihood in the sample. In practice, we propose to simply replace p by $\tilde{p} = p^{1/T}$ in Algorithm 1.

For the temperature scheme, we opted for a sinusoidal pattern with a decreasing hull (sine cardinal) following [20]: $T(\kappa) = 1 + b \frac{sin(\kappa)}{\kappa}$, $\kappa = \Delta + 2\pi \frac{K}{p}$, where b can be seen as the amplitude of the oscillations, Δ as a phase delay, and p as a period, K is the iteration number. The use of this tempered scheme allows for an alternation between exploratory phases (high temperature) and exploitation phases (low temperature). The values of the hyperparameters were empirically set to $b = 1, \Delta = 0, p = N_{iter}/100$ after several attempts.

3.4   Initialization Method

With the same practical considerations, we had to find an initialization method which would improve the odds of convergence towards the global optimum. Random or manual initialization of the model parameters $(\theta_0^c)_c$ was not satisfying, as we will see in the experiments.

We opted for an initialization as close to the clusters as possible. We first fit a disease course mapping model (without mixture) on the whole data. This yields a set of parameters $(\theta_{init}, z_{pop,init}, (z_{i,init}))$. Then we use a Gaussian mixture model (GMM) on the estimated individual parameters $z_{i,init}$. The GMM allows us to identify L clusters within the individual data. The parameters of each mode c in the GMM combined with the population parameters θ_{init} produce new population parameters for a disease course mapping model which represent the mode: for instance the new t_0^c is the shift of $t_{0,init}$ by the mean value of τ_i in the mode. This provides initialization parameters for as many disease course mapping models as there are modes in the GMM, and we use these initialization parameters for the clusters of the mixture model.

Please note that the use of a *post hoc* clustering on the estimated parameters is not equivalent to the joint estimation in the mixture model, so this initialization method does not directly give the right cluster parameters. Indeed, we can only produce clusters such that $\forall c, \mathbf{v}^c \in Span(\mathbf{v}_{init})$, which is a strong limit to the posterior analysis of a one-class model.

4   Results and Discussion

4.1   Simulated Data

Univariate Model. We first show that the mixture model accurately recovers the ground truth parameters on simulated data. We generated data by creating two unimodal disease course mapping models with chosen population parameters. We fix the first model with $t_0 = 70$, $\sigma_\tau = 2$, $\sigma_\xi = 0.1$, $\log(v_0) = -2$, $\log(g_0) = 1$. For the second model we change the values of t_0 and v_0. We use the Kullback-Leibler divergence to determine the difference between the two model distributions. We then assume the two clusters have equal prevalence and we create 512 individuals, which consists in randomly attributing the individual to a cluster and sample individual parameters according to the distribution of the cluster. Next we arbitrarily decide the number (7 in average) and time of the "visits" for each individual, and we compute the values associated to these timepoints. Finally we add a small Gaussian noise ($\sigma = 0.01$) to the output.

A simplified version of the model consists in assuming that there is no sources in the ICA, leading to an univariate model with no space-shifts. In this case, the only individual parameters left are the time-related ones: $(\xi_i)_i$ and $(\tau_i)_i$. This special case of the model converges more easily since there are less parameters to estimate, which allows us to initialize the model without having to first fit a single model. We evaluated the class estimation with the area under the ROC curve (ROC AUC) metric. For the evaluation of population and individual parameters, we computed the absolute error between the ground truth parameters of each cluster and the parameters of the closest estimated cluster, this error being normalized by the standard deviation of the parameter. Figure 1 shows the reconstruction metrics on simulated data as a function of the Kullback-Leibler divergence between clusters. With the ROC AUC, we are able to see that the mixture perfectly separates two clusters, once the two clusters are different enough. The estimation errors for population parameters increases slightly as the clusters get farther from each other, which is understandable since the algorithm needs to do more exploration. The mean error on individual parameters shows a very stable curve. The reconstruction is limited by the noise of the generated data. In all the univariate experiments, the estimated parameters allowed the model to reach a L2 loss close to the noise level. The consistent errors for individual

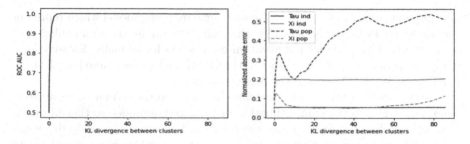

Fig. 1. Evaluation metrics for the reconstruction of true parameters. Left: ROC AUC for the estimated cluster probabilities of individuals π_i^c. Right: Absolute error between estimated parameters and ground truth, normalized by parameter standard deviation.

parameters seemingly correspond to the range in which individual parameters differences can be mistaken for noise.

Multivariate Model. In the previous experiment, the results show consistent performance on a simplified univariate model. However when we add multiple sources, the number of parameters increases drastically and convergence might be more challenging in practice. We generated a dataset as in the first experiment but with two sources and three-dimensional observations. We first fitted a single disease course mapping model on the generated dataset, yielding $(\theta_{init}, z_{pop,init})$. We then fitted several mixture models to compare the different initialization methods, with or without the tempered scheme. Final results are shown in Table 1. Each model estimation takes about 5 min for 4,000 iterations

Table 1. Performances of models. Single: single disease course mapping model; Random: random initialization; Init: initialization for both clusters at $(\theta_{init}, z_{pop,init})$; GMM: the initialization method described previously using a GMM on $(z_{i,init})_i$; True: perfect initialization at the ground truth parameters. Fit: log-likelihood related to the observations. Regularization: log-likelihood related to parameters' distribution.

Model	ROC AUC	Fit ($log\ q$)	Regularization ($log\ p$)	BIC
Single	–	42288	–3662	–38494
Random non-tempered	0.50	25922	–1439	–24212
Random tempered	0.50	36813	–3622	–32920
Init non-tempered	0.53	36523	–3637	–32615
Init tempered	0.56	40034	–3882	–35881
GMM non-tempered	**0.99**	**45787**	**–2914**	**–42602**
GMM tempered	**0.99**	**46871**	**–3068**	**–43532**
True non-tempered	1.00	53613	–2735	–50607
True tempered	1.00	53571	–2280	–51020

which is the number of iterations required in this setup for the log-likelihood to stabilize.

The table shows that the tempered version allows for a better fit at the cost of regularization overall. Random initialization does not work. "Init" shows a better fit but is not able to cluster the individuals. "GMM" initialization is the best method in the absence of better heuristics.

4.2   Applications on Alzheimer's Disease Data

Experiment Without MCI. We apply the method to the ADNI dataset[1]. We first build a model considering only stable Alzheimer's disease (AD) patients and stable controls. Our data was comprised of 400 AD (mean MMSE: 21.7, mean age: 75.9) and 695 controls (mean MMSE: 29, mean age: 75.8), with approximately 5 visits per patient. We select 8 features that are most relevant to the progression of AD based on a medical expert's advice, which included cognitive scores, MRI-derived regional volumes and biomarkers level. We then fit a single disease course mapping model on it. The posterior analysis of individual parameters highlights the need to take heterogeneity into account. The posterior distribution of the couple (τ_i, ξ_i) is shown in Fig. 2.

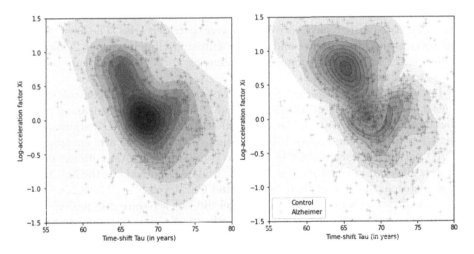

Fig. 2. Scatter plot of individual parameters, with kernel density estimation. Left: KDE on all AD and control patients. Right: KDE estimated separately for AD and controls.

The GMM on the individual parameters provides two initial clusters for our mixture model. Optimal number of clusters was decided based on the Bayesian Information Criterion (BIC). The results of the mixture model are shown in

---

[1] http://adni.loni.usc.edu/.

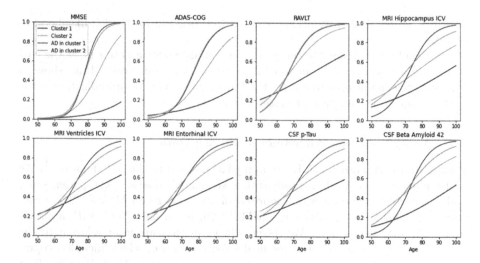

Fig. 3. Average trajectories in time. AD patients in both clusters have a similar cognitive evolution as shown by the cognitive scores (MMSE, RAVLT and ADAS-COG) whereas AD patients of cluster 1 (green) have a faster progression on MRI-based and CSF biomarkers than AD patients of cluster 2 (red). (Color figure online)

Fig. 3. The two clusters have very distinct average trajectories. The most obvious difference is the much earlier and rapid cognitive decline in cluster 2 compared to the cluster 1, while the progression of imaging and CSF biomarkers is only a few years earlier in cluster 2.

Interestingly, the clustering does not correspond to AD and controls classes. Cluster 1 contains 88% of all controls and 65% of AD cases, meaning cluster 2 accounts for a minority of the data and contains mostly AD patients. Since average trajectory takes controls into account, we plotted the average trajectory of AD patients in each cluster in order to compare them. AD patients in both clusters show rapid cognitive degradation, while AD patients in the first cluster show a steeper increase of their imaging and CSF levels.

To understand why the mixture model did not separate AD patients from controls, we estimated one model on AD patients only and one model on controls only. We then computed the log-likelihood of our models. Results are shown in Table 2. They confirm that the mixture model explains the variability seen in the data better than prior categorisation based on diagnosis. We further estimated a mixture with the initial clusters being AD and controls, and the algorithm still converged towards a similar version to the one presented in Fig. 3.

Several studies report an association between the atrophy rates of particular brain regions and cognitive decline [22,23], which lead to the identification of disease subtypes based on the differences in regional atrophies. Our analysis suggest that such associations are not systematic: similar pathological processes may lead to distinct pattern of cognitive decline, like similar cognitive decline may have distinct pathological processes.

Table 2. Log-likelihood of models

Model	Fit ($log\ q$)	Regularization ($log\ p$)	Total log-likelihood
Mixture	38100	−10391	27708
AD + Controls	37226	−9772	27454

Estimating MCI Patients. We performed individual personalization of MCI in the previous model, i.e. we estimated individual parameters including likelihood to belong to each cluster while keeping population parameters fixed. The distribution of MCI patients in the two clusters confirmed our hypothesis that cluster 2 is a specific subtype of AD: MCI associated to cluster 2 are mostly converters (66%) while 80% of non-converters are in cluster 1.

Conclusion. We proposed a mixture for a disease course mapping model which has been validated on simulated data. We also introduced an heuristic initialization method to ensure convergence without extensive parameter search. The application to an Alzheimer's disease cohort suggests two subtypes of the disease associated with distinct relationship between cognitive decline and progression of imaging and CSF biomarkers.

References

1. Laird, N.M., Ware, J.H.: Random-effects models for longitudinal data. Biometrics **38**(4), 963–974 (1982)
2. Jack, C.R., et al.: Update on hypothetical model of Alzheimer's disease biomarkers. Lancet Neurol. **12**(2), 207–216 (2013)
3. Taddé, B.O., Jacqmin-Gadda, H., Dartigues, J.F., Commenges, D., Proust-Lima, C.: dynamic modeling of multivariate dimensions and their temporal relationships using latent processes: application to Alzheimer's disease. Biometrics **76**(3), 886–899 (2020)
4. Marinescu, R.V., et al.: DIVE: a spatiotemporal progression model of brain pathology in neurodegenerative disorders. NeuroImage **192**, 166–177 (2019)
5. Schiratti, J.B., Allassonnière, S., Colliot, O., Durrleman, S.: A Bayesian mixed-effects model to learn trajectories of changes from repeated manifold-valued observations. J. Mach. Learn. Res. **18**, 4840–4872 (2017)
6. Lavielle, M., Mbogning, C.: An improved SAEM algorithm for maximum likelihood estimation in mixtures of non linear mixed effects models. Stat. Comput. **24**(5), 693–707 (2014)
7. Fonteijn, H.M., et al.: An event-based model for disease progression and its application in familial Alzheimer's disease and Huntington's disease. Neuroimage **60**(3), 1880–1889 (2012)
8. Archetti, D., et al.: Multi-study validation of data-driven disease progression models to characterize evolution of biomarkers in Alzheimer's disease. NeuroImage: Clin. **24**, 101954 (2019)

9. Bilgel, M., Jedynak, B.M.: Predicting time to dementia using a quantitative template of disease progression. Alzheimer's Dement. Diagn. Assess. Dis. Monit. **11**(1), 205–215 (2019)
10. Young, A.L., et al.: Uncovering the heterogeneity and temporal complexity of neurodegenerative diseases with subtype and stage inference. Nat. Commun. **9**, 1–16 (2018)
11. McCullagh, P.: Generalized Linear Models. Routledge, Boca Raton (October 2018)
12. Jedynak, B.M., et al.: A computational neurodegenerative disease progression score: method and results with the Alzheimer's disease neuroimaging initiative cohort. Neuroimage **63**(3), 1478–1486 (2012)
13. Couronné, R., Vidailhet, M., Corvol, J.C., Lehéricy, S., Durrleman, S.: Learning disease progression models with longitudinal data and missing values. In: ISBI 2019 - International Symposium on Biomedical Imaging (April 2019)
14. Louis, M., Couronné, R., Koval, I., Charlier, B., Durrleman, S.: Riemannian geometry learning for disease progression modelling. In: Chung, A.C.S., Gee, J.C., Yushkevich, P.A., Bao, S. (eds.) IPMI 2019. LNCS, vol. 11492, pp. 542–553. Springer, Cham (2019). https://doi.org/10.1007/978-3-030-20351-1_42
15. Koval, I., et al.: Statistical learning of spatiotemporal patterns from longitudinal manifold-valued networks. In: Descoteaux, M., Maier-Hein, L., Franz, A., Jannin, P., Collins, D.L., Duchesne, S. (eds.) MICCAI 2017. LNCS, vol. 10433, pp. 451–459. Springer, Cham (2017). https://doi.org/10.1007/978-3-319-66182-7_52
16. Mehdipour Ghazi, M., et al.: Training recurrent neural networks robust to incomplete data: application to Alzheimer's disease progression modeling. Med. Image Anal. **53**, 39–46 (2019)
17. Delyon, B., Lavielle, M., Moulines, E.: Convergence of a stochastic approximation version of the EM algorithm. Ann. Stat. **27**(1), 94–128 (1999)
18. Kuhn, E., Lavielle, M.: Coupling a stochastic approximation version of EM with an MCMC procedure. ESAIM: Probab. Stat. **8**, 115–131 (2004)
19. Allassonnière, S., Kuhn, E., Trouvé, A.: Construction of Bayesian deformable models via a stochastic approximation algorithm: a convergence study. Bernoulli **16**(1), 641–678 (2010)
20. Allassonniere, S., Chevallier, J., Oudard, S.: Learning spatiotemporal piecewise-geodesic trajectories from longitudinal manifold-valued data. In: Guyon, I., et al. (eds.) Advances in Neural Information Processing Systems. vol. 30, pp. 1152–1160. Curran Associates, Inc. (2017)
21. Debavelaere, V., Durrleman, S., Allassonnière, S.: Learning the clustering of longitudinal shape data sets into a mixture of independent or branching trajectories. Int. J. Comput. Vis. **128**(12), 2794–2809 (2020). https://doi.org/10.1007/s11263-020-01337-8
22. Zhang, X., et al.: Bayesian model reveals latent atrophy factors with dissociable cognitive trajectories in Alzheimer's disease. PNAS **113**(42), E6535–E6544 (2016)
23. Risacher, S.L., et al.: For the Alzheimer's disease neuroimaging initiative: Alzheimer disease brain atrophy subtypes are associated with cognition and rate of decline. Neurology **89**(21), 2176–2186 (2017)

Learning Transition Times in Event Sequences: The Temporal Event-Based Model of Disease Progression

Peter A. Wijeratne$^{(\boxtimes)}$ ⓘ and Daniel C. Alexander ⓘ,
for the Alzheimer's Disease Neuroimaging Initiative

Centre for Medical Image Computing, Department of Computer Science,
University College London, London, UK
{p.wijeratne,d.alexander}@ucl.ac.uk

Abstract. Progressive diseases worsen over time and can be characterised by sequences of events that correspond to changes in observable features of disease progression. Here we connect ideas from two formerly separate methodologies – event-based and hidden Markov modelling – to derive a new generative model of disease progression: the Temporal Event-Based Model (TEBM). TEBM can uniquely infer the most likely group-level sequence and timing of events (*natural history*) from mixed data types. Moreover, it can infer and predict individual-level trajectories (*prognosis*) even when data are missing, giving it high clinical utility. Here we derive TEBM and provide an inference scheme based on the expectation maximisation algorithm. We use imaging, clinical and biofluid data from the Alzheimer's Disease Neuroimaging Initiative to demonstrate the validity and utility of our model. First, we train TEBM to uncover a new sequence and timing of events in Alzheimer's disease, which are inferred to occur over a period of ∼17.6 years. Next, we demonstrate the utility of TEBM in predicting clinical progression, and that TEBM provides improved utility over a comparative disease progression model. Finally, we demonstrate that TEBM maintains predictive accuracy with up to 50% missing data. These results support the clinical validity of TEBM and its broader utility in real-world medical applications.

Keywords: Bayesian network · Markov jump process · Disease progression model · Prognosis · Dementia

1 Introduction

Progressive diseases such as Alzheimer's disease (AD) are characterised by monotonic deterioration in functional, cognitive and physical abilities over a period of

Data used in preparation of this article were obtained from the Alzheimer's Disease Neuroimaging Initiative (ADNI) database (adni.loni.usc.edu). As such, the investigators within the ADNI contributed to the design and implementation of ADNI and/or provided data but did not participate in analysis or writing of this report.

© Springer Nature Switzerland AG 2021
A. Feragen et al. (Eds.): IPMI 2021, LNCS 12729, pp. 583–595, 2021.
https://doi.org/10.1007/978-3-030-78191-0_45

years to decades [1]. AD has a long prodromal phase before symptoms become manifest (~20 years), which presents an opportunity for therapeutic intervention if individuals can be identified at an early stage in their disease trajectory [2]. Clinical trials for disease-modifying therapies in AD would also benefit from methods that can stratify participants, both in terms of individual-level disease stage and rate of progression [3].

Data-driven models of disease progression can be used to learn hidden information, such as individual-level stage, from observed data [4]. Broadly speaking, disease progression models can be categorised as regression-based or state-space models. Recent examples of regression-based methods include Bayesian mixed-effects models [5,6]; and a time-reparametrised Gaussian Process Progression Model (GPPM) [7]. However, [5,6] require strong assumptions of sigmoidal forms for trajectory dynamics, which may not reflect the true form in the data. The GPPM removes the sigmoidal assumption and allows for non-parametric dynamics, but requires regularisation to avoid over-fitting which introduces additional complexity, and does not learn individual-level rates of progression.

A state-space model of disease progression was proposed by [8], who derived a modified continuous time hidden Markov model (CTHMM), which they used to learn a set of disease states and transition times between these states from electronic health record data. However, CTHMMs fit distribution parameters for each state directly, which increases the number of model parameters that need to be inferred with the number of states. This in turn increases the likelihood of over-fitting [9], which is a well known problem for Markov models when data are sparse and/or the model is complex [10].

An event-based model (EBM) of disease progression was first proposed by [11]. The EBM defines disease progression as a monotonically ordered sequence of binary abnormality events, and as such is essentially a state-space model. Unlike a hidden Markov model, the EBM uses the monotonicity assumption to define a prior form to the distributions generating the data in each hidden state, which simplifies the inference problem. The robustness and predictive utility of the EBM was demonstrated by [12] and extended by [13] to enable both subtype (i.e., multiple sequence) and stage inference (SuStaIn). The simplicity, interpretability and utility of EBM and SuStaIn has made them popular tools for revealing new disease insights [12–20], for validating new features of disease progression (*biomarkers*) [21], and for patient stratification [13,20].

However, EBM and SuStaIn are formulated for cross-sectional data, and hence can only infer the sequence of events but not their transition times, and cannot account for individual-level time series data. Previous work has attempted to address the problem of estimating transition times in an *ad hoc* manner by first fitting an EBM and then correlating its predictions with a separate longitudinal model [16]. However, this approach provides only an approximation of time between events that is confounded by differing model assumptions. As such there is demand for a single unified method that generalises the EBM to accommodate longitudinal data and to simultaneously infer both the order and timing of events.

Here we address this problem, which is long-standing in the field of disease progression modelling [11, 22]. We connect ideas from two formerly separate methodologies – event-based and hidden Markov modelling – to derive a new generative temporal event-based model (TEBM) of disease progression. As a disease progression model, TEBM provides a natural framework to integrate mixed data types, such as imaging and clinical markers, in an informative manner. TEBM therefore has strong clinical utility, as it learns an interpretable group-level model of how mixed biomarkers change over time. Such a model for AD was first hypothesised by [23], and [6, 7, 16] all reported trajectories of various biomarker changes, but TEBM is the first to provide a single unified methodology for learning data-driven sequences and transition times in progressive diseases. As such, this paper has three main contributions.

1. We derive TEBM by generalising the EBM to longitudinal data. TEBM inherits the capabilities of EBM, which can *i*) learn an interpretable sequence of events underlying disease progression; *ii*) learn an individual-level disease stage; *iii*) handle partially missing data (when an individual does not have measurements for every feature). In addition, TEBM can uniquely *iv*) learn transition times; *v*) learn an individual-level probability of progression.
2. We devise a novel algorithm for inference of the TEBM parameters.
3. We apply TEBM to data from the Alzheimer's Disease Neuroimaging Initiative (ADNI) to reveal a new sequence and timing of imaging, clinical and biofluid events in Alzheimer's disease, and to demonstrate TEBM's improved utility over a CTHMM, and its performance in the presence of missing data.

2 Theory

2.1 Temporal Event-Based Model

To formulate TEBM, we make three assumptions, namely *i*) monotonic biomarker change; *ii*) a consistent event sequence across the whole sample; and *iii*) Markov (memoryless) stage transitions. We can write the TEBM joint distribution over all variables in a hierarchical Bayesian framework:

$$P(S, \theta, k, Y) = P(S) \cdot P(\theta|S) \cdot P(k|\theta, S) \cdot P(Y|k, \theta, S). \tag{1}$$

Here S is the hidden sequence of events, θ are the distribution parameters generating the data, k is the hidden disease stage, and Y are the observed data. Graphical models of CTHMM, EBM and TEBM are shown in Fig. 1. Note that we have assumed conditional independence of S from k; that is, the complete set of disease progression stages is independent of the time of observation. Assuming independence between observed features $i = 1, ..., I$, if a patient $j = 1, ..., J$ is at latent stage $k_{j,t} = 0, ..., N$ in the progression model, the likelihood of their data $Y_{j,t}$ observed at time $t = 1, ..., T_j$ is given by:

$$P(Y_{j,t}|k_{j,t}, \theta, S) = \prod_{i=1}^{I} P(Y_{i,j,t}|k_{j,t}, \theta_i, S). \tag{2}$$

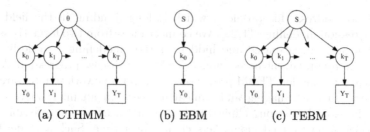

(a) CTHMM   (b) EBM   (c) TEBM

Fig. 1. Graphical models for (a) CTHMM, (b) EBM, and (c) TEBM. Hidden variables are denoted by circles, observations by squares. S: sequence of events; θ: distribution parameters; k: disease stage; Y: observed data; T: observed time.

Here θ_i are the distribution parameters for feature i, defined by a hidden set of events $S = (s(1), ..., S(N))$. Following [11], we enforce the monotonicity assumption by requiring S to be ordered, which is equivalent to requiring that feature i is monotonic at the group-level. This assumption is necessary to allow snapshots from different individuals to inform on the full event ordering. Next, we assume a Markov jump process [24] between time-points:

$$P(Y_j|k_j, \theta, S) = P(k_{j,t=0}) \prod_{t=1}^{T_j} P(k_{j,t}|k_{j,t-1}) \prod_{t=0}^{T_j} \prod_{i=1}^{I} P(Y_{i,j,t}|k_{j,t}, \theta_i, S). \qquad (3)$$

To obtain an event-based model, we now define prior values for the distribution parameters θ for each stage k in sequence S. Following [12] we choose a two-component Gaussian mixture model to describe the data likelihood:

$$\prod_{i=1}^{I} P(Y_{i,j,t}|k_{j,t}, \theta_i, S) = \prod_{i=1}^{k_{j,t}} P(Y_{i,j,t}|k_{j,t}, \theta_i^p, S) \prod_{i=k_{j,t}+1}^{I} P(Y_{i,j,t}|k_{j,t}, \theta_i^c, S). \qquad (4)$$

Here $\theta_i^p = [\mu_i^p, \sigma_i^p, w_i^p]$ and $\theta_i^c = [\mu_i^c, \sigma_i^c, w_i^c]$ are the mean, μ, standard deviation, σ, and mixture weights, w, for the patient and control distributions, respectively. Note that these distributions are fit prior to inference, which requires our data to contain labels for patients and controls (see Sect. 3); however, once θ_i^p and θ_i^c have been fit, the model can infer S without any labels. One of the strengths of the mixture model approach is that when feature data are missing, the two probabilities on the RHS of Eq. 4 can simply be set equal.

To obtain the total data likelihood, we marginalize over the hidden stage k and assume independence between measurements from different individuals j (dropping indices j, t in the sum for notational simplicity):

$$P(Y|\theta, S) = \prod_{j=1}^{J} \left[\sum_{k=0}^{N} P(k_{j,t=0}) \prod_{t=1}^{T_j} P(k_{j,t}|k_{j,t-1}) \right.$$

$$\left. \prod_{t=0}^{T_j} \prod_{i=1}^{k_{j,t}} P(Y_{i,j,t}|k_{j,t}, \theta_i^p, S) \prod_{i=k_{j,t}+1}^{I} P(Y_{i,j,t}|k_{j,t}, \theta_i^c, S) \right]. \qquad (5)$$

We can now use Bayes' theorem to obtain the posterior distribution over S. We note that Eq. 5 is the time generalisation of the models presented by [11,12,14], and for $T_j = 1$ it reduces to those models.

With this definition made, we now make the usual Markov assumptions [24] to obtain the form of the $N \times N$ dimensional transition generator matrix $Q_{a,b}$:

$$expm(\Delta Q)_{a,b} = P(k_{j,t} = a|k_{j,t-1} = b, \Delta) \equiv A_{a,b}(\Delta). \qquad (6)$$

Here we assume a homogeneous continuous-time process, τ, and a fixed time interval, Δ, that is matrix exponentially distributed, $\Delta \sim expm(\Delta)$, between stages a, b. Note that as we are only considering Δ constant, $A_{a,b}$ is independent of time, i.e., $A_{a,b}(\Delta) \equiv A_{a,b}$. The N dimensional initial stage probability vector π_a is defined as:

$$\pi_a = P(k_{j,t=0} = a). \qquad (7)$$

Finally, the expected duration of each stage (sojourn time), δ_k, is given by:

$$\delta_k = \sum_{\delta=1}^{\infty} \delta P_k(\delta) = \frac{1}{1 - p_{kk}}. \qquad (8)$$

Here $P_k(\delta)$ is the probability density function of δ in stage k, and p_{kk} are the diagonal elements of the transition matrix $A_{a,b}$.

2.2   Inference

We aim to learn the sequence $\overline{S}$, initial probability $\overline{\pi}_a$, and transition matrix $\overline{A}_{a,b}$, that maximise the complete data log likelihood, $\mathcal{L}(\overline{S}, \overline{\pi}, \overline{A}) = \log P(Y|S, \pi, A; \theta)$. As described in Sect. 2, we first obtain θ by fitting Gaussian mixture models to the feature distributions of the patient and control sub-groups. We then use a nested inference scheme based on iteratively optimising the sequence S, and fitting the initial probability π_a and transition matrix $A_{a,b}$, to find a local (possibly global) maximum via a nested application of the Expectation-Maximisation (EM) algorithm. At the first EM step, S is optimised for the current values of the initial probability π_a' and transition matrix $A_{a,b}'$, by permuting the position of every event separately while keeping the others fixed. At the second step, π_a and $A_{a,b}$ are fitted for the current sequence S' using the standard forward-backward algorithm [24]. Here we apply only a single EM pass, as iterative updating of π_a and $A_{a,b}$ can cause over-fitting for sparse [10] and noisy data.

2.3 Staging

After fitting $\overline{S}$, $\overline{\pi}_a$ and $\overline{A}_{a,b}$, we infer the most likely Markov chain (i.e., trajectory) for each individual using the standard Viterbi algorithm [24]. We can use TEBM to predict individual-level future stage by multiplying the transition matrix, $\overline{A}_{a,b}$, with the posterior probability for the individual at time t, and selecting the maximum likelihood stage:

$$\arg\max_k P(k_{t+1} = b|\overline{S}) = \arg\max_k P(k_t = a|\overline{S}) \cdot \overline{A}_{a,b}. \tag{9}$$

We can also use TEBM to define an individual-level 'probability of progression' that leverages the full information from the posterior, which we define as the normalised ratio of the predicted and inferred posteriors:

$$P(k_t, k_{t+1}|\overline{S}) = 1 - \frac{1}{I}\sum_b \frac{P(k_t = a|\overline{S}) \cdot \overline{A}_{a,b}}{P(k_t = a|\overline{S}) \cdot \overline{A}_{a,b} + P(k_t = b|\overline{S})}. \tag{10}$$

For a forward-only transition matrix, Eq. 10 will equal zero if the predicted and inferred posteriors are equal (i.e., zero probability of progression), and non-zero otherwise.

3 Experiments and Results

3.1 Alzheimer's Disease Data

We use data from the ADNI study, a longitudinal multi-centre observational study of AD [25]. We select 468 participants (119 CN: cognitively normal; 297 MCI: mild cognitive impairment; 29 AD: manifest AD; 23 NA: not available), and three time-points per participant (baseline and follow-ups at 12 and 24 months). Individuals were allowed to have partially missing data at any time-point; we refer to this dataset as 'Dataset 1'. To facilitate direct comparison between TEBM and CTHMM (the latter of which cannot handle partially missing data by default), we also select a subset of 368 individuals without partially missing data at any time-point, but who can now have different numbers of time-points; we refer to this dataset as 'Dataset 2'. We train on a mix of 12 clinical, imaging and biofluid features. The clinical data are three cognitive markers: ADAS-13, Rey Auditory Verbal Learning Test (RAVLT) and Mini-Mental State Examination (MMSE). The imaging data are T1-weighted 3T structural magnetic resonance imaging (MRI) scans, post-processed to produce regional volumes using the GIF segmentation tool [26]. We select a set of sub-cortical and cortical regional volumes with reported sensitivity to AD pathology, namely the hippocampus, ventricles, entorhinal, mid-temporal, and fusiform, and the whole brain [27]. The biofluid data are three cerebrospinal fluid markers: amyloid-β_{1-42} (ABETA), phosphorylated tau (PTAU) and total tau (TAU). The ADNI dataset used in this paper is freely available upon registering with an ADNI account and downloading the TADPOLE challenge dataset.

3.2 Model Training

We compare the TEBM and CTHMM models. To ensure fair comparison, we impose a constraint on both models by placing a 2nd order forward-backward prior on the transition matrix. For TEBM, we fit Gaussian mixture models to the distributions of AD (patients) and CN (controls) sub-groups (as in [12]) prior to performing inference, and use 16 start-points for the EM algorithm. For CTHMM, we apply the standard forward-backward algorithm and iterate the likelihood to convergence within 10^{-3} of the total model likelihood. We initialise the CTHMM prior mean and covariance matrices from the training data, using standard k-means and the feature covariance, respectively. Finally, we optimise the number of states in the CTHMM to obtain the maximum likelihood fit. TEBM is implemented and parallelised in Python and is available open source[1]. The code takes 3 min to train TEBM with 4 start-points on Dataset 1 using a 4-core 2.7 GHz Intel® Core™ i7-7500U CPU (i.e., 1 start-point per core).

3.3 TEBM Parameters

We train TEBM on Dataset 1 to infer $\overline{S}$, $\overline{\pi}$ and $\overline{A}$. Figure 2 shows (a) the Gaussian mixture models for each feature, (b) the initial probability density distribution $\overline{\pi}$; and (c) the event-based transition matrix, $\overline{A}$, with stages ordered by $\overline{S}$. The Gaussian mixture models demonstrate smooth transition probabilities between patient and control distributions (denoted by 'p(event occurred)'), indicating suitable fits. The initial probability distribution is most dense around the earliest stages ($k_{j,t=0} \leq 6$), which reflects the large proportion of CN and MCI individuals in the cohort. The event-based transition matrix is diagonally-dominant, with smooth transitions between stages and predominantly larger forward than backward probabilities, supporting the monotonicity hypothesis.

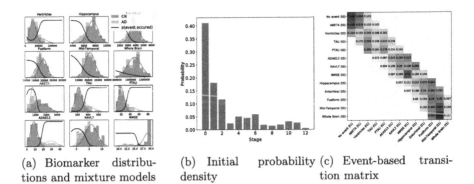

(a) Biomarker distributions and mixture models

(b) Initial probability density

(c) Event-based transition matrix

Fig. 2. TEBM parameters inferred from ADNI. (a) Gaussian mixture models fit to distributions of CN (green) and AD (red) groups. (b) Initial probability density, $\overline{\pi}$, inferred by TEBM. (c) Event-based transition matrix, $\overline{A}$, inferred by TEBM. Events are ordered by the most likely ordering, $\overline{S}$. (Color figure online)

---

[1] https://github.com/pawij/tebm.

3.4   Alzheimer's Disease Timeline

We use TEBM to infer the group-level sequence and time between events from Dataset 1, the latter of which is not possible using EBM. Figure 3 shows the corresponding order and timeline of events, and stages for two representative patients estimated by TEBM. This timeline is the first of its type in the field of AD progression modelling, and reveals a chain of observable events occurring over an inferred period of ~17.6 years. The ordering largely agrees with previous model-based analyses [12,16], and TEBM provides additional information on the time between events. Early changes in biofluid measures (ABETA, TAU, PTAU) over a relatively short timescale have been proposed in a recent hypothetical model of AD biomarker trajectories [23], though no actual timing information is reported. We also observe early neurodegeneration (represented here by the ventricles), followed by a chain of cognitive and structural brain volume changes, with change across the whole brain occurring last.

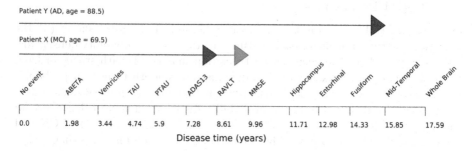

Fig. 3. AD timeline inferred by TEBM. The order of events on the horizontal axis is given by $\overline{S}$, and the mean time between events is calculated from $\overline{A}$. Baseline stage (solid arrow) and predicted next stage (shaded arrow, if different to baseline) estimated by TEBM for two example patients from the MCI and AD groups are shown.

3.5   Individual Trajectories

We demonstrate that TEBM can stratify individuals by progression rate and provide a prediction of future stage with uncertainty, which is not possible using EBM. We use TEBM to infer the most likely stage sequence, and predict the most likely next (i.e., unseen) stage over the following year for three individuals. The next most likely unseen stage is predicted according to Eq. 9, with uncertainty estimated by sampling from the posterior. Figure 4 shows three individual trajectories, which were randomly selected from three categories according to their change in stage: stable-stable (no change in stage); progressive-stable (observed increase in stage followed by no predicted change); and progressive-progressive (observed increase in stage followed by predicted increase in stage). These examples highlight the utility of TEBM for clinical applications that aim to stratify by progression rate. If one were to stratify progression rates according to only observed data, they would be inclined to group individual (a) as stable, (b) as rapidly progressive, and (c) as moderately progressive. However, TEBM predicts that individual (b) remains stable for the following year, while individual (c) increases in stage, making the latter more suitable for observing changes over the following year. As such, TEBM provides additional utility in clinical applications (e.g., prognosis) and clinical trial design (e.g., cohort enrichment).

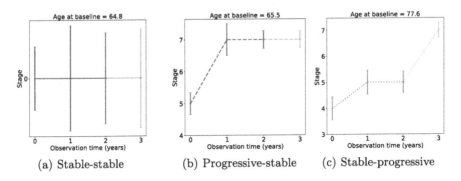

(a) Stable-stable   (b) Progressive-stable   (c) Stable-progressive

Fig. 4. TEBM individual-level staging. Solid lines represent within-sample inference, and dotted lines represent prediction. Uncertainty was estimated using 100 samples from the posterior at each time-point.

3.6 Prediction of Progression Rate

We now demonstrate TEBM's ability to predict future rate of progression, which is not possible using EBM. Specifically, we examine the relationship between the rate of change in MMSE – a key cognitive test score used for patient inclusion in AD clinical trials – and the individual-level probability of progression predicted by TEBM (Eq. 10). We train TEBM on 25% of Dataset 1, but use only the baseline measurement from each individual in the test set to predict future progression; this best reflects a baseline clinical trial. Furthermore, we utilise TEBM to select a subset of individuals with a baseline stage = 7, corresponding to abnormal MMSE; this is necessary as individuals at earlier stages are less likely to exhibit abnormal MMSE and hence add noise. We find a nearly significant dependency of MMSE rate of change on TEBM probability of progression (Fig. 5),

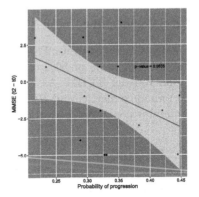

Fig. 5. Dependency of change in MMSE on TEBM probability of progression, for individuals starting at TEBM stage = 7 (abnormal MMSE).

and in the expected direction, using a linear fixed effects model ($\beta = -20.4$, $p = 0.06$).

3.7   Comparative Model Performance

We train TEBM and CTHMM to infer individual-level stage sequences and hence compare predictive accuracy on a common task. Specifically, we use base-line stage as a predictor of conversion from CN to MCI, or MCI to AD, over a period of two years. Here predicted converters are defined as people with a stage greater than a threshold stage. We calculate the area under the receiver operating characteristic curve (AU-ROC), and perform 10-fold cross-validation to estimate prediction uncertainty. Table 1(a) shows that TEBM performs sub-stantially better than CTHMM using the same dataset. We also find that TEBM performs better on Dataset 1 than 2, indicating the model benefits when trained on more individuals with more time-points and partially missing data, rather than fewer individuals with fewer time-points and complete data. Note EBM can also infer baseline stage; we find it returns similar performance as TEBM.

Table 1. Model performance for the task of predicting conversion.

(a) TEBM and CTHMM performance for the task of predicting conversion. Only Dataset 2 is reported for CTHMM as it cannot handle partially missing data.

Model	AU-ROC
TEBM (Dataset 1)	0.755 ± 0.12
TEBM (Dataset 2)	0.717 ± 0.15
CTHMM (Dataset 2)	0.489 ± 0.22

(b) TEBM performance for the task of predicting conversion with pre-defined partially missing data, using Dataset 2.

% missing	AU-ROC
25%	0.756 ± 0.12
33%	0.729 ± 0.13
50%	0.723 ± 0.17

3.8   Performance with Missing Data

Finally, we demonstrate TEBM's ability to handle missing data. We randomly discard 25%, 33% or 50% of the feature data from each individual in Dataset 2 and re-train TEBM. As in Sect. 3.7, we use prediction of conversion as the performance metric, and 10-fold cross-validation. Table 1(b) shows that TEBM maintains consistent performance with up to 50% missing data.

4   Discussion

In this paper we have introduced TEBM, a new generative state-space model of disease progression that combines the strengths of two formerly separate method-ologies – a priori structure from event-based modelling with temporal informa-tion from hidden Markov modelling – to provide a method that can learn tran-sition times in event sequences. The mathematical innovation of our work is to reformulate the EBM in a CTHMM framework (or conversely, the CTHMM in an event-based framework). To our knowledge this is the first such model of its type. We also applied TEBM to reveal a new sequence and timing of key patho-logical events in AD, and to demonstrate its utility in prediction of conversion and progression at the individual level in the presence of missing data.

TEBM is particularly applicable to clinical trials, where it could be used to inform biomarker and cohort selection criteria. In terms of clinical practice, a key corollary benefit of TEBM's formulation is that it can infer probabilistic estimates of group- and individual-level progression from datasets with missing data, both in terms of observed features and time-points. This gives it high utility in real-world medical applications, where missing data are present in most (if not all) patient studies, and in clinical applications where resources are scarce and/or it is too expensive to observe a patient multiple times.

Future technical work on TEBM will be focused on relaxing its assumptions, namely i) monotonic biomarker change; ii) a consistent event sequence across the whole sample; and iii) Markov (memoryless) stage transitions. In addition[2], the assumption of fixed time intervals will be relaxed in future work to accommodate variable intervals between observations, following [28]. Assumption i) is both a limitation and a strength: it allows us to simplify our model at the expense of requiring monotonic biomarker change; as shown here, for truly monotonic clinical, imaging and biofluid markers it only provides benefits. However for non-monotonic markers – such as brain connectivity – either the model or data would need to be adapted. Assumptions ii) and iii) could be relaxed by combining TEBM with (for example) subtype modelling [13] and semi-Markov modelling [29], respectively. In particular, TEBM can be directly integrated into the SuStaIn framework proposed by [13], which would allow us to capture the well-reported heterogeneity in AD and produce timelines such as Fig. 3 for separate subtypes. This opens up the prospect of developing a probabilistic model that can parsimoniously cluster temporal patterns of disease progression, and hence identify clinically-interpretable longitudinal subtypes.

References

1. Masters, C.L., Bateman, R., Blennow, K., et al.: Alzheimer's disease. Nat. Rev. Dis. Primers **1**, 15056 (2015)
2. Dubois, B., Hampel, H., Feldman, H.H., et al.: Preclinical alzheimer's disease: definition, natural history, and diagnostic criteria. Alzheimers Dement **12**(3), 292–323 (2016)
3. Cummings, J., Lee, G., Ritter, A., et al.: Alzheimer's disease drug development pipeline: 2019. Alzheimer's Dement. **5**, 272–293 (2019)
4. Oxtoby, N.P., Alexander, D.C.: Imaging plus x: multimodal models of neurodegenerative disease. Curr. Opin. Neurol. **30**(4), 371–379 (2019)
5. Schiratti, J.B., Allassonnière, S., Colliot, O., et al.: A Bayesian mixed-effects model to learn trajectories of changes from repeated manifold-valued observations. J. Mach. Learn. Res. **18**, 1–33 (2017)
6. Li, D., Iddi, S., Aisen, P.S., et al.: The relative efficiency of time-to-progression and continuous measures of cognition in presymptomatic Alzheimer's disease. Alzheimer's Dement. Transl. Res. Clin. Interv. **5**, 308–318 (2019)

---

[2] We note that while the requirement of a control sample for fitting the TEBM mixture model distributions could also be deemed a limitation, it is arguably a strength as it allows us to informatively leverage control data; a key issue highlighted by [8].

7. Lorenzi, M., Filippone, M., Frisoni, G.B., et al.: Probabilistic disease progression modeling to characterize diagnostic uncertainty: application to staging and prediction in Alzheimer's disease. NeuroImage **190**, 56–68 (2019)

8. Wang, X., Sontag, D., Wang, F.: Unsupervised learning of disease progression models. In: Proceedings of the 20th ACM SIGKDD International Conference on Knowledge Discovery and Data Mining (2014)

9. Lever, J., Krzywinski, M., Altman, N.: Model selection and overfitting. Nat. Methods **13**, 703–704 (2016)

10. Ghahramani, Z.: An introduction to hidden Markov models and Bayesian networks. Int. J. Pattern Recognit. Artif. Intell. **15**, 9–42 (2001)

11. Fonteijn, H.M., Clarkson, M.J., Modat, M., et al.: An event-based disease progression model and its application to familial alzheimer's disease. IPMI **6801**, 748–759 (2011)

12. Young, A.L., Oxtoby, N.P., Daga, P., et al.: A data-driven model of biomarker changes in sporadic Alzheimer's disease. Brain **137**, 2564–2577 (2014)

13. Young, A.L., Marinescu, R.V., Oxtoby, N.P., et al.: Uncovering the heterogeneity and temporal complexity of neurodegenerative diseases with subtype and stage inference. Nat. Commun. **9**, 1–16 (2018)

14. Fonteijn, H.M., Modat, M., Clarkson, M.J., et al.: An event-based model for disease progression and its application in familial alzheimer's disease and huntington's disease. NeuroImage **60**, 1880–1889 (2012)

15. Marinescu, R.V., Young, A.L., Oxtoby, N.P., et al.: A data-driven comparison of the progression of brain atrophy in posterior cortical atrophy and alzheimer's disease. Alzheimer's Dement. **12**, 401–402 (2016)

16. Oxtoby, N.P., Young, A.L., Cash, D.M., et al.: Data-driven models of dominantly-inherited alzheimer's disease progression. Brain **141**, 1529–1544 (2018)

17. Eshaghi, A., Marinescu, R.V., Young, A.L., et al.: Progression of regional grey matter atrophy in multiple sclerosis. Brain **141**, 1665–1677 (2018)

18. Firth, N.C., Startin, C.M., Hithersay, R., et al.: Aging related cognitive changes associated with alzheimer's disease in down syndrome. Ann. Clin. Transl. Neurol. **5**, 1665–1677 (2018)

19. Wijeratne, P.A., Young, A.L., Oxtoby, N.P., et al.: An image-based model of brain volume biomarker changes in hungtington's disease. Ann. Clin. Transl. Neurol. **5**, 570–582 (2018)

20. Young, A.L., Bragman, F.J.S., Rangelov, B., et al.: Disease progression modeling in chronic obstructive pulmonary disease. AJRCCM **201**(3), 294–302 (2019)

21. Byrne, L.M., Rodrigues, F.B., Johnson, E.B., et al.: Evaluation of mutant huntingtin and neurofilament proteins as potential markers in Huntington's disease. Sci. Transl. Med. **10**, eaat7108 (2018)

22. Huang, J., Alexander, D.C.: Probabilistic event cascades for alzheimer's disease. In: Advances in Neural Information Processing Systems 25 (2012)

23. Jack, C.R., Holtzman, D.M.: Biomarker modeling of alzheimer's disease. Neuron **80**(6), 1347–1358 (2013)

24. Rabiner, L.R.: A tutorial on hidden markov models and selected applications in speech recognition. IEEE **77**, 257–286 (1989)

25. Mueller, S.G., Weiner, M.W., Thal, L.J., et al.: The alzheimer's disease neuroimaging initiative. Neuroimaging Clin. N. Am. **15**, 869–877 (2005)

26. Cardoso, M.J., Modat, M., Wolz, R., et al.: Geodesic information flows: spatially-variant graphs and their application to segmentation and fusion. IEEE Trans. Med. Imaging **34**, 1976–1988 (2015)

27. Frisoni, G.B., Fox, N.C., Jack, C.R., et al.: The clinical use of structural MRI in alzheimer disease. Nat. Rev. Neurol. **6**(2), 67–77 (2010)

28. Metzner, P., Horenko, I., Schütte, C.: Generator estimation of markov jump processes based on incomplete observations non-equidistant in time. Phys. Rev. E. Stat. Nonlin. Soft. Matter Phys. **76**, 066702 (2007)

29. Alaa, A.M., van der Schaar, M.: A hidden absorbing semi-markov model for informatively censored temporal data: learning and inference. J. Mach. Learn. Res. **70**, 60–69 (2018)

Learning with Few or Low Quality Labels

Knowledge Distillation with Adaptive Asymmetric Label Sharpening for Semi-supervised Fracture Detection in Chest X-Rays

Yirui Wang[1]([✉]) [iD], Kang Zheng[1], Chi-Tung Cheng[3], Xiao-Yun Zhou[1], Zhilin Zheng[2], Jing Xiao[2], Le Lu[1], Chien-Hung Liao[3], and Shun Miao[1]

[1] PAII Inc., Bethesda, MD, USA
[2] Ping An Technology, Shenzhen, China
[3] Chang Gung Memorial Hospital, Linkou, Taiwan, ROC

Abstract. Exploiting available medical records to train high-performance computer-aided diagnosis (CAD) models via the semi-supervised learning (SSL) setting is emerging to tackle the prohibitively high labor costs involved in large-scale medical image annotations. Despite the extensive attention received on SSL, previous methods failed to 1) account for the low disease prevalence in medical records and 2) utilize the image-level diagnosis indicated from the medical records. Both issues are unique to SSL for CAD models. In this work, we propose a new knowledge distillation method that effectively exploits large-scale image-level labels extracted from the medical records, augmented with limited expert annotated region-level labels, to train a rib and clavicle fracture CAD model for chest X-ray (CXR). Our method leverages the teacher-student model paradigm and features a novel adaptive asymmetric label sharpening (AALS) algorithm to address the label imbalance problem that specially exists in the medical domain. Our approach is extensively evaluated on all CXR (N = 65,845) from the trauma registry of Chang Gung Memorial Hospital over a period of 9 years (2008–2016), on the most common rib and clavicle fractures. The experiment results demonstrate that our method achieves the state-of-the-art fracture detection performance, *i.e.*, an area under the receiver operating characteristic curve (AUROC) of 0.9318 and a free-response receiver operating characteristic (FROC) score of 0.8914 on the rib fractures, significantly outperforming previous approaches by an AUROC gap of 1.63% and an FROC improvement by 3.74%. Consistent performance gains are also observed for clavicle fracture detection.

Keywords: Knowledge distillation · Adaptive Asymmetric Label Sharpening · Semi-supervised Learning · Fracture detection · Chest X-ray

© Springer Nature Switzerland AG 2021
A. Feragen et al. (Eds.): IPMI 2021, LNCS 12729, pp. 599–610, 2021.
https://doi.org/10.1007/978-3-030-78191-0_46

1 Introduction

Computer-aided diagnosis (CAD) of medical images has been extensively studied in the past decade. In recent years, substantial progress has been made in developing deep learning-based CAD systems to diagnose a wide range of pathologies, *e.g.*, lung nodule diagnosis in chest computed tomography (CT) images [18], mass and calcification characterization in mammography [13], liver fibrosis assessment in ultrasound [7], bone fracture detection/classification in radiography [17]. The state-of-the-art CAD solutions are typically developed based on large-scale expert annotations (*e.g.*, 128,175 labeled images for diabetic retinopathy detection [3], 14,021 labeled cases for skin condition diagnosis [11]). However, the labor cost of large-scale annotations in the medical area is prohibitively high due to the required medical expertise, which hinders the development of deep learning-based CAD solutions for applications where such large-scale annotations are not yet available. In this work, we aim to develop a cost-effective semi-supervised learning (SSL) solution to *train a reliable, robust and accurate fracture detection model for chest X-ray (CXR) using limited expert annotations and abundant clinical diagnosis records.*

While expert annotations are expensive to obtain, medical records can often be efficiently/automatically collected retrospectively at a large scale from a hospital's information system. Motivated by the availability of retrospective medical records, a few large-scale X-ray datasets with natural language processing (NLP) generated image-level labels are collected and publicly released, *e.g.*, ChestXray-14 [16], CheXpert [5]. Previous works have subsequently investigated weakly-supervised learning to train CAD models using purely image-level labels [12,17]. However, since the image-level labels lack localization supervision, these methods often cannot deliver sufficient diagnosis and localization accuracy for clinical usage [8]. In addition, the public CXR datasets rely only on radiology reports, which are known to have substantial diagnostic errors and inaccuracies [2].

A more promising and practical strategy for training CAD models is to use large-scale image-level labels extracted from the *clinical diagnosis reports* with a small number of expert annotated region-level labels. Different from radiology diagnoses made by the radiologist based on a single image modality, clinical diagnoses are made by the primary doctor considering all sources of information, *e.g.*, patient history, symptoms, multiple image modalities. Therefore, clinical diagnoses offer more reliable image-level labels for training CAD models. Previous SSL methods (*e.g.*, Π-model [6], Mean Teacher [14], Mix-Match [1]) have studied a similar problem setup, *i.e.*, training classification/segmentation models using a combination of labeled and unlabeled images.

However, these general-purpose SSL methods assume that no label information is given for the *unlabeled* set. Therefore, they fail to take advantage of the clinical diagnosis reports that are available in our application. In addition, there is a unique data imbalance challenge in training CAD models using clinical diagnoses. In particular, due to the low prevalence of fractures in CXRs, the image-level diagnostic labels are imbalanced toward more negative (*e.g.*, 1:10 ratio). The region-level labeled positives and image-level diagnostic negatives are even more imbalanced (*e.g.*, 1:100 ratio). As a result, a specifically-designed SSL method is required to fully exploit the clinical diagnoses with imbalanced data distribution to effectively train CAD models.

To bridge this gap, we propose an effective SSL solution for fracture detection in CXR that better accounts for the imbalanced data distribution and exploits the image-level labels of the unannotated data. We adopt the teacher-student mechanism, where a teacher model is employed to produce pseudo ground-truths (GTs) on the image-level diagnostic positive images for supervising the training of the student model. Different from previous knowledge distillation methods where the pseudo GTs are directly used or processed with symmetric sharpening/softening, we propose an *adaptive asymmetric label sharpening (AALS)* to account for the teacher model's low sensitivity caused by the imbalanced data distribution and to encourage positive detection responses on the image-level positive CXRs. The proposed method is evaluated on a real-world scenario dataset of all (N = 65,843) CXR images taken in the trauma center of Chang Gung Memorial Hospital from 2008 to 2016. Experiments demonstrate that our method reports an area under the receiver operating characteristic curve (AUROC) of 0.9318/0.9646 and an free-response receiver operating characteristic (FROC) score of 0.8914/0.9265 on the rib/clavicle fracture detection. Compared to state-of-the-art methods, our method significantly improves the AUROC by 1.63%/0.86% and the FROC by 3.74%/3.81% on rib/clavicle fracture detection, respectively.

2   Method

Problem Setup. We develop a fracture detection model using a combination of image-level and region-level labeled CXRs. While the image-level labels can be obtained efficiently at a large scale by mining a hospital's image archive and clinical records, the region-level labels are more costly to obtain as they need to be manually annotated by experts. We collected 65,845 CXRs from the trauma registry of a medical center. Diagnosis code and keyword matching of the clinical records are used to obtain image-level labels, resulting in 6,792 positive and 59,051 negative CXRs. Among positive CXRs, 808 CXRs with positive diagnoses are annotated by experts to provide region-level labels in the form of bounding-box. The sets of region-level labeled, image-level positive and image-level negative CXRs are denoted by $\mathcal{R}$, $\mathcal{P}$ and $\mathcal{N}$, respectively. Our method aims to *effectively exploit both the region-level labels and the image-level labels under an extremely imbalanced positive/negative ratio.*

2.1   Knowledge Distillation Learning

Similar to recent CAD methods [8], we train a neural network to produce a probability map that indicates the location of the detected fracture. Since the shape and scale of fractures can vary significantly, we employ feature pyramid network (FPN) [9] with a ResNet-50 backbone to tackle the scale variation challenge

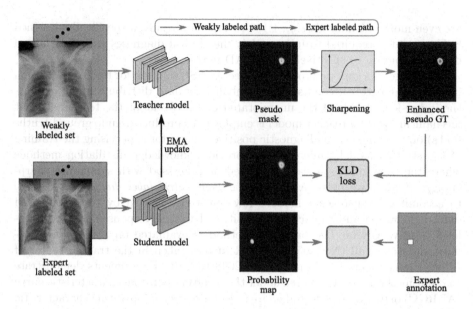

Fig. 1. An overview of the proposed knowledge distillation with AALS. The student model is trained via back-propagation. The teacher model is updated by the exponential moving average (EMA).

by fusing multi-scale features. The training consists of two steps: 1) supervised pre-training and 2) semi-supervised training. In the pre-training step, a fracture detection model is trained via supervised learning using $\mathcal{R} \cup \mathcal{N}$. In the semi-supervised training step, $\mathcal{P}$ are further exploited to facilitate the training.

Supervised Pre-training. We train the network using only CXRs in $\mathcal{R}$ and $\mathcal{N}$, where pixel-level supervision signals can be generated. Specifically, for CXRs in $\mathcal{R}$, GT masks are generated by assigning *one* to the pixels within the bounding-boxes and *zero* elsewhere. For CXRs in $\mathcal{N}$, GT masks with all *zeros* are generated. During training, we use the pixel-wise binary cross-entropy (BCE) loss between the predicted probability map and the generated GT mask, written as:

$$\mathcal{L}_{sup} = \sum_{x \in (\mathcal{R} \cup \mathcal{N})} \mathrm{BCE}\left(f_\theta(x), y\right), \tag{1}$$

where x and y denote the CXR and its pixel-level supervision mask. $f_\theta(x)$ denotes the probability map output of the network parameterized by θ. Due to the extreme imbalance between $\mathcal{R}$ and $\mathcal{N}$ (*e.g.*, 808 vs. 59,861), the pre-trained model tends to have a low detection sensitivity, *i.e.*, producing low probabilities on fracture sites.

Semi-supervised Training. To effectively leverage $\mathcal{P}$ in training, we adopt a teacher-student paradigm where the student model learns from the pseudo GT produced by the teacher model on $\mathcal{P}$. The teacher and student models share the same network architecture, i.e., ResNet-50 with FPN, and are both initialized using the pre-trained weights from the supervised learning step. Inspired by the Mean Teacher method [14], we train the student model via back propagation and iteratively update the teacher model using the exponential moving average (EMA) of the student model weights during training. Denoting the weights of the teacher and student models at training step t as θ'_t and θ_t, respectively, the weights of the teacher model are updated following:

$$\theta'_t = \alpha\theta'_{t-1} + (1-\alpha)\theta_t, \tag{2}$$

where α is a smoothing coefficient to control the pace of knowledge update. α is set to 0.999 in all our experiments, following [14].

CXRs in the region-level labeled set ($\mathcal{R}$), image-level labeled positive set ($\mathcal{P}$) and image-level labeled negative set ($\mathcal{N}$) are all used to train the teacher-student model. The training mechanism is illustrated in Fig. 1. For CXRs in $\mathcal{R}$ and $\mathcal{N}$, the same supervised loss $\mathcal{L}_{sup}$ is used. For CXRs in $\mathcal{P}$, the teacher model is applied to produce a pseudo GT map, which is further processed by an AALS operator. The sharpened pseudo GT of image x is denoted as

$$y' = S(f_{\theta'_t}(x)), \tag{3}$$

where $f_{\theta'_t}$ denotes the teacher model at the t-th step, $S(\cdot)$ denotes AALS. The KL divergence between the sharpened pseudo GT y' and the student model's prediction $f_{\theta_t}(x)$ is calculated as an additional loss:

$$\mathcal{L}_{semi} = \sum_{x \in \mathcal{P}} \text{KLDiv}\Big(S\left(f_{\theta'_t}(x)\right), f_{\theta_t}(x) \Big). \tag{4}$$

The total loss used to train the student network is

$$\mathcal{L} = \mathcal{L}_{sup} + \mathcal{L}_{semi}. \tag{5}$$

2.2   Adaptive Asymmetric Label Sharpening

In previous knowledge distillation models, the pseudo GTs are produced on unlabeled data to supervise the student model. Since no prior knowledge is given for the unlabeled data, the pseudo GTs are either directly used [14], or processed with symmetric softening [4] or sharpening [1]. In our problem setup, we have important prior knowledge that can be exploited: 1) image-level positive CXRs contain visible fracture sites, 2) due to the imbalanced positive/negative ratio, the pseudo GT tends to have low sensitivity (i.e., low probabilities at fracture sites). Therefore, when the maximum value of the pseudo GT map is low, we are motivated to enhance the activation via AALS:

$$S(y') = \text{expit}\big(a \cdot \text{logit}(y') + (1-a) \cdot \text{logit}(t)\big), \tag{6}$$

where $\text{expit}(\cdot)$ and $\text{logit}(\cdot)$ denote Sigmoid function and its inverse. a and t control the strength and center of the sharpening operator, respectively. The

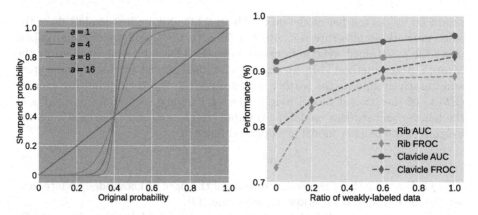

Fig. 2. Asymmetric label sharpening function at $t = 0.4$ with different a.

Fig. 3. Model performance using a subset of $\mathcal{P}$.

effects of a and t are shown in Fig. 2. Since the asymmetric sharpening aims to enhance the low probabilities in the pseudo GT, $t < 0.5$ should be used ($t = 0.4$ is used in our experiments). Since there are still many fracture sites missed in y' (*i.e.* with low probability values) due to the imbalanced training data, we use $\max(S(y'), y')$ as the label sharpening function in our final solution to avoid over penalization of the student model's activation on fracture sites with low probability values in y'.

The sharpening strength a is dynamically selected based on the maximum probability in the pseudo GT map, written as:

$$a = a_0 - (a_0 - 1)y'_{max}, \tag{7}$$

where y'_{max} is the maximum probability in the pseudo GT map, a_0 is a hyperparameter that controls the largest sharpening strength allowed. The sharpening strength a is negatively correlated with the maximum probability y'_{max}. When y'_{max} approaches 1, a approaches its minimum value 1, making $S(\cdot)$ an identity mapping. When y'_{max} decreases, a increases toward a_0, leading to stronger sharpening of the pseudo GT. A dynamic a is required because the sharpening operator is asymmetric. If a constant $a > 1$ is used, the sharpening operation will always enlarge the activation area in the pseudo GT map, which drives the model to produce probability maps with overly large activation areas. With the adaptive sharpening strength, when a fracture site is confidently detected in a CXR (*i.e.*, y'_{max} approaches 1), the sharpening operation degenerates to identity mapping to avoid consistently expanding the activation area.

2.3   Implementation Details

We trained our model on a workstation with a single Intel Xeon E5-2650 v4 CPU @ 2.2 GHz, 128 GB RAM, 4 NVIDIA Quadro RTX 8000 GPUs. All methods

Table 1. Fracture classification and localization performance comparison with state-of-the-art models. AUROC is reported for classification performance. FROC score is reported for localization performance.

Method	Rib fracture		Clavicle fracture	
	AUROC	FROC	AUROC	FROC
CheXNet [12]	0.8867	–	0.9555	–
RetinaNet [10]	0.8609	0.4654	0.8610	0.7985
FCOS [15]	0.8646	0.5684	0.8847	0.8471
Li *et al.* [8]	0.8446	–	0.9560	–
Π-Model [6]	0.8880	0.7703	0.9193	0.8536
Temporal Ensemble [6]	0.8924	0.7915	0.9132	0.8204
Mean Teacher [14]	0.9155	0.8540	0.9474	0.8884
Supervised pre-training	0.9025	0.7267	0.9174	0.7967
Ours	**0.9318**	**0.8914**	**0.9646**	**0.9265**
	(+1.63%)	(+3.74%)	(+0.86%)	(+3.81%)

are implemented in Python 3.6 and PyTorch v1.6. We use the ImageNet pre-trained weights to initialize the backbone network. Adam optimizer is employed in all methods. A learning rate of $4e-5$, a weight decay of 0.0001 and a batch size of 48 are used to train the model for 25 epochs. All images are padded to be square and resized to 1024×1024 for network training and inference. We randomly perform rotation, horizontal flipping, intensity and contrast jittering to augment the training data. The trained model is evaluated on the validation set after every training epoch, and the one with the highest validation AUROC is selected as the best model for inference.

3 Experiments

3.1 Experimental Settings

Dataset. We collected 65,843 CXRs of unique patients that were admitted to the trauma center of Chang Gung Memorial Hospital from 2008 to 2016. Based on the clinical diagnosis records, the CXRs are assigned image-level labels for rib and clavicle fractures. In total, we obtained 6,792 ($\mathcal{R} \cup \mathcal{P}$) CXRs with positive labels for at least one type of fracture and 59,051 ($\mathcal{N}$) CXRs with negative labels for both fracture types. 808 ($\mathcal{R}$) image-level positive CXRs are randomly selected for expert annotation by two experienced trauma surgeons. The annotations are confirmed by the best available information, including the original CXR images, radiologist reports, clinical diagnoses, and advanced imaging modality findings (if available). All experiments are conducted using five-fold cross-validation with a 70%/10%/20% training, validation, and testing split, respectively.

FCOS   CheXNet   Li et al.   Mean Teacher   Ours

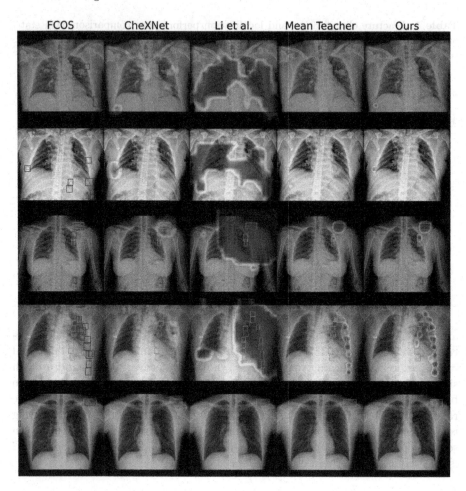

Fig. 4. Examples of the fracture detection results. GT and FCOS detected fracture bounding-boxes are shown in green and blue colors.

Evaluation Metrics. We evaluate both fracture classification and localization performances. The widely used classification metric AUROC is used to assess the classification performance. For object detection methods, the maximum classification score of all predicted bounding-boxes is taken as the classification score. For methods producing probability map, the maximum value of the probability map is taken as the classification score. We also assess the fracture localization performance of different methods. Since our method only produces probability map, standard FROC metric based on bounding-box predictions is infeasible. Thus, we report a modified FROC metric to evaluate the localization performance of all compared methods. A fracture site is considered as recalled if the center of its bounding-box is activated. And the activated pixels outside bounding-boxes are regarded as false positives. Thus, the modified FROC measures the fracture recall and the average ratio of false positive pixels per image. To calculate the modified FROC for object detection methods, we convert their predicted bounding-boxes into a binary mask using different thresholds, with the pixels within the predicted box as positive, and the pixels outside the box as negative. To quantify the localization performance, we calculate an FROC score as an average of recalls at ten false positive ratios from 1% to 10%.

Compared Methods. We compare the proposed method with baseline methods in the following three categories. 1) **Weakly-supervised methods:** We evaluate *CheXNet* [12], a representative state-of-the-art X-ray CAD method trained purely using image-level labels. 2) **Object detection methods:** We evaluate two state-of-the-art object detection methods: an anchor-based detector *RetinaNet* [10] and an anchor-free detector *FCOS* [15]. 3) **Semi-supervised methods:** We evaluate three popular knowledge distillation methods, Π-*Model* [6], *Temporal Ensemble* [6] and *Mean Teacher* [14], and a state-of-the-art medical image SSL method by Li *et al.* [8]. For all evaluated methods, ResNet-50 is employed as the backbone network. FPN is employed in the two detection methods, RetinaNet and FCOS.

3.2   Comparison with Baseline Methods

Table 1 summarizes the quantitative results of all compared methods and the proposed method. On the more challenging rib fracture detection task, Mean Teacher is the most competitive baseline method, measuring an AUROC of 0.9155 and an FROC score of 0.8540. Our proposed method measures an AUROC of 0.9318 and an FROC score of 0.8914, which significantly outperforms Mean Teacher by a 1.63% gap on the AUROC, and a 3.74% gap on the FROC score. The ROC and FROC curves of the evaluated methods are shown in Fig. 5. On the easier clavicle fracture detection task, CheXNet and Li *et al.* [8] report the highest AUROCs (*i.e.*, above 0.95) among the baseline methods. Mean Teacher delivers the strongest FROC score of 0.8884 among the baseline methods. Our proposed method also outperforms all baseline methods on the clavicle fracture detection task, reporting an AUROC of 0.9646 and an FROC of 0.9265.

We note that the three knowledge distillation methods, Π-Model, Temporal Ensemble and Mean Teacher, perform stronger than the supervised detection methods. The advantage is more significant on the easier clavicle fracture detection task. This is mainly because clavicle fractures have simpler geometric property and similar visual patterns, where knowledge distillation methods can effectively learn from the pseudo GT of unlabeled data. However, on the more complex rib fracture detection, the advantage of knowledge distillation methods is much less significant. Due to the complex visual patterns of rib fracture and the limited region-labeled positive data, the pseudo GT maps have a low sensitivity (*i.e.*, the supervised pre-trained model reports a low FROC score of 0.7267), which limits the knowledge transferred to the distilled model. Using the proposed AALS, our method effectively transfers more knowledge to the student model, hence achieving significantly improved performance compared to the previous knowledge distillation methods.

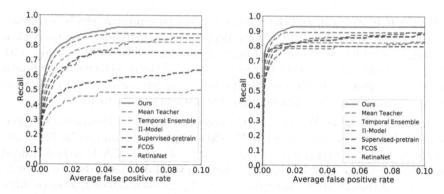

Fig. 5. FROC curves of rib fracture (left) and clavicle fracture (right) detection results using different methods.

We observed that CheXNet and Li *et al.* [8] significantly outperform baseline knowledge distillation methods on the clavicle fracture AUROC metric, but no performance advantage is observed on the rib fracture AUROC. This is because CheXNet and Li *et al.* [8] specifically use the positive image-level label, while the baseline knowledge distillation methods do not. In particular, CheXNet is trained via weakly-supervised learning purely using image-level labels. Li *et al.* [8] exploits image-level positive labels in a multi-instance learning manner. In contrast, the baseline knowledge distillation methods treat the image-level positive images as unlabeled data. While weakly-supervised learning and multi-instance learning are effective on learning the simpler clavicle fractures, they are less effective on more complex rib fractures. In addition, CheXNet and Li *et al.* [8] also produce poor localization performances. CheXNet provides localization visualization via class activation maps (CAM). Since the CAM values are not comparable across images, the FROC cannot be calculated for CheXNet results. As Li *et al.* [8] consistently produces overly large activation areas, it does not report meaningful FROC scores. For both CheXNet and Li *et al.* [8], we qualitatively verified that their localization performances are worse than other methods, as demonstrated by the examples shown in Fig. 4.

3.3   Ablation Study

We validate our proposed AALS by conducting experiments with different sharpening strengths a_0 and centers t, respectively. First, to analyze the effect of the label sharpening center t, we evaluate AALS with $t = 0.2, 0.3, 0.4, 0.5$ and summarize the results in Table 2. Using $t = 0.4$ achieves the best detection performance, measuring the highest/second highest AUROC score of 0.9318/0.9646, and the highest FROC score of 0.8914/0.9265, on rib/clavicle fracture detection. Note that for clavicle fracture classification, the best AUROC score of 0.9661 achieved at $t = 0.2$ is only marginally better than that of $t = 0.4$. The sharpening center behaves as a trade-off between sensitivity and specificity. We note that our

Table 2. Study of the sharpening bias.

t	Rib fracture		Clavicle fracture	
	AUROC	FROC	AUROC	FROC
0.2	0.9289	0.8902	**0.9661**	0.9236
0.3	0.9261	0.8888	0.9611	0.9168
0.4	**0.9318**	**0.8914**	0.9646	**0.9265**
0.5	0.9271	0.8848	0.9577	0.9106

Table 3. Study of the sharpening strength.

a_0	Rib fracture		Clavicle fracture	
	AUROC	FROC	AUROC	FROC
1	0.9222	0.8783	0.9550	0.9036
4	**0.9318**	**0.8914**	**0.9646**	**0.9265**
8	0.9283	0.8884	0.9606	0.9090
16	0.9302	0.8911	0.9620	0.9185

method consistently outperforms baseline methods using all four t values. Second, we fix the center $t = 0.4$ and evaluate $a_0 = 1, 4, 8, 16$ to study the impact of the sharpening strength. As summarized in Table 3, label sharpening with strength $a_0 = 4$ results in the best detection performance. For $a_0 = 1$, no label sharpening is applied, which results in degraded performance. For $a_0 = 8, 16$, the label sharpening becomes overly aggressive (as shown in Fig. 2), which also causes false positives in sharpened pseudo GT and hence slight performance degradation.

We further conduct an experiment to study the involvement of image-level positive set $\mathcal{P}$. Figure 3 shows the classification and detection performances for rib and clavicle using a subset of $\mathcal{P}$ with different ratios (0%, 20%, 60%, 100%), where 0% and 100% correspond to the supervised pre-training student model and the proposed method, respectively. We observe that larger $\mathcal{P}$ improves both the classification AUROC and detection FROC scores. This verifies the motivation of our method that CAD model training can benefit from utilizing image-level labels from clinical diagnoses. It also suggests a potential of our method to further improve its performance by incorporating more data with clinical diagnoses without additional annotation efforts.

4   Conclusion

In this paper, we introduced a specifically-designed SSL method to exploit both limited expert annotated region-level labels and large-scale image-level labels mined from the clinical diagnoses records for training a fracture detection model on CXR. We demonstrated that by accounting for the imbalanced data distribution and exploiting the clinical diagnoses, the proposed AALS scheme can effectively improve the effectiveness of knowledge distillation on only image-level labeled data. On a large-scale real-world scenario dataset, our method reports the state-of-the-art performance and outperforms previous methods by substantial margins. Our method offers a promising solution to exploit potentially unlimited and automatically mined clinical diagnosis data to facilitate CAD model training.

References

1. Berthelot, D., Carlini, N., Goodfellow, I., Papernot, N., Oliver, A., Raffel, C.A.: Mixmatch: a holistic approach to semi-supervised learning. In: NeurIPS, pp. 5049–5059 (2019)
2. Brady, A.P.: Error and discrepancy in radiology: inevitable or avoidable? Insights Imaging **8**(1), 171–182 (2016). https://doi.org/10.1007/s13244-016-0534-1
3. Gulshan, V., et al.: Development and validation of a deep learning algorithm for detection of diabetic retinopathy in retinal fundus photographs. Jama **316**(22), 2402–2410 (2016)
4. Hinton, G., Vinyals, O., Dean, J.: Distilling the knowledge in a neural network. stat **1050**, 9 (2015)
5. J, I., et al.: Chexpert: a large chest radiograph dataset with uncertainty labels and expert comparison. AAAI **33**, 590–597 (2019)
6. Laine, S., Aila, T.: Temporal ensembling for semi-supervised learning. In: ICLR (2017)
7. Li, B., et al.: Reliable liver fibrosis assessment from ultrasound using global hetero-image fusion and view-specific parameterization. In: Martel, A.L., et al. (eds.) MICCAI 2020, Part III. LNCS, vol. 12263, pp. 606–615. Springer, Cham (2020). https://doi.org/10.1007/978-3-030-59716-0_58
8. Li, Z., et al.: Thoracic disease identification and localization with limited supervision. In: CVPR, pp. 8290–8299 (2018)
9. Lin, T.Y., Dollár, P., Girshick, R., He, K., Hariharan, B., Belongie, S.: Feature pyramid networks for object detection. In: CVPR, pp. 2117–2125 (2017)
10. Lin, T.Y., Goyal, P., Girshick, R., He, K., Dollár, P.: Focal loss for dense object detection. In: ICCV, pp. 2980–2988 (2017)
11. Liu, Y., et al.: A deep learning system for differential diagnosis of skin diseases. Nat. Med. **26**, 1–9 (2020)
12. Rajpurkar, P., et al.: Chexnet: Radiologist-level pneumonia detection on chest x-rays with deep learning. arXiv preprint arXiv:1711.05225 (2017)
13. Shen, L., Margolies, L.R., Rothstein, J.H., Fluder, E., McBride, R., Sieh, W.: Deep learning to improve breast cancer detection on screening mammography. Sci. Rep. **9**(1), 1–12 (2019)
14. Tarvainen, A., Valpola, H.: Mean teachers are better role models: weight-averaged consistency targets improve semi-supervised deep learning results. In: NeurIPS, pp. 1195–1204 (2017)
15. Tian, Z., Shen, C., Chen, H., He, T.: FCOS: Fully convolutional one-stage object detection. In: ICCV, pp. 9627–9636 (2019)
16. Wang, X., Peng, Y., Lu, L., Lu, Z., Bagheri, M., Summers, R.M.: Chestx-ray8: hospital-scale chest x-ray database and benchmarks on weakly-supervised classification and localization of common thorax diseases. In: CVPR, pp. 2097–2106 (2017)
17. Wang, Y., et al.: Weakly supervised universal fracture detection in pelvic x-rays. In: Shen, D., et al. (eds.) MICCAI 2019, Part VI. LNCS, vol. 11769, pp. 459–467. Springer, Cham (2019). https://doi.org/10.1007/978-3-030-32226-7_51
18. Xie, Y., et al.: Knowledge-based collaborative deep learning for benign-malignant lung nodule classification on chest CT. IEEE TMI **38**(4), 991–1004 (2018)

Semi-Supervised Screening of COVID-19 from Positive and Unlabeled Data with Constraint Non-Negative Risk Estimator

Zhongyi Han[1], Rundong He[1], Tianyang Li[2], Benzheng Wei[2(✉)], Jian Wang[3], and Yilong Yin[1(✉)]

[1] School of Software, Shandong University, Jinan 250101, China
ylyin@sdu.edu.cn
[2] Center for Medical Artificial Intelligence, Shandong University of Traditional Chinese Medicine, Qingdao 266112, China
wbz99@sina.com
[3] School of Automotive Engineering, Shandong Jiaotong University, Jinan 250357, China

Abstract. With the COVID-19 pandemic bringing about a severe global crisis, our health systems are under tremendous pressure. Automated screening plays a critical role in the fight against this pandemic, and much of the previous work has been very successful in designing effective screening models. However, they would lose effectiveness under the semi-supervised learning environment with only positive and unlabeled (PU) data, which is easy to collect clinically. In this paper, we report our attempt towards achieving semi-supervised screening of COVID-19 from PU data. We propose a new PU learning method called Constraint Non-Negative Positive Unlabeled Learning (cnPU). It suggests the constraint non-negative risk estimator, which is more robust against overfitting than previous PU learning methods when giving limited positive data. It also embodies a new and efficient optimization algorithm that can make the model learn well on positive data and avoid overfitting on unlabeled data. To the best of our knowledge, this is the first work that realizes PU learning of COVID-19. A series of empirical studies show that our algorithm remarkably outperforms state of the art in real datasets of two medical imaging modalities, including X-ray and computed tomography. These advantages endow our algorithm as a robust and useful computer-assisted tool in the semi-supervised screening of COVID-19.

Keywords: COVID-19 screening · Positive unlabled learning

1 Introduction

Large-scale screening of COVID-19 plays an integral and critical role in the global fight against this epidemic. The SARS-Cov-2, a novel virus, is the culprit with the human-to-human transmission, causing an ongoing global severe

© Springer Nature Switzerland AG 2021
A. Feragen et al. (Eds.): IPMI 2021, LNCS 12729, pp. 611–623, 2021.
https://doi.org/10.1007/978-3-030-78191-0_47

crisis. According to WHO, it has attacked 220 countries, areas, or territories that involve more than 69,143,017 confirmed COVID-19 cases and more than 1,576,516 confirmed deaths until 12 December 2020. What's worse is that the daily increment of COVID-19 remains outperform 200,000. As we enter the post-pandemic period, the outbreak prevention and control of the severe COVID-19 epidemic become the new norm. Medical images are widely used for COVID-19 screening in clinical practice because chest computed tomography (CT) and X-ray can represent the infection areas [11]. However, manual screening of medical images is impractical and unsatisfactory with the global shortage of medical resources. 90% of countries have reported disruption of essential health services since the COVID-19 pandemic [31]. Efficient large-scale screening strategies of COVID-19 patients are necessary to be developed. Therefore, medical image-based automated screening of COVID-19, the main topic of our analysis, is urgently contributed to help the clinic relieve the tremendous pressure on health systems.

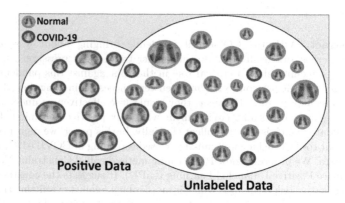

Fig. 1. The objective of this paper is to learn COVID-19 screening models with the positive (P) and unlabeled (U) medical data, which are particularly common in clinical settings due to the high false-negative rate of COVID-19 nucleic acid detection kits.

Prominent theoretical advance and effective algorithms have been achieved in the medical image-based automated screening of COVID-19. Generally speaking, pioneering screening works mainly involve chest X-ray-based studies [18] and chest CT-based attempts [11]. While previous works have achieved significant successes, they do not apply to the semi-supervised scenario where only positive and unlabeled (PU) data are available. PU data analysis is known as positive and unlabeled learning, also called learning from positive and unlabeled examples. As shown in Fig. 1, given a set of examples of a positive class (P), and a set of unlabeled examples (U) that contains examples of both positive class and negative class (N), the objective of PU learning is to build a binary classifier to classify test examples into class P or N [21]. The reason for PU learning on COVID-19 screening stands for three-fold. Firstly, PU data of COVID-19 medical images objectively exist in the clinic because the false-negative rate of nucleic acid detection kits is high [30]. Patients with a positive nucleic acid detection result can be identified as COVID-19, but patients with a negative nucleic acid detection result may be positive. Secondly, PU data are more accessible to collect than fully labeled data because there are many unlabeled medical imaging data. Finally, PU learning for COVID-19 has greater research significance and is more challenging than supervised learning. However, how to conduct in-deep analysis and construct a robust COVID-19 screening algorithm is still an open problem.

A straightforward way is to use prominent PU learning methods to screen COVID-19 patients from medical image data. However, they have some limitations when facing this new problem. According to the way of processing U data, existing PU learning methods can be divided into sample selection methods [19,22] and unbiased PU learning techniques [5,7]. Sample selection methods aim to heuristically select high confidence negative examples from U data and perform ordinary supervised (PN) learning. Unbiased PU (**uPU**) learning methods construct unbiased risk estimators aiming to achieve robust empirical risk minimization. Although unbiased PU learning is the current state of the art, it often gives negative empirical risks. The non-negative PU (**nnPU**) learning is suggested with non-negative risk estimators [17]. However, it still faces overfitting issues because the negative risk constraint is too loose and too late.

To cope with this crucial issue, we propose a new PU learning method called Constraint Non-Negative Positive Unlabeled Learning (**cnPU**). It contains a newly-designed constraint non-negative risk estimator that not only makes the U risk hold non-negative but also controls the dynamic equilibrium between P and U risks. Our analysis reveals that when the risk of U data drops fast, the classifier trends to overfitting. Thus, we introduce a constraint λ to limit U risk's decreased speed, keeping P and U risks in dynamic equilibrium to mitigate overfitting. Comparing with our cnPU method, uPN does not design any constraint on empirical risk, such that uPU easily suffers from overfitting. The nnPU does invert negative values of U risks only after they reach negative values; however, it is too late to control U risks, and the classifier has suffered from overfitting already. Our cnPU also improves the optimization way of nnPU. When the U risk occurs negative values, nnPU only optimizes U risk's negated value; however, it will lead the classifier to fit well on U data but perform worse on P data. In order to mitigate this phenomenon, cnPU simultaneously optimizes U and P risks when the U risk becomes negative. It can increase the positive risk's influence factor such that the classifier can fit nicely on the positive examples.

Our main contributions are concluded as follows:

- To the best of our knowledge, for the first time, we achieve the semi-supervised screening of COVID-19 from positive and unlabeled medical data.
- The presented constraint non-negative positive unlabeled learning approach is capable of mitigating the overfitting problem by controlling the dynamic equilibrium between positive and unlabeled risks.

2   Related Work

2.1   Automated COVID-19 Screening

At the beginning of this pandemic, many researchers worldwide have devoted themselves to analyzing clinical data of COVID-19, and have achieved many useful results. These pioneering works about intelligent COVID-19 data analyses include but not limited to automated screening [9,29], lesion segmentation [10], infection quantification [28], and patient severity assessment [13]. Among them, automated screening draws the most attention.

Many pioneering screening works have joined in the global fight and designed various useful screening models, including chest X-ray based and chest CT based works. X-ray-based works leverage 2D CNNs to make decisions directly [8,18]. CT-based works including lesion patch-based methods [29,30], 2D slice-based methods [9,10], and 3D scan-based methods [11]. As far as we know, existing methods have not yet the practical scenario of semi-supervised screening of COVID-19 where only the positive and unlabeled imaging data are available.

2.2   Positive Unlabeled Learning

PU learning can be dated back to 1998 [4]. The pioneering study also demonstrated that positive and unlabeled examples help to learning [3]. After that, several novel methods have been proposed and can be categorized into three types. The first category is the sample selection method that firstly identifies reliable negative or positive examples and then adopts supervised learning techniques [19]. The second category is the weighted PU learning methods that, for example, place higher penalties on misclassified positive examples [5,7]. The third category is the class prior estimation method that estimates the class prior to positive classes [14]. PU learning has been widely applied to disease gene identification [24], drug discovery [23], and recommender systems [25]. As we mentioned before, only positive labeled medical data of COVID-19 can be accurately collected, together with a large amount of unlabeled data, because the availability, stability, and reproducibility of the COVID-19 nucleic acid detection kits are questionable [30]. It exactly meets the setting of PU learning.

The most related work is unbiased PU learning that views U data as weighted P and N data simultaneously, which leads to unbiased risk estimation [7]. One milestone is the study that proposes the first unbiased risk estimator [6]. It gives in-depth theoretical analysis that demonstrates that for an equal number of positive and unlabeled samples, the convergence rate is no worse than $2\sqrt{2}$ times the fully supervised case. However, the unbiased risk estimator ofter encounters overfitting because it will give negative empirical risks if the trained model is very flexible, such as deep neural networks. To cope with this problem, the non-negative risk estimator that keeps the U risk not goes negative is proposed [17]. However, it still encounters the overfitting problem because it is too late to control U risks, and the classifier has suffered from overfitting already. Our proposed method further resolves this issue and exceeds previous methods significantly.

3   Methodology

This section presents the necessary notations and underlying PU learning assumptions, giving the unbiased PU learning methods, and then introducing the newly-proposed constraint non-negative PU learning method.

3.1   Learning Set-Up

We first consider the familiar positive-negative (PN) learning setting where the learner receives a sample of m labeled training examples $\{(x_i, y_i)\}_{i=1}^m$ drawn from a joint distribution $p(x, y)$ defined on $\mathcal{X} \times \mathcal{Y}$, where $\mathcal{X}$ is the feature set and $\mathcal{Y}$ is the label set. $\mathcal{X}$ is a set of medical images and $\mathcal{Y}$ is $\{-1, +1\}$ (a.k.a. negative and positive) in binary classification for COVID-19 screening.

We denote by $\ell : \mathcal{Y} \times \mathcal{Y} \to \mathbb{R}$ a loss function defined over pairs of labels. For binary classification, we denote by $f : \mathcal{X} \to \mathbb{R}^2$ a scoring function, which induces a labeling function $h_f : \mathcal{X} \to \mathcal{Y}$ where $h_f : x \to \arg\max_{y \in \mathcal{Y}}[f(x)]_y$. For any distribution $p(x, y)$ on $\mathcal{X} \times \mathcal{Y}$ and any labeling function $h \in \mathcal{H}$, we denote by $R(h) = \mathbb{E}_{(x,y) \sim p(x,y)} \ell(h(x), y)$ the expected risk. The objective is to select a hypothesis f out of a hypothesis set $\mathcal{F}$ with a small expected risk $R(h_f)$ on the target distribution. The empirical risk is $\hat{R}(h) = \frac{1}{m} \sum_{i=1}^m \ell(h(x_i), y_i)$.

In PU learning, we do not have negative data. The training instances $X = \{x_i\}^m$ draw from marginals of $p(x, y)$ consists of two parts, positive instances X_p and unlabeled instances X_u. X_p contains m_p instances sampled from $p(x|\mathcal{Y} = +1)$ and X_u contains m_u instances sampled from $p(x)$. We denote by $\pi_p = p(\mathcal{Y} = +1)$ the class-prior probability. Most methods of PU learning assumed that π_p is known already [22], because it can be estimated from P and U data [2,14]. Same as them, we assume that π_p is known throughout this paper. We also require to assume that the PU data meet separability [22] and smoothness [20].

3.2   Unbiased PU Learning

In PN learning, the unbiased expected risk can be revised as

$$R_{pn}(h) = \pi_p \mathbb{E}_{x \sim p(x|\mathcal{Y}=+1)} \ell(h(x; \theta), +1) + \\ (1 - \pi_p) \mathbb{E}_{x \sim p(x|\mathcal{Y}=-1)} \ell(h(x; \theta), -1), \tag{1}$$

and the unbiased empirical risk is

$$\hat{R}_{pn}(h) = \underbrace{\frac{\pi_p}{m_p} \sum_{i=1}^{m_p} \ell(h(x; \theta), +1)}_{\pi_p \hat{R}_p^+(h)} + \underbrace{\frac{1 - \pi_p}{m_n} \sum_{i=1}^{m_n} \ell(h(x; \theta), -1)}_{(1-\pi_p) \hat{R}_n^-(h)}, \tag{2}$$

where m_n is the training instances number of negative class, and θ denotes the parameters of screening model h. In short, $\hat{R}_{pn}(h) = \pi_p \hat{R}_p^+(h) + (1 - \pi_p) \hat{R}_n^-(h)$.

In PU learning, negative examples X_n is unaccessible such that the $\hat{R}_n^-$ cannot be estimated; however, it can be approximated indirectly thanks to prominent methods [6,26]. Denote by $\hat{R}_u$ the empirical risk of unlabeled data, the negative risk $\hat{R}_n$ can be indirectly approximated by $(1 - \pi_p)\hat{R}_n(h) = \hat{R}_u^-(h) - \pi_p\hat{R}_p^-(h)$, in which $\hat{R}_p^-(h) = \frac{1}{m_p}\sum_{i=1}^{m_p} \ell(h(x;\theta), -1)$. Finally, the PU learning risk $\hat{R}_{pu}(h)$ can be approximated by

$$\hat{R}_{pu}(h) = \pi_p\hat{R}_p^+(h) + (\hat{R}_u^-(h) - \pi_p\hat{R}_p^-(h)), \tag{3}$$

which is the risk of unbiased PU (uPU) method [6]. The labels of training U data can be viewd as -1, i.e. $\hat{R}_u^-(h) = \frac{1}{m_u}\sum_{i=1}^{m_u} \ell(h(x;\theta), -1)$. [27] suggests that uPU has good theoretical advantages that the estimation error bounds (EEB) of $\hat{h}_{pu}$ is tigher than EEB of $\hat{h}_{pn}$ when $\pi_p/\sqrt{m_p} + 1/\sqrt{m_u} < \pi_n/\sqrt{m_n}$ if (a) ℓ satisfies symmetry and is Lipschitz continuous; (b) the Rademacher complexity of $\mathcal{H}$ decays in $\mathcal{O}(1/\sqrt{m})$ for data of size m drawn from $p(x)$, $p_p(x)$ or $p_n(x)$ [17]. $\hat{h}_{pu}$ and $\hat{h}_{pn}$ are the empirical risk minimizers of $\hat{R}_{pu}$ and $\hat{R}_{pn}$, respectively.

When the second term of Eq. 3 trends to negative, the model, such as flexible enough deep networks, always turns to overfit. For improving uPU, a natural idea is to avoid the second term to be negative. Non-negative unbiased PU learning (nnPU) with the non-negative risk estimator is thus proposed to optimize a non-negative version of Eq. 3 by

$$\hat{R}_{pu}(h) = \pi_p\hat{R}_p^+(h) + max\{0, (\hat{R}_u^-(h) - \pi_p\hat{R}_p^-(h))\}, \tag{4}$$

which explicitly constrains the training risk of uPU to be non-negative. The nnPU can mitigate overfitting to a certain extent.

3.3   Constraint Non-Negative PU Learning

In this subsection, based on our analysis, we propose the constraint non-negative risk estimator and give a new and effective optimization algorithm.

While the nnPU learning method is intuitive, as mentioned before, there are still two serious issues. Firstly, non-negativity is just a primary constraint. The nnPU does invert negative values of U risks only after reaching negative values; however, it is too late to control U risks. The classifier has suffered from overfitting already. When the trainable models are flexible enough deep networks, the risk of U data $\hat{R}_u^-(h)$ would decline too quickly. Accordingly, the speed of overfitting will also increase. Secondly, the optimization way of nnPU has a problem that it only minimizes the inverse value of $\hat{R}_u^-(h)$ when the value of $\hat{R}_u^-(h)$ becomes negative. However, it will lead the classifier to fit well on U data but performs worse on P data. We define the constraint non-negative risk estimator and design the new optimization algorithm to resolve the above issues.

To avoid $\hat{R}_u$ decline too quickly, we introduce a constraint factor λ. The constraint non-negative risk estimator of our constraint non-negative PU learning (cnPU) is given by

$$\tilde{R}_{pu}(h) = \pi_p\hat{R}_p^+(h) + max\{\lambda\pi_p\hat{R}_p^+(h), (\hat{R}_u^-(h) - \pi_p\hat{R}_p^-(h))\}. \tag{5}$$

Algorithm 1: Constraint non-negative PU learning with stochastic optimization.

---

input : training data (X_p, X_u); $0 \leq \lambda \leq 1$ and $0 \leq \gamma \leq 1$

output: model parameter θ for $h(x; \theta)$

1 Let $\mathcal{A}$ be an external SGD-like stochastic optimization algorithm such as [16]

2 **while** no stopping criterion has been met:

3   Shuffle (X_p, X_u) into N mini-batches, and denote by (X_p^i, X_u^i) the i-th mini-batch

4   **for** $i = 1$ **to** N:

5   **if** $\hat{R}_u^- (h; X_u^i) - \pi_p \hat{R}_p^- (h; X_p^i)$

6       $\geq \lambda \pi_p \hat{R}_p^+ (h; X_p^i)$

7   Set gradient $\nabla_\theta \hat{R}_{pu} (h; X_p^i, X_u^i)$

8   Update θ by $\mathcal{A}$ with its current step size η

9   **else** :

10   Set gradient

11      $\nabla_\theta \left(\pi_p \hat{R}_p^+ (h; X_p^i) + \lambda \pi_p \hat{R}_p^+ (h; X_p^i) \right)$

12   Update θ by $\mathcal{A}$ with a discounted step size $\gamma\eta$

The proposed cnPU provides point-to-point remedial measures for the nnPU. On the one hand, since the value of $\hat{R}_p^+$ always be positive, the cnPU meets the non-negativity. When $\tau = \frac{\hat{R}_u^- - \pi_p \hat{R}_p^-}{\pi_p \hat{R}_p^+} < \lambda$, cnPU prioritizes the risk of $\hat{R}_p^+$. The constraint of τ can successfully avoid $\hat{R}_u$ decline too quickly. On the other hand, cnPU also controls the dynamic equilibrium between $\pi_p \hat{R}_p^+$ and $\hat{R}_u^- - \pi_p \hat{R}_p^-$. Equilibrium is an important indicator of a good algorithm, such as generative adversarial networks [1]. In summary, these advantages make cnPU perform well on the semi-supervised screening of COVID-19.

From an optimization perspective, the faster the risk decreases, the greater the probability of falling into overfitting. Generally speaking, the optimization algorithm of cnPU adopts a stopping criterion when $\hat{R}_u^-$ decline too quickly, so that the screening model can learn well on positive data and avoid overfitting on unlabeled data. Specifically, the optimization algorithm is shown in Algorithm 1.

3.4   Theoretical Analyses

Since $\hat{R}_{pu}(h)$ in Eq. 3 is strictly unbiased [6], and $\tilde{R}_{pu}(h) \geq \hat{R}_{pu}(h)$ when labeling function h is fixed, $\tilde{R}_{pu}(h)$ is biased in general. We should show the exponential decay of the bias such that the optimal estimator can be suggested. Fix h, and partition all possible (X_p, X_u) into $\mathcal{Q}^+(h) = \{(X_p, X_u) | \hat{R}_u^- - \pi_p \hat{R}_p^-(h) \geq \lambda \pi_p \hat{R}_p^+(h)\}$ and $\mathcal{Q}^-(h) = \{(X_p, X_u) | \hat{R}_u^- - \pi_p \hat{R}_p^-(h) < \lambda \pi_p \hat{R}_p^+(h)\}$. Since $\tilde{R}_{pu}(h) = \hat{R}_{pu}(h)$ on $\mathcal{Q}^+(h)$ and $\tilde{R}_{pu}(h) \neq \hat{R}_{pu}(h)$ on $\mathcal{Q}^-(h)$, we should analyze $\Pr(\mathcal{Q}^-) = \Pr\{\tilde{R}_{pu}(h) \neq \hat{R}_{pu}(h)\}$. Assume there is $C_h > 0$ such that $\sup_{h \in \mathcal{H}} \|h\|_\infty \leq C_h$ and $\sup_{|t| \leq C_h} \max_y \ell(t, y) \leq C_\ell$. Based on [17], we derive the following Lemma to analyze the biasdness degree of our risk estimator.

Lemma 1 (Biasedness). *The following three conditions are equivalent: 1) the probability measure of $Q^-(h)$ is non-zero; 2) $\tilde{R}_{pu}(h)$ differs from $\hat{R}_{pu}(h)$ with a non-zero probability over repeated sampling of (X_p, X_u); 3) the bias of $\tilde{R}_{pu}(h)$ is positive. Importantly, by assuming that there is $\alpha > 0$ such that $R_n^- \geq \alpha$, the probability measure of $Q^-(h)$ can be bounded by*

$$Pr(Q^-(h)) = exp(-2(\alpha/C_\ell)^2/((1+\lambda^2)\pi_p^2/n_p + 1/n_u)). \quad (6)$$

From Lemma 1, we can see the exponential decay of the bias with the increase of n_p and n_u. Since generalization error can measure the prediction ability of learning algorithm on unknown data, we derive the bound to dissect the consistency between the empirical risk $\tilde{R}_{pu}(h)$ and expected risk $R(h)$ following [17].

Theorem 1 (Consistency). *Assume that $R_n^-(h) \geq \alpha \geq 0$ and $0 \leq \ell(t, \pm 1) \leq C_\ell$. As $n_p, n_u \to 0$, the unconsistency decays exponentially:*

$$0 \leq \mathbb{E}[\tilde{R}_{pu}(h)] - R(h) \leq (1+\lambda)C_\ell\pi_p e^{(-2(\alpha/C_\ell)^2/((1+\lambda^2)\pi_p^2/n_p + 1/n_u))}, \quad (7)$$

Morever, for any $\delta > 0$, let $C_\delta = C_\ell\sqrt{ln(2/\delta)/2}$, then we have with probability at least $1 - \delta$,

$$|\tilde{R}_{pu}(h) - R(h)| \leq C_\delta\sqrt{4(1+\lambda^2)\pi_p^2/n_p + 1/n_u} + (1+\lambda)C_\ell\pi_p\triangle_h, \quad (8)$$

where $\triangle_h = e^{(-2(\alpha/C_\ell)^2/((1+\lambda^2)\pi_p^2/n_p + 1/n_u))}$.

Theorem 1 indicates that for fixed h, $\tilde{R}_{pu}(h) \to R(h)$ in $\mathcal{O}_p(2\pi_p\sqrt{(1+\lambda^2)/n_p} + 1/\sqrt{n_u})$. Thus, the proposed constraint non-negative risk estimator is a biased yet optimal estimator to the risk. In addition, both Lemma 1 and Theorem 1 indicate that value of λ should not be set too large.

4 Experiments

4.1 Setup

COVID-CT is a two-class chest CT dataset [32], including 349 COVID-19 CT scans and 387 non-COVID-19 CT scans. XCOV is a two-class chest X-ray dataset, including 239 COVID-19 X-rays[1] and 1,619 healthy X-rays[2]. XCOV-Four is a four-class chest X-ray dataset, including 239 COVID-19 X-rays, 1,619 healthy X-rays, 1,300 bacterial pneumonia X-rays, and 1,273 viral pneumonia X-rays [15]. We viewed COVID-19 as a positive class while the other classes as a negative class. To generate standard PU datasets, we set the class priors of XCOV, XCOVFour, and COVID-CT to 0.1, 0.1, 0.42 by considering the amount

---

[1] https://github.com/ieee8023/covid-chestxray-dataset.
[2] https://www.kaggle.com/andrewmvd/convid19-x-rays.

of COVID-19 images, respectively. We also verified the generality on MNIST and CIFAR-10.

We compared **cnPU** with state-of-the-art methods: **PN** (ResNet-50 [12]), **uPU** [6], **nnPU** [17], and a sample selection approach **SPUL** [33]. We implemented our algorithm in Pytorch. We optimized the estimator using deep neural networks (ResNet-50) by Adam [16] with initial learning rate of 1e-5 and training epoch of 50. The training images are resized to $224 \times 224 \times 3$. We normalized the pixel values to a range of -1 to 1. The λ and γ are set to 0.4 and 1, respectively. Each experiment was repeated 10 times to obtain mean accuracy.

Table 1. Accuracy (%) on the three COVID-19 datasets and two natural datasets.

Method	XCOV	XCOVFour	COVID-CT	MNIST	CIFAR-10
PN	89.94±0.03	90.50±0.05	58.83±0.07	50.77±0.03	62.80±0.02
SPUL	69.97±0.08	69.48±0.12	50.29±0.09	58.58±1.30	64.57±0.10
uPU	90.50±0.06	90.81±0.09	60.29±0.11	61.92±1.33	60.17±0.11
nnPU	95.81±0.09	94.72±0.08	75.14±0.12	92.41±0.66	85.31±0.18
cnPU-OP	96.37±0.04	96.37±0.11	78.68±0.09	92.93±0.20	86.70±0.80
cnPU	**97.49±0.03**	**98.31±0.08**	**81.62±0.11**	**93.22±0.08**	**87.44±0.12**

4.2 Results

As reported in Table 1, cnPU achieves much higher accuracy than competitors (increase about 2% or more, e.g., when cnPU is used to screen COVID-19 from CT scans, the accuracy is incremented from 58.83% to 81.62%) on various datasets and PU learning methods. Our algorithm remarkably outperforms the state-of-the-art work nnPU by 1.68%, 3.59%, and 6.48% on the three COVID-19 datasets, respectively. These improvements explicitly verify the efficacy of the constraint non-negative risk estimator on COVID-19 screening from PU data.

As shown in Fig. 2, the solid lines indicate the test error curves, and the dotted lines denote the training error curves of different PU learning methods on XCOV and COVID-CT datasets. Obviously, if the model does not overfit, the training error curve should close to zero. Moreover, the closer the test error curve is to zero, the better the result. We can see that cnPU is much better than competitors and makes a remarkable performance boost.

4.3 Insight Analyses

We dissect the strengths of the constraint non-negative risk estimator. Firstly, we explore the test error concerning different values of the constraint factor λ in Fig. 3(a). When $\lambda \to 0$, the cnPU gradually degenerates into nnPU and will suffer from overfitting. Thus λ value cannot be set too small. However, both

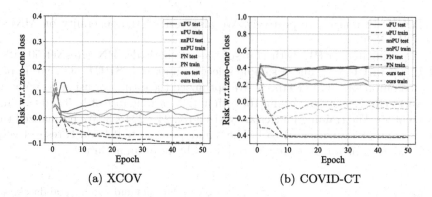

Fig. 2. Training and test error curves. The closer the curve is to 0, the better the result.

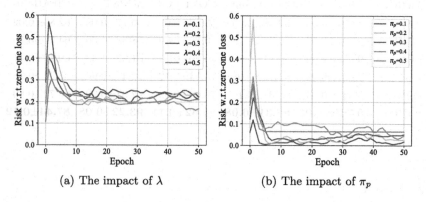

Fig. 3. Test error curves of different constraint factor λ (a) and class priors π_p (b).

Lemma 1 and Theorem 1 indicate that λ value should not be set too large. The best performance from $\lambda = 0.4$ explicitly suggests we should consider these two situations comprehensively. Secondly, we verify the importance of the new optimization algorithm 1. After removing the optimization of $R_p^+(h)$ when the value of $R_u^-(h)$ becomes negative, cnPU decreases a lot, as reported in Table 1 (see cnPU-OP). From the optimization perspective, these results justify our claim that equilibrium between P and U risks is essential for a robust algorithm. Thirdly, we provide a broader spectrum for more in-depth analysis by which Fig. 3(b) show that cnPU has performed consistently on various class priors.

Our algorithm has strong generality on natural datasets. Following the settings on MNIST and CIFAR-10 of nnPU [17], cnPU achieves 93.22% of accuracy on the MNIST dataset, which outperforms the uPU by 31.3%; cnPU achieves 87.44% of accuracy on the CIFAR-10 dataset, which remarkably outperforms nnPU by 27.27%. In addition, cnPU has acceptable scalability and time performance. The average testing time on X-ray images are 0.00186s of cnPU, 0.00185s of nPU, 00186s of nnPU, and 0.0277s of SPUL on a Titan X GPU machine.

5   Conclusion

We presented a new analysis of semi-supervised screening of COVID-19 from positive and unlabeled data, an under-explored but more realistic scenario. We also proposed the constraint non-negative positive unlabeled learning. It contains the constraint non-negative risk estimator, which is theory-induced and more robust against overfitting than previous PU learning methods. It has also improved in terms of risk optimization. Numerous experimental results have shown that it can achieve more accurate results. In-depth analyses revealed that our algorithm has the potential to assist in clinical COVID-19 screening and does not require fully-labeled data for training, which significantly reduces the heavy workload of radiologists and contributes to the rapid large-scale screening of COVID-19.

Acknowledgment. This work was funded by the National Natural Science Foundation of China (No. 61872225, No. 61876098), the Natural Science Foundation of Shandong Province (Nos. ZR2020KF013, ZR2019ZD04, ZR2020ZD44), the Introduction and Cultivation Program for Young Creative Talents in Colleges and Universities of Shandong Province (No. 173), and the National Key R&D Program of China (No. 2018YFC0830100, No. 2018YFC0830102).

References

1. Arora, S., Ge, R., Liang, Y., Ma, T., Zhang, Y.: Generalization and equilibrium in generative adversarial nets (gans). CoRR abs/1703.00573 (2017). http://arxiv.org/abs/1703.00573
2. Christoffel, M., Niu, G., Sugiyama, M.: Class-prior estimation for learning from positive and unlabeled data. In: Asian Conference on Machine Learning, pp. 221–236 (2016)
3. De Comité, F., Denis, F., Gilleron, R., Letouzey, F.: Positive and unlabeled examples help learning. In: Watanabe, O., Yokomori, T. (eds.) ALT 1999. LNCS (LNAI), vol. 1720, pp. 219–230. Springer, Heidelberg (1999). https://doi.org/10.1007/3-540-46769-6_18
4. Denis, F.Ç.: PAC learning from positive statistical queries. In: Richter, M.M., Smith, C.H., Wiehagen, R., Zeugmann, T. (eds.) ALT 1998. LNCS (LNAI), vol. 1501, pp. 112–126. Springer, Heidelberg (1998). https://doi.org/10.1007/3-540-49730-7_9
5. Du Plessis, M., Niu, G., Sugiyama, M.: Convex formulation for learning from positive and unlabeled data. In: International Conference on Machine Learning, pp. 1386–1394 (2015)
6. Du Plessis, M.C., Niu, G., Sugiyama, M.: Analysis of learning from positive and unlabeled data. Adv. Neural Inf. Process. Syst. **27**, 703–711 (2014)
7. Elkan, C., Noto, K.: Learning classifiers from only positive and unlabeled data. In: Proceedings of the 14th ACM SIGKDD International Conference on Knowledge Discovery and Data Mining, pp. 213–220 (2008)
8. Ghoshal, B., Tucker, A.: Estimating uncertainty and interpretability in deep learning for coronavirus (covid-19) detection. arXiv preprint arXiv:2003.10769 (2020)
9. Gozes, O., Frid-Adar, M., Sagie, N., Zhang, H., Ji, W., Greenspan, H.: Coronavirus detection and analysis on chest CT with deep learning. arXiv:2004.02640 (2020)

10. Gozes, O., et al.: Rapid AI development cycle for the coronavirus (covid-19) pandemic: Initial results for automated detection & patient monitoring using deep learning CT image analysis. arXiv preprint arXiv:2003.05037 (2020)

11. Han, Z., et al.: Accurate screening of covid-19 using attention-based deep 3D multiple instance learning. IEEE Trans. Med. Imaging **39**(8), 2584–2594 (2020)

12. He, K., Zhang, X., Ren, S., Sun, J.: Deep residual learning for image recognition. In: Proceedings of the IEEE Conference on Computer Vision and Pattern Recognition, pp. 770–778 (2016)

13. Huang, L., et al.: Serial quantitative chest CT assessment of covid-19: deep-learning approach. Radiol. Cardiothorac. Imaging **2**(2), e200075 (2020)

14. Kato, M., Xu, L., Niu, G., Sugiyama, M.: Alternate estimation of a classifier and the class-prior from positive and unlabeled data. arXiv preprint:1809.05710 (2018)

15. Kermany, D.S., et al.: Identifying medical diagnoses and treatable diseases by image-based deep learning. Cell **172**(5), 1122–1131 (2018)

16. Kingma, D.P., Ba, J.: Adam: A method for stochastic optimization (2014)

17. Kiryo, R., Niu, G., Du Plessis, M.C., Sugiyama, M.: Positive-unlabeled learning with non-negative risk estimator. In: Advances in Neural Information Processing Systems, pp. 1675–1685 (2017)

18. Li, T., Han, Z., Wei, B., Zheng, Y., Hong, Y., Cong, J.: Robust screening of covid-19 from chest x-ray via discriminative cost-sensitive learning. arXiv preprint arXiv:2004.12592 (2020)

19. Li, X., Liu, B.: Learning to classify texts using positive and unlabeled data. IJCAI **3**, 587–592 (2003)

20. Li, X., Liu, B., Ng, S.K.: Learning to identify unexpected instances in the test set. IJCAI **7**, 2802–2807 (2007)

21. Liu, B., Dai, Y., Li, X., Lee, W.S., Yu, P.S.: Building text classifiers using positive and unlabeled examples. In: Third IEEE International Conference on Data Mining, pp. 179–186. IEEE (2003)

22. Liu, B., Lee, W.S., Yu, P.S., Li, X.: Partially supervised classification of text documents. ICML **2**, 387–394 (2002)

23. Liu, Y., et al.: Computational drug discovery with dyadic positive-unlabeled learning. In: Proceedings of the 2017 SIAM International Conference on Data Mining, pp. 45–53. SIAM (2017)

24. Mordelet, F., Vert, J.P.: Prodige: prioritization of disease genes with multitask machine learning from positive and unlabeled examples. BMC Bioinformatics **12**(1), 389 (2011)

25. Peng, T., Zuo, W., He, F.: SVM based adaptive learning method for text classification from positive and unlabeled documents. Knowl. Inf. Syst. **16**(3), 281–301 (2008)

26. Plessis, M.D., Niu, G., Sugiyama, M.: Convex formulation for learning from positive and unlabeled data. In: Proceedings of Machine Learning Research, vol. 37, pp. 1386–1394. PMLR, Lille, France (Jul 2015). http://proceedings.mlr.press/v37/plessis15.html

27. Ritchie, D., Thomas, A., Hanrahan, P., Goodman, N.: Neurally-guided procedural models: amortized inference for procedural graphics programs using neural networks. In: Lee, D., Sugiyama, M., Luxburg, U., Guyon, I., Garnett, R. (eds.) Advances in Neural Information Processing Systems, vol. 29, pp. 622–630. Curran Associates, Inc. (2016). https://proceedings.neurips.cc/paper/2016/file/40008b9a5380fcacce3976bf7c08af5b-Paper.pdf

28. Shan, F., et al.: Lung infection quantification of covid-19 in CT images with deep learning. arXiv preprint arXiv:2003.04655 (2020)

29. Shi, F., et al.: Large-scale screening of covid-19 from community acquired pneumonia using infection size-aware classification. arXiv preprint arXiv:2003.09860 (2020)
30. Wang, S., et al.: A deep learning algorithm using CT images to screen for Corona virus disease (COVID-19). Eur. Radiol. 1–9 (2021). https://doi.org/10.1007/s00330-021-07715-1
31. WHO: Pulse survey on continuity of essential health services during the covid-19 pandemic (2020)
32. Zhao, J., Zhang, Y., He, X., Xie, P.: Covid-CT-dataset: a CT scan dataset about covid-19. arXiv preprint arXiv:2003.13865 (2020)
33. Zhu, C., Liu, B., Yu, Q., Liu, X., Yu, W.: A spy positive and unlabeled learning classifier and its application in HR SAR image scene interpretation. In: 2012 IEEE Radar Conference, pp. 0516–0521. IEEE (2012)

Deep MCEM for Weakly-Supervised Learning to Jointly Segment and Recognize Objects Using Very Few Expert Segmentations

Akshay V. Gaikwad[(⊠)] and Suyash P. Awate[(⊠)]

Department of Computer Science and Engineering, Indian Institute of Technology
(IIT) Bombay, Mumbai, India
{akshayg,suyash}@cse.iitb.ac.in

Abstract. Typical methods for semantic image segmentation rely on large training sets comprising pixel-level segmentations and pixel-level classifications. In medical applications, a large number of training images with per-pixel segmentations are difficult to obtain. In addition, many applications involve images or image tiles containing a single object/region of interest, where the image/tile-level information about object/region class is readily available. We propose a novel deep-neural-network (DNN) framework for *joint segmentation and recognition* of objects relying on *weakly-supervised* learning from training sets having *very few expert segmentations*, but with object-class labels available for all images/tiles. For weakly-supervised learning, we propose a variational-learning framework relying on *Monte Carlo expectation maximization* (MCEM), inferring a posterior distribution on the missing segmentations. We design an effective Metropolis-Hastings posterior *sampler* coupled with sample *reparametrizations* to enable end-to-end learning. Our DNN first produces probabilistic segmentations of objects, and then their probabilistic classifications. Results on two publicly available real-world datasets show the benefits of our strategies of (i) joint object segmentation and recognition as well as (ii) weakly-supervised MCEM-based learning.

Keywords: Joint segmentation and recognition · Weak supervision · Missing segmentations · Variational monte-carlo EM · Reparametrization

1 Introduction and Related Work

For semantic image segmentation, typical methods use deep-neural-network (DNN) models that learn using *full supervision* and a *large training set* of images

The authors are grateful for support from the Infrastructure Facility for Advanced Research and Education in Diagnostics grant funded by Department of Biotechnology (DBT), Government of India (BT/INF/22/SP23026/2017).

A. Feragen et al. (Eds.): IPMI 2021, LNCS 12729, pp. 624–636, 2021.
https://doi.org/10.1007/978-3-030-78191-0_48

having pixel-level segmentation and pixel-level classification. For example, in the R-CNN family of methods, learning a Mask-R-CNN [3] requires a large training set of images with bounding-boxes, pixel-wise object segmentations, as well as object-class labels. During learning, such methods cannot leverage images that only have image-level object-class labels without any segmentations. Similarly, typical methods using fully convolutional DNNs, e.g., U-Net [14], FCN [10], and DeepLabV3 [2], rely on large expert-segmented training sets and full supervision.

For medical applications, it is often infeasible to obtain a large number of expert segmentations because of limitations on experts' time and budgets. In addition, many applications involve images or image tiles with a single object/region of interest (e.g., a single organ or a structure or an abnormal region), where the image-level information about object/region class is readily available (i) at a small fraction of expert time and effort, compared to pixel-level segmentations, and (ii) within typical clinical protocols. Thus, we propose a novel DNN framework for *joint segmentation and recognition* of objects relying on *weakly-supervised* learning from small training sets having *very few expert segmentations*, but with object-class labels available for all images/tiles.

A class of semi-supervised methods for semantic-segmentation [7,15] rely on *pre-trained* DNNs using large high-quality training sets. These semi-supervised methods assume that a part of the training set is devoid of any kind of expert labels, i.e., neither pixel-level segmentations nor image/region-level class labels. In contrast, our framework leverages weakly labeled data that includes images with image-level class-labels available. These semi-supervised methods [7,15] cannot leverage training-set images with only image-level class labels available.

Some other semantic-segmentation methods [1,4,6,8,11,16,17] rely on semi-supervised/weakly-supervised learning. Class activation map (CAM) based methods like [4,6] uses a DNN pair, where, unlike our method, a DNN first outputs object labels and then another DNN segments the objects in the image, leveraging class-specific activation maps to restrict the search space during semi-supervised segmentation. The methods in [1] and [17] propose sequential heuristical schemes relying on a well-trained classifier (using very large image sets) to simulate missing segmentations, unlike our scheme that proposes variational MCEM to leverage a small training set along with a tiny set of expert segmentations. [16] uses a reconstruction based mechanism for abnormal region segmentation and uses the class label information to tune the segmentation probabilities. Unlike this method, our method has a DNN for generating segmentations and a DNN for classification and the class labels are not restricted to binary values. Unlike [1,6,16,17], our weak-supervision variational framework leverages the image-level class-label information in the entire training set to infer a posterior distribution on the missing segmentations. Methods like [8] use region annotations as weak labels, whereas our framework assumes only image-level class-label as weak labels. [11] leverage the images in training set with only image-level class labels available, but, unlike our approach, their fully-convolutional DNN for direct pixel-wise classification uses a conditional random field (CRF) model to couple with the image-level label data. In contrast to [1,4,6,8,11,16,17], our framework relies on DNNs to produce a probabilistic segmentation of an object/region in the image which is then recognized as belonging to a specific class, thereby leading to a probabilistic semantic image segmentation.

This paper makes novel contributions. We propose a novel DNN framework for *joint segmentation and recognition* of objects relying on *weakly-supervised* learning from training sets having *very few expert segmentations*, but with object-class labels available for all images/tiles. For weakly-supervised learning, we propose a variational-learning framework relying on *Monte Carlo expectation maximization* (MCEM), inferring a posterior distribution on the missing segmentations. We design an effective Metropolis-Hastings (MH) *sampler* for the posterior distribution, coupled with sample *reparametrizations* to enable end-to-end learning. Our DNN first produces probabilistic segmentations of objects, and then their probabilistic classifications. Results on two publicly available real-world datasets show the benefits of our strategies of (i) joint object segmentation and recognition, and (ii) weakly-supervised MCEM-based variational learning.

2   Methods

We describe our novel framework with weakly-supervised DNN learning based on MCEM, for the joint tasks of object segmentation and recognition. Our variational framework jointly learns a segmenter DNN and a recognizer DNN. It assumes that image-level class-label information is present for every image in the training set, but that expert segmentations for objects of interest are available for only a small subset of images in the training set. For training-set images with missing segmentations, the framework infers a posterior distribution of segmentations. It also leverages image-level class-label information to improve the inference of the missing segmentations, the segmenter, and the recognizer.

Let random field X model the *input image* that contains an object of interest. Let binary random field Z model the *binary segmentation* image, of the same

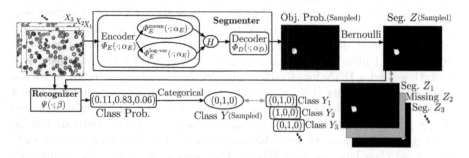

Fig. 1. Our DNN framework for joint segmentation and recognition of objects with variational MCEM-based weakly-supervised learning from training sets having very few expert segmentations, but with object-class labels available for all images/tiles.

size as image X, which indicates the location of the object of interest. The object belongs to one of $K > 1$ classes, e.g., the object can be a certain kind of a biological entity (e.g., a cell or a structure or an organ) that can belong to K different medical types, e.g., different classes within normal and/or abnormal conditions. Let binary random vector Y model the *class label* for each object of interest, as a one-hot vector. Let the joint distribution $P(X, Y, Z)$ model the statistical dependencies between the input image X, its object segmentation Z, and the object-class label Y. During *learning*, we model $P(X, Y, Z)$ through the conditional distributions of the object's segmentation $P(Z|X)$ and class $P(Y|Z, X)$. During *inference*, for input image $x \sim P(X)$, we infer a distribution of object segmentations $z \sim P(Z|x)$ and the object-class probability $P(Y|x)$ (Fig. 1).

In the *fully-supervised learning* mode, a DNN would rely on a training set of triples $\{(X_s, Y_s, Z_s)\}_{s=1}^S$ where X_s is an input image, and Z_s and Y_s are the associated object-segmentation image and the object-class label, respectively. However, obtaining high-quality expert segmentations Z for images X is laborious and expensive. Thus, in practice, a large subset of the training set will be devoid of the segmentations Z and only comprise a set of pairs $\{(X_u, Y_u)\}_{u=1}^U$. This paper focuses on the *weakly-supervised learning* mode, where the training set $\mathcal{T} := \{(x_s, y_s, z_s)\}_{s=1}^S \cup \{(x_u, y_u)\}_{u=1}^U$, with $S \ll (S + U)$.

2.1 DNN-Based Variational Model for Object Segmentation

We propose a DNN-based statistical model $P(Z|X)$ to segment the object in the input image X. At pixel v, let the segmentation-image value $Z[v] = 1$ indicate the presence of the object at pixel v in image X; $Z[v] = 0$ indicates otherwise. Let the DNN model $P(Z|X)$ comprise 2 parts: the encoder mapping $\Phi_E(\cdot; \alpha_E)$ parameterized by weights α_E and the decoder mapping $\Phi_D(\cdot; \alpha_D)$ parameterized by weights α_D. Let random vector H model the mapped vectors in the *latent space*. The encoder $\Phi_E(\cdot; \alpha_E)$ maps the image X to a factored multivariate Gaussian distribution over H, with factor means as $\Phi_E^{\text{mean}}(X; \alpha_E)$ and factor log-variances as $\Phi_E^{\text{log-var}}(X; \alpha_E)$. We model the latent-space distribution of H as $P(H|X; \alpha_E) := G(H; \Phi_E^{\text{mean}}(X; \alpha_E), \Phi_E^{\text{log-var}}(X; \alpha_E))$, where $G(\cdot; \mu, \lambda)$ is the multivariate Gaussian with mean μ and a diagonal covariance matrix with (positive) diagonal elements as exponentials of the components of the vector λ. The decoder $\Phi_D(\cdot; \alpha_D)$ maps latent-space random-vector instances h to per-pixel *probability maps* underlying the segmentation. We model the distribution on the binary segmentation image Z using Bernoulli distribution factors with parameters given by $\Phi_D(H; \alpha_D)$ as $P(Z|H, X; \alpha_D) := \prod_{v=1}^V (\Phi_D(H, X; \alpha_D)[v])^{Z[v]} (1 - \Phi_D(H, X; \alpha_D)[v])^{1-Z[v]}$. Thus, $P(Z|X; \alpha) = \int_h P(Z|h, X; \alpha_D) P(h|X; \alpha_E) dh$, where $\alpha := \alpha_E \cup \alpha_D$. Sampling binary segmentations Z from $P(Z|X; \alpha)$ is equivalent to first sampling H from the associated latent-space Gaussian parameterized by the encoder output, and then sampling Z from the associated Bernoulli distributions parameterized by the decoder output. Note: the Gaussian distribution $G(H; \Phi_E^{\text{mean}}(X; \alpha_E), \Phi_E^{\text{log-var}}(X; \alpha_E))$ over latent space implicitly model a distribution over the segmentation probability maps using the nonlinear transformation $\Phi_D(H, X; \alpha_D)$ on H; this models dependencies between inter-pixel probabilities and inter-pixel segmentation labels.

2.2   DNN-Based Statistical Model to Recognize a Segmented Object

We propose a DNN-based statistical model $P(Y|Z, X)$ to recognize the object indicated by the segmentation image Z for input image X. For index k, let $Y[k] = 1$ indicate that the object belongs to class k; $Y[k] = 0$ indicates otherwise. Let a DNN model a mapping $\Psi(\cdot; \beta)$, parameterized by weights β, from the image pair (X, Z) to a vector of parameters $\Psi(X, Z; \beta)$ underlying Bernoulli random variables within Y. At index k, let the parameter be $\Psi(X, Z; \beta)[k]$. We model $P(Y|Z, X; \beta) := \prod_{k=1}^{K}(\Psi(X, Z; \beta)[k])^{Y[k]}(1-\Psi(X, Z; \beta)[k])^{1-Y[k]}$. During learning, promoting $\log P(Y|Z, X; \beta)$ penalizes the cross entropy between the (true) one-hot encoding Y and the DNN-output probabilities $\Psi(X, Z; \beta)$.

2.3   MCEM for Weakly-Supervised Segmenter-Recognizer Learning

Given training-set $\mathcal{T}$, we propose a MCEM framework for joint DNN learning of the object segmenter and the recognizer. Let the set of DNN *parameters* be $\theta := \alpha \cup \beta$. For each image X_u, we model the missing segmentation Z_u as a *hidden* random field. For images X_s and X_u, we model the missing latent-space representations as H_s and H_v, respectively. The *complete data* is $\mathcal{T}^{\text{complete}} := \{(x_s, y_s, z_s, H_s)\}_{s=1}^{S} \cup \{(x_u, y_u, Z_u, H_u)\}_{u=1}^{U}$. The complete-data likelihood is $P(\mathcal{T}^{\text{complete}}; \theta) := \prod_{s=1}^{S} P(x_s, y_s, z_s, H_s; \theta) \prod_{u=1}^{U} P(x_u, y_u, Z_u, H_u; \theta)$.

E Step. At iteration i, with parameter estimates θ^i, EM minorizes the log-likelihood function using the expected complete-data log-likelihood over the posterior $\prod_{u=1}^{U} P(Z_u, H_u|x_u, y_u; \theta^i) \prod_{s=1}^{S} P(H_s|x_s, y_s, z_s; \theta^i)$ on the missing segmentations Z_u and the missing latent-space encodings H_u and H_s, i.e.,

$$Q(\theta; \theta^i) := E_{\prod_{u=1}^{U} P(Z_u, H_u|x_u, y_u; \theta^i) \prod_{s=1}^{S} P(H_s|x_s, y_s, z_s; \theta^i)}$$
$$\left[\sum_{u=1}^{U} \log P(x_u, y_u, Z_u, H_u; \theta) + \sum_{s=1}^{S} \log P(x_s, y_s, z_s, H_s; \theta) \right]. \quad (1)$$

MCEM approximates the analytically intractable expectation as a Monte Carlo average using an independent and identically distributed (i.i.d.) sample $\{(z_u^t, h_u^t) \sim P(Z_u, H_u|x_u, y_u; \theta^i)\}_{t=1}^{T} \cup \{h_s^t \sim P(H_s|x_s, y_s, z_s; \theta^i)\}_{t=1}^{T}$, to give $\widehat{Q}(\theta; \theta^i) :=$

$$\sum_{u=1}^{U} \frac{1}{T} \sum_{t=1}^{T} \log P(x_u, y_u, z_u^t, h_u^t; \theta) + \sum_{s=1}^{S} \frac{1}{T} \sum_{t=1}^{T} \log P(x_s, y_s, z_s, h_s^t; \theta). \quad (2)$$

We sample segmentation images z_u^t and latent-space encodings h_u^t and h_s^t, from $P(Z_u, H_u|x_u, y_u; \theta^i)$ and $P(H_s|x_s, y_s, z_s; \theta^i)$, using a MH sampler incorporating an efficient proposal distribution, as described later in Sect. 2.4. Furthermore, for the sampled (z_u^t, h_u^t) and h_s^t, we propose reparameterizations that enable gradient-based optimization algorithms, like backpropagation, for θ.

M Step. At iteration i, EM maximizes $\widehat{Q}(\theta; \theta^i)$ over parameters θ leading to the updated parameters θ^{i+1}. Selecting a sufficiently large Monte Carlo sample, MCEM inherits the behaviour of EM that leads to convergence to a stationary point of the log-likelihood function of the observed training set $\mathcal{T}$.

2.4   Efficient MH Sampling of Missing Segmentations and Encodings

Within iteration i of MCEM, we propose a MH sampling algorithm to (i) sample missing segmentations z_u and encodings h_u from the posterior $P(Z_u, H_u | x_u, y_u; \theta^i)$, and (ii) sample the encodings h_s from the posterior $P(H_s | x_s, y_s, z_s; \theta^i)$.

Given a current state, the MH sampling strategy is a MCMC method that first generates a candidate by sampling from a proposal distribution and then, based on some probability, either updates the state to the candidate or retains the current state. For sampling from $P(Z_u, H_u | x_u, y_u; \theta^i)$, we now consider several strategies to generate candidates and propose one that is computationally straightforward and leads to a good probability of acceptance of the generated candidate. First, it is well known that the naive strategy of sampling from simple prior models, e.g., $P(Z_u, H_u) = P(Z_u)P(H_u)$ with fixed covariances within Z_u and H_u, is inefficient. In our case, a simple proposal distribution $P(Z_u)$ for discrete Z_u (e.g., using model based) would typically lead to an unrealistic model of the higher-order spatial dependencies within the segmentation image Z. On the other hand, modeling a realistic prior distribution is difficult because of the unavailability of the required observations for the hidden variables Z and H. Second, some schemes aim to improve the aforementioned strategy by adapting the covariance of the proposal distribution to the local structure of the (posterior) distribution that we desire to sample from. However, such schemes often add significant complexity that may be especially challenging in our context of a Markov random field model. Thus, we design an improved proposal distribution that leverages the DNN model learned at iteration i.

Bayes rule factors $P(Z_u, H_u | x_u, y_u; \theta^i)$, upto a normalizing constant, into $P(y_u | x_u, Z_u; \beta^i) P(Z_u | H_u, x_u; \alpha_D^i) P(H_u | x_u; \alpha_E^i)$, where the first factor is modeled by the recognizer $\Psi(\cdot; \beta^i)$, the second factor is modeled by the segmenter's decoder $\Phi_D(\cdot; \alpha_D^i)$, and the third factor is modeled by segmenter's encoder $\Phi_E(\cdot; \alpha_E^i)$. Within the Markov chain in the MH sampler, when the current encoding (state) is h and the segmentation (state) is z, we propose to use the asymmetric candidate-proposal distribution $P(Z_u | H_u, x_u; \alpha_D^i) P(H_u | x_u; \alpha_E^i)$ to draw a candidate encoding (state) h' and a candidate segmentation (state) z'. Sampling the encoding from $P(H_u | x_u; \alpha_E^i)$ and, in turn, the segmentation from $P(Z_u | H_u, x_u; \alpha_D^i)$ is computationally efficient and effective because it needs only a single forward pass through the segmenter. Also, this proposal distribution is informed by the (training) data, unlike sampling from some prior distribution, and is thus more effective in generating candidates that have a good acceptance probability. The MH sampler's acceptance probability for a candidate (h', z') is

$$\min\left(1, \frac{P(z', h'|x_u, y_u; \theta^i)}{P(z, h|x_u, y_u; \theta^i)} \frac{P(z, h|x_u; \alpha^i)}{P(z', h'|x_u; \alpha^i)}\right) = \min\left(1, \frac{P(y_u|x_u, z'; \beta^i)}{P(y_u|x_u, z; \beta^i)}\right). \quad (3)$$

Thus, at iteration i, while the candidate generation relies on the learned segmenter $\Phi(\cdot; \alpha^i)$, the candidate acceptance relies on the learned recognizer $\Psi(\cdot; \beta^i)$. In this way, for those images x_u with missing segmentations Z_u, the corresponding observed class-labels y_u help the MCEM to select an informative segmentation sample $\{z_u^t\}_{t=1}^T$ that, in turn, improves the learning of the recognizer mapping $\Psi(\cdot; \beta)$ and the segmenter mapping $\Phi(\cdot; \alpha)$.

In this paper, we sample each encoding-segmentation pair (h_u^t, z_u^t) by (i) initializing the Markov chain to a state from the previous iteration $t-1$ and (ii) running the Markov chain through a burn-in period, using a different pseudo-random number sequence for each t. In this paper, for the specific datasets used, we find that a burn-in of 10 iterations and a sample size $T = 20$ works reasonably.

While sampling $h \sim P(H|x; \alpha_E^i)$, we reparameterize its d-th component as $h[d] := \Phi_E^{\text{mean}}(X; \alpha_E)[d] + \eta \exp(\Phi_E^{\text{log-var}}(X; \alpha_E)[d])$, where η is a random draw from a standard normal distribution. Reparameterizing h in terms of the parameters α_E allows backpropagating loss-function gradients through h to α_E. Similarly, when sampling z from $P(Z|H; \alpha_D^i)$, at pixel v, we can exactly sample $z[v]$ from a Bernoulli distribution, i.e., a categorical distribution with 2 classes with probabilities $\gamma_1(H; \alpha_D)[v] := \Phi_D(H; \alpha_D)[v]$ and $\gamma_2(H; \alpha_D)[v] := 1 - \Phi_D(H; \alpha_D)[v]$, by (i) drawing 2 scalars $\{g_1, g_2\}$ independently from a Gumbel distribution with location parameter 0 and scale parameter 1 and then (ii) taking $\arg\max_k(\log\gamma_k(H; \alpha_D)[v] + g_k)$. We approximate the non-differentiable function $\arg\max_k(\cdot)$ by the softmax function to give a K-length representation of the categorical variable, with k-th component $= \exp((\log\gamma_k(H; \alpha_D)[v] + g_k)/\tau)/\sum_{k=1}^K \exp((\log\gamma_k(H; \alpha_D)[v] + g_k)/\tau)$, where $\tau > 0$ is a real-valued free parameter that balances the ease of differentiability with the fidelity of the approximation. Thus, for binary segmentation, $z[v] := \exp((\log\gamma_1(H; \alpha_D)[v] + g_1)/\tau)/\sum_{k=1}^2 \exp((\log\gamma_k(H; \alpha_D)[v] + g_k)/\tau)$, We tune τ using a continuation scheme, starting with a large $\tau = 5$ (making the loss function smoother) and gradually reducing ($\Delta\tau = 0.1$) to $\tau = 0.1$ (making the loss function closer to the $\arg\max_k(\cdot)$ function). Reparameterizing z in terms of the parameters α_D allows backpropagating loss-function gradients through z.

We use an analogous strategy for sampling from $P(H_s|x_s, y_s, z_s; \theta^i)$, where H_s is associated with those images x_s for which an expert segmentation z_s is available. Here, Bayes rule refactors $P(H_s|x_s, y_s, z_s; \theta^i)$ into the (un-normalized) product $P(H_s|x_s; \alpha_E^i)P(z_s|H_s, x_s; \alpha_D^i)$, where, at iteration i, the first factor is modeled by the DNN mapping $\Phi_E(\cdot; \alpha_E^i)$ underlying the segmenter's encoder, and the second factor is modeled by the DNN mapping $\Phi_D(\cdot; \alpha_D^i)$ underlying the segmenter's decoder. Thus, in this case, the candidate generation relies on the learned segmenter's encoder model $\Phi_E(\cdot; \alpha_E^i)$ at that iteration, and the candidate acceptance relies on the segmenter's decoder model $\Phi_D(\cdot; \alpha_D^i)$ at that iteration.

We propose to reparameterize h as before to enable the backpropagation of the loss-function gradients through h to the parameters α_E.

2.5   Deep-MCEM Based Inference Strategy for Test Images

After the weakly-supervised joint training outputs optimal parameters θ^*, we can apply the framework to segment the object in a test image x' and recognize the class for the segmented object. We propose to infer the per-pixel expected segmentation probability $P(Z[v] = 1|x'; \alpha^*)$ as an expectation of the probabilities (produced by the variational segmenter) over the distribution of latent-space encodings H, i.e., $P(Z[v] = 1|x'; \alpha^*) :=$

$$E_{P(H|x';\alpha_E^*)}[P(Z[v] = 1|H, x'; \alpha_D^*)] \approx \frac{1}{T} \sum_{t=1}^{T} P(Z[v] = 1|h^t, x'; \alpha_D^*), \quad (4)$$

with independently sampled $h^t \sim P(H|x'; \alpha_E^*)$. For each class $k \in [1, K]$, we propose to infer the expected class probability $P(Y[k] = 1|x'; \beta^*)$ as an expectation of the class probabilities (produced by the recognizer) over the distribution of segmentations produced by the variational segmenter, i.e., $P(Y[k] = 1|x'; \beta^*) :=$

$$E_{P(H,Z|x';\alpha^*)}[P(Y[k] = 1|H, Z, x'; \beta^*)] \approx \frac{1}{T} \sum_{t=1}^{T} P(Y[k] = 1|z^t, x'; \beta^*), \quad (5)$$

with T independently sampled pairs $(h^t, z^t) \sim P(H, Z|x'; \alpha^*)$. Sampling from $P(H, Z|x'; \alpha^*)$ is computationally efficient, as we discussed in Sect. 2.4, such that it entails (i) a single forward-pass through the segmenter's encoder to get the distribution $P(H|x'; \alpha_E^*)$ for H, followed by draws from a standard normal to sample h, and (ii) a single forward-pass through the segmenter's decoder to the distribution $P(Z|H, x'; \alpha_D^*)$ for Z, followed by Bernoulli draws to sample z. In this paper, we use a sample size of $T = 20$ for computational efficiency.

Outputs. The expected probability of pixel v belonging to the background (i.e., absence of object) is $p_v^0 := 1 - P(Z[v] = 1|x'; \alpha^*)$. The expected probability of pixel v belonging to an object of class k is $p_v^k := P(Z[v] = 1|x'; \alpha^*)P(Y[k] = 1|x'; \beta^*)$. The hard per-pixel classification assigns, at pixel v, a class label k^* that maximizes the expected class probability, i.e., $\arg\max_{k=0,\cdots,K}(p_v^k)$.

3   Results and Discussion

We use 2 publicly available datasets to evaluate 4 methods by varying the number of the training-set images having expert segmentations; we change the percentage $100 \cdot S/(S + U)\%$ from 10 (very low; $S \ll U$) to 100 ($S \gg U = 0$). We evaluate performance using mean intersection-over-union (mean-IoU; equivalently mean-Jaccard) between the hard per-pixel classifications output by the learned models (e.g., as described in Sect. 2.5) and those provided by the expert.

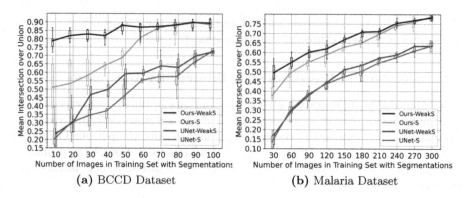

(a) BCCD Dataset   **(b)** Malaria Dataset

Fig. 2.   Results on BCCD and Malaria Datasets: Quantitative Analysis. Performance of object segmentation and recognition (in terms of mean-IoU on the test set) between the semantic segmentation (hard per-pixel labels) and the expert semantic segmentation, at varying levels of supervision (10% to 100%) ranging from a training set T. The box plots show the variability in the test-set performance over randomly selected sets of S images with expert segmentations in the training set T (50 repeats).

Methods. We compare 2 methods within our framework described in Sect. 2 for joint object segmentation and recognition, i.e., methods that produce an object segmentation ($P(Z[v] = 1|x'; \alpha^*)$) coupled with image-level recognition ($P(Y[k] = 1|x'; \beta^*)$), which then translates to per-pixel probabilistic classification (p_v^k): (i) *Ours-S*: fully-supervised learning where the training set comprises only S images having both expert segmentations and image-level labels, and (ii) *Ours-WeakS*: weakly-supervised learning where in addition to the aforementioned S images, the training set has U images with image-level labels and without expert segmentations. For Ours-S, and Ours-WeakS: the segmenter $\Phi(\cdot; \alpha)$ relies on the U-Net architecture for binary segmentation [14]; the recognizer $\Psi(\cdot; \beta)$ relies on the ResNet architecture [5]. In this paper, we implement the recognizer mapping $\Psi(X, Z; \beta)$ to use the reparameterized segmentation Z as a *spatial-attention* map that gets (point-wise) multiplied with the input image X; coarser-scale representations (i.e., Gaussian smoothed and subsampled) get (point-wise) multiplied with the first three intermediate representations in the recognizer. We compare with two baselines for semantic segmentation: (i) *UNet* [14]: fully-supervised learning of direct per-pixel classification using a training set of S images with expert-provided per-pixel classifications; (ii) *UNet-WeakS* [11]: U-Net extended to leverage weakly-supervised learning where in addition to the aforementioned S images, the training set has U images with image-level labels without expert segmentations. For consistency, all methods rely on U-Net, with latent space of dimension 28*28*256, a well-studied architecture for medical image segmentation. To train all models, we use data augmentation and stochastic gradient descent [9,13] (lr 0.01; momentum 0.9).

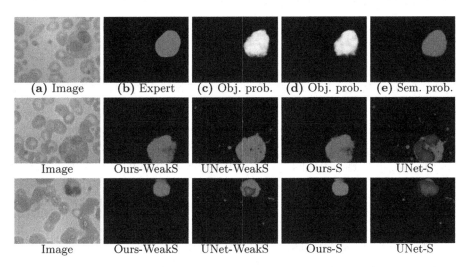

Fig. 3. Results on BCCD Dataset: Qualitative Analysis at Level of Supervision with $S = 10$ and $U = 90$. **(a)** Test Image x'. **(b)** Expert-given object segmentation (foreground) and object class (eosinophil; denoted by green); background color is black. **(c)**–**(d)** Sampled object-segmentation probability maps $\Phi_D(h^t; \alpha_D)$, output by Ours-WeakS, by sampling latent-space encodings h^t from $P(H|x'; \alpha_E^*)$. **(e)** Expected semantic segmentation probability map, output by Ours-WeakS, showing expected per-pixel class probabilities p_v^k (each color channel represents p_v^k for a specific class k). The next two rows show per-pixel class probabilities output by all methods. (Color figure online)

Datasets. The *BCCD histopathology* dataset (`github.com/Shenggan/BCCD_Dataset`) has 410 image tiles showing blood cells including white blood cells (WBCs) of four classes, i.e., eosinophil, lymphocyte, monocyte, and neutrophil. Because of very limited examples of monocytes usable (even) for evaluation in the test set, we merge it with the lymphocyte class, leading to $K = 3$ classes. We randomly select the training set $\mathcal{T}$ with cardinality $S + U = 100$ image tiles, the validation set with 50 tiles (to tune free parameters for all methods), and the test set with 260 tiles. The *Malaria parasite histopathology* dataset (`data.broadinstitute.org/bbbc/BBBC041`) has 1364 image tiles showing Giemsa-stained red blood cells (RBCs), with some infected by the malarial parasite plasmodium vivax. The infected cells belong to four classes, i.e., gametocyte, ring, schizont, and trophozoite. Because of very limited examples of gametocytes usable (even) for evaluation in the test set, we merge it with the schizont class, leading to $K = 3$ classes. We randomly select (i) a training set $\mathcal{T}$ (of cardinality $S + U$) of 300 image tiles (each containing an infected RBC), (ii) a validation set of 100 tiles, and (iii) a test set with 300 tiles. Both datasets give a bounding-box around each object of interest; we obtain per-pixel expert segmentation within each bounding box. Histopathology slides from multiple clinical sites, despite using standard staining protocols, are naturally susceptible to significant staining variation. Thus, we perform stain normalization using [12].

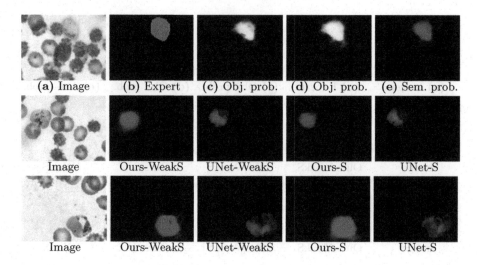

Fig. 4. Results on Malaria Dataset: Qualitative Analysis at Level of Supervision with $S = 30$ and $U = 270$. **(a)** Test Image x'. **(b)** Expert-given object segmentation (foreground) and object class (trophozoite; denoted by green); background color is black. **(c)–(d)** Sampled object-segmentation probability maps $\Phi_D(h^t; \alpha_D)$, output by Ours-WeakS, by sampling latent-space encodings h^t from $P(H|x'; \alpha_E^*)$. **(e)** Expected semantic segmentation probability map, output by Ours-WeakS, showing expected per-pixel class probabilities p_v^k (each color channel represents p_v^k for a specific class k). The next two rows show per-pixel class probabilities output by all methods. (Color figure online)

Evaluation. When very few expert segmentations are available, i.e., when $S \ll U$, Ours-WeakS clearly outperforms all other methods for both datasets, quantitatively (Fig. 2) and qualitatively (Fig. 3, Fig. 4). Ours-WeakS improves over Ours-S (in both segmentation and recognition) for upto 60% supervision by leveraging the extra information in the training set in the form of images x_u with object-class labels y_u (despite the missing expert segmentations for images x_u), which is especially so at very low levels of supervision, e.g., 10% and 20%. Quantitatively (Fig. 2), Ours-S outperforms UNet-S in all fully supervised settings, i.e., when the training set has only S images including both expert segmentations and class labels. This shows the benefits of our joint segmentation and recognition framework that first produces an object segmentation and then use that for object-level recognition, thereby indirectly translating to per-pixel probabilistic classification (p_v^k). This is unlike the baseline methods that learn to directly output per-pixel probabilistic classifications, leading to semantic segmentations that get fragmented into multiple classes (Fig. 3, Fig. 4), especially when learning using a tiny set of S expert segmentations. UNet-WeakS [11] leverages the weak supervision in terms of the image-level class label information at mid-levels of supervision, e.g., 50% and 60%, and hence performs better than UNet-S. Benefits of UNet-WeakS are seen over UNet-S (Fig. 3, Fig. 4), where UNet-WeakS corrects some of the pixels incorrectly segmented and classified by UNet-S. These results show, especially when training with very few expert segmentations, the benefits of (i) our joint object-segmentation and object-level recognition strategy (e.g., Ours-WeakS, Ours-S) over direct per-pixel classification (e.g., UNet-WeakS, UNet-S), and (ii) weakly-supervised learning (e.g., Ours-WeakS, UNet-WeakS) over fully-supervised learning that is restricted to a smaller training set (e.g., Ours-S, UNet-S).

4   Conclusion

This paper proposed a novel MCEM based variational DNN framework for joint segmentation and recognition of objects relying on weakly-supervised learning with training sets with very few expert segmentations (but object-class labels available for all images). The framework produces probabilistic semantic segmentation by producing probabilistic segmentations of objects that are then recognized as belonging to a specific class. The end-to-end variational learning underlying MCEM relies on computationally efficient and effective sampling, by designing candidate-proposal distributions for the missing segmentations (and the segmenter's latent-space encodings) coupled with suitable sample reparametrizations to enable end-to-end gradient propagation. The weak supervision leverages the image-level class-label information for the entire training set to infer a posterior distribution on the missing segmentations. Results on two publicly available real-world datasets show the benefits of our strategies of end-to-end object segmentation and recognition as well as weakly-supervised MCEM-based learning. The proposed framework assumes a image/tile has a single object of interest.

References

1. Ahn, J., Cho, S., Kwak, S.: Weakly supervised learning of instance segmentation with inter-pixel relations. In: IEEE Computer Vision and Pattern Recognition, pp. 2204–2213 (2019)
2. Chen, L., Zhu, Y., Papandreou, G., Schroff, F., Adam, H.: Encoder-decoder with atrous separable convolution for semantic image segmentation. In: European Conference on Computer Vision, pp. 833–851 (2018)
3. Girshick, R., Donahue, J., Darrell, T., Malik, J.: Rich feature hierarchies for accurate object detection and semantic segmentation. In: IEEE Computer Vision and Pattern Recognition, pp. 580–587 (2014)
4. Guo, H., Xu, M., Chi, Y., Zhang, L., Hua, X.-S.: Weakly supervised organ localization with attention maps regularized by local area reconstruction. In: Martel, A.L., et al. (eds.) MICCAI 2020, Part I. LNCS, vol. 12261, pp. 243–252. Springer, Cham (2020). https://doi.org/10.1007/978-3-030-59710-8_24
5. He, K., Zhang, X., Ren, S., Sun, J.: Deep residual learning for image recognition. In: IEEE Computer Vision and Pattern Recognition, pp. 770–778 (2016)
6. Hong, S., Noh, H., Han, B.: Decoupled deep neural network for semi-supervised semantic segmentation. In: Neural Information Processing Systems, pp. 1495–1503 (2015)

7. Hung, W., Tsai, Y., Liou, Y., Linand, Y., Yang, M.: Adversarial learning for semi-supervised semantic segmentation. In: British Machine Vision Conference, p. 65 (2018)

8. Kervadec, H., Dolz, J., Tang, M., Granger, E., Boykov, Y., Ayed, I.: Constrained-CNN losses for weakly supervised segmentation. Med. Image Ana. **54**, 88–99 (2019)

9. LeCun, Y., Bottou, L., Orr, G.B., Müller, K.-R.: Efficient backprop. In: Orr, G.B., Müller, K.-R. (eds.) Neural Networks: Tricks of the Trade. LNCS, vol. 1524, pp. 9–50. Springer, Heidelberg (1998). https://doi.org/10.1007/3-540-49430-8_2

10. Long, J., Shelhamer, E., Darrell, T.: Fully convolutional networks for semantic segmentation. In: IEEE Computer Vision and Pattern Recognition, pp. 3431–3440 (2015)

11. Papandreou, G., Chen, L., Murphy, K., Yuille, A.: Weakly-and semi-supervised learning of a deep convolutional network for semantic image segmentation. In: International Conference on Computer Vision, pp. 1742–1750 (2015)

12. Reinhard, E., Ashikhmin, M., Gooch, B., Shirley, P.: Color transfer between images. IEEE Comp. Gra. App. **21**(5), 34–41 (2001)

13. Robbins, H., Monro, S.: A stochastic approximation method. Anna. Math. Stat. **22**, 400–407 (1951)

14. Ronneberger, O., Fischer, P., Brox, T.: U-Net: convolutional networks for biomedical image segmentation. In: Navab, N., Hornegger, J., Wells, W.M., Frangi, A.F. (eds.) MICCAI 2015, Part III. LNCS, vol. 9351, pp. 234–241. Springer, Cham (2015). https://doi.org/10.1007/978-3-319-24574-4_28

15. Souly, N., Spampinato, C., Shah, M.: Semi supervised semantic segmentation using generative adversarial network. In: International Conference on Computer Vision, pp. 5688–5696 (2017)

16. Tardy, M., Mateus, D.: Looking for abnormalities in mammograms with self-and weakly supervised reconstruction. IEEE Trans. Med. Imaging **PP**, 1 (2021)

17. Zhou, Y., et al.: Collaborative learning of semi-supervised segmentation and classification for medical images. In: IEEE Computer Vision and Pattern Recognition, pp. 2088–2079 (2019)

Weakly Supervised Deep Learning for Aortic Valve Finite Element Mesh Generation from 3D CT Images

Daniel H. Pak[1]([✉]), Minliang Liu[2], Shawn S. Ahn[1], Andrés Caballero[2],
John A. Onofrey[3], Liang Liang[4], Wei Sun[2], and James S. Duncan[1,3]

[1] Biomedical Engineering, Yale University, New Haven, CT, USA
daniel.pak@yale.edu
[2] Biomedical Engineering, Georgia Institute of Technology, Atlanta, GA, USA
[3] Radiology and Biomedical Imaging, Yale School of Medicine, New Haven, CT, USA
[4] Computer Science, University of Miami, Miami-Dade County, FL, USA

Abstract. Finite Element Analysis (FEA) is useful for simulating Transcather Aortic Valve Replacement (TAVR), but has a significant bottleneck at input mesh generation. Existing automated methods for imaging-based valve modeling often make heavy assumptions about imaging characteristics and/or output mesh topology, limiting their adaptability. In this work, we propose a deep learning-based deformation strategy for producing aortic valve FE meshes from noisy 3D CT scans of TAVR patients. In particular, we propose a novel image analysis problem formulation that allows for training of mesh prediction models using segmentation labels (i.e. weak supervision), and identify a unique set of losses that improve model performance within this framework. Our method can handle images with large amounts of calcification and low contrast, and is compatible with predicting both surface and volumetric meshes. The predicted meshes have good surface and correspondence accuracy, and produce reasonable FEA results.

Keywords: Weakly supervised deep learning · Shape deformation · Aortic valve modeling

1 Introduction

Transcatheter Aortic Valve Replacement (TAVR) is an emerging minimally invasive treatment option for aortic stenosis [22]. In recent years, studies have explored Finite Element Analysis (FEA) for simulating TAVR from pre-operative patient images, and have shown promising results for predicting patient outcome and finding better treatment strategies [3]. However, there exists a significant bottleneck at producing FE meshes from patient images, as the manual process takes several hours for each patient and requires expert knowledge about the anatomy as well as the meshing techniques and requirements.

© Springer Nature Switzerland AG 2021
A. Feragen et al. (Eds.): IPMI 2021, LNCS 12729, pp. 637–648, 2021.
https://doi.org/10.1007/978-3-030-78191-0_49

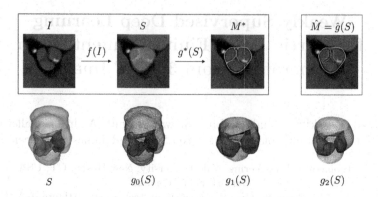

Fig. 1. Top row: $I \rightarrow S \rightarrow M$ progression, where blue box shows the desired sequence and red box shows a faulty output using marching cubes, a common choice for $\hat{g}(S)$. Bottom row: different meshes using the same segmentation based on the choice of $g(S)$. Y: aortic root/wall and R, G, B: valve leaflets. (Color figure online)

Automated solutions for aortic valve modeling have been proposed. Ionasec et al. [7] and Liang et al. [11] used a combination of landmark and boundary detection driven by intensity-based features to produce valve meshes with a predefined topology. Pouch et al. [16] used multi-atlas segmentation and medial modeling to match the template mesh to the predicted segmentation. Ghesu et al. [5] used marginal space deep learning to localize an aortic wall template mesh and subsequently deformed it along the surface normal. Although various approaches have demonstrated success with valve modeling, they have drawbacks such as heavy reliance on intensity changes along the valve structures, extensive assumptions about valve geometry, and limited adaptability to FE meshes due to assumptions about the output mesh topology.

To address these issues, we propose a deep learning-based deformation strategy for predicting FE meshes from noisy 3D CT scans of TAVR patients. Our main contributions are three-fold: (1) We propose a novel image analysis problem formulation that allows for weakly supervised training of image-to-mesh prediction models, where training is performed with segmentation labels instead of mesh labels. (2) We make minimal assumptions in defining this formulation, so it can easily adapt to various imaging conditions and desired output mesh topology (even from surface mesh to volumetric mesh). (3) We identify a unique set of losses that improves model performance within this framework.

2   Methods

2.1   Possible Problem Formulation: Meshing from Segmentation

Let I be an image, and let S and M be the corresponding segmentation and mesh outputs, respectively. Considering the sequential generation steps $I \rightarrow S \rightarrow M$, we can define two mapping functions $f(I) = S$ and $g(S) = M$ (Fig. 1).

The most common choices for $f(I)$ and $g(S)$ are the inside volume a structure and marching cubes, respectively. However, for thin structures such as valve leaflets, naïve surface meshing fails to provide the desired open surface meshes with accurate attachment points (Fig. 1). It is also problematic for the aortic wall, which requires tube-like openings. Therefore, to obtain the correct surface, we must extract structural information from S via curve fitting [11], medial modeling [16], or manual labeling. This makes it extremely difficult to define a general $g(S)$ without making heavy assumptions about the anatomy and output mesh even when provided with manually defined S during test time.

2.2 Proposed Problem Formulation: Mesh Template Matching

Instead of solving for $g(S)$, we propose a problem formulation that we refer to as Mesh Template Matching (MTM), summarized schematically in Fig. 2. Here, we find the deformation field ϕ^*:

$$\phi^* = \arg\min_{\phi} \mathcal{L}(M, M_0, \phi) \tag{1}$$

where M and M_0 are target and template meshes, respectively. We use a convolutional neural network (CNN) as our function approximator $h_\theta(I; S_0, M_0) = \phi$ where I is the image, S_0 is the segmentation template (paired to M_0), and θ is the network parameters. Then, we solve for θ that minimizes the loss:

$$\theta^* = \arg\min_{\theta} \left[\mathbb{E}_{(I,M)\sim D}[\mathcal{L}(M, M_0, h_\theta(I; S_0, M_0))] \right] \tag{2}$$

where D is the training set distribution. We propose two different variations of MTM, as detailed below.

2.2.1 MTM

For the vanilla MTM, we initially defined $\mathcal{L}$ from Eq. 1 as:

$$\mathcal{L}(M, M_0, \phi) = \mathcal{L}_{acc}(M, \phi(M_0)) + \lambda \mathcal{L}_{smooth}(\phi) \tag{3}$$

where $\phi(M_0)$ is the deformed template, $\mathcal{L}_{acc}$ is the spatial accuracy loss, and $\mathcal{L}_{smooth}$ is the field smoothness loss with a scaling hyperparameter λ. From here, we removed the need for ground truth M with the following steps:

$$\arg\min_{\phi} \mathcal{L}(M, M_0, \phi) = \arg\min_{\phi}[\mathcal{L}_{acc}(M, \phi(M_0)) \quad\quad + \lambda \mathcal{L}_{smooth}] \tag{4}$$

$$= \arg\min_{\phi}[\mathcal{L}_{acc}(g^*(S), \phi(g^*(S_0)) \quad\quad + \lambda \mathcal{L}_{smooth}] \tag{5}$$

$$\approx \arg\min_{\phi}[\mathcal{L}_{acc}(\hat{g}(S), \phi(\hat{g}(S_0))) \quad\quad + \lambda \mathcal{L}_{smooth}] \tag{6}$$

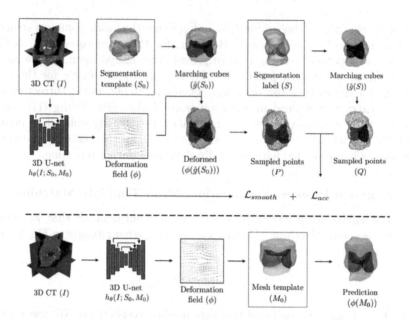

Fig. 2. Training (above dotted line) and inference steps (below dotted line) for the vanilla MTM. Blue box represents paired image-segmentation training samples and red box represents fixed templates. Note that M_0 can freely change topology as long as its surface is in close proximity to $\hat{g}(S_0)$ surface. MTMgeo is similar, but instead of $\mathcal{L}_{smooth}$, we calculate $\mathcal{L}_{geo}$ using $\phi(M_0)$ during training. (Color figure online)

where g^* is the ideal meshing function (for which the topology is defined by the template mesh), $\hat{g}$ is marching cubes, and S and S_0 are target and template segmentation volumes. Our key approximation step (Eq. 6) makes two important assumptions: (1) g^* mesh surface is in close proximity to $\hat{g}$ mesh surface by Euclidean distance and (2) ϕ is smooth with respect to Euclidean space. The first assumption is reasonable because ground truth meshes are often created using segmentation labels as intermediate steps, and the second assumption is enforced by $\mathcal{L}_{smooth}$ and the choice of ϕ (discussed further in Sect. 2.3).

Common choices for the spatial accuracy loss are mean surface distance (e.g. Chamfer distance) and volume overlap (e.g. Dice). Since Dice and other segmentation losses are typically lenient towards errors in segmentation boundaries (and we need accuracy at boundaries for meshes), we used the Chamfer distance:

$$\mathcal{L}_{acc}(P,Q) = \frac{1}{|P|}\sum_{\mathbf{p}\in P}\min_{\mathbf{q}\in Q}\|\mathbf{p}-\mathbf{q}\|_2^2 + \frac{1}{|Q|}\sum_{\mathbf{q}\in Q}\min_{\mathbf{p}\in P}\|\mathbf{q}-\mathbf{p}\|_2^2 \qquad (7)$$

where P and Q are points sampled on surfaces of $\phi(\hat{g}(S_0))$ and $\hat{g}(S)$, respectively. We experimented with adding Dice [13] to the loss, but observed no significant improvement in performance.

For field smoothness loss, we used the bending energy term to penalize non-affine fields [19]:

$$
\mathcal{L}_{smooth} = \frac{1}{V} \int_0^X \int_0^Y \int_0^Z \left[\left(\frac{\partial^2 \phi}{\partial x^2}\right)^2 + \left(\frac{\partial^2 \phi}{\partial y^2}\right)^2 + \left(\frac{\partial^2 \phi}{\partial z^2}\right)^2 \right.
$$
$$
\left. + 2\left(\frac{\partial^2 \phi}{\partial xy}\right)^2 + 2\left(\frac{\partial^2 \phi}{\partial xz}\right)^2 + 2\left(\frac{\partial^2 \phi}{\partial yz}\right)^2 \right] dx\, dy\, dz \tag{8}
$$

where V is the total number of voxels and X, Y, Z are the number of voxels in each dimension. We experimented with adding gradient magnitude [1] and field magnitude [10] to the loss, but observed no significant improvement in performance.

2.2.2 MTMgeo

For the second variation of MTM, referred to as MTMgeo, we replaced $\mathcal{L}_{smooth}$ with $\mathcal{L}_{geo}$ to preserve various desired geometric qualities of the deformed template mesh:

$$
\mathcal{L}(M, M_0, \phi) = \mathcal{L}_{acc}(M, \phi(M_0)) + \mathcal{L}_{geo}(M_0, \phi(M_0)) \tag{9}
$$

where we apply identical steps as Eq. 4–7 to get:

$$
\arg\min_\phi \mathcal{L}(M, M_0, \phi) \approx \arg\min_\phi [\mathcal{L}_{acc}(P, Q) + \mathcal{L}_{geo}] \tag{10}
$$

The geometric quality loss is a weighted sum of three different losses:

$$
\mathcal{L}_{geo}(M_0, \phi(M_0)) = \lambda_0\, \mathcal{L}_{norm} + \lambda_1\, \mathcal{L}_{lap} + \lambda_2\, \mathcal{L}_{edge} \tag{11}
$$

where λ_i are scaling hyperparameters, $\mathcal{L}_{norm}$ is face normal consistency loss, $\mathcal{L}_{lap}$ is Laplacian smoothing loss, and $\mathcal{L}_{edge}$ is edge correspondence loss.

$$
\mathcal{L}_{norm} = \frac{1}{|\mathcal{N}_f|} \sum_{(\mathbf{n}_{fi}, \mathbf{n}_{fj}) \in \mathcal{N}_f} 1 - \frac{< \mathbf{n}_{fi}, \mathbf{n}_{fj} >}{\|\mathbf{n}_{fi}\|_2 \|\mathbf{n}_{fj}\|_2} \tag{12}
$$

$\mathbf{n}_{fi}$ is the normal vector calculated at a given face and $\mathcal{N}_f$ is the set of all pairs of neighboring faces' normals within $\phi(M_0)$.

$$
\mathcal{L}_{lap} = \frac{1}{|V|} \sum_{\mathbf{v}_i \in \phi(V)} \left\| \frac{1}{|\mathcal{N}(\mathbf{v}_i)|} \sum_{\mathbf{v}_j \in \mathcal{N}(\mathbf{v}_i)} \mathbf{v}_i - \mathbf{v}_j \right\|_2 \tag{13}
$$

$\mathcal{N}(\mathbf{v}_i)$ represents neighbors of $\mathbf{v}_i$. The norm represents the magnitude of the differential coordinates, which approximates the local mean curvature.

$$
\mathcal{L}_{edge} = \frac{1}{|\varepsilon|} \sum_{(\mathbf{v}_i, \mathbf{v}_j) \in \varepsilon} \left(\frac{\|\mathbf{v}_i - \mathbf{v}_j\|_2}{\max\limits_{(\mathbf{v}_i', \mathbf{v}_j') \in \varepsilon} \|\mathbf{v}_i' - \mathbf{v}_j'\|_2} - \frac{\|\phi(\mathbf{v}_i) - \phi(\mathbf{v}_j))\|_2}{\max\limits_{(\mathbf{v}_i', \mathbf{v}_j') \in \varepsilon} \|\phi(\mathbf{v}_i') - \phi(\mathbf{v}_j')\|_2} \right)^2 \tag{14}
$$

Our proposed edge correspondence loss is different from the edge length loss [6,23] in that it allows meshes to change sizes more freely, as long as the edge length ratio stays consistent before and after deformation. This is beneficial for medical FE meshing tasks where (1) patients have organs of different sizes and (2) consistent edge ratio helps convert between triangular and quadrilateral faces. The latter is important because quadrilateral faces are desired in FEA for more accurate simulation results, but many mesh-related algorithms and libraries are only compatible with triangular faces.

2.3   Deformation Field

As mentioned in Sect. 2.2.1, the choice of ϕ is important for applying the key approximation step in MTM. Our approach is to learn a diffeomorphic B-spline deformation field from which we interpolate displacement vectors at each node of the template mesh. By requiring the result to adhere to topology-preserving diffeomorphism, we help prevent mesh intersections that can commonly occur with node-specific displacements. Also, when the field is calculated in the reverse direction for deforming a template image/segmentation to prevent hole artifacts, the invertible property of diffeomorphism allows for much more accurate field calculation. The B-spline aspect helps generate smooth fields, which prevents erratic changes in field direction or magnitude for nearby interpolation points.

3   Experiments and Results

3.1   Data Acquisition and Preprocessing

We used an aortic valve dataset consisting of 88 CT scans from 74 different patients, all with tricuspid valves. Of the 88 total scans, 73 were collected from transcatheter aortic valve replacement (TAVR) patients at the Hartford hospital, and the remaining 15 were from the training set of the MM-WHS public dataset [25]. From the Hartford images, we randomly chose some patients to include more than one random time point from the ~10 time points collected over the cardiac cycle. The 88 images were randomly split into 40, 10, 38 for training, validation, and testing sets, respectively, with no patient overlap between the training and testing sets. We pre-processed all CT scans by converting to Hounsfield units (HU), thresholding, and renormalizing to [0, 1]. We resampled all images to fix the spatial resolution at $1 \times 1 \times 1 \, mm^3$, and cropped and rigidly aligned them using three manually annotated landmark points to focus on the aortic valve, resulting in final images with [64, 64, 64] voxels.

We focused on 4 aortic valve components: the aortic root/wall (for segmentation/mesh, respectively) and the 3 leaflets. The ground truth segmentation labels (for training) and mesh labels (for testing) for all 4 components were obtained via manual and semi-automated annotations by human experts in 3D slicer [4]. We first obtained the segmentation labels using the brush tool and the robust statistics segmenter. Then, using the segmentation as guidance, we manually defined

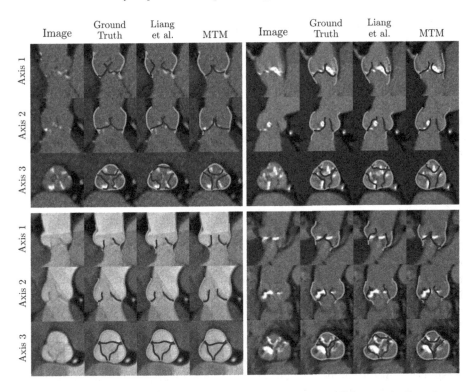

Fig. 3. Cross sectional display of CT images and meshes at 3 different viewing planes. Each block of images (separated by white space) represents a different test set patient. Y: aortic wall and R, G, B: valve leaflets (Color figure online)

the boundary curves of the aortic wall and the leaflets, while denoting key landmark points of commissures and hinges. We then applied thin plate spline to deform mesh templates from a shape dictionary to the defined boundaries, and further adjusted nodes along the surface normals, using a combination of manually marked points on surface and intensity gradient-based objective, similar to [11]. The surface mesh template was created by further processing one of the ground truth meshes with a series of remeshing and stitching steps. The final template surface mesh was a single connected component mesh with 12186 nodes and 18498 faces, consisting of both triangular and quadrilateral faces.

3.2   Implementation Details

We used Pytorch [15] to implement a variation of a 3D U-net [18] as our function approximator $h_\theta(I; S_0, M_0)$. Since the network architecture is not the focus of this paper, we kept it consistent between all deep learning-based methods for fair comparison. The basic Conv unit was Conv3D-InstanceNorm-LeakyReLu, and the network had 4 encoding layers of ConvStride2-Conv with residual connections and dropout, and 4 decoding layers of Concatenation-Conv-Conv-Upsampling-Conv. The base number of filters was 16, and was doubled at each encoding layer and halved at each decoding layer. The output of the U-net was a $3 \times 64 \times 64 \times 64$ tensor, which we interpolated to obtain a $3 \times 24 \times 24 \times 24$ tensor that we then used to displace the control points of a 3D diffeomorphic third-order B-spline transformation to obtain a dense displacement field using the Airlab registration library [20]. The Chamfer distance and geometric quality losses were implemented using Pytorch3D [17] with modifications. We used the Adam optimizer [9] with a fixed learning rate of 1e$-$4, batch size of 1, and 2000 training epochs. The models were trained with B-spline deformation augmentation step over 2000 epochs, resulting in 80k training samples and around 24 h of training time on a single NVIDIA GTX 1080 Ti.

3.3   Evaluation Metrics

For spatial accuracy, we evaluated the Chamfer distance (mean surface accuracy) and the Hausdorff distance (worst-case surface accuracy) between ground truth meshes and predicted surface meshes. The Chamfer distance was calculated using 10k sampled points on each mesh surface using Pytorch3D [17], and the Hausdorff distance was calculated using the meshes themselves using IGL [8]. For correspondence error, we evaluated the Euclidean distance between hand-labeled landmarks (3 commissures and 3 hinges) and specific node positions on the predicted meshes (e.g. commissure #1, was node #81 on every predicted mesh, etc.). Additionally, for bare minimum FEA viability, we used CGAL [12] to check for self-intersections and degenerate edges/faces of predicted volumetric meshes with no post-processing.

3.4   Comparison with an Image Intensity Gradient-Based Approach

We compared our method against the semi-automated version of [11], which uses manually delineated boundaries to first position the template meshes and refines them using an image gradient-based objective (Fig. 3). This approach performs very well under ideal imaging conditions, where there are clear intensity changes along the valve components, but it tends to make large errors in images with high calcification and low contrast. On the other hand, MTM does not particularly favor one condition or another, as long as enough variations exist in training images. However, this could also mean that it could make errors for "easy" images if the model has not seen a similar training image. We chose to not include Liang et al. [11] for evaluation metric comparisons because (1) it uses manually delineated boundaries, which skews both surface distance and correspondence errors and (2) we used some of its meshes as ground truth without any changes, when the images are in good condition (e.g. Fig. 3 bottom left).

3.5   Comparison with Other Deformation Strategies

We chose three deformation-based methods for comparison: Voxelmorph [1], U-net + Robust Point Matching (RPM) [2], and TETRIS [10] (Table 1, Fig. 4).

Table 1. Summary of evaluation metrics, mean ± standard deviation across all test set patients and all 4 valve components. "Bad" column: percentage of predicted test set meshes with self-intersection or degeneracy with no post-processing. Lower is better for all metrics.

	Chamfer (mm)	Hausdorff (mm)	Commissure error (mm)	Hinge error (mm)	Bad (%)
Voxelmorph	3.01 ± 1.38	9.51 ± 3.04	6.80 ± 3.93	7.15 ± 4.36	100.00
U-net + RPM	0.99 ± 0.32	4.57 ± 1.59	2.25 ± 1.27	2.38 ± 1.15	76.32
TETRIS	0.95 ± 0.30	4.35 ± 1.99	1.84 ± 1.10	2.32 ± 1.38	5.26
MTMgeo (ours)	0.82 ± 0.26	4.48 ± 2.43	**1.49 ± 0.94**	2.33 ± 1.07	10.53
MTM (ours)	**0.80 ± 0.24**	**4.04 ± 1.86**	1.57 ± 1.05	**2.30 ± 1.36**	**0.00**

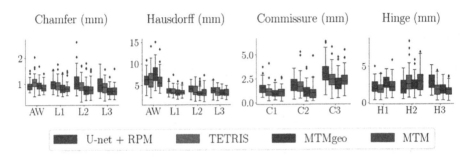

Fig. 4. Component-specific evaluation metrics (summarized in Table 1) for the four best performing methods. AW: aortic wall, L1, L2, L3: 3 leaflets, C1, C2, C3: 3 commissure points, H1, H2, H3: 3 hinge points

Voxelmorph [1] uses a CNN-predicted deformation field to perform intensity-based registration with an atlas image. Given a paired image-mesh template, we first trained for image registration and used the resulting field to deform the mesh to the target image. Since there is no guidance for the network to focus on the valve components, the resulting deformation is optimized for larger structures around the valve rather than the leaflets, leading to poor mesh accuracy.

U-net + RPM [2,18] is a sequential model where we trained a U-net for voxel-wise segmentation and used its output as the target shape for registration with a template mesh. RPM (implemented in [14]) performs optimization during test time, which requires longer time and expert knowledge for parameter tuning during model deployment. It also produces suboptimal results, possibly due to the segmentation output and point sampling not being optimized for matching with the template mesh.

TETRIS [10] uses a CNN-predicted deformation field to deform a segmentation prior to optimize for segmentation accuracy. Using a paired segmentation-mesh template, we first trained for template-deformed segmentation and used the resulting field to deform the mesh. Since the field is not diffeomorphic and calculated in the reverse direction to prevent hole artifacts, we used VTK's

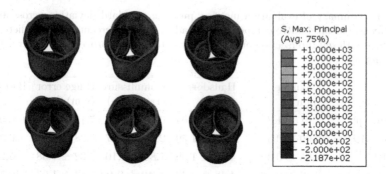

Fig. 5. FEA results using MTM-predicted meshes from 6 test set patients. Values indicate maximum principal stress in the aortic wall and leaflets during diastole.

implementation of Newton's method [21] to get the inverse deformation field for the template mesh. The inaccuracies at the segmentation boundaries and errors due to field inversion lead to suboptimal performance.

MTM consistently outperforms all other deformation strategies in terms of spatial accuracy and produces less degenerate meshes (Table 1, Fig. 4). The accuracy values are also comparable to those in [7,11], which use cleaner images, heavier assumptions about valve structure, and/or ground truth meshes for training. MTMgeo arguably performs similarly to MTM, suggesting that we may be able to replace field smoothness penalty with other mesh-related losses to refine the results for specific types of meshes. This may be especially useful for training with volumetric meshes, where we might want to dynamically adjust the thickness of different structures based on the imaging characteristics.

3.6 FEA Results

Volumetric FE meshes were produced by applying the MTM-predicted deformation field to a template volumetric mesh, which was created by applying a simple offset + stitch operation from the template surface mesh. We set aortic wall and leaflet thicknesses to 1.5 cm and 0.8 cm, respectively, and used C3D15 and C3D20 elements. FEA simulations were performed with an established protocol, similar to those in [11,24]. Briefly, to compute stresses on the aortic wall and leaflets during valve closing, an intraluminal pressure (P = 16 kPa) was applied to the upper surface of the leaflets and coronary sinuses, and a diastolic pressure (P = 10 kPa) was applied to the lower portion of the leaflets and intervalvular fibrosa. The maximum principal stresses in the aortic wall and leaflets were approximately 100–500 kPa (Fig. 5), consistent with previous studies [11,24]. This demonstrates MTM-predicted meshes' suitability for FEA simulations.

3.7 Limitations and Future Works

Although MTM shows promise, it has much room for improvement. First, the current setup requires 3 manual landmark points during preprocessing for cropping and rigid alignment. We will pursue end-to-end learning using 3D whole-heart images via region proposal networks, similar to [13]. Second, our model does not produce calcification meshes, which are important for proper simulation because calcification and valve components have different material properties. We will need a non-deformation strategy for predicting calcification meshes since their size and position vary significantly between patients. Third, the restriction to smooth and diffeomorphic field prevents large variations in valve shapes. We will continue exploring the possibility of extending our framework to node-specific displacement vectors.

4 Conclusion

We presented a weakly supervised deep learning approach for predicting aortic valve FE meshes from 3D patient images. Our method only requires segmentation labels and a paired segmentation-mesh template during training, which are easier to obtain than mesh labels. Our trained model can predict meshes with good spatial accuracy and FEA viability.

Acknowledgments and Conflict of Interest. This work was supported by the NIH R01HL142036 grant. Dr. Wei Sun is a co-founder and serves as the Chief Scientific Advisor of Dura Biotech. He has received compensation and owns equity in the company.

References

1. Balakrishnan, G., Zhao, A., Sabuncu, M.R., Guttag, J., Dalca, A.V.: Voxelmorph: a learning framework for deformable medical image registration. IEEE Trans. Med. Imaging **38**(8), 1788–1800 (2019)
2. Chui, H., Rangarajan, A.: A new point matching algorithm for non-rigid registration. Comput. Vis. Image Underst. **89**(2–3), 114–141 (2003)
3. Dowling, C., Firoozi, S., Brecker, S.J.: First-in-human experience with patient-specific computer simulation of TAVR in bicuspid aortic valve morphology. JACC Cardiovasc. Interven. **13**(2), 184–192 (2020)
4. Fedorov, A., et al.: 3D slicer as an image computing platform for the quantitative imaging network. Magn. Reson. Imaging **30**(9), 1323–1341 (2012)
5. Ghesu, F.C., et al.: Marginal space deep learning: efficient architecture for volumetric image parsing. IEEE Trans. Med. imaging **35**(5), 1217–1228 (2016)
6. Gkioxari, G., Malik, J., Johnson, J.: Mesh R-CNN. In: Proceedings of the IEEE International Conference on Computer Vision, pp. 9785–9795 (2019)
7. Ionasec, R.I., et al.: Patient-specific modeling and quantification of the aortic and mitral valves from 4-D cardiac CT and tee. IEEE Trans. Med. Imaging **29**(9), 1636–1651 (2010)

8. Jacobson, A., Panozzo, D., et al.: libigl: A simple C++ geometry processing library (2018). https://libigl.github.io/
9. Kingma, D.P., Ba, J.: Adam: A method for stochastic optimization. arXiv preprint arXiv:1412.6980 (2014)
10. Lee, M.C.H., Petersen, K., Pawlowski, N., Glocker, B., Schaap, M.: Tetris: template transformer networks for image segmentation with shape priors. IEEE Trans. Med. Imaging 38(11), 2596–2606 (2019)
11. Liang, L., et al.: Machine learning-based 3-D geometry reconstruction and modeling of aortic valve deformation using 3-D computed tomography images. Int. J. Numer. Methods Biomed. Eng. 33(5), e2827 (2017)
12. Loriot, S., Rouxel-Labbé, M., Tournois, J., Yaz, I.O.: Polygon mesh processing. In: CGAL User and Reference Manual. CGAL Editorial Board, 5.1.1 edn. (2020). https://doc.cgal.org/5.1.1/Manual/packages.html#PkgPolygonMeshProcessing
13. Pak, D.H., Caballero, A., Sun, W., Duncan, J.S.: Efficient aortic valve multilabel segmentation using a spatial transformer network. In: 2020 IEEE 17th International Symposium on Biomedical Imaging (ISBI), pp. 1738–1742. IEEE (2020)
14. Papademetris, X., et al.: Bioimage suite: an integrated medical image analysis suite: an update. Insight J. 2006, 209 (2006)
15. Paszke, A., et al.: Automatic differentiation in pytorch (2017)
16. Pouch, A.M., et al.: Medially constrained deformable modeling for segmentation of branching medial structures: application to aortic valve segmentation and morphometry. Med. Image Anal. 26(1), 217–231 (2015)
17. Ravi, N., et al.: Accelerating 3D deep learning with pytorch3d. arXiv:2007.08501 (2020)
18. Ronneberger, O., Fischer, P., Brox, T.: U-Net: convolutional networks for biomedical image segmentation. In: Navab, N., Hornegger, J., Wells, W.M., Frangi, A.F. (eds.) MICCAI 2015, Part III. LNCS, vol. 9351, pp. 234–241. Springer, Cham (2015). https://doi.org/10.1007/978-3-319-24574-4_28
19. Rueckert, D., Sonoda, L.I., Hayes, C., Hill, D.L., Leach, M.O., Hawkes, D.J.: Non-rigid registration using free-form deformations: application to breast MR images. IEEE Trans. Med. Imaging 18(8), 712–721 (1999)
20. Sandkühler, R., Jud, C., Andermatt, S., Cattin, P.C.: Airlab: Autograd image registration laboratory. arXiv preprint arXiv:1806.09907 (2018)
21. Schroeder, W.J., Lorensen, B., Martin, K.: The Visualization Toolkit: An Object-Oriented Approach to 3D Graphics. Kitware, NewYork (2004)
22. Sun, W., Martin, C., Pham, T.: Computational modeling of cardiac valve function and intervention. Annu. Rev. Biomed. Eng. 16, 53–76 (2014)
23. Wang, N., Zhang, Y., Li, Z., Fu, Y., Liu, W., Jiang, Y.G.: Pixel2Mesh: generating 3D mesh models from single RGB images. In: Proceedings of the European Conference on Computer Vision (ECCV), pp. 52–67 (2018)
24. Wang, Q., Primiano, C., McKay, R., Kodali, S., Sun, W.: CT image-based engineering analysis of transcatheter aortic valve replacement. JACC Cardiovasc. Imaging 7(5), 526–528 (2014)
25. Zhuang, X., Shen, J.: Multi-scale patch and multi-modality atlases for whole heart segmentation of MRI. Med. Image Anal. 31, 77–87 (2016)

Continual Active Learning for Efficient Adaptation of Machine Learning Models to Changing Image Acquisition

Matthias Perkonigg$^{(\boxtimes)}$ (iD), Johannes Hofmanninger (iD), and Georg Langs (iD)

Department of Biomedical Imaging and Image-guided Therapy, Computational
Imaging Research Lab (CIR), Medical University of Vienna, Vienna, Austria
{matthias.perkonigg,johannes.hofmanninger,georg.langs}@meduniwien.ac.at
https://www.cir.meduniwien.ac.at/

Abstract. Imaging in clinical routine is subject to changing scanner protocols, hardware, or policies in a typically heterogeneous set of acquisition hardware. Accuracy and reliability of deep learning models suffer from those changes as data and targets become inconsistent with their initial static training set. Continual learning can adapt to a continuous data stream of a changing imaging environment. Here, we propose a method for continual active learning on a data stream of medical images. It recognizes shifts or additions of new imaging sources - *domains* -, adapts training accordingly, and selects optimal examples for labelling. Model training has to cope with a limited labelling budget, resembling typical real world scenarios. We demonstrate our method on T1-weighted magnetic resonance images from three different scanners with the task of brain age estimation. Results demonstrate that the proposed method outperforms naive active learning while requiring less manual labelling.

Keywords: Continual learning · Active learning · Domain adaptation

1 Introduction

The frequently changing scanner hardware, imaging protocols, and heterogeneous composition of acquisition routines in the clinical environment hamper the longevity and utility of deep learning models. After initial training on a static data set they need to be continuously adapted to the changing characteristics of the data stream acquired in imaging departments. This is challenging, since training on a data stream without a continual learning strategy can lead to *catastrophic forgetting* [14], when adapting a model to a new domain or task leads to a deterioration of performance on preceding domains or tasks. Additionally, for continual learning in a medical context manual labelling is required for new cases. However, labelling is expensive and time-consuming, requiring extensive medical knowledge. Here, active learning is a possible solution, where the aim is to identify samples from an unlabelled distribution that are most informative if

© Springer Nature Switzerland AG 2021
A. Feragen et al. (Eds.): IPMI 2021, LNCS 12729, pp. 649–660, 2021.
https://doi.org/10.1007/978-3-030-78191-0_50

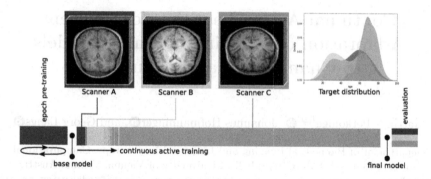

Fig. 1. Experimental setup: a model is pre-trained on scanner A and then subsequently updated on a data stream gradually including data of scanner B and scanner C. The model has to recognize the domain shifts, and identify cases whose annotation will contribute best to the model accuracy. The final model is evaluated on test sets of all three scanners.

labelled next. Keeping the number of cases requiring labelling as low as possible is a key challenge in active learning with medical images [2].

Most currently proposed continual active learning methods either do not take domain shifts in the training distributions into account or assume knowledge about the domain membership of data points. However, due to the variability in how meta data is encoded knowledge about the domain membership can not be assumed in clinical practice [5]. Therefore, we need a technique to reliably detect domain shifts in a continuous data stream. Combining continual and active learning with the detection of domain shifts can ensure that models perform well on a growing repertoire of image acquisition technology, while at the same time minimizing the resource requirements, and day to day effort necessary for continued model training.

Contribution. We propose an online active learning method in a setting where the domain membership (i.e. which scanner an image was acquired with) is unknown and in which we learn continuously from a data stream, by selecting an informative set of training examples to be annotated. Figure 1 illustrates the experimental setup reflecting this scenario. A model is pre-trained on data of one scanner. Subsequently, our method observes a continual stream and automatically detects if domain shifts occur, activating the learning algorithm to incorporate knowledge about the new domain in the form of labelled training examples. We evaluate the model on data from all observed domains, to assess if the model performs well on a specific task for all observed scanners. The proposed algorithm combines online active learning and novel domain recognition for continual learning. The proposed Continual Active Learning for Scanner Adaptation (CASA) approach uses a rehearsal method and an active labelling approach without any prior knowledge of the domain membership of each data sample. CASA learns on a stream of radiology images with a limited labelling budget, which is desirable to keep the required expert effort low.

Related Work. Our work is related to three research areas: First, continual learning with the goal to adapt a deep learning system to a continual stream of data while mitigating catastrophic forgetting. Second, active learning, which aims to wisely select samples to be labelled by an oracle to keep the number of required labels low. Third, domain adaptation, with the goal of adapting knowledge learned on one domain to a new target domain. An overview of **continual learning** in medical imaging is given in [16]. Here, we focus on the group of continual learning methods closest related to ours, namely *rehearsal and pseudo-rehearsal methods*, which store a subset of training samples and periodically use them for training. Our memory interprets different domains as images having a different style, this is closely related to [6]. They use a dynamic memory which updates the subset for training without assuming domain knowledge based on a gram-matrix based distance. Furthermore, [15] incrementally add different anatomy to a segmentation network by keeping a representative set of images from previous tasks and adding a new segmentation head for each new task. [9] used the pseudo-rehearsal technique Learning-without-Forgetting (LwF) [11] on a domain adaptation problem on chest X-Ray. A detailed review and discussion of **active learning** and human-in-the-loop systems in medical imaging can be found [2]. Also [16] describes how continual learning approaches combined with human-in-the-loop algorithms can be useful in clinical practice. The setting in which our method operates is closely related to *stream-based selective sampling* as described in [2], where a continual stream of unannotated data is assumed. There, the decision of whether or not labelling is required is made for every item on the stream independently. However, the authors claim that this family of methods have limited benefits due to the isolated decision for each sample. In this work, we alleviate this limitation by taken collected information about the data distribution observed into account. In the area of **domain adaptation**, various approaches were proposed to adapt to continuously shifting domains. [19] proposed an approach for semantic segmentation in street scenes under different lightning conditions. [1,8] proposed replay methods for continuous domain adaptation and showed performance in benchmark data sets (rotated MNIST [1] and Office-31 [8] respectively). In the area of medical imaging an approach for lung segmentation in X-rays with shifting domains was proposed in [18].

2   Method

The proposed method CASA is a continual *rehearsal method* with active sample selection. We assume an unlabelled, continual image data stream S with unknown domain shifts. There exists an oracle that can be queried and returns a task label $y = \mathbf{o}(x) \mid x \in S$. In a clinical setting this oracle would be a radiologist who labels an image. Since expert annotations are expensive, label generation by the oracle is limited by the label-budget β. The goal of CASA is to train a task network on such a data stream with the restriction of β, while mitigating catastrophic forgetting. We achieve that by detecting *pseudo-domains*, defined as groups of images similar in terms of style. The identification of pseudo-domains

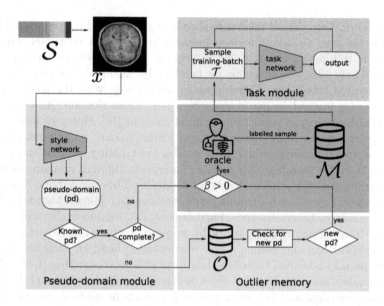

Fig. 2. Overview of the *CASA* algorithm. Each sample from the data stream is processed by the pseudo-domain module to decide whether its routed to the oracle or to the outlier memory. Whenever a new item is added to the outlier memory it is evaluated if a new pseudo-domain (pd) should be created. The oracle labels a sample and stores it in the training memory, from which the task module trains a network. Binary decision alternatives resulting in discarding the sample are left out for clarity of the figure.

helps to keep a diverse set of training examples. The proposed approach consists of two modules and two memories, which are connected by the CASA-Algorithm, described in the following.

2.1 CASA Training Scheme

Before starting continual training, the task module is pre-trained on a labelled data set $\mathcal{L} = \{\langle i_1, l_1 \rangle, \dots, \langle i_L, l_L \rangle\}$, of image-label pairs $\langle i, l \rangle$ of a particular scanner. This pre-training is done in a conventional epoch based training procedure to start continual training on a model which performs well for a given scanner.

After pre-training is finished, continual training follows the scheme depicted in Fig. 2. As a first step, an *input-mini-batch* $\mathcal{B} = \{x_1, \dots, x_B\}$ is drawn from $\mathcal{S}$ and the *pseudo-domain module* decides for each image $x \in \mathcal{B}$ to add it to one of the memories ($\mathcal{O}$ or $\mathcal{M}$) or discard the image. $\mathcal{M}$ is defined as a fixed size M samples holding *training memory* of labelled data $\mathcal{M} = \{\langle m_1, n_1, d_1 \rangle \dots, \langle m_M, n_M, d_M \rangle\}$, where m is the image, n the corresponding task label and d the *pseudo-domain* the image was assigned to. Task labels n are generated by calling the *oracle* $\mathbf{o}(x)$. Pseudo-domains d are defined and assigned by the process described in Sect. 2.2. $\mathcal{M}$ is initialized with a random subset of $\mathcal{L}$ before starting continual training. The *outlier memory* $\mathcal{O} = \{\langle o_1, c_1 \rangle \ldots, \langle o_n, c_n \rangle\}$ holds a set of unlabelled images. Here, o is an image and c is a count how long (measured in training steps) the image is a member of $\mathcal{O}$.

If there are pseudo-domains for which training is not completed, a training step is done by sampling a *training-mini-batches* $\mathcal{T} = \{\langle t_1, u_1 \rangle, \ldots, \langle t_T, u_T \rangle\}$ of size T from $\mathcal{M}$ and then training the task module for one step on $\mathcal{T}$. This process continues with the next $\mathcal{B}$ drawn from $\mathcal{S}$ until the end of $\mathcal{S}$.

2.2   Pseudo-domain Module

The pseudo-domain module is responsible to evaluate the style of an image x and assignment of x to a pseudo-domain. Pseudo-domains are defined as groups of images that are similar in terms of style. Since our method does not assume direct domain (i.e. scanner and/or protocol) knowledge, we use the procedure described below to identify pseudo-domains as part of continual learning. We define the set of pseudo-domains as $\mathcal{D} = \{\langle \mathbf{i_1}, \bar{p}_1 \rangle \ldots \langle \mathbf{i_D}, \bar{p}_D \rangle\}$. Where $\mathbf{i_j}$ is a trained *Isolation Forest (IF)* [17] used as one-class anomaly detection for the pseudo-domain $j \in \{1, \ldots, D\}$. We use IFs, because of their simplicity and the good performance on small sample sizes. $\bar{p}_j$ is the running average of a classification or regression performance metric of the target task calculated on the last P elements of pseudo-domain j that have been labelled by the *oracle*. The performance metric is measured before training on the sample. $\bar{p}_j$ is used to evaluate if the pseudo-domain completed training, that is $\bar{p}_j > k$ for classification tasks and $\bar{p}_j < k$ for regression tasks, where k is a fixed performance threshold. CASA then uses pseudo-domains to assess if training for a specific style is needed and to diversify the memory $\mathcal{M}$.

Pseudo-domain Assignment. To assign an image to an existing pseudo-domain we use a *style network*, which is pre-trained on a different dataset (not necessarily related to the task) and not updated during training. From this network we evaluate the style of an image based on the gram matrix $G^l \in \mathbb{R}^{N_l \times N_l}$, where N_l is the number of feature maps in layer l. Following [4,6] $G_{ij}^l(x)$ is defined as the inner product between the vectorized activations $\mathbf{f}_{il}(x)$ and $\mathbf{f}_{jl}(x)$ of two feature maps i and j in a layer l given a sample image x:

$$G_{ij}^l(x) = \frac{1}{N_l M_l} \mathbf{f}_{il}(x)^\top \mathbf{f}_{jl}(x) \tag{1}$$

where M_l denotes the number of elements in the vectorized feature map. Based on the gram matrix we define a *gram embedding* $\mathbf{e}(x)$: For a set of convolutional layers $\mathcal{C}$ of the style network, we calculate the gram matrices $(G^l \mid l \in \mathcal{C})$ and apply a dimensionality reduction using Sparse Random Projection (SRP) [10]. The isolation forests in $\mathcal{D}$ are trained on those embeddings $\mathbf{e}(x)$. We assign an image x to the pseudo-domain maximizing the decision function of $\mathbf{i_d}$:

$$\mathbf{p}(x) = \begin{cases} \arg\max_d \mathbf{i_d}(\mathbf{e}(x)) & \text{if } \max_d[\mathbf{i_d}(\mathbf{e}(x))] > 0 \\ -1, & \text{otherwise} \end{cases} \mid d \in \{1, \ldots, D\} \qquad (2)$$

If $\mathbf{p}(x) = -1$ the image is added to the outlier memory $\mathcal{O}$ from which new pseudo-domains are detected (see Sect. 2.5). If the pseudo-domain $\mathbf{p}(x)$ is known and have completed training we discard the image, otherwise it is added to $\mathcal{M}$ according to the strategy described in Sect. 2.4.

2.3   Task Module

The task module is responsible for learning the target task (e.g. age estimation in brain MRI), the main component of this module is the *task network* $(\mathbf{t}(x) \mapsto y)$, learning a mapping from input image x to target label y. This module is pre-trained on a labelled data set $\mathcal{L}$. During continual training, the module is updated by drawing n training-input-batches $\mathcal{T}$ from $\mathcal{M}$ and performing a training step on each of the batches. At the end of training the aim of CASA is that the task module performs well on images of all scanners available in $\mathcal{S}$ without suffering catastrophic forgetting.

2.4   Training Memory

The M sized training memory $\mathcal{M}$ is balanced between the pseudo-domains currently in $\mathcal{D}$. Each of the D pseudo-domains can occupy up to $\frac{M}{D}$ elements in the memory. If a new pseudo-domain is added to $\mathcal{D}$ (see Sect. 2.5) a random subset of elements of all previous domain are flagged for deletion, so that only $\frac{M}{D}$ are kept protected in $\mathcal{M}$. If a new element $e = \langle m_k, n_k, d_k \rangle$ is to be inserted to $\mathcal{M}$ and $\frac{M}{D}$ is not reached an element currently flagged for deletion is replaced by e. Otherwise the element will replace the one in $\mathcal{M}$, which is of the same pseudo-domain and minimizes the distance between the gram embeddings. Formally we replace the element with index:

$$\xi(i) = (\mathbf{e}(m_k) - \mathbf{e}(m_j))^2 \mid n_k = n_j, \ j \in \{1, \ldots, M\}. \qquad (3)$$

2.5   Outlier Memory and Pseudo-domain Identification

The outlier memory $\mathcal{O}$ holds candidate examples that do not fit an already identified domain, and might form a new domain. Examples are stored until they are assigned a new pseudo-domain or if a fixed number of training steps is reached. If no new pseudo-domain is discovered for an image it is considered a 'real' outlier and removed from the outlier memory. Within $\mathcal{O}$ we discover new pseudo-domains to add to $\mathcal{D}$. The discovery process is started when $|\mathcal{O}| = o$, where o is a fixed threshold. A check if a dense region is present in the memory is done by calculating the pairwise euclidean distances of all elements in $\mathcal{O}$. If there is a group of images where the distances are below a threshold t a new IF

(i_n) is fitted to the gram embeddings of the dense region and the set of pseudo-domains $\mathcal{D}$ is updated by adding $\langle \mathbf{i_n}, \bar{p}_n \rangle$. For all elements belonging to the new pseudo-domain labels are queried from the oracle and they are transferred from $\mathcal{O}$ to $\mathcal{M}$.

3   Experiments and Results

We evaluated our method on the task of brain age estimation on T1-weighted magnetic resonance imaging (MRI) and compare CASA to different baseline techniques, described in Sect. 3.2. First, we evaluate the task performance on all domains to show how the mean absolute error between predictions and ground truth changes on the validation set (Sect. 3.4). Furthermore, we evaluate the ability of continual learning to improve accuracy on existing domains by adding new domains *backward transfer* (BWT), and the contribution of previous domains in the training data to improving the accuracy on new domains *forward transfer* (FWT) [12]. BWT measure how learning a new domain influences the performance on previous tasks, FWT quantifies the influence on future tasks. Negative BWT values indicate catastrophic forgetting, thus avoiding negative BWT is especially important for continual learning. In Sect. 3.5, we analyze the memory elements at the end of training to evaluate if the detected pseudo-domains match the real domains determined by the scanner types.

3.1   Data Set

We use data pooled from two different data sets containing three different scanners. We use the IXI data set[1] and data from OASIS-3 [7]. From IXI we use data from a Philips Gyroscan Intera 1.5T and a Philips Intera 3.0T scanner, from OASIS-3 we use data from a Siemens TrioTim 3.0T scanner.

Table 1. Data: Splitting of the data into a pre-train, continual, validation, and test set. The number of cases in each split are shown.

Scanner	1.5T IXI	3.0T IXI	3.0T OASIS	Total
Pre-train	201	0	0	201
Continual	52	146	1504	1702
Validation	31	18	187	236
Test	31	18	187	236

Data was split into base pre-train, continual training, validation and test set (see Table 1). Images are resized to $64 \times 128 \times 128$ and normalized to a range between 0 and 1.

3.2   Methods Compared in the Evaluation

We compared four methods in our evaluation:

1. *Joint model*: a model trained in a standard, epoch-based approach on samples from all scanners in the experiment jointly.

---

[1] https://brain-development.org/ixi-dataset/.

2. *Scanner models*: a separate model for each scanner in the experiment trained with standard epoch-based training. The evaluation for a scanner is done for each scanner setting separately.
3. *Naive AL*: a naive continuously trained, active learning approach of labelling every n-th label from the data stream, where n depends on the labelling budget β.
4. *CASA (proposed method)*: The method described in this work. The settings for experimental parameters for CASA are described in Sect. 3.3.

The joint and scanner specific models (1, 2) require the whole training data set to be labelled and available at once, thus they are an upper limit to which our method is compared to. Naive AL and CASA use an oracle to label specific samples only. The comparison with naive AL evaluates the gains of our method of choosing samples to label by detecting domain shifts. Note, that as the goal of our experiments is to show the impact of CASA in comparison to baseline active continual learning strategies and not to develop the best network for brain age estimation we do not compare to state-of-the-art brain age estimation methods.

3.3   Experimental Setup

The task model is a simple feed-forward network as described in [3] and provided on github[2]. The style network used in the pseudo-domain module is a 3D-ModelGenesis model pre-trained on computed tomography images on the lung [20]. We run experiments with different parameter settings evaluating the influence of the memory size M, the task performance threshold k, and the labelling budget β, expressed as a fraction of the continuous training set. We test the influence of β with different settings $\beta = \frac{1}{20}$ (n = 85), $\frac{1}{10}$ (n = 170), $\frac{1}{8}$ (n = 212) and $\frac{1}{5}$ (n = 340). For the performance threshold, we tested $k = 5.0$ and $k = 7.0$, to demonstrate the influence of k on the labelling need of CASA. Values for k are set after observing the performance of the baseline models. The main performance measure for brain age estimation we use is the mean absolute error (MAE) between predicted and true age.

3.4   Model Accuracy Across Domains

Figure 3 shows how the mean absolute error on the validation set, of CASA and the naive AL approach changes during training. Adaption to new domains is much faster when using our approach, even if the labeling budget is low (e.g. $\beta = \frac{1}{20}$). Furthermore, as seen from the curves training is more stable. Lower values are reached for CASA in comparison to naive AL at the end of training across all scanners for the validation set.

In Table 2 different parameter settings are compared. The performance gap between CASA and naive AL trained with $M = 128$ is especially large for images of 3.0T IXI. There, our approach successfully identified the new domain

---

[2] https://github.com/nkdinsdale/Unlearning_for_MRI_harmonisation.

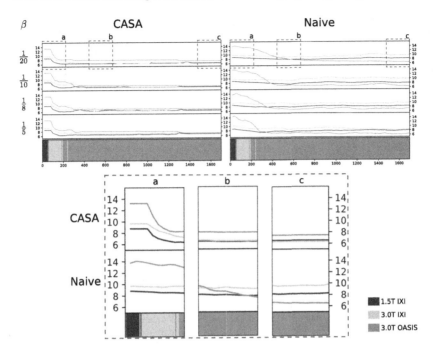

Fig. 3. Evaluation for $M = 128$ and $k = 5.0$ with different β. Y-axis shows the mean absolute error (MAE, lower is better) of the model on the validation set. Zoomed in sections of training steps of particular interest for $\beta = \frac{1}{20}$: (a): CASA detects the domain shift to 3.0T IXI and trains on the new domain, this also leads to a big forward transfer for 3.0T OASIS. Naive AL only takes every 20-th image for training, thus failing to adapt to 3.0T IXI. (b): CASA is relatively stable, while naive AL incorporates more knowledge about 3.0T OASIS images and start to overfit on those, while showing slight forgetting for 1.5T IXI and 3.0T IXI (c): At the end of the continuous stream CASA show an equal performance for all three scanners, while naive AL leads to good performance on the last domain, but significantly poorer results on previous domains.

as a pseudo-domain, and trained the model accordingly. Naive AL takes every n-th element according to β, thus samples from scanner 3.0T IXI are seen less often and the model cannot adapt to this domain. The advantage of CASA increases as the labelling budget is reduced. Evaluating two different memory sizes $M = 64$ and $M = 128$ shows, that CASA could not gain performance over a naive AL approach when M is small. Comparing CASA with $k = 7.0$ to $k = 5.0$ demonstrates, that a more challenging choice of k leads to better overall performance, furthermore CASA takes more advantage of a larger β when $k = 5.0$.

The BWT and FWT comparison in Table 2 shows positive values for all approaches. Since the task remains the same and only the imaging domains change, this is an expected behaviour. Backward transfer is similar between CASA and naive AL over all settings. For approaches with $M = 128$ we see a

Table 2. Results for age estimation on a test set reported as mean absolute error (MAE, lower is better, ± indicates the interval of results with 3 independent runs with different seeds). The table compares CASA, naive active learning (NAL), individual scanner models (ScM), and a joint model trained from all data (JM). The column *Labelled* denotes the amount of labelling by the oracle needed during training.

β	Labelled	Meth.	M	k	1.5T IXI	3.0T IXI	3.0T OASIS	BWT	FWT
$\frac{1}{20}$	[74–85]	CASA	128	5.0	6.29 ± 0.26	6.22 ± 0.54	6.51 ± 0.81	0.98 ± 0.15	6.06 ± 0.78
	[70–85]	CASA	128	7.0	6.11 ± 0.22	7.27 ± 0.14	6.24 ± 0.20	0.87 ± 0.27	5.57 ± 0.65
	85	NAL	128	–	6.89 ± 0.28	9.88 ± 0.49	5.98 ± 0.11	0.76 ± 0.28	3.69 ± 0.72
$\frac{1}{10}$	[90–170]	CASA	128	5.0	6.03 ± 0.40	6.57 ± 0.58	5.75 ± 0.47	1.07 ± 0.42	5.57 ± 0.86
	[74–75]	CASA	128	7.0	5.89 ± 0.07	6.93 ± 0.39	6.45 ± 0.12	0.79 ± 0.10	5.84 ± 0.92
	170	NAL	128	–	6.71 ± 0.28	9.08 ± 0.23	5.72 ± 0.15	1.06 ± 0.23	3.93 ± 0.81
$\frac{1}{8}$	[91–212]	CASA	128	5.0	6.65 ± 0.28	6.38 ± 0.89	5.86 ± 0.45	0.78 ± 0.46	6.05 ± 0.96
	[74–75]	CASA	128	7.0	6.14 ± 0.12	7.34 ± 0.13	6.88 ± 0.63	0.52 ± 0.23	5.55 ± 0.77
	212	NAL	128	–	7.02 ± 0.17	9.29 ± 0.23	6.64 ± 0.27	0.81 ± 0.08	4.07 ± 0.85
$\frac{1}{5}$	[91–112]	CASA	128	5.0	6.20 ± 0.28	6.68 ± 0.33	5.94 ± 0.20	0.74 ± 0.03	5.94 ± 0.79
	[69–110]	CASA	128	7.0	5.99 ± 0.16	7.09 ± 0.45	6.16 ± 0.29	1.07 ± 0.06	5.64 ± 0.92
	340	NAL	128	–	6.34 ± 0.40	8.06 ± 0.28	5.57 ± 0.13	0.90 ± 0.32	4.27 ± 1.09
$\frac{1}{20}$	[62–66]	CASA	64	7.0	6.70 ± 0.52	9.51 ± 0.67	5.95 ± 0.05	1.30 ± 0.51	3.39 ± 0.69
	85	NAL	64	–	6.53 ± 0.23	9.49 ± 0.26	6.20 ± 0.33	1.30 ± 0.51	3.74 ± 0.70
$\frac{1}{10}$	[63–69]	CASA	64	7.0	6.61 ± 0.29	9.07 ± 0.33	5.99 ± 0.19	1.54 ± 0.25	3.47 ± 0.71
	170	NAL	64	–	6.39 ± 0.32	8.57 ± 0.44	5.61 ± 0.15	1.41 ± 0.19	4.00 ± 1.01
$\frac{1}{8}$	[63–64]	CASA	64	7.0	6.21 ± 0.17	9.00 ± 0.06	6.01 ± 0.23	1.83 ± 0.05	3.39 ± 0.72
	212	NAL	64	–	6.64 ± 0.22	9.18 ± 0.10	6.49 ± 0.22	1.27 ± 0.16	3.80 ± 0.76
$\frac{1}{5}$	[62–67]	CASA	64	7.0	6.44 ± 0.54	9.57 ± 0.44	5.77 ± 0.30	1.38 ± 0.11	3.42 ± 0.83
	340	NAL	64	–	6.09 ± 0.16	8.32 ± 0.07	5.10 ± 0.13	0.98 ± 0.14	4.21 ± 0.83
		ScM			6.61 ± 0.71	8.22 ± 0.95	6.62 ± 0.97		
		JM			9.88 ± 0.30	7.14 ± 1.35	5.85 ± 0.33		

clear FWT gap between CASA and naive AL. This shows that CASA is able choose meaningful samples that are also helpful for subsequent tasks.

3.5 Evaluation of the Memory and Pseudo-Domains

Here, we analyze the memory for the parameter settings $\beta = \frac{1}{10}$, $k = 5.0$ and $M = 128$. Other parameter settings show similar trends. The final training memory $\mathcal{M}$ with CASA consists of 47 1.5T IXI, 36 3.0T IXI and 45 3.0T OASIS images. In comparison for naive AL 96 1.5T IXI, 7 3.0T IXI and 25 3.0T OASIS images are stored in the memory. This demonstrates that with CASA the memory is more diverse and captures all three scanners equally, while for naive AL images from 3.0T IXI are heavily underrepresented. Detecting and balancing between the pseudo-domains as done in CASA is beneficial to represent the diversity of the training data.

Figure 4 illustrates the capability of pseudo-domain detection to match real domains. We detect 5 pseudo-domains with the parameter setting mentioned above. Each pseudo-domain is present mainly in a single scanner, with the third scanner being represented by three pseudo-domains (2, 3 and 4). This might be related to appearance variability within a scanner. We plot a t-distributed

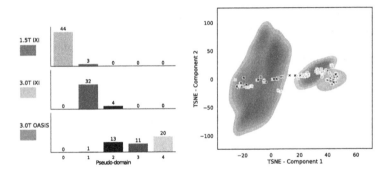

Fig. 4. Detected pseudo-domains capture scanner differences: *Left:* Distribution of pseudo-domains in $\mathcal{M}$ after training over 3 scanners. *Right:* TSNE embedding of the gram embeddings for the whole training set, with marked position of elements in $\mathcal{M}$.

Stochastic Neighbor Embedding (TSNE) [13] for the gram embeddings of all samples in the training set. The shaded areas represent the density of samples from the individual scanners. The markers show where the elements $m \in \mathcal{M}$ are located in the embedding of the whole data set and their assignments to pseudo-domains. This embedding demonstrates that samples in the final $\mathcal{M}$ are distributed over the embedding space, with areas with high sampling density for the under represented scanner 3.0T IXI and less dense areas for 3.0T OASIS with more samples.

4 Conclusion

We propose a continual active learning method for the adaptation of deep learning models to changing image acquisition technology. It detects emerging domains corresponding to new imaging characteristics, and optimally assigns training examples for labeling in a continuous stream of imaging data. Continual learning is necessary to enable models that cover a changing set of scanners. Experiments show that the proposed approach improves model accuracy over all domains, avoids catastrophic forgetting, and exploits a limited budget of annotations well.

Acknowledgments. This work was supported by Novartis Pharmaceuticals Corporation and received funding by the European Union's Horizon 2020 research and innovation programme under the Marie Skłodowska-Curie grant agreement No 765148.

References

1. Bobu, A., Tzeng, E., Hoffman, J., Darrell, T.: Adapting to continuously shifting domains. In: ICLR Workshop (2018)

2. Budd, S., Robinson, E.C., Kainz, B.: A Survey on Active Learning and Human-in-the-Loop Deep Learning for Medical Image Analysis (2019)

3. Dinsdale, N.K., Jenkinson, M., Namburete, A.I.: Unlearning Scanner Bias for MRI Harmonisation in Medical Image Segmentation. Commun. Comput. Inf. Sci. CCIS **1248**, 15–25 (2020)

4. Gatys, L., Ecker, A., Bethge, M.: A neural algorithm of artistic style. J. Vis. **16**(12), 326 (2016)

5. Gonzalez, C., Sakas, G., Mukhopadhyay, A.: What is Wrong with Continual Learning in Medical Image Segmentation? (2020). http://arxiv.org/abs/2010.11008

6. Hofmanninger, J., Perkonigg, M., Brink, J.A., Pianykh, O., Herold, C., Langs, G.: Dynamic memory to alleviate catastrophic forgetting in continuous learning settings. In: Martel, A.L., et al. (eds.) MICCAI 2020. LNCS, vol. 12262, pp. 359–368. Springer, Cham (2020). https://doi.org/10.1007/978-3-030-59713-9_35

7. LaMontagne, P.J., et al.: OASIS-3: Longitudinal Neuroimaging, Clinical, and Cognitive Dataset for Normal Aging and Alzheimer Disease. medRxiv p. 2019.12.13.19014902 (2019). https://doi.org/10.1101/2019.12.13.19014902

8. Lao, Q., Jiang, X., Havaei, M., Bengio, Y.: Continuous Domain Adaptation with Variational Domain-Agnostic Feature Replay (2020)

9. Lenga, M., Schulz, H., Saalbach, A.: Continual Learning for Domain Adaptation in Chest X-ray Classification. In: Conference on Medical Imaging with Deep Learning (MIDL) (2020)

10. Li, P., Hastie, T.J., Church, K.W.: Very sparse stable random projections for dimension reduction. In: Proceedings of the ACM SIGKDD International Conference on Knowledge Discovery and Data Mining, pp. 440–449 (2007)

11. Li, Z., Hoiem, D.: Learning without forgetting. IEEE Trans. Pattern Anal. Mach. Intell. **40**(12), 2935–2947 (2018)

12. Lopez-Paz, D., Ranzato, M.: Gradient episodic memory for continual learning. In: Advances in Neural Information Processing Systems, pp. 6468–6477 (2017)

13. Maaten, L.v.d., Hinton, G.: Visualizing data using t-SNE. J. Mach. Learn. Res. **9**, 2579–2605 (2008)

14. McCloskey, M., Cohen, N.J.: Catastrophic interference in connectionist networks: the sequential learning problem. In: Psychology of Learning and Motivation - Advances in Research and Theory, vol. 24, pp. 109–165 (1989)

15. Ozdemir, F., Fuernstahl, P., Goksel, O.: Learn the new, keep the old: extending pretrained models with new anatomy and images. In: Frangi, A.F., Schnabel, J.A., Davatzikos, C., Alberola-López, C., Fichtinger, G. (eds.) MICCAI 2018. LNCS, vol. 11073, pp. 361–369. Springer, Cham (2018). https://doi.org/10.1007/978-3-030-00937-3_42

16. Pianykh, O.S., et al.: Continuous learning AI in radiology: implementation principles and early applications. Radiology **297**(1), 6–14 (2020)

17. Tony Liu, F., Ming Ting, K., Zhou, Z.H.: Isolation Forest. In: International Conference on Data Mining (2008)

18. Venkataramani, R., Ravishankar, H., Anamandra, S.: Towards continuous domain adaptation for medical imaging. In: Proceedings - International Symposium on Biomedical Imaging, vol. 2019-April, pp. 443–446. IEEE Computer Society (4 2019)

19. Wu, Z., Wang, X., Gonzalez, J., Goldstein, T., Davis, L.: ACE: adapting to changing environments for semantic segmentation. In: Proceedings of the IEEE International Conference on Computer Vision, pp. 2121–2130 (2019)

20. Zhou, Z., Sodha, V., Pang, J., Gotway, M.B., Liang, J.: Models Genesis. Medical Image Analysis p. 101840 (2020). https://doi.org/10.1016/j.media.2020.101840

Multimodal Self-supervised Learning for Medical Image Analysis

Aiham Taleb[1]([✉])(iD), Christoph Lippert[1](iD), Tassilo Klein[2](iD), and Moin Nabi[2](iD)

[1] Hasso-Plattner Institute, Potsdam University, Potsdam, Germany
{aiham.taleb,christoph.lippert}@hpi.de
[2] SAP AI Research, Berlin, Germany
{tassilo.klein,m.nabi}@sap.com

Abstract. Self-supervised learning approaches leverage unlabeled samples to acquire generic knowledge about different concepts, hence allowing for annotation-efficient downstream task learning. In this paper, we propose a novel self-supervised method that leverages multiple imaging modalities. We introduce the *multimodal* puzzle task, which facilitates representation learning from multiple image modalities. The learned modality-agnostic representations are obtained by confusing image modalities at the data-level. Together with the Sinkhorn operator, with which we formulate the puzzle solving optimization as permutation matrix inference instead of classification, they allow for efficient solving of multimodal puzzles with varying levels of complexity. In addition, we also propose to utilize generation techniques for multimodal data augmentation used for *self-supervised pretraining*, instead of downstream tasks directly. This aims to circumvent quality issues associated with synthetic images, while improving data-efficiency and the representations learned by self-supervised methods. Our experimental results show that solving our multimodal puzzles yields better semantic representations, compared to treating each modality independently. Our results also highlight the benefits of exploiting synthetic images for self-supervised pretraining. We showcase our approach on three segmentation tasks, and we outperform many solutions and our results are competitive to state-of-the-art.

Keywords: Self supervised learning · Multimodal images analysis

1 Introduction

Modern medical diagnostics heavily rely on the analysis of multiple imaging modalities, e.g. for differential diagnosis. However, to leverage the data for supervised machine learning approaches, it requires annotation of large numbers of training examples. Generating expert annotations of patient multimodal data at scale is non-trivial, expensive, time-consuming, and is associated with risks on privacy leakages. Consequently, scarcity of data annotations is one of the main impediments for machine learning applications in medical imaging. Self-supervised learning provides a viable solution when labeled training data is

© Springer Nature Switzerland AG 2021
A. Feragen et al. (Eds.): IPMI 2021, LNCS 12729, pp. 661–673, 2021.
https://doi.org/10.1007/978-3-030-78191-0_51

scarce. In these approaches, the supervisory signals are derived from the data itself, typically by the unsupervised learning of a proxy task. Subsequently, the obtained models facilitate data-efficient supervised fine-tuning on target real-world downstream tasks, hence reducing the burden of manual annotation.

Many self-supervised methods utilize the spatial context as a rich supervisory signal to learn effective data representations. However, these approaches neglect an important characteristic of medical images: their multimodality, e.g. MRI and CT. From an anatomical perspective, multimodality is essential because differences in the physical properties of organs and tissues are translated in a complementary fashion across multiple modalities. Examples of such cases are numerous [9]: soft body tissues are better encoded in MRI, but CT scans capture bone structures better. Likewise, specific brain tissues or tumors are better seen in specific MRI modalities, and so on. Thus, we propose to include multiple imaging modalities in our multimodal Jigsaw puzzle task, to integrate the cross-modal information in learned representations using a modality confusion loss.

While the learned representations by our multimodal puzzles prove useful in several downstream tasks when trained and fine-tuned using *realistic* multimodal images, as shown in Sects. 4.2 and 4.3. We also propose to utilize a cross-modal generation step to enhance the quantities of multimodal samples used in training the puzzle solver. Not only this step allows for better adoption of our multimodal puzzles in real-world scenarios, but also demonstrates the possibility of utilizing *synthetic* images for self-supervised *pretraining*, instead of downstream task training. This step is motivated by clinical scenarios, where data is often non-registered, and the quantities of modalities may vary, i.e. creating a modality imbalance problem. By introducing this step in our pipeline, the imbalance issue is alleviated, as shown in Sect. 4.4.

Our Contributions are two-fold. First, a novel self-supervised multimodal puzzle-solving task, which mixes multiple imaging modalities at the data-level, allowing for combining the cross-modal complementary information about different concepts in the data. Second, we propose to exploit cross-modal image generation (translation) for self-supervised tasks, instead of downstream tasks directly. Our results show that exploiting inexpensive solutions similar to ours can provide gains in medical image analysis, particularly in low data regimes.

2 Related Work

Self-supervised learning methods differ in the supervision source used to create the proxy tasks. Common supervision sources include the spatial context [8,18], image colors [28], clustering [5], image rotation prediction [11], image reconstruction [29], and contrastive learning [7,19]. We propose a novel spatial context derived across multiple imaging modalities, encouraging the model to learn modality-agnostic notions from the data. Noroozi *et al.* [18] proposed to solve Jigsaw puzzles on natural images. In contrast to our approach, their method relies on a single imaging modality, limiting its ability to capture vital cross-modal information. In addition, their method requires massive memory and compute resources, even for small puzzles. We improve the computational tractability by employing the Sinkhorn operator [21] as an analog to the Softmax in permutation tasks, allowing to solve more complex puzzles. This operator casts puzzle solving as a permutation matrix inference instead of classification. In their method, the choice of a fixed permutation set as classification targets limits the self-supervised task complexity. Instead, by defining our task as a matrix inference, the model searches among *all* permutations.

Solving jigsaw puzzles can be employed in a multi-task fashion, e.g. [4, 22], as a secondary task for domain adaptation. In this scenario, the model is expected to confuse the modalities/domains at the *feature-level*, similar to the late modality fusion [3]. In contrast, we fuse the modalities in our generated puzzles, i.e. performing a *data-level* early fusion. As opposed to our approach, their approach is likely to fail when the modality difference is high, as shown in our experiments.

In the medical context, self-supervision has been applied to depth estimation in medical image registration [16], body part recognition [27], and in disc degeneration using spinal MRIs [14]. These works make assumptions about input data, resulting in engineered solutions that hardly generalize to other target tasks. Our proposed approach avoids such assumptions about the data. Instead, our results show that it may operate on different imaging modalities, even when spatially unregistered. In more related works, Tajbakhsh *et al.* [23] use orientation prediction from medical images as a proxy task, Zhou *et al.* [29] employ image reconstruction techniques, and Taleb *et al.* [24] extend several self-supervised methods to 3D medical scans. Zhuang *et al.* [31] develop a proxy task for solving 3D jigsaw puzzles, in an attempt to simulate Rubik's cube solving. Since their work extends the 2D puzzles of Noroozi *et al.* [18] to 3D, it incurs similar computational costs, only the issue is exacerbated here as 3D puzzles require more computations. We follow this line of research, and we exploit multiple imaging modalities and improve puzzle solving efficiency in our proxy task.

Image-to-image translation using Generative Adversarial Networks [13, 30] has found several use cases in the medical domain. Many works have attempted to translate across medical imaging modalities [25, 26]. While the goal of these methods is to improve the cross-modal generation quality, we view it as orthogonal to our goal. Similar to [10], we utilize cross-modal translation methods to improve the performance on downstream tasks, e.g. segmentation, through augmentation. However, especially for clinical applications, one can doubt the quality of synthetic images. Hence, as opposed to the above works, we circumvent this issue by employing these images for pretraining purposes only.

3   Method

Our method processes multimodal images, as is the case in many medical imaging datasets [9]. We assume no prior knowledge about what modalities are being used in our models, i.e. the modalities can vary from one task to another.

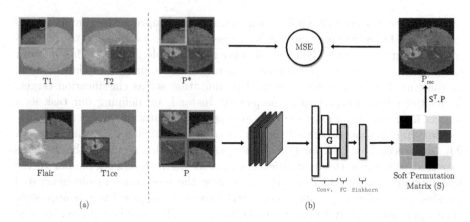

T1   T2   P*   P_rec

                                                                  S^T.P

Flair   T1ce   P   G   Soft Permutation
                                                                  Matrix (S)
                                          Conv. FC Sinkhorn

(a)   (b)

Fig. 1. Schematic illustration showing the proposed multimodal puzzles. (a) Assuming we have four modalities (this number can vary), (b) these images are then used to construct multimodal jigsaw puzzles, drawing patches from the modalities randomly.

3.1 Multimodal Puzzle Construction

Solving a jigsaw puzzle entails two steps. First, the image is cut into puzzle pieces (patches or tiles), which are shuffled according to a certain permutation. Second, these shuffled pieces are assembled such that the original image is restored. If N is the number of puzzle pieces, then there exist $N!$ of possible arrangements. In a conventional puzzle, the tiles originate from one image at a time, i.e. the computational complexity is $O(N!)$. On the other hand, we propose a *multimodal* jigsaw puzzle, which simultaneously learns the in-depth representation of how organs compose, along with the cross-modal spatial relationships. Hence, the tiles can stem from M different modalities. As a result, the computational complexity is increased to $O(N!^M)$. This quickly becomes prohibitively expensive due to: i) factorial growth in the number of permutations $N!$, ii) exponential growth in the number of modalities M. To reduce the computational burden, we use two tricks. First, we employ the Sinkhorn operator, which efficiently addresses the factorial growth. Second, we employ a feed-forward network G that learns a rich cross-modal representation, which cancels out the exponential factor M.

3.2 Puzzle-Solving with Sinkhorn Networks

To efficiently solve our multimodal jigsaw puzzle task, we train a network that can learn a permutation. A permutation matrix of size $N \times N$ corresponds to one permutation of the numbers 1 to N. Every row and column, therefore, contains precisely a single 1 with 0s everywhere else, which is a non-differentiable parameterization. However, it can be approximated in terms of a differentiable relaxation, the so-called Sinkhorn operator [21]. The Sinkhorn operator iteratively normalizes rows and columns of any real-valued matrix to obtain a "soft" permutation matrix, which is doubly stochastic. Formally, for an arbitrary N

dimensional square matrix X, the Sinkhorn operator $S(X)$ is defined as:

$$S^0(X) = exp(X),$$
$$S^i(X) = \mathcal{T}_R(\mathcal{T}_C(S^{i-1}(X))), \tag{1}$$
$$S(X) = \lim_{i \to \infty} S^i(X).$$

where $\mathcal{T}_R(X) = X \oslash (X \mathbf{1}_N \mathbf{1}_N^\top)$ and $\mathcal{T}_C(X) = X \oslash (\mathbf{1}_N \mathbf{1}_N^\top X)$ are the row and column normalization operators, respectively. The element-wise division is denoted by $\oslash$, and $\mathbf{1}_N^\top \in \mathbb{N}^N$ is an N dimensional vector of ones.

Assuming an input set of patches $P = \{p_1, p_2, ..., p_N\}$, where $P \in \mathbb{R}^{N \times l \times l}$ represents a puzzle that consists of N square patches, and l is the patch length. We process each patch in P with a network G, which produces a single output feature vector with length N per patch. By concatenating together these feature vectors obtained for all region sets, we obtain an $N \times N$ matrix, which the Sinkhorn operator converts to the soft permutation matrix $S \in [0, 1]^{N \times N}$. Formally, the network G learns the mapping $G : P \to S$, by minimizing the mean squared error (MSE) between the sorted ground-truth patch set P^* and the reconstructed version P_{rec} of the scrambled input. Then, S is applied to the scrambled input P to reconstruct the image P_{rec}, as in the formula:

$$\mathcal{L}_{puzzle}(\theta, P, P^*) = \sum_{i=1}^{K} \left\| P_i^* - S_{\theta, P_i}^T . P_i \right\|^2, \tag{2}$$

where θ are the network parameters, and K is the total number of training puzzles. The network parameters in G encode the cross-modal representations of different tissue structures. Therefore, they can be employed in downstream tasks by fine-tuning them on target domains in an annotation-efficient regime. Our approach is depicted in Fig. 1.

3.3 Cross-modal Generation

Multimodal medical scans exist in several curated datasets, and in pairs of aligned (or registered) scans. However, in many real-world scenarios, obtaining such data in large quantities can be challenging. To address this, we add an explicit cross-modal generation step using CycleGAN [30]. This model also uses a cycle-consistency loss, which relaxes the alignment (pairing) constraint across the two modalities, requiring no prior expensive registration. This step allows for leveraging the richness of multimodal representations obtained by our proposed puzzle-solving task. In our experiments, we generate samples of the smaller modality (in number of samples) using the larger modality. Then, we construct our multimodal puzzles using a mix of real and generated multimodal data. As we show in our related experiments in Sect. 4.4, this yields better representations compared to using a single modality only when creating puzzles.

4   Experimental Results

In Sect. 4.1, we provide details about the datasets. In Sect. 4.2, we evaluate the learned representations by assessing their impact on downstream tasks performance. Also, we compare to baselines from state-of-the-art. In Sect. 4.3, we assess the obtained benefits in data-efficiency. Finally, in Sect. 4.4, we analyze how data generation affects the learned representations. The experiments in the Sects. 4.3 and 4.4 are performed in ablation mode.

4.1   Datasets

We consider three multimodal medical imaging datasets. The first is the Brain Tumor Image Segmentation Benchmark (**BraTS**) [1,17], which contains multimodal MRI scans for 285 training and 66 validation cases. All cases include four MRI modalities: T1, T1Gd, T2, and T2-FLAIR volumes. The second is for **Prostate** segmentation [20], which consists of 48 multimodal MRI cases (32 for training, and 16 for testing). Segmentation masks of the prostate were produced from T2 scans and ADC maps. The third is for **Liver** segmentation from the CHAOS [15] dataset, which consists of 40 multimodal cases (20 for training, and 20 for testing). This dataset contains CT and MRI (T2) modalities, where each case has one scan per modality. The modalities in this benchmark are also non-registered, making it a pertinent test-bed for our multimodal puzzles.

4.2   Transfer Learning Results[1]

Brain Tumor Segmentation. This task involves segmenting 3 regions of brain tumor: a) whole tumor (WT), b) tumor core (TC), and c) enhanced tumor (ET).

Baselines: apart from the `Single-modal` baseline, all of the baselines use multimodal data for pretraining[2]: i) `From Scratch`: provides an insight into the benefits of pretraining, as opposed to learning the target task directly. ii) `Single-modal`: studies the impact of pretraining using a single modality as input. We employ the best modality for each task, i.e. Flair for whole tumor, T2 for tumor core, and T1ce for enhanced tumor. iii) `Isensee et al.` [12]: This model ranks among the tops in the BraTS 2018 challenge. 2D `Isensee` is a 2D version of their network, for better comparability. iv) `Chang et al.` [6]: Trained multiple versions of 2D U-Nets and formed an ensemble, which requires significantly more compute time and resources than our single model. v) `JiGen` [4]: is a multi-tasking approach, which solves jigsaw puzzles as a secondary task. It aims to analyze the benefits of data-level modality confusion (ours), as opposed to feature-level (JiGen). vi) `Models Genesis` [29]: is a self-supervised method that uses image reconstruction. We compare to the 2D version (2D `MG`).

---

[1] We Evaluate on *realistic* data in this section, using a 5-fold cross validation approach.

[2] In fine-tuning, we use the same multimodal data across all models.

Evaluation Metrics. The reported metrics are the average dice scores for the Whole Tumor (WT), the Tumor Core (TC), and the Enhanced Tumor (ET).

Discussion. The results of our `multi-modal` method compared to the above baselines are shown in Table 1. Our method outperforms both the `from scratch` and `single-modal` baselines, confirming the benefits of pretraining using our multimodal approach. In addition, our method outperforms the baselines of `Chang et al.` [6] and `2D Isensee et al.` [12], even though the latter uses co-training with additional datasets and augmentation techniques. This supports the benefits of initializing CNNs with our multimodal puzzles. We also outperform 2D Models Genesis (`2D MG`) [29] in this downstream task, supporting the effectiveness of our pretraining method. Compared to `JiGen` [4], we also find that our approach of performing the modality confusion in the data-level is superior to modality confusion in the feature-level, in this downstream task.

Table 1. Results on three segmentation benchmarks

Dataset	BraTS			Prostate				Liver
Model	Dice			Dice		NSD		Dice
	ET	WT	TC	C	P	C	P	
From scratch	68.12	80.54	77.29	68.98	86.15	94.57	97.84	89.98
Single-modal	78.26	87.01	82.52	69.48	87.42	92.97	97.21	92.01
Registered	–	–	–	–	–	–	–	95.09
Chang [6]	75.90	89.05	82.24	–	–	–	–	–
2D Isensee [12]	78.92	88.42	83.73	–	–	–	–	–
2D MG [29]	79.21	88.82	83.60	73.85	87.77	94.61	98.59	95.01
JiGen [4]	78.75	88.15	83.32	69.98	86.82	92.67	96.13	93.18
Ours (Multi-modal)	**79.65**	**89.74**	**84.48**	**75.11**	**88.79**	**94.95**	**98.65**	**95.10**

Prostate Segmentation. The target of this task is to segment two regions of the prostate: central gland and peripheral zone.

  Baselines apart from `Single-modal`, all use multimodal data. We evaluate similarly to brain tumor segmentation, and we compare to the same baselines, only here we train on prostate data: i) `From Scratch`. ii) `Single-modal`: on MRI (T2). iii) `JiGen` [4]. iv) `Models Genesis (2D MG)` [29].

Evaluation Metrics. We compute the average Dice score and the normalized surface distance (NSD), for both prostate regions (**C**entral and **P**eripheral).

Discussion. The results of our `multi-modal` method compared to the above baselines are shown in Table 1. Our method outperforms both `from scratch` and `single-modal` baselines in this task, too, supporting the advantages of pretraining using our method. We also outperform 2D Models Genesis (`2D MG`) [29] in this task, supporting the effectiveness of our pretraining method. Our method outperforms `JiGen` [4] when trained on this task too. We observe a larger gap in performance between our approach and JiGen in this task, compared to brain tumor segmentation. We posit that this is due to the more significant difference between the modalities in this task, which can be seen clearly in Fig. 3, and is caused by the underlying physics. ADC maps measure water diffusion within organ tissues (the prostate exhibits lower diffusion). BraTS modalities are variants of T1- and T2-weighted MRI, which only differ in scanner configurations.

Liver Segmentation. Using unregistered abdominal CT and MRI scans.

Baselines apart from `Single-modal`, all use multimodal data. We evaluate similarly to brain tumor segmentation, and we compare to the same baselines, only here we train on liver data: i) `From Scratch`. ii) `Single-modal`: we employ CT to create the puzzles. iii) `JiGen` [4]. iv) `2D Models Genesis (2D MG)` [29]. v) `Registered`: to assess the influence of registration on our method, we register the modalities in this baseline (using VoxelMorph [2])[3].

Evaluation Metrics. We compute the average dice score (Dice) for liver.

Discussion. The results of our `multimodal` method compared to the above baselines are shown in Table 1. Our method outperforms both `from scratch` and `single-modal` baselines in this task too, supporting the advantages of pre-training using our method. We outperform 2D Models Genesis (`2D MG`) [29] only marginally in this task, and we believe this is because Models Genesis was pre-trained on Chest CT. Also, our method outperforms `JiGen` [4], when trained on this task too. The results against the `Registered` baseline are almost on par with the our method (trained on non-registered data). This result highlights our multimodal puzzles' generalization ability to non-registered modalities.

4.3   Low-Shot Learning Results

In this set of experiments, we assess how our self-supervised task benefits data-efficiency, by measuring the performance on downstream tasks at different labeling rates, i.e. fine-tuning pre-trained models on corresponding sample sizes. We randomly select subsets of patients at 1%, 10%, 50%, and 100% of the total training set size. For each subset, we compare the performance of our `multimodal` model to the baselines `from scratch` and `single-modal`. As shown in Fig. 2, our method outperforms both. The performance gap to the `single-modal` baseline confirms the benefits of using our *multimodal* puzzles. In a low-data regime of 1% of the dataset size, the margin to the `from scratch` baseline appears larger. This case, in particular, suggests the potential for generic unsupervised features applicable to medical imaging tasks, and has consequences on annotation efficiency. We report these results on *realistic* data. The `single-modal` baselines use: FLAIR for BraTS, T2 for Prostate, and CT for Liver.

---

[3] Our aim is to benchmark our method against a proven image registration method.

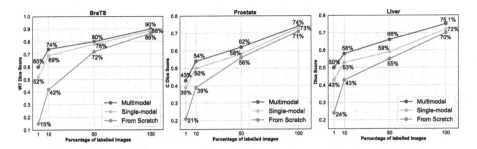

Fig. 2. Results in the low-shot scenario. Our method improves data-efficiency.

4.4 Cross-modal Generation Results

We study in these experiments the effect of the cross-modal generation step, which is motivated by the imbalance in imaging modality quantities. Hence, in this set of experiments, we perform this step in a semi-supervised fashion, assuming small multimodal and large single-modal subsets. We evaluate at multimodal subset sizes of 1%, 10%, and 50% of the total number of patients in each benchmark. We assume a reference modality[4], which is often abundant in practice, to generate the other modalities. In BraTS, since we have four MRI modalities, we train three GANs and convert T2-MRI to T1-, T1CE-, and FLAIR-MRI. In Prostate, we use T2-weighted MRI scans to generate the ADC diffusion-weighted scans. In CHAOS, we use the CT modality to generate T2 MRI.

Discussion. This step is justified if it provides a performance boost over the `single-modal` baseline, i.e. training on puzzles from one modality. The presented results of `Our method` in Table 2 clearly show an improvement on all benchmarks, when training our puzzle solver on a mixture of synthetic and realistic multimodal data. Even when we use only 1% of dataset sizes, the generator appears to capture the important characteristics of the generated modality. The qualitative results in Fig. 3 confirm the quality of generated images. In addition, the results in Table 2 support the benefits of using the synthetic data for self-supervised pretraining, instead of `Downstream training` directly.

---

[4] Alternatively, all modalities can be generated from each other, requiring many GANs.

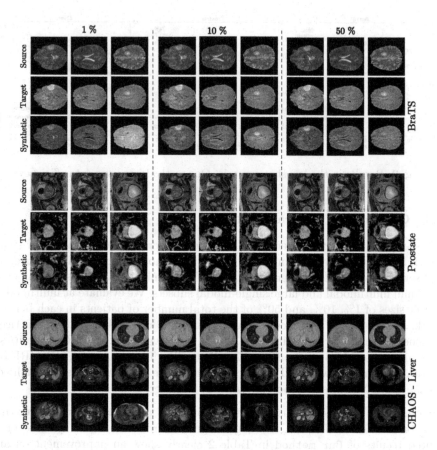

Fig. 3. Qualitative results of CycleGAN at different multimodal data rates, which affects generation quality. Here, translation is from T2 to FLAIR in BraTS, T2 to ADC in Prostate, and CT to T2-MRI in CHAOS (its targets are obtained with VoxelMorph)

Table 2. Segmentation results (in dice score). The rates are sizes of multimodal subsets

Model	BraTS			Prostate		CHAOS
	ET	WT	TC	C	P	Liver
Single-modal	72.12	82.72	79.61	69.48	87.42	92.01
Downstream training (1%)	65.40	74.11	69.24	55.24	71.23	80.31
Downstream training (10%)	69.28	78.72	71.58	62.65	76.18	83.65
Downstream training (50%)	72.92	81.20	78.36	66.34	80.24	87.58
Our method (1%)	73.12	82.42	80.01	61.87	82.67	82.71
Our method (10%)	74.19	85.71	81.33	67.67	84.37	86.26
Our method (50%)	**76.23**	**87.04**	**82.38**	**73.45**	**87.92**	**93.85**

5   Conclusion and Future Work

In this work, we proposed a self-supervised *multimodal* Jigsaw puzzle-solving task. This approach allows for learning rich semantic representations that facilitate downstream task solving in the medical imaging context. The proposed multimodal puzzles outperform their single-modal counterparts, confirming the advantages of including multiple modalities when constructing jigsaw puzzles. We also showed competitive results to state-of-the-art in three medical imaging benchmarks. One of which has unregistered modalities, further supporting the effectiveness of our approach in producing rich data representations. In addition, our approach further reduces the cost of manual annotation required for downstream tasks, and our results in the low-data regime support this benefit. We also evaluated a cross-modal translation method as part of our framework, which when used in conjunction with our method, it showed performance gains even when using few multimodal samples to train the generative model. Finally, we demonstrated the benefits of multimodality in our multimodal jigsaw puzzles, and we aim to generalize this idea to other self-supervised tasks. In addition, we believe generalizing our multimodal puzzles to the 3D context should improve the learned representations, and we deem this as a future work.

References

1. Bakas, S., et al.: Advancing the cancer genome atlas glioma MRI collections with expert segmentation labels and radiomic features. Sci. Data **4**, 1–13 (2017)
2. Balakrishnan, G., Zhao, A., Sabuncu, M., Guttag, J., Dalca, A.: Voxelmorph: a learning framework for deformable medical image registration. IEEE Trans. Med. Imaging 1 (2019). https://doi.org/10.1109/TMI.2019.2897538
3. Baltrušaitis, T., Ahuja, C., Morency, L.P.: Multimodal machine learning: a survey and taxonomy. IEEE Trans. Pattern Anal. Mach. Intell. **41**(2), 423–443 (2019)
4. Carlucci, F.M., D'Innocente, A., Bucci, S., Caputo, B., Tommasi, T.: Domain generalization by solving jigsaw puzzles. In: CVPR, IEEE (2019)
5. Caron, M., Bojanowski, P., Joulin, A., Douze, M.: Deep clustering for unsupervised learning of visual features. In: The European Conference on Computer Vision (ECCV). Springer, Munich, Germany (September 2018)
6. Chang, Y.J., Lin, Z.S., Yang, T.L., Huang, T.Y.: Automatic segmentation of brain tumor from 3d MR images using a 2d convolutional neural networks. In: Pre-Conference Proceedings of the 7th MICCAI BraTS Challenge, Springer (2018)
7. Chen, T., Kornblith, S., Norouzi, M., Hinton, G.: A simple framework for contrastive learning of visual representations (2020)
8. Doersch, C., Gupta, A., Efros, A.A.: Unsupervised visual representation learning by context prediction. In: ICCV, pp. 1422–1430. IEEE, USA (2015)
9. Eisenberg, R., Margulis, A.: A Patient's Guide to Medical Imaging. Oxford University Press, New York (2011)
10. Fu, C., et al.: Three dimensional fluorescence microscopy image synthesis and segmentation. In: IEEE Conference on Computer Vision and Pattern Recognition Workshops (CVPRW) (06 2018). https://doi.org/10.1109/CVPRW.2018.00298
11. Gidaris, S., Singh, P., Komodakis, N.: Unsupervised representation learning by predicting image rotations. CoRR arXiv abs/1803.07728 (2018)

12. Isensee, F., Kickingereder, P., Wick, W., Bendszus, M., Maier-Hein, K.H.: No new-net. In: Crimi, A., Bakas, S., Kuijf, H., Keyvan, F., Reyes, M., van Walsum, T. (eds.) BrainLes 2018. LNCS, vol. 11384, pp. 234–244. Springer, Cham (2019). https://doi.org/10.1007/978-3-030-11726-9_21

13. Isola, P., Zhu, J., Zhou, T., Efros, A.A.: Image-to-image translation with conditional adversarial networks. In: 2017 IEEE Conference on Computer Vision and Pattern Recognition (CVPR), pp. 5967–5976. IEEE, Honolulu, Hawaii, USA (2017)

14. Jamaludin, A., Kadir, T., Zisserman, A.: Self-supervised learning for spinal MRIs. In: Cardoso, M.J., et al. (eds.) DLMIA/ML-CDS -2017. LNCS, vol. 10553, pp. 294–302. Springer, Cham (2017). https://doi.org/10.1007/978-3-319-67558-9_34

15. Kavur, A.E., Selver, M.A., Dicle, O., Barış, M., Gezer, N.S.: CHAOS - Combined (CT-MR) Healthy Abdominal Organ Segmentation Challenge Data (April 2019). https://doi.org/10.5281/zenodo.3362844

16. Li, H., Fan, Y.: Non-rigid image registration using self-supervised fully convolutional networks without training data. In: ISBI, pp. 1075–1078. IEEE (April 2018)

17. Menze, B.H., et al.: The multimodal brain tumor image segmentation benchmark (brats). IEEE Trans. Med. Imaging **34**(10), 1993–2024 (2015)

18. Noroozi, M., Favaro, P.: Unsupervised learning of visual representations by solving jigsaw puzzles. In: Leibe, B., Matas, J., Sebe, N., Welling, M. (eds.) ECCV 2016. LNCS, vol. 9910, pp. 69–84. Springer, Cham (2016). https://doi.org/10.1007/978-3-319-46466-4_5

19. van den Oord, A., Li, Y., Vinyals, O.: Representation learning with contrastive predictive coding. CoRR arXiv abs/1807.03748 (2018)

20. Simpson, A.L., et al.: A large annotated medical image dataset for the development and evaluation of segmentation algorithms. CoRR arXiv abs/1902.09063 (2019)

21. Sinkhorn, R.: A relationship between arbitrary positive matrices and doubly stochastic matrices. Ann. Math. Stat. **35**(2), 876–879 (1964)

22. Sun, Y., Tzeng, E., Darrell, T., Efros, A.A.: Unsupervised domain adaptation through self-supervision (2019)

23. Tajbakhsh, N., et al.: Surrogate supervision for medical image analysis: Effective deep learning from limited quantities of labeled data. In: 2019 IEEE 16th International Symposium on Biomedical Imaging (ISBI 2019), pp. 1251–1255 (2019)

24. Taleb, A., et al.: 3d self-supervised methods for medical imaging. In: NeurIPS (2020)

25. Wolterink, J.M., Dinkla, A.M., Savenije, M.H.F., Seevinck, P.R., van den Berg, C.A.T., Išgum, I.: Deep MR to CT synthesis using unpaired data. In: Tsaftaris, S.A., Gooya, A., Frangi, A.F., Prince, J.L. (eds.) SASHIMI 2017. LNCS, vol. 10557, pp. 14–23. Springer, Cham (2017). https://doi.org/10.1007/978-3-319-68127-6_2

26. Yang, H., et al.: Unpaired brain MR-to-CT synthesis using a structure-constrained CycleGAN. In: Stoyanov, D., et al. (eds.) DLMIA/ML-CDS -2018. LNCS, vol. 11045, pp. 174–182. Springer, Cham (2018). https://doi.org/10.1007/978-3-030-00889-5_20

27. Zhang, P., Wang, F., Zheng, Y.: Self-supervised deep representation learning for fine-grained body part recognition. In: ISBI, pp. 578–582. IEEE (April 2017)

28. Zhang, R., Isola, P., Efros, A.A.: Colorful image colorization. In: Leibe, B., Matas, J., Sebe, N., Welling, M. (eds.) ECCV 2016. LNCS, vol. 9907, pp. 649–666. Springer, Cham (2016). https://doi.org/10.1007/978-3-319-46487-9_40

29. Zhou, Z., et al.: Models genesis: generic autodidactic models for 3D medical image analysis. In: Shen, D., et al. (eds.) MICCAI 2019. LNCS, vol. 11767, pp. 384–393. Springer, Cham (2019). https://doi.org/10.1007/978-3-030-32251-9_42

30. Zhu, J., Park, T., Isola, P., Efros, A.A.: Unpaired image-to-image translation using cycle-consistent adversarial networks. In: 2017 IEEE International Conference on Computer Vision (ICCV), pp. 2242–2251. IEEE, Venice, Italy (2017)

31. Zhuang, X., Li, Y., Hu, Y., Ma, K., Yang, Y., Zheng, Y.: Self-supervised feature learning for 3D medical images by playing a Rubik's cube. In: Shen, D., et al. (eds.) MICCAI 2019. LNCS, vol. 11767, pp. 420–428. Springer, Cham (2019). https:// doi.org/10.1007/978-3-030-32251-9_46

Uncertainty Quantification and Generative Modelling

Spatially Varying Label Smoothing: Capturing Uncertainty from Expert Annotations

Mobarakol Islam[(✉)] and Ben Glocker

BioMedIA Group, Department of Computing, Imperial College London, London, UK
{m.islam20,b.glocker}@imperial.ac.uk

Abstract. The task of image segmentation is inherently noisy due to ambiguities regarding the exact location of boundaries between anatomical structures. We argue that this information can be extracted from the expert annotations at no extra cost, and when integrated into state-of-the-art neural networks, it can lead to improved calibration between soft probabilistic predictions and the underlying uncertainty. We built upon label smoothing (LS) where a network is trained on 'blurred' versions of the ground truth labels which has been shown to be effective for calibrating output predictions. However, LS is not taking the local structure into account and results in overly smoothed predictions with low confidence even for non-ambiguous regions. Here, we propose Spatially Varying Label Smoothing (SVLS), a soft labeling technique that captures the structural uncertainty in semantic segmentation. SVLS also naturally lends itself to incorporate inter-rater uncertainty when multiple labelmaps are available. The proposed approach is extensively validated on four clinical segmentation tasks with different imaging modalities, number of classes and single and multi-rater expert annotations. The results demonstrate that SVLS, despite its simplicity, obtains superior boundary prediction with improved uncertainty and model calibration.

1 Introduction

Understanding the prediction uncertainty is crucial in critical decision-making tasks like medical diagnosis. Despite impressive performance of deep neural networks, the output predictions of such models are often poorly calibrated and over-confident [10,16,20,25]. There is evidence that strategies such as label smoothing (LS) [20,25,29] and temperature scaling [10,15,16] are useful for calibration and uncertainty quantification for independent class prediction tasks such as image classification. Semantic segmentation, however, is a highly structured problem where pixel-wise class predictions intrinsically depend on the spatial relationship of neighboring objects. In medical images boundaries between anatomical regions are often ambiguous or ill-defined due to image noise, low contrast or the presence of pathology which should be taking into account during model training. Disagreement between experts annotators is also quite common

© Springer Nature Switzerland AG 2021
A. Feragen et al. (Eds.): IPMI 2021, LNCS 12729, pp. 677–688, 2021.
https://doi.org/10.1007/978-3-030-78191-0_52

and poses a challenge to the definition of 'ground truth' in terms of hard segmentation labels. This requires mechanisms for aggregating multiple annotations in a reliable and sensible way that is able to capture the underlying uncertainty. Previous work fuses labels by using different techniques such as majority voting [12] or STAPLE [32]. However, these techniques do not carry the inter-rater variability through to the model predictions. Other approaches are integrating uncertainty in segmentation directly as part of the model's ability to make probabilistic predictions [5,14,19]. Nair et al. [21] use Monte Carlo dropout [9] to estimate uncertainty for multiple sclerosis lesion segmentation. Jungo et al. [13] analyse the uncertainty and calibration of brain tumor segmentation using U-Net-like [27] architectures. These techniques are complementary to what we propose here and could be considered in a combined approach.

The utility of model uncertainty is directly related to model calibration which indicates how well the confidence estimates of a probabilistic classifier reflects the true error distribution. A predictive model should not only be accurate but also well-calibrated such that the provided confidence (or uncertainty) becomes useful in practice. Various calibration techniques [10] such as Platt scaling [26], temperature scaling with dropout variational inference [16], non-parametric calibration [33], Dirichlet calibration [15], and also label smoothing [20,25] have been proposed to improve calibration of output predictions.

Label smoothing is an intriguingly simple technique which can both incorporate information about ambiguities in expert labels and improve model calibration. LS flattens the hard labels by assigning a uniform distribution over all other classes, which prevents over-confidence in the assigned label during training. LS has been shown to improve performance in deep learning models applied to different applications, including classification [29], recognition [30] and language modeling [7]. Recently, Müller et al. [20] show that LS can significantly improve model calibration with a class separating effect on the learned feature representations.

In semantic segmentation, however, the benefit of LS is less clear. The notion of structured prediction via pixel-wise classification with underlying spatial dependencies, limits LS ability to perform as well as in image classification. This is because LS flattens the training labels with a uniform distribution without considering spatial consistency. Moreover, both convolution and pooling techniques in a fully convolutional network are performed on local spatially-varying patches. Therefore, simply generating pixel-wise soft labels that ignore the underlying structure may be insufficient for capturing uncertainty in semantic segmentation, as demonstrated empirically in our experiments.

We propose a simple yet effective mechanism, *Spatially Varying Label Smoothing* (SVLS), for incorporating structural label uncertainty by capturing ambiguity about object boundaries in expert segmentation maps. SVLS does not require any additional annotations, and extracts uncertainty information directly from available expert annotation. Training a state-of-the-art neural network with SVLS target labels results in improved model calibration where uncertainty estimates for the target predictions do more faithfully represent seg-

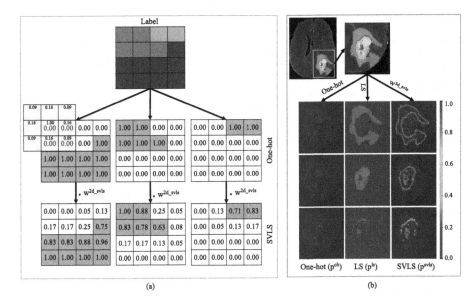

Fig. 1. SVLS label generation and comparison with one-hot and LS. (a) A toy example of calculating the SVLS soft labels from expert segmentations. 'Replicate' padding of the size 1 is for the calculation; (b) A visualization comparing the target labelmaps of one-hot, LS and SVLS for a multi-class brain tumour segmentation. One-hot and LS ignore the underlying spatial structure, whereas SVLS captures boundary uncertainty while preserving high confidence inside structures.

mentation accuracy. SVLS also naturally lends itself to the case where multiple expert annotations are available. To demonstrate the effectiveness of SVLS, we present results on four different clinical tasks including MRI segmentation of brain tumours and prostate zones, and CT segmentation of kidney tumours and lung nodules.

2   Spatially Varying Label Smoothing

In semantic segmentation, a commonly used loss function is cross-entropy, $CE = -\sum_{c=1}^{N} p_c^{oh} \log(\hat{p}_c)$, where p_c^{oh} is the target label probability (or one-hot encoding), $\hat{p}_c$ is the predicted likelihood probability, with N being the number of classes. In label smoothing (LS), the target probability is uniformly downscaled with a weight factor α to generate soft labels from the one-hot encoding, as

$$p_c^{ls} = p_c^{oh}(1 - \alpha) + \frac{\alpha}{N} \tag{1}$$

Simply replacing the original targets p_c^{oh} with LS targets p_c^{ls} in the CE loss allows us to train a neural network for image segmentation with soft target labels.

The LS approach originally proposed for image classification distributes the label uncertainty uniformly across classes and independently of the underlying

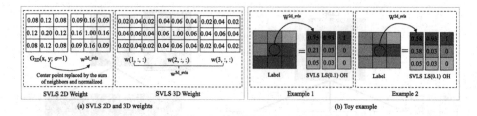

Fig. 2. (a) SVLS weights for 2D and 3D. The weights are obtained by re-weighting the center point with the sum of surrounding weights in Gaussian kernel. (b) Two examples of SVLS compared to LS and one-hot labels in two different toy structures. SVLS considers the spatial variation of the pixels and assigns label probabilities accordingly. LS and one-hot ignore the local structure. The center pixel in example 1 has higher probability of being part of the red class than in example 2 due to the spatial context.

spatial structure. For semantic segmentation, which is commonly formulated as dense pixel-wise classification, it is important to consider that the individual predictions are actually not independent, and neither are the class labels. The likelihood of the co-occurrence of different classes is spatially varying, in particular, near object boundaries which typically exhibit higher uncertainty [6,28,31,34]. In order to take these aspects into account, we introduce Spatially Varying Label Smoothing (SVLS) which is an adaptation of LS for the task of semantic segmentation. SVLS determines the probability of the target class based on neighboring pixels. This is achieved by designing a weight matrix with a Gaussian kernel which is applied across the one-hot encoded expert labelmaps to obtain soft class probabilities. The SVLS weight matrix, w^{svls}, is obtained by taking the weights from a discrete spatial Gaussian kernel $G_{ND}(\vec{x}; \sigma) = \frac{1}{(\sqrt{2\pi\sigma^2})^N} e^{-\frac{|\vec{x}|^2}{2\sigma^2}}$, with σ set to 1. The center weight is replaced by the sum of the surrounding weights, and we then normalize all weights by dividing with the center weight such that the center weight is equal to one. The motivation of this weight matrix is based on the intuition of giving an equal contribution to the central label and all surrounding labels combined. In most cases, the central class label would define which class is assigned the highest label probability in the SVLS soft labels. However, note that the weight matrix has an interesting property, which concerns cases where the central pixel has a class label in the expert annotation that is different from another label that may be present in all surrounding pixels. Such isolated, central class labels can be safely assumed to correspond to label noise, and in such cases the weights on the surrounding labels would result in an equal class probability.

Figure 2(a) shows the 2D and 3D versions of SVLS weights. The weight matrix convolves over the one-hot labels to obtain the SVLS soft labels.

$$p^{svls}_{c(i,j,k)} = \frac{1}{\sum w^{svls}} \sum_{x=1}^{3} \sum_{y=1}^{3} \sum_{z=1}^{3} p_{c(i-x,j-y,k-z)} w^{svls}_{(x,y,z)} \qquad (2)$$

where $p_c^{svls}(i,j,k)$ are soft probabilities after passing proposed weight in the position of (i,j,k) of the one-hot target for class c. A single 'replicate' padding is required to maintain label consistency around the image. A visual illustration of calculating SVLS weights is presented in Fig. 1(a). The resulting SVLS label probabilities for each class are similar to one-hot within homogeneous areas and thus preserve high confidence in non-ambiguous regions while uncertainty is captured near object boundaries. Figure 1(b) shows a visualization comparing the label probabilities of one-hot, LS and SVLS for brain tumor example, demonstrating how SVLS captures uncertainty at the tumor boundaries. The resulting SVLS soft labels are then simply plugged into the standard CE loss:

$$CE^{svls} = -\sum_{c=1}^{N} p_c^{svls} \log(\hat{p}_c) \qquad (3)$$

Figure 2(b) illustrates two examples of SVLS labels over LS and one-hot labels in different toy structures. LS and one-hot ignore the local structure where SVLS considers the spatial variation and assigns higher probability to the center pixel in example 1 to be part of the red class based on the spatial context.

2.1 Multi-rater SVLS

In cases where multiple expert annotations are available per image, we introduce a simple extension to SVLS which aggregates uncertainty information across annotations (mSVLS). Here we apply SVLS to each annotation independently before averaging the resulting soft label probabilities. This captures the uncertainty within each expert segmentation and also the variation across the different raters. If there are D number of experts and $p_{c(j)}^{svls}$ is the SVLS target probability for the jth rater, and D_c number of raters that annotate it as a class then mSVLS probabilities are obtained by simple averaging:

$$\overline{p}_c^{svls} = \frac{1}{D} \sum_{j=1}^{D_c} p_{c(j)}^{svls} \qquad (4)$$

Figure 3 illustrates and compares mSVLS with averaging the one-hot encodings of expert annotations (mOH). The toy example demonstrates how important information about nearby class labels is lost in mOH soft labels, while mSVLS is able to capture the uncertainty across classes and experts.

3 Experiments

3.1 Datasets

For experimental validation of SVLS, we use three multi-class segmentation datasets including BraTS 2019, KiTS 2019, ProstateX plus one multi-rater dataset, LIDC-IDRI, for binary segmentation. The datasets are described in more detail in the following.

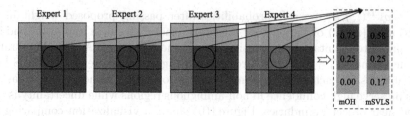

Fig. 3. A toy example showing how to aggregate SVLS soft labels over multiple expert annotations. We apply SVLS to each expert annotation and then average the soft labels to capture inter-rater variability (mSVLS). This is compared to a pixel-wise, independent aggregation of multi-rater one-hot (mOH) labels which would assign zero probability to the blue class despite its presence in the immediate neighborhood.

BraTS 2019. The BraTS dataset consists of multi-channel MRI for the task of segmenting glioma tumors. There are 335 cases with corresponding annotations in the 2019 training set [2–4]. Each case consists of four MR sequences including FLAIR, T1, T1-contrast, and T2 with image sizes of $155 \times 240 \times 240$. The reference annotations include the necrotic and non-enhancing core, edema and enhancing tumor. All scans are provided pre-processed with skull-stripping, co-registration to a fixed template, and resampling to $1\,mm^3$ isotropic voxel resolution. We conduct all experiments by splitting the dataset into 269/66 for training and testing. The images are center cropped to size $128 \times 192 \times 192$.

KiTS 2019. The kidney tumor segmentation challenge (KiTS) [11] consists of 210 CT scans with varying resolutions and image sizes. We resample all cases to a common resolution of $3.22 \times 1.62 \times 1.62\,mm$ and center crop to image size $80 \times 160 \times 160$. We split the dataset into 168/42 for training and testing. The annotations include the kidney and the tumor regions.

ProstateX. The SPIE-AAPM-NCI ProstateX challenge dataset [18] consists of 98 T2w MRI scans and corresponding annotations for four anatomical prostate zones including the peripheral zone (PZ), transition zone (TZ), distal prostatic urethra (DPU), anterior fibromuscular stroma (AFS). All image volumes are resampled into $3 \times 0.5 \times 0.5\,mm$ and center cropped to image size $24 \times 320 \times 320$. The dataset is split into 78/20 for training and testing.

LIDC-IDRI. The LIDC-IDRI [1] is a lung CT dataset for nodule segmentation. There are in total 1018 CT scans from which 887 scans contain 4 sets of annotations generated by 12 radiologists. We choose 669 cases for training and the remaining 218 cases for testing. Each CT volume is resampled to $1\,mm^3$ voxel spacing and image sizes of $90 \times 90 \times 90$ centered around the nodule annotation. The PyLIDC library[1] is used to perform all pre-processing steps.

---

[1] https://pylidc.github.io/.

3.2   Implementation Details and Baselines

We follow the common pre-processing and data augmentation techniques for all datasets and experiments. The images are center cropped and randomly rotated during data augmentation. A state-of-the-art 3D UNet [8] architecture is used to conduct all experiments with a baseline PyTorch implementation adopted from a publicly available repository[2]. We use Adam as the optimization method with a learning rate and weight decay set to 1×10^{-4}. For comparison, we train models on one-hot target labels and LS soft labels with three different values for the α parameter, namely 0.1, 0.2 and 0.3 (cf. Equation (1)).

4   Results

4.1   Evaluation Metrics

We evaluate the segmentation accuracy using the Dice Similarity Coefficient (DSC) and Surface DSC (SD) [23]. DSC $(= \frac{2|T \cap P|}{|T| + |P|})$ quantifies the overlap between the target reference segmentation T and predicted output P. SD assesses the overlap of object boundaries under a specified tolerance level. To evaluate model calibration, we calculate the Expected Calibration Error (ECE) [10], Thresholded Adaptive Calibration Error (TACE) [24] (with a threshold of 10^{-3}) and plot the reliability diagrams [22].

4.2   Multi-class Image Segmentation

We conduct experiments comparing a state-of-the-art neural network for multi-class image segmentation trained with and without LS and SVLS using CE loss as the training objective. The results are summarized in Table 1, Fig. 5(a–c) and Fig. 4. We observe a significant improvement of model calibration in terms of ECE, TACE, and confidence frequency plots as well as better segmentation accuracy for LS and SVLS over the baseline model trained with one-hot target labels. The improvement in the boundary regions is highlighted by the SD metric. In Table 1, the SD score is calculated with a tolerance level of 2 mm, and SVLS shows 2–4% improvement in accuracy over the baseline using one-hot labels across all three datasets, BraTS 2019, KiTS 2019 and ProstateX. SVLS and LS both improve model calibration seen by improved ECE scores with LS obtaining best ECE on BraTS and ProstateX. SVLS shows best results for model calibration under the TACE metric over all datasets.

The reliability diagrams also indicate better model calibration for SVLS as shown in Fig. 5(a–c). Optimal calibration between confidence and accuracy would be obtained when aligning with the dashed line (bottom row). For the baseline, we observe that the accuracy is always lower than the confidence, indicating that the model trained on one-hot labels yields overconfident predictions. Figure 4 visualizes the prediction and corresponding probability maps. The prediction probability of SVLS shows reasonable uncertainty in boundary regions between classes and anatomical regions.

---

[2] https://github.com/wolny/pytorch-3dunet

Table 1. Segmentation results for models trained with one-hot hard labels and LS and SVLS soft labels. Dice similarity coefficient (DSC), Surface DSC (SD), Expected Calibration Error (ECE), and Thresholded Adaptive Calibration Error (TACE) metrics are used to evaluate the segmentation accuracy and model calibration. Top two models with highest performance are highlighted as bold and best model is also underlined.

			One-hot	LS (0.1)	LS (0.2)	LS (0.3)	SVLS
BraTS 2019	DSC	WT	0.892 ± 0.074	0.893 ± 0.070	**0.896 ± 0.064**	0.893 ± 0.068	**0.894 ± 0.065**
		ET	0.814 ± 0.151	**0.822 ± 0.154**	0.817 ± 0.147	0.801 ± 0.186	0.816 ± 0.134
		TC	0.862 ± 0.126	**0.873 ± 0.130**	**0.863 ± 0.131**	0.858 ± 0.163	0.862 ± 0.119
	SD	WT	0.894 ± 0.074	0.913 ± 0.119	0.912 ± 0.120	**0.92 ± 0.113**	**0.940 ± 0.086**
		ET	0.930 ± 0.162	**0.950 ± 0.121**	0.943 ± 0.143	0.928 ± 0.159	**0.952 ± 0.107**
		TC	0.862 ± 0.179	**0.891 ± 0.168**	**0.881 ± 0.179**	0.872 ± 0.190	0.880 ± 0.163
	ECE/TACE		0.073/0.0041	**0.065/0.0025**	0.096/0.0049	0.146/0.0073	**0.063/0.0040**
KiTS 2019	DSC	Kidney	**0.924 ± 0.048**	**0.924 ± 0.040**	0.917 ± 0.052	0.922 ± 0.045	0.915 ± 0.044
		Tumor	0.472 ± 0.395	**0.496 ± 0.376**	0.461 ± 0.382	0.482 ± 0.382	**0.491 ± 0.382**
		Comp	0.698 ± 0.221	**0.710 ± 0.208**	0.689 ± 0.217	0.702 ± 0.213	**0.703 ± 0.213**
	SD	Kidney	0.962 ± 0.077	0.960 ± 0.065	0.943 ± 0.098	**0.967 ± 0.076**	0.963 ± 0.076
		Tumor	0.608 ± 0.393	**0.637 ± 0.353**	0.545 ± 0.38	0.617 ± 0.399	**0.634 ± 0.399**
		Comp	0.785 ± 0.235	**0.798 ± 0.209**	0.744 ± 0.239	0.792 ± 0.238	**0.799 ± 0.238**
	ECE/TACE		0.052/0.0043	**0.042/0.0032**	0.085/0.0063	0.134/0.0095	**0.036/0.0031**
ProstateX	DSC	PZ	**0.716 ± 0.087**	0.684 ± 0.097	0.694 ± 0.098	**0.709 ± 0.094**	0.706 ± 0.082
		TZ	0.850 ± 0.062	0.843 ± 0.071	0.850 ± 0.068	**0.850 ± 0.062**	**0.852 ± 0.056**
		DPU	**0.591 ± 0.169**	0.589 ± 0.191	0.579 ± 0.181	0.577 ± 0.208	**0.621 ± 0.163**
		AFS	**0.472 ± 0.110**	0.462 ± 0.097	0.426 ± 0.144	0.466 ± 0.160	**0.467 ± 0.133**
	SD	PZ	0.855 ± 0.106	0.840 ± 0.121	0.828 ± 0.112	**0.858 ± 0.098**	**0.877 ± 0.083**
		TZ	**0.948 ± 0.05**	0.920 ± 0.063	0.916 ± 0.075	**0.947 ± 0.031**	0.935 ± 0.041
		DPU	0.767 ± 0.170	0.792 ± 0.182	0.737 ± 0.188	**0.808 ± 0.205**	**0.796 ± 0.192**
		AFS	0.918 ± 0.099	0.888 ± 0.102	**0.930 ± 0.069**	0.900 ± 0.116	**0.930 ± 0.066**
	ECE/TACE		0.105/0.0025	**0.042/0.0019**	0.061/0.0038	0.106/0.0057	0.091/**0.0012**

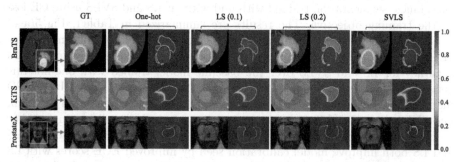

Fig. 4. Predicted segmentations with probability maps for BraTS, KiTS, and ProstateX for one-hot, LS and SVLS. We observe reasonable boundary uncertainty for SVLS while preserving high confidence within non-ambiguous regions.

4.3 Multiple Expert Annotations

To evaluate the performance of mSVLS, we run experiments by training models on different sets of expert annotations. The compared models are trained with individual expert annotations, all pairs of annotations, multi-rater one-hot labels (mOH) and mSVLS, evaluated against each available expert annotation,

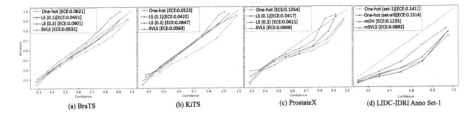

(a) BraTS   (b) KiTS   (c) ProstateX   (d) LIDC-IDRI Anno Set-1

Fig. 5. (a–c) Reliability diagrams showing calibration between confidence and accuracy for different models. LS and SVLS have lower expected calibration error (ECE). (d) Reliability diagram on the LIDC-IDRI dataset where multiple expert annotations are available. We show one-hot on annotation set-1, all, multi-rater one-hot (mOH) and mSVLS where the latter shows significantly improved calibration compared to others.

Table 2. Quantitative comparison for LIDC-IDRI with multiple expert annotations. Dice Similarity Coefficient (DSC), Surface DSC (SD), Expected Calibration Error (ECE), and Thresholded Adaptive Calibration Error (TACE) are calculated to compare the performance of one-hot, LS, and mSVLS. Top two models with highest performance are highlighted as bold and best model is also underlined.

		One-hot (Set 1)	One-hot (Set 2)	One-hot (Set 3)	One-hot (ALL)	mOH	mSVLS
DSC	Set 1	0.687 ± 0.181	0.676 ± 0.192	0.669 ± 0.206	**0.691 ± 0.175**	0.690 ± 0.180	**0.692 ± 0.171**
	Set 2	0.674 ± 0.185	0.652 ± 0.195	0.651 ± 0.218	**0.683 ± 0.173**	0.675 ± 0.188	**0.680 ± 0.183**
	Set 3	0.684 ± 0.179	0.670 ± 0.194	0.666 ± 0.205	0.686 ± 0.172	**0.687 ± 0.180**	**0.688 ± 0.181**
	Set 4	0.679 ± 0.182	0.655 ± 0.197	0.662 ± 0.213	**0.694 ± 0.172**	0.682 ± 0.183	**0.686 ± 0.174**
SD	Set 1	0.914 ± 0.171	0.892 ± 0.177	0.910 ± 0.192	**0.936 ± 0.145**	0.924 ± 0.158	**0.941 ± 0.132**
	Set 2	0.905 ± 0.172	0.880 ± 0.178	0.897 ± 0.202	**0.927 ± 0.150**	0.915 ± 0.157	**0.932 ± 0.139**
	Set 3	0.915 ± 0.171	0.890 ± 0.180	0.905 ± 0.198	**0.935 ± 0.153**	0.923 ± 0.162	**0.936 ± 0.148**
	Set 4	0.914 ± 0.168	0.884 ± 0.182	0.905 ± 0.198	**0.934 ± 0.148**	0.921 ± 0.156	**0.939 ± 0.134**
ECE/TACE	Set 1	0.141/0.0032	0.1457/0.0035	0.1646/0.0042	0.1314/0.0029	**0.1234/0.0022**	**0.0892/0.0028**
	Set 2	0.123/0.0037	0.1304/0.0041	0.1401/0.0044	0.1152/0.0033	**0.0993/0.0024**	**0.0692/0.0030**
	Set 3	0.1271/0.0031	0.1341/0.0039	0.1409/0.0035	0.1195/0.0030	**0.1053/0.0025**	**0.0748/0.0028**
	Set 4	0.1098/0.0029	0.1212/0.0039	0.1301/0.0033	0.1032/0.0025	**0.0948/0.0022**	**0.0653/0.0025**

separately. Table 2 shows the results for the metrics DSC, SD, ECE and TACE. mSVLS shows overall best performance in most cases. The model calibration is illustrated in Fig. 5(d) in terms of confidence frequency distribution (top) and ECE (bottom). In the reliability diagram, the curve for mSVLS is closer to optimal model calibration (dashed line).

Figure 6 indicates the qualitative segmentation performance and corresponding prediction probability map. mSVLS produces reasonable uncertainty at the boundary while being confident in non-ambiguous regions. The one-hot and mOH baselines show uniform confidence levels across the structure boundaries, ignoring spatial variability among the expert annotations.

5   Discussion

We propose a novel, simple yet effective approach for capturing uncertainty from expert annotations which also improves model calibration in semantic segmentation. Promising results are demonstrated on four different datasets, including

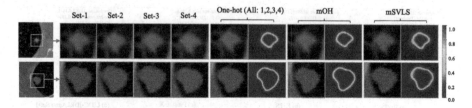

Fig. 6. Comparison of all four sets of annotations and corresponding CT scan (left five columns) and model predictions and probability maps for one-hot encoding (trained with the fusion of all sets), multi-rater one-hot (mOH), and multi-rater SVLS (mSVLS) on LIDC-IDRI dataset (right three pairs of columns, respectively). mSVLS shows reasonable boundary uncertainty and high confidence within the structure compared to the one-hot and mOH showing uniform confidence levels across structure boundaries.

CT and MRI data, and multi-class and binary segmentation tasks. We also demonstrate how SVLS can capture expert variation when multiple annotations are available. SVLS is straightforward to integrate into any existing segmentation approach, as it only requires a pre-processing on the one-hot encodings before training. Here, we trained all models with a cross-entropy loss, but other losses such as boundary losses [17] can be considered. We like to highlight that SVLS is complementary to other works on estimating uncertainty in image segmentation, and can be considered in combination, e.g., with approaches that incorporate uncertainty as part of the output predictions [5,19].

An interesting aspect that should be explored further is the effect of label smoothing on the separation of the learned latent representations for different classes. In [20], it was shown that traditional LS has a similar effect as contrastive learning pushing the latent representations away from each other. This may be interesting in the context of domain adaptation and robustness on variations in the input data, for example, when images at test time come from a different distribution (e.g., different scanner). The effect of SVLS on the learned latent representations and how it impacts generalization is part of future work.

Acknowledgements. This research has received funding from the European Research Council (ERC) under the European Union's Horizon 2020 research and innovation programme (grant agreement No 757173, project MIRA).

References

1. Armato III, S.G., et al.: Data from LIDC-IDRI. the cancer imaging archive. 2015. https://doi.org/10.7937/K9/TCIA.2015.LO9QL9SX
2. Bakas, S., et al.: Segmentation labels and radiomic features for the pre-operative scans of the TCGA-LGG collection. Cancer Imaging Arch. **286**, (2017)
3. Bakas, S., et al.: Advancing the cancer genome atlas glioma MRI collections with expert segmentation labels and radiomic features. Sci. Data **4**, 1–13 (2017)
4. Bakas, S., et al.: Identifying the best machine learning algorithms for brain tumor segmentation, progression assessment, and overall survival prediction in the brats challenge. arXiv preprint arXiv:1811.02629 (2018)

5. Baumgartner, C.F., et al.: PHiSeg: capturing uncertainty in medical image segmentation. In: Shen, D., et al. (eds.) MICCAI 2019. LNCS, vol. 11765, pp. 119–127. Springer, Cham (2019). https://doi.org/10.1007/978-3-030-32245-8_14

6. Boutry, N., Chazalon, J., Puybareau, E., Tochon, G., Talbot, H., Géraud, T.: Using separated inputs for multimodal brain tumor segmentation with 3D U-net-like architectures. In: Crimi, A., Bakas, S. (eds.) BrainLes 2019. LNCS, vol. 11992, pp. 187–199. Springer, Cham (2020). https://doi.org/10.1007/978-3-030-46640-4_18

7. Chorowski, J., Jaitly, N.: Towards better decoding and language model integration in sequence to sequence models. arXiv preprint arXiv:1612.02695 (2016)

8. Çiçek, Ö., Abdulkadir, A., Lienkamp, S.S., Brox, T., Ronneberger, O.: 3D U-net: learning dense volumetric segmentation from sparse annotation. In: Ourselin, S., Joskowicz, L., Sabuncu, M.R., Unal, G., Wells, W. (eds.) MICCAI 2016. LNCS, vol. 9901, pp. 424–432. Springer, Cham (2016). https://doi.org/10.1007/978-3-319-46723-8_49

9. Gal, Y., Ghahramani, Z.: Dropout as a bayesian approximation. arXiv preprint arXiv:1506.02157 (2015)

10. Guo, C., Pleiss, G., Sun, Y., Weinberger, K.Q.: On calibration of modern neural networks. arXiv preprint arXiv:1706.04599 (2017)

11. Heller, N., et al.: The kits19 challenge data: 300 kidney tumor cases with clinical context, CT semantic segmentations, and surgical outcomes. arXiv preprint arXiv:1904.00445 (2019)

12. Iglesias, J.E., Sabuncu, M.R.: Multi-atlas segmentation of biomedical images: a survey. Med. Image Anal. **24**(1), 205–219 (2015)

13. Jungo, A., Balsiger, F., Reyes, M.: Analyzing the quality and challenges of uncertainty estimations for brain tumor segmentation. Front. Neurosci. **14**, 282 (2020)

14. Jungo, A., et al.: On the effect of inter-observer variability for a reliable estimation of uncertainty of medical image segmentation. In: Frangi, A.F., Schnabel, J.A., Davatzikos, C., Alberola-López, C., Fichtinger, G. (eds.) MICCAI 2018. LNCS, vol. 11070, pp. 682–690. Springer, Cham (2018). https://doi.org/10.1007/978-3-030-00928-1_77

15. Kull, M., Nieto, M.P., Kängsepp, M., Silva Filho, T., Song, H., Flach, P.: Beyond temperature scaling: Obtaining well-calibrated multi-class probabilities with dirichlet calibration. In: Advances in Neural Information Processing Systems, pp. 12316–12326 (2019)

16. Laves, M.H., Ihler, S., Kortmann, K.P., Ortmaier, T.: Well-calibrated model uncertainty with temperature scaling for dropout variational inference. arXiv preprint arXiv:1909.13550 (2019)

17. Lee, H.J., Kim, J.U., Lee, S., Kim, H.G., Ro, Y.M.: Structure boundary preserving segmentation for medical image with ambiguous boundary. In: Proceedings of the IEEE/CVF Conference on Computer Vision and Pattern Recognition, pp. 4817–4826 (2020)

18. Litjens, G., Debats, O., Barentsz, J., Karssemeijer, N., Huisman, H.: Computer-aided detection of prostate cancer in MRI. IEEE Trans. Med. Imaging **33**(5), 1083–1092 (2014)

19. Monteiro, M., et al.: Stochastic segmentation networks: Modelling spatially correlated aleatoric uncertainty. arXiv preprint arXiv:2006.06015 (2020)

20. Müller, R., Kornblith, S., Hinton, G.E.: When does label smoothing help? In: Advances in Neural Information Processing Systems, pp. 4694–4703 (2019)

21. Nair, T., Precup, D., Arnold, D.L., Arbel, T.: Exploring uncertainty measures in deep networks for multiple sclerosis lesion detection and segmentation. Med. Image Anal. **59**, 101557 (2020)

22. Niculescu-Mizil, A., Caruana, R.: Predicting good probabilities with supervised learning. In: Proceedings of the 22nd International Conference on Machine Learning, pp. 625–632 (2005)
23. Nikolov, S., et al.: Deep learning to achieve clinically applicable segmentation of head and neck anatomy for radiotherapy. arXiv preprint arXiv:1809.04430 (2018)
24. Nixon, J., Dusenberry, M.W., Zhang, L., Jerfel, G., Tran, D.: Measuring calibration in deep learning. In: CVPR Workshops, pp. 38–41 (2019)
25. Pereyra, G., Tucker, G., Chorowski, J., Kaiser, Ł., Hinton, G.: Regularizing neural networks by penalizing confident output distributions. arXiv preprint arXiv:1701.06548 (2017)
26. Platt, J.: Probabilistic outputs for support vector machines and comparisons to regularized likelihood methods. Adv. Large Margin Classifiers 10(3), 61–74 (1999)
27. Ronneberger, O., Fischer, P., Brox, T.: U-net: convolutional networks for biomedical image segmentation. In: Navab, N., Hornegger, J., Wells, W.M., Frangi, A.F. (eds.) MICCAI 2015. LNCS, vol. 9351, pp. 234–241. Springer, Cham (2015). https://doi.org/10.1007/978-3-319-24574-4_28
28. Rottmann, M., Schubert, M.: Uncertainty measures and prediction quality rating for the semantic segmentation of nested multi resolution street scene images. In: Proceedings of the IEEE Conference on Computer Vision and Pattern Recognition Workshops (2019)
29. Szegedy, C., Vanhoucke, V., Ioffe, S., Shlens, J., Wojna, Z.: Rethinking the inception architecture for computer vision. In: Proceedings of the IEEE Conference on Computer Vision and Pattern Recognition, pp. 2818–2826 (2016)
30. Vaswani, A., et al.: Attention is all you need. In: Advances in Neural Information Processing Systems, pp. 5998–6008 (2017)
31. Vu, M.H., Nyholm, T., Löfstedt, T.: TuNet: end-to-end hierarchical brain tumor segmentation using cascaded networks. In: Crimi, A., Bakas, S. (eds.) BrainLes 2019. LNCS, vol. 11992, pp. 174–186. Springer, Cham (2020). https://doi.org/10.1007/978-3-030-46640-4_17
32. Warfield, S.K., Zou, K.H., Wells, W.M.: Simultaneous truth and performance level estimation (staple): an algorithm for the validation of image segmentation. IEEE Trans. Med. Imaging 23(7), 903–921 (2004)
33. Wenger, J., Kjellström, H., Triebel, R.: Non-parametric calibration for classification. In: International Conference on Artificial Intelligence and Statistics, pp. 178–190 (2020)
34. Wickstrøm, K., Kampffmeyer, M., Jenssen, R.: Uncertainty and interpretability in convolutional neural networks for semantic segmentation of colorectal polyps. Med. Image Anal. 60, 101619 (2020)

Quantile Regression for Uncertainty Estimation in VAEs with Applications to Brain Lesion Detection

Haleh Akrami[1(✉)], Anand Joshi[1], Sergul Aydore[2], and Richard Leahy[1]

[1] University of Southern California, Los Angeles, USA
{akrami,ajoshi}@usc.edu, leahy@sipi.usc.edu
[2] Amazon Web Service, New York, USA
sergulaydore@gmail.com

Abstract. The Variational AutoEncoder (VAE) has become one of the most popular models for anomaly detection in applications such as lesion detection in medical images. The VAE is a generative graphical model that is used to learn the data distribution from samples and then generate new samples from this distribution. By training on normal samples, the VAE can be used to detect inputs that deviate from this learned distribution. The VAE models the output as a conditionally independent Gaussian characterized by means and variances for each output dimension. VAEs can therefore use reconstruction probability instead of reconstruction error for anomaly detection. Unfortunately, joint optimization of both mean and variance in the VAE leads to the well-known problem of shrinkage or underestimation of variance. We describe an alternative VAE model, Quantile-Regression VAE (QR-VAE), that avoids this variance shrinkage problem by estimating conditional quantiles for the given input image. Using the estimated quantiles, we compute the conditional mean and variance for input images under the Gaussian model. We then compute reconstruction probability using this model as a principled approach to outlier or anomaly detection. We also show how our approach can be used for heterogeneous thresholding of images for detecting lesions in brain images.

1   Introduction

Inference based on deep learning methods that do not take into account uncertainty can lead to over-confident predictions, particularly with limited training data [15]. Quantifying uncertainty is particularly important in critical applications such as clinical diagnosis, where a realistic assessment of uncertainty is essential in determining disease status and appropriate treatment. Here we address the important problem of learning uncertainty in order to perform statistically-informed inference.

This work is supported by the following grants: R01-NS074980, W81XWH-18-1-0614, R01-NS089212, and R01-EB026299.

© Springer Nature Switzerland AG 2021
A. Feragen et al. (Eds.): IPMI 2021, LNCS 12729, pp. 689–700, 2021.
https://doi.org/10.1007/978-3-030-78191-0_53

Unsupervised learning approaches such as the Variational autoencoder (VAE) [9] and its variants can approximate the underlying distribution of high-dimensional data. VAEs are trained using the variational lower bound of the marginal likelihood of data as the objective function. They can then be used to generate samples from the data distribution, where probabilities at the output are modeled as parametric distributions such as Gaussian or Bernoulli that are conditionally independent across output dimensions [9].

VAEs are popular for anomaly detection. Once the distribution of anomaly-free samples is learned, during inference we can compute the reconstruction error between a given image and its reconstruction to identify abnormalities [1]. Decisions on the presence of outliers in the image are often based on empirically chosen thresholds. An and Cho [2] proposed to use reconstruction probability rather than the reconstruction error to detect outliers. This allows a more principled approach to anomaly detection since inference is based on quantitative statistical measures and can include corrections for multiple comparisons.

For determining the reconstruction probability, we need to predict both conditional mean and variance using VAEs for each of the output dimensions. The estimated variance represents an aleatoric uncertainty associated with the conditional variance of the estimates given the data [15]. Estimating the variance is more challenging than estimating the mean in generative networks due to the unbounded likelihood [17]. In the case of VAEs, if the conditional mean network prediction is nearly perfect (zero reconstruction error), then maximizing the log-likelihood pushes the estimated variance towards zero in order to maximize likelihood. This also makes VAEs susceptible to overfitting the training data - near perfect reconstruction on the training data and very small uncertainty. However this near-zero variance does not reflect the true performance of the VAE on the test data. For this reason, near-zero variance estimates, with the log-likelihood approaching an infinite supremum, do not lead to a good generative model. It has been shown that there is a strong link between this likelihood blow-up and the mode-collapse phenomenon [13,15]. In fact, in this case, the VAE behaves much like a deterministic autoencoder [5].

While the classical formulation of VAEs allows both mean and variance estimates [9], because of the variance shrinkage problem, most if not all implementations of VAE, including the standard implementations in PyTorch and Tensorflow libraries, estimate only the mean with the variance assumed constant [17]. Here we describe an approach that overcomes the variance shrinkage problem in VAEs using quantile regression (QR) in place of variance estimation. We then demonstrate this new QR-VAE by computing reconstruction probabilities for a brain lesion detection task.

Related Work: A few recent papers have targeted the variance shrinkage problem. Among these, Detlefsen et al. 2019 [7] describe reliable estimation of the variance using Comb-VAE, a locally aware mini-batching framework that includes a scheme for unbiased weight updates for the variance network. In an alternative approach Stirn and Knowles 2020, [18] suggest treating variance variationally, assuming a Student's t-likelihood for the posterior to prevent optimization instabilities and assume a Gamma prior for the precision parameter of this distribution. The resulting Kullback–Leibler (KL) divergence induces gradients that prevent the variance from approaching zero [18].

Our Contribution: To obtain a probabilistic threshold and address the variance shrinkage problem, we suggest an alternative and attractively simple solution: assuming the output of the VAE has a Gaussian distribution, we quantify uncertainty in VAE estimates using conditional quantile regression (QR-VAE). The aim of conditional quantile regression [10] is to estimate a quantile of interest. Here we use these quantiles to compute variance, thus sidestepping the shrinkage problem. It has been shown that quantile regression is able to capture aleatoric uncertainty [19]. We demonstrate the effectiveness of our method quantitatively and qualitatively on simulated and brain MRI datasets. Our approach is computationally efficient and does not add any complication to training or sampling procedures. In contrast to the VAE loss function, the QR-VAE loss function does not have an interaction term between quantiles and therefore shrinkage does not happen.

2   Background

2.1   Variance Shrinkage Problem in Variational Autoencoders

Let $x_i \in \mathbb{R}^D$ be an observed sample of random variable X where $i \in \{1, \cdots, N\}$, D is the number of features and N is the number of samples; and let z_i be an observed sample for latent variable Z. Given a sample x_i representing the input data, the VAE is a probabilistic graphical model that estimates the posterior distribution $p_\theta(Z|X)$ as well as the model evidence $p_\theta(X)$, where θ are the generative model parameters [9]. The VAE approximates the posterior distribution of Z given X by a tractable parametric distribution and minimizes the ELBO(evidence lower bound) loss [2]. It consists of the encoder network that computes $q_\phi(Z|X)$, and the decoder network that computes $p_\theta(X|Z)$ [22], where ϕ and θ are model parameters. The marginal likelihood of an individual data point can be rewritten as follows:

$$\log p_\theta(x_i) = D_{KL}(q_\phi(Z|x_i), p_\theta(Z|x_i)) + L(\theta, \phi; x_i), \tag{1}$$

where

$$L(\theta, \phi; x_i) = \mathbb{E}_{q_\phi(Z|x_i)}[\log(p_\theta(x_i|Z))] - D_{KL}(q_\phi(Z|x_i)||p_\theta(Z)). \tag{2}$$

The first term (log-likelihood) in Eq. 2 can be interpreted as the *reconstruction loss* and the second term (KL divergence) as the *regularizer*. The total loss over all samples can be written as:

$$L(\theta, \phi, X) = L_{REC} + L_{KL} \tag{3}$$

where $L_{REC} := \mathbb{E}_{q_\phi(Z|X)}[\log(p_\theta(X|Z))]$ and $L_{KL} := D_{KL}(q_\phi(Z|X)||p_\theta(Z))$.

Assuming the posterior distribution is Gaussian and using a 1-sample approximation [17], the likelihood term simplifies to:

$$L_{REC} = \sum_i \frac{-1}{2} \log(\sigma_\theta^2(z_i)) - \frac{(x_i - \mu_\theta(z_i))^2}{2\sigma_\theta^2(z_i)} \tag{4}$$

where $p(Z) = \mathcal{N}(0, I)$ (I is identity matrix), $p_\theta(X|Z) = \mathcal{N}(X|\mu_\theta(Z), \sigma_\theta(Z))$, and $q_\phi(Z|X) = \mathcal{N}(Z|\mu_\phi(X), \sigma_\phi(X))$. Optimizing VAEs Optimizing VAEs over mean and variance with a Gaussian posterior is difficult [17]. If the model has sufficient capacity that there exists (ϕ, θ) for which $\mu_\theta(z)$ provides a sufficiently good reconstruction, then the second term pushes the variance to zero before the term $\frac{-1}{2} \log(\sigma_\theta^2(x_i)))$ catches up [5,17].

One practical example of this behavior is in speech processing applications [5]. The input is a spectral envelope which is a relatively smooth 1D curve. Representing this as a 2D image produces highly structured and simple training images. As a result, the model quickly learns how to accurately reconstruct the input. Consequently, reconstruction errors are small and the estimated variance becomes vanishingly small. Another example is 2D reconstruction of MRI images where the images from neighbouring 2D slices are highly correlated leading again to variance shrinkage [20]. To overcome this problem, variance estimation networks can be avoided using a Bernoulli distribution or by simply setting variance to a constant value [17].

2.2 Conditional Quantile Regression

In contrast to classical parameter estimation where the goal is to estimate the conditional mean of the response variable given the feature variable, the goal of quantile regression is to estimate conditional quantiles based on the data [23]. The most common application of quantile regression models is in cases in which a parametric likelihood cannot be specified [23].

Quantile regression can be used to estimate the conditional median (0.5 quantile) or other quantiles of the response variable conditioned on the input data. The α-th conditional quantile function is defined as $q_\alpha(x) := \inf\{y \in \mathbb{R} : F(y|X = x) \geq \alpha\}$ where $F = P(Y \leq y)$ is a strictly monotonic cumulative distribution function. Similar to classical regression analysis which estimates the conditional mean, the α-th quantile regression $(0 < \alpha < 1)$ seeks a solution to the following minimization problem for input x and output y [10,23]:

$$\arg \min_\theta \sum_i \rho_\alpha(y_i - f_\theta(x_i)) \tag{5}$$

where x_i are the inputs, y_i are the responses, ρ_α is the *check function* or *pinball loss* [10] and f is the model paramaterized by θ. The goal is to estimate the parameter θ of the model f. The *pinball loss* is defined as:

$$\rho_\alpha(y, \hat{y}) := \begin{cases} \alpha(y - \hat{y}) & \text{if } (y - \hat{y}) > 0 \\ (1-\alpha)(y - \hat{y}) & \text{otherwise.} \end{cases} \tag{6}$$

Due to its simplicity and generality, quantile regression is widely applicable in classical regression and machine learning to obtain a conditional prediction interval [16]. It can be shown that minimization of the loss function in Eq. 5 is equivalent to maximization of the likelihood function formed by combining independently distributed asymmetric Laplace densities [23]:

$$\arg\max_{\theta} L(\theta) = \frac{\alpha(1-\alpha)}{\sigma} \exp\left\{\frac{-\sum_i \rho_\alpha(y_i - f_\theta(x_i))}{\sigma}\right\}$$

where σ is the scale parameter. Individual quantiles can be shown to be ML estimates of Laplacian density. In this paper we estimate two quantiles jointly and therefore our loss function can be seen as a summation of two Laplacian likelihoods.

3   Proposed Approach: Uncertainty Estimation for Autoencoders with Quantile Regression (QR-VAE)

Instead of estimating the conditional mean and conditional variance directly at each pixel (or feature), the outputs of our QR-VAE are multiple quantiles of the output distributions at each pixel. This is achieved by replacing the Gaussian likelihood term in the VAE loss function with the quantile loss (check or pinball loss). For the QR-VAE, if we assume a Gaussian output, then only two quantiles are needed to fully characterize the Gaussian distribution. Specifically, we estimate the median and 0.15-th quantile, which corresponds to one standard deviation from the mean. Our QR-VAE ouputs, Q_L (low quantile) and Q_H (high quantile), are then used to calculate the mean and the variance. To find these conditional quantiles, fitting is achieved by minimization of the pinball loss for each quantile. The resulting reconstruction loss for the proposed model can be calculated as:

$$L_{REC} = \sum_i \rho_L(x_i - f_{\theta_L}(x_i)) + \sum \rho_H(x_i - f_{\theta_H}(x_i))$$

where θ_L and θ_H are the parameters of the models corresponding to the quantiles Q_L and Q_H, respectively. These quantiles are estimated for each output pixel or dimension.

We reduce the chance of quantile crossing by limiting the flexibility of independent quantile regression since both quantiles are estimated simultaneously rather than training separate networks for each quantile [16]. Note that the estimated quantiles share network parameters except for the last layer.

4   Experiments and Results

We evaluate our proposed approach on (i) A simulated dataset for density estimation and (ii) Lesion detection in a brain imaging dataset. We compare our results qualitatively and quantitatively, using KL divergence between the learned distribution and the original distribution, for the simulated data with Comb-VAE [17] and VAE as baselines. We compare our lesion detection results with the VAE which estimates both mean and variance. The area under the receiver operating characteristic curve (AUC) is used as a performance metric. We also performed the lesion detection task by directly estimating a 95% confidence interval.

4.1 Simulations

Following [17], we first evaluate variance estimation using VAE, Comb-VAE, and QR-VAE on a simulated dataset. The two moon dataset inspires the data generation process for this simulation[1]. First, we generate 500 points in $\mathbb{R}^2$ in a two-moon manner to generate a known two-dimensional latent space. These are then mapped to four dimensions (v_1, v_2, v_3, v_4) using the following equations:

$$v_1(z_1, z_2) = z_1 - z_2 + \epsilon\sqrt{0.03 + 0.05(3 + z_1)}$$

$$v_2(z_1, z_2) = z_1^2 - \frac{1}{2}z_2 + \epsilon\sqrt{0.03 + 0.03||z_1||_2}$$

$$v_3(z_1, z_2) = z_1 z_2 - z_1 + \epsilon\sqrt{0.03 + 0.05||z_1||_2}$$

$$v_4(z_1, z_2) = z_1 + z_2 + \epsilon\sqrt{0.03 + \frac{0.03}{0.02 + ||z_1||_2}}$$

where ϵ is sampled from a normal distribution. For more details about the simulation, please refer to [17][2]. After training the models, we first sample from z using a Gaussian prior, and input that sample to the decoder to generate parameters of the posterior $p_\theta(x|z)$, and then sample again from the posteriors using the estimated means and variances from the decoder. The distribution of these generated samples represents the learned distribution in the generative model.

In Fig. 1, we plot the pairwise joint distribution for the input data as well as the generated samples using various models. We used Gaussian kernel density estimation to model the distributions from 1000 samples in each case. We observe that the standard VAE underestimates the variance resulting in insufficient learning of the data distribution. The samples from our QR-VAE model capture a data distribution more similar to the ground truth than either standard VAE or Comb-VAE. Our model also outperforms VAE and Comb-VAE in terms of KL divergence between input samples and generated samples as can be seen in Fig. 1. The KL-divergence is calculated using universal-divergence, which estimates the KL divergence based on k-nearest-neighbor (k-NN) distance [21][3].

4.2 Unsupervised Lesion Detection

Finally, we demonstrate utility of the proposed QR-VAE for a medical imaging application of detecting brain lesions. Multiple automatic lesion detection

---

[1] https://scikit-learn.org/stable/modules/generated/sklearn.datasets.make_moons.

[2] https://github.com/SkafteNicki/john/blob/master/toy_vae.py.

[3] https://pypi.org/project/universal-divergence.

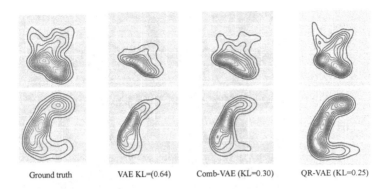

Fig. 1. Pairwise joint distribution of the ground truth and generated distributions. Top: v_1 vs. v_2 dimensions. Bottom: v_2 vs v_3 dimensions. From left to right: original distribution and distributions computed using VAE, Comb-VAE and QR-VAE, respectively. We also list the KL divergence between the learned distribution and the original distribution in each case.

approaches have been developed to assist clinicians in identifying and delineating lesions caused by congenital malformations, tumors, stroke or brain injury. The VAE is a popular framework among the class of unsupervised methods [3,6,14]. After training a VAE on a lesion free dataset, presentation of a lesioned brain to the VAE will typically result in reconstruction of a lesion-free equivalent. The error between input and output images can therefore be used to detect and localize lesions. However, selecting an appropriate threshold that differentiates lesion from noise is a difficult task. Furthermore, using a single global threshold across the entire image will inevitably lead to a poor trade-off between true and false positive rates. Using the QR-VAE, we can compute the conditional mean and variance of each output pixel. This allows a more reliable and statistically principled approach for detecting anomalies by thresholding based on computed p-values. Further, this approach also allows us to correct for multiple comparisons.

The network architectures of the VAE and QR-VAE are chosen based on previously established architectures [11]. Both the VAE and QR-VAE consist of three consecutive blocks of convolutional layer, a batch normalization layer, a rectified linear unit (ReLU) activation function and a fully-connected layer in the bottleneck for the encoder. The decoder includes three consecutive blocks of deconvolutional layers, a batch normalization layer and ReLU followed by the output layer that has 2 separate deconvolution layers (for each output) with sigmoid activations. For the VAE, the outputs represent mean and variance while for QR-VAE the outputs represent two quantiles from which the conditional mean and variance are computed at each voxel. The size of the input layer is $3 \times 64 \times 64$ where the first dimension represents three different MRI contrasts: T1-weighted, T2-weighted, and FLAIR for each image.

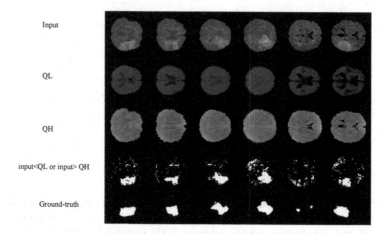

Input

QL

QH

input<QL or input> QH

Ground-truth

Fig. 2. Model-free lesion detection for ISLES dataset using $Q_L = Q_{0.025}$ and $Q_H = Q_{0.975}$. For lesion detection, we consider the pixels outside the $[Q_L, Q_H]$ interval as outliers. Estimated quantiles are the outputs of QR-VAE.

Training Data. For training we use 20 central axial slices of brain MRI datasets from a combination of 119 subjects from the Maryland MagNeTS study [8] of neurotrauma and 112 subjects from the TrackTBI-Pilot [24] dataset, both available for download from https://fitbir.nih.gov. We use 2D slices rather than 3D images to make sure we had a large enough dataset for training the VAE. These datasets contain T1, T2, and FLAIR images for each subject, and have sparse lesions. We have found that in practice both VAEs have some robustness to lesions in these training data so that they are sufficient for the network to learn to reconstruct lesion-free images as required for our anomaly detection task. The three imaging modalities (T1, T2, FLAIR) were rigidly co-registered within subject and to the MNI brain atlas reference and re-sampled to 1mm isotropic resolution. Skull and other non-brain tissue were removed using BrainSuite (https://brainsuite.org). Subsequently, we reshaped each sample into 64×64 dimensional images and performed histogram equalization to a lesion free reference.

Testing Data. We evaluated the performance of our model on a test set consisting of 20 central axial slices of 15 subjects from the ISLES (The Ischemic Stroke Lesion Segmentation) database [12] for which ground truth, in the form of manually-segmented lesions, is also provided. We performed similar preprocessing as for the training set.

Model-Free Anomaly Detection. For simplicity, we first performed the lesion detection task using the QR-VAE without the Gaussian assumption as shown in Fig. 2. We trained the QR-VAE to estimate the $Q_{0.025}$ and $Q_{0.975}$ quantiles. We then used these quantiles directly to threshold the input images for anomalies. This leads to a 5% (per pixel) false positive rate. This method

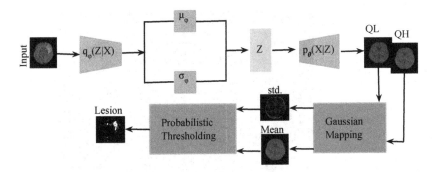

Fig. 3. Estimating two quantiles in the ISLES dataset using QR-VAE. Using the Gaussian assumption for the posterior, there is 1-1 mapping from these quantiles to mean and standard deviation.

is simple and avoids the need for validation data to determine an appropriate threshold. However, without access to p-values we are unable to determine a threshold that can be used to correct for multiple comparisons by controlling the false-disovery or family-wise error rate.

Gaussian Model for Anomaly Detection. In a second experiment, we trained a VAE with a Gaussian posterior and the QR-VAE as summarized in Fig. 3, in both cases estimating conditional mean and variance. Specifically, we estimated the $Q_{0.15}$ and $Q_{0.5}$ quantiles for the QR-VAE and mapped these values to pixel-wise mean and variance. We then used these means and variances to convert image intensities to p-values. Since we are applying the threshold separately at each pixel, there is the potential for a large number of false positives simply because of the number of tests performed. For example, thresholding at an $\alpha = 0.05$ significance level could result in up to 5% of the pixels being detected as anomalies. In practice the false positive rate is likely to be lower because of spatial correlations between pixels. To avoid an excessive number of false positives we threshold based on corrected p-values calculated to control the False Discovery Rate (FDR), that is the fraction of detected anomalies that are false positives [4]. We chose the thresholds corresponding to an FDR corrected p-value of 0.05. As shown in Fig. 4, the VAE underestimates the variance, so that most of the brain shows significant p-values, even with FDR correction. On the other hand, the QR-VAE's thresholded results detect anomalies that reasonably match the ground truth. To produce a quantitative measure of performance, we also computed the area under the ROC curve (AUC) for VAE and QR-VAE. To do this we first computed z-score images by subtracting the mean and normalizing by standard deviation. We then applied a median filtering with a 7×7 window. By varying the threshold on the resulting images and comparing it to ground truth, we obtained AUC values of 0.56 for the VAE and 0.94 for the QR-VAE. All quantitative measurements computed on a voxel-wise basis.

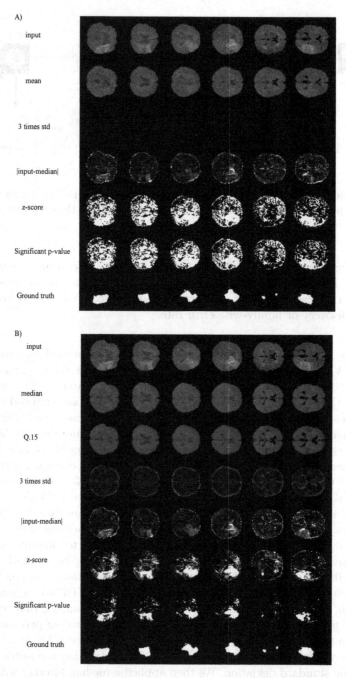

Fig. 4. Lesion detection for the ISLES dataset. A) VAE with mean and variance estimation B) QR-VAE. First, we normalize the error value using the pixel-wise model's estimates of mean and variance. The resulting z score is then converted to an FDR-corrected p-value and the images are thresholded at a significance level of 0.05. The bottom rows are ground truth based on expert manual segmentation of lesions.

5 Conclusion

VAE is a popular framework for anomaly detection in medical images, especially for unsupervised lesion detection [3,6,14]. VAEs can be used to estimate reconstruction probability instead of reconstruction error for anomaly detection tasks. For calculating reconstruction probability, VAE models the output as a conditionally independent Gaussian characterized by means and variances for each output dimension. Simultaneous estimation of the mean and the variance in VAE underestimates the true variance leading to instabilities in optimization [17]. For this reason, classical VAE formulations that include both mean and variance estimates are rarely used in practice. Typically, only the mean is estimated with variance assumed constant [17]. To address this problem in variance estimation, we proposed an alternative quantile-regression model (QR-VAE) for improving the quality of variance estimation. We used quantile regression and leveraged the Guassian assumption to obtain the mean and variance by estimating two quantiles. We showed that our approach outperforms VAE as well as a Comb-VAE which is an alternative approach for addressing the same issue, in a synthetic as well as real world dataset. Our approach also has a more straightforward implementation compared to Comb-VAE. As a demonstrative application, we used our QR-VAE model to obtain a probabilistic heterogeneous threshold for a brain lesion detection task. This threshold results in a completely unsupervised lesion (or anomaly) detection method that avoids the need for a labeled validation dataset for principled selection of an appropriate threshold to control the false discovery rate. Beyond the current application we note that Quantile regression is applicable to deep learning models for medical imaging applications beyond the VAE and anomaly detection as the pinball loss function is easy to implement and optimize and can be applied to a broader range of network architectures and cost functions.

References

1. Aggarwal, C.C.: Outlier analysis. Data Mining, pp. 237–263. Springer, Cham (2015). https://doi.org/10.1007/978-3-319-14142-8_8
2. An, J., Cho, S.: Variational autoencoder based anomaly detection using reconstruction probability. Spec. Lect. IE **2**(1), 1–18 (2015)
3. Baur, C., Wiestler, B., Albarqouni, S., Navab, N.: Deep autoencoding models for unsupervised anomaly segmentation in brain MR images. In: Crimi, A., Bakas, S., Kuijf, H., Keyvan, F., Reyes, M., van Walsum, T. (eds.) BrainLes 2018. LNCS, vol. 11383, pp. 161–169. Springer, Cham (2019). https://doi.org/10.1007/978-3-030-11723-8_16
4. Benjamini, Y., Hochberg, Y.: Controlling the false discovery rate: a practical and powerful approach to multiple testing. J. Roy. Stat. Soc. B (Methodological) **57**(1), 289–300 (1995)
5. Blaauw, M., Bonada, J.: Modeling and transforming speech using variational autoencoders. In: Morgan, N. (ed.) Interspeech 2016; 2016 Sep 8–12; San Francisco, CA, ISCA; 2016. pp. 1770–1774 (2016)

6. Chen, X., Konukoglu, E.: Unsupervised detection of lesions in brain MRI using constrained adversarial auto-encoders. arXiv preprint arXiv:1806.04972 (2018)
7. Detlefsen, N.S., Jørgensen, M., Hauberg, S.: Reliable training and estimation of variance networks. arXiv preprint arXiv:1906.03260 (2019)
8. Gullapalli, R.P.: Investigation of prognostic ability of novel imaging markers for traumatic brain injury (TBI). BALTIMORE UNIV MD, Technical Report (2011)
9. Kingma, D.P., Welling, M.: Auto-encoding variational bayes. arXiv preprint arXiv:1312.6114 (2013)
10. Koenker, R., Bassett Jr, G.: Regression quantiles. Econometrica: J. Econometric Soc. **46**, 33–50 (1978)
11. Larsen, A.B.L., Sønderby, S.K., Larochelle, H., Winther, O.: Autoencoding beyond pixels using a learned similarity metric. arXiv preprint arXiv:1512.09300 (2015)
12. Maier, O., et al.: ISLES 2015-a public evaluation benchmark for ischemic stroke lesion segmentation from multispectral MRI. Med. Image Anal. **35**, 250–269 (2017)
13. Mattei, P.A., Frellsen, J.: Leveraging the exact likelihood of deep latent variable models. In: Advances in Neural Information Processing Systems, pp. 3855–3866 (2018)
14. Pawlowski, N., et al.: Unsupervised lesion detection in brain CT using Bayesian convolutional autoencoders. Open Review (2018)
15. Reinhold, J.C., et al.: Validating uncertainty in medical image translation. arXiv preprint arXiv:2002.04639 (2020)
16. Rodrigues, F., Pereira, F.C.: Beyond expectation: deep joint mean and quantile regression for spatiotemporal problems. IEEE Trans. Neural Netw. Learn. Syst. **31**(12), 5377–5389 (2020)
17. Skafte, N., Jørgensen, M., Hauberg, S.: Reliable training and estimation of variance networks. In: Advances in Neural Information Processing Systems, pp. 6323–6333 (2019)
18. Stirn, A., Knowles, D.A.: Variational variance: Simple and reliable predictive variance parameterization. arXiv preprint arXiv:2006.04910 (2020)
19. Tagasovska, N., Lopez-Paz, D.: Single-model uncertainties for deep learning. In: Advances in Neural Information Processing Systems, pp. 6417–6428 (2019)
20. Volokitin, A., et al.: Modelling the distribution of 3D brain MRI using a 2D slice VAE. In: Martel, A.L., et al. (eds.) MICCAI 2020. LNCS, vol. 12267, pp. 657–666. Springer, Cham (2020). https://doi.org/10.1007/978-3-030-59728-3_64
21. Wang, Q., Kulkarni, S.R., Verdú, S.: Divergence estimation for multidimensional densities via k-nearest-neighbor distances. IEEE Trans. Inf. Theor. **55**(5), 2392–2405 (2009)
22. Wingate, D., Weber, T.: Automated variational inference in probabilistic programming. arXiv preprint arXiv:1301.1299 (2013)
23. Yu, K., Moyeed, R.A.: Bayesian quantile regression. Stat. Prob. Lett. **54**(4), 437–447 (2001)
24. Yue, J.K., et al.: Transforming research and clinical knowledge in traumatic brain injury pilot: multicenter implementation of the common data elements for traumatic brain injury. J. Neurotrauma **30**(22), 1831–1844 (2013)

A Probabilistic Framework for Modeling the Variability Across Federated Datasets

Irene Balelli[(✉)] [ID], Santiago Silva [ID], Marco Lorenzi [ID],
and for the Alzheimer's Disease Neuroimaging Initiative

Université Côte D'Azur, Inria Sophia Antipolis-Méditeranée, Epione Research
Project, 2004 Route des Lucioles, 06902 Valbonne, France
{irene.balelli,santiago-smith.silva-rincon,marco.lorenzi}@inria.fr

Abstract. We propose a novel federated learning paradigm to model
data variability among heterogeneous clients in multi-centric studies.
Our method is expressed through a hierarchical Bayesian latent variable
model, where client-specific parameters are assumed to be realization
from a global distribution at the master level, which is in turn estimated
to account for data bias and variability across clients. We show that
our framework can be effectively optimized through expectation maximization over latent master's distribution and clients' parameters. We
tested our method on the analysis of multi-modal medical imaging data
and clinical scores from distributed clinical datasets of patients affected
by Alzheimer's disease. We demonstrate that our method is robust when
data is distributed either in iid and non-iid manners: it allows to quantify
the variability of data, views and centers, while guaranteeing high-quality
data reconstruction as compared to the state-of-the-art autoencoding
models and federated learning schemes.

Keywords: Federated learning · Hierarchical generative model ·
Heterogeneity

1 Introduction

The analysis of medical imaging datasets for the study of neurodegenerative diseases, requires the joint modeling of multiple *views*, such as clinical scores and

Data used in preparation of this article were obtained from the Alzheimer's Disease
Neuroimaging Initiative (ADNI) database (adni.loni.usc.edu). As such, the investigators within the ADNI contributed to the design and implementation of ADNI and/or
provided data but did not participate in analysis or writing of this report. A complete
listing of ADNI investigators can be found at: http://adni.loni.usc.edu/wp-content/
uploads/how_to_apply/ADNI_Acknowledgement_List.pdf
This work received financial support by the French government, through the 3IA Côte
d'Azur Investments in the Future project managed by the National Research Agency
(ANR) with the reference number ANR-19-P3IA-0002, and by the ANR JCJC project
Fed-BioMed, ref. num. 19-CE45-0006-01. The authors are grateful to the OPAL infrastructure from Université Côte D'Azur for providing resources and support.

© Springer Nature Switzerland AG 2021
A. Feragen et al. (Eds.): IPMI 2021, LNCS 12729, pp. 701–714, 2021.
https://doi.org/10.1007/978-3-030-78191-0_54

multi-modal medical imaging data. These views are generated through different processes for data acquisition, as for instance Magnetic Resonance Imaging (MRI) or Positron Emission Tomography (PET). Each view provides a specific information about the pathology, and the joint analysis of all views is necessary to improve diagnosis, for the discovery of pathological relationships or for predicting the disease evolution. Nevertheless, the integration of *multi-views* data, accounting for their mutual interactions and their joint variability, presents a number of challenges.

When dealing with high dimensional and noisy data it is crucial to be able to extract an informative lower dimensional representation to disentangle the relationships among observations, accounting for the intrinsic heterogeneity of the original complex data structure. From a statistical perspective, this implies the estimation of a model of the joint variability across views, or equivalently the development of a joint *generative model*, assuming the existence of a common latent variable generating all views.

Several data assimilation methods based on dimensionality reduction have been developed [4], and successfully applied to a variety of domains. The main goal of these methods is to identify a suitable lower dimensional latent space, where some key characteristics of the original dataset are preserved after projection. The most basic among such methods is Principal Component Analysis (PCA) [7], where data are projected over the axes of maximal variability. More flexible approaches are Auto-Encoders [18], enabling to learn a low-dimensional representation minimizing the reconstruction error.

In some cases, Bayesian counterparts of the original dimensionality reduction methods have been developed, such as Probabilistic Principal Component Analysis (PPCA) [16], based on factor analysis, or, more recently, Variational Auto-Encoders (VAEs) [9]. VAEs are machine learning algorithms based on a generative function which allows probabilistic data reconstruction from the latent space. Encoder and decoder can be flexibly parametrized by neural networks (NNs), and efficiently optimized through Stochastic Gradient Descent (SGD). The added values of a Bayesian formulation is to provide a tool for sampling further observations from the estimated data distribution, and quantify the uncertainty of data and parameters. In addition, Bayesian model selection criteria such as the Watanabe-Akaike Information Criteria (WAIC) [5] allow to perform automatic model selection.

Multi-centric biomedical studies offer a great opportunity to significantly increase the quantity and quality of available data, hence to improve the statistical reliability of their analysis. Nevertheless, in this context, three main data-related challenges should be considered. 1) *Statistical heterogeneity* of *local datasets* (*i.e.* center-specific datasets): observations may be non-identically distributed across centers with respect to some characteristic affecting the output (*e.g.* diagnosis). Additional variability in local datasets can also come from data collection and acquisition bias [8]. 2) *Missing not at random views*: not all views are usually available for each center. 3) *Privacy* concerns: privacy-preserving laws are currently enforced to ensure the protection of personal data (*e.g.* the European General Data Protection Regulation - GDPR[1]), preventing the centralized analysis of data collected in multiple biomedical centers [3,6]. These limitations impose the need for extending data assimilation methods to handle decentralized heterogeneous data and missing views in local datasets.

Federated learning (FL) is an emerging paradigm specifically developed for the decentralized training of machine learning models. In order to guarantee data privacy, FL methods are conceived in such a way to avoid any sensitive data transfer among centers: raw data are processed within each center, which only shares local parameters with the master. The standard aggregation method in FL is Federated Averaging (FedAvg) [14], which combines local models via weighted averaging. However, this aggregation scheme is sensitive to statistical heterogeneity, which naturally arises in federated datasets [11], for example when dealing with multi-view data, or when data are not uniformly represented across data centers (e.g. non-iid distributed). In this case a faithful representation of the variability across centers is not guaranteed.

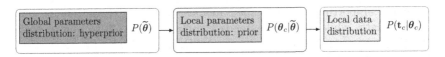

Fig. 1. Hierarchical structure of Fed-mv-PPCA. Global parameters $\widetilde{\theta}$ characterize the distribution of the local θ_c, which parametrize the local data distribution in each center.

We present here the Federated multi-view PPCA (Fed-mv-PPCA), a novel FL framework for data assimilation of heterogeneous multi-view datasets. Our framework is designed to account for the heterogeneity of federated datasets through a fully Bayesian formulation. Fed-mv-PPCA is based on a hierarchical dependency of the model's parameters to handle different sources of variability in the federated dataset (Fig. 1). The method is based on a linear generative model, assuming Gaussian latent variables and noise, and allows to account for missing views and observations across datasets. In practice, we assume that there exists an ideal global distribution of each parameter, from which local parameters are generated to account for the local data distribution in each center. The code developed in Python is publicly available at https://gitlab.inria.fr/epione/federated-multi-views-ppca.

---

[1] https://gdpr-info.eu/.

The paper is organized as follows: in Sect. 2 we provide a brief overview of the state-of-the-art and highlight the advancements provided by Fed-mv-PPCA. In Sect. 3 we describe Fed-mv-PPCA and in Sect. 4 we show results with applications to synthetic data and to data from the Alzheimer's Disease Neuroimaging Initiative dataset (ADNI). Section 5 concludes the paper with a brief discussion.

2   State of the Art

The method presented in this paper falls within two main categories: Bayesian methods for data assimilation, and FL methods for heterogeneous datasets. Several methods for dimensionality reduction based on generative models have been developed in the past years, starting from the seminal work of PPCA [16], to Bayesian Canonical Correlation Analysis (CCA) [10], which has been extended to include multiple views and missing modalities [13], up to more complex methods based on multi-variate association models [15], developed, for example, to integrate multi-modal brain imaging data and high-throughput genomics data. More recent methods for the probabilistic analysis of multi-views datasests include the multi channel Variational Autoencoder (mc-VAE) [1] and Multi-Omics Factor Analysis (MOFA) [2]. MOFA generalizes PPCA for the analysis of multiple-omics data types, supporting different noise models to adapt to continuous, binary and count data, while mc-VAE extends the classic VAE [9] to jointly account for multiple-views data. Additionally, mc-VAE can handle sparse datasets: data reconstruction in testing can be inferred from available views, if some are missing.

Despite the possibility of performing data assimilation and integrate multiple views offered by the above methods, these approaches have not been conceived to handle federated datasets.

Statistical heterogeneity is a key challenge in FL and, more generally, in multi-centric studies [11]. To tackle this problem, Li et al. recently proposed the FedProx algorithm [12], which improves FedAvg by allowing for partial local work (*i.e.* adapting the number of local epochs) and by introducing a proximal term to the local objective function to avoid divergence due to data heterogeneity. Other methods have been developed under the Bayesian non-parametric formalism, such as [19], where the local parameters of NNs are federated depending on neurons similarities.

Despite significant improvements in the handling of statistical heterogeneity have been made since the development of FedAvg, state-of-the-art FL methods are currently essentially formulated for training schemes based on stochastic gradient descent, with principal applications to NNs based models. Beyond the specific application to NNs, we still lack of a consistent Bayesian framework for the estimation of local and global data variability, as part of a global optimization model, while accounting for data heterogeneity. This provides us motivation for the development of Fed-mv-PPCA, a Bayesian framework for data assimilation from heterogeneous multi-views federated datasets.

3   Federated Multi-views PPCA

3.1   Problem Setup

We consider C independent centers. Each center $c \in \{1, \ldots, C\}$ disposes of its private local dataset $T_c = \{\mathbf{t}_{c,n}\}_n$, with $|T_c| = N_c$. We assume that a total of K distinct views have been measured across all centers, and we allow missing views in some local dataset (*i.e.* some local dataset could be incomplete, including only measurements for $K_c < K$ views). For every $k \in \{1, \ldots, K\}$, the dimension of the kth-view (*i.e.* the number of features defining the kth-view) is d_k, and we define $d := \sum_{k=1}^{K} d_k$. We denote by $\mathbf{t}_{c,n}^{(k)}$ the raw data of subject n in center c corresponding to the kth-view, hence $\mathbf{t}_{c,n} = \left(\mathbf{t}_{c,n}^{(1)}, \ldots, \mathbf{t}_{c,n}^{(K)} \right)$.

3.2   Modeling Assumptions

The main assumption at the basis of Fed-mv-PPCA is the existence of a hierarchical structure underlying the data distribution. In particular, we suppose that there exist global parameters $\widetilde{\boldsymbol{\theta}}$, following a distribution $P(\widetilde{\boldsymbol{\theta}})$, able to describe the global data variability, *i.e.* the ensemble of local datasets. For each center, local parameters $\boldsymbol{\theta}_c$ are generated from $P(\boldsymbol{\theta}_c|\widetilde{\boldsymbol{\theta}})$, to account for the specific variability of the local dataset. Finally, local data $\mathbf{t}_c$ are obtained from their local distribution $P(\mathbf{t}_c|\boldsymbol{\theta}_c)$. Given the federated datasets, Fed-mv-PPCA provides a consistent Bayesian framework to solve the inverse problem and estimate the model's parameters across the entire hierarchy.

We assume that in each center c, the local data corresponding to the kth-view, $\mathbf{t}_{c,n}^{(k)}$, follows the generative model:

$$\mathbf{t}_{c,n}^{(k)} = W_c^{(k)} \mathbf{x}_{c,n} + \boldsymbol{\mu}_c^{(k)} + \boldsymbol{\varepsilon}_c^{(k)}, \tag{1}$$

where $\mathbf{x}_{c,n} \sim \mathcal{N}(0, \mathbb{I}_q)$ is a q-dimensional latent variable, and $q < \min_k(d_k)$ is the dimension of the latent-space. $W_c^{(k)} \in \mathbb{R}^{d_k \times q}$ provides the linear mapping between latent space and observations for the kth-view, $\boldsymbol{\mu}_c^{(k)} \in \mathbb{R}^{d_k}$ is the offset of the data corresponding to view k, and $\boldsymbol{\varepsilon}_c^{(k)} \sim \mathcal{N}\left(0, \sigma_c^{(k)^2} \mathbb{I}_{d_k}\right)$ is a Gaussian noise for the kth-view. This formulation induces a Gaussian distribution over $\mathbf{t}_{c,n}^{(k)}$, implying:

$$\mathbf{t}_{c,n}^{(k)} \sim \mathcal{N}(\boldsymbol{\mu}_c^{(k)}, C_c^{(k)}), \tag{2}$$

where $C_c^{(k)} = W_c^{(k)} W_c^{(k)^T} + \sigma_c^{(k)^2} \mathbb{I}_{d_k} \in \mathbb{R}^{d_k \times d_k}$. Finally, a compact formulation for $\mathbf{t}_{c,n}$ (*i.e.* considering all views concatenated) can be derived from Eq. (1):

$$\mathbf{t}_{c,n} = W_c \mathbf{x}_{c,n} + \boldsymbol{\mu}_c + \Psi_c, \tag{3}$$

where $W_c, \boldsymbol{\mu}_c$ are obtained by concatenating all $W_c^{(k)}, \boldsymbol{\mu}_c^{(k)}$, and Ψ_c is a block diagonal matrix, where the kth-block is given by $\boldsymbol{\varepsilon}_c^{(k)}$. The local parameters describing the center-specific dataset thus are $\boldsymbol{\theta}_c := \left\{ \boldsymbol{\mu}_c^{(k)}, \ W_c^{(k)}, \sigma_c^{(k)^2} \right\}$. According to our hierarchical formulation, we assume that each local parameter in $\boldsymbol{\theta}_c$ is a realization of a common global prior distribution described by $\widetilde{\boldsymbol{\theta}} := \left\{ \widetilde{\boldsymbol{\mu}}^{(k)}, \sigma_{\widetilde{\mu}^{(k)}}, \widetilde{W}^{(k)}, \sigma_{\widetilde{W}^{(k)}}, \widetilde{\alpha}^{(k)}, \widetilde{\beta}^{(k)} \right\}$. In particular we assume that $\boldsymbol{\mu}_c^{(k)}$ and $W_c^{(k)}$ are normally distributed, while the variance of the Gaussian error, $\sigma_c^{(k)^2}$, follows an inverse-gamma distribution. Formally:

$$\boldsymbol{\mu}_c^{(k)} | \widetilde{\boldsymbol{\mu}}^{(k)}, \sigma_{\widetilde{\mu}^{(k)}} \sim \mathcal{N}\left(\widetilde{\boldsymbol{\mu}}^{(k)}, \sigma_{\widetilde{\mu}^{(k)}}^2 \mathbb{I}_{d_k} \right), \tag{4}$$

$$W_c^{(k)} | \widetilde{W}^{(k)}, \sigma_{\widetilde{W}^{(k)}} \sim \mathcal{MN}_{k,q}\left(\widetilde{W}^{(k)}, \mathbb{I}_{d_k}, \sigma_{\widetilde{W}^{(k)}}^2 \mathbb{I}_q \right), \tag{5}$$

$$\sigma_c^{(k)^2} | \widetilde{\alpha}^{(k)}, \widetilde{\beta}^{(k)} \sim \text{Inverse-Gamma}(\widetilde{\alpha}^{(k)}, \widetilde{\beta}^{(k)}), \tag{6}$$

where $\mathcal{MN}_{k,q}$ denotes the matrix normal distribution of dimension $d_k \times q$.

3.3   Proposed Framework

The assumptions made in Sect. 3.2 allow to naturally define an optimization scheme based on Expectation Maximization (EM) locally, and on Maximum Likelihood estimation (ML) at the master level (Algorithm 1). Figure 2 shows the graphical model of Fed-mv-PPCA.

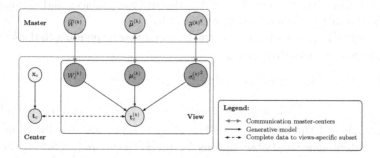

Fig. 2. Graphical model of Fed-mv-PPCA. Thick double-sided red arrows relate nodes which are shared between center and master, while plain black arrows define the relations between the local dataset and the generative model parameters. Grey filled circles correspond to raw data: the dashed double-sided arrow simply highlights the complexity of the dataset, composed by multiple views.

Algorithm 1: Fed-mv-PPCA algorithm

Input : Rounds R; Iterations I; Latent space dimension q
Output: Global parameters $\widetilde{\boldsymbol{\theta}}$

for $r = 1, \ldots, R$ do
   if $r = 1$ then
      Each center c initializes randomly local parameters $\boldsymbol{\theta}_c$;
      I iterations of EM estimation to optimize $\boldsymbol{\theta}_c$;
   else
      Each center initializes $\boldsymbol{\theta}_c$ using $P(\boldsymbol{\theta}_c|\widetilde{\boldsymbol{\theta}})$;
      I iterations of MAP estimation (EM + prior) to optimize $\boldsymbol{\theta}_c$ using
      $\widetilde{\boldsymbol{\theta}}$ as prior;
   end
   Each center c returns $\boldsymbol{\theta}_c$ to the master;
   The master collects $\boldsymbol{\theta}_c$, $c = 1, \ldots, C$ and estimates $\widetilde{\boldsymbol{\theta}}$ through ML;
   The master sends $\widetilde{\boldsymbol{\theta}}$ to all centers
end

With reference to Algorithm 1, the optimization of Fed-mv-PPCA is as follows:

Optimization. The master collects the local parameters $\boldsymbol{\theta}_c$ for $c \in \{1, \ldots, C\}$ and estimates the ML updated global parameters characterizing the prior distributions of Eqs. (4) to (6). Updated global parameters $\widetilde{\boldsymbol{\theta}}$ are returned to each center, and serve as priors to update the MAP estimation of the local parameters $\boldsymbol{\theta}_c$, through the M step on the functional $\mathbf{E}_{p(\mathbf{x}_{c,n}|\mathbf{t}_{c,n})} \ln \left(p(\mathbf{t}_{c,n}, \mathbf{x}_{c,n}|\boldsymbol{\theta}_c) p(\boldsymbol{\theta}_c|\widetilde{\boldsymbol{\theta}}) \right)$, where:

$$p(\mathbf{x}_{c,n}|\mathbf{t}_{c,n}) \sim \mathcal{N} \left(\Sigma_c^{-1} W_c^T \Psi_c^{-1}(\mathbf{t}_{c,n} - \boldsymbol{\mu}_c), \Sigma_c^{-1} \right), \Sigma_c := (\mathbb{I}_q + W_c^T \Psi_c^{-1} W_c)$$

and

$$\langle \ln \left(p(\mathbf{t}_{c,n}, \mathbf{x}_{c,n}|\boldsymbol{\theta}_c) \right) \rangle = -\sum_{n=1}^{N_c} \left\{ \sum_{k=1}^{K} \left[\frac{d_k}{2} \ln \left(\sigma_c^{(k)^2} \right) + \frac{1}{2\sigma_c^{(k)^2}} \|\mathbf{t}_{c,n}^{(k)} - \boldsymbol{\mu}_c^{(k)}\|^2 + \right. \right.$$
$$\frac{1}{2\sigma_c^{(k)^2}} tr \left(W_c^{(k)^T} W_c^{(k)} \langle \mathbf{x}_{c,n} \mathbf{x}_{c,n}^T \rangle \right)$$
$$\left. \left. -\frac{1}{\sigma_c^{(k)^2}} \langle \mathbf{x}_{c,n} \rangle^T W_c^{(k)^T} \left(\mathbf{t}_{c,i}^{(k),g} - \boldsymbol{\mu}_c^{(k)} \right) \right] + \frac{1}{2} tr \left(\langle \mathbf{x}_{c,n} \mathbf{x}_{c,n}^T \rangle \right) \right\},$$

Initialization. The latent-space dimension q, the number of local iterations I for EM and the number of communication rounds R (*i.e.* number of complete cycles centers-master) are user-defined parameters. For sake of simplicity, we set here the same number of local iterations for every center. Note that this constraint can be easily adapted to take into account systems heterogeneity among centers, as well as the size of each local dataset. At the first round, each center initializes randomly every local parameter and performs EM through I iterations, maximizing the functional $\langle \ln\left(p(\mathbf{t}_{c,n}, \mathbf{x}_{c,n}|\boldsymbol{\theta}_c)\right)\rangle$.

4   Applications

4.1   Materials

In the preparation of this article we used two datasets.

Synthetic Dataset (SD): we generated 400 observations from (1), consisting of $k = 3$ views of dimension $d_1 = 15, d_2 = 8, d_3 = 10$. Each view was generated from a common 5-dimensional latent space. We randomly chose parameters $W^{(k)}, \boldsymbol{\mu}^{(k)}, \sigma^{(k)}$. Finally, to simulate heterogeneity, a randomly chosen subsample composed by 250 observations was shifted in the latent space by a randomly generated vector: this allowed to simulate the existence of two distinct groups in the population.

Alzheimer's Disease Neuroimaging Initiative dataset (ADNI).[2]: we consider 311 participants extracted from the ADNI dataset, among cognitively normal (NL) (104 subjects) and patients diagnosed with AD (207 subjects). All participants are associated with multiple data views: cognitive scores including MMSE, CDR-SB, ADAS-Cog-11 and RAVLT (CLINIC), Magnetic resonance imaging (MRI), Fluorodeoxyglucose-PET (FDG) and AV45-Amyloid PET (AV45) images. MRI morphometrical biomarkers were obtained as regional volumes using the cross-sectional pipeline of FreeSurfer v6.0 and the Desikan-Killiany parcellation. Measurements from AV45-PET and FDG-PET were estimated by co-registering each modality to their respective MRI space, normalizing by the cerebellum uptake and by computing regional amyloid load and glucose hypometabolism using PetSurfer pipeline and the same parcellation. Features were corrected beforehand with respect to intra-cranial volume, sex and age using a multivariate linear model. Data dimensions for each view are: $d_{\text{CLINIC}} = 7$, $d_{\text{MRI}} = 41$, $d_{\text{FDG}} = 41$ and $d_{\text{AV45}} = 41$.

4.2   Benchmark

We compare our method to two state-of-the art data assimilation methods: Variational Autoencoder (VAE) [9] and multi-channel VAE (mc-VAE) [1]. In order to obtain the federated version of VAE and mc-VAE we used FedAvg [14], which is specifically conceived for stochastic gradient descent optimization.

---

[2] The ADNI project was launched in 2003 as a public-private partnership, led by Principal Investigator Michael W. Weiner, MD. The primary goal of ADNI was to test whether serial magnetic resonance imaging (MRI), positron emission tomography (PET), other biological markers, and clinical and neuropsychological assessments can be combined to measure the progression of early Alzheimer's disease (AD) (see www.adni-info.org for up-to-date information).

4.3   Results

We apply Fed-mv-PPCA to both SD and ADNI datasets, and quantify the quality of reconstruction and identification of the latent space with respect to the increasing number of centers, C, and the increasing data heterogeneity. We investigate also the ability of Fed-mv-PPCA in estimating the data variability and predicting the distribution of missing views. To this end, we consider 4 different scenarios of data distribution across multiple centers, detailed in Table 1.

Table 1. Distribution of datasets across centers.

Scenario	Description
IID	Data are iid distributed across C centers with respect to groups and all subjects dispose of a complete data raw
G	Data are non-iid distributed with respect to groups across C centers: $C/3$ centers includes subjects from both groups; $C/3$ centers only subjects from group 1 (AD in the ADNI case); $C/3$ centers only subjects from group 2 (NL for ADNI). All views have been measured in each center
K	$C/3$ centers dispose of all observations; in $C/3$ centers the second view (MRI for ADNI) is missing; in $C/3$ centers the third view (FDG for ADNI) is missing. Data are iid distributed across C centers with respect to groups
G/K	Data are non-iid distributed (scenario G) and there are missing views (scenario K)

Model Selection. The latent space dimension q is an user defined parameter, with the only constraint $q < \min_k\{d_k\}$. To assess the optimal q, we consider the IID scenario and let q vary. We perform 10 times a 3-fold Cross Validation (3-CV), and split the train dataset across 3 centers. For every test, we perform 100 rounds each consisting of 15 iterations for local optimization. The resulting models are compared using the WAIC criterion. In addition, we consider the Mean Absolute reconstruction Error (MAE) in an hold-out test dataset: the MAE is obtained by evaluating the mean absolute distance between real data and data reconstructed using the global distribution. Figure 3 shows the evolution of WAIC and MAE with respect to the latent space dimension.

Concerning the SD dataset, the WAIC suggests $q = 5$ latent dimensions, hence demonstrating the ability of Fed-mv-PPCA to correctly recover the ground truth latent space dimension used to generate the data. Analogously, the MAE improves drastically up to the dimension $q = 5$, and subsequently stabilizes. For ADNI, the MAE improves for increasing latent space dimensions, and we obtain the best WAIC score for $q = 6$, suggesting that a high-capacity model is preferable to describe this larger dimensional dataset. Despite the agreement of

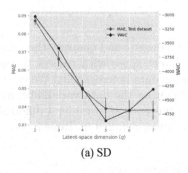
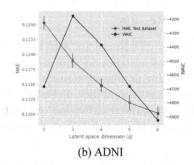

(a) SD   (b) ADNI

Fig. 3. WAIC score and MAE for (a) the SD dataset and (b) the ADNI dataset. In both figures, the left y-axis scaling describes the MAE while the right y-axis scaling corresponds to the WAIC score.

MAE and WAIC for both datasets, the WAIC has the competitive advantage of providing a natural and automatic model selection measure in Bayesian models, which does not require testing data, conversely to MAE.

In the following experiments, we set the latent space dimension $q = 5$ for the SD dataset and $q = 6$ for the ADNI dataset.

Increasing Heterogeneity Across Datasets. To test the robustness of Fed-mv-PPCA's results, for each scenario of Table 1, we split the global dataset in C centers, hence we perform 3-CV in each center to obtain local train and test datasets. We compare our method to VAE and mc-VAE. To keep the modeling setup consistent across methods, both auto-encoders were tested by considering linear encoding and decoding mappings [1]. For all methods we consider the MAE in both the train and test datasets, as well as the accuracy score in the Latent Space (LS) discriminating the groups (synthetically defined in SD or corresponding to the clinical diagnosis in ADNI). The classification was performed via Linear Discriminant Analysis (LDA) on the individual projection of test data in the latent space. In what follows we present a detailed description of results corresponding to the ADNI dataset. Results for the SD dataset are in line with what we observe for ADNI, and confirm that our method outperforms VAE and mc-VAE both in reconstruction and in discrimination (not shown for space limitations).

IID Distribution. We consider the IID scenario and split the train dataset across 1 to 6 centers. Table 2 shows that results from Fed-mv-PPCA are stable when passing from a centralized to a federated setting, and when considering an increasing number of centers C. We only observe a degradation of the MAE in the train dataset, but this does not affect the performance of Fed-mv-PPCA in reconstructing the test data. Moreover, irrespective of the number of training centers, Fed-mv-PPCA outperforms VAE and mc-VAE both in reconstruction and in preserving subjects separation in the latent space.

Table 2. Heterogeneous distribution of ADNI dataset.

Scenario	Centers	Method	MAE train	MAE test	Accuracy in LS
IID	1	**Fed-mv-PPCA**	**0.0804±0.0003**	**0.1113±0.0012**	**0.8839±0.0293**
		VAE	0.1061±0.0277	0.1350±0.0380	0.7364±0.0246
		mc-VAE	0.1392±0.0197	0.1678±0.0279	0.8327±0.0303
	3	**Fed-mv-PPCA**	**0.1059±0.0019**	**0.1102±0.0011**	**0.8962±0.0181**
		VAE	0.1183±0.0355	0.1206±0.0340	0.8681±0.0170
		mc-VAE	0.1606±0.0234	0.1567±0.0216	0.8746±0.0084
	6	**Fed-mv-PPCA**	**0.1258±0.0041**	**0.1116±0.0014**	**0.8930±0.0179**
		VAE	0.1340±0.0433	0.1176±0.0342	0.8071±0.0339
		mc-VAE	0.1837±0.0281	0.1569±0.0200	0.8811±0.0236
G	3	**Fed-mv-PPCA**	**0.1090±0.0041**	**0.1112±0.0013**	**0.8586±0.0272**
		VAE	0.1185±0.0372	0.1194±0.0359	0.7588±0.0581
		mc-VAE	0.1654±0.0262	0.1613±0.0251	0.7985±0.0522
	6	**Fed-mv-PPCA**	**0.1312±0.0113**	**0.1126±0.0014**	**0.8538±0.0354**
		VAE	0.1386±0.0453	0.1188±0.0360	0.7608±0.0492
		mc-VAE	0.1909±0.0323	0.1600±0.0238	0.7872±0.0476
K	3	Fed-mv-PPCA	0.1056±0.0118	0.1300±0.0154	0.8713±0.0227
	6		0.1220±0.0108	0.1287±0.0103	0.8642±0.0162
G/K	3	Fed-mv-PPCA	0.1020±0.0087	0.1301±0.0110	0.7098±0.0329
	6		0.1246±0.0147	0.1313±0.0105	0.7172±0.0315

Heterogeneous Distribution. We simulate an increasing degree of heterogeneity in 3 to 6 local datasets, to further challenge the models in properly recovering the global data. In particular, we consider both a non-iid distribution of subjects across centers, and missing not at random views in some local dataset. It is worth noting that scenarios implying datasets with missing views cannot be handled by VAE nor by mc-VAE, hence in these cases we reported only results obtained with our method.

In Table 2 we report the average MAEs and Accuracy in the latent space for each scenario, obtained over 10 tests for the ADNI dataset. Fed-mv-PPCA is robust despite an increasing degree of heterogeneity in the local datasests. We observe a slight deterioration of the MAE in the test dataset in the more challenging non-iid cases (scenarios K and G/K), while we note a drop of the classification accuracy in the most heterogeneous setup (G/K). Nevertheless, Fed-mv-PPCA demostrates to be more stable and to perform better than VAE and mc-VAE when statistical heterogeneity is introduced.

Figure 4 (a) shows the sampling posterior distribution of the latent variables, while in Fig. 4 (b) we plot the predicted global distribution of the corresponding original space against observations, for the G/K scenario and considering 3 training centers. We notice that the variability of centers is well captured, in spite of the heterogeneity of the distribution in the latent space. In particular center 2 and center 3 have two clearly distinct means: this is due to the fact that subjects in these centers belong to two distinct groups (AD in center 2 and NL in center 3). Despite this, Fed-mv-PPCA is able to reconstruct correctly all views,

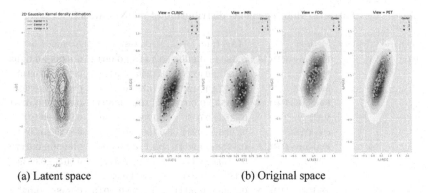

(a) Latent space   (b) Original space

Fig. 4. G/K scenario. First two dimensions for (a) sampling from posterior distribution of latent variables $\mathbf{x}_{c,n}$, and (b) predicted distribution $\mathbf{t}_{c,n}^{(k)}$ against real data.

even if 2 views are completely missing in some local datasets (MRI is missing in center 2 and FDG in center 3).

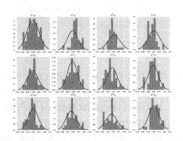

Fig. 5. G/K scenario. Predicted testing distribution (blue curve) of sample features of the missing MRI view against real data (histogram).

After convergence of Fed-mv-PPCA, each center is supplied with global distributions for each parameter: data corresponding to each view can therefore be simulated, even if some are missing in the local dataset. Considering the same simulation in the challenging G/K scenario as in Fig. 4, in Fig. 5 we plot the global distribution of some randomly selected features of a missing imaging view in the test center, against ground truth density histogram, from the original data. The global distribution provides an accurate description of the missing MRI view.

5   Conclusions

In spite of the large amount of currently available multi-site biomedical data, we still lack of reliable analysis methods to be applied in multi-centric applications. To tackle this challenge, Fed-mv-PPCA proposes a hierarchical generative model to perform data assimilation of federated heterogeneous multi-view data. The Bayesian approach allows to naturally handle statistical heterogeneity across centers and missing views in local datasets, while providing an interpretable model of data variability. Our applications demonstrate that Fed-mv-PPCA is robust with respect to an increasing degree of heterogeneity across training centers, and provides high-quality data reconstruction, outperforming competitive methods in all scenarios. Further extensions of this work will focus on identifying formal privacy guarantees for Fed-mv-PPCA, to prevent potential private information leakage from the shared statistics, in particular in case of small local datasets sizes and/or in presence of outliers. To this end, an extension of the proposed framework including Bayesian differential privacy [17] can be foreseen. Other improvements of Fed-mv-PPCA will focus on accounting for sparsity on the reconstruction weights.

References

1. Antelmi, L., Ayache, N., Robert, P., Lorenzi, M.: Sparse multi-channel variational autoencoder for the joint analysis of heterogeneous data. In: Proceedings of the 36th International Conference on Machine Learning, ICML 2019. Proceedings of Machine Learning Research, vol. 97, 9-15 June 2019, Long Beach, California, USA, pp. 302–311. PMLR (2019). http://proceedings.mlr.press/v97/antelmi19a.html
2. Argelaguet, R., et al.: Multi-omics factor analysis-a framework for unsupervised integration of multi-omics data sets. Mol. Syst. Biol. **14**(6), e8124 (2018)
3. Chassang, G.: The impact of the EU general data protection regulation on scientific research. Ecancermedical sci. **11**, (2017)
4. Cunningham, J.P., Ghahramani, Z.: Linear dimensionality reduction: survey, insights, and generalizations. J. Mach. Learn. Res. **16**(1), 2859–2900 (2015)
5. Gelman, A., Hwang, J., Vehtari, A.: Understanding predictive information criteria for bayesian models. Stat. Comput. **24**(6), 997–1016 (2014)
6. Iyengar, A., Kundu, A., Pallis, G.: Healthcare informatics and privacy. IEEE Internet Comput. **22**(2), 29–31 (2018)
7. Jolliffe, I.T.: Principal components in regression analysis. In: Principal component analysis, pp. 129–155. Springer, New York (1986) https://doi.org/10.1007/978-1-4757-1904-8_8
8. Kalter, J., Sweegers, M.G., Verdonck-de Leeuw, I.M., Brug, J., Buffart, L.M.: Development and use of a flexible data harmonization platform to facilitate the harmonization of individual patient data for meta-analyses. BMC Res. Notes **12**(1), 164 (2019)
9. Kingma, D.P., Welling, M.: Stochastic gradient VB and the variational autoencoder. In: Second International Conference on Learning Representations. In: ICLR, vol. 19 (2014)
10. Klami, A., Virtanen, S., Kaski, S.: Bayesian canonical correlation analysis. J. Mach. Learn. Res. **14**, 965–1003 (2013)
11. Li, T., Sahu, A.K., Talwalkar, A., Smith, V.: Federated learning: challenges, methods, and future directions. IEEE Signal Process. Mag. **37**(3), 50–60 (2020)
12. Li, T., Sahu, A.K., Zaheer, M., Sanjabi, M., Talwalkar, A., Smith, V.: Federated optimization in heterogeneous networks. arXiv preprint arXiv:1812.06127 (2018)
13. Matsuura, T., Saito, K., Ushiku, Y., Harada, T.: Generalized bayesian canonical correlation analysis with missing modalities. In: Proceedings of the European Conference on Computer Vision (ECCV)(2018)
14. McMahan, B., Moore, E., Ramage, D., Hampson, S., y Arcas, B.A.: Communication-efficient learning of deep networks from decentralized data. In: Artificial Intelligence and Statistics, pp. 1273–1282. PMLR (2017)
15. Shen, L., Thompson, P.M.: Brain imaging genomics: integrated analysis and machine learning. Proc. IEEE **108**(1), 125–162 (2019)

16. Tipping, M.E., Bishop, C.M.: Probabilistic principal component analysis. J. Royal Stat. Soc. Ser. B (Statistical Methodology) **61**(3), 611–622 (1999)
17. Triastcyn, A., Faltings, B.: Federated learning with bayesian differential privacy. In: 2019 IEEE International Conference on Big Data (Big Data), pp. 2587–2596. IEEE (2019)
18. Wang, Y., Yao, H., Zhao, S.: Auto-encoder based dimensionality reduction. Neurocomputing **184**, 232–242 (2016)
19. Yurochkin, M., Agarwal, M., Ghosh, S., Greenewald, K., Hoang, N., Khazaeni, Y.: Probabilistic federated neural matching (2018)

Is Segmentation Uncertainty Useful?

Steffen Czolbe[1]([✉]), Kasra Arnavaz[1], Oswin Krause[1], and Aasa Feragen[2]

[1] Department of Computer Science, University of Copenhagen, Copenhagen, Denmark
{per.sc,kasra,oswin.krause}@di.ku.dk
[2] Technical University of Denmark, DTU Compute, Kongens Lyngby, Denmark
afhar@dtu.dk

Abstract. Probabilistic image segmentation encodes varying prediction confidence and inherent ambiguity in the segmentation problem. While different probabilistic segmentation models are designed to capture different aspects of segmentation uncertainty and ambiguity, these modelling differences are rarely discussed in the context of applications of uncertainty. We consider two common use cases of segmentation uncertainty, namely assessment of segmentation quality and active learning. We consider four established strategies for probabilistic segmentation, discuss their modelling capabilities, and investigate their performance in these two tasks. We find that for all models and both tasks, returned uncertainty correlates positively with segmentation error, but does not prove to be useful for active learning.

Keywords: Image segmentation · Uncertainty quantification · Active learning

1 Introduction

Image segmentation – the task of delineating objects in images – is one of the most crucial tasks in image analysis. As image acquisition methods can introduce noise, and experts disagree on ground truth segmentations in ambiguous cases, predicting a single segmentation mask can give a false impression of certainty. Uncertainty estimates inferred from the segmentation model can give some insight into the confidence of any particular segmentation mask, and highlight areas of likely segmentation error to the practitioner. It adds transparency to the segmentation algorithm and communicates this uncertainty to the user. This is particularly important in medical imaging, where segmentation is often used to understand and treat disease. Consequently, quantification of segmentation uncertainty has become a popular topic in biomedical imaging [6,11].

Training segmentation networks requires large amounts of annotated data, which are costly and cumbersome to attain. Active learning aims to save the

---

Code available at github.com/SteffenCzolbe/probabilistic_segmentation.

S. Czolbe and K. Arnavaz—contributed equally.

© Springer Nature Switzerland AG 2021
A. Feragen et al. (Eds.): IPMI 2021, LNCS 12729, pp. 715–726, 2021.
https://doi.org/10.1007/978-3-030-78191-0_55

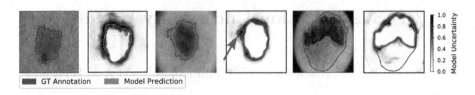

Fig. 1. Segmentation uncertainty is often interpreted as probable segmentation error, as seen near the lesion boundary in the first two examples. In the third example, however, model bias leads to a very certain, yet incorrect segmentation.

annotator's time by employing an optimal data gathering strategy. Some active learning methods use uncertainty estimates to select the next sample to annotate [7,9,10]. While several potential such data gathering strategies exist [13,16], a consistent solution remains to be found [8].

While several methods have been proposed to quantify segmentation uncertainty [4,6,11], it is rarely discussed what this uncertainty represents, whether it matches the user's interpretation, and if it can be used to formulate a data-gathering strategy. We compare the performance of several well-known probabilistic segmentation algorithms, assessing the quality and use cases of their uncertainty estimates. We consider two segmentation scenarios: An unambiguous one, where annotators agree on one underlying true segmentation, and an ambiguous one, where a set of annotators provide potentially strongly different segmentation maps, introducing variability in the ground truth annotation.

We investigate the degree to which the inferred uncertainty correlates with segmentation error, as this is how reported segmentation uncertainty would typically be interpreted by practitioners. We find that uncertainty estimates of the models coincide with likely segmentation errors and strongly correlate with the uncertainty of a set of expert annotators. Surprisingly, the model architecture used does not have a strong influence on the quality of estimates, with even a deterministic U-Net [12] giving good pixel-level uncertainty estimates.

Second, we study the potential for uncertainty estimates to be used for selecting samples for annotation in active learning. Reducing the cost of data annotation is of utmost importance in biomedical imaging, where data availability is fast-growing, while annotation availability is not. We find that there are many pitfalls to an uncertainty-based data selection strategy. In our experiment with multiple annotators, the images with the highest model uncertainty were precisely those images where the annotators were also uncertain. Labeling these ambiguous images by a group of expert annotators yielded conflicting ground truth annotations, providing little certain evidence for the model to learn from.

2   Modelling Segmentation Uncertainty

Image segmentation seeks to estimate a well-defined binary[1] segmentation $g \colon \Omega \to \{0,1\}$ for a discrete image domain Ω. Typically, a predictive model $h(\mathbf{x},\mathbf{w})$ with parameters $\mathbf{w}$, such as a neural network, is fitted to binary annotation data $a \colon \Omega \to \{0,1\}$ by minimizing a loss $\mathcal{L}(a, h(\mathbf{x},\mathbf{w}))$. Here, $\mathbf{x} \in \mathbb{R}^{\Omega}$ is the image, and $\mathbf{y} = h(\mathbf{x},\mathbf{w})$ defines an image of pixel-wise segmentation probabilities, such as the un-thresholded softmax output of a segmentation network h.

Typically, the annotation is assumed to be error-free, that is $a = g$, and predictors are typically trained on a single annotation per image. We assume that the trained neural network $h(\mathbf{x},\mathbf{w})$ satisfies

$$h(\mathbf{x},\mathbf{w}) = g(\mathbf{x}) + b + err \ ,$$

where b and err denote bias and segmentation error. Segmentation uncertainty is often interpreted as correlating with this error, although this is primarily realistic for small bias. Such segmentation tasks are called *unambiguous*; we consider a running example of skin lesion segmentation from dermoscopic images [3,15], where the lesion boundary is clearly visible in the image (Fig. 1).

Recent work has considered *ambiguous* segmentation tasks [6,11], where there is no accessible "ground truth" segmentation, either because the data is not sufficient to estimate the segmentation, or because there is subjective disagreement. Examples include lesions in medical imaging, where the boundary can be fuzzy due to gradual infiltration of tissue, or where experts disagree on whether a tissue region is abnormal or not.

In such tasks, we make no assumption on the underlying segmentation g or the errors err, but regard the observed annotations as samples from an unknown "ground truth" distribution $p(a|\mathbf{x})$ over annotations a conditioned on the image $\mathbf{x}$. The goal of segmentation is to estimate the distribution $p(a|\mathbf{x})$, or its proxy distribution $p(\mathbf{y}|\mathbf{x})$ over pixel-wise class probabilities $\mathbf{y} \colon \Omega \to [0,1]$, as accurately as possible for a given image $\mathbf{x}$. If successful, such a model can sample coherent, realistic segmentations from the distribution, and estimate their variance and significance. As a running example of an ambiguous segmentation task, we consider lung lesions [1,2,6]. For such tasks, predictors are typically trained on multiple annotators, who may disagree both on the segmentation boundary and on whether there is even an object to segment.

From the uncertainty modelling viewpoint, these two segmentation scenarios are rather different. Below, we discuss differences in uncertainty modelling for the two scenarios and four well-known uncertainty quantification methods.

3   Probabilistic Segmentation Networks

A probabilistic segmentation model seeks to model the distribution $p(\mathbf{y}|\mathbf{x})$ over segmentations given an input image $\mathbf{x}$. Here, our annotated dataset $(\mathbf{X}, \mathbf{A})$ con-

---

[1] For simplicity, we consider binary segmentation; the generalization to multi-class segmentation is straightforward.

sists of the set $\mathbf{X}$ of N images $\{\mathbf{x}_n \mid n = 1, ..., N\}$, and L annotations are available per image, so that $\mathbf{A} = \{a_n^{(l)} \sim p(\mathbf{y}|\mathbf{x}_n) \mid (n, l) = (1, 1), ..., (N, L)\}$.

Taking a Bayesian view, we seek the distribution

$$p(\mathbf{y}|\mathbf{x}, \mathbf{X}, \mathbf{A}) = \int p(\mathbf{y}|\mathbf{x}, \mathbf{w})p(\mathbf{w}|\mathbf{X}, \mathbf{A}, h)\, d\mathbf{w} \ , \tag{1}$$

over segmentations $\mathbf{y}$ given image $\mathbf{x}$ and data $(\mathbf{X}, \mathbf{A})$, which can be obtained by marginalization with respect to the weights $\mathbf{w}$ of the model h.

In most deep learning applications, our prior belief over the model h, denoted $p(h)$, is modelled by a Dirac delta distribution indicating a single architecture with no uncertainty. In the context of uncertain segmentation models, however, we would like to model uncertainty in the parameters $\mathbf{w}$. Denoting our prior belief over the parameters $\mathbf{w}$ by $p(\mathbf{w}|h)$, Bayes' theorem gives

$$p(\mathbf{w}|\mathbf{X}, \mathbf{A}, h) = \frac{p(\mathbf{w}|h)p(\mathbf{A}|\mathbf{X}, \mathbf{w}, h)}{p(\mathbf{A}|\mathbf{X}, h)}, \tag{2}$$

where the likelihood update function is given by

$$p(\mathbf{A}|\mathbf{X}, \mathbf{w}, h) = \exp\left(\sum_{n=1}^{N}\sum_{l=1}^{L} \mathbf{A}^{(l)} \log\left(h(\mathbf{x}_n, \mathbf{w})\right) + (1 - \mathbf{A}^{(l)})\log\left(1 - h(\mathbf{x}_n, \mathbf{w})\right)\right)$$

and normalizing constant

$$p(\mathbf{A}|\mathbf{X}, h) = \int p(\mathbf{w}|h)p(\mathbf{A}|\mathbf{X}, \mathbf{w}, h)\, d\mathbf{w} \ .$$

This integral is generally intractable, making it impossible to obtain the proper posterior (2). Below, we discuss how empirical approximations $\hat{p}(\mathbf{y}|\mathbf{x}, \mathbf{X}, \mathbf{A})$ to the distribution $p(\mathbf{y}|\mathbf{x}, \mathbf{X}, \mathbf{A})$ found in (1) are performed in four common segmentation models. Note that both p and $\hat{p}$ can be degenerate, depending on the number of annotations available and models used (Fig. 2).

U-Net with Softmax Output. The well established U-Net [12] architecture with a softmax output layer yields class-likelihood estimates. As the model is deterministic, $p(h|\mathbf{X}, \mathbf{A})$ is degenerate. Parameters are selected by a maximum a posteriori (MAP) estimate i.e. $p(\mathbf{w}|\mathbf{X}, \mathbf{A}, h) \approx \delta(\mathbf{w} - \hat{\mathbf{w}})$ in which $\hat{\mathbf{w}} = \text{argmax}\, p(\mathbf{w}|\mathbf{X}, \mathbf{A}, h)$. The model output (1) is approximated by the degenerate distribution $\hat{p}(\mathbf{y}|\mathbf{x}, \mathbf{X}, \mathbf{A}) \approx p(\mathbf{y}|\mathbf{x}, \hat{\mathbf{w}})$. The softmax output layer predicts a pixel-wise class probability distribution $p(\mathbf{y}_{(i,j)}|\mathbf{x}, \mathbf{X}, \mathbf{A})$. As no co-variance or dependencies between pixel-wise estimates are available, segmentation masks sampled from the pixel-wise probability distributions are often noisy [11]. An alternative approach followed by our implementation is the thresholding of pixel-wise probability values, which leads to a single, coherent segmentation map.

Ensemble Methods. combine multiple models to obtain better predictive performance than that obtained by the constituent models alone, while also allowing the sampling of distinct segmentation maps from the ensemble. We combine M U-Net models $h(\mathbf{x}, \mathbf{w}^{(m)})$ where, if labels from multiple annotators are available, each constituent model is trained on a disjoint label set $\mathbf{A}^{(m)}$. When trained on datasets with a single label, all constituent models are trained on the same data and their differences stem from randomized initialization and training. Treating the models as samples, we obtain an empirical distribution approximating (1) by drawing from the constituent models at random.

Monte-Carlo Dropout. [4] is a Bayesian approximation technique based on dropout, where samples from the posterior over dropout weights give a better approximation of the true posterior than a MAP estimation. Given a selected model h, one can approximate (1) as $\hat{p}(\mathbf{y}|\mathbf{x}, \mathbf{X}, \mathbf{A}) \approx 1/R \sum_{r=1}^{R} p(\mathbf{y}|\mathbf{x}, \mathbf{w}^{(r)})$ when $\mathbf{w}^{(r)} \sim p(\mathbf{w}|\mathbf{X}, \mathbf{A}, h)$. Since $p(\mathbf{w}|\mathbf{X}, \mathbf{A}, h)$ is intractable, it is approximated [4] by a variational distribution $p(\theta)$ as $\theta_i = w_i \cdot z_i, z_i \sim \text{Bernoulli}(p_i)$, where p_i is the probability of keeping the weight w_i in a standard dropout scheme.

The Probabilistic U-Net. [6] fuses the output of a deterministic U-Net with latent samples from a conditional variational auto-encoder modelling the variation over multiple annotators. Test-time segmentations are formed by sampling a latent $\mathbf{z}$, which is propagated with the image through the U-Net. Predictions are made as $\hat{p}(\mathbf{y}|\mathbf{x}, \mathbf{X}, \mathbf{A}) \approx p(\mathbf{y}|\mathbf{x}, \mathbf{z}^{(i)}, \hat{\mathbf{w}})$, with $\mathbf{z}^{(i)} \sim p_{\text{prior}}(\mathbf{z}|\mathbf{x})$.

4 Experiments

4.1 Data

Practical applications of uncertainty in segmentation tasks differ both in the type of ambiguity, and the availability of expert annotations. We select two representative datasets for our evaluation.

The **ISIC18** dataset consists of skin lesion images with a single annotation available [3,15], and is used as an example of unambiguous image segmentation. We rescale the images to 256×256 pixels and split the dataset into 1500 samples for the train-set and 547 each for the validation and test sets.

The **LIDC-IDRI** lung cancer dataset [1,2] contains 1018 lung CT scans from 1010 patients. For each scan, 4 radiologists (out of 12) annotated abnormal lesions. Anonymized annotations were shown to the other annotators, who were allowed to adjust their own masks. Significant disagreement remains between the annotators: Among the extracted patches where at least one annotator marked a lesion, an average of 50% of the annotations are blank. We pre-processed the images as in [6], resampled to 0.5mm resolution, and cropped the CT-slices with lesions present to 128×128 pixels. The dataset is split patient-wise into three groups, 722 for the training-set and 144 each for the validation and test sets.

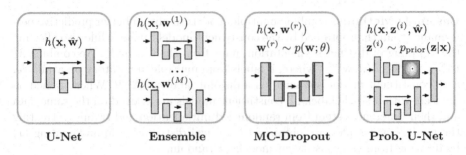

Fig. 2. Schematic overview (adapted from [6]) of the evaluated models. Blue: residual blocks . Orange: Dropout layers essential to the networks' functionality. (Color figure online)

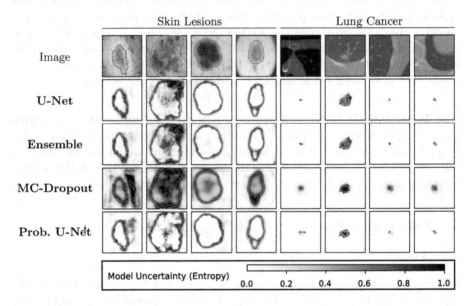

Fig. 3. Segmentation uncertainty. Samples from the test set of the two datasets. Images in row one, model uncertainty (entropy) heat-maps in rows 2–5. Outline of mean ground truth annotations in Blue, mean model predictions in Orange. (Color figure online)

4.2   Model Tuning and Training

To allow for a fair evaluation, we use the same U-Net backbone of four encoder and decoder blocks for all models. Each block contains an up-/down-sampling layer, three convolution layers, and a residual skip-connection. The ensemble consists of four identical U-Nets. The latent-space encoders of the probabilistic U-Net are similar to the encoding branch of the U-Nets, and we choose a six-dimensional latent space size, following the original paper's recommendation.

All models were trained with binary cross-entropy. The probabilistic U-Net has an additional β-weighted KL-divergence loss to align the prior and posterior distributions, as per [6]. The optimization algorithm was Adam, with a learning rate of 10^{-4} for most models, except the probabilistic U-Net and MC-Dropout models on the skin lesion dataset, where a lower learning rate of 10^{-5} gave better results. We utilized early stopping to prevent over-fitting, and define the stopping criteria as 10 epochs without improvement of the validation loss, 100 epochs for models trained with the reduced learning rate. For the MC-Dropout and probabilistic U-Net models we performed a hyper-parameter search over the dropout probability p and the loss function weighting factor β, selecting the configuration with the lowest generalized energy distance on the validation set. We arrived at $p = 0.5$, $\beta = 0.0005$.

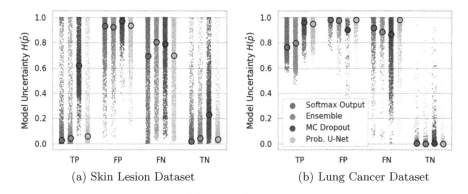

(a) Skin Lesion Dataset   (b) Lung Cancer Dataset

Fig. 4. Pixelwise uncertainty by prediction correctness (true positive, false positive, false negative, true negative). The scatter plot shows individual pixels, with the median circled. For the lung cancer dataset, we discarded pixels with annotator disagreement.

4.3 Uncertainty Estimation

For all models, our uncertainty estimates are based on non-thresholded pixel-wise predictions. For the U-Net, we take the final softmax predictions; for the remaining models we average across 16 non-thresholded samples. We quantify the *pixel-wise* uncertainty of the model by the entropy

$$\mathrm{H}(p(\mathbf{y}_{(i,j)}|\mathbf{x},\mathbf{X},\mathbf{A})) = \sum_{c \in C} p(\mathbf{y}_{(i,j)} = c|\mathbf{x},\mathbf{X},\mathbf{A}) \log_2 \frac{1}{p(\mathbf{y}_{(i,j)} = c|\mathbf{x},\mathbf{X},\mathbf{A})}$$

with $p(\mathbf{y}_{(i,j)} = c|\mathbf{x})$ as the pixel-wise probability to predict class $c \in C$. We plot the resulting uncertainty map for random images $\mathbf{x}$ from both datasets in Fig. 3. For visual reference, we overlay the mean expert annotation in Blue, and the mean model prediction in Orange. Darker shades indicate higher uncertainty.

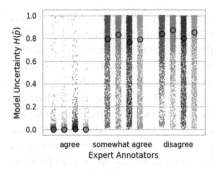
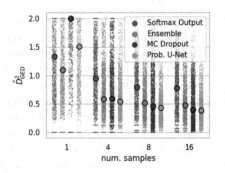

Fig. 5. Pixel-wise model uncertainty on the lung cancer dataset, grouped by agreement of expert annotations. Experts agree: $H(p) = 0$, somewhat agree $0 < H(p) < 1$, disagree $H(p) = 1$.

Fig. 6. Generalized energy distance of models on the lung cancer dataset, approximation by 1 to 16 samples, median highlighted. Lower distances are better.

We quantitatively assess the quality of uncertainty estimates by examining their relation to segmentation error in Fig. 4. On both datasets, models are more certain when they are correct (true positive, true negative) compared to when they are incorrect (false positive, false negative). A repeated measure correlation test finds a significant ($\alpha = 0.01$) correlation between segmentation error and model uncertainty on both datasets, for all methods. The relation holds, but is less strong, for MC-dropout on the skin dataset, which retains high uncertainty even when it is correct. On the lung cancer dataset, all models have high uncertainty on true positive predictions. This might be caused by the imbalance of the dataset, where the positive class is strongly outweighed by the background and annotators often disagree. We tried training the models with a class-occurrence weighted loss function, which did produce true positive predictions with higher certainty but suffered an overall higher segmentation error.

We assess the correlation of model uncertainty with the uncertainty of the annotators on the lung cancer dataset in Fig. 5. For all models, this correlation is significant ($\alpha = 0.01$) . The median model uncertainty is very low (< 0.1) when all annotators agree, but high (> 0.7) when they disagree. There is a minor difference in model uncertainty between partial agreement (annotators split 3 – 1) and full disagreement (annotators split 2 – 2).

4.4   Sampling Segmentation Masks

Figure 7 shows segmentation masks **y** sampled from the trained models $\hat{p}(\mathbf{y}|\mathbf{x})$. The U-Net model is fully deterministic and does not offer any variation in samples. The sample diversity of the ensemble is limited by the number of constituent models (four in our experiment). The MC-Dropout and probabilistic U-Net allow fully random sampling and achieve a visually higher diversity. On the skin lesion dataset, where only one export annotation per image is available, models still

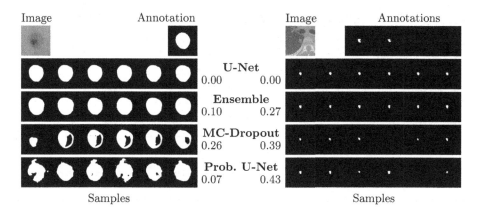

Fig. 7. Samples from the probabilistic models. First row: image and ground truth annotations from the skin dataset (left) and lung nodule dataset (right). Following rows: samples $\mathbf{y} \sim \hat{p}(\mathbf{y}|\mathbf{x}, \mathbf{X}, \mathbf{A})$ drawn from the various models. Sample diversity over the entire dataset shown next to the model name.

produce diverse predictions. On the lung cancer dataset, samples from the MC-Dropout and probabilistic U-Net represent the annotator distribution well.

We measure the distance between the model distribution $\hat{p}(\mathbf{y}|\mathbf{x}, \mathbf{X}, \mathbf{A})$ and the annotator distribution $p(\mathbf{y}|\mathbf{x})$ with the Generalized Energy Distance [6,11, 14]. The distance measure is calculated as

$$D^2_{GED}(p, \hat{p}) = 2\mathbb{E}_{y \sim p, \hat{y} \sim \hat{p}} [d(y, \hat{y})] - \mathbb{E}_{y, y' \sim p} [d(y, y')] - \mathbb{E}_{\hat{y}, \hat{y}' \sim \hat{p}} [d(\hat{y}, \hat{y}')] \ . \quad (3)$$

We use $1 - \text{IoU}(\cdot, \cdot)$ as the distance d. A low D^2_{GED} indicates similar distributions of segmentations. We approximate the metric by drawing up to 16 samples from both distributions, and sample with replacement. The results are shown in Fig. 6. We observe that the annotator distribution is best approximated by the probabilistic U-Net, with MC-dropout and Ensemble closely behind; these pairwise ranks are significant ($\alpha = 0.01$) with left-tailed t-tests. A deterministic U-Net architecture is not able to reproduce the output distribution. Our results are consistent with [6], verifying our implementation. Following [11], we use the last term of (3) to assess the diversity of samples drawn from the model and note them in Fig. 7. They reinforce the qualitative observations of sample diversity.

4.5   Uncertainty Estimates for Active Learning

Instead of training the models with all available data $\{\mathbf{X}, \mathbf{A}\}$, we now start with a small random subset $\{\mathbf{X}_0, \mathbf{A}_0\}$. We train the model with this subset at iteration $t = 0$, and then add a set of k images from $\{\mathbf{X}, \mathbf{A}\}$ to form $\{\mathbf{X}_{t+1}, \mathbf{A}_{t+1}\}$. Samples are selected based on the sum of pixel-wise entropies [7]. We repeat for T iterations, benchmarking against a random sample selection strategy.

For both skin lesion and lung cancer datasets, we start with a training size of 50 images, add $k = 25$ images at each iteration, and repeat $T = 10$ times.

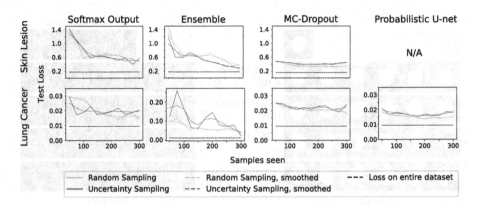

Fig. 8. Learning curves for the four algorithms on both datasets. Note that the probabilisitic U-net only applies to the ambiguous segmentation.

The models are trained for 5000 gradient updates with a batch size of 16 and 32 for the respective datasets. Since annotations are costly and to speed up computations, no validation-loss based early stopping is used. The experimental setup has been picked to ensure meaningful model uncertainties for the data selection policy and to ensure convergence within each active learning iteration.

The learning curves in Fig. 8 show that random-based sampling leads to a faster reduction in test loss over the uncertainty-based sampling strategy for both datasets. We further investigated the samples selected by the uncertainty-based strategy by looking at the images which caused a large increase in the test error. One such image is shown in Fig. 9.

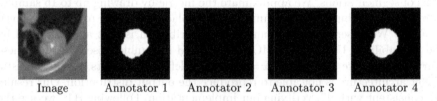

Fig. 9. An example of the ambiguous samples frequently selected for inclusion into the training set under the uncertainty-based data gathering strategy. This unseen sample was selected when 150 annotations were revealed. The group of expert annotators provided disagreeing segmentation masks, confirming the model uncertainty but providing little additional information to learn from.

5   Discussion and Conclusion

Our results in Fig. 4 show that there is a clear relation between uncertainty estimates and segmentation error. The examples in Fig. 3 further highlight that areas of high uncertainty are not merely distributed around class boundaries, but also encompass areas with ambiguous labels. Figure 5 shows that the uncertainty estimates obtained from the model are a good representation of the uncertainty of a group of expert annotators. We conclude that pixel-wise model uncertainty estimates give the practitioner a good indication of possible errors in the presented segmentation mask, allowing those predictions to be examined with care.

The learning curves in Fig. 8 show that estimated uncertainty is not generally useful for selecting active learning samples, for any model or dataset. Our results depend on using the sum of pixel-wise entropies as a per-image entropy, which is correct for the softmax model, but only an approximation for the other models. This might impact our results. For the Lung Cancer dataset, all models estimate high uncertainty for the positive class, and the active learner thus selects images with a large foreground, skewing the proportion of classes represented in the training set. Furthermore, the selected images often have high annotator disagreement, illustrated in Fig. 9. If the active learner prefers sampling ambiguous images, it will be presented with inconsistent labels leading to harder learning conditions and poor generalisation. This may stem from an incorrect active learning assumption that annotations are noise-free and unambiguous, which is often not true. In conclusion, for a fixed budget of annotated images, we find no advantage in uncertainty-based active learning.

We observed similar behaviour of pixel-wise uncertainty estimates across all four segmentation models. The models differ in their ability to generate a distribution of distinct and coherent segmentation masks, with only the MC-dropout and probabilistic U-Net offering near unlimited diversity (see Fig. 7). But these models are harder to implement, more resource-intensive to train, and require hyperparameter tuning. The choice of model is ultimately application dependent, but our experiments show that even a simple U-net is competitive for the common task of assessing segmentation error. This agrees with [5], which compared uncertainty quantification models for unambiguous segmentation.

Our division of segmentation tasks into ambiguous and unambiguous considers it as "unambiguous" when a fundamentally ambiguous segmentation task is covered by a single annotator – or potentially several annotators, but with only one annotator per image, as for the Skin Lesion dataset. Even if the underlying task *is* ambiguous, the models considered in this paper inherently assume that it is *not*, as there is no mechanism to detect annotator variance when every image is only annotated once. More fundamental modelling of segmentation ambiguity and uncertainty thus remains a highly relevant open problem.

To conclude – is segmentation uncertainty useful? We find that uncertainty, even in the simplest models, reliably gives practitioners an indication of areas of an image that might be ambiguous, or wrongly segmented. Using uncertainty estimates to reduce the annotation load has proven challenging, with no significant advantage over a random strategy.

Acknowledgements. Our data was extracted from the "ISIC 2018: Skin Lesion Analysis Towards Melanoma Detection" grand challenge datasets [3,15]. The authors acknowledge the National Cancer Institute and the Foundation for the National

Institutes of Health, and their critical role in the creation of the free publicly available LIDC/IDRI Database used here. This work was funded in part by the Novo Nordisk Foundation (grants no. NNF20OC0062606 and NNF17OC0028360) and the Lundbeck Foundation (grant no. R218-2016-883).

References

1. Armato III, S.G., et al.: The lung image database consortium (LIDC) and image database resource initiative (IDRI): a completed reference database of lung nodules on CT scans. Med. Phys. **38**(2), 915–931 (2011)
2. Clark, K., et al.: The cancer imaging archive (TCIA): maintaining and operating a public information repository. J. Digit. Imaging **26**(6), 1045–1057 (2013)
3. Codella, N.C., et al.: Skin lesion analysis toward melanoma detection: a challenge at the 2017 international symposium on biomedical imaging (ISBI), hosted by the international skin imaging collaboration (ISIC). In: 2018 IEEE 15th International Symposium on Biomedical Imaging, pp. 168–172 (2018)
4. Gal, Y., Ghahramani, Z.: Dropout as a Bayesian approximation: representing model uncertainty in deep learning. In: International Conference on Machine Learning, pp. 1050–1059 (2016)
5. Jungo, A., Reyes, M.: Assessing reliability and challenges of uncertainty estimations for medical image segmentation. In: Shen, D., et al. (eds.) MICCAI 2019. LNCS, vol. 11765, pp. 48–56. Springer, Cham (2019). https://doi.org/10.1007/978-3-030-32245-8_6
6. Kohl, S., et al.: A probabilistic u-net for segmentation of ambiguous images. Adv. Neural Inf. Process. Syst. **31**, 6965–6975 (2018)
7. Lewis, D.D., Catlett, J.: Heterogeneous uncertainty sampling for supervised learning. In: Machine Learning Proceedings 1994, pp. 148–156. Elsevier (1994)
8. Loog, M., Yang, Y.: An empirical investigation into the inconsistency of sequential active learning. In: 2016 23rd International Conference on Pattern Recognition (ICPR), pp. 210–215. IEEE (2016)
9. MacKay, D.J.: The evidence framework applied to classification networks. Neural Comput. **4**(5), 720–736 (1992)
10. MacKay, D.J.: Information-based objective functions for active data selection. Neural Comput. **4**(4), 590–604 (1992)
11. Monteiro, M., et al.: Stochastic segmentation networks: modelling spatially correlated aleatoric uncertainty. In: Larochelle, H., Ranzato, M., Hadsell, R., Balcan, M.F., Lin, H. (eds.) Advances in Neural Information Processing Systems, vol. 33, pp. 12756–12767 (2020)
12. Ronneberger, O., Fischer, P., Brox, T.: U-net: convolutional networks for biomedical image segmentation. In: Navab, N., Hornegger, J., Wells, W.M., Frangi, A.F. (eds.) MICCAI 2015. LNCS, vol. 9351, pp. 234–241. Springer, Cham (2015). https://doi.org/10.1007/978-3-319-24574-4_28
13. Settles, B.: Active learning literature survey. University of Wisconsin-Madison Department of Computer Sciences. Technical report (2009)
14. Székely, G.J., Rizzo, M.L.: Energy statistics: a class of statistics based on distances. J. Stat. Plan. Infer. **143**(8), 1249–1272 (2013)
15. Tschandl, P., Rosendahl, C., Kittler, H.: The HAM10000 dataset, a large collection of multi-source dermatoscopic images of common pigmented skin lesions. Sci. Data **5**, 180161 (2018)
16. Yang, Y., Loog, M.: A benchmark and comparison of active learning for logistic regression. Pattern Recogn. **83**, 401–415 (2018)

Deep Learning

Principled Ultrasound Data Augmentation for Classification of Standard Planes

Lok Hin Lee$^{(\boxtimes)}$⬤, Yuan Gao⬤, and J. Alison Noble⬤

Department of Engineering Science, University of Oxford, Oxford, UK
{lokhin.lee,yuan.gao2,alison.noble}@eng.ox.ac.uk

Abstract. Deep learning models with large learning capacities often overfit to medical imaging datasets. This is because training sets are often relatively small due to the significant time and financial costs incurred in medical data acquisition and labelling. Data augmentation is therefore routinely used to expand the availability of training data and to increase generalization. However, augmentation strategies are often chosen on an ad-hoc basis without justification. In this paper, we present an augmentation policy search method with the goal of improving model classification performance. We include in the augmentation policy search additional transformations that are commonly used in medical image analysis and evaluate their performance. In addition, we extend the augmentation policy search to include non-linear mixed-example data augmentation strategies. Using these learned policies, we show that principled data augmentation for medical image model training can lead to significant improvements in ultrasound standard plane detection, with an average F1-score improvement of 7.0% overall over naive data augmentation strategies in ultrasound fetal standard plane classification. We find that the learned representations of ultrasound images are better clustered and defined with optimized data augmentation.

Keywords: Data augmentation · Deep learning · Fetal ultrasound

1 Introduction

The benefits of data augmentation for training deep learning models are well documented in a variety of tasks, including image recognition [19,22,23] and regression problems [11,21]. Data augmentation acts to artificially increase the size and variance of a given training dataset by adding transformed copies of the training examples. This is particularly evident in the context of medical imaging, where data augmentation is used to combat class imbalance [9], increase model generalization [10,17], and expand training data [8,26]. This is usually done with transformations to the input image that are determined based on expert knowledge and cannot be easily transferred to other problems and domains. In ultrasound, this usually manifests as data augmentation strategies consisting of

© Springer Nature Switzerland AG 2021
A. Feragen et al. (Eds.): IPMI 2021, LNCS 12729, pp. 729–741, 2021.
https://doi.org/10.1007/978-3-030-78191-0_56

small rotations, translations and scalings [1]. However, whilst it is appealing to base augmentation strategies on "expected" variations in input image presentation, recent work has found that other augmentation strategies that generate "unrealistic looking" training images [18,23] have led to improvements in generalization capability. There has therefore been great interest in developing data augmentation strategies to automatically generate transformations to images and labels that would lead to the greatest performance increase in a neural network model. In this paper, inspired by the RandAugment [6] augmentation search policy, we automatically look for augmentation policies that outperform standard augmentation strategies in ultrasound imaging based on prior knowledge and extend our algorithm to include mixed-example data augmentation [23] in the base policy search. We evaluate the proposed method on second-trimester fetal ultrasound plane detection, and find that a randomly initialized network with our augmentation policy achieves performance competitive with methods that require external labelled data for network pre-training and self-supervised methods. We also evaluate our method on a fine-tuning a pre-trained model, and find that using an optimized augmentation policy during training improves final performance.

Contributions: Our contributions are three fold: 1) We investigate the use of an augmentation search policy with hyperparameters that does not need expensive reinforcement learning policies and can be tuned with simple grid search; 2) We extend this augmentation search policy to combinations that include mixed-example based data augmentation and include common medical imaging transformations; 3) We explain the performance of optimal augmentation strategies by looking at their affinity, diversities and effect on final model performance.

Related Work: Medical image datasets are difficult and expensive to acquire. There has therefore been previous work that seeks to artificially expand the breadth of training data available in medical image classification [10,15], segmentation [9,20] and regression [8].

Original Data Manipulation: Zeshan et al. [15] evaluate the performance of eight different affine and pixel level transformations by training eight different CNNs for predicting mammography masses and find that ensembling the trained models improves the classification performance significantly. Nalepa et al. [20] elastically deform brain MRI scans using diffeomorphic mappings and find that tumour segmentation is improved. However, in the above works, specific augmentations and parameters are selected arbitrarily and are task and modality dependent. In contrast, we propose an automated augmentation policy search method that can out perform conventional medical imaging augmentation baselines.

Artificial Data Generation: Florian et al. [8] generates new training samples in by linearly combining existing training examples in regression. Models trained to estimate the volume of white matter hyperintensities had performance comparable to networks trained with larger datasets. Zach et al. [9] also linearly combine training examples and target labels linearly inspired by mix-up [25] but focus on pairing classes with high and low incidence together, which was found to be beneficial for tasks with high class imbalance such as in brain tumor segmentation. Maayan et al. [10] train a conditional generative adversarial network (cGAN) to generate different types of liver lesions and use the synthesized samples to train a classification network. Dakai et al. [17] use a cGAN to synthesize 3D lung nodules of different sizes and appearances at multiple locations of a lung CT scan. These generated samples were then used to finetune a pretrained lung nodule segmentation network that improved segmentation of small peripheral nodules. However, cGAN-based methods are difficult to train and have significant computational costs during augmentation.

Automated Augmentation Policy Search: There are augmentation policy search methods in the natural image analysis [5,13,18] that learn a series of transformations which are parameterized by their magnitudes and probability. However, these searches are expensive, and cannot be run on the full training dataset as the hyperparameter search for each transformation require significant computational resources. RandAugment (RA) [6] finds that transformations can have a shared magnitude and probability of application and achieve similar performance, without expensive reinforcement learning. However, RA is limited to single-image transformations. We therefore explore the use of an extended RA policy search with additional transformations that are more specific to medical imaging, and expand its capabilities to include mixed-example image examples to include artificial data in model training.

2   Methods

In this section we describe our proposed framework for augmentation policy search, depicted in Fig. 1 which consists of three key procedures i) data generation, ii) data augmentation, iii) policy searching and interpretation.

Mixed-Example Data Augmentation: The original dataset $D = \{(X_i, Y_i)\}$ consists of a series of i ultrasound frames X and their associated classes Y. We first generate a paired dataset $D_{paired} = \{(x_1, x_2)_{\frac{i}{2}}, (y_1, y_2)_{\frac{i}{2}}\}$ by pairing examples from different classes. Examples of artificial data are then generated using non-linear methods [23], which are found to be more effective than linear intensity averaging (mix-up) [25]. As illustrated in Fig. 2, instead of pixel-wise averaging, the bottom λ_1 fraction of image x_1 is vertically concatenated with the top $1 - \lambda_1$ fraction of image x_2. Similarly, the right λ_2 fraction of image x_1 is horizontally concatenated with the left $1 - \lambda_2$ fraction of image x_2. After the concatenations, the resulted images are combined to produce an image $\tilde{x}$ in which the top-left is from x_1, the bottom right is from x_2, and the top-right and bottom-left are mixed between the two. Moreover, instead of linear pixel averaging, we treat each image as a zero-mean waveform and normalize mixing coefficients with image intensity energies [24]. Formally, given initial images $x_{1,2}$ with image

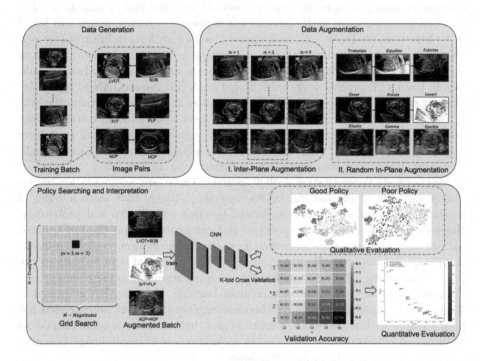

Fig. 1. Overview of our proposed learning framework.

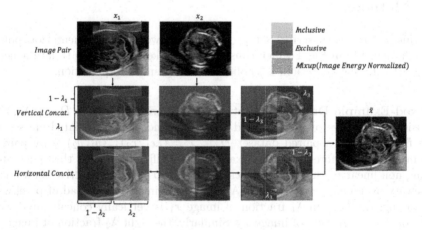

Fig. 2. The procedure for non-linear mixed-example data augmentation using an image pair and the final artificial mixed-example image.

intensity means and standard deviations of $\mu_{1,2}$ and $\sigma_{1,2}$, the generated artificial mixed-example image $\tilde{x}$ is:

$$\tilde{x} = \begin{cases} x_1(i,j) - \mu_1 & \text{if } i \leq \lambda_1 H \text{ and } j \leq \lambda_2 W \\ \frac{c}{\phi}[x_1(i,j) - \mu_1] + \frac{1-c}{\phi}[x_2(i,j) - \mu_2] & \text{if } i \leq \lambda_1 H \text{ and } j > \lambda_2 W \\ \frac{1-c}{\phi}[x_1(i,j) - \mu_1] + \frac{c}{\phi}[x_2(i,j) - \mu_2] & \text{if } i > \lambda_1 H \text{ and } j \leq \lambda_2 W \\ x_2(i,j) - \mu_2 & \text{if } i > \lambda_1 H \text{ and } j > \lambda_2 W \end{cases}$$

where c is the mixing coefficient $(1 + \frac{\sigma_1}{\sigma_2} \cdot \frac{1-\lambda_3}{\lambda_3})^{-1}$ and ϕ is the normalization term defined as $\sqrt{c^2 + (1-c)^2}$. The row index and column index is represented by i,j and the height and width of the images are represented by H, W.

We sample $\lambda_{1,2,3} \sim Beta(m/10, m/10)$ where m is a learnt hyperparameter varied from 0–10. As m approaches 10, λ values are more uniformly distributed across 0–1 and artificial images are more interpolated. The ground truth label after interpolation is determined by the mixing coefficients and can be calculated with:

$$\tilde{y} = (\lambda_3 \lambda_1 + (1 - \lambda_3)\lambda_2)y_1 + (\lambda_3(1 - \lambda_1) + (1 - \lambda_3)(1 - \lambda_2))y_2$$

Original Data Augmentation: Augmentation transformations are then applied to the mixed images. Inspired by [6], we do not learn specific magnitudes and probabilities of applying each transformation in a given transformation list. Each augmentation policy is instead defined only by n, which is the number of transformations from the list an image undergoes, and m, which is the magnitude distortion of each transformation. Note that m is a shared hyperparameter with the mixed-example augmentation process. We investigate the inclusion in the transformation list transformations commonly used in ultrasound image analysis augmentation: i) grid distortions and elastic transformation [4] and ii) speckle noise [2]. The transformation list then totals 18 transformations, examples of which can be seen in Fig. 3. The mapping between m and transformation magnitude follows the convention in [5].

Optimization: We define f and θ as a convolutional neural network (CNN) and its parameters. As depicted in Fig. 1, we train a CNN with the augmented mini-batch data $\tilde{x}^i$ and obtain the predicted output class scores $f_\theta(\tilde{x}^i)$. These are converted into class probabilities $p(\tilde{x}^i)$ with the softmax function. The KL-divergence between $f_\theta(\tilde{x}^i)$ and $\tilde{y}^i$ is then minimized with back-propagation and stochastic gradient descent

$$L = \frac{1}{B} D_{KL}(\tilde{y}^i \parallel p(\tilde{x}^i)) = \frac{1}{B} \sum_{i=1}^{B} \sum_{j=1}^{C} \tilde{y}_j^i log \frac{\tilde{y}_j^i}{\{p(\tilde{x}^i)\}_j}$$

where B is the batch size, C is the number of classes and L is the loss.

Due to the limited search space, the hyperparameters n and m that produce the optimum classification performance can be found using grid search as seen in Fig. 1. The best performing m, n tuple is used during final model evaluation.

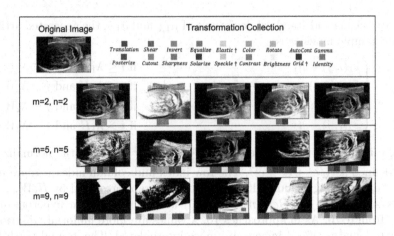

Fig. 3. Examples of how each transformation and augmentation policy affect input images. Each color represents a transformation, and augmented image is transformed using a number of transformations (n) at a magnitude of (m). †: our additional transformations.

Quantifying Augmentation Effects: We investigate how augmentation improves model generalization and quantify how different augmentation policies affect augmented data distributions and model performance. We adopt a two dimensional metric - affinity and diversity [12] to do this. Affinity quantifies the distribution shift of augmented data with respect to the unaugmented distribution captured by a baseline model; the diversity quantifies complexity of the augmented data. Given training and validation datasets, D_t and D_v, drawn from the original dataset D, we can generate an augmented validation dataset $D(m, n)'_v$ derived from D_v using m, n as hyperparameters for the augmentation policy. The affinity A for this augmentation policy is then:

$$A = \mathbb{E}[L(D'_v)] - \mathbb{E}[L(D_v)]$$

where $\mathbb{E}[L(D)]$ represents the expected value of the loss computed on the dataset D loss of a model trained on D_t.

The diversity, D, of the augmentation policy a is computed on the augmented training dataset D'_t with respect to the expected final training loss, L_t, as:

$$D = \mathbb{E}[L(D'_t)]$$

Intuitively, the greater the difference in loss between an augmented validation dataset and the original dataset on a model trained with unaugmented data, the greater the distribution shift of the augmented validation dataset. Similarly, the greater the final training loss of a model on augmented data, the more complexity and variation there is in the final augmented dataset.

3   Experiments and Results

We use a clinically acquired dataset consisting of ultrasound second-trimester fetal examinations. A GE Voluson E8 scanner was used for ultrasound image acquisition. For comparison with previous work [7,16], fetal ultrasound images were labelled into 14 categories. Four cardiac view classes (4CH, 3VV, LVOT, RVOT) corresponding to the four chamber view, three vessel view, left and right ventricular outflow tracts respectively; the brain transcerebellar and transventricular views (TC, TV); two fetal spine sagittal and coronal views (SpineSag, SpineCor); the kidney, femur, abdominal circumference standard planes, profile view planes and background images. The standard planes from 135 routine ultrasound clinical scans were labelled, and 1129 standard plane frames were extracted. A further 1127 background images were also extracted and three-fold cross validation was used to verify the performance of our network.

Network Implementation: A SE-ResNeXt-50 [14] backbone is used for the classification task. Networks were trained with an SGD optimizer with learning rate of 10^{-3}, a momentum of 0.9 and a weight decay of 10^{-4}. Networks were trained for a minimum of 150 epochs, and training was halted if there was 20 continuous epochs without improvement in validation accuracy. Models were implemented with PyTorch and trained on a NVIDIA GTX 1080 Ti. Random horizontal and vertical flipping were used in all RA policies as a baseline augmentation. Models were trained with a batch size of 50. We evaluated the performance of networks trained with augmentation policies with values of m, n where $m, n = \{1, 3, 5, 7, 9\}$ and used a simple grid search for augmentation strategies to find optimal m, n values.

Table 1. Results for standard plane detection (mean ± std %). The best performing augmentation strategies are marked in **bold** for each metric.

	Random Initialization				Initialized with external data			
	No Aug.	SN Pol.	RA [6]	Mix. RA (ours)	Siam. Init. [16]	Saliency [7]	SonoNet [3,7]	SonoNet + Mix.RA (ours)
Precision	56.5±1.2	70.4±2.3	74.7±1.8	**75.1±1.8**	75.8±1.9	79.5±1.7	82.3±1.3	**86.3±1.3**
Recall	55.1±1.2	64.9±1.6	72.2±2.3	**73.4±1.9**	76.4±2.7	75.1±3.4	**87.3±1.1**	85.1±1.3
F1-Score	55.4±1.2	67.0±1.3	72.8±1.8	**74.0±1.8**	75.7±2.0	76.6±2.6	84.5±0.9	**85.4±1.5**

Results on CNNs with Random Initialization: The effectiveness of our mixed-example augmentation search policy algorithm (*Mix. RA*) on SE-ResNeXt-50 models that are randomly initialized is compared with models trained with the baseline RandAugment (*RA*) augmentation search policy; a commonly used augmentation strategy (*SN Pol.*) in line with that found in [7], where images are augmented with random horizontal flipping, rotation ±10°, aspect ratio changes ±10%, cropping and changing brightness ±25% and image cropping 95 − 100%; and no augmentation (*No. Aug.*).

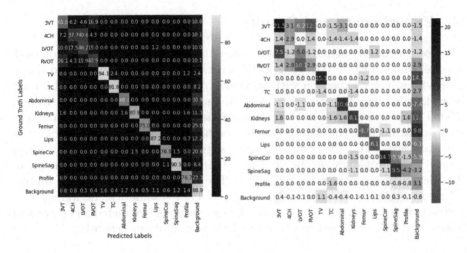

Fig. 4. Confusion matrix for *Mix. RA* (left) and the difference in precision between *Mix. RA* and *SN Pol*.

From Table 1 we can see that the proposed method *Mix. RA* outperforms all other augmentation methods on every metric with random network initialization, including the baseline *RA* augmentation policy search (Fig. 4).

To better understand how *Mix. RA* outperforms naive augmentation, we show the confusion matrix for the best performing model *Mix. Aug* and the difference in confusion matrix between it and naive augmentation *SN Pol*. We find that in general, heart plane classification is improved with a mean increase in macro F1-Score of 4.0%. Other anatomical planes with the exception of the femur plane also show consistent increases in performance with movement of probability mass away from erroneously classified background images to the correct classes suggesting the model is able to recognize greater variation in each anatomical class.

The t-SNE embeddings of the penultimate layer seen in Fig. 5 can also be used to visualize the differences in feature spaces in trained networks with different augmentation policies. Compared to the model trained with no augmentation, our best performing policy leads to a better separation of the abdominal and profile standard planes from the background class as well as clearer decision boundaries between anatomical classes. The two brain views (TC, TV) and the demarcation of the boundary between the kidney view and abdominal plane view is also better defined.

Between the best performing policy $m, n = (5, 3)$ and an underperforming policy $m, n = (7, 7)$, we find that profile planes are better separated from the background class and the abdominal planes better separated from the kidney views, which suggests that the optimum m, n value increases network recognition of salient anatomical structures. However, in all three cases, the cardiac views remain entangled. This can be attributed to the difficulty of the problem, as even human expert sonographers cannot consistently differentiate between different cardiac standard plane images. We also find that the background class also

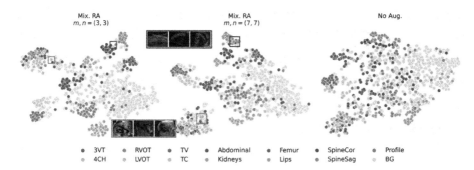

Fig. 5. t-SNE embeddings for different augmentation policies. The boxes represent the regions from which example images are taken from. The blue and purple boxes contain examples of the (SpineCor, SpineSag, and BG) and (3VT, RVOT, BG) classes respectively taken from the highlighted positions in the t-SNE embedding. Best viewed in color. (Color figure online)

contains examples of the anatomies in each class, but in sub-optimal plane views, which leads to confusion during classification. This difficulty is illustrated in example background images in Fig. 5 where the heart and spine are visible in the BG class.

Pre-trained Networks: We also compare our work to methods where networks were initialized with external data as seen in the right of Table 1. Baseline methods of self-supervised pre-training using video data [16] *(Siam. Init.)*, multimodal saliency prediction [7] *(Saliency)* and Sononet *(Sononet)* [3] were used to initialize the models and the models fine-tuned on our dataset. Using our augmentation policy during fine-tuning of a pre-trained SonoNet network further increased the performance of standard plane classification with an increase in final F1-score of 0.9% when $m, n = (5, 1)$. This reduction in optimum transformation magnitude may be due to the change in network architecture from SE-ResNeXt-50 to a Sononet, as the smaller Sononet network may not be able to capture representations the former is able to. Furthermore, we find that augmentation policy with a randomly initialized network *Mix. RA* approaches the performance of the *Siam. Init.* and *Saliency* pre-trained networks. This is despite the fact that the *Siam. Init.* requires additional 135 US videos for network self-supervised initialization, and *Saliency* required external multi-modal data in the form of sonographer gaze.

Ablation Study: To better understand the individual contributions to the *Mix. RA* augmentation search policy, we show the results of an ablation study on the components of *Mix. RA* in Table 2.

It can be seen that both including Speckle noise transformations and deformation (Grid, Elastic) transformations lead to increased classifier performance for standard plane classification of +0.1% and +0.3% respectively with further

Table 2. Ablation study on the individual components of our *Mix. RA* policy search algorithm on training of a randomly initialized CNN for ultrasound standard plane detection. All metrics are macro-averages due to the class imbalance. The *Linear Mix. RA* is included as a baseline mixed-example augmentation strategy.

	No Aug.	SN Pol.	RA	RA + Speckle ①	RA + Deform. ②	Ext. RA ① + ②	Linear Mix. RA ① + ②	Non-Linear Mix. RA ① + ②
Precision	56.5±1.2	70.4±2.3	73.9±1.7	74.6±1.7	74.6±1.7	74.0±2.4	74.6±1.6	**75.1±1.8**
Recall	55.1±1.2	64.9±1.6	72.9±2.0	72.1±1.8	72.9±1.8	**74.5±1.3**	73.2±1.5	73.4±1.9
F1-Score	55.4±1.2	67.0±1.3	72.8±1.8	72.9±1.7	73.2±1.2	73.6±1.3	73.7±1.6	**74.0±1.8**

improvement when both are combined together with *Ext. RA*. We find that both *RA* and *Ext. RA* had an optimal $m, n = (5, 3)$, suggesting that the magnitude ranges for our additional transformations are well matched to the original transformation list. This performance increase is further boosted when mixed-example augmentation is introduced on top of *Ext. RA*, with non-linear mixed-example augmentations outperforming a linear mix-up based method.

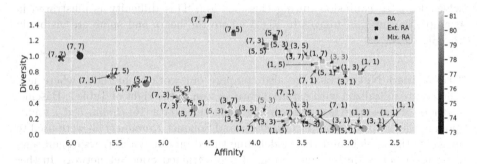

Fig. 6. Affinity and diversity metrics for *RA*, *Ext. RA* and *Mix. RA* augmentation policy search algorithms. Each point represents a (m, n) value in hyperparameter space. Best performing m, n values are highlighted in red for each policy search method. Color represents final F1-Score on a randomly initialized CNN. (Color figure online)

Affinity and Diversity: The affinity and diversity of the augmentation policies is shown in Fig. 6. We find that there exists a "sweet spot" of affinity and diversity using non-mixed class augmentation strategies at an affinity distance of ∼3.8 and diversity of ∼0.25 which maximized model performance, corresponding to $m, n = (5, 3)$. At high m, n values, affinity distance is too high and the distribution of the augmented data is too far away from the validation data, decreasing model performance. However, at low m, n values, the diversity of the augmented data decreases and the model sees too little variation in input data.

It can also be seen that the *Mix. RA* augmented dataset showed a reduced affinity distance to the original dataset than the *Ext. RA* dataset at the same

$m, n = (5, 3)$ value, implying that our proposed transforms shifts augmented images to be more similar to the original images. Moreover, using a mixed-example data augmentation strategy drastically increased diversity for any given value of data distribution affinity, which improved final model performance. The best performing mixed-example augmentation policy $m, n = (3, 3)$ reduced the magnitude of each transformation compared to the optimal non-linear augmentation policy. This suggests that mixed-example augmentation acts to increase the diversity of training images which reduces the magnitude required during further processing.

4   Conclusion

The results have shown that we can use a simple hyper-parameter grid search method to find an augmentation strategy that significantly outperforms conventional augmentation methods. For standard plane classification, the best performing augmentation policy had an average increase in F1-Score of 7.0% over that of a standard ultrasound model augmentation strategy. Our augmentation policy method is competitive with the *Siam. Init.* [16] despite the latter needing additional external data for pre-training. Our method also improves the performance of a Sononet pre-trained model when fine-tuned using our augmentation policy search method. From t-SNE plots and confusion matrix differences, we can see that the performance increase is from better classification of background-labelled planes. It should be noted that a large degree of misclassification was due to standard planes being mis-classified into background images or vice-versa, and qualitative evaluation of t-SNE clusters show that this was due to background labelled images containing sub-optimal views of labelled anatomical structures. The ablation study also shows that our additional transformations and non-linear mixed example augmentation improve model performance. The evaluation using affinity and diversity indicate that the hyperparameter search involves a trade-off between diversity and affinity. We find that using non-linear mixed-class data augmentation drastically increases diversity without further increasing affinity, which helps explain the increase in model performance. In conclusion, we have shown that our augmentation policy search method outperforms standard manual choice of augmentation. The augmentation policy search method presented does not have any inference-time computational cost, and has the potential to be applied in other medical image settings where training data is insufficient and costly to acquire.

Acknowledgements. We acknowledge the Croucher Foundation, ERC (ERC-ADG-2015 694 project PULSE), the EPSRC (EP/R013853/1, EP/T028572/1) and the MRC (MR/P027938/1).

References

1. Zaman, A., Park, S.H., Bang, H., Park, C., Park, I., Joung, S.: Generative approach for data augmentation for deep learning-based bone surface segmentation from ultrasound images. Int. J. Comput. Assist. Radiol. Surg. **15**(6), 931–941 (2020). https://doi.org/10.1007/s11548-020-02192-1
2. Bargsten, L., Schlaefer, A.: Specklegan: a generative adversarial network with an adaptive speckle layer to augment limited training data for ultrasound image processing. In: ICARS (2020)
3. Baumgartner, C.F., et al.: SonoNet: real-time detection and localisation of fetal standard scan planes in freehand ultrasound. In: IEEE TMI (2017)
4. Buslaev, A., Iglovikov, V.I., et al.: Albumentations: Fast and flexible image augmentations. MDPI (2020)
5. Cubuk, E.D., Zoph, B., Mane, D., Vasudevan, V., Le, Q.V.: Autoaugment: learning augmentation strategies from data. In: CVPR (2019)
6. Cubuk, E.D., Zoph, B., Shlens, J., Le, Q.V.: Randaugment: practical automated data augmentation with a reduced search space. In: CVPR (2020)
7. Droste, R., et al.: Ultrasound image representation learning by modeling sonographer visual attention. IPMI (2019)
8. Dubost, F., Bortsova, G., Adams, H., Ikram, M.A., Niessen, W., Vernooij, M., de Bruijne, M.: Hydranet: data augmentation for regression neural networks. In: Shen, D., Liu, T., Peters, T.M., Staib, L.H., Essert, C., Zhou, S., Yap, P.-T., Khan, A. (eds.) MICCAI 2019. LNCS, vol. 11767, pp. 438–446. Springer, Cham (2019). https://doi.org/10.1007/978-3-030-32251-9_48
9. Eaton-Rosen, Z., Bragman, F., et al.: Improving data augmentation for medical image segmentation. In: MIDL (2018)
10. Frid-Adar, M., Diamant, I., et al.: Gan-based synthetic medical image augmentation for increased cnn performance in liver lesion classification. Neurocomputing (2018)
11. Gan, Z., Henao, R., Carlson, D., Carin, L.: Learning deep sigmoid belief networks with data augmentation. In: Proceedings of Machine Learning Research (PMLR) (2015)
12. Gontijo-Lopes, R., Smullin, S.J., Cubuk, E.D., Dyer, E.: Affinity and diversity: quantifying mechanisms of data augmentation (2020)
13. Ho, D., Liang, E., et al.: Population based augmentation: efficient learning of augmentation policy schedules. In: ICML (2019)
14. Hu, J., et al.: Squeeze-and-excitation networks. In: IPAMI (2020)
15. Hussain, Z., Gimenez, F., Yi, D., Rubin, D.: Differential data augmentation techniques for medical imaging classification tasks. AMIA (2017)
16. Jiao, J., et al.: Self-supervised representation learning for ultrasound video. In: IEEE 17th International Symposium on Biomedical Imaging (2020)
17. Jin, D., Xu, Z., Tang, Y., Harrison, A.P., Mollura, D.J.: CT-realistic lung nodule simulation from 3D conditional generative adversarial networks for robust lung segmentation. In: Frangi, A.F., Schnabel, J.A., Davatzikos, C., Alberola-López, C., Fichtinger, G. (eds.) MICCAI 2018. LNCS, vol. 11071, pp. 732–740. Springer, Cham (2018). https://doi.org/10.1007/978-3-030-00934-2_81
18. Lim, S., Kim, I., Kim, T., Kim, C., Kim, S.: Fast autoaugment. In: Advances in Neural Information Processing Systems (NeurIPs) (2019)
19. Luke, T., Geoff, N.: Improving deep learning using generic data augmentation. In: IEEE Symposium Series on Computational Intelligence (2018)

20. Nalepa, J., et al.: Data augmentation via image registration. In: ICIP (2019)
21. Ohno, H.: Auto-encoder-based generative models for data augmentation on regression problems (2019)
22. Ryo, T., Takashi, M.: Data augmentation using random image cropping and patches for deep CNNs. In: IEEE TCSVT (2020)
23. Summers, C., Dinneen, M.J.: Improved mixed-example data augmentation. In: IEEE Winter Conference on Applications of Computer Vision (WACV) (2019)
24. Tokozume, Y., Ushiku, Y., Harada, T.: Between-class learning for image classification. In: CVPR (2018)
25. Zhang, H., Cisse, M., Dauphin, Y.N., Lopez-Paz, D.: mixup: beyond empirical risk minimization. In: ICLR (2018)
26. Zhao, A., Balakrishnan, G., et al.: Data augmentation using learned transformations for one-shot medical image segmentation. In: CVPR (2019)

Adversarial Regression Learning for Bone Age Estimation

Youshan Zhang$^{(\boxtimes)}$ and Brian D. Davison

Computer Science and Engineering, Lehigh University, Bethlehem, PA, USA
{yoz217,bdd3}@lehigh.edu

Abstract. Estimation of bone age from hand radiographs is essential to determine skeletal age in diagnosing endocrine disorders and depicting the growth status of children. However, existing automatic methods only apply their models to test images without considering the discrepancy between training samples and test samples, which will lead to a lower generalization ability. In this paper, we propose an adversarial regression learning network (*ARLNet*) for bone age estimation. Specifically, we first extract bone features from a fine-tuned Inception V3 neural network and propose regression percentage loss for training. To reduce the discrepancy between training and test data, we then propose adversarial regression loss and feature reconstruction loss to guarantee the transition from training data to test data and vice versa, preserving invariant features from both training and test data. Experimental results show that the proposed model outperforms state-of-the-art methods.

Keywords: Adversarial learning · Dataset shift · Bone age estimation

1 Introduction

Skeletal age estimation from hand radiology images is extensively used in endocrinological disease diagnosis, judgment of children's growth, and genetic disorder diagnoses [1]. Bone age basically reflects the appearance of the hand. As children grow, their bones become longer and change from cartilage to proper bones, such that we can estimate how old a child is based on the average age of children with similar bone images.

Bone age assessment starts with taking X-ray images of children's hands. For decades, the assessment of bone age was usually based on manual visual assessment of bone development of palms and wrists [2,3]. Hence, it is tedious and error prone. Therefore, it is necessary to develop an accurate automatic bone age algorithm. Recently, deep neural networks have become widely used in the medical field. Automatic bone age estimation using deep learning methods is much faster than manual labeling, while accuracy exceeds conventional methods [4]. Most existing deep learning based methods take advantage of well-trained models on ImageNet datasets such as VGG16 [5], ResNet50 [6], or Inception V3 [7] for feature extraction, and add a regression layer to output bone age.

© Springer Nature Switzerland AG 2021
A. Feragen et al. (Eds.): IPMI 2021, LNCS 12729, pp. 742–754, 2021.
https://doi.org/10.1007/978-3-030-78191-0_57

Although many methods achieve effective results in bone age estimation, they still suffer from one challenge: models are only optimized with training data, while the differences between training and test samples are omitted. Such models hence have a lower generalization ability to test samples if they are different from training data. To address this challenge, we aggregate three different loss functions in one framework: regression percentage error loss, adversarial regression loss, and feature reconstruction loss.

The contributions of this paper are three-fold:

1. To reduce the data discrepancy, we first extract features from a fine-tuned Inception V3 neural network and propose a regression percentage error loss, which addresses both individual prediction error and mean prediction error;
2. To the best of our knowledge, we are the first to propose an adversarial regression loss to reduce the data difference during the training;
3. The proposed feature reconstruction loss is able to maintain the feature consistency information of training and test samples.

Extensive experiments are conducted on a large-scale Bone-Age dataset and achieve superior results over state-of-the-art methods. Our architecture is also successfully applied to another regression task: face age estimation.

2   Related Work

In recent decades, bone age estimation has changed from manual assessment to automatic estimation algorithms. Deep learning methods have proved to be better than traditional machine learning methods in estimating in bone age.

Halabi et al. [8] reported the best five models for bone age estimation of the Radiological Society of North America (RSNA) challenge. The best model utilized the Inception V3 architecture concatenated with gender information. Data augmentation was leveraged to prevent overfitting and improve performance. The best performance achieves an error of 4.2 months (mean absolute difference, or MAD) in the challenge. Iglovikov et al. [9] first used a dilated U-net to segment hand, and then they removed the background and normalized images. They finally calculated the affine transformations to register images. The bone age assessment model consists of a VGG-style regression model and classification model. The classification model aimed to output the bone age class, while the regression model output the bone age. The model achieved 4.20 months MAD. Chen et al. [10] proposed an attention-guided approach to automatically localize the discriminative regions to estimate bone age. They then aggregated different regions for bone age assessment. Their model achieved 4.7 months MAD. Similarly, Escoba et al. [1] developed an approach to focus on local analysis of anatomical ROIs. They presented the additional bounding boxes and ROIs annotations during training and proposed a hand detection and hand pose estimation model to extract local information for bone age estimation. Pan et al. [11] combined four different less-correlated and relatively high-performing models, and they found that creating a ensemble model based on several weak models convincingly outperformed single-model prediction for bone age assessment.

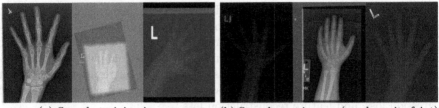

(a) Sample training images   (b) Sample test images (can be quite faint)

Fig. 1. Some bone radiology images from training and test data (differences between the training and test samples cause the difficulty of transfer learning).

Transfer learning applies existing knowledge to a new domain. Although many methods take advantage of pre-trained ImageNet models to estimate the bone age, they do not consider the differences between training and testing data, which can sometimes be quite obvious, as shown in Fig. 1. The discrepancy of data (named data shift/bias) will cause a vulnerability in the trained model, which causes poorer generalization on test data [12,13]. Transductive transfer learning uses both labeled training samples and unlabeled test samples to train the model and then uses a trained model to infer the label of the unlabeled test set. Hence, the data bias is mitigated via such a paradigm, which can improve the performance of the test data [14]. In this paper, we propose adversarial regression learning to estimate bone age and simultaneously reduce the data shift between training and test datasets.

3   Method

3.1   Motivation

As shown in Fig. 1, we observe differences between training and test data. Unlike previous work that only optimizes the model based on training data, we utilize the idea of transductive learning—we train the neural network using both the labeled training and unlabeled test data, which reduces the discrepancy between them. We adopt learning theory from [15] that the test risk can be minimized via bounding the training risk and discrepancy between them as follows.

Theorem 1. Let h be a hypothesis, $\epsilon_{tr}(h)$ and $\epsilon_{te}(h)$ represents the training and test risk (or error), respectively.

$$\epsilon_{te}(h) \leq \epsilon_{tr}(h) + d_{\mathcal{H}}(\mathcal{D}_{tr}, \mathcal{D}_{te}) + C \tag{1}$$

where $d_{\mathcal{H}}(\mathcal{D}_{tr}, \mathcal{D}_{te})$ is the $\mathcal{H}$-divergence of training and test data, C is the adaptability to quantify the error in an ideal hypothesis space of training and test data, which should be a sufficiently small constant.

3.2   Problem

Bone age estimation is a regression problem. Given training data $\mathcal{X}_{tr}$ (including bone radiology image and gender information) with its labels $\mathcal{Y}_{tr} \in (0, \mathbb{R}^+)^{N_{tr}}$ and test data $\mathcal{X}_{te}$ without its labels ($\mathcal{Y}_{te} \in (0, \mathbb{R}^+)^{N_{te}}$ for evaluation only), the goal in bone age estimation is to learn a regressor $\mathcal{R}$ to minimize the test data risk and reduce the discrepancy between training and test data.

For most existing models, in the absence of data shift, regression models simply learn a regressor $\mathcal{R}$ that performs the task on training data, and minimizes the loss function in Eq. 2:

$$\mathcal{L}_{tr}(\mathcal{X}_{tr}, \mathcal{Y}_{tr}) = \mathbb{E}[\ell(\mathcal{R}(\mathcal{X}_{tr}), \mathcal{Y}_{tr})], \tag{2}$$

where $\mathbb{E}[\cdot]$ is the expectation and ℓ can be any appropriate loss function. Equation 2 only minimizes the training risk $\epsilon_{tr}(h)$.

We define ℓ as the regression percentage error loss, $\ell = \mathcal{L}_{\mathcal{P}} = \mathcal{L}_{\mathcal{M}} + \alpha \mathcal{L}_{\mathcal{D}}$, where $\mathcal{L}_{\mathcal{M}}$ is the mean absolute percentage error loss, $\mathcal{L}_{\mathcal{D}}$ is the proposed absolute mean discrepancy loss and α is the balance factor between two loss functions. Specifically, $\mathcal{L}_{\mathcal{M}} = \frac{1}{N_{tr}} \sum_{i=1}^{N_{tr}} |\frac{\mathcal{Y}_{tr_i} - \mathcal{Y}'_{tr_i}}{\mathcal{Y}_{tr_i}}|$, $\mathcal{L}_{\mathcal{D}} = |\frac{\overline{\mathcal{Y}_{tr}} - \overline{\mathcal{Y}'_{tr}}}{\overline{\mathcal{Y}_{tr}}}|$, where $\overline{\mathcal{Y}_{tr}}$ and $\overline{\mathcal{Y}'_{tr}}$ denote the mean actual and predicted bone age in training dataset. For training data, such a loss ℓ can capture both individual and mean percentage error.

In Eq. 2, the loss of training data did not reduce the data shift issue. Therefore, previous works have lower generalization to the test data. To mitigate the effects of data shift, we follow previous adversarial learning [16,17] to map samples across different domains to a common space, and then invariant features are maintained. Hence, our model can learn on the training data, while retaining high generalization ability on test data.

In our framework, we employ a two-stage data discrepancy reduction procedure. We first extract bone features from any pre-trained or fine-tuned network. The distribution of training and test data are initially aligned, which reduced the discrepancy between them. We then use adversarial regression learning to find invariant features to further reduce the differences between training and test data. $d_{\mathcal{H}}(\mathcal{D}_{tr}, \mathcal{D}_{te}) \approx Dist(\mathcal{X}_{tr}, \mathcal{X}_{te}) + Dist(G(\mathcal{X}_{tr}), G(\mathcal{X}_{te}))$, specifically,

$$Dist(\mathcal{X}_{tr}, \mathcal{X}_{te}) = ||\frac{1}{N_{tr}} \sum_{i=1}^{N_{tr}} G(\mathcal{X}_{tr}^i) - \frac{1}{N_{te}} \sum_{j=1}^{N_{te}} G(\mathcal{X}_{te}^j)||_{\mathcal{H}}$$

$$Dist(G(\mathcal{X}_{tr}), G(\mathcal{X}_{te})) = ||\frac{1}{N_{tr}} \sum_{i=1}^{N_{tr}} \Phi(G(\mathcal{X}_{tr}^i)) - \frac{1}{N_{te}} \sum_{j=1}^{N_{te}} \Phi(G(\mathcal{X}_{te}^j))||_{\mathcal{H}}$$

where G is feature extractor from any pre-trained or fine-tuned neural network, and Φ is feature extractor from adversarial regression learning in Sect. 3.3. $\mathcal{H}$ is the Reproducing Kernel Hilbert Space (RKHS) space.

3.3   Adversarial Regression Learning

Adversarial learning is widely used to mitigate data shift issues [16,17]. It minimizes the domain discrepancy by a feature extractor and a domain discriminator.

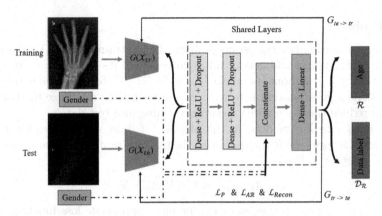

Fig. 2. The architecture of our proposed adversarial regression learning network (*ARLNet*). Training and test features are first extracted via G. Then, $G(\mathcal{X}_{tr})$ and $G(\mathcal{X}_{te})$ are fed into shared layers. The concatenate layer combines features from preceding layers and the gender. The weights of shared layers are updated by labeled training and unlabeled test data. $\Phi_{tr \to te}$ and $\Phi_{te \to tr}$ is the reconstruction from training data to test data and from test data to training data using hidden reconstruction layers (the detailed reconstruction layers are in Fig. 3). $\mathcal{L}_P$: regression percentage error loss, $\mathcal{L}_{AR}$: adversarial regression loss, $\mathcal{L}_{Recon}$: feature reconstruction loss, $\mathcal{R}$: regressor and $\mathcal{D}_{\mathcal{R}}$: data regressor

The domain discriminator aims to distinguish the source domain from the target domain, while the feature extractor aims to learn domain-invariant representations to fool the domain discriminator. Given data representations from feature extractor G, we can learn a discriminator D, which can distinguish the two domains using the following binary cross-entropy loss function:

$$\mathcal{L}_A(G(\mathcal{X}_{tr}), G(\mathcal{X}_{te})) = -\mathbb{E}_{x_{tr} \sim G(\mathcal{X}_{tr})}[\log D(x_{tr})] - \mathbb{E}_{x_{te} \sim G(\mathcal{X}_{te})}[\log(1 - D(x_{te}))] \tag{3}$$

However, adversarial learning is typically applied in classification problems. The binary cross-entropy in Eq. 3 is also frequently used in improving the accuracy of classification problems. The cross-entropy loss is not proper to indicate the data difference in a regression problem. Therefore, we need a regression loss function to distinguish the training and test datasets, and we adopt the adversarial learning for the regression problem as follows.

$$\mathcal{L}_{AR}(\Phi_{tr \to te}, G(\mathcal{X}_{tr}), G(\mathcal{X}_{te})) = \mathbb{E}_{x \sim (\mathcal{X}_{tr} \cup \mathcal{X}_{te})}[\ell(\mathcal{D}_{\mathcal{R}}(x), \mathcal{Y}_{\mathcal{DL}})]$$
$$= \frac{1}{n_{tr} + n_{te}} \sum_{k=1}^{n_{tr}+n_{te}} |\frac{y_{\mathcal{DL}}^k - y_{\mathcal{DL}}^{k'}}{y_{\mathcal{DL}}^k + \epsilon}| + |\frac{\overline{y_{\mathcal{DL}}} - \overline{y_{\mathcal{DL}}'}}{\overline{y_{\mathcal{DL}}} + \epsilon}| \tag{4}$$

where $\mathcal{L}_{AR}$ is adversarial regression loss, $\Phi_{tr \to te}$ is the mapping from training to test data; $\mathcal{D}_{\mathcal{R}}$ is the adapted data regressor, and $\mathcal{X}_{tr} \cup \mathcal{X}_{te}$ contains all training and test samples; $\mathcal{Y}_{\mathcal{DL}}$ is the data label in Fig. 2, specifically, 0 is the label for the training data and 1 is the label for the test data; $y_{\mathcal{DL}}^{k'}$ is the prediction of data

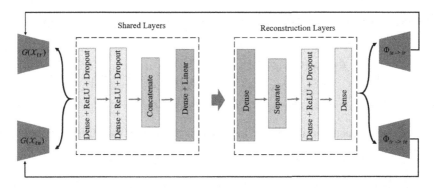

Fig. 3. Feature reconstruction layers ($\mathcal{L}_{Recon}$). The shared layers are optimized by both $G(\mathcal{X}_{tr})$ and $G(\mathcal{X}_{te})$. For $G(\mathcal{X}_{tr})$, the output from reconstruction layers should be closer to $G(\mathcal{X}_{tr})$, but it is under the conversion of $\Phi_{te \to tr}$ since the shared layers are also optimized by $G(\mathcal{X}_{te})$, it is hence from te to tr. Similarly, the output of reconstruction layer for $G(\mathcal{X}_{te})$ is under the conversion of $\Phi_{tr \to te}$.

label; $\overline{\mathcal{Y}_{DL}}$ and $\overline{\mathcal{Y}'_{DL}}$ denote the mean actual and predicted values of training or test dataset and ϵ is a small number (1e-9) to prevent division by 0. $\mathcal{L}_{AR}$ can measure how well-matched the training and test data are from both individual and overall differences. A perfect regression model would have an adversarial regression loss of 0.

To this end, the data regressor $\mathcal{D}_{R}$ learns the data discrepancy by maximizing adversarial regression loss $\mathcal{L}_{AR}$ with the fixed Φ, and the feature extractor Φ aims to learn domain-invariant representations via minimizing $\mathcal{L}_{AR}$ with the optimal regressor $\mathcal{R}$. Equation 4 guarantees that $tr \to te$, that is, given training samples, it will learn a map from training to test samples, while minimizing the $\mathcal{L}_{tr}(\mathcal{X}_{tr}, \mathcal{Y}_{tr})$ in Eq. 2. However, Eq. 4 only guarantees training data close to test data, and it does not ensure that $\Phi_{te \to tr}$ maintains the features of the training samples. We hence introduce another mapping from test data to training data $\Phi_{te \to tr}$ and train it with the same adversarial regression loss as in $\Phi_{tr \to te}$ as shown in Eq. 5. The only difference is that the 1 is the new data label for training data, and 0 is the new data label for test data.

$$\mathcal{L}_{AR}(\Phi_{te \to tr}, G(\mathcal{X}_{tr}), G(\mathcal{X}_{te})) \tag{5}$$

Therefore, we define the adversarial regression loss as:

$$\begin{aligned} \mathcal{L}_{AR}(G(\mathcal{X}_{tr}), G(\mathcal{X}_{te})) &= \mathcal{L}_{AR}(\Phi_{tr \to te}, G(\mathcal{X}_{tr}), G(\mathcal{X}_{te})) \\ &+ \mathcal{L}_{AR}(\Phi_{te \to tr}, G(\mathcal{X}_{tr}), G(\mathcal{X}_{te})) \end{aligned} \tag{6}$$

To encourage the training and test information to be preserved during the adversarial regression learning, we propose a feature reconstruction loss in our model. Details of the feature reconstruction layers are shown in Fig. 3; the reconstruction layers are right behind the shared layers, and it aims to reconstruct extracted features and maintain feature consistency during the conversion process without losing features. The feature reconstruction loss is defined as:

$$
\begin{aligned}
&\mathcal{L}_{Recon}(\Phi_{tr \to te}, \Phi_{te \to tr}, G(\mathcal{X}_{tr}), G(\mathcal{X}_{te})) \\
&= \mathbb{E}_{x_{tr} \sim G(\mathcal{X}_{tr})}[\ell'(\Phi_{te \to tr}(\Phi_{tr \to te}(x_{tr})) - x_{tr})] \\
&+ \mathbb{E}_{x_{te} \sim G(\mathcal{X}_{te})}[\ell'(\Phi_{tr \to te}(\Phi_{te \to tr}(x_{te})) - x_{te})]
\end{aligned} \tag{7}
$$

where ℓ' is the mean square error loss, which calculates the difference between true features and reconstructed features.

3.4   Overall Objective

We combine the three loss functions to formalize our objective function:

$$
\begin{aligned}
\mathcal{L}(\mathcal{X}_{tr}, \mathcal{X}_{te}, \mathcal{Y}_{tr}, \Phi_{tr \to te}, \Phi_{te \to tr}) = \mathcal{L}_{tr}(\mathcal{X}_{tr}, \mathcal{Y}_{tr}) + \beta \mathcal{L}_{AR}(G(\mathcal{X}_{tr}), G(\mathcal{X}_{te})) \\
+ \gamma \mathcal{L}_{Recon}(\Phi_{tr \to te}, \Phi_{te \to tr}, G(\mathcal{X}_{tr}), G(\mathcal{X}_{te})),
\end{aligned} \tag{8}
$$

where β and γ are trade-off parameters. Our model ultimately solves the following optimization problem. It minimizes the difference during the transition from the training to test data and from test to training data. Meanwhile, it maximizes the identification ability of training or test data.[1]

$$
\arg \min_{\substack{\Phi_{tr \to te} \\ \Phi_{te \to tr}}} \min \max_{\mathcal{D}_{tr}, \mathcal{D}_{te}} \mathcal{L}(\mathcal{X}_{tr}, \mathcal{X}_{te}, \mathcal{Y}_{tr}, \Phi_{tr \to te}, \Phi_{te \to tr})
$$

4   Experiments

We primarily validate our methods using the Bone-Age dataset. To demonstrate the generalizability of the architecture of *ARLNet*, we also evaluate our approach on the task of predicting age using two face datasets.

4.1   Datasets

Bone-Age includes data from the 2017 Pediatric Bone Age Challenge, which is organized by the Radiological Society of North America (RSNA). The statistics of the Bone-Age dataset are shown in Table 1 (Note that the test data is clearly different from the training data.) It also includes gender information associated with the bone age.

Face-Age is from the UTKFace dataset, which contains 9780 images with ages from 1 to 116. It also includes gender information with its associated images (more details can be found in Zhang et al. [18]). We also consider age regression in this dataset. The statistics of Face-Age dataset are shown in Table 2.

---

[1] Source code is available at https://github.com/YoushanZhang/Adversarial-Regression-Learning-for-Bone-Age-Estimation.

Table 1. Statistics of Bone-Age dataset

Bone-Age	# Total	# Male	# Female	Bone ages
Training set	12611	6833	5778	10.8 ± 3.5
Validation set	1425	773	652	10.8 ± 3.5
Test set	200	100	100	8.8 ± 3.6

Table 2. Statistics of Face-Age dataset

Face-Age	# Total	# Male	# Female	Face ages
Training set	4890	2183	2707	29.43 ± 24.79
Test set	4890	2189	2701	29.41 ± 24.76

MORPH II is from MORPH database, which contains more than 55,000 face images of 13,000 individuals aged from 16 to 77 years. It includes images with detailed age, gender, and many ethnicities). We followed the training/testing settings of Shen et al. [19] in the experiments, which selects 5,492 images of Caucasians. The final performance is reported using five-fold cross-validation.

4.2   Implementation Details

In the Bone-Age dataset, the features are extracted from an Inception V3 neural network through the last fully connected layer. We attach a regression layer to output the bone age, and gender is also another input for the model. One represented feature vector has the size of 1×1000 and is corresponding to one bone image. For the Bone-Age dataset, the represented feature vectors for training, validation, and test data have a size of 11611×1000, 1425×1000, and 200×1000, respectively. Similarly, we extract features from the last fully connected layer in a pre-trained Inception V3 neural network for the Face-Age dataset. The size of feature vectors of training and test data is 4890×1000. For MORPH II, the size of feature vectors of training and test data are 4394×1000, and 1098×1000, respectively. We then train the model based on these extracted feature vectors. The parameters of *ARLNet* are first tuned based on the performance of the validation dataset of the Bone-Age dataset. We then applied these parameters to test data of Bone-Age, Face-Age and MORPH II datasets.

The numbers of units of the dense layer in shared layers are 512, 8, and 1, while the numbers of units in the reconstruction layers are opposite (1, 8, and 512). The dropout rate is 0.5. Our implementation is based on Keras and the parameters settings are $\alpha = 10$, $\beta = \gamma = 0.5$, learning rate: $\eta = 0.0001$, batch size = 128, number of iterations is 300 and the optimizer is Adam. We first train the regression model using the percentage error loss on the labeled training data. Next, we perform adversarial regression learning using the extracted features and feature reconstruction loss, which yields the learned parameters for the feature transformations $\Phi_{tr \to te}$ and $\Phi_{te \to tr}$. We also compare our results with 15 state-of-the-art methods (including both traditional methods and deep neural networks). All re-implemented methods are marked in bold in Tables 3 and 4.

4.3 Evaluation

We use mean absolute error to evaluate our model: $MAE = \frac{1}{N}\sum_{i=1}^{N}(|y_i - \hat{y}_i|)$, where y is the provided age, and $\hat{y}$ is the predicted age.

Bone-Age. The comparison of MAE is listed in Table 3. We find that *ARLNet* has the lowest MAE versus all other approaches (23% reduction from the best baseline). Specifically, online software has the worst performance among all methods. It is a pruned version of Inception V3 [8], which excludes gender information, and the difference in performance between the two models is significant (more than 65% reduction). The MAE of Inception V3 is 4.20 months, while MAE of the pruned version is 12.35 months. This demonstrates that gender is important in predicting bone age. The performance of online software could be regarded as a lower bound. SVR is a traditional method, and its performance relies on the extracted features; it also does not consider the discrepancy between training and test data. GSM has better results than the SVR model since it samples more data between training and test data, which reduces the discrepancy between them. The performance of pre-trained models (VGG16 and Xception) also leads to higher MAE values. The is because the pre-trained model is trained based on the ImageNet dataset, while it does not contain information from bone images. In addition, we observe that two similar methods, DANN and ADDA, also have high MAE values. There are two possible reasons. First, the feature extraction layers of DANN and ADDA models are too shallow to extract detailed information for radiology bone images. Second, the adversarial learning of these two models only considers the transition from training data to test data.

Face-Age. The comparison of MAE is listed in Table 4. *ARLNet* again has the lowest MAE value, outperforming all others (24% reduction than the best baseline). We notice that results from Inception V3 are close to our model since our model is based on extracted features from the pre-trained Inception V3. However, our model has lower MAE than Inception V3 model, which demonstrates that the adversarial regression learning is useful in the regression problem. We find that the SVR model is better than some neural networks (VGG16 and Googlenet) since SVR uses the features from the Inception V3 model. SVR normally has a higher error than the fine-tuned IncetionV3 network. In addition, the performance of two domain adaptation methods (DANN and ADDA) have results close to that of our model. The underlying reason is that face images are easier to find data discrepancy and extract features since images are RGB images, while radiology bone images are significantly different from RGB images, it is difficult for these two methods to extract fine-grained bone features.

MORPH II. Table 4 also compares performance between *ARLNet* and state-of-the-art methods. ARLNet achieves the best performance, reducing the error rate by 17.1% compared to the best baseline model (DCNN), suggesting that adversarial regression learning is effective in reducing the discrepancy between training and test data, and achieves lower MAE.

Table 3. Results comparison of Bone-Age dataset

Methods	MAE
Online software [20]	12.35
SVR [21]	10.70
VGG16 [5]	7.57
GSM [14]	6.06
DANN [16]	5.26
ADDA [17]	4.91
Xception [22]	4.39
ResNet50 [4]	6.00
U-Net-VGG [9]	4.97
Ice Module [8]	4.40
Inception V3 [8]	4.20
Ensembles Models [11]	3.93
ARLNet	**3.01**

Table 4. MAE comparison on Face-Age and MORPH II datasets

Methods	Face-Age	MORPH II
VGG16 [5]	10.40	5.37
VGG19 [5]	9.64	4.93
SVR [21]	9.10	5.77
ResNet50 [6]	8.64	4.02
Xception [22]	8.49	3.88
Inception V3 [22]	8.36	3.65
GSM [14]	8.06	3.35
DANN [16]	6.26	3.01
ADDA [17]	5.91	2.73
ARN [23]	–	3.00
DRFs [19]	–	2.91
DCNN [24]	–	2.75
ARLNet	**4.50**	**2.28**

5 Discussion

There are three reasons that our model outperforms state-of-the-art methods. First, the proposed percentage loss ℓ is able to consider both the individual and mean percentage error. Second, we propose adversarial regression loss, which can maintain transition from training data to test data and transition from test data to training data. Third, we propose feature reconstruction loss, which further guarantees the consistency of training and test samples.

Table 5. Ablation experiments of effects of different loss functions of Bone-Age dataset

Methods	MAE
$ARLNet-\mathcal{L}_D - \mathcal{L}_{AR} - \mathcal{L}_{Recon}$	4.52
$ARLNet-\mathcal{L}_M - \mathcal{L}_{AR} - \mathcal{L}_{Recon}$	4.38
$ARLNet-\mathcal{L}_D - \mathcal{L}_{Recon}$	4.17
$ARLNet-\mathcal{L}_M - \mathcal{L}_{Recon}$	4.03
$ARLNet - \mathcal{L}_{AR} - \mathcal{L}_{Recon}$	3.91
$ARLNet - \mathcal{L}_{AR}$	3.45
$ARLNet - \mathcal{L}_{Recon}$	3.26
$ARLNet$	**3.01**

Ablation Study. To better demonstrate the performance of our model, we report the effects of different loss functions on classification accuracy in Table 5 ($\mathcal{L}_\mathcal{D}$: absolute mean discrepancy loss, $\mathcal{L}_\mathcal{M}$: mean absolute percentage error loss, and $\mathcal{L}_{\mathcal{AR}}$: adversarial regression loss and $\mathcal{L}_{Recon}$: feature reconstruction loss). "$ARLNet - \mathcal{L}_D - \mathcal{L}_{AR} - \mathcal{L}_{Recon}$" is implemented without absolute mean discrepancy loss, adversarial regression loss, and feature reconstruction loss. It is a simple model, which only considers the labeled training data using mean absolute percentage error loss. "$ARLNet - \mathcal{L}_{AR} - \mathcal{L}_{Recon}$" reports results without performing the additional adversarial regression loss and feature reconstruction loss. "$ARLNet - \mathcal{L}_{Recon}$" trains the model with percentage error loss and adversarial regression loss without the feature reconstruction loss. We observe that with the increasing of the number of loss functions, the robustness of our model keeps improving. Therefore, we can conclude that all these different loss functions are important in maximizing regression performance.

What can we learn from ARLNet? As shown in the ablation study, we know the effects of different loss functions. The adversarial regression loss has a dominant effect on the final results. Differing from traditional machine learning that only optimizes models using training data, our *ARLNet* considers transductive learning [14], and reduces the discrepancy between training and test data. It will be useful to include the test data during the training without any labels. Although there are no labels for the test data, the discrepancy between training samples and test samples is minimized, the test risk is thus reduced if there is a difference between training and test data. Therefore, the performance of the model will be improved if we feed the test data during the training processes with ARL.

6   Conclusion

We have presented an adversarial regression learning network (*ARLNet*) for bone age estimation that reduces the discrepancy between training and test data. In particular, we consider the problem from the traditional training protocol to adversarial regression learning. The adversarial regression learning consists of adversarial regression and feature reconstruction losses. The adversarial regression loss can push the prototype of bone ages computed in either training or test data close in the embedding space, and maintain invariant representations across two datasets. In addition, the proposed feature reconstruction loss further guarantees the structure and content from training and test data, and it will take the decision of regressor into account to align feature distribution, which leads to domain-invariant representations. Our approach provides a more than 20% error reduction over the state of the art in two age regression tasks.

References

1. Escobar, M., González, C., Torres, F., Daza, L., Triana, G., Arbeláez, P.: Hand pose estimation for pediatric bone age assessment. In: Shen, D., et al. (eds.) MICCAI 2019. LNCS, vol. 11769, pp. 531–539. Springer, Cham (2019). https://doi.org/10.1007/978-3-030-32226-7_59

2. Bayer, L.M.: Radiographic atlas of skeletal development of the hand and wrist. Calif. Med. **91**(1), 53 (1959)
3. Tanner, J.M., et al.: Assessment of skeletal maturity and prediction of adult height (TW2 method). Saunders London (2001)
4. Larson, D.B., Chen, M.C., Lungren, M.P., Halabi, S.S., Stence, N.V., Langlotz, C.P.: Performance of a deep-learning neural network model in assessing skeletal maturity on pediatric hand radiographs. Radiology **287**(1), 313–322 (2018)
5. Simonyan, K., Zisserman, A.: Very deep convolutional networks for large-scale image recognition. In: International Conference on Learning Representations (2015)
6. He, K., Zhang, X., Ren, S., Sun, J.: Deep residual learning for image recognition. In: Proceedings of the IEEE Conference on Computer Vision and Pattern Recognition (CVPR), pp. 770–778 (2016)
7. Szegedy, C., Vanhoucke, V., Ioffe, S. , Shlens, J., Wojna, Z.: Rethinking the inception architecture for computer vision. In: Proceedings of the IEEE Conference on Computer Vision and Pattern Recognition, pp. 2818–2826 (2016)
8. Halabi, S.S., et al.: The RSNA pediatric bone age machine learning challenge. Radiology **290**(2), 498–503 (2019)
9. Iglovikov, V.I., Rakhlin, A., Kalinin, A.A., Shvets, A.A.: Paediatric bone age assessment using deep convolutional neural networks. In: Stoyanov, D., et al. (eds.) DLMIA/ML-CDS -2018. LNCS, vol. 11045, pp. 300–308. Springer, Cham (2018). https://doi.org/10.1007/978-3-030-00889-5_34
10. Chen, C., Chen, Z., Jin, X., Li, L., Speier, W., Arnold, C.W.: Attention-guided discriminative region localization for bone age assessment. arXiv preprint arXiv:2006.00202 (2020)
11. Pan, I., Thodberg, H.H., Halabi, S.S., Kalpathy-Cramer, J., Larson, D.B.: Improving automated pediatric bone age estimation using ensembles of models from the 2017 RSNA machine learning challenge. Radiol. Artif. Intell. **1**(6), e190053 (2019)
12. Zhang, Y., Davison, B.D.: Impact of imagenet model selection on domain adaptation. In: Proceedings of the IEEE Winter Conference on Applications of Computer Vision Workshops, pp. 173–182 (2020)
13. Zhang, Y., Davison, B.D.: Domain adaptation for object recognition using subspace sampling demons. Multimed. Tools Appl., 1–20 (2020). https://doi.org/10.1007/s11042-020-09336-0
14. Zhang, Y., Xie, S., Davison, B.D.: Transductive learning via improved geodesic sampling. In: Proceedings of the 30th British Machine Vision Conference (2019)
15. Ben-David, S., et al.: A theory of learning from different domains. Mach. Learn.151–175 (2009). https://doi.org/10.1007/s10994-009-5152-4
16. Ghifary, M., Kleijn, W.B., Zhang, M.: Domain adaptive neural networks for object recognition. In: Pham, D.-N., Park, S.-B. (eds.) PRICAI 2014. LNCS (LNAI), vol. 8862, pp. 898–904. Springer, Cham (2014). https://doi.org/10.1007/978-3-319-13560-1_76
17. Tzeng, E., Hoffman, J., Saenko, K., Darrell, T.: Adversarial discriminative domain adaptation. In Proceedings of the IEEE Conference on Computer Vision and Pattern Recognition, pp. 7167–7176 (2017)
18. Zhang, Z., Song, Y., Qi, H.: Age progression/regression by conditional adversarial autoencoder. In: Proceedings of the IEEE Conference on Computer Vision and Pattern Recognition, pp. 5810–5818 (2017)
19. Shen, W., Guo, Y., Wang, Y., Zhao, K., Wang, B., Yuille, A.L.: Deep regression forests for age estimation. In: Proceedings of the IEEE Conference on Computer Vision and Pattern Recognition, pp. 2304–2313 (2018)

20. Cicero, M., Bilbily, A.: Machine learning and the future of radiology: how we won the 2017 RSNA ML challenge, November 2017. https://www.16bit.ai/blog/ml-and-future-of-radiology. Accessed 24 June 2020

21. Drucker, H., Burges, C.J.C., Kaufman, L., Smola, A.J., Vapnik, V.: Support vector regression machines. In: Advances in Neural Information Processing Systems, pp. 155–161 (1997)

22. Chollet, F.: Xception: deep learning with depthwise separable convolutions. In: Proceedings IEEE Conference on Computer Vision and Pattern Recog., pp. 1251–1258 (2017)

23. Agustsson, E., Timofte, R., Van Gool, L.: Anchored regression networks applied to age estimation and super resolution. In: Proceedings of the IEEE International Conference on Computer Vision, pp. 1643–1652 (2017)

24. Dornaika, F., Bekhouche, S.E., Arganda-Carreras, I.: Robust regression with deep CNNs for facial age estimation: an empirical study. Expert Syst. Appl. **141**, (2020)

Learning Image Quality Assessment by Reinforcing Task Amenable Data Selection

Shaheer U. Saeed[1]([✉]), Yunguan Fu[1,2], Zachary M. C. Baum[1], Qianye Yang[1], Mirabela Rusu[3], Richard E. Fan[4], Geoffrey A. Sonn[3,4], Dean C. Barratt[1], and Yipeng Hu[1]

[1] Centre for Medical Image Computing, Wellcome/EPSRC Centre for Interventional and Surgical Sciences and Department of Medical Physics and Biomedical Engineering, University College London, London, UK
shaheer.saeed.17@ucl.ac.uk
[2] InstaDeep, London, UK
[3] Department of Radiology, Stanford School of Medicine, Stanford, CA, USA
[4] Department of Urology, Stanford School of Medicine, Stanford, CA, USA

Abstract. In this paper, we consider a type of image quality assessment (IQA) as a task-specific measurement, which can be used to select images that are more amenable to a given target task, such as image classification or segmentation. We propose to train simultaneously two neural networks for image selection and a target task using reinforcement learning. A controller network learns an image selection policy by maximising an accumulated reward based on the target task performance on the controller-selected validation set, whilst the target task predictor is optimised using the training set. The trained controller is therefore able to reject images that lead to poor accuracy in the target task. In this work, we show that controller-predicted IQA can be significantly different from task-specific quality labels manually defined by humans. Furthermore, we demonstrate that it is possible to learn effective IQA without a "clean" validation set, thereby avoiding the requirement for human labels of task amenability. Using 6712, labelled and segmented, clinical ultrasound images from 259 patients, experimental results on holdout data show that the proposed IQA achieved a mean classification accuracy of 0.94 ± 0.01 and a mean segmentation Dice of 0.89 ± 0.02, by discarding 5% and 15% of the acquired images, respectively. The significantly improved performance was observed for both tested tasks, compared with the respective 0.90 ± 0.01 and 0.82 ± 0.02 from networks without considering task amenability. This enables IQA feedback during real-time ultrasound acquisition among many other medical imaging applications.

Keywords: Reinforcement learning · Medical image quality assessment · Deep learning · Task amenability

© Springer Nature Switzerland AG 2021
A. Feragen et al. (Eds.): IPMI 2021, LNCS 12729, pp. 755–766, 2021.
https://doi.org/10.1007/978-3-030-78191-0_58

1   Introduction

Image quality assessment (IQA) has been developed in the field of medical image computing and image-guided intervention as it is important to ensure that the intended diagnostic, therapeutic or navigational tasks can be performed reliably. It is intuitive that low-quality images can result in inaccurate diagnoses or measurements obtained from medical images [1,2], but there has been little evidence that such corroboration can be quantified, between completion of a specific clinical application and a single general-purpose IQA methodology. Chow and Paramesran [3] also pointed out that measures of image quality may not indicate diagnostic accuracy. We further argue that a general-purpose approach for medical image quality assessment is both challenging and potentially counterproductive. For example, various artefacts, such as reflections and shadows, may not be present near regions of clinical interest, yet a "good quality" image might still have inadequate field-of-view for the clinical task. In this work, we investigate the type of image quality which indicates how well a specific downstream target task performs and refer to this quality as *task amenability*.

Current IQA approaches in clinical practice rely on subjective human interpretation of a set of *ad hoc* criteria [3]. Automating IQA methods, for example, by computing dissimilarity to empirical references [3], typically can provide an objective and repeatable measurement, but requires robust mathematical models to approximate the underlying statistical and physical principles of good-quality image generation process or known mechanisms that reduce image quality (e.g. [4,5]). Recent deep-learning-based IQA approaches provide fast inference using expert labels of image quality for training [2,6–8]. However, besides the potentially high variability in these human-defined labels, to what extent they reflect task amenability - i.e. their usefulness for a specific task - is still an open question. In particular, a growing number of these target tasks have been modelled and automated by, for example, neural networks, which may result in different or unknown task amenability.

In this work, we focus on a specific use scenario of the task-specific IQA, in which images are selected by the measured task-specific image quality, such that the selected subset of high-quality images leads to improved target classification or segmentation accuracy. This image selection by task amenability has many clinical applications, such as meeting a clinically-defined accuracy requirement by removing the images with poor task amenability and maximising task performance given a predefined tolerance on how many images with poor amenability can be rejected and discarded. The rejected images may be re-acquired immediately in applications such as the real-time ultrasound imaging investigated in this work. The IQA feedback during scanning also provides an indirect measure of user skills, though skill assessment is not discussed further in this paper.

Furthermore, we propose to train a *controller network* and a *task predictor network* together for selecting task amenable images and for completing the target task, respectively. We highlight that optimising the controller is dependent on the task predictor being optimised. This may therefore be considered a meta-learning problem that maximises the target task performance with respect to the controller-selected images.

Reinforcement learning (RL) has increasingly been used for meta-learning problems, such as augmentation policy search [9,10], automated loss function search [11] and training data valuation [12]. Common in these approaches, a target task is optimised with a controller which modifies parameters associated with this target task. The parameter modification action is followed by a reward signal computed based on the target task performance, which is subsequently used to optimise the controller. This allows the controller to learn the parameter setting that results in a better performed target task. The target application can be image classification, regression or segmentation, while the task-associated parameter modification actions include transforming training data for data augmentation [9,10], selecting convolution filters for network architecture search [13] and sampling training data for data valuation [12]. Among these recent developments, the data valuation approach [12] shares some interesting similarities with our proposed IQA method, but with several important differences in the reward formulation by weighting/sampling validation set, the availability of "clean" high-quality image data, in addition to the different RL algorithms and other methodological details described in Sect. 2. For medical imaging applications, the RL-based meta-learning has also been proposed, for instance, to search for optimal weighting between different ultrasound modalities for the downstream breast cancer detection [14] and to optimise hyper-parameters for a subsequent 3D medical image segmentation [15], using the REINFORCE algorithm [16] and the proximal policy optimization algorithm [17], respectively.

In this work, we propose using RL to train the controller and task predictor for assessing medical image quality with respect to two common medical image analysis tasks. Using medical ultrasound data acquired from prostate cancer patients, the two tasks are a) classifying 2D ultrasound images that contain prostate glands from those that do not and b) segmenting the prostate gland. These two tasks are not only the basis of several computational applications, such as 3D volume reconstruction, image registration and tumour detection, but are also directly useful for navigating ultrasound image acquisition during surgical procedures, such as ultrasound-guided biopsy and therapies. Our experiments were designed to investigate the following research questions: 1) Can the task performance be improved on holdout test data selected by the trained controller network, compared with the same task predictor network based on supervised training and non-selective test data? 2) Does the trained controller provide a different or better measure of task amenability, compared with human labels of image quality which indicate amenability to the same tasks? 3) What is the trade-off between quantity of rejected images and improvement in task performance?

The contributions are summarised as follows: We a) propose to formulate task-specific IQA to learn task amenable data selection; b) propose a novel RL-based approach to quantify the task amenability, using different reward formulations with and without the need for human labels of task amenability; and c) present experiments to demonstrate the efficacy of the proposed IQA approach using real medical ultrasound images in two different downstream target tasks.

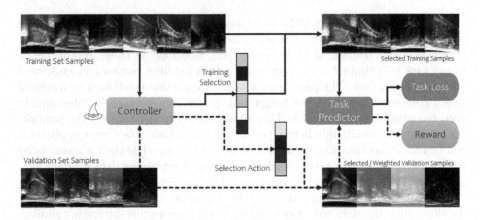

Fig. 1. Illustration of the training for controller and task predictor networks.

2   Method

2.1   Image Quality Assessment by Task Amenability

The proposed IQA consists of two parametric functions, task predictor and controller, illustrated in Fig. 1. The task predictor $f(\cdot; w) : \mathcal{X} \rightarrow \mathcal{Y}$, with parameters w, outputs a prediction $y \in \mathcal{Y}$ for a given image sample $x \in \mathcal{X}$. The controller $h(\cdot; \theta) : \mathcal{X} \rightarrow [0, 1]$, with parameters θ, generates an image quality score for a sample x, measuring task amenability of the sample. $\mathcal{X}$ and $\mathcal{Y}$ denote the image and label domains specific to a certain task, respectively.

Let $\mathcal{P}_X$ and $\mathcal{P}_{XY}$ be the image distribution and the joint image-label distribution, with probability density functions $p(x)$ and $p(x, y)$, respectively. The task predictor is optimised by minimising a weighted loss function $L_f : \mathcal{Y} \times \mathcal{Y} \rightarrow \mathbb{R}_{\geq 0}$:

$$\min_{w} \mathbb{E}_{(x,y) \sim \mathcal{P}_{XY}} [L_f(f(x; w), y) h(x; \theta)], \tag{1}$$

where L_f measures how well the task is performed by the predictor $f(x; w)$, given label y. It is weighted by the controller-measured task amenability on the same image x, as mistakes (high loss) on images with lower task amenability ought to be less weighted - with a view to rejecting them, and vice versa. The controller is optimised by minimising a weighted metric function $L_h : \mathcal{Y} \times \mathcal{Y} \rightarrow \mathbb{R}_{\geq 0}$:

$$\min_{\theta} \mathbb{E}_{(x,y) \sim \mathcal{P}_{XY}} [L_h(f(x; w), y) h(x; \theta)], \tag{2}$$

$$\text{s.t.} \quad \mathbb{E}_{x \sim \mathcal{P}_X} [h(x; \theta)] \geq c > 0 \tag{3}$$

such that the controller is encouraged to predict lower quality scores for images with higher metric values (lower task performance), as the weighted sum is minimised. The intuition is that making correct predictions on low-quality images tends to be more difficult. The constraint prevents the trivial solution $h \equiv 0$.

Thus, learning the proposed task-specific IQA can be assembled as the following minimisation problem:

$$\min_{\theta} \mathbb{E}_{(x,y)\sim\mathcal{P}_{XY}}[L_h(f(x;w^*),y)h(x;\theta)], \qquad (4a)$$

$$\text{s.t.} \qquad w^* = \arg\min_{w} \mathbb{E}_{(x,y)\sim\mathcal{P}_{XY}}[L_f(f(x;w),y)h(x;\theta)], \qquad (4b)$$

$$\mathbb{E}_{x\sim\mathcal{P}_X}[h(x;\theta)] \geq c > 0. \qquad (4c)$$

To facilitate a sampling or selection action (see Sect. 2.3) by controller-predicted task amenability scores, Eq. (4) is re-written as:

$$\min_{\theta} \mathbb{E}_{(x,y)\sim\mathcal{P}^h_{XY}}[L_h(f(x;w^*),y)], \qquad (5a)$$

$$\text{s.t.} \qquad w^* = \arg\min_{w} \mathbb{E}_{(x,y)\sim\mathcal{P}^h_{XY}}[L_f(f(x;w),y)], \qquad (5b)$$

$$\mathbb{E}_{x\sim\mathcal{P}^h_X}[1] \geq c > 0. \qquad (5c)$$

where the data x and (x,y) are sampled from the controller-selected or -sampled distributions $\mathcal{P}^h_X$ and $\mathcal{P}^h_{XY}$, with probability density functions $p^h(x) \propto p(x)h(x;\theta)$ and $p^h(x,y) \propto p(x,y)h(x;\theta)$, respectively.

2.2   The Reinforcement Learning Algorithm

In this work, an RL agent interacting with an environment is considered as a finite-horizon Markov decision process with $(\mathcal{S},\mathcal{A},p,r,\pi,\gamma)$. $\mathcal{S}$ is the state space and $\mathcal{A}$ is a continuous action space. $p : \mathcal{S} \times \mathcal{S} \times \mathcal{A} \to [0,1]$ is the state transition distribution conditioned on state-actions, e.g. $p(s_{t+1} \mid s_t, a_t)$ denotes the probability of the next state $s_{t+1} \in \mathcal{S}$ given the current state $s_t \in \mathcal{S}$ and action $a_t \in \mathcal{A}$. $r : \mathcal{S} \times \mathcal{A} \to \mathbb{R}$ is the reward function and $R_t = r(s_t, a_t)$ denotes the reward given s_t and a_t. $\pi(a_t \mid s_t) : \mathcal{S} \times \mathcal{A} \in [0,1]$ is the policy represents the probability of performing action a_t given s_t. The constant $\gamma \in [0,1]$ discounts the accumulated rewards starting from time step t: $Q^\pi(s_t, a_t) = \sum_{k=0}^{T}\gamma^k R_{t+k}$. A sequence $(s_1, a_1, R_1, s_2, a_2, R_2, \ldots, s_T, a_T, R_T)$ is thereby created with the RL agent training, with the objective to learn a parameterised policy π_θ which maximises the expected return $J(\theta) = \mathbb{E}_{\pi_\theta}[Q^\pi(s_t, a_t)]$.

Two different algorithms have been considered in our experiments, REIN-FORCE [16] and Deep Deterministic Policy Gradient (DDPG) [18]. Based on initial results indicating little difference in performance between the two, all the results presented in this paper are based on DDPG, with which a noticeably more efficient and stable training was observed. Further investigation into the choice of RL algorithms remains interesting in future work. While the REINFORCE computes policy gradient to update the controller parameters directly, DDPG is an actor-critic algorithm, with an off-policy critic $Q(s_t, a_t; \theta^Q) : \mathcal{S} \times \mathcal{A} \to \mathbb{R}$ and a deterministic actor $\mu(s_t; \theta^\mu) : \mathcal{S} \to \mathcal{A}$. To maximise the performance function $J(\theta^\mu) = \mathbb{E}_\mu[Q^\pi(s_t, \mu(s_t; \theta^\mu))]$, the variance-reduced policy gradient is used to update the controller: $\nabla_{\theta^\mu} J(\theta^\mu) = \mathbb{E}_\mu[\nabla_{\theta^\mu}\mu(s_t; \theta^\mu)\nabla_a Q^\pi(s_t, a)|_{a=\mu(s_t;\theta^\mu)}],$

which can be approximated by sampling the behaviour policy $\beta(s_t) \neq \mu(s_t; \theta^\mu)$:

$$\nabla_{\theta^\mu} J(\theta^\mu) \approx \mathbb{E}_\beta[\nabla_{\theta^\mu} \mu(s_t; \theta^\mu) \nabla_a Q(s_t, a; \theta^Q)|_{a=\mu(s_t; \theta^\mu)}], \qquad (6)$$

where the critic $Q(s_t, a_t; \theta^Q)$ is updated with respect to minimising:

$$\mathbb{E}_\beta[(R_t + \gamma Q(s_{t+1}, a_{t+1}; \theta^Q) - Q(s_t, a_t; \theta^Q))^2]. \qquad (7)$$

Copies of the actor $Q'(s_t, a_t; \theta^{Q'})$ and critic $\mu'(s_t; \theta^{\mu'})$ are used to compute moving averages during parameter updates, $\theta^{Q'} \leftarrow \tau\theta^Q + (1 - \tau)\theta^{Q'}$ and $\theta^{\mu'} \leftarrow \tau\theta^\mu + (1 - \tau)\theta^{\mu'}$, respectively (with $\tau = 0.001$). A random noise $\mathcal{N}$ is added to $\mu(s_t; \theta^\mu)$ for exploration where $\mathcal{N}$ is the Ornstein-Uhlenbeck process [19], with the scale and mean reversion rate parameters set to 0.2 and 0.15, respectively.

2.3   Image Quality Assessment with Reinforcement Learning

In this section, the IQA in Eq.(5) is formulated as a RL problem and solved by the algorithm described in Sect. 2.2. The pseudo-code is provided in Algorithm 1. A finite dataset together with the task predictor is considered the environment. At time step t, the observed state from the environment $s_t = (f(\cdot; w_t), \mathcal{B}_t)$ consists of the predictor $f(\cdot; w_t)$ and a mini-batch of samples $\mathcal{B}_t = \{(x_i, y_i)\}_{i=1}^B$ from a training dataset $\mathcal{D}_{\text{train}} = \{(x_i, y_i)\}_{i=1}^N$. The agent is the controller $h(\cdot; \theta)$ that outputs sampling probabilities $\{h(x_i; \theta)\}_{i=1}^B$. The action $a_t = \{a_t^i\}_{i=1}^B \in \{0, 1\}^B$ is the sample selection decision, by which (x_i, y_i) is selected if $a_t^i = 1$ for training the predictor. The policy $\pi_\theta(a_t \mid s_t)$ is thereby defined as:

$$\log \pi_\theta(a_t \mid s_t) = \sum_{i=1}^D h(x_i; \theta)a_t^i + (1 - h(x_i; \theta)(1 - a_t^i)) \qquad (8)$$

The unclipped reward $\tilde{R}_t$ is calculated based on the predictor's performance $\{l_{j,t}\}_{j=1}^M = \{L_h(f(x_j; w_t), y_j)\}_{j=1}^M$ on a validation dataset $\mathcal{D}_{\text{val}} = \{(x_j, y_j)\}_{j=1}^M$ and the controller's outputs $\{h_j\}_{j=1}^M = \{h(x_j; \theta)\}_{j=1}^M$. Three definitions for reward computation are considered in this work:

1. $\tilde{R}_{\text{avg},t} = -\frac{1}{M}\sum_{j=1}^M l_{j,t}$, the average performance.
2. $\tilde{R}_{\text{w},t} = -\frac{1}{M}\sum_{j=1}^M l_{j,t}h_j$, the weighted sum.
3. $\tilde{R}_{\text{sel},t} = -\frac{1}{M'}\sum_{j'=1}^{M'} l_{j',t}$, the average of the selected M' samples.

where $\{j'\}_{j'=1}^{M'} \subseteq \{j\}_{j=1}^M$ and $h_{j'} \leq h_{k'}, \forall k' \in \{j'\}^c, \forall j' \in \{j'\}$, i.e. the unclipped reward $\tilde{R}_{\text{sel},t}$ is the average of $\{l_{j'}\}$ from the subset of $M' = \lfloor(1 - s^{rej})M\rfloor$ samples, by removing the first $s^{rej} \times 100\%$ samples, after sorting h_j in decreasing order. It is important to note that, for the first reward definition $\tilde{R}_{\text{avg},t}$ without being weighted or selected by the controller, the validation set requires pre-selected "high-amenability" data. In this work, additional human labels of task amenability were used for generating such a clean fixed validation set (details in Sect. 3). During training, the clipped reward $R_t = \tilde{R}_t - \bar{R}_t$ is used with a moving average $\bar{R}_t = \alpha_R \bar{R}_{t-1} + (1 - \alpha_R)\tilde{R}_t$, where α_R is a hyper-parameter set to 0.9.

Algorithm 1: Image quality assessment by task amenability

Data: Training dataset $\mathcal{D}_{\text{train}}$ and validation dataset $\mathcal{D}_{\text{val}}$.
Result: Task predictor $f(\cdot; w)$ and controller $h(\cdot; \theta)$.

while *not converged* **do**
    for $k \leftarrow 1$ **to** K **do**
        for $t \leftarrow 1$ **to** T **do**
            Sample a mini-batch $\mathcal{B}_t = \{(x_i, y_i)\}_{i=1}^{B}$ from $\mathcal{D}_{\text{train}}$;
            Compute selection probabilities $\{h(x_i; \theta_t)\}_{i=1}^{B}$;
            Sample actions $a_t = \{a_t^i\}_{i=1}^{B}$ w.r.t. $a_t^i \sim \text{Bernoulli}(h(x_i; \theta))$;
            Selected samples $\mathcal{B}_{t,\text{selected}}$ from $\mathcal{B}_t$;
            Update predictor $f(\cdot; w_t)$ using $\mathcal{B}_{t,\text{selected}}$;
            Compute reward R_t;
        end
        Collect one episode $\{\mathcal{B}_t, a_t, R_t\}_{t=1}^{T}$;
    end
    Update controller $h(\cdot; \theta)$ using reinforcement learning algorithm;
end

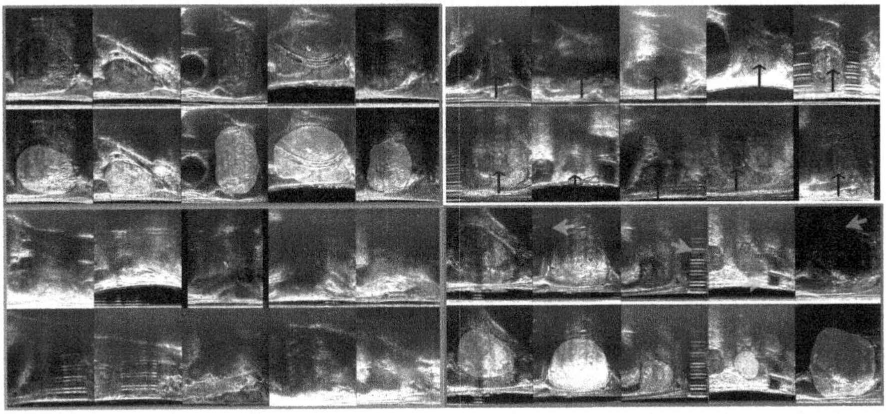

Fig. 2. Examples of ultrasound images in this study. **Top-left** (green): task-amenable images that contain prostate gland (shaded in red); **Bottom-left** (red): images with poor task amenability where recognising the prostate (for classification) and delineating its boundary (for segmentation) is difficult; **Top-right** (yellow), images that likely contain prostate glands (blue arrows) but identifying the complete gland boundaries for segmentation is challenging; and **Bottom-right** (blue): images that contain visible noise and artefacts (orange arrows), but may be amenable to both classification and segmentation tasks. (Color figure online)

3 Experiment

Transrectal ultrasound images were acquired from 259 patients, at the beginning stages of the ultrasound-guided biopsy procedures, as part of the clinical trials

(NCT02290561, NCT02341677). For each subject, a range of 50–120 2D frames were acquired with the side-firing transducer of a bi-plane transperineal ultrasound probe (C41L47RP, HI-VISION Preirus, Hitachi Medical Systems Europe), during manual positioning of a digital transperineal stepper (D&K Technologies GmbH, Barum, Germany) or rotating of the stepper with recorded relative angles, for navigating ultrasound view and scanning entire gland, respectively. For feasibility in manual labelling, the ultrasound images were sampled at approximately every 4 degrees, resulting in 6712 total images.

Prostate glands, where visible, were segmented in all images by three trained biomedical engineering researchers. Two sets of task labels were curated for individual images: classification labels (binary scalar indicating prostate presence) and segmentation labels (binary mask of the gland). In this work, a single label for each of the two tasks was obtained by consensus over all three observers, based on majority voting at image-level and pixel-level, respectively.

As discussed in Sect. 1, the task-specific image quality of interest for the classification task and the segmentation task can be different. Therefore, additional two binary labels were assigned for each image to represent the human label of task amenability, based on the observer assessment of whether the image quality adversely affects the completion of each task (see examples in Fig. 2).

The labelled images were randomly split, at the patient-level, into train, validation, and holdout sets with 4689, 1023, and 1000 images from 178, 43, and 38 subjects, respectively.

The proposed RL framework was evaluated on both tasks. The three reward definitions proposed in Sect. 2.3 were compared together with two *non-selective baseline* networks for classification and segmentation trained on all training data. For comparison purposes, they share the same network architectures and training strategies as the task predictors in the RL algorithms. For the classification tasks, Alex-Net [20,21] was trained with a cross-entropy loss and a reward based on classification accuracy (Acc.), i.e. classification correction rate. For segmentation tasks, U-Net [22] was trained with a pixel-wise cross-entropy loss and a mean binary Dice score to form the reward. For the purpose of this work, the reported experimental results are based on empirically configured networks and RL hyperparameters that were unchanged, unless specified, from the default values in the original Alex-Net, U-Net and DDPG algorithms. It is perhaps noteworthy that, based on our initial experiments, changing these configurations seems unlikely to alter the conclusions summarised in Sect. 4, but future research may be required to confirm this and further optimise their performance.

Based on the holdout set, a mean Acc. and a mean binary Dice were computed to evaluate the trained task predictor networks, in classification and segmentation tasks, respectively, with different percentages of the holdout set removed according to the trained controller networks. Selection is not applicable to the baseline networks. Standard deviation (St.D.) is also reported to measure the inter-patient variance. Paired two-sample t-test results at a significance level of $\alpha = 0.05$ are reported for comparisons.

4   Result

To evaluate the trained controllers, the 2×2 contingency tables in Fig. 3 compare subjective task amenability labels with controller predictions. For the purpose of comparison, 5% and 15% of images were removed from the holdout set by the trained controller, for the classification and segmentation tasks, respectively. The results of the selective reward $\tilde{R}_{\mathrm{sel},t}$ with $s^{rej} = 5\%$ and $s^{rej} = 15\%$ are used as examples, for the two respective tasks. Thereby, agreement and disagreement are quantified between images assessed by the proposed IQA and the same images assessed by the subjective human labels of task amenability, denoted as predicted low/high and subjective low/high, respectively. In classifying prostate presence, the rewards based on fixed-, weighted- and selective validation sets resulted in agreed 75%, 70% and 43% low task amenability samples, with Cohen's kappa values of 0.75, 0.51 and 0.30, respectively. In the segmentation task, the three rewards have 65%, 58% and 49% agreed low task amenability samples, with Cohen's kappa values of 0.63, 0.48 and 0.37, respectively.

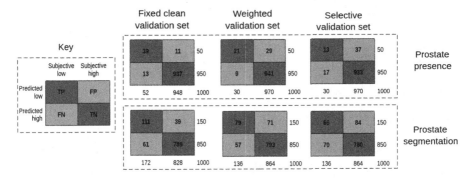

Fig. 3. Contingency tables comparing subjective labels to controller predictions for the different reward computation strategies.

Table 1. Comparison of results on the controller-selected holdout set.

Task	Reward computation strategy	Mean ± St.D
Prostate presence (Acc.)	Non-selective baseline	0.897 ± 0.010
	$\tilde{R}_{\mathrm{avg},t}$, fixed validation set	0.935 ± 0.014
	$\tilde{R}_{\mathrm{w},t}$, weighted validation set	0.926 ± 0.012
	$\tilde{R}_{\mathrm{sel},t}$, selective validation set	0.913 ± 0.012
Prostate segmentation (Dice)	Non-selective baseline	0.815 ± 0.018
	$\tilde{R}_{\mathrm{avg},t}$, fixed validation set	0.890 ± 0.017
	$\tilde{R}_{\mathrm{w},t}$, weighted validation set	0.893 ± 0.018
	$\tilde{R}_{\mathrm{sel},t}$, selective validation set	0.865 ± 0.014

To evaluate the task performances on the trained-controller-selected hold-out set, the Acc. and Dice are summarised in Table 1. The average training time was approximately 12 h on a single Nvidia Quadro P5000 GPU. In both tasks, all three proposed RL-based IQA algorithms provide statistically significant improvements, compared with the non-selective baseline counterparts, with all *p-values<0.001*. For both tasks, the results from the reward definition based on the selective validation set led to relatively inferior performances compared with the other two reward definitions, with statistical significance (*p-values<0.001*). Interestingly, no statistical significance was found between the reward definitions based on fixed- and weighted validation sets, for the classification (*p-value=0.06*) or segmentation (*p-value=0.49*) tasks, despite the disagreement summarised in Fig. 3. Figure 4a and 4b plot mean performance against (holdout) rejection ratio for the three reward computation strategies. The peak classification Acc. are 0.935, 0.932 and 0.913 at 5%, 10% and 5% rejection ratios, for the fixed-, weighted- and selective reward formulations, respectively, while the peak segmentation Dice are 0.891, 0.893 and 0.866 at 20%, 15% and 20% rejection ratios, respectively.

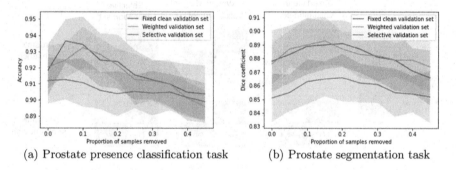

(a) Prostate presence classification task   (b) Prostate segmentation task

Fig. 4. Plots of the task performance (in respective Acc. and Dice metrics) against the ratios of removed holdout samples in each tasks.

5   Discussion and Conclusion

An interesting observation when inspecting Fig. 4 is that, in both tasks, the task performance peaked before decreasing as more samples were discarded for most tested methods. This seems counter-intuitive as the controller was trained to select task amenable data. While it remains an open question, we consider the following potential contributing factors: the variance of predictions, the possible over-fitting of the RL algorithms, the potentially non-monotonic relation between the optimal predictions conditioned on different values of s^{rej}, and the limitation of the datasets which may be considered of above-average quality (therefore higher amenability which limits potential performance improvement). Importantly, the significant improvement over the non-selective baseline networks demonstrated the efficacy of the proposed IQA approach.

The proposed weighted and selective reward formulations learned effective IQA without human labels of task amenability, which can be subjective and costly. Although the selective strategy performed moderately in this experiment, it may not be a general case for different datasets or applications and potentially provides a means to specify the desirable rejection rate. Moreover, tuning this additional rejection ratio hyper-parameter could potentially impact performance and investigating this relationship remains interesting in future work.

In summary, this paper has formulated IQA as a measure of task amenability, which can be learned by the proposed RL algorithm with and without human labels. The proposed IQA has been demonstrated and analysed with experiments based on clinical ultrasound images from prostate cancer patients.

Acknowledgements. This work is supported by the Wellcome/EPSRC Centre for Interventional and Surgical Sciences [203145Z/16/Z], the CRUK International Alliance for Cancer Early Detection (ACED) [C28070/A30912; C73666/A31378], EPSRC CDT in i4health [EP/S021930/1], the Departments of Radiology and Urology, Stanford University, the Natural Sciences and Engineering Research Council of Canada Postgraduate Scholarships-Doctoral Program (ZMCB), the University College London Overseas and Graduate Research Scholarships (ZMCB), GE Blue Sky Award (MR), and the generous philanthropic support of our patients (GAS).

References

1. Davis, H., Russell, S., Barriga, E., Abramoff, M., Soliz, P.: Vision-based, real-time retinal image quality assessment. In: 2009 22nd IEEE International Symposium on Computer-Based Medical Systems, pp. 1–6 (2009)
2. Wu, L., Cheng, J., Li, S., Lei, B., Wang, T., Ni, D.: FUIQA: fetal ultrasound image quality assessment with deep convolutional networks. IEEE Trans. Cybern. **47**(5), 1336–1349 (2017)
3. Chow, L.S., Paramesran, R.: Review of medical image quality assessment. Biomed. Sig. Process. Control **27**, 145–154 (2016)
4. Loizou, C.P., Pattichis, C.S., Pantziaris, M., Tyllis, T., Nicolaides, A.: Quality evaluation of ultrasound imaging in the carotid artery based on normalization and speckle reduction filtering. Med. Biol. Eng. Comput. **44**, 414 (2006). https://doi.org/10.1007/s11517-006-0045-1
5. Köhler, T., Budai, A., Kraus, M.F., Odstrčilik, J., Michelson, G., Hornegger, J.: Automatic no-reference quality assessment for retinal fundus images using vessel segmentation. In: Proceedings of the 26th IEEE International Symposium on Computer-Based Medical Systems, pp. 95–100 (2013)
6. Zago, G.T., Andreão, R.V., Dorizzi, B., Ottoni, E., Salles, T.: Retinal image quality assessment using deep learning. Comput. Biol. Med. **103**, 64–70 (2018)
7. Esses, S.J., et al.: Automated image quality evaluation of T2-weighted liver MRI utilizing deep learning architecture. J. Magn. Reson. Imaging **47**(3), 723–728 (2018)
8. Baum, Z.M.C.: Image quality assessment for closed-loop computer-assisted lung ultrasound. arXiv: 2008.08840 (2020)
9. Cubuk, E.D., Zoph, B., Mane, D., Vasudevan, V., Le, Q.V.: AutoAugment: learning augmentation policies from data. arXiv: 1805.09501 (2019)

10. Zhang, X., Wang, Q., Zhang, J., Zhong, Z.: Adversarial autoAugment. arXiv: 1912.11188 (2019)
11. Li, C., et al.: AM-LFS: AutoML for loss function search. In: 2019 ICCV, pp. 8409–8418 (2019)
12. Yoon, J., Arik, S., Pfister, T.: Data valuation using reinforcement learning. arXiv: 1909.11671 (2020)
13. Zoph, B., Le, Q.V.: Neural architecture search with reinforcement learning. arXiv: 1611.01578 (2017)
14. Wang, J., et al.: Auto-weighting for breast cancer classification in multimodal ultrasound. In: Matyel, A.L., et al. (eds.) MICCAI 2020. LNCS, vol. 12266, pp. 190–199. Springer, Cham (2020). https://doi.org/10.1007/978-3-030-59725-2_19
15. Yang, D., Roth, H., Xu, Z., Milletari, F., Zhang, L., Xu, D.: Searching learning strategy with reinforcement learning for 3D medical image segmentation. In: Shen, D., et al. (eds.) MICCAI 2019. LNCS, vol. 11765, pp. 3–11. Springer, Cham (2019). https://doi.org/10.1007/978-3-030-32245-8_1
16. Williams, R.J.: Simple statistical gradient-following algorithms for connectionist reinforcement learning. Mach. Learn. **8**, 229–256 (1992)
17. Schulman, J., Wolski, F., Dhariwal, P., Radford, A., Klimov, O.: Proximal policy optimization algorithms. arXiv: 1707.06347 (2017)
18. Lillicrap, T.P., et al.: Continuous control with deep reinforcement learning. arXiv: 1509.02971 (2019)
19. Uhlenbeck, G.E., Ornstein, L.S.: On the theory of the brownian motion. Phys. Rev. **36**(5), 823–841 (1930)
20. Krizhevsky, A., Sutskever, I., Hinton, G.: Imagenet classification with deep convolutional neural networks. In: NeurIPS (2012)
21. Bressem, K.K., Adams, L.C., Erxleben, C., Hamm, B., Niehues, S.M., Vahldiek, J.L.: Comparing different deep learning architectures for classification of chest radiographs. Scientific Report. **10** (2020)
22. Ronneberger, O., Fischer, P., Brox, T.: U-net: convolutional networks for biomedical image segmentation. In: Navab, N., Hornegger, J., Wells, W.M., Frangi, A.F. (eds.) MICCAI 2015. LNCS, vol. 9351, pp. 234–241. Springer, Cham (2015). https://doi.org/10.1007/978-3-319-24574-4_28

Collaborative Multi-agent Reinforcement Learning for Landmark Localization Using Continuous Action Space

Klemens Kasseroller[1] , Franz Thaler[2] , Christian Payer[1] ,
and Darko Štern[2(✉)]

[1] Institute of Computer Graphics and Vision, Graz University of Technology,
Graz, Austria
[2] Gottfried Schatz Research Center: Biophysics, Medical University of Graz,
Graz, Austria
darko.stern@medunigraz.at

Abstract. We propose a reinforcement learning (RL) based approach for anatomical landmark localization in medical images, where the agent can move in arbitrary directions with a variable step size. Using a continuous action space reduces the average number of steps required to locate a landmark by more than 30 times compared to localization using discrete actions. Our approach outperforms a state-of-the-art RL method based on a discrete action space and is inline with state-of-the-art supervised regression based methods. Furthermore, we extend our approach to a multi-agent setting, where we allow collaboration between agents to enable learning of the landmarks' spatial configuration. The results of the multi-agent RL based approach show that the position of occluded landmarks can be successfully estimated based on the relative position predicted for the visible landmarks.

Keywords: Reinforcement learning · Landmark localization · Collaborative multi-agent · Continuous action space

1 Introduction

Automatic localization of anatomical landmarks is an important step for a wide range of applications in medical image analysis, e.g. for registration or to initialize segmentation algorithms. Nevertheless, accurate anatomical landmark localization is also a challenging task due to anatomical and image intensity variations. Current state-of-the-art methods for anatomical landmark localization are based on supervised learning of Convolutional Neural Networks (CNNs) to either directly regress landmark coordinates [7] or their heatmap representation [11]. However, CNN based methods suffer from two major limitations. Either they require large amounts of memory to store the intermediate network outputs of the whole image on the GPU or, using patch-based approaches, depend on

© Springer Nature Switzerland AG 2021
A. Feragen et al. (Eds.): IPMI 2021, LNCS 12729, pp. 767–778, 2021.
https://doi.org/10.1007/978-3-030-78191-0_59

an additional model for global guidance. Differently to supervised learning, reinforcement learning (RL) based approaches have the advantage, that the RL agent is able to internally keep a representation of the environment, i.e. the content of the medical images. Applied to a medical task such as anatomical landmark localization, this internal representation of the anatomy allows the RL agent to navigate through the image from any arbitrary starting position, without the need of an additional model for global guidance. Furthermore, by learning from patches, RL eliminates the need of storing the large intermediate network outputs of the whole image in GPU memory, which is a challenge, especially when working with large 3D volumes. Finally, the navigation through images based on the perception of local image information is similar to the way a physician localizes anatomical structures in a medical image. Indeed, the physician, based on their prior knowledge in human anatomy, can estimate the position of an anatomical structure relative to other structures in the image.

Anatomical landmark localization was first formulated as a RL task by Ghesu et al. [4]. In this approach, they utilized a Deep Q-Network (DQN) agent [10] to observe a sub-image and move with a fixed one-pixel step size on the four principal directions through the 2D image or on the six principal directions through the volumetric image. Since the agent is restricted to a discrete action space with a fixed step size, during inference the DQN approach needs a large number of steps before localizing the target landmark. Ghesu et al. [5] tackle this problem with a multi-scale framework to cover a larger field of view (FOV) and accordingly take large action steps. Their implementation, however, uses a separate neural network for each scale. Alansary et al. [1], similarly, use a multi-scale approach, where a single neural network is used for all scales to reduce training time. To localize multiple landmarks simultaneously, the same group extended their work by sharing the weights between convolution layers of multiple DQN agents [12] and by additionally combining the extracted information in the fully-connected layers before generating the actions [6]. A mutual challenge of all DQN-based approaches for landmark localization is the identification of the optimal stopping criterion of the agent. For that purpose, Maicas et al. [9] proposes an additional trigger action, which increases the action space of the DQN agent and consequently the complexity of the approach. A better-accepted approach is proposed in [4] where oscillation within a local neighborhood is used as an indicator for termination, however, this limits the accuracy of the method and prolongs inference time.

To overcome the above-mentioned limitations of DQN-based approaches, in this work, we propose a continuous action space for localizing anatomical landmarks. By allowing the agent to move in an arbitrary direction with variable step size, we reduce the number of steps the agent needs to localize the target landmark, which effectively speeds up inference time while improving the accuracy. To implement a continuous action space, we utilize an actor-critic approach proposed in [8]. In our setup, the problem of the stopping criterion is intrinsically addressed, since the agent stops moving when the movement displacement falls below the pixel size. Furthermore, inspired by multi-agent RL [2], we extend our single-landmark/single-agent approach by introducing multiple agents to localize multiple landmarks simultaneously. Finally, we introduce communication between agents by providing every agent with it's relative position to the other agents. This allows learning of a spatial configuration between landmarks, which serves as regularization and provides an estimate of landmarks' position even in the case where landmarks are missing or occluded.

2 Method

Anatomical landmark localization can be formulated as a Markov Decision Process (MDP) by defining an environment, states, actions and a reward function. The environment is the medical image I in which the agent navigates to localize the target landmark. The position in the environment is the state $\mathbf{s} \in \mathbb{R}^D$ of the agent, where D is the number of image dimensions. The environment observed by the agent at the state $\mathbf{s}$ is the observation $o(\mathbf{s}) \subset I$, which is restricted to a local image patch around $\mathbf{s}$. To allow the agent to move in arbitrary directions with a varying step size, we defined a continuous action space similarly as in [8]. We represent the action $\mathbf{a}$ as a vector with $\mathbf{a} = [a_1, \cdots, a_D]^T \in \mathbb{R}^D$. Which action the agent takes after observing the state $\mathbf{s}$ is defined by the policy π. The agent's state after taking

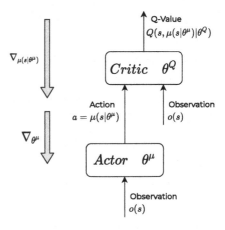

Fig. 1. Basic principle of the actor-critic architecture which allows continuous actions [8]. The actor network predicts an action and the critic network predicts a Q-value to evaluate the action.

an action is obtained by adding the action vector $\mathbf{a}$ to the current state $\mathbf{s}$, i.e. $\mathbf{s}' = \mathbf{s} + \mathbf{a}$. The reward function r for taking action $\mathbf{a}$ is defined as:

$$r = ||\mathbf{s} - \mathbf{g}|| - ||\mathbf{s}' - \mathbf{g}||, \tag{1}$$

where $\mathbf{g}$ is the position of the target landmark and $||\cdot||$ is the Euclidean distance.

The MDP can be solved by sampling experience tuples of the form $\langle \mathbf{s}, \mathbf{a}, r, \mathbf{s}' \rangle$ to determine the Q-function which can be written recursively as a Bellman equation:

$$Q_{t+1}(\mathbf{s}, \mathbf{a}) = \mathbb{E}[r + \max_{\mathbf{a}'} Q_t(\mathbf{s}', \mathbf{a}')] \tag{2}$$

with recursive step t. Differently from the DQN approach [10], where a single network can be used to model the Q-function due to the discrete action space, we use an actor-critic architecture as in [8] to allow continuous actions, see Fig. 1.

Thus, a critic network parameterized with θ^Q is modeling the Q-function, while a second, actor network μ parameterized with θ^μ is used to learn the policy π. During inference only the actor network is used to generate the new position of the agent.

To improve the stability of the training we use *soft updates* for both, critic Q and actor μ network as in [8]. Thus, we update the parameters of the target network $\theta_T^{\{Q,\mu\}}$ with parameters of the current network $\theta_C^{\{Q,\mu\}}$. An alternating procedure is used to optimize the parameters of both critic θ^Q and actor network θ^μ. By keeping the parameters of the actor network fixed, we optimize the critic parameters θ^Q using the Bellman loss:

$$\underset{\theta_C^Q}{\arg\max} \frac{1}{N} \sum_i^N \left[r_i + \gamma Q(\mathbf{s}_i', \mu(\mathbf{s}_i'|\theta_T^\mu)|\theta_T^Q) \right.$$
$$\left. - Q(\mathbf{s}_i, \mu(\mathbf{s}_i|\theta_T^\mu)|\theta_C^Q) \right]^2, \tag{3}$$

where N is the size of the mini-batch and $\gamma \in [0,1]$ is the discount factor used to weigh future rewards; the parameters θ_T^Q and θ_C^Q refer to the target and current network parameters of the critic respectively.

To optimize the parameters θ^μ of the actor network, we keep the parameters of critic θ^Q fixed and maximize the expected Q-value by using the chain rule to compute the gradient:

$$\nabla_{\theta_C^\mu} Q(\theta_C^Q, \theta_C^\mu) \approx \frac{1}{N} \sum_i^N \left[\nabla_{\mu(\mathbf{s}_i|\theta^\mu)} Q(\mathbf{s}_i, \mu(\mathbf{s}_i)|\theta_C^Q) \nabla_{\theta_C^\mu} \mu(\mathbf{s}_i|\theta_C^\mu) \right]. \tag{4}$$

Differently from DQN [10], where the stopping criterion is usually determined by state oscillation, in the proposed approach with continuous action space we can define the stopping criterion as an action with an absolute length below one pixel.

So far we introduced an agent that performs a single action and therefore can only detect one landmark at a time. To simultaneously localize multiple landmarks in an image during inference, multiple agents have to be trained individually, each one trained for a different landmark. However, in such an approach no communication among agents exists. In this work we propose an approach for multi landmark localization inspired by a collaborative multi-agent system. Thus, the input to the actor network are now multiple observations, each corresponding to different agents, see Fig. 2. The actor network independently predicts the next action for each agent. Together with the observation of each agent, these actions are used as input to the critic network to predict a single Q-value optimized using Eq. 3. To allow collaboration between multiple agents and thus, to learn the spatial configuration of the landmarks, the position of each agent relative to each other is additionally provided to the actor and critic network. To this end, we define a list of pairwise offsets $\mathbf{D}$ in the following form:

$$\mathbf{D} = \{\mathbf{s}^i - \mathbf{s}^j | i, j \in K, i \neq j\}, \tag{5}$$

where K is the number of agents.

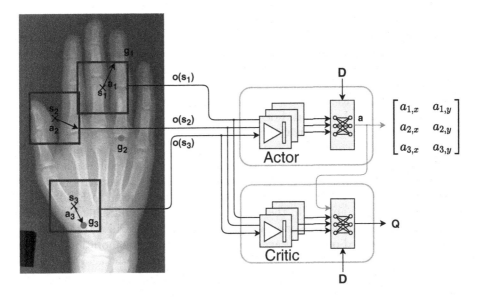

Fig. 2. Schematic representation of our proposed method for landmark localization. One observation per agent is used as input to the actor network which predicts the next actions. To allow collaboration, we additionally provide the list of pairwise offsets **D** (Eq. 5) to the network to enable learning of the spatial configuration of the anatomical landmarks. During training, an additional critic network is used which approximates the Q-function.

3 Experimental Setup

Dataset. We used a publicly available dataset of hand radiographs [3] acquired from different X-ray scanners to compare our method to both state-of-the-art RL and supervised learning based approaches for anatomical landmark localization. The dataset consists of 895 images with an average size of 156 × 2169 pixels. Since the images do not contain information about the physical resolution, we follow [11] and assume a wrist width of 50 mm from which we calculate a physical resolution for each image. We downsample all images to a common long-axis size of 512 pixels and split the dataset with the ratio 80:20 into 716 images for training and 179 images for testing. Due to the long training time needed for RL based approaches, we used five representative landmarks from the 37 landmarks provided by the authors of [11].

Implementation Details. In our single-agent approach, the actor network consists of three consecutive convolution-pooling-convolution blocks followed by three fully-connected layers, after which a final fully-connected layer yields the network output. All convolution layers use an isotropic kernel size of 3 and ReLU activation, the number of filters of the first convolution layer is 32 and is doubled after every pooling layer. We employ average pooling with an isotropic kernel size of 2 and zero padding. In the first three fully-connected layers we utilize 256 output neurons and ReLU activation, while the final fully-connected layer uses no activation function and directly outputs the predicted action. The actor and critic network are identical with following exceptions: the actor's prediction is provided as an additional input at the first fully-connected layer of the critic network, and the critic network predicts a single Q-value. This approach we named Single-Agent Landmark Localization (SALL).

In the multi-agent approach, the observation of the agent is processed individually in a unique convolution path, resulting in one parallel convolution path per agent. These paths are concatenated before the first fully-connected layer to generate the action of all agents simultaneously. The list of pairwise offsets D is provided as input to the first fully-connected layer as shown in Fig. 2. Same as with single-agent approach, the critic network of the multi-agent approach outputs a single Q-value. We named our multi-agent approached MALL. Additionally, we evaluated our multi-agent approach without collaboration between agents by omitting the pairwise offsets D from the input to the actor and critic network. We named this approach in our experiments $MALL_{noSC}$ where SC stands for spatial configuration.

During training, the agent is initialized at a random position within the image. The agent progresses to the next image, if the distance between target and the agent's current position is below one pixel or if the maximum number of steps is reached, i.e. 300 for DQN and 100 otherwise, leaving enough space for the agent to explore the entire state space. Furthermore, we limit the maximum step size per action to a distance of 50 pixels in each direction and we round the agent's position to the position of the closest pixel. If the agent overshoots the image bounds, it's position is moved to the closest position at the image border, out of bounds pixels of the observation are set to zero. Similarly to Lillicrap et al. [8], our actor network receives exploration noise from a Gaussian distribution during training. As hyperparameters we used $\gamma = 0.85$, a replay memory size of 10^5, an exploration noise with a variance of 0.15, a soft update ratio of 0.125 and Adam optimizer with a learning rate of 10^{-5} and 10^{-3} for the actor and critic respectively. We trained for 30k episodes, the training time for the single-agent approaches was around three days and for the multi-agent approaches around 10 days on a workstation with Nvidia® Titan V GPU.

Evaluation. We divide our experiments into single-landmark localization experiments, where we train five SALL networks independently each predicting a different landmark, and multi-landmark localization experiments, where we train MALL as well as $MALL_{noSC}$ network to predict five landmarks simultaneously. For comparison, we use our implementation of DQN [4] and the original code of a state-of-the-art supervised learning based approach using heatmap regression, Spatial Configuration-Net (SCN) [11]. To ensure deterministic results and a fair comparison for all experiments, we use the center of the image as the agent's initial position during inference. We compute the point error (PE) as the Euclidean distance between the agent's final position and target landmark in mm to evaluate the prediction accuracy. We present the average PE for all validation samples per landmark as well as it's overall average. Furthermore, we also determine the average number of steps the agent needs to localize the target landmark.

4 Results

The accuracy of the evaluated RL and supervised learning based approaches for landmark localization are presented in Table 1, separately for each landmark as well as all landmarks combined. In the same table we also show the average number of steps needed to terminate the RL based methods. The cumulative error distribution for all evaluated methods is shown in Fig. 3 again for each landmark separately as well as all landmarks combined. In Fig. 4 we show the results as error vectors drawn relative to the groundtruth landmark position of the respective image for all evaluated methods. In the same figure, we also show the results of the evaluated methods when the image is partially occluded starting from the landmark positioned between the metacarpal and phalanges bones simulated by uniform noise.

5 Discussion

In this work, we proposed a RL method for anatomical landmark localization using a continuous action space that allows the agent to move in an arbitrary direction with variable step size. This is different to existing state-of-the-art RL methods that use a discrete action space and a fixed step size, leading to a large number of steps and consequently long inference time to localize a landmark. As shown in Table 1, DQN [4], a state-of-the-art RL method for landmark localization, needs in average 193 forward passes of observation patches extracted from the inference image to localize a landmark. In contrast to that, our SALL method requires in average only 6.2 passes to reach the landmark. Hence, our experiments have shown that utilization of a continuous action space decreases the inference time by more than 30 times, which can be of high importance in e.g. time critical or energy efficient applications.

Our method has also shown to be more accurate compared to DQN, see Table 1 and Fig. 3, 4. While the average PE of the DQN method is 1.19 ± 0.9 mm our method is able to localize landmarks with an average PE of 0.86 ± 0.74 mm. This trend can be seen for all landmarks individually, while the largest difference can be observed for landmark 0, where our SALL method is 0.5 mm more accurate than DQN. One of the reasons why DQN is limited in accuracy is the stopping criterion, which is usually defined by oscillation of the agent and leads to ambiguity between the oscillating locations. This ambiguity is intrinsically resolved by our method, since the stopping criterion is predefined by a minimal displacement of the agent's position.

In comparison to the state-of-the-art SCN [11] method based on supervised learning and heatmap regression, our SALL method has shown inline results, see

Table 1. Average point error (PE) of all evaluated approaches for landmark localization in mm, separately for each landmark (LM) and all landmarks combined (All), as well as the average number of steps required to terminate the RL based approaches during inference.

Algorithm		LM 0	LM 1	LM 2	LM 3	LM 4	All
SCN [11]	PE	**0.27 ± 0.17**	**0.37 ± 0.21**	**0.64 ± 0.49**	**1.09 ± 0.93**	1.15 ± 0.9	**0.7 ± 0.73**
	#steps	-	-	-	-	-	-
DQN [4]	PE	0.94 ± 0.46	0.87 ± 0.81	0.83 ± 0.54	1.9 ± 1.16	1.42 ± 0.84	1.19 ± 0.9
	#steps	253.6	85.8	177.5	219.1	229.3	193.0
SALL	PE	0.4 ± 0.35	0.52 ± 0.32	0.82 ± 0.53	1.44 ± 0.97	**1.09 ± 0.75**	0.86 ± 0.74
	#steps	5.8	4.9	5.9	7.0	7.3	6.2
MALL$_{noSC}$	PE	1.41 ± 0.88	1.32 ± 0.71	1.82 ± 1.03	2.02 ± 1.14	1.71 ± 0.97	1.66 ± 0.99
	#steps	31.8	31.8	31.8	31.8	31.8	31.8
MALL	PE	1.35 ± 1.03	1.22 ± 0.72	1.63 ± 0.94	2.04 ± 1.2	1.78 ± 1.03	1.6 ± 1.04
	#steps	27.7	27.7	27.7	27.7	27.7	27.7

Table 1 and Fig. 3, 4. Although SALL achieves a better performance on landmark 4, a possible reason why SALL did not outperform SCN might be due to defining the agent's position on a pixel level, which can be improved by allowing subpixel predictions. Furthermore, to achieve a high accuracy, a heatmap-based CNN method like SCN has to store the intermediate network outputs of the whole image in GPU memory which is a challenge, especially when working with large 3D volumes. Since our RL method processes local image patches extracted around the agent's position, we are expecting similar performance for both 2D and 3D landmark localization tasks.

In this work, we additionally extend our single-agent approach (SALL) to a multi-agent approach (MALL) that is capable to simultaneously localize multiple landmarks. Differently to the recent work [6,12], where the weights are shared between convolution layers of multiple DQN agents, our method has a separate convolutional path per agent before generating the action of every agent using fully-connected layers. Furthermore, in our method, we establish direct communication between agents by providing each agent with it's relative position to all other agents. This communication between agents allows learning of the spatial configuration of anatomical landmarks, which is common in medical applications. Our experiments with partly occluded images (Fig. 4, right) show that both, heatmap based SCN [11] as well as the RL based DQN [4] are not able to localize the occluded landmark. The same behaviour is also shown by our single-agent RL method (SALL). It is interesting to see, that our multi-agent RL approach without list of pairwise offsets **D** (MALL$_{noSC}$) is failing to localize not only occluded but also visible landmarks when a large part of the image is replaced by random noise. A reason could be that the information extracted from each agent's observation is combined in the actor before an action of each agent is generated. Thus, corrupted observations of individual agents strongly affect the performance of all other agents due to common fully-connected layers in the actor. Nevertheless, we would also expect a similar behaviour from other approaches that utilize a single network to generate the actions of multiple agents

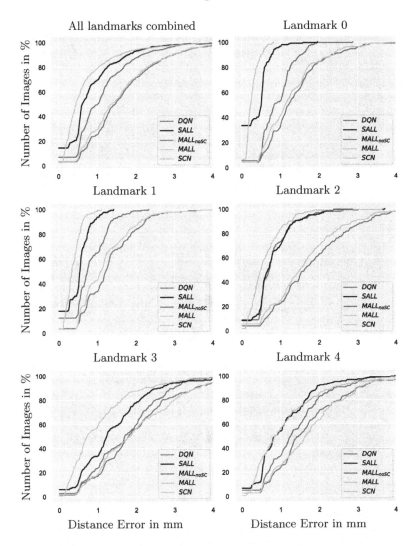

Fig. 3. Cumulative error distribution for all evaluated methods shown for all landmarks combined as well as for each landmark separately.

like [6]. Differently, when a list of pairwise offsets is provided to our multi-agent RL approach (MALL), it is able to not only localize the visible landmarks but also to use the information on their position to estimate the relative position of the occluded landmarks, see Fig. 4. Thus, our RL approach is able to successfully integrate the spatial configuration of the anatomical landmarks without the need of an additional model for global regularization, like statistical shape models or graphical models.

Additionally to evaluation of the proposed approach on volumetric images, in our future work we are planning to further investigate our multi-agent network

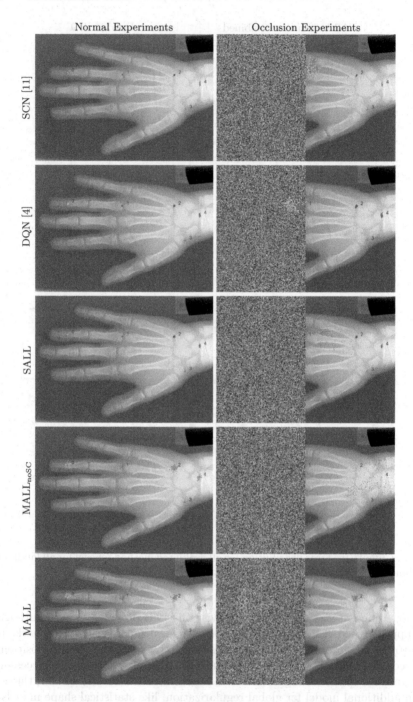

Fig. 4. Prediction results of all test images drawn on a single representative image as error vectors relative to the groundtruth landmark position of the respective image for the normal experiments (left) and the occlusion experiments (right). Each row corresponds to the method noted on the left.

architecture to improve the accuracy of the method. Namely, the average PE of MALL (1.6 ± 1.04 mm) is larger compared to SALL (0.86 ± 0.74 mm), which can be explained by an increased complexity of the MALL network compared to the SALL network. To improve the accuracy of MALL, the number of episodes can be increased, however, we trained both methods for the same number of episodes due to the long training time of MALL. A possible improvement to the MALL architecture is to use shared weights in each agent's convolutional path similarly to [6,12], which would reduce the number of parameters and consequently also the training time.

6   Conclusion

In conclusion, our proposed RL based approach allows the agent to move in arbitrary directions with a variable step size to localize an anatomical landmark in medical images. Our results show, that the proposed continuous action space reduces the number of steps necessary to localize the landmark by more than 30 times in average compared to a state-of-the-art RL approach based on discrete actions. This consequently decreases the number of forward passes needed to localize the landmark, which can be of high importance in time critical or energy efficient applications. Moreover, compared to methods using a fixed step size, where the stopping criterion is often defined by oscillation of the agent's position and thus, limiting the accuracy of the method and prolonging inference time, the stopping criterion in the continuous action space is intrinsically defined by a minimal displacement of the agent's position. Furthermore, the movement with a variable step size is also more similar to how a physician advances through a medical image, since the proposed agent is able to adapt the step size depending on the distance from the anatomy of interest.

Our single-agent RL based method has shown a higher accuracy than DQN, a state-of-the-art RL approach for landmark localization. Compared to the state-of-the-art supervised learning based SCN approach, our single-agent RL approach achieved inline results. However, in contrast to SCN, our RL approach only requires patches and not the whole image as input, which can be beneficial when working with large volumetric images. In our extension to our multi-agent RL based approach, we also introduced communication among agents by providing each agent with it's relative position to the other agents which allowed learning of the spatial configuration of the landmarks. Thus, the results of our multi-agent RL based approach show that the position of the occluded landmarks can be successfully estimated based on the relative position predicted for the visible landmarks.

References

1. Alansary, A., et al.: Evaluating reinforcement learning agents for anatomical landmark detection. Med. Image Anal. **53**, 156–164 (2019)

2. Foerster, J., Assael, I.A., de Freitas, N., Whiteson, S.: Learning to communicate with deep multi-agent reinforcement learning. Adv. Neural Inf. Process. Syst. **29**, 1–9 (2016)
3. Gertych, A., Zhang, A., Sayre, J., Pospiech-Kurkowska, S., Huang, H.: Bone age assessment of children using a digital hand atlas. Comput. Med. Imaging Grap. **31**(4–5), 322–331 (2007)
4. Ghesu, F.C., Georgescu, B., Mansi, T., Neumann, D., Hornegger, J., Comaniciu, D.: An artificial agent for anatomical landmark detection in medical images. In: Ourselin, S., Joskowicz, L., Sabuncu, M.R., Unal, G., Wells, W. (eds.) MICCAI 2016. LNCS, vol. 9902, pp. 229–237. Springer, Cham (2016). https://doi.org/10.1007/978-3-319-46726-9_27
5. Ghesu, F.C., et al.: Multi-scale deep reinforcement learning for real-time 3D-landmark detection in CT scans. IEEE Trans. Pattern Anal. Mach. Intell. **41**(1), 176–189 (2017)
6. Leroy, G., Rueckert, D., Alansary, A.: Communicative reinforcement learning agents for landmark detection in brain images. In: Kia, S.M., et al. (eds.) MLCN/RNO-AI -2020. LNCS, vol. 12449, pp. 177–186. Springer, Cham (2020). https://doi.org/10.1007/978-3-030-66843-3_18
7. Li, J., Wang, Y., Mao, J., Li, G., Ma, R.: End-to-end coordinate regression model with attention-guided mechanism for landmark localization in 3D medical images. In: Liu, M., Yan, P., Lian, C., Cao, X. (eds.) MLMI 2020. LNCS, vol. 12436, pp. 624–633. Springer, Cham (2020). https://doi.org/10.1007/978-3-030-59861-7_63
8. Lillicrap, T.P., et al.: Continuous control with deep reinforcement learning. In: International Conference on Learning Representations (2016)
9. Maicas, G., Carneiro, G., Bradley, A.P., Nascimento, J.C., Reid, I.: Deep reinforcement learning for active breast lesion detection from DCE-MRI. In: Descoteaux, M., Maier-Hein, L., Franz, A., Jannin, P., Collins, D.L., Duchesne, S. (eds.) MICCAI 2017. LNCS, vol. 10435, pp. 665–673. Springer, Cham (2017). https://doi.org/10.1007/978-3-319-66179-7_76
10. Mnih, V., et al.: Human-level control through deep reinforcement learning. Nature **518**(7540), 529–533 (2015)
11. Payer, C., Štern, D., Bischof, H., Urschler, M.: Regressing heatmaps for multiple landmark localization using CNNs. In: International Conference on Medical Image Computing and Computer-Assisted Intervention, pp. 230–238 (2016)
12. Vlontzos, A., Alansary, A., Kamnitsas, K., Rueckert, D., Kainz, B.: Multiple landmark detection using multi-agent reinforcement learning. In: International Conference on Medical Image Computing and Computer-Assisted Intervention, pp. 262–270 (2019)

Author Index

Printed in the United States
by Baker & Taylor Publisher Services